HOW TO PREPARE FOR THE GRADUATE RECORD EXAMINATION

GRE

GENERAL TEST

EIGHTH EDITION

SAMUEL C. BROWNSTEIN
MITCHEL WEINER
SHARON WEINER GREEN
Author of Special Chapter on Mathematics
STEPHEN HILBERT

BARRON'S

New York • London • Toronto • Sydney

All inquiries should be addressed to:
Barron's Educational Series, Inc.
250 Wireless Boulevard
Hauppauge, New York 11788

Library of Congress Catalog Card No. 88–14516

International Standard Book No. 0-8120-3884-3

Library of Congress Cataloging in Publication Data

Brownstein, Samuel C., 1909-
    Barron's how to prepare for the graduate record examination : GRE
general test / Samuel Brownstein, Mitchel Weiner, Sharon Weiner
Green : author of special chapter on mathematics, Stephen Hilbert.—
—8th ed.
      p.   cm.
    ISBN 0-8120-3884-3
    1. Graduate record examination—Study guides.   I. Weiner,
Mitchel, 1907-   .   II. Green, Sharon.   III. Barron's Educational
Series, Inc.   IV. Title.   V. Title: How to prepare for the graduate
record examination.   VI. Title: GRE general test.
LB2367.4.B76 1988   88-14516
378'.1664—dc19   CIP

PRINTED IN THE UNITED STATES OF AMERICA

90 100 9 8 7 6 5

Contents

Acknowledgments

The Sample GRE Questions in Chapter 1 and GRE test directions are reprinted by permission of Educational Testing Service, the copyright owner. Permission to reprint the GRE material does not constitute review or endorsement by Educational Testing Service or the Graduate Record Examinations Board of this publication as a whole or of any other testing information it may contain.

The authors gratefully acknowledge the following for permission to reprint reading passages:

From *Black Americans in the Roosevelt Era* by John B. Kirby. Copyright 1980, University of Tennessee Press.

From *The Uses of Enchantment*, by Bruno Bettelheim. Copyright © 1975, 1976 by Bruno Bettelheim. Reprinted by permission of Alred A. Knopf, Inc.

From "The Subduction of the Lithosphere" by M. Nafi Toksoz, *Scientific American*, November 1975. Reprinted in *Volcanoes and the Earth's Interior*, W. H. Freeman & Co. All rights reserved.

From *Black History and the Historical Profession, 1915-1980* by August Meier and Elliot Rudwick. Copyright 1986, University of Illinois Press.

From *From Slavery to Freedom: A History of Negro Americans*, by John Hope Franklin. Copyright 1947, © 1956, 1967 by Alfred A. Knopf, Inc. Reprinted by permission of Alfred A. Knopf, Inc.

From *The Indian in America* by Wilcomb E. Washburn, copyright © 1975 by Wilcomb E. Washburn. Reprinted by permission of Harper & Row

Excerpted from "Learning by Instinct," by James L. Gould and Peter Marler, *Scientific American*, January 1987. Copyright © 1987 by Scientific American, Inc. All rights reserved.

From "Medicine's Home Front" in *The Economist*, June 1987, Vol. 303.

From *Century of Struggle* by Eleanor Flexner, Revised Edition. Copyright 1959, 1975, 1987 by Eleanor Flexner. Published by Harvard University Press. Reprinted by permission.

Elaine Showalter, *A Literature of Their Own: British Women Novelists from Brontë to Lessing*. Copyright © 1977 by Princeton University Press. Excerpt, pp. 10–12 reprinted with permission of Princeton University Press.

From *Literary Women* by Ellen Moers. Copyright 1977 by Oxford University Press.

From *The English Novel: Form and Function* by Dorothy Van Ghent. Copyright 1953, Harper & Row Publishers, Inc.

From "W.E.B. Du Bois: Protagonist of the Afro-American Protest" by Elliot Rudwick, in *Black Leaders of the Twentieth Century*, edited by John Hope Franklin and August Meier. Copyright 1982, University of Illinois Press.

From *Eyes on the Prize: America's Civil Rights Years*, edited by Clayborne Carson et al. Copyright 1987 by Penguin Books.

Excerpted from "The Birth of Massive Stars" by Michael Zeilik, *Scientific American*, April 1978. Copyright © 1978 by Scientific American, Inc. All rights reserved.

Excerpted from "Science and the Citizen, *Scientific American*, November 1979. Copyright © 1979 by Scientific American, Inc. All rights reserved.

Excerpted from "How Bird Eggs Breathe" by Hermann Rahn, Amos Ar, and Charles V. Paganelli in *Scientific American*, February 1979. Copyright © 1979 by Scientific American, Inc. All rights reserved.

Excerpted from "The Quantum Theory and Reality" by Bernard d'Espagnat, *Scientific American*, November 1979. Copyright © 1979 by Scientific American, Inc. All rights reserved.

Excerpted from "Transposable Genetic Elements" by Stanley N. Cohen and James A. Shapiro, *Scientific American*, February 1980. Copyright © 1980 by Scientific American, Inc. All rights reserved.

Excerpted from "The Crest of the East Pacific Rise" by Ken C. Macdonald and Bruce P. Luyendyk, *Scientific American*, May 1981. Reprinted in *Volcanoes and the Earth's Interior*, W.H. Freeman & Co. All rights reserved.

Excerpted from "Learning by Instinct" by James L. Gould and Peter Marler, *Scientific American*, January 1987. Copyright © 1987 by Scientific American, Inc. All rights reserved.

Excerpted from "Mimicry in Plants" by Spencer C.H. Barrett, *Scientific American*, September 1987. Copyright © 1987 by Scientific American, Inc. All rights reserved.

Ladislas Segy "African Sculpture" Dover Publications, New York 1958.

From "So Many Female Rivals" by Christine Froula (*The New York Times Book Review*, February 7, 1988). Copyright © 1988 by The New York Times Company. Reprinted by permission.

From *The Madwoman in the Attic* by Sandra M. Gilbert and Susan Gubar, © 1979 by Yale University Press.

Preface

As prospective graduate students concerned with professional advancement, you know the importance of using good tools and drawing on solid research. In this Eighth Edition of *Barron's How to Prepare for the GRE*, we offer you both.

This revision contains the fruits of our close study of *all* recent GRE General Tests made public by the Graduate Record Examinations Board. We have scrutinized hundreds of actual GRE questions, traced dozens of GRE reading passages to their sources, analyzed subsets of questions by order of difficulty and question type. In process, we have come up with the following features, which should make this Eighth Edition particularly helpful to you:

Actual GRE Questions Analyzed

The Eighth Edition takes you step by step through dozens of verbal and mathematical questions from actual published GREs, showing you how to solve them and how to avoid going wrong.

Testing Tactics

The Eighth Edition provides you with dozens of new, high-lighted testing tactics that will help you attack the different types of questions on the GRE.

High-Frequency Word List

The Eighth Edition gives you a new 300-word High Frequency Word List, 300 words from *abate* to *zealot* that have been shown by computer analysis to occur and reoccur on actual published GREs, plus Barron's 3,500 Master Word List, *the* college-level vocabulary list for over thirty years.

Comprehensive Mathematics Review

The Eighth Edition presents you with extensive mathematical review materials that provide a refresher course for students primarily involved in non-scientific disciplines.

GRE-Modeled Tests

The Eighth Edition offers you a full-length Diagnostic Test geared to the current GRE, a diagnostic test that will enable you to pinpoint your areas of weakness right away and concentrate your review on subjects in which you need most work, plus 5 additional Model Tests, all with answers completely explained, that in format, difficulty, and content echo today's GRE.

This Eighth Edition represents a major revision of what has long been a standard text. As such, it is a sign of Barron's ongoing commitment to making this book America's outstanding GRE study guide. We, the authors, are indebted to our publisher, Manuel H. Barron, for making this commitment, and to our editor, Judy Makover, for making this commitment *work*.

TIMETABLE FOR THE GRADUATE RECORD EXAMINATION

IMPORTANT NOTE: This is a typical format only. The GRE you take may be slightly different. The order of the sections will probably vary.

Total Time: 3 hours, 40 minutes

Section	Time Allowed	Description
1	30 minutes	*Verbal Ability* 7 sentence completion questions 9 analogy questions 11 reading comprehension questions 11 antonym questions
2	30 minutes	*Verbal Ability* 7 sentence completion questions 9 analogy questions 11 reading comprehension questions 11 antonym questions
3	30 minutes	*Quantitative Ability* 15 quantitative comparison questions 10 discrete quantitative (standard multiple-choice) questions 5 data interpretation questions (tables/graphs)
		10-minute break
4	30 minutes	*Quantitative Ability* 15 quantitative comparison questions 10 discrete quantitative (standard multiple-choice) questions 5 data interpretation questions
5	30 minutes	*Analytical Ability* 19 analytical reasoning questions 6 logical reasoning questions
6	30 minutes	*Analytical Ability* 19 analytical reasoning questions 6 logical reasoning questions
7	30 minutes	*Verbal, Quantitative,* or *Analytical Ability*

1 What You Need to Know About the GRE

- ■ **An Overview of the GRE General Test**
- ■ **Commonly Asked Questions About the GRE**
- ■ **GRE Test Format**
- ■ **The Verbal Sections**
- ■ **The Quantitative Sections**
- ■ **The Analytical Sections**
- ■ **Testing Tactics**
- ■ **Sample GRE Questions**

An Overview of the GRE General Test

The GRE General Test is a multiple-choice examination designed to measure the verbal, quantitative, and analytical skills you have developed in the course of your academic career. Because there is a strong correlation between high GRE scores and the probability of success in graduate school, many graduate and professional schools require that their applicants take the GRE General Test. (They may also require their applicants to take the appropriate GRE Subject Test; these are offered in seventeen fields.)

There are seven sections on the GRE: two verbal sections, two quantitative sections, two sections testing analytical ability, and one experimental section in one of the three tested areas; this experimental section is not counted in the scoring. The verbal sections measure your ability to use words as tools in reasoning: you are tested not only on the extent of your vocabulary but on your ability to discern the relationships that exist both within written passages and among individual groups of words. The quantitative sections measure your ability to use and reason with numbers or mathematical concepts; you are tested not on advanced mathematical theory but on general concepts expected to be part of everyone's academic background. The analytical sections measure your ability to make rational assessments about unfamiliar, fic-

titious relationships and to think through arguments logically. You are given thirty minutes to answer the questions in each section; you may not go back to a section once the time for that section has elapsed.

There are three very important points you should be aware of:

1. Each question is worth the same number of points. Whether it was easy or difficult, whether it took you 10 seconds or 2 minutes to answer, you get the same number of points for each question answered correctly.

2. In each group of questions, the questions tend to go from easy to more difficult. This means that the first analogy question in a group will probably be easier than the seventh analogy question in that group, and so on. (An exception to this is the reading comprehension questions, which are not ordered by level of difficulty.)

3. The GRE General Test does *not* penalize you for incorrect answers. Leave no question unanswered. When uncertain about an answer, guess — and mark your guesses. You can always come back to them if you have time.

Keep these three points in mind as you learn more about what's on the test, and the tactics and strategies that will help you maximize your test score.

Commonly Asked Questions About the GRE

How Does the GRE Differ from Other Tests?

Most tests students take are achievement tests. They attempt to find out how much the student learned, usually in a specific subject, and how well he or she can apply that information. Without emphasis on memorized information, the GRE General Test measures verbal, mathematical, and analytical reasoning ability that you have developed both in and out of school.

How Can I Determine Which Is the Experimental Section?

Do not waste time in the examination room trying to identify which is the experimental section. Do your best on all seven sections. Some claim that most often the last section is the experimental part. Others claim that the section with unusual questions is the one that does not count. Ignore the claims: you have no sure way to tell. If you do encounter a series of questions that seem strange, do your best. Either these are experimental and will not count, in which case you have no reason to worry about them, or they will count, in which case they probably will seem just as strange and troublesome to your fellow examinees.

Should I Guess?

Yes, definitely on the *General* Test. Unlike the Subject Tests, which have a guessing penalty, the General Test simply gives credit for correct answers; it does not penalize ones that are incorrect. If you are running out of time, eliminate any answer choices you feel sure are wrong. Then go ahead and guess. On the General Test, guessing at an answer is ALWAYS better than not responding at all.

Is It Advisable to Begin by Doing All the Easy Questions First?

Yes, but don't devote too much time to any one question, even if you think it should be an easy one for you. Usually, the earlier questions of each type, except for the reading comprehension questions, are easier than the later ones. Most tests begin with "warm-up" questions. But what is easy for one person may be hard for another, so it is good advice not to get bogged down with any one question. Remember, all questions carry the same point value. After a reasonable amount of time, guess. Just make sure you make a note of your guesses in your test booklet, so that you can come back to them if you have time.

How Important Is Scrap Work on the GRE?

Scrap work on the GRE is important only to the degree that it is helpful to you. You may write in the test booklet as much as you choose. Don't hesitate to mark key words or phrases in the verbal and analytical sections. Do any necessary mathematical calculations on or near the problem. Since scrap work is not scored, keep it down to a minimum to save time. Be careful not to do any scrap work or leave any stray markings on your answer sheet. The machine that scores the test may mistake a stray mark for a second answer and give you no credit for a question.

Use your test booklet as your guessing guide. Circle any questions to which you want to return. Cross out any answer choices you are *sure* are wrong, so that you don't have to spend time considering them again.

When and Where Is the Test Given?

The GRE is given five times a year at test centers throughout the world. Tests fall on Saturdays in February, April, June, October, and December. In June, only the General Test is given. On the other four dates, the General Test is given in the morning and the Subject Tests are given in the afternoon. Candidates whose religious convictions prohibit their taking tests on Saturday may arrange for Monday dates.

In New York State, where public disclosure of standardized tests is required by law, a curtailed testing schedule is in effect.

Your college counseling office will have information about the exact test dates and should be able to provide you with a registration form. If a registration form is not available at your school, request one by mail from Graduate Record Examinations, Educational Testing Service, CN 6000, Princeton, NJ 08541-6000. You will receive with it a copy of the current GRE Information Bulletin, a helpful booklet containing sample questions and information about services and fees.

How and When Are GRE Scores Reported?

The General Test raw score, the number of correct answers, is converted to a score on a scale of 200 to 800. With no correct answers at all, a student would still have a score of 200. With one or two unanswered or incorrectly answered questions, a student could still have a score of 800. Separate scores (from 200 to 800) are given in the verbal, quantitative, and analytical reasoning sections. Your score report will include both your scaled scores and your percentile rank indicating the percent of examinees scoring below your scaled scores on the General Test.

You should receive your score report in the mail approximately six weeks after the test date.

GRE Test Format

The following seven sections are on the test. You will be given 30 minutes to complete each of them.

   38-question verbal section

   38-question verbal section

   30-question quantitative section

   30-question quantitative section

   25-question analytical section

   25-question analytical section

   an experimental section (which can resemble in content any of the six sections described above)

These sections always appear on the GRE, but their order varies. The organization within each section does not vary greatly; they will tend to be organized as outlined below:

Verbal Section

1–7 sentence completion questions

8–16 analogy questions

17–27 reading comprehension questions

28–38 antonym questions

Quantitative Section

1–15 quantitative comparison questions

16–20 discrete quantitative (standard multiple-choice) questions

21–25 data interpretation questions (tables/graphs)

26–30 discrete quantitative (standard multiple-choice) questions

Analytical Section*

1–5 analytical reasoning questions

6–8 logical reasoning questions

9–22 analytical reasoning questions

23–25 logical reasoning questions

---

*The distribution of questions in the analytical ability section varies slightly from section to section. Listed here is one of several possible formats. The total number of analytical reasoning questions (19) and logical reasoning questions (6), however, does not vary from section to section.

The Verbal Sections

The two verbal sections contain four types of questions: sentence completions, analogies, reading comprehension questions, and antonyms. Your academic success will depend on your verbal abilities — especially your ability to understand scholarly prose and to work with specialized and technical vocabulary.

As in all GRE sections, the questions in the verbal sections progress from easy to difficult within each group of the same type of question. In other words, the first antonym question will probably be easier than the last antonym question; the first analogy question will probably be easier than the last analogy question, and the first sentence completion question will probably be easier than the last sentence completion question. Reading comprehension questions, however, are not arranged in order of difficulty. They are arranged according to the logic and organization of the passage on which they are based.

Although the amount of time spent on each type of question varies from person to person, in general, antonyms take the least time, then analogies, then sentence completions, and, finally, reading comprehension. Since reading comprehension questions take much longer to answer (you have to spend time reading the passage before you can tackle the questions), you should do these questions last.

Sentence Completion Questions

The sentence completion questions ask you to choose the best way to complete a sentence from which one or two words have been omitted. These questions test a combination of reading comprehension skills and vocabulary. You must be able to recognize the logic, style, and tone of the sentence so that you will be able to choose the answer that makes sense in this context. You must also be able to recognize differences in usage. The sentences cover a wide variety of topics from a number of academic fields. They do not, however, test specific academic knowledge. You may feel more comfortable if you are familiar with the topic the sentence is discussing, but you should be able to handle any of the sentences using your knowledge of the English language.

See Chapter 3 for sentence completion question tactics and practice exercises that will help you handle these questions.

Analogy Questions

Analogy questions test your understanding of the relationships among words and ideas. You are given one pair of words and must choose another pair that is related in the same way. Many relationships are possible. The two terms in the pair can be synonyms; one term can be a cause, the other the effect; one can be a tool, the other the worker who uses the tool.

See Chapter 4 for analogy question tactics and practice exercises that will help you handle these questions.

Reading Comprehension Questions

Reading comprehension questions test your ability to understand and interpret what you read. This is probably the most important ability you will need in graduate school and afterward.

As we already noted, reading comprehension questions take more time than any other questions on the test because you have to read a passage before you can answer them. Therefore, you should do the reading comprehension questions last.

Although the passages may encompass any subject matter, you do not need to know anything about the subject discussed in the passage in order to answer the questions on that passage. The purpose of the questions is to test your reading ability, not your knowledge of history, science, literature, or art. It is true, however, that you might feel more comfortable reading a passage on a topic with which you are familiar. You should, therefore, skim the passages in each section before you start working on the reading comprehension questions, and then start with the questions on the passage with which you feel most comfortable.

See Chapter 5 for reading comprehension tactics and practice exercises that will help you handle these questions.

Antonym Questions

The antonym questions are always the last group of questions in a verbal section. They are the most straightforward vocabulary questions on the test. You are given a word and must choose, from the five choices that follow it, the best antonym (opposite). The vocabulary in this section may well include words that are totally unfamiliar to you.

See Chapter 6 for antonym testing tactics and practice exercises that will help you handle these questions.

The Quantitative Sections

The two quantitative (mathematics) sections have a total of 60 questions: 30 quantitative comparison questions, 20 discrete quantitative questions (these are actually standard multiple-choice questions), and 10 data interpretation questions. These questions assume that you have had, and remember, arithmetic, elementary algebra, and geometry. You do not need to know any more · advanced mathematics. You will be asked to use graphic, spatial, numerical, and symbolic techniques in a variety of problems. The questions are intended to show how well you understand elementary mathematics, how well you can apply your knowledge to solve problems, and how good your mathematical instincts are—how well you can use nonroutine ways of thinking. In one sense, you need some insight to spot the right approach for solving any mathematical question. More important, on the GRE, is the ability to see which answer must be correct, or at least which answers are impossible, without actually solving the problem. This is basically the ability to apply mathematical rules and principles that you already know. For example, imagine that you are asked to multiply $27,654 \times 3,042$. You should see right away that the answer will have to end in 8. When the multiplicand ends in a 4 and the multiplier ends in a 2, then the product must end with an 8. This is a typical illustration of saving time with insight rather than doing lengthy, time-consuming computation, which, incidentally, may lead to computational errors. So not only is it a time-saver, it may also be an error-saver.

Quantitative Comparison Questions

In quantitative comparison questions, you are given two quantities. Sometimes you are also given information about one or both of them. Then you must decide whether one of the quantities is greater than the other, or whether they are equal. Sometimes there will not be enough information for you to be able to make a decision.

These questions reflect the contemporary emphasis on inequalities in school mathematics courses. In general, these questions require less time than the other mathematics questions, since they require less reading and, usually, less computation. These are the only questions on the GRE that have only four answer choices.

The testing tactics and practice exercises in Chapter 8 will help you handle these questions.

Discrete Quantitative Questions

The discrete quantitative questions are like the math questions you are familiar with from math textbooks and other standardized tests. They will only cover math concepts that you have learned in school, so if a question seems unusual to you, keep in mind that you probably know the necessary facts, formulas, and concepts to work it out.

The testing tactics and practice exercises in Chapter 9 will help you handle these questions.

Data Interpretation Questions

As you might guess from their name, data interpretation questions are based on information given in graphs or tables. This type of question tests your ability to integrate data, to determine what information is needed to answer a question, or to calculate that you lack sufficient data to answer a question.

The testing tactics and practice exercises in Chapter 10 will help you handle these questions.

The Analytical Sections

The two analytical ability sections have a total of 50 questions, 38 of which are analytical reasoning questions and 12 of which are logical reasoning questions. Your task is to analyze a passage or set of conditions, reasoning out its implications, and then answer a question or group of questions based upon it. Each section begins with several relatively easy analytical reasoning questions followed by three relatively easy logical reasoning questions. These "warm-up" questions are then followed by a second set of analytical reasoning questions and three final logical reasoning ones.

Analytical Reasoning Questions

In analytical reasoning questions, the test-makers make up an arbitrary set of conditions and leave it to you to figure out the relationships ruling them. On the basis of the statements given, you are to make deductions about

these relationships. Often it is useful to make charts or diagrams to clarify the relationships and point up conflicts between the statements that have been made. You do not need to have training in formal logic to handle these questions; however, a liking for puzzles may help. Pay particular attention to key words: absolute terms like *always*, *exactly*, and *never*; and relative terms like *sometimes*, *approximately*, and *almost*.

The review of analytical reasoning techniques and practice exercises in Chapter 12 will help you handle these questions.

Logical Reasoning Questions

In logical reasoning questions, you are presented with an argument and must be able to spot its point, recognize the assumptions that lie behind it, and evaluate its worth. You must have a sense of what *necessarily follows* from a given statement as distinguished from what a statement merely suggests without proof. You must be careful here to avoid being influenced by your own personal opinions: your job is to test the argument for its logical soundness, not to testify or bear witness to the argument's ultimate truth.

The review of logical reasoning techniques and practice arguments in Chapter 12 will help you handle these questions.

Testing Tactics

The easiest way to answer a question correctly is to know the answer. If you know what all the words in an antonym question mean, you won't have any trouble choosing the right answer. If you know exactly how to solve a mathematics question and make no mistakes in arithmetic, you won't have any trouble choosing the right answer. However, some sensible strategies will help you maximize your score.

The tactics in this chapter apply to all sections of the test. In later chapters you will find tactics that apply specifically to each type of question.

Tactic 1

Know what to expect. By the time you have finished with this preparation program, you will be familiar with all the kinds of questions that are going to appear on the GRE. You should also be aware of how long it is going to take. There are seven sections on the test. Each one is half-an-hour long, and there is supposed to be a ten-minute break midway through the session.

Tactic 2

Memorize the directions for each type of question. These don't change. The test time you would spend reading the directions can be better spent answering the questions.

Tactic 3

Don't get bogged down on any one question. By the time you get to the actual GRE, you should have a fair idea of how much time to spend on each question. If a question is taking too long, guess and go on to the next question. This is no time to show the world that you can stick to a job no matter how long it takes. All the machine that grades the test will notice is the blank spaces on your answer sheet. However, before you do move on, circle the question so that you can locate it quickly if you have time to come back to it at the end.

Tactic 4

On the other hand, don't rush.   Since your score will depend on how many *correct* answers you give *within a definite period* of time, speed and accuracy both count. Don't fall into the common errors born of haste. Read *all the answer choices*, not just some. Make sure you are answering *the question asked* and not one it may have reminded you of or one you thought was going to be asked. Underline key words like "not" and "except" to make sure that you do not end up trying to answer the exact opposite of the question asked.

Tactic 5

Eliminate as many wrong answers as you can. Deciding between two choices is easier than deciding among five. Even if you have to guess, every answer you eliminate improves your chances of guessing correctly.

Tactic 6

Change answers only if you have a reason for doing so.   It's usually best not to change based on a hunch or a whim.

Tactic 7

Answer every question.   There is no penalty for incorrect answers on the General Test. It's folly to leave any question unanswered.

Tactic 8

Remember that you are allowed to write in the test book.   You can write anything you want in the test book. You can and should do your mathematical computations and analytical diagrams in the booklet. There is absolutely no need to try to do them in your head. And if it helps you to doodle while you think, then doodle away. What you write in the test booklet does not matter to anyone.

Tactic 9

Be careful not to make any stray marks on the answer sheet.   This test is graded by a machine, and a machine cannot tell the difference between an accidental mark and a filled-in answer. When the machine sees two marks, it calls the answer wrong.

Tactic 10

Check frequently to make sure that you are answering the questions in the right spots. No machine is going to notice that you made a mistake early in the test, answered question 4 in the space for question 5, and all your subsequent answers are the right answers, but in the wrong spots.

Tactic 11

Get a good night's sleep.   The best way to prepare for any test you ever take is to get a good night's sleep before the test so you are well rested and alert.

Tactic 12

Allow plenty of time for getting to the test site.   Taking a test is pressure enough. You don't need the extra tension that comes from worrying about whether you will get there on time.

Tactic 13

Bring four sharpened number 2 pencils to the test.   The *GRE Information Bulletin* tells you to bring three or four sharpened number 2 pencils to the test. Why skimp? They don't weigh much, and this might be the one day in the decade when two or even three pencil points decide to break. And bring full-size pencils, not little stubs. They are easier to write with, and you might as well be comfortable.

Tactic 14

Wear comfortable clothes.   This is a test, not a fashion show. And bring a sweater. The test room may be hot, or it may be cold. You can't change the room, but you can put on a sweater.

Tactic 15

Bring an accurate watch. The room in which you take the test may not have a clock, and some proctors are not very good about posting the time on the blackboard. Each time you begin a test section, write down in your booklet the time according to your watch. That way you will always know how much time you have left.

Sample GRE Questions*

The purpose of this section is to familiarize you with the kinds of questions that appear on the GRE by reprinting questions from recent GREs with the permission of Educational Testing Service. Knowing what to expect when you take the examination is an important step in preparing for the test and succeeding in it.

Verbal Section

Sentence Completion Questions

Directions: Each sentence below has one or two blanks, each blank indicating that something has been omitted. Beneath the sentence are five lettered words or sets of words. Choose the word or set of words for each blank that best fits the meaning of the sentence as a whole.

1. The paradoxical aspect of the myths about Demeter, when we consider the predominant image of her as a tranquil and serene goddess, is her ------- search for her daughter.

    (A) extended   (B) agitated   (C) comprehensive
    (D) motiveless   (E) heartless

2. Since she believed him to be both candid and trustworthy, she refused to consider the possibility that his statement had been -------.

    (A) irrelevant   (B) facetious   (C) mistaken
    (D) critical   (E) insincere

3. During the 1960's assessments of the family shifted remarkably, from general endorsement of it as a worthwhile, stable institution to widespread ------ it as an oppressive and bankrupt one whose ------- was both imminent and welcome.

    (A) flight from..restitution
    (B) fascination with..corruption
    (C) rejection of..vogue
    (D) censure of..dissolution
    (E) relinquishment of..ascent

4. The sheer bulk of data from the mass media seems to overpower us and drive us to ------- accounts for an easily and readily digestible portion of news.

    (A) insular
    (B) investigative
    (C) synoptic
    (D) subjective
    (E) sensational

5. People should not be praised for their virtue if they lack the energy to be -------; in such cases, goodness is merely the effect of -------.

    (A) depraved..hesitation
    (B) cruel..effortlessness
    (C) wicked..indolence
    (D) unjust..boredom
    (E) iniquitous..impiety

Analogy Questions

Directions: In each of the following questions, a related pair of words or phrases is followed by five lettered pairs of words or phrases. Select the lettered pair that best expresses a relationship similar to that expressed in the original pair.

6. AMORPHOUSNESS : DEFINITION ::
    (A) lassitude : energy
    (B) spontaneity : awareness
    (C) angularity : intricacy
    (D) rectitude : drabness
    (E) precision : uniformity

7. PHILATELIST : STAMPS ::
    (A) numismatist : coins
    (B) astrologer : predictions
    (C) geneticist : chromosomes
    (D) cartographer : maps
    (E) pawnbroker : jewelry

8. PROCTOR : SUPERVISE ::
    (A) prophet : rule
    (B) profiteer : consume
    (C) profligate : demand
    (D) prodigal : squander
    (E) prodigy : wonder

9. FLAG : VIGOR ::
    (A) endure : courage
    (B) tire : monotony
    (C) question : perception
    (D) waver : resolution
    (E) flatter : charm

10. EMBROIDER : CLOTH ::
    (A) chase : metal
    (B) patch : quilt
    (C) gild : gold
    (D) carve : knife
    (E) stain : glass

*GRE questions selected from **Practicing to Take the GRE General Test—No. 4** and **Practicing to Take the GRE General Test—No. 5**. Graduate record Examinations Board, 1986 and 1987. Reprinted by permission of Educational Testing Service, the copyright owner of the sample questions. Permission to reprint the GRE material does not constitute review or endorsement by Educational Testing Service or the Graduate Record Examinations Board of this publication as a whole or of any other testing information it may contain.

Reading Comprehension Questions

<u>Directions:</u> The passage is followed by questions based on its content. After reading the passage, choose the best answer to each question. Answer all questions following the passage on the basis of what is <u>stated</u> or <u>implied</u> in the passage.

Visual recognition involves storing and retrieving memories. Neural activity, triggered by the eye, forms an image in the brain's memory system that constitutes an internal representation of the viewed object. When an object is encountered again, it is matched with its internal representation and thereby recognized. Controversy surrounds the question of whether recognition is a parallel, one-step process or a serial, step-by-step one. Psychologists of the Gestalt school maintain that objects are recognized as wholes in a parallel procedure: the internal representation is matched with the retinal image in a single operation. Other psychologists have proposed that internal representation features are matched serially with an object's features. Although some experiments show that, as an object becomes familiar, its internal representation becomes more holistic and the recognition process correspondingly more parallel, the weight of evidence seems to support the serial hypothesis, at least for objects that are not notably simple and familiar.

11. The author is primarily concerned with

    (A) explaining how the brain receives images
    (B) synthesizing hypotheses of visual recognition
    (C) examining the evidence supporting the serial-recognition hypotheses
    (D) discussing visual recognition and some hypotheses proposed to explain it
    (E) reporting on recent experiments dealing with memory systems and their relationship to neural activity

12. According to the passage, Gestalt psychologists make which of the following suppositions about visual recognition?

    I.   A retinal image is in exactly the same form as its internal representation.
    II. An object is recognized as a whole without any need for analysis into component parts.
    III. The matching of an object with its internal representation occurs in only one step.

    (A) II only
    (B) III only
    (C) I and III only
    (D) II and III only
    (E) I, II, and III

13. It can be inferred from the passage that the matching process in visual recognition is

    (A) not a neural activity
    (B) not possible when an object is viewed for the very first time
    (C) not possible if a feature of a familiar object is changed in some way
    (D) only possible when a retinal image is received in the brain as a unitary whole
    (E) now fully understood as a combination of the serial and parallel processes

14. In terms of its tone and form, the passage can best be characterized as

    (A) a biased exposition
    (B) a speculative study
    (C) a dispassionate presentation
    (D) an indignant denial
    (E) a dogmatic explanation

Antonym Questions

<u>Directions:</u> Each question below consists of a word printed in capital letters, followed by five lettered words or phrases. Choose the lettered word or phrase that is most nearly <u>opposite</u> in meaning to the word in capital letters.

15. SYNCHRONOUS ::
    (A) off-key   (B) out-of-shape
    (C) without pity   (D) out-of-phase
    (E) without difficulty

16. LIST :   (A) be upside down
    (B) be upright   (C) slide backward
    (D) sway to and fro   (E) lie flat

17. TRACTABLE :   (A) distraught   (B) irritating
    (C) ruthless   (D) headstrong   (E) lazy

18. PERFIDY :   (A) thoroughness   (B) generosity
    (C) gratitude   (D) tact   (E) loyalty

19. REDOUBTABLE :   (A) unsurprising
    (B) unambiguous   (C) unimpressive
    (D) inevitable   (E) immovable

Quantitative Section
Quantitative Comparison Questions

<u>Directions:</u> Each of the following questions consists of two quantities, one in Column A and one in Column B. You are to compare the two quantities and choose

> A if the quantity in Column A is greater;
> B if the quantity in Column B is greater;
> C if the two quantities are equal;
> D if the relationship cannot be determined from the information given.

<u>Note:</u> Since there are only four choices, NEVER MARK (E).

<u>Common Information:</u> In a question, information concerning one or both of the quantities to be compared is centered above the two columns. A symbol that appears in both columns represents the same thing in Column A as it does in Column B.

Column A	Column B
1. The least common denominator of $\frac{1}{2}, \frac{1}{3},$ and $\frac{1}{4}$	15

Column A	Column B
2. $2 + \sqrt{3}$	$1 + \sqrt{4}$

Column A	Column B
3. $(2.3)(12.45)$	$(0.23)(124.5)$

Column A	Column B
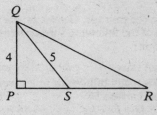	
4. $2x + y$	$2y + x$

In $\triangle RST$, $RS = ST$ and the measure of $\angle RST$ is 20

Column A	Column B
5. The measure of $\angle TRS$	$80°$

Discrete Quantitative Questions

<u>Directions:</u> Each of the following questions has five answer choices. For each of these questions, select the best of the answer choices given.

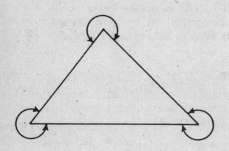

6. In the triangle above, the sum of the measures of the three marked angles is

(A) 540°
(B) 630°
(C) 720°
(D) 810°
(E) 900°

7. In the figure above, the area of triangular region PQR is 36. What is the area of triangular region SQR?

(A) 30   (B) 24   (C) 18   (D) 15   (E) 12

8. If the ratio of x to y is 9 times the ratio of y to x, then $\frac{x}{y}$ could be

(A) 9   (B) 3   (C) 1   (D) $\frac{1}{3}$ (E) $\frac{1}{9}$

9. Two microphones are located 100 meters apart and each is 130 meters from the same listening station. If a transmitter is located halfway between the two microphones, what is the distance, in meters, between the transmitter and the listening station?

   (A) 120   (B) 124   (C) 125
   (D) 128   (E) 130

10. A phone call from City X to City Y costs $1.00 for the first 3 minutes and $0.20 for each additional minute. If r is an integer greater than 3, a phone call r minutes long will cost how many <u>dollars</u>?

    (A) $\frac{3r}{5}$ (B) $\frac{r-10}{5}$ (C) $\frac{r-3}{5}$

    (D) $\frac{r+2}{5}$ (E) $\frac{r+15}{5}$

Data Interpretation Questions

<u>Questions 11–15</u> refer to the following graphs.

DOMESTIC AIR CARRIERS: OPERATING REVENUES,
MILES FLOWN, AND NUMBER OF PASSENGERS CARRIED,
1960 TO 1975

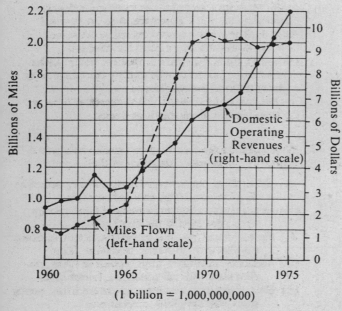

(1 billion = 1,000,000,000)

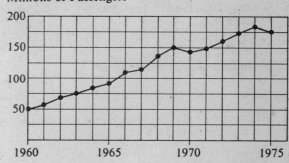

<u>Note</u>: Graphs drawn to scale.

11. In 1965 how many billions of miles were flown by domestic air carriers?

    (A) 0.95   (B) 1.05   (C) 1.2
    (D) 2.5   (E) 3.0

12. In which of the following years were there more passengers carried by domestic air carriers than in the year before and the year after?

    (A) 1961   (B) 1965   (C) 1970
    (D) 1972   (E) 1974

13. In 1969 what was the ratio of dollars of domestic operating revenues to miles flown?

    (A) $\frac{4}{1}$ (B) $\frac{3}{1}$ (C) $\frac{3}{2}$ (D) $\frac{2}{3}$ (E) $\frac{1}{4}$

14. In billions of miles, approximately what was the average (arithmetic mean) number of miles flown per year by domestic air carriers from 1965 to 1970, inclusive?

    (A) 1.0   (B) 1.5   (C) 2.0
    (D) 4.5   (E) 6.0

15. From 1960 to 1975, what was the percent increase in the number of passengers carried by domestic air carriers?

    (A) 125%
    (B) 175%
    (C) 250%
    (D) 350%
    (E) 450%

Analytical Ability Section

Analytical Reasoning Questions

Directions: Each question or group of questions is based on a passage or set of conditions. In answering some of the questions, it may be useful to draw a rough diagram. For each question, select the best answer choice given.

Question 1–4

A cryptanalyst must translate into letters all of the digits included in the following two lines of nine symbols each:

> 9 3 3 4 5 6 6 6 7
> 2 2 3 3 4 4 5 7 8

The cryptanalyst has already determined some of the rules governing the decoding:

> Each of the digits from 2 to 9 represents exactly one of the eight letters A, E, I, O, U, R, S, and T, and each letter is represented by exactly one of the digits.
> If a digit occurs more than once, it represents the same letter on each occasion.
> The letter T and the letter O are each represented exactly 3 times.
> The letter I and the letter A are each represented exactly two times.
> The letter E is represented exactly four times.

1. If 2 represents R and 7 represents A, then 5 must represent

    (A) I
    (B) O
    (C) S
    (D) T
    (E) U

2. Which of the following is a possible decoding of the five-digit message 4 6 5 3 6?

    (A) O-T-A-E-T
    (B) O-T-E-U-T
    (C) O-O-S-E-O
    (D) T-O-I-E-T
    (E) T-O-R-E-T

3. If 9 represents a vowel, it must represent which of the following?

    (A) A
    (B) E
    (C) I
    (D) O
    (E) U

4. If 8 represents a vowel, which of the following must represent a consonant?

    (A) 2
    (B) 4
    (C) 5
    (D) 7
    (E) 9

Questions 5–7

An instructor regularly offers a six-week survey course on film genres. Each time the course is given, she covers six of the following eight genres: adventure films, *cinéma noir*, detective films, fantasy films, horror films, musical comedies, silent films, and westerns. She will discuss exactly one genre per week according to the following conditions:

> Silent films are always covered, and always in the first week.
> Westerns and adventure films are always covered, with westerns covered in the week immediately preceding the week adventure films are covered.
> Musical comedies are never covered in the same course in which fantasy films are covered.
> If detective films are covered, they are covered after westerns are covered, with exactly one of the other genres covered between them.
> *Cinéma noir* is not covered unless detective films are covered in one of the previous weeks.

5. Which of the following is an acceptable schedule of genres for weeks one through six of the course?

    (A) Silent films, westerns, adventure films, detective films, horror films, musical comedies
    (B) Silent films, westerns, adventure films, horror films, detective films, fantasy films
    (C) Fantasy films, musical comedies, detective films, *cinéma noir*, westerns, adventure films
    (D) Westerns, adventure films, detective films, *cinéma noir*, musical comedies, horror films
    (E) Detective films, westerns, adventure films, horror films, fantasy films, *cinéma noir*

6. If musical comedies are covered the week immediately preceding the week westerns are covered, which of the following can be true?

    (A) Adventure films are covered the second week.
    (B) *Cinéma noir* is covered the fourth week.
    (C) Detective films are covered the third week.
    (D) Fantasy films are covered the fifth week.
    (E) Horror films are covered the sixth week.

7. Which of the following will NEVER be covered in the sixth week of the course?

    (A) *Cinéma noir*
    (B) Fantasy films
    (C) Horror films
    (D) Musical comedies
    (E) Westerns

Logical Reasoning Questions

Directions: Each question or group of questions is based on a passage or set of conditions. In answering some of the questions, it may be useful to draw a rough diagram. For each question, select the best answer choice given.

8. A study of illusionistic painting inevitably begins with the Greek painter Zeuxis. In an early work, which is the basis for his fame, he painted a bowl of grapes that was so lifelike that birds pecked at the fruit. In an attempt to expand his achievement to encompass human figures, he painted a boy carrying a bunch of grapes. When birds immediately came to peck at the fruit, Zeuxis judged that he had failed.

    Zeuxis' judgment that he had failed in his later work was based on an assumption. Which of the following can have served as that assumption?

    (A) People are more easily fooled by illusionistic techniques than are birds.
    (B) The use of illusionistic techniques in painting had become commonplace by the time Zeuxis completed his later work.
    (C) The grapes in the later painting were even more realistic than the ones in the earlier work.
    (D) Birds are less likely to peck at fruit when they see that a human being is present.
    (E) After the success of his early work, Zeuxis was unable to live up to the expectations of the general public.

9. Dormitories range from two to six stories in height. If a dormitory room is above the second floor, it has a fire escape.

    If the statements above are true, which of the following must also be true?

    (A) Second-floor dormitory rooms do not have fire escapes.
    (B) Third-floor dormitory rooms do not have fire escapes.
    (C) Only dormitory rooms above the second floor have fire escapes.
    (D) Fourth-floor dormitory rooms have fire escapes.
    (E) Some two-story dormitories do not have fire escapes.

10. It is important to teach students to use computers effectively. Therefore, students should be taught computer programming in school.

    Which of the following, if true, most weakens the argument above?

    (A) Only people who use computers effectively are skilled at computer programming.
    (B) Only people skilled at computer programming use computers effectively.
    (C) Some people who use computers effectively cannot write computer programs.
    (D) Some schools teach computer programming more effectively than others.
    (E) Most people who are able to program computers use computers effectively.

11. The Census Bureau reported that the median family income, after adjustment for inflation, increased 1.6 percent in 1983. Poverty normally declines when family income goes up, but the national poverty rate remained at its highest level in eighteen years in 1983. The Census Bureau offered two possible explanations: the lingering effects of the deep and lengthy 1981–1982 recession, and increases in the number of people living in families headed by women and in the number of adults not living with any relatives. Both groups are likely to be poorer than the population as a whole.

    Which of the following conclusions can be properly drawn from this report?

    (A) The national poverty rate has increased steadily over the last eighteen years.
    (B) The national poverty rate will increase when there are lingering effects of an earlier recession.
    (C) The median family income can increase even though the family income of some subgroups within the population declines or fails to increase.
    (D) The category of adults not living with any relatives is the most critical group in the determination of whether the economy has improved.
    (E) The median family income is affected more by the changes in family patterns than by the extent of expansion or recession of the national economy.

12. Literary historians today have rejected conventional analyses of the development of English Renaissance drama. They no longer accept the idea that the sudden achievement of Elizabethan playwrights was a historical anomaly, a sort of magical rediscovery of ancient Greek dramatic form applied to contemporary English subject matter. Instead, most students of the theater now view Elizabethan drama as being organically related to traditional local drama, particularly medieval morality plays.

    Which of the following is NOT consistent with the passage above?

    (A) England had a dramatic tradition before the Renaissance period.
    (B) Elizabethan drama, once thought to be a sudden blossoming forth of creativity, is now seen as part of a historical continuum.
    (C) Historians' views of the antecedents of English Renaissance drama have changed considerably.
    (D) Current scholarship applies an evolutionary model to English Renaissance drama.
    (E) Although English Renaissance drama treats English subject matter, its source of form and method is classical Greek drama.

Answer Key

Verbal Section

1.	B	6.	A	11.	D	16.	B
2.	E	7.	A	12.	D	17.	D
3.	D	8.	D	13.	B	18.	E
4.	C	9.	D	14.	C	19.	C
5.	C	10.	A	15.	D		

Quantitative Section

1.	B	6.	E	11.	A
2.	A	7.	A	12.	E
3.	C	8.	B	13.	B
4.	B	9.	A	14.	B
5.	C	10.	D	15.	C

Analytical Ability Section

1.	A	5.	A	9.	D
2.	A	6.	E	10.	C
3.	E	7.	E	11.	C
4.	E	8.	D	12.	E

2

A DIAGNOSTIC TEST

- ■ **Diagnostic Test**
- ■ **Answer Key**
- ■ **Self-Appraisal**
- ■ **Answer Explanations**

This chapter contains a simulated full-length GRE test. Like the actual GRE which you'll be taking soon, this Diagnostic Test has 7 sections: 2 verbal, 2 quantitative (math), 2 analytical, and 1 experimental (which in this case is another quantitative section). Each section has the same number and type of questions as you'll find on the actual GRE. And each section should be completed in 30 minutes. Taking this Diagnostic Test will provide you with a fairly accurate evaluation of what your GRE score would be barring any special preparation.

After taking the test, score your answers and evaluate your results, using the self-rating guides provided. (Be sure to also read the answer explanations for questions you answered incorrectly and questions you answered correctly but found difficult.)

You should now be in a position to approach your review program realistically and allot your time for study. For example, you should know which topics in mathematics

require review and drill. You should also know which of your verbal and analytical skills require concentrated study.

Simulate Test Conditions

Find a quiet place to work, in order to simulate examination conditions. Keep an accurate record of your time. If you complete a section before the suggested time has elapsed, check your work over and do not start another section. Don't be worried, however, if you are not able to answer all questions in the allotted time. This may also occur on the actual test. No one is expected to know the answers to all questions on an aptitude test. Read the questions carefully. Work carefully and as rapidly as possible. Do not spend too much time on questions that seem difficult for you. However, since this is a multiple-choice test, with no penalty imposed for guessing, answer every question even if you have to guess.

Answer Sheet – Diagnostic Test

Start with number 1 for each new section.
If a section has fewer than 38 questions, leave the extra spaces blank.

Section 1

1. Ⓐ Ⓑ Ⓒ Ⓓ Ⓔ	11. Ⓐ Ⓑ Ⓒ Ⓓ Ⓔ	21. Ⓐ Ⓑ Ⓒ Ⓓ Ⓔ	31. Ⓐ Ⓑ Ⓒ Ⓓ Ⓔ
2. Ⓐ Ⓑ Ⓒ Ⓓ Ⓔ	12. Ⓐ Ⓑ Ⓒ Ⓓ Ⓔ	22. Ⓐ Ⓑ Ⓒ Ⓓ Ⓔ	32. Ⓐ Ⓑ Ⓒ Ⓓ Ⓔ
3. Ⓐ Ⓑ Ⓒ Ⓓ Ⓔ	13. Ⓐ Ⓑ Ⓒ Ⓓ Ⓔ	23. Ⓐ Ⓑ Ⓒ Ⓓ Ⓔ	33. Ⓐ Ⓑ Ⓒ Ⓓ Ⓔ
4. Ⓐ Ⓑ Ⓒ Ⓓ Ⓔ	14. Ⓐ Ⓑ Ⓒ Ⓓ Ⓔ	24. Ⓐ Ⓑ Ⓒ Ⓓ Ⓔ	34. Ⓐ Ⓑ Ⓒ Ⓓ Ⓔ
5. Ⓐ Ⓑ Ⓒ Ⓓ Ⓔ	15. Ⓐ Ⓑ Ⓒ Ⓓ Ⓔ	25. Ⓐ Ⓑ Ⓒ Ⓓ Ⓔ	35. Ⓐ Ⓑ Ⓒ Ⓓ Ⓔ
6. Ⓐ Ⓑ Ⓒ Ⓓ Ⓔ	16. Ⓐ Ⓑ Ⓒ Ⓓ Ⓔ	26. Ⓐ Ⓑ Ⓒ Ⓓ Ⓔ	36. Ⓐ Ⓑ Ⓒ Ⓓ Ⓔ
7. Ⓐ Ⓑ Ⓒ Ⓓ Ⓔ	17. Ⓐ Ⓑ Ⓒ Ⓓ Ⓔ	27. Ⓐ Ⓑ Ⓒ Ⓓ Ⓔ	37. Ⓐ Ⓑ Ⓒ Ⓓ Ⓔ
8. Ⓐ Ⓑ Ⓒ Ⓓ Ⓔ	18. Ⓐ Ⓑ Ⓒ Ⓓ Ⓔ	28. Ⓐ Ⓑ Ⓒ Ⓓ Ⓔ	38. Ⓐ Ⓑ Ⓒ Ⓓ Ⓔ
9. Ⓐ Ⓑ Ⓒ Ⓓ Ⓔ	19. Ⓐ Ⓑ Ⓒ Ⓓ Ⓔ	29. Ⓐ Ⓑ Ⓒ Ⓓ Ⓔ	
10. Ⓐ Ⓑ Ⓒ Ⓓ Ⓔ	20. Ⓐ Ⓑ Ⓒ Ⓓ Ⓔ	30. Ⓐ Ⓑ Ⓒ Ⓓ Ⓔ	

Section 2

1. Ⓐ Ⓑ Ⓒ Ⓓ Ⓔ	11. Ⓐ Ⓑ Ⓒ Ⓓ Ⓔ	21. Ⓐ Ⓑ Ⓒ Ⓓ Ⓔ	31. Ⓐ Ⓑ Ⓒ Ⓓ Ⓔ
2. Ⓐ Ⓑ Ⓒ Ⓓ Ⓔ	12. Ⓐ Ⓑ Ⓒ Ⓓ Ⓔ	22. Ⓐ Ⓑ Ⓒ Ⓓ Ⓔ	32. Ⓐ Ⓑ Ⓒ Ⓓ Ⓔ
3. Ⓐ Ⓑ Ⓒ Ⓓ Ⓔ	13. Ⓐ Ⓑ Ⓒ Ⓓ Ⓔ	23. Ⓐ Ⓑ Ⓒ Ⓓ Ⓔ	33. Ⓐ Ⓑ Ⓒ Ⓓ Ⓔ
4. Ⓐ Ⓑ Ⓒ Ⓓ Ⓔ	14. Ⓐ Ⓑ Ⓒ Ⓓ Ⓔ	24. Ⓐ Ⓑ Ⓒ Ⓓ Ⓔ	34. Ⓐ Ⓑ Ⓒ Ⓓ Ⓔ
5. Ⓐ Ⓑ Ⓒ Ⓓ Ⓔ	15. Ⓐ Ⓑ Ⓒ Ⓓ Ⓔ	25. Ⓐ Ⓑ Ⓒ Ⓓ Ⓔ	35. Ⓐ Ⓑ Ⓒ Ⓓ Ⓔ
6. Ⓐ Ⓑ Ⓒ Ⓓ Ⓔ	16. Ⓐ Ⓑ Ⓒ Ⓓ Ⓔ	26. Ⓐ Ⓑ Ⓒ Ⓓ Ⓔ	36. Ⓐ Ⓑ Ⓒ Ⓓ Ⓔ
7. Ⓐ Ⓑ Ⓒ Ⓓ Ⓔ	17. Ⓐ Ⓑ Ⓒ Ⓓ Ⓔ	27. Ⓐ Ⓑ Ⓒ Ⓓ Ⓔ	37. Ⓐ Ⓑ Ⓒ Ⓓ Ⓔ
8. Ⓐ Ⓑ Ⓒ Ⓓ Ⓔ	18. Ⓐ Ⓑ Ⓒ Ⓓ Ⓔ	28. Ⓐ Ⓑ Ⓒ Ⓓ Ⓔ	38. Ⓐ Ⓑ Ⓒ Ⓓ Ⓔ
9. Ⓐ Ⓑ Ⓒ Ⓓ Ⓔ	19. Ⓐ Ⓑ Ⓒ Ⓓ Ⓔ	29. Ⓐ Ⓑ Ⓒ Ⓓ Ⓔ	
10. Ⓐ Ⓑ Ⓒ Ⓓ Ⓔ	20. Ⓐ Ⓑ Ⓒ Ⓓ Ⓔ	30. Ⓐ Ⓑ Ⓒ Ⓓ Ⓔ	

Section 3

1. Ⓐ Ⓑ Ⓒ Ⓓ Ⓔ	11. Ⓐ Ⓑ Ⓒ Ⓓ Ⓔ	21. Ⓐ Ⓑ Ⓒ Ⓓ Ⓔ	31. Ⓐ Ⓑ Ⓒ Ⓓ Ⓔ
2. Ⓐ Ⓑ Ⓒ Ⓓ Ⓔ	12. Ⓐ Ⓑ Ⓒ Ⓓ Ⓔ	22. Ⓐ Ⓑ Ⓒ Ⓓ Ⓔ	32. Ⓐ Ⓑ Ⓒ Ⓓ Ⓔ
3. Ⓐ Ⓑ Ⓒ Ⓓ Ⓔ	13. Ⓐ Ⓑ Ⓒ Ⓓ Ⓔ	23. Ⓐ Ⓑ Ⓒ Ⓓ Ⓔ	33. Ⓐ Ⓑ Ⓒ Ⓓ Ⓔ
4. Ⓐ Ⓑ Ⓒ Ⓓ Ⓔ	14. Ⓐ Ⓑ Ⓒ Ⓓ Ⓔ	24. Ⓐ Ⓑ Ⓒ Ⓓ Ⓔ	34. Ⓐ Ⓑ Ⓒ Ⓓ Ⓔ
5. Ⓐ Ⓑ Ⓒ Ⓓ Ⓔ	15. Ⓐ Ⓑ Ⓒ Ⓓ Ⓔ	25. Ⓐ Ⓑ Ⓒ Ⓓ Ⓔ	35. Ⓐ Ⓑ Ⓒ Ⓓ Ⓔ
6. Ⓐ Ⓑ Ⓒ Ⓓ Ⓔ	16. Ⓐ Ⓑ Ⓒ Ⓓ Ⓔ	26. Ⓐ Ⓑ Ⓒ Ⓓ Ⓔ	36. Ⓐ Ⓑ Ⓒ Ⓓ Ⓔ
7. Ⓐ Ⓑ Ⓒ Ⓓ Ⓔ	17. Ⓐ Ⓑ Ⓒ Ⓓ Ⓔ	27. Ⓐ Ⓑ Ⓒ Ⓓ Ⓔ	37. Ⓐ Ⓑ Ⓒ Ⓓ Ⓔ
8. Ⓐ Ⓑ Ⓒ Ⓓ Ⓔ	18. Ⓐ Ⓑ Ⓒ Ⓓ Ⓔ	28. Ⓐ Ⓑ Ⓒ Ⓓ Ⓔ	38. Ⓐ Ⓑ Ⓒ Ⓓ Ⓔ
9. Ⓐ Ⓑ Ⓒ Ⓓ Ⓔ	19. Ⓐ Ⓑ Ⓒ Ⓓ Ⓔ	29. Ⓐ Ⓑ Ⓒ Ⓓ Ⓔ	
10. Ⓐ Ⓑ Ⓒ Ⓓ Ⓔ	20. Ⓐ Ⓑ Ⓒ Ⓓ Ⓔ	30. Ⓐ Ⓑ Ⓒ Ⓓ Ⓔ	

Section 4

1. Ⓐ Ⓑ Ⓒ Ⓓ Ⓔ	11. Ⓐ Ⓑ Ⓒ Ⓓ Ⓔ	21. Ⓐ Ⓑ Ⓒ Ⓓ Ⓔ	31. Ⓐ Ⓑ Ⓒ Ⓓ Ⓔ
2. Ⓐ Ⓑ Ⓒ Ⓓ Ⓔ	12. Ⓐ Ⓑ Ⓒ Ⓓ Ⓔ	22. Ⓐ Ⓑ Ⓒ Ⓓ Ⓔ	32. Ⓐ Ⓑ Ⓒ Ⓓ Ⓔ
3. Ⓐ Ⓑ Ⓒ Ⓓ Ⓔ	13. Ⓐ Ⓑ Ⓒ Ⓓ Ⓔ	23. Ⓐ Ⓑ Ⓒ Ⓓ Ⓔ	33. Ⓐ Ⓑ Ⓒ Ⓓ Ⓔ
4. Ⓐ Ⓑ Ⓒ Ⓓ Ⓔ	14. Ⓐ Ⓑ Ⓒ Ⓓ Ⓔ	24. Ⓐ Ⓑ Ⓒ Ⓓ Ⓔ	34. Ⓐ Ⓑ Ⓒ Ⓓ Ⓔ
5. Ⓐ Ⓑ Ⓒ Ⓓ Ⓔ	15. Ⓐ Ⓑ Ⓒ Ⓓ Ⓔ	25. Ⓐ Ⓑ Ⓒ Ⓓ Ⓔ	35. Ⓐ Ⓑ Ⓒ Ⓓ Ⓔ
6. Ⓐ Ⓑ Ⓒ Ⓓ Ⓔ	16. Ⓐ Ⓑ Ⓒ Ⓓ Ⓔ	26. Ⓐ Ⓑ Ⓒ Ⓓ Ⓔ	36. Ⓐ Ⓑ Ⓒ Ⓓ Ⓔ
7. Ⓐ Ⓑ Ⓒ Ⓓ Ⓔ	17. Ⓐ Ⓑ Ⓒ Ⓓ Ⓔ	27. Ⓐ Ⓑ Ⓒ Ⓓ Ⓔ	37. Ⓐ Ⓑ Ⓒ Ⓓ Ⓔ
8. Ⓐ Ⓑ Ⓒ Ⓓ Ⓔ	18. Ⓐ Ⓑ Ⓒ Ⓓ Ⓔ	28. Ⓐ Ⓑ Ⓒ Ⓓ Ⓔ	38. Ⓐ Ⓑ Ⓒ Ⓓ Ⓔ
9. Ⓐ Ⓑ Ⓒ Ⓓ Ⓔ	19. Ⓐ Ⓑ Ⓒ Ⓓ Ⓔ	29. Ⓐ Ⓑ Ⓒ Ⓓ Ⓔ	
10. Ⓐ Ⓑ Ⓒ Ⓓ Ⓔ	20. Ⓐ Ⓑ Ⓒ Ⓓ Ⓔ	30. Ⓐ Ⓑ Ⓒ Ⓓ Ⓔ	

Section 5

1. Ⓐ Ⓑ Ⓒ Ⓓ Ⓔ	11. Ⓐ Ⓑ Ⓒ Ⓓ Ⓔ	21. Ⓐ Ⓑ Ⓒ Ⓓ Ⓔ	31. Ⓐ Ⓑ Ⓒ Ⓓ Ⓔ
2. Ⓐ Ⓑ Ⓒ Ⓓ Ⓔ	12. Ⓐ Ⓑ Ⓒ Ⓓ Ⓔ	22. Ⓐ Ⓑ Ⓒ Ⓓ Ⓔ	32. Ⓐ Ⓑ Ⓒ Ⓓ Ⓔ
3. Ⓐ Ⓑ Ⓒ Ⓓ Ⓔ	13. Ⓐ Ⓑ Ⓒ Ⓓ Ⓔ	23. Ⓐ Ⓑ Ⓒ Ⓓ Ⓔ	33. Ⓐ Ⓑ Ⓒ Ⓓ Ⓔ
4. Ⓐ Ⓑ Ⓒ Ⓓ Ⓔ	14. Ⓐ Ⓑ Ⓒ Ⓓ Ⓔ	24. Ⓐ Ⓑ Ⓒ Ⓓ Ⓔ	34. Ⓐ Ⓑ Ⓒ Ⓓ Ⓔ
5. Ⓐ Ⓑ Ⓒ Ⓓ Ⓔ	15. Ⓐ Ⓑ Ⓒ Ⓓ Ⓔ	25. Ⓐ Ⓑ Ⓒ Ⓓ Ⓔ	35. Ⓐ Ⓑ Ⓒ Ⓓ Ⓔ
6. Ⓐ Ⓑ Ⓒ Ⓓ Ⓔ	16. Ⓐ Ⓑ Ⓒ Ⓓ Ⓔ	26. Ⓐ Ⓑ Ⓒ Ⓓ Ⓔ	36. Ⓐ Ⓑ Ⓒ Ⓓ Ⓔ
7. Ⓐ Ⓑ Ⓒ Ⓓ Ⓔ	17. Ⓐ Ⓑ Ⓒ Ⓓ Ⓔ	27. Ⓐ Ⓑ Ⓒ Ⓓ Ⓔ	37. Ⓐ Ⓑ Ⓒ Ⓓ Ⓔ
8. Ⓐ Ⓑ Ⓒ Ⓓ Ⓔ	18. Ⓐ Ⓑ Ⓒ Ⓓ Ⓔ	28. Ⓐ Ⓑ Ⓒ Ⓓ Ⓔ	38. Ⓐ Ⓑ Ⓒ Ⓓ Ⓔ
9. Ⓐ Ⓑ Ⓒ Ⓓ Ⓔ	19. Ⓐ Ⓑ Ⓒ Ⓓ Ⓔ	29. Ⓐ Ⓑ Ⓒ Ⓓ Ⓔ	
10. Ⓐ Ⓑ Ⓒ Ⓓ Ⓔ	20. Ⓐ Ⓑ Ⓒ Ⓓ Ⓔ	30. Ⓐ Ⓑ Ⓒ Ⓓ Ⓔ	

Section 6

1. Ⓐ Ⓑ Ⓒ Ⓓ Ⓔ	11. Ⓐ Ⓑ Ⓒ Ⓓ Ⓔ	21. Ⓐ Ⓑ Ⓒ Ⓓ Ⓔ	31. Ⓐ Ⓑ Ⓒ Ⓓ Ⓔ
2. Ⓐ Ⓑ Ⓒ Ⓓ Ⓔ	12. Ⓐ Ⓑ Ⓒ Ⓓ Ⓔ	22. Ⓐ Ⓑ Ⓒ Ⓓ Ⓔ	32. Ⓐ Ⓑ Ⓒ Ⓓ Ⓔ
3. Ⓐ Ⓑ Ⓒ Ⓓ Ⓔ	13. Ⓐ Ⓑ Ⓒ Ⓓ Ⓔ	23. Ⓐ Ⓑ Ⓒ Ⓓ Ⓔ	33. Ⓐ Ⓑ Ⓒ Ⓓ Ⓔ
4. Ⓐ Ⓑ Ⓒ Ⓓ Ⓔ	14. Ⓐ Ⓑ Ⓒ Ⓓ Ⓔ	24. Ⓐ Ⓑ Ⓒ Ⓓ Ⓔ	34. Ⓐ Ⓑ Ⓒ Ⓓ Ⓔ
5. Ⓐ Ⓑ Ⓒ Ⓓ Ⓔ	15. Ⓐ Ⓑ Ⓒ Ⓓ Ⓔ	25. Ⓐ Ⓑ Ⓒ Ⓓ Ⓔ	35. Ⓐ Ⓑ Ⓒ Ⓓ Ⓔ
6. Ⓐ Ⓑ Ⓒ Ⓓ Ⓔ	16. Ⓐ Ⓑ Ⓒ Ⓓ Ⓔ	26. Ⓐ Ⓑ Ⓒ Ⓓ Ⓔ	36. Ⓐ Ⓑ Ⓒ Ⓓ Ⓔ
7. Ⓐ Ⓑ Ⓒ Ⓓ Ⓔ	17. Ⓐ Ⓑ Ⓒ Ⓓ Ⓔ	27. Ⓐ Ⓑ Ⓒ Ⓓ Ⓔ	37. Ⓐ Ⓑ Ⓒ Ⓓ Ⓔ
8. Ⓐ Ⓑ Ⓒ Ⓓ Ⓔ	18. Ⓐ Ⓑ Ⓒ Ⓓ Ⓔ	28. Ⓐ Ⓑ Ⓒ Ⓓ Ⓔ	38. Ⓐ Ⓑ Ⓒ Ⓓ Ⓔ
9. Ⓐ Ⓑ Ⓒ Ⓓ Ⓔ	19. Ⓐ Ⓑ Ⓒ Ⓓ Ⓔ	29. Ⓐ Ⓑ Ⓒ Ⓓ Ⓔ	
10. Ⓐ Ⓑ Ⓒ Ⓓ Ⓔ	20. Ⓐ Ⓑ Ⓒ Ⓓ Ⓔ	30. Ⓐ Ⓑ Ⓒ Ⓓ Ⓔ	

Section 7

1. Ⓐ Ⓑ Ⓒ Ⓓ Ⓔ	11. Ⓐ Ⓑ Ⓒ Ⓓ Ⓔ	21. Ⓐ Ⓑ Ⓒ Ⓓ Ⓔ	31. Ⓐ Ⓑ Ⓒ Ⓓ Ⓔ
2. Ⓐ Ⓑ Ⓒ Ⓓ Ⓔ	12. Ⓐ Ⓑ Ⓒ Ⓓ Ⓔ	22. Ⓐ Ⓑ Ⓒ Ⓓ Ⓔ	32. Ⓐ Ⓑ Ⓒ Ⓓ Ⓔ
3. Ⓐ Ⓑ Ⓒ Ⓓ Ⓔ	13. Ⓐ Ⓑ Ⓒ Ⓓ Ⓔ	23. Ⓐ Ⓑ Ⓒ Ⓓ Ⓔ	33. Ⓐ Ⓑ Ⓒ Ⓓ Ⓔ
4. Ⓐ Ⓑ Ⓒ Ⓓ Ⓔ	14. Ⓐ Ⓑ Ⓒ Ⓓ Ⓔ	24. Ⓐ Ⓑ Ⓒ Ⓓ Ⓔ	34. Ⓐ Ⓑ Ⓒ Ⓓ Ⓔ
5. Ⓐ Ⓑ Ⓒ Ⓓ Ⓔ	15. Ⓐ Ⓑ Ⓒ Ⓓ Ⓔ	25. Ⓐ Ⓑ Ⓒ Ⓓ Ⓔ	35. Ⓐ Ⓑ Ⓒ Ⓓ Ⓔ
6. Ⓐ Ⓑ Ⓒ Ⓓ Ⓔ	16. Ⓐ Ⓑ Ⓒ Ⓓ Ⓔ	26. Ⓐ Ⓑ Ⓒ Ⓓ Ⓔ	36. Ⓐ Ⓑ Ⓒ Ⓓ Ⓔ
7. Ⓐ Ⓑ Ⓒ Ⓓ Ⓔ	17. Ⓐ Ⓑ Ⓒ Ⓓ Ⓔ	27. Ⓐ Ⓑ Ⓒ Ⓓ Ⓔ	37. Ⓐ Ⓑ Ⓒ Ⓓ Ⓔ
8. Ⓐ Ⓑ Ⓒ Ⓓ Ⓔ	18. Ⓐ Ⓑ Ⓒ Ⓓ Ⓔ	28. Ⓐ Ⓑ Ⓒ Ⓓ Ⓔ	38. Ⓐ Ⓑ Ⓒ Ⓓ Ⓔ
9. Ⓐ Ⓑ Ⓒ Ⓓ Ⓔ	19. Ⓐ Ⓑ Ⓒ Ⓓ Ⓔ	29. Ⓐ Ⓑ Ⓒ Ⓓ Ⓔ	
10. Ⓐ Ⓑ Ⓒ Ⓓ Ⓔ	20. Ⓐ Ⓑ Ⓒ Ⓓ Ⓔ	30. Ⓐ Ⓑ Ⓒ Ⓓ Ⓔ	

Remove answer sheet by cutting on dotted line

DIAGNOSTIC TEST

SECTION 1

Time—30 minutes

38 Questions

Directions: Each sentence below has one or two blanks, each blank indicating that something has been omitted. Beneath the sentence are five lettered words or sets of words. Choose the word or set of words for each blank that best fits the meaning of the sentence as a whole.

1. Any numerical description of the development of the human population cannot avoid -------, simply because there has never been a census of all the people in the world.

   (A) analysis
   (B) conjecture
   (C) disorientation
   (D) corroboration
   (E) statistics

2. Many species of intertidal fish have developed ------- abilities that enable them to ------- a particular location, generally a tide pool, that provides suitable refuge.

   (A) foraging…do without
   (B) compensatory…aspire to
   (C) natural…vanish from
   (D) singular…escape from
   (E) homing…return to

3. There are any number of theories to explain these events and, since even the experts disagree, it is ------- the rest of us in our role as responsible scholars to ------- dogmatic statements.

   (A) paradoxical for…abstain from
   (B) arrogant of…compensate with
   (C) incumbent on…refrain from
   (D) opportune for…quarrel over
   (E) appropriate for…issue forth

4. It may be useful to think of character in fiction as a function of two ------- impulses: the impulse to individualize and the impulse to -------.

   (A) analogous…humanize
   (B) disparate…aggrandize
   (C) divergent…typify
   (D) comparable…delineate
   (E) related…moralize

5. Relatively few politicians willingly forsake center stage, although a touch of ------- on their parts now and again might well increase their popularity with the voting public.

   (A) garrulity
   (B) misanthropy
   (C) self-effacement
   (D) self-dramatization
   (E) self-doubt

6. It is this tightly circumscribed choice of scene that gives to Mrs. Woolf's novels, despite her modernity of technique and insight, their odd and delicious air of -------, as of some small village world, as bright and vivid and perfect in its ------- as a miniature.

   (A) anachronism…transience
   (B) parochialism…tininess
   (C) cynicism…rusticity
   (D) intrigue…antiquity
   (E) fragility…petiteness

7. Lacking the time to examine the treatise in its entirety, the editors asked the author to provide them with ------- instead.

   (A) a compendium
   (B) a dissertation
   (C) an elaboration
   (D) a facsimile
   (E) an exegesis

Directions: In each of the following questions, a related pair of words or phrases is followed by five lettered pairs of words or phrases. Select the lettered pair that best expresses a relationship similar to that expressed in the original pair.

8. CLASP : BRACELET ::
   (A) hook : coat
   (B) buckle : belt
   (C) diamond : ring
   (D) wrist : watch
   (E) cuff : trousers

9. SEDAN : AUTOMOBILE ::
   (A) hangar : airplane
   (B) bedspread : bed
   (C) rocker : chair
   (D) rung : ladder
   (E) marble : statue

10. CIRCUITOUS : ROUTE ::
   (A) problematic : solution
   (B) devious : argument
   (C) elliptical : brevity
   (D) judicious : selection
   (E) profound : depth

11. PARDON : OFFENSE ::
    (A) repent : sin
    (B) detect : violation
    (C) arraign : indictment
    (D) forgive : wrong
    (E) surrender : fugitive

12. NONPLUSSED : BAFFLEMENT ::
    (A) discomfited : embarrassment
    (B) parsimonious : extravagance
    (C) disgruntled : contentment
    (D) despicable : contempt
    (E) surly : harassment

13. GULLY : CANYON ::
    (A) eagle : bird
    (B) cliff : granite
    (C) pebble : boulder
    (D) detour : road
    (E) shore : lake

14. HELPFUL : OFFICIOUS ::
    (A) dutiful : assiduous
    (B) effusive : gushing
    (C) gullible : incredulous
    (D) enigmatic : dumbfounded
    (E) deferential : sycophantic

15. BRONZE : PATINA ::
    (A) wood : veneer
    (B) plaque : honor
    (C) mold : yeast
    (D) iron : rust
    (E) lead : tin

16. MELLIFLUOUS : CACOPHONY ::
    (A) dulcet : euphony
    (B) compliant : obsequiousness
    (C) fragrant : noisesomeness
    (D) florid : embellishment
    (E) thrifty : parsimony

Directions: Each passage in this group is followed by questions based on its content. After reading a passage, choose the best answer to each question. Answer all questions following a passage on the basis of what is stated or implied in that passage.

James's first novels used conventional narrative techniques: explicit characterization, action which related events in distinctly phased sequences, settings firmly outlined and specifically described. But this method gradually gave way to a subtler, more deliberate, more diffuse style of accumulation of minutely discriminated details whose total significance the reader can grasp only by constant attention and sensitive inference. His later novels play down scenes of abrupt and prominent action, and do not so much offer a succession of sharp shocks as slow piecemeal additions of perception. The curtain is not suddenly drawn back from shrouded things, but is slowly moved away.

Such a technique is suited to James's essential subject, which is not human action itself but the states of mind which produce and are produced by human actions and interactions. James was less interested in what characters do, than in the moral and psychological antecedents, realizations, and consequences which attend their doings. This is why he more often speaks of "cases" than of actions. His stories, therefore, grow more and more lengthy while the actions they relate grow simpler and less visible; not because they are crammed with adventitious and secondary events, digressive relief, or supernumerary characters, as overstuffed novels of action are; but because he presents in such exhaustive detail every nuance of his situation. Commonly the interest of a novel is in the variety and excitement of visible actions building up to a climactic event which will settle the outward destinies of characters with storybook promise of permanence. A James novel, however, possesses its characteristic interest in carrying the reader through a rich analysis of the mental adjustments of characters to the realities of their personal situations as they are slowly revealed to them through exploration and chance discovery.

17. The passage supplies information for answering which of the following questions?

    (A) Did James originate the so-called psychological novel?
    (B) Is conventional narrative technique strictly chronological in recounting action?
    (C) Can novels lacking overtly dramatic incident sustain the reader's interest?
    (D) Were James's later novels more acceptable to the general public than his earlier ones?
    (E) Is James unique in his predilection for exploring psychological nuances of character?

18. According to the passage, James's later novels differ from his earlier ones in their

    (A) preoccupation with specifically described settings
    (B) ever-increasing concision and tautness of plot
    (C) levels of moral and psychological complexity
    (D) development of rising action to a climax
    (E) subordination of psychological exploration to dramatic effect

19. The author's attitude towards the novel of action appears to be one of

    (A) pointed indignation
    (B) detached neutrality
    (C) scathing derision
    (D) strong partisanship
    (E) decided disapprobation

The theory of plate tectonics describes the motions of the lithosphere, the comparatively rigid outer layer of the earth that includes all the crust and part of the underlying mantle. The lithosphere is divided into a few dozen plates of various sizes and shapes; in general the plates are in motion with respect to one another. A mid-ocean ridge is a boundary between plates where new lithospheric material is injected from below. As the plates diverge from a mid-ocean ridge they slide on a more yielding layer at the base of the lithosphere.

Since the size of the earth is essentially constant, new lithosphere can be created at the mid-ocean ridges only if an equal amount of lithospheric material is consumed elsewhere. The site of this destruction is another kind of plate boundary: a subduction zone. There one plate dives under another and is reincorporated into the mantle. Both kinds of plate boundary are associated with fault systems, earthquakes and volcanism, but the kinds of geologic activity observed at the two boundaries are quite different.

The idea of sea-floor spreading actually preceded the theory of plate tectonics. The sea-floor spreading hypothesis was formulated chiefly by Harry H. Hess of Princeton University in the early 1960s. In its original version it described the creation and destruction of ocean floor, but it did not specify rigid lithospheric plates. The hypothesis was soon substantiated by the discovery that periodic reversals of the earth's magnetic field are recorded in the oceanic crust. An explanation of this process devised by F.J. Vine and D.H. Matthews of Princeton is now generally accepted. As magma rises under the mid-ocean ridge, ferromagnetic minerals in the magma become magnetized in the direction of the geomagnetic field. When the magma cools and solidifies, the direction and the polarity of the field are preserved in the magnetized volcanic rock. Reversals of the field give rise to a series of magnetic stripes running parallel to the axis of the rift. The oceanic crust thus serves as a magnetic tape recording of the history of the geomagnetic field. Because the boundaries between stripes are associated with reversals of the magnetic field that can be dated independently, the width of the stripes indicates the rate of sea-floor spreading. (Precisely how the earth's magnetic field reverses at intervals of from 10,000 to about a million years continues to be one of the great mysteries of geology.)

It follows from the theory of sea-floor spreading that many of the most interesting geologic features of the earth's surface are to be found on the ocean floor. The investigation of such features has been furthered in recent years by the development of deep-diving manned submersibles. In particular the U.S. research submersible *Alvin*, operated by the Woods Hole Oceanographic Institution, has proved to be a valuable tool for studies of the sea bed. A geologist in the *Alvin* can collect rock samples and document in detail the setting of each rock. For the first time a marine geologist can have maps of a site as precise as those of a geologist on land.

20. The author's primary purpose in the passage is to

(A) question established data
(B) describe current explorations
(C) trace the development of a theory
(D) propose an alternative solution
(E) explain the reasons behind a phenomenon

21. The passage would be most likely to appear in a

(A) congressional report advocating the continued funding of oceanographic studies
(B) geological research report focused on the likelihood of volcanism along coastal regions
(C) pamphlet designed to acquaint visitors to Woods Hole with the capabilities of deep-diving manned submersibles
(D) scholarly monograph proposing an explanation for the periodic reversals of the earth's magnetic field
(E) scientific journal article summarizing recent advances in applying plate tectonic theory to marine geology

22. According to the passage, a mid-ocean ridge differs from a subduction zone in that

(A) it marks the boundary line between neighboring plates
(B) only the former is located on the ocean floor
(C) it is a site for the emergence of new lithospheric material
(D) the former periodically disrupts the earth's geomagnetic field
(E) it is involved with lithospheric destruction rather than lithospheric creation

23. It can be inferred from the passage that as new lithospheric material is injected from below

(A) the plates become immobilized in a kind of gridlock
(B) it is incorporated into an underwater mountain ridge
(C) the earth's total mass is altered
(D) it reverses its magnetic polarity
(E) the immediately adjacent plates sink

24. The passage contains information that would answer which of the following questions about the theory of sea-floor spreading and the history of the geomagnetic field?

I.   What is the minimum known time span between reversals of the earth's magnetic field?
II. What mechanism is responsible for the magnetic field's changes in polarity?
III. Can the pace of sea-floor spreading be determined from current geomagnetic data?

(A) I only
(B) III only
(C) I and II only
(D) I and III only
(E) I, II, and III

25. It can be inferred from the passage that a large increase in the creation of new lithospheric material would result in

    (A) at least a slight decrease in activity along the subduction zones
    (B) at the most a slight increase in activity along the subduction zones
    (C) a correspondingly large increase in activity along the subduction zones
    (D) a cessation of activity along the subduction zones
    (E) no change in the level of activity along the subduction zones

26. According to the passage, lithospheric material at the site of a subduction zone

    (A) rises and is polarized
    (B) sinks and is absorbed
    (C) slides and is injected
    (D) spreads and is reincorporated
    (E) diverges and is consumed

27. The passage most directly suggests that, before the recent underwater explorations involving manned submersibles were undertaken, marine geologists

    (A) were negligent in making charts of undersea sites
    (B) underestimated the importance of the lithospheric plates
    (C) labored under a disadvantage compared to land geologists
    (D) had adequate access to those portions of the sea bed under study
    (E) were ignorant of the sea-floor spreading hypothesis

Directions: Each question below consists of a word printed in capital letters, followed by five lettered words or phrases. Choose the lettered word or phrase that is most nearly opposite in meaning to the word in capital letters.

Since some of the questions require you to distinguish fine shades of meaning, be sure to consider all the choices before deciding which one is best.

28. DETERIORATE:
    (A) hasten
    (B) demolish
    (C) alter
    (D) unify
    (E) improve

29. EVASIVE:
    (A) frank
    (B) serene
    (C) pensive
    (D) mistaken
    (E) exuberant

30. STREW:
    (A) deflate
    (B) collect
    (C) weaken
    (D) cleanse
    (E) bolster

31. PRODIGAL:
    (A) nomad
    (B) sycophant
    (C) gifted child
    (D) economical person
    (E) antagonist

32. EQUIVOCATE:
    (A) yield
    (B) distinguish
    (C) condescend
    (D) pledge
    (E) denounce

33. CRASS:
    (A) small
    (B) refined
    (C) cheerful
    (D) modest
    (E) liberal

34. ARTIFICE:
    (A) edifice
    (B) sincerity
    (C) prejudice
    (D) creativity
    (E) affirmation

35. OPULENCE:
    (A) transience
    (B) penury
    (C) solitude
    (D) generosity
    (E) transparency

36. UNTENABLE:
    (A) false
    (B) precise
    (C) circumscribed
    (D) defensible
    (E) hypothetical

37. SEDULOUS:
    (A) pointless
    (B) weighty
    (C) lugubrious
    (D) cursory
    (E) tangential

38. DISABUSE:
    (A) maltreat
    (B) violate
    (C) cancel
    (D) deceive
    (E) involve

S T O P

IF YOU FINISH BEFORE TIME IS CALLED, YOU MAY CHECK YOUR WORK ON THIS SECTION ONLY.
DO NOT WORK ON ANY OTHER SECTION IN THE TEST.

SECTION 2

Time—30 minutes

38 Questions

Directions: Each sentence below has one or two blanks, each blank indicating that something has been omitted. Beneath the sentence are five lettered words or sets of words. Choose the word or set of words for each blank that best fits the meaning of the sentence as a whole.

1. There was so much ------- material in the argument, ideas dragged in without reference to the case, that it was singularly ------- to get the budding lawyer's point.

    (A) exceptional...unrewarding
    (B) variegated...effortless
    (C) hypothetical...superfluous
    (D) superficial...irrelevant
    (E) extraneous...difficult

2. Since the propensity to migrate has persisted in every epoch, its explanation requires a theory ------- any particular period of time.

    (A) tailored to
    (B) unconscious of
    (C) inapplicable to
    (D) independent of
    (E) anomalous in

3. The earth is a planet bathed in light; it is therefore ------- that many of the living organisms that have evolved on the earth have ------- the biologically advantageous capacity to trap light energy.

    (A) anomalous...engendered
    (B) unsurprising...developed
    (C) predictable...forfeited
    (D) problematic...exhibited
    (E) expectable...relinquished

4. According to one optimistic hypothesis, the dense concentration of entrepreneurs and services in the cities would incubate new functions, ------- them, and finally export them to other areas, and so the cities, forever breeding fresh ideas, would ------- themselves repeatedly.

    (A) immunize...perpetuate
    (B) isolate...revitalize
    (C) foster...deplete
    (D) spawn...imitate
    (E) nurture...renew

5. Man is a ------- animal, and much more so in his mind than in his body: he may like to go alone for a walk, but he hates to stand alone in his -------.

    (A) gregarious...opinions
    (B) conceited...vanity
    (C) singular...uniqueness
    (D) solitary...thoughts
    (E) nomadic...footsteps

6. Although Mrs. Proudie ------- an interest in the spiritual well-being of the parishioners, in actuality her concern for their welfare was so ------- as to be practically nonexistent.

    (A) confessed...circumstantial
    (B) manifested...exemplary
    (C) simulated...profound
    (D) feigned...negligible
    (E) expressed...moribund

7. The term *baroque*, originally applied to the lavishly and grotesquely ornamented style of architecture that succeeded the Renaissance, is used generally in literary criticism to describe excessive or grandiloquent works that lack ------- of style.

    (A) diversity
    (B) economy
    (C) prolixity
    (D) adornment
    (E) comprehension

Directions: In each of the following questions, a related pair of words or phrases is followed by five lettered pairs of words or phrases. Select the lettered pair that best expresses a relationship similar to that expressed in the original pair.

8. PROLOGUE : PLAY ::
    (A) chapter : novel
    (B) overture : opera
    (C) intermezzo : symphony
    (D) epilogue : oration
    (E) gesture : pantomime

9. SERRATIONS : SAW ::
    (A) incisions : scalpel
    (B) butchery : cleaver
    (C) mortar : trowel
    (D) cogs : gear
    (E) division : ruler

10. SPIKE : SLEDGE ::
    (A) runner : sleigh
    (B) pole : ski
    (C) nail : hammer
    (D) clip : paper
    (E) trestle : train

11. THIRST : DRIVE ::
    (A) inebriety : excess
    (B) success : ambition
    (C) indifference : passion
    (D) taste : gusto
    (E) smell : sense

12. EPHEMERAL : PERMANENCE ::
    (A) erratic : predictability
    (B) immaculate : cleanliness
    (C) commendable : reputation
    (D) spurious : emulation
    (E) mandatory : obedience

13. CHAFF : WHEAT ::
    (A) mote : dust
    (B) gold : lead
    (C) dregs : wine
    (D) loaf : bread
    (E) yolk : egg

14. OGLE : OBSERVE ::
    (A) haggle : outbid
    (B) clamor : dispute

(C) discern : perceive
(D) flaunt : display
(E) glare : glower

15. ABSTEMIOUS : ABSTINENCE ::
    (A) irascible : militancy
    (B) gregarious : reticence
    (C) truculent : dogmatism
    (D) comatose : sobriety
    (E) pusillanimous : cravenness

16. INELUCTABLE : AVOID ::
    (A) ineffable : utter
    (B) impalpable : desire
    (C) impermeable : endure
    (D) irascible : provoke
    (E) irreconcilable : estrange

Directions: Each passage in this group is followed by questions based on its content. After reading a passage, choose the best answer to each question. Answer all questions following a passage on the basis of what is stated or implied in that passage.

During the decade of 1880–1890 it was becoming increasingly evident that the factors which had brought about the existence of two separate suffrage institutions were steadily diminishing in (5) importance.

The National Woman Suffrage Association had been launched by the intellectually irrepressible Elizabeth Cady Stanton and the ever catholic Susan B. Anthony. Both were ready to work with any-(10) one, whatever their views on other matters, as long as they wholeheartedly espoused woman suffrage. Consequently in its earlier years the National was both aggressive and unorthodox. It damned both Republicans and Democrats who brushed the suf-(15) frage question aside. It was willing to take up the cudgels for distressed women whatever their circumstances, be they "fallen women," divorce cases, or underpaid seamstresses.

The American Woman Suffrage Association, by (20) contrast, took its tone and outlook from a New England which had turned its back on those fiery days when abolitionists, men and women alike, had stood up to angry mobs. Its advocacy of worthy causes was highly selective. Lucy Stone was not (25) interested in trade unionism and wished to keep the suffrage cause untarnished by concern with divorce or "the social evil." The very epitome of the American's attitude was its most distinguished convert and leader, Julia Ward Howe – erudite, honored (30) lay preacher, the revered author of "The Battle Hymn of the Republic," who cast a highly desirable aura of prestige and propriety over the women's cause.

It was not that Mrs. Howe in herself made suf-(35) frage respectable; she was a symbol of the forces that were drawing the suffrage movement into the camp of decorum. American society was becoming

rapidly polarized. The middle class was learning to identify organized labor with social turmoil. A (40) succession of strikes during the depression of 1873–1878, in textiles, mining, and railroads, culminated in the Great Railroad Strike of 1877 involving nearly 100,000 workers from the Atlantic coast to the Mississippi valley; they did not help (45) to reassure women taught by press and pulpit to identify any type of militancy with radicalism. Nor was this trend allayed by the hysteria whipped up over the Molly Maguire trials for secret conspiracy among Pennsylvania coal miners, or the alleged (50) communistic influences at work in such growing organizations as the Knights of Labor and the A.F. of L. The existence of a small number of socialists was used to smear all organized labor with the taint of "anarchism." The crowning touch took place (55) during the widespread agitation for an eight-hour day in 1886 when a bomb, thrown by a hand unknown to this day into a radical meeting in Chicago's Haymarket Square, touched off a nationwide wave of panic.

(60)   The steady trend of the suffrage movement toward the conservative and the conventional during the last twenty years of the nineteenth century must be viewed in this setting, in order to avoid the misconception that a few conservative women took (65) it over, through their own superior ability and the passivity of the former militants. Even the latter were changing their views, judging by their actions. It was one thing to challenge the proprieties at the Centennial of 1876; ten years later it (70) would have been inconceivable even to the women who took part in the demonstration. Susan Anthony herself would have thought twice about flouting Federal election laws and going to jail in an era which witnessed the Haymarket hysteria.

17. The author's primary purpose in the passage is to

    (A) contrast Susan B. Anthony with Julia Ward Howe
    (B) recount the advances in the suffrage movement from 1880–1890
    (C) account for the changes occurring in the suffrage movement from 1880–1890
    (D) explain the growing divisions within the women's movement
    (E) point out aspects of the suffrage movement which exist in contemporary feminism

18. Which of the following statements is most compatible with the early principles of the National as described in the passage?

    (A) Advocates of suffrage should maintain their distance from socially embarrassing "allies."
    (B) Marital and economic issues are inappropriate concerns for the suffrage movement.
    (C) Propriety of behavior should characterize representatives of the women's cause.
    (D) A nominal espousal of woman suffrage is worthy of suffragist support.
    (E) The concerns of all afflicted women are the concerns of the suffrage movement.

19. The passage singles out Julia Ward Howe as an example of

    (A) a venerated figurehead
    (B) an overzealous advocate
    (C) a heterodox thinker
    (D) an ordained cleric
    (E) a militant activist

20. Which of the following titles best describes the content of the passage?

    (A) Trade Unionism and the Suffrage Movement
    (B) Egalitarianism at the Close of the Nineteenth Century
    (C) Rifts in the Woman Suffrage Movement
    (D) Diminution of Radicalism in the Woman Suffrage Movement
    (E) Political Polarization in American Society

21. The author's attitude toward the public reaction to the Molly Maguire trials is that the reaction was

    (A) appropriate
    (B) disorganized
    (C) overwrought
    (D) necessary
    (E) understated

22. As used in the passage, the phrase "ever catholic" (line 8) refers primarily to Anthony's

    (A) deep religious beliefs
    (B) inclusive sympathies
    (C) willingness to work
    (D) wholehearted feminism
    (E) parochial outlook

23. The author stresses the growing anti-radical bias of the American middle class during the decade 1880–1890 in order to

    (A) question a trend that proved destructive to the suffrage movement
    (B) explain the unexpected emergence of an able body of conservative leaders
    (C) refute the contention that Anthony was unchanged by her experiences
    (D) correct a misapprehension about changes in the suffrage movement
    (E) excuse the growing lack of militancy on the part of the National

24. The passage suggests that, by 1890, attempts to effect woman suffrage by violating the proprieties and defying Federal laws would probably have been viewed even by movement members with

    (A) indifference
    (B) defiance
    (C) disapprobation
    (D) respect
    (E) optimism

Mimicry, in plants or in animals, is a three-part system. There is a model: the animal, plant or substrate being imitated. There is a mimic: the organism that imitates the model. And there is a signal receiver or dupe: the animal that cannot effectively distinguish between the model and the mimic. Mimetic traits may include morphological structures, color patterns, behaviors or other attributes of the mimic that promote its resemblance to a model. That model may be either an unrelated species or an inanimate object, such as the background against which an organism spends most of its time.

Mimicry is not an active strategy on the part of an individual plant; flowers do not deliberately trick or deceive animals into visiting them. Mimicry arises as the result of evolution through natural selection and the occurrence of random mutations that lead over many generations to the appearance of favorable characteristics. If such genetically based traits help to camouflage a plant, for example, the plant is likely to have a survival advantage over other plants that are less well camouflaged. The plant will leave more descendants, thereby passing the advantage to the next generation. For natural selection to favor the evolution of mimicry, the mimic must derive a reproductive advantage from modeling itself after another organism or object; its fitness, measured as the number of offspring produced that survive into the next generation, must be increased as the result of deception.

25. The passage provides an answer to which of the following questions?

    (A) Which mimetic trait is most effective in providing plants with a reproductive advantage?
    (B) How does plant mimicry differ from animal mimicry?

(C) To what degree is animal mimicry under voluntary control?

(D) Can dupes be trained to discriminate between the mimic and the model?

(E) In natural selection, what is the measure of a plant or animal's fitness?

26. The author would regard as examples of evolutionary mimicry all of the following EXCEPT

(A) a chameleon adapting to the coloration of a mountain ledge

(B) a harmless butterfly whose coloration matches that of an exceptionally poisonous species

(C) a plant whose appearance imitates that of a nearby nectar-producing species

(D) a kit fox imitating the hunting tactics of its mother

(E) an orchid that emits a scent like the sex pheromone of a female insect

27. It can be inferred that camouflaging a plant most likely increases its potential for survival by

(A) attracting pollinators to its vicinity

(B) lessening its visibility to predators

(C) increasing its rate of random mutation

(D) enhancing its secretion of nectar

(E) depleting its number of offspring

Directions: Each question below consists of a word printed in capital letters, followed by five lettered words or phrases. Choose the lettered word or phrase that is most nearly opposite in meaning to the word in capital letters.

Since some of the questions require you to distinguish fine shades of meaning, be sure to consider all the choices before deciding which one is best.

28. TERMINATE:
(A) depart
(B) prevent
(C) begin
(D) hasten
(E) change

29. PROTRACT:
(A) abbreviate
(B) distract
(C) reject
(D) stabilize
(E) oppose

30. VOLUBILITY:
(A) shabbiness
(B) brevity
(C) disparity
(D) subtlety
(E) lucidity

31. LATE-BLOOMING:
(A) flourishing
(B) blatant
(C) punctilious
(D) embryonic
(E) precocious

32. HONE:
(A) broaden
(B) twist
(C) dull
(D) weld
(E) break

33. PHLEGMATIC:
(A) dogmatic
(B) ardent
(C) haphazard
(D) self-assured
(E) abstracted

34. BANALITY:
(A) tentative interpretation
(B) concise summation
(C) accurate delineation
(D) laudatory remark
(E) novel expression

35. ERUDITE:
(A) unhealthy
(B) ignorant
(C) impolite
(D) indifferent
(E) imprecise

36. PLETHORA:
(A) despair
(B) denial
(C) avarice
(D) aversion
(E) scarcity

37. CURRENCY:
(A) refractoriness
(B) obsolescence
(C) artificiality
(D) insolvency
(E) fluency

38. SKIRT:
(A) embroider
(B) revert
(C) address
(D) disport
(E) brook

S T O P

IF YOU FINISH BEFORE TIME IS CALLED, YOU MAY CHECK YOUR WORK ON THIS SECTION ONLY.
DO NOT WORK ON ANY OTHER SECTION IN THE TEST.

SECTION 3

Time—30 minutes

30 Questions

Numbers: All numbers used are real numbers.

Figures: Position of points, angles, regions, etc. can be assumed to be in the order shown; and angle measures can be assumed to be positive.

Lines shown as straight can be assumed to be straight.

Figures can be assumed to lie in a plane unless otherwise indicated.

Figures that accompany questions are intended to provide information useful in answering the questions. However, unless a note states that a figure is drawn to scale, you should solve these problems NOT by estimating sizes by sight or by measurement, but by using your knowledge of mathematics (see Example 2 below).

Directions: Each of the <u>Questions 1–15</u> consists of two quantities, one in Column A and one in Column B. You are to compare the two quantities and choose

  A if the quantity in Column A is greater;
  B if the quantity in Column B is greater;
  C if the two quantities are equal;
  D if the relationship cannot be determined from the information given.

Note: Since there are only four choices, NEVER MARK (E).

Common Information: In a question, information concerning one or both of the quantities to be compared is centered above the two columns. A symbol that appears in both columns represents the same thing in Column A as it does in Column B.

	Column A	Column B	Sample Answers
Example 1:	2×6	$2 + 6$	● Ⓑ Ⓒ Ⓓ Ⓔ

Examples 2-4 refer to $\triangle PQR$.

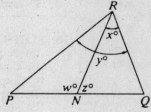

	Column A	Column B	Sample Answers
Example 2:	PN	NQ	Ⓐ Ⓑ Ⓒ ● Ⓔ
			(since equal measures cannot be assumed, even though PN and NQ appear equal)
Example 3:	x	y	Ⓐ ● Ⓒ Ⓓ Ⓔ
			(since N is between P and Q)
Example 4:	$w + z$	180	Ⓐ Ⓑ ● Ⓓ Ⓔ
			(since PQ is a straight line)

A if the quantity in Column A is greater;
B if the quantity in Column B is greater;
C if the two quantities are equal;
D if the relationship cannot be determined from the information given.

Column A	Column B

$$n > 1$$

1. $\dfrac{n + 7}{3} + \dfrac{n - 3}{4}$ $\dfrac{7n + 19}{7}$

$$.1y + .01y = 2.2$$

2. $.1y$ 20

---

3. Reciprocal of 4 $\sqrt{\dfrac{1}{16}}$

---

4. 120 $\sqrt{1440}$

---

5. 3 feet, 5 inches   1.5 yards

$$x = 6 + 7 + 8 + 9 + 10$$
$$y = 5 + 6 + 7 + 8 + 9$$

6. $5(15)$ $x + y$

In this multiplication problem each symbol represents a digit. Assume that the multiplication process is correct.

$$\begin{array}{r} 5678 \\ \times\ 73 \\ \hline 170\triangle4 \\ 3974\bigcirc \\ \hline 414494 \end{array}$$

7. value of $\triangle$ value of $\bigcirc$

Sam is older than Mary and Mary is younger than Rose.

8. Sam's age   Rose's age

$$4x = 4(14) - 4$$

9. x 14

Column A	Column B

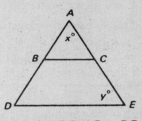

In triangle ABC, $AC = BC$
$BC \parallel DE$ and $x = 65$

10. x y

Area of $ABC = 20$ in^2
$AD = 5$ inches and $AD \perp BC$

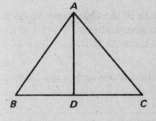

11. 4 inches   Length of DC

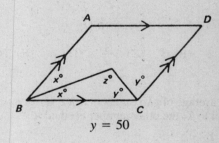

$$y = 50$$

12. $z - y$ 40

Joan covered 36 miles in 45 minutes.

13. Joan's average speed
    (in miles per hour)   48 miles per hour

A if the quantity in Column A is greater;
B if the quantity in Column B is greater;
C if the two quantities are equal;
D if the relationship cannot be determined from the information given.

Column A	Column B

$$a > b > c > d > 0$$

14. $a - d$ $b - c$

Column A	Column B

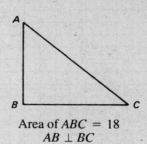

Area of $ABC = 18$
$AB \perp BC$

15.   Length of AB Length of BC

Directions: Each of the Questions 16–30 has five answer choices. For each of these questions, select the best of the answer choices given.

16. Which of the following has the largest numerical value?

    (A) $\frac{8}{.8}$ (B) $\frac{.8}{8}$ (C) $(.8)^2$ (D) $\sqrt{.8}$ (E) 0.8π

17. If $17xy + 7 = 19xy$, then $4xy =$

    (A) 2   (B) 3   (C) $3\frac{1}{2}$ (D) 7   (E) 14

18. The average of two numbers is XY. If one number is equal to X, the other number is equal to

    (A) Y
    (B) $2Y$
    (C) $XY - X$
    (D) $2XY - X$
    (E) $XY - 2X$

19. A snapshot $1\frac{7}{8}$ inches $\times$ $2\frac{1}{2}$ inches is to be enlarged so that the longer dimension will be 4 inches. What will be the length (in inches) of the shorter dimension?

    (A) $2\frac{3}{8}$ (B) $2\frac{1}{2}$ (C) 3   (D) $3\frac{3}{8}$ (E) $3\frac{1}{2}$

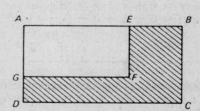

20. The length and width of rectangle $AEFG$ are each $\frac{2}{3}$ of the corresponding parts of $ABCD$. $AEB = 12$; $AGD = 6$. The area of the shaded part is

    (A) 24
    (B) 32
    (C) 36
    (D) 40
    (E) 48

Questions 21–25 refer to the following graphs.

HOMETOWN SAVINGS BANK

Number of Depositors
(in thousands)

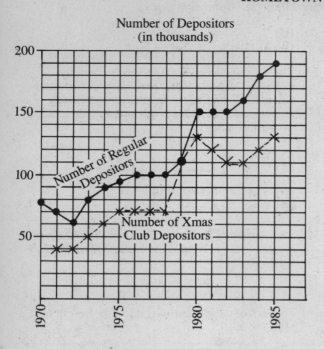

How the Savings Bank Puts
Your Money to Work For You

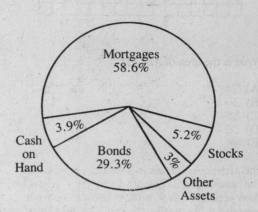

21. How many thousands of regular depositors did the bank have in 1975?

    (A) 70   (B) 85   (C) 95   (D) 100   (E) 950

22. In 1974 what was the ratio of the number of Xmas Club depositors to the number of regular depositors?

    (A) $\frac{2}{3}$ (B) $\frac{2}{1}$ (C) $\frac{1}{2}$ (D) $\frac{7}{9}$ (E) $\frac{3}{2}$

23. In which of the following years was there the greatest increase in the number of Xmas Club depositors over the previous year?

    (A) 1974
    (B) 1979
    (C) 1980
    (D) 1983
    (E) 1985

24. About how many degrees (to the nearest degree) are in the angle of the sector representing mortgages?

    (A) 59   (B) 106   (C) 211   (D) 246   (E) 318

25. The average annual interest on mortgage investments is m percent and the average annual interest on the bond investment is b percent. If the annual interest on the bond investment is x dollars, how many dollars are invested in mortgages?

    (A) $\frac{xm}{b}$

    (B) $\frac{xb}{m}$

    (C) $\frac{100xb}{m}$

    (D) $\frac{bx}{100m}$

    (E) $\frac{200x}{b}$

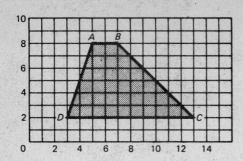

26. What is the area of *ABCD*?

(A) 24
(B) 30
(C) 35
(D) 36
(E) 48

27. The afternoon classes in a school begin at 1:00 P.M. and end at 3:52 P.M. There are 4 afternoon class periods with 4 minutes allowed between periods for passing to classes. The number of minutes in each class period is

(A) 39
(B) 40
(C) 43
(D) 45
(E) 59

28. If $x^2 + 2x - 8 = 0$, then x is either -4 or

(A) -2
(B) -1
(C) 0
(D) 2
(E) 8

29. The distance between two points is correctly expressed as either 720 statute miles or 630 nautical miles. Which of the following most closely approximates the value of one statute mile in terms of nautical miles?

(A) 0.88
(B) 0.89
(C) 0.90
(D) 1.14
(E) 1.25

30. The average of P numbers is x, and the average of N numbers is y. What is the average of all the $(P + N)$ numbers?

(A) $\dfrac{x + y}{2}$

(B) $x + y$

(C) $\dfrac{Py + Nx}{xy(P + N)}$

(D) $\dfrac{x + y}{P + N}$

(E) $\dfrac{Px + Ny}{P + N}$

S T O P

IF YOU FINISH BEFORE TIME IS CALLED, YOU MAY CHECK YOUR WORK ON THIS SECTION ONLY.
DO NOT WORK ON ANY OTHER SECTION IN THE TEST.

SECTION 4

Time—30 minutes

30 Questions

Numbers: All numbers used are real numbers.

Figures: Position of points, angles, regions, etc. can be assumed to be in the order shown; and angle measures can be assumed to be positive.

Lines shown as straight can be assumed to be straight.

Figures can be assumed to lie in a plane unless otherwise indicated.

Figures that accompany questions are intended to provide information useful in answering the questions. However, unless a note states that a figure is drawn to scale, you should solve these problems NOT by estimating sizes by sight or by measurement, but by using your knowledge of mathematics (see Example 2 below).

Directions: Each of the Questions 1–15 consists of two quantities, one in Column A and one in Column B. You are to compare the two quantities and choose

> A if the quantity in Column A is greater;
> B if the quantity in Column B is greater;
> C if the two quantities are equal;
> D if the relationship cannot be determined from the information given.

Note: Since there are only four choices, NEVER MARK (E).

Common
Information: In a question, information concerning one or both of the quantities to be compared is centered above the two columns. A symbol that appears in both columns represents the same thing in Column A as it does in Column B.

Column A	Column B	Sample Answers

Example 1: 2×6 $2 + 6$ ● Ⓑ Ⓒ Ⓓ Ⓔ

Examples 2-4 refer to $\triangle PQR$.

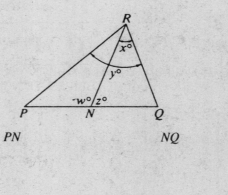

Example 2: PN NQ Ⓐ Ⓑ Ⓒ ● Ⓔ

(since equal measures cannot be assumed, even though PN and NQ appear equal)

Example 3: x y Ⓐ ● Ⓒ Ⓓ Ⓔ

(since N is between P and Q)

Example 4: $w + z$ 180   Ⓐ Ⓑ ● Ⓓ Ⓔ

(since PQ is a straight line)

A if the quantity in Column A is greater;
B if the quantity in Column B is greater;
C if the two quantities are equal;
D if the relationship cannot be determined from the information given.

Column A	Column B

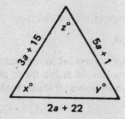

$$x = y = z$$

1. $\quad a \qquad\qquad\qquad 7$

---

2. The number of integers from -5 to $+5$ | The number of integers from $+5$ to $+15$

$$x - y = 7$$

3. $\quad x + y \qquad\qquad\qquad 14$

The area of square $ABCD$ is 25.

4. $\quad AB + BC + CD \qquad\qquad 20$

The area of isosceles right triangle ABC is 18.

5. Length of leg AB | Length of hypotenuse AC

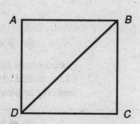

This concerns #6 and #7.

$ABCD$ is a square   Diagonal $BD = 6\sqrt{2}$

6. Perimeter of $ABCD$ $\qquad\qquad 24$

---

7. Area of ABD $\qquad\qquad\qquad 18$

Column A	Column B

In triangle ABC, $AB = BC$, and the measure of angle B = the measure of angle C.

8. The measure of angle B + the measure of angle C | The measure of angle B + the measure of angle A

$$x = 0.5$$

9. $\quad 4x \qquad\qquad\qquad x^4$

$$x > 1$$

10. $\quad \dfrac{x}{1 - x} \qquad\qquad \dfrac{1}{x - 1}$

The perimeter of triangle ABC = the perimeter of triangle DEF.

11. Area of triangle ABC | Area of triangle DEF

The sum of five consecutive integers is 35.

12. The value of the greatest of these integers $\qquad\qquad 9$

---

13. $\quad \sqrt{160} \qquad\qquad\qquad 3\sqrt{10}$

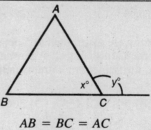

$$AB = BC = AC$$

14. $\quad 2x \qquad\qquad\qquad y$

The gasoline tank is two-thirds full with 12 gallons of gasoline.

15. The capacity of this tank | 20 gallons

Directions: Each of the Questions 16-30 has five answer choices. For each of these questions, select the best of the answer choices given.

---

16. If four cows produce 4 cans of milk in 4 days, how many days does it take eight cows to produce 8 cans of milk?

    (A) 1   (B) 2   (C) 4   (D) 8   (E) 16

17. A quart of alcohol containing $\frac{1}{2}$ pint of pure alcohol is diluted by the addition of $1\frac{1}{2}$ pints of distilled water. How much pure alcohol is contained in the diluted alcohol?

    (A) $\frac{1}{2}$ pint

    (B) $1\frac{1}{2}$ pints

    (C) 2 pints

    (D) 3 pints

    (E) $3\frac{1}{2}$ pints

18. If 20 teachers out of a faculty of 80 are transferred, what percentage of the original faculty remains?

    (A) 4   (B) 16   (C) 25   (D) 60   (E) 75

19. The total weight of three children is 152 pounds and 4 ounces. The average weight is 50 pounds and

    (A) $\frac{1}{3}$ pound

    (B) $\frac{1}{2}$ pound

    (C) $1\frac{1}{3}$ ounces

    (D) 8 ounces

    (E) 12 ounces

20. Thirty prizes were distributed to 5 percent of the original entrants in a contest. Assuming one prize per person, the number of entrants in this contest was

    (A) 15   (B) 60   (C) 150   (D) 300   (E) 600

Questions 21–25 refer to the following chart and graph.

CALORIES

Composition of Average Diet

	Grams	Calories
Carbohydrates	500	2,050
Protein	100	410
Fat	100	930

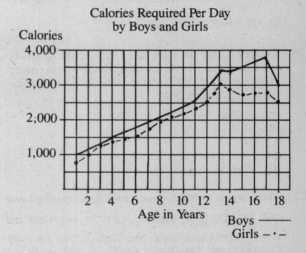

Calories Required Per Day by Boys and Girls

Boys ———
Girls – · –

21. How many calories are there in 1 gram of carbohydrate?

    (A) .2   (B) 2   (C) 4.1   (D) 10.25   (E) 1,025

22. What percent (to the nearest %) of the total calories in the average diet is derived from proteins?

    (A) 12   (B) 14   (C) 22   (D) 27   (E) 32

23. How many grams of carbohydrate (to the nearest gram) are needed to yield as many calories as 1,000 grams of fat? .

    (A) 1,110
    (B) 2,050
    (C) 2,268
    (D) 4,100
    (E) 4,536

24. Approximately how many more calories per day are required by boys than girls at age 17?

    (A)   800
    (B) 1,000
    (C) 2,500
    (D) 3,500
    (E) 4,000

25. On the basis of the graph it may be assumed that, in general, calorie requirements for boys and girls

    (A) are quite similar until age 17
    (B) are wholly dissimilar
    (C) reach their peak at about the same age
    (D) have a similar rate of increase until after age 12 to 13
    (E) are different until age 12

26. To cross a ferry the total cost T is 50 cents for the car and driver and c cents for each additional passenger in the car. What is the total cost for a car with n persons in the automobile?

    (A) $n + c$
    (B) $50 + nc$
    (C) cn
    (D) $50 + c(n - 1)$
    (E) $50 + (n + 1)c$

27. Gloria wants to make some candy using a recipe that calls for $1\frac{1}{2}$ cups of sugar, $\frac{1}{2}$ cup of boiling water and several other ingredients. She finds that she has only 1 cup of sugar. How much water will she have to use?

    (A) $\frac{1}{6}$ cup

    (B) $\frac{1}{4}$ cup

    (C) $\frac{1}{3}$ cup

    (D) $\frac{3}{4}$ cup

    (E) 1 cup

28. How many pounds of baggage are allowed for a plane passenger if the European regulations permit 20 kilograms per passenger? (1 kg = 2.2 lb)

    (A) 11   (B) 44   (C) 88   (D) 91   (E) 440

29. Which of the following statements are always true? (a, b, and c are real and not equal to zero.)

    I. $\frac{1}{a}$ is less than a

    II. $\frac{a + b}{2a}$ equals $\frac{2b}{b + a}$ when a equals b

    III. $\frac{a + c}{b + c}$ is more than $\frac{a}{b}$

    (A) II only
    (B) I and II only
    (C) I and III only
    (D) II and III only
    (E) I, II, and III

30. If $\dfrac{y}{s - t} = \dfrac{s + t}{t - s}$, then $y =$

    (A) $-s - t$
    (B) $t - s$
    (C) $t + s$
    (D) $s - t$
    (E) $t^2 - s^2$

S T O P

IF YOU FINISH BEFORE TIME IS CALLED, YOU MAY CHECK YOUR WORK ON THIS SECTION ONLY. DO NOT WORK ON ANY OTHER SECTION IN THE TEST.

SECTION 5

Time—30 minutes

25 Questions

Directions: Each question or group of questions is based on a passage or set of conditions. In answering some of the questions, it may be useful to draw a rough diagram. For each question, select the best answer choice given.

Questions 1–4

Michael attends Saddle Rock School on the 9:00-3:00 session, except on Thursdays when he is dismissed at noon so the teachers can conduct special help classes and parent conferences. Michael takes a piano lesson at home on Mondays from 3:30-4:30. On Tuesdays he goes to a karate class from 4:00-6:00. His art class meets from 4:00-6:00 on Wednesdays. He remains in school after dismissal on Fridays to participate in a ninety-minute club program.

1. The most convenient afternoon for Michael to do library research is

   (A) Tuesday
   (B) Wednesday
   (C) Thursday
   (D) Friday
   (E) Monday

2. Keeping the same 3:30-4:30 schedule, Michael can conveniently change his piano lesson to which of the following days?

   (A) Monday
   (B) Tuesday
   (C) Wednesday
   (D) Thursday
   (E) Friday

3. Michael was invited to join an advanced art class instead of his regular art class. He could accept this advancement without interfering with his other activities, if the class met on which of the following days?

   (A) Mondays and Wednesdays
   (B) Tuesdays and Wednesdays
   (C) Wednesdays and Thursdays
   (D) Thursdays and Fridays
   (E) Mondays and Thursdays

4. Michael is chosen to play for the varsity basketball team. To attend daily 5:00 practice sessions, he will have to suspend which of the following activities?

   (A) piano instruction and karate
   (B) karate and the club program
   (C) the art class and the club program
   (D) piano instruction and the art class
   (E) the art class and karate

5. Sarah: Only General Council members sit on the President's Cabinet.
   Charles: That's not true. Dr. Grogan is a General Council member and she's not on the President's Cabinet.

   Charles's response implies that he incorrectly interpreted Sarah's statement to mean that

   (A) all Cabinet members are on the General Council
   (B) Dr. Grogan sits on the President's Cabinet
   (C) all members of the General Council sit on the President's Cabinet
   (D) no General Council members are on the President's Cabinet
   (E) Dr. Grogan is not a General Council manager

6. The only unemployment problem we have is not that people can't find work, but that they won't work. Thousands of jobs go begging every day, but the unemployed are too lazy to go out and find them.

   The above argument would be more persuasive if it were established that

   (A) the majority of available jobs require unusually high levels of skill or experience or both
   (B) unemployed persons tend to be geographically clustered in regions distant from available jobs
   (C) most unemployed persons are back at work within six months
   (D) most unemployed persons do not seek work until their unemployment benefits expire
   (E) a high unemployment rate has been fostered by the government in order to control inflation

7. My father, my three uncles, and both my grandfathers became bald within five years after they began practicing law. I don't want to lose my hair, so I'm going to become a doctor.

   Which of the following most closely resembles the reasoning used in the argument above?

   (A) Every time I drink coffee before going to bed, I have trouble falling asleep. I want to sleep well tonight, so I'm going to take a sleeping pill.
   (B) All of the teenagers in my neighborhood have gotten tickets for speeding on Dole Road within the last year. I don't want to have to pay a fine, so I'm not going to speed on Dole Road.

(C) Everyone else got transferred out of our department within three years after starting work here. I don't want to work in another department, so I'm going to start working harder.

(D) The other punch press operators on my shift each were seriously injured on the job within a week after eating at Rosie's Diner. I want to maintain my safety record, so I'm going to eat at Harry's Luncheonette.

(E) The three other men in my bridge club each became irritable after they quit smoking. I want to be more pleasant, so I'm going to quit my bridge club.

Questions 8–12

The Berkeley-Sothenay Gallery displays seven paintings, one each by Degas, Ernst, Fragonard, Greuze, Hartley, Ingres, and Johns. Each has been valued by the Gallery's curator.

The value of the Johns is three times that of the Ingres.
The Greuze has the lowest valuation of any of the paintings.
The Fragonard and the Degas are valued at the same amount.
The value of the Ernst is as much as that of the Johns and the Ingres together.
The value of the Hartley is as much as that of the Fragonard, the Ernst, and the Johns together.
The value of the Degas is as much as that of the Johns and the Ernst together.

8. Which correctly lists six of the paintings in order of increasing value?

(A) Greuze, Ernst, Fragonard, Johns, Ingres, Hartley
(B) Greuze, Johns, Degas, Ernst, Fragonard, Hartley
(C) Greuze, Ernst, Johns, Degas, Fragonard, Hartley
(D) Greuze, Ingres, Johns, Degas, Ernst, Hartley
(E) Greuze, Ingres, Johns, Ernst, Fragonard, Hartley

9. The value of the Degas is

(A) twice the value of the Johns.
(B) twice the value of the Ernst.
(C) three times the value of the Johns, less the value of the Ingres.
(D) six times the value of the Ingres.
(E) half the value of the Hartley.

10. A buyer who decided not to buy the Hartley could buy for the same money

I. the Degas, the Ingres, and the Fragonard.
II. the Ernst, the Johns, and the Degas.
III. the Ingres, the Ernst, and the Johns.

(A) I only
(B) II only
(C) I and II only
(D) I and III only
(E) I, II, and III

11. If the Ernst and the Ingres together are valued at ten times the value of the Greuze, the Hartley is valued at how many times the value of the Greuze?

(A) 12
(B) 14
(C) 21
(D) 28
(E) 49

12. The paintings are bought by seven rich collectors who then trade with each other. Which trade represents an exchange of even value?

(A) The Hartley for the Degas, the Ernst, and the Ingres
(B) The Hartley and the Ernst for all the others except the Greuze
(C) The Degas and the Fragonard for the Hartley and the Ingres
(D) The Ingres, the Johns, the Ernst, and the Fragonard for the Hartley
(E) The Johns and the Ernst for the Degas and the Ingres

Questions 13–16

(1) All P and X are N.
(2) All N except P are X.
(3) No P are M.
(4) No R are N.
(5) All M are either X or R.
(6) No Q are X.

13. Which of the following statements must be true if the above six statements are true?

I. No R are P.
II. Some X are P.
III. Some X are M.

(A) I only
(B) I and II only
(C) I and III only
(D) I, II, and III
(E) Neither I, II, nor III

14. Which of the following must be false given the conditions as stated?

(A) No Q are P.
(B) Some Q are neither N nor R.
(C) Some R are X.
(D) All R are M.
(E) Some X are not M.

15. Which of the numbered statements can logically be deduced from one or more of the other statements?

(A) (2)   (B) (3)   (C) (4)   (D) (5)   (E) (6)

16. If statement (2) were shown to be false, which of the following would necessarily be true?

(A) Some M are neither X nor R.
(B) Some P are not N.
(C) Some Q are X.
(D) Some N are neither P nor X.
(E) Either some X are P or some N are neither P nor X, or both.

Questions 17–22

Four persons — Allen, Brian, Carol, and Donna—are camping at four separate campsites — Edmunds, Freeport, Grand Isle, and High Point, not necessarily in that order. The campsites are located on four separate lakes — Indian Point, Jackson, Keewaukett, and Leesville, not necessarily in that order — which are in four separate states — Maine, Nebraska, Ohio, and Pennsylvania, not necessarily in that order.

Brian is camping on Keewaukett Lake.
High Point Campsite is on Jackson Lake, which is in Nebraska.
The person at Indian Point Lake, a native of Pennsylvania, camps only in that state.
Donna is at Freeport Campsite.
Allen is camping in Ohio.

17. Brian is camping at which of the following?

(A) at Edmunds Campsite
(B) in Maine
(C) on Leesville Lake
(D) at Freeport Campsite
(E) in Nebraska

18. Indian Point Lake is the site of

(A) Freeport Campsite
(B) Allen's camp
(C) the camp in Ohio
(D) Grand Isle Campsite
(E) Carol's camp

19. On the basis of the information given, it is possible to deduce that

I.   Allen is not at High Point Campsite
II. Carol is in Pennsylvania
III. Donna is not at Edmunds Campstie

(A) I only
(B) II only
(C) III only
(D) I and III only
(E) II and III only

20. Ohio is the site of

I.   Leesville Lake
II. Freeport Campsite

(A) I only
(B) II only
(C) I and II
(D) I or II but not both
(E) Neither I nor II

21. Which is true of Leesville Lake?

(A) Carol is camping there.
(B) Donna is camping there.
(C) It is in Maine
(D) It is the site of Freeport Campsite.
(E) Allen is camping there.

22. Which cannot be determined on the basis of the information given?

(A) What state Keewaukett Lake is in
(B) Who is at Edmunds Campsite
(C) What campsite is in Pennsylvania
(D) Who is camping in Nebraska
(E) Which states Carol and Donna are in

23. Our new Model EXT Superwash Automatic Dishwasher is the most luxurious dishwasher you'll ever own. It comes in any of fourteen decorator colors. It's so quiet you'll find yourself checking to see if it's really on. And best of all, it comes in different widths and heights so that there'll be no need to redesign your present kitchen around it.

The argument above is most weakened by its failure to mention

(A) the terms of the warranty
(B) how well the dishwasher washes dishes
(C) the specific sizes available
(D) how much electricity the dishwasher uses
(E) how many dishes the dishwasher holds

24. Based solely on artifacts recently discovered in ancient Xenian tombs, archeologists claim to have reconstructed the Xenian civilization of that time. What could be more absurd? No hieroglyphs or other written records were unearthed; thus, the archeologists are claiming to have reconstructed a culture without any evidence of how the people who lived in that culture thought.

The argument above is based on which of the following assumptions?

(A) Physical artifacts do not provide evidence of how people think.
(B) Archeologists would be able to translate ancient Xenian writing if it were found.
(C) Insufficient effort was expended by the archeologists in searching for written records.
(D) Physical artifacts are of no use in trying to reconstruct a civilization.
(E) Written records are all that is needed to reconstruct a civilization.

25. I'm afraid that Roger will never be an outstanding football player again. Last year he injured his knee, and the doctors had to remove some of the cartilage.

The argument above is based upon which of the following assumptions?

I. One must have healthy knees to play football.
II. How well one plays football may be influenced by the condition of one's knees.
III. Healthy knees are necessary for a professional football career.

(A) I only
(B) II only
(C) I and II only
(D) II and III only
(E) I, II, and III

S T O P

IF YOU FINISH BEFORE TIME IS CALLED, YOU MAY CHECK YOUR WORK ON THIS SECTION ONLY. DO NOT WORK ON ANY OTHER SECTION IN THE TEST.

SECTION 6

Time — 30 minutes

25 Questions

Directions: Each question or group of questions is based on a passage or set of conditions. In answering some of the questions, it may be useful to draw a rough diagram. For each question, select the best answer choice given.

Questions 1–4

George adores classical music. He always prefers Beethoven to Bartok and Mahler to Mozart. He always prefers Haydn to Hindemith and Hindemith to Mozart. He always prefers Mahler to any composer whose name begins with B, except Beethoven, and he always chooses to listen to a composer he prefers.

1. Which of the following cannot be true?

   (A) George prefers Mahler to Bartok.
   (B) George prefers Beethoven to Mahler.
   (C) George prefers Bartok to Mozart.
   (D) George prefers Mozart to Beethoven.
   (E) George prefers Mahler to Haydn.

2. George's brother gives him one recording by each of the composers mentioned. Which of the following correctly states the order in which George must play some of the records?

   (A) Beethoven, Bartok, Mozart
   (B) Haydn, Hindemith, Mozart
   (C) Beethoven, Mahler, Bartok
   (D) Hindemith, Mahler, Mozart
   (E) Haydn, Hindemith, Mahler

3. George's mother also gives him one recording by each composer mentioned. Which of the following cannot occur?

   (A) George plays the Beethoven first.
   (B) George plays the Haydn first.
   (C) George plays the Mahler third.
   (D) George plays the Beethoven fifth.
   (E) George plays the Bartok last.

4. George's father gives him several records. If the first record he plays is by Berlioz, which of the following must be true?

   (A) There is no record by Hindemith.
   (B) There is no record by Bartok.
   (C) One of the records may be by Haydn.
   (D) If there is a record by Haydn, George will play it second.
   (E) There is no record by Beethoven.

5. The new Spanish film, *The Other Side of the Mirror,* the psychologically probing story of a pair of disturbed lovers, is clearly the best foreign film of the year, since its box office receipts show that even more people are seeing it than have seen *Double Fugue,* the highly acclaimed U.S. film on a similar theme.

The argument above is based on which of the following assumptions?

   (A) *Double Fugue* is the best U.S. film of the year.
   (B) Foreign films should be judged by standards different from those used for U.S. films.
   (C) Foreign films should be judged by the same standards used for U.S. films.
   (D) Psychologically probing stories make the best films.
   (E) The quality of a film can be measured by the number of people who go to see it.

6. By the very nature of their work, scientists must rigorously apply the scientific method. Every conclusion they reach is scrutinized by other scientists and corrected and refined as needed until it can be certified as scientifically valid. No other view of the world is derived in such a manner; neither the theologian nor the sociologist nor the artist makes use of this method. Thus, the scientific worldview must be the most accurate.

Which of the following best describes the flaw in the reasoning used in the argument above?

   (A) The author uses a single term to mean more than one thing.
   (B) The author fails to explain in detail how the scientific method works.
   (C) The truth of the author's conclusion is assumed rather than justified.
   (D) The author ignores the fact that many accepted scientific theories are later disproven.
   (E) The author attacks the people who hold other views, rather than attacking the views themselves.

7. Melinda: George has become a better boxer since he started meditating.
   Alfredo: Impossible. A boxer's most important asset is his aggressiveness.

Alfredo's statement implies that he believes that

   (A) meditation tends to make a person less aggressive
   (B) meditation has little or no effect on the person who practices it
   (C) George was previously a poor boxer because he was not aggressive enough
   (D) George has not really been meditating
   (E) mental attitude has little or nothing to do with a boxer's effectiveness

Questions 8–12

(1) At a baseball game, five men, L, M, N, O, and P, and five women, S, T, U, V, and W, occupy a row of ten seats. The men are in odd-numbered seats, starting from the left; each woman sits to the right of the man she is dating.
(2) O is V's date.
(3) W is not at the right end of the row and the man she is dating is not at the left end of the row.
(4) N is one seat from the right end of the row.
(5) The man dating W likes T best among the other women and insists on being seated to the right of T.
(6) M and his date occupy the middle pair of seats.
(7) V sits next to M.

8. Which of the following lists five persons sitting adjacent to one another, from left to right?

 (A) U, V, O, M, T
 (B) M, T, L, W, N
 (C) O, V, M, T, W
 (D) O, V, M, T, and either L or P
 (E) L or P, O, V, M, T

9. U's date may be

 (A) N or L
 (B) L or P
 (C) N or P
 (D) N, L, or P
 (E) M, N, or L

10. Which of the following cannot be determined on the basis of the information given?

 I.   Who occupies the seat farthest to the left
 II. Who occupies the seat farthest to the right
 III. Which other women are nearest T

 (A) I only
 (B) III only
 (C) I and II only
 (D) II and III only
 (E) I, II, and III

11. Which of the following could be determined exactly if the position of either L or P were given?

 (A) The identity of L's date
 (B) The identity of P's date
 (C) The identity of L's date or P's date, but not both
 (D) Which woman is not seated between two men
 (E) Who is sitting to O's left

12. In order to determine the position of T, it is necessary to use how many of the numbered statements?

 (A) 3   (B) 4   (C) 5   (D) 6   (E) 7

Questions 13–16

(1) Both B and D are prerequisites for E.
(2) Both B and C are prerequisites for F.
(3) E may occur without B only if A precedes D.
(4) A in combination with B is an alternative prerequisite for F.
(5) H will occur if E or F occurs, but not if both occur.
(6) H in combination with any two unused prerequisites for E or F will yield J.
(7) If two sets of prerequisites each sufficient to yield a result both occur, the result will not occur.
(8) Any item acts simultaneously as part of all sets of prerequisites of which it is a member and of which the other members are present.

13. J cannot occur if

 (A) A is the first item to occur
 (B) D is the first item to occur
 (C) B precedes D
 (D) A follows B or C
 (E) B and C occur simultaneously

14. B precedes D. Which of the following conditions is (are) sufficient for H to occur?

 I.   A occurs, but not before D.
 II. C occurs.
 III. A also precedes D.

 (A) I only
 (B) III only
 (C) I and II only
 (D) II and III only
 (E) I, II, and III

15. C occurs. J will occur if

 (A) B occurs
 (B) B and D occur
 (C) A precedes D
 (D) B and D occur, followed by A
 (E) A and B occur, followed by D

16. B and C occur. J will occur if

 I. A occurs
 II. D occurs before A

 (A) I only
 (B) II only
 (C) I and II only
 (D) I or II, but not both
 (E) Neither I nor II

Questions 17–22

Mathematics 11 is a prerequisite for Mathematics 101,
except for students with advanced placement in mathematics, who may take Mathematics 101 without any
prerequisite.

Chemistry 11 or 21 is a prerequisite for Chemistry 101,
except for students with advanced placement in chemistry, who may take Chemistry 101 without
prerequisite.

Physics 1, followed by Physics 11 or 21, is a prerequisite
for Physics 101 or 121. There is no advanced placement in physics, but Mathematics 11 is acceptable in
place of Physics 1.

Students who have passed Mathematics 101 may take
Mathematics 202, 211, or 221; students who have
passed Chemistry 101 may take Chemistry 201, 211, or
221, or Mathematics 201 for chemistry credit; students
who have passed Physics 101 or 121 may take Physics
201 or 221, or Chemistry 201 for physics credit.

Students who have passed three or more graduate-level
courses acceptable for credit in a given field may be
admitted to a concentration sequence in that field.
(Courses numbered 200 or higher are considered graduate-level.)

17. A student who has passed Physics 101

   I.   may be admitted to a concentration sequence in
        physics without taking Physics 121
   II. may be admitted to a concentration sequence in
        physics after taking two more physics courses
   III. must have taken Physics 1 or 11 or both

   (A) I only
   (B) III only
   (C) I and II only
   (D) I and III only
   (E) I, II, and III

18. What is the minimum number of courses in mathe-
     matics or chemistry that can satisfy the requirements
     for admission to a concentration sequence in chemis-
     try for a student without advanced placement in
     chemistry?

   (A) 3   (B) 4   (C) 5   (D) 6   (E) 7

19. How many separate ways are there to qualify for
     admission to a concentration sequence in physics?

   (A) 3   (B) 4   (C) 6   (D) 8   (E) 12

20. A student with advanced placement in mathematics
     may qualify for admission to a concentration
     sequence in chemistry by taking which of the
     following?

   I.   Mathematics 101 and 202, Chemistry 11, 201,
        and 211
   II. Chemistry 11, 101, 201, 211, and 221
   III. Mathematics 101 and 211, Chemistry 21, 101,
        201, and 221

   (A) I only
   (B) II only
   (C) III only
   (D) I and III only
   (E) II and III only

21. The maximum number of courses that must be taken
     by any student to qualify for admission to a concen-
     tration sequence is

   (A) 4   (B) 5   (C) 6   (D) 7   (E) 8

22. If all chemistry classes are cancelled following an
     explosion which destroys the chemistry building,
     which of the following must be true?

   I.   No new students will be able to qualify for
        Mathematics 201.
   II. No new students will be able to qualify for a
        concentration sequence in physics.
   III. No graduate-level courses will be open to stu-
        dents who have already passed Chemistry 101.

   (A) I only
   (B) II only
   (C) I and II only
   (D) I and III only
   (E) I, II, and III only

23. None of the stockholders in Elronco who knew
     Ortega and supported her reorganization plan voted
     for the merger with Anaco, but some of them owned
     stock in Anaco.

     If the statement above is true, each of the following
     statements may also be true EXCEPT:

   (A) No one who owned Anaco stock supported
       Ortega's reorganization plan.
   (B) Everyone who voted for the merger with Anaco
       owned Anaco stock.
   (C) Some of the Anaco stockholders knew Ortega.
   (D) Some of the Elronco stockholders who opposed
       Ortega's reorganization plan knew Ortega.
   (E) None of the Elronco stockholders voted for the
       Anaco merger.

24. Which of the following contradicts the view that
     only the smart become rich?

   (A) Brian was smart, yet he was poor his whole life.
   (B) Both "smart" and "rich" are relative terms.
   (C) Different people are smart in different ways.
   (D) Some smart people do not desire to become
       rich.
   (E) Peter is stupid, yet he amassed a large fortune
       by the age of 30.

25. Television convinces viewers that the likelihood of their becoming the victim of a violent crime is extremely high; at the same time, by its very nature, television persuades viewers to passively accept whatever happens to them.

    The argument above leads most logically to the conclusion that

    (A) people should not watch television
    (B) television promotes a feeling of helpless vulnerability in its viewers
    (C) television viewers are more likley to be victimized than other persons
    (D) the content of television programs should be changed to avoid fostering the attitudes mentioned
    (E) television viewing promotes criminal behavior

S T O P

IF YOU FINISH BEFORE TIME IS CALLED, YOU MAY CHECK YOUR WORK ON THIS SECTION ONLY.
DO NOT WORK ON ANY OTHER SECTION IN THE TEST.

SECTION 7

Time—30 minutes

30 Questions

Numbers: All numbers used are real numbers.

Figures: Position of points, angles, regions, etc. can be assumed to be in the order shown; and angle measures can be assumed to be positive.

Lines shown as straight can be assumed to be straight.

Figures can be assumed to lie in a plane unless otherwise indicated.

Figures that accompany questions are intended to provide information useful in answering the questions. However, unless a note states that a figure is drawn to scale, you should solve these problems NOT by estimating sizes by sight or by measurement, but by using your knowledge of mathematics (see Example 2 below).

Directions: Each of the Questions 1–15 consists of two quantities, one in Column A and one in Column B. You are to compare the two quantities and choose

- A if the quantity in Column A is greater;
- B if the quantity in Column B is greater;
- C if the two quantities are equal;
- D if the relationship cannot be determined from the information given.

Note: Since there are only four choices, NEVER MARK (E).

Common
Information: In a question, information concerning one or both of the quantities to be compared is centered above the two columns. A symbol that appears in both columns represents the same thing in Column A as it does in Column B.

Column A	Column B	Sample Answers

Example 1: 2×6 $2 + 6$ ● Ⓑ Ⓒ Ⓓ Ⓔ

Examples 2-4 refer to $\triangle PQR$.

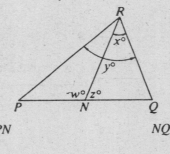

Example 2: PN NQ Ⓐ Ⓑ Ⓒ ● Ⓔ

(since equal measures cannot be assumed, even though PN and NQ appear equal)

Example 3: x y Ⓐ ● Ⓒ Ⓓ Ⓔ

(since N is between P and Q)

Example 4: $w + z$ 180   Ⓐ Ⓑ ● Ⓓ Ⓔ

(since PQ is a straight line)

A if the quantity in Column A is greater;
B if the quantity in Column B is greater;
C if the two quantities are equal;
D if the relationship cannot be determined from the information given.

Column A	Column B

$$a < b < c$$
$$d < e < f$$

1. a f

$$64 < x < 81$$

2. x 65

$KA = 6$, $BCL = 17$, and $BC = 8$

3.   Length of KL 23

The operation △ is defined by the
equation a △ $b = a^2 + b^2$

$$xy \neq 0$$

4. $(x \triangle y)^2$ $x^2 \triangle y^2$

5. $\sqrt{144}$ $\sqrt{100} + \sqrt{44}$

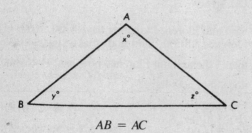

$$AB = AC$$

6. $x + y$ $x + z$

7. $\dfrac{3\sqrt{48}}{\sqrt{3}}$ 12

Column A	Column B

$$\frac{x}{4} + \frac{x}{3} = \frac{7}{12}$$

8. x -1

$$\frac{9}{a} < \frac{9}{b}$$

9. $a > 1$ $b > 1$

10.   .003%   .0003

11. $\dfrac{k}{400}$ $\dfrac{k}{4}\%$

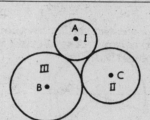

radius of I = 3 inches
radius of II = 4 inches
radius of III = 5 inches

12.   Length of perimeter of   2 feet
triangle ABC, formed
by joining the centers
of the three circles

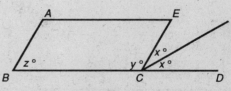

side BC of parallelogram $ABCE$ is
extended to D
$$y = 130$$

13. x z

A if the quantity in Column A is greater;
B if the quantity in Column B is greater;
C if the two quantities are equal;
D if the relationship cannot be determined from the information given.

Column A	Column B		Column A	Column B

$abc = 0$
$c = 1$

14.   1 ab

15. The average of one-   0.111
     tenth, one-hundredth,
     and one-thousandth

Directions: Each of the Questions 16–30 has five answer choices. For each of these questions, select the best of the answer choices given.

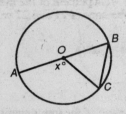

16. In the figure above, AB is the diameter and $OC = BC$. What is the value of $\frac{x}{2}$?

(A) 20   (B) 30   (C) 60   (D) 90   (E) 120

17. For which values of n and d is $\frac{n}{d} > 1$?

(A) $n = 5$ and $d = 6$
(B) $n = 3$ and $d = 2$
(C) $n = 1$ and $d = 2$
(D) $n = 1$ and $d = 1$
(E) $n = 0$ and $d = 1$

18. One-half of a number is 17 more than one-third of that number. What is the number?

(A) 52   (B) 84   (C) 102   (D) 112   (E) 204

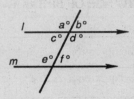

19. In the figure above, $l \parallel m$. All of the following are true EXCEPT:

(A) $c = d$
(B) $a = d$
(C) $a = e$
(D) $f = b$
(E) $f = c$

20. Sam and Florence together have $100. After giving Florence $10.00, Sam finds that he has $4.00 more than $\frac{1}{5}$ the amount Florence now has. How much does Sam now have?

(A) $18.67
(B) $20.00
(C) $21.00
(D) $27.50
(E) $35.00

Questions 21–25 refer to the following graphs.

HIGHEST LEVEL OF EDUCATION OF BRIDE-GROOMS IN 24–27 AGE GROUP

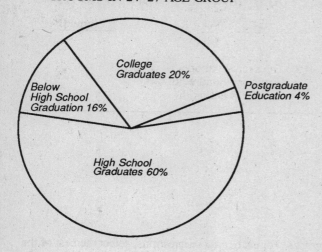

DISTRIBUTION OF 302,000 MARRIAGES ACCORDING TO AGE OF BRIDEGROOM

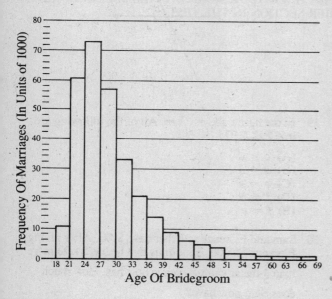

21. In one million marriages, how many thousand (to the nearest thousand) bridegrooms would you expect to be between the ages of 51 and 60?

    (A) 5
    (B) 15
    (C) 16
    (D) 17
    (E) 50

22. Which of the following best represents the percent of men who married at age 24 or younger?

    (A) 7
    (B) 10
    (C) 24
    (D) 32
    (E) 48

23. How many bridegrooms ages 24–27 received post-graduate education?

    (A)   292
    (B)   400
    (C) 2,440
    (D) 2,920
    (E) 4,000

24. If drawn accurately, how many degrees should there be in the central angle of the sector indicating the number of college graduates?

    (A) 20
    (B) 40
    (C) 60
    (D) 72
    (E) more than 72

25. Approximately what percent of the men who married were between the ages of 21 and 27 years?

    (A)   7%
    (B) 13%
    (C) 26%
    (D) 44%
    (E) 67%

26. If 0.6 is the average of the four quantities 0.2, 0.8, 1.0 and x, what is the numerical value of x?

    (A) 0.2
    (B) 0.4
    (C) 0.67
    (D) 1.3
    (E) 2.4

27. $\dfrac{a^2 - b^2}{(a - b)^2}$ is equal to

    (A) $a + b$

    (B) $a - b$

    (C) $\dfrac{a + b}{a - b}$

    (D) $\dfrac{a - b}{a + b}$

    (E) 1

28. If two items cost $c¢$, how many items can be purchased for $x¢$?

    (A) $\frac{x}{2c}$

    (B) $\frac{2c}{x}$

    (C) $\frac{2x}{c}$

    (D) $\frac{cx}{2}$

    (E) $2cx$

29. The area of square $EFGH$ is equal to the area of rectangle $ABCD$. If $GH = 6$ feet and $AD = 4$ feet, the perimeter (in feet) of the rectangle is

    (A) 13
    (B) 16
    (C) 24
    (D) 26
    (E) 36

30. The radius of a pool is twice the radius of a circular flower bed. The area of the pool is how many times the area of the flower bed?

    (A) $\frac{1}{4}$ (B) $\frac{1}{2}$ (C) 2   (D) 4   (E) 8

S T O P

IF YOU FINISH BEFORE TIME IS CALLED, YOU MAY CHECK YOUR WORK ON THIS SECTION ONLY.
DO NOT WORK ON ANY OTHER SECTION IN THE TEST.

Answer Key – Diagnostic Test

Section 1

Note: The answers to the quantitative sections are keyed to the corresponding review areas in the Mathematics Review (Chapter 11). The numbers in parentheses after each answer refer to the math topic(s) covered by that particular question.

1.	B	11.	D	21.	E	31.	D
2.	E	12.	A	22.	C	32.	D
3.	C	13.	C	23.	B	33.	B
4.	C	14.	E	24.	D	34.	B
5.	C	15.	D	25.	C	35.	B
6.	B	16.	C	26.	B	36.	D
7.	A	17.	C	27.	C	37.	D
8.	B	18.	C	28.	E	38.	D
9.	C	19.	E	29.	A		
10.	B	20.	C	30.	B		

Section 2

1.	E	11.	E	21.	C	31.	E
2.	D	12.	A	22.	B	32.	C
3.	B	13.	C	23.	D	33.	B
4.	E	14.	D	24.	C	34.	E
5.	A	15.	E	25.	E	35.	B
6.	D	16.	A	26.	D	36.	E
7.	B	17.	C	27.	B	37.	B
8.	B	18.	E	28.	C	38.	C
9.	D	19.	A	29.	A		
10.	C	20.	D	30.	B		

Section 3

1.	B (I-B)	9.	B (II-B-4)	17.	E (II-B)	25.	E (II-E, IV)
2.	B (II-B)	10.	A (III-A, D)	18.	D (I-G)	26.	D (III-H)
3.	C (I)	11.	D (III-A, D)	19.	C (II-E)	27.	B (II-C)
4.	A (I-H-4)	12.	C (III-A, D)	20.	D (III-G)	28.	D (II-B)
5.	B (II-E)	13.	C (II-C)	21.	C (IV)	29.	A (II-E)
6.	C (I-A)	14.	A (II-G)	22.	A (II-E, IV)	30.	E (I-G)
7.	B (I-A)	15.	D (III-A)	23.	B (IV)		
8.	D (II-B-4)	16.	A (I-C)	24.	C (IV-B)		

Section 4

1.	C (III-A, D)	9.	A (II-A)	17.	A (II-C)	25.	D (IV)
2.	C (I-A)	10.	B (II-A)	18.	E (I-D)	26.	D (II-C)
3.	D (II-B)	11.	D (III-G)	19.	E (I-G)	27.	C (II-E)
4.	B (III-A)	12.	C (II-B)	20.	E (II-C)	28.	B (II-E)
5.	B (III-G)	13.	A (I-H)	21.	C (IV-C)	29.	A (II-G)
6.	C (III-G)	14.	C (III-D)	22.	A (I-D, IV)	30.	A (II-A)
7.	C (III-G)	15.	B (II-C)	23.	C (II-E, IV)		
8.	C (III-D)	16.	C (II-C)	24.	B (IV)		

Section 5

1.	C	8.	E	15.	B	22.	B
2.	D	9.	E	16.	E	23.	B
3.	C	10.	B	17.	B	24.	A
4.	E	11.	D	18.	A	25.	B
5.	C	12.	B	19.	D		
6.	D	13.	A	20.	A		
7.	D	14.	C	21.	E		

Section 6

1.	D	8.	D	15.	D	22.	C
2.	B	9.	D	16.	C	23.	A
3.	D	10.	C	17.	C	24.	E
4.	E	11.	C	18.	C	25.	B
5.	E	12.	C	19.	D		
6.	C	13.	A	20.	B		
7.	A	14.	B	21.	C		

Section 7

1.	D (II-G)	9.	A (I-B)	17.	B (I-B)	25.	D (I-D, IV)
2.	D (I-A)	10.	B (I-C, D)	18.	C (II-C-1)	26.	B (I-G)
3.	A (III-B)	11.	C (I-B, D)	19.	A (III-B)	27.	C (II-A)
4.	A (I-H, II-B)	12.	C (III-F)	20.	B (II-B)	28.	C (II-E)
5.	B (I-H)	13.	B (III-C)	21.	D (IV)	29.	D (III-G)
6.	C (III-A)	14.	A (II-A)	22.	C (I-D, IV)	30.	D (III-G)
7.	C (I-H)	15.	B (I-G)	23.	D (IV)		
8.	A (II-A)	16.	C (III-P)	24.	D (III-F, D)		

Self-Appraisal

Now that you have completed the Diagnostic Test, evaluate your performance. Identify your strengths and weaknesses, and then plan a practical study program based on what you have discovered.

Use the Answer Key to check your answers. Your raw score for each section is equal to the number of correct answers you had. Compute your raw score for each ability area (verbal, quantitative, analytical) by adding your raw scores from the two sections on that area. Since on the actual GRE the experimental section does not count in your score, use only two of the three quantitative sections on this Diagnostic Test when computing your raw quantitative score.

Once you have determined your raw score for each ability area, use the conversion chart that follows to get your scaled score. Note that this conversion chart is provided to give you a rough estimate of the GRE score you would achieve if you took the test now without any further preparation. When ETS administers a GRE, a conversion chart for that particular exam is prepared based on statis-

tical data. The unofficial conversion chart presented here should only be used to give you an approximate idea of how raw scores convert into scaled scores.

Use this Diagnostic Test to identify areas you might be weak in. You may find that in some cases you had trouble with a particular question type (for example, you didn't do well on the analogy questions in either verbal section), whereas in other cases you had trouble with particular subject matter (for example, you didn't do well on any geometry questions, whether they were quantitative comparisons or discrete quantitative). Determining what it is you need to work on most will help you plan an effective study program.

Remember that, in addition to evaluating your scores and identifying weak areas, you should read all the answer explanations for questions you answered incorrectly, questions you guessed on, and questions you answered correctly but found difficult. Reviewing the answer explanations will help you understand concepts and strategies, and may point out shortcuts.

SCORE CONVERSION CHART

Raw Score	Scaled Scores		
	Verbal Score	Quantitative Score	Analytical Score
75	800		
70	770		
65	710		
60	650	800	
55	590	750	
50	540	690	800
45	490	630	770
40	450	560	700
35	410	500	620
30	360	430	550
25	320	370	470
20	280	310	400

Answer Explanations

Section 1   Verbal

1. **B.** Lacking the information derived from an actual census or population count, a numerical description of the human population would of necessity be a matter of *conjecture* (supposition based on estimate or guesswork).

2. **E.** Given that the tide pool provides suitable refuge, it is likely that the intertidal fish would seek to *return* to it. In such a case, they would be helped by the development of a *homing* instinct.

3. **C.** In a case in which experts disagree, it is *incumbent on* responsible scholars (that is, falls upon them as a scholarly duty or obligation) to *refrain from* making statements that are dogmatic or excessively assertive and arbitrary about the issue.

4. **C.** You are dealing with either similar or contradictory impulses. If the impulses are similar (that is, *analogous*, *comparable*, or *related*), the second missing word should be a synonym or near-synonym for *individualize*. If the impulses are contradictory (that is, *disparate* or *divergent*),

the second missing word should be an antonym or near-antonym for *individualize*. In this case, the latter holds true. The impulses are *divergent*; they are the impulse to individualize and the contradictory impulse to *typify* (treat characters as representatives of a type).

5. **C.** The politicians do not forsake center stage. However, if they did forsake center stage once in a while, the public might like them better for their *self-effacement* (withdrawal from attention).

6. **B.** The key phrase here is "some small village world." To be concerned only with village or parish affairs is to be *parochial*; Mrs. Woolf's novels thus have an air of *parochialism*. Again, it is a *small* world, perfect in its *tininess* as miniature paintings are perfect.
   Choice A is incorrect. It is Mrs. Woolf's choice of scene and not her choice of *period* that gives her novels their special atmosphere. (*Anachronism* has to do with chronological misplacings of persons or events.)
   Choices C and D are incorrect. Nothing in the sentence suggests *cynicism* (pessimistic disbelief) or *intrigue* (love of mystery) to be characteristic of Mrs. Woolf's work.
   Choice E, though tempting, is incorrect. A village world is not necessarily a *fragile* one; it is, however, a provincial, narrow one—in other words, a *parochial* one.

7. **A.** Because they do not have enough time to read the whole treatise, the editors ask for an abridgment or *compendium*.
   Remember, before you look at the answer choices, read the sentence and try to think of a word that makes sense.

8. **B.** A *clasp* is the fastening on a *bracelet*. A *buckle* is the fastening on a *belt*.

   (Function)

9. **C.** A *sedan* is a kind of *automobile*. A *rocker* is a kind of *chair*.

   (Class and Member)

10. **B.** By definition, a *route* that is *circuitous* follows an indirect course. Likewise, an *argument* that is *devious* follows an indirect course.

   (Defining Characteristic)

11. **D.** To *pardon* an *offense* by definition is to give up resentment for it without exacting a penalty. To *forgive* a *wrong* is to give up resentment for it without exacting a penalty.

   (Defining Characteristic)

12. A. To be *nonplussed* (totally at a loss) is to exhibit *bafflement* (perplexity). To be *discomfited* (abashed; disconcerted) is to exhibit *embarrassment*.
Beware eye-catchers. Choice D is incorrect. To be *despicable* is to be worthy of *contempt*; it is not to *exhibit* contempt.

(Synonym Variant)

13. C. A *gully* (miniature gorge or valley) is smaller than a *canyon* (deep gorge or valley). Likewise, a *pebble* is smaller than a *boulder*.

(Degree of Intensity)

14. E. To be *officious* (meddlesome) is to be *helpful* in an excessive, offensive manner. To be *sycophantic* (fawning, obsequious) is to be *deferential* (respectful) in an excessive, offensive manner.

(Manner)

15. D. *Patina* is the green coating, caused by oxidation, on *bronze* objects. *Rust* is the reddish coating, caused by oxidation, on *iron* objects.

(Defining Characteristic)

16. C. *Cacophony* (dissonance, harshness of sound) is by definition not *mellifluous* (pleasant-sounding). *Noisomeness* (stench, rankness of smell) is by definition not *fragrant* (pleasant-smelling).

(Antonym Variant)

17. C. The author states that the later novels of James play down prominent action. Thus they lack *overtly dramatic incident*. However, the author goes on to state that James's novels *do* possess interest; they carry the reader through "a rich analysis of the mental adjustments of the characters to the realities of their personal situations." It is this implicitly dramatic psychological revelation that sustains the reader's interest.

Question A is unanswerable on the basis of the passage. It is evident that James wrote psychological novels; it is nowhere stated that he originated the genre.

Question B is unanswerable on the basis of the passage. Although conventional narrative technique relates "events in distinctly phased sequences," clearly separating them, it does not necessarily recount action in *strictly* chronological order.

Question D is unanswerable on the basis of the passage. The passage does not deal with the general public's reaction to James.

Question E is unanswerable on the basis of the passage. The passage talks of qualities in James

as a novelist in terms of their being *characteristic*, not in terms of their making him *unique*.

18. C. While the stories themselves grow simpler, their moral and psychological aspects become increasingly complex.
Choice A is incorrect. The passage mentions the specific description of settings as characteristic of James's early, conventional novels, not of his later works.
Choice B is incorrect. In his later novels James grew less concerned with plot and more concerned with psychological revelation.
Choice D is incorrect. The "excitement of visible actions building up to a climactic event" is characteristic of the common novel, not of the Jamesian psychological novel.
Choice E is incorrect. The later novels tend instead to subordinate dramatic effect to psychological exploration and revelation.

19. E. The author refers to novels of action as "overstuffed" and "crammed with *adventitious* events." However, these comments, though stated with assurance, are merely made in passing. Thus, his attitude is best described as one of *decided disapprobation* or disapproval.
Choice A is incorrect. The author is not *pointedly indignant* or deeply resentful in tone. He is merely making mildly critical remarks in passing.
Choice B is incorrect. The author does make passing comments that disparage the novel of action. He is not wholly *neutral* on the topic.
Choice C is incorrect. While the author does disparage the novel of action, he does not ridicule or *deride* it sharply.
Choice D is incorrect. The author is certainly not a *strong partisan* or advocate of the novel of action.

20. C. The author indicates that the theory of plate tectonics draws upon earlier hypotheses on sea-floor spreading; he provides details about the history of these hypotheses, tracing them from their initial formulation by Hess to their explication by Vine and Matthews and finally to their confirmation by the work of the manned submersibles. Thus, he traces the development of a theory.
Choice A is incorrect. The author presents data; he does not question data.
Choice B is incorrect. The author briefly describes current explorations. However, that is not his primary purpose.
Choice D is incorrect. It is unsupported by the passage.
Choice E is incorrect. The author mentions the phenomenon of the periodic reversals of the

earth's magnetic field. However, he states this phenomenon "continues to be one of the great mysteries of geology"; he does not explain the reasons behind it.

21. E.   The entire thrust of the article is to summarize the current state of knowledge in marine geology. In addition, both the passage's free use of technical terminology and its careful provision of definitions explaining this terminology are characteristic of scientific journal articles aimed at an educated audience of non-specialists in a field.
Choice A is incorrect. The passage is expository in tone; it is not persuasive or argumentative.
Choice B is incorrect. It mentions volcanism only in passing.
Choice C is incorrect. The passage is far greater in scope.
Choice D is incorrect. The passage indicates no such explanation of "one of the great mysteries of geology" exists.

22. C.   The subduction zone is the site of the destruction or consumption of existing lithospheric material. In contrast, the mid-ocean ridge is the site of the creation or emergence of new lithospheric material.
Choice A is incorrect. Both mid-ocean ridges and subduction zones are boundaries between plates.
Choice B is incorrect. Both are located on the ocean floor.
Choice D is incorrect. It is unsupported by the passage.
Choice E is incorrect. The reverse is true.

23. B.   Choice B is correct. You are told that the new lithospheric material is injected into a mid-ocean ridge, a suboceanic mountain range. This new material does not disappear; it is added to the material already there. Thus, it is *incorporated into* the existing mid-ocean ridge.
Choice A is incorrect. "In general the plates are in motion with respect to one another." Nothing suggests that they become immobilized; indeed, they are said to diverge from the ridge, sliding as they diverge.
Choice C is incorrect. The passage specifically denies it. ("The size of the earth is essentially constant.")
Choice D is incorrect. It is the earth itself whose magnetic field reverses. Nothing in the passage suggests the new lithospheric material has any such potential.
Choice E is incorrect. At a mid-ocean ridge, the site at which new lithospheric material is injected from below, the plates diverge; they do not sink. (They sink, one plate diving under another, at a subduction zone.)

24. D.   You can determine the correct answer by the process of elimination.
Question I is answerable on the basis of the passage. The passage states that the earth's magnetic field "reverses at intervals of from 10,000 to about a million years." Therefore, you can eliminate Choice B. Question II is unanswerable on the basis of the passage. What causes the changes in polarity is still a mystery to geologists. Therefore, you can eliminate Choices C and E.
Question III is answerable on the basis of the passage. The width of the magnetic stripes "indicates the rate" or *pace* of sea-floor spreading. Therefore, you can eliminate Choice A. Only Choice D is left. It is the correct answer.

25. C.   Since the passage states that the size of the earth is essentially constant, if large amounts of new lithospheric material are being created at one point, it follows that correspondingly large amounts of lithospheric material are being destroyed at another point. Thus, an increase in activity at a mid-ocean ridge or creation point would be matched by a corresponding increase in activity at a subduction zone or destruction point.

26. B.   The third sentence of the second paragraph states that one plate dives under another (*sinks*) and is reincorporated or *absorbed* into the mantle.
Choice A is incorrect. Lithospheric material rises at mid-ocean ridges, not at subduction zones.
Choice C is incorrect. New lithospheric material is injected at a mid-ocean ridge.
Choice D is incorrect. The injection of new lithospheric material causes sea-floor spreading around the mid-ocean ridge.
Choice E is incorrect. The lithospheric plates are described as diverging from a mid-ocean ridge, not from a subduction zone.

27. C.   Until the most recent explorations, marine geologists lacked maps "as precise as those of a geologist on land." This suggests that, compared to land geologists, marine geologists were *laboring under a disadvantage*.
Choice A is incorrect. While the marine geologists lacked adequate charts, nothing in the passage suggests they had been *negligent* in their work.
Choice B is incorrect. It is unsupported by the passage.
Choice D is incorrect. The passage suggests they had *in*adequate access to the ocean floor before submersibles came into use.
Choice E is incorrect. The sea-floor spreading hypothesis has been known to marine geologists

since the 1960s. Thus, they were aware of it well before the recent explorations involving manned submersibles began.

28. E. The opposite of to *deteriorate* (become worse) is to *improve*.
Think of "deteriorating health."

29. A. The opposite of *evasive* (not direct; shifty; equivocal) is *frank* (candid; open).
Think of "evasive remarks from a politician."

30. B. The opposite of to *strew* or scatter is to *collect*.
Think of "clothes strewn all over the floor."

31. D. The opposite of a *prodigal* (spendthrift; extravagant person) is an *economical person*.
Beware eye-catchers. Choice C is incorrect. A *prodigal* is not a *prodigy* (wonder; gifted person).
Think of "a prodigal squandering his wealth."

32. D. The opposite of to *equivocate* (avoid committing oneself in what one says) is to *pledge* (bind or commit oneself solemnly).
Think of politicians "hedging and equivocating."

33. B. The opposite of *crass* (stupid; vulgar; incapable of appreciating refinement) is *refined*.
Think of "a crass blockhead."

34. B. The opposite of *artifice* (trickery; guile) is *sincerity*.
Think of being "tricked by her skillful artifice."

35. B. The opposite of *opulence* (wealth; affluence) is *penury* or extreme poverty.
Think of "luxurious opulence."

36. D. The opposite of *untenable* (not able to be supported or defended) is *defensible*.
Think of "an untenable argument."

37. D. The opposite of *sedulous* (diligent; exhibiting care) is *cursory* (hasty; inattentive).
Think of "sedulous attention to details."

38. D. The opposite of to *disabuse* (undeceive) is to *deceive*.
Beware eye-catchers. Choice A is incorrect. *Disabuse* is unrelated to physical *maltreatment* or abuse.
Think of "disabusing someone of a misapprehension."

Section 2   Verbal

1. E. The presence of *extraneous* (unrelated; irrelevant) ideas that have been dragged in would make an argument *difficult* to comprehend.
Note that the phrase set off by the commas serves to define the material referred to and thus defines the first missing word.

2. D. *Because* the tendency to migrate exists in all time periods, you cannot fully explain it on the basis of any single time period. Your explanation, like the phenomenon itself, must be *independent of* any particular period of time.
The conjunction *since* here is used as a synonym for *because*; it indicates a cause and effect relationship.

3. B. Given the ubiquity of light, it is *unsurprising* that creatures have *developed* the biologically helpful ability to make use of light energy.
Note the use of *therefore* indicating that the omitted portion of the sentence supports or continues a thought developed elsewhere in the sentence.

4. E. After incubating the new functions, the next step would be to *nurture* or foster their growth until they were ready to be sent out into the world. Their departure, however, would not diminish the cities, for by continuing to breed fresh ideas the cities would *renew* themselves.
Note the metaphoric usage of *incubate* and *breed* that influences the writer's choice of words. Cities do not literally incubate businesses or breed ideas; they only do so figuratively.

5. A. Man is *gregarious* or sociable. However, he is more in need of mental companionship than of physical companionship. The writer plays on words in his conceit that a man may like to go alone for a walk but hates to stand alone in his *opinions*.

6. D. Here the contrast is between reality and pretense. Mrs. Proudie *feigned* or pretended a great interest in the parishioners' welfare. However, her interest was *not* great but actually *negligible* or insignificant, so insignificant as to be almost nonexistent.
Note that the conjunction *although* signals the contrast here. Note also that the phrase "so negligible as to be practically nonexistent" is a cliché, a literary commonplace.

7. B. By definition, an excessive or grandiloquent literary work lacks *economy* or conciseness in verbal expression.
Note that you are dealing with a secondary meaning of *economy* here.

8. B. A *prologue* precedes a *play*. An *overture* precedes an *opera*.

(Sequence)

9. D. *Serrations* are the teeth on the edge of a *saw*. *Cogs* are the teeth on the rim of a *gear*.

(Part to Whole)

10. C. A *sledge* (large heavy hammer) strikes or pounds in a *spike* (very large nail). A *hammer* strikes or pounds in a *nail*.
Beware eye-catchers. Choice A is incorrect. *Sledge* here is related to *sledgehammers*, not to sleds or *sleighs*.

(Function)

11. E. *Thirst* is a specific example of a *drive* (state of instinctual need). *Smell* is a specific example of a *sense*.

(Class and Member)

12. A. Something *ephemeral* (fleeting; transient) lacks *permanence*. Something *erratic* (unpredictable) lacks *predictability*.

(Antonym Variant)

13. C. Just as the *wheat* is separated from the worthless straw or *chaff*, the *wine* is separated from the worthless sediment or *dregs*.

(Part to Whole)

14. D. To *ogle* is to *observe* or look at someone provocatively (in an attention-getting manner). To *flaunt* is to *display* or show off something provocatively (in an attention-getting manner).

(Manner)

15. E. Someone *abstemious* (sparing in drinking and eating) manifests *abstinence* (self-restraint in drinking and eating). Someone *pusillanimous* (cowardly) manifests *cravenness* (cowardice).

(Synonym Variant)

16. A. Something *ineluctable* (unavoidable) is impossible to *avoid*. Something *ineffable* (inexpressible) is impossible to *utter*.

(Antonym Variant)

17. C. The passage points out that in this period the differences between the two branches of the suffrage movement were diminishing in importance. Thus, it is *accounting for changes* occurring in the movement.
Choice A is incorrect. Both are mentioned (along with other suffragist leaders) in the context of the movements they led, but, while the movements are directly contrasted, Anthony and Howe are not directly contrasted.
Choice B is incorrect. The movement did not advance in this period.
Choice D is incorrect. The divisions were becoming less important, not more so, as the two branches became increasingly alike in nature.
Choice E is incorrect. It is unsupported by the passage.

18. E. The National took up the cudgels for *all* women in distress, whatever their social or economic standing.

19. A. The revered Mrs. Howe stood for the forces of propriety that were engulfing the suffragist movement. The embodiment of decorum, she was a *venerated figurehead* to be admired and respected, not a revolutionary firebrand to be followed into the battle.
Choice B is incorrect. Nothing in the passage suggests Mrs. Howe was overzealous.
Choice C is incorrect. Mrs. Howe was orthodox in her thinking, not heterodox.
Choice D is incorrect. A lay preacher is by definition not a member of the clergy. Therefore, Mrs. Howe was not an ordained cleric.
Choice E is incorrect. Mrs. Howe was characterized by a lack of militancy.

20. D. The passage focuses on describing the factors which led to the diminution or lessening of radicalism in the movement for women's suffrage.
Choice A is incorrect. The title is far too limited in scope to cover the entire passage.
Choice B is incorrect. The title is far too general to suit the passage.
Choice C is incorrect. The title is inapt: the passage focuses not on the rifts but on the diminution of radicalism which led to the closing of the rifts.
Choice E is incorrect. The title is far too broad in scope.

21. C. The author refers to the public's reaction to the Molly Maguire trials as "hysteria" that was "whipped up" or deliberately incited. Clearly, her attitude towards it is that it was *overwrought* or overexcited.
Note how the use of words that convey emotion ("hysteria") helps you to determine the author's attitude to the subject.

22. B. The passage describes Anthony as "ever catholic": very broad in sympathies; not provincial in outlook. Anthony was willing to work with anyone; her sympathies were *inclusive*, extending

sisterhood to all those who shared her espousal of woman suffrage.

Note that *catholic* here is used in its less familiar sense of "inclusive; universal," not in its common sense of "pertaining to the Roman Catholic church."

23. D. The first sentence of the final paragraph indicates that the author's concern is to avoid a misconception or *correct a misapprehension* about what caused the trend towards conservatism in the suffrage movement.

24. C. If even the radical Susan B. Anthony would have had second thoughts about flouting or disregarding Federal election laws, we may logically infer that the ordinary, not quite so militant movement member would have viewed such actions with disapproval or *disapprobation*.

25. E. The measure of a plant or animal's fitness in terms of natural selection is the number of offspring produced that survive into the next generation—its *reproductive advantage*.
Question A is unanswerable on the basis of the passage. No specific mimetic trait is cited as most effective.
Question B is unanswerable on the basis of the passage. No such difference is discussed.
Question C is unanswerable on the basis of the passage. The passage states that plant mimicry is not under voluntary control; it says nothing about the existence or non-existence of voluntary control in animal mimicry.
Question D is unanswerable on the basis of the passage. No such possibility is discussed.

26. D. In imitating its mother's hunting strategies, the kit fox is not duping any signal receiver in order to derive a reproductive advantage. It is merely developing its skills as a predator.
Choice A is incorrect. The chameleon's evolved ability to change the color of its skin renders it difficult for predators to discern. Thus, it has a better chance to produce offspring that survive into the next generation.
Choice B is incorrect. The butterfly's mimetic coloration causes it to be avoided by predators. Thus, it has a better chance to produce offspring that survive into the next generation.
Choice C is incorrect. The plant's resemblance to the nearby nectar-producing plant draws insects to it. Unable to distinguish between the model and the mimic, the insects pollinate both of them. This enables the plant to reproduce.
Choice E is incorrect. The orchid's scent, with its resemblance to the female insect's sexual attractant, draws male members of that insect species to it and thus aids in its pollination.

27. B. To *camouflage* a plant is to disguise or hide it. Its decreased visibility would be most helpful to it in hiding it from predators, thus leaving it free to produce offspring.
Choice A is incorrect. A hidden plant would be *less* likely to attract pollinators than a more visible plant would.
Choices C and D are incorrect. Neither is a logical outcome of camouflaging.
Choice E is incorrect. Depleting the number of a plant's offspring *diminishes* rather than increases the plant's potential for survival.

28. C. The opposite of to *terminate* (end) is to *begin*.
Think of "terminating someone's employment."

29. A. The opposite of to *protract* or prolong is to *abbreviate* or shorten.
Think of "protracting a lawsuit."

30. B. The opposite of *volubility* (glibness, talkativeness) is *brevity* (briefness, pithiness).
Think of "unrestrained volubility."

31. E. The opposite of *late-blooming* is maturing early or *precocious*.
Beware eye-catchers. Choice D is incorrect. Something *embryonic* is in an incipient stage; it has not yet bloomed at all.
Think of Einstein, "a late-blooming genius" who was considered not particularly intelligent as a child.

32. C. The opposite of to *hone* or sharpen is to *dull* (make blunt).
Think of "honing a razor."

33. B. The opposite of *phlegmatic* (stolid; undemonstrative) is *ardent* (passionate; eager).
Think of "phlegmatic and uncaring."

34. E. The opposite of a *banality* (commonplace; trite expression) is a *novel expression*.
Think of "the banality of a greeting card rhyme."

35. B. The opposite of *erudite* (scholarly; learned) is *ignorant*.
Think of "an erudite scholar."

36. E. The opposite of *plethora* (overabundance) is *scarcity*.
Think of "a plethora of tax forms."

37. B. The opposite of *currency* (vogue or prevalence; period of acceptance) is *obsolescence* (process of falling into disuse).
Beware eye-catchers. Choice D is incorrect. *Currency* here is unrelated to money.
Think of "the currency of an idea."

38. C.   The opposite of to *skirt* something (avoid dealing with a topic or question) is to *address* or
deal directly with it.
Think of "skirting an issue."

Section 3   Quantitative

1. B. $\dfrac{n + 7}{3} + \dfrac{n - 3}{4}$

$\dfrac{4n + 28 + 3n - 9}{12}$

$\dfrac{7n + 19}{12}$

The numerators are the same but the fraction in
Column *B* has a smaller denominator, denoting
a larger quantity.

2. B. $1y + .01y = 2.2$
$10y + 1y = 220$
$11y = 220$
$y = 20$
$.1y = 2$

3. C.   The reciprocal of 4 is $\dfrac{1}{4}$

$\sqrt{\dfrac{1}{16}} = \dfrac{1}{4}$

4. A. $\sqrt{1440}$ is a two-digit number $(37+)$ *Note*: for
this test you are required only to estimate
square roots.

5. B.   1 yard = 3 feet
(.5) or ½ yard = 1 foot, 6 inches
(1.5) or 1½ yards = 4 feet, 6 inches

6. C.   Observe $10 + 5$; $9 + 6$; $8 + 7$........
There are five additions with the sum in each
case equal to 15.

7. B. $8 \times 3 = 24, 7 \times 3 = 21 + 2 = 23$.

Therefore $\triangle = 3$. Since $8 \times 7 = 56$,

then $\bigcirc = 6$.

8. D.   Since Rose is older than Mary, she may be older
or younger than Sam.

9. B. $4x = 4(14) - 4$
$4x = 56 - 4$
$4x = 52$ and $x = 13$

10. A.   Since $x = 65$ and $AC = BC$, then the measure
of angle *ABC* is 65°, and the measure of angle
ACB is 50°. Since $BC \parallel DE$, then $y = 50°$ and
$x > y$.

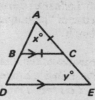

11. D.   Since $AD = 5$ and the area = 20 square
inches, we can find the value of base *BC* but not
the value of *DC*. *BC* equals 8 inches but *BD*
will be equal to *DC* only if $AB = AC$.

12. C.   Since $y = 50$, the measure of angle *DCB* is
100° and the measure of angle *ABC* is 80° since
ABCD is a parallelogram. Since $x = 40$, then z
$= 180 - 90$ or 90 and $z - y = 90 - 50$
or 40.

13. C.   Rate = Distance ÷ Time
Rate = 36 miles ÷ ¾ hour
$(36)(\frac{4}{3}) = 48$ miles per hour

14. A.   In Column A, *d*, the smallest integer, is subtracted from the integer with the largest value.

15. D. $\dfrac{BC \times AB}{2} = 18$, but any of the following may
be true: $BC > AB$, $BC < AB$, or $BC = AB$.

16. A. $\dfrac{8}{.8} = \dfrac{80}{8} = 10$

$\dfrac{.8}{8} = \dfrac{8}{80} = \dfrac{1}{10}$

$(.8)^2 = 0.64$

$\sqrt{.8} = .8+$

$0.8\pi = (.8)(3.14) = 2.5+$

17. E. $17xy + 7 = 19xy$
$7 = 2xy$
$14 = 4xy$

18. D.   Average = XY
Sum ÷ 2 = XY
Sum = $2XY$
$2XY = X + ?$
$? = 2XY - X$

19. C. This is a direct proportion.
    Let x = length of shorter dimension of enlargement.

$$\frac{\text{longer dimension}}{\text{shorter dimension}} = \frac{2\frac{1}{2}}{4} = \frac{1\frac{1}{8}}{x}$$

$$2\frac{1}{2}x = (4)(1\frac{7}{8})$$

$$\frac{5x}{2} = \frac{60}{8}$$

$$40x = 120$$

$$x = 3$$

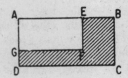

20. D. $AEB = 12 \quad AE = 8$
    $AGD = 6 \quad AG = 4$
    Area $AEFG = 32$
    Area $ABCD = 72$
    Area of shaded part = 40

21. C. Be careful to read the proper line (regular depositors). The point is midway between 90 and 100.

22. A. Number of Xmas Club depositors = 60,000
    Number of Regular depositors = 90,000
    60,000 : 90,000 or 6 : 9 or $\frac{6}{9}$ or $\frac{2}{3}$.

23. B. In 1979 there were 110,000. In the previous year there were 70,000 depositors, for an increase of 40,000 depositors. Without calculation note that the largest angle of inclination is for this period. It is greater than any other one-year period.

24. C. (58.6%) of $360° = (.586)(360°) = 210.9°$

25. E. (Amount invested)(Rate of interest) = Interest
    or, Amount invested = $\dfrac{\text{Interest}}{\text{Rate of interest}}$

    Amount invested in bonds = $\dfrac{x \text{ dollars}}{b\%}$

    or $\dfrac{x \text{ dollars}}{b/100}$

    or $x \div \dfrac{b}{100}$ or $x \cdot \left(\dfrac{100}{b}\right)$ or $(x)\left(\dfrac{100}{b}\right)$ or $\dfrac{\$100x}{b}$.

    Since the amount invested in bonds = $\dfrac{\$100x}{b}$,

the amount invested in mortgages must be 2 $\left(\dfrac{100x}{b}\right)$ dollars or $\$\dfrac{200x}{b}$ since the chart indicates that twice as much (58.6%) is invested in mortgages as is invested in bonds (28.3%).

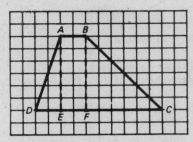

26. D. Draw altitudes AE and BF.
    Area of figure = $\triangle AED + \triangle BFC +$ rectangle $AEFB$
    Area of $\triangle AED = \dfrac{bh}{2}$
    or $\dfrac{(2 \text{ units})(6 \text{ units})}{2}$ or 6 square units.
    Area of $\triangle BCF = \dfrac{bh}{2}$ or $\dfrac{(6 \text{ units})(6 \text{ units})}{2}$
    or 18 square units.
    Area of rectange $AEFB = lw$ or (2 units)(6 units) or 12 square units.
    Sum = 36 square units.
    Or apply formula for area of trapezoid:
    Area = $\dfrac{1}{2}h(b + b_1)$
    Area = $\dfrac{1}{2}(6)(10 + 2)$
    Area = 36 square units.

27. B. Between 1 P.M. and 3:52 P.M. there are 172 minutes. There are *three* intervals between the 4 classes. 3×4 minutes, or 12 minutes, is the time spent in passing to classes. That leaves 172 − 12 or 160 minutes for instruction or 40 minutes for each class period.

28. D. Factor $x^2 + 2x - 8$ into $(x + 4)(x - 2)$. If x is either -4 or 2, $x^2 + 2x - 8 = 0$, and D is the correct answer.

29. A. This is a case of ratio and proportion.
    $\dfrac{\text{nautical}}{\text{statute}} = \dfrac{630}{720} = \dfrac{x}{1}$
    $x = .875$

30. E. (Average)(Number of cases) = sum
    $$(x)(P) = Px$$
    $$(y)(N) = Ny$$
    $$\frac{\text{Sum}}{\text{Number of cases}} = \text{average}$$
    $$\frac{Px + Ny}{P + N} = \text{average}$$

Section 4   Quantitative

1. C.   Since the triangle is equilateral
$$3a + 15 = 5a + 1 = 2a + 22$$
$$3a + 15 = 5a + 1$$
$$14 = 2a$$
$$7 = a$$

2. C.   From -5 to zero there are 5 integers and from zero to $+5$ there are 5 integers. Also, from $+5$ to $+15$ there are 10 integers.

3. A.   Since $x - y = 7$, then $x = y + 7$. x and y have many values, but x is always greater than y by 7.

4. B.   Since the area $= 25$, each side $= 5$.
The sum of three sides of the square $= 15$.

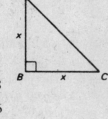

5. B. $\dfrac{x^2}{2} = 18$
$$x^2 = 36$$
$$x = 6'$$
Therefore $AC = 6\sqrt{2}$
$$6\sqrt{2} > 6$$

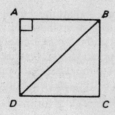

6. C. $AB = 6$
Perimeter $= 24$

7. C.   Area $= \dfrac{1}{2}(6)(6) = 18$

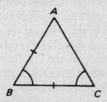

8. C. $AB = BC$ (given).
Since the measure of angle B equals the measure of angle C, $AB = AC$. Therefore ABC is equilateral and $m\angle A = m\angle B = m\angle C$ and $m\angle B + m\angle C = m\angle B + m\angle A$.

9. A. $x = 0.5$
$$4x = (0.5)(4) = 2.0$$
$$x^4 = (0.5)(0.5)(0.5)(0.5) = 0.0625$$
If you prefer to work with fractions:
$$\left(\frac{1}{2}\right)(4) = 2 \text{ and } \left(\frac{1}{2}\right)\left(\frac{1}{2}\right)\left(\frac{1}{2}\right)\left(\frac{1}{2}\right) = \frac{1}{16}$$

10. B.   The fraction in Column A has a denominator with a negative value.

11. D.   The area of the triangles is the result of the products of the base and altitude and not the value of the sides.

12. C.   Let $x =$ the first of the integers, then the sum $= x + x + 1 + x + 2 + x + 3 + x + 4 = 5x + 10$.
$5x + 10 = 35$ (given), then $5x = 25$.
$x = 5$ and the largest integer, $x + 4 = 9$.

13. A. $\sqrt{160} = \sqrt{16}\sqrt{10} = 4\sqrt{10}$

14. C.   Since the triangle is equilateral, $x = 60$ and exterior angle $y = 120$. Therefore $2x = y$.

15. B.   If $\dfrac{2}{3}$ corresponds to 12 gallons, then $\dfrac{1}{3}$ corresponds to 6 gallons, and $\dfrac{3}{3}$ corresponds to 18 gallons (Column A).

16. C.   Evidently, 4 cows produce 1 can of milk in one day. Therefore, 8 cows could produce 2 cans of milk in one day. In four days, 8 cows will be able to produce 8 cans of milk.

17. A.   Visualize the situation. The amount of pure alcohol remains the same after the dilution with water.

18. E.   Note that the question gives information about the transfer of teachers, but asks about the *remaining* teachers.
$$\frac{60}{80} = \frac{3}{4} = 75\%$$

19. E.   152 pounds and 4 ounces $= 152.25$ pounds
$152.25 \div 3 = 50.75$ pounds
$.75$ or $\dfrac{3}{4}$ pounds $= 12$ ounces

20. E.   Let $x =$ number of contestants.
$$.05x = 30$$
$$5x = 3,000$$
$$x = 600$$

21. C.   500 grams of carbohydrates $= 2,050$ calories
100 grams of carbohydrates $= 410$ calories
1 gram of carbohydrate $= 4.1$ calories

22. A.   Total calories = 3,390
     Calories from protein = 410
     $\dfrac{410}{3,390} = \dfrac{41}{339} = 12+\%$

23. C.   100 grams of fat = 930 calories
     1,000 grams of fat = 9,300 calories
     To obtain 9,300 calories from carbohydrates,
     set up a proportion, letting x = number of
     grams of carbohydrates needed.
     $\dfrac{500 \text{ grams}}{2,050 \text{ calories}} = \dfrac{x}{9,300 \text{ calories}}$
     $2,050x = (9,300)(500)$
     $\quad\quad x = 2,268$ (to the nearest gram)

24. B.   Boys at 17 require 3,750 calories per day.
     Girls at 17 require 2,750 calories per day.
     Difference = 1,000

25. D.   Observe regular increase for both sexes up to
     age 13.

26. D.   Since the driver's fee is paid with the car, the
     charge for $n - 1$ person = $c(n - 1)$ cents; cost
     of car and driver = 50¢.
     $T = 50 + c(n - 1)$

27. C.   Gloria will cut down on all constituents of the
     recipe in the ratio of $1\frac{1}{2}$:1 or 1.5:1.
     Let x = amount of boiling water Gloria will
     use.

28. B.   1 kilogram = 2.2 lb
     20 kilograms = 44 lb

29. A.   I is not correct because $\frac{1}{a}$ is not less than a if a
     is 1 or a fraction less than 1
     $\left(\text{e.g.}, \frac{1}{8} \text{ or } 8 \text{ is not less than } \frac{1}{8} \right)$. II is correct
     because $\dfrac{a + b}{2a} = \dfrac{2b}{b + a}$ reduces to $\dfrac{2b}{2b} = \dfrac{2b}{2b}$
     (which we know is correct) when $a = b$. III is
     incorrect when a is greater than b $\left(\text{e.g.}, \dfrac{3 + 1}{2 + 1} \right.$
     is not more than $\left. \dfrac{3}{2} \right)$. This statement is also not
     correct when c is negative and a is less than b
     $\left(\text{e.g., if } c \text{ is } - 1, \dfrac{2 - 1}{3 - 1} \text{ is not more than } \dfrac{2}{3} \right)$.
     The only correct answer is II.

30. A. $\dfrac{y}{s - t} = \dfrac{s + t}{t - s}$ (given)
     $\dfrac{y}{s - t} = \dfrac{-s - t}{-t + s}$ (multiplying fraction by $-\frac{1}{1}$)
     $\dfrac{y}{s - t} = \dfrac{-s - t}{s - t}$ (rearrangement of terms)
     $y = -s - t$ (multiplying by $s - t$)

Section 5   Analytical

1-4.   Summarize Michael's schedule

Monday	3:30-4:30	Piano Lesson
Tuesday	4:00-6:00	Karate
Wednesday	4:00-6:00	Art Class
Thursday	12:00-	Free
Friday	3:00-	Club Program

1. C.   Note that Thursday is a free afternoon.

2. D.   Since he must begin his piano lesson at 3:30
     P.M., Thursday is the only available day.

3. C.   Since Michael would no longer have to attend
     his original Wednesday art class, that day and
     his free Thursday afternoon would make those
     days available for his new class.

4. E.   Since karate and art meet until 6 P.M., Michael
     will have to give up these activities in order to
     be present at the 5 P.M. basketball sessions.
     After his piano lesson, he will have thirty min-
     utes to get to the basketball court. Thursday
     afternoon is free, and the Friday club program
     is dismissed by 4:30.

5. C.   This question tests an "all/only" confusion. Sar-
     ah's statement means that everyone on the Cabi-
     net is a General Council member; but there may
     be other General Council members who are not
     on the Cabinet. By giving the example of Dr.
     Grogan as a refutation of Sarah's argument,
     Charles reveals that he thought she meant that
     all General Council members were on the Cabi-
     net. Choice A is a correct restatement of Sar-
     ah's argument. B and E refer to the example
     chosen to refute Sarah's general statement; but
     Charles did not necessarily think Sarah was say-
     ing anything about Dr. Grogan specifically. D
     claims too much: by citing Grogan, Charles
     indicates only that he disagrees that *all* General
     Council members are on the Cabinet, not that
     he thinks none are.

6. D. Analyze the argument: it says that the unemployment problem has one cause, worker laziness. Anything that gives evidence for this strengthens the argument; anything that gives evidence against it or suggests another explanation weakens it. D, if true, *might* be evidence that the unemployed are lazy. Choices A, B, and E all suggest different explanations: A, that the unemployed lack the requisite skills or experience; B, that they are in the wrong places; E, that unemployment has another cause altogether. Choice B tends to weaken the idea that unemployed people are lazy.

7. D. Event X (baldness) occurs after Event Y (practicing law). The author of the argument assumes that Event Y caused Event X, and vows to avoid Event X by avoiding Event Y. This is poor reasoning, especially since the author is overlooking at least one far more probable cause for Event X, i.e., heredity. The same kind of poor reasoning is used in choice D, where Event X = injury, Event Y = eating at Rosie's, and the overlooked probable cause is unsafe working conditions. Choice B has the second closest resemblance, but here the reasoning is somewhat more plausible; speeding can lead to one's getting a speeding ticket. Choices A, C, and E all differ from the original argument in the latter portion of their reasoning.

8–12. The only problem in puzzles like this one is to rank the items correctly; the questions are then simple. Use initials, since the seven artists' names begin with different letters. Ignore G, for which no definite value is given, and start with the one whose value seems lowest. This is I. If you call I's value 1, all the others can be expressed as multiples of 1, and we get:

$$G = ?$$
$$I = 1$$
$$J = 3 \text{ times } 1 = 3$$
$$E = J + I = 3 + 1 = 4$$
$$D = J + E = 3 + 4 = 7$$
$$F = D = 7$$
$$H = F + E + J = 7 + 4 + 3 = 14$$

8. E. You can tell that the Greuze is worth least and the Hartley most without really figuring out the rest, but all choices include those values. If you've constructed a table like the one shown here, inspection gives choice E.

9. E. D = 7, H = 14. None of the other choices adds up to 7.

10. B. H = 14. Option I, D + I + F, adds up to 15. Option II, E + J + D, adds up to 14, which is right. Option III, I + E + J, adds up to 8.

11. D. E + I = 5, so the value of the Greuze, in terms of the value of the Ingres which is our base, is $\frac{1}{2}$. H = 14 or 28 times this.

12. B. H + E = 18. I + J + D + F = 18. Choice A: 14 ≠ 12. Choice C: 14 ≠ 15. Choice D: 15 ≠ 14. Choice E: 7 ≠ 8.

13–16. A diagram of the kind shown here is your best approach to this type of problem.

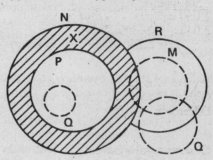

A circle inside another (like circles P and N) indicates that all members of the first (inner) group belong to the second (outer) group. Overlapping circles (like circles N and M) indicate that the groups have members in common, but neither is contained entirely within the other. Solid lines may be used for relationships that are definitely known; broken lines for relationships that are uncertain. So: statement (1) gives us the two circles N and P; statements (1) and (2) the shaded lines for X. Statement (4) gives us a circle, R, that lies entirely outside N. Why make it border N, instead of being totally separate? Because statement (3) gives us a circle, M, lying outside P, and (5) tells us M lies *inside* the areas of X and R (and outside P). But circle M is made entirely of broken lines because we can't know for sure whether it overlaps the R/N border, lies entirely within the X area of N, or lies entirely within R. Finally, statement (6) gives us a group, Q, that lies either inside P, or outside N (whether inside R or not) or both. Once you have all this admittedly complex information diagrammed, the questions are fairly easy.

13. A. I is true, because R lies entirely outside N while P is inside. II contradicts condition (2). III may or may not be true, depending on the location of M.

14. C. This is false, because R lies entirely outside N, while X lies inside. Q *may* lie within P (A) or outside both N and R (B), or both; we don't know. D may look impossible, but expand the M circle in your mind until it exactly coincides with the R circle: now, all R are M and vice versa. No stated condition prevents you from drawing the circle this way, so it is not impossible. No matter how you draw the M circle, it should be apparent that *some* X may not be M (E).

15. **B.** Statement (5), together with statement (2), indicates that no M can be P, since no X can be P. Statement (2) gives information about X not contained in any other statement; (4) excludes R from N; (5), which may look like the counterpart to (2), contains the additional information that no M are to be found outside X and R; and statement (6) contains the only information about Q.

16. **E.** Statement (2) could be untrue under either, or both, of two conditions: if some X were P, or if some N that was not P was not X. This is what choice E states. Choice D states only the second possibility; it is not necessarily true if statement (2) is false, because some X that was P would make statement (2) false even if choice D were not true. Choices A, B, and C remain false as long as statements (5), (1), and (6), respectively, are true.

Person	Campsite	Lake	State
B		K	
	H	J	N
		I	P
A			O

17–22. A four-by-four grid allows you to graph all the information. Omitting (for the moment) the statement about Donna, the other statements give you:

The other items now follow by elimination. Brian and Keewaukett Lake must be in Maine. Since Donna cannot be at High Point, she, and Freeport Campsite, must be on Indian Point Lake in Pennsylvania. Carol must be at High Point. Allen must be at Leesville, the only remaining lake. Brian and Allen must be at Edmunds and Grand Isle Campsites, but we don't know which of them is at which.

17. **B.** See above. Choice A is possible, but we can't be sure. C is a direct contradiction of the information about Brian. D and E are ruled out once everything is diagrammed.

18. **A.** See the diagram and the above discussion.

19. **D.** Allen is at Edmunds or Grand Isle (I). Carol is in Nebraska (II). Donna is at Freeport (III).

20. **A.** See the diagram.

21. **E.** See the diagram. Allen is at Leesville Lake, it is in Ohio, and it is the site of either Edmunds or Grand Isle Campsite, but not Freeport Campsite.

22. **B.** This is the item that remained ambiguous. Keewaukett is in Maine (A); Freeport Campsite is in Pennsylvania (C); Carol is in Nebraska and Donna is in Pennsylvania (D, E).

23. **B.** The ad focuses on one point, luxury; it is weakened by its failure to mention other points concerning the dishwasher's performance. B is intrinsically the most important such point; D and E are less important, because no one wants a dishwasher that does a poor job even if it holds a lot of dishes and uses very little electricity. Choice A is also not central—it is important only in case of breakdown. C points to a weakness in the arguments about luxury, but it doesn't show why these arguments are inherently weak.

24. **A.** It is claimed that the archeologists could not have understood the culture because, without written records, they have no evidence about how people thought. The assumption is that *only* written records provide such evidence, and that physical artifacts do not (A). B and C are side issues: neither one establishes what the argument assumes, that written records are the only clue to what people thought. D and E are too broad: the argument claims neither that the artifacts tell us nothing about other aspects of the civilization (D), nor that written records by themselves are sufficient to reconstruct the civilization (E).

25. **B.** Statement I is *not* assumed. The conclusion is that Roger will never be an *outstanding* football player, not that he will never play football. Statement II *is* assumed. The injured knee is cited as the reason Roger will never play outstanding football. Statement III is *not* assumed. Nothing was mentioned in the argument about Roger's playing *professional* football.

Section 6   Analytical

1–4. The only problem with this one is that George's preferences regarding Mahler, Beethoven, and Bartok cannot be related exactly to his preferences among Haydn, Hindemith, and Mozart. Note also that while he *definitely* doesn't prefer Mahler to Beethoven, he may or may not prefer Beethoven to Mahler—instead, he may like them equally. (You're never told that George always has a definite preference.) Otherwise, the questions are fairly straightforward.

1. D. George definitely prefers Mahler to Mozart, and likes Beethoven as much as, or more than, Mahler. He definitely prefers Mahler to Bartok (A) and *may* prefer Beethoven to Mahler (B). We known he prefers Mahler to Mozart and to any other composer whose name begins with B, including Bartok, but this doesn't tell us whether or not he prefers Bartok to Mozart (C). We don't know how much he likes Mahler, so he may prefer Mahler to Haydn (E).

2. B. This restates the information in the third sentence; it's the only set of preferences among three composers that we know for certain. George may or may not play Bartok before Mozart (A). We don't know that he prefers Beethoven to Mahler, just that he *doesn't* prefer Mahler to Beethoven (C). D and E may be true but may not be.

3. D. George definitely prefers Beethoven to Bartok. He also prefers Mahler to Mozart, and likes Beethoven; at least as much as Mahler. So among the six, Mozart and Bartok must come after Beethoven. All the other choices are possibilities that cannot be eliminated.

4. E. George prefers Mahler to any composer whose name begins with B (including Berlioz) *except* Beethoven; since he doesn't prefer Mahler to Beethoven but does prefer him to Berlioz, he must prefer Beethoven to Berlioz. If Berlioz is played first, there can be no Beethoven record. None of the other choices is definitely true.

5. E. Examine the structure of the argument: *The Other Side* is best *since* even more people are seeing it...The assumption is that these numbers are a valid measurement of quality (E). All other choices focus on side issues.

6. C. The author is using circular reasoning. He attempts to prove that the scientific worldview is accurate by showing that it has been verified by the scientific method; yet the validity of the scientific method is itself at issue. The author does not commit the errors mentioned in choices A and E. Although choice B is true, it is neither a flaw in nor a necessary part of the author's reasoning. Choice D is wrong because the author claims merely that the scientific worldview is the most accurate, not that it is perfect.

7. A. Alfredo replies to the claim about meditation by stating that aggressiveness is most important to a boxer. The unstated assumption is that meditation somehow lessens aggressiveness (A). B is off because, clearly, Alfredo assumes that *some* effect results from meditation. Alfredo implies nothing about how good or poor a boxer George was before, and implicitly *accepts* Melinda's

testimony that he has been meditating (C, D). E is directly contrary to Alfredo's comment about aggressiveness, which is certainly a mental attitude.

8–12. As in most logical puzzles, a diagram of some sort is the place to start. The simplest is a sketch of the ten seats (below). When you know someone is in a seat, put his/her initial in the box; if a seat is definitely occupied by either of two persons, put both initials there. If someone's position is uncertain, jot the initial below the possible seats. Skip to whichever statements yield the most definite information to start. Here, statements (2), (4), (6), and (7) give

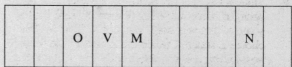

Statement (3) gives an uncertainty: We must be in seat 6 or 8. Statement (5) resolves the question: W's date cannot be M, in seat 5, because M is next to V. So W's date must be in seat 7, W must be in seat 8, and T must be M's date, in seat 6. Nothing else is known definitely. The two remaining women's seats must be occupied by S and U, and the two remaining men's seats by L and P, but we can't tell exactly who is where. Complete your diagram like this:

L	S					L			S
P	U	O	V	M	T		W	N	
							P		U

The questions are now easy.

8. D. This can be read from the diagram. Choice A reverses O and V and gives a definite location for U, which we don't know. B puts L in seat 7, when we can't know that. C and E skip a seat—the question specifies persons sitting adjacent to one another.

9. D. U may be in seat 2 or 10. N is in seat 9, and either L or P is in seat 1. Any of these could be U's date.

10. C. Look at your diagram. Exactly who is in the seats at the two ends of the row (I, II) remains uncertain. The women nearest T (III) are V on the left and W on the right.

11. C. We know that either L or P is in seat 7, but we don't know which. The other must be in seat 1. If we are told which of the two is in seat 7, we know his date is W. If we are told which of the two is in seat 1, we don't know *his* date (it could be S or U) but we know that the other's date is W.

12. D.   To determine T's position we need statement
(1), which gives the conditions for all seating;
(3), which gives the seats W may occupy; (2),
(6), and (7), which determine where O, V, and
M sit; and (5), which determines that T is to the
left of W's date and that W must be in seat 8.
The one statement that is irrelevant is (4).

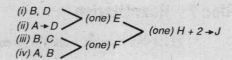

13-16.   Draw a diagram something like the one shown
here. The lowercase Roman numerals (i)-(iv)
signify the prerequisite combinations leading to
E and F. The diagram will keep conditions (1)-
(6) clear, but you will have to remember conditions (7) and (8) on your own.

13. A.   See rule (6). J can occur only if two prerequisites result in either E or F (not both), and
therefore H, and two other unused prerequisites
are also present—so it can occur only if A, B,
C, and D all occur. But if all four occur and A
occurs first, (i) and (ii) cancel each other and E
does not occur, while (iii) and (iv) also cancel
each other and F does not occur. J is possible in
the conditions given in choices B, C, D, and E.
If all four of A, B, C, and D occur, the essential
question is whether A precedes D. As long as it
does not, (ii) cannot occur, E will result from
(i), and H and J can occur.

14. B.   In option III, (ii) cancels (i), so E does not
occur, but A and B lead to F (iv), so F and
therefore H occur. In option I, (ii) does not
occur but (i) does, so E occurs, while A and B
lead to F (iv); since E and F both occur, H does
not occur.

15. D.   (i) leads to E unimpeded by (ii), which does not
occur because A does not precede D. The
occurrence of A, B, and C means that (iii) and
(iv) cancel each other and F does not occur.
Since E occurs, H occurs, and unused prerequisites A and C, plus H, yield J. In choice A, (iii)
leads to F and therefore to H, but there is only
one unused prerequisite. In choice B, (i) leads
to E and (iii) leads to F, so H does not occur. J
cannot occur without H. In choice C, (ii) leads
to E and therefore H, but there is only one
unused prerequisite. In choice E, (i) and (ii)
occur, so E cannot occur (rule 7); similarly, (iii)
and (iv) occur, so F cannot occur. Therefore, H
cannot occur.

16. C.   B and C together are (iii), so prerequisites exist
for F. If option I only occurs, (iv) will cancel
(iii) and F will not occur; but E cannot occur
without D, so neither E nor F will occur, H cannot occur, and J cannot occur. If option (ii) only
occurs, B and D or (i) will occur, E and F will
both occur, and H cannot occur; therefore J cannot occur. But if option I occurs, and therefore
F does not occur, while option II also occurs,
and therefore E occurs, H will occur, while
unused prerequisites A and C will combine
with H to yield J.

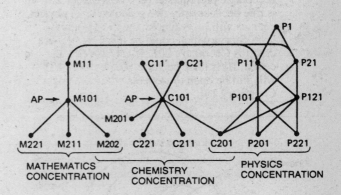

17-21.   The information given can be diagrammed in
the way shown here. Many of the questions can
then be answered by inspection of the diagram,
without even looking back at the rules as
printed.

17. C.   I is true because Physics 101 and 121 are alternative prerequisites for the 200-level courses in
Physics. II is true because Chemistry 201
counts as a graduate-level course, along with
Physics 201 and 221. III is not true because
Mathematics 11 can substitute for Physics 1,
and Physics 21 for Physics 11.

18. C.   To qualify using chemistry courses only, the
student must take Chemistry 11 *or* 21, 101, 201,
211, and 221—five in all. Using Mathematics
201 would cut one chemistry course, but to do
this the student must take at least two mathematics courses—101 and 201—so the total
becomes six.

19. D.   After the Physics 101/121 level, the student
must take Physics 201 and 221, plus Chemistry
201—but there are eight separate ways to reach
this level. You can just follow the separate lines
on the diagram: Mathematics 11 *or* Physics 1,
followed by Physics 11 *or* 21, followed by Physics 101 *or* 121.

20. **B.** I is out because Chemistry 101 must be taken to qualify for the 200-level Chemistry courses. II, though pedestrian, is just fine. III is out because Mathematics 201, not 211, satisfies the chemistry requirement.

21. **C.** In physics, one must take Mathematics 11 *or* Physics 1, Physics 11 *or* 21, Physics 101 *or* 121, and three graduate-level courses. In mathematics or chemistry, one can qualify with five courses, or four if one has advanced placement.

22. **C.** I is true because Chemistry 101 is the only acceptable prerequisite for Mathematics 201. II is true because only two graduate-level physics courses will be available; the third graduate-level course which could be taken for physics credit is Chemistry 201, which will be cancelled. III is false because Mathematics 201 will still be open to students who have taken Chemistry 101.

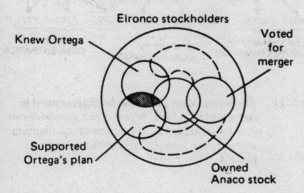

23. **A.** With a complex statement like this one, a circle diagram similar to those used in some analytical reasoning questions may be a help. In the diagram shown here, those who knew Ortega and those who supported her plan are shown as overlapping circles. The pro-merger votes are shown *not* intersecting the overlapping area (stockholders who knew Ortega *and* supported her plan); the circle for Anaco stock-owners does intersect it, and otherwise is drawn as generally as possible.
   With the aid of the diagram, you can see that choice A is impossible; choices B, D, and E are all possible, while choice C *must* be true.

24. **E.** The claim being discussed is that *only* the smart become rich, not that *all* the smart become rich. The way to disprove this view would be to point out that some stupid people also become rich (choice E). Choices B, C, and D, while possibly relevant to the issue raised, do not directly contradict the claim.

25. **B.** This choice combines the two psychological effects mentioned in the original argument.

Choices A and D are wrong because the argument states matters of (alleged) fact and does not, by itself, imply any recommendations. Choices C and E are wrong because the argument (if true) establishes that TV viewers *believe* certain things; it does not imply anything about what actually happens.

Section 7   Quantitative

1. **D.** No relationship between a and f is given.

2. **D.** The variable x may have a value between 65 and 80.

$$K \overset{\;\;6\;\;}{\rule{2cm}{0.4pt}} A \quad\quad B \overset{\;\;8\;\;}{\rule{2cm}{0.4pt}} C \quad\quad L$$
$$\underset{17}{\rule{4cm}{0.4pt}}$$

3. **A.** $KL = 23 + \text{length of } AB$
   $KL > 23$

4. **A.** $x \triangle y = x^2 + y^2$
   $(x \triangle y)^2 = (x^2 + y^2) = x^4 + 2x^2y^2 + y^4$ (Column
   $x^2 \triangle y^2 = (x^2)^2 + (y^2)^2 = x^4 + y^4$ (Column B)

5. **B.** $\sqrt{144} = 12$; $\sqrt{100} + \sqrt{44} = 10 + 6 + = 16 +$

6. **C.** Since $y = z$, because $AB = AC$, $x + y = x + z$ (if equals are added to equals the results are equal).

7. **C.** $\dfrac{3\sqrt{48}}{\sqrt{3}} \times \dfrac{\sqrt{3}}{\sqrt{3}} = \dfrac{3\sqrt{144}}{3} = \dfrac{(3)(12)}{3} = 12$

8. **A.** $\dfrac{x}{4} + \dfrac{x}{3} = \dfrac{7}{12}$
   $\dfrac{3x}{12} + \dfrac{4x}{12} = \dfrac{7}{12}$
   $3x + 4x = 7$
   $x = 1$
   $1 > -1$

9. **A.** The fraction with the larger denominator has the smaller value. Since the value of $\dfrac{9}{b}$ is greater than $\dfrac{9}{a}$, then $a > b$.

10. **B.** $0.003\% = 0.00003$
    $0.0003 > 0.00003$

11. C. $\dfrac{k}{4}\% = \dfrac{4}{100} = \dfrac{k}{4} \div 100 = \dfrac{k}{4} \times \dfrac{1}{100} = \dfrac{k}{400}$

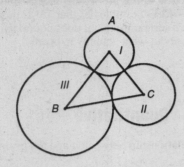

12. C. AB = 3 inches + 5 inches = 8 inches
BC = 5 inches + 4 inches = 9 inches
AC = 4 inches + 3 inches = 7 inches
                Total   24 inches = 2 feet

13. B.   Since $y = 130$, $z = 50$.
$m\angle ECD = 180° - 130° = 50°$
$2x = 50°$
$x = 25°$

14. A.   Since $abc = 0$ and $c = 1$, then either a or $b = 0$ or a and $b = 0$.

15. B. $0.1 + 0.01 + 0.001 = 0.111$ (sum)
average = $\dfrac{0.111}{3}$

$0.111 > \dfrac{0.111}{3}$

16. C.   Since $OC = BC$ and OC and OB are radii, triangle BOC is equilateral and the measure of angle $BOC = 60°$.
Therefore $x = 120$ and $\dfrac{1}{2}x = 60$.

17. B.   Select the choice in which the value of n is greater than the value of d in order to yield a value of $\dfrac{n}{d}$ greater than 1.

18. C.   Let x = the number.
$\dfrac{x}{2} = \dfrac{x}{3} + 17$
$3x = 2x + 102$
$x = 102$

19. A. $c + d = 180$ but $c \neq d$
$a = d$ (vertical angles)
$a = e$ (corresponding angles)
$f = b$ (corresponding angles)
$f = c$ (alternate interior angles)

20. B.   Let x = amount Florence had.
Let y = amount Sam had.
$x + \$10$ = amount Florence now has.
$y - \$10$ = amount Sam now has.
$x + y = \$100$

$\dfrac{x + \$10}{5} + \$4 = y - 10$

$x + \$10 + \$20 = 5y - \$50$
$x - 5y = -\$80$
$x + y = \$100$
$-x - y = -100$ [multiply by -1]
$x - 5y = -\$80$
$-6y = -\$180$ [subtraction]
$y = \$30$ (amount Sam had)
$\$30 - \$10 = \$20$ (amount Sam now has)

21. D. $6,000 : 302,000 :: x : 1,000,000$
$302,000x =$
$6,000 \times 1,000,000 = 6,000,000,000$
$x = \dfrac{60,000}{3}$ (rounded off) $= 20,000$
The closest number is 17.

22. C. $18 - 21$ group = $11,000$
$21 - 24$ group = $61,000$
         Total   = $72,000$
$\dfrac{72,000}{302,000} = 23 + \%$

23. D. $(73,000)(.04) = 2,920$

24. D.   20% or $\dfrac{1}{5}$ of $360° = 72°$

25. D.   Total between 21 and 27 :
$61,000 + 73,000 = 134,000$
$\dfrac{134,000}{302,000} = \dfrac{134}{302} = \dfrac{44}{100}$ (approx.) $= 44\%$

26. B.   Sum = $(0.6)(4)$ or 2.4.
$0.2 + 0.8 + 1 = 2$.
$x = 2.4 - 2$ or 0.4

27. C. $\dfrac{a^2 - b^2}{(a - b)^2} = \dfrac{(a + b)(a - b)}{(a - b)(a - b)} = \dfrac{a + b}{a - b}$

28. C.   This is a ratio problem.
$\dfrac{\text{number of items}}{\text{cost in ¢}} = \dfrac{2}{c} = \dfrac{?}{x}$
$c(?) = 2x$
$(?) = \dfrac{2x}{c}$

E ———— 6' ———— F   A ———————— 9' ———————— B

6' | 6' | 4' | | 4'

H ———— 6' ———— G   D ———————— 9' ———————— C

29. D.   Area of square = 36 square feet.
         Area of rectangle = 36 square feet.
         Since $AD = 4$, $DC = 9$ feet,
         and the perimeter of $ABCD = 26$ feet.

30. D.   Since the formula for the area of a circle is πr^2,
         any change in r will affect the area by the
         square of the amount of the change. Since the
         radius is doubled, the area will be four times as
         much $(2)^2$.

3 Sentence Completion Questions

- Testing Tactics
- Practice Exercises
- Answer Key

GRE sentence completion questions test your ability to use your vocabulary and recognize logical consistency among the elements in a sentence. You need to know more than the dictionary definitions of the words involved. You need to know how the words fit together to make logical and stylistic sense.

Sentence completion questions actually measure one part of reading comprehension. If you can recognize how the different parts of a sentence affect one another, you should do well at choosing the answer that best completes the meaning of the sentence or provides a clear, logical statement of fact. The ability to recognize irony and humor will also stand you in good stead, as will the ability to recognize figurative language and to distinguish between formal and informal levels of speech.

Because the sentence completion questions contain many clues that help you to answer them correctly (far more clues than the antonyms provide, for example), and because analyzing them helps you warm up for the reading passages later on in the test, answer them first. Then go on to tackle the analogies, the antonyms, and, finally, the time-consuming reading comprehension section.

GRE sentence completion questions may come from any of a number of different fields—art, literature, history, philosophy, botany, astronomy, geology, etc. You cannot predict what subject matter the sentences on your test will have. However, you can predict what general pattern they will follow.

1. Each GRE verbal section begins with seven sentence completion questions.

2. In each set of sentence completion questions, the first one or two are relatively simple to answer; the last one or two, relatively hard.

A look at the GRE's published tables showing the percentages of examinees answering each question cor-

rectly supports this point. In general, from 80–90 percent of the examinees taking a given test will answer the first sentence completion question in a set correctly. On the average, only approximately 35 percent of the examinees taking a given test will answer the last question in that set correctly.

What makes the hard questions hard?

1. **Vocabulary Level.** Sentences contain words like *intransigence, nonplussed, harbingers*. Answer choices include words like *penchant, abeyance, eclectic*. Questions employ unfamiliar secondary meanings of words—*brook* as a verb, *economy* with the meaning of *restraint*

2. **Grammatical Complexity.** Sentences combine the entire range of grammatical possibilities—subordinate clauses, relative clauses, prepositional phrases, gerunds, infinitives, etc.—in convoluted ways. The more complex the sentence, the more difficult it is for you to spot the key words that can unlock its meaning.

3. **Tone.** Sentences reflect the writer's attitude towards his subject matter. It is simple enough to comprehend material that is presented neutrally. It is far more difficult to comprehend material that is ironic, condescending, playful, somber or similarly complex in tone.

4. **Style.** Ideas may be expressed in different manners—ornately or sparely, poetically or prosaically, formally or informally, journalistically or academically, originally or imitatively. An author's style depends on such details as word choice, imagery, repetition, rhythm, sentence structure and length. Many of the most difficult GRE questions hinge on questions of style.

Work through the following tactics and learn the techniques that will help you with vocabulary, grammatical complexity, tone, and style.

Testing Tactics

Before You Look at the Choices, Read the Sentence and Think of a Word That Makes Sense

Your problem is to find the word that best completes the sentence in both thought and style. Before you look at the answer choices, see if you can come up with a word that makes logical sense in the context. Then look at all five choices. If the word you thought of is one of your five choices, select that as your answer. If the word you thought of is not one of your five choices, look for a synonym of that word. Select the synonym as your answer.

This tactic is helpful because it enables you to get a sense of the sentence as a whole without being distracted by any misleading answers among the answer choices. You are free to concentrate on spotting key words or phrases in the body of the sentence and to call on your own "writer's intuition" in arriving at a stylistically apt choice of word.

See how the process works in an example from a recent GRE.

> Since she believed him to be both candid and trustworthy, she refused to consider the possibility that his statement had been -------.
>
> (A) irrelevant   (B) facetious   (C) mistaken
> (D) critical   (E) insincere

This sentence presents a simple case of cause and effect. The key phrase here is *candid and trustworthy*. The woman has found the man to be frank and honest. *Therefore*, she refuses to believe he can say something _____ . What words immediately come to mind? *Dishonest, evasive, hypocritical*? The missing word is, of course, *insincere*. The woman expects openness (*candid*) and sincerity (*trustworthy*). The correct answer is Choice E.

Practice Tactic 1 extensively to develop your intuitive sense of the *mot juste*—the exactly right word. However, do not rely on Tactic 1 alone. On the test, always follow up Tactic 1 with Tactic 2.

Look at All the Possible Answers Before You Make Your Final Choice

Never decide on an answer before you have read all the choices. You are looking for the word that *best* fits the meaning of the sentence as a whole. In order to be sure you have not been hasty in making your decision, substitute all the answer choices for the missing word. Do not spend a lot of time doing so, but do try them all. That way you can satisfy yourself that you have come up with the *best* answer.

See how this tactic helps you deal with another question from a recent GRE.

> People should not be praised for their virtue if they lack the energy to be -------; in such cases, goodness is merely the effect of -------.
>
> (A) depraved..hesitation
> (B) cruel..effortlessness
> (C) wicked..indolence
> (D) unjust..boredom
> (E) iniquitous..impiety

On the basis of a loose sense of this sentence's meaning, you might be tempted to select Choice A. After all, this sentence basically tells you why you should not praise certain people for virtue. Clearly, you should not call people virtuous merely because they *hesitate* to perform a *depraved* or wicked act. However, this reading of the sentence is inadequate: it fails to take into account the sentence's key phrase.

The key phrase here is *lack...energy*. Lack energy for what? The first word of each answer choice is a synonym for *bad*. Thus, goodness is a result of a lack of the necessary energy to be bad. Examine the second word of each answer choice, eliminating those words that carry no suggestion of such a lack of energy. Does indecision or *hesitation* suggest a lack of energy? No, it suggests a lack of decisiveness. Does *effortlessness* or absence of strain suggest a lack of energy? No, it suggests a lack of difficulty. Does *boredom* or monotony suggest a lack of energy? No, it suggests a lack of interest. Does ungodliness or *impiety* suggest a lack of energy? No, it suggests a lack of reverence. Only one word suggests a lack of energy—*indolence*. Since goodness results from a lack of the energy to be bad, it is *merely* the effect of laziness or *indolence*.

Note the satiric tone of this epigram, and the use of *merely* to point up that this so-called goodness is no goodness at all.

In Double-Blank Sentences, Go Through the Answers, Testing the *First* Word in Each Choice (and Eliminating Those That Don't Fit)

In a sentence completion question with two blanks, read through the entire sentence to get a sense of it as a whole. Then insert the first word of each answer pair in the sentence's first blank. Ask yourself whether this particular word makes sense in this blank. If the initial word of an answer pair makes no sense in the sentence, you can eliminate that answer pair. (*Note:* Occasionally this tactic will not work. In the previous question, for example, the first words of all five answer pairs were near-synonyms. However, the tactic frequently pays off, as it does in the following example from a recent GRE.)

> During the 1960's assessments of the family shifted remarkably, from general endorsement of it as a worthwhile, stable institution to widespread ------- it as an oppressive and bankrupt one whose ------- was both imminent and welcome.
>
> (A) flight from..restitution
> (B) fascination with..corruption
> (C) rejection of..vogue
> (D) censure of..dissolution
> (E) relinquishment of..ascent

For a quick, general sense of the sentence, strip it of all its modifying phrases. What remains? *Assessments*

shifted remarkably from endorsement (approval, support) to _____.

Since *endorsement* or approval is highly positive, the shift most likely is in the negative direction of condemnation or disapproval. The phrase *oppressive and bankrupt* supports this conclusion. Your first missing word must be a synonym for *disapproval*.

Now eliminate the misfits. Choices A, B, and E fail to meet the test: *flight*, *fascination*, and *relinquishment* are not synonyms for *disapproval*. Consider them no further. Choice C, *rejection*, and Choice D, *censure*, however, both express disapprobation; they require a second look.

To decide between Choices C and D, consider the second blank. If you viewed the family as a cruel and worthless institution, what destiny for it would you welcome? You would welcome its *dissolution*, its destruction, not its popularity or *vogue*. The correct answer is clearly Choice D.

Remember, in double-blank sentences, the right answer must correctly fill **both** blanks. A wrong answer choice often includes one correct and one incorrect answer. ALWAYS test both words.

Watch for Signal Words That Link One Part of the Sentence to Another

Writers use transitions to link their ideas logically. These transitions or signal words are clues that can help you figure out what the sentence actually means.

GRE sentences often contain several signal words, combining them in complex ways.

Cause and Effect Signals

Look for words or phrases explicitly indicating that one thing **causes** another or logically determines another.

Cause and Effect Signal Words

accordingly	in order to
because	so...that
consequently	therefore
given	thus
hence	when...then
if...then	

Support Signals

Look for words or phrases explicitly indicating that the omitted portion of the sentence **supports** or **continues a thought** developed elsewhere in the sentence. In such cases, a synonym or near-synonym for another word in the sentence may provide the correct answer.

Support Signal Words

additionally	furthermore
also	indeed
and	likewise
as well	moreover
besides	too

Contrast Signals (Explicit)

Look for function words or phrases (conjunctions, sentence adverbs, etc.) that explicitly indicate a **contrast** between one idea and another, setting up a reversal of a thought. In such cases, an antonym or near-antonym for another word in the sentence may provide the correct answer.

Explicit Contrast Signal Words

albeit	nevertheless
although	nonetheless
but	notwithstanding
despite	on the contrary
even though	on the other hand
however	rather than
in contrast	still
in spite of	while
instead of	yet

Contrast Signals (Implicit)

Look for content words whose meaning inherently indicates a contrast. These words can turn a situation on its head. They indicate that something unexpected, possibly even unwanted, has occurred.

Implicit Contrast Signal Words

anomaly	anomalous	anomalously
illogic	illogical	illogically
incongruity	incongruous	incongruously
irony	ironic	ironically
paradox	paradoxical	paradoxically
surprise	surprising	surprisingly
	unexpected	unexpectedly

Note the function of such a contrast signal word in the following GRE question.

> The paradoxical aspect of the myths about Demeter, when we consider the predominant image of her as a tranquil and serene goddess, is her ------- search for her daughter.
>
> (A) extended
> (B) agitated
> (C) comprehensive
> (D) motiveless
> (E) heartless

The ruling image of Demeter is one of tranquillity; we normally think of her as calm and serene. One aspect of the myths about her, however, is *paradoxical*: it contradicts the customary image of her as always calm. This contradictory aspect is her search for her daughter, which is not calm but *agitated*. The correct answer is Choice B.

Tactic 5

Use Your Knowledge of Word Parts and Parts of Speech to Get at the Meanings of Unfamiliar Words

If a word used by the author is unfamiliar, or if an answer choice is unknown to you, two approaches are helpful.

1. Break the word down into its component parts—prefixes, suffixes, roots—to see whether they provide a clue to its meaning. For example, in the preceding GRE question, the word *predominant* contains two major word parts. *Pre-* here means exceedingly; *domin-* means to rule or command. A *predominant* image, therefore, is a prevailing image, one that has commanding influence or strength.

2. Change the unfamiliar word from one part of speech to another. If the noun *precocity* is unfamiliar to you, think of the adjective *precocious* (maturing early). If the verb *appropriate* is unfamiliar to you, think of the common noun *appropriation* or the still more common noun *misappropriation* (as in the misappropriation of funds).

Note the application of this tactic in the following GRE example.

> The sheer bulk of data from the mass media seems to overpower us and drive us to ------- accounts for an easily and readily digestible portion of news.
>
> (A) insular
> (B) investigative
> (C) synoptic
> (D) subjective
> (E) sensational

First, eliminate any answer choices that are obviously incorrect. If you feel overwhelmed by massive amounts of data provided by the news media, it seems logical that you would seek out *brief* summaries of the news instead.

You would not be particularly tempted to seek out *investigative, subjective,* or *sensational* accounts, since none of these are necessarily brief. Thus, you may rule out Choices B, D and E.

The two answer choices remaining may be unfamiliar to you. Analyze them, using what you know of related words. Choice A, *insular*, is related to the noun *peninsula*, a piece of land that juts out so far into the water that it is *almost* an *island*. Thus, an insular account is an islander's account, one that reflects the narrow viewpoint of an isolated, detached writer. Choice C, *synoptic*, is related to the noun *synopsis* (abridgment or summary). A synoptic account provides a summary, a brief but broad overview. Thus, the correct answer is *synoptic*, Choice C.

Break Down Complex Sentences into Simpler Components

In analyzing long, complex sentence completion items, you may find it useful to simplify the sentences by breaking them down. Rephrase dependent clauses and long participial phrases, turning them into simple sentences.

See how this tactic helps you to analyze the following sentence from a recent GRE.

> In failing to see that the judge's pronouncement merely ------- previous decisions rather than actually establishing a precedent, the novice law clerk ------ the scope of the justice's judgment.
>
> (A) synthesized..limited
> (B) overturned..misunderstood
> (C) endorsed..nullified
> (D) qualified..overemphasized
> (E) recapitulated..defined

What do we know?

1. The judge's pronouncement did NOT set a precedent. (Note the use of *rather than* to signal the contrast.)

2. Rather than setting a precedent, the judge's pronouncement did something RELATIVELY UNIMPORTANT to the earlier decisions. (Note the use of *merely* to signal the relative unimportance of what the judge did.)

3. The new law clerk did not understand that the judge had done something relatively unimportant. (He *failed to see.*)

What follows? Because the new clerk failed to see that the judge had done something minor, the clerk believed that the judge had done something major. In other words, the clerk *overemphasized* the scope of what the judge had done. The correct answer is Choice D.

Note that in sentence completion questions a choice may be complicated by an *unusual word order*, such as:

1. *placing the subject after the verb:*
   To the complaints window *strode* the angry *customer*.

2. *placing the subject after an auxiliary of the verb:*
   Only by unending search *could* some few Havana *cigars* be found.

3. *inverting the subject and verb to give the sense of "if":*
   Were defeat to befall him, today's dear friends would be tomorrow's acquaintances, and next week's strangers.

4. *placing a negative word or phrase first, which usually requires at least part of the verb to follow:*
   Never have I encountered so demanding a test!

In all these instances, rephrase the sentence to make it more straightforward. For example:

The angry customer strode to the complaints window.

Some few Havana cigars could be found only by unending search.

If defeat were to befall him, today's dear friends would be tomorrow's acquaintances, and next week's strangers.

I have never encountered so demanding a test!

Tactic 7

If a Sentence Contains a Metaphor, Check to See Whether That Metaphor Controls the Writer's Choice of Words (and Your Answer Choice)

Writers sometimes indulge in extended metaphors, complex analogies that imaginatively identify one object with another. In the following example from a recent GRE, the effect of words on the shape of our thoughts is compared to a common geologic process.

> It is strange how words shape our thoughts and trap us at the bottom of deeply ------- canyons of thinking, their imprisoning sides carved out by the ------- of past usage.
>
> (A) cleaved..eruptions
> (B) rooted..flood
> (C) incised..river
> (D) ridged..ocean
> (E) notched..mountains

Note how many words in this sentence contribute to the image of the canyon—*bottom, imprisoning sides, sides carved out.* This should alert you that the canyon metaphor greatly affects the writer's choice of words.

The extended metaphor of the canyon unifies this sentence. In choosing an answer, it is necessary to complete the sentence in such a way as to develop that metaphor fully. Choice B does not: one might describe a tree or a tooth as deeply *rooted*, but not a canyon. Similarly, Choice D fails. A canyon is a deep narrow valley with precipitous sides; one would not describe it as deeply *ridged*. Canyons are carved out of the rock. How? Are they *cleaved, incised,* even *notched*? To choose the correct answer, you must know some elementary geology, plus the precise meanings of these three verbs. To cleave something is to split it in two parts *by means of a cutting blow.* Erosion, the process which creates canyons, involves no cutting blows. To notch something is to *indent* or nick it. It seems almost paradoxical to describe something as *deeply* notched. In contrast, to incise something is to cut into it, to carve it, to *erode* it, in geological terms. A look at the second word of the answer pair confirms the choice. *Rivers* carve out canyons, *incising* them by erosion. Choice C completes the metaphor; it is the correct answer choice.

Practice Exercises

Sentence Completion Exercise A

Directions: Each sentence below has one or two blanks, each blank indicating that something has been omitted. Beneath the sentence are five lettered words or sets of words. Choose the word or set of words for each blank that best fits the meaning of the sentence as a whole.

1. Normally an individual thunderstorm lasts about 45 minutes, but under certain conditions the storm may -------, becoming ever more severe, for as long as four hours.

   (A) wane
   (B) moderate
   ✓(C) persist
   (D) vacillate
   (E) disperse

2. Perhaps because something in us instinctively distrusts such displays of natural fluency, some readers approach John Updike's fiction with -------.

   (A) indifference
   ✓(B) suspicion
   (C) veneration
   (D) recklessness
   (E) bewilderment

3. We lost confidence in him because he never ------- the grandiose promises he had made.

   (A) forgot about
   (B) reneged on
   (C) tired of
   ✓(D) delivered on
   (E) retreated from

4. Ms. Sutcliffe's helpful notes on her latest wine discoveries and her no-nonsense warnings to consumers about ------- wines provide ------- guide to the numbing array of wines of Burgundy.

   (A) excellent…a useful
   (B) overrated…an inadequate
   ✓(C) overpriced…a trusty
   (D) unsatisfactory…a spotty
   (E) vintage…an unreliable

5. We were amazed that a man who had been hereto-fore the most ------- of public speakers could, in a single speech, electrify an audience and bring them cheering to their feet.

   (A) enthralling
   (B) accomplished
   (C) pedestrian ✓
   (D) auspicious
   (E) masterful

6. If you are trying to make a strong impression on your audience, you cannot do so by being understated, tentative, or ------.

   (A) hyperbolic
   (B) restrained ✓
   (C) argumentative
   (D) authoritative
   (E) passionate

7. Despite the mixture's ------ nature, we found that by lowering its temperature in the laboratory we could dramatically reduce its tendency to vaporize.

   (A) resilient
   (B) volatile
   (C) homogeneous
   (D) insipid
   (E) acerbic

8. No other artist rewards the viewer with more sheer pleasure than Miró: he is one of those blessed artists who combine profundity and ------.

   (A) education
   (B) wisdom
   (C) faith
   (D) fun
   (E) depth

9. Some Central Intelligence Agency officers have ------ their previous statements denying any involve-ment on their part with the contra aid network and are now revising their earlier testimony.

   (A) justified
   (B) recanted
   (C) repeated
   (D) protracted
   (E) heeded

10. New concerns about growing religious tension in northern India were ------ this week after at least fifty people were killed and hundreds were injured or arrested in rioting between Hindus and Moslems.

   (A) lessened
   (B) invalidated
   (C) restrained
   (D) dispersed
   (E) fueled

11. In a happy, somewhat boisterous celebration of the origins of the United States, the major phase of the Constitution's Bicentennial got off to ------ start on Friday.

   (A) a slow
   (B) a rousing
   (C) a reluctant
   (D) an indifferent
   (E) a quiet

12. In one shocking instance of ------ research, one of the nation's most influential researchers in the field of genetics reported on experiments that were never carried out and published deliberately ------ scientific papers on his nonexistent work.

   (A) comprehensive...abstract
   (B) theoretical...challenging
   (C) fraudulent...deceptive
   (D) derivative...authoritative
   (E) erroneous...impartial

13. Measurement is, like any other human endeavor, a complex activity, subject to error, not always used ------, and frequently misinterpreted and ------.

   (A) mistakenly...derided
   (B) erratically...analyzed
   (C) systematically...organized
   (D) innovatively...refined
   (E) properly...misunderstood

14. In a revolutionary development in technology, sev-eral manufacturers now make biodegradable forms of plastic: some plastic six-pack rings, for example, gradually ------ when exposed to sunlight.

   (A) harden
   (B) stagnate
   (C) inflate
   (D) propagate
   (E) decompose

15. To alleviate the problem of contaminated chicken, the study panel recommends that the federal govern-ment shift its inspection emphasis from cursory bird-by-bird visual checks to a more ------ random sam-pling for bacterial and chemical contamination.

   (A) rigorous
   (B) perfunctory
   (C) symbolic
   (D) discreet
   (E) dubious

16. Her novel published to universal acclaim, her literary gifts acknowledged by the chief figures of the Harlem Renaissance, her reputation as yet ------ by envious slights, Hurston clearly was at the ------ of her career.

    (A) undamaged...ebb
    (B) untarnished...zenith
    (C) untainted...extremity
    (D) blackened...mercy
    (E) unmarred...brink

17. To the dismay of the student body, the class president was ------ berated by the principal at a school assembly.

    (A) ignominiously
    (B) privately
    (C) magnanimously
    (D) fortuitously
    (E) inconspicuously

18. Aimed at curbing European attempts to seize territory in the Americas, the Monroe Doctrine was a warning to ------ foreign powers.

    (A) pertinacious
    (B) credulous
    (C) remote
    (D) overt
    (E) predatory

19. When Frazer's editors at Macmillan tried to ------ his endless augmentations, he insisted on a type size so small and a page so packed as to approach illegibility; and if that proved ------, thinner paper.

    (A) protract...unwarranted
    (B) expurgate...satisfactory
    (C) reprimand...irrelevant
    (D) restrict...insufficient
    (E) revise...idiosyncratic

20. The authority of voice in Frazer's writing strikes many readers today as ------ colonialism; his prose seems as invulnerable and expansive as something on which the sun was presumed never to set.

    (A) consonant with
    (B) independent of
    (C) ambivalent toward
    (D) cognizant of
    (E) detrimental to

Sentence Completion Exercise B

Directions: Each sentence below has one or two blanks, each blank indicating that something has been omitted. Beneath the sentence are five lettered words or sets of words. Choose the word or set of words for each blank that best fits the meaning of the sentence as a whole.

1. Baldwin's brilliant *The Fire Next Time* is both so eloquent in its passion and so searching in its ------ that it is bound to ------ any reader.

    (A) bitterness...embarrass
    (B) romanticism...appall
    (C) candor...unsettle
    (D) indifference...disappoint
    (E) conception...bore

2. Unlike other examples of ------ verse, Milton's *Lycidas* does more than merely mourn for the death of Edward King; it also denounces corruption in the Church in which King was ordained.

    (A) satiric
    (B) elegiac
    (C) free
    (D) humorous
    (E) didactic

3. Few other plants can grow beneath the canopy of the sycamore tree, whose leaves and pods produce a natural herbicide that leaches into the surrounding soil, ------ other plants that might compete for water and nutrients.

    (A) inhibiting
    (B) distinguishing
    (C) nourishing
    (D) encouraging
    (E) refreshing

4. We now know that what constitutes practically all of matter is empty space; relatively enormous ------ in which revolve infinitesimal particles so small that they have never been seen or photographed.

    (A) crescendos
    (B) enigmas
    (C) areas
    (D) abstractions
    (E) voids

5. The officers threatened to take ------ if the lives of their men were ------ by the conquered natives.

    (A) liberties...irritated
    (B) measures...enhanced
    (C) pains...destroyed
    (D) reprisals...endangered
    (E) affront...enervated

6. Despite an affected ------ which convinced casual observers that he was indifferent about his painting and enjoyed only frivolity, Warhol cared deeply about his art and labored at it ------.

    (A) nonchalance...diligently
    (B) empathy...methodically
    (C) fervor...secretly
    (D) gloom...intermittently
    (E) hysteria...sporadically

7. Because she had a reputation for ------ we were surprised and pleased when she greeted us so ------.

    (A) insolence...irately
    (B) insouciance...cordially
    (C) graciousness...amiably
    (D) arrogance...disdainfully
    (E) querulousness...affably

8. The child was so spoiled by her indulgent parents
that she pouted and became ------ when she did not
receive all of their attention.

    (A) discreet
    (B) suspicious
    (C) elated
    (D) sullen
    (E) tranquil

9. Just as disloyalty is the mark of the renegade, ------
is the mark of the ------.

    (A) timorousness...hero
    (B) temerity...coward
    (C) avarice...philanthropist
    (D) cowardice...craven
    (E) vanity...flatterer

10. He became quite overbearing and domineering once
he had become accustomed to the ------ shown to soldiers by the natives; he enjoyed his new sense of
power and self-importance.

    (A) disrespect
    (B) apathy
    (C) deference
    (D) culpability
    (E) enmity

11. The ------ of time had left the castle ------; it towered
above the village, looking much as it must have done
in Richard the Lion-Hearted's time.

    (A) repairs...destroyed
    (B) remoteness...alone
    (C) lack...defended
    (D) status...lonely
    (E) ravages...untouched

12. One of the most ------ educators in New York, Dr.
Shalala ignited a controversy in 1984 by calling the
city public schools a "rotten barrel" in need of ------
reform.

    (A) disputatious...little
    (B) outspoken...systemic
    (C) caustic...partial
    (D) indifferent...pretentious
    (E) sycophantic...superficial

13. The newest fiber-optic cables that carry telephone
calls cross-country are made of glass so ------ that a

piece 100 miles thick is clearer than a standard
windowpane.

    (A) fragile
    (B) immaculate
    (C) tangible
    (D) transparent
    (E) iridescent

14. The reasoning in this editorial is so ------ that we
cannot see how anyone can be deceived by it.

    (A) coherent
    (B) astute
    (C) cogent
    (D) specious
    (E) dispassionate

15. The ------ of evidence was on the side of the plaintiff
since all but one witness testified that his story was
correct.

    (A) paucity
    (B) propensity
    (C) accuracy
    (D) brunt
    (E) preponderance

16. Glendon provides a dark underside to Frederick Jackson Turner's frontier thesis that saw rugged individualism as the essence of American society—an
individualism which she sees ------ atomism.

    (A) antithetical toward
    (B) skeptical of
    (C) degenerating into
    (D) aspiring to
    (E) renewed by

17. Chatwin has devoted his life to a kind of Grail quest,
hoping to prove—by study and direct experience
with primitive people—that human nature is gentle
and defensive rather than ------, and that man is
------, not a predator.

    (A) belligerent...an apostate
    (B) martial...a crusader
    (C) aggressive...a pilgrim
    (D) truculent...a gladiator
    (E) pugnacious...a pawn

18. The texts as we have them were written down and
edited carefully by Christians proud of their ancestors but unable to bear the thought of their indulging
in heathen practices; thus, all references to the
ancient religion of the Celts were ------, if not ------.

    (A) deleted...expunged
    (B) muddied...suppressed
    (C) labored...denigrated
    (D) aggrieved...overawed
    (E) obscure...ironic

19. Because Inspector Morse could not contain his scorn for the police commissioner, he was imprudent enough to make ------ remarks about his superior officer.

   (A) ambiguous
   (B) dispassionate
   (C) unfathomable
   (D) interminable
   (E) scathing

20. In Japanese art, profound emotion is frequently couched in images of nature, observed with ------ conditioned by life in a land of dramatic seasonal change, where perils of earthquake and typhoon make nature's bounty ------ and its processes awesome and beautiful.

   (A) an intimacy...precarious
   (B) a fidelity...munificent
   (C) a skill...excessive
   (D) an indifference...chancy
   (E) a sensitivity...distinctive

Sentence Completion Exercise C

Directions: Each sentence below has one or two blanks, each blank indicating that something has been omitted. Beneath the sentence are five lettered words or sets of words. Choose the word or set of words for each blank that best fits the meaning of the sentence as a whole.

1. A ------ statement is an ------ comparison: it does not compare things explicitly, but suggests a likeness between them.

   (A) sarcastic...unfair
   (B) blatant...overt
   (C) sanguine...inherent
   (D) metaphorical...implied
   (E) bellicose...ardent

2. Modern architecture has discarded the ------ trimming on buildings and has concentrated on an almost Greek simplicity of line.

   (A) flamboyant
   (B) austere
   (C) inconspicuous
   (D) aesthetic
   (E) derivative

3. If you are seeking ------ that will resolve all our ailments, you are undertaking an impossible task.

   (A) a precedent
   (B) a panacea
   (C) an abstraction
   (D) a direction
   (E) a contrivance

4. I have no ------ motive in offering this advice; I seek no personal advantage or honor.

   (A) nominal
   (B) altruistic
   (C) incongruous
   (D) disinterested
   (E) ulterior

5. This park has been preserved in all its ------ wildness so that visitors in future years may see how people lived during the eighteenth century.

   (A) hedonistic
   (B) prospective
   (C) esoteric
   (D) untrammeled
   (E) pristine

6. Though he was theoretically a friend of labor, his voting record in Congress ------ that impression.

   (A) implied
   (B) created
   (C) confirmed
   (D) belied
   (E) maintained

7. The orator was so ------ that the audience became ------.

   (A) soporific...drowsy
   (B) inaudible...elated
   (C) pompous...bombastic
   (D) dramatic...affable
   (E) convincing...moribund

8. If you carry this ------ attitude to the conference, you will ------ any supporters you may have at this moment.

   (A) belligerent...delight
   (B) truculent...alienate
   (C) conciliatory...defer
   (D) supercilious...attract
   (E) ubiquitous...delight

9. The ------ pittance the widow receives from the government cannot keep her from poverty.

   (A) magnanimous
   (B) indulgent
   (C) meticulous
   (D) munificent
   (E) niggardly

10. Harriman, Kennan, and Acheson were part of that inner ------ of the American diplomatic establishment whose distinguished legacy ------ U.S. foreign policy to this day.

   (A) circle...grieves
   (B) sanctum...absorbs
   (C) core...dominates
   (D) life...biases
   (E) coterie...exacerbates

11. The young man was quickly promoted when his employers saw how ------ he was.

    (A) indigent
    (B) indifferent
    (C) assiduous
    (D) lethargic
    (E) cursory

12. For Miró, art became a ------- ritual: paper and pencils were holy objects to him and he worked as though he were performing a religious rite.

    (A) superficial
    (B) sacred
    (C) banal
    (D) cryptic
    (E) futile

13. Because it arrives so early in the season, before many other birds, the robin has been called the ------- of spring.

    (A) hostage
    (B) autocrat
    (C) compass
    (D) newcomer
    (E) harbinger

14. Shy and hypochondriacal, Madison was uncomfortable at public gatherings; his character made him a most ------- lawmaker and practicing politician.

    (A) conscientious
    (B) unlikely
    (C) fervent
    (D) gregarious
    (E) effective

15. The tapeworm is an example of ------- organism, one that lives within or on another creature, deriving some or all of its nutrients from its host.

    (A) a hospitable
    (B) an exemplary
    (C) a parasitic
    (D) an autonomous
    (E) a protozoan

16. In place of the more general debate about abstract principles of government that most delegates probably expected, the Constitutional Convention put ------- proposals on the table.

    (A) theoretical
    (B) vague
    (C) concrete
    (D) tentative
    (E) redundant

17. Overindulgence ------- character as well as physical stamina.

    (A) strengthens
    (B) stimulates
    (C) debilitates
    (D) maintains
    (E) provides

18. We must try to understand his momentary ------- for he has ------- more strain and anxiety than any among us.

    (A) outcry...described
    (B) senility...understood
    (C) vision...forgotten
    (D) generosity...desired
    (E) aberration...undergone

19. He is ------- opponent; you must respect and fear him at all times.

    (A) a redoubtable
    (B) a disingenuous
    (C) a pugnacious
    (D) an insignificant
    (E) a craven

20. Your ------- tactics may compel me to cancel the contract as the job must be finished on time.

    (A) dilatory
    (B) offensive
    (C) repugnant
    (D) infamous
    (E) confiscatory

Sentence Completion Exercise D

Directions: Each sentence below has one or two blanks, each blank indicating that something has been omitted. Beneath the sentence are five lettered words or sets of words. Choose the word or set of words for each blank that best fits the meaning of the sentence as a whole.

1. Truculent in defending their rights of sovereignty under the Articles of Confederation, the newly-formed states ------- constantly.

    (A) apologized   (B) digressed   (C) conferred
     (D) acquiesced   (E) squabbled

2. If the Titanic had hit the iceberg head on, its watertight compartments might have saved it from -------, but it swerved to avoid the iceberg, and in the collision so many compartments were opened to the sea that disaster was -------.

    (A) foundering...inevitable
    (B) sinking...escaped
    (C) damage...limited
    (D) buoyancy...unavoidable
    (E) collapse...averted

3. Written in an amiable style, the book provides a comprehensive overview of European wines that should prove inviting to both the virtual ------- and the experienced connoisseur.

   (A) prodigal
   (B) novice
   (C) zealot
   (D) miser
   (E) glutton

4. The members of the religious sect ostracized the ------- who had abandoned their faith.

   (A) coward
   (B) suppliant
   (C) litigant
   (D) recreant
   (E) proselyte

5. I am not attracted by the ------- life of the -------, always wandering through the countryside, begging for charity.

   (A) proud…almsgiver
   (B) noble…philanthropist
   (C) affluent…mendicant
   (D) natural…philosopher
   (E) peripatetic…vagabond

6. Her true feelings ------- themselves in her sarcastic asides; only then was her ------- revealed.

   (A) concealed…sweetness
   (B) manifested…bitterness
   (C) hid…sarcasm
   (D) developed…anxiety
   (E) grieved…charm

7. They fired upon the enemy from behind trees, walls, and any other ------- point they could find.

   (A) conspicuous
   (B) definitive
   (C) vantage
   (D) exposed
   (E) indefensible

8. Critics of the movie version of *The Color Purple* ------- its saccharine, overoptimistic mood as out of keeping with the novel's more ------- tone.

   (A) applauded…somber
   (B) condemned…hopeful
   (C) acclaimed…positive
   (D) denounced…sanguine
   (E) decried…acerbic

9. We need more men of culture and enlightenment; we have too many ------- among us.

   (A) visionaries
   (B) students
   (C) philistines
   (D) pragmatists
   (E) philosophers

10. The sugar dissolved in water -------; finally all that remained was an almost ------- residue on the bottom of the glass.

    (A) quickly…lumpy
    (B) immediately…fragrant
    (C) gradually…imperceptible
    (D) subsequently…glassy
    (E) spectacularly…opaque

11. Alec Guinness has few equals among English-speaking actors, and now in his autobiography he reveals himself to be an uncommonly ------- prose stylist as well.

    (A) ambivalent
    (B) infamous
    (C) supercilious
    (D) felicitous
    (E) pedestrian

12. Traffic speed limits are set at a level that achieves some balance between the danger of ------- speed and the desire of most people to travel as quickly as possible.

    (A) marginal
    (B) normal
    (C) prudent
    (D) inadvertent
    (E) excessive

13. Although the economy suffers downturns, it also has strong ------- and self-correcting tendencies.

    (A) unstable
    (B) recidivist
    (C) inauspicious
    (D) recuperative
    (E) self-destructive

14. It is foolish to vent your spleen on ------- object; still, you make ------- enemies that way.

    (A) an inanimate…fewer
    (B) an immobile…bitter
    (C) an interesting…curious
    (D) an insipid…dull
    (E) a humane…more

15. Since Cyrano de Bergerac did not wish to be under an obligation to any man, he refused to be a ------- of Cardinal Richelieu.

    (A) proselytizer
    (B) mentor
    (C) protégé
    (D) benefactor
    (E) predecessor

16. The leader of the group is the passionately committed Crimond, whose ------- politics is inversely proportional to his disciples' ------- political faith.

    (A) retreat from...remote
    (B) penchant for...ardent
    (C) indifference to...jaundiced
    (D) engagement in...lapsed
    (E) disinclination for...problematic

17. After the Japanese attack on Pearl Harbor on December 7, 1941, Japanese-Americans were ------- of being spies for Japan, although there was no ------- to back up this accusation.

    (A) acquitted...buttress
    (B) tired...witness
    (C) reminded...reason
    (D) suspected...evidence
    (E) exonerated...money

18. More than one friendly whale has nudged a boat with such ------- that passengers have been knocked overboard.

    (A) enthusiasm
    (B) lethargy
    (C) hostility
    (D) serenity
    (E) animosity

19. The mind of a bigot is like the pupil of the eye: the more light you pour upon it, the more it will -------.

    (A) blink
    (B) veer
    (C) stare
    (D) reflect
    (E) contract

20. We have become so democratic in our habits of thought that we are convinced that truth is determined through ------- of facts.

    (A) a hierarchy
    (B) a transcendance
    (C) a plebiscite
    (D) a repeal
    (E) an ignorance

Sentence Completion Exercise E

<u>Directions:</u> Each sentence below has one or two blanks, each blank indicating that something has been omitted. Beneath the sentence are five lettered words or sets of words. Choose the word or set of words for each blank that <u>best</u> fits the meaning of the sentence as a whole.

1. Studded starfish are well protected from most ------- and parasites by ------- surface whose studs are actually modified spines.

    (A) dangers...a vulnerable
    (B) predators...an armored
    (C) threats...a fragile
    (D) challenges...an obtuse
    (E) exigencies...a brittle

2. Chaotic in conception but not in -------, Kelly's canvases are as neat as the proverbial pin.

    (A) conceit
    (B) theory
    (C) execution
    (D) origin
    (E) intent

3. After having worked in the soup kitchen feeding the hungry, the volunteer began to see her own good fortune as ------- and her difference from the ------- as chance rather than destiny.

    (A) an omen...homeless
    (B) a fluke...impoverished
    (C) a threat...destitute
    (D) a reward...indigent
    (E) a lie...affluent

4. Some students are ------- and want to take only the courses for which they see immediate value.

    (A) theoretical
    (B) impartial
    (C) pragmatic
    (D) idealistic
    (E) opinionated

5. Unlike the Shakespearean plays that lit up the English stage, the "closet dramas" of the nineteenth century were meant to be ------- rather than -------.

    (A) seen..acted
    (B) read...staged
    (C) quiet...raucous
    (D) sophisticated...urbane
    (E) produced...performed

6. Japan's industrial success is ------- in part to its tradition of group effort and -------, as opposed to the emphasis on personal achievement that is a prominent aspect of other industrial nations.

    (A) responsive...independence
    (B) related...introspection
    (C) equivalent...solidarity
    (D) subordinate...individuality
    (E) attributed...cooperation

7. I was so bored with the verbose and redundant style of Victorian novelists that I welcomed the change to the ------- style of Hemingway.

    (A) prolix
    (B) consistent
    (C) terse
    (D) logistical
    (E) florid

8. As ------- head of the organization, he attended social functions and civic meetings but had no ------- in the formulation of company policy.

    (A) titular…voice
    (B) hypothetical…vote
    (C) former…pride
    (D) nominal…competition
    (E) actual…say

9. His listeners enjoyed his ------- wit but his victims often ------- at its satire.

    (A) lugubrious…suffered
    (B) caustic…laughed
    (C) kindly…smarted
    (D) subtle…smiled
    (E) trenchant…winced

10. The first forty years of life give us the text: the next thirty supply the -------.

    (A) abridgement
    (B) bibliography
    (C) commentary
    (D) epitaph
    (E) title

11. The distinctive qualities of African music were not appreciated or even ------- by Westerners until fairly recently.

    (A) deplored
    (B) revered
    (C) ignored
    (D) neglected
    (E) perceived

12. It is only to the vain that all is vanity; and all is ------- only to those who have never been ------- themselves.

    (A) arrogance…proud of
    (B) deception…sincere with
    (C) cowardice…afraid for
    (D) indolence…bored by
    (E) solitude…left to

13. No act of ------- was more pronounced than his refusal of any rewards for his discovery.

    (A) abeyance
    (B) submission
    (C) egoism
    (D) denunciation
    (E) abnegation

14. The evil of class and race hatred must be eliminated while it is still in an ------ state; otherwise it may grow to dangerous proportions.

    (A) amorphous
    (B) embryonic
    (C) uncultivated
    (D) overt
    (E) independent

15. Unlike the gregarious Capote, who was never happier than when he was in the center of a crowd of celebrities, Faulkner, in later years, grew somewhat ------- and shunned company.

    (A) congenial
    (B) decorous
    (C) dispassionate
    (D) reclusive
    (E) ambivalent

16. She is a pragmatist, as ------- to base her future on impractical dreams as she would be to build a castle on shifting sand.

    (A) determined
    (B) disinclined
    (C) quick
    (D) apt
    (E) diligent

17. We are ------- the intellects of the past; or, rather, like children we take it for granted that somebody must supply us with our supper and our -------.

    (A) ungrateful to…ideas
    (B) dependent on…repose
    (C) unfaithful to…needs
    (D) fortunate in…allowance
    (E) generous to…wants

18. This island is a colony; however, in most matters, it is ------- and receives no orders from the mother country.

    (A) submissive
    (B) amorphous
    (C) distant
    (D) autonomous
    (E) aloof

19. Although eighteenth-century English society as a whole did not encourage learning for its own sake in women, nonetheless it illogically ------- women's sad lack of education.

    (A) palliated
    (B) postulated
    (C) decried
    (D) brooked
    (E) vaunted

20. Faced with these massive changes, the government keeps its own counsel; although generally benevolent, it has always been ------- regime.

    (A) an altruistic
    (B) an unpredictable
    (C) a reticent
    (D) a sanguine
    (E) an indifferent

Answer Key

Sentence Completion Exercise A

1.	C	6.	B	11.	B	16.	B
2.	B	7.	B	12.	C	17.	A
3.	D	8.	D	13.	E	18.	E
4.	C	9.	B	14.	E	19.	D
5.	C	10.	E	15.	A	20.	A

Sentence Completion Exercise B

1.	C	6.	A	11.	E	16.	C
2.	B	7.	E	12.	B	17.	C
3.	A	8.	D	13.	D	18.	B
4.	E	9.	D	14.	D	19.	E
5.	D	10.	C	15.	E	20.	A

Sentence Completion Exercise C

1.	D	6.	D	11.	C	16.	C
2.	A	7.	A	12.	B	17.	C
3.	B	8.	B	13.	E	18.	E
4.	E	9.	E	14.	B	19.	A
5.	E	10.	C	15.	C	20.	A

Sentence Completion Exercise D

1.	E	6.	B	11.	D	16.	E
2.	A	7.	C	12.	E	17.	D
3.	B	8.	E	13.	D	18.	A
4.	D	9.	C	14.	A	19.	E
5.	E	10.	C	15.	C	20.	C

Sentence Completion Exercise E

1.	B	6.	E	11.	E	16.	B
2.	C	7.	C	12.	B	17.	A
3.	B	8.	A	13.	E	18.	D
4.	C	9.	E	14.	B	19.	C
5.	B	10.	C	15.	D	20.	C

4 Analogy Questions

- ■ **Testing Tactics**
- ■ **Practice Exercises**
- ■ **Answer Key**

Analogy questions ask you to determine the relationship between a pair of words and then recognize a similar or parallel relationship between a different pair of words. You are given one pair of words and must choose from the five answer choices another pair that is related in the same way. The relationship between the words in the original pair will always be specific and precise, as will the relationship between the words in the correct answer pair.

In each GRE verbal section the set of sentence completion questions is followed by eight analogy questions. In each set of analogy questions, the first one or two are relatively simple; the last one or two, relatively hard.

Analogies come from a wide variety of fields. You need to know that musicians study in conservatories and ministers in seminaries, that panegyrics praise and elegies lament. You need to be aware of catalysts and conundrums, augers and auguries, and know in which contexts these words are found. You are not, however, dealing with these words in isolation; you are always dealing with them in relationship to other words.

Once you have analyzed analogy questions, you will find that they fall into certain patterns. You should be able to answer them reasonably rapidly. Tackle them after you have warmed up with the sentence completion questions. Then skip to the antonyms.

Note how a GRE analogy question is set up. First you have the two capitalized words linked by a symbol. Take a look at a few examples.

FRESCO : WALL
A fresco is related to a wall. **How?** A fresco or mural painting is painted on a wall.

STAMMER : TALK
Stammer is related to talk. **How?** To stammer is to talk haltingly, even inarticulately. It is to talk in a defective or faulty *manner*.

TILE : MOSAIC
Tile is related to mosaic. **How?** A mosaic is made up of tiles. Notice the wording of the last sentence. You could also have said "Tiles are the pieces that make up a mosaic" and maintained the word order of the analogy. Sometimes, however, it is easier to express a relationship if you reverse the order of the words.

Next you come to the five answer choices. See if you can tell which pair best expresses a relationship similar to the relationship of tile to mosaic.

> TILE : MOSAIC ::   (A) hoop : embroidery
> (B) wick : candle   (C) whalebone : scrimshaw
>   (D) easel : painting   (E) knot : macrame

The correct answer is Choice E: macrame is made up of knots. Just as the tiles in a mosaic make a pattern, so too the knots in a piece of macrame make a pattern.

Some of the analogy questions on the GRE are as clear-cut as this. Others are more complex. To answer them correctly involves far more than knowing single meanings of individual words: it involves knowing the usual contexts in which they are found, and their connotations as well. Master the tactics that immediately follow. Then proceed to the practice exercises containing both relatively simple and challenging analogies at the chapter's end.

Testing Tactics

Tactic 1

Before you Look at the Choices, Try to State the Relationship Between the Capitalized Words in a Clear Sentence

In answering an analogy question, your first problem is to determine the exact relationship between the two capitalized words. *Before you look at the answer pairs*, make up a sentence that illustrates how these capitalized words are related. Then test the possible answers by seeing how well they fit in your sentence.

Try this tactic on the following two questions from recent GREs.

> DELUGE : DROPLET ::   (A) beach : wave
> (B) desert : oasis   (C) blizzard : icicle
>   (D) landslide : pebble   (E) cloudburst : puddle

A *deluge* (drenching rain or flood) is made up of *droplets*. A *landslide* or fall of rocks is made up of *pebbles*. Choice D is correct.

Don't let Choice E fool you: while a cloudburst, like a deluge, is a drenching rain, it is not made up of puddles; rather, it leaves puddles in its aftermath.

> PHILATELIST : STAMPS ::
> (A) numismatist : coins
> (B) astrologer : predictions
> (C) geneticist : chromosomes
> (D) cartographer : maps
> (E) pawnbroker : jewelry

A *philatelist* collects *stamps*. A *numismatist* collects *coins*. Choice A is correct.

Note how difficult this question would be if you did not know that a philatelist is a stamp collector. You might have guessed that a philatelist primarily *studies* stamps (as, for example, a geneticist studies chromosomes) or even *makes* stamps (as a cartographer makes maps). Knowing the primary relationship between the capitalized words, however, you can go through the answer choices eliminating any pairs that do not express the same relationship. Thus, you can eliminate Choice B: an astrologer may possibly collect predictions; but his primary, dictionary-defined, role is to make predictions, to foretell human affairs by studying the positions of the stars. Similarly, you can eliminate Choice E: a pawnbroker does not collect jewelry; he takes jewelry (and many other sorts of personal property) as a pledge to secure the repayment of money he lends. You can eliminate Choice C as well: a geneticist studies chromosomes. This process of elimination leaves you with two relatively unfamiliar words— *numismatist* and *cartographer*—and a fifty percent chance of guessing the answer correctly.

If you are not sure of the answer, *always* rule out answer choices that you *know* cannot be correct, and then guess among the choices that are left.

Tactic 2

If More Than One Answer Fits the Relationship in Your Sentence, Look for A Narrower Approach

When you try to express the relationship between the two capitalized words in sentence form, occasionally you come up with too simple a sentence, one that fails to include enough details to particularize your analogy. In such cases, more than one answer may fit the relationship, and you will have to analyze the original pair again.

Consider this actual analogy question from the GRE.

> BOUQUET : FLOWERS ::   (A) forest : trees
> (B) husk : corn   (C) mist : rain
>   (D) woodpile : logs   (E) drift : snow

"A bouquet is made up of flowers." You have stated a relationship between the capitalized words in a sentence, but you have not stated a relationship that is precise enough. After all, forests are made up of trees, woodpiles are made up of logs, and even drifts are made of snow. You need to focus on some aspect of the relationship between the original pair of words that corresponds to an aspect of only *one* of the answer pairs. Go back to the original pair of words for more details. A bouquet is made up of flowers that have been *picked* and *gathered* into a bunch. In contrast, a forest is a tract of land covered with densely growing trees. A drift is a mass of snow driven together by the wind. Neither the relationship in Choice A nor that in Choice E exactly parallels the relationship between the word pair BOUQUET:FLOWERS. Choice D, however, is perfect: a woodpile is made up of logs that have been *cut* and *gathered* into a stack.

In answering analogy questions on the GRE, pay special attention to how a dictionary would define the words

involved. Do not settle for what "may be" a good relationship. Precision is important in analogies: a bouquet is not simply made up of flowers, it is made up of flowers that have been cut. Strive to identify the relationship that exists "by definition."

Consider Secondary Meanings of Words As Well As Their Primary Meanings

Frequently, the test-makers attempt to mislead you by using familiar words in relatively uncommon ways. When an apparently familiar word seems incongruous in a particular analogy, consider other definitions of that word.

See how this tactic applies to two examples from recent GREs.

AMORPHOUSNESS : DEFINITION ::
(A) lassitude : energy
(B) spontaneity : awareness
(C) angularity : intricacy
(D) rectitude : drabness
(E) precision : uniformity

What relationship exists between *amorphousness* and *definition*? *Amorphousness* means formlessness or shapelessness; an amorphous idea lacks form or shape. But what does formlessness have to do with *definition*? After all, a definition is a statement of the meaning of a word or phrase.

Look closely at the term *definition*. When you define a word, you distinguish its essential characteristics; you make its features clear. *Definition* in fact possesses a secondary meaning: "sharp demarcation of outlines or limits; distinctness of outline or detail." With this meaning in mind, you can state the essential relationship between the capitalized words: *amorphousness* is a lack of *definition*. Analogously, *lassitude* (listlessness, weariness) is a lack of *energy*. The correct answer is Choice A.

EMBROIDER : CLOTH ::   (A) chase : metal
(B) patch : quilt   (C) gild : gold
  (D) carve : knife   (E) stain : glass

Ostensibly, this is a simple analogy. One embroiders cloth to ornament it, embellishing it with needlework. The relationship between the capitalized words is clear. However, only 9% of the examinees who answered this question answered it correctly. The problem lies not in the original analogy but in the answer pairs.

Consider the answer choices closely. Choices B, C, D, and E are clear enough: one patches a quilt, either repairing it or putting it together (patch has both senses); one gilds something, overlaying it with gold; one carves with a knife; one stains glass, imparting color to it. Several of these straightforward choices have something to do with ornamentation, but none seems precisely right. But how does one *chase* metal? Certainly not the way one chases an ambulance! Among the straight forward answer choices, Choice A seems strangely out of place.

When an item in an analogy strikes you as out of place, take a second look. Remember that the test-makers usually place more difficult analogies toward the end of the analogy section. Therefore, if one of the final analogy questions in a set looks simple, *suspect a trap*. In this case, the trap is a double one. Choice B, *patch : quilt*, is an eye-catcher: because embroidery and quilt-making both are related to sewing, Choice B has an immediate appeal. Choose it and you fall into the test-makers' trap. Choice A, the odd-seeming choice, is the real answer: *chase*, as used here, means to ornament a metal surface, as silversmiths decorate silver with hammered patterns; chasing metal, thus, is directly analogous to embroidering cloth.

Watch Out for Errors Caused By Eye-Catchers

When you look at answer choices, do you find that certain ones seem to leap right off the page? For instance, when you were looking for an analogy similar to

EMBROIDER : CLOTH, did the terms related to stitchery catch your eye? These words are eye-catchers. They look good—but not if you take a second glance.

In an analogy you have two capitalized words that relate in a particular way. In creating eye-catchers, the test-makers tempt you with pairs of words that are related, but in a grammatically or logically different way. See how eye-catchers work in an example from a published GRE.

PROCTOR : SUPERVISE ::   (A) prophet : rule
(B) profiteer : consume   (C) profligate : demand
(D) prodigal : squander   (E) prodigy : wonder

Just as there are many possible relationships linking word pairs, there are many possible ways an eye-catcher may attract your eye. First, an answer choice may some-how remind you in subject matter of one or both of the terms in the original pair. Thus, Choice A is an eye-catcher: *rule* reminds you of *supervise*; both words feel as if they belong in the same set of words, the same *semantic field*. Second, the answer choice may masquer-ade as a clearcut, precise, dictionary-perfect analogy and yet not be one. Thus, Choice E is an eye-catcher: while there is a clear relationship between the nouns *prodigy* and *wonder*, there is no such clear relationship between the noun *prodigy* and the verb *wonder*. See how this works:

Noun/Noun	A *prodigy* (marvel) is a *wonder*.	CLEAR ANALOGY
Noun/Verb	A *prodigy wonders* (ponders; marvels).	VAGUE ANALOGY

A prodigy excites wonder in others; he is not necessarily astonished or full of wonder himself. The relationship is vague. Eliminate vague analogies when you find them; their only function is to catch your eye.

You have ruled out Choice E; you are suspicious of Choice A. How do you determine the correct answer? In this case, ask yourself **who is doing what to whom.** A *proctor* (monitor) by definition *supervises* students or examinees. You can eliminate Choices A, B, and C because no necessary relationship links the words in these pairs. Prophets prophesy; they do not rule. Profit-eers sell goods (at excessive prices) that others con-sume. Profligates waste their fortunes; they do not necessarily demand.

The correct answer is Choice D. Just as a *proctor super-vises* students, a *prodigal* or wastrel *squanders* wealth.

Look At the Answer Choices to Determine a Word's Part of Speech

Look at the capitalized words. What parts of speech are they? Words often have several forms. You may think of *run* as a verb, for example, but in the phrases "a run in her stocking" and "hit a home run" *run* is a noun.

The GRE plays on this confusion in testing your verbal ability. When you look at a capitalized word, you may not know whether you are dealing with a noun, a verb, or an adjective. *Harbor*, for example, is a very common noun; in "to harbor a fugitive," to give refuge to a runaway, it is a much less common verb.

If you suspect that a capitalized word may represent more than one part of speech, don't worry. Grammatical information built into the question can help you recognize analogy types and spot the use of unfamiliar or second-ary meanings of words. In GRE analogy questions, the relationship between the parts of speech of the capital-ized words and the parts of speech of the answer choices is identical. If your capitalized words are a noun and a verb, each of your answer pairs will be a noun and a verb. If they are an adjective and a noun, each of your answer pairs will be an adjective and a noun. If you can recognize the parts of speech in a single answer pair, you

know the parts of speech of every other answer pair and of the original pair as well. See how this tactic works in a somewhat difficult question from a recently published GRE.

FLAG : VIGOR ::   (A) endure : courage
(B) tire : monotony   (C) question : perception
(D) waver : resolution   (E) flatter : charm

At first glance, you might think that both *flag* and *vigor* were nouns; *flag*, after all, is a common noun, and *vigor* ends in *-or*, a common noun suffix. However, *endure* is clearly a verb. Simply from looking at the first answer choice, you know *flag* is a verb, not a noun.

What occurs when someone or something flags? Think of an American flag when the breeze dies down. The ban-ner hangs limp; it droops. In a word, the flag *flags*. By extension, the verb *flag* has come to mean to slacken or decline; when vigor flags, it becomes less firm. Only one answer choice conveys this sense of something firm weakening: Choice D. If one's resolution wavers, it declines.

Tactic 6

Familiarize Yourself with Common Analogy Types

Analogies tend to fall into certain basic types. If you can discover no apparent relationship between the two capitalized words, try establishing a relationship between them based on those types commonly used on this test.

Common Analogy Types

Definition

REFUGE : SHELTER
A *refuge* (place of asylum) by definition *shelters*.

TAXONOMIST : CLASSIFY
A *taxonomist*, a person who specializes in classification, by definition *classifies*.

HAGGLER : BARGAIN
A *haggler*, a person who argues over prices, by definition *bargains*.

Defining Characteristic

TIGER : CARNIVOROUS
A *tiger* is defined as a *carnivorous* or meat-eating animal.

ENTOMOLOGIST : INSECTS
An *entomologist* is defined as a person who studies *insects*.

APIARY : BEE
An *apiary* is defined as a home for *bees*.

Class and Member

REPTILE: IGUANA
An iguana is an example of a *reptile*.

METAPHYSICS : PHILOSOPHY
Metaphysics belongs to the field of *philosophy*.

SONNET : POEM
A *sonnet* is a specific kind of *poem*.

Antonyms

Antonyms are words that are opposite in meaning. Both words belong to the same part of speech.

CONCERNED : INDIFFERENT
Indifferent means *unconcerned*.

WAX : WANE
Wax, to grow larger, and *wane*, to dwindle, are opposites.

ANARCHY : ORDER
Anarchy is the opposite of *order*.

Antonym Variants

In an Antonym Variant, the words are not strictly antonyms; their meanings, however, are opposed. Take the adjective *nervous*. A strict antonym for the adjective *nervous* would be the adjective *poised*. However, where an Antonym would have the adjective *poised*, an Antonym Variant analogy has the noun *poise*. It looks like this:

NERVOUS : POISE
Nervous means lacking in *poise*.

INIQUITOUS : VIRTUE
Something *iniquitous* lacks *virtue*. It is the opposite of virtuous.

ABSTINENT : GORGE
Abstinent or sparing in eating means not inclined to cram or *gorge*.

Synonyms

Synonyms are words that have the same meaning. Both words belong to the same part of speech.

MAGNIFICENT : GRANDIOSE
Grandiose means *magnificent*.

RATIOCINATE : THINK
To *ratiocinate* is to *think*.

RECIDIVIST : BACKSLIDER
A *recidivist* or habitual offender is a *backslider*.

Synonym Variants

In a Synonym Variant, the words are not strictly synonymous; their meanings, however, are similar. Take the adjective *willful*. A strict synonym for the adjective *willful* would be the adjective *unruly*. However, where a Synonym would have the adjective *unruly*, a Synonym Variant analogy has the noun *unruliness*. It looks like this:

WILLFULL : UNRULINESS
Willful means exhibiting *unruliness*.

VERBOSE : WORDINESS
Someone *verbose* is wordy; he or she exhibits *wordiness*.

SOLICITOUS : CONCERN
Someone *solicitous* is concerned; he or she shows *concern*.

Degree of Intensity

FOND : DOTING
Fond is less extreme than *doting*.

FLURRY : BLIZZARD
A *flurry* or shower of snow is less extreme than a *blizzard*.

GRASPING : RAPACIOUS
To be *grasping* is less extreme than to be *rapacious*.

Part to Whole

ISLAND : ARCHIPELAGO
Many *islands* make up an *archipelago*.

SHARD : POTTERY
A *shard* is a fragment of *pottery*.

CANTO : POEM
A *canto* is part of a *poem*.

Function
ASYLUM : REFUGE
An *asylum* provides *refuge* or protection.

BALLAST : STABILITY
Ballast provides *stability*.

LULL : STORM
A *lull* temporarily interrupts a *storm*.

Manner
MUMBLE : SPEAK
To *mumble* is to *speak* indistinctly.

STRUT : WALK
To *strut* is to *walk* proudly.

STRAINED : WIT
Wit that is *strained* is forced in manner.

Action and Its Significance
WINCE : PAIN
A *wince* is a sign that one feels *pain*.

BLUSH : DISCOMFITURE
A *blush* signifies *discomfiture* or embarrassment.

PROSTRATION : SUBMISSIVENESS
Prostration (assuming a prostrate position, face to the ground) is a sign of *submissiveness* or abasement.

Worker and Article Created
POET : SONNET
A *poet* creates a *sonnet*.

ARCHITECT : BLUEPRINT
An *architect* designs a *blueprint*.

MASON : WALL
A *mason* builds a *wall*.

Worker and Tool
PAINTER : BRUSH
A *painter* uses a *brush*.

SICKLE : REAPER
A *reaper* uses a *sickle* to cut the grain.

CARPENTER : VISE
A *carpenter* uses a *vise* to hold the object being worked on.

Worker and Action
ACROBAT : CARTWHEEL
An *acrobat* performs a *cartwheel*.

FINANCIER : INVEST
A *financier invests*.

TENOR : ARIA
A *tenor* sings an *aria*.

Worker and Workplace
MUSICIAN : CONSERVATORY
A *musician* studies at a *conservatory*.

SCULPTOR : ATELIER
A *sculptor* works in an *atelier* or studio.

MINER : QUARRY
A *miner* works in a *quarry* or pit.

Tool and Its Action
DRILL : BORE
A *drill* is a tool used to *bore* holes.

CROWBAR : PRY
A *crowbar* is a tool used to *pry* things apart.

SIEVE : SIFT
A *sieve* is a tool used to strain or *sift*.

Less Common Analogy Types
Cause and Effect
SOPORIFIC : SLEEPINESS
A *soporific* causes *sleepiness*.

Sex
DOE : STAG
A *doe* is a female deer; a *stag*, a male deer.

Age
COLT : STALLION
A *colt* is a young *stallion*.

Time Sequence
CORONATION : REIGN
The *coronation* precedes the *reign*.

Spatial Sequence
ROOF : FOUNDATION
The *roof* is the highest point of a house; the *foundation*, the lowest point.

Symbol and Quality It Represents
DOVE : PEACE
A *dove* is the symbol of *peace*.

Practice Exercises

Analogy Exercise A

Directions: In each of the following questions, a related pair of words or phrases is followed by five lettered pairs of words or phrases. Select the lettered pair that best expresses a relationship similar to that expressed in the original pair.

1. MASON : WALL ::   (A) artist : easel
   (B) fisherman : trout   (C) author : book
   (D) congressman : senator   (E) sculptor : mallet

2. FIRE : ASHES ::   (A) accident : delay
   (B) wood : splinters   (C) water : waves
   (D) regret : melancholy   (E) event : memories

3. GOOSE : GANDER :: (A) duck : drake
   (B) hen : chicken   (C) sheep : flock
   (D) dog : kennel   (E) horse : bridle

4. CARPENTER : SAW ::
   (A) stenographer : typewriter   (B) painter : brush
   (C) lawyer : brief   (D) seamstress : scissors
   (E) runner : sneakers

5. CAPTAIN : SHOAL ::   (A) lawyer : litigation
   (B) pilot : radar   (C) soldier : ambush
   (D) doctor : hospital   (E) corporal : sergeant

6. HORNS : BULL ::   (A) mane : lion
   (B) wattles : turkey   (C) antlers : stag
   (D) hoofs : horse   (E) wings : eagle

7. JUDGE : COURTHOUSE ::   (A) carpenter : bench
   (B) lawyer : brief   (C) architect : blueprint
   (D) physician : infirmary   (E) landlord : studio

8. HELMET : HEAD ::   (A) pedal : foot
   (B) gun : hand   (C) breastplate : chest
   (D) pendant : neck   (E) knapsack : back

9. GULLIBLE : DUPED ::   (A) credible : cheated
   (B) careful : cautioned   (C) malleable : molded
   (D) myopic : misled   (E) articulate : silenced

10. DUNGEON : CONFINEMENT ::
    (A) church : chapel   (B) school : truancy
    (C) asylum : refuge   (D) hospital : mercy
    (E) courthouse : remorse

11. HERMIT : GREGARIOUS ::
    (A) miser : penurious
    (B) ascetic : hedonistic
    (C) coward : pusillanimous
    (D) scholar : literate
    (E) crab : crustacean

12. MENDACITY : HONESTY ::
    (A) courage : cravenness
    (B) truth : beauty
    (C) courage : fortitude
    (D) unsophistication : ingenuousness
    (E) turpitude : depravity

13. MARATHON : STAMINA ::
    (A) relay : independence
    (B) hurdle : perseverance
    (C) sprint : celerity
    (D) jog : weariness
    (E) ramble : directness

14. NAIVE : INGENUE ::
    (A) ordinary : genuis
    (B) venerable : celebrity
    (C) urbane : sophisticate
    (D) crafty : artisan
    (E) modest : braggart

15. RETOUCH : PHOTOGRAPH ::
    (A) hang : painting   (B) finger : fabric
    (C) retract : statement   (D) compose : melody
    (E) refine : style

16. INDIGENT : WEALTH ::
    (A) contented : happiness
    (B) aristocratic : stature
    (C) smug : complacency
    (D) emaciated : nourishment
    (E) variegated : variety

17. SHALE : GEOLOGIST ::
    (A) catacombs : entomologist
    (B) aster : botanist
    (C) obelisk : fireman
    (D) love : philologist
    (E) reef : astrologer

18. DIDACTIC : TEACH ::   (A) sophomoric : learn
    (B) satiric : mock   (C) reticent : complain
    (D) chaotic : rule   (E) apologetic : deny

19. HACKNEYED : ORIGINAL ::
    (A) mature : juvenile   (B) trite : morbid
    (C) withdrawn : reserved   (D) evasive : elusive
    (E) derivative : traditional

20. AUGER : CARPENTER ::
    (A) studio : sculptor   (B) awl : cobbler
    (C) seam : seamstress   (D) cement : mason
    (E) apron : chef

Analogy Exercise B

<u>Directions:</u> In each of the following questions, a related pair of words or phrases is followed by five lettered pairs of words or phrases. Select the lettered pair that best expresses a relationship similar to that expressed in the original pair.

1. MUSTER : CREW ::
    (A) convene : committee
    (B) demobilize : troops
    (C) dominate : opposition
    (D) cheer : team
    (E) dismiss : jury

2. DWELL : DENIZEN ::   (A) shun : outcast
    (B) inherit : heir   (C) squander : miser
      (D) obey : autocrat   (E) patronize : protégé

3. MEANDERING : DIRECTNESS ::
    (A) menacing : ambition
    (B) affable : permissiveness
    (C) digressive : conciseness
    (D) circuitous : rotation
    (E) aboveboard : openness

4. CEMENT : TROWEL ::   (A) lawn : rake
    (B) conflagration : match   (C) paint : brush
      (D) floor : polish   (E) wallpaper : ladder

5. PIGHEADED : YIELD ::
    (A) lionhearted : retreat   (B) lilylivered : flee
      (C) dogged : pursue   (D) featherbrained : giggle
        (E) eagle-eyed : discern

6. ALARM : TRIGGER ::   (A) prison : escape
    (B) tunnel : dig   (C) criminal : corner
      (D) fright : allay   (E) trap : spring

7. QUOTATION : QUOTATION MARKS ::
    (A) remark : colon
    (B) sentence : period
    (C) aside : parentheses
    (D) clause : semicolon
    (E) interjection : exclamation point

8. SIGNATURE : ILLUSTRATION ::
    (A) byline : column   (B) alias : charge
      (C) credit : purchase   (D) note : scale
        (E) reference : recommendation

9. SCALES : JUSTICE ::   (A) weights : measures
    (B) laws : courts   (C) torch : liberty
      (D) laurel : peace   (E) balance : equity

10. SURPRISE : EXCLAMATION ::
     (A) insolence : bow   (B) dismay : groan
       (C) happiness : grimace   (D) deference : nod
         (E) contentment : mutter

11. APOSTATE : RELIGION ::
     (A) potentate : kingdom   (B) traitor : country
       (C) bureacrat : government   (D) jailor : law
         (E) teacher : education

12. FOX : CUNNING ::   (A) dog : playful
     (B) hyena : amusing   (C) beaver : industrious
       (D) vixen : cute   (E) colt : sturdy

13. PERJURY : OATH ::   (A) plagiarism : authority
     (B) embezzlement : trust   (C) disrespect : age
       (D) testimony : court   (E) jury : vow

14. EULOGY : BLAME ::   (A) elegy : loss
     (B) satire : mockery   (C) tirade : abuse
       (D) simile : likeness   (E) benediction : curse

15. PRIDE : LIONS ::   (A) gaggle : geese
     (B) honor : thieves   (C) snarl : wolves
       (D) arrogance : kings   (E) lair : bears

16. RANGE : MOUNTAINS ::   (A) atlas : maps
     (B) plain : prairie   (C) string : beads
       (D) novel : short stories   (E) sea : rivers

17. EXCESSIVE : MODERATION ::
     (A) extensive : duration
     (B) arbitrary : courage
     (C) impulsive : reflection
     (D) distinguished : reverence
     (E) expensive : cost

18. DEADBEAT : PAY ::   (A) killjoy : lament
     (B) spoilsport : refrain   (C) daredevil : risk
       (D) diehard : quit   (E) turncoat : betray

19. MENDICANT : IMPECUNIOUS ::
     (A) critic : quizzical   (B) complainer : petulant
       (C) physician : noble   (D) liar : compulsive
         (E) philanthropist : prodigal

20. SNICKER : DISRESPECT ::
     (A) whimper : impatience   (B) chortle : glee
       (C) frown : indifference   (D) sneer : detachment
         (E) glower : cheerfulness

Analogy Exercise C

Directions: In each of the following questions, a related pair of words or phrases is followed by five lettered pairs of words or phrases. Select the lettered pair that best expresses a relationship similar to that expressed in the original pair.

1. MYTH : LEGENDARY ::   (A) sermon : lengthy
(B) anecdote : witty   (C) fable : didactic
(D) epic : comic   (E) allegory : obscure

2. TIRADE : ABUSIVE ::
(A) monologue : lengthy
(B) aphorism : boring
(C) prologue : conclusive
(D) encomium : laudatory
(E) critique : insolent

3. EXPEDITIOUS : SPEED ::
(A) astute : wisdom
(B) decorous : impropriety
(C) thoughtful : inanity
(D) haggard : sturdiness
(E) portable : frailty

4. ANNOTATE : TEXT ::
(A) enact : law   (B) prescribe : medication
(C) caption : photograph   (D) abridge : novel
(E) censor : film

5. DRUDGERY : IRKSOME ::
(A) encumbrance : burdensome
(B) journey : wearisome
(C) ambivalence : suspicious
(D) compliance : forced
(E) dissonance : harmonious

6. IMPROMPTU : REHEARSAL ::
(A) practiced : technique   (B) makeshift : whim
(C) offhand : premeditation   (D) glib : fluency
(E) numerical : calculation

7. ELISION : SYLLABLES ::
(A) contraction : letters   (B) thesis : ideas
(C) diagnosis : symptoms   (D) almanac : facts
(E) abacus : numbers

8. STICKLER : INSIST ::   (A) mumbler : enunciate
(B) trickster : risk   (C) haggler : concede
(D) laggard : outlast   (E) braggart : boast

9. DETRITUS : GLACIER ::   (A) thaw : snowfall
(B) snow : ice cap   (C) silt : river
(D) range : mountain   (E) foliage : tree

10. DESCRY : DISTANT ::   (A) mourn : lost
(B) whisper : muted   (C) discern : subtle
(D) destroy : flagrant   (E) entrap : hostile

11. HORSE : CORRAL ::   (A) oyster : reef
(B) dog : muzzle   (C) sheep : flock
(D) pig : sty   (E) deer : stag

12. RUBBER : ELASTIC ::   (A) paper : brittle
(B) diamond : hard   (C) satin : sheer
(D) metal : heavy   (E) dust : allergic

13. REAM : PAPER ::   (A) carton : milk
(B) statue : marble   (C) tablet : clay
(D) ink : pen   (E) cord : wood

14. HOBBLE : WALK ::   (A) gallop : run
(B) stammer : speak   (C) stumble : fall
(D) sniff : smell   (E) amble : stroll

15. DETECTIVE : INFORMER ::
(A) spy : counterspy   (B) reporter : source
(C) author : editor   (D) architect : draftsman
(E) sailor : mutineer

16. SCULPTOR : STONE ::   (A) essayist : words
(B) painter : turpentine   (C) composer : symphony
(D) logger : timber   (E) etcher : acid

17. MASTHEAD : NEWSPAPER ::
(A) footnote : essay   (B) credits : film
(C) spine : book   (D) ream : paper
(E) advertisement : magazine

18. FRAYED : FABRIC ::   (A) thawed : ice
(B) renovated : building   (C) frazzled : nerves
(D) watered : lawn   (E) cultivated : manner

19. INDOLENT : WORK ::   (A) decisive : act
(B) gullible : cheat   (C) perceptive : observe
(D) theatrical : perform   (E) taciturn : speak

20. INFALLIBLE : ERROR ::   (A) irreversible : cure
(B) invulnerable : emotion   (C) impeccable : flaw
(D) intolerable : defect   (E) immovable : choice

Analogy Exercise D

Directions: In each of the following questions, a related pair of words or phrases is followed by five lettered pairs of words or phrases. Select the lettered pair that best expresses a relationship similar to that expressed in the original pair.

1. INFRACTION : LAW ::
(A) interruption : continuity
(B) renovation : structure
(C) establishment : order
(D) enactment : amendment
(E) punishment : crime

2. LACHRYMOSE : TEARS ::
   (A) effusive : requests   (B) ironic : jests
   (C) morose : speeches   (D) profound : sighs
   (E) verbose : words

3. MOISTEN : DRENCH ::   (A) enclose : confine
   (B) prick : stab   (C) disregard : ignore
   (D) scrub : polish   (E) heat : chill

4. WITCH : COVEN ::   (A) ogre : castle
   (B) seer : prophecy   (C) actor : troupe
   (D) fairy : spell   (E) doctor : medicine

5. CONTINENT : ISLAND ::   (A) ocean : lake
   (B) isthmus : peninsula   (C) cape : cove
   (D) river : canal   (E) plateau : plain

6. SKINFLINT : STINGY ::
   (A) daredevil : alert
   (B) braggart : carefree
   (C) blackguard : protective
   (D) spendthrift : weak
   (E) diehard : stubborn

7. STORY : BUILDING ::   (A) plot : outline
   (B) rung : ladder   (C) cable : elevator
   (D) foundation : skyscraper   (E) spire : church

8. CANONIZE : SAINT ::   (A) train : athlete
   (B) guard : dignitary   (C) deify : sinner
   (D) lionize : celebrity   (E) humanize : scholar

9. STARE : GLANCE ::   (A) participate : observe
   (B) scorn : admire   (C) hunt : stalk
   (D) gulp : sip   (E) confide : tell

10. PERFORATE : HOLES ::   (A) speckle : spots
    (B) evaporate : perfume   (C) decorate : rooms
    (D) filter : water   (E) repent : sins

11. PUGNACIOUS : BATTLE ::   (A) timorous : beg
    (B) loquacious : drink   (C) tenacious : persist
    (D) veracious : lie   (E) wicked : survive

12. CLEARSIGHTED : PERSPICACITY ::
    (A) daring : temerity
    (B) reserved : impulsiveness
    (C) transparent : opacity
    (D) severe : clemency
    (E) lethargic : energy

13. PLEAD : SUPPLIANT ::
    (A) disperse : rioter
    (B) shun : outcast
    (C) revere : elder
    (D) beg : philanthropist
    (E) translate : interpreter

14. EPIGRAM : PITHY ::   (A) allegory : lengthy
    (B) saga : heroic   (C) anecdote : humorous
    (D) elegy : satiric   (E) proverb : modern

15. BOLT : FABRIC ::   (A) lock : key
    (B) book : paper   (C) roll : film
    (D) needle : thread   (E) light : lamp

16. PROOF : ALCOHOL ::   (A) cream : milk
    (B) canteen : water   (C) tanker : oil
    (D) octane : gasoline   (E) pulp : juice

17. INCUBATOR : INFANT ::
    (A) henhouse : chicken   (B) greenhouse : plant
    (C) archives : document   (D) cooler : wine
    (E) hive : bee

18. CITADEL : DEFENSE ::
    (A) chapel : refreshment
    (B) gazebo : refuge
    (C) marina : contemplation
    (D) warehouse : storage
    (E) rampart : supervision

19. RANCID : TASTE ::   (A) tepid : temperature
    (B) glossy : look   (C) rank : smell
    (D) dulcet : sound   (E) savory : odor

20. TRYST : CLANDESTINE ::
    (A) reverie : dreamy
    (B) acquaintanceship : brief
    (C) expectation : hopeless
    (D) glance : resentful
    (E) journey : leisurely

Analogy Exercise E

Directions: In each of the following questions, a related pair of words or phrases is followed by five lettered pairs of words or phrases. Select the lettered pair that best expresses a relationship similar to that expressed in the original pair.

1. WHISPER : SPEAK ::   (A) brush : touch
   (B) skip : walk   (C) listen : hear
   (D) request : ask   (E) whimper : whine

2. ELUSIVE : CAPTURE ::
   (A) persuasive : convince   (B) elastic : stretch
   (C) headstrong : control   (D) sensible : decide
   (E) gullible : trick

3. LINEAGE : PERSON :   (A) foliage : tree
   (B) derivation : word   (C) adolescence : child
   (D) title : book   (E) landscape : portrait

4. IMPANEL : JUROR ::   (A) accuse : defendant
   (B) convict : culprit   (C) testify : witness
   (D) enroll : student   (E) involve : bystander

5. PECCADILLO : TRIFLING ::
   (A) pariah : popular   (B) diagnosis : accurate
   (C) notion : farfetched   (D) squabble : petty
   (E) pursuit : trivial

6. PHYSIQUE : STURDY ::   (A) intellect : noble
   (B) punctuality : tardy   (C) investment : sound
   (D) fabric : worn   (E) technique : inept

7. TRAILER : MOTION PICTURE ::
   (A) truck : cargo   (B) theater : play
   (C) edition : novel   (D) commercial : product
   (E) libretto : opera

8. SIGN : ZODIAC ::   (A) poster : billboard
   (B) letter : alphabet   (C) prediction : prophecy
   (D) signal : beacon   (E) rhyme : almanac

9. LUMINARY : ILLUSTRIOUS ::
   (A) zealot : intense   (B) miser : prodigal
   (C) atheist : devout   (D) dignitary : conceited
   (E) celebrity : wealthy

10. BUFFOON : DIGNITY ::
    (A) braggart : modesty
    (B) blackguard : strength
    (C) laughingstock : ridicule
    (D) imposter : identification
    (E) gambler : risk

11. ROUT : DEFEAT ::   (A) ovation : applause
    (B) triumph : failure   (C) grief : loss
    (D) pathway : ruin   (E) memory : oblivion

12. METAPHOR : FIGURATIVE ::
    (A) fable : contemporary
    (B) adage : paradoxical
    (C) precept : instructive
    (D) irony : dramatic
    (E) epic : literal

13. CALUMNY : ASPERSIONS ::
    (A) approbation : praise
    (B) slander : mockery
    (C) approval : criticism
    (D) expectation : threats
    (E) satire : lamentations

14. LAST : SHOE ::   (A) cuff : trousers
    (B) finale : curtain   (C) pattern : glove
    (D) buckle : belt   (E) strap : slip

15. INDOLENT : SLOTH ::   (A) wrathful : ire
    (B) arrogant : acuity   (C) covetous : enigma
    (D) gluttonous : loyalty   (E) impatient : apathy

16. GROVEL : SERVILITY ::   (A) titter : arrogance
    (B) fume : anger   (C) yawn : civility
    (D) preen : modesty   (E) snivel : hypocrisy

17. DELICATE : FASTIDIOUS ::
    (A) hard-working : diligent
    (B) altruistic : mercenary
    (C) demonstrative : effusive
    (D) deceptive : fallacious
    (E) blithe : melancholy

18. RICOCHET : BULLET ::   (A) soar : falcon
    (B) aim : crossbow   (C) pierce : dart
    (D) carom : ball   (E) catapult : missile

19. JUGGERNAUT : INEXORABLE ::
    (A) cosmonaut : worldly
    (B) colossus : gigantic
    (C) demagogue : liberal
    (D) philistine : cultivated
    (E) despot : immaculate

20. APOCRYPHAL : AUTHENTICITY ::
    (A) nefarious : wickedness
    (B) dogmatic : assertiveness
    (C) hypocritical : integrity
    (D) perspicacious : discernment
    (E) deceptive : artifice

Answer Key

Analogy Exercise A

1.	C	6.	C	11.	B	16.	D
2.	E	7.	D	12.	A	17.	B
3.	A	8.	C	13.	C	18.	B
4.	D	9.	C	14.	C	19.	A
5.	C	10.	C	15.	E	20.	B

Analogy Exercise B

1.	A	6.	E	11.	B	16.	C
2.	B	7.	C	12.	C	17.	C
3.	C	8.	A	13.	B	18.	D
4.	C	9.	C	14.	E	19.	B
5.	A	10.	B	15.	A	20.	B

Analogy Exercise C

1.	C	6.	C	11.	D	16.	A
2.	D	7.	A	12.	B	17.	B
3.	A	8.	E	13.	E	18.	C
4.	C	9.	C	14.	B	19.	E
5.	A	10.	C	15.	B	20.	C

Analogy Exercise D

1.	A	6.	E	11.	C	16.	D
2.	E	7.	B	12.	A	17.	B
3.	B	8.	D	13.	E	18.	D
4.	C	9.	D	14.	B	19.	C
5.	A	10.	A	15.	C	20.	A

Analogy Exercise E

1.	A	6.	C	11.	A	16.	B
2.	C	7.	D	12.	C	17.	C
3.	B	8.	B	13.	A	18.	D
4.	D	9.	A	14.	C	19.	B
5.	D	10.	A	15.	A	20.	C

5 Reading Comprehension Questions

■ **Testing Tactics**
■ **Practice Exercises**
■ **Answer Key**

GRE reading comprehension questions test your ability to understand what you read—both content and technique. Each verbal section on the GRE includes two passages, one short, one long, the short passage followed by three or four questions, the long passage followed by seven or eight. One passage deals with the **sciences** (including medicine, botany, zoology, chemistry, physics, geology, astronomy); the other deals with the **humanities** (including art, literature, music, philosophy, folklore), or with the **social sciences** (including history, economics, sociology, government). Each test generally contains a passage that is "**ethnic**" in content: whether it is a history passage or a passage on music, art, or literature, it deals with concerns of a particular minority group (including women).

The verbal sections follow two basic patterns.

Section A	Example
1 Science Passage (150 – 200 words)	Geology—Physical Science
1 Non-Science Passage (500–600 words)	Women'sSuffrage Movement—Social Sciences
Section B	
1 Science Passage (500 – 600 words)	DNA—Biological Science
1 Non-Science Passage (150 – 200 words)	Thomas Hardy— Literature

The GRE tends to take its reading passages from *Scientific American*, from prestigious university presses (Harvard, Princeton, Oxford), from scholarly journals. Often the test-makers hit academically "hot" topics—sociobiology, plate tectonics, damage to the ozone layer, Arthurian romance, the status of women's literature—that have aroused controversy over the past two decades. Frequently they edit these passages to make them more demanding both in vocabulary level and in grammatical complexity.

Some of the reading comprehension questions on the GRE are factual, asking you about specific details in the passages. Others ask you to interpret the passages, to make judgments about them. Still others ask you to recognize various techniques used by the authors or possible applications of their ideas to other circumstances. Many of the questions include lengthy and complex statements, as lengthy and complex as any sentences in the passage. All require you to read closely, as does the text. Be sure, in answering reading comprehension questions, that you read *all* the answer choices before deciding which is correct.

Unlike the antonym, analogy, and sentence completion questions, the reading comprehension questions following each passage are not arranged in order of difficulty. They tend to be arranged to reflect the way the passage's content is organized. (A question based on information found at the beginning of the passage generally will come before a question based on information at the passage's end.) If you are stumped by a tough reading question, do not skip the other questions on that passage. A tough question may be just one question away from an easy one.

Testing Tactics

Save the Reading Comprehension Questions for Last

To answer an antonym question takes you seconds; to answer a reading comprehension question takes minutes of going over the passage before you ever get to the questions at all.

On the GRE, you get the same points for answering a "quick and easy" question correctly as you do for answering a time-consuming one. The more questions you answer correctly, the higher your score will be. Therefore, it makes sense for you to tackle the quick-to-answer questions—the sentence completions, the analogies, the antonyms—*first*. Get as many of them right as you can, and then settle down to answering the reading questions, knowing you've done everything possible to maximize your score.

One word of caution: Remember that the reading questions typically occur toward the end of the section, just before the antonyms. If you plan to skip them and come back to them later, *be very careful in marking your answer sheet.*

Tackle Passages with Familiar Subjects Before Passages with Unfamiliar Ones

Just as it is common sense to tackle quick-to-answer questions before time-consuming ones, it is also common sense to tackle reading passages with familiar subjects before reading passages with unfamiliar ones. If you know very little about the physics of elementary particles or are uninterested in it, you are all too likely to run into trouble reading a passage about quantum theory.

It is hard to concentrate when you read about something wholly unfamiliar to you. Give yourself a break. If you find one reading passage interests you or deals with a topic in which you are well grounded, attack that passage first. There is nothing wrong with skipping questions. Just remember to check the numbering of your answer sheet. You should, of course, go back to the questions you skipped if you have time. If you find you are running out of time, simply guess at random: you get no points for empty spaces on your answer sheet.

First Read the Passage, Then Read the Questions

Students often ask whether it is better to read the passage first or the questions first. Those who want to read the questions before reading the passage think it will save time. Ninety-nine times out of a hundred they are wrong.

Reading the questions before you read the passage will not save you time. It will cost you time. If you read the questions first, when you turn to the passage you will have a number of question words and phrases dancing around in your head. These phrases might possibly focus you; more likely, they will distract you. You will be so involved in trying to spot the places they occur in the passage that you will not be able to concentrate on comprehending the passage as a whole. Why increase your anxiety and decrease your capacity to think? First read the passage, using the following technique:

1. Read as rapidly as you can with understanding, but do not force yourself. Do not worry about the time element. If you worry about not finishing the test, you will begin to take short cuts and miss the correct answer in your haste. Remember, if you have followed Tactic 1 and answered the quick questions first, you have already maximized your score and made the best use of your time.

2. As you read the opening sentences, try to anticipate what the passage will be about. Whom or what is the author talking about?

3. As you continue reading, try to identify what *kind* of writing this is, what *techniques* are being used, who its intended *audience* may be, and what *feeling* (if any) the author has toward his subject. Try to retain names, dates, and places for quick reference later. In particular, try to remember where in the passage the author makes *major points*. Then, when you start looking for the phrase or sentence that will justify your choice of answer, you will be able to save time by going back to that section of the passage immediately without having to reread the entire selection. (This is particularly important in dealing with the two 500 – 600 word passages on the test.)

4. Your first reading of the passage should give you a general impression of the theme of the passage and of the location of its major subdivisions. In order to answer each question properly, *you must go back to the passage* to verify your choice of answer. Do not rely on memory, and, above all, do not rely on knowledge gained outside of the passage.

5. Underline sparingly, if at all. You may want to circle key words in question stems (words like EXCEPT and LEAST, which the test-makers capitalize for emphasis, and which restrict your answer choice) or put an asterisk (*) or check mark in the margin next to an important word or phrase. You do not, however, want to underline everything in sight, making the passage harder to read.

6. Then read the first question. You may remember where the answer to that question is to be found. If so, go directly to that part of the reading selection. If not, read the entire selection again. Do not jump around, hoping to encounter the answer by chance. Decide on your answer, or, if you cannot be certain you have identified the correct answer, guess. Then go on to the next question.

If you have reservations about this tactic, feel free to try other approaches doing some of the practice exercises at the end of this chapter. Compare the scores you get using each approach. Reading is a highly individual skill. See what approach works best for you. The important thing is to know yourself and to feel comfortable with what you do.

Learn to Spot the Major Reading Question Types

Just as it will help you to know the common types of analogies found on the GRE, it will also help you to familiarize yourself with the major types of reading questions on the test.

If you can recognize just what a given question is asking for, you will be better able to tell which reading tactic to apply.

Here are six categories of reading questions you are sure to face:

1. **Main Idea** Questions that test your ability to find the central thought of a passage or to judge its significance often take one of the following forms:

   The main point of the passage is to...
   The passage is primarily concerned with...
   The author's primary purpose in this passage is to...
   The chief theme of the passage can best be described as...
   Which of the following titles best states the central idea of the passage?
   Which of the following statements best expresses the main idea of the passage?

2. **Finding Specific Details** Questions that test your ability to understand what the author states *explicitly* are often worded:

   According to the author...

   The author states all of the following EXCEPT
   According to the passage, which of the following is true of the...
   The passage supplies information that would answer which of the following questions?
   Which of the following statements is (are) best supported by the passage?
   Which of the following is NOT cited in the passage as evidence of...

3. **Drawing Inferences** Questions that test your ability to go beyond the author's explicit statements and see what these statements imply may be worded:

   It can be inferred from the passage that...
   The author implies that...
   The passage suggests that...
   Which of the following statements about...can be inferred from the passage?

4. **Application to Other Situations** Questions that test your ability to recognize how the author's ideas might apply to other situations often are worded:

   With which of the following statements would the author of the passage be most likely to agree?
   With which of the following aphorisms would the author be in strongest agreement?
   The author's argument would be most weakened by the discovery of which of the following?
   The author's contention would be most clearly

strengthened if which of the following were found to be true?
Which of the following examples could best be substituted for the author's example of...
Which of the following statements would be most likely to begin the paragraph immediately following the passage?
The author is most probably addressing which of the following audiences?

5. **Tone/Attitude** Questions that test your ability to sense an author's emotional state often take the form:

The author's attitude toward the problem can best be described as
The author regards the idea that...with
The author's tone in the passage is that of a person attempting to
Which of the following best describes the author's tone in the passage?

6. **Technique** Questions that test your ability to recognize a passage's method of organization or technique

often are worded:

Which of the following best describes the development of this passage?
In presenting the argument, the author does all of the following EXCEPT...
The relationship between the second paragraph and the first paragraph can best be described as...
In the passage, the author makes the central point primarily by...
The organization of the passage can best be described as...

7. **Determining the Meaning of Words from Their Context** Questions that test your ability to work out the meaning of unfamiliar words from their context often are worded:

As it is used in the passage, the term...can best be described as
The phrase...is used in the passage to mean that
As used by the author, the term...refers to
The author uses the phrase...to describe

When Asked to Find the Main Idea, Be Sure to Check the Opening and Summary Sentences of Each Paragraph

Authors typically provide readers with a sentence that expresses a paragraph's main idea succinctly. Although such *topic sentences* may appear anywhere in the paragraph, most often they are either the passage's opening or closing sentence.

Note that in GRE reading passages topic sentences are sometimes implied rather than stated directly. If you cannot find a topic sentence, ask yourself these questions:

1. Who or what is this passage about?
   (The subject of the passage can be a *person*, *place*, or *thing*. It can be something abstract, such as an *idea*. It can even be a *process*, or something in motion, for which no single-word synonym exists.)

2. What aspect of this subject is the author talking about?

3. What is the author trying to get across about this aspect of the subject?
   (Decide the most important thing that is being said about the subject. Either the subject must be *doing* something, or something is *being done* to it.)

Read the following natural science passage from a recent GRE and apply this tactic.

When the same parameters and quantitative theory are used to analyze both termite colonies and troops of rhesus macaques, we will have a unified science of sociobiol-

ogy. Can this ever really happen? As my own studies have advanced, I have been increasingly impressed with the functional similarities between insect and vertebrate societies and less so with the structural differences that seem, at first glance, to constitute such an immense gulf between them. Consider for a moment termites and macaques. Both form cooperative groups that occupy territories. In both kinds of society there is a well-marked division of labor. Members of both groups communicate to each other hunger, alarm, hostility, caste status or rank, and reproductive status. From the specialist's point of view, this comparison may at first seem facile — or worse. But it is out of such deliberate oversimplification that the beginnings of a general theory are made.

[Adapted by ETS from *Sociobiology* by Edward O. Wilson.]

Now look at the GRE's main idea question on this passage.

Which of the following best summarizes the author's main point?

(A) Oversimplified comparisons of animal societies could diminish the likelihood of developing a unified science of sociobiology.

(B) Understanding the ways in which animals as different as termites and rhesus macaques resemble each other requires training in both biology and sociology.

(C) Most animals organize themselves into societies that exhibit patterns of group behavior similar to those of human societies.

(D) Animals as different as termites and rhesus macaques follow certain similar and predictable patterns of behavior.

(E) A study of the similarities between insect and vertebrate societies could provide the basis for a unified science of sociobiology.

Look at the opening and summary sentences of the passage: "When the same parameters and quantitative theory are used to analyze both termite colonies and troops of rhesus macaques, we will have a unified science of sociobiology....it is out of such deliberate oversimplification that the beginnings of a general theory are made." First, is there a person, place, thing, idea, or process that is common to both sentences? Are there any words in the last sentence that repeat something in the first? *A general theory* repeats the idea of *a unified science* of sociobiology. The paragraph's subject seems to be the unified science of sociobiology. Note as well the words pointing to expectations for the future—*will have*, *beginnings*. The tone of both sentences appears positive: when certain conditions are met, then a specific result will follow—we will have a unified science or general theory of sociobiol-

ogy. This result, however, is not guaranteed: it can come about only if the conditions are met.

Now turn to the answer choices. What does Choice A say about a unified science of sociobiology? It states some things could make it less likely, not more likely, to come about. Choice A is incorrect; it contradicts the passage's sense that a unified science of sociobiology is a *likely* outcome. Choices B, C, and D also may be incorrect: not one of them mentions a unified science of sociobiology. On closer inspection, Choice B proves incorrect: it makes an unsupported statement that one needs biological and sociological training to understand the resemblances between insects and vertebrates. Choice C also proves incorrect: it goes far beyond what the passage actually states. Where the passage speaks in terms of termites and rhesus macaques, Choice C speaks in terms of *most* animals and extends the comparison to include humans as well. Choice D, while factually correct according to the passage, is incorrect because it is too narrow in scope. It ignores the author's main point: it fails to include the author's interest in the possibility that a study of such similar patterns of behavior might lead to a general theory of sociobiology. The correct answer is Choice E. It is the only statement that speaks of a unified science of sociobiology as a likely possibility.

When Asked to Choose a Title, Watch Out for Choices That Are Too Specific or Too Broad

An appropriate title for a passage must express the central theme developed in the passage. It should be neither too broad nor too narrow in scope; it should be specific and yet comprehensive enough to include all the essential ideas presented. For a passage of two or more paragraphs, it should express the thoughts of ALL the paragraphs.

When you are trying to select the best title for a passage, watch out for words that come straight out of the passage. They may not always be your best choice.

This second question on the sociobiology passage is a title question. Note how it resembles questions on the passage's purpose or main idea.

Which of the following is the best title for the passage?

(A) Deceptive Comparisons: Oversimplification in Biological Research

(B) An Uncanny Likeness: Termites and Rhesus Macaques

(C) Structural Dissimilarities Between Insects and Vertebrates

(D) Arguments against a Science of Sociobiology

(E) Sociobiology: Intimations of a General Theory

Choice A is incorrect: it is at once too narrow and too broad. It is too narrow in that the passage refers to *oversimplification* only in passing. It is too broad in that the passage emphasizes sociobiology, not the whole realm of biological research. It is also misleading: the passage never asserts that the deliberate oversimplification of the comparison between termites and macaques is intended to deceive.

Choice B is incorrect: it is too narrow. True, the author discusses the resemblance between termite and macaque societies; however, this likeness is not his subject. He discusses it to provide an example of the sort of comparison that may lay the groundwork for a potential science of sociobiology.

Choice C is also incorrect because it is not inclusive enough. It fails to mention the potential science of sociobiology. In addition, while the passage refers to *structural differences* between insect and vertebrate societies, it stresses structural similarities, not structural dissimilarities.

Choices D and E both mention the theory of sociobiology. Which is the better title for the piece? Clearly, Choice E. The author is not arguing against the potential science of sociobiology; he is discussing favorably the likelihood of sociobiology's emergence as a unified science. Thus, he finds in the termite-macaque comparison *intimations* or hints of an incipient general theory.

When Asked to Determine Questions of Attitude, Mood, or Tone, Look for Words that Convey Emotion, Express Values, or Paint Pictures

In determining the attitude, mood, or tone of an author, examine the specific diction used. Is the author using adjectives to describe the subject? If so, are they words like *fragrant, tranquil, magnanimous*—words with positive connotations? Or are they words like *fetid, ruffled, stingy*—words with negative connotations?

When we speak, our tone of voice conveys our mood—frustrated, cheerful, critical, gloomy, angry. When we write, our images and descriptive phrases get our feelings across.

The second GRE question on the Wilson passage is an attitude question. Note the range of feelings in the answer choices.

> The author's attitude toward the possibility of a unified theory in sociobiology is best described as which of the following?
>
> (A) Guarded optimism
> (B) Unqualified enthusiasm
> (C) Objective indifference
> (D) Resignation
> (E) Dissatisfaction

How does the author feel about the possibility of a unified theory of sociobiology? The answer choices range from actively negative (*dissatisfaction*) to actively positive (*unqualified enthusiasm*), with passively negative (*resignation*), neutral (*objective indifference*), and cautiously positive (*guarded optimism*) in between.

Wilson's attitude toward the possibility of a unified theory of sociobiology is implicit in his choice of words. It is clear that he views this possibility positively. The whole thrust of his argument is that the current studies of the similarities between insect and vertebrate societies could mark the beginnings of such a unified theory and that the specialist should not dismiss these studies as facile or simpleminded. Note, however, in the second sentence how Wilson's specific choice of words conveys his feelings and value judgments. He describes his own studies as having "advanced"—not as having merely continued, but as having progressed and ultimately improved. He implies that he knows better now than he did in earlier years and deprecates less advanced viewpoints with the negative phrases "at first glance" and "seem."

Wilson is certainly not unhappy or *dissatisfied* with this potential unified theory, nor is he merely longsuffering or *resigned* to it. Similarly, he is not *objectively indifferent* to it; he actively involves himself in arguing the case for sociobiology. Thus, you can eliminate Choices C, D, and E. But how do you decide between the two positive terms, *optimism* and *enthusiasm*, Choice A and Choice B? To decide between them, you must look carefully at the adjectives modifying them. Is Wilson's enthusiasm unconditional or *unqualified*? Not absolutely. His opening sentence states a basic condition that must be met before there can be a unified science of sociobiology: the same parameters and quantitative theory must be used to analyze insect and vertebrate societies. *Unqualified enthusiasm* seems to overstate his attitude. Choice B appears incorrect. What of Choice A? Is Wilson's optimism cautious or *guarded*? Yes. He is aware that specialists may well find fault with the sociobiologist's conclusions; he uses terms that convey values, first the negative "facile—or worse" to suggest the specialist's negative attitude towards sociobiology, then the positive "deliberate" to suggest his more positive response. The correct answer is Choice A.

When Asked About Specific Details in the Passage, Spot Key Words in the Question and Scan the Passage to Find Them (or Their Synonyms).

In developing the main idea of a passage, a writer will make statements to support his or her point. To answer questions about such supporting details, you *must* find a word or group of words in the passage supporting your choice of answer. The words "according to the passage" or "according to the author" should focus your attention on what the passage explicitly states. Do not be misled into choosing an answer (even one that makes good sense) if you can not find it supported by the text.

Detail questions often ask about a particular phrase or line. In such cases, use the following technique:

1. Look for key words (nouns or verbs) in the answer choices.

2. Run your eye down the passage, looking for those key words or their synonyms. (This is *scanning*. It is what you do when you look up someone's number in the phone directory.)

3. When you find a key word or its synonym, reread the sentence to make sure the test-makers haven't used the original wording to mislead you.

Read the following *Scientific American* passage from a recently-published GRE and apply this tactic.

Visual recognition involves storing and retrieving memories. Neural activity, triggered by the eye, forms an image in the brain's memory system that constitutes an internal representation of the viewed object. When an object is encountered again, it is matched with its internal representation and thereby recognized. Controversy surrounds the question of whether recognition is a parallel, one-step process or a serial, step-by-step one. Psychologists of the Gestalt school maintain that objects are recognized as wholes in a parallel procedure: the internal representation is matched with the retinal image in a single operation. Other psychologists have proposed that internal representation features are matched serially with an object's features. Although some experiments show that, as an object becomes familiar, its internal representation becomes more holistic and the recognition process correspondingly more parallel, the weight of evidence seems to support the serial hypothesis, at least for objects that are not notably simple and familiar.

[Adapted by ETS from "Eye Movements and Visual Perception" by David Noton and Lawrence Stark, *Scientific American*, June, 1971]

Now look at a GRE question on a specific detail in the passage.

You can arrive at the correct answer to this question by elimination.

According to the passage, Gestalt psychologists make which of the following suppositions about visual recognition?

I. A retinal image is in exactly the same form as its internal representation.
II. An object is recognized as a whole without any need for analysis into component parts.
III. The matching of an object with its internal representation occurs in only one step.

(A) II only
(B) III only
(C) I and III only
(D) II and III only
(E) I, II, and III

First, quickly scan the passage looking for the key word *Gestalt*. The sentence mentioning Gestalt psychologists states they maintain that objects are recognized as wholes in a parallel procedure. The sentence immediately preceding defines a parallel procedure as one that takes only one step.

Now examine the statements. Do Gestalt psychologists maintain that a retinal image is in exactly the same form as its internal representation? Statement I is unsupported by the passage. Therefore, you can eliminate Choices C and E.

Statement II is supported by the passage: lines 8–12 indicate that Gestalt psychologists believe objects are recognized as wholes. Therefore, you can eliminate Choice B.

Statement III is supported by the passage: lines 8–12 indicate that Gestalt psychologists believe matching is a parallel process that occurs in one step. Therefore, you can eliminate Choice A.

Only Choice D is left. It is the correct answer.

Note how necessary it is to point to specific lines in the passage when you answer questions on specific details.

When Asked to Make Inferences, Base Your Answers on What the Passage Implies, Not What It States Directly

Inference questions require you to use your own judgment. You must not take anything directly stated by the author as an inference. Instead, you must look for clues in the passage that you can use in deriving your own conclusion. You should choose as your answer a statement that is a logical development of the information the author has provided.

Try this relatively easy GRE inference question, based on the previous passage about visual recognition.

It can be inferred from the passage that the matching process in visual recognition is

(A) not a neural activity
(B) not possible when an object is viewed for the very first time
(C) not possible if a feature of a familiar object is changed in some way
(D) only possible when a retinal image is received in the brain as a unitary whole
(E) now fully understood as a combination of the serial and parallel processes

Go through the answer choices, eliminating any choices that obviously contradict what the passage states or implies. Remember that in answering inference questions you must go beyond the obvious, beyond what the authors explicitly state, to look for logical implications of what they say.

Choice A is incorrect. Nothing in the passage suggests that the matching process is not a neural activity. Rather, the entire process of visual recognition, including the matching of images, should involve neural activity.

Choice D is incorrect. It can be eliminated because it directly contradicts information in the passage stating that recognition most likely is a serial or step-by-step process rather than a parallel one grasping an image as a unitary whole.

Choice E is incorrect. It is clear from the passage that the matching process is *not* fully understood: the weight of the evidence *seems* to support the serial hypothesis, but controversy still surrounds the entire question.

Choices B and C are left. Which is a possible inference? Choice B seems a possible inference. Although the author never says so, it seems logical that you could not match an object if you had never seen it before. After all, if you had never seen the object before, you would have no prior internal representation of it and would have nothing with which to match it. What of Choice C? Nothing in the passage mentions changing the features of a familiar object. Therefore, *on the basis of the passage* you have no way to deduce whether matching would or would not be possible if such a change took place. There is not enough information in the passage to justify Choice C as an inference. The correct answer is Choice B.

Another, more difficult GRE inference question is based on the previous excerpt from Wilson's *Sociobiology*. Review the passage briefly and see how you do with a question that only 16 percent of the examinees answered correctly.

When the same parameters and quantitative theory are used to analyze both termite colonies and troops of rhesus macaques, we will have a unified science of sociobiology. Can this ever really happen? As my own studies have advanced, I have been increasingly impressed with the functional similarities between insect and vertebrate societies and less so with the structural differences that seem, at first glance, to constitute such an immense gulf between them. Consider for a moment termites and macaques. Both form cooperative groups that occupy territories. In both kinds of society there is a well-marked division of labor. Members of both groups communicate to each other hunger, alarm, hostility, caste status or rank, and reproductive status. From the specialist's point of view, this comparison may at first seem facile — or worse. But it is out of such deliberate oversimplification that the beginnings of a general theory are made.

In discussing insect and vertebrate societies, the author suggests which of the following?

(A) A distinguishing characteristic of most insect and vertebrate societies is a well-marked division of labor.
(B) The caste structure of insect societies is similar to that of vertebrate societies.
(C) Most insect and vertebrate societies form cooperative groups in order to occupy territory.
(D) The means of communication among members of insect societies is similar to that among members of vertebrate societies.
(E) There are significant structural differences between insect and vertebrate societies.

The reason so many examinees answered this question incorrectly is simple: they confused statements made about specific insect and vertebrate societies with statements made about insect and vertebrate societies in general. They did not see that, in the fourth sentence, the author switches from talking about insect and vertebrate societies in general and considers termites and macaques in specific.

Go through the answer choices one by one. Does the author suggest that a marked division of labor distinguishes *most* insect and vertebrate societies? No. He merely states that it is a characteristic of termite and rhesus macaque societies. Choice A is incorrect: you cannot justify leaping from a single type of insect (*termites*) and a single type of vertebrate (*rhesus macaques*) to most insects and most vertebrates.

Does the author suggest that the caste structure of insect societies is similar to that of vertebrate societies? No. He merely states that termites and macaques both can communicate caste status or rank. Choice B is incorrect. You cannot assume that the caste structure of insect societies is similar to that of vertebrate societies just because termites and rhesus macaques both have some way to communicate caste status or rank.

Does the author suggest that *most* insect and vertebrate societies form cooperative groups in order to occupy territory? No. He merely states that termites and macaques form cooperative groups that occupy territories. Choice C is incorrect: again, you cannot justify leaping from termites and rhesus macaques to most insects and most vertebrates.

Does the author suggest that the means of communication among members of insect societies is similar to that among members of vertebrate societies? No. He merely states that communication among termites and macaques serves similar ends; he says nothing about their means of communication, nor about those means of communication used by other insects and vertebrates. Choice D is incorrect.

The correct answer is Choice E. In the passage, the author states that he has grown less impressed "with the structural differences that seem, at first glance, to constitute such an immense gulf between" insect and verte-brate societies. This suggests that, even though Wilson may be unimpressed with them, these differences exist and are *significant*.

When Asked to Apply Ideas from the Passage to a New Situation, Put Yourself in the Author's Place

GRE application questions require you to do three things:

1. *Reason*—If X is true, then Y must also be true.

2. *Perceive Feelings*—If the author feels this way about subject A, he or she probably feels a certain way about subject B.

3. *Sense a Larger Structure*—This passage is part of an argument for a proposal, or part of a description of a process, or part of a critique of a hypothesis.

Like inference questions, application questions require you to go beyond what the author explicitly states. Application questions, however, ask you to go well beyond a simple inference, using clues in the passage to interpret possible reasons for actions and possible outcomes of events. Your concern is to comprehend how the author's ideas might apply to other situations, or be affected by them. To do so, you have to put yourself in the author's place.

Imagine you are the author. What are you arguing for? Given what you have just stated in the passage, what would you want to say next? What might hurt your argument? What might make it stronger? What kind of audience would appreciate what you have to say? Whom are you trying to convince? If you involve yourself personally with the passage, you will be better able to grasp it in its entirety and see its significance.

Answer the following application question based on the previous passage from *Sociobiology*.

Which of the following statements would be most likely to begin the paragraph immediately following the passage?

(A) I have raised a problem in ethical philosophy in order to characterize the essence of the discipline of sociobiology.
(B) It may not be too much to say that sociology and the other social sciences are the last branches of biology waiting to be integrated into neo-Darwinist evolutionary theory.
(C) Although behavioral biology is traditionally spoken of as if it were a unified subject, it is now emerging as two distinct disciplines centered on neurophysiology and sociobiology, respectively.
(D) The formulation of a theory of sociobiology constitutes, in my opinion, one of the great manageable problems of biology for the next twenty or thirty years.
(E) In the past, the development of sociobiology has been slowed by too close an identification with ethology and behavioral psychology.

As you know from answering the previous main idea and attitude questions, Wilson's point is that students of insect and vertebrate societies may be on the verge of devising a general theory of sociobiology. He is optimistic about the likelihood of developing this unified science. At the same time, he is guarded: he does not wish to overstate his case.

Put yourself in Wilson's place. What would you be likely to say next? You have just been talking optimistically about the prospects for putting together a general theory. What would be more natural than to talk in terms of a time frame? Choice D, with its optimistic yet careful view of the formulation of a theory of sociobiology as "one of the great *manageable* problems of biology for the next twenty or thirty years," seems a logical extension of what Wilson has just been saying. While Choices A, B, C, and E all touch on sociobiology in some way, none of them follows as naturally from his immediate argument.

Tactic 11

When Asked to Give the Meaning of an Unfamiliar Word, Look for Nearby Context Clues

When a question in the reading comprehension part of an examination asks for the meaning of a word, that meaning can usually be deduced from the word's context. The purpose of this kind of question is to determine how well you can extract meaning from the text, not how extensive your general vocabulary is.

Sometimes the unknown word is a common word used in one of its special or technical meanings. For example:

He *threw* the pot in an hour. The wheel turned busily and the shape grew quickly as his fingers worked the wet, spinning clay. (*Throw* here means to shape on a potter's wheel.)

At other times, the unknown word may bear a deceptive resemblance to a known word.

He fell *senseless* to the ground. (He was unconscious. He did not fall foolishly or nonsensically to the ground.)

Just because you know *one* meaning of a word, do not assume that you know its meaning as it is used in a particular passage. You must look within the passage for clues. Often authors will use an unfamiliar word and then immediately define it within the same sentence. The two words or groups of words are juxtaposed—set beside one another—to make their relationship clear. Commas, hyphens, and parentheses may be used to signal this relationship.

1. The *rebec*, a medieval stringed instrument played with a bow, has only three strings.

2. *Paleontologists*—students of fossil remains—explore the earth's history.

3. Most mammals are *quadrupeds* (four-footed animals).

Often an unfamiliar word in one clause of a sentence will be defined or clarified in the sentence's other clause.

1. The early morning dew had frozen, and everything was covered with a thin coat of *rime*.

2. Cowards, we use *euphemisms* when we cannot bear the truth, calling our dead "the dear departed," as if they have just left the room.

Refer once more to the *Scientific American* passage to answer the following question.

Visual recognition involves storing and retrieving memories. Neural activity, triggered by the eye, forms an image in the brain's memory system that constitutes an internal representation of the
(5) viewed object. When an object is encountered again, it is matched with its internal representation and thereby recognized. Controversy surrounds the question of whether recognition is a parallel, one-step process or a serial, step-by-step one. Psychol-
(10) ogists of the Gestalt school maintain that objects are recognized as wholes in a parallel procedure: the internal representation is matched with the retinal image in a single operation. Other psychologists have proposed that internal representation
(15) features are matched serially with an object's features. Although some experiments show that, as an object becomes familiar, its internal representation becomes more holistic and the recognition process correspondingly more parallel, the weight of evi-
(20) dence seems to support the serial hypothesis, at least for objects that are not notably simple and familiar.

[Adapted by ETS from "Eye Movements and Visual Perception" by David Noton and Lawrence Stark, *Scientific American*, June, 1971]

Which of the following phrases could best be substituted for "becomes more holistic" (lines 17–18) without substantially changing the author's meaning?

(A) increases in complexity
(B) grows less fragmented
(C) diminishes in magnitude
(D) reflects its image
(E) becomes unclear

What words or phrases in the vicinity of "becomes more holistic" give you a clue to the phrase's meaning? The phrase immediately following, "[becomes] more parallel." If the recognition process becomes more parallel as an object becomes more familiar, then matching takes place in one step in which all the object's features are simultaneously transformed into a single internal representation. Thus, to say that an object's internal representation becomes more holistic is to say that it becomes more *integrated* or whole. The correct answer is Choice B.

Look at the words in the immediate vicinity of the word or phrase you are defining. They will give you a sense of the meaning of the unfamiliar word.

Tactic 12

Familiarize Yourself with the Technical Terms Used to Describe a Passage's Organization

Another aspect of understanding the author's point is understanding how the author organizes what he has to say. You have to understand how the author makes his point, figure out whether he begins with his thesis or main idea or works up to it gradually. Often this means observing how the opening sentence or paragraph relates to the passage as a whole.

Here is a technique question based on the last two sentences of the passage from *Sociobiology*. Those lines are repeated here so that you can easily refer to them.

From the specialist's point of view, this comparison may at first seem facile — or worse. But it is out of such deliberate oversimplification that the beginnings of a general theory are made.

Which of the following statements best describes the organization of the author's discussion of the importance of the termite/macaque comparison in the development of a unified science of sociobiology (lines 14–17)?

(A) He provides an example of a comparison and then rejects its implications.

(B) He concedes that current data are insufficient and modifies his initial assertion of their importance.

(C) He acknowledges hypothetical objections to the comparison, but concludes by reaffirming its significance.

(D) He cites critical appraisals of the comparison, but refrains from making an appraisal of his own.

(E) He notes an ambiguity in the comparison, but finally concedes its validity.

Consider the first clause of each answer choice.

In his comment on how things may seem from the specialist's point of view, does the author *provide an example* of a comparison? No. He refers to a comparison he made earlier. Therefore, you can eliminate Choice A.

Does he *concede the insufficiency* of current data? Not quite. He states that some people may quarrel with the comparison because it seems facile to them; he does not grant that they are right or that the data is inadequate. Therefore, you can eliminate Choice B.

Does he *acknowledge hypothetical objections* to the comparison? Definitely. Make a note to come back later to Choice C.

Does he *cite critical appraisals* of the comparison? Possibly. Again, make a note of Choice D.

Does he *note an ambiguity* in the comparison? No. He notes an objection to the comparison; he mentions no ambiguities within it. Therefore, you can eliminate Choice E.

Now consider the second clause of Choices C and D. Does the author *refrain from making an appraisal* of the comparison? No. He calls it a deliberate oversimplification that may bear fruit. Choice D is incorrect. Does the author conclude by *reaffirming the significance* of the termite/macaque comparison? Clearly he does: his final point is that such oversimplified comparisons can provide the basis for an important general theory. The correct answer is Choice C.

Practice Exercises

Reading Comprehension Exercise A

Directions: Each passage in this group is followed by questions based on its content. After reading a passage, choose the best answer to each question. Answer all questions following a passage on the basis of what is <u>stated</u> or <u>implied</u> in that passage.

One phase of the business cycle is the *expansion phase*. This phase is a two-fold one, including recovery and prosperity. During the recovery period there is ever-growing expansion of existing
(5) facilities, and new facilities for production are created. More businesses are created and older ones expanded. Improvements of various kinds are made. There is an ever increasing optimism about the future of economic growth. Much capital is

(10) invested in machinery or "heavy" industry. More labor is employed. More raw materials are required. As one part of the economy develops, other parts are affected. For example, a great expansion in automobiles results in an expansion of
(15) the steel, glass, and rubber industries. Roads are required; thus the cement and machinery industries are stimulated. Demand for labor and materials results in greater prosperity for workers and sup-

pliers of raw materials, including farmers. This
(20) increases purchasing power and the volume of
goods bought and sold. Thus prosperity is diffused
among the various segments of the population.
This prosperity period may continue to rise and rise
without an apparent end. However, a time comes
(25) when this phase reaches a peak and stops spiralling
upwards. This is the end of the expansion phase.

1. Which of the following statements is the best example of the optimism mentioned in line 8 of the passage as being part of the expansion phase?

(A) Public funds are designated for the construction
of new highways designed to stimulate
tourism.
(B) Industrial firms allocate monies for the purchase
of machine tools.
(C) The prices of agricultural commodities are
increased at the producer level.
(D) Full employment is achieved at all levels of the
economy.
(E) As technology advances, innovative businesses
replace antiquated firms.

2. It can be inferred from the passage that the author
believes that

(A) when consumers lose their confidence in the
market, a recession follows
(B) cyclical ends to business expansion are normal
(C) luxury goods such as jewelry are unaffected by
industrial expansion
(D) with sound economic policies, prosperity can
become a fixed pattern
(E) the creation of new products is essential for
prosperity

3. Which of the following statements would be most
likely to begin the paragraph immediately following
the passage?

(A) Union demands may also have an effect on business cycles.
(B) Some industries are, by their very nature, cyclical, having regular phases of expansion and
recession.
(C) Inflation is a factor that must be taken into consideration in any discussion of the expansion
phase.
(D) The farmer's role during the expansion phase is
of vital importance.
(E) The other phase of the business cycle is called
the recession phase.

The history of mammals dates back at least to
Triassic time. Development was retarded, however, until the sudden acceleration of evolutional
change that occurred in the oldest Paleocene. This
(5) led in Eocene time to increase in average size,
larger mental capacity, and special adaptations for
different modes of life. In the Oligocene Epoch,

there was further improvement, with some appearance of some new lines and extinction of others.
(10) Miocene and Pliocene time was marked by culmination of several groups and continued approach
toward modern characters. The peak of the career
of mammals in variety and average large size was
attained in the Miocene.
(15) The adaptation of mammals to almost all possible modes of life parallels that of the reptiles in
Mesozoic time, and except for greater intelligence,
the mammals do not seem to have done much better than corresponding reptilian forms. The bat is
(20) doubtless a better flying animal than the pterosaur,
but the dolphin and whale are hardly more fishlike
than the ichthyosaur. Many swift-running mammals of the plains, like the horse and the antelope,
must excel any of the dinosaurs. The tyrannosaur
(25) was a more ponderous and powerful carnivore than
any flesh-eating mammal, but the lion or tiger is
probably a more efficient and dangerous beast of
prey because of a superior brain. The significant
point to observe is that different branches of the
(30) mammals gradually fitted themselves for all sorts
of life, grazing on the plains and able to run swiftly
(horse, deer, bison), living in rivers and swamps
(hippopotamus, beaver), dwelling in trees (sloth,
monkey), digging underground (mole, rodent),
(35) feeding on flesh in the forest (tiger) and plain
(wolf), swimming in the sea (dolphin, whale, seal)
and flying in the air (bat). Man is able by mechanical means to conquer the physical world and to
adapt himself to almost any set of conditions.
(40) This adaptation produces gradual changes of
form and structure. It is biologically characteristic
of the youthful, plastic stage of a group. Early in its
career, an animal assemblage seems to possess
capacity for change, which, as the unit becomes
(45) old and fixed, disappears. The generalized types of
organisms retain longest the ability to make adjustments when required, and it is from them that new,
fecund stocks take origin—certainly not from any
specialized end products. So, in the mammals, we
(50) witness the birth, plastic spread in many directions,
increasing specialization, and in some branches,
the extinction, which we have learned from observation of the geologic record of life is a characteristic of the evolution of life.

4. Which of the following would be the most appropriate title for the passage?

(A) From Dinosaur to Man
(B) Adaptation and Extinction
(C) The Superiority of Mammals
(D) The Geologic Life Span
(E) Man, Conqueror of the Physical World

5. It can be inferred from the passage that the chronological order of the geologic periods is

(A) Paleocene, Miocene, Triassic, Mesozoic
(B) Paleocene, Triassic, Mesozoic, Miocene
(C) Miocene, Paleocene, Triassic, Mesozoic
(D) Mesozoic, Oligocene, Paleocene, Miocene
(E) Mesozoic, Paleocene, Eocene, Miocene

6. It can be inferred from the passage that the pterosaur

    (A) resembled the bat
    (B) was a Mesozoic mammal
    (C) was a flying reptile
    (D) lived in the sea
    (E) evolved during the Miocene period

7. According to the passage, the greatest number of forms of mammalian life is found in the

    (A) Triassic period
    (B) Eocene period
    (C) Oligocene epoch
    (D) Pliocene period
    (E) Miocene period

8. Which of the following statements, if true, would weaken the statement made by the author in lines 15–19?

    (A) Tryannosaur has been found to have a larger brain than was previously thought.
    (B) Mammals will become extinct within the next thousand years.
    (C) Forms of flying ichthyosaurs have recently been discovered.
    (D) The tiger has now been proved to be more powerful than the carnivorous reptiles.
    (E) Computers have been developed that can double human mental capacity.

9. It can be inferred from the passage that the evidence the author uses in discussing the life of past time periods was

    (A) developed by Charles Darwin
    (B) uncovered by the author
    (C) negated by more recent evidence
    (D) never definitely established
    (E) based on fossil remains

10. With which of the following observations about human existence would the author be most likely to agree?

    (A) It's a cruel world
    (B) All the world's a stage
    (C) The more things change, the more they remain the same
    (D) Footprints in the sands of time
    (E) A short life, but a merry one

For me, scientific knowledge is divided into mathematical sciences, natural sciences or sciences dealing with the natural world (physical and biological sciences), and sciences dealing with mankind (psychology, sociology, all the sciences of cultural achievements, every kind of historical knowledge). Apart from these sciences is philosophy, about which we will talk shortly. In the first place, all this is pure or theoretical knowledge, sought only for the purpose of understanding, in order to fulfill the need to understand that is intrinsic and consubstantial to man. What distinguishes man from animal is that he knows and needs to know. If man did not know that the world existed, and that the world was of a certain kind, that he was in the world and that he himself was of a certain kind, he wouldn't be man. The technical aspects of applications of knowledge are equally necessary for man and are of the greatest importance, because they also contribute to defining him as man and permit him to pursue a life increasingly more truly human.

But even while enjoying the results of technical progress, he must defend the primacy and autonomy of pure knowledge. Knowledge sought directly for its practical applications will have immediate and foreseeable success, but not the kind of important result whose revolutionary scope is in large part unforeseen, except by the imagination of the Utopians. Let me recall a well-known example. If the Greek mathematicians had not applied themselves to the investigation of conic sections, zealously and without the least suspicion that it might someday be useful, it would not have been possible centuries later to navigate far from shore. The first men to study the nature of electricity could not imagine that their experiments, carried on because of mere intellectual curiosity, would eventually lead to modern electrical technology, without which we can scarcely conceive of contemporary life. Pure knowledge is valuable for its own sake, because the human spirit cannot resign itself to ignorance. But, in addition, it is the foundation for practical results that would not have been reached if this knowledge had not been sought disinterestedly.

11. The author points out that the Greeks who studied conic sections

    (A) invented modern mathematical applications
    (B) were interested in navigation
    (C) were unaware of the value of their studies
    (D) worked with electricity
    (E) were forced to resign themselves to failure

12. The title below that best expresses the ideas of this passage is

    (A) Technical Progress
    (B) A Little Learning Is a Dangerous Thing
    (C) Man's Distinguishing Characteristics
    (D) Learning for Its Own Sake
    (E) The Difference Between Science and Philosophy

13. It can be inferred from the passage that to the author man's need to know is chiefly important in that it

    (A) allows the human race to progress technically
    (B) encompasses both the physical and social sciences
    (C) demonstrates human vulnerability
    (D) defines his essential humanity
    (E) has increased as our knowledge of the world has grown

When you first saw a piece of African art, it impressed you as a unit; you did not see it as a collection of shapes or forms. This, of course, means that the shapes and volumes within the sculpture
(5) itself were coordinated so successfully that the viewer was affected emotionally.

It is entirely valid to ask how, from a purely artistic point of view, this unity was achieved. And we must also inquire whether there is a recurrent pat-
(10) tern or rules or a plastic language and vocabulary which is responsible for the powerful communication of emotion which the best African sculpture achieves. If there is such a pattern or rules, are these rules applied consciously or instinctively to obtain
(15) so many works of such high artistic quality?

It is obvious from the study of art history that an intense and unified emotional experience, such as the Christian credo of the Byzantine or 12th or 13th century Europe, when expressed in art forms, gave
(20) great unity, coherence, and power to art. But such an integrated feeling was only the inspirational element for the artist, only the starting point of the creative act. The expression of this emotion and its realization in the work could be done only with dis-
(25) cipline and thorough knowledge of the craft. And the African sculptor was a highly trained workman. He started his apprenticeship with a master when a child, and he learned the tribal styles and the use of tools and the nature of woods so thoroughly that his
(30) carving became what Boas calls "motor action." He carved automatically and instinctively.

The African carver followed his rules without thinking of them; indeed, they never seem to have been formulated in words. But such rules existed,
(35) for accident and coincidence can not explain the common plastic language of African sculpture. There is too great a consistency from one work to another. Yet, although the African, with amazing insight into art, used these rules, I am certain that
(40) he was not conscious of them. This is the great mystery of such a traditional art: talent, or the ability certain people have, without conscious effort, to follow the rules which later the analyst can discover only from the work of art which has already been
(45) created.

14. The author is primarily concerned with

(A) discussing how African sculptors achieved their effects
(B) listing the rules followed in African art
(C) relating African art to the art of 12th or 13th century Europe
(D) integrating emotion and realization
(E) expressing the beauty of African art

15. According to the passage, one of the outstanding features of African sculpture is

(A) its esoteric subject matter
(B) the emotional content of the work
(C) the education or training of the artists
(D) its "foreignness" when compared to western art
(E) its high degree of conscious control

16. The author uses the phrase "plastic language" in lines 10 and 36 to refer to African art's

(A) mass reproduction
(B) unrealistic qualities
(C) modernistic orientation
(D) sculptural symbols
(E) repetitive nature

17. The information in the passage suggests that an African carver might best be compared to a

(A) chef following a recipe
(B) fluent speaker of English who is just beginning to study French
(C) batter who hits a homerun in his or her first baseball game
(D) concert pianist performing a well-rehearsed concerto
(E) writer who is grammatically expert but stylistically uncreative

18. Which of the following does the passage imply about art?

(A) Content is more important than form.
(B) There is no room for untrained artists.
(C) Form is more important then content.
(D) Western artists are overly concerned with technique.
(E) Great art must be consistent.

19. The author's presentation of the material includes all of the following EXCEPT

(A) comparison
(B) cause and effect
(C) rhetorical questioning
(D) direct quotation
(E) concrete example

20. Which of the following titles best expresses the content of the passage?

(A) The Apprenticeship of the African Sculptor
(B) The History of African Sculpture
(C) How African Art Achieves Unity
(D) Analyzing African Art
(E) The Unconscious Rules of African Art

Reading Comprehension Exercise B

Directions: Each passage in this group is followed by questions based on its content. After reading a passage, choose the best answer to each question. Answer all questions following a passage on the basis of what is stated or implied in that passage.

Both plants and animals of many sorts show remarkable changes in form, structure, growth habits, and even mode of reproduction in becoming adapted to different climatic environment, types of
(5) food supply, or mode of living. This divergence in response to evolution is commonly expressed by altering the form and function of some part or parts of the organism, the original identity of which is clearly discernible. For example, the creeping foot
(10) of the snail is seen in related marine pteropods to be modified into a flapping organ useful for swimming, and is changed into prehensile arms that bear suctorial disks in the squids and other cephalopods. The limbs of various mammals are modified
(15) according to several different modes of life – for swift running (cursorial) as in the horse and antelope, for swinging in trees (arboreal) as in the monkeys, for digging (fossorial) as in the moles and gophers, for flying (volant) as in the bats, for
(20) swimming (aquatic) as in the seals, whales and dolphins, and for other adaptations. The structures or organs that show main change in connection with this adaptive divergence are commonly identified readily as homologous, in spite of great altera-
(25) tions. Thus, the finger and wristbones of a bat and whale, for instance, have virtually nothing in common except that they are definitely equivalent elements of the mammalian limb.

1. Which of the following is the most appropriate title for the passage, based on its content?

   (A) Adaptive Divergence
   (B) Evolution
   (C) Unusual Structures
   (D) Changes in Organs
   (E) Our Changing Bodies

2. The author provides information that would answer which of the following questions?

   I. What factors cause change in organisms?
   II. What is the theory of evolution?
   III. How are horses' legs related to seals' flippers?

   (A) I only
   (B) II only
   (C) I and II only
   (D) I and III only
   (E) I, II, and III

3. Which of the following words could best be substituted for "homologous" (line 24) without substantially changing the author's meaning?

   (A) altered
   (B) mammalian
   (C) corresponding
   (D) divergent
   (E) tactile

4. The author's style can best be described as

   (A) humorous
   (B) objective
   (C) patronizing
   (D) esoteric
   (E) archaic

Plato — who may have understood better what forms the mind of man than do some of our contemporaries who want their children exposed only to "real" people and everyday events — knew what intellectual experiences make for true humanity. He suggested that the future citizens of his ideal republic begin their literary education with the telling of myths, rather than with mere facts or so-called rational teachings. Even Aristotle, master of pure reason, said: "The friend of wisdom is also a friend of myth."

Modern thinkers who have studied myths and fairy tales from a philosophical or psychological viewpoint arrive at the same conclusion, regardless of their original persuasion. Mircea Eliade, for one, describes these stories as "models for human behavior [that,] by that very fact, give meaning and value to life." Drawing on anthropological parallels, he and others suggest that myths and fairy tales were derived from, or given symbolic expression to, initiation rites or other rites of passage — such as metaphoric death of an old, inadequate self in order to be reborn on a higher plane of existence. He feels that this is why these tales meet a strongly felt need and are carriers of such deep meaning.

Other investigators with a depth-psychological orientation emphasize the similarities between the fantastic events in myths and fairy tales and those in adult dreams and daydreams — the fulfillment of wishes, the winning out over all competitors, the destruction of enemies — and conclude that one attraction of this literature is its expression of that which is normally prevented from coming to awareness.

There are, of course, very significant differences between fairy tales and dreams. For example, in dreams more often than not the wish fulfillment is disguised, while in fairy tales much of it is openly expressed. To a considerable degree, dreams are the result of inner pressures which have found no relief, of problems which beset a person to which he knows no solution and to which the dream finds none. The fairy tale does the opposite: it projects the relief of all pressures and not only offers ways to solve problems but promises that a "happy" solution will be found.

We cannot control what goes on in our dreams. Although our inner censorship influences what we may dream, such control occurs on an unconscious level. The fairy tale, on the other hand, is very much the result of common conscious and unconscious content having been shaped by the conscious mind, not of one particular person, but the consensus of many in regard to what they view as universal human problems, and what they accept as desirable solutions. If all these elements were not present in a fairy tale, it would not be retold by generation after generation. Only if a fairy tale met the conscious and unconscious requirements of many people was it repeatedly retold, and listened to with great interest. No dream of a person could arouse such persistent interest unless it was worked into a myth, as was the story of the pharaoh's dream as interpreted by Joseph in the Bible.

5. It can be inferred from the passage that the author's interest in fairy tales centers chiefly on their

   (A) literary qualities
   (B) historical background
   (C) factual accuracy
   (D) psychological relevance
   (E) ethical weakness

6. According to the passage, fairy tales differ from dreams in which of the following characteristics?

   I.   The communal nature of their creation
   II. Their convention of a happy ending
   III. Their enduring general appeal

   (A) I only
   (B) II only
   (C) I and II only
   (D) II and III only
   (E) I, II, and III

7. It can be inferred from the passage that Mircea Eliade is most likely

   (A) a writer of children's literature
   (B) a student of physical anthropology
   (C) a twentieth-century philosopher
   (D) an advocate of practical education
   (E) a contemporary of Plato

8. Which of the following best describes the author's attitude toward fairy tales?

   (A) Reluctant fascination
   (B) Wary skepticism
   (C) Scornful disapprobation
   (D) Indulgent tolerance
   (E) Open approval

9. The author quotes Plato and Aristotle primarily in order to

   (A) define the nature of myth
   (B) contrast their opposing points of view
   (C) support the point that myths are valuable
   (D) prove that myths originated in ancient times
   (E) give an example of depth psychology

10. The author mentions all of the following as reasons for reading fairy tales EXCEPT

   (A) emotional catharsis
   (B) behavioral paradigm
   (C) uniqueness of experience
   (D) sublimation of aggression
   (E) symbolic satisfaction

The stability that had marked the Iroquois Confederacy's generally pro-British position was shattered with the overthrow of James II in 1688, the colonial uprisings that followed in Massachusetts, New York, and Maryland, and the commencement of King William's War against Louis XIV of France. The increasing French threat to English hegemony in the interior of North America was signalized by French-led or French-inspired attacks on the Iroquois and on outlying colonial settlements in New York and New England. The high point of the Iroquois response was the spectacular raid of August 5, 1689, in which the Iroquois virtually wiped out the French village of Lachine, just outside Montreal. A counterraid by the French on the English village of Schenectady in March, 1690, instilled an appropriate measure of fear among the English and their Iroquois allies.

The Iroquois position at the end of the war, which was formalized by treaties made during the summer of 1701 with the British and the French, and which was maintained throughout most of the eighteenth century, was one of "aggressive neutrality" between the two competing European powers. Under the new system the Iroquois initiated a peace policy toward the "far Indians," tightened their control over the nearby tribes, and induced both English and French to support their neutrality toward the European powers by appropriate gifts and concessions.

By holding the balance of power in the sparsely settled borderlands between English and French settlements, and by their willingness to use their power against one or the other nation if not appropriately treated, the Iroquois played the game of European power politics with effectiveness. The system broke down, however, after the French became convinced that the Iroquois were compromising the system in favor of the English and launched a full-scale attempt to establish French physical and juridical presence in the Ohio Valley, the heart of the borderlands long claimed by the Iroquois. As a consequence of the ensuing Great War for Empire, in which Iroquois neutrality was dissolved and European influence moved closer, the play-off system lost its efficacy and a system of direct bargaining supplanted it.

11. The author's primary purpose in this passage is to

    (A) denounce the imperialistic policies of the French
    (B) disprove the charges of barbarism made against the Iroquois
    (C) expose the French government's exploitation of the Iroquois balance of power
    (D) describe and assess the effect of European military power on Iroquois policy
    (E) show the inability of the Iroquois to engage in European-style diplomacy

12. It can be inferred from the passage that the author's attitude toward the Iroquois leadership can best be described as one of

    (A) suspicion of their motives
    (B) respect for their competence
    (C) indifference to their fate
    (D) dislike of their savagery
    (E) pride in their heritage

13. With which of the following statements would the author be LEAST likely to agree?

    (A) The Iroquois were able to respond effectively to French acts of aggression.
    (B) James II's removal from the throne caused dissension to break out among the colonies.
    (C) The French begrudged the British their alleged high standing among the Iroquois.
    (D) Iroquois negotiations involved playing one side against the other.
    (E) The Iroquois ceased to hold the balance of power early in the eighteenth century.

14. The author attributes such success as the Iroquois policy of aggressive neutrality had to

    (A) their readiness to fight either side
    (B) ties of loyalty to the British
    (C) French physical presence in the borderlands
    (D) the confusion of the European forces
    (E) European reliance on formal treaties

Of the 197 million square miles making up the surface of the globe, 71 per cent is covered by the interconnecting bodies of marine water; the Pacific Ocean alone covers half the Earth and averages near 14,000 feet in depth. The *continents*—Eurasia, Africa, North America, South America, Australia, and Antarctica—are the portions of the *continental masses* rising above sea level. The submerged borders of the continental masses are the *continental shelves*, beyond which lie the deep-sea basins.

The oceans attain their greatest depths not in their central parts, but in certain elongated furrows, or long narrow troughs, called *deeps*. These profound troughs have a peripheral arrangement, notably around the borders of the Pacific and Indian oceans. The position of the deeps near the continental masses suggests that the deeps, like the highest mountains, are of recent origin, since otherwise they would have been filled with waste from the lands. This suggestion is strengthened by the fact that the deeps are frequently the sites of world-shaking earthquakes. For example, the "tidal wave" that in April, 1946, caused widespread destruction along Pacific coasts resulted from a strong earthquake on the floor of the Aleutian Deep.

The topography of the ocean floors is none too well known, since in great areas the available soundings are hundreds or even thousands of miles apart. However, the floor of the Atlantic is becoming fairly well known as a result of special surveys since 1920. A broad, well-defined ridge—the Mid-Atlantic ridge—runs north and south between Africa and the two Americas, and numerous other major irregularities diversify the Atlantic floor. Closely spaced soundings show that many parts of the oceanic floors are as rugged as mountainous regions of the continents. Use of the recently perfected method of echo sounding is rapidly enlarging our knowledge of submarine topography. During World War II great strides were made in mapping submarine surfaces, particularly in many parts of the vast Pacific basin.

The continents stand on the average 2870 feet—slightly more than half a mile—above sea level. North America averages 2300 feet; Europe averages only 1150 feet; and Asia, the highest of the larger continental subdivisions, averages 3200 feet. The highest point on the globe, Mount Everest in the Himalayas, is 29,000 feet above the sea; and as the greatest known depth in the sea is over 35,000 feet, the maximum *relief* (that is, the difference in altitude between the lowest and highest points) exceeds 64,000 feet, or exceeds 12 miles. The continental masses and the deep-sea basins are relief features of the first order; the deeps, ridges, and volcanic cones that diversify the sea floor, as well as the plains, plateaus, and mountains of the continents, are relief features of the second order. The lands are unendingly subject to a complex of activities summarized in the term *erosion*, which first sculptures them in great detail and then tends to reduce them ultimately to sea level. The modeling of the landscape by weather, running water, and other agents is apparent to the keenly observant eye and causes thinking people to speculate on what must be the final result of the ceaseless wearing down of the lands. Long before there was a science of geology, Shakespeare wrote "the revolution of the times makes mountains level."

15. Which of the following would be the most appropriate title for the passage?

    (A) Features of the Earth's Surface
    (B) Marine Topography
    (C) The Causes of Earthquakes
    (D) Primary Geologic Considerations
    (E) How to Prevent Erosion

16. It can be inferred from the passage that the largest ocean is the

   (A) Atlantic
   (B) Pacific
   (C) Indian
   (D) Antarctic
   (E) Arctic

17. The "revolution of the times" as used in the final sentence means

   (A) the passage of years
   (B) the current rebellion
   (C) the science of geology
   (D) the action of the ocean floor
   (E) the overthrow of natural forces

18. According to the passage, the peripheral furrows or *deeps* are found

   (A) only in the Pacific and Indian oceans
   (B) near earthquakes
   (C) near the shore
   (D) in the center of the ocean
   (E) to be 14,000 feet in depth in the Pacific

19. The passage contains information that would answer which of the following questions?

   I.   What is the highest point on North America?
   II. Which continent is, on the average, 1150 feet above sea level?
   III. How deep is the deepest part of the ocean?

   (A) I only
   (B) II only
   (C) III only
   (D) I and II only
   (E) II and III only

20. From this passage, it can be inferred that earthquakes

   (A) occur only in the peripheral furrows
   (B) occur more frequently in newly formed land or sea formations
   (C) are a prime cause of soil erosion
   (D) will ultimately "make mountains level"
   (E) are caused by the weight of the water

Reading Comprehension Exercise C

<u>Directions:</u>   Each passage in this group is followed by questions based on its content. After reading a passage, choose the best answer to each question. Answer all questions following a passage on the basis of what is <u>stated</u> or <u>implied</u> in that passage.

An essay which appeals chiefly to the intellect is Francis Bacon's "Of Studies." His careful tripartite division of studies expressed succinctly in aphoris-tic prose demands the complete attention of the
(5) mind of the reader. He considers studies as they should be: for pleasure, for self-improvement, for business. He considers the evils of excess study: laziness, affectation, and preciosity. Bacon divides books into three categories: those to be read in part,
(10) those to be read cursorily, and those to be read with care. Studies should include reading which gives depth, speaking which adds readiness of thought, and writing which trains in preciseness. Somewhat mistakenly, the author ascribes certain virtues to
(15) individual fields of study: wisdom to history, wit to poetry, subtlety to mathematics and depth to natu-ral philosophy. Bacon's four-hundred-word essay, studded with Latin phrases and highly compressed in thought, has intellectual appeal indeed.

1. Which of the following is the most appropriate title for the passage, based on its content?

   (A) Francis Bacon and the Appeal of the Essay
   (B) "Of Studies": A Tripartite Division
   (C) An Intellectual Exercise: Francis Bacon's "Of Studies"
   (D) The Categorization of Books According to Bacon
   (E) A Method for Reading Books

2. Which of the following words could best be substi-tuted for "aphoristic" (line 3) without substantially changing the author's meaning?

   (A) abstruse
   (B) pithy
   (C) tripartite
   (D) proverbial
   (E) realistic

3. The passage suggests that the author would be most likely to agree with which of the following statements?

   (A) "Of Studies" belongs in the category of works that demand to be read with care.
   (B) Scholars' personalities are shaped by the aca-demic discipline in which they are engaged.
   (C) It is an affectation to use foreign words in one's writing.
   (D) An author can be more persuasive in a long work than in a shorter one.
   (E) Studies should be undertaken without thought of personal gain.

Rocks which have solidified directly from molten materials are called igneous rocks. Igneous rocks are commonly referred to as primary rocks because they are the original source of material found in sedimentaries and metamorphics. Igneous rocks compose the greater part of the earth's crust, but they are generally covered at the surface by a relatively thin layer of sedimentary or metamorphic rocks. Igneous rocks are distinguished by the following characteristics: (1) they contain no fossils; (2) they have no regular arrangement of layers; and (3) they are nearly always made up of crystals.

Sedimentary rocks are composed largely of minute fragments derived from the disintegration of existing rocks and in some instances from the remains of animals. As sediments are transported, individual fragments are assorted according to size. Distinct layers of such sediments as gravels, sand, and clay build up, as they are deposited by water and occasionally wind. These sediments vary in size with the material and the power of the eroding agent. Sedimentary materials are laid down in layers called strata.

When sediments harden into sedimentary rocks, the names applied to them change to indicate the change in physical state. Thus, small stones and gravel cemented together are known as conglomerates; cemented sand becomes sandstone; and hardened clay becomes shale. In addition to these, other sedimentary rocks such as limestone frequently result from the deposition of dissolved material. The ingredient parts are normally precipitated by organic substances, such as shells of clams or hard skeletons of other marine life.

Both igneous and sedimentary rocks may be changed by pressure, heat, solution, or cementing action. When individual grains from existing rocks tend to deform and interlock, they are called metamorphic rocks. For example, granite, an igneous rock, may be metamorphosed into a gneiss or a schist. Limestone, a sedimentary rock, when subjected to heat and pressure may become marble, a metamorphic rock. Shale under pressure becomes slate.

4. The primary purpose of the passage is to

   (A) differentiate between and characterize igneous and sedimentary rocks
   (B) explain the factors that may cause rocks to change in form
   (C) show how the scientific names of rocks reflect the rocks' composition
   (D) define and describe several diverse kinds of rocks
   (E) explain why rocks are basic parts of the earth's structure

5. All of the following are sedimentary rocks EXCEPT

   (A) shale
   (B) gravel
   (C) sand
   (D) limestone
   (E) schist

6. The passage would be most likely to appear in a

   (A) technical article for geologists
   (B) teaching manual accompanying an earth science text
   (C) pamphlet promoting conservation of natural resources
   (D) newspaper feature explaining how oil is found
   (E) nonfiction book explaining where to find results

7. The relationship between igneous and sedimentary rocks may best be compared to the relationship between

   (A) leaves and compost
   (B) water and land
   (C) DNA and heredity
   (D) nucleus and cell wall
   (E) sand and clay

8. The passage contains information that would answer which of the following questions?

   I.   Which elements form igneous rocks?
   II. What produces sufficient pressure to alter a rock?
   III. Why is marble called a metamorphic rock?

   (A) I only   (B) III only   (C) I and II only
   (D) II and III only   (E) I, II, and III

9. Which of the following methods is NOT used by the author?

   (A) inclusion of concrete examples
   (B) classification and discussion
   (C) comparison and contrast
   (D) observation and hypothesis
   (E) cause and effect

10. The author's tone in the passage can best be described as

   (A) meditative
   (B) objective
   (C) ironic
   (D) concerned
   (E) bombastic

Although vocal cords are lacking in cetaceans, phonation is undoubtedly centered in the larynx.

The toothed whales or odontocetes (sperm whale and porpoises) are much more vociferous than the
(5) whalebone whales, or mysticetes. In this country observers have recorded only occasional sounds from two species of mysticetes (the humpback and right whale). A Russian cetologist reports hearing sounds from at least five species of whalebone
(10) whales but gives no details of the circumstances or descriptions of the sounds themselves. Although comparison of the sound-producing apparatus in the two whale groups cannot yet be made, it is interesting to note that the auditory centers of the
(15) brain are much more highly developed in the odontocetes than in the mysticetes, in fact, to a degree unsurpassed by any other mammalian group.

11. The passage contains information that would answer which of the following questions?

    I.   What are odontocetes and mysticetes?
    II. In which part of the body do whales produce sounds?
    III. In which animals is the auditory center of the brain most developed?

    (A) I only   (B) II only   (C) I and II only
    (D) II and III only   (E) I, II, and III

12. The author's attitude toward the observations reported by the Russian cetologist mentioned in lines 8–11 is best described as one of

    (A) admiration
    (B) indignation
    (C) surprise
    (D) skepticism
    (E) pessimism

13. It can be inferred from the passage that

    (A) animals with more highly developed auditory apparatuses tend to produce more sounds
    (B) animals without vocal cords tend to produce as much sound as those with vocal cords
    (C) highly intelligent animals tend to produce more sound than less intelligent species
    (D) the absence of vocal cords has hindered the adaptation of cetaceans
    (E) sound is an important means of communication among whales

---

Like her white friends Eleanor Roosevelt and Aubrey Williams, Mary Bethune believed in the fundamental commitment of the New Deal to assist the black American's struggle and in the need for
(5) blacks to assume responsibilities to help win that struggle. Unlike those of her white liberal associates, however, Bethune's ideas had evolved out of a long experience as a "race leader." Founder of a small black college in Florida, she had become
(10) widely known by 1935 as an organizer of black women's groups and as a civil and political rights activist. Deeply religious, certain of her own capabilities, she held a relatively uncluttered view of what she felt were the New Deal's and her own
(15) people's obligations to the cause of racial justice. Unafraid to speak her mind to powerful whites, including the President, or to differing black factions, she combined faith in the ultimate willingness of whites to discard their prejudice and bigotry
(20) with a strong sense of racial pride and commitment to Negro self-help.
    More than her liberal white friends, Bethune argued for a strong and direct black voice in initiating and shaping government policy. She pursued
(25) this in her conversations with President Roosevelt, in numerous memoranda to Aubrey Williams, and in her administrative work as head of the National Youth Administration's Office of Negro Affairs.

With the assistance of Williams, she was success-
(30) ful in having blacks selected to NYA posts at the national, state, and local levels. But she also wanted a black presence throughout the federal government. At the beginning of the war she joined other black leaders in demanding appointments to
(35) the Selective Service Board and to the Department of the Army; and she was instrumental in 1941 in securing Earl Dickerson's membership on the Fair Employment Practices Committee. By 1944, she was still making appeals for black representation in
(40) "all public programs, federal, state, and local," and "in policy-making posts as well as rank and file jobs."
    Though recognizing the weakness in the Roosevelt administration's response to Negro needs,
(45) Mary Bethune remained in essence a black partisan champion of the New Deal during the 1930s and 1940s. Her strong advocacy of administration policies and programs was predicated on a number of factors: her assessment of the low status of black
(50) Americans during the Depression; her faith in the willingness of some liberal whites to work for the inclusion of blacks in the government's reform and recovery measures; her conviction that only massive federal aid could elevate the Negro economi-
(55) cally; and her belief that the thirties and forties were producing a more self-aware and self-assured black population. Like a number of her white friends in government, Bethune assumed that the preservation of democracy and black people's "full
(60) integration into the benefits and the responsibilities" of American life were inextricably tied together. She was convinced that, with the help of a friendly government, a militant, aggressive "New Negro" would emerge out of the devastation of
(65) depression and war, a "New Negro" who would "save America from itself," who would lead America toward the full realization of its democratic ideas.

14. The author's main purpose in this passage is to do which of the following?

    (A) Criticize Mary Bethune for adhering too closely to New Deal policies
    (B) Argue that Mary Bethune was too optimistic in her assessment of race relations
    (C) Demonstrate Mary Bethune's influence on black progress during the Roosevelt years
    (D) Point out the weaknesses of the white liberal approach to black needs
    (E) Summarize the attainments of blacks under the auspices of Roosevelt's New Deal

15. It can be inferred from the passage that Aubrey Williams was which of the following?

    I.   A man with influence in the National Youth Administration
    II. A white liberal
    III. A man of strong religious convictions

    (A) I only   (B) II only   (C) I and II only
    (D) II and III only   (E) I, II, and III

16. The author mentions Earl Dickerson (line 37) primarily in order to

    (A) cite an instance of Bethune's political impact
    (B) contrast his career with that of Bethune
    (C) introduce the subject of a subsequent paragraph
    (D) provide an example of Bethune's "New Negro"
    (E) show that Dickerson was a leader of his fellow blacks

17. It can be inferred from the passage that Bethune believed the "New Negro" would "save America from itself" (lines 65–66) by

    (A) joining the army and helping America overthrow its Fascist enemies
    (B) helping America accomplish its egalitarian ideals
    (C) voting for administration anti-poverty programs
    (D) electing other blacks to government office
    (E) expressing a belief in racial pride

18. The tone of the author's discussion of Bethune is best described as

    (A) adulatory
    (B) sentimental
    (C) ironic
    (D) objective
    (E) recriminatory

19. The author uses all the following techniques in the passage EXCEPT

    (A) comparison and contrast
    (B) development of an extended analogy
    (C) direct quotation
    (D) general statement and concrete examples
    (E) reiteration of central ideas

20. Which of the following statements about the New Deal does the passage best support?

    (A) It was strongly committed to justice for all races.
    (B) It encouraged black participation in making policy decisions.
    (C) It was actively involved in military strategy.
    (D) It was primarily the province of Eleanor Roosevelt.
    (E) It shaped programs for economic aid and growth.

Reading Comprehension Exercise D

Directions: Each passage in this group is followed by questions based on its content. After reading a passage, choose the best answer to each question. Answer all questions following a passage on the basis of what is stated or implied in that passage.

"The emancipation of women," James Joyce told one of his friends, "has caused the greatest revolution in our time in the most important relationship there is—that between men and women." Other modernists agreed: Virginia Woolf, claiming that in about 1910 "human character changed," and, illustrating the new balance between the sexes, urged, "Read the 'Agamemnon,' and see whether...your sympathies are not almost entirely with Clytemnestra." D.H. Lawrence wrote, "perhaps the deepest fight for 2000 years and more, has been the fight for women's independence."

But if modernist writers considered women's revolt against men's domination one of their "greatest" and "deepest" themes, only recently—in perhaps the past 15 years—has literary criticism begun to catch up with it. Not that the images of sexual antagonism that abound in modern literature have gone unremarked; far from it. But what we are able to see in literary works depends on the perspectives we bring to them, and now that women —enough to make a difference—are reforming canons and interpreting literature, the landscapes of literary history and the features of individual books have begun to change.

1. According to the passage, women are changing literary criticism by

    (A) noting instances of hostility between men and women
    (B) seeing literature from fresh points of view
    (C) studying the works of early twentieth-century writers
    (D) reviewing books written by feminists
    (E) resisting masculine influence

2. The author quotes James Joyce, Virginia Woolf, and D.H. Lawrence primarily in order to show that

    (A) these were feminist writers
    (B) although well-meaning, they were ineffectual
    (C) before the twentieth century, there was little interest in women's literature
    (D) modern literature is dependent on the women's movement
    (E) the interest in feminist issues is not new

3. The author's attitude toward women's emancipation can best be described as one of

    (A) ambivalence
    (B) fervor
    (C) detachment
    (D) endorsement
    (E) reservation

4. Which of the following titles best describes the content of the passage?

    (A) Modernist Writers and the Search for Equality
    (B) The Meaning of Literary Works
    (C) Toward a New Criticism
    (D) Women in Literature, from 1910 On
    (E) Transforming Literature

Ocean water plays an indispensable role in supporting life. The great ocean basins hold about 300 million cubic miles of water. From this vast amount, about 80,000 cubic miles of water are sucked into the atmosphere each year by evaporation and returned by precipitation and drainage to the ocean. More than 24,000 cubic miles of rain descend annually upon the continents. This vast amount is required to replenish the lakes and streams, springs and water tables on which all flora and fauna are dependent. Thus, the hydrosphere permits organic existence.

The hydrosphere has strange characteristics because water has properties unlike those of any other liquid. One anomaly is that water upon freezing expands by about 9 percent, whereas most liquids contract on cooling. For this reason, ice floats on water bodies instead of sinking to the bottom. If the ice sank, the hydrosphere would soon be frozen solidly, except for a thin layer of surface melt water during the summer season. Thus, all aquatic life would be destroyed and the interchange of warm and cold currents, which moderates climate, would be notably absent.

Another outstanding characteristic of water is that water has a heat capacity which is the highest of all liquids and solids except ammonia. This characteristic enables the oceans to absorb and store vast quantities of heat, thereby often preventing climatic extremes. In addition, water dissolves more substances than any other liquid. It is this characteristic which helps make oceans a great storehouse for minerals which have been washed down from the continents. In several areas of the world these minerals are being commercially exploited. Solar evaporation of salt is widely practiced, potash is extracted from the Dead Sea, and magnesium is produced from sea water along the American Gulf Coast.

5. The author's main purpose in this passage is to

    (A) describe the properties and uses of water
    (B) illustrate the importance of conserving water
    (C) explain how water is used in commerce and industry
    (D) reveal the extent of the earth's ocean masses
    (E) compare water with other liquids

6. According to the passage, fish can survive in the oceans because

    (A) they do not need oxygen
    (B) ice floats
    (C) evaporation and condensation create a water cycle
    (D) there are currents in the oceans
    (E) water absorbs heat

7. Which of the following characteristics of water does the author mention in the passage?

    I.   Water expands when it is frozen.
    II. Water is a good solvent.
    III. Water can absorb heat.

    (A) I only   (B) II only   (C) I and II only
    (D) II and III only   (E) I, II, and III

8. According to the passage, the hydrosphere is not

    (A) responsible for all forms of life
    (B) able to modify weather
    (C) a source of natural resources
    (D) in danger of freezing over
    (E) the part of the earth covered by water

9. The author's tone in the passage can best be described as

    (A) dogmatic
    (B) dispassionate
    (C) speculative
    (D) biased
    (E) fascinated

10. The author organizes the passage by

    (A) comparison and contrast
    (B) juxtaposition of true and untrue ideas
    (C) general statements followed by examples
    (D) hypothesis and proof
    (E) definition of key terms

11. Which of the following statements would be most likely to begin the paragraph immediately following the passage?

    (A) Water has the ability to erode the land.
    (B) Magnesium is widely used in metallurgical processes.
    (C) Now let us consider the great land masses.
    (D) Another remarkable property of ice is its strength.
    (E) Droughts and flooding are two types of disasters associated with water.

The opposite of adaptive divergence is an interesting and fairly common expression of evolution.
Whereas related groups of organisms take on
widely different characters in becoming adapted to
(5) unlike environments in the case of adaptive divergence, we find that unrelated groups of organisms
exhibit adaptive convergence when they spot similar modes of life or become suited for special sorts
of environments. For example, invertebrate marine
(10) animals living firmly attached to the sea bottom or
to some foreign object tend to develop a subcy-
lindrical or conical form. This is illustrated by
coral individuals, by many sponges, and even by
the diminutive tubes of bryozoans. Adaptive con-
(15) vergence in taking this coral-like form is shown by
some brachiopods and pelecypods that grew in
fixed position. More readily appreciated is the
streamlined fitness of most fishes for moving
swiftly through water; they have no neck, the con-
(20) tour of the body is smoothly curved so as to give
minimum resistance, and the chief propelling organ
is a powerful tail fin. The fact that some fossil reptiles (Ichthyosaurs) and modern mammals (whales,
dolphins) are wholly fishlike in form is an expres-
(25) sion of adaptive convergence, for these air breathing reptiles and mammals, which are highly
efficient swimmers, are not closely related to
fishes. Unrelated or distantly related organisms that
develop similarity of form are sometimes desig-
(30) nated as homeomorphs (having same form).

12. The author mentions dolphins and Ichthyosaurs
(lines 22–23) as examples of

(A) modern mammalian life forms that are aquatic
(B) species of slightly greater mobility than
    brachiopods
(C) air-breathing reptiles closely related to fish
(D) organisms that have evolved into a fishlike form
(E) invertebrate and vertebrate marine animals

13. According to the passage, adaptive convergence and
adaptive divergence are

(A) manifestations of evolutionary patterns
(B) hypotheses unsupported by biological
    phenomena
(C) ways in which plants and animals adjust to a
    common environment
(D) demonstrated by brachiopods and pelecypods
(E) compensatory adjustments made in response to
    an unlike environment

14. It can be inferred that in the paragraph immediately
preceding this passage the author discussed

(A) marine intelligence
(B) adaptive divergence
(C) air-breathing reptiles
(D) environmental impacts
(E) organisms with similar forms

Nearly two thousand years have passed since a census
decreed by Caesar Augustus became part of the greatest
story ever told. Many things have changed in the inter-
vening years. The hotel industry worries more about
overbuilding than overcrowding, and if they had to meet
an unexpected influx, few inns would have a manger to
accommodate the weary guests. Now it is the census
taker that does the traveling in the fond hope that a
highly mobile population will stay put long enough to
get a good sampling. Methods of gathering, recording,
and evaluating information have presumably been
improved a great deal. And where then it was the modest
purpose of Rome to obtain a simple head count as an
adequate basis for levying taxes, now batteries of complicated statistical series furnished by governmental
agencies and private organizations are eagerly scanned
and interpreted by sages and seers to get a clue to future
events. The Bible does not tell us how the Roman census
takers made out, and as regards our more immediate
concern, the reliability of present-day economic forecasting, there are considerable differences of opinion.
They were aired at the celebration of the 125th anniver-
sary of the American Statistical Association. There was
the thought that business forecasting might well be on its
way from an art to a science, and some speakers talked
about newfangled computers and high-falutin mathematical systems in terms of excitement and endearment
which we, at least in our younger years when these
things mattered, would have associated more readily
with the description of a fair maiden. But others pointed
to the deplorable record of highly esteemed forecasts
and forecasters with a batting average below that of the
Mets, and the President-elect of the Association cautioned that "high powered statistical methods are usually
in order where the facts are crude and inadequate, the
exact contrary of what crude and inadequate statisticians
assume." We left his birthday party somewhere between
hope and despair and with the conviction, not really
newly acquired, that proper statistical methods applied
to ascertainable facts have their merits in economic forecasting as long as neither forecaster nor public is
deluded into mistaking the delineation of probabilities
and trends for a prediction of certainties of mathematical
exactitude.

15. The passage would be most likely to appear in

(A) a journal of biblical studies
(B) an introductory college textbook on statistics
(C) the annual report of the American Statistical
    Association
(D) a newspaper review of a recent professional
    festivity
(E) the current bulletin of the census bureau

16. According to the passage, taxation in Roman times
was based on

(A) mobility
(B) wealth
(C) population
(D) census takers
(E) economic predictions

17. The author refers to the Romans primarily in order to

    (A) prove the superiority of modern sampling methods to ancient ones
    (B) provide a historical framework for the passage
    (C) relate an unfamiliar concept to a familiar one
    (D) show that statistical forecasts have not significantly improved
    (E) cite an authority to support the thesis of the passage

18. The author refers to the Mets primarily in order to

    (A) show that sports do not depend on statistics
    (B) provide an example of an unreliable statistic
    (C) contrast verifiable and unverifiable methods of record keeping
    (D) indicate the changes in attitudes from Roman days to the present
    (E) illustrate the failure of statistical predictions

19. On the basis of the passage, it can be inferred that the author would agree with which of the following statements?

    (A) Computers have significantly improved the application of statistics in business.
    (B) Statistics is not, at the present time, a science.
    (C) It is useless to try to predict the economy.
    (D) Most mathematical systems are inexact.
    (E) Statisticians should devote themselves to the study of probability.

20. The author's tone can best be described as

    (A) jocular
    (B) scornful
    (C) pessimistic
    (D) objective
    (E) humanistic

Reading Comprehension Exercise E

Directions: Each passage in this group is followed by questions based on its content. After reading a passage, choose the best answer to each question. Answer all questions following a passage on the basis of what is <u>stated</u> or <u>implied</u> in that passage.

    Observe the dilemma of the fungus: it is a plant, but it possesses no chlorophyl. While all other plants put the sun's energy to work for them combining the nutrients of ground and air into the body
(5) structure, the chlorophylless fungus must look elsewhere for an energy supply. It finds it in those other plants which, having received their energy free from the sun, relinquish it at some point in their cycle either to other animals (like us humans)
(10) or to fungi.
    In this search for energy the fungus has become the earth's major source of rot and decay. Wherever you see mold forming on a piece of bread, or a pile of leaves turning to compost, or a blown-down
(15) tree becoming pulp on the ground, you are watching a fungus action the earth would be piled high with the dead plant life of past centuries. In fact, certain plants which contain resins that are toxic to fungi will last indefinitely;
(20) specimens of the redwood, for instance, can still be found resting on the forest floor centuries after having been blown down.

1. Which of the following words best describes the fungus as depicted in the passage?

    (A) Unevolved
    (B) Sporadic
    (C) Enigmatic
    (D) Parasitic
    (E) Toxic

2. The passage states all the following about fungi EXCEPT:

    (A) They are responsible for the decomposition of much plant life.
    (B) They cannot live completely apart from other plants.
    (C) They are vastly different from other plants.
    (D) They are poisonous to resin-producing plants.
    (E) They cannot produce their own store of energy.

3. The author's statement that "you are watching a fungus eating" (lines 15–16) is best described as

    (A) figurative
    (B) ironical
    (C) parenthetical
    (D) erroneous
    (E) contradictory

4. The author is primarily concerned with

    (A) warning people of the dangers of fungi
    (B) writing a humorous essay on fungi
    (C) relating how most plants use solar energy
    (D) describing the actions of fungi
    (E) explaining the long life of some redwoods

The establishment of the Third Reich influenced events in American history by starting a chain of events which culminated in war between Germany and the United States. The complete destruction of democracy, the persecution of Jews, the war on religion, the cruelty and barbarism of the Nazis, and especially, the plans of Germany and her allies, Italy and Japan, for world conquest caused great indignation in this country and brought on fear of another world war. While speaking out against Hitler's atrocities, the American people generally favored isolationist policies and neutrality. The Neutrality Acts of 1935 and 1936 prohibited trade with any belligerents or loans to them. In 1937 the President was empowered to declare an arms embargo in wars between nations at his discretion.

American opinion began to change somewhat after President Roosevelt's "quarantine the aggressor" speech at Chicago (1937) in which he severely criticized Hitler's policies. Germany's seizure of Austria and the Munich Pact for the partition of Czechoslovakia (1938) also aroused the American people. The conquest of Czechoslovakia in March, 1939 was another rude awakening to the menace of the Third Reich. In August, 1939 came the shock of the Nazi-Soviet Pact and in September the attack on Poland and the outbreak of European war. The United States attempted to maintain neutrality in spite of sympathy for the democracies arrayed against the Third Reich. The Neutrality Act of 1939 repealed the arms embargo and permitted "cash and carry" exports of arms to belligerent nations. A strong national defense program was begun. A draft act was passed (1940) to strengthen the military services. A Lend-Lease Act (1941) authorized the President to sell, exchange, or lend materials to any country deemed necessary by him for the defense of the United States. Help was given to Britain by exchanging certain overage destroyers for the right to establish American bases in British territory in the Western Hemisphere. In August, 1941, President Roosevelt and Prime Minister Churchill met and issued the Atlantic Charter which proclaimed the kind of a world which should be established after the war. In December, 1941, Japan launched the unprovoked attack on the United States at Pearl Harbor. Immediately thereafter, Germany declared war on the United States.

5. The author is primarily concerned with

(A) evaluating various legislative efforts to strengthen national defense
(B) summarizing the events that led up to America's involvement in the war
(C) criticizing the atrocities perpetrated by the Third Reich
(D) explaining a basic distinction between American and German policy
(E) describing the social and psychological effects of war

6. During the years 1933–36, American foreign policy may best be described as being one of

(A) overt belligerence
(B) deliberate uninvolvement
(C) moral indignation
(D) veiled contempt
(E) reluctant admiration

7. According to the passage, the United States, while maintaining neutrality, showed its sympathy for the democracies by which of the following actions?

I.   It came to the defense of Poland.
II.   It conscripted recruits for the armed forces.
III. It supplied weapons to friendly countries.

(A) I only   (B) III only   (C) I and II only
(D) II and III only   (E) I, II, and III

8. According to the passage, all of the following events occurred in 1939 EXCEPT

(A) the invasion of Poland
(B) the invasion of Czechoslovakia
(C) the annexation of Austria
(D) passage of the Neutrality Act
(E) the beginning of the war in Europe

9. With which of the following statements would the author of the passage be most likely to agree?

(A) American neutrality during the 1930s was a natural consequence of the course of world events.
(B) Every nation should be free to determine its own internal policy without interference.
(C) The United States, through its aggressive actions, invited an attack on its territory.
(D) Americans were slow to realize the full danger posed by Nazi Germany.
(E) President Roosevelt showed undue sympathy for Britain.

10. Which of the following best decribes the organization of the passage?

(A) The author presents a thesis and then lists events that support that thesis in chronological order.
(B) The author presents a thesis and then cites examples that support the thesis as well as evidence that tends to negate it.
(C) The author summarizes a historical study and then discusses an aspect of the study in detail.
(D) The author describes historical events and then gives a personal interpretation of them.
(E) The author cites noted authorities as a means of supporting his or her own opinion.

Not a few of Jane Austen's personal acquaintances might have echoed Sir Samuel Egerton Brydges, who noticed that "she was fair and handsome, slight and elegant, but with cheeks a little too full," while "never suspect[ing] she was an authoress." For this novelist whose personal obscurity was more complete than that of any other famous writer was always quick to insist either on complete anonymity or on the propriety of her limited craft, her delight in delineating just "3 or 4 Families in a Country Village." With her self-deprecatory remarks about her inability to join "strong manly, spirited sketches, full of Variety and Glow" with her "little bit (two Inches wide) of Ivory," Jane Austen perpetuated the belief among her friends that her art was just an accomplishment "by a lady," if anything "rather too light and bright and sparkling." In this respect she resembled one of her favorite contemporaries, Mary Brunton, who would rather have "glid[ed] through the world unknown" than been "suspected of literary airs — to be shunned, as literary women are, by the more pretending of their own sex, and abhorred, as literary women are, by the more pretending of the other! —my dear, I would sooner exhibit as a ropedancer."

Yet, decorous though they might first seem, Austen's self-effacing anonymity and her modest description of her miniaturist art also imply a criticism, even a rejection, of the world at large. For, as Gaston Bachelard explains, the miniature "allows us to be world conscious at slight risk." While the creators of satirically conceived diminutive landscapes seem to see everything as small because they are themselves so grand, Austen's analogy for her art—her "little bit (two Inches wide) of Ivory"—suggests a fragility that reminds us of the risk and instability outside the fictional space. Besides seeing her art metaphorically, as her critics would too, in relation to female arts severely devalued until quite recently (for painting on ivory was traditionally a "ladylike" occupation), Austen attempted through self-imposed novelistic limitations to define a secure place, even as she seemed to admit the impossibility of actually inhabiting such a small space with any degree of comfort. And always, for Austen, it is women—because they are too vulnerable in the world at large—who must acquiesce in their own confinement, no matter how stifling it may be.

11. The passage primarily focuses on

(A) Jane Austen's place in English literature
(B) the literary denigration of female novelists
(C) the implications of Austen's attitude to her work
(D) critical evaluations of the novels of Jane Austen
(E) social rejection of professional women in the 18th–19th centuries

12. According to the passage, Austen concentrated on a limited range of subjects because

(A) she had a limited degree of experience in life
(B) her imagination was incapable of creating other worlds
(C) women in her time were discouraged from writing about significant topics
(D) she wanted to create a special niche for her talents
(E) she did not wish to be acknowledged as an author

13. Which of the following best expresses the relationship of the first sentence to the rest of the passage?

(A) Specific instance followed by generalizations
(B) Assertion followed by analysis
(C) Objective statement followed by personal opinion
(D) Quotation from an authority followed by conflicting views
(E) Challenge followed by debate

The atmosphere is a mixture of several gases. There are about ten chemical elements which remain permanently in gaseous form in the atmosphere under all natural conditions. Of these permanent gases, oxygen makes up about 21 per cent and nitrogen about 78 per cent. Several other gases, such as argon, carbon dioxide, hydrogen, neon, krypton, and xenon, comprise the remaining one per cent of the volume of dry air. The amount of water vapor, and its variations in amount and distribution is of extraordinary importance in weather changes. Atmospheric gases hold in suspension great quantities of dust, pollen, smoke, and other impurities which are always present in considerable, but variable amounts.

The atmosphere has no definite upper limits but gradually thins until it becomes imperceptible. Until recently it was assumed that the air above the first few miles gradually grew thinner and colder at a constant rate. It was also assumed that upper air had little influence on weather changes. Recent studies of the the upper atmophere, currently being conducted by earth satellites and missile probings, have shown these assumptions to be incorrect. The atmosphere has three well-defined strata.

The layer of the air next to the earth, which extends upward for about ten miles, is known as the *troposphere*. On the whole, it makes up about 75 per cent of all the weight of the atmosphere. It is the warmest part of the atmosphere because most of the solar radiation is absorbed by the earth's surface which warms the air immediately surrounding it. A steady decrease of temperature with increasing elevation is a most striking characteristic. The upper layers are colder because of their greater distance from the earth's surface and rapid radiation of heat into space. The temperatures within the troposphere decrease about 3.5 degrees per 1,000 feet increase in altitude. Within the troposphere, winds and air currents distribute heat and moisture. Strong winds, called jet streams, are located at the upper levels of the troposphere. These jet streams are both complex and widespread in occurrence. They normally show a wave-shaped pattern and move from west to east at velocities of 150 mph, but velocities as high as 400 mph have been noted. The influences of changing locations and strengths of jet streams upon weather conditions and patterns are no doubt considerable. Current intensive research may eventually reveal their true significance.

Above the troposphere to a height of about 50 miles is a zone called the *stratosphere*. The stratosphere is separated from the troposphere by a zone of uniform temperatures called the tropopause. Within the lower portions of the stratosphere is a layer of ozone gases which filters out most of the ultraviolet rays from the sun. The ozone layer varies with air pressure. If this zone were not there, the full blast of the sun's ultraviolet light would burn our skins, blind our eyes, and eventually result in our destruction. Within the stratosphere, the temperature and atmospheric composition are relatively uniform.

The layer upward of about 50 miles is the most fascinating but the least known of these three strata. It is called the *ionosphere* because it consists of electrically charged particles called ions, thrown from the sun. The northern lights (*aurora borealis*) originates within this highly charged portion of the atmosphere. Its effect upon weather conditions if any, is as yet, unknown.

14. Which of the following titles best expresses the ideas of the passage?

(A) The Makeup of the Atmosphere
(B) Studying the Atmosphere
(C) Atmosphere and Weather
(D) Temperature in the Stratosphere
(E) The Sun's Rays

15. The passage supplies information that would answer which of the following questions?

I. How do the troposphere and the stratosphere differ?
II. How does the ionosphere affect the weather?
III. How do earth satellites study the atmosphere?

(A) I only   (B) III only   (C) I and II only
(D) I and III only   (E) I, II , and III

16. According to the passage, life as we know it exists on the earth because the atmosphere

(A) contains a layer of ozone gases
(B) contains electrically charged particles
(C) is warmest at the bottom
(D) carries the ultraviolet rays of the sun
(E) provides the changes in weather

17. It can be inferred from the passage that a jet plane will usually have its best average rate of speed on its run from

(A) New York to San Francisco
(B) Los Angeles to New York
(C) Boston to Miami
(D) Bermuda to New York
(E) London to Washington, D.C.

18. It can be inferred from the passage that at the top of Jungfrau, which is 12,000 feet above the town of Interlaken in Switzerland, the temperature is usually

(A) below freezing
(B) about 42 degrees colder than on the ground
(C) warmer than in Interlaken
(D) affected by the ionosphere
(E) about 75 degrees colder than in Interlaken

19. The passage states that the troposphere is the warmest part of the atmosphere because it

(A) is closest to the sun
(B) contains electrically charged particles
(C) radiates heat into space
(D) has winds and air current that distribute the heat
(E) is warmed by the earth's heat

20. According to the passage, the atmosphere consists of all of the following EXCEPT

(A) 21 percent oxygen
(B) a definite amount of water vapor
(C) ten permanent elements
(D) less than 1 percent of xenon
(E) considerable waste products

Answer Key

Reading Comprehension Exercise A

1.	B	6.	C	11.	C	16.	D
2.	B	7.	E	12.	D	17.	D
3.	E	8.	A	13.	D	18.	C
4.	B	9.	E	14.	A	19.	E
5.	E	10.	D	15.	B	20.	E

Reading Comprehension Exercise B

1.	A	6.	E	11.	D	16.	B
2.	D	7.	C	12.	B	17.	A
3.	C	8.	E	13.	E	18.	C
4.	B	9.	C	14.	A	19.	E
5.	D	10.	C	15.	A	20.	B

Reading Comprehension Exercise C

1.	C	6.	B	11.	C	16.	A
2.	B	7.	A	12.	B	17.	B
3.	A	8.	B	13.	A	18.	D
4.	D	9.	D	14.	C	19.	B
5.	E	10.	B	15.	C	20.	E

Reading Comprehension Exercise D

1.	B	6.	B	11.	A	16.	C
2.	E	7.	E	12.	D	17.	D
3.	D	8.	D	13.	A	18.	E
4.	C	9.	B	14.	B	19.	B
5.	A	10.	C	15.	D	20.	A

Reading Comprehension Exercise E

1.	D	6.	B	11.	C	16.	A
2.	D	7.	D	12.	A	17.	B
3.	A	8.	C	13.	B	18.	B
4.	B	9.	D	14.	C	19.	E
5.	B	10.	A	15.	A	20.	B

6 Antonym Questions

- **Testing Tactics**
- **Practice Exercises**
- **Answer Key**

Your task in answering antonym questions is straightforward: you are given a word and must choose, from the five choices that follow it, the best antonym (opposite). Antonym questions range from relatively easy ones at the beginning of a set to extremely difficult ones at the set's end. Do not expect to recognize every word—not even professional writers would recognize all of them.

The eleven antonym questions always make up the last group of questions in a verbal section. Do not, however, answer them last. Right after you have finished answering the analogy questions, skip to the antonyms and go through them quickly. Answer them all, but do not take too long answering any given one. The time you save by answering the antonym questions quickly will help you when you get to the time-consuming reading comprehension ones.

Testing Tactics

Tactic 1 — Think of a Context for the Capitalized Word

Take a quick look at the word in capital letters. If you don't recollect its meaning right away, try to think of a phrase or sentence in which you have heard it used. The context may help you come up with the word's meaning. For example:

> MAGNIFY: (A) forgive   (B) comprehend   (C) extract   (D) diminish   (E) electrify

The term "magnifying glass" should immediately come to mind. A magnifying glass enlarges things. The opposite of enlarging something is to make it smaller or *diminish* it. The answer is D.

Now apply this tactic to a question from a recent GRE.

> ABERRANT: (A) attractive   (B) predictive   (C) blissful   (D) normal   (E) precise

What phrase comes to your mind? "Aberrant behavior." "Aberrant data." In both cases you should have an impression of something deviating from what is expected, an impression of something *abnormal*, in fact. Aberrant behavior strays from the norm; aberrant, thus, is an antonym for *normal*. The correct answer is Choice D.

Tactic 2 — Before You Look at the Choices, Think Of Antonyms for the Capitalized Word

Suppose your word is *industrious*, hard-working. What opposites come to your mind? You might come up with *lazy*, *idle*, *slothful*, *inactive*—all words that mean lacking industry and energy.

Now look at the choices:

> INDUSTRIOUS: (A) stupid   (B) harsh   (C) indolent   (D) complex   (E) inexpensive

121

Lazy, idle, and slothful all are synonyms for *indolent*. Your correct answer is Choice C.

This tactic will help you even when you have to deal with unfamiliar words among your answer choices. Suppose you do not know the meaning of the word *indolent*. You know that one antonym for your key word *industrious* is *lazy*. Therefore, you know that you are looking for a word that means the same as *lazy*. At this point you can go through the answer choices eliminating answers that don't work. Does *stupid* mean the same as *lazy*? No, smart people can be lazy, too. Does *harsh* mean the same as *lazy*? No, harsh means cruel or rough. Does *indolent* mean the same as *lazy*? You don't know; you should check the other choices and then come back. Does *complex* mean the same as *lazy*? No, *complex*

means complicated or intricate. Does *inexpensive* mean the same as *lazy*? No. So what is left? *Indolent*. Once again, your correct answer is Choice C.

Apply this tactic to a question from a recent GRE:

> GARRULITY: (A) servility (B) forbearance
> (C) peacefulness (D) constancy
> (E) taciturnity

Garrulity means talkativeness. In thinking of possible antonyms for *garrulity*, you may have come up with words like *untalkativeness*, *curtness*, and *reticence*, words signifying briefness of speech. *Untalkativeness*, *curtness*, and *reticence* are all synonyms for *taciturnity*. The correct answer is Choice E.

Read All the Choices Before You Decide Which Is Best

On the GRE you are working under time pressure. You may be tempted to mark down the first answer that feels right and ignore the other choices given. Don't do it. Consider each answer. Only in this way can you be sure to distinguish between two possible answers and come up with the best answer for the question.

Words have shades of meaning. In matching a word with its opposite, you must pay attention to these shades of meaning. Try this example from an actual GRE test to see how it works.

> TRACTABLE: (A) distraught (B) irritating
> (C) ruthless (D) headstrong (E) lazy

Suppose you have only a vague sense of the meaning of *tractable*. You associate it with such vaguely positive terms as *gentle*, *docile*, *amiable*. For this reason, you stop short when you come to Choice C. Reasoning that

someone gentle and docile is *not* ruthless or merciless, you look no further and mark down Choice C.

Choice C, however, is incorrect. True, a tractable person is docile and easily guided, even mild. Someone who lacks docility, however, is not necessarily ruthless. Such a person is difficult to guide, obstinate, in fact *headstrong*. The correct answer is Choice D.

> PERFIDY: (A) thoroughness (B) generosity
> (C) gratitude (D) tact (E) loyalty

Perfidy means treachery; someone perfidious betrays those who have faith in him. Choice C has an immediate appeal: someone perfidious is ungrateful for the trust shown him; in committing *perfidy*, he lacks *gratitude*. However, strictly speaking, in committing perfidy, the traitor's crime is not thanklessness but *disloyalty*. The best antonym for perfidy is Choice E, *loyalty*.

Look at the Answer Choices to Determine the Main Word's Part Of Speech

Look at the capitalized word. What part of speech is it? Words often exist in several forms. You may think of *run* as a verb, for example, but in the phrases "a run in her stocking" and "hit a home run" *run* is a noun.

The GRE plays on this confusion in testing your verbal ability. When you look at a particular capitalized word, you may not know whether you are dealing with a noun, a verb, or an adjective. *Harbor*, for example, is a very common noun; in "to harbor a fugitive," to give refuge to a runaway, it is a much less common verb.

If you suspect that a capitalized word may have more than one part of speech, don't worry. Just look at the first couple of answer choices and see what part of speech they are. That part of speech will be the capitalized word's part of speech.

In GRE Antonym Questions, **all** *the answer choices have the same part of speech.* You can always tell what that part of speech is by a quick glance at the first answer choice or two.

See how this tactic works in answering a relatively simple question from a published GRE.

> CARDINAL: (A) abstract   (B) elusive
> (C) subtle   (D) minor   (E) miniature

Are you dealing with *cardinal* the noun or *cardinal* the adjective?

A quick look at the answers assures you that they are all adjectives. *Cardinal* here is neither a church leader nor a bird. The adjective *cardinal* means central or principal in importance, as in "the cardinal element" of a plan. Its opposite is *minor*. The correct answer is Choice D.

Now try a second example from a recent GRE.

> APPROPRIATE: (A) create a void
> (B) rectify an error   (C) sanction
>   (D) surrender   (E) lend

Is the word in capitals the adjective *appropriate* (suitable, proper) or the verb *appropriate* (to set aside, acquire)?

A quick look at the answer choices reveals that it is a verb. (The *-ate* and *-ify* word endings are common verb endings.) One definition of the verb *appropriate* is to take something or make it particularly one's own, as in *appropriating money* or *appropriating land*. Thus, its opposite is to yield or *surrender* something, Choice D.

Consider Secondary Meanings of the Capitalized Word as Well as Its Primary Meaning

If none of the answer choices seems right to you, take another look at the capitalized word. It may have more than one meaning. The GRE often constructs questions that make use of secondary, less well-known meanings of deceptively familiar words. Take, for example, this typical GRE question.

> LIST: (A) be upside down   (B) be upright
> (C) slide backward   (D) sway to and fro
>   (E) lie flat

List here has nothing to do with making lists or enumerating. It has to do with moving. When it *lists* to starboard, a ship simply leans to one side or tilts. The best antonym for this meaning of *list* is Choice B, *be upright*.

Try a second, more difficult GRE question involving a less familiar meaning of a familiar word.

> REDUNDANT: (A) consistent   (B) complex
> (C) diffuse   (D) insightful   (E) economical

Only 38% of the examinees tested on this question answered it correctly. Why?

The problem lies not in the capitalized word but in the answer choices. *Redundant* means superfluous, repetitive, wordy. Thus, its antonym means succinct and concise. Not immediately spotting succinct or concise among the answer choices, and looking for a positive term to contrast with *redundant*, some examinees may settle for Choice A, *consistent*, or Choice D, *insightful*. In doing so, they fail to consider that words have secondary meanings. In this case, *economical* does not mean thrifty or profitable, as in *an economical housewife* or *an economical business venture*. Instead, it means sparing in quantity, as in *an economical use of words*. The correct answer is Choice E.

Break Down Unfamiliar Words into Recognizable Parts

When you come upon a totally unfamiliar word, don't give up. Break it down and see if you recognize any of its parts. Pay particular attention to prefixes—word parts added to the beginning of a word—and to roots, the building blocks of the language.

Look once more at the following question from the GRE.

> ABERRANT: (A) attractive   (B) predictive
> (C) blissful   (D) normal   (E) precise

Suppose you had never seen *aberrant* before. You have seen dozens of other words beginning with *ab-*: *absent*, *abnormal*, *abduct*. Take *abduct*. What do you do when you abduct someone? You kidnap him, or steal him away. *Ab-* means *away*.

What about the root, *err*? To *err* is to be wrong or to wander, as in wandering from the right path. Thus, *aberrant* means *wandering away*, straying from what is right or normal, and its opposite is of course Choice D, *normal*.

Now try a second example from a recently-published GRE.

SYNCHRONOUS:
(A) off-key
(B) out-of-shape
(C) without pity
(D) out-of-phase
(E) without difficulty

Syn- means together. *Chron-* means time. Something *synchronous* must have to do with occurring together in time, like the *synchronous* movements of swimmers keeping time with one another. The antonym for *synchronous* thus is Choice D, *out-of-phase*.

The word part approach can help you interpret new words you encounter. However, apply it cautiously. In many words the roots, prefixes, and suffixes have lost their original meanings. In others, the same root occurs, but with markedly differing effects. It would not do to call a *philanthropist* a *philanderer*, for instance, though both words contain the root for love.

If you find the word part approach appealing, try to spend some time working with the Basic Word Parts List in Chapter 7. Remember, however, there is no substitute for learning the exact meaning of a word as it is used today.

Tactic 7

In Eliminating Answer Choices, Test Words for Their Positive or Negative Connotations

When you are dealing with a partially unfamiliar word, a word that you cannot define or use in a sentence but that you know you have seen previously, try to remember in what sort of context you have seen that word. Did it have positive connotations, or did it have a negative feel? If you are certain the capitalized word has positive connotations, then, since you are looking for its antonym, you *know* the correct answer must have negative ones. Thus, you can eliminate any answer choices that have positive connotations and guess among the answer choices that are negative in tone.

See how this approach applies in the following example from a recent GRE.

CHARY: (A) brisk   (B) bold   (C) untidy
(D) ungenerous   (E) unfriendly

You cannot define *chary*. You would hesitate to use it in a sentence of your own. And yet, you are sure the word has a slightly negative feel to it. A person is *chary about* something. You have a sense of someone holding back.

Look at the answer choices. Which of them have negative connotations? *Untidy*? *Ungenerous*? *Unfriendly*? Eliminate all three. You have narrowed down your choices to *brisk* and *bold*, both words that have a positive feel. You are in an excellent position to guess. As it turns out, *chary* means hesitant or reluctant to proceed. Its opposite is Choice B, *bold*.

Tactic 8

Watch Out for Errors Caused by Eye-Catchers

When you look at answer choices, do you find that certain ones seem to leap right off the page? These words are eye-catchers. They look good—but be sure to take a second look.

Try these next GRE antonym questions to see just how an eye-catcher works. First, an easy one.

GAUCHENESS: (A) probity   (B) sophistry
(C) acumen   (D) polish   (E) vigor

What comes to mind when you think of synonyms for *gauche* (socially awkward)? *Unsophisticated*? This common association of *gaucheness* with lack of sophistication can hurt you here, for it may cause your eye to be attracted by Choice B, *sophistry*, the eye-catcher here.

Sophistry (superficially plausible, but actually specious reasoning) is not a synonym for *sophistication* or worldliness. Both words share a common root, however, and resemble one another enough that someone unsure of the correct answer might select *sophistry* as a sort of "educated guess." The only way to avoid this error is to read all the answer choices carefully and note that *sophistication's* true synonym here is *polish*.

Here's a more difficult GRE example. See if you can spot the eye-catcher.

REDOUBTABLE: (A) unsurprising
(B) unambiguous   (C) unimpressive
(D) inevitable   (E) immovable

Only 17% of the test-takers who attempted this question (the last in its set) answered it correctly. Why? Once more an early answer choice has been set up to tempt you. In this case, the presence of the familiar word *doubt*

in the unfamiliar word *redoubtable* suggests that *redoubtable* has something to do with uncertainty. You know that *ambiguous* means uncertain in meaning. Thus, Choice B, *unambiguous* is particularly appealing here. It is particularly appealing, and it is wrong.

Doubt in *redoubtable* is used in the sense not of uncertainty but of fear. *A redoubtable foe* causes fear; such a person is awesome or impressive. Someone *unimpressive* causes no such fear.

When you reach the final antonyms of a set, be wary. Suspect questions whose answers seem too easy. There are no easy answers when you get to the last questions of a set.

Practice Exercises

Antonym Exercise A

Directions: Each question below consists of a word printed in capital letters, followed by five lettered words or phrases. Choose the lettered word or phrase that is most nearly opposite in meaning to the word in capital letters.

Since some of the questions require you to distinguish fine shades of meaning, be sure to consider all the choices before deciding which one is best.

1. MOURNFUL : (A) informal   (B) sympathetic
(C) private   (D) appropriate   (E) joyous

2. SCAD : (A) parsimony   (B) allocation
(C) dearth   (D) restraint   (E) provision

3. GRANDIOSE: (A) docile   (B) unlikely to occur
(C) simple and unimposing   (D) light in weight
(E) uncommunicative

4. ENTRENCH : (A) defy   (B) oust
(C) extinguish   (D) squander   (E) intercede

5. LACKLUSTER : (A) superficial
(B) courteous   (C) vibrant
(D) complex   (E) abundant

6. CENSURE : (A) augment   (B) eradicate
(C) enthrall   (D) commend   (E) reform

7. TRANSIENCE: (A) slowness   (B) permanence
(C) lack of caution   (D) desire for perfection
(E) original nature

8. DESICCATE : (A) lengthen   (B) hallow
(C) exonerate   (D) saturate   (E) anesthetize

9. PROTRUSION : (A) deep recess
(B) strong dislike   (C) growing scarcity
(D) illusion   (E) chaos

10. ENTICE : (A) repel   (B) authorize
(C) baffle   (D) misplace   (E) diminish

11. ORTHODOXY : (A) renown   (B) trepidation
(C) unconventionality   (D) inquisitiveness
(E) remoteness

12. SUMPTUOUS : (A) dank   (B) frequent
(C) partial   (D) restrained   (E) open

13. DISSOLUTION : (A) retribution
(B) compliance   (C) futility
(D) persuasion   (E) establishment

14. IRK : (A) pry   (B) tinge
(C) beguile   (D) convince   (E) soothe

15. LIMBER : (A) sturdy   (B) orderly
(C) durable   (D) stiff   (E) gloomy

16. OBLIQUITY : (A) praise
(B) straightforwardness   (C) conformity
(D) self-righteousness   (E) depreciation

17. SLUR : (A) sensitivity   (B) sacrifice
(C) understatement   (D) challenge
(E) commendation

18. APOTHEOSIS: (A) departure from tradition
(B) impatience with stupidity
(C) demotion from glory
(D) surrender to impulse
(E) cause for grief

19. ENERVATE :   (A) narrate   (B) enrage
    (C) accomplish   (D) invigorate   (E) acquiesce

20. NIGGARDLY :   (A) appropriate   (B) generous
    (C) complete   (D) radiant   (E) ongoing

Antonym Exercise B

Directions: Each question below consists of a word printed in capital letters, followed by five lettered words or phrases. Choose the lettered word or phrase that is most nearly opposite in meaning to the word in capital letters.

Since some of the questions require you to distinguish fine shades of meaning, be sure to consider all the choices before deciding which one is best.

1. HEDGE :

    (A) act on impulse
    (B) refuse to represent
    (C) state without qualification
    (D) make a foolish comment
    (E) establish a connection

2. ABROGATE :   (A) transgress   (B) signify
   (C) alleviate   (D) question   (E) ratify

3. INDUSTRY :   (A) cleanliness   (B) pragmatism
   (C) sloth   (D) promptness   (E) abasement

4. SPUNK :   (A) success   (B) timidity
   (C) growing awareness   (D) lack of intelligence
    (E) loss of prestige

5. SAGE :   (A) zealot   (B) miser
   (C) braggart   (D) fool   (E) tyrant

6. ADMONITION :   (A) premonition
   (B) hallucination   (C) escape
    (D) commendation   (E) trepidation

7. CHARY :   (A) lugubrious   (B) brash
   (C) indifferent   (D) graceful   (E) scornful

8. STUPEFY :   (A) lie   (B) bend
   (C) enliven   (D) talk nonsense
    (E) consider thoughtfully

9. COGENT :   (A) contemplative
   (B) unpersuasive   (C) expository   (C) stable
    (D) inconceivable

10. FICKLE :   (A) spotless   (B) industrious
    (C) welcome   (D) urgent   (E) loyal

11. COMPLY :   (A) simplify   (B) strive
    (C) rebel   (D) unite   (E) appreciate

12. CREDIT :   (A) believe false
    (B) treat as equal   (C) make more difficult
     (D) underemphasize   (E) forget

13. STILTED :   (A) informal
    (B) verbose   (C) secretive
     (D) senseless   (E) tentative

14. UNGAINLY :   (A) slender
    (B) graceful   (C) restrained
     (D) inaccurate   (E) unnoticed

15. QUIXOTIC :   (A) slow
    (B) abstemious   (C) pragmatic
     (D) benevolent   (E) grave

16. DISPARITY: (A) timidity   (B) complacency
    (C) bigotry   (D) likeness   (E) influence

17. CRITICAL: (A) unimportant   (B) uncertain
    (C) silent   (D) coherent   (E) destructive

18. SOBRIETY: (A) influence   (B) nonchalance
    (C) holiness   (D) civility   (E) mirth

19. RESTIVENESS: (A) completeness
    (B) conviction   (C) concern   (D) docility
     (E) petulance

20. HALLOW :   (A) keep silence
    (B) prove incorrect   (C) accuse openly
     (D) desecrate   (E) instigate

Antonym Exercise C

Directions: Each question below consists of a word printed in capital letters, followed by five lettered words or phrases. Choose the lettered word or phrase that is most nearly opposite in meaning to the word in capital letters.

Since some of the questions require you to distinguish fine shades of meaning, be sure to consider all the choices before deciding which one is best.

1. HARBINGER: (A) ascetic   (B) miser
    (C) counselor   (D) follower   (E) braggart

2. SPUR: (A) embitter   (B) discourage
    (C) impress   (D) mislead   (E) ignore

3. DISJOINTED: (A) responsible   (B) connected
    (C) implied   (D) useful   (E) imprecise

4. MEALYMOUTHED: (A) hungry
    (B) indefinite   (C) tightlipped   (D) sincere
     (E) apathetic

5. PREVARICATE: (A) postulate
    (B) emphasize   (C) support in theory
     (D) consider thoughtfully   (E) state truthfully

6. LUMINARY: (A) impostor   (B) nonentity
    (C) pilgrim   (D) braggart   (E) mutineer

7. TESTY: (A) erroneous   (B) uncommunicative
(C) even-tempered   (D) quick-witted
(E) industrious

8. NEFARIOUS: (A) lackadaisical   (B) eccentric
(C) exemplary   (D) corrigible   (E) hypocritical

9. BEGRUDGE: (A) mourn silently   (B) grant
freely   (C) hunger for   (D) advance rapidly
(E) fight back

10. BILK: (A) reduce in size   (B) make famous
(C) roughen   (D) renovate   (E) pay in full

11. COMPOSE: (A) disturb   (B) reveal
(C) strengthen   (D) isolate   (E) prevent

12. OCCLUDE: (A) determine   (B) transcend
(C) surround   (D) open   (E) regulate

13. AMBIGUITY: (A) extent   (B) success
(C) clarity   (D) normality   (E) expression

14. AMELIORATION: (A) prevention
(B) aggravation   (C) distraction
(D) indifference   (E) dissuasion

15. CAVIL: (A) discern   (B) disclose
(C) introduce   (D) flatter   (E) commend

16. SKEPTICAL: (A) theoretical   (B) indifferent
(C) ready to believe   (D) eager for change
(E) lost in thought

17. FLEDGLING: (A) experienced person
(B) shy onlooker   (C) social outcast
(D) fugitive   (E) adversary

18. CRASS: (A) boastful   (B) temporary
(C) cheerful   (D) refined   (E) extensive

19. RECALCITRANT: (A) tractable   (B) erratic
(C) intuitive   (D) vigorous   (E) rambling

20. PROTRACT: (A) defy   (B) supplement
(C) postpone   (D) shorten   (E) design

Antonym Exercise D

<u>Directions:</u> Each question below consists of a word
printed in capital letters, followed by five lettered words
or phrases. Choose the lettered word or phrase that is
most nearly <u>opposite</u> in meaning to the word in capital
letters.

Since some of the questions require you to distinguish
fine shades of meaning, be sure to consider all the
choices before deciding which one is best.

1. PRIM: (A) rare   (B) careful
(C) unnecessary   (D) improper   (E) decisive

2. REPUGNANCE: (A) attraction   (B) lethargy
(C) blame   (D) virtue   (E) awe

3. NETTLE: (A) disentangle   (B) mollify
(C) magnify   (D) muffle   (E) recompense

4. REPLETE: (A) unwrinkled   (B) devoid
(C) vulgar   (D) matchless   (E) unsympathetic

5. UNASSUAGED: (A) presumed   (B) deceptive
(C) singular   (D) faulty   (E) soothed

6. PALTRY: (A) munificent   (B) improvident
(C) random   (D) cautious   (E) obsolete

7. CONCLUSIVE: (A) difficult to express
(B) bringing bad luck   (C) easy to solve
(D) lacking merit   (E) open to question

8. RESOURCEFULNESS: (A) wealth
(B) gratitude   (C) melancholy
(D) incompetence   (E) frustration

9. DISSUADE: (A) extol   (B) exhort
(C) intensify   (D) complicate   (E) precede

10. SPLENETIC: (A) lackluster   (B) heartless
(C) diffident   (D) constant   (E) cordial

11. VIRULENCE: (A) pallor   (B) orderliness
(C) femininity   (D) harmlessness
(E) cowardice

12. ADHERENT: (A) fugitive   (B) dissembler
(C) opponent   (D) educator   (E) witness

13. OSCILLATE: (A) entreat   (B) intensify
(C) remain fixed   (D) expand gradually
(E) wither away

14. ASPERITY: (A) gentility   (B) superiority
(C) kindness   (D) clarity   (E) vagueness

15. UNSCATHED: (A) honest   (B) gathered
(C) injured   (D) cleansed   (E) forgiven

16. FETTER: (A) diminish   (B) enervate
(C) liberate   (D) return   (E) cure

17. AUTONOMY: (A) dependence   (B) animation
(C) renown   (D) altruism   (E) antipathy

18. SLACK: (A) rough   (B) active   (C) liberal
(D) dependent   (E) familiar

19. RECOIL :   (A) plunge forward
(B) cease firing   (C) skirt an issue
(D) facilitate   (E) surrender

20. ENCUMBER :   (A) disburden
(B) perform easily   (C) challenge boldly
(D) observe with care   (E) suppress

Antonym Exercise E

<u>Directions:</u> Each question below consists of a word printed in capital letters, followed by five lettered words or phrases. Choose the lettered word or phrase that is most nearly <u>opposite</u> in meaning to the word in capital letters.

Since some of the questions require you to distinguish fine shades of meaning, be sure to consider all the choices before deciding which one is best.

1. OPACITY :   (A) iridescence   (B) firmness
   (C) transparence   (D) poverty   (E) slum

2. PREDILECTION :   (A) postponement
   (B) afterthought   (C) lamentation
    (D) reoccurrence   (E) aversion

3. SEEDY :   (A) elegant   (B) intricate
   (C) tranquil   (D) irregular   (E) slow

4. BOGGLE :   (A) disentangle
   (B) repudiate   (C) ascertain
    (D) remain unruffled   (E) lack planning

5. HIDEBOUND :   (A) strong-willed
   (B) open-minded   (C) thin-skinned
    (D) tenderhearted   (E) scatterbrained

6. CASTIGATE :   (A) diminish   (B) imitate
   (C) compare   (D) reward   (E) misjudge

7. GAMBOL :   (A) dodge   (B) masquerade
   (C) digress   (D) plod   (E) vex

8. RAUCOUS :   (A) orderly   (B) absorbent
   (C) mellifluous   (D) contentious   (E) buoyant

9. TAPER :   (A) emphasize   (B) restore
   (C) split   (D) broaden   (E) modify

10. HIGH-HANDED :   (A) dejected
    (B) reasonable   (C) hard-handed
    (D) short-handed   (E) dynamic

11. DIMINUTION :   (A) measurement
    (B) proximity   (C) augmentation
    (D) orderliness   (E) inclination

12. DISTEND :   (A) tell the truth
    (B) respond as expected   (C) approximate
    (D) collect   (E) shrink

13. EMBROIL:
    (A) disengage
    (B) remonstrate
    (C) refute thoroughly
    (D) answer hypothetically
    (E) consider genuinely

14. VOUCHSAFE :   (A) postpone   (B) dissemble
    (C) endanger   (D) prohibit   (E) justify

15. JETTISON :   (A) salvage   (B) decelerate
    (C) muffle   (D) distract   (E) anchor

16. STOIC :   (A) savant   (B) herald
    (C) whiner   (D) victor   (E) bystander

17. GAMELY :   (A) fearfully   (B) diligently
    (C) clumsily   (D) gloomily   (E) respectfully

18. CRESTFALLEN :   (A) haughty   (B) impolite
    (C) frivolous   (D) tentative   (E) rough

19. DESULTORY :   (A) apologetic
    (B) independent   (C) laudatory
    (D) questionable   (E) methodical

20. PULCHRITUDE :   (A) antipathy
    (B) unsightliness   (C) inexperience
    (D) languor   (E) rancor

Answer Key

Antonym Exercise A

1.	E	6.	D	11.	C	16.	B
2.	C	7.	B	12.	D	17.	E
3.	C	8.	D	13.	E	18.	C
4.	B	9.	A	14.	E	19.	D
5.	C	10.	A	15.	D	20.	B

Antonym Exercise B

1.	C	6.	D	11.	C	16.	D
2.	E	7.	B	12.	A	17.	A
3.	C	8.	C	13.	A	18.	E
4.	B	9.	B	14.	B	19.	D
5.	D	10.	E	15.	C	20.	D

Antonym Exercise C

1.	D	6.	B	11.	A	16.	C
2.	B	7.	C	12.	D	17.	A
3.	B	8.	C	13.	C	18.	D
4.	D	9.	B	14.	B	19.	A
5.	E	10.	E	15.	E	20.	D

Antonym Exercise D

1.	D	6.	A	11.	D	16.	C
2.	A	7.	E	12.	C	17.	A
3.	B	8.	D	13.	C	18.	B
4.	B	9.	B	14.	C	19.	A
5.	E	10.	E	15.	C	20.	A

Antonym Exercise E

1.	C	6.	D	11.	C	16.	C
2.	E	7.	D	12.	E	17.	A
3.	A	8.	C	13.	A	18.	A
4.	D	9.	D	14.	D	19.	E
5.	B	10.	B	15.	A	20.	B

7 REVIEWING VOCABULARY

- **GRE High-Frequency Words**
- **Master Word List**
- **Basic Word Parts**

Now that you have mastered the appropriate strategies for dealing with the four basic types of questions on the Graduate Record Examination that test your verbal ability, you have the opportunity to spend some time refining your vocabulary and acquainting yourself with the fine shades of meaning that words possess. Studies show that while the average high school graduate recognizes about 50,000 words, the average college graduate recognizes around 70,000. That indicates that during your four years of college you have rapidly acquired about 20,000 new words (many of them technical terms from a variety of disciplines), some of which may have connotations and nuances that still escape you.

The best way to develop a powerful vocabulary is to read extensively and well. However, it is possible to finetune your vocabulary by exploring unabridged dictionaries, in which usage notes make clear the fine distinctions between related words, and by studying high-level vocabulary lists, such as our 3,500 word Master Word List.

The following chapter presents the Master Word List and a Basic Word Parts List, a chart of prefixes, roots, and suffixes that may provide you with clues to the meaning of unfamiliar words. In addition, the chapter begins with the GRE High-Frequency Word List, 300 words that have occurred and reoccurred on GREs published in the 1980s.

The GRE High-Frequency Word List

How many of the following words do you think you know? Half? Even more? First, check off those words that you recognize. Then, look up all 300 words and their definitions in our Master Word List. Pay particular attention to the following:

1. Words you recognize but cannot use in a sentence or define. You have a feel for these words—you are on the brink of knowing them. Effort you put into mastering these "borderline" words will pay off soon.

2. Words you thought you knew—but didn't. See whether any of them are defined in an unexpected way. If they are, make a special note of them. As you know from the preceding chapters, the GRE often stumps students with questions based on unfamiliar meanings of familiar-looking words.

In the course of your undergraduate career, you have undoubtedly developed your own techniques for building your vocabulary. One familiar technique—flash cards—often is used less than effectively. Students either try to cram too much information onto a flash card or try to cram too many flash cards into a practice session. If you wish to work with flash cards, try following these suggestions:

Writing the Flash Card   Be brief—but include all the information you need. On one side write the word. On the other side write a *concise* definition—two or three words at most—for each major meaning of the word you want to learn. Include an antonym, too: the synonym-antonym associations can help you remember both words. To fix the word in your mind, use it in a short phrase. Then write that phrase down.

Memorizing the Flash Card   Carry a few of your flash cards with you every day. Look them over whenever you have a spare moment or two. Work in short bursts. Try going through five flash cards at a time, shuffling through them rapidly so that you can build up your rapid sight recognition of the words for the test. You want these words and their antonyms to spring to your mind instantaneously.

Test your memory: don't look at the back of the card unless you must. Go through your five cards several times a day. Then, when you have mastered two or three of the cards and have them down pat, set those cards aside and add a couple of new ones to your working pile. That way you will always be working with a limited group, but you won't be wasting time reviewing words you already recognize on sight.

Never try to master a whole stack of flash cards in one long cram session. It won't work.

GRE High-Frequency Words

abate
aberrant
abeyance
abstain
abstemious
abstruse
adulation
adulterate
aggregate
alleviate
ambiguous
ambivalence
anachronism
analogous
anarchy
anomalous
antipathy
apathy
apostate
approbation
appropriate (V)
armada
ascetic
assiduous
assuage
attenuate
audacious
augment
auspicious
austere
autonomous
aver
aviary
ballast
banal
bane
belie
brook (V)
burgeon
burnish
buttress
cacophony
cajole
capricious
carping
castigation
centrifuge
chauvinist
coda
collusion
compendium

conciliatory
condescend
condone
conducive
connoisseur
contentious
conundrum
credulity
cynical
dearth
debase
decorum
deference
delineate
demographic
denigrate
deprecate
derelict (ADJ)
derision
derivative
desiccate
despotism
desultory
diaphanous
dichotomy
diffidence
diffusion
dilemma
diligence
disavowal
discerning
discomfit
discordant
discrepancy
discrete
disingenuous
disinterested
disjointed
disparage
disparate
disseminate
dissolution
dissonance
distraught
diverge
divest
docile
doggerel
dogmatic
droll
ductility

eclectic
efficacy
elegy
elicit
embellish
emissary
empirical
emulate
endemic
enervate
enigmatic
enmity
ensconce
ephemeral
equanimity
equivocate
erudite
eulogy
euphony
evanescent
exculpate
exigency
expunge
extrapolation
extricate
facetious
fallacious
fawning
fecundity
felicitous
fervor
fetter (V)
flag (V)
fledgling
flout
frugality
garner
garrulity
gist
gratuitous
gregarious
hermetic
hiatus
homogeneous
hybrid
hyperbole
hypocritical
hypothetical
imminent
immutable
impassive

impede
imperiousness
impervious
implement (V)
impromptu
improvident
imprudent
incarcerate
inchoate
incisive
incongruity
indigence
indiscriminate
indolence
inequity
inertia
ingenuous
inherent
inimical
insouciant
insularity
interdict
intransigence
intrinsically
invective
irascible
irate
itinerary
judicious
lachrymose
laconic
lampoon
lassitude
laudatory
legend
lethargic
levity
lucid
malleable
mendicant
metamorphosis
mitigate
mollify
moribund
multifarious
munificent
neophyte
nexus
obdurate
officious
opaque

oscillate
ostentatious
panegyric
paradox
paragon
parody
parsimonious
partisan
pathological
paucity
pedantic
penchant
penury
perfidy
perfunctory
permeable
pervasive
phlegmatic
piquant
placate
platitude
plethora
pragmatic
precipitate (ADJ)
precipitate (V)
precocious
presumptuous
pretentious
probity
problematic
prodigal
prodigy
profligate
prolific
propensity
propitiate
proscribe
pundit
pungency
qualified
ramification
rancor
ratiocination
recant
recondite
redoubtable
refractory
refute
relinquish
render
reparation

reprobate	sinuous	strut (N)	tenacity	ubiquitous
rescind	skeptic	substantiate	tendentious	usurp
resolution	sloth	substantive	tenet	vacillation
reticent	sophistry	supplant	torpor	vacuous
salacious	soporific	supposition	torque	venerate
salubrious	spurious	surreptitious	tractable	viscous
scapegoat	stigma	sycophant	trenchant	visionary
scrupulous	stolidity	tacit	truculence	welter (N)
shard	striated	taciturn	turbid	zealot

The 3,500 Master Word List

The 3,500 Master Word List begins on the following page. As a graduate student you should be familiar with the majority of these words. You do not, however, need to memorize every word.

The best way to enlarge your vocabulary is to read extensively in a variety of fields. You can, however, assess the extent of your vocabulary by exploring specialized word lists such as this.

For those of you who wish to work your way through the word list and feel the need for a plan, we recommend that you follow the procedure described below in order to use the lists and the exercises most profitably:

1. Allot a definite time each day for the study of a list.

2. Devote at least one hour to each list.

3. First go through the list looking at the short, simple-looking words (6 letters at most). Mark those you don't know. In studying, pay particular attention to them.

4. Go through the list again looking at the longer words. Pay particular attention to words with more than one meaning and familiar-looking words which have unusual definitions that come as a surprise to you. Many tests make use of these secondary definitions.

5. List unusual words on index cards which you can shuffle and review from time to time. (Use the flash card technique described earlier in this chapter.)

6. Use the illustrative sentences in the list as models and make up new sentences of your own.

7. Take the test which follows each list at least one day after studying the words. In this way, you will check your ability to remember what you have studied.

8. If you can answer correctly 12 of the 15 questions in the test, you may proceed to the next list; if you cannot answer this number, restudy the list.

9. Keep a record of your guesses and of your success as a guesser.

For each word, the following is provided:

1. The word (printed in heavy type).

2. Its part of speech (abbreviated).

3. A brief definition.

4. A sentence illustrating the word's use.

5. Whenever appropriate, related words are provided, together with their parts of speech.

The word lists are arranged in strict alphabetical order. In each word list, High-Frequency words are marked with a square bullet (■).

Master Word List

Word List 1   abase-adroit

abase v. lower; humiliate. His refusal to *abase* himself in the eyes of his followers irritated the king, who wanted to humiliate him.

abash v. embarrass. He was not at all *abashed* by her open admiration.

■ **abate** v. subside or moderate. Rather than leaving immediately, they waited for the storm to *abate*.

abbreviate v. shorten. Because we were running out of time, the lecturer had to *abbreviate* her speech.

abdicate v. renounce; give up. When Edward VIII *abdicated* the British throne, he surprised the entire world.

■ **aberrant** ADJ. abnormal or deviant. Given the *aberrant* nature of the data, we came to doubt the validity of the entire experiment. Also N.

aberration N. wandering or straying; in optics, failure of rays to focus. In designing a good lens for a camera, the problem of correcting chromatic and rectilinear *aberration* was a serious one.

abettor N. encourager. She was accused of being an aider and *abettor* of the criminal. abet, v.

■ **abeyance** N. suspended action. The deal was held in *abeyance* until her arrival.

abhor v. detest; hate. She *abhorred* all forms of bigotry. abhorrence, N.

abjure v. renounce upon oath. He *abjured* his allegiance to the king. abjuration, N.

ablution N. washing. His daily *ablutions* were accompanied by loud noises that he humorously labeled "Opera in the Bath."

abnegation N. repudiation; self-sacrifice. No act of *abnegation* was more pronounced than his refusal of any rewards for his discovery.

abolish v. cancel; put an end to. The president of the college refused to *abolish* the physical education requirement. abolition, N.

abominate v. loathe; hate. Moses scolded the idol worshippers in the tribe because he *abominated* the custom. abominable, ADJ.

aboriginal ADJ., N. being the first of its kind in a region; primitive; native. Her studies of the primitive art forms of the *aboriginal* Indians were widely reported in the scientific journals. aborigines, N.

abortive ADJ. unsuccessful; fruitless. We had to abandon our *abortive* attempts.

abrade v. wear away by friction; erode. The skin of her leg was *abraded* by the sharp rocks. abrasion, N.

abridge v. condense or shorten. Because the publishers felt the public wanted a shorter version of *War and Peace,* they proceeded to *abridge* the novel.

abrogate v. abolish. He intended to *abrogate* the decree issued by his predecessor.

abscond v. depart secretly and hide. The teller *absconded* with the bonds and was not found.

absolve v. pardon (an offense). The father confessor *absolved* him of his sins. absolution, N.

■ **abstain** v. refrain; withhold from participation. After considering the effect of alcohol on his athletic performance, he decided to *abstain* from drinking while he trained for the race.

■ **abstemious** ADJ. sparing in eating and drinking; temperate. The drunkards mocked him because of his *abstemious* habits.

abstinence N. restraint from eating or drinking. The doctor recommended total *abstinence* from salted foods. abstain, v.

abstract ADJ. theoretical; not concrete; nonrepresentational. To him, hunger was an *abstract* concept; he had never missed a meal.

■ **abstruse** ADJ. obscure; profound; difficult to understand. She read *abstruse* works in philosophy.

abusive ADJ. coarsely insulting; physically harmful. An *abusive* parent damages a child both mentally and physically.

abut v. border upon; adjoin. Where our estates *abut,* we must build a fence.

abysmal ADJ. bottomless. His arrogance is exceeded only by his *abysmal* ignorance.

accede v. agree. If I *accede* to this demand for blackmail, I am afraid that I will be the victim of future demands.

accelerate v. move faster. In our science class, we learn how falling bodies *accelerate*.

accessible ADJ. easy to approach; obtainable. We asked our guide whether the ruins were *accessible* on foot.

accessory N. additional object; useful but not essential thing. She bought an attractive handbag as an accessory for her dress. also ADJ.

acclimate v. adjust to climate. One of the difficulties of our present air age is the need of travelers to *acclimate* themselves to their new and often strange environments.

acclivity N. sharp upslope of a hill. The car could not go up the *acclivity* in high gear.

accolade N. award of merit. In Hollywood, an "Oscar" is the highest *accolade*.

accomplice N. partner in crime. Because he had provided the criminal with the lethal weapon, he was arrested as an *accomplice* in the murder.

accord N. agreement. She was in complete *accord* with the verdict.

accost v. approach and speak first to a person. When the two young men *accosted* me, I was frightened because I thought they were going to attack me.

accoutre v. equip. The fisherman was *accoutred* with the best that the sporting goods store could supply. accoutrements, N.

accretion N. growth; increase. The *accretion* of wealth marked the family's rise in power.

accrue v. come about by addition. You must pay the interest which has *accrued* on your debt as well as the principal sum. accrual, N.

acerbity N. bitterness of speech and temper. The meeting of the United Nations Assembly was marked with such *acerbity* that little hope of reaching any useful settlement of the problem could be held.

acetic ADJ. vinegary. The salad had an exceedingly *acetic* flavor.

acidulous ADJ. slightly sour; sharp, caustic. James was unpopular because of his sarcastic and *acidulous* remarks.

acknowledge v. recognize; admit. When pressed for an answer, she *acknowledged* the existence of another motive for the crime.

acme N. top; pinnacle. His success in this role marked his *acme* as an actor.

acoustics N. science of sound; quality that makes a room easy or hard to hear in. Carnegie Hall is liked by music lovers because of its fine *acoustics*.

acquiesce v. assent; agree passively. Although she appeared to *acquiesce* to her employer's suggestions, I could tell she had reservations about the changes he wanted made.

acquiescence N. submission; compliance. It is impossible to obtain their *acquiescence* to the proposal because it is abhorrent to their philosophy.

acquiescent ADJ. accepting passively. His *acquiescent* manner did not indicate the extent of his reluctance to join the group. acquiesce, v.

acquittal N. deliverance from a charge. His *acquittal* by the jury surprised those who had thought him guilty. acquit, v.

acrid ADJ. sharp; bitterly pungent. The *acrid* odor of burnt gunpowder filled the room after the pistol had been fired.

acrimonious ADJ. stinging; caustic. His tendency to utter *acrimonious* remarks alienated his audience. acrimony, N.

actuarial ADJ. calculating; pertaining to insurance statistics. According to recent *actuarial* tables, life expectancy is greater today than it was a century ago.

actuate v. motivate. I fail to understand what *actuated* you to reply to this letter so nastily.

acuity N. sharpness. In time his youthful *acuity* of vision failed him, and he needed glasses.

acumen N. mental keenness. His business *acumen* helped him to succeed where others had failed.

adage N. wise saying; proverb. There is much truth in the old *adage* about fools and their money.

adamant ADJ. hard; inflexible. He was *adamant* in his determination to punish the wrongdoer. adamancy, N.

adapt v. alter; modify. Some species of animals have become extinct because they could not *adapt* to a changing environment.

addiction N. compulsive, habitual need. His *addiction* to drugs caused his friends much grief.

addle ADJ. rotten; muddled; crazy. This *addle*-headed plan is so preposterous that it does not deserve any consideration. also v.

adduce v. present as evidence. When you *adduce* material of this nature, you must be sure of your sources.

adept ADJ. expert at. She was *adept* at the fine art of irritating people. also N.

adhere v. stick fast. I will *adhere* to this opinion until proof that I am wrong is presented. adhesion, N.

adjunct N. something attached to but holding an inferior position. I will entertain this concept as an *adjunct* to the main proposal.

adjuration N. solemn urging. Her *adjuration* to tell the truth did not change the witnesses' testimony.

adjure v. request solemnly. I must *adjure* you to consider this matter carefully as it is of utmost importance to all of us.

admonish v. warn; reprove. He *admonished* his listeners to change their wicked ways. admonition, N.

admonition N. warning. After repeated rejections of its *admonitions,* the country was forced to issue an ultimatum.

adorn v. decorate. Wall paintings and carved statues *adorned* the temple. adornment, N.

adroit ADJ. skillful. His *adroit* handling of the delicate situation pleased his employers.

Test

Word List 1   *Synonyms*

Each of the questions below consists of a word in capital letters, followed by five lettered words or phrases. Choose the lettered word or phrase that is most nearly similar in meaning to the word in capital letters and write the letter of your choice on your answer paper.

1. ABASE (A) incur (B) tax (C) ground floor (D) humility (E) humiliate
2. ABERRATION (A) deviation (B) abhorrence (C) dislike (D) absence (E) anecdote
3. ABETTOR (A) conception (B) one who wagers (C) encourager (D) evidence (E) protection

4. ABEYANCE (A) obedience (B) discussion (C) excitement (D) suspended action (E) editorial
5. ABJURE (A) discuss (B) renounce (C) run off secretly (D) perjure (E) project
6. ABLUTION (A) censure (B) forgiveness (C) mutiny (D) survival (E) washing
7. ABNEGATION (A) blackness (B) self-denial (C) selfishness (D) cause (E) effect
8. ABORIGINES (A) first designs (B) absolutions (C) finales (D) concepts (E) primitive inhabitants
9. ABORTIVE (A) unsuccessful (B) consuming (C) financing (D) familiar (E) fruitful
10. ABSTINENCE (A) restrained eating or drinking (B) vulgar display (C) deportment (D) reluctance (E) population
11. ABSTRUSE (A) profound (B) irrespective (C) suspended (D) protesting (E) not thorough
12. ABUT (A) stimulate (B) grasp (C) oppose (D) widen (E) adjoin
13. ABYSMAL (A) bottomless (B) eternal (C) meteoric (D) diabolic (E) internal
14. ACCEDE (A) fail (B) compromise (C) correct (D) consent (E) mollify
15. ACCLIVITY (A) index (B) report (C) upslope of a hill (D) character (E) negotiator

Word List 2   adulation–amend

■ **adulation** N. flattery; admiration. He thrived on the *adulation* of his henchmen. adulate, V.

■ **adulterate** V. make impure by mixing with baser substances. It is a crime to *adulterate* foods without informing the buyer.

adulterated ADJ. made impure or spoiled by the addition of inferior materials. The health authorities ordered the sale of the meat stopped because they found it *adulterated*.

advent N. arrival. Most Americans were unaware of the *advent* of the Nuclear Age until the news of Hiroshima reached them.

adventitious ADJ. accidental; casual. He found this *adventitious* meeting with his friend extremely fortunate.

adverse ADJ. unfavorable; hostile. *Adverse* circumstances compelled him to close his business.

adversity N. poverty; misfortune. We must learn to meet *adversity* gracefully.

advert V. refer to. Since you *advert* to this matter so frequently, you must regard it as important.

advocate V. urge; plead for. The abolitionists *advocated* freedom for the slaves. also N.

aegis N. shield; defense. Under the *aegis* of the Bill of Rights, we enjoy our most treasured freedoms.

aeon N. long period of time; an age. It has taken *aeons* for our civilization to develop.

aesthetic ADJ. artistic; dealing with or capable of appreciation of the beautiful. Because of his *aesthetic* nature, he was emotionally disturbed by ugly things. aesthete, N.

affable ADJ. courteous. Although he held a position of responsibility, he was an *affable* individual and could be reached by anyone with a complaint.

affected ADJ. artificial; pretended. His *affected* mannerisms irritated many of us who had known him before his promotion. affectation, N.

affidavit N. written statement made under oath. The court refused to accept his statement unless he presented it in the form of an *affidavit*.

affiliation N. joining; associating with. His *affiliation* with the political party was of short duration for he soon disagreed with his colleagues.

affinity N. kinship. She felt an *affinity* with all who suffered their pains were her pains.

affirmation N. solemn pledge by one who refuses to take an oath. The Constitution of this country provides for oath or *affirmation* by officeholders.

affluence N. abundance; wealth. Foreigners are amazed by the *affluence* and luxury of the American way of life.

affray N. public brawl. He was badly mauled by the fighters in the *affray*.

agape ADJ. openmouthed. She stared, *agape*, at the many strange animals in the zoo.

agenda N. items of business at a meeting. We had so much difficulty agreeing upon an *agenda* that there was very little time for the meeting.

agglomeration N. collection; heap. It took weeks to assort the *agglomeration* of miscellaneous items she had collected on her trip.

aggrandize V. increase or intensify. The history of the past quarter century illustrates how a President may *aggrandize* his power to act aggressively in international affairs without considering the wishes of Congress.

■ **aggregate** ADJ. sum; total. The *aggregate* wealth of this country is staggering to the imagination. also V, N.

aghast ADJ. horrified. He was *aghast* at the nerve of the speaker who had insulted his host.

agility N. nimbleness. The *agility* of the acrobat amazed and thrilled the audience.

agitate V. stir up; disturb. Her fiery remarks *agitated* the already angry mob.

agitation N. strong feeling; excitement. We felt that he was responsible for the *agitation* of the mob because of the inflammatory report he had issued.

agnostic N. one who is skeptical of the existence or knowability of a god or any ultimate reality. The *agnostic* demanded proof before she would accept the statement of the minister. also ADJ.

agrarian ADJ. pertaining to land or its cultivation. The country is gradually losing its *agrarian* occupation and turning more and more to an industrial point of view.

alacrity N. cheerful promptness. He demonstrated his eagerness to serve by his *alacrity* in executing the orders of his master.

albeit CONJ. although. *Albeit* fair, she was not sought after.

alchemy N. medieval chemistry. The changing of baser metals into gold was the goal of the students of *alchemy*. alchemist, N.

alias N. an assumed name. John Smith's *alias* was Bob Jones. also ADV.

alienate V. make hostile; separate. Her attempts to *alienate* the two friends failed because they had complete faith in each other.

alimentary ADJ. supplying nourishment. The *alimentary* canal in our bodies is so named because digestion of foods occurs there.

alimony N. payment by a husband to his divorced wife. Mrs. Jones was awarded $200 monthly *alimony* by the court when she was divorced from her husband.

allay V. calm; pacify. The crew tried to *allay* the fears of the passengers by announcing that the fire had been controlled.

allege V. state without proof. It is *alleged* that she had worked for the enemy. allegation, N.

allegory N. story in which characters are used as symbols; fable. *Pilgrim's Progress* is an *allegory* of the temptations and victories of man's soul. allegorical, ADJ.

■ **alleviate** V. relieve. This should *alleviate* the pain; if it does not, we shall have to use stronger drugs.

alliteration N. repetition of beginning sound in poetry. "The furrow followed free" is an example of *alliteration*.

allocate V. assign. Even though the Red Cross had *allocated* a large sum for the relief of the sufferers of the disaster, many people perished.

alloy N. a mixture as of metals. *Alloys* of gold are used more frequently than the pure metal.

allude V. refer indirectly. Try not to *allude* to this matter in his presence because it annoys him to hear of it.

allure V. entice; attract. *Allured* by the song of the sirens, the helmsman steered the ship toward the reef. also N.

allusion N. indirect reference. The *allusions* to mythological characters in Milton's poems bewilder the reader who has not studied Latin.

alluvial ADJ. pertaining to soil deposits left by rivers, etc. The farmers found the *alluvial* deposits at the mouth of the river very fertile.

aloof ADJ. apart; reserved. Shy by nature, she remained *aloof* while all the rest conversed.

aloft ADV. upward. The sailor climbed *aloft* into the rigging.

altercation N. wordy quarrel. Throughout the entire *altercation,* not one sensible word was uttered.

altruistic ADJ. unselfishly generous; concerned for others. In providing tutorial assistance and college scholarships for hundreds of economically disadvantaged youths, Eugene Lang performed a truly *altruistic* deed. altruism, N.

amalgamate V. combine; unite in one body. The unions will attempt to *amalgamate* their groups into one national body.

amass V. collect. The miser's aim is to *amass* and hoard as much gold as possible.

amazon N. female warrior. Ever since the days of Greek mythology we refer to strong and aggressive women as *amazons*.

ambidextrous ADJ. capable of using either hand with equal ease. A switch-hitter in baseball should be naturally *ambidextrous*.

ambience N. environment; atmosphere. She went to the restaurant not for the food but for the *ambience*.

■ **ambiguous** ADJ. unclear or doubtful in meaning. His *ambiguous* instructions misled us; we did not know which road to take. ambiguity, N.

amble N. moving at an easy pace. When she first mounted the horse, she was afraid to urge the animal to go faster than a gentle *amble*. also V.

■ **ambivalence** N. the state of having contradictory or conflicting emotional attitudes. Torn between loving her parents one minute and hating them the next, she was confused by the *ambivalence* of her feelings. ambivalent, ADJ.

ambrosia N. food of the gods. *Ambrosia* was supposed to give immortality to any human who ate it.

ambulatory ADJ. able to walk. He was described as an *ambulatory* patient because he was not confined to his bed.

ameliorate V. improve. Many social workers have attempted to *ameliorate* the conditions of people living in the slums.

amenable ADJ. readily managed; willing to be led. He was *amenable* to any suggestions which came from those he looked up to; he resented advice from his inferiors.

amend V. correct; change, generally for the better. Hoping to *amend* his condition, he left Vietnam for the United States.

Test

Word List 2   *Antonyms*

Each of the questions below consists of a word in capital letters, followed by five lettered words or phrases. Choose the lettered word or phrase that is most nearly opposite in meaning to the word in capital letters and write the letter of your choice on your answer paper.

16. ADULATION (A) youth (B) purity (C) brightness (D) defense (E) criticism

17. ADVOCATE (A) define (B) oppose (C) remove
    (D) inspect (E) discern
18. AFFABLE (A) rude (B) ruddy (C) needy
    (D) useless (E) conscious
19. AFFECTED (A) weary (B) unfriendly (C) divine
    (D) unfeigned (E) slow
20. AFFLUENCE (A) poverty (B) fear (C) persuasion
    (D) consideration (E) neglect
21. AGILITY (A) awkwardness (B) solidity (C) temper
    (D) harmony (E) warmth
22. ALACRITY (A) slowness (B) plenty (C) filth
    (D) courtesy (E) despair
23. ALLEVIATE (A) endure (B) worsen (C) enlighten
    (D) maneuver (E) humiliate

24. ALLURE (A) hinder (B) repel (C) ignore
    (D) leave (E) wallow
25. ALOOF (A) triangular (B) gregarious
    (C) comparable (D) honorable (E) savory
26. AMALGAMATE (A) equip (B) separate
    (C) generate (D) materialize (E) repress
27. AMBIGUOUS (A) salvageable (B) corresponding
    (C) responsible (D) clear (E) auxiliary
28. AMBLE (A) befriend (B) hasten (C) steal
    (D) browse (E) prattle
29. AMBULATORY (A) convalescent (B) conservatory
    (C) bedridden (D) emergency (E) congenital
30. AMELIORATE (A) make slow (B) make sure
    (C) make young (D) make worse (E) make able

Word List 3   amenities-apothecary

amenities N. agreeable manners; courtesies. She observed the social *amenities*.

amiable ADJ. agreeable; lovable. His *amiable* disposition pleased all who had dealings with him.

amicable ADJ. friendly. The dispute was settled in an *amicable* manner with no harsh words.

amiss ADJ. wrong; faulty. Seeing her frown, he wondered if anything were *amiss*. also ADV.

amity N. friendship. Student exchange programs such as the Experiment in International Living were established to promote international *amity*.

amnesia N. loss of memory. Because she was suffering from *amnesia*, the police could not get the young girl to identify herself.

amnesty N. pardon. When his first child was born, the king granted *amnesty* to all in prison.

amoral ADJ. nonmoral. The *amoral* individual lacks a code of ethics; he should not be classified as immoral.

amorous ADJ. moved by sexual love; loving. Don Juan was known for his *amorous* adventures.

amorphous ADJ. shapeless. She was frightened by the *amorphous* mass which had floated in from the sea.

amortization N. act of reducing a debt through partial payments. Your monthly payments to the bank include provisions for taxes, interest on the principal, and *amortization* of the mortgage.

amphibian ADJ. able to live both on land and in water. Frogs are classified as *amphibian*. also N.

amphitheater N. oval building with tiers of seats. The spectators in the *amphitheater* cheered the gladiators.

ample ADJ. abundant. He had *ample* opportunity to dispose of his loot before the police caught up with him.

amplify V. enlarge. Her attempts to *amplify* her remarks were drowned out by the jeers of the audience.

amputate V. cut off part of body; prune. When the doctors decided to *amputate* his leg to prevent the spread of gangrene, he cried that he preferred death to incapacity.

amuck ADV. in a state of rage. The police had to be called in to restrain him after he ran *amuck* in the department store.

amulet N. charm; talisman. Around her neck she wore the *amulet* that the witch doctor had given her.

■ **anachronism** N. an error involving time in a story. The reference to clocks in *Julius Caesar* is an *anachronism*.

analgesic ADJ. causing insensitivity to pain. The *analgesic* qualities of this lotion will provide temporary relief.

■ **analogous** ADJ. comparable. She called our attention to the things that had been done in an *analogous* situation and recommended that we do the same.

analogy N. similarity; parallelism. Your *analogy* is not a good one because the two situations are not similar.

anarchist N. person who rebels against the established order. Only the total overthrow of all governmental regulations would satisfy the *anarchist*.

■ **anarchy** N. absence of governing body; state of disorder. The assassination of the leaders led to a period of *anarchy*.

anathema N. solemn curse. He heaped *anathema* upon his foe.

anathematize V. curse. The high priest *anathematized* the heretic.

ancillary ADJ. serving as an aid or accessory; auxiliary. In an *ancillary* capacity he was helpful; however, he could not be entrusted with leadership. also N.

andirons N. metal supports in a fireplace for cooking utensils or logs. She spent many hours in the department stores looking for a pair of ornamental *andirons* for her fireplace.

anemia N. condition in which blood lacks red corpuscles. The doctor ascribes her tiredness to *anemia*. anemic, ADJ.

anesthetic N. substance that removes sensation with or without loss of consciousness. His monotonous voice acted like an *anesthetic*; his audience was soon asleep. anesthesia, N.

angular ADJ. sharp-cornered; stiff in manner. His features, though *angular*, were curiously attractive.

animadversion N. critical remark. He resented the *animadversions* of his critics, particularly because he realized they were true.

animated ADJ. lively. Her *animated* expression indicated a keenness of intellect. animation, N.

animosity N. active enmity. He incurred the *animosity* of the ruling class because he advocated limitations of their power.

animus N. hostile feeling or intent. The *animus* of the speaker became obvious to all when he began to indulge in sarcastic and insulting remarks.

annals N. records; history. In the *annals* of this period, we find no mention of democratic movements.

anneal V. reduce brittleness and improve toughness by heating and cooling. After the glass is *annealed,* it will be less subject to chipping and cracking.

annihilate V. destroy. The enemy in its revenge tried to *annihilate* the entire population.

annotate V. comment; make explanatory notes. In the appendix to the novel, the critic sought to *annotate* many of the more esoteric references.

annuity N. yearly allowance. The *annuity* he set up with the insurance company supplements his social security benefits so that he can live very comfortably without working.

annul V. make void. The parents of the eloped couple tried to *annul* the marriage.

anodyne N. drug that relieves pain; opiate. His pain was so great that no *anodyne* could relieve it.

anoint V. consecrate. The prophet Samuel *anointed* David with oil, crowning him king of Israel.

■ **anomalous** ADJ. abnormal; irregular. He was placed in the *anomalous* position of seeming to approve procedures which he despised.

anomaly N. irregularity. A bird that cannot fly is an *anomaly.*

anonymity N. state of being nameless; anonymousness. The donor of the gift asked the college not to mention him by name; the dean readily agreed to respect his *anonymity.*

anonymous ADJ. having no name. She tried to ascertain the identity of the writer of the *anonymous* letter.

antagonism N. active resistance. We shall have to overcome the *antagonism* of the natives before our plans for settling this area can succeed.

antagonistic ADJ. hostile; opposed. Despite his lawyers' best efforts to stop him, the angry prisoner continued to make *antagonistic* remarks to the judge.

antecede V. precede. The invention of the radiotelegraph *anteceded* the development of television by a quarter of a century.

antediluvian ADJ. antiquated; ancient. The *antediluvian* customs had apparently not changed for thousands of years. also N.

anthropoid ADJ. manlike. The gorilla is the strongest of the *anthropoid* animals. also N.

anthropologist N. a student of the history and science of mankind. *Anthropologists* have discovered several relics of prehistoric man in this area.

anthropomorphic ADJ. having human form or characteristics. Primitive religions often have deities with *anthropomorphic* characteristics.

anticlimax N. letdown in thought or emotion. After the fine performance in the first act, the rest of the play was an *anticlimax*. anticlimactic, ADJ.

■ **antipathy** N. aversion; dislike. His extreme *antipathy* to dispute caused him to avoid argumentative discussions with his friends.

antiseptic N. substance that prevents infection. It is advisable to apply an *antiseptic* to any wound, no matter how slight or insignificant. also ADJ.

antithesis N. contrast; direct opposite of or to. This tyranny was the *antithesis* of all that he had hoped for, and he fought it with all his strength.

apathetic ADJ. indifferent. He felt *apathetic* about the conditions he had observed and did not care to fight against them. apathy, N.

■ **apathy** N. lack of caring; indifference. A firm believer in democratic government, she could not understand the *apathy* of people who never bothered to vote.

ape V. imitate or mimic. He was suspended for a week because he had *aped* the principal in front of the whole school.

aperture N. opening; hole. She discovered a small *aperture* in the wall, through which the insects had entered the room.

apex N. tip; summit; climax. He was at the *apex* of his career.

aphasia N. loss of speech due to injury or illness. After the automobile accident, the victim had periods of *aphasia* when he could not speak at all or could only mumble incoherently.

aphorism N. pithy maxim. An *aphorism* differs from an adage in that it is more philosophical or scientific. aphoristic, ADJ.

apiary N. a place where bees are kept. Although he spent many hours daily in the *apiary,* he was very seldom stung by a bee.

aplomb N. poise. His nonchalance and *aplomb* in times of trouble always encouraged his followers.

apocalyptic ADJ. prophetic; pertaining to revelations. His *apocalyptic* remarks were dismissed by his audience as wild surmises.

apocryphal ADJ. not genuine; sham. Her *apocryphal* tears misled no one.

apogee N. highest point. When the moon in its orbit is furthest away from the earth, it is at its *apogee*.

apoplexy N. stroke; loss of consciousness followed by paralysis. He was crippled by an attack of *apoplexy*.

■ **apostate** N. one who abandons his religious faith or political beliefs. Because he switched from one party to another, his former friends shunned him as an *apostate*. apostasy, N.

apothecary N. druggist. In the *apothecaries'* weight, twelve ounces equal one pound.

Test

Word List 3   *Antonyms*

Each of the questions below consists of a word in capital letters, followed by five lettered words or phrases. Choose the lettered word or phrase that is most nearly opposite in meaning to the word in capital letters and write the letter of your choice on your answer paper.

31. AMICABLE (A) penetrating (B) compensating (C) unfriendly (D) zig-zag (E) inescapable
32. AMORAL (A) unusual (B) unfriendly (C) ethical (D) suave (E) firm
33. AMORPHOUS (A) nauseous (B) obscene (C) providential (D) definite (E) happy
34. AMPLIFY (A) distract (B) infer (C) publicize (D) decrease (E) pioneer
35. ANALOGOUS (A) not comparable (B) not capable (C) not culpable (D) not corporeal (E) not congenial
36. ANATHEMATIZE (A) locate (B) deceive (C) regulate (D) radiate (E) bless

37. ANEMIC (A) pallid (B) cruel (C) red-blooded (D) ventilating (E) hazardous
38. ANIMATED (A) worthy (B) dull (C) humorous (D) lengthy (E) realistic
39. ANIMUS (A) pterodactyl (B) bastion (C) giraffe (D) grimace (E) favor
40. ANOMALY (A) desperation (B) requisition (C) registry (D) regularity (E) radiation
41. ANONYMOUS (A) desperate (B) signed (C) defined (D) expert (E) written
42. ANTEDILUVIAN (A) transported (B) subtle (C) isolated (D) celebrated (E) modern
43. ANTIPATHY (A) profundity (B) objection (C) willingness (D) abstention (E) fondness
44. ANTITHESIS (A) velocity (B) maxim (C) similarity (D) acceleration (E) reaction
45. APHASIA (A) volubility (B) necessity (C) pain (D) crack (E) prayer

---

Word List 4   apothegm-astigmatism

apothegm N. pithy, compact saying. Proverbs are *apothegms* that have become familiar sayings.

apotheosis N. deification; glorification. The *apotheosis* of a Roman emperor was designed to insure his eternal greatness.

appall V. dismay; shock. We were *appalled* by the horrifying conditions in the city's jails.

apparition N. ghost; phantom. Hamlet was uncertain about the identity of the *apparition* that had appeared and spoken to him.

appease V. pacify; soothe. We have discovered that, when we try to *appease* our enemies, we encourage them to make additional demands.

appellation N. name; title. He was amazed when the witches hailed him with his correct *appellation*.

append V. attach. I shall *append* this chart to my report.

apposite ADJ. appropriate; fitting. He was always able to find the *apposite* phrase, the correct expression for every occasion.

appraise V. estimate value of. It is difficult to *appraise* the value of old paintings; it is easier to call them priceless. appraisal, N.

apprehend V. arrest (a criminal); dread; perceive. The police will *apprehend* the culprit and convict him before long.

apprehensive ADJ. fearful; discerning. His *apprehensive* glances at the people who were walking in the street revealed his nervousness.

apprise V. inform. When he was *apprised* of the dangerous weather conditions, he decided to postpone his trip.

■ **approbation** N. approval. She looked for some sign of *approbation* from her parents.

■ **appropriate** V. acquire; take possession of for one's own use. The ranch owners *appropriated* the lands that had originally been set aside for the Indians' use.

appurtenances N. subordinate possessions. He bought the estate and all its *appurtenances*.

apropos PREP. with reference to; regarding. I find your remarks *apropos* of the present situation timely and pertinent. also ADJ. and ADV.

aptitude N. fitness; talent. The counselor gave him an *aptitude* test before advising him about the career he should follow.

aquiline ADJ. curved, hooked. He can be recognized by his *aquiline* nose, curved like the beak of the eagle.

arable ADJ. fit for plowing. The land was no longer *arable*; erosion had removed the valuable topsoil.

arbiter N. a person with power to decide a dispute; judge. As an *arbiter* in labor disputes, she has won the confidence of the workers and the employers.

arbitrary ADJ. fixed or definite; imperious; tyrannical; despotic. Any *arbitrary* action on your part will be resented by the members of the board whom you do not consult.

arbitrate V. act as judge. She was called upon to *arbitrate* the dispute between the union and the management.

arcade N. a covered passageway, usually lined with shops. The *arcade* was popular with shoppers because it gave them protection from the summer sun and the winter rain.

arcane ADJ. secret; mysterious. What was *arcane* to us was clear to the psychologist.

archaeology N. study of artifacts and relics of early mankind. The professor of *archaeology* headed an expedition to the Gobi Desert in search of ancient ruins.

archaic ADJ. antiquated. ''Methinks,'' ''thee,'' and ''thou'' are *archaic* words which are no longer part of our normal vocabulary.

archetype N. prototype; primitive pattern. The Brooklyn Bridge was the *archetype* of the many spans that now connect Manhattan with Long Island and New Jersey.

archipelago N. group of closely located islands. When he looked at the map and saw the *archipelagoes* in the South Seas, he longed to visit them.

archives N. public records; place where public records are kept. These documents should be part of the *archives* so that historians may be able to evaluate them in the future.

ardor N. heat; passion; zeal. His *ardor* was contagious; soon everyone was eagerly working.

arduous ADJ. hard; strenuous. Her *arduous* efforts had sapped her energy.

argot N. slang. In the *argot* of the underworld, she ''was taken for a ride.''

aria N. operatic solo. At her Metropolitan Opera audition, Marian Anderson sang an *aria* from *Norma*.

arid ADJ. dry; barren. The cactus has adapted to survive in an *arid* environment.

■ **armada** N. fleet of warships. Queen Elizabeth's navy was able to defeat the mighty *armada* that threatened the English coast.

aromatic ADJ. fragrant. Medieval sailing vessels brought *aromatic* herbs from China to Europe.

arraign V. charge in court; indict. After his indictment by the Grand Jury, the accused man was *arraigned* in the County Criminal Court.

arrant ADJ. thorough; complete; unmitigated. ''*Arrant* knave,'' an epithet found in books dealing with the age of chivalry, is a term of condemnation.

array V. marshal; draw up in order. His actions were bound to *array* public sentiment against him. also N.

array V. clothe; adorn. She liked to watch her mother *array* herself in her finest clothes before going out for the evening. also N.

arrears N. being in debt. He was in *arrears* with his payments on the car.

arrogance N. pride; haughtiness. The *arrogance* of the nobility was resented by the middle class.

arrogate V. claim without reasonable grounds. I am afraid that the manner in which he *arrogates* power to himself indicates that he is willing to ignore Constitutional limitations.

arroyo N. gully. Until the heavy rains of the past spring, this *arroyo* had been a dry bed.

articulate ADJ. effective; distinct. Her *articulate* presentation of the advertising campaign impressed her employer. also V.

artifacts N. products of primitive culture. Archaeologists debated the significance of the *artifacts* discovered in the ruins of Asia Minor and came to no conclusion.

artifice N. deception; trickery. The Trojan War proved to the Greeks that cunning and *artifice* were often more effective than military might.

artisan N. a manually skilled worker. Artists and *artisans* alike are necessary to the development of a culture.

ascendancy N. controlling influence. President Marcos failed to maintain his *ascendancy* over the Philippines.

ascertain V. find out for certain. Please *ascertain* her present address.

■ **ascetic** ADJ. practicing self-denial; austere. The wealthy young man could not understand the *ascetic* life led by the monks. also N.

asceticism N. doctrine of self-denial. We find *asceticism* practiced in many monasteries.

ascribe V. refer; attribute; assign. I can *ascribe* no motive for her acts.

aseptic ADJ. preventing infection; having a cleansing effect. Hospitals succeeded in lowering the mortality rate as soon as they introduced *aseptic* conditions.

ashen ADJ. ash-colored. Her face was *ashen* with fear.

asinine ADJ. stupid. Your *asinine* remarks prove that you have not given this problem any serious consideration.

askance ADV. with a sideways or indirect look. Looking *askance* at her questioner, she displayed her scorn.

askew ADV. crookedly; slanted; at an angle. When he placed his hat *askew* upon his head, his observers laughed.

asperity N. sharpness (of temper). These remarks, spoken with *asperity,* stung the boys to whom they had been directed.

aspersion N. slanderous remark. Do not cast *aspersions* on her character.

aspirant N. seeker after position or status. Although I am an *aspirant* for public office, I am not willing to accept the dictates of the party bosses. also ADJ.

aspiration N. noble ambition. Man's *aspirations* should be as lofty as the stars.

assail V. assault. He was *assailed* with questions after his lecture.

assay V. analyze; evaluate. When they *assayed* the ore, they found that they had discovered a very rich vein. also N.

assent V. agree; accept. It gives me great pleasure to *assent* to your request.

assessment N. estimation. I would like to have your *assessment* of the situation in South Africa.

■ **assiduous** ADJ. diligent. He worked *assiduously* at this task for weeks before he felt satisfied with his results. assiduity, N.

assimilate V. absorb; cause to become homogeneous. The manner in which the United States was able to *assimilate* the hordes of immigrants during the nineteenth and the early part of the twentieth centuries will always be a source of pride.

■ **assuage** V. ease; lessen (pain). Your messages of cheer should *assuage* her suffering. assuagement, N.

asteroid N. small planet. *Asteroids* have become commonplace to the readers of interstellar travel stories in science fiction magazines.

astigmatism N. eye defect which prevents proper focus. As soon as his parents discovered that the boy suffered from *astigmatism,* they took him to the optometrist for corrective glasses.

Test

Word List 4   *Synonyms and Antonyms*

Each of the following questions consists of a word in capital letters, followed by five lettered words or phrases. Choose the lettered word or phrase which is most nearly similar or the opposite of the word in capital letters and write the letter of your choice on your answer paper.

46. APPEASE (A) agitate (B) qualify (C) display (D) predestine (E) interrupt
47. APPOSITE (A) inappropriate (B) diagonal (C) exponential (D) unobtrusive (E) discouraging
48. APPREHEND (A) obviate (B) set free (C) shiver (D) understand (E) contrast
49. APTITUDE (A) sarcasm (B) inversion (C) adulation (D) lack of talent (E) gluttony
50. AQUILINE (A) watery (B) hooked (C) refined (D) antique (E) rodentlike
51. ARCHAIC (A) youthful (B) cautious (C) antiquated (D) placated (E) buttressed
52. ARDOR (A) zeal (B) paint (C) proof (D) group (E) excitement
53. ARROGATE (A) swindle (B) balance (C) claim (D) perjure (E) effect
54. ARROYO (A) crevice (B) gully (C) value (D) food (E) fabric
55. ARTIFICE (A) spite (B) exception (C) anger (D) candor (E) loyalty
56. ARTISAN (A) educator (B) decider (C) sculptor (D) discourser (E) unskilled laborer
57. ASCERTAIN (A) amplify (B) master (C) discover (D) retain (E) explode
58. ASPERITY (A) anguish (B) absence (C) innuendo (D) good temper (E) snake
59. ASSUAGE (A) stuff (B) describe (C) wince (D) worsen (E) introduce
60. ASTEROID (A) Milky Way (B) radiance (C) large planet (D) rising moon (E) setting moon

Word List 5   astral-barb

astral ADJ. relating to the stars. She was amazed at the number of *astral* bodies the new telescope revealed.

astringent ADJ. binding; causing contraction. The *astringent* quality of the unsweetened lemon juice made swallowing difficult. also N.

astronomical ADJ. enormously large or extensive. The government seems willing to spend *astronomical* sums on weapons development.

astute ADJ. wise; shrewd. That was a very *astute* observation. I shall heed it.

asunder ADV. into parts; apart. Their points of view are poles *asunder*.

asylum N. place of refuge or shelter; protection. The refugees sought *asylum* from religious persecution in a new land.

atavism N. resemblance to remote ancestors rather than to parents; deformity returning after passage of two or more generations. The doctors ascribed the child's deformity to an *atavism*.

atelier N. workshop; studio. Stories of Bohemian life in Paris are full of tales of artists' starving or freezing in their *ateliers*.

atheistic ADJ. denying the existence of God. His *atheistic* remarks shocked the religious worshippers.

athwart PREP. across; in opposition. His tendency toward violence was *athwart* the philosophy of the peace movement. also ADV.

atone V. make amends for; pay for. He knew no way in which he could *atone* for his brutal crime.

atrocity N. brutal deed. In time of war, many *atrocities* are committed by invading armies.

atrophy N. wasting away. Polio victims need physiotherapy to prevent the *atrophy* of affected limbs. also V.

■ **attenuate** V. make thin; weaken. By withdrawing their forces, the generals hoped to *attenuate* the enemy lines.

attest V. testify, bear witness. Having served as a member of the Grand Jury, I can *attest* that our system of indicting individuals is in need of improvement.

attribute N. essential quality. His outstanding *attribute* was his kindness.

attribute V. ascribe; explain. I *attribute* her success in science to the encouragement she received from her parents.

attrition N. gradual wearing down. They decided to wage a war of *attrition* rather than to rely on an all-out attack.

atypical ADJ. not normal. You have taken an *atypical* case. It does not prove anything.

■ **audacious** ADJ. daring; bold. Audiences cheered as Luke Skywalker and Princess Leia made their *audacious,* death-defying leap to freedom and escaped Darth Vader's troops. audacity, N.

audit N. examination of accounts. When the bank examiners arrived to hold their annual *audit,* they discovered the embezzlements of the chief cashier. also V.

■ **augment** V. increase. How can we hope to *augment* our forces when our allies are deserting us?

augury N. omen; prophecy. He interpreted the departure of the birds as an *augury* of evil. augur, V.

august ADJ. impressive; majestic. Visiting the palace at Versailles, she was impressed by the *august* surroundings in which she found herself.

aureole N. sun's corona; halo. Many medieval paintings depict saintly characters with *aureoles* around their heads.

auroral ADJ. pertaining to the aurora borealis. The *auroral* display was particularly spectacular that evening.

auscultation N. act of listening to the heart or lungs to discover abnormalities. The science of *auscultation* was enhanced with the development of the stethoscope.

■ **auspicious** ADJ. favoring success. With favorable weather conditions, it was an *auspicious* moment to set sail.

■ **austere** ADJ. strict, stern. His *austere* demeanor prevented us from engaging in our usual frivolous activities.

austerity N. sternness; severity; lack of luxuries. The *austerity* and dignity of the court were maintained by the new justices, who were a strict and solemn group.

authenticate V. prove genuine. An expert was needed to *authenticate* the original Van Gogh painting, distinguishing it from its imitation.

authoritarian ADJ. favoring or exercising total control; non-democratic. The people had no control over their own destiny; they were forced to obey the dictates of the *authoritarian* regime. also N.

authoritative ADJ. having the weight of authority; dictatorial. We accepted her analysis of the situation as *authoritative.*

autocrat N. monarch with supreme power. He ran his office like an *autocrat,* giving no one else any authority. autocracy, N.

automaton N. mechanism which imitates actions of humans. Long before science fiction readers became aware of robots, writers were presenting stories of *automatons* who could outperform men.

■ **autonomous** ADJ. self-governing. This island is a colony; however, in most matters, it is *autonomous* and receives no orders from the mother country. autonomy, N.

autopsy N. examination of a dead body; post-mortem. The medical examiner ordered an *autopsy* to determine the cause of death. also V.

auxiliary ADJ. helper, additional or subsidiary. To prepare for the emergency, they built an *auxiliary* power station. also N.

avarice N. greediness for wealth. King Midas's *avarice* has been famous for centuries. avaricious, ADJ.

avatar N. incarnation. In Hindu mythology, the *avatar* of Vishnu is thoroughly detailed.

■ **aver** V. state confidently. I wish to *aver* that I am certain of success.

averse ADJ. reluctant. He was *averse* to revealing the sources of his information.

aversion N. firm dislike. Their mutual *aversion* was so great that they refused to speak to one another.

avert V. prevent; turn away. She *averted* her eyes from the dead cat on the highway.

■ **aviary** N. enclosure for birds. The *aviary* at the zoo held nearly 300 birds.

avid ADJ. greedy; eager for. He was *avid* for learning and read everything he could get. avidity, N.

avocation N. secondary or minor occupation. His hobby proved to be so fascinating and profitable that gradually he abandoned his regular occupation and concentrated on his *avocation.*

avow V. declare openly. I must *avow* that I am innocent.

avuncular ADJ. like an uncle. *Avuncular* pride did not prevent him from noticing his nephew's shortcomings.

awe N. solemn wonder. The tourists gazed with *awe* at the tremendous expanse of the Grand Canyon.

awry ADV. distorted; crooked. He held his head *awry,* giving the impression that he had caught cold in his neck during the night. also ADJ.

axiom N. self-evident truth requiring no proof. Before a student can begin to think along the lines of Euclidean geometry, he must accept certain principles or *axioms.*

azure ADJ. sky blue. *Azure* skies are indicative of good weather.

babble V. chatter idly. The little girl *babbled* about her doll. also N.

bacchanalian ADJ. drunken. Emperor Nero attended the *bacchanalian* orgy.

badger V. pester; annoy. She was forced to change her telephone number because she was *badgered* by obscene phone calls.

badinage N. teasing conversation. Her friends at work greeted the news of her engagement with cheerful *badinage.*

baffle V. frustrate; perplex. The new code *baffled* the enemy agents.

bagatelle N. trifle. Trying to reassure Roxanne about his wound, Cyrano claimed it was a mere *bagatelle.*

baleful ADJ. deadly; destructive. The drought was a *baleful* omen.

bait V. harass; tease. The soldiers *baited* the prisoners, terrorizing them.

balk V. foil. When the warden learned that several inmates were planning to escape, he took steps to *balk* their attempt.

■ **ballast** N. heavy substance used to add stability or weight. The ship was listing badly to one side; it was necessary to shift the *ballast* in the hold to get her back on an even keel. also V.

balm N. something that relieves pain. Friendship is the finest *balm* for the pangs of disappointed love.

balmy ADJ. mild; fragrant. A *balmy* breeze refreshed us after the sultry blast.

■ **banal** ADJ. hackneyed; commonplace; trite. His frequent use of clichés made his essay seem *banal.* banality, N.

bandanna N. large, bright-colored handkerchief. She could be identified by the gaudy *bandanna* she wore as a head covering.

bandy V. discuss lightly; exchange blows or words. The President refused to *bandy* words with the reporters at the press conference.

■ **bane** N. cause of ruin. Lack of public transportation is the *bane* of urban life.

baneful ADJ. ruinous; poisonous. His *baneful* influence was feared by all.

bantering ADJ. good-natured ridiculing. They resented his *bantering* remarks because they thought he was being sarcastic.

barb N. sharp projection from fishhook, etc. The *barb* from the fishhook caught in his finger as he grabbed the fish. barbed, ADJ.

Test

Word List 5   *Synonyms*

Each of the questions below consists of a word in capital letters, followed by five lettered words or phrases. Choose the lettered word or phrase that is most nearly similar in meaning to the word in capital letters and write the letter of your choice on your answer paper.

61. ASTUTE (A) sheer (B) noisy (C) astral (D) unusual (E) clever
62. ATROCITY (A) endurance (B) fortitude (C) session (D) heinous act (E) hatred
63. ATROPHY (A) capture (B) waste away (C) govern (D) award prize (E) defeat
64. ATTENUATE (A) appear (B) be absent (C) weaken (D) testify (E) soothe
65. ATYPICAL (A) superfluous (B) fortitude (C) unusual (D) clashing (E) lovely
66. AUDACITY (A) boldness (B) asperity (C) strength (D) stature (E) anchorage
67. AUGMENT (A) make noble (B) anoint (C) increase (D) harvest (E) reach
68. AUXILIARY (A) righteous (B) prospective (C) assistant (D) archaic (E) mandatory
69. AVARICE (A) easiness (B) greed (C) statement (D) invoice (E) power
70. AVATAR (A) hedge (B) hypnosis (C) incarnation (D) perfume (E) disaster
71. AWRY (A) recommended (B) commiserating (C) startled (D) crooked (E) psychological
72. BALEFUL (A) doubtful (B) virtual (C) deadly (D) conventional (E) virtuous
73. BALMY (A) venturesome (B) dedicated (C) mild (D) fanatic (E) memorable
74. BANAL (A) philosophical (B) trite (C) dramatic (D) heedless (E) discussed
75. BANEFUL (A) intellectual (B) thankful (C) decisive (D) poisonous (E) remorseful

Word List 6   bard-bludgeon

bard N. poet. The ancient *bard* Homer sang of the fall of Troy.

baroque ADJ. highly ornate. They found the *baroque* architecture amusing.

barrage N. barrier laid down by artillery fire. The company was forced to retreat through the *barrage* of heavy cannons.

barrister N. counselor-at-law. Galsworthy started as a *barrister,* but, when he found the practice of law boring, turned to writing.

barterer N. trader. The *barterer* exchanged trinkets for the natives' furs.

bask V. luxuriate; take pleasure in warmth. *Basking* on the beach, she relaxed so completely that she fell asleep.

bassoon N. reed instrument of the woodwind family. In the orchestra, the *bassoon* is related to the oboe and the clarinet.

bastion N. fortress; defense. Once a *bastion* of democracy, under its new government the island became a dictatorship.

bate V. let down; restrain. Until it was time to open the presents, the children had to *bate* their curiosity. bated, ADJ.

bauble N. trinket; trifle. The child was delighted with the *bauble* she had won in the grab bag.

bawdy ADJ. indecent; obscene. She took offense at his *bawdy* remarks.

beatific ADJ. giving bliss; blissful. The *beatific* smile on the child's face made us very happy.

beatitude N. blessedness; state of bliss. Growing closer to God each day, the mystic achieved a state of indescribable *beatitude*.

bedizen V. dress with vulgar finery. The witch doctors were *bedizened* in all their gaudiest costumes.

bedraggle V. wet thoroughly. We were so *bedraggled* by the severe storm that we had to change into dry clothing. bedraggled, ADJ.

befuddle V. confuse thoroughly. His attempts to clarify the situation succeeded only in *befuddling* her further.

begrudge V. resent. I *begrudge* every minute I have to spend attending meetings.

beguile V. amuse; delude; cheat. He *beguiled* himself during the long hours by playing solitaire.

behemoth N. huge creature; monstrous animal. Sportscasters nicknamed the linebacker "The *Behemoth.*"

beholden ADJ. obligated; indebted. Since I do not wish to be *beholden* to anyone, I cannot accept this favor.

behoove V. suited to; incumbent upon. In this time of crisis, it *behooves* all of us to remain calm and await the instructions of our superiors.

belabor V. beat soundly; assail verbally. He was *belaboring* his opponent during the debate.

belated ADJ. delayed. He apologized for his *belated* note of condolence to the widow of his friend and explained that he had just learned of her husband's untimely death.

beleaguer V. besiege. As soon as the city was *beleaguered,* life became more subdued as the citizens began their long wait for outside assistance. beleaguered, ADJ.

■ **belie** V. contradict; give a false impression. His coarse, hard-bitten exterior *belied* his innate sensitivity.

belittle V. disparage; depreciate. Although I do not wish to *belittle* your contribution, I feel we must place it in its proper perspective.

bellicose ADJ. warlike. His *bellicose* disposition alienated his friends.

belligerent ADJ. quarrelsome. Whenever he had too much to drink, he became *belligerent* and tried to pick fights with strangers.

benediction N. blessing. The appearance of the sun after the many rainy days was like a *benediction*.

benefactor N. gift giver; patron. Scrooge later became Tiny Tim's *benefactor* and gave him gifts.

beneficiary N. person entitled to benefits or proceeds of an insurance policy or will. You may change your *beneficiary* as often as you wish.

benevolent ADJ. generous; charitable. His *benevolent* nature prevented him from refusing any beggar who accosted him. benevolence, N.

benighted ADJ. overcome by darkness. In the *benighted* Middle Ages, intellectual curiosity was discouraged by the authorities.

benign ADJ. kindly; favorable; not malignant. The old man was well liked because of his *benign* attitude toward friend and stranger alike.

benignity N. state of being kind, benign, gracious. We have endowed our Creator with a *benignity* which permits forgiveness of our sins and transgressions.

benison N. blessing. Let us pray that the *benison* of peace once more shall prevail among the nations of the world.

berate V. scold strongly. He feared she would *berate* him for his forgetfulness.

bereavement N. state of being deprived of something valuable or beloved. His friends gathered to console him upon his sudden *bereavement*.

bereft ADJ. deprived of; lacking. The foolish gambler soon found himself *bereft* of funds.

berserk ADV. frenzied. Angered, he went *berserk* and began to wreck the room.

beset V. harass; trouble. Many problems *beset* the American public school system.

besmirch V. soil, defile. The scandalous remarks in the newspaper *besmirch* the reputations of every member of the society.

bestial ADJ. beastlike; brutal. We must suppress our *bestial* desires and work for peaceful and civilized ends.

bestow V. confer. He wished to *bestow* great honors upon the hero.

bête noire N. aversion; person or thing strongly disliked or avoided. Going to the opera was his personal *bête noire* because high-pitched sounds irritated him.

betroth V. become engaged to marry. The announcement that they had become *betrothed* surprised their friends who had not suspected any romance. betrothal, N.

bevy N. large group. The movie actor was surrounded by a *bevy* of starlets.

bicameral ADJ. two-chambered, as a legislative body. The United States Congress is a *bicameral* body.

bibulous ADJ. inclined to drink; affected by alcohol. We could not help laughing at his *bibulous* farewells.

bicker V. quarrel. The children *bickered* morning, noon, and night, exasperating their parents.

biennial ADJ. every two years. The group held *biennial* meetings instead of annual ones.

bifurcated ADJ. divided into two branches; forked. With a *bifurcated* branch and a piece of elastic rubber, he made a crude but effective slingshot.

bigotry N. stubborn intolerance. Brought up in a democratic atmosphere, the student was shocked by the *bigotry* and narrowness expressed by several of his classmates.

bilious ADJ. suffering from indigestion; irritable. His *bilious* temperament was apparent to all who heard him rant about his difficulties.

bilk V. swindle; cheat. The con man specialized in *bilking* insurance companies.

bivouac N. temporary encampment. While in *bivouac,* we spent the night in our sleeping bags under the stars. also V.

bizarre ADJ. fantastic; violently contrasting. The plot of the novel was too *bizarre* to be believed.

blanch V. bleach; whiten. Although age had *blanched* his hair, he was still vigorous and energetic.

bland ADJ. soothing; mild. She used a *bland* ointment for her sunburn. blandness, N.

blandishment N. flattery. Despite the salesperson's *blandishments,* the customer did not buy the outfit.

blasé ADJ. bored with pleasure or dissipation. Your *blasé* attitude gives your students an erroneous impression of the joys of scholarship.

blasphemous ADJ. profane; impious. The people in the room were shocked by his *blasphemous* language.

blatant ADJ. loudly offensive. I regard your remarks as *blatant* and ill-mannered. blatancy, N.

blazon V. decorate with an heraldic coat of arms. *Blazoned* on his shield were the two lambs and the lion, the traditional coat of arms of his family. also N.

bleak ADJ. cold; cheerless. The Aleutian Islands are *bleak* military outposts.

blighted ADJ. suffering from a disease; destroyed. The extent of the *blighted* areas could be seen only when viewed from the air.

blithe ADJ. gay; joyous. Shelley called the skylark a "*blithe* spirit" because of its happy song.

bloated ADJ. swollen or puffed as with water or air. Her *bloated* stomach came from drinking so much water.

bludgeon N. club; heavy-headed weapon. His walking stick served him as a *bludgeon* on many occasions. also V.

Test

Word List 6 *Antonyms*

Each of the questions below consists of a word in capital letters, followed by five lettered words or phrases. Choose the lettered word or phrase that is most nearly opposite in meaning to the word in capital letters and write the letter of your choice on your answer paper.

76. BAROQUE (A) polished (B) constant (C) transformed (D) simple (E) aglow
77. BEATIFIC (A) glorious (B) dreadful (C) theatrical (D) crooked (E) handsome
78. BELITTLE (A) disobey (B) forget (C) magnify (D) extol (E) envy
79. BELLICOSE (A) peaceful (B) navel (C) amusing (D) piecemeal (E) errant
80. BENIGN (A) tenfold (B) peaceful (C) blessed (D) wavering (E) malignant
81. BENISON (A) curse (B) bachelor (C) wedding (D) orgy (E) tragedy

82. BERATE (A) grant (B) praise (C) refer (D) purchase (E) deny
83. BESTIAL (A) animated (B) noble (C) zoological (D) clear (E) dusky
84. BIGOTRY (A) arrogance (B) approval (C) mourning (D) promptness (E) tolerance
85. BIZARRE (A) roomy (B) veiled (C) subdued (D) triumphant (E) outspoken
86. BLANCH (A) bleach (B) scatter (C) darken (D) analyze (E) subdivide
87. BLAND (A) caustic (B) meager (C) soft (D) uncooked (E) helpless
88. BLASÉ (A) fiery (B) clever (C) intriguing (D) slim (E) ardent
89. BLEAK (A) pale (B) sudden (C) dry (D) narrow (E) cheerful
90. BLITHE (A) spiritual (B) profuse (C) cheerless (D) hybrid (E) comfortable

Word List 7 blunder-canter

blunder N. error. The criminal's fatal *blunder* led to his capture. also V.

blurt V. utter impulsively. Before she could stop him, he *blurted* out the news.

bode V. foreshadow; portend. The gloomy skies and the sulphurous odors from the mineral springs seemed to *bode* evil to those who settled in the area.

bogus ADJ. counterfeit; not authentic. The police quickly found the distributors of the *bogus* twenty-dollar bills.

boisterous ADJ. violent; rough; noisy. The unruly crowd became even more *boisterous* when he tried to quiet them.

bolster V. support; prop up. I do not intend to *bolster* your

hopes with false reports of outside assistance; the truth is that we must face the enemy alone. also N.

bombastic ADJ. pompous; using inflated language. The orator's *bombastic* manner left the audience unimpressed. bombast, N.

boorish ADJ. rude; clownish. Your *boorish* remarks to the driver of the other car were not warranted by the situation and served merely to enrage him.

bouillon N. clear beef soup. The cup of *bouillon* served by the stewards was welcomed by those who had been chilled by the cold ocean breezes.

bountiful ADJ. generous; showing bounty. She distributed gifts in a *bountiful* and gracious manner.

bourgeois N. middle class. The French Revolution was inspired by the *bourgeois*, who resented the aristocracy. also ADJ.

bowdlerize V. expurgate. After the film editors had *bowdlerized* the language in the script, the motion picture's rating was changed from "R" to "PG."

brackish ADJ. somewhat saline. He found the only wells in the area were *brackish;* drinking the water made him nauseated.

braggadocio N. boasting. He was disliked because his manner was always full of *braggadocio*.

braggart N. boaster. Modest by nature, she was no *braggart*, preferring to let her accomplishments speak for themselves.

bravado N. swagger; assumed air of defiance. The *bravado* of the young criminal disappeared when he was confronted by the victims of his brutal attack.

brazen ADJ. insolent. Her *brazen* contempt for authority angered the officials.

brazier N. open pan in which live coals are burned. On chilly nights, the room was warmed by coals burning in *braziers* set in the corners of the room.

breach N. breaking of contract or duty; fissure; gap. They found a *breach* in the enemy's fortifications and penetrated their lines. also V.

breadth N. width; extent. We were impressed by the *breadth* of her knowledge.

brevity N. conciseness. *Brevity* is essential when you send a telegram or cablegram; you are charged for every word.

brindled ADJ. tawny or grayish with streaks or spots. He was disappointed in the litter because the puppies were *brindled;* he had hoped for animals of a uniform color.

bristling ADJ. rising like bristles; showing irritation. The dog stood there, *bristling* with anger.

brittle ADJ. easily broken; difficult. My employer's *brittle* personality made it difficult for me to get along with her.

broach V. open up. He did not even try to *broach* the subject of poetry.

brocade N. rich, figured fabric. The sofa was covered with expensive *brocade*.

brochure N. pamphlet. This *brochure* on farming was issued by the Department of Agriculture.

brooch N. ornamental clasp. She treasured the *brooch* because it was an heirloom.

■ **brook** V. tolerate; endure. The dean would *brook* no interference with his disciplinary actions. (secondary meaning)

brusque ADJ. blunt; abrupt. She was offended by his *brusque* reply.

bucolic ADJ. rustic; pastoral. The meadow was the scene of *bucolic* gaiety.

buffoonery N. clowning. Jimmy Durante's *buffoonery* was hilarious.

bugaboo N. bugbear; object of baseless terror. If we become frightened by such *bugaboos,* we are no wiser than the birds who fear scarecrows.

bullion N. gold and silver in the form of bars. Much *bullion* is stored in the vaults at Fort Knox.

bulwark N. earthwork or other strong defense; person who defends. The navy is our principal *bulwark* against invasion.

bumptious ADJ. self-assertive. His classmates called him a show-off because of his *bumptious* airs.

bungle V. spoil by clumsy behavior. I was afraid you would *bungle* this assignment but I had no one else to send.

bureaucracy N. government by bureaus. Many people fear that the constant introduction of federal agencies will create a government by *bureaucracy*.

■ **burgeon** V. grow forth; send out buds. In the spring, the plants that *burgeon* are a promise of the beauty that is to come.

burlesque V. give an imitation that ridicules. In his caricature, he *burlesqued* the mannerisms of his adversary. also N.

burly ADJ. husky; muscular. The *burly* mover lifted the packing crate with ease.

■ **burnish** V. make shiny by rubbing; polish. The *burnished* metal reflected the lamplight.

buskin N. thick-soled half boot worn by actors of Greek tragedy. Wearing the *buskin* gave the Athenian tragic actor a larger-than-life appearance and enhanced the intensity of the play.

■ **buttress** N. support or prop. The huge cathedral walls were supported by flying *buttresses*. also V.

buxom ADJ. plump; vigorous; jolly. The soldiers remembered the *buxom* nurse who had always been so pleasant to them.

cabal N. small group of persons secretly united to promote their own interests. The *cabal* was defeated when their scheme was discovered.

cache N. hiding place. The detectives followed the suspect until he led them to the *cache* where he had stored his loot. also V.

■ **cacophony** N. discord. Some people seem to enjoy the *cacophony* of an orchestra that is tuning up. cacophonous, ADJ.

cadaver N. corpse. In some states, it is illegal to dissect *cadavers*.

cadaverous ADJ. like a corpse; pale. By his *cadaverous* appearance, we could see how the disease had ravaged him.

■ **cajole** V. coax; wheedle. I will not be *cajoled* into granting you your wish. cajolery, N.

calamity N. disaster; misery. As news of the *calamity* spread, offers of relief poured in to the stricken community.

caliber N. ability; capacity. A man of such *caliber* should not be assigned such menial tasks.

calligraphy N. beautiful writing; excellent penmanship. As we examine ancient manuscripts, we become impressed with the *calligraphy* of the scribes.

callous ADJ. hardened; unfeeling. He had worked in the hospital for so many years that he was *callous* to the suffering in the wards. callus, N.

callow ADJ. youthful; immature. In that youthful movement, the leaders were only a little less *callow* than their immature followers.

calorific ADJ. heat-producing. Coal is much more *calorific* than green wood.

calumniate V. slander. Shakespeare wrote that love and friendship were subject to envious and *calumniating* time.

calumny N. malicious misrepresentation; slander. He could endure his financial failure, but he could not bear the *calumny* that his foes heaped upon him.

camaraderie N. good-fellowship. What he loved best about his job was the sense of *camaraderie* he and his co-workers shared.

cameo N. shell or jewel carved in relief. Tourists are advised not to purchase *cameos* from the street peddlers of Rome who sell poor specimens of the carver's art.

canard N. unfounded rumor; exaggerated report. It is almost impossible to protect oneself from such a base *canard*.

candor N. frankness. The *candor* and simplicity of his speech impressed all; it was clear he held nothing back. candid, ADJ.

canine ADJ. related to dogs; dog-like. Some days the *canine* population of Berkeley seems almost to outnumber the human population.

canker N. any ulcerous sore; any evil. Poverty is a *canker* in the body politic; it must be cured.

canny ADJ. shrewd; thrifty. The *canny* Scotsman was more than a match for the swindlers.

cant N. jargon of thieves; pious phraseology. Many listeners were fooled by the *cant* and hypocrisy of his speech.

cantankerous ADJ. ill humored; irritable. Constantly complaining about his treatment and refusing to cooperate with the hospital staff, he was a *cantankerous* patient.

cantata N. story set to music, to be sung by a chorus. The choral society sang the new *cantata* composed by its leader.

canter N. slow gallop. Because the racehorse had outdistanced its competition so easily, the reporter wrote that the race was won in a *canter*. also V.

Test

Word List 7   *Synonyms*

Each of the questions below consists of a word in capital letters, followed by five lettered words or phrases. Choose the lettered word or phrase that is most nearly similar in meaning to the word in capital letters and write the letter of your choice on your answer paper.

91. BOISTEROUS (A) conflicting (B) noisy (C) testimonial (D) grateful (E) adolescent
92. BOMBASTIC (A) sensitive (B) pompous (C) rapid (D) sufficient (E) expensive
93. BOORISH (A) brave (B) oafish (C) romantic (D) speedy (E) dry
94. BOUILLON (A) insight (B) chowder (C) gold (D) clear soup (E) stew
95. BRACKISH (A) careful (B) salty (C) chosen (D) tough (E) wet
96. BRAGGADOCIO (A) weaponry (B) boasting (C) skirmish (D) encounter (E) position
97. BRAZEN (A) shameless (B) quick (C) modest (D) pleasant (E) melodramatic
98. BRINDLED (A) equine (B) pathetic (C) hasty (D) spotted (E) mild tasting
99. BROCHURE (A) opening (B) pamphlet (C) censor (D) bureau (E) pin
100. BUCOLIC (A) diseased (B) repulsive (C) rustic (D) twinkling (E) cold
101. BUXOM (A) voluminous (B) indecisive (C) convincing (D) plump (E) bookish
102. CACHE (A) lock (B) hiding place (C) tide (D) automobile (E) grappling hook
103. CACOPHONY (A) discord (B) dance (C) applause (D) type of telephone (E) rooster
104. CALLOW (A) youthful (B) holy (C) mild (D) colored (E) seated
105. CANDID (A) vague (B) outspoken (C) experienced (D) anxious (E) sallow

Word List 8   canto-champ

canto N. division of a long poem. Dante's poetic masterpiece *The Divine Comedy* is divided into *cantos*.

canvass V. determine votes, etc. After *canvassing* the sentiments of his constituents, the congressman was confident that he represented the majority opinion of his district. also N.

capacious ADJ. spacious. In the *capacious* areas of the railroad terminal, thousands of travelers lingered while waiting for their train.

caparison N, V. showy harness or ornamentation for a horse; put showy ornamentation on a horse. The audience admired the *caparison* of the horses as they made their entrance into the circus ring.

capillary ADJ. having a very fine bore. The changes in surface tension of liquids in *capillary* vessels is of special interest to physicists. also N.

capitulate V. surrender. The enemy was warned to *capitulate* or face annihilation.

caprice N. whim. Do not act on *caprice*. Study your problem.

■ **capricious** ADJ. fickle; incalculable. The storm was *capricious* and changed course constantly.

caption N. title; chapter heading; text under illustration. I find the *captions* which accompany these cartoons very clever and humorous. also V.

captious ADJ. faultfinding. His criticisms were always *captious* and frivolous, never offering constructive suggestions.

carafe N. glass water bottle; decanter. With each dinner, the patron receives a *carafe* of red or white wine.

carat N. unit of weight for precious stones; measure of fineness of gold. He gave her a three-*carat* diamond mounted in an eighteen-*carat* gold band.

carcinogenic ADJ. causing cancer. Many supposedly harmless substances have been revealed to be *carcinogenic*.

cardinal ADJ. chief. If you want to increase your word power, the *cardinal* rule of vocabulary-building is to read.

careen V. lurch; sway from side to side. The taxicab *careened* wildly as it rounded the corner.

caricature N. distortion; burlesque. The *caricatures* he drew always emphasized a personal weakness of the people he burlesqued. also V.

carillon N. a set of bells capable of being played. The *carillon* in the bell tower of the Coca-Cola pavilion at the New York World's Fair provided musical entertainment every hour.

carmine N. rich red. *Carmine* in her lipstick made her lips appear black in the photographs.

carnage N. destruction of life. The *carnage* that can be caused by atomic warfare adds to the responsibilities of our statesmen.

carnal ADJ. fleshly. The public was more interested in *carnal* pleasures than in spiritual matters.

carnivorous ADJ. meat-eating. The lion is a *carnivorous* animal. carnivore, N.

carousal N. drunken revel. The party degenerated into an ugly *carousal*.

■ **carping** ADJ. finding fault. A *carping* critic disturbs sensitive people. carp, V.

carrion N. rotting flesh of a dead body. Buzzards are nature's scavengers; they eat the *carrion* left behind by other predators.

carte blanche N. unlimited authority or freedom. Use your own discretion in this matter; I give you *carte blanche*.

cartographer N. map-maker. Though not a professional *cartographer*, Tolkien was able to construct a map of his fictional world.

caryatid N. sculptured column of a female figure. The *caryatids* supporting the entablature reminded the onlooker of the columns he had seen in the Acropolis at Athens.

cascade N. small waterfall. We could not appreciate the beauty of the many *cascades* as we made detours around each of them to avoid getting wet. also V.

caste N. one of the hereditary classes in Hindu society. The differences created by *caste* in India must be wiped out if true democracy is to prevail in that country.

■ **castigation** N. punishment; severe criticism. Sensitive even to mild criticism, Woolf could not bear the *castigation* which she found in certain reviews. castigate, V.

casualty N. serious or fatal accident. The number of automotive *casualties* on this holiday weekend was high.

casuistry N. subtle or sophisticated reasoning resulting in minute distinctions. You are using *casuistry* to justify your obvious violation of decent behavior.

cataclysm N. deluge; upheaval. A *cataclysm* such as the French Revolution affects all countries. cataclysmic, ADJ.

catalyst N. agent which brings about a chemical change while it remains unaffected and unchanged. Many chemical reactions cannot take place without the presence of a *catalyst*.

catapult N. slingshot; a hurling machine. Airplanes are sometimes launched from battleships by *catapults*. also V.

cataract N. great waterfall; eye abnormality. She gazed with awe at the mighty *cataract* known as Niagara Falls.

catastrophe N. calamity. The Johnstown flood was a *catastrophe*.

catechism N. book for religious instruction; instruction by question and answer. He taught by engaging his pupils in a *catechism* until they gave him the correct answer.

catharsis N. purging or cleansing of any passage of the body. Aristotle maintained that tragedy created a *catharsis* by purging the soul of base concepts.

cathartic N. purgative. Some drugs act as laxatives when taken in small doses but act as *cathartics* when taken in much larger doses.

catholic ADJ. broadly sympathetic; liberal. He was extremely *catholic* in his taste and read everything he could find in the library.

caucus N. private meeting of members of a party to select officers or determine policy. At the opening of Congress, the members of the Democratic Party held a *caucus* to elect the Majority Leader of the House and the Party Whip.

caustic ADJ. burning; sarcastically biting. The critic's *caustic* remarks angered the hapless actors who were the subjects of his sarcasm.

cauterize V. burn with hot iron or caustic. In order to prevent infection, the doctor *cauterized* the wound.

cavalcade N. procession; parade. As described by Chaucer, the *cavalcade* of Canterbury pilgrims was a motley group.

cavil V. make frivolous objections. I respect your sensible criticisms, but I dislike the way you *cavil* about unimportant details. also N.

cede V. transfer; yield title to. I intend to *cede* this property to the city.

celerity N. speed; rapidity. Hamlet resented his mother's *celerity* in remarrying within a month after his father's death.

celestial ADJ. heavenly. She spoke of the *celestial* joys that awaited virtuous souls in the hereafter.

celibate ADJ. unmarried; abstaining from sexual intercourse. The perennial bachelor vowed to remain *celibate*. celibacy, N.

censor N. overseer of morals; person who reads to eliminate inappropriate remarks. Soldiers dislike having their mail read by a *censor* but understand the need for this precaution. also V.

censorious ADJ. critical. *Censorious* people delight in casting blame.

censure V. blame; criticize. He was *censured* for his inappropriate behavior. also N.

centaur N. mythical figure, half man and half horse. I was particularly impressed by the statue of the *centaur* in the Roman Hall of the museum.

centigrade ADJ. measure of temperature used widely in Europe. On the *centigrade* thermometer, the freezing point of water is zero degrees.

centrifugal ADJ. radiating; departing from the center. Many automatic drying machines remove excess moisture from clothing by *centrifugal* force.

■ **centrifuge** N. machine that separates substances by whirling them. At the dairy, we employ a *centrifuge* to separate cream from milk.

centripetal ADJ. tending toward the center. Does *centripetal* force or the force of gravity bring orbiting bodies to the earth's surface?

centurion N. Roman army officer. Because he was in command of a company of one hundred soldiers, he was called a *centurion*.

cerebral ADJ. pertaining to the brain or intellect. The content of philosophical works is *cerebral* in nature and requires much thought.

cerebration N. thought. Mathematics problems sometimes require much *cerebration*.

ceremonious ADJ. marked by formality. Ordinary dress would be inappropriate at so *ceremonious* an affair.

cessation N. stopping. The workers threatened a *cessation* of all activities if their demands were not met. cease, V.

cession N. yielding to another; ceding. The *cession* of Alaska to the United States is discussed in this chapter.

chafe V. warm by rubbing; make sore by rubbing. The collar *chafed* his neck. also N.

chaff N. worthless products of an endeavor. When you separate the wheat from the chaff, be sure you throw out the *chaff*.

chaffing ADJ. bantering; joking. Sometimes his flippant and *chaffing* remarks annoy us.

chagrin N. vexation; disappointment. Her refusal to go with us filled us with *chagrin*.

chalice N. goblet; consecrated cup. In a small room adjoining the cathedral, many ornately decorated *chalices* made by the most famous European goldsmiths were on display.

chameleon N. lizard that changes color in different situations. Like the *chameleon*, he assumed the political thinking of every group he met.

champ V. chew noisily. His dining companions were amused by the way he *champed* his food.

Test

Word List 8   *Antonyms*

Each of the questions below consists of a word in capital letters, followed by five lettered words or phrases. Choose the lettered word or phrase that is most nearly similar in meaning to the word in capital letters and write the letter of your choice on your answer paper.

106. CAPACIOUS (A) warlike (B) cordial (C) curious (D) not spacious (E) not capable

107. CAPRICIOUS (A) satisfied (B) insured (C) photographic (D) scattered (E) steadfast

108. CAPTIOUS (A) tolerant (B) capable (C) frivolous (D) winning (E) recollected

109. CARNAL (A) impressive (B) minute (C) spiritual (D) actual (E) private

110. CARNIVOROUS (A) gloomy (B) tangential (C) productive (D) weak (E) vegetarian

111. CAROUSAL (A) awakening (B) sobriety (C) acceleration (D) direction (E) production

112. CARPING (A) acquiescent (B) mean (C) limited (D) farming (E) racing

113. CARTE BLANCHE (A) capitalistic (B) investment (C) importance (D) restriction (E) current

114. CATHOLIC (A) religious (B) pacific (C) narrow (D) weighty (E) funny

115. CELERITY (A) assurance (B) state (C) acerbity (D) delay (E) infamy

116. CELIBATE (A) investing (B) married (C) retired (D) commodious (E) dubious

117. CENSURE (A) process (B) enclose (C) interest (D) praise (E) penetrate

118. CENTRIFUGAL (A) centripetal (B) ephemeral (C) lasting (D) barometric (E) algebraic

119. CESSATION (A) premium (B) gravity (C) beginning (D) composition (E) apathy

120. CHAFFING (A) achieving (B) serious (C) capitalistic (D) sneezing (E) expensive

Word List 9   champion-colander

champion V. support militantly. Martin Luther King, Jr., won the Nobel Peace Prize because he *championed* the oppressed in their struggle for equality.

chaotic ADJ. in utter disorder. He tried to bring order into the *chaotic* state of affairs. chaos, N.

charisma N. divine gift; great popular charm or appeal of a political leader. Political commentators have deplored the importance of a candidate's *charisma* in these days of television campaigning.

charlatan N. quack; pretender to knowledge. Because he was unable to substantiate his claim that he had found a cure for the dread disease, he was called a *charlatan* by his colleagues.

chary ADJ. cautiously watchful. She was *chary* of her favors because she had been hurt before.

chase V. ornament a metal surface by indenting. With his hammer, he carefully *chased* an intricate design onto the surface of the chalice. (secondary meaning)

chasm N. abyss. They could not see the bottom of the *chasm*.

chassis N. framework and working parts of an automobile. Examining the car after the accident, the owner discovered that the body had been ruined but that the *chassis* was unharmed.

chaste ADJ. pure. Her *chaste* and decorous garb was appropriately selected for the solemnity of the occasion. chastity, N.

chasten V. discipline; punish in order to correct. Whom God loves, God *chastens.*

chastise V. punish. I must *chastise* you for this offense.

chattel N. personal property. When he bought his furniture on the installment plan, he signed a *chattel* mortgage.

■ **chauvinist** N. blindly devoted patriot. A *chauvinist* cannot recognize any faults in his country, no matter how flagrant they may be. chauvinistic, ADJ.

checkered ADJ. marked by changes in fortune. During his *checkered* career he had lived in palatial mansions and in dreary boardinghouses.

cherubic ADJ. angelic; innocent-looking. With her cheerful smile and rosy cheeks, she was a particularly *cherubic* child.

chicanery N. trickery. Your deceitful tactics in this case are indications of *chicanery.*

chide V. scold. Grandma began to *chide* Steven for his lying.

chimerical ADJ. fantastic; highly imaginative. Poe's *chimerical* stories are sometimes too morbid for reading in bed. chimera, N.

chiropodist N. one who treats disorders of the feet. The *chiropodist* treated the ingrown nail on the boy's foot.

chivalrous ADJ. courteous; faithful; brave. *Chivalrous* behavior involves noble words and good deeds.

choleric ADJ. hot-tempered. His flushed, angry face indicated a *choleric* nature.

choreography N. art of dancing. Martha Graham introduced a form of *choreography* which seemed awkward and alien to those who had been brought up on classic ballet.

chronic ADJ. long established as a disease. The doctors were finally able to attribute his *chronic* headaches and nausea to traces of formaldehyde gas in his apartment.

churlish ADJ. boorish; rude. Dismayed by his *churlish* manners at the party, the girls vowed never to invite him again.

ciliated ADJ. having minute hairs. The paramecium is a *ciliated*, one-celled animal.

cipher N. nonentity; worthless person or thing. She claimed her ex-husband was a total *cipher* and wondered why she had ever married him.

circlet N. small ring; band. This tiny *circlet* is very costly because it is set with precious stones.

circuitous ADJ. roundabout. Because of the traffic congestion on the main highways, she took a *circuitous* route. circuit, N.

circumlocution N. indirect or roundabout expression. He was afraid to call a spade a spade and resorted to *circumlocutions* to avoid direct reference to his subject.

circumscribe V. limit; confine. Although I do not wish to *circumscribe* your activities, I must insist that you complete this assignment before you start anything else.

circumspect ADJ. prudent; cautious. Investigating before acting, she tried always to be *circumspect.*

circumvent V. outwit; baffle. In order to *circumvent* the enemy, we will make two preliminary attacks in other sections before starting our major campaign.

citadel N. fortress. The *citadel* overlooked the city like a protecting angel.

cite V. quote; commend. She could *cite* passages in the Bible from memory. citation, N.

clairvoyant ADJ., N. having foresight; fortuneteller. Cassandra's *clairvoyant* warning was not heeded by the Trojans. clairvoyance, N.

clamber V. climb by crawling. She *clambered* over the wall.

clamor N. noise. The *clamor* of the children at play outside made it impossible for her to take a nap. also V.

clandestine ADJ. secret. After avoiding their chaperon, the lovers had a *clandestine* meeting.

clangor N. loud, resounding noise. The blacksmith was accustomed to the *clangor* of hammers on steel.

clarion ADJ. shrill, trumpetlike sound. We woke to the *clarion* call of the bugle.

claustrophobia N. fear of being locked in. His fellow classmates laughed at his *claustrophobia* and often threatened to lock him in his room.

clavicle N. collarbone. Even though he wore shoulder pads, the football player broke his *clavicle* during a practice scrimmage.

cleave v. split asunder. The lightning *cleaves* the tree in two. cleavage, N.

cleft N. split. Erosion caused a *cleft* in the huge boulder. also ADJ.

clemency N. disposition to be lenient; mildness, as of the weather. The lawyer was pleased when the case was sent to Judge Smith's chambers because Smith was noted for her *clemency* toward first offenders.

cliché N. phrase dulled in meaning by repetition. High school compositions are often marred by such *clichés* as "strong as an ox."

clientele N. body of customers. The rock club attracted a young, stylish *clientele*.

climactic ADJ. relating to the highest point. When he reached the *climactic* portions of the book, he could not stop reading. climax, N.

clime N. region; climate. His doctor advised him to move to a milder *clime*.

clique N. small exclusive group. She charged that a *clique* had assumed control of school affairs.

cloister N. monastery or convent. The nuns lived in the *cloister*.

cloven ADJ. split. Popular legends maintain that the devil has *cloven* hooves.

coadjutor N. assistant; colleague. He was assigned as *coadjutor* of the bishop.

coalesce v. combine; fuse. The brooks *coalesce* into one large river.

cockade N. decoration worn on hat. Members of that brigade can be recognized by the green and white *cockade* in their helmets.

■ **coda** N. concluding section of a musical or literary composition. The piece concluded with a distinctive *coda* that strikingly brought together various motifs.

coddle v. to treat gently. Don't *coddle* the children so much; they need a taste of discipline.

codicil N. supplement to the body of a will. This *codicil* was drawn up five years after the writing of the original will.

coercion N. use of force. They forced him to obey, but only under great *coercion*. coerce, v.

coeval ADJ. living at the same time as; contemporary. *Coeval* with the dinosaur, the pterodactyl flourished during the Mesozoic era.

cog N. tooth projecting from a wheel. On steep slopes, *cog* railways are frequently used to prevent slipping.

cogent ADJ. convincing. She presented *cogent* arguments to the jury.

cogitate v. think over. *Cogitate* on this problem; the solution will come.

cognate ADJ. allied by blood; of the same or kindred nature. In the phrase "die a thousand deaths," the word "death" is a *cognate* object.

cognizance N. knowledge. During the election campaign, the two candidates were kept in full *cognizance* of the international situation.

cognomen N. family name. He asked the court to change his *cognomen* to a more American-sounding name.

cohere v. stick together. Solids have a greater tendency to *cohere* than liquids.

cohesion N. force which keeps parts together. In order to preserve our *cohesion*, we must not let minor differences interfere with our major purposes.

cohorts N. armed band. Caesar and his Roman *cohorts* conquered almost all of the known world.

coincident ADJ. occurring at the same time. Some people find the *coincident* events in Hardy's novels annoying.

colander N. utensil with perforated bottom used for straining. Before serving the spaghetti, place it in a *colander* to drain it.

Test

Word List 9 *Synonyms*

Each of the questions below consists of a word in capital letters, followed by five lettered words or phrases. Choose the lettered word or phrase that is most nearly similar in meaning to the word in capital letters and write the letter of your choice on your answer paper.

121. CHASTE (A) loyal (B) timid (C) curt (D) pure (E) outspoken
122. CHIDE (A) unite (B) fear (C) record (D) skid (E) scold
123. CHIMERICAL (A) developing (B) brief (C) distant (D) economical (E) fantastic
124. CHOLERIC (A) musical (B) episodic (C) hotheaded (D) global (E) seasonal
125. CHURLISH (A) marine (B) economical (C) impolite (D) compact (E) young
126. CILIATED (A) foolish (B) swift (C) early (D) constructed (E) hairy
127. CIRCUITOUS (A) indirect (B) complete (C) obvious (D) aware (E) tortured
128. CITE (A) galvanize (B) visualize (C) locate (D) quote (E) signal
129. CLANDESTINE (A) abortive (B) secret (C) tangible (D) doomed (E) approved
130. CLAUSTROPHOBIA (A) lack of confidence (B) fear of spiders (C) love of books (D) fear of grammar (E) fear of closed places
131. CLEFT (A) split (B) waterfall (C) assembly (D) parfait (E) surplus
132. CLICHÉ (A) increase (B) vehicle (C) morale (D) platitude (E) pique
133. COERCE (A) recover (B) total (C) force (D) license (E) ignore

134. COGNIZANCE (A) policy (B) knowledge (C) advance (D) omission (E) examination

135. COGNOMEN (A) family name (B) dwarf (C) suspicion (D) kind of railway (E) pseudopod

Word List 10   collaborate-congenital

collaborate v. work together. Two writers *collaborated* in preparing this book.

collage N. work of art put together from fragments. Scraps of cloth, paper doilies, and old photographs all went into her *collage*.

collate v. examine in order to verify authenticity; arrange in order. They *collated* the newly found manuscripts to determine their age.

collateral N. security given for loan. The sum you wish to borrow is so large that it must be secured by *collateral*.

collation N. a light meal. Tea sandwiches and cookies were offered at the *collation*.

collier N. worker in coal mine; ship carrying coal. The extended cold spell has prevented the *colliers* from delivering the coal to the docks as scheduled.

colloquial ADJ. pertaining to conversational or common speech. Your use of *colloquial* expressions in a formal essay such as the one you have presented spoils the effect you hope to achieve.

colloquy N. informal discussion. I enjoy our *colloquies*, but I sometimes wish that they could be made more formal and more searching.

■ **collusion** N. conspiring in a fraudulent scheme. The swindlers were found guilty of *collusion*.

colossal ADJ. huge. Radio City Music Hall has a *colossal* stage.

comatose ADJ. in a coma; extremely sleepy. The long-winded orator soon had his audience in a *comatose* state.

combustible ADJ. easily burned. After the recent outbreak of fires in private homes, the fire commissioner ordered that all *combustible* materials be kept in safe containers. also N.

comely ADJ. attractive; agreeable. I would rather have a poor and *comely* wife than a rich and homely one.

comestible N. something fit to be eaten. The roast turkey and other *comestibles*, the wines, and the excellent service made this Thanksgiving dinner particularly memorable.

comeuppance N. rebuke; deserts. After his earlier rudeness, we were delighted to see him get his *comeuppance*.

comity N. courtesy; civility. A spirit of *comity* should exist among nations.

commandeer v. to draft for military purposes; to take for public use. The policeman *commandeered* the first car that approached and ordered the driver to go to the nearest hospital.

commemorative ADJ. remembering; honoring. The new *commemorative* stamp honors the late Martin Luther King, Jr.

commensurate ADJ. equal in extent. Your reward will be *commensurate* with your effort.

commiserate v. feel or express pity or sympathy for. Her friends *commiserated* with the widow.

commodious ADJ. spacious and comfortable. After sleeping in small roadside cabins, they found their hotel suite *commodious*.

communal ADJ. held in common; of a group of people. When they were divorced, they had trouble dividing their *communal* property.

compact N. agreement; contract. The signers of the Mayflower *Compact* were establishing a form of government.

compact ADJ. tightly packed; firm; brief. His short, *compact* body was better suited to wrestling than to basketball.

compatible ADJ. harmonious; in harmony with. They were *compatible* neighbors, never quarreling over unimportant matters. compatibility, N.

■ **compendium** N. brief comprehensive summary. This text can serve as a *compendium* of the tremendous amount of new material being developed in this field.

compensatory ADJ. making up for; repaying. Can a *compensatory* education program make up for the inadequate schooling he received in earlier years?

compilation N. listing of statistical information in tabular or book form. The *compilation* of available scholarships serves a very valuable purpose.

complacent ADJ. self-satisfied. There was a *complacent* look on his face as he examined his paintings. complacency, N.

complaisant ADJ. trying to please; obliging. The courtier obeyed the king's orders in a *complaisant* manner.

complement N. that which completes. A predicate *complement* completes the meaning of the subject. also v.

compliance N. readiness to yield; conformity in fulfilling requirements. The design for the new school had to be in *compliance* with the local building code.

compliant ADJ. yielding. He was *compliant* and ready to conform to the pattern set by his friends.

complicity N. participation; involvement. You cannot keep your *complicity* in this affair secret very long; you would be wise to admit your involvement immediately.

component N. element; ingredient. I wish all the *components* of my stereo system were working at the same time.

comport v. bear one's self; behave. He *comported* himself with great dignity.

composure N. mental calmness. Even the latest work crisis failed to shake her *composure*.

comprehensive ADJ. thorough; inclusive. This book provides a *comprehensive* review of verbal and math skills for the SAT.

compress v. close; squeeze; contract. She *compressed* the package under her arm.

compromise v. adjust; endanger the interests or reputation of. Your presence at the scene of the dispute *compromises* our claim to neutrality in this matter. also N.

compunction N. remorse. The judge was especially severe in his sentencing because he felt that the criminal had shown no *compunction* for his heinous crime.

compute v. reckon; calculate. He failed to *compute* the interest, so his bank balance was not accurate.

concatenate v. link as in a chain. It is difficult to understand how these events could *concatenate* as they did without outside assistance.

concave ADJ. hollow. The back-packers found partial shelter from the storm by huddling against the *concave* wall of the cliff.

conceit N. whimsical idea; extravagant metaphor. He was an entertaining companion, always expressing himself in amusing *conceits* and witty turns of phrase.

concentric ADJ. having a common center. The target was made of *concentric* circles.

conception N. beginning; forming of an idea. At the first *conception* of the work, he was consulted. conceive, v.

concession N. an act of yielding. Before they could reach an agreement, both sides had to make certain *concessions.*

conch N. large seashell. In this painting we see a Triton blowing on his *conch.*

■ conciliatory ADJ. reconciling; soothing. She was still angry despite his *conciliatory* words. conciliate, v.

concise ADJ. brief and compact. The essay was *concise* and explicit. concision, conciseness, N.

conclave N. private meeting. He was present at all their *conclaves* as an unofficial observer.

conclusive ADJ. decisive; ending all debate. When the stolen books turned up in John's locker, we finally had *conclusive* evidence of the identity of the mysterious thief.

concoct v. prepare by combining; make up in concert. How did the inventive chef ever *concoct* such a strange dish? concoction, N.

concomitant N. that which accompanies. Culture is not always a *concomitant* of wealth. also ADJ.

concordat N. agreement, usually between the papal authority and the secular. One of the most famous of the agreements between a Pope and an emperor was the *Concordat* of Worms in 1122.

concur v. agree. Did you *concur* with the decision of the court or did you find it unfair?

concurrent ADJ. happening at the same time. In America, the colonists were resisting the demands of the mother country; at the *concurrent* moment in France, the middle class was sowing the seeds of rebellion.

■ condescend v. bestow courtesies with a superior air. The king *condescended* to grant an audience to the friends of the condemned man. condescension, N.

condign ADJ. adequate; deservedly severe. The public approved the *condign* punishment for the crime.

condiments N. seasonings; spices. Spanish food is full of *condiments.*

condole v. express sympathetic sorrow. His friends gathered to *condole* with him over his loss. condolence, N.

■ condone v. overlook; forgive. We cannot *condone* your recent criminal cooperation with the gamblers.

■ conducive ADJ. helpful; contributive. Rest and proper diet are *conducive* to good health.

conduit N. aqueduct; passageway for fluids. Water was brought to the army in the desert by an improvised *conduit* from the adjoining mountain.

confidant N. trusted friend. He had no *confidants* with whom he could discuss his problems at home.

confiscate v. seize; commandeer. The army *confiscated* all available supplies of uranium.

conflagration N. great fire. In the *conflagration* that followed the 1906 earthquake, much of San Francisco was destroyed.

confluence N. flowing together; crowd. They built the city at the *confluence* of two rivers.

conformity N. harmony; agreement. In *conformity* with our rules and regulations, I am calling a meeting of our organization.

confound v. confuse; puzzle. No mystery could *confound* Sherlock Holmes for long.

congeal v. freeze; coagulate. His blood *congealed* in his veins as he saw the dread monster rush toward him.

congenial ADJ. pleasant; friendly. My father loved to go out for a meal with *congenial* companions.

congenital ADJ. existing at birth. His *congenital* deformity disturbed his parents.

Test

Word List 10   *Synonyms and Antonyms*

Each of the following questions consists of a word in capital letters, followed by five lettered words or phrases. Choose the lettered word or phrase which is most nearly similar or the opposite of the word in capital letters and write the letter of your choice on your answer paper.

136. COLLATION (A) furor (B) emphasis (C) distillery (D) spree (E) lunch
137. COLLOQUIAL (A) burnt (B) polished (C) political (D) gifted (E) problematic
138. COLLOQUY (A) dialect (B) diversion (C) announcement (D) discussion (E) expansion

139. COMATOSE (A) cozy (B) restrained (C) alert (D) dumb (E) grim

140. COMBUSTIBLE (A) flammable (B) industrious (C) waterproof (D) specific (E) plastic

141. COMESTIBLE (A) vigorous (B) fit to be eaten (C) liquid (D) beautiful (E) circumvented

142. COMMISERATE (A) communicate (B) expand (C) repay (D) diminish (E) sympathize

143. COMMODIOUS (A) numerous (B) yielding (C) leisurely (D) limited (E) expensive

144. COMPLIANT (A) numerous (B) veracious (C) soft (D) adamant (E) livid

145. CONCILIATE (A) defend (B) activate (C) integrate (D) quarrel (E) react

146. CONCOCT (A) thrive (B) wonder (C) intrude (D) drink (E) invent

147. CONDONE (A) build (B) evaluate (C) pierce (D) infuriate (E) overlook

148. CONFISCATE (A) discuss (B) discover (C) seize (D) exist (E) convey

149. CONFORMITY (A) agreement (B) ambition (C) confinement (D) pride (E) restraint

150. CONGENITAL (A) slight (B) obscure (C) thorough (D) existing at birth (E) classified

---

Word List 11   conglomeration-countermand

conglomeration N. mass of material sticking together. In such a *conglomeration* of miscellaneous statistics, it was impossible to find a single area of analysis.

congruence N. correspondence of parts; harmonious relationship. The student demonstrated the *congruence* of the two triangles by using the hypotenuse-arm theorem.

conifer N. pine tree; cone-bearing tree. According to geologists, the *conifers* were the first plants to bear flowers.

conjecture N. surmise; guess. I will end all your *conjectures;* I admit I am guilty as charged. also V.

conjugal ADJ. pertaining to marriage. Their dreams of *conjugal* bliss were shattered as soon as their temperaments clashed.

conjure V. summon a devil; practice magic; imagine; invent. He *conjured* up an image of a reformed city and had the voters completely under his spell.

connivance N. pretense of ignorance of something wrong; assistance; permission to offend. With the *connivance* of his friends, he plotted to embarrass the teacher. connive, V.

■ **connoisseur** N. person competent to act as a judge of art, etc.; a lover of an art. She had developed into a *connoisseur* of fine china.

connotation N. suggested or implied meaning of an expression. Foreigners frequently are unaware of the *connotations* of the words they use.

connubial ADJ. pertaining to marriage or the matrimonial state. In his telegram, he wished the newlyweds a lifetime of *connubial* bliss.

consanguinity N. kinship. The lawsuit developed into a test of the *consanguinity* of the claimant to the estate.

conscientious ADJ. scrupulous; careful. A *conscientious* editor, she checked every definition for its accuracy.

consecrate V. dedicate; sanctify. We shall *consecrate* our lives to this noble purpose.

consensus N. general agreement. The *consensus* indicates that we are opposed to entering into this pact.

consequential ADJ. pompous; self-important. Convinced of his own importance, the actor strutted about the dressing room with a *consequential* air.

consonance N. harmony; agreement. Her agitation seemed out of *consonance* with her usual calm.

consort V. associate with. We frequently judge people by the company with whom they *consort.*

consort N. husband or wife. The search for a *consort* for the young Queen Victoria ended happily.

conspiracy N. treacherous plot. Brutus and Cassius joined in the *conspiracy* to kill Julius Caesar.

constituent N. supporter. The congressman received hundreds of letters from angry *constituents* after the Equal Rights Amendment failed to pass.

constraint N. compulsion; repression of feelings. There was a feeling of *constraint* in the room because no one dared to criticize the speaker. constrain, V.

construe V. explain; interpret. If I *construe* your remarks correctly, you disagree with the theory already advanced.

consummate ADJ. complete. I have never seen anyone who makes as many stupid errors as you do; you must be a *consummate* idiot. also V.

contagion N. infection. Fearing *contagion,* they took great steps to prevent the spread of the disease.

contaminate V. pollute. The sewage system of the city so *contaminated* the water that swimming was forbidden.

contempt N. scorn; disdain. I will not tolerate those who show *contempt* for the sincere efforts of this group. contemptuous, contemptible, ADJ.

■ **contentious** ADJ. quarrelsome. We heard loud and *contentious* noises in the next room.

contest V. dispute. The defeated candidate attempted to *contest* the election results.

context N. writings preceding and following the passage quoted. Because these lines are taken out of *context,* they do not convey the message the author intended.

contiguous ADJ. adjacent to; touching upon. The two countries are *contiguous* for a few miles; then they are separated by the gulf.

continence N. self-restraint; sexual chastity. She vowed to lead a life of *continence.* continent, ADJ.

contingent ADJ. conditional. The continuation of this contract is *contingent* on the quality of your first output. contingency, N.

contortions N. twistings; distortions. As the effects of the opiate wore away, the *contortions* of the patient became more violent and demonstrated how much pain she was enduring.

contraband N, ADJ. illegal trade; smuggling. The Coast Guard tries to prevent traffic in *contraband* goods.

contravene V. contradict; infringe on. I will not attempt to *contravene* your argument for it does not affect the situation.

contrite ADJ. penitent. Her *contrite* tears did not influence the judge when he imposed sentence. contrition, N.

controvert V. oppose with arguments; contradict. To *controvert* your theory will require much time but it is essential that we disprove it.

contumacious ADJ. disobedient; resisting authority. The *contumacious* mob shouted defiantly at the police. contumacy, N.

contusion N. bruise. She was treated for *contusions* and abrasions.

■ **conundrum** N. riddle. During the long car ride, she invented *conundrums* to entertain the children.

convene V. assemble. Because much needed legislation had to be enacted, the governor ordered the legislature to *convene* in special session by January 15.

conventional ADJ. ordinary; typical. His *conventional* upbringing left him wholly unprepared for his wife's eccentric family.

converge V. come together. Marchers *converged* on Washington for the great Peace March.

conversant ADJ. familiar with. The lawyer is *conversant* with all the evidence.

converse N. opposite. The inevitable *converse* of peace is not war but annihilation.

convex ADJ. curving outward. He polished the *convex* lens of his telescope.

conveyance N. vehicle; transfer. During the transit strike, commuters used various kinds of *conveyances*.

conviction N. strongly held belief. Nothing could shake his *conviction* that she was innocent. (secondary meaning)

convivial ADJ. festive; gay; characterized by joviality. The *convivial* celebrators of the victory sang their college songs.

convoke V. call together. Congress was *convoked* at the outbreak of the emergency. convocation, N.

convoluted ADJ. coiled around; involved; intricate. His argument was so *convoluted* that few of us could follow it intelligently.

copious ADJ. plentiful. She had *copious* reasons for rejecting the proposal.

coquette N. flirt. Because she refused to give him an answer to his proposal of marriage, he called her a *coquette*. also V.

cordial ADJ. gracious; heartfelt. Our hosts greeted us at the airport with a *cordial* welcome and a hearty hug.

cordon N. extended line of men or fortifications to prevent access or egress. The police *cordon* was so tight that the criminals could not leave the area. also V.

cormorant N. greedy, rapacious bird. The *cormorants* spend their time eating the fish which they catch by diving. also ADJ.

cornice N. projecting molding on building (usually above columns). Because the *cornice* stones had been loosened by the storms, the police closed the building until repairs could be made.

corollary N. consequence; accompaniment. Brotherly love is a complex emotion, with sibling rivalry its natural *corollary*.

corporeal ADJ. bodily; material. He was not a churchgoer; he was interested only in *corporeal* matters.

corpulent ADJ. very fat. The *corpulent* man resolved to reduce. corpulence, N.

correlation N. mutual relationship. He sought to determine the *correlation* that existed between ability in algebra and ability to interpret reading exercises. correlate, V., N.

corroborate V. confirm. Unless we find a witness to *corroborate* your evidence, it will not stand up in court.

corrosive ADJ. eating away by chemicals or disease. Stainless steel is able to withstand the effects of *corrosive* chemicals. corrode, V.

corrugated ADJ. wrinkled; ridged. She wished she could smoothe away the wrinkles from his *corrugated* brow.

corsair N. pirate; pirate ship. The *corsairs,* preying on shipping in the Mediterranean, were often inspired by racial and religious hatreds as well as by the desire for money and booty.

cortege N. procession. The funeral *cortege* proceeded slowly down the avenue.

coruscate V. glitter; scintillate. His wit is the kind that *coruscates* and startles all his listeners.

cosmic ADJ. pertaining to the universe; vast. *Cosmic* rays derive their name from the fact that they bombard the earth's atmosphere from outer space. cosmos, N.

coterie N. group that meets socially; select circle. After his book had been published, he was invited to join the literary *coterie* that lunched daily at the hotel.

countenance V. approve; tolerate. He refused to *countenance* such rude behavior on their part.

countermand V. cancel; revoke. The general *countermanded* the orders issued in his absence.

Test

Word List 11   *Synonyms*

Each of the questions below consists of a word in capital letters, followed by five lettered words or phrases. Choose the lettered word or phrase that is most nearly similar in meaning to the word in capital letters and write the letter of your choice on your answer paper.

151. CONJECTURE (A) magic (B) guess (C) position (D) form (E) place
152. CONNOISSEUR (A) gourmand (B) lover of art (C) humidor (D) delinquent (E) interpreter
153. CONSANGUINITY (A) kinship (B) friendship (C) bloodletting (D) relief (E) understanding
154. CONSENSUS (A) general agreement (B) project (C) insignificance (D) sheaf (E) crevice
155. CONSTRUE (A) explain (B) promote (C) reserve (D) erect (E) block
156. CONTAMINATE (A) arrest (B) prepare (C) pollute (D) beam (E) inform

157. CONTENTIOUS (A) squealing (B) surprising (C) quarrelsome (D) smug (E) creative
158. CONTINENCE (A) humanity (B) research (C) embryology (D) bodies of land (E) self-restraint
159. CONTRABAND (A) purpose (B) rogue (C) rascality (D) difficulty (E) smuggling
160. CONTRITE (A) smart (B) penitent (C) restful (D) recognized (E) perspiring
161. CONTROVERT (A) turn over (B) contradict (C) mind (D) explain (E) swing
162. CONVENE (A) propose (B) restore (C) question (D) gather (E) motivate
163. CONVERSANT (A) ignorant (B) speaking (C) incorporated (D) familiar (E) pedantic
164. COPIOUS (A) plentiful (B) cheating (C) dishonorable (D) adventurous (E) inspired
165. CORPULENT (A) regenerate (B) obese (C) different (D) hungry (E) bloody

Word List 12   counterpart-decelerate

counterpart N. a thing that completes another; things very much alike. Night and day are *counterparts*.

coup N. highly successful action or sudden attack. As the news of his *coup* spread throughout Wall Street, his fellow brokers dropped by to congratulate him.

couple V. join; unite. The Flying Karamazovs *couple* expert juggling and amateur joking in their nightclub act.

courier N. messenger. The publisher sent a special *courier* to pick up the manuscript.

covenant N. agreement. We must comply with the terms of the *covenant*.

covert ADJ. secret; hidden; implied. She could understand the *covert* threat in the letter.

covetous ADJ. avaricious; eagerly desirous of. The child was *covetous* by nature and wanted to take the toys belonging to his classmates. covet, V.

cower V. shrink quivering, as from fear. The frightened child *cowered* in the corner of the room.

coy ADJ. shy; modest; coquettish. She was *coy* in her answers to his offer.

cozen V. cheat; hoodwink; swindle. He was the kind of individual who would *cozen* his friends in a cheap card game but remain eminently ethical in all his business dealings.

crabbed ADJ. sour; peevish. The *crabbed* old man was avoided by the children because he scolded them when they made noise.

crass ADJ. very unrefined; grossly insensible. The philosophers deplored the *crass* commercialism.

craven ADJ. cowardly. Her *craven* behavior in this critical period was criticized by her comrades.

credence N. belief. Do not place any *credence* in his promises.

credo N. creed. I believe we may best describe his *credo* by saying that it approximates the Golden Rule.

■ **credulity** N. belief on slight evidence. The witch doctor took advantage of the *credulity* of the superstitious natives. credulous, ADJ.

creed N. system of religious or ethical belief. In any loyal American's *creed*, love of democracy must be emphasized.

crepuscular ADJ. pertaining to twilight. Bats are *crepuscular* creatures since they begin their flights as soon as the sun begins to sink below the horizon.

crescendo N. increase in the volume or intensity, as in a musical passage; climax. The overture suddenly changed from a quiet pastoral theme to a *crescendo* featuring blaring trumpets and clashing cymbals.

crestfallen ADJ. dejected; dispirited. We were surprised at his reaction to the failure of his project; instead of being *crestfallen*, he was busily engaged in planning new activities.

crevice N. crack; fissure. The mountain climbers found footholds in the tiny *crevices* in the mountainside.

cringe V. shrink back, as if in fear. The dog *cringed*, expecting a blow.

criterion N. standard used in judging. What *criterion* did you use when you selected this essay as the prizewinner? criteria, PL.

crone N. hag. The toothless *crone* frightened us when she smiled.

crotchety ADJ. eccentric; whimsical. Although he was reputed to be a *crotchety* old gentleman, I found his ideas substantially sound and sensible.

cruet N. small glass bottle for vinegar, oil, etc. The waiter preparing the salad poured oil and vinegar from two *cruets* into the bowl.

crux N. crucial point. This is the *crux* of the entire problem.

crypt N. secret recess or vault, usually used for burial. Until recently, only bodies of rulers and leading statesmen were interred in this *crypt*.

cryptic ADJ. mysterious; hidden; secret. His *cryptic* remarks could not be interpreted.

cubicle N. small chamber used for sleeping. After his many hours of intensive study in the library, he retired to his *cubicle*.

cuisine N. style of cooking. French *cuisine* is noted for its use of sauces and wines.

cul-de-sac N. blind alley; trap. The soldiers were unaware that they were marching into a *cul-de-sac* when they entered the canyon.

culinary ADJ. relating to cooking. Many chefs attribute their *culinary* skill to the wise use of spices.

cull V. pick out; reject. Every month the farmer *culls* the nonlaying hens from his flock and sells them to the local butcher. also N.

culmination N. attainment of highest point. His inauguration as President of the United States marked the *culmination* of his political career.

culpable ADJ. deserving blame. Corrupt politicians who condone the activities of the gamblers are equally *culpable*.

culvert N. artificial channel for water. If we build a *culvert* under the road at this point, we will reduce the possibility of the road's being flooded during the rainy season.

cumbersome ADJ. heavy; hard to manage. He was burdened down with *cumbersome* parcels.

cupidity N. greed. The defeated people could not satisfy the *cupidity* of the conquerors, who demanded excessive tribute.

curator N. superintendent; manager. The members of the board of trustees of the museum expected the new *curator* to plan events and exhibitions which would make the museum more popular.

curmudgeon N. churlish, miserly individual. Although he was regarded by many as a *curmudgeon*, a few of us were aware of the many kindnesses and acts of charity which he secretly performed.

curry V. dress; treat leather; seek favor. The courtier *curried* favors of the king.

cursive ADJ. flowing, running. In normal writing we run our letters together in *cursive* form; in printing, we separate the letters.

cursory ADJ. casual; hastily done. A *cursory* examination of the ruins indicates the possibility of arson; a more extensive study should be undertaken.

curtail V. shorten; reduce. During the coal shortage, we must *curtail* our use of this vital commodity.

■ **cynical** ADJ. skeptical or distrustful of human motives. *Cynical* at all times, he was suspicious of all altruistic actions of others. cynic, N.

cynosure N. the object of general attention. As soon as the movie star entered the room, she became the *cynosure* of all eyes.

dais N. raised platform for guests of honor. When he approached the *dais*, he was greeted by cheers from the people who had come to honor him.

dally V. trifle with; procrastinate. Laertes told Ophelia that Hamlet could only *dally* with her affections.

dank ADJ. damp. The walls of the dungeon were *dank* and slimy.

dappled ADJ. spotted. The sunlight filtering through the screens created a *dappled* effect on the wall.

dastard N. coward. This sneak attack is the work of a *dastard*. dastardly, ADJ.

daub V. smear (as with paint). From the way he *daubed* his paint on the canvas, I could tell he knew nothing of oils. also N.

daunt V. intimidate. Your threats cannot *daunt* me.

dauntless ADJ. bold. Despite the dangerous nature of the undertaking, the *dauntless* soldier volunteered for the assignment.

dawdle V. loiter; waste time. Inasmuch as we must meet a deadline, do not *dawdle* over this work.

deadlock N. standstill; stalemate. The negotiations had reached a *deadlock*. also V.

deadpan ADJ. wooden; impersonal. We wanted to see how long he could maintain his *deadpan* expression.

■ **dearth** N. scarcity. The *dearth* of skilled labor compelled the employers to open trade schools.

debacle N. breaking up; downfall. This *debacle* in the government can only result in anarchy.

■ **debase** V. reduce to lower state. Do not *debase* yourself by becoming maudlin. debasement, N.

debauch V. corrupt; make intemperate. A vicious newspaper can *debauch* public ideals. debauchery, N.

debenture N. bond issued to secure a loan. The manager of the company urged that the company try to raise money by issuing *debentures* rather than by selling stock.

debilitate V. weaken; enfeeble. Overindulgence *debilitates* character as well as physical stamina.

debonair ADJ. friendly; aiming to please. The *debonair* youth was liked by all who met him, because of his cheerful and obliging manner.

debris N. rubble. A full year after the earthquake in Mexico City, they were still carting away the *debris*.

debutante N. young woman making formal entrance into society. As a *debutante*, she was often mentioned in the society columns of the newspapers.

decadence N. decay. The moral *decadence* of the people was reflected in the lewd literature of the period.

decant V. pour off gently. Be sure to *decant* this wine before serving it.

decapitate v. behead. They did not hang Lady Jane Grey; they *decapitated* her.

decelerate v. slow down. Seeing the emergency blinkers in the road ahead, he *decelerated* quickly.

Test

Word List 12 *Antonyms*

Each of the questions below consists of a word in capital letters, followed by five lettered words or phrases. Choose the lettered word or phrase that is most nearly opposite in meaning to the word in capital letters and write the letter of your choice on your answer paper.

166. COY (A) weak (B) airy (C) brazen (D) old (E) tiresome
167. COZEN (A) amuse (B) treat honestly (C) prate (D) shackle (E) vilify
168. CRAVEN (A) desirous (B) direct (C) bold (D) civilized (E) controlled
169. CRUX (A) affliction (B) spark (C) events (D) trivial point (E) belief
170. CRYPTIC (A) tomblike (B) futile (C) famous (D) candid (E) indifferent
171. CUPIDITY (A) anxiety (B) tragedy (C) generosity (D) entertainment (E) love
172. CURTAIL (A) mutter (B) lengthen (C) express (D) burden (E) shore
173. CYNICAL (A) trusting (B) effortless (C) conclusive (D) gallant (E) vertical
174. DANK (A) dry (B) guiltless (C) warm (D) babbling (E) reserved
175. DASTARD (A) illegitimacy (B) hero (C) presence (D) warmth (E) idol
176. DAUNTLESS (A) stolid (B) cowardly (C) irrelevant (D) peculiar (E) particular
177. DEARTH (A) life (B) abundance (C) brightness (D) terror (E) width
178. DEBACLE (A) progress (B) refusal (C) masque (D) cowardice (E) traffic
179. DEBILITATE (A) bedevil (B) repress (C) strengthen (D) animate (E) deaden
180. DEBONAIR (A) awkward (B) windy (C) balmy (D) strong (E) stormy

Word List 13   deciduous-dermatologist

deciduous ADJ. falling off as of leaves. The oak is a *deciduous* tree.

decimate v. kill, usually one out of ten. We do more to *decimate* our population in automobile accidents than we do in war.

decipher v. decode. I could not *decipher* the doctor's handwriting.

declivity N. downward slope. The children loved to ski down the *declivity*.

decolleté ADJ. having a low-necked dress. Current fashion decrees that evening gowns be *decolleté* this season; bare shoulders are again the vogue.

decomposition N. decay. Despite the body's advanced state of *decomposition,* the police were able to identify the murdered man.

■ decorum N. propriety; seemliness. Shocked by the unruly behavior, the teacher criticized the class for its lack of *decorum.* decorous, ADJ.

decoy N. lure or bait. The wild ducks were not fooled by the *decoy.* also v.

decrepit ADJ. worn out by age. The *decrepit* car blocked traffic on the highway.

decrepitude N. state of collapse caused by illness or old age. I was unprepared for the state of *decrepitude* in which I had found my old friend; he seemed to have aged twenty years in six months.

decry v. disparage. Do not attempt to increase your stature by *decrying* the efforts of your opponents.

deducible ADJ. derived by reasoning. If we accept your premise, your conclusions are easily *deducible*.

defalcate v. misuse money held in trust. Legislation was passed to punish brokers who *defalcated* their clients' funds.

defamation N. harming a person's reputation. Such *defamation* of character may result in a slander suit.

default N. failure to do. As a result of her husband's failure to appear in court, she was granted a divorce by *default.* also v.

defeatist ADJ. attitude of one who is ready to accept defeat as a natural outcome. If you maintain your *defeatist* attitude, you will never succeed. also N.

defection N. desertion. The children, who had made him an idol, were hurt most by his *defection* from our cause.

■ deference N. courteous regard for another's wish. In *deference* to his desires, the employers granted him a holiday. defer, v.

defile v. pollute; profane. The hoodlums *defiled* the church with their scurrilous writing.

definitive ADJ. final; complete. Carl Sandburg's *Abraham Lincoln* may be regarded as the *definitive* work on the life of the Great Emancipator.

deflect v. turn aside. His life was saved when his cigarette case *deflected* the bullet.

defray v. pay the costs of. Her employer offered to *defray* the costs of her postgraduate education.

deft ADJ. neat; skillful. The *deft* waiter uncorked the champagne without spilling a drop.

defunct ADJ. dead; no longer in use or existence. The lawyers sought to examine the books of the *defunct* corporation.

degraded ADJ. lowered in rank; debased. The *degraded* wretch spoke only of his past glories and honors.

deify v. turn into a god; idolize. Admire the rock star all you want; just don't *deify* him.

deign v. condescend. He felt that he would debase himself if he *deigned* to answer his critics.

delete v. erase; strike out. If you *delete* this paragraph, the composition will have more appeal.

deleterious ADJ. harmful. Workers in nuclear research must avoid the *deleterious* effects of radioactive substances.

deliberate v. consider; ponder. Offered the new job, she asked for time to *deliberate* before she told them her decision.

■ **delineate** v. portray. He is a powerful storyteller, but he is weakest when he attempts to *delineate* character. delineation, N.

deliquescent ADJ. capable of absorbing moisture from the air and becoming liquid. Since this powder is extremely *deliquescent*, it must be kept in a hermetically sealed container until it is used.

delirium N. mental disorder marked by confusion. The drunkard in his *delirium* saw strange animals.

delude v. deceive. Do not *delude* yourself into believing that he will relent.

deluge N. flood; rush. When we advertised the position, we received a *deluge* of applications.

delusion N. false belief; hallucination. This scheme is a snare and a *delusion*.

delusive ADJ. deceptive; raising vain hopes. Do not raise your hopes on the basis of his *delusive* promises.

delve v. dig; investigate. *Delving* into old books and manuscripts is part of a researcher's job.

demagogue N. person who appeals to people's prejudice; false leader of people. He was accused of being a *demagogue* because he made promises which aroused futile hopes in his listeners.

demean v. degrade; humiliate. He felt that he would *demean* himself if he replied to the scurrilous letter.

demeanor N. behavior; bearing. His sober *demeanor* quieted the noisy revelers.

demented ADJ. insane. She became increasingly more *demented* and had to be hospitalized.

demesne N. domain; land over which a person has full sovereignty. The lord of the manor proudly surveyed his *demesne*.

demise N. death. Upon the *demise* of the dictator, a bitter dispute about succession to power developed.

■ **demographic** ADJ. related to population balance. In conducting a survey, one should take into account *demographic* trends in the region.

demolition N. destruction. One of the major aims of the air force was the complete *demolition* of all means of transportation by bombing of rail lines and terminals. demolish, N.

demoniac ADJ. fiendish. The Spanish Inquisition devised many *demoniac* means of torture. demon, N.

demotic ADJ. pertaining to the people. He lamented the passing of aristocratic society and maintained that a *demotic* society would lower the nation's standards.

demur v. delay; object. To *demur* at this time will only worsen the already serious situation; now is the time for action.

demure ADJ. grave; serious; coy. She was *demure* and reserved.

■ **denigrate** v. blacken. All attempts to *denigrate* the character of our late President have failed; the people still love him and cherish his memory.

denizen N. inhabitant of. Ghosts are *denizens* of the land of the dead who return to earth.

denotation N. meaning; distinguishing by name. A dictionary will always give us the *denotation* of a word; frequently, it will also give us its connotation.

denouement N. outcome; final development of the plot of a play. The play was childishly written; the *denouement* was obvious to sophisticated theatergoers as early as the middle of the first act.

denounce v. condemn; criticize. The reform candidate *denounced* the corrupt city officers for having betrayed the public's trust. denunciation, N.

depict v. portray. In this book, the author *depicts* the slave owners as kind and benevolent masters.

depilate v. remove hair. Many women *depilate* their legs with a razor; some use a cream.

deplete v. reduce; exhaust. We must wait until we *deplete* our present inventory before we order replacements.

deplore v. regret. Although I *deplore* the vulgarity of your language, I defend your right to express yourself freely.

deploy v. move troops so that the battle line is extended at the expense of depth. The general ordered the battalion to *deploy* in order to meet the offensive of the enemy.

depose v. dethrone; remove from office. The army attempted to *depose* the king and set up a military government.

deposition N. testimony under oath. He made his *deposition* in the judge's chamber.

depravity N. corruption; wickedness. The *depravity* of the tyrant's behavior shocked all. deprave, v.

■ **deprecate** v. disapprove regretfully. I must *deprecate* your attitude and hope that you will change your mind.

deprecatory ADJ. disapproving. Your *deprecatory* criticism has offended the author.

depreciate v. lessen in value. If you neglect this property, it will *depreciate*.

depredation N. plundering. After the *depredations* of the invaders, the people were penniless.

deranged ADJ. insane. He had to be institutionalized because he was mentally *deranged*.

■ derelict ADJ. abandoned. The *derelict* craft was a menace to navigation. also N.

deride V. scoff at. The people *derided* his grandiose schemes.

■ derision N. ridicule. They greeted his proposal with *derision* and refused to consider it seriously. derisive, ADJ.

■ derivative ADJ. unoriginal; derived from another source. Although her early poetry was clearly *derivative* in nature, the critics thought she had promise and eventually would find her own voice.

dermatologist N. one who studies the skin and its diseases. I advise you to consult a *dermatologist* about your acne.

Test

Word List 13   *Synonyms*

Each of the questions below consists of a word in capital letters, followed by five lettered words or phrases. Choose the lettered word or phrase that is most nearly similar in meaning to the word in capital letters and write the letter of your choice on your answer paper.

181. DECIMATE (A) kill (B) disgrace (C) search (D) collide (E) deride

182. DECLIVITY (A) trap (B) quadrangle (C) quarter (D) activity (E) downward slope

183. DECOLLETÉ (A) flavored (B) demure (C) flowery (D) low-necked (E) sweet

184. DECREPIT (A) momentary (B) emotional (C) suppressed (D) worn out (E) unexpected

185. DECREPITUDE (A) feebleness (B) disease (C) coolness (D) melee (E) crowd

186. DEFALCATE (A) abscond (B) elope (C) observe (D) panic (E) invest

187. DEFECTION (A) determination (B) desertion (C) invitation (D) affection (E) reservation

188. DEFILE (A) manicure (B) ride (C) pollute (D) assemble (E) order

189. DEGRADED (A) surprised (B) lowered (C) ascended (D) learned (E) prejudged

190. DELETERIOUS (A) delaying (B) experimental (C) harmful (D) graduating (E) glorious

191. DELUGE (A) confusion (B) deception (C) flood (D) mountain (E) weapon

192. DENIGRATE (A) refuse (B) blacken (C) terrify (D) admit (E) review

193. DENOUEMENT (A) action (B) scenery (C) resort (D) character (E) solution

194. DEPRAVITY (A) wickedness (B) sadness (C) heaviness (D) tidiness (E) seriousness

195. DERANGED (A) insane (B) announced (C) neighborly (D) alphabetical (E) surrounded

Word List 14   derogatory-disgruntle

derogatory ADJ. expressing a low opinion. I resent your *derogatory* remarks.

descant V. discuss fully. He was willing to *descant* upon any topic of conversation, even when he knew very little about the subject under discussion. also N.

descry V. catch sight of. In the distance, we could barely *descry* the enemy vessels.

desecrate V. profane; violate the sanctity of. The soldiers *desecrated* the temple.

■ desiccate V. dry up. A tour of this smokehouse will give you an idea of how the pioneers used to *desiccate* food in order to preserve it.

desideratum N. that which is desired. Our first *desideratum* must be the establishment of peace; we can then attempt to remove the causes of the present conflict.

desolate V. rob of joy; lay waste to; forsake. The bandits *desolated* the countryside, burning farms and carrying off the harvest.

despicable ADJ. contemptible. Your *despicable* remarks call for no reply.

despise V. scorn. I *despise* your attempts at a reconciliation at this time and refuse to meet you.

despoil V. plunder. If you do not yield, I am afraid the enemy will *despoil* the countryside.

despondent ADJ. depressed; gloomy. To the dismay of his parents, he became more and more *despondent* every day. despondency, N.

■ despotism N. tyranny. The people rebelled against the *despotism* of the king.

destitute ADJ. extremely poor. The illness left the family *destitute*.

desuetude N. disused condition. The machinery in the idle factory was in a state of *desuetude*.

■ desultory ADJ. aimless; jumping around. The animals' *desultory* behavior indicated that they had no awareness of their predicament.

detached ADJ. emotionally removed; calm and objective; indifferent. A psychoanalyst must maintain a *detached* point of view and stay uninvolved with her patients' personal lives. detachment, N. (secondary meaning)

detergent N. cleansing agent. Many new *detergents* have replaced soap.

determinate ADJ. having a fixed order of procedure; invariable. At the royal wedding, the procession of the nobles followed a *determinate* order of precedence.

deterrent N. something that discourages; hindrance. Does the threat of capital punishment serve as a *deterrent* to potential killers?

detonation N. explosion. The *detonation* of the bomb could be heard miles away.

detraction N. slandering; aspersion. He is offended by your frequent *detractions* of his ability as a leader.

detrimental ADJ. harmful; damaging. Your acceptance of her support will ultimately prove *detrimental* rather than helpful to your cause. detriment, N.

deviate V. turn away from. Do not *deviate* from the truth; you must face the facts.

devious ADJ. going astray; erratic. Your *devious* behavior in this matter puzzles me since you are usually direct and straightforward.

devoid ADJ. lacking. He was *devoid* of any personal desire for gain in his endeavor to secure improvement in the community.

devolve V. deputize; pass to others. It *devolved* upon us, the survivors, to arrange peace terms with the enemy.

devotee N. enthusiastic follower. A *devotee* of the opera, he bought season tickets every year.

devout ADJ. pious. The *devout* man prayed daily.

dexterous ADJ. skillful. The magician was so *dexterous* that we could not follow him as he performed his tricks.

diabolical ADJ. devilish. This scheme is so *diabolical* that I must reject it.

diadem N. crown. The king's *diadem* was on display at the museum.

dialectic N. art of debate. I am not skilled in *dialectic* and, therefore, cannot answer your arguments as forcefully as I wish.

■ **diaphanous** ADJ. sheer; transparent. They saw the burglar clearly through the *diaphanous* curtain.

diatribe N. bitter scolding; invective. During the lengthy *diatribe* delivered by his opponent he remained calm and self-controlled.

■ **dichotomy** N. branching into two parts. The *dichotomy* of our legislative system provides us with many safeguards.

dictum N. authoritative and weighty statement. She repeated the statement as though it were the *dictum* of the most expert worker in the group.

didactic ADJ. teaching; instructional. The *didactic* qualities of his poetry overshadow its literary qualities; the lesson he teaches is more memorable than the lines.

■ **diffidence** N. shyness. You must overcome your *diffidence* if you intend to become a salesperson.

■ **diffusion** N. wordiness; spreading in all directions like a gas. Your composition suffers from a *diffusion* of ideas; try to be more compact. diffuse, ADJ. and V.

digression N. wandering away from the subject. His book was marred by his many *digressions*. digress, V.

dilapidated ADJ. ruined because of neglect. We felt that the *dilapidated* building needed several coats of paint. dilapidation, N.

dilate V. expand. In the dark, the pupils of your eyes *dilate*.

dilatory ADJ. delaying. Your *dilatory* tactics may compel me to cancel the contract.

■ **dilemma** N. problem; choice of two unsatisfactory alternatives. In this *dilemma*, he knew no one to whom he could turn for advice.

dilettante N. aimless follower of the arts; amateur; dabbler. He was not serious in his painting; he was rather a *dilettante*.

■ **diligence** N. steadiness of effort; persistent hard work. Her employers were greatly impressed by her *diligence* and offered her a partnership in the firm.

dilute V. make less concentrated; reduce in strength. She preferred her coffee *diluted* with milk.

diminution N. lessening; reduction in size. The blockaders hoped to achieve victory as soon as the *diminution* of the enemy's supplies became serious.

dint N. means; effort. By *dint* of much hard work, the volunteers were able to place the raging forest fire under control.

dipsomaniac N. one who has a strong craving for intoxicating liquor. The picture *The Lost Weekend* was an excellent portrayal of the struggles of the *dipsomaniac*.

dire ADJ. disastrous. People ignored her *dire* predictions of an approaching depression.

dirge N. lament with music. The funeral *dirge* stirred us to tears.

disabuse V. correct a false impression; undeceive. I will attempt to *disabuse* you of your impression of my client's guilt; I know he is innocent.

disapprobation N. disapproval; condemnation. The conservative father viewed his daughter's radical boyfriend with *disapprobation*.

disarray N. a disorderly or untidy state. After the New Year's party, the once orderly house was in total *disarray*.

■ **disavowal** N. denial; disclaiming. His *disavowal* of his part in the conspiracy was not believed by the jury. disavow, V.

disband V. dissolve; disperse. The chess club *disbanded* after its disastrous initial season.

disburse V. pay out. When you *disburse* money on the company's behalf, be sure to get a receipt.

discernible ADJ. distinguishable; perceivable. The ships in the harbor were not *discernible* in the fog.

■ **discerning** ADJ. mentally quick and observant; having insight. Because he was considered the most *discerning* member of the firm, he was assigned the most difficult cases. discern, V. discernment, N.

disclaim V. disown; renounce claim to. If I grant you this privilege, will you *disclaim* all other rights?

disclose V. reveal. Although competitors offered him

bribes, he refused to *disclose* any information about his company's forthcoming product. disclosure, N.

■ **discomfit** v. put to rout; defeat; disconcert. This ruse will *discomfit* the enemy. discomfiture, N. discomfited, ADJ.

disconcert v. confuse; upset; embarrass. The lawyer was *disconcerted* by the evidence produced by her adversary.

disconsolate ADJ. sad. The death of his wife left him *disconsolate.*

■ **discordant** ADJ. inharmonious; conflicting. She tried to unite the *discordant* factions.

discount v. disregard. Be prepared to *discount* what he has to say about his ex-wife.

■ **discrepancy** N. lack of consistency; difference. The police noticed some *discrepancies* in his description of the crime and did not believe him.

■ **discrete** ADJ. separate; unconnected. The universe is composed of *discrete* bodies.

discretion N. prudence; ability to adjust actions to circumstances. Use your *discretion* in this matter and do not discuss it with anyone. discreet, ADJ.

discrimination N. ability to see differences; prejudice. They feared he lacked sufficient *discrimination* to judge complex works of modern art. (secondary meaning) discriminating, ADJ.

discursive ADJ. digressing; rambling. They were annoyed and bored by her *discursive* remarks.

disdain v. treat with scorn or contempt. You make enemies of all you *disdain.* also N.

disgruntle v. make discontented. The passengers were *disgruntled* by the numerous delays.

Test

Word List 14   *Antonyms*

Each of the questions below consists of a word in capital letters, followed by five lettered words or phrases. Choose the lettered word or phrase that is most nearly opposite in meaning to the word in capital letters and write the letter of your choice on your answer paper.

196. DEROGATORY (A) roguish (B) immediate (C) opinionated (D) praising (E) conferred

197. DESECRATE (A) desist (B) integrate (C) confuse (D) intensify (E) consecrate

198. DESPICABLE (A) steering (B) worthy of esteem (C) inevitable (D) featureless (E) incapable

199. DESTITUTE (A) affluent (B) dazzling (C) stationary (D) characteristic (E) explanatory

200. DEVOID (A) latent (B) eschewed (C) full of (D) suspecting (E) evident

201. DEVOUT (A) quiet (B) dual (C) impious (D) straightforward (E) wrong

202. DIABOLICAL (A) mischievous (B) lavish (C) seraphic (D) azure (E) red

203. DIATRIBE (A) mass (B) range (C) eulogy (D) elegy (E) starvation

204. DIFFIDENCE (A) sharpness (B) boldness (C) malcontent (D) dialogue (E) catalog

205. DILATE (A) procrastinate (B) contract (C) conclude (D) participate (E) divert

206. DILATORY (A) narrowing (B) prompt (C) enlarging (D) portentous (E) sour

207. DIMINUTION (A) expectation (B) context (C) validity (D) appreciation (E) difficulty

208. DIPSOMANIAC (A) realist (B) thief (C) teetotaller (D) pyromaniac (E) swimmer

209. DISABUSE (A) crash (B) violate (C) renege (D) control (E) deceive

210. DISCONSOLATE (A) examining (B) thankful (C) theatrical (D) joyous (E) prominent

Word List 15   dishabille-duplicity

dishabille N. in a state of undress. Because he was certain that he would have no visitors, he lounged around the house in a state of *dishabille,* wearing only his pajamas and a pair of old bedroom slippers.

disheartened ADJ. lacking courage and hope. His failure to pass the bar exam *disheartened* him.

disheveled ADJ. untidy. Your *disheveled* appearance will hurt your chances in this interview.

disinclination N. unwillingness. Some mornings I feel a great *disinclination* to get out of bed.

■ **disingenuous** ADJ. not naive; sophisticated. Although he was young, his remarks indicated that he was *disingenuous.*

disinter v. dig up; unearth. They *disinterred* the body and held an autopsy.

■ **disinterested** ADJ. unprejudiced. The only *disinterested* person in the room was the judge.

■ **disjointed** ADJ. disconnected. His remarks were so *disjointed* that we could not follow his reasoning.

dismantle v. take apart. When the show closed, they *dismantled* the scenery before storing it.

dismember v. cut into small parts. When the Austrian Empire was *dismembered,* several new countries were established.

■ **disparage** v. belittle. Do not *disparage* anyone's contribution; these little gifts add up to large sums.

■ **disparate** ADJ. basically different; unrelated. It is difficult, if not impossible, to organize these *disparate* elements into a coherent whole.

disparity N. difference; condition of inequality. The *disparity* in their ages made no difference at all.

dispassionate ADJ. calm; impartial. In a *dispassionate* analysis of the problem, he carefully examined the causes of the conflict and proceeded to suggest suitable remedies.

disperse V. scatter. The police fired tear gar into the crowd to disperse the protesters.

dispersion N. scattering. The *dispersion* of this group throughout the world may be explained by their expulsion from their homeland.

dispirited ADJ. lacking in spirit. The coach used all the tricks at his command to buoy up the enthusiasm of his team, which had become *dispirited* at the loss of the star player.

disport V. amuse. The popularity of Florida as a winter resort is constantly increasing; each year, thousands more *disport* themselves at Miami and Palm Beach.

disputatious ADJ. argumentative; fond of argument. People avoided discussing contemporary problems with him because of his *disputatious* manner.

disquisition N. a formal systematic inquiry; an explanation of the results of a formal inquiry. In his *disquisition,* he outlined the steps he had taken in reaching his conclusions.

dissection N. analysis; cutting apart in order to examine. The *dissection* of frogs in the laboratory is particularly unpleasant to some students.

dissemble V. disguise; pretend. Even though you are trying to *dissemble* your motive in joining this group, we can see through your pretense.

■ **disseminate** V. scatter (like seeds). The invention of the radio has helped propagandists to *disseminate* their favorite doctrines very easily.

dissertation N. formal essay. In order to earn a graduate degree from many of our universities, a candidate is frequently required to prepare a *dissertation* on some scholarly subject.

dissimulate V. pretend; conceal by feigning. She tried to *dissimulate* her grief by her exuberant attitude.

dissipate V. squander. The young man quickly *dissipated* his inheritance and was soon broke.

dissolution N. disintegration; looseness in morals. The profligacy and *dissolution* of life in Caligula's Rome appall some historians. dissolute, ADJ.

■ **dissonance** N. discord. Some contemporary musicians deliberately use *dissonance* to achieve certain effects.

dissuade V. advise against. He could not *dissuade* his friend from joining the conspirators.

dissuasion N. advice against. All his powers of *dissuasion* were useless; they failed to heed his warning.

distaff ADJ. female. His ancestors on the *distaff* side were equally as famous as his father's progenitors.

distant ADJ. reserved or aloof; cold in manner. His *distant* greeting made me feel unwelcome from the start. (secondary meaning)

distend V. expand; swell out. I can tell when he is under stress by the way the veins *distend* on his forehead.

distortion N. twisting out of shape. It is difficult to believe the newspaper accounts of this event because of the *distortions* and exaggerations written by the reporters.

distrait ADJ. absentminded. Because of his concentration on the problem, the professor often appeared *distrait* and unconcerned about routine.

■ **distraught** ADJ. upset; distracted by anxiety. The *distraught* parents frantically searched the ravine for their lost child.

diurnal ADJ. daily. A farmer cannot neglect his *diurnal* tasks at any time; cows, for example, must be milked regularly.

diva N. operatic singer; prima donna. Although world famous as a *diva,* she did not indulge in fits of temperament.

■ **diverge** V. vary; go in different directions from the same point. The spokes of the wheel *diverge* from the hub.

divergent ADJ. differing; deviating. The two witnesses presented the jury with remarkably *divergent* accounts of the same episode. divergence, N.

divers ADJ. several; differing. We could hear *divers* opinions of his ability.

diverse ADJ. differing in some characteristics; various. There are *diverse* ways of approaching this problem.

diversion N. act of turning aside; pastime. After studying for several hours, he needed a *diversion* from work. divert, V.

diversity N. variety; dissimilitude. The *diversity* of colleges in this country indicates that many levels of ability are being cared for.

■ **divest** V. strip; deprive. He was *divested* of his power to act and could no longer govern. divestiture, N.

divination N. foreseeing the future with aid of magic. I base my opinions not on any special gift of *divination* but on the laws of probability.

divulge V. reveal. I will not tell you this news because I am sure you will *divulge* it prematurely.

■ **docile** ADJ. obedient; easily managed. As *docile* as he seems today, that old lion was once a ferocious, snarling beast. docility, N.

docket N. program as for trial; book where such entries are made. The case of Smith vs. Jones was entered in the *docket* for July 15. also V.

document V. provide written evidence. She kept all the receipts from her business trip in order to *document* her expenses for the firm. also N.

doddering ADJ. shaky; infirm from old age. Although he is not as yet a *doddering* and senile old man, his ideas and opinions no longer can merit the respect we gave them years ago.

doff V. take off. A gentleman used to *doff* his hat to a lady.

■ **doggerel** N. poor verse. Although we find occasional snatches of genuine poetry in her work, most of her writing is mere *doggerel*.

■ **dogmatic** ADJ. positive; arbitrary. Do not be so *dogmatic* about that statement; it can be easily refuted.

doldrums N. blues; listlessness; slack period. Once the excitement of meeting her deadline was over, she found herself in the *doldrums*.

dolorous ADJ. sorrowful. He found the *dolorous* lamentations of the bereaved family emotionally disturbing and he left as quickly as he could.

dolt N. stupid person. I thought I was talking to a mature audience; instead, I find myself addressing a pack of *dolts* and idiots.

domicile N. home. Although his legal *domicile* was in New York City, his work kept him away from his residence for many years. also V.

domineer V. rule over tyrannically. Students prefer teachers who guide, not ones who *domineer*.

dormant ADJ. sleeping; lethargic; torpid. Sometimes *dormant* talents in our friends surprise those of us who never realized how gifted our acquaintances really are. dormancy, N.

dorsal ADJ. relating to the back of an animal. A shark may be identified by its *dorsal* fin, which projects above the surface of the ocean.

dotage N. senility. In his *dotage,* the old man bored us with long tales of events in his childhood.

doughty ADJ. courageous. Many folk tales have sprung up about this *doughty* pioneer who opened up the New World for his followers.

dour ADJ. sullen; stubborn. The man was *dour* and taciturn.

douse V. plunge into water; drench; extinguish. They *doused* each other with hoses and water balloons.

dowdy ADJ. slovenly; untidy. She tried to change her *dowdy* image by buying a new fashionable wardrobe.

dregs N. sediment; worthless residue. The *dregs* of society may be observed in this slum area of the city.

■ **droll** ADJ. queer and amusing. He was a popular guest because his *droll* anecdotes were always entertaining.

dross N. waste matter; worthless impurities. Many methods have been devised to separate the valuable metal from the *dross*.

drone N. idle person; male bee. Content to let his wife support him, the would-be writer was in reality nothing but a *drone*.

drone V. talk dully; buzz or murmur like a bee. On a gorgeous day, who wants to be stuck in a classroom listening to the teacher *drone*.

drudgery N. menial work. Cinderella's fairy godmother rescued her from a life of *drudgery*.

dubious ADJ. doubtful. He has the *dubious* distinction of being the lowest man in his class.

■ **ductility** N. malleability; flexibility; ability to be drawn out. Copper wire has many industrial uses because of its extreme *ductility*.

duenna N. attendant of young female; chaperone. Their romance could not flourish because of the presence of her *duenna*.

dulcet ADJ. sweet sounding. The *dulcet* sounds of the birds at dawn were soon drowned out by the roar of traffic passing our motel.

duplicity N. double-dealing; hypocrisy. People were shocked and dismayed when they learned of his *duplicity* in this affair, as he had always seemed honest and straightforward.

Test

Word List 15   *Synonyms and Antonyms*

Each of the following questions consists of a word in capital letters, followed by five lettered words or phrases. Choose the lettered word or phrase which is most nearly similar or the opposite of the word in capital letters and write the letter of your choice on your answer paper.

211. DISINGENUOUS (A) uncomfortable (B) eventual (C) naive (D) complex (E) enthusiastic

212. DISINTERESTED (A) prejudiced (B) horrendous (C) affected (D) arbitrary (E) bored

213. DISJOINTED (A) satisfied (B) carved (C) understood (D) connected (E) evicted

214. DISPARITY (A) resonance (B) elocution (C) relief (D) difference (E) symbolism

215. DISPASSIONATE (A) sensual (B) immoral (C) inhibited (D) impartial (E) scientific

216. DISPIRITED (A) current (B) dented (C) drooping (D) removed (E) dallying

217. DISSIPATE (A) economize (B) clean (C) accept (D) anticipate (E) withdraw

218. DISTEND (A) bloat (B) adjust (C) exist (D) materialize (E) finish

219. DISTRAIT (A) clever (B) industrial (C) absentminded (D) narrow (E) crooked

220. DIVULGE (A) look (B) refuse (C) deride (D) reveal (E) harm

221. DOFF (A) withdraw (B) take off (C) remain (D) control (E) start

222. DOGMATIC (A) benign (B) canine (C) impatient (D) petulant (E) arbitrary

223. DOTAGE (A) senility (B) silence (C) sensitivity (D) interest (E) generosity

224. DOUR (A) sullen (B) ornamental (C) grizzled (D) lacking speech (E) international

225. DROLL (A) rotund (B) amusing (C) fearsome (D) tiny (E) strange

Word List 16   durance-encroachment

durance N. restraint; imprisonment. The lecturer spoke of a "durance vile" to describe his years in the prison camp.

duress N. forcible restraint, especially unlawfully. The hostages were held under duress until the prisoners' demands were met.

dwindle V. shrink; reduce. They spent so much money that their funds dwindled to nothing.

dynamic ADJ. active; efficient. A dynamic government is necessary to meet the demands of a changing society.

dyspeptic ADJ. suffering from indigestion. All the talk about rich food made him feel dyspeptic. dyspepsia, N.

earthy ADJ. unrefined; coarse. His earthy remarks often embarrassed the women in his audience.

ebb V. recede; lessen. His fortunes began to ebb during the Recession. also N.

ebullient ADJ. showing excitement; overflowing with enthusiasm. His ebullient nature could not be repressed; he was always exuberant. ebullience, N.

eccentric ADJ. odd; whimsical; irregular. The comet passed close by the earth in its eccentric orbit.

eccentricity N. oddity; idiosyncrasy. Some of his friends tried to account for his rudeness to strangers as the eccentricity of genius.

ecclesiastic ADJ. pertaining to the church. The minister donned his ecclesiastic garb and walked to the pulpit. also N.

eclat N. brilliance; glory. To the delight of his audience, he completed his task with eclat and consummate ease.

■ **eclectic** ADJ. selective; composed of elements drawn from disparate sources. His style of interior decoration was eclectic: bits and pieces of furnishings from widely divergent periods, strikingly juxtaposed to create a unique decor. eclecticism, N.

eclipse V. darken; extinguish; surpass. The new stock market high eclipsed the previous record set in 1985.

ecologist N. a person concerned with the interrelationship between living organisms and their environment. The ecologist was concerned that the new dam would upset the natural balance of the creatures living in Glen Canyon.

ecstasy N. rapture; joy; any overpowering emotion. The announcement that the war had ended brought on an ecstasy of joy that resulted in many uncontrolled celebrations.

edify V. instruct; correct morally. Although his purpose was to edify and not to entertain his audience, many of his listeners were amused and not enlightened.

educe V. draw forth; elicit. She could not educe a principle that would encompass all the data.

eerie ADJ. weird. In that eerie setting, it was easy to believe in ghosts and other supernatural beings.

efface V. rub out. The coin had been handled so many times that its date had been effaced.

effectual ADJ. efficient. If we are to succeed, we must seek effectual means of securing our goals.

effeminate ADJ. having womanly traits. His voice was high-pitched and effeminate.

effervesce V. bubble over; show excitement. Some of us cannot stand the way she effervesces over trifles.

effervescence N. inner excitement; exuberance. Nothing depressed her for long; her natural effervescence soon reasserted itself. effervescent, ADJ.

effete ADJ. worn out; exhausted; barren. The literature of the age reflected the effete condition of the writers; no new ideas were forthcoming.

■ **efficacy** N. power to produce desired effect. The efficacy of this drug depends on the regularity of the dosage. efficacious, ADJ.

effigy N. dummy. The mob showed its irritation by hanging the judge in effigy.

efflorescent ADJ. flowering. Greenhouse gardeners are concerned with the coinciding of the plants' efflorescent period with certain holidays.

effluvium N. noxious smell. Air pollution has become a serious problem in our major cities; the effluvium and the poisons in the air are hazards to life.

effrontery N. shameless boldness. She had the effrontery to insult the guest.

effulgent ADJ. brilliantly radiant. The effulgent rays of the rising sun lit the sky.

effusion N. pouring forth. The critics objected to her literary effusion because it was too flowery.

effusive ADJ. pouring forth; gushing. Her effusive manner of greeting her friends finally began to irritate them.

egoism N. excessive interest in one's self; belief that one should be interested in one's self rather than in others. His egoism prevented him from seeing the needs of his colleagues.

egotism N. conceit; vanity. She thought so much of herself that we found her egotism unwarranted and irritating.

egregious ADJ. gross; shocking. She was an egregious liar and we could never believe her.

egress N. exit. Barnum's sign "To the Egress" fooled many people who thought they were going to see an animal and instead found themselves in the street.

ejaculation N. exclamation. He could not repress an ejaculation of surprise when he heard the news.

elaboration N. addition of details; intricacy. Tell what happened simply, without any elaboration. elaborate, V.

elation N. a rise in spirits; exaltation. She felt no elation at finding the purse because it was empty.

■ **elegy** N. poem or song expressing lamentation. On the death of Edward King, Milton composed the elegy "Lycidas." elegiacal, ADJ.

■ **elicit** V. draw out by discussion. The detectives tried to elicit where he had hidden his loot.

elixir N. cure-all; something invigorating. The news of her chance to go abroad acted on her like an *elixir*.

eloquence N. expressiveness; persuasive speech. The crowds were stirred by Martin Luther King's *eloquence*.

elucidate V. explain; enlighten. He was called upon to *elucidate* the disputed points in his article.

elusive ADJ. evasive; baffling; hard to grasp. His *elusive* dreams of wealth were costly to those of his friends who supported him financially. elude, V.

elusory ADJ. tending to deceive expectations; elusive. He argued that the project was an *elusory* one and would bring disappointment to all.

elysian ADJ. relating to paradise; blissful. An afternoon sail on the bay was for her an *elysian* journey.

emaciated ADJ. thin and wasted. His long period of starvation had left him *emaciated*.

emanate V. issue forth. A strong odor of sulphur *emanated* from the spring.

emancipate V. set free. At first, the attempts of the Abolitionists to *emancipate* the slaves were unpopular in New England as well as in the South.

■ **embellish** V. adorn. His handwriting was *embellished* with flourishes.

embezzlement N. stealing. The bank teller confessed his *embezzlement* of the funds.

emblazon V. deck in brilliant colors. *Emblazoned* on his shield was his family coat of arms.

embroil V. throw into confusion; involve in strife; entangle. He became *embroiled* in the heated discussion when he tried to arbitrate the dispute.

embryonic ADJ. undeveloped; rudimentary. The evil of class and race hatred must be eliminated while it is still in an *embryonic* state; otherwise, it may grow to dangerous proportions.

emend V. correct; correct by a critic. The critic *emended* the book by selecting the passages which he thought most appropriate to the text.

emendation N. correction of errors; improvement. Please initial all the *emendations* you have made in this contract.

emeritus ADJ. retired but retained in an honorary capacity. As professor *emeritus,* he retained all his honors without having to meet the obligations of daily assignments.

emetic N. substance causing vomiting. The use of an *emetic* like mustard is useful in cases of poisoning.

eminent ADJ. high; lofty. After his appointment to this *eminent* position, he seldom had time for his former friends.

■ **emissary** N. agent; messenger. The Secretary of State was sent as the President's special *emissary* to the conference on disarmament.

emollient N. soothing or softening remedy. He applied an *emollient* to the inflamed area. Also ADJ.

emolument N. salary; compensation. In addition to the *emolument* this position offers, you must consider the social prestige it carries with it.

■ **empirical** ADJ. based on experience. He distrusted hunches and intuitive flashes; he placed his reliance entirely on *empirical* data.

empyreal ADJ. celestial; fiery. The scientific advances of the twentieth century have enabled man to invade the *empyreal* realm of the eagle.

■ **emulate** V. rival; imitate. As long as our political leaders *emulate* the virtues of the great leaders of this country, we shall flourish.

enamored ADJ. in love. Narcissus became *enamored* of his own beauty.

embed V. enclose; place in something. Tales of actual historical figures like King Alfred have become *embedded* in legends.

enclave N. territory enclosed within an alien land. The Vatican is an independent *enclave* in Italy.

encomiastic ADJ. praising; eulogistic. Some critics believe that his *encomiastic* statements about Napoleon were inspired by his desire for material advancement rather than by an honest belief in the Emperor's genius. encomium, N.

encomium N. praise; eulogy. He was sickened by the *encomiums* and panegyrics expressed by speakers who had previously been among the first to vilify the man they were now honoring.

encompass V. surround. Although we were *encompassed* by enemy forces, we were cheerful for we were well stocked and could withstand a siege until our allies joined us.

encroachment N. gradual intrusion. The *encroachment* of the factories upon the neighborhood lowered the value of the real estate.

Test

Word List 16   *Synonyms*

Each of the questions below consists of a word in capital letters, followed by five lettered words or phrases. Choose the lettered word or phrase that is most nearly similar in meaning to the word in capital letters and write the letter of your choice on your answer paper.

226. DWINDLE (A) blow (B) inhabit (C) spin (D) lessen (E) combine

227. ECSTASY (A) joy (B) speed (C) treasure (D) warmth (E) lack

228. EDIFY (A) mystify (B) suffice (C) improve (D) erect (E) entertain

229. EFFACE (A) countenance (B) encourage (C) recognize (D) blackball (E) rub out

230. EFFIGY (A) requisition (B) organ (C) charge (D) accordion (E) dummy

231. EGREGIOUS (A) pious (B) shocking (C) anxious (D) sociable (E) gloomy

232. EGRESS (A) entrance (B) bird (C) exit (D) double (E) progress

233. ELATED (A) debased (B) respectful (C) drooping (D) gay (E) charitable

234. ELUSIVE (A) deadly (B) eloping (C) evasive (D) simple (E) petrified

235. EMACIATED (A) garrulous (B) primeval (C) vigorous (D) disparate (E) thin

236. EMBELLISH (A) doff (B) don (C) balance (D) adorn (E) equalize

237. EMEND (A) cherish (B) repose (C) correct (D) assure (E) worry

238. EMENDATION (A) correction (B) interpretation (C) exhumation (D) inquiry (E) fault

239. EMINENT (A) purposeful (B) high (C) delectable (D) curious (E) urgent

240. EMANCIPATE (A) set free (B) take back (C) make worse (D) embolden (E) run away

---

Word List 17 encumber-eulogistic

encumber V. burden. Some people *encumber* themselves with too much luggage when they take short trips.

endearment N. fond statement. Your gifts and *endearments* cannot make me forget your earlier insolence.

endemic ADJ. prevailing among a specific group of people or in a specific area or country. This disease is *endemic* in this part of the world; more than 80 percent of the population are at one time or another affected by it.

endive N. species of leafy plant used in salads. The salad contained *endive* in addition to the ingredients she usually used.

endorse V. approve; support. Everyone waited to see which one of the rival candidates for the city council the mayor would *endorse*. (secondary meaning) endorsement, N.

endue V. provide with some quality; endow. He was *endued* with a lion's courage.

energize V. invigorate; make forceful and active. We shall have to *energize* our activities by getting new members to carry on.

enervate V. weaken. The hot days of August are *enervating*.

enervation N. lack of vigor; weakness. She was slow to recover from her illness; even a short walk to the window left her in a state of *enervation*.

engender V. cause; produce. To receive praise for real accomplishments *engenders* self-confidence in a child.

engross V. occupy fully. John was so *engrossed* in his studies that he did not hear his mother call.

enhance V. advance; improve. Your chances for promotion in this department will be *enhanced* if you take some more courses in evening school.

enigma N. puzzle. Despite all attempts to decipher the code, it remained an *enigma*.

enigmatic ADJ. obscure; puzzling. Many have sought to fathom the *enigmatic* smile of the *Mona Lisa*.

enjoin V. command; order; forbid. The owners of the company asked the court to *enjoin* the union from picketing the plant.

enmity N. ill will; hatred. At Camp David President Carter labored to bring an end to the *enmity* that prevented Egypt and Israel from living in peace.

ennui N. boredom. The monotonous routine of hospital life induced a feeling of *ennui* which made him moody and irritable.

enormity N. hugeness (in a bad sense). He did not realize the *enormity* of his crime until he saw what suffering he had caused.

enrapture V. please intensely. The audience was *enraptured* by the freshness of the voices and the excellent orchestration.

ensconce V. settle comfortably. The parents thought that their children were *ensconced* safely in the private school and decided to leave for Europe.

ensue V. follow. The evils that *ensued* were the direct result of the miscalculations of the leaders.

enthrall V. capture; enslave. From the moment he saw her picture, he was *enthralled* by her beauty.

entice V. lure; attract; tempt. She always tried to *entice* her baby brother into mischief.

entity N. real being. As soon as the Charter was adopted, the United Nations became an *entity* and had to be considered as a factor in world diplomacy.

entomology N. study of insects. I found *entomology* the least interesting part of my course in biology; studying insects bored me.

entrance V. put under a spell; carry away with emotion. Shafts of sunlight on a wall could *entrance* her and leave her spellbound.

entreat V. plead; ask earnestly. She *entreated* her father to let her stay out till midnight.

entree N. entrance; a way in. Because of his wealth and social position, he had *entree* into the most exclusive circles.

entrepreneur N. businessman; contractor. Opponents of our present tax program argue that it discourages *entrepreneurs* from trying new fields of business activity.

enunciate V. speak distinctly. How will people understand you if you do not *enunciate*?

environ V. enclose; surround. In medieval days, Paris was *environed* by a wall. environs, N.

ephemeral ADJ. short-lived; fleeting. The mayfly is an *ephemeral* creature.

epicure N. connoisseur of food and drink. *Epicures* frequent this restaurant because it features exotic wines and dishes.

epicurean N. person who devotes himself to pleasures of the senses, especially to food. This restaurant is famous for its menu, which can cater to the most exotic whim of the *epicurean*. also ADJ.

epigram N. witty thought or saying, usually short. Poor Richard's *epigrams* made Benjamin Franklin famous.

epilogue N. short speech at conclusion of dramatic work. The audience was so disappointed in the play that many did not remain to hear the *epilogue*.

epitaph N. inscription in memory of a dead person. In his will, he dictated the *epitaph* he wanted placed on his tombstone.

epithet N. descriptive word or phrase. Homer's writings were featured by the use of such *epithets* as "rosy-fingered dawn."

epitome N. summary; concise abstract. This final book is the *epitome* of all his previous books. epitomize, V.

epoch N. period of time. The glacial *epoch* lasted for thousands of years.

equable ADJ. tranquil; steady; uniform. After the hot summers and cold winters of New England, he found the climate of the West Indies *equable* and pleasant.

■ **equanimity** N. calmness of temperament. In his later years, he could look upon the foolishness of the world with *equanimity* and humor.

equestrian N. rider on horseback. These paths in the park are reserved for *equestrians* and their steeds. also ADJ.

equilibrium N. balance. After the divorce, he needed some time to regain his *equilibrium*.

equine ADJ. resembling a horse. His long, bony face had an *equine* look to it.

equinox N. period of equal days and nights; the beginning of Spring and Autumn. The vernal *equinox* is usually marked by heavy rainstorms.

equipage N. horse-drawn carriage. The *equipage* drew up before the inn and the passengers stepped out.

equipoise N. balance; balancing force; equilibrium. The high wire acrobat used his pole as an *equipoise* to overcome the swaying caused by the wind.

equitable ADJ. fair; impartial. I am seeking an *equitable* solution to this dispute, one which will be fair and acceptable to both sides.

equity N. fairness; justice. Our courts guarantee *equity* to all.

equivocal ADJ. doubtful; ambiguous. Macbeth was misled by the *equivocal* statements of the witches.

■ **equivocate** V. lie; mislead; attempt to conceal the truth. The audience saw through his attempts to *equivocate* on the subject under discussion and ridiculed his remarks.

erode V. eat away. The limestone was *eroded* by the dripping water. erosion, N.

erotic ADJ. pertaining to passionate love. The *erotic* pas-

sages in this novel should be removed as they are merely pornographic.

errant ADJ. wandering. Many a charming tale has been written about the knights-*errant* who helped the weak and punished the guilty during the Age of Chivalry.

erratic ADJ. odd; unpredictable. Investors become anxious when the stock market appears *erratic*.

erroneous ADJ. mistaken; wrong. I thought my answer was correct, but it was *erroneous*.

■ **erudite** ADJ. learned; scholarly. His *erudite* writing was difficult to read because of the many allusions which were unfamiliar to most readers. erudition, N.

erudition N. high degree of knowledge and learning. Although they respected his *erudition*, the populace refused to listen to his words of caution and turned to less learned leaders.

escapade N. prank; flighty conduct. The headmaster could not regard this latest *escapade* as a boyish joke and expelled the young man.

eschew V. avoid. He tried to *eschew* all display of temper.

escutcheon N. shield-shaped surface on which coat of arms is placed. His traitorous acts placed a shameful blot on the family *escutcheon*.

esoteric ADJ. known only to the chosen few. Those students who had access to his *esoteric* discussions were impressed by the breadth of his knowledge.

espionage N. spying. In order to maintain its power, the government developed a system of *espionage* which penetrated every household.

espouse V. adopt; support. She was always ready to *espouse* a worthy cause.

esprit de corps N. comradeship; spirit. West Point cadets are proud of their *esprit de corps*.

esteem V. respect; value; judge. I esteem Ezra Pound both for his exciting poetry and for his acute comments on literature. also N.

estranged ADJ. separated; alienated. The *estranged* wife sought a divorce. estrangement, N.

ethereal ADJ. light; heavenly; fine. Visitors were impressed by her *ethereal* beauty, her delicate charm.

ethnic ADJ. relating to races. Intolerance between *ethnic* groups is deplorable and usually is based on lack of information.

ethnology N. study of man. Sociology is one aspect of the science of *ethnology*.

etymology N. study of word parts. A knowledge of *etymology* can help you on many English tests.

eugenic ADJ. pertaining to the improvement of race. It is easier to apply *eugenic* principles to the raising of race horses or prize cattle than to the development of human beings.

eulogistic ADJ. praising. To everyone's surprise, the speech was *eulogistic* rather than critical in tone.

Test

Word List 17   *Antonyms*

Each of the questions below consists of a word in capital letters, followed by five lettered words or phrases. Choose the lettered word or phrase that is most nearly opposite in meaning to the word in capital letters and write the letter of your choice on your answer paper.

241. ENERVATE (A) strengthen (B) sputter (C) arrange (D) scrutinize (E) agree
242. ENHANCE (A) degrade (B) doubt (C) scuff (D) gasp (E) agree
243. ENNUI (A) hate (B) excitement (C) seriousness (D) humility (E) kindness
244. ENUNCIATE (A) pray (B) request (C) deliver (D) wait (E) mumble
245. EPHEMERAL (A) sensuous (B) passive (C) popular (D) distasteful (E) eternal
246. EQUABLE (A) flat (B) decisive (C) stormy (D) rough (E) scanty

247. EQUANIMITY (A) agitation (B) stirring (C) volume (D) identity (E) luster
248. EQUILIBRIUM (A) imbalance (B) peace (C) inequity (D) directness (E) urgency
249. EQUITABLE (A) able to leave (B) able to learn (C) unfair (D) preferable (E) rough
250. EQUIVOCAL (A) mistaken (B) quaint (C) azure (D) clear (E) universal
251. ERRATIC (A) unromantic (B) free (C) popular (D) steady (E) unknown
252. ERRONEOUS (A) accurate (B) dignified (C) curious (D) abrupt (E) round
253. ERUDITE (A) professorial (B) stately (C) short (D) unknown (E) ignorant
254. ETHEREAL (A) long-lasting (B) earthy (C) ill (D) critical (E) false
255. EULOGISTIC (A) pretty (B) critical (C) brief (D) stern (E) free

Word List 18   eulogy-faculty

■ **eulogy** N. praise. All the *eulogies* of his friends could not remove the sting of the calumny heaped upon him by his enemies. eulogize, V.

euphemism N. mild expression in place of an unpleasant one. The expression "he passed away" is a *euphemism* for "he died."

■ **euphony** N. sweet sound. Noted for its *euphony* even when it is spoken, the Italian language is particularly pleasing to the ear when sung. euphonious, ADJ.

euthanasia N. mercy killing. Many people support *euthanasia* for terminally-ill patients who wish to die.

■ **evanescent** ADJ. fleeting; vanishing. For a brief moment, the entire skyline was bathed in an orange-red hue in the *evanescent* rays of the sunset.

evasive ADJ. not frank; eluding. Your *evasive* answers convinced the judge that you were withholding important evidence. evade, V.

evince V. show clearly. When he tried to answer the questions, he *evinced* his ignorance of the subject matter.

eviscerate V. disembowel; remove entrails. The medicine man *eviscerated* the animal and offered the entrails to the angry gods.

evoke V. call forth. He *evoked* much criticism by his hostile manner.

ewer N. water pitcher. The primitive conditions of the period were symbolized by the porcelain *ewer* and basin in the bedroom.

exacerbate V. worsen; embitter. This latest arrest will *exacerbate* the already existing discontent of the people and enrage them.

exaction N. exorbitant demand; extortion. The colonies rebelled against the *exactions* of the mother country.

exasperate V. vex. Johnny often *exasperates* his mother with his pranks.

exchequer N. treasury. He had been Chancellor of the *Exchequer* before his promotion to the office he now holds.

excision N. act of cutting away. With the *excision* of the dead and dying limbs of this tree, you have not only improved its appearance but you have enhanced its chances of bearing fruit.

excoriate V. flay; abrade. These shoes are so ill-fitting that they will *excoriate* the feet and create blisters.

■ **exculpate** V. clear from blame. He was *exculpated* of the crime when the real criminal confessed.

execrable ADJ. very bad. The anecdote was in *execrable* taste and shocked the audience.

execrate V. curse; express abhorrence for. The world *execrates* the memory of Hitler and hopes that genocide will never again be the policy of any nation.

execute V. put into effect; carry out. The choreographer wanted to see how well she could *execute* a pirouette. (secondary meaning) execution, N.

exegesis N. explanation, especially of Biblical passages. I can follow your *exegesis* of this passage to a limited degree; some of your reasoning eludes me.

exemplary ADJ. serving as a model; outstanding. Her *exemplary* behavior was praised at Commencement.

exertion N. effort; expenditure of much physical work. The *exertion* spent in unscrewing the rusty bolt left her exhausted.

exhort V. urge. The evangelist will *exhort* all sinners in his audience to reform.

exhume V. dig out of the ground; remove from a grave. Because of the rumor that he had been poisoned, his body was *exhumed* in order that an autopsy might be performed.

■ **exigency** N. urgent situation. In this *exigency*, we must look for aid from our allies.

exiguous ADJ. small; minute. Grass grew there, an *exiguous* outcropping among the rocks.

exodus N. departure. The *exodus* from the hot and stuffy city was particularly noticeable on Friday evenings.

ex officio ADJ. by virtue of one's office. The Mayor was *ex officio* chairman of the committee that decided the annual tax rate. also ADV.

exonerate V. acquit; exculpate. I am sure this letter naming the actual culprit will *exonerate* you.

exorbitant ADJ. excessive. The people grumbled at his *exorbitant* prices but paid them because he had a monopoly.

exorcise V. drive out evil spirits. By incantation and prayer, the medicine man sought to *exorcise* the evil spirits which had taken possession of the young warrior.

exotic ADJ. not native; strange. Because of his *exotic* headdress, he was followed in the streets by small children who laughed at his strange appearance.

expatiate V. talk at length. At this time, please give us a brief resumé of your work; we shall permit you to *expatiate* later.

expatriate N. exile; someone who has withdrawn from his native land. Henry James was an American *expatriate* who settled in England.

expedient ADJ. suitable; practical; politic. A pragmatic politician, he was guided by what was *expedient* rather than by what was ethical. expediency, N.

expedite V. hasten. We hope you will be able to *expedite* delivery because of our tight schedule.

expeditiously ADV. rapidly and efficiently. Please adjust this matter as *expeditiously* as possible as it is delaying important work.

expertise N. specialized knowledge; expert skill. Although she was knowledgeable in a number of fields, she was hired for her particular *expertise* in computer programming.

expiate V. make amends for (a sin). He tried to *expiate* his crimes by a full confession to the authorities.

expletive N. interjection; profane oath. The sergeant's remarks were filled with *expletives* that offended the new recruits.

explicit ADJ. definite; open. Your remarks are *explicit*; no one can misinterpret them.

exploit N. deed or action, particularly a brave deed. Raoul Wallenberg was noted for his *exploits* in rescuing Jews from Hitler's forces.

exploit V. make use of, sometimes unjustly. Cesar Chavez fought attempts to *exploit* migrant farmworkers in California. exploitation, N.

expostulation N. remonstrance. Despite the teacher's scoldings and *expostulations*, the class remained unruly.

■ **expunge** V. cancel; remove. If you behave, I will *expunge* this notation from your record.

expurgate V. clean; remove offensive parts of a book. The editors felt that certain passages in the book had to be *expurgated* before it could be used in the classroom.

extant ADJ. still in existence. Although the authorities suppressed the book, many copies are *extant* and may be purchased at exorbitant prices.

extemporaneous ADJ. not planned; impromptu. Because his *extemporaneous* remarks were misinterpreted, he decided to write all his speeches in advance.

extenuate V. weaken; mitigate. It is easier for us to *extenuate* our own shortcomings than those of others.

extirpate V. root up. The Salem witch trials were a misguided attempt to *extirpate* superstition and heresy.

extol V. praise; glorify. The astronauts were *extolled* as the pioneers of the Space Age.

extort V. wring from; get money by threats, etc. The blackmailer *extorted* money from his victim.

extradition N. surrender of prisoner by one state to another. The lawyers opposed the *extradition* of their client on the grounds that for more than five years he had been a model citizen.

extraneous ADJ. not essential; external. Do not pad your paper with *extraneous* matters; stick to essential items only.

■ **extrapolation** N. projection; conjecture. Based on their *extrapolation* from the results of the primaries on Super Tuesday, the networks predicted that George Bush would be the Republican candidate for the presidency. extrapolate, V.

■ **extricate** V. free; disentangle. He found that he could not *extricate* himself from the trap.

extrinsic ADJ. external; not inherent; foreign. Do not be fooled by *extrinsic* causes. We must look for the intrinsic reason.

extrovert N. person interested mostly in external objects and actions. A good salesman is usually an *extrovert*, who likes to mingle with people.

extrude V. force or push out. Much pressure is required to *extrude* these plastics.

exuberant ADJ. abundant; effusive; lavish. His speeches were famous for his *exuberant* language and vivid imagery.

exude V. discharge; give forth. The maple syrup is obtained from the sap that *exudes* from the trees in early spring. exudation, N.

exult V. rejoice. We *exulted* when our team won the victory.

fabricate V. build; lie. Because of the child's tendency to *fabricate*, we had trouble believing her.

facade N. front of the building. The *facade* of the church had often been photographed by tourists because it was more interesting than the rear.

facet N. small plane surface (of a gem); a side. The stonecutter decided to improve the rough diamond by providing it with several *facets*.

■ **facetious** ADJ. humorous; jocular. Your *facetious* remarks are not appropriate at this serious moment.

facile ADJ. easy; expert. Because he was a *facile* speaker, he never refused a request to address an organization.

facilitate V. make less difficult. He tried to *facilitate* matters at home by getting a part-time job.

facsimile N. copy. Many museums sell *facsimiles* of the works of art on display.

faction N. party; clique; dissension. The quarrels and bick-

ering of the two small *factions* within the club disturbed the majority of the members.

factious ADJ. inclined to form factions; causing dissension. Your statement is *factious* and will upset the harmony that now exists.

factitious ADJ. artificial; sham. Hollywood actresses often create *factitious* tears by using glycerine.

factotum N. handyman; person who does all kinds of work. Although we had hired him as a messenger, we soon began to use him as a general *factotum* around the office.

faculty N. mental or bodily powers; teaching staff. As he grew old, he feared he might lose his *faculties* and become useless to his employer.

Test

Word List 18   *Antonyms*

Each of the questions below consists of a word in capital letters, followed by five lettered words or phrases. Choose the lettered word or phrase that is most nearly opposite in meaning to the word in capital letters and write the letter of your choice on your answer paper.

256. EUPHONIOUS (A) strident (B) lethargic (C) literary (D) significant (E) merry
257. EVASIVE (A) frank (B) correct (C) empty (D) fertile (E) watchful
258. EXASPERATE (A) confide (B) formalize (C) placate (D) betray (E) bargain
259. EXCORIATE (A) scandalize (B) encourage (C) avoid (D) praise (E) vanquish
260. EXCULPATE (A) blame (B) prevail (C) acquire (D) ravish (E) accumulate
261. EXECRABLE (A) innumerable (B) philosophic (C) physical (D) excellent (E) meditative

262. EXECRATE (A) disobey (B) enact (C) perform (D) acclaim (E) fidget
263. EXHUME (A) decipher (B) sadden (C) integrate (D) admit (E) inter
264. EXODUS (A) neglect (B) consent (C) entry (D) gain (E) rebuke
265. EXONERATE (A) forge (B) accuse (C) record (D) doctor (E) reimburse
266. EXORBITANT (A) moderate (B) partisan (C) military (D) barbaric (E) counterfeit
267. EXTEMPORANEOUS (A) rehearsed (B) hybrid (C) humiliating (D) statesmanlike (E) picturesque
268. EXTRANEOUS (A) modern (B) decisive (C) essential (D) effective (E) expressive
269. EXTRINSIC (A) reputable (B) inherent (C) swift (D) ambitious (E) cursory
270. EXTROVERT (A) clown (B) hero (C) ectomorph (D) neurotic (E) introvert

Word List 19   fain-flinch

fain ADV. gladly. The knight said, "I would *fain* be your protector."

■ **fallacious** ADJ. misleading. Your reasoning must be *fallacious* because it leads to a ridiculous answer.

fallible ADJ. liable to err. I know I am *fallible,* but I feel confident that I am right this time.

fallow ADJ. plowed but not sowed; uncultivated. Farmers have learned that it is advisable to permit land to lie *fallow* every few years.

falter V. hesitate. When told to dive off the high board, she did not *falter,* but proceeded at once.

fanaticism N. excessive zeal. The leader of the group was held responsible even though he could not control the *fanaticism* of his followers. fantastic, ADJ., N.

fancied ADJ. imagined; unreal. You are resenting *fancied* insults. No one has ever said such things about you.

fancier N. breeder or dealer of animals. The dog *fancier* exhibited her prize collie at the annual Kennel Club show.

fanciful ADJ. whimsical; visionary. This is a *fanciful* scheme because it does not consider the facts.

fanfare N. call by bugles or trumpets. The exposition was opened with a *fanfare* of trumpets and the firing of cannon.

fantastic ADJ. unreal; grotesque; whimsical. Your fears are *fantastic* because no such animal as you have described exists.

farce N. broad comedy; mockery. Nothing went right; the entire interview degenerated into a *farce*. farcical, ADJ.

fastidious ADJ. difficult to please; squeamish. The waitresses disliked serving him dinner because of his very *fastidious* taste.

fatalism N. belief that events are determined by forces beyond one's control. With *fatalism,* he accepted the hardships that beset him. fatalistic, ADJ.

fathom V. comprehend; investigate. I find his motives impossible to *fathom.*

fatuous ADJ. foolish; inane. He is far too intelligent to utter such *fatuous* remarks.

fauna N. animals of a period or region. The scientist could visualize the *fauna* of the period by examining the skeletal remains and the fossils.

faux pas N. an error or slip (in manners or behavior). Your tactless remarks during dinner were a *faux pas.*

■ **fawning** ADJ. courting favor by cringing and flattering. She was constantly surrounded by a group of *fawning* admirers who hoped to win some favor. fawn, V.

fealty N. loyalty; faithfulness. The feudal lord demanded *fealty* of his vassals.

feasible ADJ. practical. This is an entirely *feasible* proposal. I suggest we adopt it.

febrile ADJ. feverish. In his *febrile* condition, he was subject to nightmares and hallucinations.

■ **fecundity** N. fertility; fruitfulness. The *fecundity* of his mind is illustrated by the many vivid images in his poems.

feign V. pretend. Lady Macbeth *feigned* illness in the courtyard although she was actually healthy.

feint N. trick; shift; sham blow. The boxer was fooled by his opponent's *feint* and dropped his guard. also V.

■ **felicitous** ADJ. apt; suitably expressed; well chosen. He was famous for his *felicitous* remarks and was called upon to serve as master-of-ceremonies at many a banquet. felicity, N.

fell ADJ. cruel; deadly. The newspapers told of the tragic spread of the *fell* disease.

felon N. person convicted of a grave crime. A convicted *felon* loses the right to vote.

ferment N. agitation; commotion. The entire country was in a state of *ferment.*

ferret V. drive or hunt out of hiding. She *ferreted* out their secret.

fervent ADJ. ardent; hot. She felt that the *fervent* praise was excessive and somewhat undeserved.

fervid ADJ. ardent. Her *fervid* enthusiasm inspired all of us to undertake the dangerous mission.

■ **fervor** N. glowing ardor. Their kiss was full of the *fervor* of first love.

fester V. generate pus. When her finger began to *fester,* the doctor lanced it and removed the splinter which had caused the pus to form.

festive ADJ. joyous; celebratory. Their wedding in the park was a *festive* occasion.

fete V. honor at a festival. The returning hero was *feted* at a community supper and dance. also N.

fetid ADJ. malodorous. The neglected wound became *fetid.*

fetish N. object supposed to possess magical powers; an object of special devotion. The native wore a *fetish* around his neck to ward off evil spirits.

■ **fetter** V. shackle. The prisoner was *fettered* to the wall.

fiasco N. total failure. Our ambitious venture ended in a *fiasco* and we were forced to flee.

fiat N. command. I cannot accept government by *fiat;* I feel that I must be consulted.

fickle ADJ. changeable; faithless. He discovered she was *fickle* and went out with many men.

fictitious ADJ. imaginary. Although this book purports to be a biography of George Washington, many of the incidents are *fictitious.*

fidelity N. loyalty. A dog's *fidelity* to its owner is one of the reasons why that animal is a favorite household pet.

fiduciary ADJ. pertaining to a position of trust. In his will, he stipulated that the bank act in a *fiduciary* capacity and manage his estate until his children became of age. also N.

figment N. invention; imaginary thing. That incident never took place; it is a *figment* of your imagination.

filch V. steal. The boys *filched* apples from the fruit stand.

filial ADJ. pertaining to a son or daughter. Many children forget their *filial* obligations and disregard the wishes of their parents.

finale N. conclusion. It is not until we reach the *finale* of this play that we can understand the author's message.

finesse N. delicate skill. The *finesse* and adroitness of the surgeon impressed the observers in the operating room.

finicky ADJ. too particular; fussy. The old lady was *finicky* about her food and ate very little.

finite ADJ. limited. It is difficult for humanity with its *finite* existence to grasp the infinite.

firebrand N. hothead; troublemaker. The police tried to keep track of all the local *firebrands* when the President came to town.

fissure N. crevice. The mountain climbers secured footholds in tiny *fissures* in the rock.

fitful ADJ. spasmodic; intermittent. After several *fitful* attempts, he decided to postpone the start of the project until he felt more energetic.

flaccid ADJ. flabby. His sedentary life had left him with *flaccid* muscles.

■ **flag** V. droop; grow feeble. When the opposing hockey team scored its third goal only minutes into the first quarter, the home team's spirits *flagged.* flagging, ADJ.

flagellate V. flog; whip. The Romans used to *flagellate* criminals with a whip that had three knotted strands.

flagrant ADJ. conspicuously wicked. We cannot condone such *flagrant* violations of the rules.

flail V. thresh grain by hand; strike or slap. In medieval times, warriors *flailed* their foe with a metal ball attached to a handle.

flair N. talent. She has an uncanny *flair* for discovering new artists before the public has become aware of their existence.

flamboyant ADJ. ornate. Modern architecture has discarded the *flamboyant* trimming on buildings and emphasizes simplicity of line.

flaunt V. display ostentatiously. She is not one of those actresses who *flaunt* their physical charms; she can act.

flay V. strip off skin; plunder. The criminal was condemned to be *flayed* alive.

fleck V. spot. Her cheeks, *flecked* with tears, were testimony to the hours of weeping.

■ **fledgling** ADJ. inexperienced. While it is necessary to provide these *fledgling* poets with an opportunity to present

their work, it is not essential that we admire everything they write. also N.

fleece N. wool coat of a sheep. They shear sheep of their *fleece,* which they then comb into separate strands of wool.

fleece V. rob; plunder. The tricksters *fleeced* him of his inheritance.

flick N. light stroke as with a whip. The horse needed no encouragement; only one *flick* of the whip was all the jockey had to apply to get the animal to run at top speed.

flinch V. hesitate; shrink. He did not *flinch* in the face of danger but fought back bravely.

Test

Word List 19   *Synonyms and Antonyms*

Each of the following questions consists of a word in capital letters, followed by five lettered words or phrases. Choose the lettered word or phrase which is most nearly similar or the opposite of the word in capital letters and write the letter of your choice on your answer paper.

271. FANCIFUL (A) imaginative (B) knowing (C) elaborate (D) quick (E) lusty
272. FATUOUS (A) fatal (B) natal (C) terrible (D) sensible (E) tolerable
273. FEASIBLE (A) theoretical (B) impatient (C) constant (D) present (E) impractical
274. FECUNDITY (A) prophecy (B) futility (C) fruitfulness (D) need (E) dormancy
275. FEIGN (A) deserve (B) condemn (C) condone (D) attend (E) pretend
276. FELL (A) propitious (B) illiterate (C) catastrophic (D) futile (E) inherent

277. FERMENT (A) stir up (B) fill (C) ferret (D) mutilate (E) banish
278. FIASCO (A) cameo (B) mansion (C) pollution (D) success (E) gamble
279. FICKLE (A) fallacious (B) tolerant (C) loyal (D) hungry (E) stupid
280. FILCH (A) milk (B) purloin (C) itch (D) cancel (E) resent
281. FINITE (A) bounded (B) established (C) affirmative (D) massive (E) finicky
282. FLAIL (A) succeed (B) harvest (C) knife (D) strike (E) resent
283. FLAIR (A) conflagration (B) inspiration (C) bent (D) egregiousness (E) magnitude
284. FLAMBOYANT (A) old-fashioned (B) restrained (C) impulsive (D) cognizant (E) eloquent
285. FLEDGLING (A) weaving (B) bobbing (C) beginning (D) studying (E) flaying

Word List 20   flippancy-gaff

flippancy N. trifling gaiety. Your *flippancy* at this serious moment is offensive. flippant, ADJ.

floe N. mass of floating ice. The ship made slow progress as it battered its way through the ice *floes.*

flora N. plants of a region or era. Because she was a botanist, she spent most of her time studying the *flora* of the desert.

florid ADJ. flowery; ruddy. His complexion was even more *florid* than usual because of his anger.

flotilla N. small fleet. It is always an exciting and interesting moment when the fishing *flotilla* returns to port.

flotsam N. drifting wreckage. Beachcombers eke out a living by salvaging the *flotsam* and jetsam of the sea.

flourish V. grow well; prosper; decorate with ornaments. The orange trees *flourished* in the sun.

■ **flout** V. reject; mock. The headstrong youth *flouted* all authority; he refused to be curbed.

fluctuation N. wavering. Meteorologists watch the *fluctuations* of the barometer in order to predict the weather.

fluency N. smoothness of speech. He spoke French with *fluency* and ease.

fluster V. confuse. The teacher's sudden question *flustered* him and he stammered his reply.

fluted ADJ. having vertical parallel grooves (as in a pillar). All that remained of the ancient building were the *fluted* columns.

flux N. flowing; series of changes. While conditions are in such a state of *flux,* I do not wish to commit myself too deeply in this affair.

foible N. weakness; slight fault. We can overlook the *foibles* of our friends; no one is perfect.

foil N. contrast. In "Star Wars," dark, evil Darth Vader is a perfect *foil* for fair-haired, naive Luke Skywalker.

foil V. defeat; frustrate. In the end, Skywalker is able to *foil* Vader's diabolical schemes.

foist V. insert improperly; palm off. I will not permit you to *foist* such ridiculous ideas upon the membership of this group.

foment V. stir up; instigate. This report will *foment* dissension in the club.

foolhardy ADJ. rash. Don't be *foolhardy*. Get the advice of experienced people before undertaking this venture.

foppish ADJ. vain about dress and appearance. He tried to imitate the *foppish* manner of the young men of the court.

foray N. raid. The company staged a midnight *foray* against the enemy outpost.

forbearance N. patience. We must use *forbearance* in dealing with him because he is still weak from his illness.

foreboding N. premonition of evil. Caesar ridiculed his wife's *forebodings* about the Ides of March.

forensic ADJ. suitable to debate or courts of law. In her best *forensic* manner, the lawyer addressed the jury.

foresight N. ability to foresee future happenings; prudence. A wise investor, she had the *foresight* to buy land just before the current real estate boom.

formality N. adherence to established rules or procedures. Signing this position is a mere *formality*; it does not obligate you in any way.

formidable ADJ. menacing; threatening. We must not treat the battle lightly for we are facing a *formidable* foe.

forte N. strong point or special talent. I am not eager to play this rather serious role, for my *forte* is comedy.

fortitude N. bravery; courage. He was awarded the medal for his *fortitude* in the battle.

fortuitous ADJ. accidental; by chance. There is no connection between these two events; their timing is extremely *fortuitous*.

foster V. rear; encourage. According to the legend, Romulus and Remus were *fostered* by a she-wolf. also ADJ.

fracas N. brawl, melee. The military police stopped the *fracas* in the bar and arrested the belligerents.

fractious ADJ. unruly. The *fractious* horse unseated its rider.

frailty N. weakness. We had to pity the sick old woman because of her *frailty*.

franchise N. right granted by authority. The city issued a *franchise* to the company to operate surface transit lines on the streets for ninety-nine years. also V.

frantic ADJ. wild. At the time of the collision, many people became *frantic* with fear.

fraudulent ADJ. cheating; deceitful. The government seeks to prevent *fraudulent* and misleading advertising.

fraught ADJ. filled. Since this enterprise is *fraught* with danger, I will ask for volunteers who are willing to assume the risks.

fray N. brawl. The three musketeers were in the thick of the *fray*.

freebooter N. buccaneer. This town is a rather dangerous place to visit as it is frequented by pirates, *freebooters,* and other plunderers.

frenetic ADJ. frenzied; frantic. His *frenetic* activities convinced us that he had no organized plan of operation.

frenzied ADJ. madly excited. As soon as they smelled smoke, the *frenzied* animals milled about in their cages.

fresco N. painting on plaster (usually fresh). The cathedral is visited by many tourists who wish to admire the *frescoes* by Giotto.

freshet N. sudden flood. Motorists were warned that spring *freshets* had washed away several small bridges and that long detours would be necessary.

fret V. to be annoyed or vexed. To *fret* over your poor grades is foolish; instead, decide to work harder in the future.

friction N. clash in opinion; rubbing against. At this time when harmony is essential, we cannot afford to have any *friction* in our group.

frieze N. ornamental band on a wall. The *frieze* of the church was adorned with sculpture.

frigid ADJ. intensely cold. Alaska is in the *frigid* zone.

fritter V. waste. He could not apply himself to any task and *frittered* away his time in idle conversation.

frivolity N. lack of seriousness. We were distressed by his *frivolity* during the recent grave crisis. frivolous, ADJ.

frolicsome ADJ. prankish; gay. The *frolicsome* puppy tried to lick the face of its master.

frond N. fern leaf; palm or banana leaf. After the storm the beach was littered with the *fronds* of palm trees.

froward ADJ. disobedient; perverse; stubborn. Your *froward* behavior has alienated many of us who might have been your supporters.

frowzy ADJ. slovenly; unkempt; dirty. Her *frowzy* appearance and her cheap decorations made her appear ludicrous in this group.

fructify V. bear fruit. This peach tree should *fructify* in three years.

■ **frugality** N. thrift. In these difficult days, we must live with *frugality* or our money will be gone.

fruition N. bearing of fruit; fulfillment; realization. This building marks the *fruition* of all our aspirations and years of hard work.

frustrate V. thwart; defeat. We must *frustrate* this dictator's plan to seize control of the government.

fulcrum N. support on which a lever rests. If we use this stone as a *fulcrum* and the crowbar as a lever, we may be able to move this boulder.

fulgent ADJ. beaming; radiant. In the *fulgent* glow of the early sunrise, everything seemed bright and gleaming.

fulminate V. thunder; explode. The people against whom she *fulminated* were innocent of any wrongdoing.

fulsome ADJ. disgustingly excessive. His *fulsome* praise of the dictator annoyed his listeners.

functionary N. official. As his case was transferred from one *functionary* to another, he began to despair of ever reaching a settlement.

funereal ADJ. sad; solemn. I fail to understand why there is such a *funereal* atmosphere; we have lost a battle, not a war.

furor N. frenzy; great excitement. The story of her embezzlement of the funds created a *furor* on the Stock Exchange.

furtive ADJ. stealthy; sneaky. The boy gave a *furtive* look at his classmate's test paper.

fusion N. union; coalition. The opponents of the political party in power organized a *fusion* of disgruntled groups and became an important element in the election.

fustian ADJ. pompous; bombastic. Several in the audience were deceived by her *fustian* style; they mistook pomposity for erudition.

futile ADJ. ineffective; fruitless. Why waste your time on *futile* pursuits?

gadfly N. animal-biting fly; an irritating person. Like a *gadfly,* he irritated all the guests at the hotel; within forty-eight hours, everyone regarded him as an annoying busybody.

gaff N. hook; barbed fishing spear. When he attempted to land the sailfish, he was so nervous that he dropped the *gaff* into the sea. also V.

Test

Word List 20   *Synonyms*

Each of the questions below consists of a word in capital letters, followed by five lettered words or phrases. Choose the lettered word or phrase that is most nearly similar in meaning to the word in capital letters and write the letter of your choice on your answer paper.

286. FLORID (A) ruddy (B) rusty (C) ruined (D) patient (E) poetic
287. FOIL (A) bury (B) frustrate (C) shield (D) desire (E) gain
288. FOMENT (A) spoil (B) instigate (C) interrogate (D) spray (E) maintain
289. FOOLHARDY (A) strong (B) unwise (C) brave (D) futile (E) erudite
290. FOPPISH (A) scanty (B) radical (C) orthodox (D) dandyish (E) magnificent
291. FORAY (A) excursion (B) contest (C) ranger (D) intuition (E) fish
292. FORMIDABLE (A) dangerous (B) outlandish (C) grandiloquent (D) impenetrable (E) venerable
293. FOSTER (A) speed (B) fondle (C) become infected (D) raise (E) roll
294. FRANCHISE (A) subway (B) kiosk (C) license (D) reason (E) fashion
295. FRITTER (A) sour (B) chafe (C) dissipate (D) cancel (E) abuse
296. FRUGALITY (A) foolishness (B) extremity (C) indifference (D) enthusiasm (E) economy
297. FULGENT (A) dizzy (B) empty (C) diverse (D) shining (E) dreamy
298. FUROR (A) excitement (B) worry (C) flux (D) anteroom (E) lover
299. FURTIVE (A) underhanded (B) coy (C) brilliant (D) quick (E) abortive
300. GADFLY (A) humorist (B) nuisance (C) scholar (D) bum (E) thief

Word List 21   gainsay-gossamer

gainsay V. deny. She was too honest to *gainsay* the truth of the report.

gait N. manner of walking or running; speed. The lame man walked with an uneven *gait*.

galaxy N. the Milky Way; any collection of brilliant personalities. The deaths of such famous actors as Clark Gable, Gary Cooper and Spencer Tracy demonstrate that the *galaxy* of Hollywood superstars is rapidly disappearing.

gall N. bitterness; nerve. The knowledge of his failure filled him with *gall*.

gall V. annoy; chafe. Their taunts *galled* him.

galleon N. large sailing ship. The Spaniards pinned their hopes on the *galleon,* the large warship; the British, on the smaller and faster pinnace.

galvanize V. stimulate by shock; stir up. The entire nation was *galvanized* into strong military activity by the news of the attack on Pearl Harbor.

gambit N. opening in chess in which a piece is sacrificed. The player was afraid to accept his opponent's *gambit* because he feared a trap which as yet he could not see.

gambol V. skip; leap playfully. Watching children *gamboling* in the park is a pleasant experience. also N.

gamely ADV. Because he had fought *gamely* against a much superior boxer, the crowd gave him a standing ovation when he left the arena.

gamester N. gambler. An inveterate *gamester,* she was willing to wager on the outcome of any event, even one which involved the behavior of insects.

gamut N. entire range. In this performance, the leading lady was able to demonstrate the complete *gamut* of her acting ability.

gape V. open widely. The huge pit *gaped* before him; if he stumbled, he would fall in.

garbled ADJ. mixed up; based on false or unfair selection.

The *garbled* report confused many readers who were not familiar with the facts. garble, V.

gargantuan ADJ. huge; enormous. The *gargantuan* wrestler was terrified of mice.

gargoyle N. waterspout carved in grotesque figures on building. The *gargoyles* adorning the Cathedral of Notre Dame in Paris are amusing in their grotesqueness.

garish ADJ. gaudy. She wore a *garish* rhinestone necklace.

■ **garner** V. gather; store up. She hoped to *garner* the world's literature in one library.

garnish V. decorate. Parsley was used to *garnish* the boiled potato. also N.

■ **garrulity** N. talkativeness. The man who married a dumb wife asked the doctor to make him deaf because of his wife's *garrulity* after her cure.

garrulous ADJ. loquacious; wordy. Many members avoided the company of the *garrulous* old gentleman because his constant chatter on trivial matters bored them.

gasconade N. bluster; boastfulness. Behind his front of *gasconade* and pompous talk, he tried to hide his inherent uncertainty and nervousness. also V.

gastronomy N. science of preparing and serving good food. One of the by-products of his trip to Europe was his interest in *gastronomy;* he enjoyed preparing and serving foreign dishes to his friends.

gauche ADJ. clumsy; boorish. Such remarks are *gauche* and out of place; you should apologize for making them.

gaudy ADJ. flashy; showy. Her *gaudy* taste in clothes appalled us.

gaunt ADJ. lean and angular; barren. His once round face looked surprisingly *gaunt* after he had lost weight.

gauntlet N. leather glove. Now that we have been challenged, we must take up the *gauntlet* and meet our adversary fearlessly.

gazette N. official periodical publication. He read the *gazettes* regularly for the announcement of his promotion.

genealogy N. record of descent; lineage. He was proud of his *genealogy* and constantly referred to the achievements of his ancestors.

generality N. vague statement. This report is filled with *generalities;* you must be more specific in your statements.

generic ADJ. characteristic of a class or species. You have made the mistake of thinking that his behavior is *generic;* actually, very few of his group behave the way he does.

genesis N. beginning; origin. Tracing the *genesis* of a family is the theme of "Roots."

geniality N. cheerfulness; kindliness; sympathy. This restaurant is famous and popular because of the *geniality* of the proprietor who tries to make everyone happy.

genre N. style of art illustrating scenes of common life. His painting of fisher folk at their daily tasks is an excellent illustration of *genre* art.

genteel ADJ. well-bred; elegant. We are looking for a man with a *genteel* appearance who can inspire confidence by his cultivated manner.

gentility N. those of gentle birth; refinement. Her family was proud of its *gentility* and elegance.

gentry N. people of standing; class of people just below nobility. The local *gentry* did not welcome the visits of the summer tourists and tried to ignore their presence in the community.

genuflect V. bend the knee as in worship. A proud democrat, he refused to *genuflect* to any man.

germane ADJ. pertinent; bearing upon the case at hand. The lawyer objected that the testimony being offered was not *germane* to the case at hand.

germinal ADJ. pertaining to a germ; creative. Such an idea is *germinal;* I am certain that it will influence thinkers and philosophers for many generations.

germinate V. cause to sprout; sprout. After the seeds *germinate* and develop their permanent leaves, the plants may be removed from the cold frames and transplanted to the garden.

gerrymander V. change voting district lines in order to favor a political party. The illogical pattern of the map of this congressional district is proof that the State Legislature *gerrymandered* this area in order to favor the majority party. also N.

gestate V. evolve, as in prenatal growth. While this scheme was being *gestated* by the conspirators, they maintained complete silence about their intentions.

gesticulation N. motion; gesture. Operatic performers are trained to make exaggerated *gesticulations* because of the large auditoriums in which they appear.

ghastly ADJ. horrible. The murdered man was a *ghastly* sight.

gibber V. speak foolishly. The demented man *gibbered* incoherently.

gibbet N. gallows. The bodies of the highwaymen were left dangling from the *gibbet* as a warning to other would-be transgressors.

gibe V. mock. As you *gibe* at their superstitious beliefs, do you realize that you, too, are guilty of similarly foolish thoughts?

giddy ADJ. light-hearted; dizzy. He felt his *giddy* youth was past.

gig N. two-wheeled carriage. As they drove down the street in their new *gig*, drawn by the dappled mare, they were cheered by the people who recognized them.

gingerly ADV. very carefully. To separate egg whites, first crack the egg *gingerly*.

■ **gist** N. essence. She was asked to give the *gist* of the essay in two sentences.

glaze V. cover with a thin and shiny surface. The freezing rain *glazed* the streets and made driving hazardous. also N.

glean V. gather leavings. After the crops had been harvested by the machines, the peasants were permitted to *glean* the wheat left in the fields.

glib ADJ. fluent. He is a *glib* and articulate speaker.

gloaming N. twilight. The snow began to fall in the *gloaming* and continued all through the night.

gloat V. express evil satisfaction; view malevolently. As you *gloat* over your ill-gotten wealth, do you think of the many victims you have defrauded?

glossary N. brief explanation of words used in the text. I have found the *glossary* in this book very useful; it has eliminated many trips to the dictionary.

glossy ADJ. smooth and shining. I want this photograph printed on *glossy* paper, not matte.

glower V. scowl. The angry boy *glowered* at his father.

glut V. overstock; fill to excess. The many manufacturers *glutted* the market and could not find purchasers for the many articles they had produced. also N.

glutinous ADJ. sticky; viscous. Molasses is a *glutinous* substance.

glutton N. someone who eats too much. You can be a gourmet without being a *glutton.*

gluttonous ADJ. greedy for food. The *gluttonous* boy ate all the cookies.

gnarled ADJ. twisted. The *gnarled* oak tree had been a landmark for years and was mentioned in several deeds.

gnome N. dwarf; underground spirit. In medieval mythology, *gnomes* were the special guardians and inhabitants of subterranean mines.

goad V. urge on. He was *goaded* by his friends until he yielded to their wishes. also N.

gorge V. stuff oneself. The gluttonous guest *gorged* himself with food as though he had not eaten for days.

gory ADJ. bloody. The audience shuddered as they listened to the details of the *gory* massacre.

gossamer ADJ. sheer; like cobwebs. Nylon can be woven into *gossamer* or thick fabrics. also N.

Test

Word List 21   *Synonyms*

Each of the questions below consists of a word in capital letters, followed by five lettered words or phrases. Choose the lettered word or phrase that is most nearly similar in meaning to the word in capital letters and write the letter of your choice on your answer paper.

301. GALLEON (A) liquid measure (B) ship (C) armada (D) company (E) printer's proof
302. GARISH (A) sordid (B) flashy (C) prominent (D) lusty (E) thoughtful
303. GARNER (A) prevent (B) assist (C) collect (D) compute (E) consult
304. GARNISH (A) paint (B) garner (C) adorn (D) abuse (E) banish
305. GARRULITY (A) credulity (B) senility (C) loquaciousness (D) speciousness (E) artistry
306. GARRULOUS (A) arid (B) hasty (C) sociable (D) quaint (E) talkative
307. GASCONADE (A) transparency (B) cleanliness (C) bluster (D) imposture (E) seizure
308. GAUCHE (A) rigid (B) awkward (C) swift (D) tacit (E) needy
309. GAUNT (A) victorious (B) tiny (C) stylish (D) haggard (E) nervous
310. GENUFLECT (A) falsify (B) trick (C) project (D) bend the knee (E) pronounce correctly
311. GERMANE (A) bacteriological (B) Middle European (C) prominent (D) warlike (E) relevant
312. GERMINAL (A) creative (B) excused (C) sterilized (D) primitive (E) strategic
313. GIST (A) chaff (B) summary (C) expostulation (D) expiation (E) chore
314. GLIB (A) slippery (B) fashionable (C) antiquated (D) articulate (E) anticlimactic
315. GNOME (A) fury (B) giant (C) dwarf (D) native (E) alien

Word List 22   gouge-hiatus

gouge V. tear out. In that fight, all the rules were forgotten; the adversaries bit, kicked, and tried to *gouge* each other's eyes out.

gourmand N. epicure; person who takes excessive pleasure in food and drink. The *gourmand* liked the French cuisine.

gourmet N. connoisseur of food and drink. The *gourmet* stated that this was the best onion soup she had ever tasted.

granary N. storehouse for grain. We have reason to be thankful, for our crops were good and our *granaries* are full.

grandiloquent ADJ. pompous; bombastic; using high-sounding language. The politician could never speak simply; she was always *grandiloquent.*

grandiose ADJ. imposing; impressive. His *grandiose* manner impressed those who met him for the first time.

granulate V. form into grains. Sugar that has been *granulated* dissolves more readily than lump sugar. granule, N.

graphic ADJ. pertaining to the art of delineating; vividly described. I was particularly impressed by the *graphic* presentation of the storm.

grapple V. wrestle; come to grips with. He *grappled* with the burglar and overpowered him.

gratify v. please. Her parents were *gratified* by her success.

gratis ADJ. free. The company offered to give one package *gratis* to every purchaser of one of their products. also ADJ.

■ **gratuitous** ADJ. given freely; unwarranted. I resent your *gratuitous* remarks because no one asked for them.

gratuity N. tip. Many service employees rely more on *gratuities* than on salaries for their livelihood.

gravity N. seriousness. We could tell we were in serious trouble from the *gravity* of her expression. (secondary meaning) grave, ADJ.

■ **gregarious** ADJ. sociable. She was not *gregarious* and preferred to be alone most of the time.

grimace N. a facial distortion to show feeling such as pain, disgust, etc. Even though he remained silent, his *grimace* indicated his displeasure. also v.

grisly ADJ. ghastly. She shuddered at the *grisly* sight.

grotesque ADJ. fantastic; comically hideous. On Halloween people enjoy wearing *grotesque* costumes.

grotto N. small cavern. The Blue *Grotto* in Capri can be entered only by small boats rowed by natives through a natural opening in the rocks.

grovel v. crawl or creep on ground; remain prostrate. Even though we have been defeated, we do not have to *grovel* before our conquerors.

grudging ADJ. unwilling; reluctant; stingy. We received only *grudging* support from the mayor despite his earlier promises of aid.

gruel N. liquid food made by boiling oatmeal, etc., in milk or water. Our daily allotment of *gruel* made the meal not only monotonous but also unpalatable.

grueling ADJ. exhausting. The marathon is a *grueling* race.

gruesome ADJ. grisly. People screamed when her *gruesome* appearance was flashed on the screen.

gruff ADJ. rough-mannered. Although he was blunt and *gruff* with most people, he was always gentle with children.

guffaw N. boisterous laughter. The loud *guffaws* that came from the closed room indicated that the members of the committee had not yet settled down to serious business. also v.

guile N. deceit; duplicity. She achieved her high position by *guile* and treachery.

guileless ADJ. without deceit. He is naive, simple, and *guileless;* he cannot be guilty of fraud.

guise N. appearance; costume. In the *guise* of a plumber, the detective investigated the murder case.

gullible ADJ. easily deceived. He preyed upon *gullible* people, who believed his stories of easy wealth.

gustatory ADJ. affecting the sense of taste. This food is particularly *gustatory* because of the spices it contains.

gusto N. enjoyment; enthusiasm. He accepted the assignment with such *gusto* that I feel he would have been satisfied with a smaller salary.

gusty ADJ. windy. The *gusty* weather made sailing precarious.

guttural ADJ. pertaining to the throat. *Guttural* sounds are produced in the throat or in the back of the tongue and palate.

habiliments N. garb; clothing. Although not a minister, David Belasco used to wear clerical *habiliments*.

hackles N. hairs on back and neck of a dog. The dog's *hackles* rose and he began to growl as the sound of footsteps grew louder.

hackneyed ADJ. commonplace; trite. The English teacher criticized her story because of its *hackneyed* and unoriginal plot.

haggard ADJ. wasted away; gaunt. After his long illness, he was pale and *haggard*.

haggle v. argue about prices. I prefer to shop in a store that has a one-price policy because, whenever I *haggle* with a shopkeeper, I am never certain that I paid a fair price for the articles I purchased.

halcyon ADJ. calm; peaceful. In those *halcyon* days, people were not worried about sneak attacks and bombings.

hale ADJ. healthy. After a brief illness, he was soon *hale*.

hallowed ADJ. blessed; consecrated. She was laid to rest in *hallowed* ground.

hallucination N. delusion. I think you were frightened by a *hallucination* which you created in your own mind.

hamper v. obstruct. The minority party agreed not to *hamper* the efforts of the leaders to secure a lasting peace.

hap N. chance; luck. In his poem *Hap*, Thomas Hardy objects to the part chance plays in our lives.

haphazard ADJ. random; by chance. His *haphazard* reading left him unacquainted with the authors of the books.

hapless ADJ. unfortunate. This *hapless* creature had never known a moment's pleasure.

harangue N. noisy speech. In her lengthy *harangue*, the principal berated the offenders. also v.

harbor v. provide a refuge for; hide. The church *harbored* illegal aliens who were political refugees.

harass v. to annoy by repeated attacks. When he could not pay his bills as quickly as he had promised, he was *harassed* by his creditors.

harbinger N. forerunner. The crocus is an early *harbinger* of spring.

harping N. tiresome dwelling on a subject. After he had reminded me several times about what he had done for me, I told him to stop *harping* on my indebtedness to him. harp, v.

harridan N. shrewish hag. Most people avoided the *harridan* because they feared her abusive and vicious language.

harrow v. break up ground after plowing; torture. I don't want to *harrow* you at this time by asking you to recall the details of your unpleasant experience.

harry v. raid. The guerrilla band *harried* the enemy nightly.

haughtiness N. pride; arrogance. I resent his *haughtiness* because he is no better than we are.

hauteur N. haughtiness. His snobbishness is obvious to all who witness his *hauteur* when he talks to those whom he considers his social inferiors.

hawser N. large rope. The ship was tied to the pier by a *hawser*.

hazardous ADJ. dangerous. Your occupation is too *hazardous* for insurance companies to consider your application.

hazy ADJ. slightly obscure. In *hazy* weather, you cannot see the top of this mountain.

heckler N. person who harasses others. The *heckler* kept interrupting the speaker with rude remarks. heckle, v.

hedonism N. belief that pleasure is the sole aim in life. *Hedonism* and asceticism are opposing philosophies of human behavior.

heedless ADJ. not noticing; disregarding. He drove on, *heedless* of the warnings placed at the side of the road that it was dangerous.

hegira flight, especially Mohammed's flight from Mecca to Medina. Mohammed began his *hegira* when he was 53 years old.

heinous ADJ. atrocious; hatefully bad. Hitler's *heinous* crimes will never be forgotten.

herbivorous ADJ. grain-eating. Some *herbivorous* animals have two stomachs for digesting their food.

heresy N. opinion contrary to popular belief; opinion con-

trary to accepted religion. He was threatened with excommunication because his remarks were considered to be pure *heresy*.

heretic N. person who maintains opinions contrary to the doctrines of the church. She was punished by the Spanish Inquisition because she was a *heretic*.

■ **hermetic** ADJ. obscure and mysterious; occult. It is strange to consider that modern chemistry originated in the *hermetic* teachings of the ancient alchemists. (secondary meaning)

hermetically ADV. sealed by fusion so as to be airtight. After these bandages are sterilized, they are placed in *hermetically* sealed containers.

hermitage N. home of a hermit. Even in his remote *hermitage* he could not escape completely from the world.

heterogeneous ADJ. dissimilar. In *heterogeneous* groupings, we have an unassorted grouping, while in homogeneous groupings we have people or things which have common traits.

hew V. cut to pieces with ax or sword. The cavalry rushed into the melee and *hewed* the enemy with their swords.

■ **hiatus** N. gap; pause. Except for a brief two-year *hiatus*, during which she enrolled in the Peace Corps, Ms. Clements has devoted herself to her medical career.

Test

Word List 22   *Antonyms*

Each of the questions below consists of a word in capital letters, followed by five lettered words or phrases. Choose the lettered word or phrase that is most nearly opposite in meaning to the word in capital letters and write the letter of your choice on your answer paper.

316. GRANDIOSE (A) false (B) ideal (C) proud (D) simple (E) functional
317. GRATUITOUS (A) warranted (B) frank (C) ingenuous (D) frugal (E) pithy
318. GREGARIOUS (A) antisocial (B) anticipatory (C) glorious (D) horrendous (E) similar
319. GRISLY (A) suggestive (B) doubtful (C) untidy (D) pleasant (E) bearish
320. GULLIBLE (A) incredulous (B) fickle (C) tantamount (D) easy (E) stylish
321. GUSTO (A) noise (B) panic (C) atmosphere (D) gloom (E) distaste

322. GUSTY (A) calm (B) noisy (C) fragrant (D) routine (E) gloomy
323. HACKNEYED (A) carried (B) original (C) banned (D) timely (E) oratorical
324. HAGGARD (A) shrewish (B) inspired (C) plump (D) maidenly (E) vast
325. HALCYON (A) wasteful (B) prior (C) subsequent (D) puerile (E) martial
326. HAPHAZARD (A) safe (B) indifferent (C) deliberate (D) tense (E) conspiring
327. HAPLESS (A) cheerful (B) consistent (C) fortunate (D) considerate (E) shapely
328. HEGIRA (A) return (B) harem (C) oasis (D) panic (E) calm
329. HERETIC (A) sophist (B) believer (C) interpreter (D) pacifist (E) owner
330. HETEROGENEOUS (A) orthodox (B) pagan (C) unlikely (D) similar (E) banished

Word List 23   hibernal-imbue

hibernal ADJ. wintry. Bears prepare for their long *hibernal* sleep by overeating.

hibernate V. sleep throughout the winter. Bears are one of the many species of animals that *hibernate*. hibernation, N.

hierarchy N. body divided into ranks. It was difficult to step out of one's place in this *hierarchy*.

hieroglyphic N. picture writing. The discovery of the Rosetta Stone enabled scholars to read the ancient Egyptian *hieroglyphics*.

hilarity N. boisterous mirth. This *hilarity* is improper on this solemn day of mourning.

hindmost ADJ. furthest behind. The coward could always be found in the *hindmost* lines whenever a battle was being waged.

hindrance N. block; obstacle. Stalled cars along the highway are a *hindrance* to traffic that tow trucks should remove without delay. hinder, V.

hireling N. one who serves for hire [usually used contemptuously]. In a matter of such importance, I do not wish to deal with *hirelings;* I must meet with the chief.

hirsute ADJ. hairy. He was a *hirsute* individual with a heavy black beard.

histrionic ADJ. theatrical. He was proud of his *histrionic* ability and wanted to play the role of Hamlet. histrionics, N.

hoary ADJ. white with age. The man was *hoary* and wrinkled when he was 70.

hoax N. trick; practical joke. Embarrassed by the *hoax,* he reddened and left the room. also V.

hogshead N. large barrel. On the trip to England, the ship carried munitions; on its return trip, *hogsheads* filled with French wines and Scotch liquors.

holocaust N. destruction by fire. Citizens of San Francisco remember that the destruction of the city was caused not by the earthquake but by the *holocaust* that followed.

holster N. pistol case. Even when he was not in uniform, he carried a *holster* and pistol under his arm.

homage N. honor; tribute. In her speech she tried to pay *homage* to a great man.

homespun ADJ. domestic; made at home. *Homespun* wit like *homespun* cloth was often coarse and plain.

homily N. sermon; serious warning. His speeches were always *homilies,* advising his listeners to repent and reform.

■ **homogeneous** ADJ. of the same kind. Educators try to put pupils of similar abilities into classes because they believe that this *homogeneous* grouping is advisable. homogeneity, N.

hone V. sharpen. To make shaving easier, he *honed* his razor with great care.

hoodwink V. deceive; delude. Having been *hoodwinked* once by the fast-talking salesman, he was extremely cautious when he went to purchase a used car.

horde N. crowd. Just before Christmas the stores are filled with *hordes* of shoppers.

hortatory ADJ. encouraging; exhortive. The crowd listened to his *hortatory* statements with ever-growing excitement; finally they rushed from the hall to carry out his suggestions.

horticultural ADJ. pertaining to cultivation of gardens. When he bought his house, he began to look for flowers and decorative shrubs, and began to read books dealing with *horticultural* matters.

hostelry N. inn. Travelers interested in economy should stay at *hostelries* and pensions rather than fashionable hotels.

hovel N. shack; small, wretched house. He wondered how poor people could stand living in such a *hovel.*

hover V. hang about; wait nearby. The police helicopter *hovered* above the accident.

hoyden N. boisterous girl. Although she is now a *hoyden,* I am sure she will outgrow her tomboyish ways and quiet down.

hubbub N. confused uproar. The marketplace was a scene of *hubbub* and excitement; in all the noise, we could not distinguish particular voices.

hubris N. arrogance; excessive self-conceit. Filled with *hubris,* Lear refused to heed his friends' warnings.

hue N. color; aspect. The aviary contained birds of every possible *hue.*

hue and cry N. outcry. When her purse was snatched, she raised such a *hue and cry* that the thief was captured.

humane ADJ. kind. His *humane* and considerate treatment of the unfortunate endeared him to all.

humdrum ADJ. dull; monotonous. After his years of adventure, he could not settle down to a *humdrum* existence.

humid ADJ. damp. She could not stand the *humid* climate and moved to a drier area.

humility N. humbleness of spirit. He spoke with a *humility* and lack of pride that impressed his listeners.

hummock N. small hill. The ascent of the *hummock* is not difficult and the view from the hilltop is ample reward for the effort.

humus N. substance formed by decaying vegetable matter. In order to improve his garden, he spread *humus* over his lawn and flower beds.

hurtle V. crash; rush. The runaway train *hurtled* towards disaster.

husbandry N. frugality; thrift; agriculture. He accumulated his small fortune by diligence and *husbandry.* husband, V.

hustings N. meetings particularly to choose candidates. Congress adjourned so that the members could attend to their political *hustings.*

■ **hybrid** N. mongrel; mixed breed. Mendel's formula explains the appearance of *hybrids* and pure species in breeding. also ADJ.

hydrophobia N. rabies; fear of water. A dog that bites a human being must be observed for symptoms of *hydrophobia.*

■ **hyperbole** N. exaggeration; overstatement. This salesman is guilty of *hyperbole* in describing his product; it is wise to discount his claims. hyperbolic, ADJ.

hyperborean ADJ. situated in extreme north; arctic; cold. The *hyperborean* blasts brought snow and ice to the countryside.

hypercritical ADJ. excessively exacting. You are *hypercritical* in your demands for perfection; we all make mistakes.

hypochondriac N. person unduly worried about his health; worrier without cause about illness. The doctor prescribed chocolate pills for his patient who was a *hypochondriac.*

■ **hypocritical** ADJ. pretending to be virtuous; deceiving. I resent his *hypocritical* posing as a friend for I know he is interested only in his own advancement. hypocrisy, N.

■ **hypothetical** ADJ. based on assumptions or hypotheses. Why do we have to consider *hypothetical* cases when we have actual case histories which we may examine? hypothesis, N.

ichthyology N. study of fish. Jacques Cousteau's programs about sea life have advanced the cause of *ichthyology.*

icon N. religious image; idol. The *icons* on the walls of the church were painted in the 13th century.

iconoclastic ADJ. attacking cherished traditions. George Bernard Shaw's *iconoclastic* plays often startled more conventional people. iconoclasm, N.

ideology N. ideas of a group of people. That *ideology* is dangerous to this country because it embraces undemocratic philosophies.

idiom N. special usage in language. I could not understand their *idiom* because literal translation made no sense.

idiosyncrasy N. peculiarity; eccentricity. One of his personal *idiosyncrasies* was his habit of rinsing all cutlery given him in a restaurant.

idiosyncratic ADJ. private; peculiar to an individual. Such behavior is *idiosyncratic;* it is as easily identifiable as a signature.

idolatry N. worship of idols; excessive admiration. Such *idolatry* of singers of country music is typical of the excessive enthusiasm of youth.

idyllic ADJ. charmingly carefree; simple. Far from the city, she led an *idyllic* existence in her rural retreat.

igneous ADJ. produced by fire; volcanic. Lava, pumice, and other *igneous* rocks are found in great abundance around Mount Vesuvius near Naples.

ignoble ADJ. of lowly origin; unworthy. This plan is inspired by *ignoble* motives and I must, therefore, oppose it.

ignominious ADJ. disgraceful. The country smarted under the *ignominious* defeat and dreamed of the day when it would be victorious. ignominy, N.

illimitable ADJ. infinite. Man, having explored the far corners of the earth, is now reaching out into *illimitable* space.

illusion N. misleading vision. It is easy to create an optical *illusion* in which lines of equal length appear different.

illusive ADJ. deceiving. This is only a mirage; let us not be fooled by its *illusive* effect.

illusory ADJ. deceptive; not real. Unfortunately, the costs of running the lemonade stand were so high that Tom's profits proved *illusory.*

imbecility N. weakness of mind. I am amazed at the *imbecility* of the readers of these trashy magazines.

imbibe V. drink in. The dry soil *imbibed* the rain quickly.

imbroglio N. a complicated situation; perplexity; entanglement. He was called in to settle the *imbroglio* but failed to bring harmony into the situation.

imbrue V. drench, stain, especially with blood. As the instigator of this heinous murder, he is as much *imbrued* in blood as the actual assassin.

imbue V. saturate, fill. His visits to the famous Gothic cathedrals *imbued* him with feelings of awe and reverence.

Test

Word List 23   *Antonyms*

Each of the questions below consists of a word in capital letters, followed by five lettered words or phrases. Choose the lettered word or phrase that is most nearly opposite in meaning to the word in capital letters and write the letter of your choice on your answer paper.

331. HIBERNAL (A) musical (B) summerlike (C) local (D) seasonal (E) discordant
332. HILARITY (A) gloom (B) heartiness (C) weakness (D) casualty (E) paucity
333. HIRSUTE (A) scaly (B) bald (C) erudite (D) quiet (E) long
334. HORTATORY (A) inquiring (B) denying (C) killing (D) frantic (E) dissuading
335. HOYDEN (A) burden (B) light (C) demure girl (D) game (E) traffic
336. HUBBUB (A) calm (B) fury (C) capital (D) axle (E) wax
337. HUMMOCK (A) unmusical (B) scorn (C) wakefulness (D) vale (E) vestment
338. HUSBANDRY (A) sportsmanship (B) dishonesty (C) wastefulness (D) friction (E) cowardice
339. HYBRID (A) productive (B) special (C) purebred (D) oafish (E) genius
340. HYPERBOLE (A) velocity (B) climax (C) curve (D) understatement (E) expansion
341. HYPERBOREAN (A) sultry (B) pacific (C) noteworthy (D) western (E) wooded
342. HYPERCRITICAL (A) tolerant (B) false (C) extreme (D) inarticulate (E) cautious
343. HYPOTHETICAL (A) rational (B) fantastic (C) wizened (D) opposed (E) axiomatic
344. IGNOBLE (A) produced by fire (B) worthy (C) given to questioning (D) huge (E) known
345. ILLUSIVE (A) not deceptive (B) not certain (C) not obvious (D) not coherent (E) not brilliant

Word List 24   immaculate-incessant

immaculate ADJ. pure; spotless. The West Point cadets were *immaculate* as they lined up for inspection.

■ **imminent** ADJ. impending; near at hand. The *imminent* battle will soon determine our success or failure in this conflict.

immobility N. state of being immovable. Modern armies cannot afford the luxury of *immobility*, as they are vulnerable to attack while standing still.

immolate V. offer as a sacrifice. The tribal king offered to *immolate* his daughter to quiet the angry gods.

immune ADJ. exempt. He was fortunately *immune* from the disease and could take care of the sick.

immure V. imprison; shut up in confinement. For the two weeks before the examination, the student *immured* himself in his room and concentrated upon his studies.

■ **immutable** ADJ. unchangeable. Scientists are constantly seeking to discover the *immutable* laws of nature.

impair V. worsen; diminish in value. This arrest will *impair* her reputation in the community.

impale V. pierce. He was *impaled* by the spear hurled by his adversary.

impalpable ADJ. imperceptible; intangible. The ash is so fine that it is *impalpable* to the touch but it can be seen as a fine layer covering the window ledge.

impasse N. predicament from which there is no escape. In this *impasse*, all turned to prayer as their last hope.

■ **impassive** ADJ. without feeling; not affected by pain. The American Indian has been incorrectly depicted as an *impassive* individual, undemonstrative and stoical.

impeach V. charge with crime in office; indict. The angry congressman wanted to *impeach* the President for his misdeeds.

impeccable ADJ. faultless. He was proud of his *impeccable* manners.

impecunious ADJ. without money. Now that he was wealthy, he gladly contributed to funds to assist the *impecunious* and the disabled.

■ **impede** V. hinder; block. The special prosecutor determined that the Attorney General, though inept, had not intentionally set out to *impede* the progress of the investigation.

impediment N. hindrance; stumbling-block. She had a speech *impediment* that prevented her speaking clearly.

impending ADJ. nearing; approaching. The entire country was saddened by the news of his *impending* death.

impenitent ADJ. not repentant. We could see by his brazen attitude that he was *impenitent*.

■ **imperiousness** N. lordliness; domineering manner; arrogance. His *imperiousness* indicated that he had long been accustomed to assuming command. imperious, ADJ.

impermeable ADJ. impervious; not permitting passage through its substance. This new material is *impermeable* to liquids.

impertinent ADJ. insolent. I regard your remarks as *impertinent* and I resent them.

imperturbability N. calmness. We are impressed by his *imperturbability* in this critical moment and are calmed by it.

imperturbable ADJ. calm; placid. He remained *imperturbable* and in full command of the situation in spite of the hysteria and panic all around him.

■ **impervious** ADJ. not penetrable; not permitting passage through. You cannot change their habits for their minds are *impervious* to reasoning.

impetuous ADJ. violent; hasty; rash. We tried to curb his *impetuous* behavior because we felt that in his haste he might offend some people.

impetus N. moving force. It is a miracle that there were any survivors since the two automobiles that collided were traveling with great *impetus*.

impiety N. irreverence; wickedness. We must regard your blasphemy as an act of *impiety*.

impinge V. infringe; touch; collide with. How could they be married without *impinging* on one another's freedom?

impious ADJ. irreverent. The congregation was offended by her *impious* remarks.

implacable ADJ. incapable of being pacified. Madame Defarge was the *implacable* enemy of the Evremonde family.

implausible ADJ. unlikely; unbelievable. Though her alibi seemed *implausible*, it in fact turned out to be true.

■ **implement** V. supply what is needed; furnish with tools. I am unwilling to *implement* this plan until I have assurances that it has the full approval of your officials. also N.

implication N. that which is hinted at or suggested. If I understand the *implications* of your remark, you do not trust our captain.

implicit ADJ. understood but not stated. It is *implicit* that you will come to our aid if we are attacked.

imply V. suggest a meaning not expressed; signify. Even though your statement does not declare that you are at war with that country, your actions *imply* that that is the actual situation.

impolitic ADJ. not wise. I think it is *impolitic* to raise this issue at the present time because the public is too angry.

imponderable ADJ. weightless. I can evaluate the data gathered in this study; the *imponderable* items are not so easily analyzed.

import N. significance. I feel that you have not grasped the full *import* of the message sent to us by the enemy.

importunate ADJ. urging; demanding. He tried to hide from his *importunate* creditors until his allowance arrived.

importune V. beg earnestly. I must *importune* you to work for peace at this time.

imposture N. assuming a false identity; masquerade. She was imprisoned for her *imposture* of a doctor.

impotent ADJ. weak; ineffective. Although he wished to break the nicotine habit, he found himself *impotent* in resisting the craving for a cigarette.

imprecate V. curse; pray that evil will befall. To *imprecate* Hitler's atrocities is not enough; we must insure against any future practice of genocide.

impregnable ADJ. invulnerable. Until the development of the airplane as a military weapon, the fort was considered *impregnable*.

imprimatur N. permission to print or publish a book. The publication of the book was delayed until the *imprimatur* of the State Education Committee was granted.

■ **impromptu** ADJ. without previous preparation. Her listeners were amazed that such a thorough presentation could be made in an *impromptu* speech.

impropriety N. state of being inappropriate. Because of the *impropriety* of his costume, he was denied entrance into the dining room.

■ **improvident** ADJ. thriftless. He was constantly being warned to mend his *improvident* ways and begin to "save for a rainy day." improvidence, N.

improvise V. compose on the spur of the moment. She would sit at the piano and *improvise* for hours on themes from Bach and Handel.

■ **imprudent** ADJ. lacking caution; injudicious. It is *imprudent* to exercise vigorously and become overheated when you are unwell.

impugn V. doubt; challenge; gainsay. I cannot *impugn* your honesty without evidence.

impunity N. freedom from punishment. The bully mistreated everyone in the class with *impunity* for he felt that no one would dare retaliate.

imputation N. charge; reproach. You cannot ignore the *imputations* in his speech that you are the guilty party.

impute V. attribute; ascribe. If I wished to *impute* blame to the officers in charge of this program, I would come out and state it definitely and without hesitation.

inadvertently ADV. carelessly; unintentionally; by oversight. She *inadvertently* omitted two questions on the examination and mismarked her answer sheet.

inalienable ADJ. not to be taken away; nontransferable. The Declaration of Independence mentions the *inalienable* rights that all of us possess.

inane ADJ. silly; senseless. Such comments are *inane* because they do not help us solve our problem. inanity, N.

inanimate ADJ. lifeless. She was asked to identify the still and *inanimate* body.

inarticulate ADJ. speechless; producing indistinct speech. He became *inarticulate* with rage and uttered sounds without meaning.

incandescent ADJ. strikingly bright; shining with intense heat. If you leave on an *incandescent* light bulb, it quickly grows too hot to touch.

incantation N. singing or chanting of magic spells; magical formula. Uttering *incantations* to make the brew more potent, the witch doctor stirred the liquid in the caldron.

incapacitate V. disable. During the winter, many people were *incapacitated* by respiratory ailments.

■ **incarcerate** V. imprison. The warden will *incarcerate* the felon after conviction.

incarnadine V. stain crimson or blood-color. After killing Duncan, Macbeth cries that his hands are so bloodstained that they would "the multitudinous seas *incarnadine.*"

incarnate ADJ. endowed with flesh; personified. Your attitude is so fiendish that you must be a devil *incarnate.*

incarnation N. act of assuming a human body and human nature. The *incarnation* of Jesus Christ is a basic tenet of Christian theology.

incendiary N. arsonist. The fire spread in such an unusual manner that the fire department chiefs were certain that it had been set by an *incendiary.* also ADJ.

incense V. enrage; infuriate. Unkindness to children *incensed* her.

incentive N. spur; motive. Students who dislike school must be given an *incentive* to learn.

inception N. start; beginning. She was involved with the project from its *inception.*

incessant ADJ. uninterrupted. The crickets kept up an *incessant* chirping which disturbed our attempts to fall asleep.

Test

Word List 24   *Synonyms and Antonyms*

Each of the following questions consists of a word in capital letters, followed by five lettered words or phrases. Choose the lettered word or phrase which is most nearly similar or the opposite of the word in capital letters and write the letter of your choice on your answer paper.

346. IMMOLATE (A) debate (B) scour (C) sacrifice (D) sanctify (E) ratify
347. IMMUTABLE (A) silent (B) changeable (C) articulate (D) loyal (E) varied
348. IMPAIR (A) separate (B) make amends (C) make worse (D) falsify (E) cancel
349. IMPALPABLE (A) obvious (B) combined (C) high (D) connecting (E) lost
350. IMPASSIVE (A) active (B) demonstrative (C) perfect (D) anxious (E) irritated
351. IMPECCABLE (A) unmentionable (B) quotable (C) blinding (D) faulty (E) hampering
352. IMPECUNIOUS (A) affluent (B) afflicted (C) affectionate (D) affable (E) afraid
353. IMPERVIOUS (A) impenetrable (B) perplexing (C) chaotic (D) cool (E) perfect
354. IMPETUOUS (A) rash (B) inane (C) just (D) flagrant (E) redolent
355. IMPOLITIC (A) campaigning (B) advisable (C) aggressive (D) legal (E) fortunate
356. IMPORTUNE (A) export (B) plead (C) exhibit (D) account (E) visit
357. IMPROMPTU (A) prompted (B) appropriate (C) rehearsed (D) foolish (E) vast

358. INALIENABLE (A) inherent (B) repugnant
     (C) closed to immigration (D) full (E) accountable
359. INANE (A) passive (B) wise (C) intoxicated
     (D) mellow (E) silent

360. INCARCERATE (A) inhibit (B) acquit (C) account
     (D) imprison (E) force

Word List 25   inchoate-ingenious

■ **inchoate** ADJ. recently begun; rudimentary; elementary. Before the Creation, the world was an *inchoate* mass.

incidence N. falling on a body; a casual occurrence. We must determine the angle of *incidence* of the rays of light.

incipient ADJ. beginning; in an early stage. I will go to sleep early for I want to break an *incipient* cold.

■ **incisive** ADJ. cutting; sharp. His *incisive* remarks made us see the fallacy in our plans.

incite V. arouse to action. The demagogue *incited* the mob to take action into its own hands.

inclement ADJ. stormy; unkind. I like to read a good book in *inclement* weather.

inclusive ADJ. tending to include all. This meeting will run from January 10 to February 15 *inclusive*.

incognito ADV. with identity concealed; using an assumed name. The monarch enjoyed traveling through the town *incognito* and mingling with the populace. also ADJ.

incoherence N. lack of relevance; lack of intelligibility. The bereaved father sobbed and stammered, caught up in the *incoherence* of his grief.

incommodious ADJ. not spacious. In their *incommodious* quarters, they had to improvise for closet space.

incompatible ADJ. inharmonious. The married couple argued incessantly and finally decided to separate because they were *incompatible*. incompatibility, N.

■ **incongruity** N. lack of harmony; absurdity. The *incongruity* of his wearing sneakers with formal attire amused the observers.

incongruous ADJ. not fitting; absurd. These remarks do not have any relationship to the problem at hand; they are *incongruous* and should be stricken from the record.

inconsequential ADJ. of trifling significance. Your objections are *inconsequential* and may be disregarded.

incontinent ADJ. lacking self-restraint; licentious. His *incontinent* behavior off stage shocked many people and they refused to attend the plays and movies in which he appeared.

incontrovertible ADJ. indisputable. We must yield to the *incontrovertible* evidence which you have presented and free your client.

incorporeal ADJ. immaterial; without a material body. We must devote time to the needs of our *incorporeal* mind as well as our corporeal body.

incorrigible ADJ. uncorrectable. Because he was an *incorrigible* criminal, he was sentenced to life imprisonment.

incredulity N. a tendency to disbelief. Your *incredulity* in the face of all the evidence is hard to understand.

incredulous ADJ. withholding belief; skeptical. The *incredulous* judge refused to accept the statement of the defendant.

increment N. increase. The new contract calls for a 10 percent *increment* in salary for each employee for the next two years.

incriminate V. accuse. The evidence gathered against the racketeers *incriminates* some high public officials as well.

incubate V. hatch; scheme. Inasmuch as our supply of electricity is cut off, we shall have to rely on the hens to *incubate* these eggs.

incubus N. burden; mental care; nightmare. The *incubus* of financial worry helped bring on her nervous breakdown.

inculcate V. teach. In an effort to *inculcate* religious devotion, the officials ordered that the school day begin with the singing of a hymn.

incumbent N. officeholder. The newly elected public official received valuable advice from the present *incumbent*. also ADJ.

incur V. bring upon oneself. His parents refused to pay any future debts he might *incur*.

incursion N. temporary invasion. The nightly *incursions* and hit-and-run raids of our neighbors across the border tried the patience of the country to the point where we decided to retaliate in force.

indefatigable ADJ. tireless. He was *indefatigable* in his constant efforts to raise funds for the Red Cross.

indemnify V. make secure against loss; compensate for loss. The city will *indemnify* all home owners whose property is spoiled by this project.

indenture V. bind as servant or apprentice to master. Many immigrants could come to America only after they had *indentured* themselves for several years. also N.

indicative ADJ. suggestive; implying. A lack of appetite may be *indicative* of a major mental or physical disorder.

indict V. charge. If the grand jury *indicts* the suspect, he will go to trial.

indifferent ADJ. unmoved; lacking concern. Because she felt no desire to marry, she was *indifferent* to his constant proposals.

■ **indigence** N. poverty. Neither the economists nor the political scientists have found a way to wipe out the inequities of wealth and eliminate *indigence* from our society. indigent, ADJ., N.

indigenous ADJ. native. Tobacco is one of the *indigenous* plants which the early explorers found in this country.

indignation N. anger at an injustice. He felt *indignation* at the ill-treatment of helpless animals.

indignity N. offensive or insulting treatment. Although he seemed to accept cheerfully the *indignities* heaped upon him, he was inwardly very angry.

■ **indiscriminate** ADJ. choosing at random; confused. She disapproved of her son's *indiscriminate* television viewing and decided to restrict him to educational programs.

indisputable ADJ. too certain to be disputed. In the face of these *indisputable* statements, I withdraw my complaint.

indissoluble ADJ. permanent. The *indissoluble* bonds of marriage are all too often being dissolved.

indite V. write; compose. Cyrano *indited* many letters for Christian.

■ **indolence** N. laziness. He outgrew his youthful *indolence* to become a model of industry and alertness on the job. indolent, ADJ.

indomitable ADJ. unconquerable. The founders of our country had *indomitable* willpower.

indubitably ADV. beyond a doubt. Because her argument was *indubitably* valid, the judge accepted it.

induce V. persuade; bring about. They tried to *induce* labor because the baby was overdue.

inductive ADJ. pertaining to induction or proceeding from the specific to the general. The discovery of the planet Pluto is an excellent example of the results that can be obtained from *inductive* reasoning.

indulgent ADJ. humoring; yielding; lenient. An *indulgent* parent may spoil a child by creating an artificial atmosphere of leniency.

inebriety N. habitual intoxication. Because of his *inebriety*, he was discharged from his position as family chauffeur.

ineffable ADJ. unutterable; cannot be expressed in speech. Such *ineffable* joy must be experienced; it cannot be described.

ineluctable ADJ. irresistible; not to be escaped. He felt that his fate was *ineluctable* and refused to make any attempt to improve his lot.

inept ADJ. unsuited; absurd; incompetent. The constant turmoil in the office proved that she was an *inept* administrator.

■ **inequity** N. unfairness. In demanding equal pay for equal work, women protest the basic *inequity* of a system that allots greater financial rewards to men.

inert ADJ. inactive; lacking power to move. Faced with the growing corruption scandal, the bureaucracy was *inert* and did nothing.

■ **inertia** N. state of being inert or indisposed to move. Our *inertia* in this matter may prove disastrous; we must move to aid our allies immediately.

inevitable ADJ. unavoidable. Death and taxes are both *inevitable*.

inexorable ADJ. relentless; unyielding; implacable. After listening to the pleas for clemency, the judge was *inexorable* and gave the convicted man the maximum punishment allowed by law.

infallible ADJ. unerring. We must remember that none of us is *infallible*; we all make mistakes.

infamous ADJ. notoriously bad. Jesse James was an *infamous* outlaw.

infantile ADJ. childish; infantile. When will he outgrow such *infantile* behavior?

infer V. deduce; conclude. We must be particularly cautious when we *infer* that a person is guilty on the basis of circumstantial evidence.

inference N. conclusion drawn from data. I want you to check this *inference* because it may have been based on insufficient information.

infernal ADJ. pertaining to hell; devilish. They could think of no way to hinder his *infernal* scheme.

infidel N. unbeliever. The Saracens made war against the *infidels*.

infinitesimal ADJ. very small. In the twentieth century, physicists have made their greatest discoveries about the characteristics of *infinitesimal* objects like the atom and its parts.

infirmity N. weakness. Her greatest *infirmity* was lack of willpower.

inflated ADJ. exaggerated; pompous; enlarged (with air or gas). His claims about the new product were inflated; it did not work as well as he had promised.

influx N. flowing into. The *influx* of refugees into the country has taxed the relief agencies severely.

infraction N. violation. Because of his many *infractions* of school regulations, he was suspended by the dean.

infringe V. violate; encroach. I think your machine *infringes* on my patent and I intend to sue.

ingenious ADJ. clever. He came up with an *ingenious* use for styrofoam packing balls.

Test

Word List 25 *Synonyms*

Each of the questions below consists of a word in capital letters, followed by five lettered words or phrases. Choose the lettered word or phrase that is most nearly similar in meaning to the word in capital letters and write the letter of your choice on your answer paper.

361. INCLEMENT (A) unfavorable (B) abandoned (C) kindly (D) selfish (E) active
362. INCOMPATIBLE (A) capable (B) reasonable (C) faulty (D) indifferent (E) alienated
363. INCONSEQUENTIAL (A) disorderly (B) insignificant (C) subsequent (D) insufficient (E) preceding

364. INCONTINENT (A) insular (B) complaisant (C) crass (D) wanton (E) false

365. INCORRIGIBLE (A) narrow (B) straight (C) inconceivable (D) unreliable (E) unreformable

366. INCRIMINATE (A) exacerbate (B) involve (C) intimidate (D) lacerate (E) prevaricate

367. INCULCATE (A) exculpate (B) educate (C) exonerate (D) prepare (E) embarrass

368. INDIGENT (A) lazy (B) pusillanimous (C) penurious (D) affluent (E) contrary

369. INDIGNITY (A) pomposity (B) bombast (C) obeisance (D) insult (E) message

370. INDOLENCE (A) sloth (B) poverty (C) latitude (D) aptitude (E) anger

371. INDUBITABLY (A) flagrantly (B) doubtfully (C) carefully (D) carelessly (E) certainly

372. INEBRIETY (A) revelation (B) drunkenness (C) felony (D) starvation (E) gluttony

373. INEPT (A) outward (B) spiritual (C) foolish (D) clumsy (E) abundant

374. INFALLIBLE (A) final (B) unbelievable (C) perfect (D) inaccurate (E) inquisitive

375. INFIRMITY (A) disability (B) age (C) inoculation (D) hospital (E) unity

---

Word List 26   ingenue-invidious

ingenue N. an artless girl; an actress who plays such parts. Although she was forty, she still insisted that she be cast as an *ingenue* and refused to play more mature roles.

■ **ingenuous** ADJ. naive; young; unsophisticated. These remarks indicate that you are *ingenuous* and unaware of life's harsher realities.

ingrate N. ungrateful person. You are an *ingrate* since you have treated my gifts with scorn.

ingratiate V. become popular with. He tried to *ingratiate* himself into her parents' good graces.

■ **inherent** ADJ. firmly established by nature or habit. His *inherent* love of justice compelled him to come to their aid.

inhibit V. prohibit; restrain. The child was not *inhibited* in her responses. inhibition, N.

■ **inimical** ADJ. unfriendly; hostile. She felt that they were *inimical* and were hoping for her downfall.

inimitable ADJ. matchless; not able to be imitated. We admire Auden for his *inimitable* use of language; he is one of a kind.

iniquitous ADJ. unjust; wicked. I cannot approve of the *iniquitous* methods you used to gain your present position. iniquity, N.

initiate V. begin; originate; receive into a group. The college is about to *initiate* a program in reducing math anxiety among students.

injurious ADJ. harmful. Smoking cigarettes can be *injurious* to your health.

inkling N. hint. This came as a complete surprise to me as I did not have the slightest *inkling* of your plans.

innate ADJ. inborn. His *innate* talent for music was soon recognized by his parents.

innocuous ADJ. harmless. Let him drink it; it is *innocuous* and will have no ill effect.

innovation N. change; introduction of something new. She loved *innovations* just because they were new.

innovative ADJ. novel; introducing a change. The establishment of our GRE computer data base has enabled us to come up with some *innovative* tactics for doing well on the GRE.

innuendo N. hint; insinuation. I resent the *innuendos* in your statement more than the statement itself.

inopportune ADJ. untimely; poorly chosen. A rock concert is an *inopportune* setting for a quiet conversation.

inordinate ADJ. unrestrained; excessive. She had an *inordinate* fondness for candy.

insatiable ADJ. not easily satisfied; greedy. His thirst for knowledge was *insatiable;* he was always in the library.

inscrutable ADJ. incomprehensible; not to be discovered. I fail to understand the reasons for your outlandish behavior; your motives are *inscrutable*.

insensate ADJ. without feeling. She lay there as *insensate* as a log.

insidious ADJ. treacherous; stealthy; sly. The fifth column is *insidious* because it works secretly within our territory for our defeat.

insinuate V. hint; imply. What are you trying to *insinuate* by that remark?

insipid ADJ. tasteless; dull. I am bored by your *insipid* talk.

insolent ADJ. haughty and contemptuous. I resent your *insolent* manner.

insolvent ADJ. bankrupt; lacking money to pay. When rumors that he was *insolvent* reached his creditors, they began to press him for payment of the money due them. insolvency, N.

insomnia N. wakefulness; inability to sleep. He refused to join us in a midnight cup of coffee because he claimed it gave him *insomnia*.

■ **insouciant** ADJ. indifferent; without concern or care. Your *insouciant* attitude at such a critical moment indicates that you do not understand the gravity of the situation.

instigate V. urge; start; provoke. I am afraid that this statement will *instigate* a revolt.

insubordinate ADJ. disobedient. The *insubordinate* private was confined to the barracks.

■ **insularity** N. narrow-mindedness; isolation. The *insularity* of the islanders manifested itself in their suspicion of anything foreign. insular, ADJ.

insuperable ADJ. insurmountable; invincible. In the face of *insuperable* difficulties they maintained their courage and will to resist.

insurgent ADJ. rebellious. We will not discuss reforms until the *insurgent* troops have returned to their homes. also N.

insurrection N. rebellion; uprising. Given the current state of affairs in South Africa, an *insurrection* seems unavoidable.

integrate V. make whole; combine; make into one unit. She tried to *integrate* all their activities into one program.

integrity N. wholeness; purity; uprightness. The beloved preacher was a man of great *integrity*.

integument N. outer covering or skin. The turtle takes advantage of its hard *integument* and hides within its shell when threatened.

intellect N. higher mental powers. He thought college would develop his *intellect*.

intelligentsia N. the intelligent and educated classes [often used derogatorily]. She preferred discussions about sports and politics to the literary conversations of the *intelligentsia*.

inter V. bury. They are going to *inter* the body tomorrow at Broadlawn Cemetery.

■ **interdict** V. prohibit; forbid. Civilized nations must *interdict* the use of nuclear weapons if we expect our society to live.

interim N. meantime. The company will not consider our proposal until next week; in the *interim,* let us proceed as we have in the past.

interlocutory ADJ. conversational; intermediate, not final. This *interlocutory* decree is only a temporary setback; the case has not been settled.

interloper N. intruder. The merchant thought of his competitors as *interlopers* who were stealing away his trade.

interment N. burial. *Interment* will take place in the church cemetery at 2 P.M. Wednesday.

interminable ADJ. endless. Although his speech lasted for only twenty minutes, it seemed *interminable* to his bored audience.

intermittent ADJ. periodic; on and off. Our picnic was marred by *intermittent* rains.

internecine ADJ. mutually destructive. The rising death toll on both sides indicates the *internecine* nature of this conflict.

interpolate V. insert between. She talked so much that I could not *interpolate* a single remark.

interstices N. chinks; crevices. The mountain climber sought to obtain a foothold in the *interstices* of the cliff.

intervene V. come between. She *intervened* in the argument between her two sons.

intimate V. hint. She *intimated* rather than stated her preferences.

intimidation N. fear. A ruler who maintains his power by *intimidation* is bound to develop clandestine resistance.

intractable ADJ. unruly; refractory. The horse was *intractable* and refused to enter the starting gate.

■ **intransigence** N. state of stubborn unwillingness to compromise. The *intransigence* of both parties in the dispute makes an early settlement almost impossible to obtain.

intransigent ADJ. refusing any compromise. The strike settlement has collapsed because both sides are *intransigent*.

intrepid ADJ. fearless. For his *intrepid* conduct in battle, he was promoted.

■ **intrinsically** ADV. essentially; inherently; naturally. Although my grandmother's china has *intrinsically* little value, I shall always cherish it for the memories it evokes. intrinsic, ADJ.

introspective ADJ. looking within oneself. We all have our *introspective* moments during which we examine our souls.

introvert N. one who is introspective; inclined to think more about oneself. In his poetry, he reveals that he is an *introvert* by his intense interest in his own problems. also V.

intrude V. trespass; enter as an uninvited person. She hesitated to *intrude* on their conversation.

intuition N. power of knowing without reasoning. She claimed to know the truth by *intuition.* intuitive, ADJ.

inundate V. overflow; flood. The tremendous waves *inundated* the town.

inured ADJ. accustomed; hardened. She became *inured* to the Alaskan cold.

invalidate V. weaken; destroy. The relatives who received little or nothing sought to *invalidate* the will by claiming that the deceased had not been in his right mind when he had signed the document.

■ **invective** N. abuse. He had expected criticism but not the *invective* which greeted his proposal.

inveigh V. denounce; utter censure or invective. He *inveighed* against the demagoguery of the previous speaker and urged that the audience reject his philosophy as dangerous.

inveigle V. lead astray; wheedle. She was *inveigled* into joining the club after an initial reluctance.

inverse ADJ. opposite. There is an *inverse* ratio between the strength of light and its distance.

invert V. turn upside down or inside out. When he *inverted* his body in a hand stand, he felt the blood rush to his head.

inveterate ADJ. deep-rooted; habitual. She is an *inveterate* smoker and cannot stop the habit.

invidious ADJ. designed to create ill will or envy. We disregarded her *invidious* remarks because we realized how jealous she was.

Test

Word List 26   *Synonyms*

Each of the questions below consists of a word in capital letters, followed by five lettered words or phrases. Choose the lettered word or phrase that is most nearly similar in meaning to the word in capital letters and write the letter of your choice on your answer paper.

376. INGENUOUS (A) clever (B) stimulating (C) naive (D) worried (E) cautious

377. INIMICAL (A) antagonistic (B) anonymous (C) fanciful (D) accurate (E) seldom

378. INNOCUOUS (A) not capable (B) not dangerous (C) not eager (D) not frank (E) not peaceful

379. INSINUATE (A) resist (B) suggest (C) report (D) rectify (E) lecture

380. INSIPID (A) witty (B) flat (C) wily (D) talkative (E) lucid

381. INTEGRATE (A) tolerate (B) unite (C) flow (D) copy (E) assume

382. INTER (A) bury (B) amuse (C) relate (D) frequent (E) abandon

383. INTERDICT (A) acclaim (B) dispute (C) prohibit (D) decide (E) fret

384. INTERMITTENT (A) heavy (B) fleet (C) occasional (D) fearless (E) responding

385. INTRACTABLE (A) culpable (B) flexible (C) unruly (D) efficient (E) base

386. INTRANSIGENCE (A) lack of training (B) stubbornness (C) novelty (D) timidity (E) cupidity

387. INTREPID (A) cold (B) hot (C) understood (D) callow (E) courageous

388. INTRINSIC (A) extrinsic (B) abnormal (C) above (D) abandoned (E) basic

389. INUNDATE (A) abuse (B) deny (C) swallow (D) treat (E) flood

390. INVEIGH (A) speak violently (B) orate (C) disturb (D) apply (E) whisper

Word List 27   invincible-laity

invincible ADJ. unconquerable. Superman is *invincible*.

inviolability N. security from being destroyed, corrupted or profaned. They respected the *inviolability* of her faith and did not try to change her manner of living.

invoke V. call upon; ask for. She *invoked* her advisor's aid in filling out her financial aid forms.

invulnerable ADJ. incapable of injury. Achilles was *invulnerable* except in his heel.

iota N. very small quantity. She hadn't an *iota* of common sense.

■ **irascible** ADJ. irritable; easily angered. Her *irascible* temper frightened me.

■ **irate** ADJ. angry. When John's mother found out that he had overdrawn his checking account for the third month in a row, she was so *irate* that she could scarcely speak to him.

iridescent ADJ. exhibiting rainbowlike colors. She admired the *iridescent* hues of the oil that floated on the surface of the water.

irksome ADJ. annoying; tedious. He found working on the assembly line *irksome* because of the monotony of the operation he had to perform. irk, V.

ironic ADJ. resulting in an unexpected and contrary manner. It is *ironic* that his success came when he least wanted it.

irony N. hidden sarcasm or satire; use of words that convey a meaning opposite to the literal meaning. Gradually his listeners began to realize that the excessive praise he was lavishing was merely *irony;* he was actually denouncing his opponent.

irreconcilable ADJ. incompatible; not able to be resolved. Because the separated couple were *irreconcilable*, the marriage counselor recommended a divorce.

irrefragable ADJ. not to be disproved; indisputable. The testimonies of the witnesses provide *irrefragable* proof that my client is innocent; I demand that he be released at once.

irrelevant ADJ. not applicable; unrelated. This statement is *irrelevant* and should be disregarded by the jury.

irremediable ADJ. incurable; uncorrectable. The error she made was *irremediable;* she could see no way to repair it.

irreparable ADJ. not able to be corrected or repaired. Your apology cannot atone for the *irreparable* damage you have done to her reputation.

irrepressible ADJ. unable to be restrained or held back. Her high spirits were *irrepressible*.

irresolute ADJ. uncertain how to act; weak. She had no respect for him because he seemed weak-willed and *irresolute*.

irreverent ADJ. lacking proper respect. The worshippers resented her *irreverent* remarks about their faith.

irrevocable ADJ. unalterable. Let us not brood over past mistakes since they are *irrevocable*.

isotope N. varying form of an element. The study of the *isotopes* of uranium led to the development of the nuclear bomb.

iterate V. utter a second time; repeat. I will *iterate* the warning I have previously given to you.

itinerant ADJ. wandering; traveling. He was an *itinerant* peddler and traveled through Pennsylvania and Virginia selling his wares. also N.

■ **itinerary** N. plan of a trip. Before leaving for his first visit to France and England, he discussed his *itinerary* with people who had been there and with his travel agent.

jaded ADJ. fatigued; surfeited. He looked for exotic foods to stimulate his *jaded* appetite.

jargon N. language used by special group; gibberish. We tried to understand the *jargon* of the peddlers in the marketplace but could not find any basis for comprehension.

jaundiced ADJ. yellowed; prejudiced; envious. She gazed at the painting with *jaundiced* eyes; she knew it was better than hers.

jaunt N. trip; short journey. He took a quick *jaunt* to Atlantic City.

jaunty ADJ. stylish; perky; carefree. She wore her beret at a *jaunty* angle.

jejune ADJ. lacking interest; barren; meager. The plot of the play is *jejune* and fails to capture the interest of the audience.

jeopardy N. exposure to death or danger. She cannot be placed in double *jeopardy*.

jeremiad N. lament; complaint. His account of the event was a lengthy *jeremiad*, unrelieved by any light moments.

jettison V. throw overboard. In order to enable the ship to ride safely through the storm, the captain had to *jettison* much of his cargo.

jingoism N. extremely aggressive and militant patriotism. We must be careful to prevent a spirit of *jingoism* from spreading at this time; the danger of a disastrous war is too great.

jocose ADJ. giving to joking. The salesman was so *jocose* that many of his customers suggested that he become a "stand-up" comic.

jocular ADJ. said or done in jest. Do not take my *jocular* remarks seriously.

jocund ADJ. merry. Santa Claus is always vivacious and *jocund*.

jollity N. gaiety; cheerfulness. The festive Christmas dinner was a merry one, and old and young alike joined in the general *jollity*.

jostle V. shove; bump. In the subway he was *jostled* by the crowds.

jovial ADJ. good-natured; merry. A frown seemed out of place on his invariably *jovial* face.

jubilation N. rejoicing. There was great *jubilation* when the armistice was announced.

■ **judicious** ADJ. sound in judgment; wise. At a key moment in his life, he made a *judicious* investment that was the foundation of his later wealth.

juggernaut N. irresistible crushing force. Nothing could survive in the path of the *juggernaut*.

juncture N. crisis; joining point. At this critical *juncture*, let us think carefully before determining the course we shall follow.

junket N. a merry feast or picnic. The opposition claimed that her trip to Europe was merely a political *junket*.

junta N. group of men joined in political intrigue; cabal. As soon as he learned of its existence, the dictator ordered the execution of all of the members of the *junta*.

jurisprudence N. science of law. He was more a student of *jurisprudence* than a practitioner of the law.

juxtapose V. place side by side. Comparison will be easier if you *juxtapose* the two objects.

kaleidoscope N. tube in which patterns made by the reflection in mirrors of colored pieces of glass, etc., produce interesting symmetrical effects. People found a new source of entertainment while peering through the *kaleidoscope*; they found the ever-changing patterns fascinating.

ken N. range of knowledge. I cannot answer your question since this matter is beyond my *ken*.

kindle V. start a fire; inspire. Her teacher's praise *kindled* a spark of hope inside her.

kindred ADJ. related; belonging to the same family. Tom Sawyer and Huck Finn were two *kindred* spirits. also N.

kiosk N. summer house; open pavilion. She waited at the subway *kiosk*.

kinetic ADJ. producing motion. Designers of the electric automobile find that their greatest obstacle lies in the development of light and efficient storage batteries, the source of the *kinetic* energy needed to propel the vehicle.

kismet N. fate. *Kismet* is the Arabic word for "fate."

kith N. familiar friends. He always helped both his *kith* and kin.

kleptomaniac N. person who has a compulsive desire to steal. They discovered that the wealthy customer was a *kleptomaniac* when they caught her stealing some cheap trinkets.

knavery N. rascality. We cannot condone such *knavery* in public officials.

knead V. mix; work dough. Her hands grew strong from *kneading* bread.

knell N. tolling of a bell at a funeral; sound of the funeral bell. "The curfew tolls the *knell* of parting day." also V.

knoll N. little round hill. Robert Louis Stevenson's grave is on a *knoll* in Samoa.

labyrinth N. maze. Tom and Betty were lost in the *labyrinth* of secret caves.

lacerate V. mangle; tear. Her body was *lacerated* in the automobile crash.

■ **lachrymose** ADJ. producing tears. His voice has a *lachrymose* quality which is more appropriate at a funeral than a class reunion.

lackadaisical ADJ. affectedly languid. He was *lackadaisical* and indifferent about his part in the affair.

lackey N. footman; toady. The duke was followed by his *lackeys*.

lackluster ADJ. dull. We were disappointed by the *lackluster* performance.

■ **laconic** ADJ. brief and to the point. Many of the characters portrayed by Clint Eastwood are *laconic* types: strong men of few words.

laggard ADJ. slow; sluggish. The sailor had been taught not to be *laggard* in carrying out orders. lag, N., V.

lagoon N. shallow body of water near a sea; lake. They enjoyed their swim in the calm *lagoon*.

laity N. laymen; persons not connected with the clergy. The *laity* does not always understand the clergy's problems.

Test

Word List 27 *Antonyms*

Each of the questions below consists of a word in capital letters, followed by five lettered words or phrases. Choose the lettered word or phrase that is most nearly opposite in meaning to the word in capital letters and write the letter of your choice on your answer paper.

391. IRKSOME (A) interesting (B) lazy (C) tireless (D) few (E) too many
392. IRRELEVANT (A) lacking piety (B) fragile (C) congruent (D) pertinent (E) varied
393. IRREPARABLE (A) legible (B) correctable (C) proverbial (D) concise (E) legal
394. IRREVERENT (A) related (B) mischievous (C) respective (D) pious (E) violent
395. JADED (A) upright (B) stimulated (C) aspiring (D) applied (E) void
396. JAUNDICED (A) whitened (B) inflamed (C) quickened (D) aged (E) unbiased
397. JEJUNE (A) youthful (B) ancient (C) strong (D) fictional (E) interesting
398. JEREMIAD (A) prophecy (B) proposition (C) praise (D) overture (E) explanation
399. JETTISON (A) salvage (B) submerge (C) descend (D) decelerate (E) repent
400. JOCULAR (A) arterial (B) bloodless (C) verbose (D) serious (E) blind
401. JUDICIOUS (A) punitive (B) unwise (C) criminal (D) licit (E) temporary
402. KITH (A) outfit (B) strangers (C) brothers (D) ceramics tool (E) quality
403. LACHRYMOSE (A) cheering (B) smooth (C) passionate (D) curt (E) tense
404. LACKADAISICAL (A) monthly (B) possessing time (C) ambitious (D) pusillanimous (E) intelligent
405. LACONIC (A) milky (B) verbose (C) wicked (D) flagrant (E) derelict

Word List 28 lambent-lout

lambent ADJ. flickering; softly radiant. They sat quietly before the *lambent* glow of the fireplace.

laminated ADJ. made of thin plates or scales. The desk was covered with a sheet of *laminated* plastic.

■ **lampoon** V. ridicule. This article *lampoons* the pretensions of some movie moguls. also N.

languid ADJ. weary; sluggish; listless. Her siege of illness left her *languid* and pallid.

languish V. lose animation; lose strength. In stories, love-lorn damsels used to *languish* and pine away.

languor N. lassitude; depression. His friends tried to overcome the *languor* into which he had fallen by taking him to parties and to the theater.

lank ADJ. long and thin. *Lank*, gaunt, Abraham Lincoln was a striking figure.

lapidary N. worker in precious stones. She employed a *lapidary* to cut the large diamond.

larceny N. theft. Because of the prisoner's record, the district attorney refused to reduce the charge from grand *larceny* to petit *larceny*.

largess N. generous gift. Lady Bountiful distributed *largess* to the poor.

lascivious ADJ. lustful. The *lascivious* books were banned by the clergy.

■ **lassitude** N. languor; weariness. The hot, tropical weather created a feeling of *lassitude* and encouraged drowsiness.

latent ADJ. dormant; hidden. Her *latent* talent was discovered by accident.

lateral ADJ. coming from the side. In order to get good plant growth, the gardener must pinch off all *lateral* shoots.

latitude N. freedom from narrow limitations. I think you have permitted your son too much *latitude* in this matter.

laudable ADJ. praiseworthy; commendable. His *laudable* deeds will be remembered by all whom he aided.

■ **laudatory** ADJ. expressing praise. The critics' *laudatory* comments helped to make her a star.

lave V. wash. The running water will *lave* away all stains.

lavish ADJ. liberal; wasteful. The actor's *lavish* gifts pleased her. also V.

lax ADJ. careless. We dislike restaurants where the service is *lax* and inattentive.

lecherous ADJ. impure in thought and act; lustful; unchaste. He is a *lecherous* and wicked old man.

lechery N. gross lewdness; lustfulness. In his youth he led a life of *lechery* and debauchery; he did not mend his ways until middle age.

lectern N. reading desk. The chaplain delivered his sermon from a hastily improvised *lectern*.

leeway N. room to move; margin. When you set a deadline, allow a little *leeway*.

legacy N. a gift made by a will. Part of my *legacy* from my parents is an album of family photographs.

■ **legend** N. explanatory list of symbols on a map. The *legend* at the bottom of the map made it clear which symbols stood for rest areas along the highway and which stood for public camp sites. (secondary meaning)

legerdemain N. sleight of hand. The magician demonstrated his renowned *legerdemain.*

leniency N. mildness; permissiveness. Considering the gravity of the offense, we were surprised by the *leniency* of the sentence.

leonine N. like a lion. He was *leonine* in his rage.

lesion N. unhealthy change in structure; injury. Many *lesions* are the result of disease.

lethal ADJ. deadly. It is unwise to leave *lethal* weapons where children may find them.

■ **lethargic** ADJ. drowsy; dull. The stuffy room made her *lethargic.*

■ **levity** N. lightness. Such *levity* is improper on this serious occasion.

lewd ADJ. lustful. They found his *lewd* stories objectionable.

lexicographer N. compiler of a dictionary. The new dictionary is the work of many *lexicographers* who spent years compiling and editing the work.

lexicon N. dictionary. I cannot find this word in any *lexicon* in the library.

liaison N. officer who acts as go-between for two armies. As the *liaison,* he had to avoid offending the leaders of the two armies. also ADJ.

libation N. drink. He offered a *libation* to the thirsty prisoner.

libelous ADJ. defamatory; injurious to the good name of a person. He sued the newspaper because of its *libelous* story.

libertine N. debauched person, roué. Although she was aware of his reputation as a *libertine,* she felt she could reform him and help him break his dissolute way of life.

libidinous ADJ. lustful. They objected to his *libidinous* behavior.

libido N. emotional urges behind human activity. The psychiatrist maintained that suppression of the *libido* often resulted in maladjustment and neuroses.

libretto N. text of an opera. The composer of an opera's music is remembered more frequently than the author of its *libretto.*

licentious ADJ. wanton; lewd; dissolute. The *licentious* monarch helped bring about his country's downfall.

lieu N. instead of. They accepted his check in *lieu* of cash.

lilliputian ADJ. extremely small. The model was built on a *lilliputian* scale. also N.

limber ADJ. flexible. Hours of ballet classes kept him *limber.*

limbo N. region near heaven or hell where certain souls are kept; a prison (slang). Among the divisions of Hell are Purgatory and *Limbo.*

limn V. portray; describe vividly. He was never satisfied with his attempts to *limn* her beauty on canvas.

limpid ADJ. clear. A *limpid* stream ran through his property.

lineage N. descent; ancestry. He traced his *lineage* back to Mayflower days.

lineaments N. features of the face. She quickly sketched the *lineaments* of his face.

linguistic ADJ. pertaining to language. The modern tourist will encounter very little *linguistic* difficulty as English has become an almost universal language.

lionize V. treat as a celebrity. She enjoyed being *lionized* and adored by the public.

liquidate V. settle accounts; clearup. He was able to *liquidate* all his debts in a short period of time.

lissom ADJ. agile; lithe. As a young boy, he was *lissom* and graceful; he gave promise of developing into a fine athlete.

listless ADJ. lacking in spirit or energy. We had expected him to be full of enthusiasm and were surprised by his *listless* attitude.

litany N. supplicatory prayer. On this solemn day, the congregation responded to the prayers of the priest during the *litany* with fervor and intensity.

lithe ADJ. flexible; supple. Her figure was *lithe* and willowy.

litigation N. lawsuit. Try to settle this amicably; I do not want to start *litigation.* litigant, N.

litotes N. understatement for emphasis. To say, "He little realizes," when we mean that he does not realize at all, is an example of the kind of understatement we call *litotes.*

livid ADJ. lead-colored; black and blue; enraged. His face was so *livid* with rage that we were afraid that he might have an attack of apoplexy.

loath ADJ. averse; reluctant. They were both *loath* for him to go.

loathe V. detest. We *loathed* the wicked villain.

lode N. metal-bearing vein. If this *lode* which we have discovered extends for any distance, we have found a fortune.

lofty ADJ. very high. They used to tease him about his *lofty* ambitions.

loiter V. hang around; linger. The policeman told him not to *loiter* in the alley.

loll V. lounge about. They *lolled* around in their chairs watching television.

longevity N. long life. When he reached ninety, the old man was proud of his *longevity.*

lope V. gallop slowly. As the horses *loped* along, we had an opportunity to admire the ever-changing scenery.

loquacious ADJ. talkative. She is very *loquacious* and can speak on the telephone for hours.

lout N. clumsy person. The delivery boy is an awkward *lout.*

Test

Word List 28 *Antonyms*

Each of the questions below consists of a word in capital letters, followed by five lettered words or phrases. Choose the lettered word or phrase that is most nearly opposite in meaning to the word in capital letters and write the letter of your choice on your answer paper.

406. LAMPOON (A) darken (B) praise (C) abandon (D) sail (E) fly
407. LANGUOR (A) vitality (B) length (C) embarrassment (D) wine (E) avarice
408. LATENT (A) trim (B) forbidding (C) execrable (D) early (E) obvious
409. LAVISH (A) hostile (B) unwashed (C) timely (D) decent (E) frugal
410. LAUDATORY (A) dirtying (B) disclaiming (C) defamatory (D) inflammatory (E) debased
411. LAX (A) salty (B) strict (C) shrill (D) boring (E) cowardly

412. LECHERY (A) trust (B) compulsion (C) zeal (D) addiction (E) purity
413. LETHARGIC (A) convalescent (B) beautiful (C) enervating (D) invigorating (E) interrogating
414. LEVITY (A) bridge (B) dam (C) praise (D) blame (E) solemnity
415. LILLIPUTIAN (A) destructive (B) proper (C) gigantic (D) elegant (E) barren
416. LIMPID (A) erect (B) turbid (C) tangential (D) timid (E) weary
417. LITHE (A) stiff (B) limpid (C) facetious (D) insipid (E) vast
418. LIVID (A) alive (B) mundane (C) positive (D) undiscolored (E) vast
419. LOATH (A) loose (B) evident (C) deliberate (D) eager (E) tiny
420. LOQUACIOUS (A) taciturn (B) sentimental (C) soporific (D) soothing (E) sedate

Word List 29 lubricity-maunder

lubricity N. slipperiness; evasiveness. He exasperated the reporters by his *lubricity;* they could not pin him down to a definite answer.

lucent ADJ. shining. The moon's *lucent* rays silvered the river.

■ **lucid** ADJ. bright; easily understood. His explanation was *lucid* and to the point.

lucrative ADJ. profitable. He turned his hobby into a *lucrative* profession.

lucre N. money. Preferring *lucre* to fame, he wrote stories of popular appeal.

ludicrous ADJ. laughable; trifling. Let us be serious; this is not a *ludicrous* issue.

lugubrious ADJ. mournful. The *lugubrious* howling of the dogs added to our sadness.

lull N. moment of calm. Not wanting to get wet, they waited under the awning for a *lull* in the rain.

luminous ADJ. shining; issuing light. The sun is a *luminous* body.

lunar ADJ. pertaining to the moon. *Lunar* craters can be plainly seen with the aid of a small telescope.

lupine ADJ. like a wolf. She was terrified of his fierce, *lupine* smile.

lurid ADJ. wild; sensational. The *lurid* stories he told shocked his listeners.

luscious ADJ. pleasing to taste or smell. The ripe peach was *luscious.*

luster N. shine; gloss. The soft *luster* of the silk in the dim light was pleasing.

lustrous ADJ. shining. Her large and *lustrous* eyes gave a touch of beauty to an otherwise drab face.

luxuriant ADJ. fertile; abundant; ornate. Farming was easy in this *luxuriant* soil.

macabre ADJ. gruesome; grisly. The city morgue is a *macabre* spot for the uninitiated.

macerate V. waste away. Cancer *macerated* his body.

Machiavellian ADJ. crafty; double-dealing. I do not think he will be a good ambassador because he is not accustomed to the *Machiavellian* maneuverings of foreign diplomats.

machinations N. schemes. I can see through your wily *machinations.*

madrigal N. pastoral song. His program of folk songs included several *madrigals* which he sang to the accompaniment of a lute.

maelstrom N. whirlpool. The canoe was tossed about in the *maelstrom.*

magnanimous ADJ. generous. The philanthropist was most *magnanimous.*

magnate N. person of prominence or influence. The steel *magnate* decided to devote more time to city politics.

magniloquent ADJ. boastful, pompous. In their stories of the trial, the reporters ridiculed the *magniloquent* speeches of the defense attorney.

magnitude N. greatness; extent. It is difficult to comprehend the *magnitude* of his crime.

maim V. mutilate; injure. The hospital could not take care of all who had been wounded or *maimed* in the railroad accident.

maladroit ADJ. clumsy; bungling. In his usual *maladroit* way, he managed to upset the cart and spill the food.

malaise N. uneasiness; distress. She felt a sudden vague *malaise* when she heard sounds at the door.

malapropism N. comic misuse of a word. Mrs. Warren's funniest *malapropism* occurs when she accuses Skitterby of being "a snare and an Andalusian."

malcontent N. person dissatisfied with existing state of affairs. He was one of the few *malcontents* in Congress; he constantly voiced his objections to the Presidential program. also ADJ.

malediction N. curse. The witch uttered *maledictions* against her captors.

malefactor N. criminal. We must try to bring these *malefactors* to justice.

malevolent ADJ. wishing evil. We must thwart his *malevolent* schemes.

malicious ADJ. dictated by hatred or spite. The *malicious* neighbor spread the gossip.

malign V. speak evil of; defame. Because of her hatred of the family, she *maligns* all who are friendly to them.

malignant ADJ. having an evil influence; virulent. This is a *malignant* disease; we may have to use drastic measures to stop its spread.

malingerer N. one who feigns illness to escape duty. The captain ordered the sergeant to punish all *malingerers* and force them to work.

mall N. public walk. The *Mall* in Central Park has always been a favorite spot for Sunday strollers.

■ **malleable** ADJ. capable of being shaped by pounding. Gold is a *malleable* metal.

malodorous ADJ. foul-smelling. The compost heap was most *malodorous* in summer.

mammal N. a vertebrate animal whose female suckles its young. Many people regard the whale as a fish and do not realize that it is a *mammal*.

mammoth ADJ. gigantic. The *mammoth* corporations of the twentieth century are a mixed blessing.

manacle V. restrain; handcuff. The police immediately *manacled* the prisoner so he could not escape. also N.

mandate N. order; charge. In his inaugural address, the President stated that he had a *mandate* from the people to seek an end to social evils such as poverty, poor housing, etc. also V.

mandatory ADJ. obligatory. These instructions are *mandatory;* any violation will be severely punished.

mangy ADJ. shabby; wretched. We finally threw out the *mangy* rug that the dog had destroyed.

maniacal ADJ. raving mad. His *maniacal* laughter frightened us.

manifest ADJ. understandable; clear. His evil intentions were *manifest* and yet we could not stop him. also V.

manifesto N. declaration; statement of policy. This statement may be regarded as the *manifesto* of the party's policy.

manifold ADJ. numerous; varied. I cannot begin to tell you how much I appreciate your *manifold* kindnesses.

manipulate V. operate with the hands. How do you *manipulate* these puppets?

manumit V. emancipate; free from bondage. Enlightened slave owners were willing to *manumit* their slaves and thus put an end to the evil of slavery in the country.

marauder N. raider; intruder. The sounding of the alarm frightened the *marauders*.

marital ADJ. pertaining to marriage. After the publication of his book on *marital* affairs, he was often consulted by married people on the verge of divorce.

maritime ADJ. bordering on the sea; nautical. The *Maritime* Provinces depend on the sea for their wealth.

marred ADJ. damaged; disfigured. She had to refinish the *marred* surface of the table. mar, V.

marrow N. soft tissue filling the bones. The frigid cold chilled the traveler to the *marrow*.

marsupial N. one of a family of mammals that nurse their offspring in a pouch. The most common *marsupial* in North America is the opossum.

martial ADJ. warlike. The sound of *martial* music is always inspiring.

martinet N. strict disciplinarian. The commanding officer was a *martinet* who observed each regulation to the letter.

masochist N. person who enjoys his own pain. The *masochist* begs, "Hit me." The sadist smiles and says, "I won't."

masticate V. chew. We must *masticate* our food carefully and slowly in order to avoid stomach disorders.

maternal ADJ. motherly. Many animals display *maternal* instincts only while their offspring are young and helpless.

matriarch N. woman who rules a family or larger social group. The *matriarch* ruled her gypsy tribe with a firm hand.

matricide N. murder of a mother by a child. A crime such as *matricide* is inconceivable.

matrix N. mold or die. The cast around the *matrix* was cracked.

maudlin ADJ. effusively sentimental. I do not like such *maudlin* pictures. I call them tearjerkers.

maul V. handle roughly. The rock star was *mauled* by his over-excited fans.

maunder V. talk incoherently; utter drivel. You do not make sense; you *maunder* and garble your words.

Test

Word List 29   *Synonyms and Antonyms*

Each of the following questions consists of a word in capital letters, followed by five lettered words or phrases. Choose the lettered word or phrase which is most nearly similar or the opposite of the word in capital letters and write the letter of your choice on your answer paper.

421. LUGUBRIOUS (A) frantic (B) cheerful (C) burdensome (D) oily (E) militant
422. LURID (A) dull (B) duplicate (C) heavy (D) painstaking (E) intelligent
423. MACABRE (A) musical (B) frightening (C) chewed (D) wicked (E) exceptional
424. MAGNILOQUENT (A) loquacious (B) bombastic (C) rudimentary (D) qualitative (E) minimizing
425. MAGNITUDE (A) realization (B) fascination (C) enormity (D) gratitude (E) interference
426. MALADROIT (A) malicious (B) starving (C) thirsty (D) tactless (E) artistic
427. MALEDICTION (A) misfortune (B) hap (C) fruition (D) correct pronunciation (E) benediction
428. MALEFACTOR (A) quail (B) lawbreaker (C) beneficiary (D) banker (E) female agent
429. MALEVOLENT (A) kindly (B) vacuous (C) ambivalent (D) volatile (E) primitive
430. MALIGN (A) intersperse (B) vary (C) emphasize (D) frighten (E) eulogize
431. MALLEABLE (A) brittle (B) blatant (C) brilliant (D) brownish (E) basking
432. MANIACAL (A) demoniac (B) saturated (C) sane (D) sanitary (E) handcuffed
433. MANIFEST (A) limited (B) obscure (C) faulty (D) varied (E) vital
434. MANUMIT (A) print (B) impress (C) enslave (D) endeavor (E) fail
435. MARTIAL (A) bellicose (B) celibate (C) divorced (D) quiescent (E) planetary

Word List 30   mausoleum-misnomer

mausoleum N. monumental tomb. His body was placed in the family *mausoleum.*

mauve ADJ. pale purple. The *mauve* tint in the lilac bush was another indication that Spring had finally arrived.

maverick N. rebel; nonconformist. To the masculine literary establishment, George Sand with her insistence on wearing trousers and smoking cigars was clearly a *maverick* who fought her proper womanly role.

mawkish ADJ. sickening; insipid. Your *mawkish* sighs fill me with disgust.

maxim N. proverb; a truth pithily stated. Aesop's fables illustrate moral *maxims.*

mayhem N. injury to body. The riot was marked not only by *mayhem,* with its attendant loss of life and limb, but also by arson and pillage.

meander V. to wind or turn in its course. It is difficult to sail up this stream because of the way it *meanders* through the countryside.

meddlesome ADJ. interfering. He felt his marriage was suffering because of his *meddlesome* mother-in-law.

mediate V. settle a dispute through the services of an outsider. Let us *mediate* our differences rather than engage in a costly strike.

mediocre ADJ. ordinary; commonplace. We were disappointed because he gave a rather *mediocre* performance in this role.

meditation N. reflection; thought. She reached her decision only after much *meditation.*

medley N. mixture. The band played a *medley* of Gershwin tunes.

megalomania N. mania for doing grandiose things. Developers who spend millions trying to build the world's tallest skyscraper suffer from *megalomania.*

mélange N. medley; miscellany. This anthology provides a *mélange* of the author's output in the fields of satire, criticism and political analysis.

melee N. fight. The captain tried to ascertain the cause of the *melee* that had broken out among the crew members.

mellifluous ADJ. flowing smoothly; smooth. Italian is a *mellifluous* language.

memento N. token; reminder. Take this book as a *memento* of your visit.

memorialize V. commemorate. Let us *memorialize* his great contribution by dedicating this library in his honor.

mendacious ADJ. lying; false. He was a pathological liar, and his friends learned to discount his *mendacious* stories.

■ **mendicant** N. beggar. From the moment we left the ship, we were surrounded by *mendicants* and peddlers.

menial ADJ. suitable for servants; low. I cannot understand why a person of your ability and talent should engage in such *menial* activities. also N.

mentor N. teacher. During this very trying period, she could not have had a better *mentor,* for the teacher was sympathetic and understanding.

mercantile ADJ. concerning trade. I am more interested in the opportunities available in the *mercantile* field than I am in those in the legal profession.

mercenary ADJ. interested in money or gain. I am certain that your action was prompted by *mercenary* motives. also N.

mercurial ADJ. fickle; changing. He was of a *mercurial* temperament and therefore unpredictable.

meretricious ADJ. flashy; tawdry. Her jewels were inexpensive but not *meretricious*.

meringue N. a pastry decoration made of whites of eggs. The lemon *meringue* pie is one of our specialties.

mesa N. high, flat-topped hill. The *mesa*, rising above the surrounding countryside, was the most conspicuous feature of the area.

mesmerize V. hypnotize. The incessant drone seemed to *mesmerize* him and place him in a trance.

metallurgical ADJ. pertaining to the art of removing metals from ores. During the course of his *metallurgical* research, the scientist developed a steel alloy of tremendous strength.

■ **metamorphosis** N. change of form. The *metamorphosis* of caterpillar to butterfly is typical of many such changes in animal life. metamorphose, V.

metaphor N. implied comparison. "He soared like an eagle" is an example of a simile; "He is an eagle in flight," a *metaphor*.

metaphysical ADJ. pertaining to speculative philosophy. The modern poets have gone back to the fanciful poems of the *metaphysical* poets of the seventeenth century for many of their images. metaphysics, N.

mete V. measure; distribute. He tried to be impartial in his efforts to *mete* out justice.

meteoric ADJ. swift; momentarily brilliant. We all wondered at his *meteoric* rise to fame.

methodical ADJ. systematic. An accountant must be *methodical* and maintain order among his financial records.

meticulous ADJ. excessively careful. He was *meticulous* in checking his accounts and never made mistakes.

metropolis N. large city. Every evening this terminal is filled with the thousands of commuters who are going from this *metropolis* to their homes in the suburbs.

mettle N. courage; spirit. When challenged by the other horses in the race, the thoroughbred proved its *mettle* by its determination to hold the lead.

mews N. group of stables built around a courtyard. Let us visit the *mews* to inspect the newly purchased horse.

miasma N. swamp gas; odor of decaying matter. I suspect that this area is infested with malaria as I can readily smell the *miasma*.

microcosm N. small world. In the *microcosm* of our small village, we find illustrations of all the evils that beset the universe.

mien N. demeanor; bearing. She had the gracious *mien* of a queen.

migrant ADJ. changing its habitat; wandering. These *migrant* birds return every spring. also N.

migratory ADJ. wandering. The return of the *migratory* birds to the northern sections of this country is a harbinger of spring.

milieu N. environment; means of expression. His *milieu* is watercolor although he has produced excellent oil paintings and lithographs.

militant ADJ. combative; bellicose. Although at this time he was advocating a policy of neutrality, one could usually find him adopting a more *militant* attitude. also N.

militate V. work against. Your record of lateness and absence will *militate* against your chances of promotion.

millennium N. thousand-year period; period of happiness and prosperity. I do not expect the *millennium* to come during my lifetime.

mimicry N. imitation. Her gift for *mimicry* was so great that her friends said that she should be in the theater.

minaret N. slender tower attached to a mosque. From the balcony of the *minaret* we obtained an excellent view of the town and the neighboring countryside.

minatory ADJ. threatening. All abusive and *minatory* letters received by the mayor and other public officials were examined by the police.

mincing ADJ. affectedly dainty. Yum-Yum walked across the stage with *mincing* steps.

minion N. a servile dependent. He was always accompanied by several of his *minions* because he enjoyed their subservience and flattery.

minuscule ADJ. extremely small. Why should I involve myself with a project with so *minuscule* a chance for success?

minutiae N. petty details. She would have liked to ignore the *minutiae* of daily living.

mirage N. unreal reflection; optical illusion. The lost prospector was fooled by a *mirage* in the desert.

mire V. entangle; stick in swampy ground. Their rear wheels became *mired* in mud. also N.

mirth N. merriment; laughter. Sober Malvolio found Sir Toby's *mirth* improper.

misadventure N. mischance; ill luck. The young explorer met death by *misadventure*.

misanthrope N. one who hates mankind. We thought the hermit was a *misanthrope* because he shunned our society.

misapprehension N. error; misunderstanding. To avoid *misapprehension*, I am going to ask all of you to repeat the instructions I have given.

miscegenation N. intermarriage between races. Some states passed laws against *miscegenation*.

miscellany N. mixture of writings on various subjects. This is an interesting *miscellany* of nineteenth-century prose and poetry.

mischance N. ill luck. By *mischance*, he lost his week's salary.

miscreant N. wretch; villain. His kindness to the *miscreant* amazed all of us who had expected to hear severe punishment pronounced.

misdemeanor N. minor crime. The culprit pleaded guilty to a *misdemeanor* rather than face trial for a felony.

miserly ADJ. stingy; mean. The *miserly* old man hoarded his coins not out of prudence but out of greed. miser, N.

misgivings N. doubts. Hamlet described his *misgivings* to Horatio but decided to fence with Laertes despite his foreboding of evil.

mishap N. accident. With a little care you could have avoided this *mishap*.

misnomer N. wrong name; incorrect designation. His tyrannical conduct proved to all that his nickname, King Eric the Just, was a *misnomer*.

Test

Word List 30 *Synonyms*

Each of the questions below consists of a word in capital letters, followed by five lettered words or phrases. Choose the lettered word or phrase that is most nearly similar in meaning to the word in capital letters and write the letter of your choice on your answer paper.

436. MAWKISH (A) sentimental (B) true (C) certain (D) devious (E) carefree
437. MEDIOCRE (A) average (B) bitter (C) medieval (D) industrial (E) agricultural
438. MELEE (A) heat (B) brawl (C) attempt (D) weapon (E) choice
439. MELLIFLUOUS (A) porous (B) honeycombed (C) strong (D) smooth (E) viscous
440. MENIAL (A) intellectual (B) clairvoyant (C) servile (D) arrogant (E) laudatory
441. MENTOR (A) guide (B) genius (C) talker (D) philosopher (E) stylist

442. MESMERIZE (A) remember (B) hypnotize (C) delay (D) bore (E) analyze
443. METICULOUS (A) steadfast (B) recent (C) quaint (D) painstaking (E) overt
444. MIASMA (A) dream (B) noxious fumes (C) scenario (D) quantity (E) total
445. MILITANT (A) combative (B) dramatic (C) religious (D) quaint (E) paternal
446. MINION (A) monster (B) quorum (C) majority (D) host (E) dependent
447. MIRAGE (A) dessert (B) illusion (C) water (D) mirror (E) statement
448. MISANTHROPE (A) benefactor (B) philanderer (C) man-hater (D) aesthete (E) epicure
449. MISCHANCE (A) gamble (B) ordinance (C) aperture (D) anecdote (E) adversity
450. MISDEMEANOR (A) felony (B) peccadillo (C) indignity (D) fiat (E) illiteracy

Word List 31 misogamy-natal

misogamy N. hatred of marriage. He remained a bachelor not because of *misogamy* but because of ill fate: his fiancee died before the wedding.

misogynist N. hater of women. She accused him of being a *misogynist* because he had been a bachelor all his life.

missile N. object to be thrown or projected. Scientists are experimenting with guided *missiles*.

missive N. letter. The ambassador received a *missive* from the Secretary of State.

mite N. very small object or creature; small coin. Gnats are annoying *mites* that sting.

■ **mitigate** V. appease. Nothing he did could *mitigate* her wrath; she was unforgiving.

mnemonic ADJ. pertaining to memory. He used *mnemonic* tricks to master new words.

mobile ADJ. movable; not fixed. The *mobile* blood bank operated by the Red Cross visited our neighborhood today. mobility, N.

mode N. prevailing style. She was not used to their lavish *mode* of living.

modicum N. limited quantity. Although his story is based on a *modicum* of truth, most of the events he describes are fictitious.

modish ADJ. fashionable. She always discarded all garments which were no longer *modish*.

modulation N. toning down; changing from one key to another. When she spoke, it was with quiet *modulation* of voice.

mogul N. powerful person. The oil *moguls* made great profits when the price of gasoline rose.

moiety N. half; part. There is a slight *moiety* of the savage in her personality which is not easily perceived by those who do not know her well.

molecule N. the smallest part of a homogeneous substance. In chemistry, we study how atoms and *molecules* react to form new substances.

■ **mollify** V. soothe. We tried to *mollify* the hysterical child by promising her many gifts.

molt V. shed or cast off hair or feathers. The male robin *molted* in the spring.

molten ADJ. melted. The city of Pompeii was destroyed by volcanic ash rather than by *molten* lava flowing from Mount Vesuvius.

momentous ADJ. very important. On this *momentous* occasion, we must be very solemn.

momentum N. quantity of motion of a moving body; impetus. The car lost *momentum* as it tried to ascend the steep hill.

monarchy N. government under a single ruler. England today remains a *monarchy*.

monastic ADJ. related to monks. Wanting to live a religious life, he took his *monastic* vows.

monetary ADJ. pertaining to money. She was in complete charge of all *monetary* matters affecting the household.

monolithic ADJ. solidly uniform; unyielding. The patriots sought to present a *monolithic* front.

monotheism N. belief in one God. Abraham was the first to proclaim his belief in *monotheism*.

monotony N. sameness leading to boredom. He took a clerical job, but soon grew to hate the *monotony* of his daily routine.

monumental ADJ. massive. Writing a dictionary is a *monumental* task.

moodiness N. fits of depression or gloom. We could not discover the cause of her recurrent *moodiness*.

moor N. marshy wasteland. These *moors* can only be used for hunting; they are too barren for agriculture.

moot ADJ. debatable. Our tariff policy is a *moot* subject.

moratorium N. legal delay of payment. If we declare a *moratorium* and delay collection of debts for six months, I am sure the farmers will be able to meet their bills.

morbid ADJ. given to unwholesome thought; gloomy. These *morbid* speculations are dangerous; we must lighten our thinking by emphasis on more pleasant matters.

mordant ADJ. biting; sarcastic; stinging. Actors feared the critic's *mordant* pen.

mores N. customs. The *mores* of Mexico are those of Spain with some modifications.

morganatic ADJ. describing a marriage between a member of a royal family and a commoner in which it is agreed that any children will not inherit title, etc. Refusing the suggestion of a *morganatic* marriage, the king abdicated from the throne when he could not marry the woman he loved.

■ **moribund** ADJ. at the point of death. The doctors called the family to the bedside of the *moribund* patient.

morose ADJ. ill-humored; sullen. When we first meet Hamlet, we find him *morose* and depressed.

mortician N. undertaker. The *mortician* prepared the corpse for burial.

mortify V. humiliate; punish the flesh. She was so *mortified* by her blunder that she ran to her room in tears.

mote N. small speck. The tiniest *mote* in the eye is very painful.

motif N. theme. This simple *motif* runs throughout the entire score.

motley ADJ. parti-colored; mixed. The captain had gathered a *motley* crew to sail the vessel.

mottled ADJ. spotted. When he blushed, his face took on a *mottled* hue.

mountebank N. charlatan; boastful pretender. The patent medicine man was a *mountebank*.

muddle V. confuse; mix up. His thoughts were *muddled* and chaotic. also N.

muggy ADJ. warm and damp. August in New York City is often *muggy*.

mugwump N. defector from a party. When he refused to support his party's nominees, he was called a *mugwump* and deprived of his seniority privileges in Congress.

mulct V. defraud a person of something. The lawyer was accused of trying to *mulct* the boy of his legacy.

■ **multifarious** ADJ. varied; greatly diversified. A career woman and mother, she was constantly busy with the *multifarious* activities of her daily life.

multiform ADJ. having many forms. Snowflakes are *multiform* but always hexagonal.

multilingual ADJ. having many languages. Because they are bordered by so many countries, the Swiss people are *multilingual*.

multiplicity N. state of being numerous. He was appalled by the *multiplicity* of details he had to complete before setting out on his mission.

mundane ADJ. worldly as opposed to spiritual. He was concerned only with *mundane* matters, especially the daily stock market quotations.

■ **munificent** ADJ. very generous. The *munificent* gift was presented to the bride by her rich uncle. munificence, N.

murkiness N. darkness; gloom. The *murkiness* and fog of the waterfront that evening depressed me.

murrain N. plague; cattle disease. "A *murrain* on you" was a common malediction in that period.

muse V. ponder. For a moment he *mused* about the beauty of the scene, but his thoughts soon changed as he recalled his own personal problems. also N.

musky ADJ. having the odor of musk. She left a trace of *musky* perfume behind her.

muster V. gather; assemble. Washington *mustered* his forces at Trenton.

musty ADJ. stale; spoiled by age. The attic was dark and *musty*.

mutable ADJ. changing in form; fickle. His opinions were *mutable* and easily influenced by anyone who had any powers of persuasion.

muted ADJ. silent; muffled; toned down. In the funeral parlor, the mourners' voices had a *muted* quality. mute, V.

mutilate V. maim. The torturer threatened to *mutilate* his victim.

mutinous ADJ. unruly; rebellious. The captain had to use force to quiet his *mutinous* crew.

myopic ADJ. nearsighted. In thinking only of your present needs and ignoring the future, you are being rather *myopic*.

myriad N. very large number. *Myriads* of mosquitoes from the swamps invaded our village every twilight. also ADJ.

nadir N. lowest point. Although few people realized it, the Dow-Jones averages had reached their *nadir* and would soon begin an upward surge.

naiveté N. quality of being unsophisticated. I cannot believe that such *naiveté* is unassumed in a person of her age and experience. naive, ADJ.

narcissist N. conceited person. A *narcissist* is his own best friend.

nascent ADJ. incipient; coming into being. If we could identify these revolutionary movements in their *nascent* state,

we would be able to eliminate serious trouble in later years.

natal ADJ. pertaining to birth. He refused to celebrate his *natal* day because it reminded him of the few years he could look forward to.

Test

Word List 31   *Synonyms*

Each of the questions below consists of a word in capital letters, followed by five lettered words or phrases. Choose the lettered word or phrase that is most nearly similar in meaning to the word in capital letters and write the letter of your choice on your answer paper.

451. MODISH (A) sentimental (B) stylish (C) vacillating (D) contrary (E) adorned

452. MOLLIFY (A) avenge (B) attenuate (C) attribute (D) mortify (E) appease

453. MONETARY (A) boring (B) fascinating (C) fiscal (D) stationary (E) scrupulous

454. MOOT (A) visual (B) invisible (C) controversial (D) anticipatory (E) obsequious

455. MORDANT (A) dying (B) trenchant (C) fabricating (D) controlling (E) avenging

456. MORIBUND (A) dying (B) appropriate (C) leather bound (D) answering (E) undertaking

457. MOTLEY (A) active (B) disguised (C) variegated (D) somber (E) sick

458. MUGGY (A) attacking (B) fascinating (C) humid (D) characteristic (E) gelid

459. MULCT (A) swindle (B) hold (C) record (D) print (E) fertilize

460. MULTILINGUAL (A) variegated (B) polyglot (C) multilateral (D) polyandrous (E) multiplied

461. MUNDANE (A) global (B) futile (C) spatial (D) heretic (E) worldly

462. MUNIFICENT (A) grandiose (B) puny (C) philanthropic (D) poor (E) gracious

463. MUSTY (A) flat (B) necessary (C) indifferent (D) nonchalant (E) vivid

464. MYOPIC (A) visionary (B) nearsighted (C) moral (D) glassy (E) blind

465. NASCENT (A) incipient (B) ignorant (C) loyal (D) treacherous (E) unnamed

Word List 32   natation-obsidian

natation N. swimming. The Red Cross emphasizes the need for courses in *natation*.

nauseate V. cause to become sick; fill with disgust. The foul smells began to *nauseate* him.

nautical ADJ. pertaining to ships or navigation. The Maritime Museum contains many models of clipper ships, logbooks, anchors and many other items of a *nautical* nature.

nave N. main body of a church. The *nave* of the cathedral was empty at this hour.

neap ADJ. lowest. We shall have to navigate very cautiously over the reefs as we have a *neap* tide this time of the month.

nebulous ADJ. vague; hazy; cloudy. She had only a *nebulous* memory of her grandmother's face.

necrology N. obituary notice; list of the dead. The *necrology* of those buried in this cemetery is available in the office.

necromancy N. black magic; dealings with the dead. Because he was able to perform feats of *necromancy,* the natives thought he was in league with the devil.

nefarious ADJ. very wicked. He was universally feared because of his many *nefarious* deeds.

negation N. denial. I must accept his argument since you have been unable to present any *negation* of his evidence.

negligence N. carelessness. *Negligence* can prove costly near complicated machinery.

nemesis N. revenging agent. Captain Bligh vowed to be Christian's *nemesis.*

neologism N. new or newly coined word or phrase. As we invent new techniques and professions, we must also invent *neologisms* such as "microcomputer" and "astronaut" to describe them.

■ neophyte N. recent convert; beginner. This mountain slope contains slides that will challenge experts as well as *neophytes.*

nepotism N. favoritism (to a relative). John left his position with the company because he felt that advancement was based on *nepotism* rather than ability.

nether ADJ. lower. Tradition locates hell in the *nether* regions.

nettle V. annoy; vex. Do not let him *nettle* you with his sarcastic remarks.

■ nexus N. connection. I fail to see the *nexus* which binds these two widely separated events.

nib N. beak; pen point. The *nibs* of fountain pens often became clotted and corroded.

nicety N. precision; minute distinction. I cannot distinguish between such *niceties* of reasoning.

niggardly ADJ. meanly stingy; parsimonious. The *niggardly* pittance the widow receives from the government cannot keep her from poverty.

niggle V. spend too much time on minor points; carp. Let's not *niggle* over details. niggling, ADJ.

nihilism N. denial of traditional values; total skepticism. *Nihilism* holds that existence has no meaning.

nirvana N. in Buddhist teachings, the ideal state in which the individual loses himself in the attainment of an impersonal beatitude. He tried to explain the concept of *nirvana* to his skeptical students.

nocturnal ADJ. done at night. Mr. Jones obtained a watchdog to prevent the *nocturnal* raids on his chicken coops.

noisome ADJ. foul smelling; unwholesome. I never could stand the *noisome* atmosphere surrounding the slaughter houses.

nomadic ADJ. wandering. Several *nomadic* tribes of Indians would hunt in this area each year.

nomenclature N. terminology; system of names. She struggled to master scientific *nomenclature*.

nominal ADJ. in name only; trifling. He offered to drive her to the airport for only a *nominal* fee.

nonage N. immaturity. She was embarrassed by the *nonage* of her contemporaries who never seemed to grow up.

nonchalance N. indifference; lack of interest. Few people could understand how he could listen to the news of the tragedy with such *nonchalance;* the majority regarded him as callous and unsympathetic.

noncommittal ADJ. neutral; unpledged; undecided. We were annoyed by his *noncommittal* reply for we had been led to expect definite assurances of his approval.

nonentity N. nonexistence; person of no importance. Of course you are a *nonentity;* you will continue to be one until you prove your value to the community.

nonplus V. bring to a halt by confusion. In my efforts to correct this situation I felt *nonplussed* by the stupidity of my assistants.

non sequitur N. a conclusion that does not follow from the facts stated. Your term paper is full of *non sequiturs;* I cannot see how you reached the conclusions you state.

nosegay N. fragrant bouquet. These spring flowers will make an attractive *nosegay*.

nostalgia N. homesickness; longing for the past. The first settlers found so much work to do that they had little time for *nostalgia*.

nostrum N. questionable medicine. No quack selling *nostrums* is going to cheat me.

notorious ADJ. outstandingly bad; unfavorably known. Captain Kidd was a *notorious* pirate. notoriety, N.

novelty N. something new; newness. The computer is no longer a *novelty* around the office. novel, ADJ.

novice N. beginner. Even a *novice* can do good work if he follows these simple directions.

noxious ADJ. harmful. We must trace the source of these *noxious* gases before they asphyxiate us.

nuance N. shade of difference in meaning or color. The unskilled eye of the layman has difficulty in discerning the *nuances* of color in the paintings.

nubile ADJ. marriageable. Mrs. Bennet, in *Pride and Prejudice* by Jane Austen, was worried about finding suitable husbands for her five *nubile* daughters.

nugatory ADJ. futile; worthless. This agreement is *nugatory* for no court will enforce it.

nullify V. to make invalid. Once the contract was *nullified,* it no longer had any legal force.

numismatist N. person who collects coins. The *numismatist* had a splendid collection of antique coins.

nuptial ADJ. related to marriage. Their *nuptial* ceremony was performed in Golden Gate Park.

nurture V. bring up; feed; educate. We must *nurture* the young so that they will develop into good citizens.

nutrient ADJ. providing nourishment. During the convalescent period, the patient must be provided with *nutrient* foods. also N.

oaf N. stupid, awkward person. He called the unfortunate waiter a clumsy *oaf*.

obdurate ADJ. stubborn. He was *obdurate* in his refusal to listen to our complaints.

obeisance N. bow. She made an *obeisance* as the king and queen entered the room.

obelisk N. tall column tapering and ending in a pyramid. Cleopatra's Needle is an *obelisk* in New York City's Central Park.

obese ADJ. fat. It is advisable that *obese* people try to lose weight.

obfuscate V. confuse; muddle. Do not *obfuscate* the issues by dragging in irrelevant arguments.

obituary ADJ. death notice. I first learned of her death when I read the *obituary* column in the newspaper. also N.

objective ADJ. not influenced by emotions; fair. Even though he was her son, she tried to be *objective* about his behavior.

objective N. goal; aim. A degree in medicine was her ultimate *objective*.

objurgate V. scold; rebuke severely. I am afraid she will *objurgate* us publicly for this offense.

objurgation N. severe rebuke; scolding. *Objurgations* and even threats of punishment did not deter the young hoodlums.

oblation N. the Eucharist; pious donation. The wealthy man offered *oblations* so that the Church might be able to provide for the needy.

obligatory ADJ. binding; required. It is *obligatory* that books borrowed from the library be returned within two weeks.

oblique ADJ. slanting; deviating from the perpendicular or from a straight line. The sergeant ordered the men to march "Oblique Right."

obliquity N. departure from right principles; perversity. His moral decadence was marked by his *obliquity* from the ways of integrity and honesty.

obliterate v. destroy completely. The tidal wave *obliterated* several island villages.

oblivion N. forgetfulness. Her works had fallen into a state of *oblivion;* no one bothered to read them. oblivious, ADJ.

obloquy N. slander; disgrace; infamy. I resent the *obloquy* that you are casting upon my reputation.

obnoxious ADJ. offensive. I find your behavior *obnoxious;* please mend your ways.

obscure ADJ. dark; vague; unclear. Even after I read the poem a fourth time, its meaning was still *obscure.* obscurity, N.

obscure v. darken; make unclear. At times he seemed purposely to *obscure* his meaning, preferring mystery to clarity.

obsequious ADJ. slavishly attentive; servile; sycophantic. Nothing is more disgusting to me than the *obsequious* demeanor of the people who wait upon you.

obsequy N. funeral ceremony. Hundreds paid their last respects at his *obsequies.*

obsession N. fixed idea; continued brooding. This *obsession* with the supernatural has made him unpopular with his neighbors.

obsidian N. black volcanic rock. The deposits of *obsidian* on the mountain slopes were an indication that the volcano had erupted in ancient times.

Test

Word List 32   *Antonyms*

Each of the questions below consists of a word in capital letters, followed by five lettered words or phrases. Choose the lettered word or phrase that is most nearly opposite in meaning to the word in capital letters and write the letter of your choice on your answer paper.

466. NEBULOUS (A) starry (B) clear (C) cold (D) fundamental (E) porous

467. NEFARIOUS (A) various (B) lacking (C) benign (D) pompous (E) futile

468. NEGATION (A) postulation (B) hypothecation (C) affirmation (D) violation (E) anticipation

469. NEOPHYTE (A) veteran (B) satellite (C) desperado (D) handwriting (E) violence

470. NIGGARDLY (A) protected (B) biased (C) prodigal (D) bankrupt (E) placated

471. NOCTURNAL (A) harsh (B) marauding (C) patrolling (D) daily (E) fallow

472. NOISOME (A) quiet (B) dismayed (C) fragrant (D) sleepy (E) inquisitive

473. NOTORIOUS (A) fashionable (B) renowned (C) inactive (D) intrepid (E) invincible

474. OBDURATE (A) yielding (B) fleeting (C) finite (D) fascinating (E) permanent

475. OBESE (A) skillful (B) cadaverous (C) clever (D) unpredictable (E) lucid

476. OBJURGATION (A) elegy (B) oath (C) model (D) praise (E) approval

477. OBLIGATORY (A) demanding (B) optional (C) facile (D) friendly (E) divorced

478. OBLOQUY (A) praise (B) rectangle (C) circle (D) dialogue (E) cure

479. OBSEQUIOUS (A) successful (B) democratic (C) supercilious (D) ambitious (E) lamentable

480. OBSESSION (A) whim (B) loss (C) phobia (D) delusion (E) feud

Word List 33   obsolete-pacifist

obsolete ADJ. outmoded. That word is *obsolete;* do not use it.

obstetrician N. physician specializing in delivery of babies. In modern times, the delivery of children has passed from the midwife to the more scientifically trained *obstetrician.*

obstinate ADJ. stubborn. We tried to persuade him to give up smoking, but he was *obstinate* and refused to change.

obstreperous ADJ. boisterous; noisy. The crowd became *obstreperous* and shouted their disapproval of the proposals made by the speaker.

obtrude v. push into prominence. The other members of the group object to the manner in which you *obtrude* your opinions into matters of no concern to you.

obtrusive ADJ. pushing forward. I found her a very *obtrusive* person, constantly seeking the center of the stage.

obtuse ADJ. blunt; stupid. Because he was so *obtuse,* he could not follow the teacher's reasoning and asked foolish questions.

obviate v. make unnecessary; get rid of. I hope this contribution will *obviate* any need for further collections of funds.

Occident N. the West. It will take time for the *Occident* to understand the ways and customs of the Orient.

occlude v. shut; close. A blood clot *occluded* an artery to the heart.

occult ADJ. mysterious; secret; supernatural. The *occult* rites of the organization were revealed only to members. also N.

oculist N. physician who specializes in treatment of the eyes. In many states, an *oculist* is the only one who may apply medicinal drops to the eyes for the purpose of examining them.

odious ADJ. hateful. I find the task of punishing you most *odious.*

odium N. repugnance; dislike. I cannot express the *odium* I feel at your heinous actions.

odoriferous ADJ. giving off an odor. The *odoriferous* spices stimulated her jaded appetite.

odorous ADJ. having an odor. This variety of hybrid tea rose is more *odorous* than the one you have in your garden.

odyssey N. long, eventful journey. The refugee's journey from Cambodia was a terrifying *odyssey.*

offal N. waste; garbage. In America, we discard as *offal* that which could feed families in less fortunate parts of the world.

offertory N. collection of money at religious ceremony; part of the Mass during which offerings are made. The donations collected during the *offertory* will be assigned to our mission work abroad.

■ **officious** ADJ. meddlesome; excessively trying to please. Browning informs us that the Duke resented the bough of cherries some *officious* fool brought to please the Duchess.

ogle V. glance coquettishly at; make eyes at. Sitting for hours at the sidewalk cafe, the old gentleman would *ogle* the young girls and recall his youthful romances.

olfactory ADJ. concerning the sense of smell. The *olfactory* organ is the nose.

oligarchy N. government by a few. The feudal *oligarchy* was supplanted by an autocracy.

ominous ADJ. threatening. These clouds are *ominous;* they portend a severe storm.

omnipotent ADJ. all-powerful. The monarch regarded himself as *omnipotent* and responsible to no one for his acts.

omnipresent ADJ. universally present; ubiquitous. On Christmas Eve, Santa Claus is *omnipresent.*

omniscient ADJ. all-knowing. I do not pretend to be *omniscient,* but I am positive about this fact.

omnivorous ADJ. eating both plant and animal food; devouring everything. Some animals, including man, are *omnivorous* and eat both meat and vegetables; others are either carnivorous or herbivorous.

onerous ADJ. burdensome. He asked for an assistant because his work load was too *onerous.*

onomatopoeia N. words formed in imitation of natural sounds. Words like "rustle" and "gargle" are illustrations of *onomatopoeia.*

onslaught N. vicious assault. We suffered many casualties during the unexpected *onslaught* of the enemy troops.

onus N. burden; responsibility. The emperor was spared the *onus* of signing the surrender papers; instead, he relegated the assignment to his generals.

opalescent ADJ. iridescent. The Ancient Mariner admired the *opalescent* sheen on the water.

■ **opaque** ADJ. dark; not transparent. The *opaque* window kept the sunlight out of the room. opacity, N.

opiate N. sleep producer; deadener of pain. By such opi-

ates, she made the people forget their difficulties and accept their unpleasant circumstances.

opportune ADJ. timely; well chosen. You have come at an *opportune* moment for I need a new secretary.

opportunist N. individual who sacrifices principles for expediency by taking advantage of circumstances. I do not know how he will vote on this question as he is an *opportunist.*

opprobrious ADJ. disgraceful. I find your conduct so *opprobrious* that I must exclude you from classes.

opprobrium N. infamy; vilification. He refused to defend himself against the slander and *opprobrium* hurled against him by the newspapers; he preferred to rely on his record.

optician N. maker and seller of eyeglasses. The patient took the prescription given him by his oculist to the *optician.*

optimist N. person who looks on the good side. The pessimist says the glass is half-empty; the *optimist* says it is half-full.

optimum ADJ. most favorable. If you wait for the *optimum* moment to act, you may never begin your project. also N.

optional ADJ. not compulsory; left to one's choice. I was impressed by the range of *optional* accessories for my microcomputer that were available. option, N.

optometrist N. one who fits glasses to remedy visual defects. Although an *optometrist* is qualified to treat many eye disorders, she may not use medicines or surgery in her examinations.

opulence N. wealth. Visitors from Europe are amazed and impressed by the *opulence* of this country.

opus N. work. Although many critics hailed his Fifth Symphony as his major work, he did not regard it as his major *opus.*

oracular ADJ. foretelling; mysterious. Oedipus could not understand the *oracular* warning he received.

oratorio N. dramatic poem set to music. The Glee Club decided to present an *oratorio* during their recital.

ordain V. command; arrange; consecrate. The king *ordained* that no foreigner should be allowed to enter the city.

ordinance N. decree. Passing a red light is a violation of a city *ordinance.*

orient V. get one's bearings; adjust. Philip spent his first day in Denver *orienting* himself to the city.

orientation N. act of finding oneself in society. Freshman *orientation* provides the incoming students with an opportunity to learn about their new environment and their place in it.

orifice N. mouthlike opening; small opening. The Howe Caverns were discovered when someone observed that a cold wind was issuing from an *orifice* in the hillside.

orison N. prayer. Hamlet greets Ophelia with the request, "Nymph, in thy *orisons,* be all my sins remembered.".

ornate ADJ. excessively decorated; highly decorated. Furniture of the Baroque period can be recognized by its *ornate* carvings.

ornithologist N. scientific student of birds. Audubon's drawings of American bird life have been of interest not only to the *ornithologists* but also to the general public.

ornithology N. study of birds. Audubon's studies of American birds greatly influenced the course of *ornithology*.

orotund ADJ. having a round, resonant quality; inflated speech. The politician found that his *orotund* voice was an asset when he spoke to his constituents.

orthodox ADJ. traditional; conservative in belief. Faced with a problem, he preferred to take an *orthodox* approach rather than shock anyone. orthodoxy, N.

orthography N. correct spelling. Many of us find English *orthography* difficult to master because so many of our words are not written phonetically.

■ **oscillate** V. vibrate pendulumlike; waver. It is interesting to note how public opinion *oscillates* between the extremes of optimism and pessimism.

ossify V. change or harden into bone. When he called his opponent a "bonehead," he implied that his adversary's brain had *ossified* and that he was not capable of clear thinking.

ostensible ADJ. apparent; professed; pretended. Although the *ostensible* purpose of this expedition is to discover new lands, we are really interested in finding new markets for our products.

■ **ostentatious** ADJ. showy; pretentious. The real hero is modest, never *ostentatious*. ostentation, N.

ostracize V. exclude from public favor; ban. As soon as the newspapers carried the story of his connection with the criminals, his friends began to *ostracize* him. ostracism, N.

oust V. expel; drive out. The world wondered if Aquino would be able to *oust* Marcos from office.

overt ADJ. open to view. According to the United States Constitution, a person must commit an *overt* act before he may be tried for treason.

overweening ADJ. presumptuous; arrogant. His *overweening* pride in his accomplishments was not justified.

ovine ADJ. like a sheep. How *ovine* these true-believers were, following their shepherds thoughtlessly.

ovoid ADJ. egg-shaped. At Easter she had to cut out hundreds of brightly colored *ovoid* shapes.

pachyderm N. thick-skinned animal. The elephant is probably the best-known *pachyderm*.

pacifist N. one opposed to force; antimilitarist. The *pacifists* urged that we reduce our military budget and recall our troops stationed overseas.

Test

Word List 33　*Antonyms*

Each of the questions below consists of a word in capital letters, followed by five lettered words or phrases. Choose the lettered word or phrase that is most nearly opposite in meaning to the word in capital letters and write the letter of your choice on your answer paper.

481. OBSOLETE (A) heated (B) desolate (C) renovated (D) frightful (E) automatic
482. OBSTREPEROUS (A) turbid (B) quiet (C) remote (D) lucid (E) active
483. OBTUSE (A) sheer (B) transparent (C) tranquil (D) timid (E) shrewd
484. ODIOUS (A) fragrant (B) redolent (C) fetid (D) delightful (E) puny
485. ODIUM (A) noise (B) liking (C) dominant (D) hasty (E) atrium
486. OMNIPOTENT (A) weak (B) democratic (C) despotic (D) passionate (E) late
487. OMNISCIENT (A) sophisticated (B) ignorant (C) essential (D) trivial (E) isolated
488. OPIATE (A) distress (B) sleep (C) stimulant (D) laziness (E) despair
489. OPPORTUNE (A) occasional (B) fragrant (C) fragile (D) awkward (E) neglected
490. OPPORTUNIST (A) man of destiny (B) man of principle (C) changeling (D) adversary (E) colleague
491. OPPROBRIUM (A) delineation (B) aptitude (C) majesty (D) freedom (E) praise
492. OPTIMUM (A) pessimistic (B) knowledgeable (C) worst (D) minimum (E) chosen
493. OPULENCE (A) pessimism (B) patriotism (C) potency (D) passion (E) poverty
494. OROTUND (A) not reddish (B) not resonant (C) grave (D) fragile (E) not eager
495. OVERWEENING (A) humble (B) impotent (C) avid (D) acrimonious (E) exaggerated

Word List 34　paddock-peccadillo

paddock N. saddling enclosure at race track; lot for exercising horses. The *paddock* is located directly in front of the grandstand so that all may see the horses being saddled and the jockeys mounted.

paean N. song of praise or joy. *Paeans* celebrating the victory filled the air.

painstaking ADJ. showing hard work; taking great care. The new high frequency word list is the result of *painstaking* efforts on the part of our research staff.

palatable ADJ. agreeable; pleasing to the taste. Paying taxes can never be made *palatable*.

palatial ADJ. magnificent. He proudly showed us through his *palatial* home.

palaver N. discussion; misleading speech; chatter. In spite of all the *palaver* before the meeting, the delegates were able to conduct serious negotiations when they sat down at the conference table. also V.

paleontology N. study of prehistoric life. The *paleontology* instructor had a superb collection of fossils.

palette N. board on which painter mixes pigments. At the present time, art supply stores are selling a paper *palette* which may be discarded after use.

palimpsest N. parchment used for second time after original writing has been erased. Using chemical reagents, scientists have been able to restore the original writings on many *palimpsests*.

pall V. grow tiresome. The study of word lists can eventually *pall* and put one to sleep.

pallet N. small, poor bed. The weary traveler went to sleep on his straw *pallet*.

palliate V. ease pain; make less guilty or offensive. Doctors must *palliate* that which they cannot cure.

palliation N. act of making less severe or violent. If we cannot find a cure for this disease at the present time, we can, at least, endeavor to seek its *palliation*.

pallid ADJ. pale; wan. Because his occupation required that he work at night and sleep during the day, he had an exceptionally *pallid* complexion.

palpable ADJ. tangible; easily perceptible. I cannot understand how you could overlook such a *palpable* blunder.

palpitate V. throb; flutter. As he became excited, his heart began to *palpitate* more and more erratically.

paltry ADJ. insignificant; petty. This is a *paltry* sum to pay for such a masterpiece.

panacea N. cure-all; remedy for all diseases. There is no easy *panacea* that will solve our complicated international situation.

panache N. flair; flamboyance. Many performers imitate Noel Coward, but few have his *panache* and sense of style.

pandemic ADJ. widespread; affecting the majority of people. They feared the AIDS epidemic would soon reach *pandemic* proportions.

pandemonium N. wild tumult. When the ships collided in the harbor, *pandemonium* broke out among the passengers.

pander V. cater to the low desires of others. Books which *pander* to man's lowest instincts should be banned.

■ **panegyric** N. formal praise. The modest hero blushed as he listened to the *panegyrics* uttered by the speakers about his valorous act.

panoply N. full set of armor. The medieval knight in full *panoply* found his movements limited by the weight of his armor.

panorama N. comprehensive view; unobstructed view in all directions. Tourists never forget the impact of their first *panorama* of the Grand Canyon.

pantomime N. acting without dialogue. Because he worked in *pantomime,* the clown could be understood wherever he appeared. also V.

papyrus N. ancient paper made from stem of papyrus plant. The ancient Egyptians were among the first to write on *papyrus.*

parable N. short, simple story teaching a moral. Let us apply to our own conduct the lesson that this *parable* teaches.

■ **paradox** N. statement that looks false but is actually correct; a contradictory statement. Wordsworth's "The child is father to the man" is an example of *paradox.*

■ **paragon** N. model of perfection. The class disliked him because the teacher was always pointing to him as a *paragon* of virtue.

parallelism N. state of being parallel; similarity. There is a striking *parallelism* between the twins.

parameter N. limits; independent variable. We need to define the *parameters* of the problem.

paramour N. illicit lover. She sought a divorce on the grounds that her husband had a *paramour* in another town.

paranoia N. chronic form of insanity marked by delusions of grandeur or persecution. The psychiatrists analyzed his ailment as *paranoia* when he claimed that everyone hated him.

paranoiac N. mentally unsound person suffering from delusions. Although he is obviously suffering from delusions, I hesitate to call him a *paranoiac.*

parapet N. low wall at edge of roof or balcony. The best way to attack the soldiers fighting behind the *parapets* on the roof is by bombardment from the air.

paraphernalia N. equipment; odds and ends. His desk was cluttered with paper, pen, ink, dictionary and other *paraphernalia* of the writing craft.

paraphrase V. restate a passage in one's own words while retaining thought of author. In 250 words or less, *paraphrase* this article. also N.

parasite N. animal or plant living on another; toady; sycophant. The tapeworm is an example of the kind of *parasite* that may infest the human body.

parched ADJ. extremely dry; very thirsty. The *parched* desert landscape seemed hostile to life.

paregoric N. medicine that eases pain. The doctor prescribed a *paregoric* to alleviate his suffering.

pariah N. social outcast. I am not a *pariah* to be shunned and ostracized.

parity N. equality; close resemblance. I find your analogy inaccurate because I do not see the *parity* between the two illustrations.

parlance N. language; idiom. All this legal *parlance* confuses me; I need an interpreter.

parley N. conference. The peace *parley* has not produced the anticipated truce. also V.

■ **parody** N. humorous imitation; travesty. We enjoyed the clever *parodies* of popular songs which the chorus sang.

paroxysm N. fit or attack of pain, laughter, rage. When he heard of his son's misdeeds, he was seized by a *paroxysm* of rage.

parricide N. person who murders his own father; murder of a father. The jury was shocked by the details of this vicious *parricide* and found the man who had killed his father guilty of murder in the first degree.

parry V. ward off a blow. He was content to wage a defensive battle and tried to *parry* his opponent's thrusts.

■ **parsimonious** ADJ. stingy; excessively frugal. His *parsimonious* nature did not permit him to enjoy any luxuries.

partial ADJ. (1) incomplete. In this issue we have published only a *partial* list of contributors because we lack space to acknowledge everyone. (2) biased; having a liking for something. I am extremely *partial* to chocolate eclairs.

partiality N. inclination; bias. As a judge, not only must I be unbiased, but I must also avoid any evidence of *partiality* when I award the prize.

■ **partisan** ADJ. one-sided; prejudiced; committed to a party. On certain issues of conscience, she refused to take a *partisan* stand. also N.

parturition N. delivery; childbirth. The difficulties anticipated by the obstetricians at *parturition* did not materialize; it was a normal delivery.

parvenu N. upstart; newly rich person. Although extremely wealthy, he was regarded as a *parvenu* by the aristocratic members of society.

passé ADJ. old-fashioned; past the prime. Her style is *passé* and reminiscent of the Victorian era.

passive ADJ. not active; acted upon. Mahatma Gandhi urged his followers to pursue a program of *passive* resistance as he felt that it was more effective than violence and acts of terrorism.

pastiche N. imitation of another's style in musical composition or in writing. We cannot even say that her music is a *pastiche* of this composer or that; it is, rather, reminiscent of many musicians.

pastoral ADJ. rural. In these stories of *pastoral* life, we find an understanding of the daily tasks of country folk.

patent ADJ. open for the public to read; obvious. It was *patent* to everyone that the witness spoke the truth. also N.

pathetic ADJ. causing sadness, compassion, pity; touching. Everyone in the auditorium was weeping by the time he finished his *pathetic* tale about the orphaned boy.

■ **pathological** ADJ. pertaining to disease. As we study the *pathological* aspects of this disease, we must not overlook the psychological elements.

pathos N. tender sorrow; pity; quality in art or literature that produces these feelings. The quiet tone of *pathos* that ran through the novel never degenerated into the maudlin or the overly sentimental.

patina N. green crust on old bronze works; tone slowly taken by varnished painting. Judging by the *patina* on this bronze statue, we can conclude that this is the work of a medieval artist.

patois N. local or provincial dialect. His years of study of the language at the university did not enable him to understand the *patois* of the natives.

patriarch N. father and ruler of a family or tribe. In many primitive tribes, the leader and lawmaker was the *patriarch*.

patrician ADJ. noble; aristocratic. We greatly admired her well-bred, *patrician* elegance. also N.

patricide N. person who murders his father; murder of a father. The words parricide and *patricide* have exactly the same meaning.

patrimony N. inheritance from father. As predicted by his critics, he spent his *patrimony* within two years of his father's death.

patronize V. support; act superior toward. Experts in a field sometimes appear to *patronize* people who are less knowledgeable of the subject.

■ **paucity** N. scarcity. They closed the restaurant because the *paucity* of customers made it uneconomical to operate.

peccadillo N. slight offense. If we examine these escapades carefully, we will realize that they are mere *peccadilloes* rather than major crimes.

Test

Word List 34   *Synonyms and Antonyms*

Each of the following questions consists of a word in capital letters, followed by five lettered words or phrases. Choose the lettered word or phrase which is most nearly similar or the opposite of the word in capital letters and write the letter of your choice on your answer paper.

496. PAEAN (A) serf (B) pealing (C) lien (D) lament
     (E) folly
497. PALLET (A) bed (B) pigment board (C) bench
     (D) spectrum (E) quality
498. PALLIATE (A) smoke (B) quicken (C) substitute
     (D) alleviate (E) sadden
499. PANDEMONIUM (A) calm (B) frustration
     (C) efficiency (D) impishness (E) sophistication

500. PANEGYRIC (A) medication (B) panacea
     (C) rotation (D) vacillation (E) praise
501. PARABLE (A) equality (B) allegory (C) frenzy
     (D) folly (E) cuticle
502. PARADOX (A) exaggeration (B) contradiction
     (C) hyperbole (D) invective (E) poetic device
503. PARAMOUR (A) illicit lover (B) majority
     (C) importance (D) hatred (E) clandestine affair
504. PARANOIA (A) fracture (B) statement
     (C) quantity (D) benefaction (E) sanity
505. PARIAH (A) village (B) suburb (C) outcast
     (D) disease (E) benefactor
506. PARITY (A) duplicate (B) miniature (C) golf tee
     (D) similarity (E) event

507. PARSIMONIOUS (A) grammatical (B) syntactical (C) effective (D) extravagant (E) esoteric
508. PARTIALITY (A) completion (B) equality (C) bias (D) divorce (E) reflection

509. PASSÉ (A) scornful (B) rural (C) out-of-date (D) silly (E) barbaric
510. PASTICHE (A) imitation (B) glue (C) present (D) greeting (E) family

---

Word List 35   peculate-philander

peculate V. steal; embezzle. His crime of *peculating* public funds entrusted to his care is especially damnable.

peculation N. embezzlement; theft. Her *peculations* were not discovered until the auditors found discrepancies in the financial statements.

pecuniary ADJ. pertaining to money. I never expected a *pecuniary* reward for my work in this activity.

pedagogue N. teacher; dull and formal teacher. He could never be a stuffy *pedagogue;* his classes were always lively and filled with humor.

pedant N. scholar who overemphasizes book learning or technicalities. Her insistence that the book be memorized marked the teacher as a *pedant* rather than a scholar.

■ **pedantic** ADJ. showing off learning; bookish. What you say is *pedantic* and reveals an unfamiliarity with the realities of life.

pedestrian ADJ. ordinary; unimaginative. Unintentionally boring, he wrote page after page of *pedestrian* prose.

pediatrician N. expert in children's diseases. The family doctor advised the parents to consult a *pediatrician* about their child's ailment.

pediment N. triangular part above columns in Greek buildings. The *pediment* of the building was filled with sculptures and adorned with elaborate scrollwork.

pejorative ADJ. having a deteriorating or depreciating effect on the meaning of a word. His use of *pejorative* language indicated his contempt for his audience.

pell-mell ADV. in confusion; disorderly. The excited students dashed *pell-mell* into the stadium to celebrate the victory.

pellucid ADJ. transparent; limpid; easy to understand. After reading these stodgy philosophers, I find his *pellucid* style very enjoyable.

penance N. self-imposed punishment for sin. The Ancient Mariner said, "I have *penance* done and *penance* more will do," to atone for the sin of killing the albatross.

■ **penchant** N. strong inclination; liking. He had a strong *penchant* for sculpture and owned many statues.

pendant ADJ. hanging down from something. Her *pendant* earrings glistened in the light.

pendent ADJ. suspended; jutting; pending. The *pendent* rock hid the entrance to the cave.

penitent ADJ. repentant. When he realized the enormity of his crime, he became remorseful and *penitent.* also N.

pendulous ADJ. hanging; suspended. The *pendulous* chandeliers swayed in the breeze and gave the impression that they were about to fall from the ceiling.

pennate ADJ. having wings or feathers. The *pennate* leaves of the sumac remind us of feathers.

pensive ADJ. dreamily thoughtful; thoughtful with a hint of sadness. The *pensive* youth gazed at the painting for a long time and then sighed.

penumbra N. partial shadow (in an eclipse). During an eclipse, we can see an area of total darkness and a lighter area which is the *penumbra*.

penurious ADJ. stingy; parsimonious. He was a *penurious* man, averse to spending money even for the necessities of life.

■ **penury** N. extreme poverty. We find much *penury* and suffering in this slum area.

peon N. unskilled laborer; drudge. He was doomed to be a *peon,* to live a lowly life of drudgery and toil.

percussion ADJ. striking one object against another sharply. The drum is a *percussion* instrument. also N.

perdition N. damnation; complete ruin. He was damned to eternal *perdition.*

peregrination N. journey. His *peregrinations* in foreign lands did not bring understanding; he mingled only with fellow tourists and did not attempt to communicate with the native population.

peremptory ADJ. demanding and leaving no choice. I resent your *peremptory* attitude.

perennial N. lasting. These plants are hardy *perennials* and will bloom for many years. also ADJ.

perfidious ADJ. basely false. Your *perfidious* gossip is malicious and dangerous.

■ **perfidy** N. violation of a trust. When we learned of his *perfidy,* we were shocked and dismayed.

perforce ADV. of necessity. I must *perforce* leave, as my train is about to start.

■ **perfunctory** ADJ. superficial; listless; not thorough. He overlooked many weaknesses when he inspected the factory in his *perfunctory* manner.

perigee N. point of moon's orbit when it is nearest the earth. The rocket which was designed to take photographs of the moon was launched as the moon approached its *perigee.*

perimeter N. outer boundary. To find the *perimeter* of any quadrilateral, we add the lengths of the four sides.

peripatetic ADJ. walking about; moving. The *peripatetic* school of philosophy derives its name from the fact that Aristotle walked with his pupils while discussing philosophy with them.

peripheral ADJ. marginal; outer. We lived, not in central

London, but in one of those *peripheral* suburbs that spring up on the outskirts of a great city.

periphery N. edge, especially of a round surface. He sensed that there was something just beyond the *periphery* of his vision.

peristyle N. series of columns surrounding a building or yard. The cloister was surrounded by a *peristyle* reminiscent of the Parthenon.

perjury N. false testimony while under oath. When several witnesses appeared to challenge his story, he was indicted for *perjury*.

■ **permeable** ADJ. porous; allowing passage through. Glass is *permeable* to light.

permeate V. pass through; spread. The odor of frying onions *permeated* the air.

pernicious ADJ. very destructive. He argued that these books had a *pernicious* effect on young and susceptible minds.

perpetrate V. commit an offense. Only an insane person could *perpetrate* such a horrible crime.

perpetual ADJ. everlasting. Ponce de Leon hoped to find *perpetual* youth.

peroration N. conclusion of an oration. The *peroration* was largely hortatory and brought the audience to its feet clamoring for action at its close.

perquisite N. any gain above stipulated salary. The *perquisites* attached to this job make it even more attractive than the salary indicates.

persiflage N. flippant conversation; banter. This *persiflage* is not appropriate when we have such serious problems to discuss.

personable ADJ. attractive. The man I am seeking to fill this position must be *personable* since he will be representing us before the public.

perspicacious ADJ. having insight; penetrating; astute. The brilliant lawyer was known for his *perspicacious* deductions.

perspicuity N. clearness of expression; freedom from ambiguity. One of the outstanding features of this book is the *perspicuity* of its author; her meaning is always clear.

perspicuous ADJ. plainly expressed. Her *perspicuous* comments eliminated all possibility of misinterpretation.

pert ADJ. impertinent; forward. I think your *pert* and impudent remarks call for an apology.

pertinacious ADJ. stubborn; persistent. He is bound to succeed because his *pertinacious* nature will not permit him to quit.

pertinent ADJ. suitable; to the point. The lawyer wanted to know all the *pertinent* details.

perturb V. disturb greatly. I am afraid this news will *perturb* him and cause him grief.

perturbation N. agitation. I fail to understand why such an innocent remark should create such *perturbation*.

perusal N. reading. I am certain that you have missed important details in your rapid *perusal* of this document. peruse, V.

pervade V. spread throughout. As the news of the defeat *pervaded* the country, a feeling of anger directed at the rulers who had been the cause of the disaster grew.

■ **pervasive** ADJ. pervading; spread throughout. Despite airing them for several hours, she could not rid her clothes of the *pervasive* odor of mothballs that clung to them.

perverse ADJ. stubborn; intractable. Because of your *perverse* attitude, I must rate you as deficient in cooperation.

perversion N. corruption; turning from right to wrong. Inasmuch as he had no motive for his crimes, we could not understand his *perversion*.

perversity N. stubborn maintenance of a wrong cause. I cannot forgive your *perversity* in repeating such an impossible story.

pessimism N. belief that life is basically bad or evil; gloominess. The good news we have been receiving lately indicates that there is little reason for your *pessimism*.

pestilential ADJ. causing plague; baneful. People were afraid to explore the *pestilential* swamp. pestilence, N.

petrify V. turn to stone. His sudden and unexpected appearance seemed to *petrify* her.

petty ADJ. trivial; unimportant; very small. She had no major complaints to make about his work, only a few *petty* quibbles that were almost too minor to state.

petulant ADJ. touchy; peevish. The feverish patient was *petulant* and restless.

pharisaical ADJ. pertaining to the Pharisees, who paid scrupulous attention to tradition; self-righteous; hypocritical. Walter Lippmann has pointed out that moralists who do not attempt to explain the moral code they advocate are often regarded as *pharisaical* and ignored.

phenomena N. observable facts; subjects of scientific investigation. We kept careful records of the *phenomena* we noted in the course of these experiments.

phial N. small bottle. Even though it is small, this *phial* of perfume is expensive.

philander V. make love lightly; flirt. Do not *philander* with my affections because love is too serious.

Test

Word List 35   *Antonyms*

Each of the questions below consists of a word in capital letters, followed by five lettered words or phrases. Choose the lettered word or phrase that is most nearly opposite in meaning to the word in capital letters and write the letter of your choice on your answer paper.

511. PEJORATIVE (A) positive (B) legal (C) determining (D) delighting (E) declaiming
512. PELLUCID (A) logistical (B) philandering (C) incomprehensible (D) vagrant (E) warranted
513. PENCHANT (A) distance (B) imminence (C) dislike (D) attitude (E) void
514. PENURIOUS (A) imprisoned (B) captivated (C) generous (D) vacant (E) abolished
515. PERFUNCTORY (A) official (B) thorough (C) insipid (D) vicarious (E) distinctive
516. PERIGEE (A) eclipse (B) planet (C) apogee (D) refugee (E) danger
517. PERIPATETIC (A) worldly (B) stationary (C) disarming (D) seeking (E) inherent
518. PERMEABLE (A) perishable (B) effective (C) plodding (D) impenetrable (E) lasting

519. PERNICIOUS (A) practical (B) comparative (C) harmless (D) tangible (E) detailed
520. PERPETUAL (A) momentary (B) standard (C) serious (D) industrial (E) interpretive
521. PERSPICUITY (A) grace (B) feature (C) review (D) difficulty (E) vagueness
522. PERT (A) polite (B) perishable (C) moral (D) deliberate (E) stubborn
523. PERTINACIOUS (A) vengeful (B) consumptive (C) superficial (D) skilled (E) advertised
524. PERTINENT (A) understood (B) living (C) discontented (D) puzzling (E) irrelevant
525. PETULANT (A) angry (B) moral (C) declining (D) underhanded (E) uncomplaining

Word List 36   philanthropist-precedent

philanthropist N. lover of mankind; doer of good. As he grew older, he became famous as a *philanthropist* and benefactor of the needy.

philistine N. narrow-minded person, uncultured and exclusively interested in material gain. We need more men of culture and enlightenment; we have too many *philistines* among us.

philology N. study of language. The professor of *philology* advocated the use of Esperanto as an international language.

■ **phlegmatic** ADJ. calm; not easily disturbed. The nurse was a cheerful but *phlegmatic* person.

phobia N. morbid fear. Her fear of flying was more than mere nervousness; it was a real *phobia*.

physiognomy N. face. He prided himself on his ability to analyze a person's character by studying his *physiognomy*.

physiological ADJ. pertaining to the science of the function of living organisms. To understand this disease fully, we must examine not only its *physiological* aspects but also its psychological elements.

picaresque ADJ. pertaining to rogues in literature. *Tom Jones* has been hailed as one of the best *picaresque* novels in the English language.

piebald ADJ. mottled; spotted. You should be able to identify this horse easily as it is the only *piebald* horse in the race; the others are all one color.

pied ADJ. variegated; multicolored. The *Pied* Piper of Hamelin got his name from the multicolored clothing he wore.

pillage V. plunder. The enemy *pillaged* the quiet village and left it in ruins.

pillory V. punish by placing in a wooden frame and subjecting to ridicule. Even though he was mocked and *pilloried*, he maintained that he was correct in his beliefs. also N.

pinion V. restrain. They *pinioned* his arms against his body but left his legs free so that he could move about. also N.

pinnacle N. peak. We could see the morning sunlight illuminate the *pinnacle* while the rest of the mountain lay in shadow.

pious ADJ. devout. The *pious* parents gave their children a religious upbringing. piety, N.

■ **piquant** ADJ. pleasantly tart-tasting; stimulating. The *piquant* sauce added to our enjoyment of the meal. piquancy, N.

pique N. irritation; resentment. She showed her *pique* by her refusal to appear with the other contestants at the end of the contest.

piscatorial ADJ. pertaining to fishing. He spent many happy hours at the lake in his *piscatorial* activities.

pithy ADJ. concise; meaty. I enjoy reading his essays because they are always compact and *pithy*.

pittance N. a small allowance or wage. He could not live on the *pittance* he received as a pension and had to look for an additional source of revenue.

■ **placate** V. pacify; conciliate. The teacher tried to *placate* the angry mother.

placid ADJ. peaceful; calm. After his vacation in this *placid* section, he felt soothed and rested.

plagiarism N. theft of another's ideas or writings passed off as original. The editor recognized the *plagiarism* and rebuked the culprit who had presented the manuscript as original.

plagiarize V. steal another's ideas and pass them off as one's own. The editor could tell that the writer had *plagiarized* parts of the article; he could recognize whole paragraphs from the original source.

plaintive ADJ. mournful. The dove has a *plaintive* and melancholy call.

plangent ADJ. plaintive; resounding sadly. Although we could not understand the words of the song, we got the impression from the *plangent* tones of the singers that it was a lament of some kind.

■ **platitude** N. trite remark; commonplace statement. The

platitudes in his speech were applauded by the vast majority in his audience; only a few people perceived how trite his remarks were.

platonic ADJ. purely spiritual; theoretical; without sensual desire. Although a member of the political group, she took only a *platonic* interest in its ideals and goals.

plauditory ADJ. approving; applauding. The theatrical company reprinted the *plauditory* comments of the critics in its advertisement.

plausible ADJ. having a show of truth but open to doubt; specious. Even though your argument is *plausible,* I still would like to have more proof.

plebeian ADJ. common; pertaining to the common people. His speeches were aimed at the *plebeian* minds and emotions; they disgusted the more refined.

plebiscite N. expression of the will of a people by direct election. I think this matter is so important that it should be decided not by a handful of legislators but by a *plebiscite* of the entire nation.

plenary ADJ. complete; full. The union leader was given *plenary* power to negotiate a new contract with the employers.

plenipotentiary ADJ. fully empowered. Since he was not given *plenipotentiary* powers by his government, he could not commit his country without consulting his superiors. also N.

plenitude N. abundance; completeness. Looking in the pantry, we admired the *plenitude* of fruits and pickles we had preserved during the summer.

■ **plethora** N. excess; overabundance. She offered a *plethora* of reasons for her shortcomings.

plumb ADJ. checking perpendicularity; vertical. Before hanging wallpaper it is advisable to drop a *plumb* line from the ceiling as a guide. also N. and V.

podiatrist N. doctor who treats ailments of the feet. He consulted a *podiatrist* about his fallen arches.

podium N. pedestal; raised platform. The audience applauded as the conductor made his way to the *podium.*

poignant ADJ. keen; piercing; severe. Her *poignant* grief left her pale and weak.

polemic N. controversy; argument in support of point of view. Her essays were, for the main part, *polemics* for the party's policy.

politic ADJ. expedient; prudent; well devised. Even though he was disappointed, he did not think it *politic* to refuse this offer.

polity N. form of government of nation or state. Our *polity* should be devoted to the concept that the government should strive for the good of all citizens.

poltroon N. coward. Only a *poltroon* would so betray his comrades at such a dangerous time.

polygamist N. one who has more than one spouse at a time. He was arrested as a *polygamist* when his two wives filed complaints about him.

polyglot ADJ. speaking several languages. New York City is a *polyglot* community because of the thousands of immigrants who settle there.

ponderous ADJ. weighty; unwieldy. His humor lacked the light touch; his jokes were always *ponderous.*

porphyry N. igneous rock containing feldspar or quartz crystals. The *porphyry* used by the Egyptians in their buildings was purplish in color.

portend V. foretell; presage. The king did not know what these omens might *portend* and asked his soothsayers to interpret them.

portent N. sign; omen; forewarning. He regarded the black cloud as a *portent* of evil.

portentous ADJ. ominous; serious. I regard our present difficulties and dissatisfactions as *portentous* omens of future disaster.

portly ADJ. stately; stout. The overweight gentleman was referred to as *portly* by the polite salesclerk.

posterity N. descendants; future generations. We hope to leave a better world to *posterity.*

posthumous ADJ. after death (as of child born after father's death or book published after author's death). The critics ignored his works during his lifetime; it was only after the *posthumous* publication of his last novel that they recognized his great talent.

postprandial ADJ. after dinner. The most objectionable feature of these formal banquets is the *postprandial* speech.

postulate N. self-evident truth. We must accept these statements as *postulates* before pursuing our discussions any further. also V.

potable ADJ. suitable for drinking. The recent drought in the Middle Atlantic States has emphasized the need for extensive research in ways of making sea water *potable.* also N.

potentate N. monarch; sovereign. The *potentate* spent more time at Monte Carlo than he did at home on his throne.

potential ADJ. expressing possibility; latent. This juvenile delinquent is a *potential* murderer. also N.

potion N. dose (of liquid). Tristan and Isolde drink a love *potion* in the first act of the opera.

potpourri N. heterogeneous mixture; medley. He offered a *potpourri* of folk songs from many lands.

poultice N. soothing application applied to sore and inflamed portions of the body. He was advised to apply a flaxseed *poultice* to the inflammation.

practicable ADJ. feasible. The board of directors decided that the plan was *practicable* and agreed to undertake the project.

practical ADJ. based on experience; useful. He was a *practical* man, opposed to theory.

■ **pragmatic** ADJ. practical; concerned with practical values. This test should provide us with a *pragmatic* analysis of the value of this course.

pragmatist N. practical person. No *pragmatist* enjoys becoming involved in a game which he can never win.

prate V. speak foolishly; boast idly. Let us not *prate* about our qualities; rather, let our virtues speak for themselves.

prattle V. babble. The children *prattled* endlessly about their new toys. also N.

preamble N. introductory statement. In the *Preamble* to the Constitution, the purpose of the document is set forth.

precarious ADJ. uncertain; risky. I think this stock is a *precarious* investment and advise against its purchase.

precedent N. something preceding in time which may be used as an authority or guide for future action. This decision sets a *precedent* for future cases of a similar nature.

precedent ADJ. preceding in time, rank, etc. Our discussions, *precedent* to this event, certainly did not give you any reason to believe that we would adopt your proposal.

Test

Word List 36   *Synonyms*

Each of the questions below consists of a word in capital letters, followed by five lettered words or phrases. Choose the lettered word or phrase that is most nearly similar in meaning to the word in capital letters and write the letter of your choice on your answer paper.

526. PHLEGMATIC (A) calm (B) cryptic (C) practical (D) salivary (E) dishonest
527. PHYSIOGNOMY (A) posture (B) head (C) physique (D) face (E) size
528. PIEBALD (A) motley (B) coltish (C) hairless (D) thoroughbred (E) delicious
529. PILLAGE (A) hoard (B) plunder (C) versify (D) denigrate (E) confide
530. PINION (A) express (B) report (C) reveal (D) submit (E) restrain
531. PINNACLE (A) foothills (B) card game (C) pass (D) taunt (E) peak

532. PIOUS (A) historic (B) devout (C) multiple (D) fortunate (E) authoritative
533. PIQUE (A) pyramid (B) revolt (C) resentment (D) struggle (E) inventory
534. PLACATE (A) determine (B) transmit (C) pacify (D) allow (E) define
535. PLAINTIVE (A) mournful (B) senseless (C) persistent (D) rural (E) evasive
536. PLAGIARISM (A) theft of funds (B) theft of ideas (C) belief in God (D) arson (E) ethical theory
537. PLATITUDE (A) fatness (B) bravery (C) dimension (D) trite remark (E) strong belief
538. POLEMIC (A) blackness (B) lighting (C) magnetism (D) controversy (E) grimace
539. POLTROON (A) bird (B) tavern (C) soldier (D) coward (E) politician
540. POSTPRANDIAL (A) after dark (B) on awakening (C) in summer (D) after dinner (E) in winter

Word List 37   precept-propitiate

precept N. practical rule guiding conduct. "Love thy neighbor as thyself" is a worthwhile *precept*.

preciosity N. overrefinement in art or speech. Roxane, in the play *Cyrano de Bergerac,* illustrates the extent to which *preciosity* was carried in French society.

precipice N. cliff; dangerous position. Suddenly Indiana Jones found himself dangling from the edge of a *precipice*.

■ **precipitate** ADJ. headlong; rash. Do not be *precipitate* in this matter; investigate further.

■ **precipitate** V. throw headlong; hasten. The removal of American political support appears to have *precipitated* the downfall of the Marcos regime.

precipitous ADJ. steep. This hill is difficult to climb because it is so *precipitous*.

precise ADJ. exact. If you don't give me *precise* directions and a map, I'll never find your place.

preclude V. make impossible; eliminate. This contract does not *preclude* my being employed by others at the same time that I am working for you.

■ **precocious** ADJ. advanced in development. By her rather adult manner of discussing serious topics, the child demonstrated that she was *precocious*. precocity, N.

precursor N. forerunner. Gray and Burns were *precursors* of the Romantic Movement in English literature.

predatory ADJ. plundering. The hawk is a *predatory* bird.

predecessor N. former occupant of a post. I hope I can live up to the fine example set by my late *predecessor* in this office.

predilection N. partiality; preference. Although the artist used various media from time to time, she had a *predilection* for watercolors.

preeminent ADJ. outstanding; superior. The king traveled to Boston because he wanted the *preeminent* surgeon in the field to perform the operation.

preempt V. appropriate beforehand. Your attempt to *preempt* this land before it is offered to the public must be resisted.

prefatory ADJ. introductory. The chairman made a few *prefatory* remarks before he called on the first speaker.

prehensile ADJ. capable of grasping or holding. Monkeys use not only their arms and legs but also their *prehensile* tails in traveling through the trees.

prelude N. introduction; forerunner. I am afraid that this border raid is the *prelude* to more serious attacks.

premeditate V. plan in advance. She had *premeditated* the murder for months, reading about common poisons and buying weed killer that contained arsenic.

premonition N. forewarning. We ignored these *premonitions* of disaster because they appeared to be based on childish fears.

premonitory ADJ. serving to warn. You should have visited a doctor as soon as you felt these *premonitory* chest pains.

preponderance N. superiority of power, quantity, etc. The rebels sought to overcome the *preponderance* of strength of the government forces by engaging in guerrilla tactics.

preponderate V. be superior in power; outweigh. I feel confident that the forces of justice will *preponderate* eventually in this dispute.

preposterous ADJ. absurd; ridiculous. The excuse he gave for his lateness was so *preposterous* that everyone laughed.

prerogative N. privilege; unquestionable right. The President cannot levy taxes; that is the *prerogative* of the legislative branch of government.

presage V. foretell. The vultures flying overhead *presaged* the discovery of the corpse in the desert.

presentiment N. premonition; foreboding. Hamlet felt a *presentiment* about his meeting with Laertes.

prestige N. impression produced by achievements or reputation. The wealthy man sought to obtain social *prestige* by contributing to popular charities.

■ **presumptuous** ADJ. arrogant; taking liberties. It seems *presumptuous* for one so relatively new to the field to challenge the conclusions of its leading experts. presumption, N.

■ **pretentious** ADJ. ostentatious; ambitious. I do not feel that your limited resources will permit you to carry out such a *pretentious* program.

preternatural ADJ. beyond that which is normal in nature. John's mother's total ability to tell when he was lying struck him as almost *preternatural.*

pretext N. excuse. He looked for a good *pretext* to get out of paying a visit to his aunt.

prevail V. induce; triumph over. He tried to *prevail* on her to type his essay for him.

prevaricate V. lie. Some people believe that to *prevaricate* in a good cause is justifiable and regard the statement as a "white lie."

prim ADJ. very precise and formal; exceedingly proper. Many people commented on the contrast between the *prim* attire of the young lady and the inappropriate clothing worn by her escort.

primogeniture N. seniority by birth. By virtue of *primogeniture,* the first-born child has many privileges denied his brothers and sisters.

primordial ADJ. existing at the beginning (of time); rudimentary. The Neanderthal Man is one of our *primordial* ancestors.

primp V. dress up. She *primps* for hours before a dance.

pristine ADJ. characteristic of earlier times; primitive; unspoiled. This area has been preserved in all its *pristine* wildness.

privation N. hardship; want. In his youth, he knew hunger and *privation.*

privy ADJ. secret; hidden; not public. We do not care for *privy* chamber government.

probe V. explore with tools. The surgeon *probed* the wound for foreign matter before suturing it. also N.

■ **probity** N. uprightness; incorruptibility. Everyone took his *probity* for granted; his defalcations, therefore, shocked us all.

■ **problematic** ADJ. perplexing; unsettled; questionable. Given the many areas of conflict still awaiting resolution, the outcome of the peace talks remains *problematic.*

proboscis N. long snout; nose. The elephant uses his *proboscis* to handle things and carry them from place to place.

proclivity N. inclination; natural tendency. The cross old lady has a *proclivity* to grumble.

procrastinate V. postpone; delay. It is wise not to *procrastinate;* otherwise, we find ourselves bogged down in a mass of work which should have been finished long ago.

prod V. poke; stir up; urge. If you *prod* him hard enough, he'll eventually clean his room.

■ **prodigal** ADJ. wasteful; reckless with money. The *prodigal* son squandered his inheritance. also N.

prodigious ADJ. marvelous; enormous. He marveled at her *prodigious* appetite when he saw all the food she ate.

■ **prodigy** N. marvel; highly gifted child. Menuhin was a *prodigy,* performing wonders on his violin when he was barely eight years old.

profane V. violate; desecrate. Tourists are urged not to *profane* the sanctity of holy places by wearing improper garb. also ADJ.

■ **profligate** ADJ. dissipated; wasteful; licentious. In this *profligate* company, she lost all sense of decency. also N.

profusion N. lavish expenditure; overabundant condition. Seldom have I seen food and drink served in such *profusion* as at the wedding feast.

progenitor N. ancestor. We must not forget the teachings of our *progenitors* in our desire to appear modern.

progeny N. children; offspring. He was proud of his *progeny* but regarded George as the most promising of all his children.

prognathous ADJ. having projecting jaws. His *prognathous* face made him seem more determined than he actually was.

prognosis N. forecasted course of a disease; prediction. If the doctor's *prognosis* is correct, the patient will be in a coma for at least twenty-four hours.

prognosticate V. predict. I *prognosticate* disaster unless we change our wasteful ways.

projectile N. missile. Man has always hurled *projectiles* at his enemy whether in the form of stones or of highly explosive shells.

proletarian N. member of the working class. The aristocrats feared mob rule and gave the right to vote only to the wealthy, thus depriving the *proletarians* of a voice in government. also ADJ.

■ **prolific** ADJ. abundantly fruitful. She was a *prolific* writer and wrote as many as three books a year.

prolix ADJ. verbose; drawn out. Her *prolix* arguments irritated and bored the jury. prolixity, N.

promiscuous ADJ. mixed indiscriminately; haphazard; irregular, particularly sexually. In the opera *La Boheme*, we get a picture of the *promiscuous* life led by the young artists of Paris.

promontory N. headland. They erected a lighthouse on the *promontory* to warn approaching ships of their nearness to the shore.

promulgate V. make known by official proclamation or publication. As soon as the Civil Service Commission *promul-*

gates the names of the successful candidates, we shall begin to hire members of our staff.

prone ADJ. inclined to; prostrate. She was *prone* to sudden fits of anger.

propagate V. multiply; spread. I am sure disease must *propagate* in such unsanitary and crowded areas.

propellants N. substances which propel or drive forward. The development of our missile program has forced our scientists to seek more powerful *propellants*.

■ **propensity** N. natural inclination. I dislike your *propensity* to belittle every contribution she makes to our organization.

prophylactic ADJ. used to prevent disease. Despite all *prophylactic* measures introduced by the authorities, the epidemic raged until cool weather set in. also N.

propinquity N. nearness; kinship. Their relationship could not be explained as being based on mere *propinquity*: they were more than relatives; they were true friends.

■ **propitiate** V. appease. The natives offered sacrifices to *propitiate* the gods.

Test

Word List 37 *Antonyms*

Each of the questions below consists of a word in capital letters, followed by five lettered words or phrases. Choose the lettered word or phrase that is most nearly opposite in meaning to the word in capital letters and write the letter of your choice on your answer paper.

541. PRECIPITATE (A) dull (B) anticipatory (C) cautious (D) considerate (E) welcome
542. PREFATORY (A) outstanding (B) magnificent (C) conclusive (D) intelligent (E) predatory
543. PRELUDE (A) intermezzo (B) diva (C) aria (D) aftermath (E) duplication
544. PRESUMPTION (A) assertion (B) activation (C) motivation (D) proposition (E) humility
545. PRETENTIOUS (A) ominous (B) calm (C) unassuming (D) futile (E) volatile
546. PRIM (A) informal (B) prior (C) exterior (D) private (E) cautious
547. PRISTINE (A) cultivated (B) condemned (C) irreligious (D) cautious (E) critical

548. PROBITY (A) regret (B) assumption (C) corruptibility (D) extent (E) upswing
549. PRODIGAL (A) large (B) thrifty (C) consistent (D) compatible (E) remote
550. PRODIGIOUS (A) infinitesimal (B) indignant (C) indifferent (D) indisposed (E) insufficient
551. PROFANE (A) sanctify (B) desecrate (C) define (D) manifest (E) urge
552. PROGNATHOUS (A) chewing (B) maxillary (C) receding (D) belligerent (E) impacted
553. PROLIX (A) stupid (B) indifferent (C) redundant (D) livid (E) pithy
554. PROPHYLACTIC (A) causing growth (B) causing disease (C) antagonistic (D) brushing (E) favorable
555. PROPINQUITY (A) remoteness (B) uniqueness (C) health (D) virtue (E) simplicity

Word List 38 propitious-quarry

propitious ADJ. favorable; kindly. I think it is advisable that we wait for a more *propitious* occasion to announce our plans; this is not a good time.

propound V. put forth for analysis. In your discussion, you have *propounded* several questions; let us consider each one separately.

propriety N. fitness; correct conduct. I want you to behave at this dinner with *propriety;* don't embarrass me.

propulsive ADJ. driving forward. The jet plane has a greater *propulsive* power than the engine-driven plane.

prorogue V. dismiss parliament; end officially. It was agreed that the king could not *prorogue* parliament until it had been in session for at least fifty days.

prosaic ADJ. commonplace; dull. I do not like this author because he is so unimaginative and *prosaic*.

proscenium N. part of stage in front of curtain. In the theater-in-the-round there can be no *proscenium* or *proscenium* arch.

■ **proscribe** V. ostracize; banish; outlaw. Antony, Octavius, and Lepidus *proscribed* all those who had conspired against Julius Caesar.

proselytize V. convert to a religion or belief. In these inter-faith meetings, there must be no attempt to *proselytize;* we must respect all points of view.

prosody N. the art of versification. This book on *prosody* contains a rhyming dictionary as well as samples of the various verse forms.

prostrate V. stretch out full on ground. He *prostrated* himself before the idol. also ADJ.

protean ADJ. versatile; able to take on many shapes. A remarkably *protean* actor, Alec Guinness could take on any role.

protégé N. person under the protection and support of a patron. Cyrano de Bergerac refused to be a *protégé* of Cardinal Richelieu.

protocol N. diplomatic etiquette. We must run this state dinner according to *protocol* if we are to avoid offending any of our guests.

prototype N. original work used as a model by others. The crude typewriter on display in this museum is the *prototype* of the elaborate machines in use today.

protract V. prolong. Do not *protract* this phone conversation as I expect an important business call within the next few minutes.

protrude V. stick out. His fingers *protruded* from the holes in his gloves.

provenance N. origin or source of something. I am not interested in its *provenance;* I am more concerned with its usefulness than with its source.

provender N. dry food; fodder. I am not afraid of a severe winter because I have stored a large quantity of *provender* for the cattle.

provident ADJ. displaying foresight; thrifty; preparing for emergencies. In his usual *provident* manner, he had insured himself against this type of loss.

provincial ADJ. pertaining to a province; limited. We have to overcome their *provincial* attitude and get them to become more cognizant of world problems.

provisional ADJ. tentative. The appointment is *provisional;* only on the approval of the board of directors will it be made permanent.

proviso N. stipulation. I am ready to accept your proposal with the *proviso* that you meet your obligations within the next two weeks.

provoke V. stir to anger; cause retaliation. In order to prevent a sudden outbreak of hostilities, we must not *provoke* our foe. provocation, N.

proximity N. nearness. The deer sensed the hunter's *proximity* and bounded away.

proxy N. authorized agent. Please act as my *proxy* and vote for this slate of candidates in my absence.

prude N. excessively modest person. The X-rated film was definitely not for *prudes*.

prudent ADJ. cautious; careful. A miser hoards money not because he is *prudent* but because he is greedy. prudence, N.

prune V. cut away; trim. With the help of her editor, she was able to *prune* her manuscript into publishable form.

prurient ADJ. based on lascivious thoughts. The police attempted to close the theater where the *prurient* film was being presented.

pseudonym N. pen name. Samuel Clemens' *pseudonym* was Mark Twain.

psyche N. soul; mind. It is difficult to delve into the *psyche* of a human being.

psychiatrist N. a doctor who treats mental diseases. A *psychiatrist* often needs long conferences with his patient before a diagnosis can be made.

psychopathic ADJ. pertaining to mental derangement. The *psychopathic* patient suffers more frequently from a disorder of the nervous system than from a diseased brain.

psychosis N. mental disorder. We must endeavor to find an outlet for the patient's repressed desires if we hope to combat this *psychosis*.

pterodactyl N. extinct flying reptile. The remains of *pterodactyls* indicate that these flying reptiles had a wingspan of as much as twenty feet.

puerile ADJ. childish. His *puerile* pranks sometimes offended his more mature friends.

pugilist N. boxer. The famous *pugilist* Cassius Clay changed his name to Muhammed Ali.

pugnacious ADJ. combative; disposed to fight. As a child he was *pugnacious* and fought with everyone.

puissant ADJ. powerful; strong; potent. We must keep his friendship for he will make a *puissant* ally.

pulchritude N. beauty; comeliness. I do not envy the judges who have to select this year's Miss America from this collection of female *pulchritude*.

pulmonary ADJ. pertaining to the lungs. In his researches on *pulmonary* diseases, he discovered many facts about the lungs of animals and human beings.

pulsate V. throb. We could see the blood vessels in his temple *pulsate* as he became more angry.

pummel V. beat. The severity with which he was *pummeled* was indicated by the bruises he displayed on his head and face.

punctilious ADJ. laying stress on niceties of conduct, form; precise. We must be *punctilious* in our planning of this affair, for any error may be regarded as a personal affront.

■ **pundit** N. learned Hindu; any learned man; authority on a subject. Even though he discourses on the matter like a *pundit,* he is actually rather ignorant about this topic.

■ **pungency** N. sharpness; stinging quality. The *pungency* of the cigarette smoke made me cough. pungent, ADJ.

punitive ADJ. punishing. He asked for *punitive* measures against the offender.

puny ADJ. insignificant; tiny; weak. Our *puny* efforts to stop the flood were futile.

purblind ADJ. dim-sighted; obtuse. In his *purblind* condition, he could not identify the people he saw.

purgatory N. place of spiritual expiation. In this *purgatory,* he could expect no help from his comrades.

purge V. clean by removing impurities; clear of charges. If you are to be *purged* of the charge of contempt of Congress, you must be willing to answer the questions previously asked. also N.

purloin V. steal. In the story, "The *Purloined* Letter," Poe points out that the best hiding place is often the most obvious place.

purport N. intention; meaning. If the *purport* of your speech was to arouse the rabble, you succeeded admirably. also V.

purveyor N. furnisher of foodstuffs; caterer. As *purveyor* of rare wines and viands, he traveled through France and Italy every year in search of new products to sell.

purview N. scope. The sociological implications of these inventions are beyond the *purview* of this book.

pusillanimous ADJ. cowardly; fainthearted. You should be ashamed of your *pusillanimous* conduct during this dispute.

putative ADJ. supposed; reputed. Although there are some doubts, the *putative* author of this work is Massinger.

putrid ADJ. foul; rotten; decayed. The gangrenous condition of the wound was indicated by the *putrid* smell when the bandages were removed. putrescence, N.

pyromaniac N. person with an insane desire to set things on fire. The detectives searched the area for the *pyromaniac* who had set these costly fires.

quack N. charlatan; impostor. Do not be misled by the exorbitant claims of this *quack;* he cannot cure you.

quadruped N. four-footed animal. Most mammals are *quadrupeds.*

quaff V. drink with relish. As we *quaffed* our ale, we listened to the gay songs of the students in the tavern.

quagmire N. bog; marsh. Our soldiers who served in Vietnam will never forget the drudgery of marching through the *quagmires* of the delta country.

quail V. cower; lose heart. He was afraid that he would *quail* in the face of danger.

quaint ADJ. odd; old-fashioned; picturesque. Her *quaint* clothes and old-fashioned language marked her as an eccentric.

■ **qualified** ADJ. limited; restricted. Unable to give the candidate full support, the mayor gave him only a *qualified* endorsement. (secondary meaning)

qualms N. misgivings. His *qualms* of conscience had become so great that he decided to abandon his plans.

quandary N. dilemma. When the two colleges to which he had applied accepted him, he was in a *quandary* as to which one he should attend.

quarantine N. isolation of person or ship to prevent spread of infection. We will have to place this house under *quarantine* until we determine the exact nature of the disease. also V.

quarry N. victim; object of a hunt. The police closed in on their *quarry.*

quarry V. dig into. They *quarried* blocks of marble out of the hillside.

Test

Word List 38   *Antonyms*

Each of the questions below consists of a word in capital letters, followed by five lettered words or phrases. Choose the lettered word or phrase that is most nearly opposite in meaning to the word in capital letters and write the letter of your choice on your answer paper.

556. PROPITIOUS (A) rich (B) induced (C) promoted (D) indicative (E) unfavorable
557. PROSAIC (A) pacified (B) reprieved (C) pensive (D) imaginative (E) rhetorical
558. PROTEAN (A) amateur (B) catholic (C) unchanging (D) rapid (E) unfavorable
559. PROTRACT (A) make circular (B) shorten (C) further (D) retrace (E) involve
560. PROVIDENT (A) unholy (B) rash (C) miserable (D) disabled (E) remote
561. PROVINCIAL (A) wealthy (B) crass (C) literary (D) aural (E) sophisticated
562. PSYCHOTIC (A) dangerous (B) clairvoyant (C) criminal (D) soulful (E) sane
563. PUERILE (A) fragrant (B) adult (C) lonely (D) feminine (E) masterly
564. PUGNACIOUS (A) pacific (B) feline (C) mature (D) angular (E) inactive
565. PUISSANT (A) pouring (B) fashionable (C) articulate (D) healthy (E) weak
566. PULCHRITUDE (A) ugliness (B) notoriety (C) bestiality (D) masculinity (E) servitude
567. PUNCTILIOUS (A) happy (B) active (C) vivid (D) careless (E) futile
568. PUNITIVE (A) large (B) humorous (C) rewarding (D) restive (E) languishing
569. PUSILLANIMOUS (A) poverty-stricken (B) chained (C) posthumous (D) courageous (E) strident
570. PUTATIVE (A) colonial (B) quarrelsome (C) undisputed (D) powerful (E) unremarkable

Word List 39   quay-recusant

quay N. dock; landing place. Because of the captain's carelessness, the ship crashed into the *quay*.

queasy ADJ. easily nauseated; squeamish. As the ship left the harbor, he became *queasy* and thought that he was going to suffer from seasickness.

quell V. put down; quiet. The police used fire hoses and tear gas to *quell* the rioters.

querulous ADJ. fretful; whining. His classmates were repelled by his *querulous* and complaining statements.

quibble V. equivocate; play on words. Do not *quibble*; I want a straightforward and definite answer. also N.

queue N. line. They stood patiently in the *queue* outside the movie theatre.

quiescent ADJ. at rest; dormant. After this geyser erupts, it will remain *quiescent* for twenty-four hours.

quietude N. tranquillity. He was impressed by the air of *quietude* and peace that pervaded the valley.

quintessence N. purest and highest embodiment. Noel Coward displayed the *quintessence* of wit.

quip N. taunt. You are unpopular because you are too free with your *quips* and sarcastic comments. also V.

quirk N. startling twist; caprice. By a *quirk* of fate, he found himself working for the man whom he had discharged years before.

quixotic ADJ. idealistic but impractical. His head is in the clouds; he is constantly presenting these *quixotic* schemes.

quizzical ADJ. bantering; comical; humorously serious. Will Rogers' *quizzical* remarks endeared him to his audiences.

quorum N. number of members necessary to conduct a meeting. The senator asked for a roll call to determine whether a *quorum* was present.

rabid ADJ. like a fanatic; furious. He was a *rabid* follower of the Dodgers and watched them play whenever he could go to the ball park.

raconteur N. story-teller. My father was a gifted *raconteur* with an unlimited supply of anecdotes.

ragamuffin N. person wearing tattered clothes. He felt sorry for the *ragamuffin* who was begging for food and gave him money to buy a meal.

rail V. scold; rant. You may *rail* at him all you want; you will never change him.

raiment N. clothing. "How can I go to the ball?" asked Cinderella. "I have no *raiment* fit to wear."

rakish ADJ. stylish; sporty. He wore his hat at a *rakish* and jaunty angle.

■ **ramification** N. branching out; subdivision. We must examine all the *ramifications* of this problem.

ramify V. divide into branches or subdivisions. When the plant begins to *ramify*, it is advisable to nip off most of the new branches.

ramp N. slope; inclined plane. The house was built with *ramps* instead of stairs in order to enable the man in the wheelchair to move easily from room to room and floor to floor.

rampant ADJ. rearing up on hind legs; unrestrained. The *rampant* weeds in the garden killed all the flowers which had been planted in the spring.

rampart N. defensive mound of earth. "From the *ramparts* we watched" as the fighting continued.

ramshackle ADJ. rickety; falling apart. The boys propped up the *ramshackle* clubhouse with a couple of boards.

rancid ADJ. having the odor of stale fat. A *rancid* odor filled the ship's galley and nauseated the crew.

■ **rancor** N. bitterness; hatred. Let us forget our *rancor* and cooperate in this new endeavor.

rankle V. irritate; fester. The memory of having been jilted *rankled* him for years.

rant V. rave; speak bombastically. As we heard him *rant* on the platform, we could not understand his strange popularity with many people.

rapacious ADJ. excessively grasping; plundering. Hawks and other *rapacious* birds may be killed at any time.

rapprochement N. reconciliation. Both sides were eager to effect a *rapprochement* but did not know how to undertake a program designed to bring about harmony.

rarefied ADJ. made less dense [of a gas]. The mountain climbers had difficulty breathing in the *rarefied* atmosphere. rarefy, V.

raspy ADJ. grating; harsh. The sergeant's *raspy* voice grated on the recruits' ears.

■ **ratiocination** N. reasoning; act of drawing conclusions from premises. Poe's "The Gold Bug" is a splendid example of the author's use of *ratiocination*.

rationalization N. bringing into conformity with reason. All attempts at *rationalization* at this time are doomed to failure; tempers and emotions run too high for intelligent thought to prevail.

rationalize V. reason; justify an improper act. Do not try to *rationalize* your behavior by blaming your companions.

raucous ADJ. harsh and shrill. His *raucous* laughter irritated me and grated on my ears.

ravage V. plunder; despoil. The marauding army *ravaged* the countryside.

ravening ADJ. rapacious; seeking prey. We kept our fires burning all night to frighten away the *ravening* wolves.

ravenous ADJ. extremely hungry. The *ravenous* dog upset several garbage pails in its search for food.

raze V. destroy completely. The owners intend to *raze* the hotel and erect an office building on the site.

reactionary ADJ. recoiling from progress; retrograde. His program was *reactionary* since it sought to abolish many of the social reforms instituted by the previous administration. also N.

realm N. kingdom; sphere. The *realm* of possibilities for the new invention was endless.

rebate N. discount. We offer a *rebate* of ten percent to those who pay cash.

rebuff V. snub; beat back. She *rebuffed* his invitation so smoothly that he did not realize he had been snubbed.

rebuttal N. refutation; response with contrary evidence. The defense lawyer confidently listened to the prosecutor sum up his case, sure that she could answer his arguments in her *rebuttal*.

recalcitrant ADJ. obstinately stubborn. Donkeys are reputed to be the most *recalcitrant* of animals.

■ **recant** V. repudiate; withdraw previous statement. Unless you *recant* your confession, you will be punished severely.

recapitulate V. summarize. Let us *recapitulate* what has been said thus far before going ahead.

recession N. withdrawal; retreat. The *recession* of the troops from the combat area was completed in an orderly manner.

recidivism N. habitual return to crime. Prison reformers in the United States are disturbed by the high rate of *recidivism;* the number of men serving second and third terms in prison indicates the failure of the prisons to rehabilitate the inmates.

recipient N. receiver. Although he had been the *recipient* of many favors, he was not grateful to his benefactor.

reciprocal ADJ. mutual; exchangeable; interacting. The two nations signed a *reciprocal* trade agreement.

reciprocate V. repay in kind. If they attack us, we shall be compelled to *reciprocate* and bomb their territory. reciprocity, N.

recluse N. hermit. The *recluse* lived in a hut in the forest.

reconcile V. make friendly after quarrel; correct inconsistencies. Each month we *reconcile* our checkbook with the bank statement.

■ **recondite** ADJ. abstruse; profound; secret. He read many *recondite* books in order to obtain the material for his scholarly thesis.

reconnaissance N. survey of enemy by soldiers; reconnoitering. If you encounter any enemy soldiers during your *reconnaissance,* capture them for questioning.

recourse N. resorting to help when in trouble. The boy's only *recourse* was to appeal to his father for aid.

recreant N. coward; betrayer of faith. The religious people ostracized the *recreant* who had abandoned their faith.

recrimination N. countercharges. Loud and angry *recriminations* were her answer to his accusations.

recrudescence N. reopening of a wound or sore. Keep this wound bandaged until it has completely healed to prevent its *recrudescence*.

rectify V. correct. I want to *rectify* my error before it is too late.

rectitude N. uprightness. He was renowned for his *rectitude* and integrity.

recumbent ADJ. reclining; lying down completely or in part. The command "AT EASE" does not permit you to take a *recumbent* position.

recuperate V. recover. The doctors were worried because the patient did not *recuperate* as rapidly as they had expected.

recurrent ADJ. occurring again and again. These *recurrent* attacks disturbed us and we consulted a physician.

recusant N. person who refuses to comply; applied specifically to those who refused to attend Anglican services. In that religious community, the *recusant* was shunned as a pariah.

Test

Word List 39   *Synonyms and Antonyms*

Each of the following questions consists of a word in capital letters, followed by five lettered words or phrases. Choose the lettered word or phrase which is most nearly similar or the opposite of the word in capital letters and write the letter of your choice on your answer paper.

571. QUEASY (A) toxic (B) easily upset (C) chronic (D) choleric (E) false

572. QUELL (A) boast (B) incite (C) reverse (D) wet (E) answer

573. QUIXOTIC (A) rapid (B) exotic (C) longing (D) timid (E) idealistic

574. RAGAMUFFIN (A) dandy (B) biscuit (C) exotic dance (D) light snack (E) baker

575. RAUCOUS (A) mellifluous (B) uncooked (C) realistic (D) veracious (E) anticipating

576. RAVAGE (A) rank (B) revive (C) plunder (D) pillory (E) age

577. RAZE (A) shave (B) heckle (C) finish (D) tear down (E) write

578. REACTIONARY (A) conservative (B) retrograde (C) dramatist (D) militant (E) chemical

579. REBATE (A) relinquish (B) settle (C) discount (D) cancel (E) elicit

580. RECALCITRANT (A) grievous (B) secretive (C) cowardly (D) thoughtful (E) cooperative

581. RECLUSE (A) learned scholar (B) mocker (C) social person (D) careful worker (E) daredevil

582. RECREANT (A) vacationing (B) faithful (C) indifferent (D) obliged (E) reviving

583. RECTIFY (A) remedy (B) avenge (C) create (D) assemble (E) attribute

584. RECUPERATE (A) reenact (B) engage (C) recapitulate (D) recover (E) encounter

585. RECUSANT (A) nonconformer (B) deliberator (C) abstainer (D) qualifier (E) patient

Word List 40   redolent-rescind

redolent ADJ. fragrant; odorous; suggestive of an odor. Even though it is February, the air is *redolent* of spring.

redoubtable ADJ. formidable; causing fear. The neighboring countries tried not to offend the Russians because they could be *redoubtable* foes.

redress N. remedy; compensation. Do you mean to tell me that I can get no *redress* for my injuries? also V.

redundant ADJ. superfluous; excessively wordy; repetitious. Your composition is *redundant;* you can easily reduce its length. redundancy, N.

reek V. emit (odor). The room *reeked* with stale tobacco smoke. also N.

refection N. slight refreshment. Despite our hunger, we stopped on the road for only a quick *refection*.

refectory N. dining hall. In this huge *refectory,* we can feed the entire student body at one sitting.

refraction N. bending of a ray of light. When you look at a stick inserted in water, it looks bent because of the *refraction* of the light by the water.

refractory ADJ. stubborn; unmanageable. The *refractory* horse was eliminated from the race when he refused to obey the jockey.

refulgent ADJ. radiant. We admired the *refulgent* moon and watched it for a while.

refurbish V. renovate; make bright by polishing. The flood left a deposit of mud on everything; it was necessary to *refurbish* our belongings.

refutation N. disproof of opponents' arguments. I will wait until I hear the *refutation* before deciding whom to favor.

refute V. disprove. The defense called several respectable witnesses who were able to *refute* the false testimony of the prosecution's only witness.

regal ADJ. royal. Prince Albert had a *regal* manner.

regale V. entertain. John *regaled* us with tales of his adventures in Africa.

regatta N. boat or yacht race. Many boating enthusiasts followed the *regatta* in their own yachts.

regeneration N. spiritual rebirth. Modern penologists strive for the *regeneration* of the prisoners.

regicide N. murder of a king or queen. The death of Mary Queen of Scots was an act of *regicide*.

regime N. method or system of government. When a Frenchman mentions the Old *Regime,* he refers to the government existing before the revolution.

regimen N. prescribed diet and habits. I doubt whether the results warrant our living under such a strict *regimen*.

rehabilitate V. restore to proper condition. We must *rehabilitate* those whom we send to prison.

reimburse V. repay. Let me know what you have spent and I will *reimburse* you.

reiterate V. repeat. I shall *reiterate* this message until all have understood it.

rejuvenate V. make young again. The charlatan claimed that his elixir would *rejuvenate* the aged and weary.

relegate V. banish; consign to inferior position. If we *relegate* these experienced people to positions of unimportance because of their political persuasions, we shall lose the services of valuably trained personnel.

relevancy N. pertinence; reference to the case in hand. I was impressed by the *relevancy* of your remarks; I now understand the situation perfectly. relevant, ADJ.

relinquish V. abandon. I will *relinquish* my claims to this property if you promise to retain my employees.

relish V. savor; enjoy. I *relish* a good joke as much as anyone else. also N.

remediable ADJ. reparable. Let us be grateful that the damage is *remediable*.

remedial ADJ. curative; corrective. Because he was a slow reader, he decided to take a course in *remedial* reading.

reminiscence N. recollection. Her *reminiscences* of her experiences are so fascinating that she ought to write a book.

remiss ADJ. negligent. He was accused of being *remiss* in his duty when the prisoner escaped.

remnant N. remainder. I suggest that you wait until the store places the *remnants* of these goods on sale.

remonstrate V. protest. I must *remonstrate* about the lack of police protection in this area.

remorse N. guilt; self-reproach. The murderer felt no *remorse* for his crime.

remunerative ADJ. compensating; rewarding. I find my new work so *remunerative* that I may not return to my previous employment. remuneration, N.

rend V. split; tear apart. In his grief, he tried to *rend* his garments.

render V. deliver; provide; represent. He *rendered* aid to the needy and indigent.

rendezvous N. meeting place. The two fleets met at the *rendezvous* at the appointed time. also V.

rendition N. translation; artistic interpretation of a song, etc. The audience cheered enthusiastically as she completed her *rendition* of the aria.

renegade N. deserter; apostate. Because he refused to support his fellow members in their drive, he was shunned as a *renegade*.

renege V. deny; go back on. He *reneged* on paying off his debt.

renounce V. abandon; discontinue; disown; repudiate. Joan of Arc refused to *renounce* her statements even though she knew she would be burned at the stake as a witch.

renovate v. restore to good condition; renew. They claim that they can *renovate* worn shoes so that they look like new ones.

renunciation N. giving up; renouncing. Do not sign this *renunciation* of your right to sue until you have consulted a lawyer.

reparable ADJ. capable of being repaired. Fortunately, the damages we suffered in the accident were *reparable* and our car looks brand new.

■ **reparation** N. amends; compensation. At the peace conference, the defeated country promised to pay *reparations* to the victors.

repartee N. clever reply. He was famous for his witty *repartee* and his sarcasm.

repellent ADJ. driving away; unattractive. Mosquitoes find the odor so *repellent* that they leave any spot where this liquid has been sprayed. also N.

repercussion N. rebound; reverberation; reaction. I am afraid that this event will have serious *repercussions*.

repertoire N. list of works of music, drama, etc., a performer is prepared to present. The opera company decided to include *Madame Butterfly* in its *repertoire* for the following season.

repine v. fret; complain. There is no sense *repining* over the work you have left undone.

replenish v. fill up again. The end of rationing enabled us to *replenish* our supply of canned food.

replete ADJ. filled to capacity; abundantly supplied. This book is *replete* with humorous situations.

replica N. copy. Are you going to hang this *replica* of the Declaration of Independence in the classroom or in the auditorium?

repository N. storehouse. Libraries are *repositories* of the world's best thoughts.

reprehensible ADJ. deserving blame. Your vicious conduct in this situation is *reprehensible*.

reprieve N. temporary stay. During the twenty-four-hour *reprieve*, the lawyers sought to make the stay of execution permanent. also v.

reprimand v. reprove severely. I am afraid that my parents will *reprimand* me when I show them my report card. also N.

reprisal N. retaliation. I am confident that we are ready for any *reprisals* the enemy may undertake.

reproach N. blame; censure. I want my work to be above *reproach* and without error. also v.

■ **reprobate** N. person hardened in sin, devoid of a sense of decency. I cannot understand why he has so many admirers if he is the *reprobate* you say he is.

reprobation N. severe disapproval. The students showed their *reprobation* of his act by refusing to talk with him.

reprove v. censure; rebuke. The principal *reproved* the students when they became unruly in the auditorium.

repudiate v. disown; disavow. He announced that he would *repudiate* all debts incurred by his wife.

repugnance N. loathing. She looked at the snake with *repugnance*.

repulsion N. act of driving back; distaste. The *repulsion* of the enemy forces was not accomplished bloodlessly; many of the defenders were wounded in driving the enemy back.

reputed ADJ. supposed. He is the *reputed* father of the child. also v.

requiem N. mass for the dead; dirge. They played Mozart's *Requiem* at the funeral.

requisite N. necessary requirement. Many colleges state that a student must offer three years of a language as a *requisite* for admission.

requite v. repay; revenge. The wretch *requited* his benefactors by betraying them.

■ **rescind** v. cancel. Because of public resentment, the king had to *rescind* his order.

Test

Word List 40   *Synonyms*

Each of the questions below consists of a word in capital letters, followed by five lettered words or phrases. Choose the lettered word or phrase that is most nearly similar in meaning to the word in capital letters and write the letter of your choice on your answer paper.

586. REFRACTORY (A) articulate (B) sinkable (C) vaunted (D) useless (E) unmanageable
587. REGAL (A) oppressive (B) royal (C) major (D) basic (E) entertaining
588. REITERATE (A) gainsay (B) revive (C) revenge (D) repeat (E) return
589. RELISH (A) desire (B) nibble (C) savor (D) vindicate (E) avail
590. REMISS (A) lax (B) lost (C) foolish (D) violating (E) ambitious
591. REMONSTRATE (A) display (B) restate (C) protest (D) resign (E) reiterate
592. REPARTEE (A) witty retort (B) willful departure (C) spectator (D) monologue (E) sacrifice
593. REPELLENT (A) propulsive (B) unattractive (C) porous (D) stiff (E) elastic
594. REPERCUSSION (A) reaction (B) restitution (C) resistance (D) magnificence (E) acceptance
595. REPLENISH (A) polish (B) repeat (C) reinstate (D) refill (E) refuse
596. REPLICA (A) museum piece (B) famous site (C) battle emblem (D) facsimile (E) replacement

597. REPRISAL (A) reevaluation (B) assessment (C) loss (D) retaliation (E) nonsense
598. REPROVE (A) prevail (B) rebuke (C) ascertain (D) prove false (E) scarify
599. REPUDIATE (A) besmirch (B) appropriate (C) annoy (D) reject (E) avow
600. REPUGNANCE (A) belligerence (B) tenacity (C) renewal (D) pity (E) loathing

Word List 41   rescission-sacrosanct

rescission N. abrogation; annulment. The *rescission* of the unpopular law was urged by all political parties.

reserve N. self-control; care in expressing oneself. She was outspoken and uninhibited; he was cautious and inclined to *reserve*. (secondary meaning)

residue N. remainder; balance. In his will, he requested that after payment of debts, taxes, and funeral expenses, the *residue* be given to his wife.

resignation N. submissiveness. He met all his troubles with an attitude of patient *resignation*. (secondary meaning) resigned, ADJ.

resilient ADJ. elastic; having the power of springing back. Steel is highly *resilient* and therefore is used in the manufacture of springs.

■ **resolution** N. determination. Nothing could shake his *resolution* to succeed despite all difficulties. resolute, ADJ.

resonant ADJ. echoing; resounding; possessing resonance. His *resonant* voice was particularly pleasing.

respite N. delay in punishment; interval of relief; rest. The judge granted the condemned man a *respite* to enable his attorneys to file an appeal.

resplendent ADJ. brilliant; lustrous. The toreador wore a *resplendent* costume.

responsiveness N. state of reacting readily to appeals, orders, etc. The audience cheered and applauded, delighting the performers by its *responsiveness*.

restitution N. reparation; indemnification. He offered to make *restitution* for the window broken by his son.

restive ADJ. unmanageable; fretting under control. We must quiet the *restive* animals.

restraint N. controlling force. She dreamt of living an independent life, free of all *restraints*.

resurgent ADJ. rising again after defeat, etc. The *resurgent* nation surprised everyone by its quick recovery after total defeat.

resuscitate V. revive. The lifeguard tried to *resuscitate* the drowned child by applying artificial respiration.

retaliate V. repay in kind (usually for bad treatment). Fear that we will *retaliate* immediately deters our foe from attacking us.

retentive ADJ. holding; having a good memory. The pupil did not need to spend much time in study as he had a *retentive* mind.

■ **reticent** ADJ. reserved; uncommunicative; inclined to silence. Hughes preferred *reticent* employees to loquacious ones, noting that the formers' dislike of idle chatter might ensure their discretion about his affairs. reticence, N.

reticulated ADJ. covered with a network; having the appearance of a mesh. She wore the *reticulated* stockings so popular with teenagers at that time.

retinue N. following; attendants. The queen's *retinue* followed her down the aisle.

retort N. quick sharp reply. Even when it was advisable for her to keep her mouth shut, she was always ready with a quick *retort*. also V.

retraction N. withdrawal. He dropped his libel suit after the newspaper published a *retraction* of its statement.

retrench V. cut down; economize. If they were to be able to send their children to college, they would have to *retrench*.

retribution N. vengeance; compensation; punishment for offenses. The evangelist maintained that an angry deity would exact *retribution* from the sinners.

retrieve V. recover; find and bring in. The dog was intelligent and quickly learned to *retrieve* the game killed by the hunter.

retroactive ADJ. of a law which dates back to a period before its enactment. Because the law was *retroactive* to the first of the year, we found she was eligible for the pension.

retrograde V. go backwards; degenerate. Instead of advancing, our civilization seems to have *retrograded* in ethics and culture. also ADJ.

retrospective ADJ. looking back on the past. It is only when we become *retrospective* that we can appreciate the tremendous advances made during this century.

revelry N. boisterous merrymaking. New Year's Eve is a night of *revelry*.

reverberate V. echo; resound. The entire valley *reverberated* with the sound of the church bells.

revere V. respect; honor. In Asian societies, people *revere* their elders.

reverent ADJ. respectful. His *reverent* attitude was appropriate in a house of worship.

reverie N. daydream; musing. He was awakened from his *reverie* by the teacher's question.

revile V. slander; vilify. He was avoided by all who feared that he would *revile* and abuse them if they displeased him.

revulsion N. sudden violent change of feeling; reaction. Many people in this country who admired dictatorships underwent a *revulsion* when they realized what Hitler and Mussolini were trying to do.

rhapsodize V. to speak or write in an exaggeratedly enthusiastic manner. She greatly enjoyed her Hawaiian vacation and *rhapsodized* about it for weeks.

rhetoric N. art of effective communication; insincere language. All writers, by necessity, must be skilled in *rhetoric*.

rhetorical ADJ. pertaining to effective communication; insincere in language. To win his audience, the speaker used every *rhetorical* trick in the book.

rheumy ADJ. pertaining to a discharge from nose and eyes. His *rheumy* eyes warned us that he was coming down with a cold.

ribald ADJ. wanton; profane. He sang a *ribald* song that offended many of the more prudish listeners.

rife ADJ. abundant; current. In the face of the many rumors of scandal, which are *rife* at the moment, it is best to remain silent.

rift N. opening; break. The plane was lost in the stormy sky until the pilot saw the city through a *rift* in the clouds.

rigor N. severity. Many settlers could not stand the *rigors* of the New England winters.

rime N. white frost. The early morning dew had frozen and everything was covered with a thin coat of *rime*.

risible ADJ. inclined to laugh; ludicrous. His remarks were so *risible* that the audience howled with laughter. risibility, N.

risqué ADJ. verging upon the improper; offcolor. Please do not tell your *risqué* anecdotes at this party.

roan ADJ. brown mixed with gray or white. You can distinguish this horse in a race because it is *roan* while all the others are bay or chestnut.

robust ADJ. vigorous; strong. The candidate for the football team had a *robust* physique.

rococo ADJ. ornate; highly decorated. The *rococo* style in furniture and architecture, marked by scrollwork and excessive decoration, flourished during the middle of the eighteenth century.

roil V. to make liquids murky by stirring up sediment. Be careful when you pour not to *roil* the wine; if you stir up the sediment you'll destroy the flavor.

roseate ADJ. rosy; optimistic. I am afraid you will have to alter your *roseate* views in the light of the distressing news that has just arrived.

roster N. list. They print the *roster* of players in the season's program.

rostrum N. platform for speech-making; pulpit. The crowd murmured angrily and indicated that they did not care to listen to the speaker who was approaching the *rostrum*.

rote N. repetition. He recited the passage by *rote* and gave no indication he understood what he was saying.

rotunda N. circular building or hall covered with a dome. His body lay in state in the *rotunda* of the Capitol.

rotundity N. roundness; sonorousness of speech. Washington Irving emphasized the *rotundity* of the governor by describing his height and circumference.

rout V. stampede; drive out. The reinforcements were able to *rout* the enemy. also N.

rubble N. fragments. Ten years after World War II, some of the *rubble* left by enemy bombings could still be seen.

rubicund ADJ. having a healthy reddish color; ruddy; florid. His *rubicund* complexion was the result of an active outdoor life.

ruddy ADJ. reddish; healthy-looking. His *ruddy* features indicated that he had spent much time in the open.

rudimentary ADJ. not developed; elementary. His dancing was limited to a few *rudimentary* steps.

rueful ADJ. regretful; sorrowful; dejected. The artist has captured the sadness of childhood in his portrait of the boy with the *rueful* countenance.

ruffian N. bully; scoundrel. The *ruffians* threw stones at the police.

ruminate V. chew the cud; ponder. We cannot afford to wait while you *ruminate* upon these plans.

rummage V. ransack; thoroughly search. When we *rummaged* through the trunks in the attic, we found many souvenirs of our childhood days. also N.

ruse N. trick; stratagem. You will not be able to fool your friends with such an obvious *ruse*.

rustic ADJ. pertaining to country people; uncouth. The backwoodsman looked out of place in his *rustic* attire.

rusticate V. banish to the country; dwell in the country. I like city life so much that I can never understand how people can *rusticate* in the suburbs.

ruthless ADJ. pitiless. The escaped convict was a dangerous and *ruthless* murderer.

saccharine ADJ. cloyingly sweet. She tried to ingratiate herself, speaking sweetly and smiling a *saccharine* smile.

sacerdotal ADJ. priestly. The priest decided to abandon his *sacerdotal* duties and enter the field of politics.

sacrilegious ADJ. desecrating; profane. His stealing of the altar cloth was a very *sacrilegious* act.

sacrosanct ADJ. most sacred; inviolable. The brash insurance salesman invaded the *sacrosanct* privacy of the office of the president of the company.

Test

Word List 41   *Antonyms*

Each of the questions below consists of a word in capital letters, followed by five lettered words or phrases. Choose the lettered word or phrase that is most nearly opposite in meaning to the word in capital letters and write the letter of your choice on your answer paper.

601. RESILIENT (A) pungent (B) foolish (C) worthy (D) insolent (E) unyielding

602. RESTIVE (A) buoyant (B) placid (C) remorseful (D) resistant (E) retiring

603. RETENTIVE (A) forgetful (B) accepting (C) repetitive (D) avoiding (E) fascinating
604. RETICENCE (A) fatigue (B) fashion (C) treachery (D) loquaciousness (E) magnanimity
605. RETROGRADE (A) progressing (B) inclining (C) evaluating (D) concentrating (E) directing
606. REVERE (A) advance (B) dishonor (C) age (D) precede (E) wake
607. RIFE (A) direct (B) scant (C) peaceful (D) grim (E) mature
608. ROBUST (A) weak (B) violent (C) vicious (D) villainous (E) hungry

609. ROTUNDITY (A) promenade (B) nave (C) grotesqueness (D) slimness (E) impropriety
610. RUBICUND (A) dangerous (B) pallid (C) remote (D) indicative (E) nonsensical
611. RUDDY (A) robust (B) witty (C) wan (D) exotic (E) creative
612. RUDIMENTARY (A) pale (B) polite (C) asinine (D) developed (E) quiescent
613. RUEFUL (A) trite (B) content (C) capable (D) capital (E) zealous
614. RUSTIC (A) urban (B) slow (C) corroded (D) mercenary (E) civilian
615. RUTHLESS (A) merciful (B) majestic (C) mighty (D) militant (E) maximum

Word List 42   sadistic-sepulcher

sadistic ADJ. inclined to cruelty. If we are to improve conditions in this prison, we must first get rid of the *sadistic* warden.

saffron ADJ. orange-colored; colored like the autumn crocus. The Halloween cake was decorated with *saffron*-colored icing.

saga N. Scandinavian myth; any legend. This is a *saga* of the sea and the men who risk their lives on it.

sagacious ADJ. keen; shrewd; having insight. He is much too *sagacious* to be fooled by a trick like that.

■ **salacious** ADJ. lascivious; lustful. Chaucer's monk is not pious but *salacious,* a teller of lewd tales and ribald jests.

salient ADJ. prominent. One of the *salient* features of that newspaper is its excellent editorial page.

saline ADJ. salty. The slightly *saline* taste of this mineral water is pleasant.

sallow ADJ. yellowish; sickly in color. We were disturbed by his *sallow* complexion, which was due to jaundice.

saltatory ADJ. relating to leaping. The male members of the ballet company were renowned for their *saltatory* exploits.

■ **salubrious** ADJ. healthful. Many people with hay fever move to more *salubrious* sections of the country during the months of August and September.

salutary ADJ. tending to improve; beneficial; wholesome. The punishment had a *salutary* effect on the boy, as he became a model student.

salvage V. rescue from loss. All attempts to *salvage* the wrecked ship failed. also N.

salver N. tray. The food was brought in on silver *salvers* by the waiters.

sanctimonious ADJ. displaying ostentatious or hypocritical devoutness. You do not have to be so *sanctimonious* to prove that you are devout.

sanction V. approve; ratify. Nothing will convince me to *sanction* the engagement of my daughter to such a worthless young man.

sangfroid N. coolness in a trying situation. The captain's *sangfroid* helped to allay the fears of the passengers.

sanguinary ADJ. bloody. The battle of Iwo Jima was unexpectedly *sanguinary* with many casualties.

sanguine ADJ. cheerful; hopeful. Let us not be too *sanguine* about the outcome; something could go wrong.

sapid ADJ. savory; tasty; relishable. This chef has the knack of making most foods more *sapid* and appealing.

sapient ADJ. wise; shrewd. The students enjoyed the professor's *sapient* digressions more than his formal lectures.

sarcasm N. scornful remarks; stinging rebuke. His feelings were hurt by the *sarcasm* of his supposed friends.

sarcophagus N. stone coffin, often highly decorated. The display of the *sarcophagus* in the art museum impresses me as a morbid exhibition.

sardonic ADJ. disdainful; sarcastic; cynical. The *sardonic* humor of nightclub comedians who satirize or ridicule patrons in the audience strikes some people as amusing and others as rude.

sartorial ADJ. pertaining to tailors. He was as famous for the *sartorial* splendor of his attire as he was for his acting.

sate V. satisfy to the full; cloy. Its hunger *sated,* the lion dozed.

satellite N. small body revolving around a larger one. During the first few years of the Space Age, hundreds of *satellites* were launched by Russia and the United States.

satiate V. surfeit; satisfy fully. The guests, having eaten until they were *satiated,* now listened inattentively to the speakers.

satiety N. condition of being crammed full; glutted state; repletion. The *satiety* of the guests at the sumptuous feast became apparent when they refused the delicious dessert.

satire N. form of literature in which irony, sarcasm, and ridicule are employed to attack vice and folly. *Gulliver's Travels,* which is regarded by many as a tale for children, is actually a bitter *satire* attacking man's folly.

satirical ADJ. mocking. The humor of cartoonist Gary Trudeau often is *satirical;* through the comments of the Doonesbury characters, Trudeau ridicules political corruption and folly.

satrap N. petty ruler working for a superior despot. The monarch and his *satraps* oppressed the citizens of the country.

saturate V. soak. Their clothes were *saturated* by the rain. saturation, N.

saturnine ADJ. gloomy. Do not be misled by his *saturnine* countenance; he is not as gloomy as he looks.

satyr N. half-human, half-bestial being in the court of Dionysus, portrayed as wanton and cunning. He was like a *satyr* in his lustful conduct.

saunter V. stroll slowly. As we *sauntered* through the park, we stopped frequently to admire the spring flowers.

savant N. scholar. Our faculty includes many world-famous *savants*.

savoir faire N. tact; poise; sophistication. I envy his *savoir faire*; he always knows exactly what to do and say.

savor V. have a distinctive flavor, smell, or quality. I think your choice of a successor *savors* of favoritism.

scanty ADJ. meager; insufficient. Thinking his helping of food was *scanty*, Oliver Twist asked for more.

■ **scapegoat** N. someone who bears the blame for others. After the Challenger disaster, NASA searched for *scapegoats* on whom they could cast the blame.

scarify V. make slight incisions in; scratch. He was not severely cut; the flying glass had merely *scarified* him.

scavenger N. collector and disposer of refuse; animal that devours refuse and carrion. The Oakland *Scavenger* Company is responsible for the collection and disposal of the community's garbage.

schism N. division; split. Let us not widen the *schism* by further bickering.

scintilla N. shred; least bit. You have not produced a *scintilla* of evidence to support your argument.

scintillate V. sparkle; flash. I enjoy her dinner parties because the food is excellent and the conversation *scintillates*.

scion N. offspring. The farm boy felt out of place in the school attended by the *scions* of the wealthy and noble families.

scoff V. mock; ridicule. He *scoffed* at dentists until he had his first toothache.

scourge N. lash; whip; severe punishment. They feared the plague and regarded it as a deadly *scourge*. also V.

■ **scrupulous** ADJ. conscientious; extremely thorough. I can recommend him for a position of responsibility for I have found him a very *scrupulous* young man.

scullion N. menial kitchen worker. He acted as though he were the head chef when he was actually only a *scullion*.

scurrilous ADJ. obscene; indecent. Your *scurrilous* remarks are especially offensive because they are untrue.

scurry V. move briskly. The White Rabbit had to *scurry* to get to his appointment on time.

scuttle V. sink. The sailors decided to *scuttle* their vessel rather than surrender it to the enemy.

sebaceous ADJ. oily; fatty. The *sebaceous* glands secrete oil to the hair follicles.

secession N. withdrawal. The *secession* of the Southern states provided Lincoln with his first major problem after his inauguration.

seclusion N. isolation; solitude. One moment she loved crowds; the next, she sought *seclusion*.

secular ADJ. worldly; not pertaining to church matters; temporal. The church leaders decided not to interfere in *secular* matters.

sedate ADJ. composed; grave. The parents were worried because they felt their son was too quiet and *sedate*.

sedentary ADJ. requiring sitting. Because he had a *sedentary* occupation, he decided to visit a gymnasium weekly.

sedition N. resistance to authority; insubordination. His words, though not treasonous in themselves, were calculated to arouse thoughts of *sedition*.

sedulous ADJ. diligent. The young woman was so *sedulous* that she received a commendation for her hard work.

seethe V. be disturbed; boil. The nation was *seething* with discontent as the noblemen continued their arrogant ways.

seine N. net for catching fish. When the shad run during the spring, you may see fishermen with *seines* along the banks of our coastal rivers.

seismic ADJ. pertaining to earthquakes. The Richter scale is a measurement of *seismic* disturbances.

semblance N. outward appearance; guise. Although this book has a *semblance* of wisdom and scholarship, a careful examination will reveal many errors and omissions.

senescence N. state of growing old. He did not show any signs of *senescence* until he was well past seventy.

senility N. old age; feeble mindedness of old age. Most of the decisions are being made by the junior members of the company because of the *senility* of the president.

sensual ADJ. devoted to the pleasures of the senses; carnal; voluptuous. I cannot understand what caused him to drop his *sensual* way of life and become so ascetic.

sensuous ADJ. pertaining to the physical senses; operating through the senses. He was stimulated by the sights, sounds and smells about him; he was enjoying his *sensuous* experience.

sententious ADJ. terse; concise; aphoristic. After reading so many redundant speeches, I find his *sententious* style particularly pleasing.

septic ADJ. putrid; producing putrefaction. The hospital was in such a filthy state that we were afraid that many of the patients would suffer from *septic* poisoning.

sepulcher N. tomb. Annabel Lee was buried in the *sepulcher* by the sea.

Test

Word List 42   *Antonyms*

Each of the questions below consists of a word in capital letters, followed by five lettered words or phrases. Choose the lettered word or phrase that is most nearly opposite in meaning to the word in capital letters and write the letter of your choice on your answer paper.

616. SADISTIC (A) happy (B) quaint (C) kindhearted (D) vacant (E) fortunate

617. SAGACIOUS (A) foolish (B) bitter (C) voracious (D) veracious (E) fallacious

618. SALLOW (A) salacious (B) ruddy (C) colorless (D) permitted (E) minimum

619. SALUBRIOUS (A) salty (B) bloody (C) miasmic (D) maudlin (E) wanted

620. SALVAGE (A) remove (B) outfit (C) burn (D) lose (E) confuse

621. SANCTIMONIOUS (A) hypothetical (B) paltry (C) mercenary (D) pious (E) grateful

622. SANGUINE (A) choleric (B) sickening (C) warranted (D) irritated (E) pessimistic

623. SATIETY (A) emptiness (B) warmth (C) erectness (D) ignorance (E) straight

624. SCANTY (A) collected (B) remote (C) invisible (D) plentiful (E) straight

625. SCURRILOUS (A) savage (B) scabby (C) decent (D) volatile (E) major

626. SECULAR (A) vivid (B) clerical (C) punitive (D) positive (E) varying

627. SEDENTARY (A) vicarious (B) loyal (C) accidental (D) active (E) afraid

628. SENESCENCE (A) youth (B) romance (C) doldrums (D) quintessence (E) friendship

629. SENILITY (A) virility (B) loquaciousness (C) forgetfulness (D) youth (E) majority

630. SENTENTIOUS (A) paragraphed (B) positive (C) posthumous (D) pacific (E) wordy

Word List 43   sequacious-somatic

sequacious ADJ. eager to follow; ductile. The *sequacious* members of Parliament were only too willing to do the bidding of their leader.

sequester V. retire from public life; segregate; seclude. Although he had hoped for a long time to *sequester* himself in a small community, he never was able to drop his busy round of activities in the city.

seraph N. high-ranking, six-winged angel. In "Annabel Lee" Poe maintains that the "winged *seraphs* of Heaven" envied their great love.

serendipity N. gift for finding valuable things not searched for. Many scientific discoveries are a matter of *serendipity.*

serenity N. calmness; placidity. The *serenity* of the sleepy town was shattered by a tremendous explosion.

serpentine ADJ. winding; twisting. The car swerved at every curve in the *serpentine* road.

serrated ADJ. having a sawtoothed edge. The beech tree is one of many plants that have *serrated* leaves.

serried ADJ. standing shoulder to shoulder; crowded. In these days of automatic weapons, it is suicidal for troops to charge in *serried* ranks against the foe.

servile ADJ. slavish; cringing. Uriah Heep was a very *servile* individual.

severance N. division; partition; separation. The *severance* of church and state is a basic principle of our government.

severity N. harshness; plainness. The newspapers disapproved of the *severity* of the sentence.

shackle V. chain; fetter. The criminal's ankles were *shackled* to prevent his escape. also N.

sham V. pretend. He *shammed* sickness to get out of going to school. also N.

shambles N. slaughterhouse; scene of carnage. By the time the police arrived, the room was a *shambles*.

■ **shard** N. fragment, generally of pottery. The archaeologist assigned several students the task of reassembling earthenware vessels from the *shards* he had brought back from the expedition.

sheaf N. bundle of stalks of grain; any bundle of things tied together. The lawyer picked up a *sheaf* of papers as he rose to question the witness.

sheathe V. place into a case. As soon as he recognized the approaching men, he *sheathed* his dagger and hailed them as friends.

sherbet N. flavored dessert ice. I prefer raspberry *sherbet* to ice cream since it is less fattening.

shibboleth N. watchword; slogan. We are often misled by *shibboleths.*

shimmer V. glimmer intermittently. The moonlight *shimmered* on the water as the moon broke through the clouds for a moment. also N.

shoal N. shallow place. The ship was stranded on a *shoal* and had to be pulled off by tugs.

shoddy ADJ. sham; not genuine; inferior. You will never get the public to buy such *shoddy* material.

shrew N. scolding woman. No one wanted to marry Shakespeare's Kate because she was a *shrew.*

shrewd ADJ. clever; astute. A *shrewd* investor, he took clever advantage of the fluctuations of the stock market.

sibling N. brother or sister. We may not enjoy being *siblings,* but we cannot forget that we still belong to the same family.

sibylline ADJ. prophetic; oracular. Until their destruction by fire in 83 B.C., the *sibylline* books were often consulted by the Romans.

sidereal   ADJ. relating to the stars. The study of *sidereal* bodies has been greatly advanced by the new telescope.

silt   N. sediment deposited by running water. The harbor channel must be dredged annually to remove the *silt*.

simian   ADJ. monkeylike. Lemurs are nocturnal mammals and have many *simian* characteristics, although they are less intelligent than monkeys.

simile   N. comparison of one thing with another, using the word *like* or *as*. "My love is like a red, red rose" is a *simile*.

similitude   N. similarity; using comparisons such as similes, etc. Although the critics deplored his use of mixed metaphors, he continued to write in *similitudes*.

simpering   ADJ. smirking. I can overlook his *simpering* manner, but I cannot ignore his stupidity.

simulate   V. feign. He *simulated* insanity in order to avoid punishment for his crime.

sinecure   N. well-paid position with little responsibility. My job is no *sinecure;* I work long hours and have much responsibility.

sinewy   ADJ. tough; strong and firm. The steak was too *sinewy* to chew.

sinister   ADJ. evil. We must defeat the *sinister* forces that seek our downfall.

■ **sinuous**   ADJ. winding; bending in and out; not morally honest. The snake moved in a *sinuous* manner.

sirocco   N. warm, sultry wind blown from Africa to southern Europe. We can understand the popularity of the siesta in southern Spain; when the *sirocco* blows, the afternoon heat is unbearable.

■ **skeptic**   N. doubter; person who suspends judgment until he has examined the evidence supporting a point of view. In this matter, I am a *skeptic;* I want proof. skeptical, ADJ.

skimp   V. provide scantily; live very economically. They were forced to *skimp* on necessities in order to make their limited supplies last the winter.

skinflint   N. miser. The old *skinflint* refused to give her a raise.

skittish   ADJ. lively; frisky. She is as *skittish* as a kitten playing with a piece of string.

skulduggery   N. dishonest behavior. The investigation into municipal corruption turned up new instances of *skulduggery* daily.

skulk   V. move furtively and secretly. He *skulked* through the less fashionable sections of the city in order to avoid meeting any of his former friends.

slacken   V. slow up; loosen. As they passed the finish line, the runners *slackened* their pace.

slake   V. quench; sate. When we reached the oasis, we were able to *slake* our thirst.

slander   N. defamation; utterance of false and malicious statements. Unless you can prove your allegations, your remarks constitute *slander*. also V.

slattern   N. untidy or slovenly person. If you persist in wearing such sloppy clothes, people will call you a *slattern*.

sleazy   ADJ. flimsy; unsubstantial. This is a *sleazy* material; it will not wear well.

sleeper   N. something originally of little value or importance that in time becomes very valuable. Unnoticed by the critics at its publication, the eventual Pulitzer Prize winner was a classic *sleeper*.

sleight   N. dexterity. The magician amazed the audience with his *sleight* of hand.

slither   V. slip or slide. During the recent ice storm, many people *slithered* down this hill as they walked to the station.

■ **sloth**   N. laziness. Such *sloth* in a young person is deplorable; go to work!

■ **sloth**   N. slow-moving tree-dwelling mammal. Note how well the somewhat greenish coat of the *sloth* enables it to blend in with its arboreal surrounding. (secondary meaning)

slough   V. cast off. Each spring, the snake *sloughs* off its skin.

slovenly   ADJ. untidy; careless in work habits. Such *slovenly* work habits will never produce good products.

sluggard   N. lazy person. "You are a *sluggard,* a drone, a parasite," the angry father shouted at his lazy son.

sluggish   ADJ. slow; lazy; lethargic. After two nights without sleep, she felt *sluggish* and incapable of exertion.

sluice   N. artificial channel for directing or controlling the flow of water. This *sluice* gate is opened only in times of drought to provide water for irrigation.

smattering   N. slight knowledge. I don't know whether it is better to be ignorant of a subject or to have a mere *smattering* of information about it.

smirk   N. conceited smile. Wipe that *smirk* off your face! also V.

smolder   V. burn without flame; be liable to break out at any moment. The rags *smoldered* for hours before they burst into flame.

snicker   N. half-stifled laugh. The boy could not suppress a *snicker* when the teacher sat on the tack. also V.

snivel   V. run at the nose; snuffle; whine. Don't you come *sniveling* to me complaining about your big brother.

sobriety   N. soberness. The solemnity of the occasion filled us with *sobriety*.

sobriquet   N. nickname. Despite all his protests, his classmates continued to call him by that unflattering *sobriquet*.

sodden   ADJ. soaked; dull, as if from drink. He set his *sodden* overcoat near the radiator to dry.

sojourn   N. temporary stay. After his *sojourn* in Florida, he began to long for the colder climate of his native New England home.

solace   N. comfort in trouble. I hope you will find *solace* in the thought that all of us share your loss.

solecism   N. construction that is flagrantly incorrect grammatically. I must give this paper a failing mark because it contains many *solecisms*.

solicitous ADJ. worried; concerned. The employer was very *solicitous* about the health of her employees as replacements were difficult to get.

soliloquy N. talking to oneself. The *soliloquy* is a device used by the dramatist to reveal a character's innermost thoughts and emotions.

solstice N. point at which the sun is farthest from the equator. The winter *solstice* usually occurs on December 21.

solvent ADJ. able to pay all debts. By dint of very frugal living, he was finally able to become *solvent* and avoid bankruptcy proceedings.

somatic ADJ. pertaining to the body; physical. Why do you ignore the spiritual aspects and emphasize only the corporeal and the *somatic?*

Test

Word List 43   *Synonyms and Antonyms*

Each of the following questions consists of a word in capital letters, followed by five lettered words or phrases. Choose the lettered word or phrase which is most nearly similar or the opposite of the word in capital letters and write the letter of your choice on your answer paper.

631. SERAPH (A) messenger (B) harbinger (C) demon (D) official (E) potentate
632. SERRIED (A) worried (B) embittered (C) in close order (D) fallen (E) infantile
633. SERVILE (A) moral (B) puerile (C) futile (D) foul (E) haughty
634. SHODDY (A) superior (B) barefoot (C) sunlit (D) querulous (E) garrulous
635. SIMILITUDE (A) gratitude (B) magnitude (C) likeness (D) aptitude (E) kindness
636. SINISTER (A) unwed (B) ministerial (C) good (D) returned (E) splintered

637. SKITTISH (A) tractable (B) inquiring (C) dramatic (D) vain (E) frisky
638. SLEAZY (A) fanciful (B) creeping (C) substantial (D) uneasy (E) warranted
639. SLOTH (A) penitence (B) filth (C) futility (D) poverty (E) industry
640. SLOUGH (A) toughen (B) trap (C) violate (D) cast off (E) depart
641. SLOVENLY (A) half-baked (B) loved (C) inappropriate (D) tidy (E) rapidly
642. SOBRIETY (A) inebriety (B) aptitude (C) scholasticism (D) monotony (E) aversion
643. SOBRIQUET (A) ingenue (B) livelihood (C) bar (D) epitaph (E) nickname
644. SOLSTICE (A) equinox (B) sunrise (C) pigsty (D) interstices (E) iniquity
645. SOLVENT (A) enigmatic (B) bankrupt (C) fiducial (D) puzzling (E) gilded

Word List 44   somber-sublime

somber ADJ. gloomy; depressing. From the doctor's grim expression, I could tell he had *somber* news.

somnambulist N. sleepwalker. The most famous *somnambulist* in literature is Lady Macbeth; her monologue in the sleepwalking scene is one of the highlights of Shakespeare's play.

somnolent ADJ. half asleep. The heavy meal and the overheated room made us all *somnolent* and indifferent to the speaker.

sonorous ADJ. resonant. His *sonorous* voice resounded through the hall.

sophist N. teacher of philosophy; quibbler; employer of fallacious reasoning. You are using all the devices of a *sophist* in trying to prove your case; your argument is specious.

sophistication N. artificiality; unnaturalness; act of employing sophistry in reasoning. *Sophistication* is an acquired characteristic, found more frequently among city dwellers than among residents of rural areas.

■ **sophistry** N. seemingly plausible but fallacious reasoning. Instead of advancing valid arguments, he tried to overwhelm his audience with a flood of *sophistries*.

sophomoric ADJ. immature; shallow. Your *sophomoric* remarks are a sign of your youth and indicate that you have not given much thought to the problem.

■ **soporific** ADJ. sleep producer. I do not need a sedative when I listen to one of his *soporific* speeches. also N.

sordid ADJ. filthy; base; vile. The social worker was angered by the *sordid* housing provided for the homeless.

soupçon N. suggestion; hint; taste. A *soupçon* of garlic will improve this dish.

spangle N. small metallic piece sewn to clothing for ornamentation. The thousands of *spangles* on her dress sparkled in the glare of the stage lights.

spasmodic ADJ. fitful; periodic. The *spasmodic* coughing in the auditorium annoyed the performers.

spate N. sudden flood. I am worried about the possibility of a *spate* if the rains do not diminish soon.

spatial ADJ. relating to space. It is difficult to visualize the *spatial* extent of our universe.

spatula N. broad-bladed instrument used for spreading or mixing. The manufacturers of this frying pan recommend the use of a rubber *spatula* to avoid scratching the specially treated surface.

spawn V. lay eggs. Fish ladders had to be built in the dams to assist the salmon returning to *spawn* in their native streams. also N.

specious ADJ. seemingly reasonable but incorrect. Let us not be misled by such *specious* arguments.

spectral ADJ. ghostly. We were frightened by the *spectral* glow that filled the room.

spectrum N. colored band produced when beam of light passes through a prism. The visible portion of the *spectrum* includes red at one end and violet at the other.

sphinx-like ADJ. enigmatic; mysterious. The Mona Lisa's *sphinx-like* expression has puzzled art lovers for centuries.

splenetic ADJ. spiteful; irritable; peevish. People shunned him because of his *splenetic* temper. spleen, N.

spoliation N. pillaging; depredation. We regard this unwarranted attack on a neutral nation as an act of *spoliation* and we demand that it cease at once and that proper restitution be made.

spoonerism N. accidental transposition of sounds in successive words. When the radio announcer introduced the President as Hoobert Herver, he was guilty of a *spoonerism*.

sporadic ADJ. occurring irregularly. Although there are *sporadic* outbursts of shooting, we may report that the major rebellion has been defe' ᵈ

sportive ADJ. playful. Su   ᵣtive attitude is surprising in a person as serious as   usually are.

spry ADJ. vigorously active; nimble. She was eighty years old, yet still *spry* and alert.

spume N. froth; foam. The *spume* at the base of the waterfall extended for a quarter of a mile downriver.

■ **spurious** ADJ. false; counterfeit. She tried to pay the check with a *spurious* ten-dollar bill.

spurn V. reject; scorn. The heroine *spurned* the villain's advances.

squalid ADJ. dirty; neglected; poor. It is easy to see how crime can breed in such a *squalid* neighborhood.

squander V. waste. The prodigal son *squandered* the family estate.

staccato ADJ. played in an abrupt manner; marked by abrupt sharp sound. His *staccato* speech reminded one of the sound of a machine gun.

stagnant ADJ. motionless; stale; dull. The *stagnant* water was a breeding ground for disease. stagnate, V.

staid ADJ. sober; sedate. Her conduct during the funeral ceremony was *staid* and solemn.

stalemate N. deadlock. Negotiations between the union and the employers have reached a *stalemate;* neither side is willing to budge from previously stated positions.

stalwart ADJ. strong, brawny; steadfast. His consistent support of the party has proved that he is a *stalwart* and loyal member. also N.

stamina N. strength; staying power. I doubt that she has the *stamina* to run the full distance of the marathon race.

stanch V. check flow of blood. It is imperative that we *stanch* the gushing wound before we attend to the other injuries.

stanza N. division of a poem. Do you know the last *stanza* of "The Star-Spangled Banner"?

statute N. law. We have many *statutes* in our law books which should be repealed.

statutory ADJ. created by statute or legislative action. The judicial courts review and try *statutory* crimes.

steadfast ADJ. loyal. I am sure you will remain *steadfast* in your support of the cause.

stein N. beer mug. She thought of college as a place where one drank beer from *steins* and sang songs of lost lambs.

stellar ADJ. pertaining to the stars. He was the *stellar* attraction of the entire performance.

stentorian ADJ. extremely loud. The town crier had a *stentorian* voice.

stereotyped ADJ. fixed and unvarying representation. My chief objection to the book is that the characters are *stereotyped*.

stertorous ADJ. having a snoring sound. He could not sleep because of the *stertorous* breathing of his roommates.

stilted ADJ. bombastic; inflated. His *stilted* rhetoric did not impress the college audience; they were immune to bombastic utterances.

■ **stigma** N. token of disgrace; brand. I do not attach any *stigma* to the fact that you were accused of this crime; the fact that you were acquitted clears you completely.

stigmatize V. brand; mark as wicked. I do not want to *stigmatize* this young offender for life by sending her to prison.

stint N. supply; allotted amount; assigned portion of work. He performed his daily *stint* cheerfully and willingly. also, V.

stipend N. pay for services. There is a nominal *stipend* for this position.

stoic N. person who is indifferent to pleasure or pain. The doctor called her patient a *stoic* because he had borne the pain of the examination without whimpering. also ADJ.

stoke V. to feed plentifully. They swiftly *stoked* themselves, knowing they would not have another meal until they reached camp.

■ **stolidity** N. dullness; impassiveness. The earthquake shattered his usual *stolidity;* trembling, he crouched on the no longer stable ground.

stratum N. layer of earth's surface; layer of society. Unless we alleviate conditions in the lowest *stratum* of our society, we may expect grumbling and revolt.

■ **striated** ADJ. marked with parallel bands; grooved. The glacier left many *striated* rocks. striate, V.

stricture N. critical comments; severe and adverse criticism. His *strictures* on the author's style are prejudiced and unwarranted.

strident ADJ. loud and harsh. She scolded him in a *strident* voice.

stringent ADJ. binding; rigid. I think these regulations are too *stringent*.

■ **strut** N. pompous walk. His *strut* as he marched about the parade ground revealed him for what he was: a pompous buffoon. also V.

■ **strut** N. supporting bar. The engineer calculated that the *strut* supporting the rafter needed to be reinforced. (secondary meaning)

stultify V. cause to appear foolish or inconsistent. By changing your opinion at this time, you will *stultify* yourself.

stupor N. state of apathy; daze; lack of awareness. In his *stupor,* the addict was unaware of the events taking place around him.

stygian ADJ. gloomy; hellish; deathly. They descended into the *stygian,* half-lit sub-basement.

stymie V. present an obstacle; stump. The detective was *stymied* by the contradictory evidence in the robbery investigation. also N.

suave ADJ. smooth; bland. He is the kind of individual who is more easily impressed by a *suave* approach than by threats or bluster.

suavity N. urbanity; polish. He is particularly good in roles that require *suavity* and sophistication.

subaltern N. subordinate. The captain treated his *subalterns* as though they were children rather than commissioned officers.

subjective ADJ. occurring or taking place within the subject; unreal. Your analysis is highly *subjective;* you have permitted your emotions and your opinions to color your thinking.

subjugate V. conquer; bring under control. It is not our aim to *subjugate* our foe; we are interested only in establishing peaceful relations.

sublimate V. refine; purify. We must strive to *sublimate* these desires and emotions into worthwhile activities.

sublime ADJ. exalted; noble; uplifting. Mother Teresa has been honored for her *sublime* deeds.

Test

Word List 44   *Synonyms and Antonyms*

Each of the following questions consists of a word in capital letters, followed by five lettered words or phrases. Choose the lettered word or phrase which is most nearly similar or the opposite of the word in capital letters and write the letter of your choice on your answer paper.

646. SONOROUS (A) resonant (B) reassuring (C) repetitive (D) resinous (E) sisterly
647. SOPHOMORIC (A) unprecedented (B) mature (C) insipid (D) intellectual (E) illusionary
648. SOPORIFIC (A) dining (B) caustic (C) memorial (D) awakening (E) springing
649. SPASMODIC (A) intermittent (B) fit (C) inaccurate (D) violent (E) physical
650. SPORADIC (A) seedy (B) latent (C) vivid (D) inconsequential (E) occasional
651. SPORTIVE (A) competing (B) playful (C) indignant (D) foppish (E) fundamental
652. SPURIOUS (A) genuine (B) angry (C) mitigated (D) interrogated (E) glorious
653. SQUANDER (A) fortify (B) depart (C) roam (D) preserve (E) forfeit
654. STACCATO (A) musical (B) long (C) legato (D) sneezing (E) pounded
655. STAMINA (A) patience (B) pistils (C) weakness (D) fascination (E) patina
656. STEREOTYPED (A) original (B) antique (C) modeled (D) repetitious (E) continued
657. STILTED (A) candid (B) pompous (C) modish (D) acute (E) inarticulate
658. STRINGENT (A) binding (B) reserved (C) utilized (D) lambent (E) indigent
659. SUAVITY (A) ingeniousness (B) indifference (C) urbanity (D) constancy (E) paucity
660. SUBLIME (A) unconscious (B) respected (C) exalted (D) sneaky (E) replaced

Word List 45   subliminal-tantamount

subliminal ADJ. below the threshold. We may not be aware of the *subliminal* influences which affect our thinking.

sub rosa ADV. in strict confidence; privately. I heard of this *sub rosa* and I cannot tell you about it.

subsequent ADJ. following; later. In *subsequent* lessons, we shall take up more difficult problems.

subservient ADJ. behaving like a slave; servile; obsequious. He was proud and dignified; he refused to be *subservient* to anyone.

subside V. settle down; descend; grow quiet. The doctor assured us that the fever would eventually *subside*.

subsidiary ADJ. subordinate; secondary. This information may be used as *subsidiary* evidence but is not sufficient by itself to prove your argument. also N.

subsidy N. direct financial aid by government, etc. Without this *subsidy,* American ship operators would not be able to compete in world markets.

subsistence N. existence; means of support; livelihood. In these days of inflated prices, my salary provides a mere *subsistence*.

■ **substantiate** V. verify; support. I intend to *substantiate* my statement by producing witnesses.

■ **substantive** ADJ. essential; pertaining to the substance. Although the delegates were aware of the importance of the problem, they could not agree on the *substantive* issues.

subterfuge N. pretense; evasion. As soon as we realized that you had won our support by a *subterfuge,* we withdrew our endorsement of your candidacy.

subtlety N. nicety; cunning; guile; delicacy. The *subtlety* of his remarks was unnoticed by most of his audience. subtle, ADJ.

subversive ADJ. tending to overthrow or ruin. We must destroy such *subversive* publications.

succinct ADJ. brief; terse; compact. His remarks are always *succinct* and pointed.

succor N. aid; assistance; relief. We shall be ever grateful for the *succor* your country gave us when we were in need. also V.

succulent ADJ. juicy; full of richness. The citrus foods from Florida are more *succulent* to some people than those from California. also N.

succumb V. yield; give in; die. I *succumb* to temptation whenever it comes my way.

sudorific ADJ. pertaining to perspiration. Manufacturers of deodorants have made the public conscious of the need to avoid offending people with *sudorific* odors.

suffuse V. spread over. A blush *suffused* her cheeks when we teased her about her love affair.

sully V. tarnish; soil. He felt that it was beneath his dignity to *sully* his hands in such menial labor.

sultry ADJ. sweltering. He could not adjust himself to the *sultry* climate of the tropics.

summation N. act of finding the total; summary. In his *summation,* the lawyer emphasized the testimony given by the two witnesses.

sumptuary ADJ. limiting or regulating expenditures. While no *sumptuary* law has been enacted, the public will never tolerate the expenditure of so large a sum.

sumptuous ADJ. lavish; rich. I cannot recall when I have had such a *sumptuous* Thanksgiving feast.

sunder V. separate; part. Northern and southern Ireland are politically and religiously *sundered.*

sundry ADJ. various; several. My suspicions were aroused when I read *sundry* items in the newspapers about your behavior.

superannuated ADJ. retired on pension because of age. The *superannuated* man was indignant because he felt that he could still perform a good day's work.

supercilious ADJ. contemptuous; haughty. I resent your *supercilious* and arrogant attitude.

superficial ADJ. trivial; shallow. Since your report gave only a *superficial* analysis of the problem, I cannot give you more than a passing grade.

superfluity N. excess; overabundance. We have a definite lack of sincere workers and a *superfluity* of leaders.

superimpose V. place over something else. Your attempt to *superimpose* another agency in this field will merely increase the bureaucratic nature of our government.

supernal ADJ. heavenly; celestial. His tale of *supernal* beings was skeptically received.

supernumerary N. person or thing in excess of what is necessary; extra. His first appearance on the stage was as a *supernumerary* in a Shakespearean tragedy.

supersede V. cause to be set aside; replace. This regulation will *supersede* all previous rules.

supine ADJ. lying on back. The defeated pugilist lay *supine* on the canvas.

■ **supplant** V. replace; usurp. Ferdinand Marcos was *supplanted* by Corazon Aquino as president of the Philippines.

supple ADJ. flexible; pliant. The angler found a *supple* limb and used it as a fishing rod.

suppliant ADJ. entreating; beseeching. He could not resist the dog's *suppliant* whimpering, and he gave it some food. also N.

supplicate V. petition humbly; pray to grant a favor. We *supplicate* Your Majesty to grant him amnesty.

■ **supposition** N. hypothesis; surmise. I based my decision to confide in him on the *supposition* that he would be discreet. suppose, V.

supposititious ADJ. assumed; counterfeit; hypothetical. I find no similarity between your *supposititious* illustration and the problem we are facing.

suppurate V. create pus. The surgeon refused to lance the abscess until it *suppurated.*

surcease N. cessation. He begged the doctors to grant him *surcease* from his suffering.

surfeit V. cloy; overfeed. I am *surfeited* with the sentimentality of the average motion picture film.

surly ADJ. rude; cross. Because of his *surly* attitude, many people avoided his company.

surmise V. guess. I *surmise* that he will be late for this meeting. also N.

surmount V. overcome. He had to *surmount* many obstacles in order to succeed.

surpass V. exceed. Her SAT scores *surpassed* our expectations.

■ **surreptitious** ADJ. secret. News of their *surreptitious* meeting gradually leaked out.

surrogate N. substitute. For a fatherless child, a male teacher may become a father *surrogate.*

surveillance N. watching; guarding. The FBI kept the house under constant *surveillance* in the hope of capturing all the criminals at one time.

susceptible ADJ. impressionable; easily influenced; having little resistance, as to a disease. He was a very *susceptible* young man, and so his parents worried that he might fall into bad company.

sustenance N. means of support, food, nourishment. In the tropics, the natives find *sustenance* easy to obtain, due to all the fruit trees. sustain, V.

suture N. stitches sewn to hold the cut edges of a wound or incision; material used in sewing. We will remove the *sutures* as soon as the wound heals. also V.

swarthy ADJ. dark; dusky. Despite the stereotypes, not all Italians are *swarthy;* many are fair and blond.

swathe V. wrap around; bandage. When I visited him in the hospital, I found him *swathed* in bandages.

swelter V. be oppressed by heat. I am going to buy an air conditioning unit for my apartment as I do not intend to *swelter* through another hot and humid summer.

swindler N. cheat. She was gullible and trusting, an easy victim for the first *swindler* who came along.

sybarite N. lover of luxury. Rich people are not always *sybarites;* some of them have little taste for a life of luxury.

■ **sycophant** N. servile flatterer. The king enjoyed the servile compliments and attentions of the *sycophants* in his retinue. sycophantic, ADJ.

syllogism N. logical formula utilizing a major premise, a minor premise and a conclusion. There must be a fallacy in this *syllogism;* I cannot accept the conclusion.

sylvan ADJ. pertaining to the woods; rustic. His paintings of nymphs in *sylvan* backgrounds were criticized as overly sentimental.

symmetry N. arrangement of parts so that balance is obtained; congruity. The addition of a second tower will give this edifice the *symmetry* which it now lacks.

synchronous ADJ. similarly timed; simultaneous with. We have many examples of scientists in different parts of the world who have made *synchronous* discoveries.

synthesis N. combining parts into a whole. Now that we have succeeded in isolating this drug, our next problem is to plan its *synthesis* in the laboratory. synthesize, V.

synthetic ADJ. artificial; resulting from synthesis. During the twentieth century, many *synthetic* products have replaced the natural products. also N.

■ **tacit** ADJ. understood; not put into words. We have a *tacit* agreement based on only a handshake.

■ **taciturn** ADJ. habitually silent; talking little. New Englanders are reputedly *taciturn* people.

tactile ADJ. pertaining to the organs or sense of touch. His callused hands had lost their *tactile* sensitivity.

tainted ADJ. contaminated; corrupt. Health authorities are always trying to prevent the sale and use of *tainted* food.

talisman N. charm. She wore the *talisman* to ward off evil.

talon N. claw of bird. The falconer wore a leather gauntlet to avoid being clawed by the hawk's *talons.*

tantalize V. tease; torture with disappointment. Tom loved to *tantalize* his younger brother with candy; he knew the boy was forbidden to have it.

tantamount ADJ. equal. Your ignoring their pathetic condition is *tantamount* to murder.

Test

Word List 45   *Synonyms and Antonyms*

Each of the following questions consists of a word in capital letters, followed by five lettered words or phrases. Choose the lettered word or phrase which is most nearly similar or the opposite of the word in capital letters and write the letter of your choice on your answer paper.

661. SUBLIMINAL (A) radiant (B) indifferent (C) obvious (D) domestic (E) horizontal
662. SUPERANNUATED (A) senile (B) experienced (C) retired (D) attenuated (E) accepted
663. SUPERCILIOUS (A) haughty (B) highbrow (C) angry (D) inane (E) philosophic
664. SUPERFICIAL (A) abnormal (B) portentous (C) shallow (D) angry (E) tiny
665. SUPERNUMERARY (A) miser (B) extra (C) associate (D) astronomer (E) inferiority
666. SUPPLIANT (A) intolerant (B) swallowing (C) beseeching (D) finishing (E) flexible
667. SURFEIT (A) belittle (B) cloy (C) drop (D) estimate (E) claim
668. SURREPTITIOUS (A) secret (B) snakelike (C) nightly (D) abstract (E) furnished
669. SUTURE (A) stitch (B) reflection (C) knitting (D) tailor (E) past
670. SWATHED (A) wrapped around (B) waved (C) gambled (D) rapt (E) mystified
671. SYCOPHANTIC (A) quiet (B) recording (C) servilely flattering (D) frolicsome (E) eagerly awaiting
672. SYNTHETIC (A) simplified (B) doubled (C) tuneful (D) artificial (E) fiscal
673. TACIT (A) spoken (B) allowed (C) neural (D) impertinent (E) unwanted
674. TALISMAN (A) chief (B) juror (C) medicine man (D) amulet (E) gift
675. TANTALIZE (A) tease (B) wax (C) warrant (D) authorize (E) total

Word List 46   tantrum-tome

tantrum N. fit of petulance; caprice. The child learned that he could have almost anything if he went into *tantrums.*

taper N. candle. He lit the *taper* on the windowsill.

tarantula N. venomous spider. We need an antitoxin to counteract the bite of the *tarantula*.

tarn N. small mountain lake. This mountainous area is famous for its picturesque *tarns* and larger lakes.

tarry V. delay; dawdle. We can't *tarry* if we want to get to the airport on time.

tatterdemalion N. ragged fellow. Do you expect an army of *tatterdemalions* and beggars to put up a real fight?

taurine ADJ. like a bull. The bull charged into the ring, a mighty specimen of *taurine* power.

taut ADJ. tight; ready. The captain maintained that he ran a *taut* ship.

tautological ADJ. needlessly repetitious. In the sentence "It was visible to the eye," the phrase "to the eye" is *tautological*.

tautology N. unnecessary repetition; pleonasm. "Joyful happiness" is an illustration of *tautology*.

tawdry ADJ. cheap and gaudy. He won a few *tawdry* trinkets in Coney Island.

tedium N. boredom; weariness. We hope this radio will help overcome the *tedium* of your stay in the hospital.

teleology N. belief that a final purpose or design exists for the presence of individual beings or of the universe itself. The questions propounded by *teleology* have long been debated in religious and scientific circles.

temerarious ADJ. rash. Mountain climbing at this time of year is *temerarious* and foolhardy.

temerity N. boldness; rashness. Do you have the *temerity* to argue with me?

temper V. restrain; blend; toughen. His hard times in the army only served to *temper* his strength.

temperate ADJ. restrained; self-controlled. Noted for his *temperate* appetite, he seldom gained weight.

tempo N. speed of music. I find the conductor's *tempo* too slow for such a brilliant piece of music.

temporal ADJ. not lasting forever; limited by time; secular. At one time in our history, *temporal* rulers assumed that they had been given their thrones by divine right.

temporize V. avoid committing oneself; gain time. I cannot permit you to *temporize* any longer; I must have a definite answer today.

tenacious ADJ. holding fast. I had to struggle to break his *tenacious* hold on my arm.

tenacity N. firmness; persistency; adhesiveness. It is extremely difficult to overcome the *tenacity* of a habit such as smoking.

tendentious ADJ. having an aim; biased; designed to further a cause. The editorials in this periodical are *tendentious* rather than truth-seeking.

tenebrous ADJ. dark; gloomy. We were frightened as we entered the *tenebrous* passageways of the cave.

tenet N. doctrine; dogma. The agnostic did not accept the *tenets* of their faith.

tensile ADJ. capable of being stretched. Mountain climbers must know the *tensile* strength of their ropes.

tentative ADJ. provisional; experimental. Your *tentative* plans sound plausible; let me know when the final details are worked out.

tenuous ADJ. thin; rare; slim. The allegiance of our allies is held by rather *tenuous* ties.

tenure N. holding of an office; time during which such an office is held. He has permanent *tenure* in this position and cannot be fired.

tepid ADJ. lukewarm. During the summer, I like to take a *tepid* bath, not a hot one.

tergiversation N. evasion; fickleness. I cannot understand your *tergiversation;* I was certain that you were devoted to our cause.

termagant N. shrew; scolding, brawling woman. *The Taming of the Shrew* is one of many stories of the methods used in changing a *termagant* into a demure lady.

terminate V. to bring to an end. When his contract was *terminated* unexpectedly, he desperately needed a new job.

terminology N. terms used in a science or art. The special *terminology* developed by some authorities in the field has done more to confuse the layman than to enlighten him.

terminus N. last stop of railroad. After we reached the railroad *terminus*, we continued our journey into the wilderness on saddle horses.

terrapin N. American marsh tortoise. The flesh of the diamondback *terrapin* is considered by many epicures to be a delicacy.

terrestrial ADJ. on the earth. We have been able to explore the *terrestrial* regions much more thoroughly than the aquatic or celestial regions.

terse ADJ. concise; abrupt; pithy. I admire his *terse* style of writing; he comes directly to the point.

tertiary ADJ. third. He is so thorough that he analyzes *tertiary* causes where other writers are content with primary and secondary reasons.

tesselated ADJ. inlaid; mosaic. I recall seeing a table with a *tesselated* top of bits of stone and glass in a very interesting pattern.

testator N. maker of a will. The attorney called in his secretary and his partner to witness the signature of the *testator*.

testy ADJ. irritable; short-tempered. My advice is to avoid discussing this problem with him today as he is rather *testy* and may shout at you.

tether V. tie with a rope. Before we went to sleep, we *tethered* the horses to prevent their wandering off during the night.

thaumaturgist N. miracle worker; magician. I would have to be a *thaumaturgist* and not a mere doctor to find a remedy for this disease.

theocracy N. government of a community by religious leaders. Some Pilgrims favored the establishment of a *theocracy* in New England.

theosophy N. wisdom in divine things. *Theosophy* seeks to embrace the essential truth in all religions.

therapeutic ADJ. curative. These springs are famous for their *therapeutic* and healing qualities.

thermal ADJ. pertaining to heat. The natives discovered that the hot springs gave excellent *thermal* baths and began to develop their community as a health resort. also N.

thespian ADJ. pertaining to drama. Her success in the school play convinced her she was destined for a *thespian* career. also N.

thrall N. slave; bondage. The captured soldier was held in *thrall* by the conquering army.

threnody N. song of lamentation; dirge. When he died, many poets wrote *threnodies* about his passing.

thrifty ADJ. careful about money; economical. A *thrifty* shopper compares prices before making major purchases.

throes N. violent anguish. The *throes* of despair can be as devastating as the spasms accompanying physical pain.

throng N. crowd. *Throngs* of shoppers jammed the aisles. also V.

throttle V. strangle. The criminal tried to *throttle* the old man with his bare hands.

thwart V. baffle; frustrate. He felt that everyone was trying to *thwart* his plans and prevent his success.

thyme N. aromatic plant used for seasoning. The addition of a little *thyme* will enhance the flavor of the clam chowder.

timbre N. quality of a musical tone produced by a musical instrument. We identify the instrument producing a musical sound by its *timbre*.

timidity N. lack of self-confidence or courage. If you are to succeed as a salesman, you must first lose your *timidity* and fear of failure.

timorous ADJ. fearful; demonstrating fear. His *timorous* manner betrayed the fear he felt at the moment.

tipple V. drink (alcoholic beverages) frequently. He found that his most enjoyable evenings occurred when he *tippled* with his friends at the local pub.

tirade N. extended scolding; denunciation. Long before he had finished his *tirade,* we were sufficiently aware of the seriousness of our misconduct.

titanic ADJ. gigantic. *Titanic* waves beat against the shore during the hurricane.

tithe N. tax of one-tenth. Because he was an agnostic, he refused to pay his *tithes* to the clergy. also V.

titillate V. tickle. I am here not to *titillate* my audience but to enlighten it.

titter N. nervous laugh. Her aunt's constant *titter* nearly drove her mad. also V.

titular ADJ. nominal holding of title without obligations. Although he was the *titular* head of the company, the real decisions were made by his general manager.

toady V. flatter for favors. I hope you see through those who are *toadying* you for special favors. also N.

tocsin N. alarm bell. Awakened by the sound of the *tocsin,* we rushed to our positions to await the attack.

toga N. Roman outer robe. Marc Antony pointed to the slashes in Caesar's *toga*.

tome N. large volume. He spent much time in the libraries poring over ancient *tomes*.

Test

Word List 46   *Synonyms*

Each of the questions below consists of a word in capital letters, followed by five lettered words or phrases. Choose the lettered word or phrase that is most nearly similar in meaning to the word in capital letters and write the letter of your choice on your answer paper.

676. TATTERDEMALION (A) confetti (B) crudity
     (C) stubborn individual (D) ragged fellow
     (E) artist
677. TAUTOLOGY (A) memory (B) repetition
     (C) tension (D) simile (E) lack of logic
678. TAWDRY (A) orderly (B) meretricious
     (C) reclaimed (D) filtered (E) proper
679. TEMERITY (A) timidity (B) resourcefulness
     (C) boldness (D) tremulousness (E) caution
680. TEMPORAL (A) priestly (B) scholarly (C) secular
     (D) sleepy (E) sporadic
681. TENACIOUS (A) fast running (B) intentional
     (C) obnoxious (D) holding fast (E) collecting

682. TENACITY (A) splendor (B) perseverance
     (C) tendency (D) ingratitude (E) decimation
683. TENDENTIOUS (A) biased (B) likely (C) absurd
     (D) festive (E) literary
684. TENTATIVE (A) prevalent (B) portable
     (C) mocking (D) wry (E) experimental
685. TENUOUS (A) vital (B) thin (C) careful
     (D) dangerous (E) necessary
686. TEPID (A) boiling (B) lukewarm (C) freezing
     (D) gaseous (E) cold
687. TERGIVERSATION (A) fickleness (B) conversation
     (C) altercation (D) swollen state (E) acquiescence
688. TESSELATED (A) striped (B) made of mosaics
     (C) piebald (D) uniform (E) trimmed
689. THAUMATURGIST (A) producer (B) dreamer
     (C) philosopher (D) thief (E) miracle worker
690. TITILLATE (A) hasten (B) fasten (C) stimulate
     (D) incorporate (E) enlarge .

Word List 47   tonsure-ukase

tonsure N. shaving of the head, especially by person entering religious orders. His *tonsure,* even more than his monastic garb, indicated that he was a member of the religious order.

topography N. physical features of a region. Before the generals gave the order to attack, they ordered a complete study of the *topography* of the region.

torpid ADJ. dormant; dull; lethargic. The *torpid* bear had just come out of his cave after his long hibernation.

■ **torpor** N. lethargy; sluggishness; dormancy. Nothing seemed to arouse him from his *torpor:* he had wholly surrendered himself to lethargy.

■ **torque** N. twisting force; force producing rotation. With her wrench she applied sufficient *torque* to the nut to loosen it.

torso N. trunk of statue with head and limbs missing; human trunk. This *torso,* found in the ruins of Pompeii, is now on exhibition in the museum in Naples.

tortilla N. flat cake made of cornmeal, etc. As we traveled through Mexico, we became more and more accustomed to the use of *tortillas* instead of bread.

tortuous ADJ. winding; full of curves. Because this road is so *tortuous,* it is unwise to go faster than twenty miles an hour on it.

touchstone N. stone used to test the fineness of gold alloys; criterion. What *touchstone* can be used to measure the character of a person?

touchy ADJ. sensitive; irascible. Do not discuss this phase of the problem as he is very *touchy* about it.

toxic ADJ. poisonous. We must seek an antidote for whatever *toxic* substance he has eaten. toxicity, N.

tract N. pamphlet; a region of indefinite size. The King granted William Penn a *tract* of land in the New World.

■ **tractable** ADJ. docile. You will find the children in this school very *tractable* and willing to learn.

traduce V. expose to slander. His opponents tried to *traduce* the candidate's reputation by spreading rumors about his past.

trajectory N. path taken by a projectile. The police tried to locate the spot from which the assassin had fired the fatal shot by tracing the *trajectory* of the bullet.

tranquillity N. calmness; peace. After the commotion and excitement of the city, I appreciate the *tranquillity* of these fields and forests.

transcend V. exceed; surpass. This accomplishment *transcends* all our previous efforts. transcendental, ADJ.

transcribe V. copy. When you *transcribe* your notes, please send a copy to Mr. Smith and keep the original for our files. transcription, N.

transgression N. violation of a law; sin. Forgive us our *transgressions;* we know not what we do.

transient ADJ. fleeting; quickly passing away; staying for a short time. This hotel caters to a *transient* trade because it is near a busy highway.

transition N. going from one state of action to another. During the period of *transition* from oil heat to gas heat, the furnace will have to be shut off.

translucent ADJ. partly transparent. We could not recognize the people in the next room because of the *translucent* curtains which separated us.

transmute V. change; convert to something different. He was unable to *transmute* his dreams into actualities.

transparent ADJ. permitting light to pass through freely; easily detected. Your scheme is so *transparent* that it will fool no one.

transpire V. exhale; become known; happen. In spite of all our efforts to keep the meeting a secret, news of our conclusions *transpired.*

trappings N. outward decorations; ornaments. He loved the *trappings* of success: the limousines, the stock options, the company jet.

traumatic ADJ. pertaining to an injury caused by violence. In his nightmares, he kept on recalling the *traumatic* experience of being wounded in battle.

travail N. painful labor. How long do you think a man can endure such *travail* and degradation without rebelling?

traverse V. go through or across. When you *traverse* this field, be careful of the bull.

travesty N. comical parody; treatment aimed at making something appear ridiculous. The ridiculous decision the jury has arrived at is a *travesty* of justice.

treacle N. syrup obtained in refining sugar. *Treacle* is more highly refined than molasses.

treatise N. article treating a subject systematically and thoroughly. He is preparing a *treatise* on the Elizabethan playwrights for his graduate degree.

trek N. travel; journey. The tribe made their *trek* further north that summer in search of game. also V.

tremor N. trembling; slight quiver. She had a nervous *tremor* in her right hand.

tremulous ADJ. trembling; wavering. She was *tremulous* more from excitement than from fear.

■ **trenchant** ADJ. cutting; keen. I am afraid of his *trenchant* wit for it is so often sarcastic.

trencherman N. good eater. He is not finicky about his food; he is a *trencherman.*

trepidation N. fear; trembling agitation. We must face the enemy without *trepidation* if we are to win this battle.

tribulation N. distress; suffering. After all the trials and *tribulations* we have gone through, we need this rest.

tribunal N. court of justice. The decision of the *tribunal* was final and the prisoner was sentenced to death.

tribute N. tax levied by a ruler; mark of respect. The colonists refused to pay *tribute* to a foreign despot.

trident N. three-pronged spear. Neptune is usually depicted as rising from the sea, carrying his *trident* on his shoulder.

trilogy N. group of three works. Romain Rolland's novel *Jean Christophe* was first published as a *trilogy.*

triolet N. eight-line stanza with rhyme scheme *a b aaa b a b.* The *triolet* is a difficult verse pattern because it utilizes only two rhymes in its eight lines.

trite ADJ. hackneyed; commonplace. The *trite* and predictable situations in many television programs alienate many viewers.

trivia N. trifles; unimportant matters. Too many magazines ignore newsworthy subjects and feature *trivia.*

troglodyte N. cave dweller. We know that the first men in this area were *troglodytes* by the artifacts we have discovered in the caves.

trope N. figure of speech. The poem abounds in *tropes* and alliterative expressions.

troth N. pledge of good faith especially in betrothal. He gave her his *troth* and vowed he would cherish her always.

truckle V. curry favor; act in an obsequious way. If you *truckle* to the lord, you will be regarded as a sycophant; if you do not, you will be considered arrogant.

■ **truculence** N. aggressiveness; ferocity. Tynan's reviews were noted for their caustic attacks and general tone of *truculence.* truculent, ADJ.

truism N. self-evident truth. Many a *truism* is well expressed in a proverb.

trumpery N. objects that are showy, valueless, deceptive. All this finery is mere *trumpery.*

truncate V. cut the top off. The top of a cone which has been *truncated* in a plane parallel to its base is a circle.

tryst N. meeting. The lovers kept their *tryst* even though they realized their danger.

tumbrel N. a farm tipcart. The *tumbrels* became the vehicles which transported the condemned people from the prisons to the guillotine.

tumid ADJ. swollen; pompous; bombastic. I especially dislike his *tumid* style; I prefer writing which is less swollen and bombastic.

tumult N. commotion; riot; noise. She could not make herself heard over the *tumult* of the mob.

tundra N. rolling, treeless plain in Siberia and arctic North America. Despite the cold, many geologists are trying to discover valuable mineral deposits in the *tundra.*

■ **turbid** ADJ. muddy; having the sediment disturbed. The water was *turbid* after the children had waded through it.

turbulence N. state of violent agitation. We were frightened by the *turbulence* of the ocean during the storm.

tureen N. deep table dish for holding soup. The waiters brought the soup to the tables in silver *tureens.*

turgid ADJ. swollen; distended. The *turgid* river threatened to overflow the levees and flood the countryside.

turmoil N. confusion; strife. Conscious he had sinned, he was in a state of spiritual *turmoil.*

turnkey N. jailer. By bribing the *turnkey,* the prisoner arranged to have better food brought to him in his cell.

turpitude N. depravity. A visitor may be denied admittance to this country if she has been guilty of moral *turpitude.*

tutelage N. guardianship; training. Under the *tutelage* of such masters of the instrument, she made rapid progress as a virtuoso.

tutelary ADJ. protective; pertaining to a guardianship. I am acting in my *tutelary* capacity when I refuse to grant you permission to leave the campus.

tycoon N. wealthy leader. John D. Rockefeller was a prominent *tycoon.*

tyranny N. oppression; cruel government. Frederick Douglass fought against the *tyranny* of slavery throughout his entire life.

tyro N. beginner; novice. For a mere *tyro,* you have produced some marvelous results.

■ **ubiquitous** ADJ. being everywhere; omnipresent. You must be *ubiquitous* for I meet you wherever I go.

ukase N. official decree, usually Russian. It was easy to flaunt the *ukases* issued from St. Petersburg; there was no one to enforce them.

Test

Word List 47   *Antonyms*

Each of the questions below consists of a word in capital letters, followed by five lettered words or phrases. Choose the lettered word or phrase that is most nearly opposite in meaning to the word in capital letters and write the letter of your choice on your answer paper.

691. TRACTABLE (A) unmanageable (B) irreligious (C) mortal (D) incapable (E) unreal

692. TRADUCE (A) exhume (B) increase (C) purchase (D) extol (E) donate

693. TRANQUILLITY (A) lack of sleep (B) lack of calm (C) emptiness (D) renewal (E) closeness

694. TRANSIENT (A) carried (B) close (C) permanent (D) removed (E) certain

695. TREMULOUS (A) steady (B) obese (C) young (D) healthy (E) unkempt

696. TRENCHERMAN (A) finicky eater (B) infantryman (C) angler (D) imbiber (E) pacifist

697. TREPIDATION (A) slowness (B) amputation (C) fearlessness (D) adroitness (E) death

698. TRITE (A) correct (B) original (C) distinguished (D) premature (E) certain

699. TRUCULENT (A) juicy (B) overflowing (C) peaceful (D) determined (E) false

700. TRUMPERY (A) silence (B) defeat (C) percussion (D) murder (E) valuables
701. TURBID (A) clear (B) improbable (C) invariable (D) honest (E) turgid
702. TURBULENCE (A) reaction (B) approach (C) impropriety (D) calm (E) hostility
703. TURGID (A) rancid (B) shrunken (C) cool (D) explosive (E) painful
704. TURPITUDE (A) amplitude (B) heat (C) wealth (D) virtue (E) quiet
705. TYRO (A) infant (B) rubber (C) personnel (D) idiot (E) expert

Word List 48 ulterior-vehement

ulterior ADJ. situated beyond; unstated. You must have an *ulterior* motive for your behavior, since there is no obvious reason for it.

ultimate ADJ. final; not susceptible to further analysis. Scientists are searching for the *ultimate* truths.

ultimatum N. last demand; warning. Since they have ignored our *ultimatum,* our only recourse is to declare war.

umbrage N. resentment; anger; sense of injury or insult. She took *umbrage* at his remarks and stormed away in a huff.

unanimity N. complete agreement. We were surprised by the *unanimity* with which our proposals were accepted by the different groups.

unassuaged ADJ. unsatisfied; not soothed. Her anger is *unassuaged* by your apology.

unassuming ADJ. modest. He is so *unassuming* that some people fail to realize how great a man he really is.

unbridled ADJ. violent. She had a sudden fit of *unbridled* rage.

uncanny ADJ. strange; mysterious. You have the *uncanny* knack of reading my innermost thoughts.

unconscionable ADJ. unscrupulous; excessive. She found the loan shark's demands *unconscionable* and impossible to meet.

uncouth ADJ. outlandish; clumsy; boorish. Most biographers portray Lincoln as an *uncouth* and ungainly young man.

unction N. the act of anointing with oil. The anointing with oil of a person near death is called extreme *unction.*

unctuous ADJ. oily; bland; insincerely suave. Uriah Heep disguised his nefarious actions by *unctuous* protestations of his " 'umility."

undermine V. weaken; sap. The recent corruption scandals have *undermined* many people's faith in the city government.

undulate V. move with a wavelike motion. The flag *undulated* in the breeze.

unearth V. dig up. When they *unearthed* the city, the archeologists found many relics of an ancient civilization.

unearthly ADJ. not earthly; weird. There is an *unearthly* atmosphere in her work which amazes the casual observer.

unequivocal ADJ. plain; obvious. My answer to your proposal is an *unequivocal* and absolute "No."

unerringly ADV. infallibly. My teacher *unerringly* pounced on the one typographical error in my essay.

unfaltering ADJ. steadfast. She approached the guillotine with *unfaltering* steps.

unfeigned ADJ. genuine; real. She turned so pale that I am sure her surprise was *unfeigned.*

unfledged ADJ. immature. It is hard for an *unfledged* writer to find a sympathetic publisher.

ungainly ADJ. awkward. He is an *ungainly* young man; he trips over everything.

unguent N. ointment. Apply this *unguent* to the sore muscles before retiring.

uniformity N. sameness; monotony. After a while, the *uniformity* of TV situation comedies becomes boring.

unilateral ADJ. one-sided. This legislation is *unilateral* since it binds only one party in the controversy.

unimpeachable ADJ. blameless and exemplary. Her conduct in office was *unimpeachable* and her record is spotless.

uninhibited ADJ. unrepressed. The congregation was shocked by her *uninhibited* laughter during the sermon.

unique ADJ. without an equal; single in kind. You have the *unique* distinction of being the first student whom I have had to fail in this course.

unison N. unity of pitch; complete accord. The choir sang in *unison.*

unkempt ADJ. disheveled; with uncared-for appearance. The beggar was dirty and *unkempt.*

unmitigated ADJ. harsh; severe; not lightened. I sympathize with you in your *unmitigated* sorrow.

unobtrusive ADJ. inconspicuous; not blatant. The secret service agents in charge of protecting the President tried to be as *unobtrusive* as possible.

unprecedented ADJ. novel; unparalleled. Margaret Mitchell's book *Gone with the Wind* was an *unprecedented* success.

unruly ADJ. disobedient; lawless. The only way to curb this *unruly* mob is to use tear gas.

unsavory ADJ. distasteful; morally offensive. People with *unsavory* reputations should not be allowed to work with young children.

unscathed ADJ. unharmed. They prayed he would come back from the war *unscathed.*

unseemly ADJ. unbecoming; indecent. Your levity is *unseemly* at this time of mourning.

unsullied ADJ. untarnished. I am happy that my reputation is *unsullied.*

untenable ADJ. unsupportable. I find your theory *untenable* and must reject it.

untoward ADJ. unfortunate; annoying. *Untoward* circumstances prevent me from being with you on this festive occasion.

unwitting ADJ. unintentional; not knowing. She was the *unwitting* tool of the swindlers.

unwonted ADJ. unaccustomed. He hesitated to assume the *unwonted* role of master of ceremonies at the dinner.

upbraid V. scold; reproach. I must *upbraid* him for his unruly behavior.

upshot N. outcome. The *upshot* of the rematch was that the former champion proved that he still possessed all the skills of his youth.

urbane ADJ. suave; refined; elegant. The courtier was *urbane* and sophisticated. urbanity, N.

urchin N. mischievous child (usually a boy). Get out! This store is no place for grubby *urchins!*

ursine ADJ. bearlike; pertaining to a bear. Because of its *ursine* appearance, the great panda has been identified with the bears; actually, it is closely related to the raccoon.

■ usurp V. seize power; supplant. The revolution ended when the victorious rebel leader *usurped* the throne. usurpation, N.

usury N. lending money at illegal rates of interest. The loan shark was found guilty of *usury.*

utopia N. imaginary land with perfect social and political system. Shangri-la was the name of James Hilton's Tibetan *utopia.*

uxorious ADJ. excessively devoted to one's wife. His friends laughed at him because he was so *uxorious* and submissive to his wife's desires.

■ vacillation N. fluctuation; wavering. His *vacillation* when confronted with a problem annoyed all of us who had to wait until he made his decision. vacillate, V.

■ vacuous ADJ. empty; inane. The *vacuous* remarks of the politician annoyed the audience, who had hoped to hear more than empty platitudes.

vagabond N. wanderer; tramp. In summer, college students wander the roads of Europe like carefree *vagabonds.* also ADJ.

vagary N. caprice; whim. She followed every *vagary* of fashion.

vagrant ADJ. stray; random. He tried to study, but could not collect his *vagrant* thoughts. also N.

vainglorious ADJ. boastful; excessively conceited. She was a *vainglorious* and arrogant individual.

valance N. short drapery hanging above window frame. The windows were curtainless; only the tops were covered with *valances.*

valedictory ADJ. pertaining to farewell. I found the *valedictory* address too long; leave-taking should be brief.

validate V. confirm; ratify. I will not publish my findings until I *validate* my results.

valor N. bravery. He received the Medal of Honor for his *valor* in battle.

vampire N. ghostly being that sucks the blood of the living. Children were afraid to go to sleep at night because of the many legends of *vampires.*

vanguard N. forerunners; advance forces. We are the *vanguard* of a tremendous army that is following us.

vantage N. position giving an advantage. They fired upon the enemy from behind trees, walls and any other point of *vantage* they could find.

vapid ADJ. insipid; inane. She delivered an uninspired and *vapid* address.

variegated ADJ. many-colored. He will not like this solid blue necktie as he is addicted to *variegated* clothing.

vassal N. in feudalism, one who held land of a superior lord. The lord demanded that his *vassals* contribute more to his military campaign.

vaunted ADJ. boasted; bragged; highly publicized. This much *vaunted* project proved a disappointment when it collapsed.

veer V. change in direction. After what seemed an eternity, the wind *veered* to the east and the storm abated.

vegetate V. live in a monotonous way. I do not understand how you can *vegetate* in this quiet village after the adventurous life you have led.

vehement ADJ. impetuous; with marked vigor. He spoke with *vehement* eloquence in defense of his client. vehemence, N.

Test

Word List 48   *Antonyms*

Each of the questions below consists of a word in capital letters, followed by five lettered words or phrases. Choose the lettered word or phrase that is most nearly opposite in meaning to the word in capital letters and write the letter of your choice on your answer paper.

706. UNEARTH (A) conceal (B) gnaw (C) clean (D) fling (E) react

707. UNFEIGNED (A) pretended (B) fashionable (C) wary (D) switched (E) colonial

708. UNGAINLY (A) ignorant (B) graceful (C) detailed (D) dancing (E) pedantic

709. UNIMPEACHABLE (A) fruitful (B) rampaging (C) faulty (D) pensive (E) thorough

710. UNKEMPT (A) bombed (B) washed (C) neat (D) showy (E) tawdry
711. UNRULY (A) chatting (B) obedient (C) definite (D) lined (E) curious
712. UNSEEMLY (A) effortless (B) proper (C) conducive (D) pointed (E) informative
713. UNSULLIED (A) tarnished (B) countless (C) soggy (D) papered (E) homicidal
714. UNTENABLE (A) supportable (B) tender (C) sheepish (D) tremulous (E) adequate
715. UNWITTING (A) clever (B) intense (C) sensitive (D) freezing (E) intentional

716. VACILLATION (A) remorse (B) relief (C) respect (D) steadfastness (E) inoculation
717. VALEDICTORY (A) sad (B) collegiate (C) derivative (D) salutatory (E) promising
718. VALOR (A) admonition (B) injustice (C) cowardice (D) generosity (E) repression
719. VANGUARD (A) regiment (B) rear (C) echelon (D) protection (E) loyalty
720. VAUNTED (A) unvanquished (B) fell (C) belittled (D) exacting (E) believed

Word List 49   vellum-vogue

vellum N. parchment. Bound in *vellum* and embossed in gold, this book is a beautiful example of the binder's craft.

velocity N. speed. The train went by at considerable *velocity*.

vendetta N. blood feud. The rival mobs engaged in a bitter *vendetta*.

vendor N. seller. The fruit *vendor* sold her wares from a stall on the sidewalk.

venal ADJ. capable of being bribed. The *venal* policeman accepted the bribe offered him by the speeding motorist whom he had stopped.

veneer N. thin layer; cover. Casual acquaintances were deceived by his *veneer* of sophistication and failed to recognize his fundamental shallowness.

venerable ADJ. deserving high respect. We do not mean to be disrespectful when we refuse to follow the advice of our *venerable* leader.

■ **venerate** V. revere. In China, the people *venerate* their ancestors.

venial ADJ. forgivable; trivial. We may regard a hungry man's stealing as a *venial* crime.

venison N. the meat of a deer. The hunters dined on *venison*.

vent N. a small opening; outlet. The wine did not flow because the air *vent* in the barrel was clogged.

vent V. express; utter. He *vented* his wrath on his class.

ventral V. abdominal. We shall now examine the *ventral* plates of this serpent, not the dorsal side.

ventriloquist N. someone who can make his or her voice seem to come from another person or thing. This *ventriloquist* does an act in which she has a conversation with a wooden dummy.

venturous ADJ. daring. The five *venturous* young men decided to look for a new approach to the mountain top.

venturesome ADJ. bold. A group of *venturesome* women were the first to scale Mt. Annapurna.

venue N. location. The attorney asked for a change of *venue*; he thought his client would do better if the trial were held in a less conservative county.

veracious ADJ. truthful. I can recommend him for this position because I have always found him *veracious* and reliable. veracity, N.

verbalize V. to put into words. I know you don't like to talk about these things, but please try to *verbalize* your feelings.

verbatim ADV. word for word. He repeated the message *verbatim*. also ADJ.

verbiage N. pompous array of words. After we had waded through all the *verbiage*, we discovered that the writer had said very little.

verbose ADJ. wordy. This article is too *verbose*; we must edit it.

verdant ADJ. green; fresh. The *verdant* meadows in the spring are always an inspiring sight.

verge N. border; edge. Madame Curie knew she was on the *verge* of discovering the secrets of radioactive elements. also V.

verdigris N. a green coating on copper which has been exposed to the weather. Despite all attempts to protect the statue from the elements, it became coated with *verdigris*.

verisimilitude N. appearance of truth; likelihood. Critics praised her for the *verisimilitude* of her performance as Lady Macbeth. She was completely believable.

verity N. truth; reality. The four *verities* were revealed to Buddha during his long meditation.

vermicular ADJ. pertaining to a worm. The *vermicular* burrowing in the soil helps to aerate it.

vernal ADJ. pertaining to spring. We may expect *vernal* showers all during the month of April.

vernacular N. living language; natural style. Cut out those old-fashioned thee's and thou's and write in the *vernacular*. also ADJ.

versatile ADJ. having many talents; capable of working in many fields. He was a *versatile* athlete; at college he had earned varsity letters in baseball, football, and track.

vertex N. summit. Let us drop a perpendicular line from the *vertex* of the triangle to the base.

vertiginous ADJ. giddy; causing dizziness. I do not like the rides in the amusement park because they have a *vertiginous* effect on me.

vertigo N. dizziness. We test potential plane pilots for susceptibility to spells of *vertigo*.

verve N. enthusiasm; liveliness. She approached her studies with such *verve* that it was impossible for her to do poorly.

vestige N. trace; remains. We discovered *vestiges* of early Indian life in the cave.

vex N. annoy; distress. Please try not to *vex* your mother; she is doing the best she can.

viable ADJ. capable of maintaining life. The infant, though prematurely born, is *viable* and has a good chance to survive.

viand N. food. There was a variety of *viands* at the feast.

vicarious ADJ. acting as a substitute; done by a deputy. Many people get a *vicarious* thrill at the movies by imagining they are the characters on the screen.

vicissitude N. change of fortune. I am accustomed to life's *vicissitudes*, having experienced poverty and wealth, sickness and health, and failure and success.

victuals N. food. I am very happy to be able to provide you with these *victuals;* I know you are hungry.

vie V. contend; compete. When we *vie* with each other for his approval, we are merely weakening ourselves and strengthening him.

vigilance N. watchfulness. Eternal *vigilance* is the price of liberty.

vignette N. picture; short literary sketch. *The New Yorker* published her latest *vignette*.

vilify V. slander. She is a liar and is always trying to *vilify* my reputation. vilification, N.

vindicate V. clear of charges. I hope to *vindicate* my client and return him to society as a free man.

vindictive ADJ. revengeful. She was very *vindictive* and never forgave an injury.

viper N. poisonous snake. The habitat of the horned *viper*, a particularly venomous snake, is in sandy regions like the Sahara or the Sinai peninsula.

virago N. shrew. Rip Van Winkle's wife was a veritable *virago*.

virile ADJ. manly. I do not accept the premise that a man is *virile* only when he is belligerent.

virtual ADJ. in essence; for practical purposes. She is a *virtual* financial wizard when it comes to money matters.

virtuoso N. highly skilled artist. Heifetz is a violin *virtuoso*.

virulent ADJ. extremely poisonous. The virus is highly *virulent* and has made many of us ill for days.

virus N. disease communicator. The doctors are looking for a specific medicine to control this *virus*.

visage N. face; appearance. The stern *visage* of the judge indicated that she had decided to impose a severe penalty.

visceral ADJ. felt in one's inner organs. She disliked the *visceral* sensations she had whenever she rode the roller coaster.

viscid ADJ. sticky; adhesive. Glue is a *viscid* liquid.

■ **viscous** ADJ. sticky; gluey. Melted tar is a *viscous* substance.

■ **visionary** ADJ. produced by imagination; fanciful; mystical. She was given to *visionary* schemes which never materialized. also N.

vitiate V. spoil the effect of; make inoperative. Fraud will *vitiate* the contract.

vitreous ADJ. pertaining to or resembling glass. Although this plastic has many *vitreous* qualities such as transparency, it is unbreakable.

vitriolic ADJ. corrosive; sarcastic. Such *vitriolic* criticism is uncalled for.

vituperative ADJ. abusive; scolding. He became more *vituperative* as he realized that we were not going to grant him his wish.

vivacious ADJ. animated; gay. She had always been *vivacious* and sparkling.

vivisection N. act of dissecting living animals. The Society for the Prevention of Cruelty to Animals opposed *vivisection* and deplored the practice of using animals in scientific experiments.

vixen N. female fox; ill-tempered woman. Aware that she was right once again, he lost his temper and called her a shrew and a *vixen*.

vizier N. powerful Muslim government official. The *vizier* decreed that all persons in the city were to be summoned to the ceremony.

vociferous ADJ. clamorous; noisy. The crowd grew *vociferous* in its anger and threatened to take the law into its own hands.

vogue N. popular fashion. Jeans became the *vogue* on many college campuses.

Test

Word List 49   *Synonyms and Antonyms*

Each of the following questions consists of a word in capital letters, followed by five lettered words or phrases. Choose the lettered word or phrase which is most nearly similar or the opposite of the word in capital letters and write the letter of your choice on your answer paper.

721. VENAL (A) springlike (B) honest (C) angry
  (D) indifferent (E) going

722. VENERATE (A) revere (B) age (C) reject
  (D) reverberate (E) degenerate

723. VENIAL (A) unforgivable (B) unforgettable
  (C) unmistaken (D) fearful (E) fragrant

724. VERACIOUS (A) worried (B) slight (C) alert
  (D) truthful (E) instrumental

725. VERDANT (A) poetic (B) green (C) red
  (D) autumnal (E) frequent

726. VERITY (A) sanctity (B) reverence (C) falsehood (D) rarity (E) household

727. VESTIGE (A) trek (B) trail (C) trace (D) trial (E) tract

728. VIABLE (A) moribund (B) salable (C) useful (D) foolish (E) inadequate

729. VIAND (A) wand (B) gown (C) food (D) orchestra (E) frock

730. VICARIOUS (A) substitutional (B) aggressive (C) sporadic (D) reverent (E) internal

731. VIGILANCE (A) bivouac (B) guide (C) watchfulness (D) mob rule (E) posse

732. VILIFY (A) erect (B) eulogize (C) better (D) magnify (E) horrify

733. VINDICTIVE (A) revengeful (B) fearful (C) divided (D) literal (E) convincing

734. VIRULENT (A) sensuous (B) malignant (C) masculine (D) conforming (E) approaching

735. VISAGE (A) doubt (B) personality (C) hermitage (D) face (E) armor

---

Word List 50   volatile-zephyr

volatile ADJ. evaporating rapidly; lighthearted; mercurial. Ethyl chloride is a very *volatile* liquid.

volition N. act of making a conscious choice. She selected this dress of her own *volition*.

voluble ADJ. fluent; glib. She was a *voluble* speaker, always ready to talk.

voluminous ADJ. bulky; large. Despite her family burdens, she kept up a *voluminous* correspondence with her friends.

voluptuous ADJ. gratifying the senses. The nobility during the Renaissance led *voluptuous* lives.

voracious ADJ. ravenous. The wolf is a *voracious* animal, its hunger never satisfied.

votary N. follower of a cult. She was a *votary* of every new movement in literature and art.

vouchsafe V. grant condescendingly; guarantee. I can safely *vouchsafe* you a fair return on your investment.

vulnerable ADJ. susceptible to wounds. Achilles was *vulnerable* only in his heel.

vulpine ADJ. like a fox; crafty. She disliked his sly ways, but granted him a certain *vulpine* intelligence.

vying V. contending. Why are we *vying* with each other for her favors? vie, V.

waft V. moved gently by wind or waves. Daydreaming, he gazed at the leaves which *wafted* past his window.

waggish ADJ. mischievous; humorous; tricky. He was a prankster who, unfortunately, often overlooked the damage he could cause with his *waggish* tricks.

waif N. homeless child or animal. Although he already had eight cats, he could not resist adopting yet another feline *waif*.

waive V. give up temporarily; yield. I will *waive* my rights in this matter in order to expedite our reaching a proper decision.

wallow V. roll in; indulge in; become helpless. The hippopotamus loves to *wallow* in the mud.

wan ADJ. having a pale or sickly color; pallid. Suckling asked, ''Why so pale and *wan*, fond lover?''

wane V. grow gradually smaller. From now until December 21, the winter equinox, the hours of daylight will *wane*.

wangle V. wiggle out; fake. She tried to *wangle* an invitation to the party.

wanton ADJ. unruly; unchaste; excessive. His *wanton*, drunken ways cost him many friends.

warble V. sing; babble. Every morning the birds *warbled* outside her window. also N.

warrant V. justify; authorize. Before the judge issues the injunction, you must convince her this action is *warranted*.

warranty N. guarantee; assurance by seller. The purchaser of this automobile is protected by the manufacturer's *warranty* that he will replace any defective part for five years or 50,000 miles.

warren N. tunnels in which rabbits live; crowded conditions in which people live. The tenement was a veritable *warren*, packed with people too poor to live elsewhere.

wary ADJ. very cautious. The spies grew *wary* as they approached the sentry.

wastrel N. profligate. He was denounced as a *wastrel* who had dissipated his inheritance.

wax V. increase; grow. With proper handling, his fortunes *waxed* and he became rich.

waylay V. ambush; lie in wait. They agreed to *waylay* their victim as he passed through the dark alley going home.

wean V. accustom a baby not to nurse; give up a cherished activity. He decided he would *wean* himself away from eating junk food and stick to fruits and vegetables.

weather V. endure the effects of weather or other forces. He *weathered* the changes in his personal life with difficulty, as he had no one in whom to confide.

welt N. mark from a beating or whipping. The evidence of child abuse was very clear; Jennifer's small body was covered with *welts* and bruises.

■ **welter** N. turmoil; bewildering jumble. The existing *welter* of overlapping federal and state programs cries out for immediate reform.

welter V. wallow. At the height of the battle, the casualties were so numerous that the victims *weltered* in their blood while waiting for medical attention.

wheedle V. cajole; coax; deceive by flattery. She knows she can *wheedle* almost anything she wants from her father.

whelp N. young wolf, dog, tiger, etc. This collie *whelp* won't do for breeding, but he'd make a fine pet.

whet V. sharpen; stimulate. The odors from the kitchen are *whetting* my appetite; I will be ravenous by the time the meal is served.

whimsical ADJ. capricious; fanciful; quaint. *Peter Pan* is a *whimsical* play.

whinny V. neigh like a horse. When he laughed through his nose, it sounded as if he *whinnied.*

whit N. smallest speck. There is not a *whit* of intelligence or understanding in your observations.

whorl N. ring of leaves around stem; ring. Identification by fingerprints is based on the difference in shape and number of the *whorls* on the fingers.

wily ADJ. cunning; artful. She is as *wily* as a fox in avoiding trouble.

wince V. shrink back; flinch. The screech of the chalk on the blackboard made her *wince.*

windfall N. fallen fruit; unexpected lucky event. This huge tax refund is quite a *windfall.*

winnow V. sift; separate good parts from bad. This test will *winnow* out the students who study from those who don't bother.

winsome ADJ. agreeable; gracious; engaging. By her *winsome* manner, she made herself liked by everyone who met her.

wither V. shrivel; decay. Cut flowers are beautiful for a day, but all too soon they *wither.*

witless ADJ. foolish; idiotic. Such *witless* and fatuous statements will create the impression that you are an ignorant individual.

witticism N. witty saying; facetious remark. What you regard as *witticisms* are often offensive to sensitive people.

wizardry N. sorcery; magic. Merlin amazed the knights with his *wizardry.*

wizened ADJ. withered; shriveled. The *wizened* old man in the home for the aged was still active and energetic.

wont N. custom; habitual procedure. As was his *wont,* he jogged two miles every morning before going to work.

worldly ADJ. engrossed in matters of this earth; not spiritual. You must leave your *worldly* goods behind you when you go to meet your Maker.

wraith N. ghost; phantom of a living person. It must be a horrible experience to see a ghost; it is even more horrible to see the *wraith* of a person we know to be alive.

wrangle V. quarrel; obtain through arguing; herd cattle. They *wrangled* over their inheritance.

wrath N. anger; fury. She turned to him, full of *wrath,* and said, "What makes you think I'll accept lower pay for this job than you get?"

wreak V. inflict. I am afraid he will *wreak* his vengeance on the innocent as well as the guilty.

wrench V. pull; strain; twist. She *wrenched* free of her attacker and landed a powerful kick to his kneecap.

wrest V. pull away; take by violence. With only ten seconds left to play, our team *wrested* victory from their grasp.

writhe V. squirm, twist. He was *writhing* in pain, desperate for the drug his body required.

wry ADJ. twisted; with a humorous twist. We enjoy Dorothy Parker's verse for its *wry* wit.

xenophobia N. fear or hatred of foreigners. When the refugee arrived in America, he was unprepared for the *xenophobia* he found there.

yen N. longing; urge. She had a *yen* to get away and live on her own for a while.

yeoman N. man owning small estate; middle-class farmer. It was not the aristocrat but the *yeoman* who determined the nation's policies.

yoke V. join together, unite. I don't wish to be *yoked* to him in marriage, as if we were cattle pulling a plow.

yokel N. country bumpkin. At school, his classmates regarded him as a *yokel* and laughed at his rustic mannerisms.

yore N. time past. He dreamed of the elegant homes of *yore,* but gave no thought to their inelegant plumbing.

zany ADJ. crazy; comic. I can watch the Marx brothers' *zany* antics for hours.

■ zealot N. fanatic; person who shows excessive zeal. It is good to have a few *zealots* in our group for their enthusiasm is contagious.

zenith N. point directly overhead in the sky; summit. When the sun was at its *zenith,* the glare was not as strong as at sunrise and sunset.

zephyr N. gentle breeze; west wind. When these *zephyrs* blow, it is good to be in an open boat under a full sail.

Test

Word List 50   *Synonyms*

Each of the questions below consists of a word in capital letters, followed by five lettered words or phrases. Choose the lettered word or phrase that is most nearly similar in meaning to the word in capital letters and write the letter of your choice on your answer paper.

736. VOLUBLE (A) worthwhile (B) serious (C) terminal (D) loquacious (E) circular

737. VORACIOUS (A) ravenous (B) spacious (C) truthful (D) pacific (E) tenacious

738. VOUCHSAFE (A) borrow (B) grant (C) punish (D) desire (E) qualify

739. WAIF (A) soldier (B) urchin (C) surrender (D) breeze (E) spouse

740. WANTON (A) needy (B) passive (C) rumored (D) oriental (E) unchaste

741. WARRANTY (A) threat (B) guarantee
(C) order for arrest (D) issue (E) fund

742. WASTREL (A) refuse (B) spendthrift (C) mortal
(D) tolerance (E) song

743. WAYLAY (A) ambush (B) journey (C) rest
(D) roadmap (E) song

744. WELKIN (A) bell (B) greeting (C) cloudy
(D) pressure (E) sky

745. WHINNY (A) complain (B) hurry (C) request
(D) neigh (E) gallop

746. WINDFALL (A) unexpected gain (B) widespread
destruction (C) calm (D) autumn (E) wait

747. WINSOME (A) victorious (B) gracious
(C) married (D) permanent (E) pained

748. WIZENED (A) magical (B) clever (C) shriveled
(D) swift (E) active

749. YEOMAN (A) masses (B) middle-class farmer
(C) proletarian (D) indigent person (E) man of
rank

750. ZEALOT (A) beginner (B) patron (C) fanatic
(D) murderer (E) leper

Answer Key

Test—Word List 1

1. E	6. E	11. A
2. A	7. B	12. E
3. C	8. E	13. A
4. D	9. A	14. D
5. B	10. A	15. C

Test—Word List 2

16. E	21. A	26. B
17. B	22. A	27. D
18. A	23. B	28. B
19. D	24. B	29. C
20. A	25. B	30. D

Test—Word List 3

31. C	36. E	41. B
32. C	37. C	42. E
33. D	38. B	43. E
34. D	39. E	44. C
35. A	40. D	45. A

Test—Word List 4

46. A	51. C	56. E
47. A	52. A	57. C
48. B	53. C	58. D
49. D	54. B	59. D
50. B	55. D	60. C

Test—Word List 5

61. E	66. A	71. D
62. D	67. C	72. C
63. B	68. C	73. C
64. C	69. B	74. B
65. C	70. C	75. D

Test—Word List 6

76. D	81. A	86. C
77. B	82. B	87. A
78. D	83. B	88. E
79. A	84. E	89. E
80. E	85. C	90. C

Test—Word List 7

91. B	96. B	101. D
92. B	97. A	102. B
93. B	98. D	103. A
94. D	99. B	104. A
95. B	100. C	105. B

Test—Word List 8

106. D	111. B	116. B✓
107. E	112. A	117. D
108. A	113. D	118. A
109. C	114. C	119. C ✓
110. E	115. D ✓	120. B✓

Test—Word List 9

121. D	126. E	131. A
122. E	127. A	132. D
123. E	128. D	133. C
124. C	129. B	134. B
125. C	130. E	135. A

Test—Word List 10

136. E	141. B	146. E
137. B	142. E	147. E
138. D	143. D	148. C
139. C	144. D	149. A
140. A	145. D	150. D

Test—Word List 11

151. B	156. C	161. B
152. B	157. C	162. D
153. A	158. E	163. D
154. A	159. E	164. A
155. A	160. B	165. B

Test—Word List 12

166. C	171. C	176. B
167. B	172. B	177. B
168. C	173. A	178. A
169. D	174. A	179. C
170. D	175. B	180. A

Test—Word List 13

181. A	186. A	191. C
182. E	187. B	192. B
183. D	188. C	193. E
184. D	189. B	194. A
185. A	190. C	195. A

Test—Word List 14

196. D	201. C	206. B
197. E	202. C	207. D
198. B	203. C	208. C
199. A	204. B	209. E
200. C	205. B	210. D

Test—Word List 15

211. C	216. C	221. B
212. A	217. A	222. E
213. D	218. A	223. A
214. D	219. C	224. A
215. D	220. D	225. B

Test—Word List 16

226. D	231. B	236. D
227. A	232. C	237. C
228. C	233. D	238. A
229. E	234. C	239. B
230. E	235. E	240. A

Test—Word List 17

241. A	246. C	251. D
242. A	247. A	252. A
243. B	248. A	253. E
244. E	249. C	254. B
245. E	250. D	255. B

Test—Word List 18

256. A	261. D	266. A
257. A	262. D	267. A
258. C	263. E	268. C
259. D	264. C	269. B
260. A	265. B	270. E

Test—Word List 19

271. A	276. A	281. A
272. D	277. A	282. D
273. E	278. D	283. C
274. C	279. C	284. B
275. E	280. B	285. C

Test—Word List 20

286. A	291. A	296. E
287. B	292. A	297. D
288. B	293. D	298. A
289. B	294. C	299. A
290. D	295. C	300. B

Test—Word List 21

301. B	306. E	311. E
302. B	307. C	312. E
303. C	308. B	313. B
304. C	309. D	314. D
305. C	310. D	315. C

Test—Word List 22

316. D	321. E	326. C
317. A	322. A	327. C
318. A	323. B	328. A
319. D	324. C	329. B
320. A	325. E	330. D

Test—Word List 23

331. B	336. A	341. A
332. A	337. D	342. A
333. B	338. C	343. E
334. E	339. C	344. B
335. C	340. D	345. A

Test—Word List 24

346. C	351. D	356. B
347. B	352. A	357. C
348. C	353. A	358. A
349. A	354. A	359. B
350. B	355. B	360. D

Test—Word List 25

361. A	366. B	371. E
362. E	367. B	372. B
363. B	368. C	373. D
364. D	369. D	374. C
365. E	370. A	375. A

Test—Word List 26

376. C	381. B	386. B
377. A	382. A	387. E
378. B	383. C	388. E
379. B	384. C	389. E
380. B	385. C	390. D

Test—Word List 27

391. A	396. E	401. B
392. D	397. E	402. B
393. B	398. C	403. A
394. D	399. A	404. C
395. B	400. D	405. B

Test—Word List 28

406. B	411. B	416. B
407. A	412. E	417. A
408. E	413. D	418. D
409. E	414. E	419. D
410. C	415. C	420. A

Test—Word List 29

421. B	426. D	431. A
422. A	427. E	432. C
423. B	428. B	433. B
424. B	429. A	434. C
425. C	430. E	435. A

Test—Word List 30

436. A	441. A	446. E
437. A	442. B	447. B
438. B	443. D	448. C
439. D	444. B	449. E
440. C	445. A	450. B

Test—Word List 31

451. B	456. A	461. E
452. E	457. C	462. C
453. C	458. C	463. A
454. C	459. A	464. B
455. B	460. B	465. A

Test—Word List 32

466. B	471. D	476. D
467. C	472. C	477. B
468. C	473. B	478. A
469. A	474. A	479. C
470. C	475. B	480. A

Test—Word List 33

481. C	486. A	491. E
482. B	487. B	492. C
483. E	488. C	493. E
484. D	489. D	494. B
485. B	490. B	495. A

Test—Word List 34

496. D	501. B	506. D
497. A	502. B	507. D
498. D	503. A	508. C
499. A	504. E	509. C
500. E	505. C	510. A

Test—Word List 35

511. A	516. C	521. E
512. C	517. B	522. A
513. C	518. D	523. C
514. C	519. C	524. E
515. B	520. A	525. E

Test—Word List 36

526. A	531. E	536. B
527. D	532. B	537. D
528. A	533. C	538. D
529. B	534. C	539. D
530. E	535. A	540. D

Test—Word List 37

541. C	546. A	551. A
542. C	547. A	552. C
543. D	548. C	553. E
544. E	549. B	554. B
545. C	550. A	555. A

Test—Word List 38

556. E	561. E	566. A
557. D	562. E	567. D
558. C	563. B	568. C
559. B	564. A	569. D
560. B	565. E	570. C

Test—Word List 39

571. B	576. C	581. C
572. B	577. D	582. B
573. E	578. A	583. A
574. A	579. C	584. D
575. A	580. E	585. A

Test—Word List 40

586. E	591. C	596. D
587. B	592. A	597. D
588. D	593. B	598. B
589. C	594. A	599. D
590. A	595. D	600. E

Test—Word List 41

601. E	606. B	611. C
602. B	607. B	612. D
603. A	608. A	613. B
604. D	609. D	614. A
605. A	610. B	615. A

Test—Word List 42

616. C	621. D	626. B
617. A	622. E	627. D
618. B	623. A	628. A
619. C	624. D	629. D
620. D	625. C	630. E

Test—Word List 43

631. C	636. C	641. D
632. C	637. E	642. A
633. E	638. C	643. E
634. A	639. E	644. A
635. C	640. D	645. B

Test—Word List 44

646. A	651. B	656. A
647. B	652. A	657. B
648. D	653. D	658. A
649. A	654. C	659. C
650. E	655. C	660. C

Test—Word List 45

661. C	666. C	671. C
662. C	667. B	672. D
663. A	668. A	673. A
664. C	669. A	674. D
665. B	670. A	675. A

Test—Word List 46

676. D	681. D	686. B
677. B	682. B	687. A
678. B	683. A	688. B
679. C	684. E	689. E
680. C	685. B	690. C

Test—Word List 47

691. A	696. A	701. A
692. D	697. C	702. D
693. B	698. B	703. B
694. C	699. C	704. D
695. A	700. E	705. E

Test—Word List 48

706. A	711. B	716. D
707. A	712. B	717. D
708. B	713. A	718. C
709. C	714. A	719. B
710. C	715. E	720. C

Test—Word List 49

721. B	726. C	731. C
722. A	727. C	732. B
723. A	728. A	733. A
724. D	729. C	734. B
725. B	730. A	735. D

Test—Word List 50

736. D	741. B	746. A
737. A	742. B	747. B
738. B	743. A	748. C
739. B	744. E	749. B
740. E	745. D	750. C

Basic Word Parts

Words are made up of word parts: prefixes, suffixes and roots. A knowledge of these word parts and their meanings can help you determine the meanings of unfamiliar words.

Common Prefixes

Prefixes are syllables that precede the root or stem and change or refine its meaning.

Prefix	Meaning	Illustration
ab, abs	from, away from	*abduct* lead away, kidnap *abjure* renounce *abject* degraded
ad, ac, af, ag, an, ap, ar, as, at	to, forward	*adit* entrance *adjure* request earnestly *admit* allow entrance *accord* agreement, harmony *affliction* distress *aggregation* collection *annexation* add to *apparition* ghost *arraignment* indictment *assumption* arrogance, the taking for granted *attendance* presence, the persons present
ambi	both	*ambidextrous* skilled with both hands *ambiguous* of double meaning *ambivalent* having two conflicting emotions
an, a	without	*anarchy* lack of government *anemia* lack of blood *amoral* without moral sense
ante	before	*antecedent* preceding event or word *antediluvian* ancient (before the flood) *ante-nuptial* before the wedding
anti	against, opposite	*antipathy* hatred *antiseptic* against infection *antithetical* exactly opposite

Prefix	Meaning	Illustration
arch	chief, first	*archetype* original *archbishop* chief bishop *archeology* study of first or ancient times
be	over, thoroughly	*bedaub* smear over *befuddle* confuse thoroughly *beguile* deceive, charm thoroughly
bi	two	*bicameral* composed of two houses (Congress) *biennial* every two years *bicycle* two-wheeled vehicle
cata	down	*catastrophe* disaster *cataract* waterfall *catapult* hurl (throw down)
circum	around	*circumnavigate* sail around (the globe) *circumspect* cautious (looking around) *circumscribe* limit (place a circle around)
com, co, col, con, cor	with, together	*combine* merge with *commerce* trade with *communicate* correspond with *coeditor* joint editor *collateral* subordinate, connected *conference* meeting *corroborate* confirm
contra, contro	against	*contravene* conflict with *controversy* dispute
de	down, away	*debase* lower in value *decadence* deterioration *decant* pour off
demi	partly, half	*demigod* partly divine being
di	two	*dichotomy* division into two parts *dilemma* choice between two bad alternatives
dia	across	*diagonal* across a figure *diameter* distance across a circle *diagram* outline drawing
dis, dif	not, apart	*discord* lack of harmony *differ* disagree (carry apart) *disparity* condition of inequality; difference
dys	faulty, bad	*dyslexia* faulty ability to read *dyspepsia* indigestion
ex, e	out	*expel* drive out *extirpate* root out *eject* throw out

Prefix	Meaning	Illustration
extra, extro	beyond, outside	*extracurricular* beyond the curriculum *extraterritorial* beyond a nation's bounds *extrovert* person interested chiefly in external objects and actions
hyper	above; excessively	*hyperbole* exaggeration *hyperventilate* breathe at an excessive rate
hypo	beneath; lower	*hypoglycemia* low blood sugar
in, il, im, ir	not	*inefficient* not efficient *inarticulate* not clear or distinct *illegible* not readable *impeccable* not capable of sinning; flawless *irrevocable* not able to be called back
in, il, im, ir	in, on, upon	*invite* call in *illustration* something that makes clear *impression* effect upon mind or feelings *irradiate* shine upon
inter	between, among	*intervene* come between *international* between nations *interjection* a statement thrown in
intra, intro	within	*intramural* within a school *introvert* person who turns within himself
macro	large, long	*macrobiotic* tending to prolong life *macrocosm* the great world (the entire universe)
mega	great, million	*megalomania* delusions of grandeur *megaton* explosive force of a million tons of TNT
meta	involving change	*metamorphosis* change of form
micro	small	*microcosm* miniature universe *microbe* minute organism *microscopic* extremely small
mis	bad, improper	*misdemeanor* minor crime; bad conduct *mischance* unfortunate accident *misnomer* wrong name
mis	hatred	*misanthrope* person who hates mankind *misogynist* woman-hater
mono	one	*monarchy* government by one ruler *monotheism* belief in one god
multi	many	*multifarious* having many parts *multitudinous* numerous
neo	new	*neologism* newly coined word *neophyte* beginner; novice

Prefix	Meaning	Illustration
non	not	*noncommittal* undecided *nonentity* person of no importance
ob, oc, of, op	against	*obloquy* infamy; disgrace *obtrude* push into prominence *occlude* close; block out *offend* insult *opponent* someone who struggles against; foe
olig	few	*oligarchy* government by a few
pan	all, every	*panacea* cure-all *panorama* unobstructed view in all directions
para	beyond, related	*parallel* similar *paraphrase* restate; translate
per	through, completely	*permeable* allowing passage through *pervade* spread throughout
peri	around, near	*perimeter* outer boundary *periphery* edge *periphrastic* stated in a roundabout way
poly	many	*polygamist* person with several spouses *polyglot* speaking several languages
post	after	*postpone* delay *posterity* generations that follow *posthumous* after death
pre	before	*preamble* introductory statement *prefix* word part placed before a root/stem *premonition* forewarning
prim	first	*primordial* existing at the dawn of time *primogeniture* state of being the first born
pro	forward, in favor of	*propulsive* driving forward *proponent* supporter
proto	first	*prototype* first of its kind
pseudo	false	*pseudonym* pen name
re	again, back	*reiterate* repeat *reimburse* pay back
retro	backward	*retrospect* looking back *retroactive* effective as of a past date
se	away, aside	*secede* withdraw *seclude* shut away *seduce* lead astray

Prefix	Meaning	Illustration
semi	half, partly	*semiannual* every six months *semiconscious* partly conscious
sub, suc, suf, sug, sup, sus	under, less	*subway* underground road *subjugate* bring under control *succumb* yield; cease to resist *suffuse* spread through *suggest* hint *suppress* put down by force *suspend* delay
super, sur	over, above	*supernatural* above natural things *supervise* oversee *surtax* additional tax
syn, sym, syl, sys	with, together	*synchronize* time together *synthesize* combine together *sympathize* pity; identify with *syllogism* explanation of how ideas relate *system* network
tele	far	*telemetry* measurement from a distance *telegraphic* communicated over a distance
trans	across	*transport* carry across *transpose* reverse, move across
ultra	beyond, excessive	*ultramodern* excessively modern *ultracritical* exceedingly critical
un	not	*unfeigned* not pretended; real *unkempt* not combed; disheveled *unwitting* not knowing; unintentional
under	below	*undergird* strengthen underneath *underling* someone inferior
uni	one	*unison* oneness of pitch; complete accord *unicycle* one-wheeled vehicle
vice	in place of	*vicarious* acting as a substitute *viceroy* governor acting in place of a king
with	away, against	*withhold* hold back; keep *withstand* stand up against; resist

Common Roots and Stems

Roots are basic words which have been carried over into English. *Stems* are varia- tions of roots brought about by changes in declension or conjugation.

Root or Stem	Meaning	Illustration
ac, acr	sharp	*acrimonious* bitter; caustic *acerbity* bitterness of temper *acidulate* to make somewhat acid or sour
aev, ev	age, era	*primeval* of the first age *coeval* of the same age or era *medieval* or *mediaeval* of the middle ages
ag, act	do	*act* deed *agent* doer
agog	leader	*demagogue* false leader of people *pedagogue* teacher (leader of children)
agri, agrari	field	*agrarian* one who works in the field *agriculture* cultivation of fields *peregrination* wandering (through fields)
ali	another	*alias* assumed (another) name *alienate* estrange (turn away from another)
alt	high	*altitude* height *altimeter* instrument for measuring height
alter	other	*altruistic* unselfish, considering others *alter ego* a second self
am	love	*amorous* loving, especially sexually *amity* friendship *amicable* friendly
anim	mind, soul	*animadvert* cast criticism upon *unanimous* of one mind *magnanimity* greatness of mind or spirit
ann, enn	year	*annuity* yearly remittance *biennial* every two years *perennial* present all year; persisting for several years
anthrop	man	*anthropology* study of man *misanthrope* hater of mankind *philanthropy* love of mankind; charity
apt	fit	*aptitude* skill *adapt* make suitable or fit

Root or Stem	Meaning	Illustration
aqua	water	*aqueduct* passageway for conducting water *aquatic* living in water *aqua fortis* nitric acid (strong water)
arch	ruler, first	*archaeology* study of antiquities (study of first things) *monarch* sole ruler *anarchy* lack of government
aster	star	*astronomy* study of the stars *asterisk* star-like type character (∗) *disaster* catastrophe (contrary star)
aud, audit	hear	*audible* able to be heard *auditorium* place where people may be heard *audience* hearers
auto	self	*autocracy* rule by one person (self) *automobile* vehicle that moves by itself *autobiography* story of one's own life
belli	war	*bellicose* inclined to fight *belligerent* inclined to wage war *rebellious* resisting authority
ben, bon	good	*benefactor* one who does good deeds *benevolence* charity (wishing good) *bonus* something extra above regular pay
biblio	book	*bibliography* list of books *bibliophile* lover of books *Bible* The Book
bio	life	*biography* writing about a person's life *biology* study of living things *biochemist* student of the chemistry of living things
breve	short	*brevity* briefness *abbreviate* shorten *breviloquent* marked by brevity of speech
cad, cas	to fall	*decadent* deteriorating *cadence* intonation, musical movement *cascade* waterfall
cap, capt, cept, cip	to take	*capture* seize *participate* take part *precept* wise saying (originally a command)
capit, capt	head	*decapitate* remove (cut off) someone's head *captain* chief
carn	flesh	*carnivorous* flesh-eating *carnage* destruction of life *carnal* fleshly

Root or Stem	Meaning	Illustration
ced, cess	to yield, to go	*recede* go back, withdraw *antecedent* that which goes before *process* go forward
celer	swift	*celerity* swiftness *decelerate* reduce swiftness *accelerate* increase swiftness
cent	one hundred	*century* one hundred years *centennial* hundredth anniversary *centipede* many-footed, wingless animal
chron	time	*chronology* timetable of events *anachronism* a thing out of time sequence *chronicle* register events in order of time
cid, cis	to cut, to kill	*incision* a cut (surgical) *homicide* killing of a man *fratricide* killing of a brother
cit, citat	to call, to start	*incite* stir up, start up *excite* stir up *recitation* a recalling (or repeating) aloud
civi	citizen	*civilization* society of citizens, culture *civilian* member of community *civil* courteous
clam, clamat	to cry out	*clamorous* loud *declamation* speech *acclamation* shouted approval
claud, claus, clos, clud	to close	*claustrophobia* fear of close places *enclose* close in *conclude* finish
cognosc, cognit	to learn	*agnostic* lacking knowledge, skeptical *incognito* traveling under assumed name *cognition* knowledge
compl	to fill	*complete* filled out *complement* that which completes something *comply* fulfill
cord	heart	*accord* agreement (from the heart) *cordial* friendly *discord* lack of harmony
corpor	body	*incorporate* organize into a body *corporeal* pertaining to the body, fleshly *corpse* dead body
cred, credit	to believe	*incredulous* not believing, skeptical *credulity* gullibility *credence* belief

Root or Stem	Meaning	Illustration
cur	to care	*curator* person who has the care of something *sinecure* position without responsibility *secure* safe
curr, curs	to run	*excursion* journey *cursory* brief *precursor* forerunner
da, dat	to give	*data* facts, statistics *mandate* command *date* given time
deb, debit	to owe	*debt* something owed *indebtedness* debt *debenture* bond
dem	people	*democracy* rule of the people *demagogue* (false) leader of the people *epidemic* widespread (among the people)
derm	skin	*epidermis* skin *pachyderm* thick-skinned quadruped *dermatology* study of skin and its disorders
di, diurn	day	*diary* a daily record of activities, feelings, etc. *diurnal* pertaining to daytime
dic, dict	to say	*abdicate* renounce *diction* speech *verdict* statement of jury
doc, doct	to teach	*docile* obedient; easily taught *document* something that provides evidence *doctor* learned person (originally, teacher)
domin	to rule	*dominate* have power over *domain* land under rule *dominant* prevailing
duc, duct	to lead	*viaduct* arched roadway *aqueduct* artificial waterway
dynam	power, strength	*dynamic* powerful *dynamite* powerful explosive *dynamo* engine making electrical power
ego	I	*egoist* person who is self-interested *egotist* selfish person *egocentric* revolving about self
erg, urg	work	*energy* power *ergatocracy* rule of the workers *metallurgy* science and technology of metals

Root or Stem	Meaning	Illustration
err	to wander	*error* mistake *erratic* not reliable, wandering *knight-errant* wandering knight
eu	good, well, beautiful	*eupeptic* having good digestion *eulogize* praise *euphemism* substitution of pleasant way of saying something blunt
fac, fic, fec, fect	to make, to do	*factory* place where things are made *fiction* manufactured story *affect* cause to change
fall, fals	to deceive	*fallacious* misleading *infallible* not prone to error, perfect *falsify* lie
fer, lat	to bring, to bear	*transfer* bring from one place to another *translate* bring from one language to another *conifer* bearing cones, as pine trees
fid	belief, faith	*infidel* nonbeliever, heathen *confidence* assurance, belief
fin	end, limit	*confine* keep within limits *finite* having definite limits
flect, flex	bend	*flexible* able to bend *deflect* bend away, turn aside
fort	luck, chance	*fortuitous* accidental, occurring by chance *fortunate* lucky
fort	strong	*fortitude* strength, firmness of mind *fortification* strengthening *fortress* stronghold
frag, fract	break	*fragile* easily broken *infraction* breaking of a rule *fractious* unruly, tending to break rules
fug	flee	*fugitive* someone who flees *refuge* shelter, home for someone fleeing
fus	pour	*effusive* gushing, pouring out *diffuse* widespread (poured in many directions)
gam	marriage	*monogamy* marriage to one person *bigamy* marriage to two people at the same time *polygamy* having many wives or husbands at the same time
gen, gener	class, race	*genus* group of animals with similar traits *generic* characteristic of a class *gender* class organized by sex

Root or Stem	Meaning	Illustration
grad, gress	go, step	*digress* go astray (from the main point) *regress* go backwards *gradual* step by step, by degrees
graph, gram	writing	*epigram* pithy statement *telegram* instantaneous message over great distance *stenography* shorthand (writing narrowly)
greg	flock, herd	*gregarious* tending to group together as in a herd *aggregate* group, total *egregious* conspicuously bad; shocking
helio	sun	*heliotrope* flower that faces the sun *heliograph* instrument that uses the sun's rays to send signals
it, itiner	journey, road	*exit* way out *itinerary* plan of journey
jac, jact, jec	to throw	*projectile* missile; something thrown forward *trajectory* path taken by thrown object *ejaculatory* casting or throwing out
jur, jurat	to swear	*perjure* testify falsely *jury* group of men and women sworn to seek the truth *adjuration* solemn urging
labor, laborat	to work	*laboratory* place where work is done *collaborate* work together with others *laborious* difficult
leg, lect, lig	to choose, to read	*election* choice *legible* able to be read *eligible* able to be selected
leg	law	*legislature* law-making body *legitimate* lawful *legal* lawful
liber, libr	book	*library* collection of books *libretto* the "book" of a musical play *libel* slander (originally found in a little book)
liber	free	*liberation* the fact of setting free *liberal* generous (giving freely); tolerant
log	word, study	*entomology* study of insects *etymology* study of word parts and derivations *monologue* speech by one person
loqu, locut	to talk	*soliloquy* speech by one individual *loquacious* talkative *elocution* speech

Root or Stem	Meaning	Illustration
luc	light	*elucidate* enlighten *lucid* clear *translucent* allowing some light to pass through
magn	great	*magnify* enlarge *magnanimity* generosity, greatness of soul *magnitude* greatness, extent
mal	bad	*malevolent* wishing evil *malediction* curse *malefactor* evil-doer
man	hand	*manufacture* create (make by hand) *manuscript* written by hand *emancipate* free (let go from the hand)
mar	sea	*maritime* connected with seafaring *submarine* undersea craft *mariner* seaman
mater, matr	mother	*maternal* pertaining to motherhood *matriarch* female ruler of a family, group, or state *matrilineal* descended on the mother's side
mit, miss	to send	*missile* projectile *dismiss* send away *transmit* send across
mob, mot, mov	move	*mobilize* cause to move *motility* ability to move *immovable* not able to be moved
mon, monit	to warn	*admonish* warn *premonition* foreboding *monitor* watcher (warner)
mori, mort	to die	*mortuary* funeral parlor *moribund* dying *immortal* not dying
morph	shape, form	*amorphous* formless, lacking shape *metamorphosis* change of shape *anthropomorphic* in the shape of man
mut	change	*immutable* not able to be changed *mutate* undergo a great change *mutability* changeableness, inconstancy
nat	born	*innate* from birth *prenatal* before birth *nativity* birth
nav	ship	*navigate* sail a ship *circumnavigate* sail around the world *naval* pertaining to ships

Root or Stem	Meaning	Illustration
neg	deny	*negation* denial *renege* deny, go back on one's word *renegade* turncoat, traitor
nomen	name	*nomenclature* act of naming, terminology *nominal* in name only (as opposed to actual) *cognomen* surname, distinguishing nickname
nov	new	*novice* beginner *renovate* make new again *novelty* newness
omni	all	*omniscient* all knowing *omnipotent* all powerful *omnivorous* eating everything
oper	to work	*operate* work *cooperation* working together
pac	peace	*pacify* make peaceful *pacific* peaceful *pacifist* person opposed to war
pass	feel	*dispassionate* free of emotion *impassioned* emotion-filled *impassive* showing no feeling
pater, patr	father	*patriotism* love of one's country (fatherland) *patriarch* male ruler of a family, group, or state *paternity* fatherhood
path	disease, feeling	*pathology* study of diseased tissue *apathetic* lacking feeling; indifferent *antipathy* hostile feeling
ped, pod	foot	*impediment* stumbling-block; hindrance *tripod* three-footed stand *quadruped* four-footed animal
ped	child	*pedagogue* teacher of children *pediatrician* children's doctor
pel, puls	to drive	*compulsion* a forcing to do *repel* drive back *expel* drive out, banish
pet, petit	to seek	*petition* request *appetite* craving, desire *compete* vie with others
phil	love	*philanthropist* benefactor, lover of humanity *Anglophile* lover of everything English *philanderer* one involved in brief love affairs

Root or Stem	Meaning	Illustration
pon, posit	to place	*postpone* place after *positive* definite, unquestioned (definitely placed)
port, portat	to carry	*portable* able to be carried *transport* carry across *export* carry out (of country)
poten	able, powerful	*omnipotent* all-powerful *potentate* powerful person *impotent* powerless
psych	mind	*psychology* study of the mind *psychosis* mental disorder *psychopath* mentally ill person
put, putat	to trim, to calculate	*putative* supposed (calculated) *computation* calculation *amputate* cut off
quer, ques, quir, quis	to ask	*inquiry* investigation *inquisitive* questioning *query* question
reg, rect	rule	*regicide* murder of a ruler *regent* ruler *insurrection* rebellion; overthrow of a ruler
rid, ris	to laugh	*derision* scorn *risibility* inclination to laughter *ridiculous* deserving to be laughed at
rog, rogat	to ask	*interrogate* question *prerogative* privilege
rupt	to break	*interrupt* break into *bankrupt* insolvent *rupture* a break
sacr	holy	*sacred* holy *sacrilegious* impious, violating something holy *sacrament* religious act
sci	to know	*science* knowledge *omniscient* knowing all *conscious* aware
scop	watch, see	*periscope* device for seeing around corners *microscope* device for seeing small objects
scrib, script	to write	*transcribe* make a written copy *script* written text *circumscribe* write around, limit
sect	cut	*dissect* cut apart *bisect* cut into two pieces

Root or Stem	Meaning	Illustration
sed, sess	to sit	*sedentary* inactive (sitting) *session* meeting
sent, sens	to think, to feel	*consent* agree *resent* show indignation *sensitive* showing feeling
sequi, secut, seque	to follow	*consecutive* following in order *sequence* arrangement *sequel* that which follows *non sequitur* something that does not follow logically
solv, solut	to loosen	*absolve* free from blame *dissolute* morally lax *absolute* complete (not loosened)
somn	sleep	*insomnia* inability to sleep *somnolent* sleepy *somnambulist* sleepwalker
soph	wisdom	*philosopher* lover of wisdom *sophisticated* worldly wise
spec, spect	to look at	*spectator* observer *aspect* appearance *circumspect* cautious (looking around)
spir	breathe	*respiratory* pertaining to breathing *spirited* full of life (breath)
string, strict	bind	*stringent* strict *constrict* become tight *stricture* limit, something that restrains
stru, struct	build	*constructive* helping to build *construe* analyze (how something is built)
tang, tact, ting	to touch	*tangent* touching *contact* touching with, meeting *contingent* depending upon
tempor	time	*contemporary* at same time *extemporaneous* impromptu *temporize* delay
ten, tent	to hold	*tenable* able to be held *tenure* holding of office *retentive* holding; having a good memory
term	end	*interminable* endless *terminate* end
terr	land	*terrestrial* pertaining to earth *subterranean* underground

Root or Stem	Meaning	Illustration
therm	heat	*thermostat* instrument that regulates heat *diathermy* sending heat through body tissues
tors, tort	twist	*distort* twist out of true shape or meaning *torsion* act of twisting *tortuous* twisting
tract	drag, pull	*distract* pull (one's attention) away *intractable* stubborn, unable to be dragged *attraction* pull, drawing quality
trud, trus	push, shove	*intrude* push one's way in *protrusion* something sticking out
urb	city	*urban* pertaining to a city *urbane* polished, sophisticated (pertaining to a city dweller) *suburban* outside of a city
vac	empty	*vacuous* lacking content, empty-headed *evacuate* compel to empty an area
vad, vas	go	*invade* enter in a hostile fashion *evasive* not frank; eluding
veni, vent, ven	to come	*intervene* come between *prevent* stop *convention* meeting
ver	true	*veracious* truthful *verify* check the truth *verisimilitude* appearance of truth
verb	word	*verbose* wordy *verbiage* excessive use of words *verbatim* word for word
vers, vert	turn	*vertigo* turning dizzy *revert* turn back (to an earlier state) *diversion* something causing one to turn aside
via	way	*deviation* departure from the way *viaduct* roadway (arched) *trivial* trifling (small talk at crossroads)
vid, vis	to see	*vision* sight *evidence* things seen *vista* view
vinc, vict, vanq	to conquer	*invincible* unconquerable *victory* winning *vanquish* defeat

Root or Stem	Meaning	Illustration
viv, vit	alive	*vivisection* operating on living animals *vivacious* full of life *vitality* liveliness
voc, vocat	to call	*avocation* calling, minor occupation *provocation* calling or rousing the anger of *invocation* calling in prayer
vol	wish	*malevolent* wishing someone ill *voluntary* of one's own will
volv, volut	to roll	*revolve* roll around *evolve* roll out, develop *convolution* coiled state

Common Suffixes

Suffixes are syllables which are added to a word. Occasionally, they change the meaning of the word; more frequently, they serve to change the grammatical form of the word (noun to adjective, adjective to noun, noun to verb).

Suffix	Meaning	Illustration
able, ible	capable of (adjective suffix)	*portable* able to be carried *interminable* not able to be limited *legible* able to be read
ac, ic	like, pertaining to (adjective suffix)	*cardiac* pertaining to the heart *aquatic* pertaining to the water *dramatic* pertaining to the drama
acious, icious	full of (adjective suffix)	*audacious* full of daring *perspicacious* full of mental perception *avaricious* full of greed
al	pertaining to (adjective or noun suffix)	*maniacal* insane *final* pertaining to the end *logical* pertaining to logic
ant, ent	full of (adjective or noun suffix)	*eloquent* pertaining to fluid, effective speech *suppliant* pleader (person full of requests) *verdant* green
ary	like, connected with (adjective or noun suffix)	*dictionary* book connected with words *honorary* with honor *luminary* celestial body
ate	to make (verb suffix)	*consecrate* to make holy *enervate* to make weary *mitigate* to make less severe

Suffix	Meaning	Illustration
ation	that which is (noun suffix)	*exasperation* irritation *irritation* annoyance
cy	state of being (noun suffix)	*democracy* government ruled by the people *obstinacy* stubbornness *accuracy* correctness
eer, er, or	person who (noun suffix)	*mutineer* person who rebels *lecher* person who lusts *censor* person who deletes improper remarks
escent	becoming (adjective suffix)	*evanescent* tending to vanish *pubescent* arriving at puberty
fic	making, doing (adjective suffix)	*terrific* arousing great fear *soporific* causing sleep
fy	to make (verb suffix)	*magnify* enlarge *petrify* turn to stone *beautify* make beautiful
iferous	producing, bearing (adjective suffix)	*pestiferous* carrying disease *vociferous* bearing a loud voice
il, ile	pertaining to, capable of (adjective suffix)	*puerile* pertaining to a boy or child *ductile* capable of being hammered or drawn *civil* polite
ism	doctrine, belief (noun suffix)	*monotheism* belief in one god *fanaticism* excessive zeal; extreme belief
ist	dealer, doer (noun suffix)	*fascist* one who believes in a fascist state *realist* one who is realistic *artist* one who deals with art
ity	state of being (noun suffix)	*annuity* yearly grant *credulity* state of being unduly willing to believe *sagacity* wisdom
ive	like (adjective suffix)	*expensive* costly *quantitative* concerned with quantity *effusive* gushing
ize, ise	make (verb suffix)	*victimize* make a victim of *rationalize* make rational *harmonize* make harmonious *enfranchise* make free or set free
oid	resembling, like (adjective suffix)	*ovoid* like an egg *anthropoid* resembling man *spheroid* resembling a sphere
ose	full of (adjective suffix)	*verbose* full of words *lachrymose* full of tears

Suffix	Meaning	Illustration
osis	condition (noun suffix)	*psychosis* diseased mental condition *neurosis* nervous condition *hypnosis* condition of induced sleep
ous	full of (adjective suffix)	*nauseous* full of nausea *ludicrous* foolish
tude	state of (noun suffix)	*fortitude* state of strength *beatitude* state of blessedness *certitude* state of sureness

8 Quantitative Comparison Questions

- ■ **Testing Tactics**
- ■ **Practice Exercises**
- ■ **Answer Key**

One-half of the questions on the quantitative sections of the GRE General Test are of the quantitative comparison type. These questions are designed to test your ability to reason quickly about the magnitudes of two quantities. Some questions require simple computation; others ask you to reason more and to consider special cases. In this type of question you are given two quantities, with information regarding either or both. You are asked to decide which, if either, is the greater quantity. Actually, these questions require the same basic knowledge of high school level arithmetic, plane geometry, and algebra that you need for the other types of multiple-choice questions. However, these questions involve less reading and less computation than the other types of math questions.

TESTING TACTICS

Memorize the Directions to Save Time in the Examination Room

You may expect to find the following directions:

<u>Directions:</u> Each of the <u>Questions 1–15</u> consists of two quantities, one in Column A and one in Column B. You are to compare the two quantities and choose

> A if the quantity in Column A is greater;
> B if the quantity in Column B is greater;
> C if the two quantities are equal;
> D if the relationship cannot be determined from the information given.

<u>Note:</u>   Since there are only four choices, NEVER MARK (E).

<u>Common Information:</u>   In a question, information concerning one or both of the quantities to be compared is centered above the two columns. A symbol that appears in both columns represents the same thing in Column A as it does in Column B.

Do Not Spend Too Much Time on These Questions

Quantitative comparison questions require less time than the other types of math questions. Do not spend more than 30 seconds on any one question. The following question from a recent GRE will show you how quickly these questions can be answered. This question was handled correctly by 90% of the applicants who took the test on which it appeared.

With denominators of 2, 3, and 4, the least common denominator is 12. Therefore the answer is (B), since 15 is greater than 12.

Column A	Column B
1. The least common denominator of $\frac{1}{2}, \frac{1}{3},$ and $\frac{1}{4}$	15

Expect the Early Questions to Be Relatively Easy

These are warm up questions. If you find you cannot reach an answer quickly, perhaps you missed a point. Look at the following question, which was question 7 on a recent GRE. All but 18% of those taking the test answered this question correctly.

Notice that, disregarding the decimal points, the two factors to be multiplied are the same in both Column A and Column B. Thus, with the possible exception of the position of the decimal point, the products must be the same.

The product in Column A requires 3 decimal places and so does the product in Column B, so the decimal points are in the same position and the correct answer is (C).

Column A	Column B
7. (2.3)(12.45)	(0.23)(124.5)

Do Not Spend Time with Unnecessary Computations

The following former GRE question can be solved without computation.

Column B with $\sqrt{4}$ has a value of $1 + 2$, or exactly 3. In Column A estimate $\sqrt{3}$ is between 1 and 2. Column A, then, is $2 +$ (a number greater than 1 but less than 2), which equals a number greater than 3 but less than 4. Thus Column A is more than 3 while Column B is exactly 3, and (A) is the correct answer.

Column A	Column B
5. $2 + \sqrt{3}$	$1 + \sqrt{4}$

Eliminate from Consideration Any Quantity That Appears in Both Columns

In the following question note that 6^{10} appears in both columns. Consider only the values of -2^6 and -3^6.

Column A	Column B
$6^{10} - 2^6$	$6^{10} - 3^6$

The even number (2) to the sixth power will have a positive value. The odd number (3) to the sixth power will have a larger positive value. The correct answer is (A), since subtracting a larger positive number from 6^{10} gives a smaller result.

Do Not Choose (D) If the Quantities in Both Columns Have No Variables

If the quantities in both columns have no variables, (D) cannot be the correct answer. Therefore in such cases you have only three choices. The examples cited in Tactics 2 to 5 cannot have (D) as the correct answer since none have any variables.

Consider All Types of Numbers as Possible Values for Variables

If you find the relationship between the quantities depends upon the kind of numbers you use, the correct answer is (D). You must consider whether the relationship is affected by using positive or negative values, zero, one, fractions less than one, etc. Consider this example.

Column A	Column B
$\dfrac{1}{x + y}$	$x + y$

Only for positive values of x and y will $x + y$ have greater value than $\dfrac{1}{x + y}$.

Do Not Hesitate to Mark Up a Given Diagram in Your Test Booklet

Consider this actual GRE question.

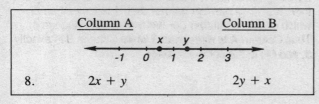

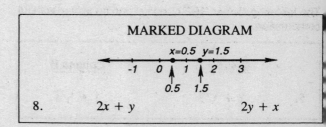

Evaluate $x = 0.5$ and $y = 1.5$.

Substitute the values. Column A: $2x + y = 1.0 + 1.5 = 2.5$. Column B: $2y + x = 3 + 0.5 = 3.5$. The correct answer is (B). Eighty percent of the candidates who took this test chose (B).

Make Rough Sketches or Diagrams to Help You Visualize the Situation Presented

The following question from a recent GRE was troublesome to almost 30% of the applicants. No diagram was given.

Note that if you are given a diagram do not assume it is drawn to scale unless the statement is made that the diagram is drawn to scale.

Column A	Column B
In $\triangle RST$, $RS = ST$ and the measure of $\angle RST$ is 20°.	
9. The measure of $\angle TRS$	80°

The correct diagram you must make looks like the one shown here.

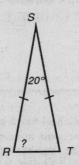

Recall that the sum of the measures in degrees of a triangle is 180. Since $RS = ST$, the measure of angle TRS = measure of angle RTS. Since the measure of angle RST is 20° then the measure of angle TRS plus the measure of angle $RTS = 160°$ and angle $TRS = \frac{1}{2}$ of 160° or 80°. The correct answer is (C).

Practice Exercise

Quantitative Comparison Exercise A

Directions: Each of the Questions 1–50 consists of two quantities, one in Column A and one in Column B. You are to compare the two quantities and choose

- A if the quantity in Column A is greater;
- B if the quantity in Column B is greater;
- C if the two quantities are equal;
- D if the relationship cannot be determined from the information given.

Note: Since there are only four choices, NEVER MARK (E).

Common Information: In a question, information concerning one or both of the quantities to be compared is centered above the two columns. A symbol that appears in both columns represents the same thing in Column A as it does in Column B.

Column A	Column B

In triangle ABC, the measure of $\angle ACB = 60°$.

1. $\angle B$ $\angle A$ D

---

2. Michael has 5 green marbles and the same number of red marbles. The number of red marbles in his collection is ½ the number of white marbles and ⅓ the number of blue ones.   Philip has 35 marbles in his collection. C

---

3. The number of posts needed by Mr. A. to hold a wire fence 120 feet long if he places posts 12 feet apart in a straight line.   Mr. B uses 10 posts to support a similar wire fence. A

$$0 < x < 10$$
$$0 < y < 12$$

4. x y D

$$a = 1 \text{ and } b = -1$$

5. $\dfrac{x(a+b)}{v}$ $\dfrac{2x(a+b)}{v}$ C

Triangle ABC

6. $AB + BC$ AC A

---

7. $\angle 4$ $\angle 3$ A

Column A | Column B

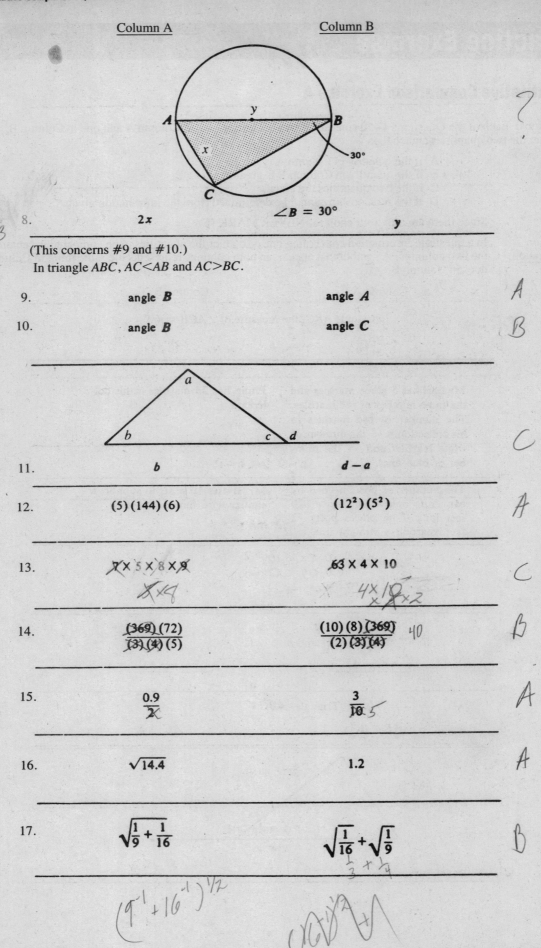

∠B = 30°

8.   2x   y

(This concerns #9 and #10.)
In triangle ABC, AC<AB and AC>BC.

9.   angle **B**   angle **A**   A

10.   angle **B**   angle **C**   B

11.   b   d − a   C

12.   (5)(144)(6) $(12^2)(5^2)$ A

13.   7 × 5 × 8 × 9   63 × 4 × 10   C

14. $\dfrac{(369)(72)}{(3)(4)(5)}$ $\dfrac{(10)(8)(369)}{(2)(3)(4)}$ B

15. $\dfrac{0.9}{2}$ $\dfrac{3}{10}$ A

16. $\sqrt{14.4}$ 1.2   A

17. $\sqrt{\frac{1}{9}+\frac{1}{16}}$ $\sqrt{\frac{1}{16}}+\sqrt{\frac{1}{9}}$ B

Column A	Column B

18. $\dfrac{1}{.5}$ $\sqrt{4}$ *C*

19. $\left(\dfrac{1}{.07}\right)^2$ $\dfrac{1}{7}$ *A*

$3^{n+2} = 27$ *AB*

20. n 3

21. $\sqrt{.16}$ $0.1\,\pi$ *A*
   .4   .314

22. $\dfrac{1}{\sqrt{25}}$ $\tfrac{1}{5}$ $\dfrac{1}{(0.5)}$ 2   *B*

$3 - 2x < 9$

23. x -3 *A*

$a < 0 \text{ and } b < 0$

24. $a - b$ $a + b$ *A*

$x > 0 \text{ and } y > 0$

$\dfrac{x}{y} > 2$ *B*

25. $2y$ x

26.   3   4 $\sqrt{9} + \sqrt{16}$ $\sqrt{49}$ 7   *C*

$\dfrac{9}{a} < \dfrac{9}{b}$ *A*

27. a b

$3^{x+1} = 81$ *B*

28. x 4

$x > 1 \text{ and } y > 1$
$x \neq y$ *C*

29. $\dfrac{x}{y} + 1$ $\dfrac{x + y}{y}$ $\dfrac{x}{y} + \dfrac{y}{y}$

$\dfrac{1+2}{3}$ $\dfrac{1}{3} + \dfrac{2}{3} = \dfrac{3}{3} = 1$

Column A	Column B

Questions 30–31 refer to $\triangle ABC$.

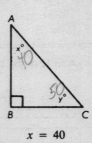

$x = 40$

30.   Length of side AB Length of side BC *A*

31. x y *B*

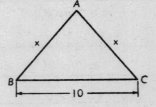

C

32. $\dfrac{BC}{AB} \cdot \dfrac{AC}{BC}$ 1

$$x^2 + 2xy + y^2 = 25$$
$$xy = 6$$

33. $x^2 + y^2$ $(x + y)^2$ *B*

$$a^2 = ab$$

34. a b *C*

$$x^2 + y^2 = 100$$

35. x y *D*

$$ab = 0$$

36. a b *D*

$$1 \text{ kilometer} = \frac{5}{8} \text{ mile}$$

37. $\dfrac{5}{8}$ kilometer   3 miles   *B*

38. $\dfrac{1274}{7}$ inches   5 yards, 2 inches   *C*

39. $(.2)^3$ $\sqrt{.64}$ *B*

Column A	Column B

40. 50% $\dfrac{1}{.02}$ B

It takes x men to complete a job in 12 days, but $x - 4$ men require A days to do the same job.

$12x$
$= (x-4)A$
$xA - 4A = 12x$
$12x - 48 = 12x$

41. A 12 $?D$ or A

$$y = \frac{k}{x}$$

42. x y D

$$\frac{a}{b} > 2$$

$$a > 0 \text{ and } b > 0$$

43. a $2b$ A

$$3^{x+1} = 81$$

44. x 4 B

The average weight of Mark, Philip, and Lori is 50 pounds.

45. Weight of Mark and Lori   Weight of Philip and Lori D

46. The distance covered going at the average rate of 40 miles per hour for three hours   120 mi   The distance covered in three hours going at 50 miles per hour for the first hour and then going at the average rate of 30 miles per hour for the next two hours   110 A

Martin is 5 times as old as Sara.

Michael's age is $\dfrac{1}{6}$ of Martin's age

47. Michael's age   Sara's age B

Questions 48–50 refer to the following figure.

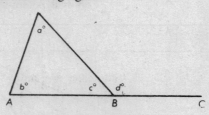

ABC is a straight line

48. $d + c$ $a + b + c$ C

49. d b A

50. $a + b$ d C

Quantitative Comparison Exercise B

<u>Directions:</u> Each of the Questions 1-50 consists of two quantities, one in Column A and one in Column B. You are to compare the two quantities and choose

A if the quantity in Column A is greater;
B if the quantity in Column B is greater;
C if the two quantities are equal;
D if the relationship cannot be determined from the information given.

<u>Note:</u>   Since there are only four choices, NEVER MARK (E).

<u>Common</u>
<u>Information:</u> In a question, information concerning one or both of the quantities to be compared is centered above the two columns. A symbol that appears in both columns represents the same thing in Column A as it does in Column B.

	<u>Column A</u>	<u>Column B</u>
1.	$\dfrac{1}{2}$	$\dfrac{1}{.02}$
2.	48	102% of 40
3.	$\sqrt{\dfrac{1}{16} + \dfrac{1}{9}}$	$\dfrac{7}{12}$
4.	0.01π	$\sqrt{0.3}$

5.

$$a > 0 \text{ and } b > 0$$

	Column A	Column B
	$a^2 + b^2$	$(a - b)^2$

6.

$$x + y = 5$$
$$x + z = 6$$

	Column A	Column B
	x	1

7. The average of $(30 + 2x - y)$ and $(10 + y)$ | The average of $(x - 120)$ and $(160 + x)$

8. Area of square with perimeter of 32 feet | Area of isosceles right triangle with hypotenuse of $10\sqrt{2}$ feet

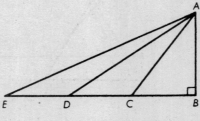

In triangle ABE, $BC = CD = DE$

9. Area of $\triangle ABC$ + Area of $\triangle ACD$ | Area of $\triangle ACD$ + Area of $\triangle ADE$

Column A	Column B
10. The length of side *AB* of square *ABCD* with a perimeter of 8 units	The length of side *KL* of square *KLMN* with area of 4 units

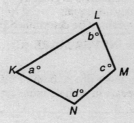

Note: Not drawn to scale.

In quadrilateral *KLMN*, *b* = 80 and *d* = 110.

11. *a*	*c*

12. The volume of a cube is 27	The volume of a cube in which the length of a diagonal of one face is $3\sqrt{2}$

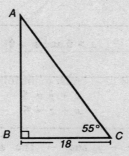

13. *AB*	*BC*

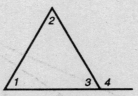

14. ∠4	∠1 + ∠2

<u>Column A</u>   <u>Column B</u>

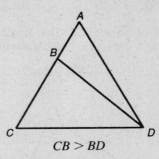

$$CB > BD$$

<u>Note</u>: Not drawn to scale.

15.   ∠ACD   ∠ADC

_____

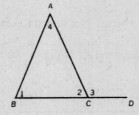

16.   ∠3   ∠1

_____

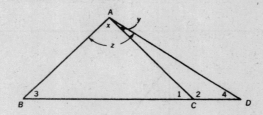

Questions 17–24 refer to the following figure.

17.   ∠3   ∠4

18.   ∠z   ∠y

19.   ∠x   ∠y

20.   ∠3   ∠2

21.   ∠x + ∠y   ∠z

22.   BC   CD

23.   ∠1 + ∠2   ∠3 + ∠4 + ∠z

24.   BC + CD   AB + AD

Column A   Column B

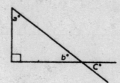

25. $(c + a)°$ $90°$

$$2a = 3b - 4$$
$$a = b$$

26. b 4

---

27. Martin's average speed if he walks 8   Michael's average speed if he walks 5
miles in 2 hours   miles in an hour and 30 minutes

$$x \neq 0$$

28. $\dfrac{2 + 3 + 4 + 5 + 6}{5x}$ $\dfrac{4}{x}$

---

29. a^5 a^4

---

x, y, and z are consecutive
integers and $x + y + z = 12$

30. xyz 60

$$b \neq -c$$
$$\frac{a}{-b - c} = \frac{-5}{c + b}$$

31. 5 a

---

32. 2 hours, 40 minutes   The elapsed time from 8:55 P.M. to
10:15 the same evening

The distance from Mark's house to the Waban school is 3 miles; the distance
from Sara's house to this school is 4 miles.

33. The distance from Mark's house to   5 miles
Sara's house

---

34. $(0.1)(\pi)$ $\sqrt{.17}$

---

35. $\dfrac{2 + 2 + 2}{2 - 2 - 2}$ $\dfrac{3 + 3 + 3}{3 - 3 - 3}$

---

36. $\sqrt{1.44}$ 0.12

Column A	Column B

$$X^2 = 100$$

37. X — 10

$$a > 0, \ x > 0, \ \text{and} \ \frac{a}{x} < 1$$

38. a — x

$$0 < a < b$$

39. $\dfrac{1}{a}$ — $\dfrac{1}{b}$

40. 105% of 500 — 50% of 1000

$$5x = 23 = y$$

41. x — y

$$X > Y \text{ and } Y > Z$$

42. $2X$ — $Y + Z$

$$x > 0 \text{ and } y > 0$$

43. $\dfrac{1}{x + y}$ — $\dfrac{\dfrac{1}{xy}}{\dfrac{1}{x} + \dfrac{1}{y}}$

44. $\sqrt{\dfrac{1}{25}}$ — $\left(\dfrac{1}{5}\right)^2$

45. 15% — $\dfrac{0.3}{2}$

$$0 < x < y < z$$

46. $\dfrac{z}{y}$ — $\dfrac{z}{x}$

47. The percentage increase from \$5 to \$7 — The percentage increase from \$7 to \$9

48. $a + 1$ — $a - 1$

$$\frac{1}{a} < 0$$

49. zero — a

$$1 \text{ kilometer} = \frac{5}{8} \text{ mile}$$

50. 1.6 kilometers — 1 mile

Answer Key

Quantitative Comparison Exercise A

1.	D	14.	B	27.	A	40.	B
2.	C	15.	A	28.	B	41.	A
3.	A	16.	A	29.	C	42.	D
4.	D	17.	B	30.	A	43.	A
5.	C	18.	C	31.	B	44.	B
6.	A	19.	A	32.	C	45.	D
7.	A	20.	B	33.	B	46.	A
8.	C	21.	A	34.	C	47.	B
9.	A	22.	B	35.	D	48.	C
10.	B	23.	A	36.	D	49.	A
11.	C	24.	A	37.	B	50.	C
12.	A	25.	B	38.	C		
13.	C	26.	C	39.	B		

Quantitative Comparison Exercise B

1.	B	14.	C	27.	A	40.	A
2.	A	15.	B	28.	C	41.	B
3.	B	16.	A	29.	D	42.	A
4.	B	17.	D	30.	C	43.	C
5.	A	18.	A	31.	C	44.	A
6.	D	19.	D	32.	A	45.	C
7.	C	20.	B	33.	D	46.	B
8.	A	21.	C	34.	B	47.	A
9.	C	22.	D	35.	C	48.	A
10.	C	23.	C	36.	A	49.	A
11.	D	24.	B	37.	D	50.	C
12.	C	25.	C	38.	B		
13.	A	26.	C	39.	A		

9 Discrete Quantitative Questions

- ■ Testing Tactics
- ■ Practice Exercises
- ■ Answer Key
- ■ Answer Explanations

The discrete quantitative questions are like the standard multiple-choice questions you have encountered in math classes and on other standardized tests. They cover basic arithmetic operations, elementary algebra, and plane geometry. They test both your knowledge of basic mathematical concepts and, in some cases, your ability to apply that knowledge, as in questions that ask you to solve a problem involving an actual or an abstract situation. The arithmetic questions deal with operations on numbers and finding powers, roots of powers, percents, and averages. The algebra questions include linear equations, factorization, inequalities, exponents, and radicals. Also, some questions test the ability to set up an equation in order to solve a problem. The topics in geometry include properties of lines, circles, triangles, rectangles, and other polygons. Also, some questions test knowledge of measurement-related concepts, the Pythagorean theorem, and knowledge of coordinate geometry.

There are 10 discrete quantitative questions in each quantitative section of the test—usually questions 16–20 and 26–30, with a set of 5 data interpretation questions in between. Generally, the first 5 discrete quantitative questions are easier than the last 5. The tactics and practice exercises that follow will help you answer these questions.

Testing Tactics

Use Your Time Wisely

You have 30 minutes for 30 questions. The 15 quantitative comparison questions should be done in 10 minutes. That leaves 20 minutes to do 5 data interpretation questions and 10 discrete quantitative questions. Thus, it is logical to expect to allow a minute or a minute and a half for each question. If you find that you are spending as much as two minutes on a question, you must come to some decision about your answer right then and there. However, mark the question in some way so that you can return to it when you have completed the section. At that time the question may read differently or perhaps some item that came up since you left the question will help you answer it. In any event do not leave it blank. There is no penalty for guessing on the GRE.

Expect to encounter relatively easy questions in the early part of the test. Don't be surprised to find a beginning question such as the following.

$$\frac{4}{3} + \frac{3}{4} =$$
(A) $\frac{1}{1}$ (B) $\frac{16}{9}$ (C) $\frac{25}{12}$ (D) $\frac{7}{12}$ (E) $\frac{7}{4}$

The basic elementary principle for this warm up question is that to add fractions the denominators must be similar. Most test takers will quickly reason that $\frac{16}{12} + \frac{9}{12} = \frac{25}{12}$, Spending only about 20 seconds to arrive at the correct answer, (C).

Avoid Lengthy Computations

Time saved on a question permits more time for the challenging questions. Remember all questions carry the same weight. In general, GRE questions do not involve lengthy, time-consuming computation. Therefore, if you come to a question that seems to require straightforward, but complex computation, look for a shortcut; there almost always is one. Consider this question. Can you arrive at the answer in less than 30 seconds, including time to read the question?

The product of 8754896 and 48933 is

(A) 428403325965
(B) 428403325966
(C) 428403325967
(D) 428403325968
(E) 428403325969

In a question such as this one, your ability to do complicated multiplication is not what is being tested; you are being tested for higher skills and insights. Observe the choices given. They vary only in the last digit. This should be your only concern. Since you are multiplying a number

ending in 6 with a number ending in 3, the product must be a number ending in 8, making Choice (D) the correct answer.

The following question also illustrates the point.

If $3x = \frac{5}{6}y$, then $5y =$

(A) $\frac{1}{2}x$ (B) $2x$ (C) $3.6x$ (D) $5x$ (E) $18x$

A time-consuming method of solving this problem would be to solve for y in terms of x and to substitute that value in $5y$. A superior method would be to multiply both sides of the equation by 6 in order to obtain a value of $5y$.

$$3x = \frac{5}{6}y$$

$$(6)(3x) = \left(\frac{5}{6}y\right)(6)$$

$$18x = 5y$$

The correct answer is (E).

Read the Questions Carefully

Read each question carefully to make sure you answer the question that was asked and not the one you expected to be asked. Also, make sure you take all relevant information into consideration and that you work with the correct units.

The following GRE question, which appeared on a recent test, is an example of how some incorrect answer choices are often answers to what you might have incorrectly anticipated the question as asking.

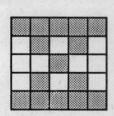

In the figure above, the number of shaded squares is what percent greater than the number of unshaded squares?

(A) 25% (B) 40% (C) 50% (D) 60% (E) 75%

If you did not read the question carefully, you might have fallen into the trap of answering the question "What percent of the squares are shaded?" You would have chosen (D) 60% as your answer, and you would have been incorrect. The question asked what percent *greater* the shaded squares are than the unshaded squares. To answer *this* question, you count the number of unshaded squares and the number of shaded squares, which come to 15 and 10, respectively. Then, you subtract 10 from 15, which gives you 5, and since 5 is 50 percent of 10, the number of shaded squares is 50 percent greater than the number of unshaded squares, and (C) is the correct answer.

The former GRE question that follows is a good example of the importance of reading the question carefully to determine what relevant information is given. Note that the answer must be given in dollars. Also, be careful not to impose a double charge for the first 3 minutes or to impose no charge at all for the first 3 minutes.

A phone call from City X to City Y costs $1.00 for the first 3 minutes and $0.20 for each additional minute. If r is an integer greater than 3, a phone call r minutes long will cost how many dollars?

(A) $\frac{3r}{5}$ (B) $\frac{r - 10}{5}$ (C) $\frac{r - 3}{5}$

(D) $\frac{r + 2}{5}$ (E) $\frac{r + 15}{5}$

If the phone call lasted r minutes and the value of r is more than 3 minutes, then the total charge is $1.00 plus $.20 for each minute beyond the first 3 minutes. There were $(r - 3)$ minutes for this phone call after the first 3 minutes. [Check: $3 + (r - 3) = r$] The total cost will be $1.00 + ($.20) $(r - 3)$ or $1.00 + 0.2r - 0.6$ or $0.2r + 0.4$ or $\frac{2r}{10} + \frac{4}{10}$ or $\frac{r}{5} + \frac{2}{5}$ or $\frac{r + 2}{5}$ dollars.

Don't Panic When Faced with a Complex Problem

When faced with a complex problem, if possible, make a sketch to help you visualize the situation. The former GRE question that follows illustrates how useful this can be.

Two microphones are located 100 meters apart and each is 130 meters from the same listening station. If a transmitter is located halfway between the two microphones, what is the distance, in meters, between the transmitter and the listening station?

(A) 120   (B) 124   (C) 125   (D) 128   (E) 130

To visualize the situation make a rough sketch, but do not spend too much time doing so.

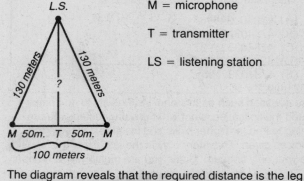

M = microphone

T = transmitter

LS = listening station

The diagram reveals that the required distance is the leg of a right triangle, with a hypotenuse of 130 and a leg of 50. Recall the 5, 12, 13 right triangle relationship or in this case the 50, 120, 130 relationship. Therefore, the correct answer is (A).

Mark Up Diagrams Given in the Test Booklet

See how this tactic works with a former GRE question.

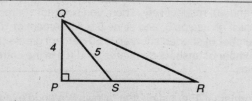

In the figure above, the area of triangular region PQR is 36. What is the area of triangular region SQR?

(A) 30   (B) 24   (C) 18   (D) 15   (E) 12

Let $PR = x$. The area of $PQR = \frac{4x}{2}$ or $2x$. $2x = 36$ and $x = 18$.

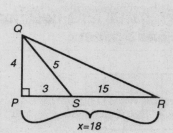

Note that right triangle QPS has a 3 - 4 - 5 relationship. Therefore $PS = 3$ and $SR = 15$. To find the area of SQR, note that the altitude is 4. The area of $SQR = \frac{(4)(15)}{2}$ or 30, so the answer is (A).

Be Prepared to Apply Basic Rules, Formulas and Concepts

Examinees are expected to have basic mathematical knowledge of arithmetic, algebra, and geometry, and to be able to apply that knowledge in some cases. The following question from a recent GRE calls for knowing the meaning of ratio and for the ability to set up and solve an equation.

If the ratio of x to y is 9 times the ratio of y to x, then $\frac{x}{y}$ could be

(A) 9 (B) 3 (C) 1 (D) $\frac{1}{3}$ (E) $\frac{1}{9}$

The ratio of y to $x = \frac{y}{x}$

$$\frac{x}{y} = 9\left(\frac{y}{x}\right)$$

$$\frac{x}{y} = \frac{9y}{x}$$

Note that since all answers have numerical values, you must solve this equation.

$x^2 = 9y^2$

$\frac{x^2}{y^2} = 9$

$\frac{x}{y} = 3$

The correct answer is (B).

The following former GRE question basically applies the principle that a circle has a measure of 360° and the sum of the measure of the angles of a triangle is 180.

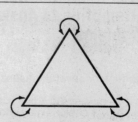

In the triangle above, the sum of the measures of the three marked angles is

(A) 540° (B) 630° (C) 720° (D) 810° (E) 900°

MARKED DIAGRAM

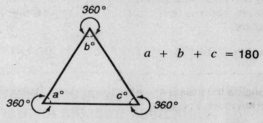

$a + b + c = 180$

Look at the marked diagram. By including the interior angles of the triangle, 3 circles appear with a total of (3)(360°) or 1080°. To answer the question subtract 180° for the angles of the triangle. The correct answer is (E).

Be Prepared for a Question with An Unusual Symbol

If you come to a question with an unusual symbol, replace the symbol with the given information. If $\hat{x}$ is defined as $\sqrt{\frac{x}{2}}$, then for any quantity you find in the circle, the circle's value is equal to $\frac{1}{2}$ the square root of that quantity.

The following is a typical problem.

If ⟨triangle a, b, c⟩ is defined to equal $\frac{ab}{c}$

and ⟨triangle a, b, c⟩ $- \frac{1}{x} = 0$, then $x =$

(A) $\frac{ab}{c}$ (B) $\frac{ac}{b}$ (C) $\frac{c}{ab}$ (D) $\frac{bc}{a}$ (E) $\frac{a}{bc}$

Solve for x to obtain the correct answer, (C).

$$\frac{ab}{c} - \frac{1}{x} = 0 \text{ (given)}$$

$$\frac{ab}{c} = \frac{1}{x} \left(\text{addition of } \frac{1}{x}\right)$$

$$\frac{c}{ab} = x \text{ (reciprocals of equals are equal)}$$

Look at the Answer Choices Before Attempting to Answer Complex Problems

This tactic is important for several reasons.

1. Looking at the answer choices may show you a quick way of solving the problem as in the first example for Tactic 1.

2. The answer choices give you an idea of how exact your figuring has to be. For example, if the choices are 3, 4, 5, 6, 7, you know you have to get a pretty exact answer, whereas if the choices are 9, 18, 40, 80, 90, you do not. This should alert you to several possibilities: you may be able to save time by estimating, there is a good chance that a shortcut is involved, and you may be able to get the correct answer by eliminating choices that just are not reasonable.

3. The answer choices show you the form that is required which will keep you from wasting time putting your answer in a form that is not given. For example, if the answers are all decimals, you do not want to compute your answer in terms of fractions.

If You Can't Answer a Question, Try to Work Back from the Answer Choices

Sometimes this is easier and faster than trying to solve the problem through other means. For example, in the following question from a recent GRE, trying out each answer choice might be easier and faster than figuring out the square root of 20,000.

> The floor of a company's storage room has an area of 20,000 square feet. If the floor is in the shape of a square, approximately how many feet long is each side?
>
> (A)   140
> (B)   450
> (C)   500
> (D) 1,000
> (E) 5,000

If you look at the answer choices, you can see that the numbers are far apart. Start with (C) 500, since it is an easy figure to multiply. Add 4 zeros to 5 × 5 or 25 and you get 250,000. Since squaring 500 gave you a much larger number than the approximately 20,000 you are looking for, don't even bother to try (D) 1,000 and (E) 5,000. Choice (B) 450 does not look likely either, since it is too close to 500, so try (A) 140. You get 19,600, which is almost 20,000, making (A) the correct answer. Note that you only did two computations to get the answer, and that one of them, 500 × 500, only took you about two seconds to do.

Practice Exercises

Discrete Quantitative Exercise A

Directions: Each of the Questions 1–25 has five answer choices. For each of these questions, select the best of the answer choices given.

---

1. In 1955, it cost $12 to purchase one hundred pounds of potatoes. In 1975, it cost $34 to purchase one hundred pounds of potatoes. The price of one hundred pounds of potatoes increased how many dollars between 1955 and 1975?

   (A) 1.20
   (B) 2.20
   (C) 3.40
   (D) 22
   (E) 34

2. A house cost Ms. Jones C dollars in 1985. Three years later she sold the house for 25% more than she paid for it. She has to pay a tax of 50% of the gain. (The gain is the selling price minus the cost.) How much tax must Ms. Jones pay?

   (A) $\frac{1}{24}C$

   (B) $\frac{C}{8}$

   (C) $\frac{1}{4}C$

   (D) $\frac{C}{2}$

   (E) $.6C$

3. If the length of a rectangle is increased by 20%, and the width of the same rectangle is decreased by 20%, then the area of the rectangle

   (A) decreases by 20%
   (B) decreases by 4%
   (C) is unchanged
   (D) increases by 20%
   (E) increases by 40%

4. Eight percent of the people eligible to vote are between 18 and 21. In an election, 85% of those eligible to vote who were between 18 and 21 actually voted. In that election, people between 18 and 21 who actually voted were what percent of those people eligible to vote?

   (A) 4.2
   (B) 6.4
   (C) 6.8
   (D) 8
   (E) 8.5

5. If n and p are both odd numbers, which of the following numbers *must* be an even number?

   (A) $n + p$
   (B) np
   (C) $np + 2$
   (D) $n + p + 1$
   (E) $2n + p$

6. It costs g cents a mile for gasoline and m cents a mile for all other costs to run a car. How many *dollars* will it cost to run the car for 100 miles?

   (A) $\dfrac{g + m}{100}$

   (B) $100g + 100m$
   (C) $g + m$
   (D) $g + .1m$
   (E) g

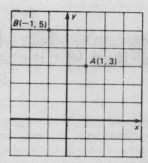

7. In the figure above, what is the length of the line segment that connects A to B?

   (A) $\sqrt{3}$
   (B) 2
   (C) $2\sqrt{2}$
   (D) 4
   (E) 8

8. A cab driver's income consists of his salary and tips. His salary is $50 a week. During one week his tips were $\frac{5}{4}$ of his salary. What fraction of his income for the week came from tips?

   (A) $\frac{4}{9}$ (B) $\frac{1}{2}$ (C) $\frac{5}{9}$ (D) $\frac{5}{8}$ (E) $\frac{5}{4}$

9. Given that x and y are real numbers, let $S(x,y) = x^2 - y^2$. Then $S(3, S(3,4)) =$

   (A) -40
   (B) -7
   (C) 40
   (D) 49
   (E) 56

10. Eggs cost 90¢ a dozen. Peppers cost 20¢ each. An omelet consists of 3 eggs and $\frac{1}{4}$ of a pepper. How much will the ingredients for 8 omelets cost?

    (A) $ .90
    (B) $1.30
    (C) $1.80
    (D) $2.20
    (E) $2.70

11. It is 185 miles from Binghamton to New York City. If a bus takes 2 hours to travel the first 85 miles, how long must the bus take to travel the final 100 miles in order to average 50 miles an hour for the entire trip?

    (A) 60 min.
    (B) 75 min.
    (C) 94 min.
    (D) 102 min.
    (E) 112 min.

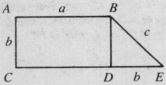

12. What is the area of the figure above, if $ABDC$ is a rectangle and BDE is an isosceles right triangle?

    (A) ab
    (B) ab^2
    (C) $b\left(a + \dfrac{b}{2}\right)$
    (D) cab
    (E) $\frac{1}{2}bc$

13. If $2x + y = 5$, then $4x + 2y =$

    (A) 5
    (B) 8
    (C) 9
    (D) 10
    (E) none of these

14. In 1967, a new sedan cost $2,500; in 1975, the same type of sedan cost $4,800. The cost of that type of sedan has increased by what percent between 1967 and 1975?

    (A) 48 (B) 52   (C) 92   (D) 152 (E) 192

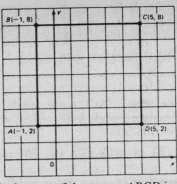

15. What is the area of the square $ABCD$ in the figure above?

    (A) 10
    (B) 18
    (C) 24
    (D) 36
    (E) 48

16. If $x + y = 6$ and $3x - y = 4$, then $x - y =$

    (A) -1
    (B) 0
    (C) 2
    (D) 4
    (E) 6

17. If $\frac{x}{y} = \frac{2}{3}$ then $\frac{y^2}{x^2}$ is equal to

    (A) $\frac{4}{9}$ (B) $\frac{2}{3}$ (C) $\frac{3}{2}$ (D) $\frac{9}{4}$ (E) $\frac{5}{2}$

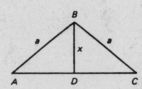

18. In the figure above, BD is perpendicular to AC. BA and BC have length a. What is the area of the triangle ABC?

    (A) $2x\sqrt{a^2 - x^2}$
    (B) $x\sqrt{a^2 - x^2}$
    (C) $a\sqrt{a^2 - x^2}$
    (D) $2a\sqrt{x^2 - a^2}$
    (E) $x\sqrt{x^2 - a^2}$

19. If two places are one inch apart on a map, then they are actually 160 miles apart. (The scale on the map is one inch equals 160 miles). If Seton is $2\frac{7}{8}$ inches from Monroe on the map, how many miles is it from Seton to Monroe?

    (A) 3
    (B) 27
    (C) 300
    (D) 360
    (E) 460

20. In the figure above, *ABCD* is a rectangle. The area of isosceles right triangle *ABE* = 7, *EC* = 3(*BE*). The area of *ABCD* is

    (A) 21 (B) 28 (C) 42 (D) 56 (E) 84

21. An automobile tire has two punctures. The first puncture by itself would make the tire flat in 9 minutes. The second puncture by itself would make the tire flat in 6 minutes. How long will it take for both punctures together to make the tire flat? (Assume the air leaks out at a constant rate.)

    (A) $3\frac{3}{5}$ minutes

    (B) 4 minutes

    (C) $5\frac{1}{4}$ minutes

    (D) $7\frac{1}{2}$ minutes

    (E) 15 minutes

22. For the integer *n*, if n^3 is odd, which of the following statements are true?

    I. *n* is odd.
    II. n^2 is odd.
    III. n^2 is even.

    (A) I only
    (B) II only
    (C) III only
    (D) I and II only
    (E) I and III only

23. There are 50 students enrolled in Business 100. Of the enrolled students, 90% took the final exam. Two-thirds of the students who took the final exam passed the final exam. How many students passed the final exam?

    (A) 30 (B) 33 (C) 34 (D) 35 (E) 45

24. If *a* is less than *b*, which of the following numbers is greater than *a* and less than *b*?

    (A) $\dfrac{(a + b)}{2}$

    (B) $\dfrac{(ab)}{2}$

    (C) $b^2 - a^2$

    (D) ab

    (E) $b - a$

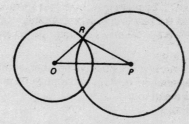

25. In the figure above, *OR* and *PR* are radii of circles. *PR* is tangent to the circle with center *O*. The length of *OP* is 4. If *OR* = 2, what is *PR*?

    (A) 2
    (B) $\dfrac{5}{2}$
    (C) 3
    (D) $2\sqrt{3}$
    (E) $3\sqrt{2}$

Discrete Quantitative Exercise B

Directions: Each of the Questions 1–25 has five answer choices. For each of these questions, select the best of the answer choices given.

1. A bus uses one gallon of gasoline to travel 15 miles. After a tune-up, the bus travels 15% farther on one gallon. How many gallons of gasoline (to the nearest tenth) will it take for the bus to travel 150 miles after a tune-up?

   (A) 8.5 (B) 8.7 (C) 8.9 (D) 9.0 (E) 10.0

2. If $x + 2y = 4$ and $\frac{x}{y} = 2$, then $x =$

   (A) 0 (B) $\frac{1}{2}$ (C) 1 (D) $\frac{3}{2}$ (E) 2

3. It costs $1,000 to make the first thousand copies of a book and *x* dollars to make each subsequent copy. If it costs a total of $7,230 to make the first 8,000 copies of a book, what is *x*?

   (A) .89
   (B) .90375
   (C) 1.00
   (D) 89
   (E) 90.375

4. If 16 workers can finish a job in three hours, how long should it take 5 workers to finish the same job?

   (A) $3\frac{1}{2}$ hours

   (B) 4 hours

   (C) 5 hours

   (D) $7\frac{1}{16}$ hours

   (E) $9\frac{3}{5}$ hours

5. A box contains 12 poles and 7 pieces of net. Each piece of net weighs .2 pounds; each pole weighs 1.1 pounds. The box and its contents together weigh 16.25 pounds. How much does the empty box weigh?

   (A) 1.2 pounds
   (B) 1.65 pounds
   (C) 2.75 pounds
   (D) 6.15 pounds
   (E) 16 pounds

6. If $a + b + c + d$ is a positive number, a minimum of x of the numbers a, b, c, and d must be positive where x is equal to

   (A) 0
   (B) 1
   (C) 2
   (D) 3
   (E) 4

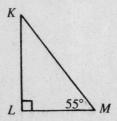

7. Consider the accompanying diagram. Which of the following statements is true?

   (A) $KM < KL$
   (B) $KM < LM$
   (C) $KL + LM < KM$
   (D) $KL < LM$
   (E) $KL > LM$

8. Which of the following numbers is the largest?

   (A) $(2 + 2 + 2)^2$
   (B) $[(2 + 2)^2]^2$
   (C) $(2 \times 2 \times 2)^2$
   (D) $2 + 2^2 + (2^2)^2$
   (E) 4^3

9. In a survey of the town of Waso, it was found that 65% of the people surveyed watched the news on television, 40% read a newspaper, and 25% read a newspaper and watched the news on television. What percent of the people surveyed neither watched the news on television nor read a newspaper?

   (A) 0%
   (B) 5%
   (C) 10%
   (D) 15%
   (E) 20%

10. A worker is paid d dollars an hour for the first 8 hours she works in a day. For every hour after the first 8 hours, she is paid c dollars an hour. If she works 12 hours in one day, what is her average hourly wage for that day?

   (A) $\dfrac{(2d + c)}{3}$

   (B) $8d + 4c$

   (C) $\dfrac{(8d + 12c)}{12}$

   (D) $\dfrac{(4d + 8c)}{12}$

   (E) $d + \left(\dfrac{1}{3}\right)c$

11. A screwdriver and a hammer currently have the same price. If the price of a screwdriver rises by 5% and the price of a hammer goes up by 3%, how much more will it cost to buy 3 screwdrivers and 3 hammers?

   (A) 3%
   (B) 4%
   (C) 5%
   (D) 8%
   (E) 24%

12. If the radius of a circle is increased by 6%, then the area of the circle is increased by

   (A) .36%
   (B) 3.6%
   (C) 6%
   (D) 12.36%
   (E) 36%

13. Given that a and b are real numbers, let $f(a,b) = ab$ and let $g(a) = a^2 + 2$. Then $f[3, g(3)] =$

   (A) $3a^2 + 2$
   (B) $3a^2 + 6$
   (C) 27
   (D) 29
   (E) 33

14. A share of stock in Ace Enterprises cost D dollars on Jan. 1, 1987. One year later, a share increased to Q dollars. The fraction by which the cost of a share of stock has increased in the year is

(A) $\dfrac{(Q - D)}{D}$

(B) $\dfrac{(D - Q)}{Q}$

(C) $\dfrac{D}{Q}$

(D) $\dfrac{Q}{D}$

(E) $\dfrac{(Q - D)}{Q}$

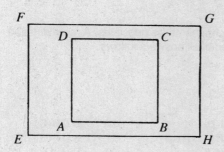

15. In the figure above, $ABCD$ is a square, $EFGH$ is a rectangle. $AB = 3$, $EF = 4$, $FG = 6$. The area of the region outside of $ABCD$ and inside $EFGH$ is

(A) 6
(B) 9
(C) 12
(D) 15
(E) 24

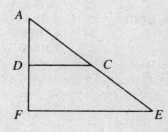

16. In the triangle above, DC is parallel to FE. $AD = DF$, $DC = 4$, and $DF = 3$. What is FE?

(A) 4
(B) 5
(C) 6
(D) 7
(E) 8

17. Which of the following fractions is the largest?

(A) $\dfrac{5}{6}$ (B) $\dfrac{11}{14}$ (C) $\dfrac{12}{15}$ (D) $\dfrac{17}{21}$ (E) $\dfrac{29}{35}$

18. How much simple interest will $2,000 earn in 18 months at an annual rate of 6%?

(A) $120
(B) $180
(C) $216
(D) $1,800
(E) $2,160

19. If $x + y > 5$ and $x - y > 3$, then which of the following gives all possible values of x and only possible values of x?

(A) $x > 3$
(B) $x > 4$
(C) $x > 5$
(D) $x < 5$
(E) $x < 3$

20. If the average (or arithmetic mean) of 6 numbers is 4.5, what is the sum of the numbers?

(A) 4.5
(B) 24
(C) 27
(D) 30
(E) cannot be determined

21. A silo is filled to capacity with W pounds of wheat. Rats eat r pounds a day. After 25 days, what percent of the silo's capacity have the rats eaten?

(A) $\dfrac{25r}{W}$

(B) $\dfrac{25r}{100W}$

(C) $2{,}500\left(\dfrac{r}{W}\right)$

(D) $\dfrac{r}{W}$

(E) $\dfrac{r}{25W}$

22. If $x^2 + 2x - 8 = 0$, then x is either -4 or

(A) -2
(B) -1
(C) 0
(D) 2
(E) 8

23. The interest charged on a loan is p dollars per $1,000 for the first month and q dollars per $1,000 for each month after the first month. How much interest will be charged during the first three months on a loan of $10,000?

(A) $30p$
(B) $30q$
(C) $p + 2q$
(D) $20p + 10p$
(E) $10p + 20q$

24. In rectangle $ACDF$, $AB = BC$ and $FE = ED$. G is any point on AF. The ratio of the area of $BCDE$ to the area of triangle GCD is

    (A) 2:1   (B) 1:2   (C) 1:1   (D) 2:3   (E) 3:2

25. If $3x = \frac{5}{6}y$, then $5y =$

    (A) $\frac{1}{2}x$
    (B) $2x$
    (C) $3.6x$
    (D) $5x$
    (E) $18x$

Answer Key

The letter following each question number is the correct answer. The numbers in parentheses refer to the sections of Chapter 11: Mathematics Review that explain the necessary mathematics principles. A more detailed explanation of all answers follows.

Discrete Quantitative Exercise A

1.	D (I-A)	8.	C (I-B)	14.	C (I-D)	20.	D (III-G)
2.	B (I-D)	9.	A (II-A)	15.	D (III-H, III-G)	21.	A (II-C)
3.	B (III-G, I-D)	10.	D (I-B)	16.	A (II-B)	22.	D (I-A)
4.	C (I-D)	11.	D (II-C)	17.	D (I-H)	23.	A (I-D, I-B)
5.	A (I-A)	12.	C (III-G, II-A, I-H)	18.	B (III-D, III-G)	24.	A (II-G)
6.	C (II-A)	13.	D (II-B)	19.	E (II-E)	25.	D (III-F, III-D)
7.	C (III-H, I-H)						

Discrete Quantitative Exercise B

1.	B (I-D)	8.	B (I-G)	14.	A (I-B)	20.	C (I-G)
2.	E (II-B)	9.	E (II-D)	15.	D (III-G)	21.	C (I-D)
3.	A (II-A)	10.	A (I-G, II-A)	16.	E (III-D)	22.	D (II-A, II-B)
4.	E (II-B)	11.	B (I-D)	17.	A (I-A, I-B, III-G)	23.	E (II-A)
5.	B (I-C)	12.	D (III-G)	18.	B (I-D)	24.	C (III-G)
6.	B (II-G, I-F)	13.	E (II-A)	19.	B (II-G)	25.	E (II-A)
7.	E (III-D)						

Answer Explanations

Discrete Quantitative Exercise A

1. D. The price increased by $34 - 12 = 22$ dollars.

2. B. She sold the house for 125% of C or $\frac{5}{4}C$. Thus, the gain is $\frac{5}{4}C - C = \frac{C}{4}$. She must pay a tax of 50% of $\frac{C}{4}$ or $\frac{1}{2}$ of $\frac{C}{4}$. Therefore, the tax is $\frac{C}{8}$. Notice that the three years has nothing to do with the problem. Sometimes a question contains unnecessary information.

3. B. The area of a rectangle is length times width. Let L and W denote the original length and width. Then the new length is $1.2L$ and the new width is $.8W$. Therefore, the new area is $(1.2L)(.8W) = .96LW$ or 96% of the original area. So the area has decreased by 4%.

4. C. Voters between 18 and 21 who voted at 85% of the 8% of eligible voters. Thus, $(.08)(.85) = .068$, so 6.8% of the eligible voters were voters between 18 and 21 who voted.

5. A. Odd numbers are of the form $2x + 1$ where x is an integer. Thus if $n = 2x + 1$ and $p = 2k + 1$, then $n + p = 2x + 1 + 2k + 1 = 2x + 2k + 2$, which is even. Using $n = 3$ and $p = 5$, all the other choices give an odd number. In general, if a problem involves odd or even numbers, try using the fact that odd numbers are of the form $2x + 1$ and even numbers of the form $2y$ where x and y are integers.

6. C. To run a car 100 miles will cost $100(g + m)$ cents. Divide by 100 to convert to dollars. The result is $g + m$.

7. C. Using the distance formula, the distance from A to B is
$\sqrt{(1 - (-1))^2 + (3 - 5)^2} = \sqrt{4 + 4} = \sqrt{8} = \sqrt{4 \times 2} = \sqrt{4}\sqrt{2} = 2\sqrt{2}$. You have to be able to simplify $\sqrt{8}$ in order to obtain the correct answer.

8. C. Tips for the week were $\frac{5}{4} \times 50$, so his total income was $50 + \frac{5}{4}(50) = \frac{9}{4}(50)$. Therefore,
tips made up $\dfrac{\frac{5}{4}(50)}{\frac{9}{4}(50)} = \dfrac{\frac{5}{4}}{\frac{9}{4}} = \dfrac{5}{9}$ of his income.

   Don't waste time figuring out the total income and the tip income. You can use the time to answer other questions.

9. A. $S(3,4) = 3^2 - 4^2 = 9 - 16 = -7$. Therefore, $S(3,S(3,4)) = S(3,-7) = 3^2 - (-7)^2 = 9 - 49 = -40$.

10. D. 8 omelets will use $8 \times 3 = 24$ eggs and $8 \times \frac{1}{4} = 2$ peppers. Since 24 is two dozen, the cost will be $(2)(90¢) + (2)(20¢) = 220¢$ or $2.20.

11. D. In order to average 50 m.p.h. for the trip, the bus must make the trip in $\frac{185}{50} = 3\frac{7}{10}$ hours, which is 222 minutes. Since 2 hours or 120 minutes were needed for the first 85 miles, the final 100 miles must be completed in $222 - 120$, which is 102 minutes.

12. C. The area of a rectangle is length times width so the area of $ABDC$ is ab. The area of a triangle is one-half of the height times the base. Since BDE is an isosceles right triangle, the base and height both are equal to b. Thus, the area of BDE is $\frac{1}{2}b^2$. Therefore, the area of the figure is
$ab + \frac{1}{2}b^2$, which is equal to $b\left(a + \frac{b}{2}\right)$. You have to express your answer as one of the possible answers, so you need to be able to simplify.

13. D. Since $4x + 2y$ is equal to $2(2x + y)$ and $2x + y = 5$, $4x + 2y$ is equal to $2(5)$ or 10.

14. C. The cost has increased by $4,800 minus $2,500 or $2,300 between 1967 and 1975. So the cost has increased by $\frac{2,300}{2,500}$, which is .92 or 92%. Answer (E) is incorrect. The price in 1975 is 192% of the price in 1967, but the *increase* is 92%.

15. D. The distance from $(-1, 2)$ to $(5, 2)$ is 6. (You can use the distance formula or just count the blocks in this case.) The area of a square is the length of a side squared, so the area is 6^2 or 36.

16. A. Since $x + y = 6$ and $3x - y = 4$, we may add the two equations to obtain $4x = 10$, or $x = 2.5$. Then, because $x + y = 6$, y must be 3.5. Therefore, $x - y = -1$.

17. D. If $\frac{x}{y}$ is $\frac{2}{3}$, then $\frac{y}{x}$ is $\frac{3}{2}$. Since $\left(\frac{y}{x}\right)^2$ is equal to
$\frac{y^2}{x^2}$, $\frac{y^2}{x^2}$ is $\left(\frac{3}{2}\right)^2$ or $\frac{9}{4}$.

18. B. The area of a triangle is $\frac{1}{2}$ altitude times base. Since BD is perpendicular to AC, x is the altitude. Using the Pythagorean theorem, $x^2 + (AD)^2 = a^2$ and $x^2 + (DC)^2 = a^2$. Thus, $AD = DC$, and $AD = \sqrt{a^2 - x^2}$. So the base is $2\sqrt{a^2 - x^2}$. Therefore, the area is $\frac{1}{2}(x)(2\sqrt{a^2 - x^2})$, which is choice B.

19. E. $1 : 160 :: 2\frac{7}{8} : x$. $x = 2\frac{7}{8}(160)$. $2\frac{7}{8}$ is $\frac{23}{8}$ so the distance from Seton to Monroe is $\frac{23}{8}(160) = 460$ miles.

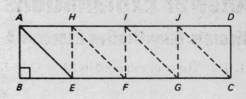

20. D. Let $EF = FG = GC$. Therefore, $BE = EF = FG = GC$. Draw perpendiculars EH, FI, GJ. Draw diagonals HF, IG, JC. The 8 triangles are equal in area since they each have the same altitude (AB or DC) and equal bases (BE, EF, FG, GC, AH, HI, IJ, JD). Since the area of $ABE = 7$, the area of $ABCD = (8)(7)$ or 56.

21. A. In each minute the first puncture will leak $\frac{1}{9}$ of the air and the second puncture will leak $\frac{1}{6}$ of the air. Together $\frac{1}{9} + \frac{1}{6} = \frac{5}{18}$. So $\frac{5}{18}$ of the air will leak out in each minute. In $\frac{18}{5}$ or $3\frac{3}{5}$ minutes the tire will be flat.

22. D. Since an even number times any number is even, and n times n^2 is odd, neither n nor n^2 can be even. Therefore, n and n^2 must both be odd for n^3 to be odd. I and II are true, and III is false.

23. A. 90% of 50 is 45, so 45 students took the final. $\frac{2}{3}$ of 45 is 30. Therefore, 30 students passed the final.

24. A. The average of two different numbers is always between the two. If $a = 2$ and $b = 3$, then $b^2 - a^2 = 5$, $ab = 6$, and $b - a = 1$ so C, D, and E must be false. If $a = \frac{1}{2}$ and $b = 1$, then $\frac{(ab)}{2} = \frac{1}{4}$, so B is also false.

25. D. Since the radius to the point of tangency is perpendicular to the tangent, OR must be perpendicular to PR. Therefore, ORP is a right triangle, and $(PO)^2 = (OR)^2 + (PR)^2$. Then, $(PR)^2 = (PO)^2 - (OR)^2$. Thus, $(PR)^2 = 4^2 - 2^2$, and $PR = \sqrt{16 - 4} = \sqrt{12} = \sqrt{4}\sqrt{3} = 2\sqrt{3}$.

Discrete Quantitative Exercise B

1. B. After the tune-up, the bus will travel $(1.15)(15) = 17.25$ miles on a gallon of gas. Therefore, it will take $(150) \div (17.25) = 8.7$ (to the nearest tenth) gallons of gasoline to travel 150 miles.

2. E. If $\frac{x}{y} = 2$, then $x = 2y$, so $x + 2y = 2y + 2y = 4y$. But $x + 2y = 4$, so $4y = 4$, or $y = 1$. Since $x = 2y$, x must be 2.

3. A. The cost of producing the first 8,000 copies is $1,000 + 7,000x$. $1,000 + 7,000x = \$7,230$. Therefore, $7,000x = 6,230$ and $x = .89$.

4. E. Assume all workers work at the same rate unless given different information. Since 16 workers take 3 hours, each worker does $\frac{1}{48}$ of the job an hour. Thus, the 5 workers will finish $\frac{5}{48}$ of the job each hour. $\frac{5}{48}x = \frac{48}{48}$. It will take $\frac{48}{5} = 9\frac{3}{5}$ hours for them to finish the job.

5. B. The 12 poles weigh $(12)(1.1) = 13.2$ pounds and the 7 pieces of net weigh $7(.2) = 1.4$ pounds, so the contents of the box weigh $13.2 + 1.4 = 14.6$ pounds. Therefore, the box by itself must weigh $16.25 - 14.6 = 1.65$ pounds.

6. B. If all the numbers were not positive, then the sum could not be positive so A is incorrect. If a, b, and c were all -1 and d were 5, then $a + b + c + d$ would be positive so C, D, and E are incorrect.

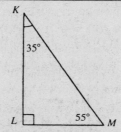

7. E. Since the measure of angle M is $55°$, the measure of angle K is $35°$. Therefore, $KL > LM$ since the larger side is opposite the larger angle.

8. B. Choice A gives 6^2 or 36. Choice B gives 4^4 or 256. Choice C is 8^2 or 64. Choice D is $2 + 4 + 16 = 22$. Choice E is 4^3 or 64.

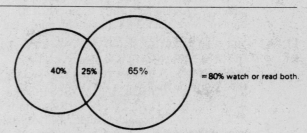

9. E. Since 25% read the newspaper and watched the news on television and 40% read the newspaper, $40\% - 25\%$ or 15% read the newspaper but did not watch the news on television. Thus $65\% + 15\%$ or 80% read the newspaper or watched the news on television, so $100\% - 80\%$ or 20% neither read the newspaper nor watched the news on television.

10. A. For the first 8 hours, she is paid a total of $8d$. For the final 4 hours $(12 - 8)$, she is paid $4c$. Therefore, her total pay is $8d + 4c$. To find the average hourly pay, divide by 12. To find the correct answer among the choices, you have to reduce the fraction. Divide the numerator by 4 and the denominator by 4.

11. B. If the price of one screwdriver increases by 5%, then the price of three screwdrivers increases by 5% (not 15%). The percentage change is the same regardless of the number sold. Since a screwdriver and a hammer currently cost the same, the screwdrivers and hammers each cost one-half of the total price. So one-half of the total is increased by 5%. The other half is increased by 3%. Therefore, the total price is increased by $\frac{1}{2}(5\%) + \frac{1}{2}(3\%)$ = 4%.

12. D. After the radius is increased by 6%, the radius will be 1.06 times the original radius. Since the area of a circle is πr^2, the new area will be $\pi(1.06r)^2 = \pi(1.1236r^2)$ or $1.1236\pi r^2$. Thus, the area has been increased by .1236 or by 12.36%.

13. E. Since $g(a) = a^2 + 2$, $g(3)$ is $3^2 + 2$ or 11. So $f[3,g(3)]$ is $f(3,11) = 3 \times 11$ or 33.

14. A. The difference in the price is $Q - D$. So the fraction by which it has increased is $\frac{Q - D}{D}$. Note that the denominator is the *original* price.

15. D. Since $ABCD$ is a square, the area of $ABCD$ is 3^2 or 9. The area of the rectangle $EFGH$ is *length* times *width* or $4 \times 6 = 24$. Thus, the area outside the square and inside the rectangle is $24 - 9$ or 15.

16. E. Since CD is parallel to EF, the triangles ACD and AEF are similar. Therefore, corresponding sides are proportional. So CD is to EF as AD is to AF. Since $AD = DF$, $\frac{AD}{AF}$ is $\frac{1}{2}$. Therefore, EF is twice CD or 8.

17. A. You need to find a common denominator for the fractions. One method is to multiply all the denominators. A quicker method is to find the least common multiple of the denominators. Since $6 = 3 \times 2$, $14 = 2 \times 7$, $15 = 3 \times 5$, $21 = 3 \times 7$, and $35 = 5 \times 7$, the least common multiple is $2 \times 3 \times 5 \times 7 = 210$. $\frac{5}{6}$ is $\frac{175}{210}$, $\frac{11}{14}$ is $\frac{165}{210}$, $\frac{12}{15}$ is $\frac{168}{210}$, $\frac{17}{21}$ is $\frac{170}{210}$, and $\frac{29}{35}$ is $\frac{174}{210}$. $\frac{5}{6}$ has the largest numerator.

18. B. 18 months is $\frac{3}{2}$ of a year. Interest = Amount × Time × Rate. $(\$2,000)\left(\frac{3}{2}\right)(.06) = \$180$.

19. B. If $x + y > 5$ and $x - y > 3$, then, since both inequalities are of the same type, the corresponding sides can be added to obtain $2x > 8$ or $x > 4$.

20. C. The average of 6 numbers is the sum of the numbers divided by 6. Thus, the sum of the numbers is the average multiplied by 6 or 4.5×6 which is 27.

21. C. After 25 days the rats have eaten $25r$ pounds of wheat. So $\frac{25r}{W}$ is the fraction of the capacity eaten by the rats. To change this to percent, multiply by 100. $\frac{25r}{W} \times 100 = 2,500\left(\frac{r}{W}\right)$.

22. D. Factor $x^2 + 2x - 8$ into $(x + 4)(x - 2)$. If x is either -4 or 2, $x^2 + 2x - 8 = 0$, and D is the correct answer.

23. E. The interest on the $10,000 for the first month will be $10p$. For the next 2 months the interest will be $20q$. The total interest is $10p + 20q$.

24. C. Area of rectangle $ACDF = (AC)(CD)$. Area of rectangle $BCDE = (BC)(CD)$ or $\left(\frac{1}{2}\right)AC$ (CD). Area of triangle $GCD = \left(\frac{1}{2}\right)$ $(AC)(CD)$.

25. E. A time-consuming method would be to solve for y in terms of x and to substitute that value in $5y$. A superior method would be to multiply both sides of the equation by 6 in order to obtain a value of $5y$.
$$3x = \frac{5}{6}y$$
$$(6)(3x) = \left(\frac{5}{6}y\right)(6)$$
$$18x = 5y$$

10 Data Interpretation Questions

- ■ **Testing Tactics**
- ■ **Practice Exercise**
- ■ **Answer Key**
- ■ **Answer Explanations**

Data interpretation questions are based on information given in tables or graphs. These questions test your ability to interpret the information presented and to select the appropriate data for answering a question. There are usually five data interpretation questions in each quantitative section. They are generally questions 21–25.

TESTING TACTICS

The five questions that follow were part of an actual GRE test. These questions will be used to illustrate the data interpretation testing tactics.

Questions 21–25 refer to the following graphs.

DOMESTIC AIR CARRIERS: OPERATING REVENUES, MILES FLOWN, AND NUMBER OF PASSENGERS CARRIED, 1960 TO 1975

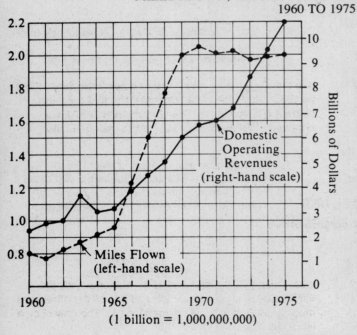

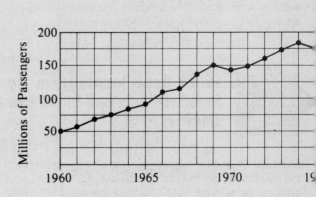

(1 billion = 1,000,000,000)

Note: Graphs drawn to scale.

21. In 1965 how many billions of miles were flown by domestic air carriers?

   (A) 0.95
   (B) 1.05
   (C) 1.2
   (D) 2.5
   (E) 3.0

22. In which of the following years were there more passengers carried by domestic air carriers than in the year before and the year after?

   (A) 1961
   (B) 1965
   (C) 1970
   (D) 1972
   (E) 1974

23. In 1969 what was the ratio of dollars of domestic operating revenues to miles flown?

   (A) $\frac{4}{1}$ (B) $\frac{3}{1}$ (C) $\frac{3}{2}$ (D) $\frac{2}{3}$ (E) $\frac{1}{4}$

24. In billions of miles, approximately what was the average (arithmetic means) number of miles flown per year by domestic air carriers from 1965 to 1970, inclusive?

   (A) 1.0
   (B) 1.5
   (C) 2.0
   (D) 4.5
   (E) 6.0

25. From 1960 to 1975, what was the percent increase in the number of passengers carried by domestic air carriers?

   (A) 125%
   (B) 175%
   (C) 250%
   (D) 350%
   (E) 450%

Get a General Picture of the Information before Reading the Question

Read the title. Then discover the details. In the case of these sample questions, note that the graph to the right deals with the number of passengers carried in the period 1960 to 1975. The more detailed graph on the left deals with two distinct factors, revenues and miles flown. To summarize then, the five questions will deal with revenues, mileage flown, and number of passengers carried for a 15-year period.

Avoid Lengthy Computations

Do no expect to be asked to do extensive computations in data interpretation questions. Most questions simply require reading the data correctly and putting it to use with common sense. For example, to obtain the correct answer for question 21, you simply have to be sure to use the broken line, which shows miles flown, and follow its 1965 reading along a horizontal line to a point just below 1.0 billion miles. The correct answer, (A), was obtained by 87 percent of the people taking the test.

Break Down lengthy Questions into Smaller Parts and Eliminate Impossible Choices

Question 24 seems lengthy, yet almost three-quarters of the candidates got the correct answer, (B). Note that the greatest value in the 1965–1970 period was 2.05. Therefore, choices (D) and (E) are impossible. The two greatest values are 2.0 and 2.05 and the other four are much less. Thus, (C) is eliminated as an average. Only the 1965 value is slightly less than 1. Since all the others are much greater than 1, this eliminates (A). The only choice left is (B).

Use Only the Information Given

Only use the information given and your knowledge of everyday facts such as the number of hours in a day to answer these questions. Do not add outside information, even if you feel it is related. In answering the five questions here, even if you happen to be quite familiar with information about domestic air carriers, you would base your answers only on the data presented in the two graphs.

Answer the Questions Asked, Not What You Think the Questions Should Be

Seventy-six percent of the people who answered question 22 correctly must have followed this advice. The questions asks for a year in which the number of passengers was greater than both the year before AND the year after. You must answer the questions asked, not what you think the question should be. To answer the questions then, the broken line must slope downwards on <u>both</u> sides of the year concerned, not just one side. Only 1974 fits this condition.

Be Careful to Use Proper Units

Notice that the units on the right scale are in billions of dollars and the miles flown are in billions of miles, but the two sides of the graphs have different scales. This is important in answering question 23 where you are asked to compare dollars of domestic operating revenues to miles flown. For the year 1969 the revenue was $6 billion and the mileage was 2 billion. The ratio was 6:2 or 3:1 or $\frac{3}{1}$.

Use Your Answer Sheet as a Straight Edge to Help You Read the Graph

To make it easier and to avoid errors, use the edge of your answer sheet to locate the position you are looking for on the graph. This is especially helpful when there are not enough lines or grids on the graph.

Make Sure Your Answer Is Reasonable

In discussing question 24 under Tactic 3, we applied the test of logic as we broke down a complicated question into smaller parts. If by some miscalculation, you had chosen either (D) or (E) as your answer, doublechecking to see whether your answer was reasonable would have shown you right away that it was not, since both choices are greater than the maximum number of miles flown in a given year, which was 2.05 in 1970.

Tactic 9

Be Prepared to Apply Basic Mathematical Rules, Principles, and Formulas

Question 25 applies a basic rule in percents, one that is often used on GRE data interpretation questions and, therefore, one that you should be sure to know before you take the test. To obtain percent increase or decrease, the difference divided by the original multiplied by 100 gives the percent changed. For example, in ques-

tion 25 there were 50 million passengers in 1960 and 175 million passengers in 1975. The difference is 125. Divide 125 million by 50 million and you get $2\frac{1}{2}$ or 2.5 or 250%, which is the correct answer.

Tactic 10

Whenever Possible Answer the Question by Visualizing Rather Than by Computing

Since one of the major benefits of graphs and tables is that they present data in a form that enables you to readily see relationships and to make quick comparisons, use this visual attribute of graphs and tables to help you answer the questions. Where possible, use your eye instead of your computational skills. For example, in

question 24, finding the approximate midpoint of the dashed line between 1965 and 1970 would give you the correct answer. You can feel safe using this visual method for questions 24 because you can see that the inclination of the line is about the same on either side of the approximate midpoint.

Practice Exercise

Directions: Each of the Questions 1–24 has five answer choices. For each of these questions, select the best of the answer choices given.

Questions 1–4 refer to the following graph.

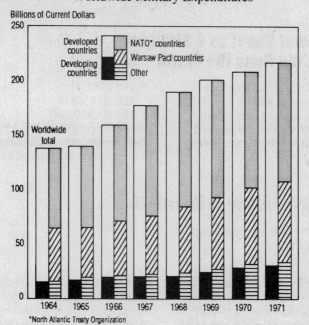

Source: Pocket Data Book U.S.A. 1973. Bureau of the Census.

1. Between 1964 and 1969, worldwide military expenditures

    (A) increased by about 50%
    (B) roughly doubled ·
    (C) increased by about 150%
    (D) almost tripled
    (E) increased by 10%

2. The average yearly military expenditure by the developing countries between 1964 and 1971 was approximately how many billions of current dollars?

    (A) 20 (B) 50 (C) 100 (D) 140 (E) 175

3. Which of the following statements can be inferred from the graph?

    I.   The NATO countries have higher incomes than the Warsaw Pact countries.

    II. Worldwide military expenditures have increased each year between 1964 and 1971.
    III. In 1972 worldwide military expenditures were more than 230 billion current dollars.

    (A) I only
    (B) II only
    (C) I and II only
    (D) II and III only
    (E) I, II, and III

4. A speaker claims that the NATO countries customarily spend $\frac{1}{3}$ of their combined incomes on military expenditures. According to the speaker, the combined incomes of the NATO countries (in billions of current dollars) in 1971 was about

    (A) 100 (B) 200 (C) 250 (D) 350 (E) 500

Questions 5–9 refer to the following table.

INCOME (IN DOLLARS)	TAX (IN DOLLARS)
0–4,000	1% of income
4,000–6,000	40 + 2% of income over 4,000
6,000–8,000	80 + 3% of income over 6,000
8,000–10,000	140 + 4% of income over 8,000
10,000–15,000	220 + 5% of income over 10,000
15,000–25,000	470 + 6% of income over 15,000
25,000–50,000	1,070 + 7% of income over 25,000

5. How much tax is due on an income of $7,500?

    (A) $75
    (B) $80
    (C) $125
    (D) $150
    (E) $225

6. Your income for a year is $26,000. You receive a raise so that next year your income will be $29,000. How much *more* will you pay in taxes next year if the tax rate remains the same?

    (A) $70
    (B) $180
    (C) $200
    (D) $210
    (E) $700

7. Joan paid $100 in taxes. If X was her income, which of the following statements is true?

    (A) $0 < X < 4,000$
    (B) $4,000 < X < 6,000$
    (C) $6,000 < X < 8,000$
    (D) $8,000 < X < 10,000$
    (E) $10,000 < X < 15,000$

8. The town of Zenith has a population of 50,000. The average income of a person who lives in Zenith is $3,700 per year. What is the total amount paid in taxes by the people of Zenith? Assume each person pays tax on $3,700.

    (A) $37
    (B) $3700
    (C) $50,000
    (D) $185,000
    (E) $1,850,000

9. A person who has an income of $10,000 pays what percent (to the nearest percent) of his or her income in taxes?

    (A) 1
    (B) 2
    (C) 3
    (D) 4
    (E) 5

Questions 10–14 refer to the following graph.

Women In the Labor Force

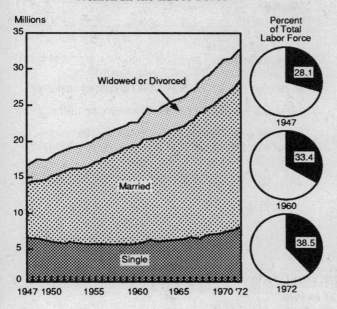

Sources: Pocket Data Book U.S.A. 1973. Bureau of the Census.

10. The total labor force in 1960 was about *y* million with *y* equal to about

    (A) 22
    (B) 65
    (C) 75
    (D) 80
    (E) 85

11. In 1947, the percent of women in the labor force who were married was about

    (A) 28
    (B) 33
    (C) 38
    (D) 50
    (E) 65

12. What was the first year when more than 20 million women were in the labor force?

    (A) 1950
    (B) 1953
    (C) 1956
    (D) 1958
    (E) 1964

13. Between 1947 and 1972, the number of women in the labor force

    (A) increased by about 50%
    (B) increased by about 100%
    (C) increased by about 150%
    (D) increased by about 200%
    (E) increased by about 250%

14. Which of the following statements about the labor force can be inferred from the graphs?

    I. Between 1947 and 1957, there were no years when more than 5 million widowed or divorced women were in the labor force.
    II. In every year between 1947 and 1972, the number of single women in the labor force has increased.
    III. In 1965, women made up more than $\frac{1}{3}$ of the total labor force.

    (A) I only
    (B) II only
    (C) I and II only
    (D) I and III only
    (E) I, II, and III

Questions 15–18 refer to the following table.

Participation in National Elections

Persons in millions. Civilian noninstitutional population as of Nov. 1. Based on post-election surveys of persons reporting whether or not they voted; differs from table 103 data which are based on actual vote counts.

Characteristic	1964 Persons of voting age	1964 Percent voted	1968 Persons of voting age	1968 Percent voted	1972 Persons of voting age	1972 Percent voted
Total	111	69	117	68	136	63
Male	52	72	54	70	64	64
Female	58	67	62	66	72	62
White	99	71	105	69	121	64
Negro and other	11	57	12	56	15	51
Negro	10	58	11	58	13	52
Region:						
North and West	78	75	82	71	94	66
South	32	57	35	60	43	55
Age:						
18–24 years	10	51	12	50	25	50
25–44 years	45	69	46	67	49	63
45–64 years	38	76	40	75	42	71
65 years and over	17	66	18	66	20	63

Source: U.S. Bureau of the Census.

15. Which of the following groups had the highest percentage of voters in 1968?

    (A) 18–24 years
    (B) Female
    (C) South
    (D) 25–44 years
    (E) Male

16. In 1972, what percent (to the nearest percent) of persons of voting age were female?

    (A) 52
    (B) 53
    (C) 62
    (D) 64
    (E) 72

17. In 1968, how many males of voting age voted?

    (A) 37,440,000
    (B) 37,800,000
    (C) 42,160,000
    (D) 62,000,000
    (E) 374,400,000

18. Let X be the number (in millions) of persons of voting age in the 25–44 year range who lived in the North and West in 1964. Which of the following includes all possible values and only possible values of X?

(A) $0 \lesseqgtr X \lesseqgtr 45$
(B) $13 \lesseqgtr X \lesseqgtr 45$
(C) $13 \lesseqgtr X \lesseqgtr 78$
(D) $45 \lesseqgtr X \lesseqgtr 78$
(E) $75 \lesseqgtr X \lesseqgtr 78$

Questions 19–21 refer to the following table.

TIMED PERIOD (in minutes)	SPEED OF A TRAIN OVER A 3-HOUR PERIOD							
	0	30	45	60	90	120	150	180
SPEED AT TIME (in m.p.h.)	40	45	47.5	50	55	60	65	70

19. How fast was the train traveling $2\frac{1}{2}$ hours after the beginning of the timed period?

(A) 50 m.p.h.
(B) 55 m.p.h.
(C) 60 m.p.h.
(D) 65 m.p.h.
(E) 70 m.p.h.

20. During the three hours shown on the table, the speed of the train

(A) increased by 25%
(B) increased by 50%
(C) increased by 75%
(D) increased by 100%
(E) increased by 125%

21. At time t, measured in minutes after the beginning of the time period, which of the following gives the speed of the train in accordance with the table?

(A) $\frac{1}{6}t$
(B) $10t$
(C) $40 + t$
(D) $40 + \frac{1}{6}t$
(E) $40 + 10t$

Questions 22–24 refer to the following table.

	% OF PROTEIN	% OF CARBOHYDRATES	% OF FAT	COST PER 100 GRAMS
FOOD A	10	20	30	$1.80
FOOD B	20	15	10	$3.00
FOOD C	20	10	40	$2.75

22. If you purchase x grams of Food A, y grams of Food B, and z grams of Food C, the cost will be

(A) $\left(\frac{9}{5}x + 3y + \frac{11}{4}z\right)\cent$
(B) $\$\left(\frac{9}{5}x + 3y + \frac{11}{4}z\right)$
(C) $\$(1.8x + 3z + 2.75y)$
(D) $(3x + 1.8y + 2.75z)\cent$
(E) $\$(x + y + z)$

23. Which of the following diets would supply the most grams of protein?

(A) 500 grams of A
(B) 250 grams of B
(C) 350 grams of C
(D) 150 grams of A and 200 grams of B
(E) 200 grams of B and 200 grams of C

24. All of the following diets would supply at least 75 grams of fat. Which of the diets costs the least?

(A) 200 grams of A, 150 grams of B
(B) 500 grams of B, 100 grams of A
(C) 200 grams of C
(D) 150 grams of A, 100 grams of C
(E) 300 grams of A

Answer Key

1.	A	7.	C	13.	B	19.	D
2.	A	8.	E	14.	A	20.	C
3.	B	9.	B	15.	E	21.	D
4.	D	10.	B	16.	B	22.	A
5.	C	11.	D	17.	B	23.	E
6.	D	12.	C	18.	B	24.	E

Answer Explanations

1. A. In 1964 military expenditures were about 140 billion and by 1969 they had increased to about 200 billion. $\frac{60}{140} = \frac{3}{7}$, which is almost 50%.

   By using a straight edge, you may see that the bar for 1969 is about half again as long as the bar for 1964.

2. A. Since the developing countries' military expenditures for every year were less than 30 billion, Choice A is the only possible answer. Notice that by reading the possible answers first, you save time. You don't need the exact answer.

3. B. I cannot be inferred since the graph indicates *only* the dollars spent on military expenditures, not the percentage of income and not total

income. II is true since each bar is higher than the previous bar to the left. III cannot be inferred since the graph gives no information about 1972. So only statement II can be inferred from the graph.

4. **D.** In 1971 the NATO countries spent over 100 billion and less than 150 billion on military expenditures. Since this was $\frac{1}{3}$ of their combined incomes, the combined income is between 300 billion and 450 billion. Thus, Choice D must be the correct answer.

5. **C.** 7,500 is in the 6,000–8,000 bracket so the tax will be 80 + 3% of the income over 6,000. Since 7,500 − 6,000 = 1,500, the income over 6,000 is 1,500. 3% of 1500 = (.03)(1500) = 45, so the tax is 80 + 45 = 125.

6. **D.** The tax on 26,000 is 1,070 + 7% of (26,000 − 25,000). Thus, the tax is 1,070 + 70 = 1,140. The tax on 29,000 is 1,070 + 7% of (29,000 − 25,000). Thus, the tax on 29,000 is 1,070 + 280 = 1,350. Therefore, you will pay 1,350 − 1,140 = $210 more in taxes next year. A faster method is to use the fact that the $3,000 raise is income over 25,000, so it will be taxed at 7%. Therefore, the tax on the extra $3,000 will be (.07)(3,000) = 210.

7. **C.** If income is less than 6,000, then the tax is less than 80. If income is greater than 8,000, then the tax is greater than 140. Therefore, if the tax is 100, the income must be between 6,000 and 8,000. You *do not* have to calculate her exact income.

8. **E.** Each person pays the tax on $3,700, which is 1% of 3,700 or $37. Since there are 50,000 people in Zenith, the total taxes are (37)(50,000) = $1,850,000.

9. **B.** The tax on 10,000 is 220, so taxes are $\frac{220}{10,000}$ = .022 = 2.2% of income. 2.2% is 2% after rounding to the nearest percent.

10. **B.** In 1960 women made up 33.4% or about $\frac{1}{3}$ of the labor force. Using the line graph, there were about 22 million women in the labor force in 1960. So the labor force was about 3(22) or 66 million. The closest answer among the choices is 65 million.

11. **D.** In 1947, there were about 16 million women in the labor force, and about 14 − 6 or 8 million of them were married. Therefore, the percent of women in the labor force who were married is $\frac{8}{16}$ or 50%.

12. **C.** Look at the possible answers first. You can use your pencil and admission card as straight edges.

13. **B.** In 1947, there were about 16 million women in the labor force. By 1972 there were about 32 million. Therefore, the number of women doubled, which is an increase of 100%. (Not of 200%.)

14. **A.** I is true since the width of the band for widowed or divorced women was never more than 5 million between 1947 and 1957. II is false since the number of single women in the labor force decreased from 1947 to 1948. III cannot be inferred since there is no information about the total labor force or women as a percent of it in 1965. Thus, only I can be inferred.

15. **E.** Look in the fourth column.

16. **B.** In 1972 there were 72 million females out of 136 million persons of voting age. $\frac{72}{136}$ = .529, which is 53% to the nearest percent.

17. **B.** In 1968, 70% of the 54 million males of voting age voted, and (.7)(54,000,000) = 37,800,000.

18. **B.** Since 78 million persons of voting age lived in the North and West in 1964, and there were 65 million persons of voting age not in the 25–44 year range, there must be at least 78 − 65 = 13 million people in the North and West in the 25–44 year range. X must be greater than or equal to 13. Since there were 45 million people of voting age in the 25–44 year range, X must be less than or equal to 45.

19. **D.** $2\frac{1}{2}$ hours is 150 minutes.

20. **C.** The train's speed increased by 70 − 40 which is 30 miles per hour. $\frac{30}{40}$ is 75%.

21. **D.** When $t = 0$, the speed is 40, so A and B are incorrect. When $t = 180$, the speed is 70, so C and E are incorrect. Choice D gives all the values that appear in the table.

22. **A.** The cost of food A is $1.80 per hundred grams or 1.8¢ a gram, so x grams cost (1.8x)¢ or $\left(\frac{9}{5}\right)x$¢. Each gram of food B costs 3¢ so y grams of food B will cost 3y¢. Each gram of food C costs 2.75¢ or $\frac{11}{4}$¢; thus, z grams of food C will cost $\left(\frac{11}{4}\right)z$¢. Therefore, the total

cost is $\left[\left(\dfrac{9}{5}\right)x + 3y + \left(\dfrac{11}{4}\right)z\right]\cancel{c}$.

23. E.   Since food A is 10% protein, 500 grams of
food A will supply 50 grams of protein. Food
B is 20% protein, so 250 grams of food B will
supply 50 grams of protein. 350 grams of food
C will supply 70 grams of protein. 150 grams
of food A and 200 grams of food B will supply
$15 + 40 = 55$ grams of protein. 200 grams of
food B and 200 grams of food C will supply 40
+ 40 or 80 grams of protein. Choice E supplies the most protein.

24. E.   The diet of choice A will cost 2($1.80) +
$\left(\dfrac{3}{2}\right)$($3) = $3.60 + $4.50 = $8.10. Choice B
will cost 5($3) + $1.80 = $16.80. Choice C
costs 2($2.75) = $5.50. Choice D costs
$\left(\dfrac{3}{2}\right)$($1.80) + $2.75 = $2.70 + $2.75 =
$5.45. The diet of Choice E costs 3($1.80) or
$5.40 so Choice E costs the least.

11 Mathematics Review

- ■ **Arithmetic**
- ■ **Algebra**
- ■ **Geometry**
- ■ **Tables and Graphs**
- ■ **Formulas**

The mathematics questions on the GRE General Test require a working knowledge of mathematical principles, including an understanding of the fundamentals of algebra, plane geometry, and arithmetic, as well as the ability to translate problems into formulas and to interpret graphs. The following review covers these areas thoroughly and will prove helpful.

Read through the review carefully. You will notice that each topic is keyed for easy reference. Each of the Practice Exercises in this chapter, as well as the Diagnostic and five Model Tests, are keyed in the same manner. Therefore, after working the mathematics problems in each area, refer to the answer key and follow the mathematics reference key so that you can focus in on those topics where you need improvement.

Review and Practice

I. Arithmetic

I–A. Whole Numbers

A-1

The numbers 0, 1, 2, 3,...are called whole numbers or positive *integers* and 0. So 75 is an integer but $4\frac{1}{3}$ is not an integer.

A-2

If the integer k divides m evenly, then we say *m is divisible by k* or *k is a factor of m*. For example, 12 is divisible by 4, but 12 is not divisible by 5. 1, 2, 3, 4, 6, 12 are all factors of 12.

If k is a factor of m, then there is another integer n such that $m = k \times n$; in this case, m is called a *multiple of k*.

Since $12 = 4 \times 3$, 12 is a multiple of 4 and also 12 is a multiple of 3. 5,10, 15, and 20 are all multiples of 5 but 15 and 5 are not multiples of 10.

Any integer is a multiple of each of its factors.

A-3

Any whole number is divisible by itself and by 1. If p is a whole number greater than 1, which has *only* p and 1 as factors, then p is called a *prime number*. 2, 3, 5, 7, 11, 13, 17, 19 and 23 are all primes. 14 is not a prime since it is divisible by 2 and by 7.

A whole number which is divisible by 2 is called an *even* number; if a whole number is not even, then it is an *odd* number. 2, 4, 6, 8, 10 are even numbers, and 1, 3, 5, 7 and 9 are odd numbers.

A collection of numbers is *consecutive* if each number is the successor of the number which precedes it. For example, 7, 8, 9 and 10 are consecutive, but 7, 8, 10, 13 are not. 4, 6, 8, 10 are consecutive even numbers. 7, 11, 13, 17 are consecutive primes. 7, 13, 19, 23 are not consecutive primes since 11 is a prime between 7 and 13.

A-4

Any whole number can be written as a product of factors which are prime numbers.

To write a number as a *product of prime factors:*

(A) Divide the number by 2 if possible; continue to divide by 2 until the factor you get is not divisible by 2.
(B) Divide the result from (A) by 3 if possible; continue to divide by 3 until the factor you get is not divisible by 3.
(C) Divide the result from (B) by 5 if possible; continue to divide by 5 until the factor you get is not divisible by 5.
(D) Continue the procedure with 7, 11, and so on, until all the factors are primes.

EXAMPLE 1: Express 24 as a product of prime factors.

(A) $24 = 2 \times 12, 12 = 2 \times 6, 6 = 2 \times 3$ so $24 = 2 \times 2 \times 2 \times 3$. Since each factor (2 and 3) is prime, $24 = 2 \times 2 \times 2 \times 3$.

EXAMPLE 2: Express 252 as a product of primes.

(A) $252 = 2 \times 126, 126 = 2 \times 63$ and 63 is not divisible by 2, so $252 = 2 \times 2 \times 63$.
(B) $63 = 3 \times 21, 21 = 3 \times 7$ and 7 is not divisible by 3. Since 7 is a prime, then $252 = 2 \times 2 \times 3 \times 3 \times 7$ and all the factors are primes.

A-5

A number m is a *common multiple* of two other numbers k and j if it is a multiple of each of them. For example, 12 is a common multiple of 4 and 6, since $3 \times 4 = 12$ and $2 \times 6 = 12$. 15 is not a common multiple of 3 and 6, because 15 is not a multiple of 6.

A number k is a *common factor* of two other numbers m and n if k is a factor of m and k is a factor of n.

The *least common multiple* (L.C.M.) of two numbers is the smallest number which is a common multiple of both numbers. To find the least common multiple of two integers k and j:

(A) Write k as a product of primes and j as a product of primes.
(B) If there are any common factors *delete* them in *one* of the products.
(C) Multiply the remaining factors; the result is the least common multiple.

EXAMPLE 1: Find the L.C.M. of 12 and 11.

(A) $12 = 2 \times 2 \times 3$, $11 = 11 \times 1$.
(B) There are no common factors.
(C) The L.C.M. is $12 \times 11 = 132$.

EXAMPLE 2: Find the L.C.M. of 27 and 63.

(A) $27 = 3 \times 3 \times 3$, $63 = 3 \times 3 \times 7$.
(B) $3 \times 3 = 9$ is a common factor so delete it once.
(C) The L.C.M. is $3 \times 3 \times 3 \times 7 = 189$.

You can find the L.C.M. of a collection of numbers in the same way except that if in step (B) the common factors are factors of more than two of the numbers, then delete the common factor in *all but one* of the products.

EXAMPLE 3: Find the L.C.M. of 27, 63 and 72.

(A) $27 = 3 \times 3 \times 3$, $63 = 3 \times 3 \times 7$, $72 = 2 \times 2 \times 2 \times 3 \times 3$.
(B) Delete 3×3 from two of the products.
(C) The L.C.M. is $3 \times 7 \times 2 \times 2 \times 2 \times 3 \times 3 = 21 \times 72 = 1,512$.

I–B. Fractions

B–1

A FRACTION is a number which represents a ratio or division of two whole numbers (integers). A fraction is written in the form $\frac{a}{b}$. The number on the top, a, is called the numerator; the number on the bottom, b, is called the denominator. The denominator tells how many equal parts there are (for example, parts of a pie); the numerator tells how many of these equal parts are taken. For example, $\frac{5}{8}$ is a fraction whose numerator is 5 and whose denominator is 8; it represents taking 5 of 8 equal parts, or dividing 8 into 5.

A fraction can not have 0 as a denominator since division by 0 is not defined.

A fraction with 1 as the denominator is the same as the whole number which is its numerator. For example, $\frac{12}{1}$ is 12, $\frac{0}{1}$ is 0.

If the numerator and denominator of a fraction are identical, the fraction represents 1. For example, $\frac{3}{3} = \frac{9}{9} = \frac{13}{13} = 1$. Any whole number, k, is represented by a fraction with a numerator equal to k times the denominator. For example, $\frac{18}{6} = 3$, and $\frac{30}{5} = 6$.

B–2

Mixed Numbers.   A mixed number consists of a whole number and a fraction. For example, $7\frac{1}{4}$ is a mixed number; it means $7 + \frac{1}{4}$ and $\frac{1}{4}$ is called the fractional part of the mixed number $7\frac{1}{4}$. Any mixed number can be changed into a fraction:

(A)   Multiply the whole number by the denominator of the fraction.
(B)   Add the numerator of the fraction to the result of step A.
(C)   Use the result of step B as the numerator and use the denominator of the fractional part of the mixed number as the denominator. This fraction is equal to the mixed number.

EXAMPLE 1:   Write $7\frac{1}{4}$ as a fraction.

(A) $4 \cdot 7 = 28$
(B) $28 + 1 = 29$
(C)   so $7\frac{1}{4} = \frac{29}{4}$

A fraction whose numerator is larger than its denominator can be changed into a mixed number.

(A)   Divide the denominator into the numerator; the result is the whole number of the mixed number.
(B)   Put the remainder from step A over the denominator; this is the fractional part of the mixed number.

EXAMPLE 2:   Change $\frac{35}{8}$ into a mixed number.

(A)   Divide 8 into 35; the result is 4 with a remainder of 3.
(B) $\frac{3}{8}$ is the fractional part of the mixed number.
(C)   So $\frac{35}{8} = 4\frac{3}{8}$.

In calculations with mixed numbers, change the mixed numbers into fractions.

B–3

Multiplying Fractions.   To multiply two fractions, multiply their numerators to form the numerator of the product. Multiply their denominators to form the denominator of the product.

In word problems, *of* usually indicates multiplication.

EXAMPLE: John saves $\frac{1}{3}$ of $240. How much does he save?

$$\frac{1}{3} \cdot \frac{240}{1} = \frac{240}{3} = \$80, \text{ the amount John saves.}$$

B–4

Dividing Fractions. One fraction is a *reciprocal* of another if their product is 1. So $\frac{1}{2}$ and 2 are reciprocals $\left(\frac{1}{2} \cdot 2 = \frac{1}{2} \cdot \frac{2}{1} = \frac{2}{2} = 1\right)$. To find the reciprocal of a fraction, simply interchange the numerator and denominator (turn the fraction upside down). This is called *inverting* the fraction. So when you invert $\frac{15}{17}$ you get $\frac{17}{15}$. When a fraction is inverted the inverted fraction and the original fraction are reciprocals. Thus $\frac{15}{17} \cdot \frac{17}{15} = \frac{255}{255} = \frac{1}{1} = 1$.

To divide one fraction (the dividend) by another fraction (the divisor), invert the divisor and multiply.

EXAMPLE 1: $\frac{5}{6} \div \frac{3}{4} = \frac{5}{6} \cdot \frac{4}{3} = \frac{20}{18}$

EXAMPLE 2: A worker makes a basket every $\frac{2}{3}$ hour. If the worker works for $7\frac{1}{2}$ hours, how many baskets will he make? We want to divide $\frac{2}{3}$ into $7\frac{1}{2}$, $7\frac{1}{2} = \frac{15}{2}$, so we want to divide $\frac{15}{2}$ by $\frac{2}{3}$. Thus

$$\frac{15}{2} \div \frac{2}{3} = \frac{15}{2} \cdot \frac{3}{2} = \frac{45}{4} = 11\frac{1}{4} \text{ baskets.}$$

B–5

Dividing and Multiplying by the Same Number. Since multiplication or division by 1 does not change the value of a number, you can multiply or divide any fraction by 1 and the fraction will remain the same. Remember that $\frac{a}{a} = 1$ for any non-zero number a. Therefore, if you multiply or divide any fraction by $\frac{a}{a}$, the result is the same as if you multiplied the numerator by a and denominator by a or divided the numerator by a and the denominator by a.

If you multiply the numerator and denominator of a fraction by the same non-zero number, the value of the fraction remains the same.

If you divide the numerator and denominator of any fraction by the same non-zero number, the value of the fraction remains the same.

Consider the fraction $\frac{3}{4}$. If we multiply 3 by 10 and 4 by 10, then $\frac{30}{40}$ must equal

$\frac{3}{4}$ (In $\frac{30}{40}$, 10 is a common factor of 30 and 40.)

When we multiply fractions, if any of the numerators and denominators have a common factor (see A–2 for factors) we can divide each of them by the common factor and the fraction remains the same. This process is called *cancelling* and can be a great time-saver.

EXAMPLE: Multiply $\frac{4}{9} \cdot \frac{75}{8}$. Since 4 is a common factor of 4 and 8, divide 4 and 8 by 4 getting $\frac{4}{9} \cdot \frac{75}{8} = \frac{1}{9} \cdot \frac{75}{2}$. Since 3 is a common factor of 9 and 75 divide 9 and 75 by 3 to get $\frac{1}{9} \cdot \frac{75}{2} = \frac{1}{3} \cdot \frac{25}{2}$. So $\frac{4}{9} \cdot \frac{75}{8} = \frac{1}{3} \cdot \frac{25}{2} = \frac{25}{6}$.

B–6
Equivalent Fractions.   Two fractions are equivalent or equal if they represent the same ratio or number. In the last section, you saw that if you multiply or divide the numerator and denominator of a fraction by the same non-zero number, the result is equivalent to the original fraction. For example, $\frac{7}{8} = \frac{70}{80}$ since $70 = 10 \times 7$ and $80 = 10 \times 8$.

> In a multiple-choice test, your answer to a problem may not be the same as any of the given choices, yet one choice may be equivalent. Therefore, you may have to express your answer as an equivalent fraction.

To find a fraction with a known denominator equal to a given fraction:

(A)   divide the denominator of the given fraction into the known denominator;

(B)   multiply the result of (A) by the numerator of the given fraction; this is the numerator of the required equivalent fraction.

EXAMPLE: Your answer is $\frac{2}{5}$ One of the test answers has a denominator of 30.

Find a fraction with denominator 30 which is equal to $\frac{2}{5}$:

(A)   5 into 30 is 6;

(B) $6 \cdot 2 = 12$ so $\frac{12}{30} = \frac{2}{5}$.

Check your result. Divide numerator and denominator by the same number. $12 \div 6 = 2$ and $30 \div 6 = 5$

B–7
Reducing a Fraction to Lowest Terms.   A fraction has been reduced to lowest terms when the numerator and denominator have no common factors.

For example, $\frac{3}{4}$ is reduced to lowest terms, but $\frac{3}{6}$ is not because 3 is a common factor of 3 and 6.

To reduce a fraction to lowest terms, cancel all the common factors of the numerator and denominator. (Cancelling common factors will not change the value of the fraction.)

For example, $\frac{100}{150} = \frac{10 \cdot 10}{10 \cdot 15} = \frac{10}{15} = \frac{5 \cdot 2}{5 \cdot 3} = \frac{2}{3}$. Since 2 and 3 have no common factors, $\frac{2}{3}$ is $\frac{100}{150}$ reduced to lowest terms. A fraction is equivalent to its reduction to lowest terms.

If you write the numerator and denominator as products of primes, it is easy to cancel all the common factors.

$$\frac{63}{81} = \frac{3 \cdot 3 \cdot 7}{3 \cdot 3 \cdot 3 \cdot 3} = \frac{7}{9}$$

B–8

Adding Fractions. If the fractions have the same denominator, then the denominator is called a *common denominator*. Add the numerators, and use this sum as the new numerator, retaining the common denominator as the denominator of the new fraction. Reduce the new fraction to lowest terms.

EXAMPLE 1: $\frac{5}{12} + \frac{3}{12} = \frac{5 + 3}{12} = \frac{8}{12} = \frac{2}{3}$

EXAMPLE 2: Jim uses 7 eggs to make breakfast and 8 eggs for supper. How many dozen eggs has he used? 7 eggs are $\frac{7}{12}$ of a dozen and 8 eggs are $\frac{8}{12}$ of a dozen. He used $\frac{7}{12} + \frac{8}{12} = \frac{7 + 8}{12} = \frac{15}{12} = \frac{5}{4} = 1\frac{1}{4}$ dozen eggs.

If the fractions don't have the same denominator, you must first find a common denominator. Multiply all the denominators together; the result is a common denominator.

EXAMPLE: To add $\frac{1}{2} + \frac{2}{3} + \frac{7}{4}$, $2 \cdot 3 \cdot 4 = 24$ is a common denominator.

There are many common denominators; the smallest one is called the *least common denominator*. For the previous example, 12 is the least common denominator.

Once you have found a common denominator, express each fraction as an equivalent fraction with the common denominator, and add as you did when the fractions had the same denominator.

EXAMPLE: $\frac{1}{2} + \frac{2}{3} + \frac{7}{4} = ?$

(A)   24 is a common denominator.

(B) $\frac{1}{2} = \frac{12}{24}, \frac{2}{3} = \frac{16}{24}, \frac{7}{4} = \frac{42}{24}.$

(C) $\frac{1}{2} + \frac{2}{3} + \frac{7}{4} = \frac{12}{24} + \frac{16}{24} + \frac{42}{24} = \frac{12 + 16 + 42}{24} = \frac{70}{24} = \frac{35}{12}.$

B–9

Subtracting Fractions. When the fractions have the same denominator, subtract the numerators and place the result over the denominator.

EXAMPLE: $\frac{3}{5} - \frac{2}{5} = \frac{3-2}{5} = \frac{1}{5}$

When the fractions have different denominators

(A)   Find a common denominator.

(B)   Express the fractions as equivalent fractions with the same denominator.

(C)   Subtract.

EXAMPLE: $\frac{3}{5} - \frac{2}{7} = ?$

(A)   A common denominator is $5 \cdot 7 = 35.$

(B) $\frac{3}{5} = \frac{21}{35}, \frac{2}{7} = \frac{10}{35}.$

(C) $\frac{3}{5} - \frac{2}{7} = \frac{21}{35} - \frac{10}{35} = \frac{21 - 10}{35} = \frac{11}{35}.$

B–10

Complex Fractions. A fraction whose numerator and denominator are themselves fractions is called a *complex fraction*. For example $\dfrac{\frac{2}{3}}{\frac{4}{5}}$ is a complex fraction. A complex fraction can always be simplified by dividing its numerator by its denominator.

EXAMPLE 1:   Simplify $\dfrac{\frac{2}{3}}{\frac{4}{5}}$.

$$\frac{2}{3} \div \frac{4}{5} = \frac{\overset{1}{2}}{3} \cdot \frac{5}{\underset{2}{4}} = \frac{1}{3} \cdot \frac{5}{2} = \frac{5}{6}$$

EXAMPLE 2:   It takes $2\frac{1}{2}$ hours to get from Buffalo to Cleveland traveling at a constant rate of speed. What part of the distance is traveled in $\frac{3}{4}$ of an hour?

$\dfrac{3/4}{2\,1/2} = \dfrac{3/4}{5/2} = \dfrac{3}{4} \cdot \dfrac{2}{5} = \dfrac{3}{2} \cdot \dfrac{1}{5} = \dfrac{3}{10}$ of the distance.

I–C.   Decimals

C–1

A collection of digits (the digits are 0,1,2, . . . ,9) after a period (called the decimal point) is called a *decimal fraction*. For example, these are all decimal fractions:

.503
.5602
.32
.4

Every decimal fraction represents a fraction. To find the fraction a decimal fraction represents:

(A) Take the fraction whose denominator is 10 and whose numerator is the first digit to the right of the decimal point.

(B) Take the fraction whose denominator is 100 and whose numerator is the second digit to the right of the decimal point.

(C) Take the fraction whose denominator is 1,000 and whose numerator is the third digit to the right of the decimal point.

(D) Continue the procedure until you have used each digit to the right of the decimal place. The denominator in each step is 10 times the denominator in the previous step.

(E) The *sum* of the fractions you have obtained in (A), (B), (C), and (D) is the fraction that the decimal fraction represents.

EXAMPLE 1:   Find the fraction .503 represents.

(A) $\dfrac{5}{10}$

(B) $\dfrac{0}{100}$

(C) $\dfrac{3}{1000}$

(D) All the digits have already been used.

(E) So $.503 = \dfrac{5}{10} + \dfrac{0}{100} + \dfrac{3}{1000} = \dfrac{500}{1000} + \dfrac{0}{1000} + \dfrac{3}{1000} = \dfrac{503}{1000}$.

EXAMPLE 2:   What fraction does .78934 represent?

(A) $\dfrac{7}{10}$

(B) $\dfrac{8}{100}$

(C) $\dfrac{9}{1000}$

(D) $\dfrac{3}{10,000}, \dfrac{4}{100,000}$

(E) So $.78934 = \dfrac{7}{10} + \dfrac{8}{100} + \dfrac{9}{1000} + \dfrac{3}{10,000} + \dfrac{4}{100,000} = \dfrac{78,934}{100,000}$.

Notice that the denominator of the last fraction you obtain in step (D) is a common denominator for all the previous denominators. Since each denominator is 10 times the previous one, the denominator of the final fraction of part (D) will be the product of r copies of 10 multiplied together (called 10^r) where r is the number of digits which appear in the decimal fraction. Therefore, a decimal fraction represents a fraction whose denominator is 10^r where r is the number of digits in the decimal fraction and whose numerator is the number represented by the digits of the decimal fraction.

EXAMPLE 3:   What fraction does .5702 represent?

There are 4 digits in .5702. Therefore, the denominator is $10 \times 10 \times 10 \times 10 = 10,000$, and the numerator is 5,702. Therefore, $.5702 = \dfrac{5,702}{10,000}$.

You can add any number of zeros to the right of a decimal fraction without changing its value.

EXAMPLE: $.3 = \dfrac{3}{10} = \dfrac{30}{100} = .30 = .30000 = \dfrac{30,000}{100,000} = .300000000 \ldots$

C–2

We call the first position to the right of the decimal point the tenths place, since the digit in that position tells you how many tenths you should take. (It is the numerator of a fraction whose denominator is 10.) In the same way, we call the second position to the right the hundredths place, the third position to the right the thousandths, and so on. This is similar to the way whole numbers are expressed, since 568 means $5 \times 100 + 6 \times 10 + 8 \times 1$. The various digits represent different numbers depending on their position: the first place to the left of the decimal point represents units, the second place to the left represents tens, and so on.

The following diagram may be helpful:

```
T   H   T   U       T   H   T
H   U   E   N       E   U   H
O   N   N   I   .   N   N   O
U   D   N   T       T   D   U
S   R   S   T       H   R   S
A   E       S       S   E   A
N   D               E   D   N
D   S               D   T   D
S                   T   H   T
                    H   S   H
                    S       S
```

Thus, 5,342.061 means 5 thousands + 3 hundreds + 4 tens + 2 + 0 tenths + 6 hundredths + 1 thousandth.

C–3

A DECIMAL is a whole number plus a decimal fraction; the decimal point separates the whole number from the decimal fraction. For example, 4,307.206 is a decimal which represents 4,307 added to the decimal fraction .206. A decimal fraction is a decimal with zero as the whole number.

C–4

A fraction whose denominator is a multiple of 10 is equivalent to a decimal. The denominator tells you the last place that is filled to the right of the decimal point. Place the decimal point in the numerator so that the number of places to the right of the decimal point corresponds to the number of zeros in the denominator. If the numerator does not have enough digits, add the appropriate number of zeros *before* the numerator.

EXAMPLE 1: Find the decimal equivalent of $\frac{5,732}{100}$.

Since the denominator is 100, you need two places to the right of the decimal point so $\frac{5,732}{100} = 57.32$.

EXAMPLE 2: What is the decimal equivalent of $\frac{57}{10,000}$?

The denominator is 10,000, so you need 4 decimal places. Since 57 only has two places, we add two zeros in front of 57; thus, $\frac{57}{10,000} = .0057$.

Do not make the error of adding the zeros to the right instead of to the left of 57; .5700 means $\frac{5,700}{10,000}$ not $\frac{57}{10,000}$.

C–5

Adding Decimals. Decimals are much easier to add than fractions. To add a collection of decimals:

(A) Write the decimals in a column with the decimal points vertically aligned.
(B) Add enough zeros to the right of the decimal point so that every number has an entry in each column to the right of the decimal point.
(C) Add the numbers in the same way as whole numbers.
(D) Place a decimal point in the sum so that it is directly beneath the decimal points in the decimals added.

EXAMPLE 1: How much is $5 + 3.43 + 16.021 + 3.1$?

(A)		(B)	
	5		5.000
	3.43		3.430
	16.021		16.021
	+ 3.1		+ 3.100

(C)
    5.000
    3.430
  16.021
+ 3.100

(D)   27.551   The answer is **27.551.**

EXAMPLE 2:   If John has $.50, $3.25, and $6.05, how much does he have altogether?

$$\begin{array}{r} \$ \ .50 \\ 3.25 \\ + \ 6.05 \\ \hline \$9.80 \end{array} \quad \text{So John has \$9.80.}$$

C–6

Subtracting Decimals.   To subtract one decimal from another:

(A) Put the decimals in a column so that the decimal points are vertically aligned.
(B) Add zeros so that every decimal has an entry in each column to the right of the decimal point.
(C) Subtract the numbers as you would whole numbers.
(D) Place the decimal point in the result so that it is directly beneath the decimal points of the numbers you subtracted.

EXAMPLE 1:   Solve $5.053 - 2.09$.

(A) $\begin{array}{r} 5.053 \\ - \ 2.09 \ \\ \end{array}$ (B) $\begin{array}{r} 5.053 \\ - \ 2.090 \\ \end{array}$

(C) $\begin{array}{r} 5.053 \\ - \ 2.090 \\ \end{array}$

(D) $\quad 2.963$ The answer is **2.963.**

EXAMPLE 2:   If Joe has $12 and he loses $8.40, how much money does he have left?

Since $12.00 - $8.40 = $3.60, he has $3.60 left.

C–7

Multiplying Decimals.   Decimals are multiplied like whole numbers. *The decimal point of the product is placed so that the number of decimal places in the product is equal to the total of the number of decimal places in all of the numbers multiplied.*

EXAMPLE 1:   What is $(5.02)(.6)$?

$(502)(6) = 3012$. There were 2 decimal places in 5.02 and 1 decimal place in .6, so the product must have $2 + 1 = 3$ decimal places. Therefore, $(5.02)(.6) = 3.012$.

EXAMPLE 2:   If eggs cost $.06 each, how much should a dozen eggs cost?

Since $(12)(.06) = .72$, a dozen eggs should cost $.72.

> **Computing Tip.** To multiply a decimal by 10, just move the decimal point to the right one place; to multiply by 100, move the decimal point two places to the right and so on.

EXAMPLE: $9,983.456 \times 100 = 998,345.6$

C–8

Dividing Decimals. To divide one decimal (the dividend) by another decimal (the divisor):

(A) Move the decimal point in the divisor to the right until there is no decimal fraction in the divisor (this is the same as multiplying the divisor by a multiple of 10).

(B) Move the decimal point in the dividend the same number of places to the right as you moved the decimal point in step (A).

(C) Divide the result of (B) by the result of (A) as if they were whole numbers.

(D) The number of decimal places in the result (quotient) should be equal to the number of decimal places in the result of step (B).

EXAMPLE 1: Divide .05 into 25.155.

(A) Move the decimal point two places to the right in .05; the result is 5.

(B) Move the decimal point two places to the right in 25.155; the result is 2515.5.

(C) Divide 5 into 25155; the result is 5031.

(D) Since there was one decimal place in the result of (B); the answer is 503.1.

The work for this example might look like this:

$$.05 \overline{\smash{)}25.15\,5} \quad 503.1$$

You can always check division by multiplying.

$$(503.1)(.05) = 25.155 \text{ so we were correct.}$$

If you write division as a fraction, example 1 would be expressed as $\dfrac{25.155}{.05}$.

You can multiply both the numerator and denominator by 100 without changing the value of the fraction, so

$$\frac{25.155}{.05} = \frac{25.155 \times 100}{.05 \ \times 100} = \frac{2515.5}{5.}$$

So step (A) and (B) always change the division of a decimal by a decimal into the division by a whole number.

To divide a decimal by a whole number, divide them as if they were whole numbers. Then place the decimal point in the quotient so that the quotient has as many decimal places as the decimal (the dividend).

EXAMPLE 2: $\dfrac{55.033}{1.1} = \dfrac{550.33}{11.} = 50.03.$

EXAMPLE 3:   If oranges cost 6¢ each, how many oranges can you buy for $2.52?

$$6¢ = \$.06,$$

so the number of oranges is

$$\dfrac{2.52}{.06} = \dfrac{252}{6} = 42.$$

Computing Tip.   To divide a decimal by 10, move the decimal point *to the left* one place; to divide by 100, move the decimal point two places to the left, and so on.

EXAMPLE: Divide 5,637.6471 by 1,000.

The answer is 5.6376471, since to divide by 1,000 you move the decimal point 3 places to the left.

C–9

Converting a Fraction into a Decimal.   To convert a fraction into a decimal, divide the denominator into the numerator. For example. $\dfrac{3}{4} = 4\overline{)3.00} = $ .75. Some fractions give an infinite decimal when you divide the denominator into the numerator, for example, $\dfrac{1}{3} = .333 \ldots$ where the three dots mean you keep on getting 3 with each step of division. .333 . . . is an *infinite decimal.*

If a fraction has an infinite decimal, use the fraction in any computation.

EXAMPLE 1:   What is $\dfrac{2}{9}$ of $3,690.90?

Since the decimal for $\dfrac{2}{9}$ is .2222 . . . use the fraction $\dfrac{2}{9}$. $\dfrac{2}{9} \times \$3,690.90 = 2 \times \$410.10 = \$820.20.$

You should know the following decimal equivalents of fractions:

$\frac{1}{100} = .01$	$\frac{1}{6} = .1666\ldots$
$\frac{1}{50} = .02$	$\frac{1}{5} = .2$
$\frac{1}{40} = .025$	$\frac{1}{4} = .25$
$\frac{1}{25} = .04$	$\frac{1}{3} = .333\ldots$
$\frac{1}{20} = .05$	$\frac{3}{8} = .375$
$\frac{1}{16} = .0625$	$\frac{2}{5} = .4$
$\frac{1}{15} = .0666\ldots$	$\frac{1}{2} = .5$
$\frac{1}{12} = .0833\ldots$	$\frac{5}{8} = .625$
$\frac{1}{10} = .1$	$\frac{2}{3} = .666\ldots$
$\frac{1}{9} = .111\ldots$	$\frac{3}{4} = .75$
$\frac{1}{8} = .125$	$\frac{7}{8} = .875$
	$\frac{3}{2} = 1.5$

Any decimal with . . . is an infinite decimal.

I–D. Percentage

D–1

PERCENT is another method of expressing fractions or parts of an object. Percents are expressed in terms of hundredths, so 100% means 100 hundredths or 1. In the same way, 50% would be 50 hundredths or $\frac{50}{100}$ or $\frac{1}{2}$.

A decimal is converted to a percent by multiplying the decimal by 100. Since multiplying a decimal by 100 is accomplished by moving the decimal point two places to the right, *you convert a decimal into a percent by moving the decimal point two places to the right.* For example, .134 = 13.4%.

If you wish to convert a percent into a decimal, you divide the percent by 100. There is a shortcut for this also. To divide by 100 you move the decimal point two places to the left.

Therefore, *to convert a percent into a decimal, move the decimal point two places to the left.* For example, 24% = .24.

A fraction is converted into a percent by changing the fraction to a decimal and then changing the decimal to a percent. A percent is changed into a fraction by first converting the percent into a decimal and then changing the decimal to a fraction. You should know the following fractional equivalents of percents.

$1\% = \dfrac{1}{100}$	$25\% = \dfrac{1}{4}$	$80\% = \dfrac{4}{5}$
$2\% = \dfrac{1}{50}$	$33\dfrac{1}{3}\% = \dfrac{1}{3}$	$83\dfrac{1}{3}\% = \dfrac{5}{6}$
$4\% = \dfrac{1}{25}$	$37\dfrac{1}{2}\% = \dfrac{3}{8}$	$87\dfrac{1}{2}\% = \dfrac{7}{8}$
$5\% = \dfrac{1}{20}$	$40\% = \dfrac{2}{5}$	$100\% = 1$
$8\dfrac{1}{3}\% = \dfrac{1}{12}$	$50\% = \dfrac{1}{2}$	$120\% = \dfrac{6}{5}$
$10\% = \dfrac{1}{10}$	$60\% = \dfrac{3}{5}$	$125\% = \dfrac{5}{4}$
$12\dfrac{1}{2}\% = \dfrac{1}{8}$	$62\dfrac{1}{2}\% = \dfrac{5}{8}$	$133\dfrac{1}{3}\% = \dfrac{4}{3}$
$16\dfrac{2}{3}\% = \dfrac{1}{6}$	$66\dfrac{2}{3}\% = \dfrac{2}{3}$	$150\% = \dfrac{3}{2}$
$20\% = \dfrac{1}{5}$	$75\% = \dfrac{3}{4}$	

Note, for example, that $133\dfrac{1}{3}\% = 1.33\dfrac{1}{3} = 1\dfrac{1}{3} = \dfrac{4}{3}$.

When you compute with percents, it is usually easier to change the percents to decimals or fractions.

EXAMPLE 1:   A company has 6,435 bars of soap. If the company sells 20% of its bars of soap, how many bars of soap did it sell?

Change 20% into .2. Thus, the company sold $(.2)(6,435) = 1287.0 = 1,287$ bars of soap. An alternative method would be to convert 20% to $\dfrac{1}{5}$. Then, $\dfrac{1}{5} \times 6,435 = 1,287$.

EXAMPLE 2:   In a class of 60 students, 18 students received a grade of B. What percent of the class received a grade of B?

$\dfrac{18}{60}$ of the class received a grade of B. $\dfrac{18}{60} = \dfrac{3}{10} = .3$ and $.3 = .30 = 30\%$, so 30% of the class received a grade of B.

EXAMPLE 3: If the population of Dryden was 10.000 in 1960 and the population of Dryden increased by 15% between 1960 and 1970, what was the population of Dryden in 1970?

The population increased by 15% between 1960 and 1970, so the increase was (.15)(10,000) which is 1,500. The population in 1970 was 10,000 + 1,500 = 11,500.

A quicker method: the population increased 15%, so the population in 1970 is 115% of the population in 1960. Therefore, the population in 1970 is 115% of 10,000 which is (1.15)(10,000) = 11,500.

D–2
Interest and Discount. Two of the most common uses of percent are in interest and discount problems.

The rate of interest is usually given as a percent. The basic formula for interest problems is:

$$\boxed{\text{INTEREST} = \text{AMOUNT} \times \text{TIME} \times \text{RATE}}$$

You can assume the rate of interest is the annual rate of interest unless the problem states otherwise; so you should express the time in years.

EXAMPLE 1: How much interest will $10,000 earn in 9 months at an annual rate of 6%?

9 months is $\frac{3}{4}$ of a year and $6\% = \frac{3}{50}$, so using the formula, the interest is $10,000 $\times \frac{3}{4} \times \frac{3}{50} = \$50 \times 9 = \$450$.

EXAMPLE 2: What annual rate of interest was paid if $5,000 earned $300 in interest in 2 years?

Since the interest was earned in 2 years, $150 is the interest earned in one year. $\frac{150}{5,000} = .03 = 3\%$, so the annual rate of interest was 3%.

This type of interest is called *simple interest.*

There is another method of computing interest called *compound interest.* In computing compound interest, the interest is periodically added to the amount (or principal) which is earning interest.

EXAMPLE 3: What will $1,000 be worth after three years if it earns interest at the rate of 5% compounded annually?

Compounded annually means that the interest earned during one year is added to the amount (or principal) at the end of each year. The interest on $1,000 at

5% for one year is $\$(1,000)(.05) = \$50$. So you must compute the interest on $\$1,050$ (not $\$1.000$) for the second year. The interest is $\$(1,050)(.05) = \$52.50$. Therefore, during the third year interest will be computed for $\$1,102.50$. During the third year the interest is $\$(1,102.50)(.05) = \$55.125 = \$55.13$. Therefore, after 3 years the original $\$1000$ will be worth $\$1,157.63$.

If you calculated simple interest on $\$1,000$ at 5% for three years, the answer would be $\$(1,000)(.05)(3) = \$150$. Therefore, using simple interest, $\$1,000$ is worth $\$1,150$ after 3 years. Notice that this is not the same as the money was worth using compound interest.

You can assume that interest means simple interest unless a problem states otherwise.

The basic formula for discount problems is:

$$\boxed{\text{DISCOUNT} = \text{COST} \times \text{RATE OF DISCOUNT}}$$

EXAMPLE 1: What is the discount if a car which cost $\$3,000$ is discounted 7%?

The discount is $\$3,000 \times .07 = \$210.00$ since 7% = .07.

If we know the cost of an item and its discounted price, we can find the rate of discount by using the formula

$$\text{rate of discount} = \frac{\text{cost} - \text{price}}{\text{cost}}$$

EXAMPLE 2. What was the rate of discount if a boat which cost $\$5,000$ was sold for $\$4,800$?

Using this formula, we find that the rate of discount equals

$$\frac{5,000 - 4,800}{5,000} = \frac{200}{5,000} = \frac{1}{25} = .04 = 4\%.$$

After an item has been discounted once, it may be discounted again. This procedure is called *successive* discounting.

EXAMPLE 3: A bicycle originally cost $\$100$ and was discounted 10%. After three months it was sold after being discounted 15%. How much was the bicycle sold for?

After the 10% discount the bicycle was selling for $\$100(.90) = \$90$. An item which costs $\$90$ and is discounted 15% will sell for $\$90(.85) = \$76.50$, so the bicycle was sold for $\$76.50$.

Notice that if you added the two discounts of 10% and 15% and treated the successive discounts as a single discount of 25%, your answer would be that the bicycle sold for $\$75$, which is incorrect. Successive discounts are *not* identical to a single discount of the sum of the discounts. The previous example shows that successive discounts of 10% and 15% are not identical to a single discount of 25%.

I–E. Rounding off Numbers

E–1

Many times an approximate answer can be found more quickly and may be more useful than the exact answer. For example, if a company had sales of $998.875.63 during a year, it is easier to remember that the sales were about $1 million.

Rounding off a number to a decimal place means finding the multiple of the representative of that decimal place which is closest to the original number. Thus, rounding off a number to the nearest hundred means finding the multiple of 100 which is closest to the original number. Rounding off to the nearest tenth means finding the multiple of $\frac{1}{10}$ which is closest to the original number.

After a number has been rounded off to a particular decimal place, all the digits to the right of that particular decimal place will be zero.

EXAMPLE 1:   Round off 9,403,420.71 to the nearest hundred.

You must find the multiple of one hundred which is closest to 9,403,420.71.

The answer is 9,403,400.

Most problems dealing with money are rounded off if the answer contains a fractional part of a cent.

To round off a number to the rth decimal place:

(A)   Look at the digit in the place to the right of the rth place;
(B)   *If the digit is 0, 1, 2, 3, or 4, change all the digits in places to the right of the* rth *place to 0 to round off the number.*
(C)   *If the digit is 5, 6, 7, 8, or 9, add 1 to the digit in the* rth *place and change all the digits in places to the right of the* rth *place to 0 to round off the number.*

EXAMPLE 2:   If 16 donuts cost $1.00, how much should three donuts cost?

Three donuts should cost $\frac{3}{16}$ of $1.00. Since $\frac{3}{16} \times 1. = .1875$, the cost would be $.1875. In practice, you would round it up to $.19 or 19¢.

Rounding off numbers can help you get quick, approximate answers. Since many questions require only rough answers, you can sometimes save time on the test by rounding off numbers.

EXAMPLE 3:   Round off 43.79 to the nearest tenth.

The place to the right of tenths is hundredths, so look in the hundredths place. Since 9 is bigger than 5, add 1 to the tenths place. Therefore, 43.79 is 43.8 rounded off to the nearest tenth.

If the digit in the rth place is 9 and you need to add 1 to the digit to round off the number to the rth decimal place, put a zero in the rth place and add 1 to the digit in the position to the left of the rth place. For example, 298 rounded off to the nearest 10 is 300; 99,752 to the nearest thousand is 100,000.

I–F. Signed Numbers

F–1

A number preceded by either a plus or a minus sign is called a SIGNED NUMBER. For example, +5, −6, −4.2, and +¾ are all signed numbers. If no sign is given with a number, a plus sign is assumed; thus, 5 is interpreted as +5.

Signed numbers can often be used to distinguish different concepts. For example, a profit of $10 can be denoted by +$10 and a loss of $10 by −$10. A temperature of 20 degrees below zero can be denoted −20°.

F–2

Signed numbers are also called DIRECTED NUMBERS. You can think of numbers arranged on a line, called a number line, in the following manner:

Take a line which extends indefinitely in both directions, pick a point on the line and call it 0, pick another point on the line to the right of 0 and call it 1. The point to the right of 1 which is exactly as far from 1 as 1 is from 0 is called 2, the point to the right of 2 just as far from 2 as 1 is from 0 is called 3, and so on. The point halfway between 0 and 1 is called ½, the point halfway between ½ and 1 is called ¾. In this way, you can identify any whole number or any fraction with a point on the line.

All the numbers which correspond to points to the right of 0 are called *positive numbers*. The sign of a positive number is +.

If you go to the left of zero the same distance as you did from 0 to 1, the point is called −1; in the same way as before, you can find $-2, -3, -\frac{1}{2}, -\frac{3}{2}$ and so on.

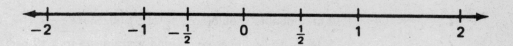

All the numbers which correspond to points to the left of zero are called *negative numbers*. Negative numbers are signed numbers whose sign is −. For example, −3, −5.15, −.003 are all negative numbers.

0 is neither positive nor negative; any nonzero number is positive or negative but not both. So $-0 = 0$.

F-3

Absolute Value. The absolute value of a signed number is the distance of the number from 0. The absolute value of any nonzero number is *positive*. For example, the absolute value of 2 is 2; the absolute value of -2 is 2. The absolute value of a number a is denoted by $|a|$, so $|-2| = 2$. The absolute value of any number can be found by dropping its sign, $|-12| = 12$, $|4| = 4$. *Thus $|-a| = |a|$ for any number a.* The only number whose absolute value is zero is zero.

F-4

Adding Signed Numbers:
Case I. Adding numbers with the *same sign:*

- (A) The sign of the sum is the same as the sign of the numbers being added.
- (B) Add the absolute values.
- (C) Put the sign from step (A) in front of the number you obtained in step (B).

EXAMPLE 1: What is $-2 + (-3.1) + (-.02)$?

- (A) The sign of the sum will be $-$.
- (B) $|-2| = 2, |-3.1| = 3.1, |-.02| = .02$, and $2 + 3.1 + .02 = 5.12$.
- (C) The answer is -5.12.

Case II. Adding *two* numbers with *different signs:*

- (A) The sign of the sum is the sign of the number which is largest in absolute value.
- (B) Subtract the absolute value of the number with the smaller absolute value from the absolute value of the number with the larger absolute value.
- (C) The answer is the number you obtained in step (B) preceded by the sign from part (A).

EXAMPLE 2: How much is $-5.1 + 3$?

- (A) The absolute value of -5.1 is 5.1 and the absolute value of 3 is 3, so the sign of the sum will be $-$.
- (B) 5.1 is larger than 3, and $5.1 - 3 = 2.1$.
- (C) The sum is -2.1.

Case III. Adding *more than two* numbers with *different signs:*

- (A) Add all the positive numbers; the result is positive (this is Case I).
- (B) Add all the negative numbers; the result is negative (this is Case I).
- (C) Add the result of step (A) to the result of step (B), by using Case II.

EXAMPLE 3:   Find the value of $5 + 52 + (-3) + 7 + (-5.1)$.

  (A) $5 + 52 + 7 = 64$.
  (B) $-3 + (-5.1) = -8.1$.
  (C) $64 + (-8.1) = 55.9$, so the answer is 55.9.

EXAMPLE 4:   If a store made a profit of $23.50 on Monday, lost $2.05 on Tuesday, lost $5.03 on Wednesday, made a profit of $30.10 on Thursday, and made a profit of $41.25 on Friday, what was its total profit (or loss) for the week? Use + for profit and − for loss.

The total is $23.50 + (-2.05) + (-5.03) + 30.10 + 41.25$ which is $94.85 + (-7.08) = 87.77$. So the store made a profit of $87.77.

F-5

Subtracting Signed Numbers.   When subtracting signed numbers:

  (A)   Change the sign of the number you are subtracting (the subtrahend).
  (B)   <u>Add</u> the result of step (A) to the number being subtracted from (the minuend) using the rules of the preceding section.

EXAMPLE 1:   Subtract 4.1 from 6.5.

  (A)   4.1 becomes −4.1.
  (B) $6.5 + (-4.1) = 2.4$.

EXAMPLE 2:   What is $7.8 - (-10.1)$?

  (A)   −10.1 becomes 10.1.
  (B) $7.8 + 10.1 = 17.9$.

So we subtract a negative number by adding a positive number with the same absolute value, and we subtract a positive number by adding a negative number of the same absolute value.

F-6

Multiplying Signed Numbers.

Case I. Multiplying two numbers:

  (A)   Multiply the absolute values of the numbers.
  (B)   If both numbers have the same sign, the result of step (A) is the answer, i.e. the product is positive. If the numbers have different signs, then the answer is the result of step (A) with a minus sign.

EXAMPLE 1: $(-5)(-12) = ?$

  (A) $5 \times 12 = 60$
  (B)   Both signs are the same, so the answer is 60.

EXAMPLE 2: $(4)(-3)=$?

(A) $4 \times 3 = 12$
(B)   The signs are different, so the answer is -12. You can remember the sign of the product in the following way:

$$(-)(-) = +$$
$$(+)(+) = +$$
$$(-)(+) = -$$
$$(+)(-) = -$$

Case II. Multiplying more than two numbers:

(A)   Multiply the first two factors using Case I.
(B)   Multiply the result of (A) by the third factor.
(C)   Multiply the result of (B) by the fourth factor.
(D)   Continue until you have used each factor.

EXAMPLE 3: $(-5)(4)(2)(-\frac{1}{2})(\frac{3}{4})=$?

(A) $(-5)(4) = -20$
(B) $(-20)(2) = -40$
(C) $(-40)(-\frac{1}{2}) = 20$
(D) $(20)(\frac{3}{4}) = 15$, so the answer is 15.

The sign of the product is $+$ if there are no negative factors or an even number of negative factors. The sign of the product is $-$ if there are an odd number of negative factors.

F–7

Dividing Signed Numbers: Divide the absolute values of the numbers; the sign of the quotient is determined by the same rules as you used to determine the sign of a product. Thus,

$$+ \div + = +$$
$$- \div - = +$$
$$+ \div - = -$$
$$- \div + = -$$

EXAMPLE 1:   Divide 53.2 by -4.

53.2 divided by 4 is 13.3. Since one of the numbers is positive and the other negative, the answer is -13.3.

EXAMPLE 2: $\frac{-5}{-2} = \frac{5}{2}$

I–G.   Averages and Medians

G–1

Mean.   The *average* or *arithmetic mean* of a collection of N numbers is the result of dividing the sum of all the numbers in the collection by N.

EXAMPLE 1: The scores of 9 students on a test were 72, 78, 81, 64, 85, 92, 95, 60, and 55. What was the average score of the students?

Since there are 9 students, the average is the total of all the scores divided by 9. So the average is $\frac{1}{9}$ of $(72 + 78 + 81 + 64 + 85 + 92 + 95 + 60 + 55)$, which is $\frac{1}{9}$ of (682) or $75\frac{7}{9}$.

EXAMPLE 2: The temperature at noon in Coldtown, U.S.A. was 5° on Monday, 10° on Tuesday, 2° below zero on Wednesday, 5° below zero on Thursday, 0° on Friday, 4° on Saturday, and 1° below zero on Sunday. What was the average temperature at noon for the week?

Use negative numbers for the temperatures below zero. The average temperature is the average of 5, 10, −2, −5, 0, 4 and −1, which is $\frac{5 + 10 + (-2) + (-5) + 0 + 4 + (-1)}{7} = \frac{11}{7} = 1\frac{4}{7}$. Therefore, the average temperature at noon for the week is $1\frac{4}{7}°$.

EXAMPLE 3: If the average annual income of 10 workers is $15,665 and two of the workers each made $20,000 for the year, what is the average annual income of the remaining 8 workers?

The total income of all 10 workers is 10 times the average income which is $156,650. The two workers made a total of $40,000, so the total income of the remaining 8 workers was $156,650 − $40,000 = $116,650. Therefore, the average annual income of the 8 remaining workers is $\frac{\$116,650}{8} = \$14,581.25$.

G–2
The Median.   The number which is in the middle if the numbers in a collection of numbers are arranged in order is called the *median*. In example 1 above, the median score was 78, and in example 2, the median temperature for the week was 0. Notice that the medians were different from the averages. In example 3, we don't have enough data to find the median although we know the average.

> *In general, the median and the average of a collection of numbers are different.*

If the collection contains an even number of numbers there is no single middle number. In such a case, the median is the average of the two middle numbers. For example, the median of 64, 66, 72, 75, 76, and 77 is the average of 72 and 75 which is 73.5.

I–H.   Powers, Exponents, and Roots

H–1
If b is any number and n is a whole number greater than 0, b^n means the product of n factors each of which is equal to b. Thus,

$$b^n = b \times b \times b \times \cdots \times b \text{ where there are } n \text{ copies of } b.$$

If $n = 1$, there is only one copy of b so $b^1 = b$. Here are some examples,

$$2^5 = 2 \times 2 \times 2 \times 2 \times 2 = 32, (-4)^3 = (-4) \times (-4) \times (-4) = -64, \frac{3^2}{4} = \frac{3 \times 3}{4} = \frac{9}{4},$$
$$1^n = 1 \text{ for any } n, 0^n = 0 \text{ for any } n.$$

b^n is read as "b raised to the nth power." b^2 is read "b squared." b^2 is always greater than 0 (positive) if b is not zero, since the product of two negative numbers is positive. b^3 is read "b cubed." b^3 can be negative or positive.

You should know the following squares and cubes:

$1^2 = 1$	$8^2 = 64$
$2^2 = 4$	$9^2 = 81$
$3^2 = 9$	$10^2 = 100$
$4^2 = 16$	$11^2 = 121$
$5^2 = 25$	$12^2 = 144$
$6^2 = 36$	$13^2 = 169$
$7^2 = 49$	$14^2 = 196$
	$15^2 = 225$
$1^3 = 1$	$3^3 = 27$
$2^3 = 8$	$4^3 = 64$
	$5^3 = 125$

If you raise a fraction, $\frac{p}{q}$, to a power, then $\left(\frac{p}{q}\right)^n = \frac{p^n}{q^n}$. For example,

$$\left(\frac{5}{4}\right)^3 = \frac{5^3}{4^3} = \frac{125}{64}.$$

EXAMPLE 1: If the value of an investment triples each year, what percent of its value today will the investment be worth in 4 years?

The value increases by a factor of 3 each year. Since the time is 4 years, there will be four factors of 3. So the investment will be worth $3 \times 3 \times 3 \times 3 = 3^4$ as much as it is today. $3^4 = 81$, so the investment will be worth 8,100% of its value today in four years.

H–2

Exponents. In the expression b^n, b is called the base and n is called the *exponent*. In the expression 2^5, 2 is the base and 5 is the exponent. The exponent tells how many factors there are.

> The *two basic formulas for problems involving exponents* are:
>
> (A) $b^n \times b^m = b^{n+m}$
> (B) $a^n \times b^n = (a \cdot b)^n$
>
> (A) and (B) are called *laws of exponents*.

EXAMPLE 1:   What is 6^3?

$$\text{Since } 6 = 3 \times 2, 6^3 = 3^3 \times 2^3 = 27 \times 8 = 216.$$

or

$$6^3 = 6 \times 6 \times 6 = 216.$$

EXAMPLE 2:   Find the value of $2^3 \times 2^2$.

Using (A), $2^3 \times 2^2 = 2^{2+3} = 2^5$ which is 32. You can check this, since $2^3 = 8$ and $2^2 = 4$; $2^3 \times 2^2 = 8 \times 4 = 32$.

H–3

Negative Exponents. $b^0 = 1$ *for any nonzero number b.* **By one of the laws of exponents (A) above,** $b^n \times b^0$ **should be** $b^{n+0} = b^n$. **If we still want (A) to be true, then** b^0 **must be 1.** (NOTE: 0^0 is not defined.)

Using the law of exponents once more, you can define b^{-n} where n is a positive number. If (A) holds, $b^{-n} \times b^n = b^{-n+n} = b^0 = 1$, so $b^{-n} = \dfrac{1}{b^n}$. *Multiplying by* b^{-n} *is the same as dividing by* b^n.

EXAMPLE 1: $2^0 = 1$

EXAMPLE 2: $2^{-3} = \dfrac{1}{2^3} = \dfrac{1}{8}$

EXAMPLE 3: $\left(\dfrac{1}{2}\right)^{-1} = \dfrac{1}{1/2} = 2$

EXAMPLE 4:   Find the value of $\dfrac{6^4}{3^3}$.

$$\frac{6^4}{3^3} = \frac{(3 \cdot 2)^4}{3^3} = \frac{3^4 \cdot 2^4}{3^3} = 3^4 \times 2^4 \times 3^{-3} = 3^4 \times 3^{-3} \times 2^4 = 3^1 \times 2^4 = 48.$$

H–4

Roots.   If you raise a number d to the nth power and the result is b, then d is called the nth root of b, which is usually written $\sqrt[n]{b} = d$. Since $2^5 = 32$, then $\sqrt[5]{32} = 2$. The second root is called the square root and is written $\sqrt{}$; the third root is called the cube root. If you read the columns of the table on page 323 from right to left, you have a table of square roots and cube roots. For example, $\sqrt{225} = 15$; $\sqrt{81} = 9$; $\sqrt[3]{64} = 4$.

There are two possibilities for the square root of a positive number; the square root of 9 is $+3$ and -3. The symbol $\sqrt{9}$ stands for the positive square root only; thus $\sqrt{9} = 3$.

Since the square of any nonzero number is positive *the square root of a negative·number is not defined as a real number.* Thus $\sqrt{-2}$ is not a real number. There are cube roots of negative numbers. $\sqrt[3]{-8} = -2$, because $(-2) \times (-2) \times (-2) = -8$.

You can also write roots as exponents; for example,

$$\sqrt[n]{b} = b^{1/n}; \text{ so } \sqrt{b} = b^{1/2}, \sqrt[3]{b} = b^{1/3}.$$

Since you can write roots as exponents, formula (B) above is especially useful.

$a^{1/n} \times b^{1/n} = (a \cdot b)^{1/n}$ or $\sqrt[n]{a \times b} = \sqrt[n]{a} \times \sqrt[n]{b}$. This formula is the basic formula for simplifying square roots, cube roots and so on. *On the test you must state your answer in a form which matches one of the choices given.*

EXAMPLE 1: $\sqrt{54} = ?$

Since $54 = 9 \times 6$, $\sqrt{54} = \sqrt{9 \times 6} = \sqrt{9} \times \sqrt{6}$. Since $\sqrt{9} = 3$, $\sqrt{54} = 3\sqrt{6}$.

You can not simplify by adding square roots unless you are taking square roots of the same number. For example,

$$\sqrt{3} + 2\sqrt{3} - 4\sqrt{3} = -\sqrt{3}, \text{ but } \sqrt{3} + \sqrt{2} \text{ is not equal to } \sqrt{5}.$$

EXAMPLE 2: Simplify $6\sqrt{12} + 2\sqrt{75} - 3\sqrt{98}$.

Since $12 = 4 \times 3$, $\sqrt{12} = \sqrt{4 \times 3} = \sqrt{4} \times \sqrt{3} = 2\sqrt{3}$;
$75 = 25 \times 3$, so $\sqrt{75} = \sqrt{25} \times \sqrt{3} = 5\sqrt{3}$;
and $98 = 49 \times 2$, so $\sqrt{98} = \sqrt{49} \times \sqrt{2} = 7\sqrt{2}$.
Therefore, $6\sqrt{12} + 2\sqrt{75} - 3\sqrt{98} = 6 \times 2\sqrt{3} + 2 \times 5\sqrt{3} - 3 \times 7\sqrt{2} = 12\sqrt{3} + 10\sqrt{3} - 21\sqrt{2} = 22\sqrt{3} - 21\sqrt{2}$.

EXAMPLE 3: Simplify $27^{1/3} \times 8^{1/3}$.

$27^{1/3} = \sqrt[3]{27} = 3$ and $8^{1/3} = \sqrt[3]{8} = 2$, so $27^{1/3} \times 8^{1/3} = 3 \times 2 = 6$. Notice that 6 is $\sqrt[3]{216}$ and $27^{1/3} \times 8^{1/3} = (27 \times 8)^{1/3} = 216^{1/3}$.

II. Algebra

II-A. Algebraic Expressions

A-1

Often it is necessary to deal with quantities which have a numerical value which is unknown. For example, we may know that Tom's salary is twice as much as

Joe's salary. If we let the value of Tom's salary be called T and the value of Joe's salary be J, then T and J are numbers which are unknown. However, we do know that the value of T must be twice the value of J, or $T = 2J$.

T and $2J$ are examples of algebraic expressions. An algebraic expression may involve letters in addition to numbers and symbols; however, *in an algebraic expression a letter always stands for a number*. Therefore, you can multiply, divide, add, subtract and perform other mathematical operations on a letter. Thus, x^2 would mean x times x. Some examples of algebraic expressions are: $2x + y$, $y^3 + 9y$, $z^3 - 5ab$, $c + d + 4$, $5x + 2y(6x - 4y + z)$. When letters or numbers are written together without any sign or symbol between them, multiplication is assumed. Thus $6xy$ means 6 times x times y. $6xy$ is called a term; terms are separated by $+$ or $-$ signs. The expression $5z + 2 + 4x^2$ has three terms, $5z$, 2, and $4x^2$. Terms are often called monomials (mono = one). If an expression has more than one term, it is called a *polynomial*, (poly = many). The letters in an algebraic expression are called *variables* or *unknowns*. When a variable is multiplied by a number, the number is called the *coefficient* of the variable. So in the expression $5x^2 + 2yz$, the coefficient of x^2 is 5, and the coefficient of yz is 2.

A–2

Simplifying Algebraic Expressions. *You must be able to recognize algebraic expressions which are equal.* It will also save time when you are working problems if you can change a complicated expression into a simpler one.

Case I. Simplifying expressions which don't contain parentheses:

(A) Perform any multiplications or divisions before performing additions or subtractions. Thus, the expression $6x + y \div x$ means add $6x$ to the quotient of y divided by x. Another way of writing the expression would be $6x + \frac{y}{x}$. This is not the same as $\frac{6x + y}{x}$.

(B) The order in which you multiply numbers and letters in a term does not matter. So $6xy$ is the same as $6yx$.

(C) The order in which you add terms does not matter; for instance, $6x + 2y - x = 6x - x + 2y$.

(D) If there are roots or powers in any terms, you may be able to simplify the term by using the laws of exponents. For example, $5xy \cdot 3x^2y = 15x^3y^2$.

(E) Combine like terms. *Like terms* (or similar terms) are terms which have exactly the same letters raised to the same powers. So x, $-2x$, $\frac{1}{3}x$ are like terms. For example, $6x - 2x + x + y$ is equal to $5x + y$. In combining like terms, you simply add or subtract the coefficients of the like terms, and the result is the coefficient of that term in the simplified expression. In our example above, the coefficients of x were $+6$, -2, and $+1$; since $6 - 2 + 1 = 5$ the coefficient of x in the simplified expression is 5.

(F) Algebraic expressions which involve divisions or factors can be simplified by using the techniques for handling fractions and the laws of exponents. Remember dividing by b^n is the same as multiplying by b^{-n}.

EXAMPLE 1: $3x^2 - 4\sqrt{x} + \sqrt{4x} + xy + 7x^2 = ?$

(D) $\sqrt{4x} = \sqrt{4}\sqrt{x} = 2\sqrt{x}.$
(E) $3x^2 + 7x^2 = 10x^2,\ -4\sqrt{x} + 2\sqrt{x} = -2\sqrt{x}.$

The original expression equals $3x^2 + 7x^2 - 4\sqrt{x} + 2\sqrt{x} + xy$. Therefore, the simplified expression is $10x^2 - 2\sqrt{x} + xy$.

EXAMPLE 2: Simplify $\dfrac{21x^4y^2}{3x^6y}$.

(F) $\dfrac{21}{3}x^4y^2x^{-6}y^{-1}.$

(B) $7x^4x^{-6}y^2y^{-1}.$

(D) $7x^{-2}y$, so the simplified term is $\dfrac{7y}{x^2}$.

EXAMPLE 3: Write $\dfrac{2x}{y} - \dfrac{4}{x}$ as a single fraction.

(F) A common denominator is xy so $\dfrac{2x}{y} = \dfrac{2x \cdot x}{y \cdot x} = \dfrac{2x^2}{xy}$, and $\dfrac{4}{x} = \dfrac{4y}{xy}$.

Therefore, $\dfrac{2x}{y} - \dfrac{4}{x} = \dfrac{2x^2}{xy} - \dfrac{4y}{xy} = \dfrac{2x^2 - 4y}{xy}$

Case II. Simplifying expressions which have parentheses:

The first rule is to perform the operations inside parentheses first. So $(6x + y) \div x$ means divide the sum of $6x$ and y by x. Notice that $(6x + y) \div x$ is different from $6x + y \div x$.

The main rule for getting rid of parentheses is the distributive law, which is expressed as $a(b + c) = ab + ac$. In other words, if any monomial is followed by an expression contained in a parenthesis, then *each* term of the expression is multiplied by the monomial. Once we have gotten rid of the parentheses, we proceed as we did in Case I.

EXAMPLE 4: $2x(6x - 4y + 2) = (2x)(6x) + (2x)(-4y) + (2x)(2) = 12x^2 - 8xy + 4x.$

> If an expression has more than one set of parentheses, get rid of the *inner parentheses first* and then *work out* through the rest of the parentheses.

EXAMPLE 5: $2x - (x + 6(x - 3y) + 4y) = ?$

To remove the inner parentheses we multiply $6(x - 3y)$ getting $6x - 18y$. Now we have $2x - (x + 6x - 18y + 4y)$ which equals $2x - (7x - 14y)$. Distribute the minus sign (multiply by -1), getting $2x - 7x - (-14y) = -5x + 14y$.

Sometimes brackets are used instead of parentheses.

EXAMPLE 6: Simplify $-3x\left[\frac{1}{2}(3x - 2y) - 2(x(3 + y) + 4y)\right]$

$$= -3x\left[\frac{1}{2}(3x - 2y) - 2(3x + xy + 4y)\right]$$

$$= -3x\left[\frac{3}{2}x - y - 6x - 2xy - 8y\right]$$

$$= -3x\left[-\frac{9}{2}x - 2xy - 9y\right]$$

$$= \frac{27}{2}x^2 + 6x^2y + 27xy.$$

A–3

Adding and Subtracting Algebraic Expressions. Since algebraic expressions are numbers, they can be added and subtracted.

> *The only algebraic terms which can be combined are like terms.*

EXAMPLE 1: $(3x + 4y - xy^2) + (3x + 2x(x - y)) = ?$

The expression $= (3x + 4y - xy^2) + (3x + 2x^2 - 2xy)$, removing the inner parentheses;

$\qquad = 6x + 4y + 2x^2 - xy^2 - 2xy$, combining like terms.

EXAMPLE 2: $(2a + 3a^2 - 4) - 2(4a^2 - 2(a + 4)) = ?$

It equals $(2a + 3a^2 - 4) - 2(4a^2 - 2a - 8)$, removing inner parentheses;

$= 2a + 3a^2 - 4 - 8a^2 + 4a + 16$, removing outer parentheses;

$= -5a^2 + 6a + 12$, combining like terms.

A–4

Multiplying Algebraic Expressions. When you multiply two expressions, you multiply *each term of the first by each term of the second.*

EXAMPLE 1: $(b - 4)(b + a) = b(b + a) - 4(b + a) = ?$

$$= b^2 + ab - 4b - 4a.$$

EXAMPLE 2: $(2h - 4)(h + 2h^2 + h^3) = ?$

$$= 2h(h + 2h^2 + h^3) - 4(h + 2h^2 + h^3)$$
$$= 2h^2 + 4h^3 + 2h^4 - 4h - 8h^2 - 4h^3$$
$$= -4h - 6h^2 + 2h^4, \text{ which is the product.}$$

If you need to multiply more than two expressions, multiply the first two expressions, then multiply the result by the third expression, and so on until you have used each factor. Since algebraic expressions can be multiplied, they can be squared, cubed, or raised to other powers.

EXAMPLE 3: $(x - 2y)^3 = (x - 2y)(x - 2y)(x - 2y)$.

Since $(x - 2y)(x - 2y) = x^2 - 2yx - 2yx + 4y^2$
$$= x^2 - 4xy + 4y^2,$$

$$\begin{aligned}(x - 2y)^3 &= (x^2 - 4xy + 4y^2)(x - 2y)\\ &= x(x^2 - 4xy + 4y^2) - 2y(x^2 - 4xy + 4y^2)\\ &= x^3 - 4x^2y + 4xy^2 - 2x^2y + 8xy^2 - 8y^3\\ &= x^3 - 6x^2y + 12xy^2 - 8y^3.\end{aligned}$$

The order in which you multiply algebraic expressions does not matter. Thus $(2a + b)(x^2 + 2x) = (x^2 + 2x)(2a + b)$.

A–5

Factoring Algebraic Expressions. If an algebraic expression is the product of other algebraic expressions, then the expressions are called factors of the original expression. For instance, we claim that $(2h - 4)$ and $(h + 2h^2 + h^3)$ are factors of $-4h - 6h^2 + 2h^4$. We can always check to see if we have the correct factors by multiplying; so by example 2 above we see that our claim is correct. We need to be able to factor algebraic expressions in order to solve quadratic equations. It also can be helpful in dividing algebraic expressions.

First remove any monomial factor which appears in every term of the expression.

Some examples:

$$3x + 3y = 3(x + y)\text{: 3 is a monomial factor.}$$
$$15a^2b + 10ab = 5ab(3a + 2)\text{: } 5ab \text{ is a monomial factor.}$$

$$\frac{1}{2}hy - 3h^3 + 4hy = h\left(\frac{1}{2}y - 3h^2 + 4y\right),$$

$$= h\left(\frac{9}{2}y - 3h^2\right)\text{: } h \text{ is a monomial factor.}$$

You may also need to factor expressions which contain squares or higher powers into factors which only contain linear terms. (Linear terms are terms in which variables are raised only to the first power.) The first rule to remember is that since $(a + b)(a - b) = a^2 + ba - ba - b^2 = a^2 - b^2$, the difference of two squares can always be factored.

EXAMPLE 1:   Factor $(9m^2 - 16)$.

$9m^2 = (3m)^2$ and $16 = 4^2$, so the factors are $(3m - 4)(3m + 4)$.

Since $(3m - 4)(3m + 4) = 9m^2 - 16$, these factors are correct.

EXAMPLE 2:   Factor $x^4y^4 - 4x^2$.

$x^4y^4 = (x^2y^2)^2$ and $4x^2 = (2x)^2$, so the factors are $x^2y^2 + 2x$ and $x^2y^2 - 2x$.

You also may need to factor expressions which contain squared terms and linear terms, such as $x^2 + 4x + 3$. The factors will be of the form $(x + a)$ and $(x + b)$. Since $(x + a)(x + b) = x^2 + (a + b)x + ab$, you must look for a pair of numbers a and b such that $a \cdot b$ is the numerical term in the expression and $a + b$ is the coefficient of the linear term (the term with exponent 1).

EXAMPLE 3:   Factor $x^2 + 4x + 3$.

You want numbers whose product is 3 and whose sum is 4. Look at the possible factors of three and check whether they add up to 4. Since $3 = 3 \times 1$ and $3 + 1$ is 4, the factors are $(x + 3)$ and $(x + 1)$. Remember to check by multiplying.

EXAMPLE 4:   Factor $y^2 + y - 6$.

Since -6 is negative, the two numbers a and b must be of opposite sign. Possible pairs of factors for -6 are -6 and $+1$, 6 and -1, 3 and -2, and -3 and 2. Since $-2 + 3 = 1$, the factors are $(y + 3)$ and $(y - 2)$. So $(y + 3)(y - 2) = y^2 + y - 6$.

EXAMPLE 5:   Factor $a^3 + 4a^2 + 4a$.

Factor out a, so $a^3 + 4a^2 + 4a = a(a^2 + 4a + 4)$. Consider $a^2 + 4a + 4$; since $2 + 2 = 4$ and $2 \times 2 = 4$, the factors are $(a + 2)$ and $(a + 2)$. Therefore, $a^3 + 4a^2 + 4a = a(a + 2)^2$.

If the term with the highest exponent has a coefficient unequal to 1, divide the entire expression by that coefficient. For example, to factor $3a^3 + 12a^2 + 12a$, factor out a 3 from each term, and the result is $a^3 + 4a^2 + 4a$ which is $a(a + 2)^2$. Thus, $3a^3 + 12a^2 + 12a = 3a(a + 2)^2$.

There are some expressions which can not be factored, for example, $x^2 + 4x + 6$. In general, if you can't factor something by using the methods given above, don't waste a lot of time on the question. Sometimes you may be able to check the answers given to find out what the correct factors are.

A–6

Division of Algebraic Expressions.   The main things to remember in division are:

(1)   When you divide a sum, you can get the same result by dividing each term and adding quotients. For example, $\dfrac{9x + 4xy + y^2}{x} = \dfrac{9x}{x} + \dfrac{4xy}{x} + \dfrac{y^2}{x} = 9 + 4y + \dfrac{y^2}{x}$.

(2)   You can cancel common factors, so the results on factoring will be helpful. For example, $\dfrac{x^2 - 2x}{x - 2} = \dfrac{x(x - 2)}{x - 2} = x$.

You can also divide one algebraic expression by another using long division.

EXAMPLE 1: $(15x^2 + 2x - 4) \div 3x - 1$.

$$
\begin{array}{r}
5x + 2 \\
3x - 1 \overline{)\,15x^2 + 2x - 4} \\
\underline{15x^2 - 5x} \\
7x - 4 \\
\underline{6x - 2} \\
x - 2
\end{array}
$$

So the answer is $5x + 2$ with a remainder of $x - 2$.

You can check by multiplying,

$$(5x + 2)(3x - 1) = 15x^2 + 6x - 5x - 2$$

$$= 15x^2 + x - 2; \text{ now add the remainder } x - 2$$

and the result is $15x^2 + x - 2 + x - 2 = 15x^2 + 2x - 4$.

Division problems where you need to use (1) and (2) are more likely than problems involving long division.

II–B.   Equations

B–1

AN EQUATION is a statement that says two algebraic expressions are equal. $x + 2 = 3, 4 + 2 = 6, 3x^2 + 2x - 6 = 0, x^2 + y^2 = z^2, \frac{y}{x} = 2 + z$, and $A = LW$ are all examples of equations. We will refer to the algebraic expressions on each side of the equals sign as the left side and the right side of the equation. Thus, in the equation $2x + 4 = 6y + x$, $2x + 4$ is the left side and $6y + x$ is the right side.

B–2

If we assign specific numbers to each variable or unknown in an algebraic expression, then the algebraic expression will be equal to a number. This is called *evaluating* the expression. For example, if you evaluate $2x + 4y^2 + 3$ for $x = -1$ and $y = 2$, the expression is equal to $2(-1) + 4 \cdot 2^2 + 3 = -2 + 4 \cdot 4 + 3 = 17$.

If we evaluate each side of an equation and the number obtained is the same for each side of the equation, then the specific values assigned to the unknowns are called a *solution of the equation*. Another way of saying this is that the choices for the unknowns satisfy the equation.

EXAMPLE 1:   Consider the equation $2x + 3 = 9$.

If $x = 3$, then the left side of the equation becomes $2 \cdot 3 + 3 = 6 + 3 = 9$, so both sides equal 9, and $x = 3$ is a solution of $2x + 3 = 9$. If $x = 4$, then the left side is $2 \cdot 4 + 3 = 11$. Since 11 is not equal to 9, $x = 4$ is *not* a solution of $2x + 3 = 9$.

EXAMPLE 2:   Consider the equation $x^2 + y^2 = 5x$.

If $x = 1$ and $y = 2$, then the left side is $1^2 + 2^2$ which equals $1 + 4 = 5$. The right side is $5 \cdot 1 = 5$, since both sides are equal to 5, $x = 1$ and $y = 2$ is a solution.

If $x = 5$ and $y = 0$, then the left side is $5^2 + 0^2 = 25$ and the right side is $5 \cdot 5 = 25$, so $x = 5$ and $y = 0$ is also a solution.

If $x = 1$ and $y = 1$, then the left side is $1^2 + 1^2 = 2$ and the right side is $5 \cdot 1 = 5$. Therefore, since $2 \neq 5$, $x = 1$ and $y = 1$ is not a solution.

There are some equations which *do not have any solutions which are real numbers*. Since the square of any real number is positive or zero, the equation $x^2 = -4$ does not have any solutions which are real numbers.

B–3

Equivalence.   One equation is *equivalent* to another equation, if they have exactly the same solutions. The basic idea in solving equations is to transform a given equation into an equivalent equation whose solutions are obvious.

The two main tools for solving equations are:

  (A)   If you add or subtract the same algebraic expression to or from *each side* of an equation, the resulting equation is equivalent to the original equation.

  (B)   If you multiply or divide both sides of an equation by the same *nonzero* algebraic expression, the resulting equation is equivalent to the original equation.

The most common type of equation is the linear equation with only one unknown. $6z = 4z - 3$, $3 + a = 2a - 4$, $3b + 2b = b - 4b$, are all examples of linear equations with only one unknown.

Using (A) and (B), you can solve a linear equation in one unknown in the following way:

  (1)   Group all the terms which involve the unknown on one side of the equation and all the terms which are purely numerical on the other side of the equation. This is called *isolating the unknown*.
  (2)   Combine the terms on each side.
  (3)   Divide each side by the coefficient of the unknown.

EXAMPLE 1:   Solve $6x + 2 = 3$ for x.

  (1)   Using (A) subtract 2 from each side of the equation. Then $6x + 2 - 2 = 3 - 2$ or $6x = 3 - 2$.
  (2) $6x = 1$.
  (3)   Divide each side by 6. Therefore, $x = \frac{1}{6}$.

You should always check your answer in the original equation.

$$\text{Since } 6\left(\frac{1}{6}\right) + 2 = 1 + 2 = 3, \ x = \frac{1}{6} \text{ is a solution.}$$

EXAMPLE 2:   Solve $3x + 15 = 3 - 4x$ for x.

  (1)   Add $4x$ to each side and subtract 15 from each side; $3x + 15 - 15 + 4x = 3 - 15 - 4x + 4x$.

(2) $7x = -12$.

(3) Divide each side by 7, so $x = \frac{-12}{7}$ is the solution.

CHECK:

$$3\left(\frac{-12}{7}\right) + 15 = \frac{-36}{7} + 15 = \frac{69}{7} \text{ and } 3 - 4\left(\frac{-12}{7}\right) = 3 + \frac{48}{7} = \frac{69}{7}.$$

If you do the same thing to each side of an equation, the result is still an equation but it may not be equivalent to the original equation. Be especially careful if you square each side of an equation. For example, $x = -4$ is an equation; square both sides and you get $x^2 = 16$ which has both $x = 4$ and $x = -4$ as solutions. *Always check your answer in the original equation.*

If the equation you want to solve involves square roots, get rid of the square roots by squaring each side of the equation. Remember to check your answer since squaring each side does not always give an equivalent equation.

EXAMPLE 3: Solve $\sqrt{4x + 3} = 5$.

Square both sides: $(\sqrt{4x + 3})^2 = 4x + 3$ and $5^2 = 25$, so the new equation is $4x + 3 = 25$. Subtract 3 from each side to get $4x = 22$ and now divide each side by 4. The solution is $x = \frac{22}{4} = 5.5$. Since $4(5.5) + 3 = 25$ and $\sqrt{25} = 5$, $x = 5.5$ is a solution to the equation $\sqrt{4x + 3} = 5$.

If an equation involves fractions, multiply through by a common denominator and then solve. Check your answer to make sure you did not multiply or divide by zero.

EXAMPLE 4: Solve $\frac{3}{a} = 9$ for a.

Multiply each side by a: the result is $3 = 9a$. Divide each side by 9, and you obtain $\frac{3}{9} = a$ or $a = \frac{1}{3}$. Since $\frac{3}{\frac{1}{3}} = 3 \cdot 3 = 9$, $a = \frac{1}{3}$ is a solution.

B–4

You may be asked to solve two equations in two unknowns. Use one equation to solve for one unknown in terms of the other; now change the second equation into an equation in only one unknown which can be solved by the methods of the preceding section.

EXAMPLE 1: Solve for x and y: $\begin{cases} \dfrac{x}{y} = 3 \\ 2x + 4y = 20. \end{cases}$

The first equation gives $x = 3y$. Using $x = 3y$, the second equation is $2(3y) + 4y = 6y + 4y$ or $10y = 20$, so $y = \frac{20}{10} = 2$. Since $x = 3y$, $x = 6$.

CHECK:

$$\frac{6}{2} = 3, \text{ and } 2 \cdot 6 + 4 \cdot 2 = 20, \text{ so } x = 6 \text{ and } y = 2 \text{ is a solution.}$$

EXAMPLE 2:   If $2x + y = 5$ and $x + y = 4$, find x and y.

Since $x + y = 4$, $y = 4 - x$, so $2x + y = 2x + 4 - x = x + 4 = 5$ and $x = 1$. If $x = 1$, then $y = 4 - 1 = 3$. So $x = 1$ and $y = 3$ is the solution.

CHECK:

$$2 \cdot 1 + 3 = 5 \text{ and } 1 + 3 = 4.$$

Sometimes we can solve two equations by adding them or by subtracting one from the other. If we subtract $x + y = 4$ from $2x + y = 5$ in example 2, we have $x = 1$. However, the previous method will work in cases when the addition method does not work.

B–5

Solving Quadratic Equations.   If the terms of an equation contain squares of the unknown as well as linear terms, the equation is called *quadratic*. Some examples of quadratic equations are $x^2 + 4x = 3$, $2z^2 - 1 = 3z^2 - 2z$, and $a + 6 = a^2 + 6$.

To solve a quadratic equation:

(A)   Group all the terms on one side of the equation so that the other side is *zero*.
(B)   Combine the terms on the nonzero side.
(C)   Factor the expression into linear expressions.
(D)   Set the linear factors equal to zero and solve.

The method depends on the fact that if a product of expressions is zero then at least one of the expressions must be zero.

EXAMPLE 1:   Solve $x^2 + 4x = -3$.

(A) $x^2 + 4x + 3 = 0$
(C) $x^2 + 4x + 3 = (x + 3)(x + 1) = 0$
(D)   So $x + 3 = 0$ or $x + 1 = 0$. Therefore, the solutions are $x = -3$ and $x = -1$.

CHECK:

$$(-3)^2 + 4(-3) = 9 - 12 = -3$$
$$(-1)^2 + 4(-1) = 1 - 4 = -3, \text{ so } x = -3 \text{ and } x = -1$$
are solutions.

A quadratic equation will usually have 2 different solutions, but it is possible for a quadratic to have only one solution or even no solution.

EXAMPLE 2:   If $2z^2 - 1 = 3z^2 - 2z$, what is z?

(A) $0 = 3z^2 - 2z^2 - 2z + 1$
(B) $z^2 - 2z + 1 = 0$
(C) $z^2 - 2z + 1 = (z - 1)^2 = 0$
(D) $z - 1 = 0$ or $z = 1$

CHECK:

$$2 \cdot 1^2 - 1 = 2 - 1 = 1 \text{ and } 3 \cdot 1^2 - 2 \cdot 1 = 3 - 2 = 1,$$
so $z = 1$ is a solution.

Equations which may not look like quadratics may be changed into quadratics.

EXAMPLE 3:   Find a if $a - 3 = \dfrac{10}{a}$.

Multiply each side of the equation by a to obtain $a^2 - 3a = 10$, which is quadratic.

(A) $a^2 - 3a - 10 = 0$
(C) $a^2 - 3a - 10 = (a - 5)(a + 2)$
(D)   So $a - 5 = 0$ or $a + 2 = 0$.

Therefore, $a = 5$ and $a = -2$ are the solutions.

CHECK:

$$5 - 3 = 2 = \frac{10}{5} \text{ so } a = 5 \text{ is a solution.}$$

$$-2 - 3 = -5 = \frac{10}{-2} \text{ so } a = -2 \text{ is a solution.}$$

You can also solve quadratic equations by using the *quadratic formula*. The quadratic formula states that the solutions of the quadratic equation $ax^2 + bx + c = 0$ are $x = \dfrac{1}{2a}[-b + \sqrt{b^2 - 4ac}]$ and $x = \dfrac{1}{2a}[-b - \sqrt{b^2 - 4ac}]$.

This is usually written $x = \dfrac{1}{2a}[-b \pm \sqrt{b^2 - 4ac}]$. Use of the quadratic formula would replace steps (C) and (D).

EXAMPLE 4:   Find x if $x^2 + 5x = 12 - x^2$.

(A) $x^2 + 5x + x^2 - 12 = 0$
(B) $2x^2 + 5x - 12 = 0$

So $a = 2$, $b = 5$ and $c = -12$. Therefore, using the quadratic formula, the solutions are $x = \frac{1}{4}[-5 \pm \sqrt{25 - 4 \cdot 2 \cdot (-12)}] = \frac{1}{4}[-5 \pm \sqrt{25 + 96}] = \frac{1}{4}[-5 \pm \sqrt{121}]$. So we have $x = \frac{1}{4}[-5 \pm 11]$. The solutions are $x = \frac{3}{2}$ and $x = -4$.

CHECK:

$$\left(\frac{3}{2}\right)^2 + 5 \cdot \frac{3}{2} = \frac{9}{4} + \frac{15}{2} = \frac{39}{4} = 12 - \frac{9}{4} = 12 - \left(\frac{3}{2}\right)^2$$
$$(-4)^2 + 5(-4) = 16 - 20 = -4 = 12 - 16 = 12 - (-4)^2$$

NOTE: If $b^2 - 4ac$ is negative, then the quadratic equation $ax^2 + bx + c = 0$ has no real solutions because negative numbers do not have real square roots.

The quadratic formula will always give you the solutions to a quadratic equation. If you can factor the equation, factoring will usually give you the solution in less time. Remember, you want to answer as many questions as you can in the time given. So factor if you can. If you don't see the factor immediately, then use the formula.

PRACTICE

1. If $r = \frac{s}{3}$ and $4r = 5t$, what is s in terms of t?

   (A) $\frac{4t}{15}$ (B) $\frac{15t}{4}$ (C) $4t$ (D) $5t$ (E) $60t$

2. If $\frac{1}{r} = 3$ and $s = 3$, what is r in terms of s?

   (A) s (B) $3 - s$ (C) $\frac{1}{s}$ (D) $-s$ (E) $9s$

3. $\frac{a}{b} = c$; $b = c$; $b = ?$

   (A) $\frac{a}{2}$ (B) $\sqrt{a}$ (C) $\frac{a}{6}$ (D) $2a$ (E) a^2

4. $z + \frac{1}{z} = 2$; $z = ?$

   (A) $\frac{1}{2}$ (B) 1 (C) $1\frac{1}{2}$ (D) 2 (E) $2\frac{1}{2}$

5. If $\frac{n}{7} + \frac{n}{5} = \frac{12}{35}$, what is the numerical value of n?

   (A) 1 (B) $\sqrt{12}$ (C) 6 (D) 17.5 (E) 35

6. $\frac{ca^2 - cb^2}{-a - b}$ is equivalent to $cb + ?$

   (A) ac (B) $-ca$ (C) 1 (D) -1 (E) c

7. $x\sqrt{.09} = 3$; $x = ?$

   (A) $\frac{1}{10}$ (B) $\frac{3}{10}$ (C) $\frac{1}{3}$ (D) 1 (E) 10

8. $7x - 5y = 13$
   $2x - 7y = 26$
   $9x - 12y = ?$

   (A) 13 (B) 26 (C) 39 (D) 40 (E) 52

9. $ab - 2cd = p$
   $ab - 2cd = q$
   $6cd - 3ab = r$
   $p = (?)r$

   (A) -3 (B) $-\frac{1}{3}$ (C) $\frac{1}{3}$ (D) 1 (E) 3

10. $\sqrt{1\frac{1}{1} + \frac{1}{4}} = ?$

   (A) $\frac{2}{3}$ (B) $\frac{1}{3}$ (C) $\frac{5}{6}$ (D) $\frac{11}{12}$ (E) $\frac{7}{6}$

11. $z + \frac{2}{z} = 2z$; $z^2 = (?)$

   (A) 0 (B) $\frac{1}{2}$ (C) 1 (D) $1\frac{1}{2}$ (E) 2

12. $\frac{\frac{1}{1}}{N} + \frac{1}{N} = ?$

   (A) 1 (B) $\frac{1}{N^2}$ (C) $\frac{1}{N}$ (D) N (E) N^2

13. If $\frac{1}{x} = \frac{a}{b}$ then x equals the

   (A) sum of a and b
   (B) product of a and b
   (C) difference of a and b
   (D) quotient of b and a
   (E) quotient a and b

14. $x^2 + y = 9$
    $x^2 - y = -1$
    $y = ?$

   (A) 1 (B) ± 3 (C) 5 (D) 8 (E) 10

15. $2x - 4y = -10$
    $5x - 3y = -3$
    $3x + y = ?$

   (A) $\frac{3}{5}$ (B) $\frac{2}{5}$ (C) -7 (D) ± 7 (E) 7

16. $5x - 3y = 3$
    $2x - 4y = -10$
    $3x + y = (?)$

   (A) -30 (B) -13 (C) -7 (D) 7 (E) 13

17. $4y - x = 10$
    $3x = 2y$
    $xy = ?$

   (A) 2 (B) 3 (C) 6 (D) 12 (E) 24

18. $3x + 10 = 9x - 20$
    $(x + 5)^2 = (?)$

   (A) 5 (B) 10 (C) 15 (D) 25 (E) 100

19. $\frac{a}{b} = c$; $b = c$. Find b in terms of a.

   (A) a (B) b (C) $\pm\sqrt{b}$ (D) $\pm\sqrt{a}$ (E) $\pm\sqrt{ac}$

20. $17xy = 22xy - 5$
    $x^2y^2 = (?)$

   (A) 0 (B) 1 (C) -5 (D) 5 (E) $7\frac{1}{2}$

ANSWER KEY

1. B	8. C	15. E
2. C	9. B	16. E
3. B	10. C	17. C
4. B	11. E	18. E
5. A	12. E	19. D
6. B	13. D	20. B
7. E	14. C	

II–C. Verbal Problems

C–1

The general method for solving word problems is to translate them into algebraic problems. The quantities you are seeking are the unknowns, which are usually represented by letters. The information you are given in the problem is then turned into equations. Words such as "is," "was," "are," and "were" mean equals, and words like "of" and "as much as" mean multiplication.

EXAMPLE 1:   A coat was sold for $75. The coat was sold for 150% of the cost of the coat. How much did the coat cost?

You want to find the cost of the coat. Let $C be the cost of the coat. You know that the coat was sold for $75 and that $75 was 150% of the cost. So $75 = 150% of $C or $75 = 1.5C$. Solving for C you get $C = \frac{75}{1.5} = 50$, so the coat cost $50.

CHECK:

$$(1.5) \$50 = \$75.$$

EXAMPLE 2:   Tom's salary is 125% of Joe's salary. Mary's salary is 80% of Joe's salary. The total of all three salaries is $61,000. What is Mary's salary?

Let M = Mary's salary, J = Joe's salary and T = Tom's salary. The first sentence says $T = 125\%$ of J or $T = \frac{5}{4}J$, and $M = 80\%$ of J or $M = \frac{4}{5}J$. The second sentence says that $T + M + J = \$61,000$. Using the information from the first sentence, $T + M + J = \frac{5}{4}J + \frac{4}{5}J + J = \frac{25}{20}J + \frac{16}{20}J + J = \frac{61}{20}J$. So $\frac{61}{20}J = 61,000$; solving for J you have $J = \frac{20}{61} \times 61,000 = 20,000$. Therefore, $T = \frac{5}{4} \times \$20,000 = \$25,000$ and $M = \frac{4}{5} \times \$20,000 = \$16,000$.

CHECK:

$$\$25,000 + \$16,000 + \$20,000 = \$61,000.$$

So Mary's salary is $16,000.

EXAMPLE 3:   Steve weighs 25 pounds more than Jim. Their combined weight is 325 pounds. How much does Jim weigh?

Let S = Steve's weight in pounds and J = Jim's weight in pounds. The first sentence says $S = J + 25$, and the second sentence becomes $S + J = 325$. Since $S = J + 25$, $S + J = 325$ becomes $(J + 25) + J = 2J + 25 = 325$. So $2J = 300$ and $J = 150$. Therefore, Jim weighs 150 pounds.

CHECK:

If Jim weighs 150 pounds, then Steve weighs
175 pounds and $150 + 175 = 325$.

EXAMPLE 4:   A carpenter is designing a closet. The floor will be in the shape of a rectangle whose length is 2 feet more than its width. How long should the closet be if the carpenter wants the area of the floor to be 15 square feet?

The area of a rectangle is length times width, usually written $A = LW$, where A is the area, L is the length, and W is the width. We know $A = 15$ and $L = 2 + W$. Therefore, $LW = (2 + W) W = W^2 + 2W$; this must equal 15. So we need to solve $W^2 + 2W = 15$ or $W^2 + 2W - 15 = 0$. Since $W^2 + 2W - 15$ factors into $(W + 5)(W - 3)$, the only possible solutions are $W = -5$ and $W = 3$. Since W represents a width, -5 cannot be the answer; therefore the width is 3 feet. The length is the width plus two feet, so the length is 5 feet. Since $5 \times 3 = 15$, the answer checks.

PRACTICE

1. How many cents are there in $2x - 1$ dimes?

  (A) $10x$ (B) $20x - 10$ (C) $19x$ (D) $\dfrac{2x - 1}{10}$

  (E) $\dfrac{x}{5} - 1$

2. How many nickels are there in c cents and q quarters?

  (A) $\dfrac{c}{5} + 5q$ (B) $5(c + q)$ (C) $5c + \dfrac{q}{5}$

  (D) $\dfrac{c + q}{5}$ (E) $c + 25q$

3. How many days are there in w weeks and w days?

  (A) $7w^2$ (B) 7   (C) $8w$ (D) $14w$ (E) $7w$

4. How many pupils can be seated in a room with s single seats and d double seats?

  (A) sd (B) $2sd$ (C) $2(s + d)$ (D) $2d + s$
  (E) $2s + d$

5. A classroom has r rows of desks with d desks in each row. On a particular day when all pupils are present 3 seats are left vacant. The number of pupils in this class is

  (A) $dr - 3$ (B) $d + r + 3$ (C) $dr + 3$

  (D) $\dfrac{r}{d} + 3$ (E) $\dfrac{d}{r} + 3$

6. A storekeeper had n loaves of bread. By noon he had s loaves left. How many loaves did he sell?

  (A) $s - n$ (B) $n - s$ (C) $n + s$ (D) $sn - s$

  (E) $\dfrac{n}{s}$

7. A man has d dollars and spends s cents. How many dollars has he left?

  (A) $d - s$ (B) $s - d$ (C) $100d - s$

  (D) $\dfrac{100d - s}{100}$ (E) $\dfrac{d - s}{100}$

8. How much change (in cents) would a woman receive if she purchases p pounds of sugar at c cents per pound after she gives the clerk a one-dollar bill?

  (A) $100 - p - c$ (B) $pc - 100$ (C) $100 - pc$
  (D) $100 - p + c$ (E) $pc + 100$

9. Sylvia is two years younger than Mary. If Mary is m years old, how old was Sylvia two years ago?

  (A) $m + 2$ (B) $m - 2$ (C) $m - 4$
  (D) $m + 4$ (E) $2m - 2$

10. A storekeeper sold n articles at $\$D$ each and thereby made a profit of r dollars. The cost to the storekeeper for each article was

  (A) $Dn - r$ (B) $D(n - r)$ (C) $\dfrac{Dn - r}{n}$

  (D) $\dfrac{D(n - r)}{n}$ (E) $\dfrac{Dn + r}{n}$

ANSWER KEY

1. B	5. A	9. C
2. A	6. B	10. C
3. C	7. D	
4. D	8. C	

C-2

Distance Problems. A common type of word problem is a distance or velocity problem. The basic formula is

$$\boxed{\text{DISTANCE TRAVELED} = \text{RATE} \times \text{TIME.}}$$

The formula is abbreviated $d = rt$.

The distance an object travels is the product of its *average* speed (rate) and the time it is traveling. This formula can be readily converted to express time in terms of distance and rate by dividing each side by r.

$$t = \frac{d}{r}$$

It can also be changed to a formula for rate by dividing it by t,

$$r = \frac{d}{t}.$$

You should memorize the original formula, $d = rt$, and know how to convert it quickly to the others.

EXAMPLE 1:   A train travels at an average speed of 50 miles per hour for $2\frac{1}{2}$ hours and then travels at a speed of 70 miles per hour for $1\frac{1}{2}$ hours. How far did the train travel in the entire 4 hours?

The train traveled for $2\frac{1}{2}$ hours at an average speed of 50 miles per hour, so it traveled $50 \times \frac{5}{2} = 125$ miles in the first $2\frac{1}{2}$ hours. Traveling at a speed of 70 miles per hour for $1\frac{1}{2}$ hours, the distance traveled will be equal to $r \times t$ where $r = 70$ m.p.h. and $t = 1\frac{1}{2}$. so the distance is $70 \times \frac{3}{2} = 105$ miles. Therefore, the total distance traveled is $125 + 105 = 230$ miles.

EXAMPLE 2:   The distance from Cleveland to Buffalo is 200 miles. A train takes $3\frac{1}{2}$ hours to go from Buffalo to Cleveland and $4\frac{1}{2}$ hours to go back from Cleveland to Buffalo. What was the average speed of the train for the round trip from Buffalo to Cleveland and back?

The train took $3\frac{1}{2} + 4\frac{1}{2} = 8$ hours for the trip. The distance of a round trip is $2(200) = 400$ miles. Since $d = rt$ then 400 miles $= r \times 8$ hours. Solve for r and you have $r = \dfrac{400 \text{ miles}}{8 \text{ hours}} = 50$ miles per hour. Therefore the average speed is 50 miles per hour.

The speed in the formula is the average speed. If you know that there are different speeds for different lengths of time, then you must use the formula more than once, as we did in example 1.

PRACTICE

1. An automobile travels at the rate of 55 miles per hour on the Pennsylvania Turnpike. How many minutes will it take to travel $\frac{1}{3}$ of a mile at this rate?
   (A) 0.2 (B) 0.72 (C) 2.2 (D) 13.5 (E) 22

2. Miguel leaves at 9:00 A.M. and stops for repairs at 9:20 A.M. If the distance covered was 18 miles, what was the average velocity for this part of the trip?
   (A) 5.4 (B) 6 (C) 54 (D) 36 (E) 60

3. A man runs y yards in m minutes. What is his rate in yards per hour?
   (A) $\frac{y}{60m}$ (B) $\frac{m}{60y}$ (C) $60my$ (D) $\frac{60y}{m}$ (E) $\frac{60m}{y}$

4. Ten minutes after a plane leaves the airport, it is reported that the plane is 40 miles away. What is the average speed of the plane, in miles per hour?
   (A) 66 (B) 240 (C) 400 (D) 600 (E) 660

5. An automobile passes City X at 9:55 A.M. and City Y at 10:15 A.M. City X is 30 miles from City Y. What is the average rate of the automobile in miles per hour?
   (A) 10 (B) 30 (C) 90 (D) 120 (E) 360

6. The distance between two cities is 1800 miles. How many gallons of gasoline will a motorist use with an automobile that uses (on the average) 1 gallon of gasoline for each 12 miles?
   (A) 150 (B) 160 (C) 216 (D) 1500 (E) 2160

7. How many miles does a car travel if it averages a rate of 35 miles per hour for 3 hours and 24 minutes?
   (A) 109 (B) 112 (C) 113 (D) 119 (E) 129

8. Two cars start towards each other from points 400 miles apart. One car travels at 40 miles an hour and the other travels at 35 miles an hour. How far apart will the two cars be after four hours of continuous traveling?
   (A) 20 (B) 40 (C) 75 (D) 100 (E) 160

9. A motorist travels for 3 hours at 40 miles per hour and then covers a distance of 80 miles in two hours and 40 minutes. His average rate for the entire trip was
   (A) 35 m.p.h. (B) 35.3 m.p.h. (C) 35.5 m.p.h.
   (D) 36 m.p.h. (E) 37 m.p.h.

10. A man driving a distance of 90 miles, averages 30 miles per hour. On the return trip he averages 45 miles per hour. His average for the round trip, in miles per hour, is
    (A) 34 (B) 36 (C) $37\frac{1}{2}$ (D) 40 (E) 75

11. The El Capitan of the Santa Fe travels a distance of 152.5 miles from La Junta to Garden City in two hours. What is the average speed in m.p.h.?
    (A) 15.25 (B) 31.5 (C) 30.5 (D) 7.1 (E) 76.3

12. The distance between Portland, Oregon, and Santa Fe, New Mexico is 1800 miles. How long would it take a train with an average speed of 60 miles per hour to make the trip? (Give answer in hours)
    (A) 30 (B) 39 (C) 48 (D) 300 (E) 480

13. A man travels for 5 hours at an average rate of 40 m.p.h. He develops some motor trouble and returns to his original starting point in 10 hours. What was his average rate on the return trip?
    (A) 10 (B) 15 (C) 20 (D) 26.6 (E) 40

14. If a man walks W miles in H hours, and then rides R miles in the same length of time, what is his average rate for the entire trip?
    (A) $\frac{R+W}{H}$ (B) $\frac{2(R+W)}{H}$ (C) $\frac{R+W}{2H}$
    (D) $\frac{H}{R-W}$ (E) $\frac{RW-H}{2}$

15. How long would it take a car traveling at 30 miles per hour to cover a distance of 44 feet? (1 mile = 5280 feet)
    (A) 1 second (B) 2.64 seconds (C) 5.2 seconds
    (D) 1 minute (E) 7.7 minutes

ANSWER KEY

1. B	*6.* A	*11.* E
2. C	*7.* D	*12.* A
3. D	*8.* D	*13.* C
4. B	*9.* B	*14.* C
5. C	*10.* B	*15.* A

C–3

Work Problems. In this type of problem you can assume all workers in the same category work at the same rate. The main idea is: If it takes k workers 1 hour to do a job then *each worker does $\frac{1}{k}$ of the job in an hour* or he works at the rate of $\frac{1}{k}$ of the job per hour. If it takes m workers h hours to finish a job then each worker does $\frac{1}{m}$ of the job in h hours so he does $\frac{1}{h}$ of $\frac{1}{m}$ in an hour. Therefore, each worker *works at the rate of $\frac{1}{mh}$ of the job per hour.*

EXAMPLE 1:   If 5 men take an hour to dig a ditch, how long should it take 12 men to dig a ditch of the same type?

Since 5 workers took an hour, each worker does $\frac{1}{5}$ of the job in an hour. So 12 workers will work at the rate of $\frac{12}{5}$ of the job per hour. Thus if T is the time it takes for 12 workers to do the job, $\frac{12}{5} \times T = 1$ job   and $T = \frac{5}{12} \times 1$, so

$$T = \frac{5}{12} \text{ hours or 25 minutes.}$$

EXAMPLE 2:   Worker A takes 8 hours to do a job. Worker B takes 10 hours to do the same job. How long should it take worker A and worker B working together, but independently, to do the same job?

Worker A works at a rate of $\frac{1}{8}$ of the job per hour, since he takes 8 hours to finish the job. Worker B finished the job in 10 hours, so he works at a rate of $\frac{1}{10}$ of the job per hour. Therefore, if they work together they should complete $\frac{1}{8} + \frac{1}{10} = \frac{18}{80} = \frac{9}{40}$, so they work at a rate of $\frac{9}{40}$ of the job per hour together. So if T is the time it takes them to finish the job, $\frac{9}{40}$ of the job per hour $\times$ T hours must equal 1 job. Therefore,

$$\frac{9}{40} \times T = 1 \text{ and } T = \frac{40}{9} = 4\frac{4}{9} \text{ hours.}$$

EXAMPLE 3:   There are two taps, tap 1 and tap 2, in a keg. If both taps are opened, the keg is drained in 20 minutes. If tap 1 is closed and tap 2 is open, the keg will be drained in 30 minutes. If tap 2 is closed and tap 1 is open, how long will it take to drain the keg?

Tap 1 and tap 2 together take 20 minutes to drain the keg, so together they drain the keg at a rate of $\frac{1}{20}$ of the keg per minute. Tap 2 takes 30 minutes to drain the keg by itself, so it drains the keg at the rate of $\frac{1}{30}$ of the keg per minute. Let r be the rate at which tap 1 will drain the keg by itself. Then $\left(r + \frac{1}{30}\right)$ of the keg per minute is the rate at which both taps together will drain the keg, so $r + \frac{1}{30} = \frac{1}{20}$. Therefore, $r = \frac{1}{20} - \frac{1}{30} = \frac{1}{60}$, and tap 1 drains the keg at the rate of $\frac{1}{60}$ of the keg per minute, so it will take 60 minutes or 1 hour for tap 1 to drain the keg if tap 2 is closed.

342 Mathematics Review

PRACTICE

1. One boy can deliver newspapers on his route in $1\frac{1}{4}$ hours. A boy who takes his place one day finds it takes him 15 minutes longer to deliver these papers. How long would it take to deliver the papers if they worked together?
   (A) $22\frac{1}{4}$ min. (B) $37\frac{1}{2}$ min. (C) 40 min.
   (D) 50 min. (E) 65 min.

2. A contractor estimates that he can paint a house in 5 days by using 6 men. If he actually uses only 5 men for the job how many days will it take to do this job?
   (A) 5 (B) $5\frac{1}{4}$ (C) $5\frac{1}{2}$ (D) 6 (E) $6\frac{1}{2}$

3. A club decided to build a cabin. The job can be done by 3 skilled workmen in 20 days or by 5 of the boys in 30 days. How many days will it take if all work together?
   (A) 10 days (B) 12 days (C) $12\frac{2}{3}$ days
   (D) 14 days (E) 5 days

4. Andrew can do a piece of work in r days and Bill, who works faster, can do the same work in s days. Which of the following expressions, if any, represents the number of days it would take the two of them to do the work if they worked together?
   (A) $\frac{r+s}{2}$ (B) $\frac{1}{r}+\frac{1}{s}$ (C) $r-s$ (D) $\frac{rs}{r+s}$
   (E) none of these

5. Four tractors working together can plow a field in 12 hours. How long will it take 6 tractors to plow a field of the same size, if all tractors work at the same rate?
   (A) 6 hrs. (B) 9 hrs. (C) 10 hrs. (D) 18 hrs.
   (E) 8 hrs.

6. A small factory with 3 machines has a job of stamping out a number of pan covers. The newest machine can do the job in 3 days, another machine can do it in 4 days, and the third machine can do it in 6 days. How many days will it take the factory to do the job, using all three machines.
   (A) $1\frac{1}{3}$ days (B) $4\frac{1}{3}$ days (C) 6 days
   (D) 13 days (E) $1\frac{4}{9}$ days

7. Steven can mow a lawn in 20 minutes and Bernard can mow the same lawn in 30 minutes. How long will it take them working together to mow the lawn?
   (A) 10 min. (B) $12\frac{1}{2}$ min. (C) 15 min.
   (D) 25 min. (E) 12 min.

8. It takes Bert an hour to do a job that Harry can do in 40 minutes. One morning they worked together for 12 minutes, then Bert went away and Harry finished the job. How long did it take him to finish?
   (A) 8 min. (B) 16 min. (C) 20 min.
   (D) 28 min. (E) 33 min.

9. One man can paint a house in r days and another man s days. If together they can do the work in d days, the

equation that expresses the amount of work done by both men in one day is
   (A) $d=\frac{1}{r+s}$ (B) $\frac{1}{r}=\frac{d}{r+s}$ (C) $\frac{1}{d}=\frac{r+s}{rs}$
   (D) $\frac{r+s}{d}=1$ (E) $\frac{d}{rs}=1$

10. Linda has m minutes of homework in each of her s subjects. What part of her homework does she complete in an hour?
    (A) $\frac{1}{ms}$ (B) $\frac{ms}{60}$ (C) $\frac{60}{ms}$ (D) $\frac{s}{60m}$ (E) $\frac{60m}{s}$

11. Sam can mow a lawn in 20 minutes, while Mark takes 10 minutes longer to mow this lawn. How long will it take them to mow the lawn if they both work together?
    (A) 10 minutes
    (B) 12 minutes
    (C) $12\frac{1}{2}$ minutes
    (D) 15 minutes
    (E) more than 15 minutes

12. It takes h hours to mow a lawn. What part of the lawn is mowed in one hour?
    (A) h (B) $\frac{h}{x}$ (C) hx (D) $\frac{1}{h}$ (E) $\frac{x}{h}$

13. If M men can complete a job in H hours, how long will it take 5 men to do this job?
    (A) $\frac{5M}{H}$ (B) $\frac{M}{5H}$ (C) $\frac{MH}{5}$ (D) $\frac{5}{MH}$
    (E) $\frac{5H}{M}$

14. Ann can type a manuscript in 10 hours. Florence can type this manuscript in 5 hours. If they both type this manuscript together it can be completed in
    (A) 2 hours 30 minutes
    (B) 3 hours
    (C) 3 hours 20 minutes
    (D) 5 hours
    (E) 7 hours 30 minutes

15. It was calculated that 75 men could complete a strip on a new highway in 20 days. When work was scheduled to commence, it was found necessary to send 25 men on another road project. How much longer will it take to complete the strip?
    (A) 10 days (B) 20 days (C) 30 days
    (D) 40 days (E) 60 days

ANSWER KEY

1.	C	6.	A	11.	B
2.	D	7.	E	12.	D
3.	B	8.	C	13.	C
4.	D	9.	C	14.	C
5.	E	10.	C	15.	A

II–D.   Counting Problems

D–1

An example of the first type of counting problem is: 50 students signed up for both English and Math. 90 students signed up for either English or Math. If 25 students are taking English but not taking Math, how many students are taking Math but not taking English?

In these problems, "either . . . or . . ." means you can take both, so the people taking both are counted among the people taking either Math or English.

You must avoid counting the same people twice in these problems. The formula is:

the number taking English or Math = the number taking English + the number taking Math − the number taking both.

You have to subtract the number taking both subjects since they are counted once with those taking English and counted again with those taking Math.

A person taking English is either taking Math or not taking Math, so there are $50 + 25 = 75$ people taking English, 50 taking English and Math and 25 taking English but not taking Math. Since 75 are taking English, $90 = 75 +$ number taking Math $- 50$; so there are $90 - 25 = 65$ people taking Math. 50 of the people taking Math are taking English so $65 - 50$ or 15 are taking Math but not English.

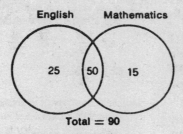

The figure shows what is given. Since 90 students signed up for English or Mathematics, 15 must be taking Mathematics but not English.

EXAMPLE 1: In a survey, 60% of those surveyed owned a car and 80% of those surveyed owned a T.V. If 55% owned both a car and a T.V., what percent of those surveyed owned a car or a T.V. but not both?

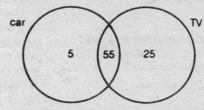

To indicate that 55% is common to both conditions, that is owning a car and a T.V., 55 appears in the area common to both circles. An additional 5% who owned cars but not T.V.s is indicated by a 5 in the circle at the left, since 60% of those surveyed owned a car. An additional 25% who owned T.V.s but not cars is indicated by a 25 in the circle at the right, since 80% owned a T.V. Therefore 30% owned a car or a T.V., but not both.

D-2

> If an event can happen in m different ways, and each of the m ways is followed by a second event which can occur in k different ways, then the first event can be followed by the second event in $m \cdot k$ different ways. This is called the *fundamental principle of counting*.

EXAMPLE 1:   If there are 3 different roads from Syracuse to Binghamton and 4 different roads from Binghamton to Scranton, how many different routes are there from Syracuse to Scranton which go through Binghamton?

There are 3 different ways to go from Syracuse to Binghamton. Once you are in Binghamton, there are 4 different ways to get to Scranton. So using the fundamental principle of counting, there are $3 \times 4 = 12$ different ways to get from Syracuse to Scranton going through Binghamton.

EXAMPLE 2:   A club has 20 members. They are electing a president and a vice president. How many different outcomes of the election are possible? (Assume the president and vice president must be different members of the club.)

There are 20 members, so there are 20 choices for president. Once a president is chosen, there are 19 members left who can be vice president. So there are $20 \cdot 19 = 380$ different possible outcomes of the election.

II–E.   Ratio and Proportion

E-1

Ratio.   A ratio is a comparison of two numbers by division. The ratio of a to b is written as $a{:}b = \dfrac{a}{b} = a \div b$. We can handle ratios as fractions, since a ratio is a fraction. In the ratio $a{:}b$, a and b are called the *terms* of the ratio. *Since* a:b *is a fraction,* b *can never be zero.* The fraction $\dfrac{a}{b}$ is usually different from the fraction $\dfrac{b}{a}$ $\left(\text{for example } \dfrac{3}{2} \text{ is not the same as } \dfrac{2}{3}\right)$ so *the order of the terms in a ratio is important.*

EXAMPLE 1:   If an orange costs 20¢ and an apple costs 12¢, what is the ratio of the cost of an orange to the cost of an apple?

The ratio is $\dfrac{20¢}{12¢} = \dfrac{5}{3}$ or 5:3. Notice that the ratio of the cost of an apple to the cost of an orange is $\dfrac{12¢}{20¢} = \dfrac{3}{5}$ or 3:5. So the order of the terms is important.

A ratio is a number, so if you want to find the ratio of two quantities they must be expressed in the same units.

EXAMPLE 2: What is the ratio of 8 inches to 6 feet?

Change 6 feet into inches. Since there are 12 inches in a foot, 6 feet $= 6 \times 12$ inches $= 72$ inches. So the ratio is $\frac{8 \text{ inches}}{72 \text{ inches}} = \frac{1}{9}$ or 1:9. If you regard ratios as fractions, the units must cancel out, that is, the two terms in a ratio must be expressed in the same unit of measure. In example 2, if you did not change units the ratio would be $\frac{8 \text{ inches}}{6 \text{ feet}} = \frac{4}{3}$ inches/feet, which is not a number.

If two numbers measure different quantities, their quotient is usually called a rate. For example, $\frac{50 \text{ miles}}{2 \text{ hours}}$ which equals 25 miles per hour is a rate of speed.

E–2

Proportion. A proportion is a statement that two ratios are equal. For example, $\frac{3}{12} = \frac{1}{4}$ is a proportion; it could also be expressed as $3:12 = 1:4$ or $3:12 :: 1:4$.

In the proportion $a:b = c:d$, the terms on the outside, (a and d), are called the *extremes*, and the terms on the inside, (b and c), are called the *means*. Since $a:b$ and $c:d$ are ratios, b and d are both different from zero, so $bd \neq 0$. Multiply each side of $\frac{a}{b} = \frac{c}{d}$ by bd; you get $(bd)\left(\frac{a}{b}\right) = ad$ and $(bd)\left(\frac{c}{d}\right) = bc$. Since $bd \neq 0$, the proportion $\frac{a}{b} = \frac{c}{d}$ is equivalent to the equation $ad = bc$. This is usually expressed in the following way.

In a proportion the product of the extremes is equal to the product of the means.

EXAMPLE 1:   Find x if $\frac{4}{5} = \frac{10}{x}$.

In the proportion $\frac{4}{5} = \frac{10}{x}$, 4 and x are the extremes and 5 and 10 are the means, so $4x = 5 \cdot 10 = 50$.

$$\text{Solve for } x \text{ and we get } x = \frac{50}{4} = 12.5.$$

Finding the products ad and bc is also called <u>cross-multiplying the proportion:</u> $\frac{a}{b} \times \frac{c}{d}$. So cross-multiplying a proportion gives two equal numbers. The proportion $\frac{a}{b} = \frac{c}{d}$ is read "a is to b as c is to d."

EXAMPLE 2:   Two numbers are in the ratio 5:4 and their difference is 10. What is the larger number?

Let m and n be the two numbers. Then $\frac{m}{n} = \frac{5}{4}$ and $m - n = 10$. Cross-multiply the proportion and you get $5n = 4m$ or $n = \frac{4}{5}m$. So $m - n = m - \frac{4}{5}m = \frac{1}{5}m = 10$ and $m = 50$, which means $n = \frac{4}{5} \cdot 50 = 40$. Therefore, the larger number is 50.

CHECK:

$$\frac{50}{40} = \frac{5}{4} \text{ and } 50 - 40 = 10.$$

Two variables, a and b, are *directly proportional* if they satisfy a relationship of the form $a = kb$, where k is a number that is a constant. The distance a car travels in two hours and its average speed for the two hours are directly proportional, since $d = 2s$ where d is the distance and s is the average speed expressed in miles per hour. Here $k = 2$. Sometimes the word *directly* is omitted, so a and b are proportional means $a = kb$.

EXAMPLE 3: If m is proportional to n and $m = 5$ when $n = 4$, what is the value of m when $n = 18$?

There are two different ways to work the problem.

I.   Since m and n are directly proportional, $m = kn$; and $m = 5$ when $n = 4$, so $5 = k \cdot 4$ which means $k = \frac{5}{4}$. Therefore, $m = \frac{5}{4}n$. So when $n = 18$,
$m = \frac{5}{4} \cdot 18 = \frac{90}{4} = 22.5$.

II. Since m and n are directly proportional, $m = kn$. If n' is some value of n, then the value of m corresponding to n' we will call m', and $m' = kn'$. So $\frac{m}{n} = k$ and $\frac{m'}{n'} = k$; therefore, $\frac{m}{n} = \frac{m'}{n'}$ is a proportion. Since $m = 5$ when $n = 4$, $\frac{m}{n} = \frac{5}{4} = \frac{m'}{18}$. Cross-multiply and we have $4m' = 90$ or
$m' = \frac{90}{4} = 22.5$.

If two quantities are proportional, you can always set up a proportion in this manner.

EXAMPLE 4: If a machine makes 3 yards of cloth in 2 minutes, how many yards of cloth will the machine make in 50 minutes?

The amount of cloth is proportional to the time the machine operates. Let y be the number of yards of cloth the machine makes in 50 minutes; then $\frac{2 \text{ minutes}}{50 \text{ minutes}} = \frac{3 \text{ yards}}{y \text{ yards}}$, so $\frac{2}{50} = \frac{3}{y}$. Cross-multiply, and you have $2y = 150$, so $y = 75$. Therefore, the machine makes 75 yards of cloth in 50 minutes.

Since a ratio is a number, the units must cancel; so put the numbers which measure the same quantity in the same ratio.

Any two units of measurement of the same quantity are directly proportional.

EXAMPLE 5: How many ounces are there in $4\frac{3}{4}$ pounds?

Let x be the number of ounces in $4\frac{3}{4}$ pounds. Since there are 16 ounces in a pound, $\dfrac{x \text{ ounces}}{16 \text{ ounces}} = \dfrac{4\frac{3}{4} \text{ pounds}}{1 \text{ pound}}$. Cross-multiply to get $x = 16 \cdot 4\frac{3}{4} = 16 \cdot \dfrac{19}{4} = 76$; so $4\frac{3}{4}$ pounds $= 76$ ounces.

You can always change units by using a proportion. You should know the following measurements:

LENGTH:	1 foot = 12 inches
	1 yard = 3 feet
AREA:	1 square foot = 144 square inches
	1 square yard = 9 square feet
TIME:	1 minute = 60 seconds
	1 hour = 60 minutes
	1 day = 24 hours
	1 week = 7 days
	1 year = 52 weeks
VOLUME:	1 quart = 2 pints
	1 gallon = 4 quarts
WEIGHT:	1 ounce = 16 drams
	1 pound = 16 ounces
	1 ton = 2000 pounds

EXAMPLE 6: On a map, it is $2\frac{1}{2}$ inches from Harrisburg to Gary. The actual distance from Harrisburg to Gary is 750 miles. What is the actual distance from town A to town B if they are 4 inches apart on the map?

Let d miles be the distance from A to B; then $\dfrac{2\frac{1}{2} \text{ inches}}{4 \text{ inches}} = \dfrac{750 \text{ miles}}{d \text{ miles}}$. Cross-multiply and we have $\left(2\frac{1}{2}\right)d = 4 \times 750 = 3,000$, so $d = \dfrac{2}{5} \times 3,000 = 1,200$. Therefore, the distance from A to B is 1,200 miles. Problems like this one are often called scale problems.

Two variables, a and b, are *indirectly proportional* if they satisfy a relationship of the form $k = ab$, where k is a number that is a constant. So the average speed of a car and the time it takes the car to travel 300 miles are indirectly proportional, since $st = 300$ where s is the speed and t is the time.

EXAMPLE 7: m is indirectly proportional to n and $m = 5$ when $n = 4$. What is the value of m when $n = 18$?

Since m and n are indirectly proportional, $m \cdot n = k$, and $k = 5 \cdot 4 = 20$ because $m = 5$ when $n = 4$. Therefore, $18m = k = 20$, so $m = \dfrac{20}{18} = \dfrac{10}{9}$ when $n = 18$.

Other examples of indirect proportion are work problems.

If two quantities are directly proportional, then when one increases, the other increases. If two quantities are indirectly proportional when one quantity increases, the other decreases.

E–3

It is also possible to compare three or more numbers by a ratio. The numbers A, B, and C are in the ratio 2:4:3 means $A:B = 2:4$, $A:C = 2:3$, and $B:C = 4:3$. The order of the terms is important. $A:B:C$ is read "A is to B is to C."

EXAMPLE 1: What is the ratio of Tom's salary to Martha's salary to Anne's salary if Tom makes $15,000, Martha makes $12,000 and Anne makes $10,000?

The ratio is 15,000:12,000:10,000 which is the same as 15:12:10. You can cancel a factor which appears in *every* term.

EXAMPLE 2: The angles of a triangle are in the ratio 5:4:3; how many degrees are there is the largest angle?

The sum of the angles in a triangle is 180°. If the angles are $a°$, $b°$, and $c°$, then $a + b + c = 180$, and $a:b:c: = 5:4:3$. You could find b in terms of a since $\frac{a}{b} = \frac{5}{4}$

and c in terms of a since $\frac{a}{c} = \frac{5}{3}$ and then solve the equation for a.

A quicker method for this type of problem is:

(1) Add all the numbers, so $5 + 4 + 3 = 12$.
(2) Use each number as the numerator of a fraction whose denominator is the result of step (1), getting $\frac{5}{12}, \frac{4}{12}, \frac{3}{12}$.
(3) Each quantity is the corresponding fraction (from step (2)), of the total.

Thus

$a = \frac{5}{12}$ of 180 or 75, $b = \frac{4}{12}$ of 180 or 60, and $c = \frac{3}{12}$ of 180 or 45.

So the largest angle is 75°.

CHECK:

$$75:60:45 = 5:4:3 \text{ and } 75 + 60 + 45 = 180.$$

PRACTICE

1. An Erlenmeyer flask can hold 0.6 liters. How many flasks are necessary to hold 3.6 liters?
   (A) 3 (B) 4.2 (C) 6 (D) 12 (E) 21.6

2. At 13° Centigrade a cubic centimeter of uranium weighs 18.7 grams. What is the weight (in grams) of 0.1 cubic centimeters of uranium at 13° Centigrade?
   (A) 1 (B) 1.87 (C) .187 (D) 100 (E) 1870

3. If the cost of 500 articles is d dollars, how many of these articles can be bought for x dollars?
   (A) $\frac{500d}{x}$ (B) $\frac{500}{dx}$ (C) $\frac{dx}{500}$ (D) $\frac{500x}{d}$ (E) $\frac{d}{500x}$

4. A man left $5,000.00 to his three sons. For every dollar Abraham received, Benjamin received $1.50 and Charles received $2.50. How much money was left to Benjamin?
   (A) $750 (B) $1000 (C) $1100 (D) $1500 (E) $3000

5. The Wey of Scotland is equivalent to 40 bushels. How many Weys are there in 4 bushels?
   (A) $\frac{1}{10}$ (B) 1 (C) 10 (D) 44 (E) 160

6. The Japanese ken is equivalent to 5.97 feet. How many feet are there in 59.7 ken?
   (A) 0.1 (B) 10 (C) 248 (D) 356 (E) 360

7. 640 acres = 1 square mile
   1 acre = 4,840 square yards
   1 square mile = ? square yards

(A) $\frac{18}{121}$ (B) $\frac{121}{16}$ (C) 1760   (D) 309,760
(E) 3,097,600

8. A bag of chicken feed will feed 18 chickens for 54 days. How long will it feed 12 chickens?

(A) 36   (B) 37   (C) 53   (D) 72   (E) 81

9. If it requires 9 men 15 days to complete a task, how long would it take to complete this task if three additional men were employed?

(A) $4\frac{3}{4}$ (B) 10   (C) $11\frac{1}{4}$ (D) 12   (E) 16

10. A man works 5 days a week and binds 35 sets of books each week. If there are 7 books in a set, what is the number of books he binds each day?

(A) 1   (B) 7   (C) 25   (D) 35   (E) 49

11. Three men invested $2,000, $3,000, and $5,000 respectively upon the formation of a partnership. The net profits at the end of the year amounted to $960.00. How much should the man who invested the least money receive as his share if the profits are divided in accordance with the amount each partner invested?

(A) $192   (B) $220   (C) $240   (D) $384   (E) $480

12. Three boys have marbles in the ratio of 19:5:3. If the boy with the least number has 9 marbles, how many marbles does the boy with the greatest number have?

(A) 27   (B) 33   (C) 57   (D) 81   (E) 171

13. Snow is accumulating f feet per minute. How much snow will fall in h hours if it continues falling at that rate?

(A) $60fh$ (B) fh (C) $\dfrac{60f}{h}$ (D) $\dfrac{60h}{f}$ (E) $\dfrac{f}{h}$

14. A diagram of a plane drawn to the scale of 0.5 inch equals 80 feet. If the length of the diagram is 4.5 inches the actual length of the plane is

(A) 320 ft.   (B) 360 ft.   (C) 640 ft.   (D) 680 ft.
(E) 720 ft.

15. Joan can wire x radios in $\frac{3}{4}$ minute. At this rate, how many radios can she wire in $\frac{3}{4}$ of an hour?

(A) $\dfrac{x}{60}$ (B) $\dfrac{60}{x}$ (C) $60x$ (D) 60   (E) $x+60$

16. If a light flashes every 6 seconds, how many times will it flash in $\frac{3}{4}$ of an hour?

(A) 225   (B) 250   (C) 360   (D) 450   (E) 480

17. Samuel, Martin, and Miguel invest $5000, $7000, and $12,000 respectively in a business. If the profits are distributed proportionately, what share of a $1111 profit should Miguel receive?

(A) $231.40   (B) $264.00   (C) $333.33   (D) $370.33
(E) $555.50

18. If there are 5 to 8 eggs in a pound, what is the maximum number of eggs in 40 pounds?

(A) 5   (B) 8   (C) 160   (D) 200   (E) 320

19. 24-carat gold is pure gold
18-carat gold is $\frac{3}{4}$ gold
20-carat gold is $\frac{5}{6}$ gold
The ratio of pure gold in 18-carat gold to 20-carat gold is

(A) 5:8   (B) 9:10   (C) 15:24   (D) 8:5   (E) 10:9

20. A cup of oatmeal weighs 3 ounces. A cup of pancake mix weighs 5 ounces. How many cups of oatmeal will have the same weight as 3 cups of pancake mix?

(A) $\frac{3}{5}$ (B) $1\frac{2}{3}$ (C) 3   (D) 5   (E) 15

ANSWER KEY

1. C	*8.* E	*15.* C
2. B	*9.* C	*16.* D
3. D	*10.* E	*17.* E
4. D	*11.* A	*18.* E
5. A	*12.* C	*19.* B
6. D	*13.* A	*20.* D
7. E	*14.* E	

II–F. Sequence and Progressions

F–1

A SEQUENCE is an ordered collection of numbers. For example, 2,4,6,8,10, . . . is a sequence. 2,4,6,8,10 are called the *terms* of the sequence. We identify the terms by their position in the sequence; so 2 is the first term, 8 is the 4th term and so on. The dots mean the sequence continues; you should be able to figure out the succeeding terms. In the example, the sequence is the sequence of even integers, and the next term after 10 would be 12.

EXAMPLE 1: What is the eighth term of the sequence 1,4,9,16,25, . . . ?

Since $1^2 = 1$, $2^2 = 4$, $3^2 = 9$, the sequence is the sequence of squares of integers, so the eighth term is $8^2 = 64$.

F-2

An *arithmetical progression* is a sequence of numbers with the property that the *difference* of any two consecutive numbers is always the same. The numbers 2,6,10,14,18,22, . . . constitute an arithmetical progression, since each term is 4 more than the term before it. 4 is called the common difference of the progression.

If d is the common difference and a is the first term of the progression, then the nth term will be a + (n − 1)d. So a progression with common difference 4 and initial term 5 will have $5 + 6(4) = 29$ as its 7th term. You can check your answer. The sequence would be 5,9,13,17,21,25,29, . . . so 29 is the seventh term.

To find the sum of the first n terms in an arithmetic progression, use the formula

$S = \frac{n}{2} \quad (a + l)$, where l is the last term.

EXAMPLE 1:   In the arithmetic progression 7, 10, 13, 16,...what is the sum of 36 terms?

First find the value of l.

$l = a + d(n − 1)$

$l = 7 + 3(35)$

$l = 112$

Apply the formula $S = \frac{n}{2} (a + l)$

$S = 18(7 + 112)$

$S = 18(119)$

$S = 2142$

Or, use the formula that combines both formulas: $S = \frac{n}{2} (2a + [n − 1]d)$

$S = 18(14 + [35]3)$

$S = 18(14 + 105)$

$S = 18(119) = 2142$

A sequence of numbers is called a *geometric progression* if the *ratio* of consecutive terms is always the same. So 3,6,12,24,48, . . . is a geometric progression since $\frac{6}{3} = 2 = \frac{12}{6} = \frac{24}{12} = \frac{48}{24}, \ldots$. *The nth term of a geometric series is* ar^{n-1} where a is the first term and r is the common ratio. If a geometric progression started with 2 and the common ratio was 3, then the fifth term should be $2 \cdot 3^4 = 2 \cdot 81 = 162$. The sequence would be 2,6,18,54,162, . . . so 162 is indeed the fifth term of the progression.

We can quickly add up the first n terms of a geometric progression which starts with a and has common ratio r. *The formula for the sum of the first n terms is* $\dfrac{ar^n - a}{r - 1}$ when $r \neq 1$. (If $r = 1$ all the terms are the same so the sum is *na*.)

EXAMPLE 1:   Find the sum of the first 7 terms of the sequence 5,10,20,40, ...

Since $\dfrac{10}{5} = \dfrac{20}{10} = \dfrac{40}{20} = 2$, the sequence is a geometric sequence with common ratio 2. The first term is 5, so $a = 5$ and the common ratio is 2. The sum of the first seven terms means $n = 7$. Thus, the sum is

$$\frac{5 \cdot 2^7 - 5}{2 - 1} = 5(2^7 - 1) = 5(128 - 1) = 5 \cdot 127 = 635.$$

CHECK:

The first seven terms are 5,10,20,40,80,160,320, and $5 + 10 + 20 + 40 + 80 + 160 + 320 = 635$.

II–G. Inequalities

G–1

A number is positive if it is greater than 0, so 1, $\dfrac{1}{1000}$, and 53.4 are all positive numbers. Positive numbers are signed numbers whose sign is +. If you think of numbers as points on a number line (see section I-F-2, page 241), positive numbers correspond to points to the right of 0.

A number is negative if it is less than 0. $-\dfrac{4}{5}$, -50, and $-.0001$ are all negative numbers. Negative numbers are signed numbers whose sign is $-$. Negative numbers correspond to points to the left of 0 on a number line.

0 is the only number which is neither positive nor negative.

$a > b$ means the number a is greater than the number b, that is $a = b + x$ where x is a positive number. If we look at a number line, $a > b$ means a is to the right of b. $a > b$ can also be read as b is less than a, which is also written $b < a$. For example, $-5 > -7.5$ because $-5 = -7.5 + 2.5$ and 2.5 is positive.

The notation $a \leq b$ means a is less than or equal to b, or b is greater than or equal to a. For example, $5 \geq 4$; also $4 \geq 4$. $a \neq b$ means a is not equal to b.

If you need to know whether one fraction is greater than another fraction, put the fractions over a common denominator and compare the numerators.

EXAMPLE 1: Which is larger, $\frac{13}{16}$ or $\frac{31}{40}$?

A common denominator is 80.

$\frac{13}{16} = \frac{65}{80}$, and $\frac{31}{40} = \frac{62}{80}$;

since $65 > 62$,

$\frac{65}{80} > \frac{62}{80}$,

so $\frac{13}{16} > \frac{31}{40}$.

G–2

Inequalities have certain properties which are similar to those of equations. We can talk about the left side and the right side of an inequality, and we can use algebraic expressions for the sides of an inequality. For example, $6x < 5x + 4$. A value for an unknown *satisfies an inequality*, if when you evaluate each side of the inequality the numbers satisfy the inequality. So if $x = 2$, then $6x = 12$ and $5x + 4 = 14$ and since $12 < 14$, $x = 2$ satisfies $6x < 5x + 4$. Two inequalities are equivalent if the same collection of numbers satisfies both inequalities.

The following basic principles are used in work with inequalities:

(A) Adding the same expression to *each* side of an inequality gives an equivalent inequality (written $a < b \leftrightarrow a + c < b + c$ where $\leftrightarrow$ means equivalent).

(B) Subtracting the same expression from *each* side of an inequality gives an equivalent inequality ($a < b \leftrightarrow a - c < b - c$).

(C) Multiplying or dividing *each* side of an inequality by the same *positive* expression gives an equivalent inequality ($a < b \leftrightarrow ca < cb$ for $c > 0$).

(D) Multiplying or dividing each side of an inequality by the same *negative* expression *reverses* the inequality ($a < b \leftrightarrow ca > cb$ for $c < 0$).

(E) If both sides of an inequality have the same sign, inverting both sides of the inequality *reverses* the inequality.

$$0 < a < b \leftrightarrow 0 < \frac{1}{b} < \frac{1}{a}$$

$$a < b < 0 \leftrightarrow \frac{1}{b} < \frac{1}{a} < 0$$

(F) If two inequalities are of the same type (both greater or both less), adding the respective sides gives the same type of inequality.

$$(a < b \text{ and } c < d, \text{ then } a + c < b + d)$$

Note that the inequalities are *not* equivalent.

(G) If $a < b$ and $b < c$ then $a < c$.

EXAMPLE 1: Find the values of x for which $5x - 4 < 7x + 2$.

Using principle (B) subtract $5x + 2$ from each side, so $(5x - 4 < 7x + 2) \leftrightarrow -6 < 2x$. Now use principle (C) and divide each side by 2, so $-6 < 2x \leftrightarrow -3 < x$.

So any x greater than -3 satisfies the inequality. It is a good idea to make a spot check. -1 is > -3; let $x = -1$ then $5x - 4 = -9$ and $7x + 2 = -5$. Since $-9 < -5$, the answer is correct for at least the particular value $x = -1$.

EXAMPLE 2:   Find the values of a which satisfy $a^2 + 1 > 2a + 4$.

Subtract $2a$ from each side, so
$(a^2 + 1 > 2a + 4) \leftrightarrow a^2 - 2a + 1 > 4$.
$a^2 - 2a + 1 = (a - 1)^2$ so
$a^2 - 2a + 1 > 4 \leftrightarrow (a - 1)^2 > 2^2$.

We need to be careful when we take the square roots of inequalities. If $q^2 > 4$ and if $q > 0$, then $q > 2$; but if $q < 0$, then $q < -2$. We must look at two cases in example 2. First, if $(a - 1) \geq 0$ then

$(a - 1)^2 > 2^2 \leftrightarrow a - 1 > 2$ or $a > 3$.
If $(a - 1) < 0$ then $(a - 1)^2 > 2^2 \leftrightarrow a - 1 < -2 \leftrightarrow a < -1$.
So the inequality is satisfied if $a > 3$ or if $a < -1$.

CHECK:

$(-2)^2 + 1 = 5 > 2(-2) + 4 = 0$, and $5^2 + 1 = 26 > 14 = 2 \cdot 5 + 4$.

Some inequalities are not satisfied by *any* real number. For example, since $x^2 \geq 0$ for all x, there is no real number x such that $x^2 < -9$.

You may be given an inequality and asked whether other inequalities follow from the original inequality. You should be able to answer such questions by using principles (A) through (G).

If there is any property of inequalities you can't remember, try out some specific numbers. If $x < y$, then what is the relation between $-x$ and $-y$? Since $4 < 5$ but $-5 < -4$, the relation is probably $-x > -y$, which is true by (D).

Probably the most common mistake is forgetting to reverse the inequalities if you multiply or divide by a negative number.

PRACTICE

1. Point P is on line segment AB. Which of the following is always true?
(A) $AP = PB$ (B) $AP > PB$ (C) $PB > AP$
(D) $AB > AP$ (E) $AB > AP + PB$

2. If $x < y$ and $a = b$ then
(A) $x + a = y + b$ (B) $x + a < y + b$
(C) $x + a > y + b$ (D) $x + a = y$
(E) $x + a = b$

3. If $x < y$ and $z = \frac{1}{2}x$ and $a = \frac{1}{2}y$ then
(A) $z > a$ (B) $a > z$ (C) $\frac{1}{2}a = \frac{1}{2}z$
(D) $2x > 2z$ (E) $2a > y$

4. If $b < d$ and $a = 2b$ and $c = 2d$ then
(A) $b = d$ (B) $a = c$ (C) $a < c$
(D) $b > d$ (E) $a > c$

5. If $p < q$ and $r < s$ then
(A) $p = r > q + s$ (B) $p + r < q + s$
(C) $pr < qs$ (D) $pr > qs$ (E) $p + r = q + s$

6. If $-1 < x \leq 1$ and x is an integer then the value of x is
(A) zero only   (B) one only   (C) one and zero
(D) one value more than one
(E) one value less than one

7. In the inequality $5x + 2 < 2x + 5$ all of the following may be a value of x except
(A) 0   (B) 1   (C) -1 (D) -2 (E) -3

8. If $a > b$ and $b > c$ then
(A) $a < c$ (B) $a > c$ (C) $a = c$
(D) $c > a$ (E) $b < a$

9. If $a > b > 1$ then which of the following is true?
  (A) $b + a > 2a$ (B) $a^2 < ab$ (C) $a - b < 0$
  (D) $a < b + 1$ (E) $a^2 > b^2$

10. If $2y > 5$ then
  (A) $y > 2.5$ (B) $y < 2.5$ (C) $y = 2.5$
  (D) $y = 10$ (E) $y = 5.2$

11. If $3x - 4 > 8$ then
  (A) $x = 4$ (B) $x = 0$ (C) $x = 4, 0$
  (D) $x > 4$ (E) $x < 4$

12. In triangle ABC $AB = AC$. All of the following statements are true except
  (A) $AB < AC + BC$ (B) $AC < AB + BC$
  (C) $BC < AB + AC$ (D) $AC + BC = AB + BC$
  (E) $BC + AC > AB + BC$

13. In triangle KLM the measure of angle $M >$ the measure of angle L. Which of the following is true?
  (A) $KM > KL$ (B) $KL > KM$ (C) $KL < KM$
  (D) $KM + LM < KL$ (E) $KL + LM < KM$

14. In triangles ABC and DEF, $AC = DF$, $BC = EF$ and $AB > DE$, then
  (A) m $\angle C =$ m $\angle F$ (B) m $\angle F >$ m $\angle C$
  (C) m $\angle F <$ m $\angle C$ (D) m $\angle A =$ m $\angle D$
  (E) m $\angle B =$ m $\angle E$

15. If $x < y$ and $a < b$, then
  (A) $a + x < b + y$ (B) $a + x > b + y$
  (C) $a = y$ (D) $x = b$ (E) $ax = by$

ANSWER KEY

1. D	6. C	11. D
2. B	7. B	12. E
3. B	8. B	13. B
4. C	9. E	14. C
5. B	10. A	15. A

III. Geometry

III-A. Angles

A-1

If two straight lines meet at a point they form an *angle*. The point is called the *vertex* of the angle and the lines are called the *sides* or *rays* of the angle. The sign for angle is $\angle$ and an angle can be denoted in the following ways:

  (A) $\angle ABC$ where B is the vertex, A is a point on one side, and C a point on the other side.

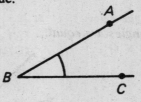

  (B) $\angle B$ where B is the vertex.

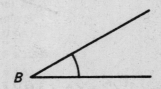

(C) $\angle 1$ or $\angle x$ where x or 1 is written inside the angle.

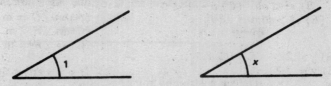

Angles are usually measured in degrees. We say that an angle equals x degrees, when its measure is x degrees. Degrees are denoted by °. An angle of 50 degrees is 50°. $60' = 1°, 60'' = 1'$ where ' is read minutes and " is read seconds.

A–2

Two angles are *adjacent* if they have the same vertex and a common side and one angle is not inside the other.

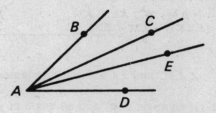

$\angle BAC$ and $\angle CAD$ are adjacent, but $\angle CAD$ and $\angle EAD$ are not adjacent.

If two lines intersect at a point, they form 4 angles. The angles opposite each other are called *vertical* angles. $\angle 1$ and $\angle 3$ are vertical angles. $\angle 2$ and $\angle 4$ are vertical angles.

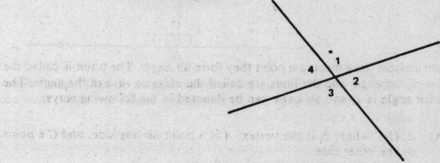

Vertical angles are equal,

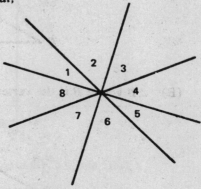

so $\angle 1 = \angle 5, \angle 2 = \angle 6, \angle 3 = \angle 7, \angle 4 = \angle 8.$

A–3

A straight angle is an angle whose sides lie on a straight line. *A straight angle equals 180°.*

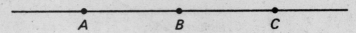

∠*ABC* is a straight angle.

If the sum of two angles is a straight angle, then the angles are *supplementary* and each angle is the supplement of the other.

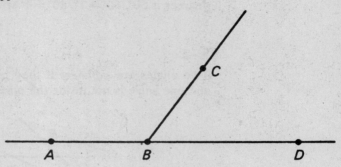

∠*ABC* and ∠*CBD* are supplementary.

If an angle of $x°$ and an angle of $y°$ are supplements, then $x + y = 180$.

If two supplementary angles are equal, they are both *right angles*. A right angle is half of a straight angle. A right angle = 90°.

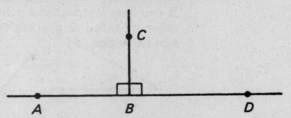

∠*ABC* = ∠*CBD* and they are both right angles. A right angle is denoted by ∟. When 2 lines intersect and all four of the angles are equal, then each of the angles is a right angle.

If the sum of two angles is a right angle, then the angles are *complementary* and each angle is the complement of the other.

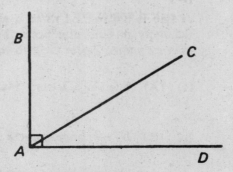

∠*BAC* and ∠*CAD* are complementary.

If an angle of $x°$ and an angle of $y°$ are complementary, then $x + y = 90$.

EXAMPLE 1:   If the supplement of angle x is three times as much as the complement of angle x, how many degrees is angle x?

Let d be the number of degrees in angle x; then the supplement of x is $(180-d)°$, and the complement of x is $(90-d)°$. Since the supplement is 3 times the complement, $180 - d = 3(90 - d) = 270 - 3d$ which gives $2d = 90$, so $d = 45$.

Therefore, angle x is $45°$.

If an angle is divided into two equal parts by a straight line, then the angle has been *bisected* and the line is called the *bisector* of the angle.

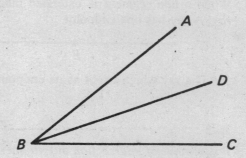

BD bisects $\angle ABC$; so $\angle ABD = \angle DBC$.

An *acute angle* is an angle less than a right angle. An *obtuse* angle is an angle greater than a right angle, but less than a straight angle.

$\angle 1$ is an acute angle, and $\angle 2$ is an obtuse angle.

III–B.   Lines

B–1

A line is understood to be a straight line. A line is assumed to extend indefinitely in both directions. *There is one and only one line between two distinct points.* There are two ways to denote a line:

(1)   (A)   by a single letter: l is a line;

(2)   (B)   by two points on the line:  AB is a line.

A *line segment* is the part of a line between two points called *endpoints*. A line segment is denoted by its endpoints.

AB is a line segment. If a point *P* on a line segment is equidistant from the endpoints, then *P* is called the *midpoint* of the line segment.

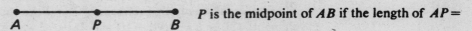

P is the midpoint of *AB* if the length of *AP* = the length of *PB*. Two line segments are equal if their lengths are equal; so *AP* = *PB* means the line segment *AP* has the same length as the line segment *PB*.

When a line segment is extended indefinitely in one direction, it is called a *ray*. A ray has one endpoint.

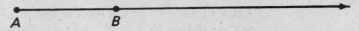

AB is a ray which has *A* as its endpoint.

B–2

P is a *point of intersection* of two lines if *P* is a point which is on both of the lines. *Two different lines can not have more than one point of intersection,* because there is only one line between two points.

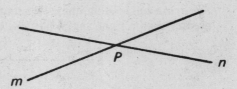

P is the point of intersection of *m* and *n*. We also say *m and n intersect at P*.

Two lines in the same plane are parallel if they do not intersect no matter how far they are extended.

m and *n* are parallel, but *k* and *l* are not parallel since if *k* and *l* are extended they will intersect. Parallel lines are denoted by the symbol ‖; so *m* ‖ *n* means *m* is parallel to *n*.

If two lines are parallel to a third line, then they are parallel to each other.

If a third line intersects two given lines, it is called a *transversal*. A transversal and the two given lines form eight angles. The four inside angles are called *interior* angles. The four outside angles are called *exterior* angles. If two angles are on opposite sides of the transversal and have different lines for their sides they are called *alternate* angles.

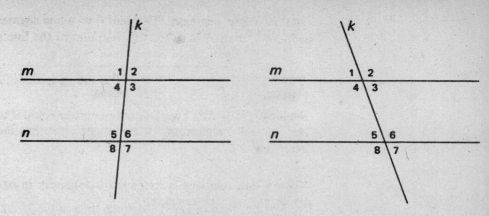

k is a transversal of the lines m and n. Angles 1, 2, 7, and 8 are the exterior angles, and angles 3, 4, 5, and 6 are the interior angles. $\angle 4$ and $\angle 6$ are an example of a pair of alternate angles. $\angle 1$ and $\angle 5$, $\angle 2$ and $\angle 6$, $\angle 3$ and $\angle 7$, and $\angle 4$ and $\angle 8$ are pairs of *corresponding* angles.

If two parallel lines are intersected by a transversal then:

(1)   Alternate interior angles are equal.
(2)   Corresponding angles are equal.
(3)   Interior angles on the same side of the transversal are supplementary.

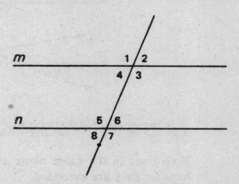

If we use the fact that vertical angles are equal, we can replace "interior" by "exterior" in (1) and (3).

m is parallel to n implies:

(1) $\angle 4 = \angle 6$ and $\angle 3 = \angle 5$
(2) $\angle 1 = \angle 5$, $\angle 2 = \angle 6$, $\angle 3 = \angle 7$ and $\angle 4 = \angle 8$
(3) $\angle 3 + \angle 6 = 180°$ and $\angle 4 + \angle 5 = 180°$

The converse is also true. Let m and n be two lines which have k as a transversal.

(1)   If a pair of alternate interior angles are equal, then m and n are parallel.
(2)   If a pair of corresponding angles are equal, then m and n are parallel.
(3)   If a pair of interior angles on the same side of the transversal are supplementary, then m is parallel to n.

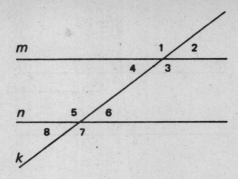

If $\angle 3 = \angle 5$, then $m \parallel n$. If $\angle 4 = \angle 6$ then $m \parallel n$. If $\angle 2 = \angle 6$ then $m \parallel n$. If $\angle 3 + \angle 6 = 180°$, then $m \parallel n$.

EXAMPLE 1:   If m and n are two parallel lines and angle 1 is 60°, how many degrees is angle 2?

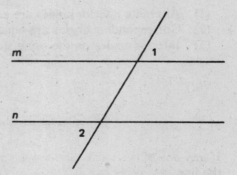

Let $\angle 3$ be the vertical angle equal to angle 2.

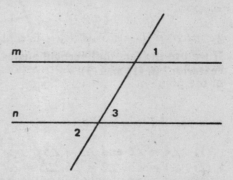

$\angle 3 = \angle 2$. Since m and n are parallel, corresponding angles are equal. Since $\angle 1$ and $\angle 3$ are corresponding angles, $\angle 1 = \angle 3$. Therefore, $\angle 1 = \angle 2$, and $\angle 2$ equals 60° since $\angle 1 = 60°$.

B–3

When two lines intersect and all four of the angles formed are equal, the lines are said to be *perpendicular*. If two lines are perpendicular, they are the sides of right angles whose vertex is the point of intersection.

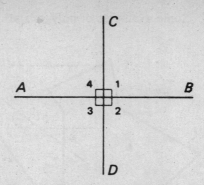

AB is perpendicular to *CD*, and angles 1, 2, 3, and 4 are all right angles. ⊥ is the symbol for perpendicular; so *AB* ⊥ *CD*.

If two lines in a plane are perpendicular to the same line, then the two lines are parallel.

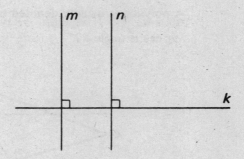

m ⊥ *k* and *n* ⊥ *k* implies that *m* ∥ *n*.

If *any one* of the angles formed when two lines intersect is a right angle, then the lines are perpendicular.

III–C. Polygons

A POLYGON is a closed figure in a plane which is composed of line segments which meet only at their endpoints. The line segments are called *sides* of the polygon, and a point where two sides meet is called a *vertex* (plural *vertices*) of the polygon.

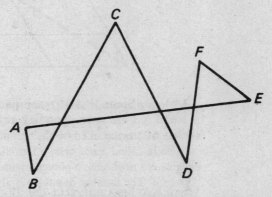

ABCDEF is not a polygon since the line segments intersect at points which are not endpoints.

Some examples of polygons are:

A polygon is usually denoted by the vertices given in order.

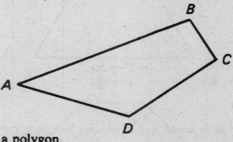

ABCD is a polygon.

A *diagonal* of a polygon is a line segment whose endpoints are nonadjacent vertices. The *altitude* from a vertex *P* to a side is the line segment with end-point *P* which is perpendicular to the side.

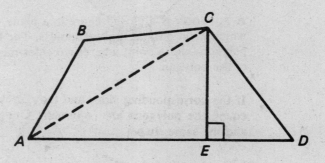

AC is a diagonal, and *CE* is the altitude from *C* to *AD*.

Polygons are classified by the number of angles or sides they have. A polygon with three angles is called a *triangle*; a four-sided polygon is a *quadrilateral*; a polygon with five angles is a *pentagon*; a polygon with six angles is a *hexagon*; an eight-sided polygon is an *octagon*. The number of angles is always equal to the number of sides in a polygon, so a six-sided polygon is a hexagon, which has six angles. The term *n*-gon refers to a polygon with *n* sides.

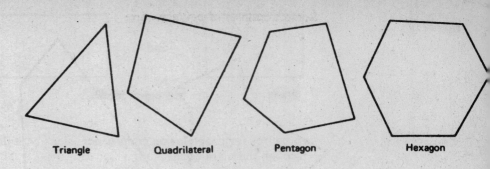

| Triangle | Quadrilateral | Pentagon | Hexagon |

If the sides of a polygon are all equal in length and if all the angles of a polygon are equal, the polygon is called a *regular* polygon.

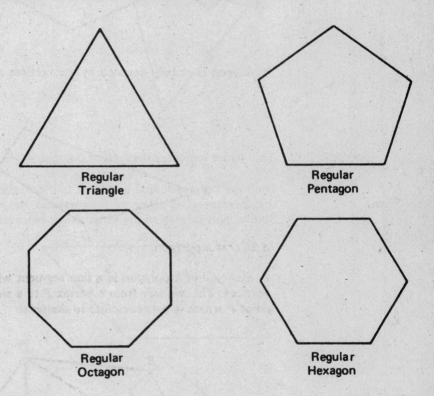

Regular
Triangle

Regular
Pentagon

Regular
Octagon

Regular
Hexagon

If the corresponding sides and the corresponding angles of two polygons are equal, the polygons are *congruent*. Congruent polygons have the same size and the same shape.

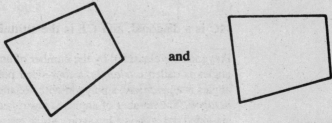

and

are congruent but

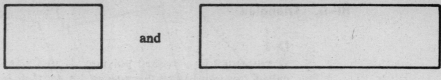

and

are not congruent.

In figures for problems on congruence, sides with the same number of strokes through them are equal.

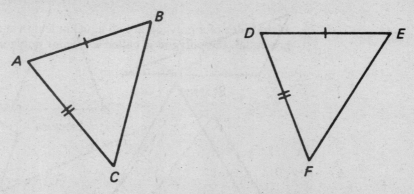

This figure indicates that $AB = DE$ and $AC = DF$.

If all the corresponding angles of two polygons are equal and the lengths of the corresponding sides are proportional, the polygons are said to be *similar*. Similar polygons have the same shape but need not be the same size.

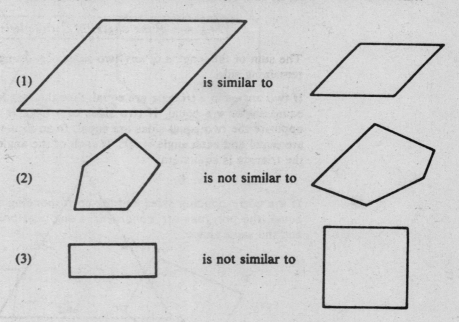

(1)   is similar to

(2)   is not similar to

(3)   is not similar to

In (3) the corresponding angles are equal, but the corresponding sides are not proportional.

The sum of all the angles of an n-gon is $(n - 2)180°$. So the sum of the angles in a hexagon is $(6 - 2)180° = 720°$.

III–D. Triangles

D–1

A TRIANGLE is a 3-sided polygon. If two sides of a triangle are equal, it is called *isosceles*. If all three sides are equal, it is an *equilateral* triangle. If all of the sides have different lengths, the triangle is *scalene*. When one of the angles in a triangle is a right angle, the triangle is a *right triangle*. If one of the angles is obtuse we have an *obtuse triangle*. If all the angles are acute, the triangle is an *acute triangle*.

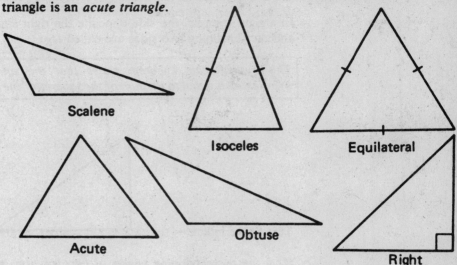

The symbol for a triangle is △; so △*ABC* means a triangle whose vertices are *A*, *B*, and *C*.

> *The sum of the angles in a triangle is 180°.*

The sum of the lengths of any two sides of a triangle must be longer than the remaining side.

If two angles in a triangle are equal, then the lengths of the sides opposite the equal angles are equal. If two sides of a triangle are equal, then the angles opposite the two equal sides are equal. In an equilateral triangle all the angles are equal and each angle = 60°. If each of the angles in a triangle is 60°, then the triangle is equilateral.

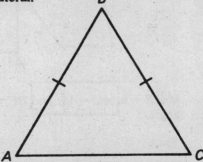

If *AB* = *BC*, then ∠*BAC* = ∠*BCA*.

If one angle in a triangle is larger than another angle, the side opposite the larger angle is longer than the side opposite the smaller angle. If one side is longer than another side, then the angle opposite the longer side is larger than the angle opposite the shorter side.

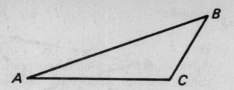

$AB > AC$ implies $\angle BCA > \angle ABC$.

In a right triangle, the side opposite the right angle is called the *hypotenuse*, and the remaining two sides are called *legs*.

> The Pythagorean Theorem states that the square of the length of the hypotenuse is equal to the sum of the squares of the lengths of the legs.

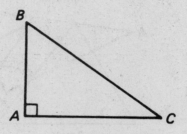

$(BC)^2 = (AB)^2 + (AC)^2$

If $AB = 4$ and $AC = 3$ then $(BC)^2 = 4^2 + 3^2 = 25$ so $BC = 5$. If $BC = 13$ and $AC = 5$, then $13^2 = 169 = (AB)^2 + 5^2$. So $(AB)^2 = 169 - 25 = 144$ and $AB = 12$.

If the lengths of the three sides of a triangle are a, b, and c and $a^2 = b^2 + c^2$, then the triangle is a right triangle where a is the length of the hypotenuse.

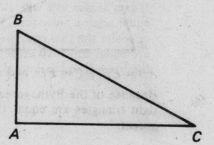

If $AB = 8$, $AC = 15$, and $BC = 17$, then since $17^2 = 8^2 + 15^2$, $\angle BAC$ is a right angle.

D–2

CONGRUENCE. Two triangles are congruent, if two pairs of corresponding sides and the corresponding *included* angles are equal. This is called *Side-Angle-Side* and is denoted by S.A.S.

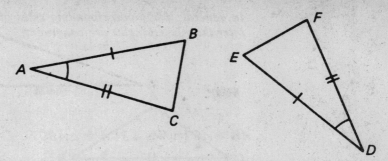

AB = DE, AC = DF and *∠BAC = ∠EDF* imply that *△ABC ≅ △DEF*. ≅ means congruent.

Two triangles are congruent if two pairs of corresponding angles and the corresponding *included* side are equal. This is called *Angle-Side-Angle* or A.S.A.

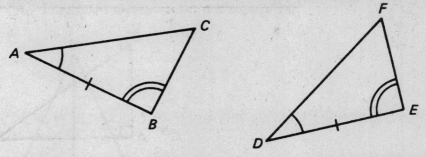

If *AB = DE, ∠BAC = ∠EDF*, and *∠CBA = ∠FED* then *△ABC ≅ △DEF*.

If all three pairs of corresponding sides of two triangles are equal, then the triangles are congruent. This is called *Side-Side-Side* or S.S.S.

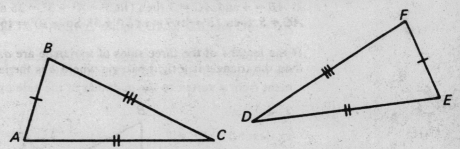

AB = EF, AC = ED, and *BC = FD* imply that *△ABC ≅ △EFD*.

Because of the Pythagorean Theorem, if any two corresponding sides of two right triangles are equal, the third sides are equal and the triangles are congruent.

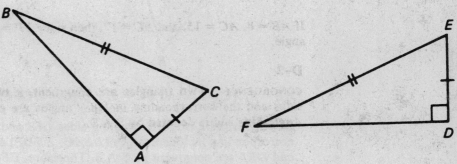

AC = DE and *BC = EF* imply *△ABC ≅ △DFE*.

In general, if two corresponding sides of two triangles are equal, we cannot infer that the triangles are congruent.

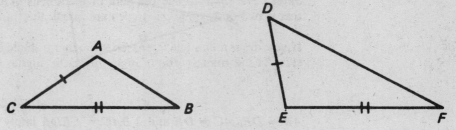

$AC = DE$ and $CB = EF$, but the triangles are not congruent.

If two sides of a triangle are equal, then the altitude to the third side divides the triangle into two congruent triangles.

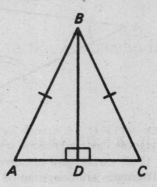

$AB = BC$ and $BD \perp AC$ implies $\triangle ADB \cong \triangle CDB$.

Therefore, $\angle ABD = \angle CBD$, so BD bisects $\angle ABC$. Since $AD = DC$, D is the midpoint of AC so BD is the median from B to AC. A *median* is the segment from a vertex to the midpoint of the side opposite the vertex.

EXAMPLE 1: $EF = ?$

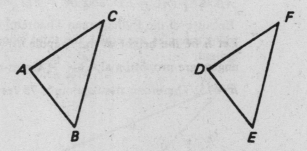

$AB = 4$, $AC = 4.5$ and $BC = 6$, $\angle BAC = \angle EDF$, $DE = 4$ and $DF = 4.5$

Since two pairs of corresponding sides (AB and DE, AC and DF) and the corresponding included angles ($\angle BAC$, $\angle EDF$) are equal, the triangles ABC and DEF are congruent by S.A.S. Therefore, $EF = BC = 6$.

D–3

Similarity. *Two triangles are similar if all three pairs of corresponding angles are equal.* Since the sum of the angles in a triangle is 180°, it follows that if two corresponding angles are equal, the third angles must be equal.

If you draw a line which passes through a triangle and is parallel to one of the sides of the triangle, the triangle formed is similar to the original triangle.

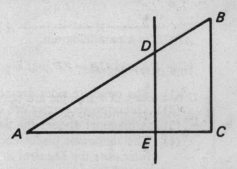

If $DE \parallel BC$ then $\triangle ADE \sim \triangle ABC$. The symbol $\sim$ means similar.

EXAMPLE 1:   A man 6 feet tall casts a shadow 4 feet long; at the same time a flagpole casts a shadow which is 50 feet long. How tall is the flagpole?

The man with his shadow and the flagpole with its shadow can be regarded as the pairs of corresponding sides of two similar triangles.

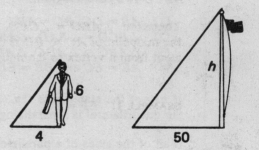

Let h be the height of the flagpole. Since corresponding sides of similar triangles are proportional, $\frac{4}{50} = \frac{6}{h}$. Cross-multiply getting $4h = 6 \cdot 50 = 300$; so $h = 75$. Therefore, the flagpole is 75 feet high.

III–E.   Quadrilaterals

A QUADRILATERAL is a polygon with four sides. The sum of the angles in a quadrilateral is 360°. If the opposite sides of a quadrilateral are parallel, the figure is a *parallelogram*.

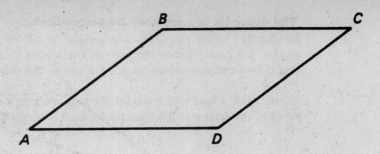

ABCD is a parallelogram.

In a parallelogram:

(1) The opposite sides are equal.
(2) The opposite angles are equal.
(3) A diagonal divides the parallelogram into two congruent triangles.
(4) The diagonals bisect each other. (A line *bisects* a line segment if it intersects the segment at the midpoint of the segment.)

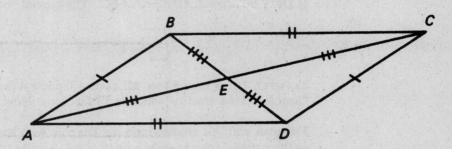

ABCD is a parallelogram.

(1) $AB = DC$, $BC = AD$.
(2) $\angle BCD = \angle BAD$, $\angle ABC = \angle ADC$.
(3) $\triangle ABC \cong \triangle ADC$, $\triangle ABD \cong \triangle CDB$.
(4) $AE = EC$ and $BE = ED$.

If *any* of the statements (1), (2), (3) and (4) are true for a quadrilateral, then the quadrilateral is a parallelogram.

If all of the sides of a parallelogram are equal, the figure is called a *rhombus*.

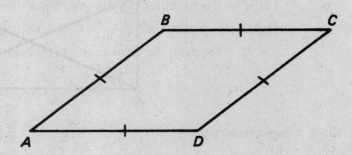

ABCD is a rhombus.

The diagonals of a rhombus are perpendicular.

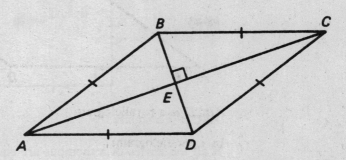

$BD \perp AC$; $\angle BEC = \angle CED = \angle AED = \angle AEB = 90°$.

If all the angles of a parallelogram are right angles, the figure is a *rectangle*.

ABCD is a rectangle.

Since the sum of the angles in a quadrilateral is 360°, if *all* the angles of a quadrilateral are equal then the figure is a rectangle. The diagonals of a rectangle are equal. The length of a diagonal can be found by using the Pythagorean Theorem.

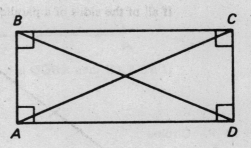

If *ABCD* is a rectangle, $AC = BD$ and $(AC)^2 = (AD)^2 + (DC)^2$.

If all the sides of a rectangle are equal, the figure is a *square*.

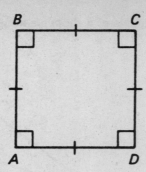

ABCD is a square.

If all the angles of a rhombus are equal, the figure is a square. The length of the diagonal of a square is $\sqrt{2}\,s$ where s is the length of a side.

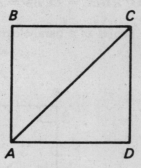

In square *ABCD*, $AC = (\sqrt{2})AD$.

A quadrilateral with two parallel sides and two sides which are not parallel is called a *trapezoid*. The parallel sides are called *bases*, and the non-parallel sides are called *legs*.

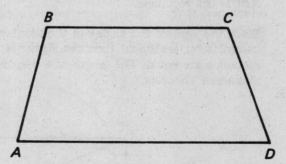

If $BC \parallel AD$ then *ABCD* is a trapezoid; *BC* and *AD* are the bases.

III–F.   Circles

A CIRCLE is a figure in a plane consisting of all the points which are the same distance from a fixed point called the *center* of the circle. A line segment from any point on the circle to the center of the circle is called a *radius* (plural: radii) of the circle. All radii of the same circle have the same length.

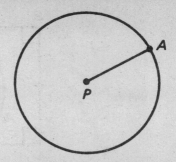

This circle has center P and radius AP.

A circle is denoted by a single letter, usually its center. Two circles with the same center are *concentric*.

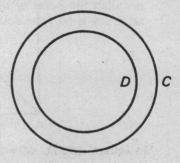

C and D are concentric circles.

A line segment whose endpoints are on a circle is called a *chord*. A chord which passes through the center of the circle is a *diameter*. *The length of a diameter is twice the length of a radius.* A diameter divides a circle into two congruent halves which are called *semicircles*.

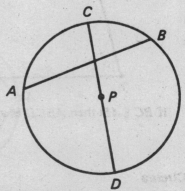

P is the center of the circle.
AB is a chord and CD is a diameter.

A diameter which is perpendicular to a chord bisects the chord.

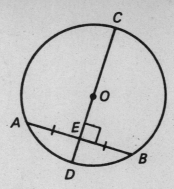

O is the center of this circle and $AB \perp CD$; then $AE = EB$.

If a line intersects a circle at one and only one point, the line is said to be a *tangent* to the circle. The point common to a circle and a tangent to the circle is called the *point of tangency*. The radius from the center to the point of tangency is perpendicular to the tangent.

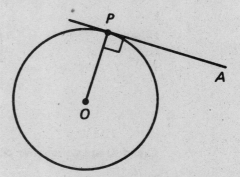

AP is tangent to the circle with center O. P is the point of tangency and $OP \perp PA$.

A polygon is *inscribed* in a circle if all of its vertices are points on the circle.

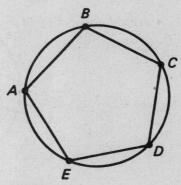

$ABCDE$ is an inscribed pentagon.

An angle whose vertex is a point on a circle and whose sides are chords of the circle is called an *inscribed angle*. An angle whose vertex is the center of a circle and whose sides are radii of the circle is called a *central angle*.

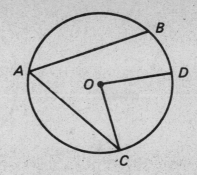

∠*BAC* is an inscribed angle.
∠*DOC* is a central angle.

An *arc* is a part of a circle.

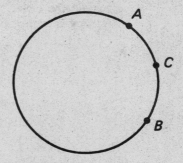

ACB is an arc. Arc *ACB* is written $\overparen{ACB}$.

If two letters are used to denote an arc, they represent the smaller of the two possible arcs. So $\overparen{AB} = \overparen{ACB}$.

An arc can be measured in degrees. The entire circle is 360°; thus an arc of 120° would be ⅓ of a circle.

A central angle is equal in measure to the arc it intercepts.

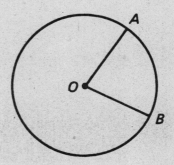

m∠*AOB* = m$\overparen{AB}$ (The measure of ∠*AOB* equals the measure of $\overparen{AB}$)

An inscribed angle is equal in measure to ½ the arc it intercepts.

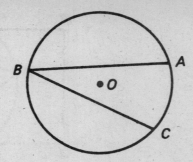

$$m\angle ABC = m\frac{1}{2}\widehat{AC}.$$

An angle inscribed in a semicircle is a *right angle*.

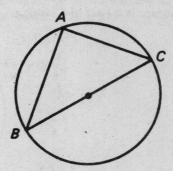

If *BC* is a diameter, then $\angle BAC$ is inscribed in a semicircle; so $m\angle BAC = 90°$.

III–G. Area and Perimeter

G–1

The area *A* of a square equals s^2, where *s* is the length of a side of the square. Thus, $A = s^2$.

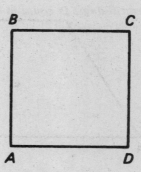

If *AD* = 5 inches, the area of square *ABCD* is 25 square inches.

The area of a rectangle equals length times width; if *L* is the length of one side and *W* is the length of a perpendicular side, then the area $A = LW$.

If $AB = 5$ feet and $AD = 8$ feet, then the area of rectangle $ABCD$ is 40 square feet.

The area of a parallelogram is base × height; $A = bh$, where b is the length of the base and h is the length of an altitude to the base.

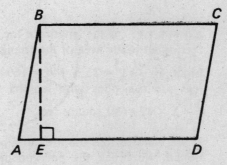

If $AD = 6$ yards and $BE = 4$ yards, then the area of the parallelogram $ABCD$ is $6 \cdot 4$ or 24 square yards.

The area of a trapezoid is the (average of the bases) × height. $A = [(b_1 + b_2)/2] h$ where b_1 and b_2 are the lengths of the parallel sides and h is the length of an altitude to one of the bases.

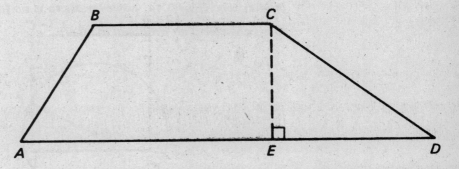

If $BC = 3$ miles, $AD = 7$ miles, and $CE = 2$ miles, then the area of trapezoid $ABCD$ is $[(3 + 7)/2] \cdot 2 = 10$ square miles.

The area of a triangle is $\frac{1}{2}$ (base × height); $A = \frac{1}{2} bh$, where b is the length of a side and h is the length of the altitude to that side.

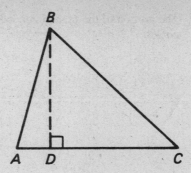

If $AC = 5$ miles and $BD = 4$ miles, then the area of the triangle is $\frac{1}{2} \times 5 \times 4 = 10$ square miles.

Since the legs of a right triangle are perpendicular to each other, the area of a right triangle is one-half the product of the lengths of the legs.

EXAMPLE 1:   If the lengths of the sides of a triangle are 5 feet, 12 feet, and 13 feet, what is the area of the triangle?

Since $5^2 + 12^2 = 25 + 144 = 169 = 13^2$, the triangle is a right triangle and the legs are the sides with lengths 5 feet and 12 feet. Therefore, the area is $\frac{1}{2} \times 5 \times 12 = 30$ square feet.

If we want to find the area of a polygon which is not of a type already mentioned, we break the polygon up into smaller figures such as triangles or rectangles, find the area of each piece, and add these to get the area of the given polygon.

The area of a circle is πr^2 where r is the length of a radius. Since $d = 2r$ where d is the length of a diameter, $A = \pi\left(\frac{d}{2}\right)^2 = \pi\frac{d^2}{4}$. π is a number which is approximately $\frac{22}{7}$ or 3.14; however, there is *no fraction which is exactly equal to* π. π *is called an* *irrational number.*

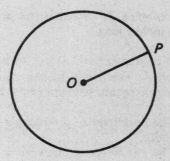

If $OP = 2$ inches, then the area of the circle with center O is $\pi 2^2$ or 4π square inches.

The portion of the plane bounded by a circle and a central angle is called a *sector* of the circle.

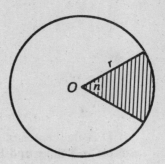

The shaded region is a sector of the circle with center O. The area of a sector with central angle $n°$ in a circle of radius r is $\frac{n}{360}\pi r^2$.

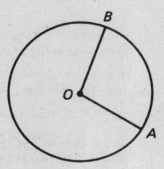

If $OB = 4$ inches and $\angle BOA = 100°$, then the area of the sector is $\frac{100}{360}\pi \cdot 4^2 =$ $\frac{5}{18} \cdot 16\pi = \frac{40}{9}\pi$ square inches.

G–2

The *perimeter* of a polygon is the sum of the lengths of the sides.

EXAMPLE 1:   What is the perimeter of a regular pentagon whose sides are 6 inches long?

A pentagon has 5 sides. Since the pentagon is regular, all sides have the same length which is 6 inches. Therefore, the perimeter of the pentagon is 5×6 which equals 30 inches or 2.5 feet.

The *perimeter of a rectangle* is $2(L + W)$ where L is the length and W is the width.
The *perimeter of a square* is $4s$ where s is the length of a side of the square.

The *perimeter of a circle* is called the *circumference* of the circle. The *circumference* of a circle is πd or $2\pi r$, where d is the length of a diameter and r is the length of a radius.

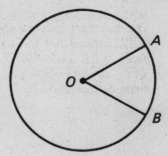

If O is the center of a circle and $OP = 5$ feet, then the circumference of the circle is $2 \times 5\pi$ or 10π feet.

The length of an arc of a circle is $(n/360)\ \pi d$ where the central angle of the arc is $n°$.

If O is the center of a circle where $OA = 5$ yards and $\angle AOB = 60°$, then the length of arc AB is $\frac{60}{360}\pi \times 10 = \frac{10}{6}\pi = \frac{5}{3}\pi$ yards.

EXAMPLE 2:　How far will a wheel of radius 2 feet travel in 500 revolutions? (Assume the wheel does not slip.)

The diameter of the wheel is 4 feet; so the circumference is 4π feet. Therefore, the wheel will travel $500 \times 4\pi$ or $2,000\pi$ feet in 500 revolutions.

III–H.　Coordinate Geometry

In coordinate geometry, every point in the plane is associated with an ordered pair of numbers called *coordinates*. Two perpendicular lines are drawn; the horizontal line is called the x-axis and the vertical line is called the y-axis. The point where the two axes intersect is called the *origin*. Both of the axes are number lines with the origin corresponding to zero (see I–6.) Positive numbers on the x-axis are to the right of the origin, negative numbers to the left. Positive numbers on the y-axis are above the origin, negative numbers below the origin. The coordinates of a point P are (x,y) if P is located by moving x units along the x-axis from the origin and then moving y units up or down. *The distance along the x-axis is always given first.*

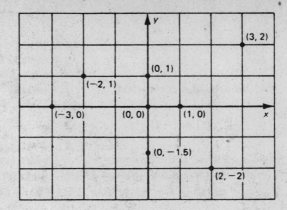

The numbers in parentheses are the coordinates of the point. Thus "$P =$ (3,2)" means that the coordinates of P are (3,2). *The distance between the point with coordinates (x,y) and the point with coordinates (a,b) is $\sqrt{(x-a)^2 + (y-b)^2}$.* You should be able to answer most questions by using the distance formula.

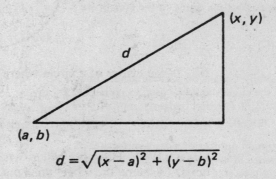

$$d = \sqrt{(x-a)^2 + (y-b)^2}$$

EXAMPLE 1:   Is $ABCD$ a parallelogram? $A = (3,2)$, $B = (1,-2)$, $C = (-2,1)$, $D = (1,5)$.

The length of AB is $\sqrt{(3-1)^2 + (2-(-2))^2} = \sqrt{2^2 + 4^2} = \sqrt{20}$. The length of CD is $\sqrt{(-2-1)^2 + (1-5)^2} = \sqrt{(-3)^2 + (-4)^2} = \sqrt{25}$. Therefore, $AB \neq CD$, so $ABCD$ cannot be a parallelogram, since in a parallelogram the lengths of opposite sides are equal.

Geometry problems occur frequently. *If you are not provided with a diagram, draw one for yourself.* Think of any conditions which will help you answer the question; perhaps you can see how to answer a different question which will lead to an answer to the original question. It may help to draw in some diagonals, altitudes, or other auxiliary lines in your diagram.

PRACTICE

$r = \dfrac{x}{2\pi}$ Area $= \pi \left(\dfrac{x}{2\pi}\right)^2 = \dfrac{\pi x^2}{4\pi^2} = \dfrac{x^2}{4\pi}$

$x = 2\pi r$

1. Using formulas
   Circumference $= 2\pi r$
   Area $= \pi r^2$
   where r = radius, find the area of a circle whose circumference is x.

   (A) $\dfrac{x^2}{4\pi^2}$ (B) $\dfrac{x^2}{4\pi}$ (C) $\dfrac{x^2}{4}$ (D) πx^2 (E) πx

2. One side of a rectangle is x inches. If the perimeter is p inches, what is the length (in inches) of the other side?

   (A) $p - x$ (B) $p - 2x$ (C) $\dfrac{p - x}{2}$

   (D) $\dfrac{p - 2x}{2}$ (E) $2p - 2x$

3. C is the midpoint of line AE. B and D are on line AE so that $AB = BC$ and $CD = DE$. What percent of AC is AD?

   (A) 33   (B) 50   (C) 66   (D) 133   (E) 150

4. A picture in an art museum is six feet wide and eight feet long. If its frame has a width of six inches, what is the ratio of the area of the frame to the area of the picture?

   (A) $\dfrac{5}{16}$ (B) $\dfrac{5}{4}$ (C) $\dfrac{4}{5}$ (D) $\dfrac{5}{12}$ (E) $\dfrac{3\frac{1}{3}}{1}$

5. To represent a family budget on a circle graph, how many degrees of the circle should be used to represent an item that is 20% of the total budget?

   (A) 20   (B) 36   (C) 60   (D) 72   (E) 90

6. What is the maximum number of glass tumblers (each with a circumference of 4π inches) that can be placed rectangularly on a table $48'' \times 32''$?

   (A) 36   (B) 48   (C) 92   (D) 96   (E) 192

7. To avoid paying a toll on a direct road, I go west 10 miles, south 5 miles, west 30 miles, and north 35 miles. The length of the toll road is (?) miles.

   (A) 30   (B) 45   (C) 50   (D) 70   (E) 85

8. The length of a rectangle is increased by 50%. By what per cent would the width have to be decreased to maintain the same area?

   (A) $33\frac{1}{3}$ (B) 50   (C) $66\frac{2}{3}$ (D) 150   (E) 200

9. Area of circle $O = 9\pi$. What is the area of $ABCD$?
   (A) 24   (B) 30   (C) 35
   (D) 36   (E) 48

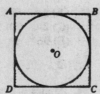

10. A man travels four miles north, twelve miles east, and then twelve miles north. How far (to the nearest mile) is he from the starting point?

    (A) 17   (B) 20   (C) 21   (D) 24   (E) 28

11. If angle DBA equals 39° and angle FBE equals 79°, then angle GBC has a measure of
    (A) 39°   (B) 51°   (C) 62°
    (D) 118°   (E) 152°

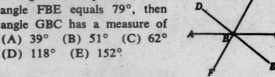

12. The length of a rectangle is l and the width is w. If the width is increased by 2 units, by how many units will the perimeter be increased?

    (A) 2   (B) 4   (C) $2w$ (D) $2w + 2$ (E) $2w + 4$

13. If the radius of a wheel is f feet, how many revolutions does the wheel make per mile? (1 mile equals 5,280 feet)

    (A) $5280f$ (B) $\dfrac{2640}{\pi f}$ (C) $5280\pi f^2$ (D) $\dfrac{\pi f}{2640}$ (E) $\dfrac{\pi f^2}{5280}$

14. The length of a wire fence around a circular flower bed is 100π feet. What is the area (in square feet) of a two-foot concrete walk surrounding this fence?
    (A) 98π (B) 100π (C) 102π (D) 202π (E) 204π

15. How many tiles (each one foot square) are necessary to form a one-foot border around the inside of a room 24 feet by 14 feet?

    (A) 36   (B) 37   (C) 72   (D) 74   (E) 76

16. When the radius of a circle is doubled the area is multiplied by
    (A) 2   (B) 2π (C) $2\pi r$ (D) 3.14   (E) 4

17. $AD = 14$
    $EF = 6$
    $BC = ?$
    (A) 8   (B) 12   (C) 20
    (D) 26   (E) 36

18. If the diagonal of a table with a square top is 6 feet, what is the area of the table top (in square feet)?
    (A) $\sqrt{18}$ (B) 9π (C) 18   (D) $18\sqrt{2}$ (E) 36

19. How many spokes are there in the wheel of a sports car if any two spokes form an angle of 15°?
    (A) 12   (B) 15   (C) 22   (D) 24   (E) 36

20. How many degrees are there in an angle formed by the hands of a clock at 2:30?
    (A) 100°   (B) 105°   (C) 110°   (D) 115°   (E) 120°

21. If $8x$ represents the perimeter of a rectangle and $2x + 3$ represents its length, what is its width?
    (A) $6x + 3$ (B) $6x - 3$ (C) 3
    (D) $2x - 3$ (E) $10x + 3$

22. Base RT of triangle RST is $\frac{4}{3}$ of altitude SV. If SV equals c, which of the following is an expression for the area of the triangle RST?

(A) $\frac{2c}{5}$ (B) $\frac{2c^2}{5}$ (C) $\frac{c^2}{2}$ (D) $\frac{4c^2}{5}$ (E) $\frac{8c^2}{5}$

23. A triangle has a base b and an altitude a. A second triangle has a base twice the altitude of the first triangle, and an altitude twice the base of the first triangle. What is the area of the second triangle?

(A) $\frac{1}{2}ab$ (B) ab (C) $2ab$ (D) $4ab$ (E) $\frac{1}{2}a^2b^2$

24. A pond 100 feet in diameter is surrounded by a circular grass walk which is 2 feet wide. How many square feet of grass are there on the walk? (Answer in terms of π.)

(A) 98π (B) 100π (C) 102π (D) 202π (E) 204π

25. What is the area of $ABCD$?
(A) 5 (B) 8 (C) 10 (D) 16 (E) 20

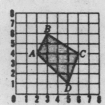

26. The distance from A to C in the square field $ABCD$ is 50 feet. What is the area of field $ABCD$ in square feet?
(A) $25\sqrt{2}$ (B) 625 (C) 1250 (D) 2500 (E) 5000

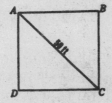

27. In the figure at the right, $ABCD$ is a square and semicircles and constructed on each side of the square. If AB is 2, what is the area of the entire figure?
(A) $2 + 4\pi$ (B) $2 - 4\pi$ (C) $4 + 8\pi$ (D) $4 - 2\pi$ (E) $4 + 2\pi$

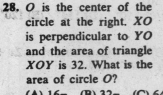

28. O is the center of the circle at the right. XO is perpendicular to YO and the area of triangle XOY is 32. What is the area of circle O?
(A) 16π (B) 32π (C) 64π (D) 128π (E) 256π

29. Square $QRST$ is inscribed in circle O.
$OV \perp TS$
$OV = 1$
The area of the shaded portion is
(A) $\pi - 4$ (B) $4\pi - 4$ (C) $2\pi - 4$ (D) $4\pi - 2$ (E) $2\pi - 2$

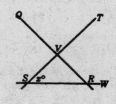

30. $QVR \perp SVT$
$\angle VSR = x°$
$\angle VRW = (?)°$
(A) $90 - x$ (B) $90 + x$ (C) $x - 90$ (D) $180 - x$ (E) 135

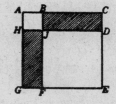

31. $ABJH, JDEF, ACEG$ are squares
$\frac{BC}{AB} = 3$
$\frac{\text{Area } BCDJ}{\text{Area } HJFG} = ?$

(A) $\frac{1}{9}$ (B) $\frac{1}{3}$ (C) 1 (D) 3 (E) 9

32. Rectangle $ABCD$ is made up of five equal squares. $AD = 30$. Find EF.
(A) 6 (B) 8 (C) 10 (D) 12 (E) 20

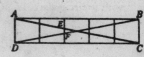

33. Radius $OA = 6.5$
Chord $AC = 5$
Area of triangle ABC equals
(A) 16 (B) 18 (C) 24 (D) 30 (E) 36

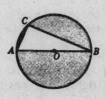

34. Angles a, b and c are in ratio of $1:3:2$. How many degrees in angle b?
(A) 30 (B) 50 (C) 60 (D) 90 (E) 100

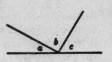

35. BC equals one half of AB. The area of right triangle ABC equals 64 square feet. Find hypotenuse AC to the nearest foot.

(A) 12 (B) 14
(C) 18 (D) 24
(E) 32

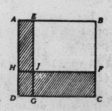

36. $ABCD$ is a square
$AE = 2$
$GC = 8$
Shaded area $= 44$
Area of $FBEJ = ?$

(A) 36 (B) 56
(C) 64 (D) 68
(E) 80

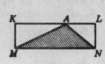

37. The area of a rectangle $KLNM$ equals 100. Base NM equals 20. What is the area of triangle ANM if A is any point on KL?

(A) 25 (B) 50 (C) 75
(D) 100 (E) cannot be determined

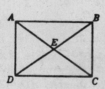

38. $ABCD$ is a rectangle.
$AD = 12$, $AB = 16$. $DE = ?$

(A) 8 (B) 10 (C) 14
(D) 15 (E) 20

39. O is the center of the circle. BC is parallel to AD.
$OA = 5$
$CB = 8$
$\dfrac{AB}{AD} = ?$

(A) $\dfrac{3}{4}$ (B) $\dfrac{4}{5}$ (C) 1

(D) $\dfrac{5}{4}$ (E) $\dfrac{4}{3}$

40. $BA = 2BC$
$EA = 2DE$
$BE = 14$
$DC = ?$

(A) 7 (B) 18 (C) 21
(D) 24 (E) 28

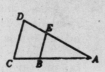

41. If angle DBG equals 79° and angle CBE equals 39° then angle GBE equals

(A) 51° (B) 62°
(C) 101° (D) 108°
(E) 202°

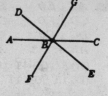

42. $\angle A = (?)°$

(A) 15 (B) 45 (C) 60
(D) 80 (E) 120

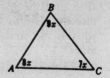

43. Four equal circles of diameter one foot touch at four points as shown in the figure. What is the area of the shaded portion (in square feet)?

(A) $1 - \dfrac{\pi}{4}$ (B) $1 - \pi$

(C) $1 - 4\pi$ (D) π (E) $\dfrac{\pi}{4}$

44. Perimeter of $ABCD = 24$
The area of the shaded portion is

(A) 27π (B) $9\pi - 36$
(C) $9\pi - 24$ (D) $36 - 9\pi$
(E) $24 - 9\pi$

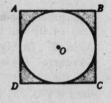

45. $ABIJ$, $BCHI$, $CDGH$, and $DEFG$ are congruent rectangles.
$AJ = 21$
$KI = ?$

(A) 3 (B) 5.25 (C) 7
(D) 10.5 (E) 14

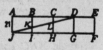

46. The area of the shaded portion is

(A) $2r^2(4 - \pi)$
(B) $2r^2(2 - 2\pi)$
(C) $2r^2(\pi - 4)$
(D) $2r^2(\pi - 2)$
(E) $r^2(2 - \pi)$

47. How many square units are there in the shaded triangle?

(A) 4 (B) 6 (C) 8
(D) 9 (E) 12

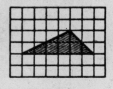

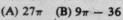

48. $AE \perp ED$ $ED = 13$
   $CD \perp ED$ $CD = 3$
   $DC \perp CB$ $CB = 2$
   $AB = ?$ $AE = 11$
   (A) 8   (B) 13   (C) 14
   (D) 15   (E) 17

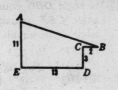

49. If an airplane starts at point R and travels 14 miles directly north to S, then 48 miles directly east to T, what is the straight line distance from T to R in miles?
   (A) 25   (B) 34   (C) 50   (D) 62   (E) 2500

50. The area of a circle with radius r is equal to the area of a rectangle with base b. Find the altitude of the rectangle in terms of π, r, and b.
   (A) $\sqrt{\pi r}$ (B) $\dfrac{2\pi r}{b}$ (C) $\pi r^2 b$ (D) $\dfrac{\pi r^2}{b}$ (E) $\dfrac{\pi r^2}{b^2}$

51. A line segment is drawn from point $(8, -2)$ to point $(4, 6)$. The coordinates of the midpoint of this line segment are
   (A) $(12, 4)$ (B) $(12, 8)$ (C) $(6, 4)$
   (D) $(6, 2)$ (E) $(6, -2)$

52. Lines joining point $(-4, 0)$ with point $(0, 5)$ with point $(4, 0)$ will form a (an)
   (A) circle   (B) right triangle   (C) rectangle
   (D) square   (E) isosceles triangle

53. Point A $(-3, -4)$ is drawn to point B $(3, 4)$. Which of the following is true?
   (A) the length of $AB = 5$ units   (B) AB is parallel to the X axis   (C) AB passes through point $(6, 8)$ (D) AB passes through origin   (E) AB is the radius of a circle with center at $(0,0)$

54. Triangle ABC has the following vertices: $A(1, 0)$, $B(5,0)$, and $C(3, 4)$. Which of the following is true?
   (A) $AB = BC$ (B) $AB = AC$ (C) $CA = CB$
   (D) $AC > BC$ (E) $AC < BC$

55. The area of a circle whose center is at $(0, 0)$ is 25π. The circle passes through all of the following points EXCEPT
   (A) $(-5, 0)$ (B) $(5, 5)$ (C) $(5, 0)$
   (D) $(0, 5)$ (E) $(0, -5)$

56. The following points are vertices of quadrilateral $ABCD$ $(0, 4)$, $(4, 0)$, $(0, -4)$ and $(-4, 0)$. The area of $ABCD$ is
   (A) 8   (B) 16   (C) 32   (D) 48   (E) 64

57. The vertices of triangle ABC are $(4, 3)$, $(4, 7)$ and $(8, 3)$. The area of triangle ABC equals
   (A) 4   (B) $4\sqrt{3}$ (C) 8   (D) 12.5
   (E) 16

58. A line segment AB is drawn from point $(2, 3)$ to point $(4, 7)$. What are the coordinates of the midpoint?
   (A) $(5, 3)$ (B) $(3, 5)$ (C) $(6, 10)$
   (D) $(2. 4)$ (E) $(4, 2)$

59. What is the distance from point $A(3, 4)$ to point $B(-3, -4)$?
   (A) 0   (B) 5   (C) 10   (D) 13   (E) 14

60. Point $P(4, 2)$ is the midpoint of line OPC, where O is at origin (O, O). The coordinates of C are
   (A) $(2, 1)$ (B) $(4, 8)$ (C) $(4, 4)$
   (D) $(8, 2)$ (E) $(8, 4)$

ANSWER KEY

1.	B	21.	D	41.	C
2.	D	22.	B	42.	C
3.	E	23.	C	43.	A
4.	A	24.	E	44.	D
5.	D	25.	C	45.	C
6.	D	26.	C	46.	A
7.	C	27.	E	47.	B
8.	A	28.	C	48.	E
9.	D	29.	C	49.	C
10.	B	30.	B	50.	D
11.	C	31.	C	51.	D
12.	B	32.	A	52.	E
13.	B	33.	D	53.	D
14.	E	34.	D	54.	C
15.	C	35.	C	55.	B
16.	E	36.	B	56.	C
17.	D	37.	B	57.	C
18.	C	38.	B	58.	B
19.	D	39.	A	59.	C
20.	B	40.	C	60.	E

IV. Tables and Graphs

IV–A. Tables

Tables are often used in reports, magazines, and newspapers to present a set of numerical facts. They enable the reader to make comparisons and to draw quick conclusions. One of the main purposes of tables is to make complicated information easier to understand. The advantage of presenting data in a table such as the one in the example that follows is that you can see the information at a glance.

When answering questions based on tables, carefully read the table title and the column headings. The table title gives you a general idea of the type and often the purpose of the information presented. The column headings tell you the specific kind of information given in that column. Both the table titles and the column headings are usually very straightforward. After all, the table is supposed to make it easy for you to grasp this information. So, in a column headed "Hourly Wage," you can expect to find just that — a list of hourly wages. You do have to be careful, however, to choose the appropriate column from which to get the information you need and to take note of the units that are used.

1. **What percent of the babies born in the U.S. in 1947 died before the age of 1 year?**

   (A) 3.22   (B) 4.7   (C) 26.7   (D) 32.2   (E) 47

To find a percent, use the information given in the rate columns. The rate is given *per thousand*. In 1947 the rate was 32.2 per thousand which is $\frac{32.2}{1000} = .0322$ or 3.22%. So the correct answer is (A). If you assumed incorrectly that the rate was per hundred, you would get the incorrect answer (D); if you looked in the wrong column you might get (B) or (E) as your answer.

2. **Which state had the most infant deaths in 1940?**

   (A) California
   (B) New Mexico
   (C) New York
   (D) Pennsylvania
   (E) Texas

Look in the numbers column under 1940. Only Texas had more than 8,000 in 1940, so the correct answer is (E). New Mexico had a *higher rate*, but the question asked for the *highest amount. Make sure you answer the question which is asked.*

3. **Which of the following statements can be inferred from the table?**

   I.   In 1950 less than $\frac{1}{20}$ of the babies born in the U.S. died before the age of 1 year.
   II. The number of infant deaths in the U.S. decreased from 1945 to 1950.
   III. More than 5% of the infant deaths in the U.S. in 1950 occurred in California.
   IV. The number of infant deaths in North America in 1950 was less than 150,000.

   (A) I only
   (B) II only
   (C) I and III only
   (D) I, III, IV only
   (E) I, II, III, IV

INFANT DEATHS (UNDER 1 YEAR OF AGE) AND RATES PER 1,000 LIVE BIRTHS, BY STATES: 1940 TO 1950

STATE	NUMBER OF INFANT DEATHS					RATE PER 1,000 LIVE BIRTHS				
	1940	1947	1948	1949	1950	1940	1947	1948	1949	1950
United States	110,984	119,173	113,169	111,531	103,825	47.0	32.2	32.0	31.3	29.2
Alabama	3,870	3,301	3,228	3,345	3,044	61.5	37.5	37.8	39.6	36.8
Arizona	983	973	1,083	1,034	953	85.5	50.8	56.4	51.0	45.8
Arkansas	1,810	1,445	1,363	1,539	1,209	47.0	29.5	28.4	33.7	26.5
California	4,403	7,233	6,885	6,574	6,115	39.2	29.4	28.6	26.8	25.0
Colorado	1,270	1,234	1,267	1,153	1,167	60.4	37.5	38.4	35.1	34.4
Connecticut	868	1,150	1,026	943	886	34.0	25.2	24.3	23.1	21.8
Delaware	217	239	214	224	235	47.7	31.0	29.5	30.4	30.7
District of Columbia	554	691	531	576	603	49.3	31.9	25.5	29.1	30.4
Florida	1,818	2,285	2,103	2,088	2,078	53.8	38.2	35.3	33.8	32.1
Georgia	3,744	3,251	3,169	3,101	3,064	57.8	34.2	34.2	33.3	33.5
Idaho	506	478	481	431	434	42.9	29.4	29.8	27.0	27.1
Illinois	4,398	5,672	5,123	5,195	4,868	35.3	28.9	27.7	27.4	25.6
Indiana	2,595	2,949	2,760	2,746	2,520	42.1	30.6	29.8	29.1	27.0
Iowa	1,636	1,817	1,610	1,591	1,555	36.5	28.5	26.6	25.7	24.8
Kansas	1,106	1,251	1,151	1,136	1,130	38.3	28.1	26.9	25.9	25.7
Kentucky	3,387	2,971	3,073	3,139	2,616	53.1	37.1	39.8	41.2	34.9
Louisiana	3,268	2,773	2,779	2,810	2,639	64.3	37.2	37.9	37.2	34.6
Maine	810	853	706	713	650	53.2	35.7	32.0	32.5	30.9
Maryland	1,590	1,794	1,537	1,636	1,465	49.1	31.6	28.8	30.5	27.0
Massachusetts	2,458	3,027	2,613	2,347	2,240	37.5	28.1	26.8	24.5	23.3
Michigan	4,032	5,080	4,639	4,545	4,230	40.7	31.5	30.0	28.9	26.3
Minnesota	1,758	2,165	1,959	1,893	1,889	33.2	28.6	26.9	25.6	25.1
Mississippi	2,869	2,448	2,474	2,631	2,385	54.4	36.8	37.9	39.6	36.7
Missouri	2,885	2,929	2,585	2,563	2,510	46.9	32.5	30.3	30.0	29.2
Montana	537	484	461	457	441	46.5	32.1	30.7	29.7	28.2
Nebraska	792	894	835	761	796	36.0	27.8	26.8	24.1	25.0
Nevada	109	134	147	118	139	51.7	33.2	39.8	32.1	37.9
New Hampshire	341	399	361	333	282	40.9	30.1	29.1	27.9	24.5
New Jersey	2,121	2,965	2,585	2,534	2,467	35.5	27.9	26.5	26.0	25.2
New Mexico	1,488	1,379	1,438	1,408	1,211	100.6	67.9	70.1	65.1	54.8
New York	7,297	9,123	8,258	7,878	7,429	37.2	28.2	27.3	26.1	24.7
North Carolina	4,631	3,938	3,858	4,113	3,674	57.6	34.9	35.3	38.1	34.5
North Dakota	593	523	487	517	453	45.1	30.6	29.4	30.7	26.6
Ohio	4,744	5,817	5,693	5,315	4,990	41.4	29.5	30.5	28.1	26.8
Oklahoma	2,238	1,733	1,731	1,531	1,514	49.9	32.3	34.4	30.8	30.2
Oregon	585	895	897	869	812	33.2	24.7	25.5	24.6	22.5
Pennsylvania	7,404	7,741	6,442	6,567	6,126	44.7	31.1	28.4	29.2	27.6
Rhode Island	410	522	444	395	450	37.9	28.2	26.3	24.0	27.8
South Carolina	3,042	2,352	2,331	2,283	2,220	68.2	39.5	40.4	39.0	38.6
South Dakota	466	511	525	448	473	38.7	30.9	32.0	26.0	26.6
Tennessee	2,954	3,144	3,098	3,331	2,961	53.5	36.3	37.7	40.2	36.4
Texas	8,675	8,161	9,131	8,628	7,630	68.3	41.1	46.2	42.7	37.4
Utah	539	545	568	535	503	40.4	25.1	27.4	25.3	23.7
Vermont	309	303	271	301	221	44.5	31.2	28.9	32.4	24.5
Virginia	3,335	3,142	3,163	3,162	2,836	58.5	36.6	38.5	38.1	34.6
Washington	992	1,643	1,537	1,530	1,522	35.2	28.1	27.5	27.1	27.3
West Virginia	2,269	2,091	2,108	2,082	1,822	53.7	38.0	40.2	39.6	36.1
Wisconsin	2,046	2,476	2,148	2,202	2,121	37.3	29.5	26.3	26.5	25.7
Wyoming	232	249	293	280	247	44.7	34.0	39.5	37.4	32.5

Source: Department of Health, Education, and Welfare, Public Health Service, National Office of Vital Statistics; annual report, *Vital Statistics of the United States.*

Source: Statistical Abstract of the U.S. 1957

Statement I can be inferred since $\frac{1}{20}$ of $1,000 = 50$ which exceeds the rate per thousand of 29.2 in 1950.

Statement II can't be inferred since the table has no information about 1945. Infant deaths decreased between 1940 and 1950, but that doesn't mean they decreased between 1945 and 1950.

Statement III can be inferred from the table. The total number of infant deaths in 1950 was 103,825, and 6,115 occurred in California. A calculation of 6,115/103,825 could be made, but it is much quicker to find 5% of 103,825 which is 5,191. Since 6,115 is greater than 5,191, more than 5% of the infant deaths in the U.S. occurred in California.

Statement IV can't be inferred, because the table only gives information about the U.S. and there are other countries in North America.

So the correct answer is (C).

IV–B.   Circle Graphs

CIRCLE GRAPHS are used to show how various sectors share in the whole. Circle graphs are sometimes called pie charts. Circle graphs usually give the percent that each sector receives.

EXAMPLE: (Refer to the graph below.)

1. The amount spent on materials in 1960 was 120% of the amount spent on

    (A)   research in 1960
    (B)   compensation in 1960
    (C)   advertising in 1970
    (D)   materials in 1970
    (E)   legal affairs in 1960

Expenditures of General Industries
By major categories

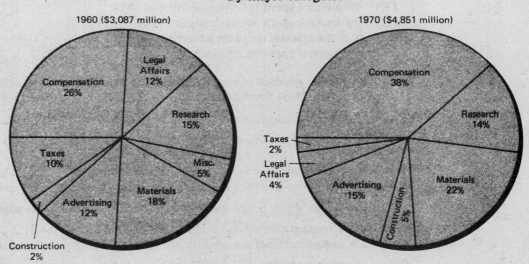

1960 ($3,087 million)   1970 ($4,851 million)

When using circle graphs to find ratios of various sectors, don't find the amounts each sector received and then the ratio of the amounts. Find the *ratio of the percents*, which is much quicker. In 1960, 18% of the expenditures were for materials. We want x where 120% of $x = 18\%$; so $x = 15\%$. Any category which received 15% of 1960 expenditures gives the correct answer, but only one of the five choices is correct. Here, the answer is (A) since research received 15% of the expenditure in

1960. Check the 1960 answers first since you need look only at the percentages, which can be done quickly. Notice that (C) is incorrect, since 15% of the expenditures for 1970 is different from 15% of the expenditures for 1960.

2. The fraction of the total expenditures for 1960 and 1970 spent on compensation was about

      (A) $\frac{1}{5}$ (D) $\frac{3}{7}$

      (B) $\frac{1}{4}$ (E) $\frac{1}{2}$

      (C) $\frac{1}{3}$

In 1960, 26% of \$3,087 million was spent on compensation and in 1970 compensation received 38% of \$4,851 million. The total expenditures for 1960 and 1970 are \$(3,087 + 4,851) million. So the exact answer is $[(.26)(3,087) + (.38)(4,851)]/(3,087 + 4,851)$. Actually calculating the answer, you will waste a lot of time. Look at the answers and think for a second.

We are taking a weighted average of 26% and 38%. To find a weighted average, we multiply each value by a weight and divide by the total of all the weights. Here 26% is given a weight of 3,087 and 38% a weight of 4,851. The following general rule is often useful in average problems: The average or weighted average of a collection of values can *never* be:

(1) less than the smallest value in the collection, or
(2) greater than the largest value in the collection.

Therefore, the answer to the question must be greater than or equal to 26% and less than or equal to 38%.

Since $\frac{1}{5} = 20\%$ and $\frac{1}{4} = 25\%$, which are both less than 26%, neither (A) nor (B) can be the correct answer. Since $\frac{3}{7} = 42\frac{6}{7}\%$ and $\frac{1}{2} = 50\%$, which are both greater than 38%, neither (D) nor (E) can be correct. Therefore, by elimination (C) is the correct answer.

3. The amount spent in 1960 for materials, advertising, and taxes was about the same as

      (A) $\frac{5}{4}$ of the amount spent for compensation in 1960
      (B) the amount spent for compensation in 1970
      (C) the amount spent on materials in 1970
      (D) $\frac{5}{3}$ of the amount spent on advertising in 1970
      (E) the amount spent on research and construction in 1970

First calculate the combined percent for materials, advertising, and taxes in 1960. Since 18% + 12% + 10% = 40%, these three categories accounted for 40% of the expenditures in 1960. You can check the one answer which involves 1960 now. Since $\frac{5}{4}$ of 26% = 32.5%, (A) is incorrect. To check the answers which involve 1970, you must know the amount spent on the three categories above in 1960. 40% of 3,087 is 1234.8; so the amount spent on the three categories in 1960 was \$1,234.8 million. You could calculate the amount spent in each of the possible answers, but there is a quicker way. Find the *approximate* percentage that 1,234.8 is of 4,851, and check this against the percentages of the answers. Since $\frac{12}{48} = \frac{1}{4}$, the amount for the 3 categories in 1960 is about 25% of the 1970 expenditures. Compensation received 38% of 1970 expenditures, so (B) is incorrect. Materials received 22%, and research and construction together received 19%; since advertising received 15%, $\frac{5}{3}$ of the amount for advertising yields 25%. So (D) is probably correct. You can check by calculating 22% of 4,851 which is 1,067.22, while 25% of 4,851 = 1,212.75. Therefore, (D) is correct.

In inference questions involving circle graphs, *do not compare different percents*. Note in question 3 that the percent of expenditures in 1960 for the three categories (40%) is *not equal* to 40% of the expenditures in 1970.

IV–C.   Line Graphs

LINE GRAPHS are used to show how a quantity changes continuously. Very often the quantity is measured as time changes. If the line goes up, the quantity is increasing; if the line goes down, the quantity is decreasing; if the line is horizontal, the quantity is not changing. To measure the height of a point on the graph, use your pencil or a piece of paper (for example, the edge of the test booklet) as a straight edge.

EXAMPLE: (Refer to the graph below.)

1.   The ratio of productivity in 1967 to productivity in 1940 was about

(A)   1:4   (B)   1:3   (C)   3:1   (D)   4:1   (E)   9:1

In 1967 productivity had an index number of 400, and the index numbers are based on 1940 = 100. So the ratio is 400:100 = 4:1. Therefore, the answer is (D). [If you used (incorrectly) output or employment (instead of productivity) you would get the wrong answer (E) or (C); if you confused the order of the ratio you would have incorrectly answered (A).]

TRENDS IN INDUSTRIAL INVESTMENT, LABOUR PRODUCTIVITY, EMPLOYMENT AND OUTPUT, 1940 TO 1967

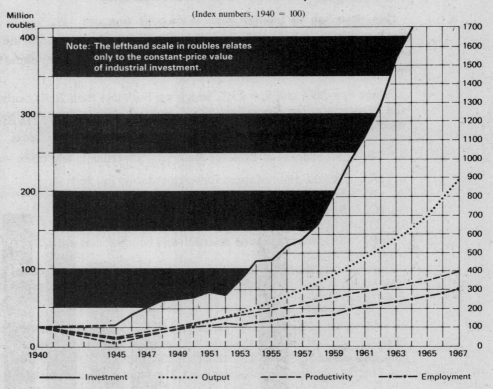

Source: United Nations Economics Bulletin for Europe

2.   If 1 rouble = $3, then the constant-price value of industrial investment in 1959 was about

(A) $1.9 million   (B) $200 million   (C) $420,000,000
(D) $570,000,000   (E) $570,000 million

In 1959, the value was about 190 million roubles. (It was a little below 200 million.) The answers are all in dollars, so multiply 190 by 3 to get $570 million or $570,000,000 (D). If you are not careful about units, you may answer (B) or (E), which are incorrect.

3. Employment was at its minimum during the year

   (A) 1940   (B) 1943   (C) 1945   (D) 1953   (E) 1967

The minimum of a quantity displayed on a line graph is the lowest place on the line. Thus in 1945, (C), the minimum value of employment was reached.

4. Between 1954 and 1965, output

   (A) decreased by about 10%   (D) increased by about 250%
   (B) stayed about the same   (E) increased by about 500%
   (C) increased by about 200%

The line for output goes up between 1954 and 1965, so output increased between 1954 and 1965. Therefore, (A) and (B) are wrong. Output was about 200 in 1954 and about 700 in 1965, so the increase was 500. Since $\frac{500}{200} = 2.5 = 250\%$, the correct answer is (D).

IV–D. Bar Graphs

Quantities can be compared by the height or length of a bar in a bar graph. A bar graph can have either vertical or horizontal bars. You can compare different quantities or the same quantity at different times. Use your pencil or a piece of paper to compare bars which are not adjacent to each other.

DISABILITY BENEFICIARIES REPORTED AS REHABILITATED:
Number, as percent of all rehabilitated clients
of State vocational rehabilitation agencies,
Years 1955–1971

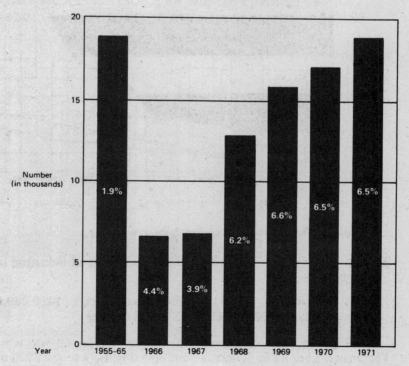

Source: Social Security Bulletin

EXAMPLE: (Refer to the graph on page 391.)

1. Between 1967 and 1971, the largest number of disability beneficiaries was reported as rehabilitated in the year.

(A)   1967
(B)   1968
(C)   1969

(D)   1970
(E)   1971

The answer is (E) since the highest bar is the bar for 1971. The percent of disability beneficiaries out of all rehabilitated clients was higher in 1969, but the *number* was lower.

2. Between 1955 and 1965, about how many clients were rehabilitated by State vocational rehabilitation agencies?

(A)   90,000
(B)   400,000
(C)   1,000,000

(D)   1,900,000
(E)   10,000,000

1.9% of those rehabilitated were disability beneficiaries, and there were about 19,000 disability beneficiaries rehabilitated. So if T is the total number rehabilitated, then 1.9% of $T = 19,000$ or $.019T = 19,000$. Thus, $T = 19,000/.019 = 1,000,000$ and the answer is (C).

IV-E.   Cumulative Graphs

You can compare several categories by a graph of the cumulative type. These are usually bar or line graphs where the height of the bar or line is divided up proportionately among different quantities.

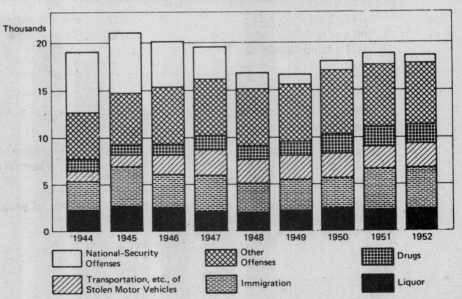

FEDERAL PRISONERS RECEIVED FROM THE COURTS, BY MAJOR OFFENSE GROUPS: Years 1944–1952

Source: Statistical Abstract of the U.S. 1953

1. In 1946, roughly what percent of the federal prisoners received from the courts were national-security offenders?

    (A) 15
    (B) 20
    (C) 25

    (D) 30
    (E) 35

The total number of prisoners in 1946 was about 20,000, and national security offenders accounted for the part of the graph from just above 15,000 to just above 20,000. Therefore, there were about $20,000 - 15,000 = 5,000$ prisoners convicted of national-security offenses. Since $5,000/20,000 = \frac{1}{4} = 25\%$, the correct answer is (C).

2. Of the combined total for the four years 1947 through 1950, the largest number of offenders were in the category

    (A) national-security offenses
    (B) other offenses
    (C) drugs

    (D) immigration
    (E) liquor

The correct answer is (B). Since other offenses have the most offenders in each year, that category must have the largest total number of offenders. [If this question specified the years 1944–1946, then (A) would be correct.]

3. Which of the following statements can be inferred from the graph?

    I.   The number of federal prisoners received from the courts decreased each year from 1946 to 1948.
    II. More than 40% of the prisoners between 1944 and 1952 came from the other offenses category.
    III. 2% of the federal prisoners received in 1952 were convicted on heroin charges.

    (A) I only
    (B) III only
    (C) I and II only

    (D) I and III only
    (E) I, II, and III

Statement I is true, since the height of the bar for each year is lower than the height of the bar for the previous year in 1946, 1947, and 1948.

Statement II is not true. For most of the years, other offenses accounted for about 25–30%, and it never was more than 40% in any year. Therefore, it could not account for more than 40% of the total.

Statement III can not be inferred. There is a category of drug offenders, but there is no information about specific drugs.

So, the correct answer is (A).

Review of Formulas

(The number next to each formula refers to the section of the chapter where the formula is discussed.)

Interest = Amount × Time × Rate   I– D–2

Discount = Cost × Rate of Discount   I– D–2

$x = \dfrac{1}{2a}\left[-b \pm \sqrt{b^2 - 4ac}\,\right]$ (quadratic formula)   II– B–5

Distance = Speed × Time   II– C–2

$a^2 + b^2 = c^2$ when a and b are the legs and c is   III– D–1
   the hypotenuse of a right triangle (Pythagorean Theorem)

Diameter of a circle = 2 × Radius   III– F

Area of a square = s^2 III– G–1

Area of a rectangle = LW III– G–1

Area of a triangle = $\frac{1}{2} bh$ III– G–1

Area of a circle = πr^2 III– G–1

Area of a parallelogram = bh III– G–1

Area of a trapezoid = $\frac{1}{2}(b_1 + b_2)h$ III– G–1

Circumference of a circle = πd III– G–2

Perimeter of a square = $4s$ III– G–2

Perimeter of a rectangle = $2(L + W)$ III– G–2

Distance between points (x,y) and (a,b) is $\sqrt{(x-a)^2 + (y-b)^2}$ III– H

12 Analytical Ability

- ■ Analytical Reasoning Tactics
- ■ Logical Reasoning Tactics
- ■ Practices Exercise
- ■ Answer Key
- ■ Answer Explanations

The analytical ability portion of the GRE is made up of two types of questions: analytical reasoning (puzzle) questions, and logical reasoning (argument analysis) questions. Typically, each analytical ability section consists of twenty-five questions. Nineteen analytical reasoning questions are divided among three to five groups containing from three to seven questions each. Six logical reasoning questions come in two sets of three, one set following the first group of analytical reasoning questions, and one set ending the section.

In dealing with analytical ability questions, you should expect to spend most of your time reading and analyzing the puzzle statements and the verbal arguments themselves. Read closely. Once you have worked out a particular structure of relationships, organizing your information in outline or diagram form, you will find the puzzle questions themselves relatively easy. Similarly, once you have critically evaluated a particular verbal argument, noting the assumptions on which it is based and the inferences which can logically be drawn from it, you will find questions concerning the reasoning displayed in that argument readily manageable.

Analytical Reasoning Tactics

Tackle Each Group of Analytical Reasoning Questions as a Unit

Analytical reasoning questions require you to think through a complicated set of conditions and to keep these conditions in mind as you answer a group of questions. It therefore makes sense for you to treat each group of questions as a unit and attempt to answer *all* the questions while you still have the conditions clearly in mind. Do not jump from one group to a second before you answer all the questions in the first group; you will lose time refamiliarizing yourself with the relationships.

Within a given group, you may find it helpful to skip from question to question. In answering the fourth question based on a particular set of conditions, you may gain an insight into the total relationship that will help you answer questions two and three.

Simplify the Information by Using Abbreviations and Symbolic Shorthand

The analytical reasoning questions are not intended to be ambiguous. Far from it—the test-makers take great pains to use language precisely and to word the set of conditions describing a particular relationship so exactly that only one interpretation works. In doing so, however, they use so many words that it is easy to get lost. To see the situation clearly, you need to work with symbols, not words.

Strip away individual names and irrelevant details that clutter up the situation. If the test-makers list a lengthy group of items, substitute initials for the individual words. If they take a dozen words to describe a relationship, try to express it in three or four letters and symbols ($\rightarrow$, $=$, $+$, etc.). In the course of taking lecture notes, you have probably worked up your own personal shorthand, a system of symbolic notation you use to get down ideas rapidly. Build on this system, adding to it any of the standard logical symbols found in the following chart.

STANDARD LOGICAL NOTATION

Linking Term	Symbol
and	$+$
or	$\lor$
not	$\sim$
if - then	$\supset$
if and only if	$\equiv$
equal to, same as	$=$
not equal to, not same as	$\neq$
greater than (taller, older, etc.)	$>$
less than (shorter, younger, etc.)	$<$

Work with these symbols <u>if and only if</u> they seem useful to you. You may prefer other symbols, such as <u>&</u> for <u>and</u>.

See how this tactic works in dealing with a set of conditions presented on a recent GRE.

Questions 20–22

An instructor regularly offers a six-week survey course on film genres. Each time the course is given, she covers six of the following eight genres: adventure films, *cinema noir*, detective films, fantasy films, horror films, musical comedies, silent films, and westerns. She will discuss exactly one genre per week according to the following conditions:

Silent films are always covered, and always in the first week.
Westerns and adventure films are always covered, with westerns covered in the week immediately preceding the week adventure films are covered.

Musical comedies are never covered in the same course in which fantasy films are covered.
If detective films are covered, they are covered after westerns are covered, with exactly one of the other genres covered between them.
Cinema noir is not covered unless detective films are covered in one of the previous weeks.

Your first task is to reduce this mass of data to manageable proportions. First, substitute initials for the names of the eight genres, as follows:

Adventure films	$=$	A
Cinema noir	$=$	C
Detective films	$=$	D
Fantasy films	$=$	F
Horror films	$=$	H
Musical comedies	$=$	M
Silent films	$=$	S
Westerns	$=$	W

Now, note down what you *know* about these genres:

S *always* 1
W $\Rightarrow$ A *always* (here $\Rightarrow$ means immediately precedes)
If F, no M
If M, no F
If C, D $\rightarrow$ C (here $\rightarrow$ means *precedes, but not necessarily immediately*)
If D, W $\Rightarrow$? $\Rightarrow$ D

Take a look at the last condition. You *know* that westerns immediately precede adventure films (W $\Rightarrow$ A *always*). Therefore, you can rewrite the last condition to read:

If D, W $\Rightarrow$ A $\Rightarrow$ D

Whenever detective films are covered, you know the exact order and identity of three of the six film genres discussed in the course.

Highlight Key Words That Limit the Situation Critically

Look at the previous example. Note the words that limit the relationships presented. Silent films are *always* covered, and *always* in the *first* week. Westerns *immediately* precede adventure films. *Exactly one* genre is covered

between westerns and detective films. *Cinema noir* is *not* covered *unless* detective films are covered. Musical comedies are *never* covered in the same course in which fantasy films are covered.

These words are critical to your understanding of the situation. Take particular note of them, underlining them or circling them to emphasize their importance.

Frequently Used Key Words

all
always
at least (*at least one member in common* — can be 1, 2, 3...)
at most (*at most two members in common* — can be 0, 1, or 2)
but
can be
cannot be
consecutive (*three consecutive days*)
directly (*directly opposite*; *directly after*)
each
every
exactly (*exactly one*; *exactly once*)
except
if
immediately (*immediately preceding*; *immediately adjacent*)
impossible
must be
never

no fewer than (*no fewer than three*—can be 3, 4, 5...)
no more than (*no more than four*—can be 0, 1, 2, 3, or 4)
none
only (*once and only once*; *if and only if*)
perfectly (*perfectly straight*; *perfectly round*)
possible
same
some
the least (*shortest, smallest, youngest, etc.*)
the most (*tallest, greatest, oldest, etc.*)
unless

Note that certain of these key words have only one function — to rule out a potential ambiguity. These words so precisely define the situation that only one interpretation is possible. Take, for example, *immediately*. What does the statement "John precedes Kenneth" tell you? It tells you that John is somewhere ahead of Kenneth. What does the statement "John immediately precedes Kenneth" tell you? It tells you the exact relationship between John and Kenneth, letting you know that John is the person who comes right before Kenneth, and that nobody else comes between Kenneth and John.

First, Eliminate Answer Choices Ruled Out by Individual Conditions; Then, Work Through Remaining Choices or Guess

Pay special note to any conditions phrased in unambiguous terms—*always, never, all, none*. Because they allow only one interpretation of the situation, you may be able to use them to rule out several answer choices at a glance.

See how a single condition allows you to eliminate three answer choices to a question based on the preceding set of course conditions.

20. Which of the following is an acceptable schedule of genres for weeks one through six of the course?

   (A) Silent films, westerns, adventure films, detective films, horror films, musical comedies

   (B) Silent films, westerns, adventure films, horror films, detective films, fantasy films

   (C) Fantasy films, musical comedies, detective films, *cinema noir*, musical comedies, horror films

   (D) Westerns, adventure films, detective films, *cinema noir*, musical comedies, horror films

   (E) Detective films, westerns, adventure films, horror films, fantasy films, *cinema noir*

What is the first condition that must be met? "S *always* 1." Therefore, every schedule of genres must begin with S, silent films. Choices A and B begin with S; they deserve further examination. Choices C, D, and E, however, begin with other genres. Eliminate them and give them no further thought.

Go back to Choice A. What pattern do you see?

S W A D H M

S is where it belongs. W A D is an acceptable pattern. In the absence of F, M is acceptable. Choice A works.

Double check yourself. Look over Choice B. Here the pattern is:

S W A H D F

Once again, S is in its place. W A meets the second condition. In the absence of M, F is acceptable. The problem lies in the placement of D. According to the rules, it can only exist in the pattern W A D. It is not enough for westerns merely to precede detective films. The fourth condition states that *exactly* one genre is covered between westerns and detective films. Given the second condition, that one genre must be adventure films. Thus, if detective films are covered, the pattern must be W A D. Choice B is incorrect. The correct answer is Choice A.

In this instance, you narrowed things down to Choices A and B and had time to work out that Choice A was correct. If you run out of time, don't worry. Just guess. By being able to eliminate some answer choices at a glance, you have improved your chance of selecting the correct choice.

Study Conditions Not Merely for What They State But for What They Imply

Analytical reasoning questions resemble the inference questions you find in reading comprehension tests. To answer them correctly, you must understand not only what the conditions state explicitly but what they imply.

See how this holds true in answering the following question on the preceding GRE example.

---

22. Which of the following will NEVER be covered in the sixth week of the course?

   (A) *Cinema noir*
   (B) Fantasy films
   (C) Horror films
   (D) Musical comedies
   (E) Westerns

Look at your list of conditions. Which of them provide information about the order in which the different genres may be covered?

S *always* 1
W ⇒ A *always* (here ⇒ means *immediately precedes*)
If C, D → C (here → means *precedes, but not necessarily immediately*)
If D, W ⇒ A ⇒ D

Consider the second condition. If westerns and adventure films are always covered, with westerns always immediately preceding adventure films, this implies that westerns can be covered in only weeks 2, 3, 4, or 5. They cannot be covered in week 1, for that is reserved for silent films (S *always* 1). Likewise, they cannot be covered in week 6, for they must be followed by adventure films. (See table.)

1	2	3	4	5	6
S	W	A			

1	2	3	4	5	6
S		W	A		

1	2	3	4	5	6
S			W	A	

1	2	3	4	5	6
S				W	A

From studying the implications of the conditions, you can see that only four basic configurations are possible. You can also see that westerns will never be covered in the sixth week of the course. The correct answer is Choice E.

Organize Information in List or Table Form

When you study a set of conditions for its implications, you wind up with a mass of information. You need to organize this information. As in the previous question, you will find it useful to list the basic conditions and to set down their implications in table form.

Apply this tactic to the following set of conditions from a recent GRE.

Questions 16–19

A cryptanalyst must translate into letters all of the digits included in the following two lines of nine symbols each:

9 3 3 4 5 6 6 6 7
2 2 3 3 4 4 5 7 8

The cryptanalyst has already determined some of the rules governing the decoding:

Each of the digits from 2 to 9 represents exactly one of the eights letters A, E, I, O, U, R, S, and T, and each letter is represented by exactly one of the digits.

If a digit occurs more than once, it represents the same letter on each occasion.

The letter T and the letter O are each represented exactly 3 times.

The letter I and the letter A are each represented exactly two times.

The letter E is represented exactly four times.

List the digits from 2 to 9. Beside each digit, note the number of times that digit occurs in the two lines being decoded.

Number of Occurrences	Digit
2 x	2
4 x	3
3 x	4
2 x	5
3 x	6
2 x	7
1 x	8
1 x	9

Next, compare the information in this table with the information already determined by the cryptanalyst. Note on the table what you can deduce from this comparison. (For example, the cryptanalyst has determined that the letter E occurs four times. Therefore, you can deduce that the letter E must be represented by the digit 3, the only digit occurring four times.)

Number of Occurrences	Digit	
2 x	2	A or I or ?
4 x	3	E
3 x	4	T or O
2 x	5	A or I or ?
3 x	6	T or O
2 x	7	A or I or ?
1 x	8	?
1 x	9	?

Unassigned Letters R, S, U

See how simple it is to answer the following GRE question by referring to this table of information.

16. If 2 represents R and 7 represents A, then 5 must represent

(A) I
(B) O
(C) S
(D) T
(E) U

Examine the chart. According to the rules determined by the cryptanalyst, 2, 5 and 7 each represent one (and only one) of three letters: A, I, and an undetermined third letter. This question identifies that third letter as R and stipulates that 2 represents R and 7 represents A. Incorporate this information into your table for the moment. The only letter of the three that remains is I. Thus, 5 *must* represent I. The correct answer is Choice A.

Number of Occurrences	Digit	
2 x	2	R (not A or I)
4 x	3	E
3 x	4	T or O
2 x	5	I
3 x	6	T or O
2 x	7	A (not R or I)
1 x	8	?
1 x	9	?

Unassigned Letters S, U

Organize Information in Map or Diagram Form

One of the best ways to deal with the information in an analytical reasoning question is to construct a simple map or diagram. This is particularly helpful when you are dealing with a problem involving the physical or temporal order of things. It is much easier to tell whether a particular route from point A to point B is possible when you actually see points A and B on a map.

Note how you can construct a map to illustrate the following set of conditions from a recent GRE.

Questions 18–22

On an island there are exactly seven towns: T, U, V, W, X, Y, and Z. All existing and projected roads on the island are two-way and run perfectly straight between one town and the next. All distances by road are distances from the main square of one town to the main square of another town. U is the same distance by road from T, V, and W as Y is from X and Z. The following are all of the currently existing roads and connections by road on the island.

Road 1 goes from T to V via U.
Road 2 goes from U directly to W.
The Triangle Road goes from X to Y, from Y on to Z, and from Z back to X.
Any main square reached by two roads is an interchange between them, and there are no other interchanges between roads.

Draw Road 1, labeling points T, U, and V.

Now draw Road 2, for simplicity's sake making it perpendicular to Road 1.

Above this diagram, and unconnected to it, construct the Triangle Road.

To indicate that they each are the same length (their main squares are the same distance apart), mark the following five line segments with equal signs: UT, UV, UW, YX, and

YZ. You now have a diagram that you can use to answer any questions about the physical relationships among the island's seven towns.

Try constructing a second diagram, this one illustrating the way in which five computers are linked.

Questions 14–18

P, Q, R, S, T are the computers in the five overseas offices of a large multinational corporation. The computers are linked in an unusual manner in order to provide increased security for the data in certain offices. Data can be directly requested only from:
  P by Q
  P by T
  Q by P
  R by P
  S by Q
  S by T
  T by R
If a computer can directly request data from another computer, then it can also pass on requests for data to that other computer.

In this situation, you are dealing not with two way streets, but with "one-way" streets. To say that T can directly request data from P does not imply that P can directly request data from T. Thus, you need to use arrows to indicate the direction in which requests for data may go.

Go through the list, connecting each pair of letters with its arrow or arrows.

Q ⟶ P   Q ⟶ P ⟵ T   Q ⟷ P ⟵ T
                                    S   S
Q ⟷ P ⟵ T   Q ⟷ P ⟵ T   Q ⟷ P ⟵ T
        │   │   │
        R   R   R

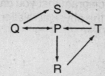

You now have a diagram that illustrates exactly how these computers are linked. Note how much information about these relationships you have. For example, you can see that several possible routes allow you to request information from computer R. P can request information directly from R. Alternatively, Q and T may also request information from R via P. Taking this process to extremes, R can even request information from itself by routing its request through T and P.

Individual questions often contain new conditions that affect the determined structure of relationships. To understand how a change in the computer linkup described affects the relationships involved, you have only to make a new diagram or alter your diagram temporarily.

See how readily you can answer the following GRE question by altering your diagram appropriately.

17. If computers Q, R, S, and T are the only ones operating, which of the following requests for data can be made, either directly or through one or more of the other computers?

(A) A request by P for data from Q
(B) A request by Q for data from R
(C) A request by Q for data from T
(D) A request by R for data from P
(E) A request by R for data from S

 Beware of Making Unwarranted Assumptions

Generally, once you have set up your table or completed your diagram based on a particular set of conditions, you should have little difficulty with the group of questions based on those conditions. Sometimes, however, you may misread one of the conditions, drawing an incorrect inference from it. For example, in a set establishing relationships of age and military rank among the members of a squad, you should not assume that a person who is older than another person must hold a higher rank than that person.

Beware of reading too much into a condition. Take the following condition:

If J is selected for a team, K must also be selected for that team.

P is non-functional. Therefore, it is out of the linkup: you must delete it and the arrows going to and from it from your diagram. Thus altered, your diagram looks like this:

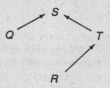

A quick glance reveals that, of the choices given, only Choice E is possible. Despite the gaps in the linkup, R can still, by going through T, request data from S.

One word of caution. When an analytical reasoning question introduces new information in the form of a stipulation—an additional condition or restriction, or, as in the question above, a suspension of one of the original conditions—be sure you add that information to your diagram or table *temporarily*: apply it to that question alone. Do *not* apply it to other questions in its group.

Or, in brief,

If J, K (J⊃K)

Do not assume on the basis of this that if K is selected for a team, J must also be selected for that team. The condition does not work both ways: it has not been imposed on both parties.

Many sets of conditions in analytical reasoning problems include such one-way conditions. The set of conditions for the film course, for example, includes the following condition:

Cinema noir is not covered unless detective films are covered in one of the previous weeks.

In other words,

If C, D → C

However, this restriction does not apply equally to C and D. The same condition has not been imposed on both genres. To say that

Cinema noir is not covered unless detective films are covered in one of the previous weeks

is *not* to say that

Detective films are not covered unless *cinema noir* is covered in one of the following weeks.

In other words,

If C, D → C does NOT imply If D, D → C

It is unfortunately very easy to introduce graphic assumptions into the construction of a diagram. For example, look at the following diagram based upon the description of road connections in the preceding discussion.

Questions 18–22

On an island there are exactly seven towns: T, U, V, W, X, Y, and Z. All existing and projected roads on the island are two-way and run perfectly straight between one town and the next. All distances by road are distances from the main square of one town to the main square of another town. U is the same distance by road from T, V, and W as Y is from X and Z. The following are all of the currently existing roads and connections by road on the island.

Road 1 goes from T to V via U.
Road 2 goes from U directly to W.
The Triangle Road goes from X to Y, from Y on to Z, and from Z back to X.
Any main square reached by two roads is an interchange between them, and there are no other interchanges between roads.

The diagram above represents the Triangle Road as an equilateral triangle: visually, XY, YZ, and XZ are equal in length. Unfortunately, this diagram embodies an assumption that may mislead you when you attempt to answer the following question.

19. It is possible that the distance by road from X to Y is *unequal* to the distance by road from

   (A) T to U
   (B) U to V
   (C) U to W
   (D) X to Z
   (E) Y to Z

The question asks that you find a road that *can differ* in length from Road XY.

It is possible that Triangle XYZ is an equilateral triangle, and that lines XY, XZ, and YZ are all equal in length. That, however, is not what you are told. You are told only that XY and YZ are equal in length, as are TU, UV, and UW. You have no information about the length of XZ. By picturing Triangle XYZ as equilateral, you assume a relationship in which all road segments are the same in length and in which no road can differ in length from Road XY. If that were the case, there would be no correct answer to the question.

The test-makers do not create questions for which no correct answers exist. If you can find no correct answer to an analytical reasoning question, go back to the original conditions and re-examine them. You will find that you have misinterpreted one or more of them.

In this case, in constructing your diagram you have assumed incorrectly that the condition defining the length of XY and YZ applies equally to XZ. It does not. XZ can be equal in length to XY. It can be greater in length than XY. It can be shorter in length than XY. Therefore, it follows that the distance by road from X to Y *can be unequal* to the distance by road from X to Z. The correct answer is Choice D.

Logical Reasoning Tactics

Look at the Question Before You Look at the Argument

Analytical reasoning questions come in groups of three to seven questions based on a single set of conditions. It makes sense to analyze the set of conditions carefully before you look at the questions based upon it. One, or at most two, logical reasoning questions, however, are based on a given argument. Rather than jumping in blindly and analyzing each and every aspect of the argument—assumptions, central point, evidence, further application, logical flaws—do no more work than necessary. Look at the question stem. Then examine the argument. Know what aspect of the argument you are to concentrate on, and concentrate on it. You will save time and effort.

See how this tactic applies to the following logical reasoning question from a recent GRE.

The Census Bureau reported that the median family income, after adjustment, increased 1.6 percent in 1983. Poverty normally declines when family income goes up, but the national poverty rate remained at its highest level in eighteen years in 1983. The Census Bureau offered two possible explanations: the lingering effects of the deep and lengthy 1981-1982 recession, and increases in the number of people living in families headed by women and in the number of adults not living with any relatives. Both groups are likely to be poorer than the population as a whole.

Which of the following conclusions can be properly drawn from this report?

(A) The national poverty rate has increased steadily over the last eighteen years.

(B) The national poverty rate will increase when there are lingering effects of an earlier recession.

(C) The median family income can increase even though the family income of some subgroups within the population declines or fails to increase.

(D) The category of adults not living with any relatives is the most critical group in the determination of whether the economy has improved.

(E) The median family income is affected more by changes in family patterns than by the extent of expansion or recession of the national economy.

Your goal is to select the answer choice that logically follows from specific facts and ideas stated in the passage. You do not have to evaluate the argument for possible flaws in logic or consider the premises on which it is based. You are looking for a proper conclusion. Therefore, you must carefully analyze each answer choice and see how it relates to the passage. You can eliminate any answer choice that contradicts what the passage states as fact. You can also eliminate any answer choice that strays from the subject of the passage or cannot be linked to specific supporting evidence in the passage.

Go through the answer choices, keeping sight of your goal while you think the argument through. Is Choice A a conclusion that can be properly drawn from what is stated in the passage? No. Choice A contradicts something the passage states as fact. In asserting that the national poverty rate has *increased steadily* over the last eighteen years, Choice A contradicts the second sentence, which states that the national poverty rate *remained at its highest level* in 1983. According to the passage, therefore, the national poverty rate did not steadily increase throughout the period in question.

Is Choice B a conclusion that can be properly drawn from what is stated in the passage? No. Choice B goes beyond what the passage states or suggests. In the third sentence, "the lingering effects of an earlier recession" are offered as a possible explanation for the failure of the national poverty rate to decline. These lingering effects are not, however, offered as evidence that the national poverty rate will increase.

Is Choice C a conclusion that can be properly drawn from what is stated in the passage? Possibly. Choice C states that the median family income *can* increase *even though* the family income of some subgroups within the population declines or fails to increase. This assertion is in keeping with the facts presented in the passage. The first sentence states the median family income has increased. The second sentence states that the national poverty level remained at its highest rate. This implies that the income of some families either failed to increase or declined. The third sentence cites two subgroups whose income is likely to fall below the national median. This is probably the correct answer choice—it appears to be a conclusion that can be drawn from the passage—but, just to be sure, you should check out the remaining answer choices, Choices D and E.

Is Choice D a conclusion that can be properly drawn from what is stated in the passage? No. Choice D goes *far* beyond what the passage suggests or states. Where the passage cites an increase in two subgroups—families headed by women, and adults not living with any relatives —as one *possible* explanation for the lack of improvement in the economy, Choice D pinpoints one of these two subgroups as *the most critical* group in determining whether the economy has improved. There is no evidence in the passage to support singling out one particular subgroup in this way. Therefore, you can eliminate Choice D.

What of Choice E? Is Choice E a conclusion that can be properly drawn from what is stated in the passage? No. Like Choice D, Choice E goes beyond what the passage states or suggests. Nothing in the passage suggests that one factor more than another affects the median family income. In fact, the passage cites changes in family pattern and the effects of recession not as influences on the median family income but as influences on the national poverty rate. Choice E clearly is incorrect.

Of the conclusions listed, the only one that can be properly drawn from the passage is Choice C.

Learn to Spot the Major Logical Reasoning Question Types

Just as it will help you to know the major types of reading questions on the GRE, it will also help you to familiarize yourself with the major types of logical reasoning questions on the test.

If you can recognize just what a given question is asking for, you'll be better able to tell which particular approach to take to the argument at hand.

Here are eight categories of logical reasoning questions you are sure to face.

1. **Assumption**   Questions that test your ability to recognize the premises on which an argument is based often take the following form:

    The conclusion above depends on which of the following assumptions?
    The author of the passage above makes which of the following assumptions?
    The author of the passage above presupposes that...
    The statement above assumes which of the following?

2. **Inference**   Questions that test your ability to go beyond the author's explicit statements and see what these statements imply may be worded:

    It can be inferred from the passage above that the author believes that...
    Which of the following is implied by the passage above?
    From the information above, which of the following can be most reasonably inferred about...

3. **Conclusion**   Questions that test your ability to determine what claim can logically be made on the basis of the evidence in the passage often take the form:

    If the statements above are true, which of the following conclusions can be properly drawn?

Choose the most logical completion for the following paragraph.
Which of the following would provide the most logical conclusion for the preceding paragraph?
The statements in the passage, if true, best support which of the following conclusions?

4. **Central Point**   Questions that test your ability to understand the thrust of an argument are often worded:

    The statement cited above conveys which of the following propositions?
    The passage above emphasizes which of the following points?
    The author in the passage above argues that...
    Which of the following expresses the point the author of the passage above makes?

5. **Support**   Questions that test your ability to recognize whether an assertion supports or undermines an argument are often worded:

    Which of the following, if true, does NOT support the claim that...
    Which of the following, if true, would additionally weaken the traditional opinion that...
    Which of the following, if true, would constitute the strongest evidence in support of the claim made above?
    The persuasiveness of the claim made above is most weakened by...

6. **Argument Evaluation**   Questions that test your ability to judge an argument often take the form:

    Which of the following would be most important to know in evaluating the accuracy of the argument above?
    Which of the following hypotheses, if true, would help resolve the apparent paradox introduced above?

If all of the statements above are correct, an explanation of their apparent contradiction is provided by...
Which of the following identifies a flaw in the speaker's reasoning?
Knowledge of which of the following would be LEAST useful in evaluating the claims made in the passage above?

7. **Application**   Questions that test your ability to apply the principles ruling one argument to another argument are often worded:

    Which of the following parallels the method of argumentation above...

The argument above is most like which of the following?
Which of the following suffers from a flaw that, in its logical aspects, is most like the difficulty described above?

8. **Technique**   Questions that test your ability to recognize an argument's method of organization or technique may be worded:

    The author's point is made primarily by...
    The labor negotiator minimizes his differences with management by...
    The passage above criticizes the authorities by...

Pay Particular Attention to Signal Words in the Question (and in the Argument As Well)

In answering logical reasoning questions, you must read closely both the argument and the question or questions based on it. When you do so, be on the lookout for certain signal words that can clarify the situation. In particular, be on the lookout for:

Cause and Effect Signal Words

The following words often signal the conclusion of an argument:

    accordingly
    consequently
    hence
    therefore
    thus

Contrast Signal Words

The following words often signal a reversal of thought within an argument or a question stem:

    although
    but
    despite
    even though
    however
    in contrast
    instead
    nevertheless
    not
    on the contrary
    on the other hand
    rather than
    unlike

See how several of these signal words function in the following logical reasoning problem from a recent GRE.

Literary historians today have rejected conventional analyses of the development of English Renaissance drama. They no longer accept the idea that the sudden achievement of Elizabethan playwrights was a historical anomaly, a sort of magical rediscovery of ancient Greek dramatic form applied to contemporary English subject matter. Instead, most students of the theater now view Elizabethan drama as being organically related to traditional local drama, particularly medieval morality plays.

Which of the following is NOT consistent with the passage above?

(A) England had a dramatic tradition before the Renaissance period.
(B) Elizabethan drama, once thought to be a sudden blossoming forth of creativity, is now seen as part of a historical continuum.
(C) Historians' views of the antecedents of English Renaissance drama have changed considerably.
(D) Current scholarship applies an evolutionary model to English Renaissance drama.
(E) Although English Renaissance drama treats English subject matter, its source of form and method is classical Greek drama.

Your job is to decide which answer choice is NOT consistent with the passage above. Therefore, you can eliminate any answer choice that *is* consistent with it.

Go through the answer choices. Is Choice A in keeping with what is stated in the passage? Yes. The concluding sentence states that Elizabethan (*i. e.*, English Renaissance) drama is viewed as "organically related" to the earlier traditional local drama. In other words, there was a dramatic tradition in England before Renaissance times.

Is Choice B in keeping with what is stated in the passage? Yes. The second sentence states that the sudden achievement of Elizabethan drama is no longer viewed as a historical anomaly. In other words, it is not seen as something abnormal, something that stands apart from history, but as part of a historical continuum. You can eliminate Choice B.

Is Choice C in keeping with what is stated in the passage? Yes. The opening sentence states that literary historians have rejected the conventional views of how English drama developed. Therefore, their views of its antecedents have changed considerably. You can eliminate Choice C.

Is Choice D in keeping with what is stated in the passage? Yes. The concluding sentence speaks of English Renaissance drama as being "organically related" to earlier dramatic forms. In other words, it developed out of or evolved from these earlier forms. The language here is that of evolutionary discourse. You can eliminate Choice D.

Is Choice E in keeping with what is stated in the passage? No. The second sentence states that literary historians have discarded the view that English Renaissance drama owes its form and method to the plays of classical Greece. Choice E asserts the very point that the passage seeks to deny. Thus, Choice E is not consistent with the passage and is the correct answer choice.

In Questions About an Argument's Assumptions, First Pinpoint the Argument's Conclusion and the Grounds on Which It Is Based

When asked about an argument's assumptions, work backwards from what is stated to what is unsaid. Start with the conclusion. Why does the argument's proponent arrive at this conclusion? What evidence supports it? When you are clear exactly what claim has been made and on what grounds it is founded, you are in a position to determine the assumptions underlying the argument. Ask yourself what there is about this particular evidence that justifies this particular claim. In process, you will uncover the argument's unstated premises.

Apply this tactic to the following GRE question.

A study of illusionistic painting inevitably begins with the Greek painter Zeuxis. In an early work, which is the basis for his fame, he painted a bowl of grapes that was so lifelike that birds pecked at the fruit. In an attempt to expand his achievement to encompass human figures, he painted a boy carrying a bunch of grapes. When birds immediately came to peck at the fruit, Zeuxis judged that he had failed.

Zeuxis' judgment that he had failed in his later work was based on an assumption. Which of the following can have served as that assumption?

(A) People are more easily fooled by illusionistic techniques than are birds.
(B) The use of illusionistic techniques in painting had become commonplace by the time Zeuxis had completed his later work.
(C) The grapes in the later painting were even more realistic than the ones in the earlier work.
(D) Birds are less likely to peck at fruit when they see that a human being is present.
(E) After the success of his early work, Zeuxis was unable to live up to the expectations of the general public.

What is Zeuxis' judgment or conclusion? His conclusion is that he failed to paint human figures with the illusion of life. Why does he draw this conclusion? What evidence does he offer to support it? He concludes that he failed to paint human figures with the illusion of life *because* birds came to peck at the fruit in one of his paintings that included a human figure. Why does he think this evidence supports his conclusion? Given this description, what assumption does he necessarily make about the behavior of birds? He assumes that birds are unlikely to peck at fruit when they realize a person is nearby. In other words, "Birds are less likely to peck at fruit when they see that a human being is present." The correct answer is Choice D.

Tactic 5

In Questions About Weakening or Strengthening an Argument, Examine the Argument for Any Unstated Assumptions It Makes

An argument is based upon certain assumptions made by its author. If an argument's basic premises are sound, that strengthens the argument. If the argument's basic premises are flawed, that weakens the argument.

Pinpoint what the argument assumes. Then compare that assumption with the answer choices. If the question asks you to choose an answer that most strengthens the argument, look for the answer choice that is most in keeping with the argument's basic assumption. If the question asks you to choose an answer that most weakens the argument, look for the answer choice that casts the most doubt on that assumption.

Apply this tactic to the following question from a recent GRE.

It is important to teach students to use computers effectively. Therefore, students should be taught computer programming in school.

Which of the following, if true, most weakens the argument above.

(A) Only people who use computers effectively are skilled at computer programming.

(B) Only people skilled at computer programming use computers effectively.

(C) Some people who use computers effectively cannot write computer programs.

(D) Some schools teach computer programming more effectively than others.

(E) Most people who are able to program computers use computers effectively.

The argument claims that, if students are to learn to use computers effectively, they should be taught computer programming in school. It clearly assumes a high correlation between knowledge of computer programming and effective computer use. It assumes at the least that people who have studied computer programming use computers effectively, and, possibly, that people who have not studied computer programming do not.

Choices B and E are in keeping with the argument's assumptions: if true, they would strengthen the argument, not weaken it. Therefore, Choices B and E are incorrect.

Choice A does not cast doubt on an assumption. It reverses it. This particular assumption, however, only works one-way. Think of it in *if-then* terms. Saying "If people are skilled at computer programming, then they can use computers effectively" does not imply "If people can use computers effectively, then they are skilled at computer programming." Likewise, the assumption "Only people skilled at computer programming use computers effectively" does not imply "Only people who use computers effectively are skilled at computer programming." Choice A is incorrect.

Choice D is also incorrect. It neither strengthens nor weakens the argument. It goes off on an entirely different track.

The correct answer is Choice C. It states that people exist who use computers effectively yet are unskilled at computer programming—they cannot write programs. It thus casts doubt upon the assumption that people unskilled at computer programming do not or cannot use computers effectively.

Tactic 6

Be on the Lookout for Common Logical Fallacies

If you've studied logic, rhetoric, philosophy, or debating, you may notice some familiar types of fallacies and logical errors turning up on the exam—for example, the *ad hominem* argument, in which the speaker attacks the personality of his or her opponent rather than criticizing the opponent's arguments; the *post hoc ergo propter hoc* argument, in which a simple association between two things is erroneously assumed to imply a cause-and-effect relationship between them; the *hasty generaliza-* *tion*, in which one or two isolated instances are taken as proof of some general rule; *circular reasoning*, in which the argument assumes the truth of what's supposed to be proven; and various kinds of *confusion of logical categories*. Technical terms like the ones just mentioned will NOT be tested or used on the exam. But you will be expected to recognize flaws like these when they appear in arguments and understand why they weaken the arguments based upon them.

Practice Exercise

Directions: Each questions or group of questions is based on a passage or set of conditions. In answering some of the questions, it may be useful to draw a rough diagram. For each question, select the best answer choice given.

Questions 1-4

An office manager must assign offices to six staff members. The available offices, numbered 1-6 consecutively, are arranged in a row, and are separated only by six-foot-high dividers. Therefore, voices, sounds, and cigarette smoke readily pass from each office to those on either side.

Miss Braun's work requires her to speak on the telephone frequently throughout the day.

Mr. White and Mr. Black often talk to one another in their work, and prefer to have adjacent offices.

Miss Green, the senior employee, is entitled to Office 5, which has the largest window.

Mr. Parker needs silence in the office(s) adjacent to his own.

Mr. Allen, Mr. White, and Mr. Parker all smoke. Miss Green is allergic to tobacco smoke and must have non-smokers in the office(s) adjacent to her own.

Unless otherwise specified, all employees maintain silence while in their offices.

1. The best location for Mr. White is in Office

   (A) 1　(B) 2　(C) 3　(D) 4　(E) 6

2. The best employee to occupy the office furthest from Mr. Black would be

   (A) Mr. Allen
   (B) Miss Braun
   (C) Miss Green
   (D) Mr. Parker
   (E) Mr. White

3. The three employees who smoke should be placed in Offices

   (A) 1, 2, and 3
   (B) 1, 2, and 4
   (C) 1, 2, and 6
   (D) 2, 3, and 4
   (E) 2, 3, and 6

4. Which of the following events, occurring one month after the assignment of offices, would be most likely to lead to a request for a change in office assignment by one or more employees?

   (A) Miss Braun's deciding that she needs silence in the office(s) adjacent to her own.
   (B) Mr. Black's contracting laryngitis.
   (C) Mr. Parker's giving up smoking.
   (D) Mr. Allen's taking over the duties formerly assigned to Miss Braun.
   (E) Miss Green's installing a noisy teletype machine in her office.

5. Excessive amounts of mercury in drinking water, associated with certain types of industrial pollution, have been shown to cause Hobson's Disease. Island R. has an economy based entirely on subsistence-level agriculture; modern industry of any kind is unknown. The inhabitants of Island R. have an unusually high incidence of Hobson's Disease.

   Which of the following can be validly inferred from the above statements?

   I.　Mercury in drinking water is actually perfectly safe.
   II.　Mercury in drinking water must have sources other than industrial pollution.
   III.　Hobson's Disease must have causes other than mercury in drinking water.

   (A) II only
   (B) III only
   (C) I or III, but not both
   (D) II or III, but not both
   (E) II or III, or both

6. Those who oppose the new water project claim to have the best interests of this community at heart. Yet they are the same people who, only three years ago, opposed the building of the new state highway, which now provides half a million commuters with fast, easy motoring every day. What could be a better argument in favor of the water project?

   Which of the following statements is most like the argument above?

   (A) Those who oppose nuclear power are unable or simply unwilling to recognize the fact that the nuclear energy industry has a safety record unparalleled by that of any other industry.
   (B) The new gun control law is a misguided and dangerous proposal, which has been denounced by every sportsmen's club and gun-owner's association in the state.
   (C) We must fight the proposed anti-pornography statute, for its principal sponsors have voted against every major piece of women's rights legislation introduced in the last twenty years.
   (D) The polls show that over 60% of the concerned parents in the state favor the school bond issue; cast your vote with the concerned majority on election day.
   (E) The so-called tax reform bill now before the state senate must be defeated; its only true beneficiaries would be the wealthy corporations, which already pay too little in taxes.

U   N

AorC | B

Questions 7–11

The office staff of the XYZ Corporation presently consists of three bookeepers (A, B, and C) and five secretaries (D, E, F, G, and H). Management is planning to open a new office in another city using three secretaries and two book-keepers of the present staff. To do so they plan to separate certain individuals who do not function well together. The following guidelines were established to set up the new office:

1. Bookkeepers A and C are constantly finding fault with one another and should not be sent as a team to the new office.
2. C and E function well alone but not as a team. They should be separated.
3. D and G have not been on speaking terms for many months. They should not go together.
4. Since D and F have been competing for promotion, they should not be a team.

7. If A is to be moved as one of the bookkeepers, which of the following CANNOT be a possible working unit?

D of the bookkeepers, F G

(A) ABDEH
(B) ABDGH
(C) ABEFH
(D) ABEGH
(E) ABFGH

AE | CFB

DGH

8. If C and F are moved to the new office, how many combinations are possible?

(A) 1   (B) 2   (C) 3   (D) 4   (E) 5

9. If C is sent to the new office which member of the staff CANNOT go with C?

(A) B   (B) D   (C) F   (D) G   (E) H

10. Under the guidelines developed, which of the following MUST go to the new office?

(A) B   (B) D   (C) E   (D) G   (E) H

11. If D goes to the new office which of the following is (are) true?

I.   C cannot go ✓
II. A cannot go
III. H must also go ✓

(A) I only
(B) II only
(C) I and II only
(D) I and III only
(E) I, II, and III

12. Fran: I want to stay out of Professor Caldwell's classes if I can. I've heard she's very strict when it comes to giving out the grades.

Sid: That's not true. My friend Phil took her class last year, and she gave him an A.

From the conversation above, it can be inferred that Sid interpreted Fran's statement to mean that Professor Caldwell

(A) makes unfair demands on her students
(B) only gives good grades to a few favored students
(C) has become increasingly strict in her grading over the past year
(D) gives out fewer good grades than most teachers in the department
(E) never gives out grades of A

13. The nursing shortage in this country is a phony one, caused by the concentration of nurses in the geographical regions with the highest paid and most generous fringe benefits for nurses. In addition, the League of American Nurses has artificaly worsened the shortage by encouraging nursing schools to keep enrollments low in order to boost nurses' salaries to even higher levels.

All of the following statements, if true, would tend to WEAKEN the argument above except:

(A) Although nurses are paid less in Texas than in Connecticut, there are 35% more nurses in Texas than in Connecticut.
(B) Nationwide, the salaries of nurses have risen at a slower rate than inflation over the last ten years.
(C) The number of students who earned degrees in nursing last year was almost double the number six years ago.
(D) Those areas of the country with the highest pay for nurses also have correspondingly higher living costs.
(E) The League of American Nurses has almost no influence on the policies of American nursing schools.

Questions 14–17

After months of talent searching for an administrative assistant to the president of the college the field of applicants has been narrowed down to five (A, B, C, D, and E). It was announced that the finalist would be chosen after a series of all-day group personal interviews were held. The examining committee agreed upon the following procedure:

1. The interviews will be held once a week.
2. No more than 3 candidates will appear at any all-day interview session.
3. Each candidate will appear at least once.
4. If it becomes necessary to call applicants for additional interviews, no more than one such applicant should be asked to appear the next week.
5. Because of a detail in the written applications, it was agreed that whenever Candidate B appears, A should also be present.
Because of travel difficulties, it was agreed that C will appear for only one interview.

14. At the first interview, the following candidates appear: A, B, and D. Which of the following combinations can be called for the interview to be held the next week?

    (A) ~~BCD~~ (B) CDE (C) ~~ABE~~
    (D) ~~ABC~~ (E) ~~ADE~~

15. Which of the following is a possible sequence of combinations for interviews in two successive weeks?

    (A) ~~ABC, BDE~~
    (B) ~~ABD, ABE~~
    (C) ADE; ABC
    (D) ~~BDE, ACD~~
    (E) ~~CDE, ABC~~

16. If A, B, and D appear at the interview and D is called for an additional interview the following week, which two candidates may be asked to appear with D?

    I.   A
    II. B
    III. C ✓
    IV. E ✓

    (A) I and II
    (B) I and III only
    (C) II and III only
    (D) II and IV only
    (E) III and IV only

17. Which of the following correctly states the procedure followed by the search committee?

    I.   After the second interview, all applicants have appeared at least once.
    II. The committee sees at least one applicant a second time.
    III. If a third session is held it is possible for all applicants to appear at least twice.

    (A) I only
    (B) II only
    (C) I and II only
    (D) III only
    (E) I and III only

Questions 18–21

To obtain a government post in the Republic of Malabar, you must either be a member of the ruling Independence Party or a personal associate of President Zamir.

Party members seeking a government post must either give a substantial donation in gold bullion to the party's campaign fund or make a televised speech denouncing President Zamir's political enemies.

Gold bullion may only be purchased at the National Bank, which only does business with those who have been certified as politically sound by the Minister of Justice.

Only those who either have been certified as politically sound by the Minister of Justice or have donated 300 hours of service to the Independence Party are allowed to make political speeches on television.

To become a personal associate of President Zamir, you must either give a substantial donation in gold bullion to the president's personal expense account or perform personal services for a member of his immediate family.

Before appointing a personal associate to a government post, President Zamir always checks to make sure that he or she has been certified as politically sound by the Minister of Justice.

18. Mr. Mizar is a member of the Independence Party. To obtain a government post, his next step must be to either

    (A) be certified as politically sound by the Minister of Justice, or give a substantial donation in gold bullion to the party's campaign fund
    (B) donate 300 hours of service to the Independence Party, or give a substantial donation in gold bullion to the president's personal expense account
    (C) be certified as politically sound by the Minister of Justice, or donate 300 hours of service to the party
    (D) perform personal services for a member of President Zamir's immediate family, or make a televised speech denouncing the president's political enemies
    (E) be certified as politically sound by the Minister of Justice, or become a personal associate of President Zamir

19. All those who wish to obtain government posts must

    I.   become personal associates of President Zamir
    II. be certified as politically sound by the Minister of Justice
    III. purchase gold bullion at the National Bank

    (A) I only
    (B) II only
    (C) III only
    (D) II and III only
    (E) Neither I, II, nor III

20. Mr. Razim has been certified as politically sound by the Minister of Justice. He may obtain a government post immediately only if he

    (A) has donated 300 hours of service to the Independence Party
    (B) is allowed to make political speeches on television
    (C) is a member of the Independence Party
    (D) is a personal associate of President Zamir
    (E) has purchased gold bullion at the National Bank

21. Becase of a financial crisis, the National Bank is closed indefinitely. Those who wish to obtain government posts during this period must

    (A) either perform some kind of services or make televised speeches denouncing President Zamir's political enemies
    (B) become members of the Independence Party
    (C) donate 300 hours of service to the Independence Party
    (D) become personal associates of President Zamir
    (E) either become members of the Independence Party or perform any services for the party

Questions 22 and 23

In a laboratory study, 160 rabbits in an experimental group were injected with Serum D, while 160 rabbits in a control group were injected with a harmless sugar solution. Within two weeks, 39% of the experimental group rabbits had contracted jungle fever, a highly contagious and usually fatal disease. Therefore, jungle fever must be caused by some substance similar to the substances found in Serum D.

22. The above argument would be most greatly strengthened if it were shown that

    (A) the normal rate of jungle fever among rabbits is less than .01%
    (B) 40% of the rabbits in the control group had also contracted jungle fever within two weeks
    (C) Serum D contains substances extracted from the root of a certain poisonous jungle wildflower
    (D) the blood of jungle fever victims invariable contains a high level of certain toxic substance also found in Serum D
    (E) nearly all the rabbits who contracted jungle fever died within two days of the appearance of the first symptoms

23. The above argument would be most seriously weakened if it were shown that

    (A) none of the substances in Serum D occurs naturally in the habitats of most species of rabbit
    (B) the rabbit in the experimental group had been kept strictly isolated from one another
    (C) jungle fever is usually found only among victims of the bite of the South American Lesser Hooded Viper
    (D) the scientists administering the injections were unaware of the contents of the solutions they were using
    (E) one of the rabbits in the experimental group had had jungle fever prior to the start of the experiment

24. Now Mesa Electronics brings tomorrow's technology to today's home stereo. The same space-age circuitry used by the Wanderer spacecraft to send images of the most distant planets back to earth has been incorporated in the new Mesa X-2700 stereo system. If your home entertainment is important to you, why settle for an old-fashioned stereo system when the Mesa X-2700 is priced at only a few dollars more?

The most serious logical weakness of this argument is its failure to

    (A) provide technical data on the manufacturing specifications of the Mesa X-2700
    (B) show the relevance of space-age circuitry to the requirements of home stereo
    (C) specify the exact price difference between the Mesa X-2700 and old-fashioned stereo systems
    (D) acknowledge the contributions of scientists in the space program to the development of the advanced circuitry mentioned
    (E) explain the precise meaning of the technical terms used

Questions 25–28

Professor Kittredge's literature seminar includes students with varied tastes in poetry. All those in the seminar who enjoy the poetry of Browning also enjoy the poetry of Eliot. Those who enjoy the poetry of Eliot despise the poetry of Coleridge.
Some of those who enjoy the poetry of Eliot also enjoy the poetry of Auden.
All those who enjoy the poetry of Coleridge also enjoy the poetry of Donne.
Some of those who enjoy the poetry of Donne also enjoy the poetry of Eliot.
Some of those who enjoy the poetry of Auden despise the poetry of Coleridge.
All those who enjoy the poetry of Donne also enjoy the poetry of Frost.

25. Miss Garfield enjoys the poetry of Donne. Which of the following must be true?

    (A) She may or may not enjoy the poetry of Coleridge.
    (B) She does not enjoy the poetry of Browning.
    (C) She enjoys the poetry of Auden.
    (D) She does enjoy the poetry of Eliot.
    (E) She enjoys the poetry of Coleridge.

26. Mr. Huxtable enjoys the poetry of Browning. He may also enjoy any of the following poets except

    (A) Auden
    (B) Coleridge
    (C) Donne
    (D) Eliot
    (E) Frost

27. Miss Inaguchi enjoys the poetry of Coleridge. Which of the following must be false?

    (A) She does not enjoy the poetry of Auden.
    (B) She enjoys the poetry of Donne.
    (C) She enjoys the poetry of Frost.
    (D) She does not enjoy the poetry of Browning.
    (E) She may enjoy the poetry of Eliot.

28. Based on the information provided, which of the following statements concerning the members of the seminar must be true?

    (A) All those who enjoy the poetry of Eliot also enjoy the poetry of Browning.
    (B) None of those who despise the poetry of Frost enjoy the poetry of Auden.
    (C) Some of those who enjoy the poetry of Auden despise the poetry of Coleridge.
    (D) None of those who enjoy the poetry of Browning despise the poetry of Donne.
    (E) Some of those who enjoy the poetry of Frost despise the poetry of Donne.

Questions 29–31

A certain city is served by six subway lines, designated by the letters A, B, and C, and the numbers 1, 2, and 3.
When it snows, morning service on the B line is delayed.
When it rains or snows, service on the A, 2, and 3 lines is delayed both morning and afternoon.
When the temperature drops below 30°F., afternoon service is cancelled on either the A line or the 3 line, but not both.
When the temperature rises above 90°F., afternoon service is cancelled on either the C line or the 3 line, but not both.
When service on the A line is delayed or cancelled, service on the C line, which connects with the A line, is delayed.
When service on the 3 line is cancelled, service on the B line, which connects with the 3 line, is delayed.

29. On January 10, with the temperature at 15°F., it snows all day. On how many lines will service be affected, including both morning and afternoon?

    (A) 2
    (B) 3
    (C) 4
    (D) 5
    (E) 6

30. On August 15, with the temperature at 97°F., it begins to rain at 1 p.m. What is the minimum number of lines on which service will be affected?

    (A) 2
    (B) 3
    (C) 4
    (D) 5
    (E) 6

31. On which of the following occasions would service on the greatest number of lines be disrupted?

    (A) A snowy afternoon with the temperature at 45° F.
    (B) A snowy morning with the temperature at 45° F.
    (C) A rainy morning with the temperature at 45° F.
    (D) A snowy afternoon with the temperature at 20° F.
    (E) A rainy afternoon with the temperature at 95° F.

Questions 32–36

Seven candidates in a gubernatorial primary election are to speak at a voters' forum. They are named Johnson, Kelleher, Lindsay, Macmillan, Nevins, Oberlander, and Pankhurst, and currently hold the offices of lieutenant governor, attorney general, state comptroller, U.S. Senator, highway commissioner, county supervisor, and schools superintendent, though not necessarily in that order.
The third speaker will be the highway commissioner.
Macmillan, who is not the county supervisor, will speak after the speaker who immediately follows Nevins.
Johnson is the state comptroller.
The lieutenant governor will speak sixth.
The attorney general will speak immediately before the county supervisor.
Pankhurst will speak immediately after Oberlander and immediately before Kelleher.
Schools Superintendent Nevins will speak fifth.

32. The first speaker will be

    (A) Oberlander
    (B) the state comptroller
    (C) Pankhurst
    (D) the county supervisor
    (E) Lindsay

33. The speaker who immediately precedes Macmillan will be

    (A) the highway commissioner
    (B) Johnson
    (C) the lieutenant governor
    (D) Kelleher
    (E) the county supervisor

34. Which of the following correctly pairs a speaker with his or her current office?

    (A) Oberlander—U.S. Senator
    (B) Kelleher—highway commissioner
    (C) Lindsay—county supervisor
    (D) Pankhurst—lieutenant governor
    (E) Macmillan—attorney general

35. Before the forum, Pankhurst drops out of the race, while a new candidate, Quigley, enters the race. If Pankhurst is dropped from the forum, while Quigley is added in the slot immediately after Lindsay, the sixth speaker will be

    (A) Kelleher   (C) Nevins   (E) Macmillan
    (B) Johnson   (D) Quigley

36. If, in addition to the changes described in question 35, the highway commissioner and the U.S. Senator agree to exchange positions in the speaking schedule, which of the following will be true?

    (A) Macmillan will speak after Oberlander and before Johnson.
    (B) Kelleher will be the only candidate to speak after Lindsay.
    (C) There will be an equal number of speakers before and after Johnson.
    (D) Only one candidate will speak after Nevins and before Kelleher.
    (E) The first and last speakers will not be changed.

Questions 37–39

A certain baseball team has four pitchers, named Miller, Craig, Hook, and Mizell. Each of the four is best known for throwing one type of pitch: fastball, curve ball, slider, or screwball.

Each of the four also uses a particular style of delivery in pitching: overhand, three-quarter, sidearm, or underhand.

Hook is best known for throwing the slider.
Neither Craig nor Mizell uses a three-quarter style of delivery.
The pitcher who uses an underhand delivery is best known for throwing the fastball.
Mizell is best known for throwing the screwball.
Miller uses an overhand delivery.

37. Which of the following correctly matches a pitcher with his best-known pitch and his style of delivery?

    (A) Miller--curve ball—three-quarter
    (B) Hook—slider—side arm
    (C) Craig—fastball—underhand
    (D) Mizell—curve ball—underhand
    (E) Miller—screwball—sidearm

38. During a game, if the starting pitcher is ineffective, he will be replaced by another pitcher. All of the following are possible pitching changes except

    (A) the curve ball pitcher being replaced by the pitcher who uses an overhand delivery
    (B) the screwball pitcher being replaced by Hook
    (C) Miller being replaced by the fastball pitcher
    (D) the slider pitcher being replaced by the pitcher who uses a sidearm delivery
    (E) Craig being replaced by the curve ball pitcher

39. In a four-game series, the manager of the team decides to pitch the fastball pitcher first, the pitcher who uses a three-quarter delivery second, the curve ball pitcher third, and the pitcher who uses a sidearm delivery fourth. In which order will the pitchers appear?

    (A) Mizell, Craig, Miller, Hook
    (B) Craig, Hook, Miller, Mizell
    (C) Miller, Craig, Hook, Mizell
    (D) Craig, Miller, Mizell, Hook
    (E) Miller, Hook, Mizell, Craig

Questions 40 and 41

As President of the National Association of Widget Manufacturers, I oppose government handouts to private business. But the present program of federal aid to the widget industry must continue. This is not a handout but rather a system of moderate cash subsidies to enable our beleaguered industry to withstand the shocks of rising costs and high interest rates, and so continue to provide useful employment to thousands of U.S Citzens.

40. The major logical weakness of the argument above is the fact that

    (A) the speaker is arguing against his own personal interest
    (B) it makes no attempt to explain the ultimate causes of rising costs and high interest rates
    (C) it draws no meaningful distinction between handouts and subsidies
    (D) it does not explain the significance of the widget industry for the U.S. economy as a whole
    (E) it offers no factual evidence to substantiate the claim that the widget industry is in danger

41. Which of the following persons would be most likely to disagree with the conclusions reached in the above argument?

    (A) The president of a medium-sized widget manufacturing firm
    (B) The patentee of a new device designed to make the widget obsolete
    (C) The federal administrator charged with coordinating the widget industry subsidy program
    (D) A congressional representative from a district containing several large widget manufacturing plants
    (E) The president of the national widget industry employees' union

42. Leafletting and speechmaking on government property should be outlawed. Radicals and fanatics have no right to use public property when peddling their unsavory views.

    The argument above is based on the assumption that

    (A) radicals and fanatics prefer using public property when disseminating their views
    (B) legal restrictions that apply to one group need not apply equally to all
    (C) the general public has a vested interest in the free exchange of varied political views
    (D) political activity that interferes with the orderly functioning of government should not be protected by law
    (E) all those who leaflet and make speeches on government property are radicals and fanatics

Answer Key

1.	C	12.	E	23.	E	33.	C
2.	D	13.	A	24.	B	34.	B
3.	A	14.	B	25.	A	35.	D
4.	D	15.	C	26.	B	36.	A
5.	E	16.	E	27.	E	37.	C
6.	C	17.	A	28.	C	38.	A
7.	B	18.	C	29.	D	39.	B
8.	A	19.	E	30.	C	40.	C
9.	B	20.	D	31.	B	41.	B
10.	A	21.	A	32.	A	42.	E
11.	D	22.	D				

Answer Explanations

1–4: Miss Green is definitely assigned to Office #5. Since no smoker may be near Miss Green, either Miss Braun or Mr. Black are the only ones that may be near #5. Mr. Black cannot go to #6 because he must be close to Mr. White. He must therefore take Office #4 and give Miss Braun #6. Mr. White may have #3 and be close to Mr. Black. Messrs. Allen and Parker have yet to be assigned. At this point the two vacancies are #1 and #2. Mr. Parker cannot be near Mr. White who often talks to Mr. Black. Mr. Parker should have #1 and leave #2 for Mr. Allen. The assignment of offices may be summarized as follows:

OFFICE #	STAFF MEMBER
1	Mr. Parker
2	Mr. Allen
3	Mr. White
4	Mr. Black
5	Miss Green
6	Miss Braun

1. C. Observe summary chart.

2. D. Observe summary chart.

3. A. Observe summary chart.

4. D. Mr. Allen is a smoker and cannot be near Miss Green who, because of seniority, must stay in #5. This would cause a complete change of assignments.

5. E. I is denied by the statement that some forms of mercury cause Hobson's Disease. II mentions the mercury in drinking water that is associated with industrial pollution. It may be concluded that mercury may get into drinking water by some other means. III alludes to the fact that this island has no industrial wastes and yet has a high incidence of this disease.

6. C. The argument presented here against proposed legislation is based upon unrelated, earlier legislation. The water project and the highway proposal is similar in logic to the anti-pornography proposal and the earlier women's rights legislation.

7–11: Summary with dotted lines indicating combinations to avoid:

BOOKKEEPERS → A B C
SECRETARIES → D E F G H

7. B. See item #3.

8. A. Since C is going, A cannot go, leaving B as the second bookkeeper. To have three secretaries, you cannot use E with C, leaving only D, F, G, and H. If D is used, F and G are ruled out. There is one and only one combination: F, G, and H with C and B.

9. B. If C goes you cannot use D. See explanation above.

10. A. Bookkeeper B has no limitations. A cannot go with C. D cannot go with F or G. E cannot go with C. Although H has no limitations, he could be left in the old office with a combination of E, F, and G. Another way of analyzing this question is to consider that to get two bookkeepers out of the three available ones, you must take either A or C but not both.

11. D. If D goes, the other two secretaries must be E and H. C cannot go with E. Therefore, A and B are the two bookkeepers.

12. E.   If the professor is strict about grades, she might possibly still make unfair demands (A) and also have favorites (B). It is possible that she acquired this tendency recently (C). It is possible that few of her students deserve good grades (D), but the fact that she NEVER gives out grades of A could quite possibly label her as being very strict when it comes to giving out grades.

13. A.   The statement in (A) may not weaken the argument. Texas is a much bigger, more heavily populated state than Connecticut. Even though there are 35% more nurses in Texas than Connecticut, the lower salary in Texas may still cause fewer nurses to go there than would otherwise go.

14. B.   According to procedure item #4, only one candidate may appear on two subsequent weeks.

15. C.   (A) violates item #5. (B) contradicts #4. (D) fails to consider #5. (E) does not take #6 into account.

16. E.   (A) is not correct; see item #4. (B) is not correct because of item #4. (C) and (D) contradict item #5.

17. A.   Since there are five applicants and three appear at each session, after the second session all applicants must have made an appearance (I).

18–21:   In solving this puzzle, a "flow chart" indicating the various steps which can lead to a government post in Malabar wil be useful. It might look something like this:

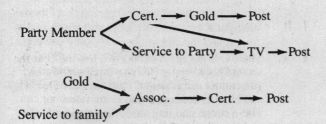

18. C.   As the chart shows, an Independence Party member has two possible routes to a government post. Therefore, as his next step, Mr. Mizar may either be certified by the Minister of Justice or donate 300 hours of service.

19. E.   To answer this question, check the chart to determine whether there is any step which is required by *all* routes to a government post. Since there is no such step, the correct answer is choice E. Note that statement II is not correct; it is possible for a party member to avoid having to be certified by the Minister of Justice by donating 300 hours of service to the party instead.

20. D.   As the chart shows, a personal associate of President Zamir who has been certified by the Minister of Justice is immediately eligible for a government post. Each of the other choices would leave some requirement unfulfilled. Choice E would be correct if Mr. Razim were known to be a party member; however, this is not stated in the question.

21. A.   According to this question, all routes to a government post which require the purchase of gold bullion have been blocked off. The only remaining routes are: the Party Member--Cert. or Services--TV route; and the Service--Assoc.--Cert. route. Both routes require either the performance of some kind of service or the making of a televised speech.

22. D.   The conclusion that some substance found in Serum D causes jungle fever would be greatly strengthened if the substance and the fever were invariably found together, as stated in choice E. Choice A does not help to establish the *cause* of the high rate of jungle fever in the experimental group. Choice B would weaken the original argument, not strengthen it. And choice C and E would neither weaken nor strengthen the argument.

23. E.   Since we are told that jungle fever is a "highly contagious" disease, choice E suggests an alternative explanation for the high rate of jungle fever in the experimental group. Choice A is irrelevant, since we have no idea whether rabbits or any particular species of rabbits are frequent victims of jungle fever in the first place. Choice B would strengthen the argument, not weaken it.

24. B.   The force of the argument presented in this advertisement lies in the attractiveness of the promise of "space-age circuitry" in the X-2700 stereo system. Choice B effectively points out the fundamental weakness of this appeal. All the other choices present features of the advertisement which might be regarded as flaws, but which are very minor in comparison to the flaw indicated in choice B.

25–28:   For a puzzle like this one, which relates various interlocking groups to one another, you'll need to draw a *circle diagram* showing the interrelationships of the groups named. Use solid lines to represent groups whose relationships are definitely established; use broken lines to represent groups about which some ambiguity exists. Your diagram should look more or less like this one:

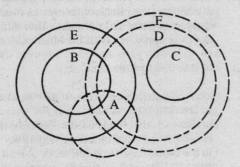

25. A. If Miss Garfield is within the circle labeled D (lovers of Donne), she may or may not be within the circle labeled C (lovers of Coleridge). Each of the other statements presents as definite fact something which may or may not be true.

26. B. As the diagram shows, the circle labeled B has no overlap with the circle labeled C. Therefore, there are no Browning-lovers who are also Coleridge-lovers. Browning-lovers may also enjoy Auden, Donne, or Frost; they *definitely* enjoy Eliot, since the circle labeled B is entirely within the circle labeled E.

27. E. All of the choices are possibly true, with the exception of choice E. Since the circle labeled C and the circle labeled E have no overlap, Miss Inaguchi definitely does not enjoy the poetry of Eliot.

28. C. Since some Auden-lovers are Eliot-lovers, and since all Eliot-lovers are Coleridge-despisers, there must be some Auden-lovers who are Coleridge-despisers.

29. D. As shown by the second, third, and sixth statements listed, the A, B, C, 2, and 3 lines will all be affected.

30. C. Combining the third, fifth, and sixth statements listed, we see that the A and 2 lines will be delayed, the 3 line will be cancelled, and the C line will be delayed (because of the delay on the A line).

31. B. On a snowy morning with the temperature at 45° F., the A, B, C, 2, and 3 lines will all be affected. Under each of the other conditions mentioned, only four lines will be affected.

32–36: Draw a chart providing spaces for the initials of the seven speakers along with abbreviations for the seven offices they hold. Start by filling in

the most definite information provided, which is found in the second, fifth, and eighth paragraphs. Your chart now looks like this:

	SPEAKER	OFFICE
1.		
2.		
3.		H.C.
4.		
5.	N.	S.S.
6.		L.G.
7.		

The third paragraph tells us that Macmillan should be placed in the seventh spot in the line-up. The sixth paragraph tells us that the attorney general will speak immediately before the county supervisor; however, looking at the chart, we see that the only two *consecutive* places still open are the first and the second, so that these two speakers must fit into those two openings. The chart now looks like this:

	SPEAKER	OFFICE
1.		A.G.
2.		C.S.
3.		H.C.
4.		
5.	N.	S.S.
6.		L.G.
7.	M.	

We can now put state comptroller Johnson into the fourth place in the line-up, since this is the only possible place for him. In addition, we know from the seventh paragraph that Oberlander, Pankhurst, and Kelleher will speak in that order, and the chart now shows only one place where three consecutive places are still open: namely, the first, second, and third places. Therefore, Oberlander, Pankhurst, and Kelleher belong in those spots. By elimination we can fill in the remaining slots. The questions are now easy.

32. A. Read directly from the chart

33. C. Read directly from the chart.

34. B. Read directly from the chart.

35. D. If Pankhurst, in the second slot, drops out, those who originally were scheduled to speak third, fourth, fifth, sixth, and seventh will now speak second, third, fourth, fifth, and sixth. If Quigley is to speak following Lindsay, who is now the fifth speaker, Quigley will speak sixth.

36. **A.** Choice A is correct, since Macmillan will now be the second speaker, and will follow Oberlander and precede Johnson. Choice B is wrong, because Quigley will also speak after Lindsay (see question 35). Choice C is wrong, because there will be only two speakers preceding Johnson but four following him. Choice D is wrong, because Lindsay and Quigley will both follow Nevins and precede Kelleher. And choice E is false because the last speaker was changed from Macmillan to Kelleher.

37–39: For this puzzle, you'll need a three-column chart listing pitchers, pitches, and styles of delivery. The information given in the second, fourth, fifth, and sixth paragraphs can be easily charted as follows:

PITCHER	PITCH	DELIVERY
H.	Sl.	
	F.	U.
Miz.	Sc.	
Mil.		O.

Now, using the process of elimination and the information in the third paragraph, you can complete the chart like this:

PITCHER	PITCH	DELIVERY
H.	Sl.	T.
C.	F.	U.
Miz.	Sc.	S.
Mil.	C.	O.

All three questions can be answered by referring to this chart.

37. **C.** Read directly from the chart.

38. **A.** Choice A is impossible, because the curve ball pitcher and the pitcher who uses an overhand delivery are one and the same. This difficulty does not apply to any of the other choices.

39. **B.** Read directly from the chart.

40. **C.** The only difference between the "handouts" which the author deplores and the "subsidies" he favors is the words used to describe them. In one case, the words used are negatively loaded; in the other, they are positive, or at least neutral. Choice A is directly contrary to fact. Choices B and E are true, but of minor importance. Choice D is probably false; the reference in the argument to the thousands of widget industry jobs does indicate the significance of the industry for the U.S. economy.

41. **B.** The persons named in choices A, C, D, and E would all have an interest in the continuation of the widget industry subsidy program. The person named in choice B, however, would oppose outside help to an industry with which he or she is in direct competition.

42. **E.** In this argument, the first sentence states the conclusion; the second sentence states the evidence. However, there is no real connection between the two statements unless the assumption given in choice E is accepted as valid.

13 Test Yourself—Five Practice Tests

■ **5 Full-Length Model Tests**
■ **Answer Keys**
■ **Answer Explanations**

This chapter is designed to give you further experience in what to expect on the verbal, quantitative, and analytical ability sections of the Graduate Record Examination General Test. These tests should serve as a basis for analysis, which for some may signal the need for further drill before taking the other tests, and for others, may indicate that preparation for this part of the test is adequate. For the best results, take these tests only after reviewing your weak areas, found as a result of completing our Diagnostic Test.

Simulate actual test conditions as you take each test. Find a quiet place to work. Keep an accurate record of your time. If you complete a section before the suggested time has elapsed, check your work and do not start another section. Don't be worried, however, if you are not able to answer all questions in the allotted time. This may also occur on the actual test. No one is expected to know the answer to all questions on an aptitude test. Read the questions carefully. Work carefully and as rapidly as possible. Do not spend too much time on questions that seem difficult for you. If time permits, go back to the ones you left out.

Remember, there is no penalty imposed for guessing. Your score is determined by the number of correct answers. Therefore, it is to your advantage to answer every question—even if you have to guess. Of course, you better your odds of answering correctly if you eliminate as many incorrect answer choices as you can and then guess from the remaining choices.

After you have devoted the specified time allowed for each section of a model examination, refer to the correct answers furnished, determine your raw score, judge your progress, and plan further study. You should then carefully study the explanations for the correct answers of those questions that gave you difficulty. If you find that a particular topic needs further review, refer to the earlier part of the book where this topic is treated before attempting to take the next model test. If you follow this procedure, by the time you complete the last test in this chapter you will feel confident about your success.

Answer Sheet – MODEL TEST 1

Start with number 1 for each new section.
If a section has fewer than 38 questions, leave the extra spaces blank.

Section 1

1. Ⓐ Ⓑ Ⓒ Ⓓ Ⓔ	11. Ⓐ Ⓑ Ⓒ Ⓓ Ⓔ	21. Ⓐ Ⓑ Ⓒ Ⓓ Ⓔ	31. Ⓐ Ⓑ Ⓒ Ⓓ Ⓔ
2. Ⓐ Ⓑ Ⓒ Ⓓ Ⓔ	12. Ⓐ Ⓑ Ⓒ Ⓓ Ⓔ	22. Ⓐ Ⓑ Ⓒ Ⓓ Ⓔ	32. Ⓐ Ⓑ Ⓒ Ⓓ Ⓔ
3. Ⓐ Ⓑ Ⓒ Ⓓ Ⓔ	13. Ⓐ Ⓑ Ⓒ Ⓓ Ⓔ	23. Ⓐ Ⓑ Ⓒ Ⓓ Ⓔ	33. Ⓐ Ⓑ Ⓒ Ⓓ Ⓔ
4. Ⓐ Ⓑ Ⓒ Ⓓ Ⓔ	14. Ⓐ Ⓑ Ⓒ Ⓓ Ⓔ	24. Ⓐ Ⓑ Ⓒ Ⓓ Ⓔ	34. Ⓐ Ⓑ Ⓒ Ⓓ Ⓔ
5. Ⓐ Ⓑ Ⓒ Ⓓ Ⓔ	15. Ⓐ Ⓑ Ⓒ Ⓓ Ⓔ	25. Ⓐ Ⓑ Ⓒ Ⓓ Ⓔ	35. Ⓐ Ⓑ Ⓒ Ⓓ Ⓔ
6. Ⓐ Ⓑ Ⓒ Ⓓ Ⓔ	16. Ⓐ Ⓑ Ⓒ Ⓓ Ⓔ	26. Ⓐ Ⓑ Ⓒ Ⓓ Ⓔ	36. Ⓐ Ⓑ Ⓒ Ⓓ Ⓔ
7. Ⓐ Ⓑ Ⓒ Ⓓ Ⓔ	17. Ⓐ Ⓑ Ⓒ Ⓓ Ⓔ	27. Ⓐ Ⓑ Ⓒ Ⓓ Ⓔ	37. Ⓐ Ⓑ Ⓒ Ⓓ Ⓔ
8. Ⓐ Ⓑ Ⓒ Ⓓ Ⓔ	18. Ⓐ Ⓑ Ⓒ Ⓓ Ⓔ	28. Ⓐ Ⓑ Ⓒ Ⓓ Ⓔ	38. Ⓐ Ⓑ Ⓒ Ⓓ Ⓔ
9. Ⓐ Ⓑ Ⓒ Ⓓ Ⓔ	19. Ⓐ Ⓑ Ⓒ Ⓓ Ⓔ	29. Ⓐ Ⓑ Ⓒ Ⓓ Ⓔ	
10. Ⓐ Ⓑ Ⓒ Ⓓ Ⓔ	20. Ⓐ Ⓑ Ⓒ Ⓓ Ⓔ	30. Ⓐ Ⓑ Ⓒ Ⓓ Ⓔ	

Section 2

1. Ⓐ Ⓑ Ⓒ Ⓓ Ⓔ	11. Ⓐ Ⓑ Ⓒ Ⓓ Ⓔ	21. Ⓐ Ⓑ Ⓒ Ⓓ Ⓔ	31. Ⓐ Ⓑ Ⓒ Ⓓ Ⓔ
2. Ⓐ Ⓑ Ⓒ Ⓓ Ⓔ	12. Ⓐ Ⓑ Ⓒ Ⓓ Ⓔ	22. Ⓐ Ⓑ Ⓒ Ⓓ Ⓔ	32. Ⓐ Ⓑ Ⓒ Ⓓ Ⓔ
3. Ⓐ Ⓑ Ⓒ Ⓓ Ⓔ	13. Ⓐ Ⓑ Ⓒ Ⓓ Ⓔ	23. Ⓐ Ⓑ Ⓒ Ⓓ Ⓔ	33. Ⓐ Ⓑ Ⓒ Ⓓ Ⓔ
4. Ⓐ Ⓑ Ⓒ Ⓓ Ⓔ	14. Ⓐ Ⓑ Ⓒ Ⓓ Ⓔ	24. Ⓐ Ⓑ Ⓒ Ⓓ Ⓔ	34. Ⓐ Ⓑ Ⓒ Ⓓ Ⓔ
5. Ⓐ Ⓑ Ⓒ Ⓓ Ⓔ	15. Ⓐ Ⓑ Ⓒ Ⓓ Ⓔ	25. Ⓐ Ⓑ Ⓒ Ⓓ Ⓔ	35. Ⓐ Ⓑ Ⓒ Ⓓ Ⓔ
6. Ⓐ Ⓑ Ⓒ Ⓓ Ⓔ	16. Ⓐ Ⓑ Ⓒ Ⓓ Ⓔ	26. Ⓐ Ⓑ Ⓒ Ⓓ Ⓔ	36. Ⓐ Ⓑ Ⓒ Ⓓ Ⓔ
7. Ⓐ Ⓑ Ⓒ Ⓓ Ⓔ	17. Ⓐ Ⓑ Ⓒ Ⓓ Ⓔ	27. Ⓐ Ⓑ Ⓒ Ⓓ Ⓔ	37. Ⓐ Ⓑ Ⓒ Ⓓ Ⓔ
8. Ⓐ Ⓑ Ⓒ Ⓓ Ⓔ	18. Ⓐ Ⓑ Ⓒ Ⓓ Ⓔ	28. Ⓐ Ⓑ Ⓒ Ⓓ Ⓔ	38. Ⓐ Ⓑ Ⓒ Ⓓ Ⓔ
9. Ⓐ Ⓑ Ⓒ Ⓓ Ⓔ	19. Ⓐ Ⓑ Ⓒ Ⓓ Ⓔ	29. Ⓐ Ⓑ Ⓒ Ⓓ Ⓔ	
10. Ⓐ Ⓑ Ⓒ Ⓓ Ⓔ	20. Ⓐ Ⓑ Ⓒ Ⓓ Ⓔ	30. Ⓐ Ⓑ Ⓒ Ⓓ Ⓔ	

Section 3

1. Ⓐ Ⓑ Ⓒ Ⓓ Ⓔ	11. Ⓐ Ⓑ Ⓒ Ⓓ Ⓔ	21. Ⓐ Ⓑ Ⓒ Ⓓ Ⓔ	31. Ⓐ Ⓑ Ⓒ Ⓓ Ⓔ
2. Ⓐ Ⓑ Ⓒ Ⓓ Ⓔ	12. Ⓐ Ⓑ Ⓒ Ⓓ Ⓔ	22. Ⓐ Ⓑ Ⓒ Ⓓ Ⓔ	32. Ⓐ Ⓑ Ⓒ Ⓓ Ⓔ
3. Ⓐ Ⓑ Ⓒ Ⓓ Ⓔ	13. Ⓐ Ⓑ Ⓒ Ⓓ Ⓔ	23. Ⓐ Ⓑ Ⓒ Ⓓ Ⓔ	33. Ⓐ Ⓑ Ⓒ Ⓓ Ⓔ
4. Ⓐ Ⓑ Ⓒ Ⓓ Ⓔ	14. Ⓐ Ⓑ Ⓒ Ⓓ Ⓔ	24. Ⓐ Ⓑ Ⓒ Ⓓ Ⓔ	34. Ⓐ Ⓑ Ⓒ Ⓓ Ⓔ
5. Ⓐ Ⓑ Ⓒ Ⓓ Ⓔ	15. Ⓐ Ⓑ Ⓒ Ⓓ Ⓔ	25. Ⓐ Ⓑ Ⓒ Ⓓ Ⓔ	35. Ⓐ Ⓑ Ⓒ Ⓓ Ⓔ
6. Ⓐ Ⓑ Ⓒ Ⓓ Ⓔ	16. Ⓐ Ⓑ Ⓒ Ⓓ Ⓔ	26. Ⓐ Ⓑ Ⓒ Ⓓ Ⓔ	36. Ⓐ Ⓑ Ⓒ Ⓓ Ⓔ
7. Ⓐ Ⓑ Ⓒ Ⓓ Ⓔ	17. Ⓐ Ⓑ Ⓒ Ⓓ Ⓔ	27. Ⓐ Ⓑ Ⓒ Ⓓ Ⓔ	37. Ⓐ Ⓑ Ⓒ Ⓓ Ⓔ
8. Ⓐ Ⓑ Ⓒ Ⓓ Ⓔ	18. Ⓐ Ⓑ Ⓒ Ⓓ Ⓔ	28. Ⓐ Ⓑ Ⓒ Ⓓ Ⓔ	38. Ⓐ Ⓑ Ⓒ Ⓓ Ⓔ
9. Ⓐ Ⓑ Ⓒ Ⓓ Ⓔ	19. Ⓐ Ⓑ Ⓒ Ⓓ Ⓔ	29. Ⓐ Ⓑ Ⓒ Ⓓ Ⓔ	
10. Ⓐ Ⓑ Ⓒ Ⓓ Ⓔ	20. Ⓐ Ⓑ Ⓒ Ⓓ Ⓔ	30. Ⓐ Ⓑ Ⓒ Ⓓ Ⓔ	

Section 4

1. Ⓐ Ⓑ Ⓒ Ⓓ Ⓔ
2. Ⓐ Ⓑ Ⓒ Ⓓ Ⓔ
3. Ⓐ Ⓑ Ⓒ Ⓓ Ⓔ
4. Ⓐ Ⓑ Ⓒ Ⓓ Ⓔ
5. Ⓐ Ⓑ Ⓒ Ⓓ Ⓔ
6. Ⓐ Ⓑ Ⓒ Ⓓ Ⓔ
7. Ⓐ Ⓑ Ⓒ Ⓓ Ⓔ
8. Ⓐ Ⓑ Ⓒ Ⓓ Ⓔ
9. Ⓐ Ⓑ Ⓒ Ⓓ Ⓔ
10. Ⓐ Ⓑ Ⓒ Ⓓ Ⓔ
11. Ⓐ Ⓑ Ⓒ Ⓓ Ⓔ
12. Ⓐ Ⓑ Ⓒ Ⓓ Ⓔ
13. Ⓐ Ⓑ Ⓒ Ⓓ Ⓔ
14. Ⓐ Ⓑ Ⓒ Ⓓ Ⓔ
15. Ⓐ Ⓑ Ⓒ Ⓓ Ⓔ
16. Ⓐ Ⓑ Ⓒ Ⓓ Ⓔ
17. Ⓐ Ⓑ Ⓒ Ⓓ Ⓔ
18. Ⓐ Ⓑ Ⓒ Ⓓ Ⓔ
19. Ⓐ Ⓑ Ⓒ Ⓓ Ⓔ
20. Ⓐ Ⓑ Ⓒ Ⓓ Ⓔ
21. Ⓐ Ⓑ Ⓒ Ⓓ Ⓔ
22. Ⓐ Ⓑ Ⓒ Ⓓ Ⓔ
23. Ⓐ Ⓑ Ⓒ Ⓓ Ⓔ
24. Ⓐ Ⓑ Ⓒ Ⓓ Ⓔ
25. Ⓐ Ⓑ Ⓒ Ⓓ Ⓔ
26. Ⓐ Ⓑ Ⓒ Ⓓ Ⓔ
27. Ⓐ Ⓑ Ⓒ Ⓓ Ⓔ
28. Ⓐ Ⓑ Ⓒ Ⓓ Ⓔ
29. Ⓐ Ⓑ Ⓒ Ⓓ Ⓔ
30. Ⓐ Ⓑ Ⓒ Ⓓ Ⓔ
31. Ⓐ Ⓑ Ⓒ Ⓓ Ⓔ
32. Ⓐ Ⓑ Ⓒ Ⓓ Ⓔ
33. Ⓐ Ⓑ Ⓒ Ⓓ Ⓔ
34. Ⓐ Ⓑ Ⓒ Ⓓ Ⓔ
35. Ⓐ Ⓑ Ⓒ Ⓓ Ⓔ
36. Ⓐ Ⓑ Ⓒ Ⓓ Ⓔ
37. Ⓐ Ⓑ Ⓒ Ⓓ Ⓔ
38. Ⓐ Ⓑ Ⓒ Ⓓ Ⓔ

Section 5

1. Ⓐ Ⓑ Ⓒ Ⓓ Ⓔ
2. Ⓐ Ⓑ Ⓒ Ⓓ Ⓔ
3. Ⓐ Ⓑ Ⓒ Ⓓ Ⓔ
4. Ⓐ Ⓑ Ⓒ Ⓓ Ⓔ
5. Ⓐ Ⓑ Ⓒ Ⓓ Ⓔ
6. Ⓐ Ⓑ Ⓒ Ⓓ Ⓔ
7. Ⓐ Ⓑ Ⓒ Ⓓ Ⓔ
8. Ⓐ Ⓑ Ⓒ Ⓓ Ⓔ
9. Ⓐ Ⓑ Ⓒ Ⓓ Ⓔ
10. Ⓐ Ⓑ Ⓒ Ⓓ Ⓔ
11. Ⓐ Ⓑ Ⓒ Ⓓ Ⓔ
12. Ⓐ Ⓑ Ⓒ Ⓓ Ⓔ
13. Ⓐ Ⓑ Ⓒ Ⓓ Ⓔ
14. Ⓐ Ⓑ Ⓒ Ⓓ Ⓔ
15. Ⓐ Ⓑ Ⓒ Ⓓ Ⓔ
16. Ⓐ Ⓑ Ⓒ Ⓓ Ⓔ
17. Ⓐ Ⓑ Ⓒ Ⓓ Ⓔ
18. Ⓐ Ⓑ Ⓒ Ⓓ Ⓔ
19. Ⓐ Ⓑ Ⓒ Ⓓ Ⓔ
20. Ⓐ Ⓑ Ⓒ Ⓓ Ⓔ
21. Ⓐ Ⓑ Ⓒ Ⓓ Ⓔ
22. Ⓐ Ⓑ Ⓒ Ⓓ Ⓔ
23. Ⓐ Ⓑ Ⓒ Ⓓ Ⓔ
24. Ⓐ Ⓑ Ⓒ Ⓓ Ⓔ
25. Ⓐ Ⓑ Ⓒ Ⓓ Ⓔ
26. Ⓐ Ⓑ Ⓒ Ⓓ Ⓔ
27. Ⓐ Ⓑ Ⓒ Ⓓ Ⓔ
28. Ⓐ Ⓑ Ⓒ Ⓓ Ⓔ
29. Ⓐ Ⓑ Ⓒ Ⓓ Ⓔ
30. Ⓐ Ⓑ Ⓒ Ⓓ Ⓔ
31. Ⓐ Ⓑ Ⓒ Ⓓ Ⓔ
32. Ⓐ Ⓑ Ⓒ Ⓓ Ⓔ
33. Ⓐ Ⓑ Ⓒ Ⓓ Ⓔ
34. Ⓐ Ⓑ Ⓒ Ⓓ Ⓔ
35. Ⓐ Ⓑ Ⓒ Ⓓ Ⓔ
36. Ⓐ Ⓑ Ⓒ Ⓓ Ⓔ
37. Ⓐ Ⓑ Ⓒ Ⓓ Ⓔ
38. Ⓐ Ⓑ Ⓒ Ⓓ Ⓔ

Section 6

1. Ⓐ Ⓑ Ⓒ Ⓓ Ⓔ
2. Ⓐ Ⓑ Ⓒ Ⓓ Ⓔ
3. Ⓐ Ⓑ Ⓒ Ⓓ Ⓔ
4. Ⓐ Ⓑ Ⓒ Ⓓ Ⓔ
5. Ⓐ Ⓑ Ⓒ Ⓓ Ⓔ
6. Ⓐ Ⓑ Ⓒ Ⓓ Ⓔ
7. Ⓐ Ⓑ Ⓒ Ⓓ Ⓔ
8. Ⓐ Ⓑ Ⓒ Ⓓ Ⓔ
9. Ⓐ Ⓑ Ⓒ Ⓓ Ⓔ
10. Ⓐ Ⓑ Ⓒ Ⓓ Ⓔ
11. Ⓐ Ⓑ Ⓒ Ⓓ Ⓔ
12. Ⓐ Ⓑ Ⓒ Ⓓ Ⓔ
13. Ⓐ Ⓑ Ⓒ Ⓓ Ⓔ
14. Ⓐ Ⓑ Ⓒ Ⓓ Ⓔ
15. Ⓐ Ⓑ Ⓒ Ⓓ Ⓔ
16. Ⓐ Ⓑ Ⓒ Ⓓ Ⓔ
17. Ⓐ Ⓑ Ⓒ Ⓓ Ⓔ
18. Ⓐ Ⓑ Ⓒ Ⓓ Ⓔ
19. Ⓐ Ⓑ Ⓒ Ⓓ Ⓔ
20. Ⓐ Ⓑ Ⓒ Ⓓ Ⓔ
21. Ⓐ Ⓑ Ⓒ Ⓓ Ⓔ
22. Ⓐ Ⓑ Ⓒ Ⓓ Ⓔ
23. Ⓐ Ⓑ Ⓒ Ⓓ Ⓔ
24. Ⓐ Ⓑ Ⓒ Ⓓ Ⓔ
25. Ⓐ Ⓑ Ⓒ Ⓓ Ⓔ
26. Ⓐ Ⓑ Ⓒ Ⓓ Ⓔ
27. Ⓐ Ⓑ Ⓒ Ⓓ Ⓔ
28. Ⓐ Ⓑ Ⓒ Ⓓ Ⓔ
29. Ⓐ Ⓑ Ⓒ Ⓓ Ⓔ
30. Ⓐ Ⓑ Ⓒ Ⓓ Ⓔ
31. Ⓐ Ⓑ Ⓒ Ⓓ Ⓔ
32. Ⓐ Ⓑ Ⓒ Ⓓ Ⓔ
33. Ⓐ Ⓑ Ⓒ Ⓓ Ⓔ
34. Ⓐ Ⓑ Ⓒ Ⓓ Ⓔ
35. Ⓐ Ⓑ Ⓒ Ⓓ Ⓔ
36. Ⓐ Ⓑ Ⓒ Ⓓ Ⓔ
37. Ⓐ Ⓑ Ⓒ Ⓓ Ⓔ
38. Ⓐ Ⓑ Ⓒ Ⓓ Ⓔ

Section 7

1. Ⓐ Ⓑ Ⓒ Ⓓ Ⓔ
2. Ⓐ Ⓑ Ⓒ Ⓓ Ⓔ
3. Ⓐ Ⓑ Ⓒ Ⓓ Ⓔ
4. Ⓐ Ⓑ Ⓒ Ⓓ Ⓔ
5. Ⓐ Ⓑ Ⓒ Ⓓ Ⓔ
6. Ⓐ Ⓑ Ⓒ Ⓓ Ⓔ
7. Ⓐ Ⓑ Ⓒ Ⓓ Ⓔ
8. Ⓐ Ⓑ Ⓒ Ⓓ Ⓔ
9. Ⓐ Ⓑ Ⓒ Ⓓ Ⓔ
10. Ⓐ Ⓑ Ⓒ Ⓓ Ⓔ
11. Ⓐ Ⓑ Ⓒ Ⓓ Ⓔ
12. Ⓐ Ⓑ Ⓒ Ⓓ Ⓔ
13. Ⓐ Ⓑ Ⓒ Ⓓ Ⓔ
14. Ⓐ Ⓑ Ⓒ Ⓓ Ⓔ
15. Ⓐ Ⓑ Ⓒ Ⓓ Ⓔ
16. Ⓐ Ⓑ Ⓒ Ⓓ Ⓔ
17. Ⓐ Ⓑ Ⓒ Ⓓ Ⓔ
18. Ⓐ Ⓑ Ⓒ Ⓓ Ⓔ
19. Ⓐ Ⓑ Ⓒ Ⓓ Ⓔ
20. Ⓐ Ⓑ Ⓒ Ⓓ Ⓔ
21. Ⓐ Ⓑ Ⓒ Ⓓ Ⓔ
22. Ⓐ Ⓑ Ⓒ Ⓓ Ⓔ
23. Ⓐ Ⓑ Ⓒ Ⓓ Ⓔ
24. Ⓐ Ⓑ Ⓒ Ⓓ Ⓔ
25. Ⓐ Ⓑ Ⓒ Ⓓ Ⓔ
26. Ⓐ Ⓑ Ⓒ Ⓓ Ⓔ
27. Ⓐ Ⓑ Ⓒ Ⓓ Ⓔ
28. Ⓐ Ⓑ Ⓒ Ⓓ Ⓔ
29. Ⓐ Ⓑ Ⓒ Ⓓ Ⓔ
30. Ⓐ Ⓑ Ⓒ Ⓓ Ⓔ
31. Ⓐ Ⓑ Ⓒ Ⓓ Ⓔ
32. Ⓐ Ⓑ Ⓒ Ⓓ Ⓔ
33. Ⓐ Ⓑ Ⓒ Ⓓ Ⓔ
34. Ⓐ Ⓑ Ⓒ Ⓓ Ⓔ
35. Ⓐ Ⓑ Ⓒ Ⓓ Ⓔ
36. Ⓐ Ⓑ Ⓒ Ⓓ Ⓔ
37. Ⓐ Ⓑ Ⓒ Ⓓ Ⓔ
38. Ⓐ Ⓑ Ⓒ Ⓓ Ⓔ

MODEL TEST 1

Directions: Each sentence below has one or two blanks, each blank indicating that something has been omitted. Beneath the sentence are five lettered words or sets of words. Choose the word or set of words for each blank that best fits the meaning of the sentence as a whole.

1. To the cynic, there are no wholly altruistic, unselfish acts; every human deed is ------- an ulterior selfish motive.

   (A) independent of
   (B) emulated by
   (C) disguised as
   (D) founded upon
   (E) similar to

2. Like the theory of evolution, the big-bang model of the universe's formation has undergone modification and -------, but it has ------- all serious challenges.

   (A) alteration...confirmed
   (B) refinement...resisted
   (C) transformation...ignored
   (D) evaluation...acknowledged
   (E) refutation...misdirected

3. We have in America a ------- speech that is neither American, Oxford English, nor colloquial English, but ------- of all three.

   (A) motley...an enhancement
   (B) hybrid...a combination
   (C) nasal...a blend
   (D) mangled...a medley
   (E) formal...a patchwork

4. It has been said that printing does as much harm as good, since it gives us bad books as well as good ones and ------- falsehood and error no less than -------.

   (A) displays...folly
   (B) flaunts...ignorance
   (C) betrays...treachery
   (D) demonstrates...pedantry
   (E) propagates...knowledge

5. A university training enables a graduate to see things as they are, to go right to the point, to disentangle a ------- of thought.

   (A) line
   (B) strand
   (C) mass
   (D) plethora
   (E) skein

6. Rather than portraying Joseph II as a radical reformer whose reign was strikingly enlightened, the play *Amadeus* depicts him as ------- thinker, too wedded to orthodox theories of musical composition to appreciate an artist of Mozart's genius.

   (A) a revolutionary
   (B) an idiosyncratic
   (C) a politic
   (D) a doctrinaire
   (E) an iconoclastic

7. While ------- in his own approach to philosophy, the scholar was, illogically, ------- his colleagues who averred that a seeker of knowledge must be free to select such doctrines as pleased him in every school.

   (A) indiscriminate...supportive of
   (B) eclectic...intolerant of
   (C) speculative...cordial to
   (D) problematical...dismissive of
   (E) theoretic...impatient with

Directions: In each of the following questions, a related pair of words or phrases is followed by five lettered pairs of words or phrases. Select the lettered pair that best expresses a relationship similar to that expressed in the original pair.

8. FANS : BLEACHERS::
   (A) cheerleaders : pompoms
   (B) audience : seats
   (C) team : goalposts
   (D) conductor : podium
   (E) referee : decision

9. AUGER : BORE::
   (A) awl : flatten
   (B) bit : grind
   (C) plane : smooth
   (D) scythe : mash
   (E) mallet : pierce

10. CHAMELEON : HERPETOLOGIST::
   (A) fungi : ecologist
   (B) salmon : ichthyologist
   (C) mongoose : ornithologist
   (D) oriole : virologist
   (E) aphid : etymologist

11. SCURRY : MOVE::
    (A) chant : sing
    (B) chatter : talk
    (C) carry : lift
    (D) sleep : drowse
    (E) limp : walk

12. SONG : CYCLE::
    (A) waltz : dance
    (B) tune : arrangement
    (C) sonnet : sequence
    (D) agenda : meeting
    (E) cadenza : aria

13. OBDURATE : FLEXIBILITY::
    (A) accurate : perception
    (B) turbid : roughness
    (C) principled : fallibility
    (D) diaphanous : transparency
    (E) adamant : submissiveness

14. SARTORIAL : TAILOR::
    (A) pictorial : spectator
    (B) thespian : designer
    (C) histrionic : singer
    (D) rhetorical : questioner
    (E) terpsichorean : dancer

15. SKIRT : ISSUE::
    (A) vest : interest
    (B) rig : wager
    (C) dodge : encounter
    (D) sweep : election
    (E) mask : purpose

16. FEUD : ACRIMONY::
    (A) scuffle : confusion
    (B) crusade : heresy
    (C) duel : brevity
    (D) scrimmage : sparring
    (E) siege : vulnerability

Directions: Each passage in this group is followed by questions based on its content. After reading a passage, choose the best answer to each question. Answer all questions following a passage on the basis of what is stated or implied in the passage.

(This passage was written prior to 1950.)

In the long run a government will always encroach upon freedom to the extent to which it has the power to do so; this is almost a natural law of politics, since, whatever the intentions of the men who exercise political power, the sheer momentum of government leads to a constant pressure upon the liberties of the citizen. But in many countries society has responded by throwing up its own defenses in the shape of social classes or organized corporations which, enjoying economic power and popular support, have been able to set limits to the scope of action of the executive. Such, for example, in England was the origin of all our liberties—won from government by the stand first of the feudal nobility, then of churches and political parties, and latterly of trade unions, commercial organizations, and the societies for promoting various causes. Even in European lands which were arbitrarily ruled, the powers of the monarchy, though absolute in theory, were in their exercise checked in a similar fashion. Indeed the fascist dictatorships of today are the first truly tyrannical governments which western Europe has known for centuries, and they have been rendered possible only because on coming to power they destroyed all forms of social organization which were in any way rivals to the state.

17. The passage can most accurately be described as a discussion of the

    (A) limited powers of monarchies
    (B) ideal of liberal government
    (C) functions of trade unions
    (D) ruthless methods of dictators
    (E) safeguards of individual liberty

18. According to the passage, the natural relationship between government and individual liberty is one of

    (A) marked indifference
    (B) secret collusion
    (C) inherent opposition
    (D) moderate complicity
    (E) fundamental interdependence

19. Fascist dictatorships differ from monarchies of recent times in

    (A) setting limits to their scope of action
    (B) effecting results by sheer momentum
    (C) rivaling the state in power
    (D) exerting constant pressure on liberties
    (E) eradicating people's organizations

20. The passage suggests which of the following about fascist dictatorships?

    (A) They represent a more efficient form of the executive.
    (B) Their rise to power came about through an accident of history.
    (C) They mark a regression to earlier despotic forms of government.
    (D) Despite superficial dissimilarities, they are in essence like absolute monarchies.
    (E) They maintain their dominance by rechanneling opposing forces in new directions.

The bird egg is a self-contained life-support system for the developing bird embryo. All the nutrients, minerals, energy sources and water utilized by the embryo during its incubation are
(5) already present in the freshly laid egg, so that the egg requires only warming by the parents and periodic turning to prevent the adhesion of the embryo to the shell membranes. Still, the egg lacks one crucial requirement: oxygen, which drives the met-
(10) abolic machinery of the embryonic cells so that they can execute the complex maneuvers of development. How does the egg breathe, taking up oxygen from the surrounding atmosphere and discharging carbon dioxide, the waste product of
(15) respiration?

Gas exchange is usually associated with the periodic inhalation of a fluid medium (air or water), which carries oxygen to the capillaries of the lungs or the gills and removes carbon dioxide from the
(20) respiratory organ with each exhalation. The lungs or the gills are driven by muscles whose rate of pumping is determined by metabolic demand and controlled by the nervous system. Yet the eggs of birds and other organisms (such as insects, spiders,
(25) amphibians and reptiles) show no respiratory movements, and there are no air currents within the egg that could transport oxygen to the capillaries of the growing embryo. Instead the egg "breathes" by diffusion through thousands of microscopic pores
(30) in the shell.

Gas moves through the pores by the passive process of diffusion: the tendency for a high concentration of a molecule to run downhill to an area of lower concentration. Diffusion takes place
(35) because of the kinetic energy of gas molecules and does not require the direct expenditure of metabolic energy by the embryo: the lower concentration of oxygen inside the egg brings new oxygen in through the pores from the outside, where the con-
(40) centration is higher. Conversely, the concentration of carbon dioxide inside the egg causes those molecules to diffuse toward the outside, where there are essentially none. These diffusion processes are governed by the available pore area of the shell, the
(45) length of the pores and the concentration differences of the gases diffusing across the shell.

The water content of the air within the egg is greater than that of the air outside it, and so the pores will also allow water molecules (which are
(50) smaller than oxygen molecules) to diffuse out. Animals have evolved many specialized adaptations for conserving water, but bird eggs seem designed to lose it at a controlled rate. Most of the energy needed for embryonic development is taken from
(55) the fat stores of the yolk, and for every gram of fat burned an almost equal mass of metabolic water is generated. Therefore the relative water content of the egg will increase during incubation unless water is lost. If the relative water content at hatch-
(60) ing is to equal that of the freshly laid egg, about 15 percent of the initial mass of the egg must be lost as water. As breeders of domestic fowl well know, this amount of water loss is essential for successful hatching.

21. The passage is primarily concerned with

(A) explaining the origin of passive diffusion as a method of respiration
(B) explaining difficulties involved in cultivating domestic fowl
(C) explaining the processes of gas and water diffusion in eggs
(D) distinguishing between passive diffusion and active respiration
(E) defining the concept of passive diffusion and explaining its uses

22. A necessary ingredient in the eggshell's suitability for gas exchange is its

(A) fragility
(B) opacity
(C) permeability
(D) adhesiveness
(E) rotundity

23. The passage contains information that would answer which of the following questions about fowl-breeding?

I. What function does turning the fertilized egg serve in the hatching process?
II. Why must the egg shed water during the hatching process?
III. What occurs when the amount of water loss during hatching exceeds 15 percent of the egg's initial mass?

(A) I only
(B) II only
(C) I and II only
(D) II and III only
(E) I, II, and III

24. The passage would be most likely to appear in

(A) an agricultural research report focused on the history of fowl-breeding practices in the United States
(B) a pamphlet designed to introduce novice breeders of domestic fowl to the advantages of current techniques
(C) a congressional report urging the appropriation of funds for research into needed improvements in egg-hatching
(D) a scientific journal article highlighting biochemical and physical principles underlying common phenomena
(E) an ornithological survey of the breeding habits of rare species of fowl

25. According to the passage, which of the following statements is true of the extent of water loss by the egg during the hatching process?

(A) It is regulated by a specialized adaptation for conserving water.
(B) It exceeds the initial mass of the egg by 15 percent.
(C) It should compensate for the egg's entire water gain during incubation.
(D) It should amount to 15 percent of the egg's water gain during incubation.
(E) It is greatest when the egg is freshly laid.

26. It can be inferred from the passage that adhesion of the embryo to the shell membranes represents

    (A) a necessary stage in embryonic development
    (B) a method of discharging carbon dioxide into the environment
    (C) a potential threat to the well-being of the embryo
    (D) a cause of water loss during incubation
    (E) a tendency for the embryo to utilize additional nutrient sources

27. The author's style can best be described as

    (A) hyperbolic
    (B) sentimental
    (C) naturalistic
    (D) esoteric
    (E) objective

Directions: Each question below consists of a word printed in capital letters, followed by five lettered words or phrases. Choose the lettered word or phrase that is most nearly *opposite* in meaning to the word in capital letters.

Since some of the questions require you to distinguish fine shades of meaning, be sure to consider all the choices before deciding which one is best.

28. DISREGARD:
    (A) admit
    (B) evade
    (C) heed
    (D) improve
    (E) prevent

29. VERACITY:
    (A) uncertainty
    (B) mendacity
    (C) plausibility
    (D) intuition
    (E) opposition

30. BEDECK:
    (A) erect
    (B) awake
    (C) isolate
    (D) cleanse
    (E) strip

31. SPURIOUS:
    (A) cautious
    (B) fantastic
    (C) modest
    (D) genuine
    (E) pertinent

32. ESTRANGE:
    (A) reconcile
    (B) feign
    (C) perplex
    (D) arbitrate
    (E) commiserate

33. PROVIDENT:
    (A) manifest
    (B) prodigal
    (C) thankful
    (D) tidy
    (E) refuted

34. CAPITULATE:
    (A) initiate
    (B) defame
    (C) exonerate
    (D) resist
    (E) repeat

35. INDIGENOUS:
    (A) affluent
    (B) parochial
    (C) alien
    (D) serene
    (E) inimical

36. SALUBRITY:
    (A) unwholesomeness
    (B) insolvency
    (C) dissatisfaction
    (D) diffidence
    (E) rigidity

37. QUAIL:
    (A) hover
    (B) tolerate
    (C) arouse enmity
    (D) become resolute
    (E) abstain from action

38. TANTAMOUNT:
    (A) not negotiable
    (B) not equivalent
    (C) not ambitious
    (D) not evident
    (E) not relevant

S T O P

IF YOU FINISH BEFORE TIME IS CALLED, YOU MAY CHECK YOUR WORK ON THIS SECTION ONLY.
DO NOT WORK ON ANY OTHER SECTION IN THE TEST.

SECTION 2

Time—30 Minutes

38 Questions

Directions: Each sentence below has one or two blanks, each blank indicating that something has been omitted. Beneath the sentence are five lettered words or sets of words. Choose the word or set of words for each blank that *best* fits the meaning of the sentence as a whole.

1. The simplest animals are those whose bodies are simplest in structure and which do the things done by all living animals, such as eating, breathing, moving, and feeling, in the most ------- way.

    (A) haphazard
    (B) bizarre
    (C) primitive
    (D) advantageous
    (E) unique

2. Although weeks remain for concessions to be made and for new approaches to be attempted, negotiations have reached such a state that management and union leaders are ------- that their differences can no longer be reconciled.

    (A) encouraged
    (B) bewildered
    (C) apprehensive
    (D) relieved
    (E) skeptical

3. Not only the ------- are fooled by propaganda; we can all be misled if we are not -------.

    (A) ignorant...cynical
    (B) gullible...wary
    (C) credulous...headstrong
    (D) illiterate...mature
    (E) fatuous...intelligent

4. When those whom he had injured accused him of being a -------, he retorted curtly that he had never been a quack.

    (A) libertine
    (B) sycophant
    (C) charlatan
    (D) plagiarist
    (E) reprobate

5. There is an essential ------- in human gestures, and when someone raises the palms of his hands together, we do not know whether it is to bury himself in prayer or to throw himself into the sea.

    (A) economy
    (B) dignity
    (C) insincerity
    (D) reverence
    (E) ambiguity

6. It is somewhat paradoxical that, nine times out of ten, the coarse word is the word that ------- an evil and the ------- word is the word that excuses it.

    (A) condemns...refined
    (B) exonerates...vulgar
    (C) contradicts...crass
    (D) condones...genteel
    (E) admits...clever

7. It has been Virginia Woolf's peculiar destiny to be declared annoyingly feminine by male critics at the same time that she has been ------- by women interested in the sexual revolution as not really eligible to be ------- their ranks.

    (A) lauded...enlisted in
    (B) emulated...counted among
    (C) neglected...helpful to
    (D) dismissed...drafted into
    (E) excoriated...discharged from

Directions: In each of the following questions, a related pair of words or phrases is followed by five lettered pairs of words or phrases. Select the lettered pair that best expresses a relationship similar to that expressed in the original pair.

8. DROPCLOTH : FURNITURE::
    (A) banner : flagpole
    (B) towel : rack
    (C) pillow : bedding
    (D) curtain : theatre
    (E) apron : clothing

9. ARCHIPELAGO : ISLAND::
    (A) arbor : bower
    (B) garden : flower
    (C) mountain : valley
    (D) sand : dune
    (E) constellation : star

10. CROW : BOASTFUL::
    (A) smirk : witty
    (B) conceal : sly
    (C) pout : sulky
    (D) blush : coarse
    (E) bluster : unhappy

11. ASCETIC : SELF-DENIAL::
    (A) nomad : dissipation
    (B) miser : affluence
    (C) zealot : fanaticism
    (D) renegade : loyalty
    (E) athlete : stamina

12. CAMOUFLAGE : DISCERN::
—(A) encipher : comprehend
(B) adorn : admire
(C) magnify : observe
(D) renovate : construct
(E) embroider : unravel

13. SEER : PROPHECY::
(A) mentor : reward
—(B) sage : wisdom
(C) pilgrim : diligence
(D) diplomat : flattery
(E) virtuoso : penance

14. BRACKET : SHELF::
(A) hammer : anvil
(B) girder : rivet
—(C) strut : rafter
(D) valve : pipe
(E) bucket : well

15. TAXONOMY : CLASSIFICATION::
—(A) etymology : derivation
(B) autonomy : authorization
(C) economy : rationalization
(D) tautology : justification
(E) ecology : urbanization

16. BRUSQUE : UNCEREMONIOUSNESS::
(A) audacious : trepidation
—(B) obstinate : intractability
(C) pert : improvidence
(D) curt : loquacity
(E) officious : inattentiveness

Directions: Each passage in this group is followed by questions based on its content. After reading a passage, choose the best answer to each question. Answer all questions following a passage on the basis of what is stated or implied in the passage.

As the works of dozens of women writers have been rescued from what E.P. Thompson calls "the enormous condescension of posterity," and consid-
(5) ered in relation to each other, the lost continent of the female tradition has risen like Atlantis from the sea of English literature. It is now becoming clear that, contrary to Mill's theory, women have had a literature of their own all along. The woman novel-
(10) ist, according to Vineta Colby, was "really neither single nor anomalous," but she was also more than a "register and spokesman for her age." She was part of a tradition that had its origins before her age, and has carried on through our own.
(15) Many literary historians have begun to reinterpret and revise the study of women writers. Ellen Moers sees women's literature as an international movement, "apart from, but hardly subordinate to the mainstream: an undercurrent, rapid and power-
(20) ful. This 'movement' began in the late eighteenth century, was multinational, and produced some of the greatest literary works of two centuries, as well as most of the lucrative pot-boilers." Patricia Meyer Spacks, in *The Female Imagination*, finds that "for readily discernible historical reasons
(25) women have characteristically concerned themselves with matters more or less peripheral to male concerns, or at least slightly skewed from them. The differences between traditional female preoccupations and roles and male ones make a differ-
(30) ence in female writing." Many other critics are beginning to agree that when we look at women writers collectively we can see an imaginative continuum, the recurrence of certain patterns, themes, problems, and images from generation to
(35) generation.
This book is an effort to describe the female lit-

erary tradition in the English novel from the generation of the Brontës to the present day, and to show how the development of this tradition is similar to
(40) the development of any literary subculture. Women have generally been regarded as "sociological chameleons," taking on the class, lifestyle, and culture of their male relatives. It can, however, be argued that women themselves have constituted a subcul-
(45) ture within the framework of a larger society, and have been unified by values, conventions, experiences, and behaviors impinging on each individual. It is important to see the female literary tradition in these broad terms, in relation to the wider evolu-
(50) tion of women's self-awareness and to the ways any minority group finds its direction of self-expression relative to a dominant society, because we cannot show a pattern of deliberate progress and accumulation. It is true, as Ellen Moers writes,
(55) that "women studied with a special closeness the works written by their own sex"; in terms of influences, borrowings, and affinities, the tradition is strongly marked. But it is also full of holes and hiatuses, because of what Germaine Greer calls the
(60) "phenomenon of the transience of female literary fame"; "almost uninterruptedly since the Interregnum, a small group of women have enjoyed dazzling literary prestige during their own lifetimes, only to vanish without trace from the records of
(65) posterity." Thus each generation of women writers has found itself, in a sense, without a history, forced to rediscover the past anew, forging again and again the consciousness of their sex. Given this perpetual disruption, and also the self-hatred that
(70) has alienated women writers from a sense of collective identity, it does not seem possible to speak of a movement.

17. The author of this passage implies that a significant element furthering the woman writer's awareness of a female literary tradition is her

(A) vulnerability to male deprecation
(B) assimilation of the values of her subculture
(C) rejection of monetary gain as an acceptable goal
(D) ability to adopt the culture of the dominant society
(E) sense that fame and prestige are evanescent

18. In the second paragraph of the passage the author's attitude toward the literary critics cited can best be described as one of

(A) irony
(B) ambivalence
(C) disparagement
(D) receptiveness
(E) awe

19. The passage supplies information for answering which of the following questions?

(A) Does the author believe the female literary tradition to be richer in depth than its masculine counterpart?
(B) Are women psychological as well as sociological chameleons?
(C) Does Moers share Greer's concern over the ephemeral nature of female literary renown?
(D) What patterns, themes, images, and problems recur sufficiently in the work of women writers to belong to the female imaginative continuum?
(E) Did Mills acknowledge the existence of a separate female literary tradition?

20. The passage suggests that it might be possible to speak of an actual female literary movement were it not for

(A) masculine suppression of feminist criticism
(B) female lack of artistic autonomy
(C) the ephemeral nature of female literary renown
(D) the absence of proper contemporary role models
(E) female rejection of disruptive male influences

21. In the first paragraph, the author makes use of all the following techniques EXCEPT

(A) extended metaphor
(B) enumeration and classification
(C) classical allusion
(D) direct quotation
(E) comparison and contrast

22. Which of the following words could best be substituted for "forging" (line 67) without substantially changing the author's meaning?

(A) counterfeiting
(B) creating
(C) exploring
(D) diverting
(E) straining

23. It can be inferred from the passage that the author considers Moers' work to be

(A) fallacious and misleading
(B) scholarly and definitive
(C) admirable, but inaccurate in certain of its conclusions
(D) popular, but irrelevant to mainstream female literary criticism
(E) idiosyncratic, but of importance historically

24. Which of the following would be the most appropriate title for the passage?

(A) A Unique Phenomenon: Nineteenth and Twentieth Century Feminine Literary Movements
(B) A Literature of Their Own: The Female Literary Tradition
(C) Adaptive Coloration: Feminine Adoption of Masculine Cultural Criteria
(D) The Emergence of the Contemporary Women's Novel
(E) Fame Versus Fortune: The Dilemma of the Woman Writer

Among the many whimsical terms introduced into the physics of elementary particles in the past two decades — such as "quark," "color," and "charm"—perhaps the most aptly chosen is "gluon." The gluon is conjectured to bind together the particles called quarks, thereby forming protons, neutrons, pions and all the other entities that are classified as hadrons, or strongly interacting particles. The adhesive strength of the gluon is thought to be so great that a quark cannot be extracted from a hadron no matter what force is brought to bear on it. Moreover, the gluon itself also seems to be permanently confined: just as the quarks cannot be prized apart, it is impossible to squeeze a drop of the glue out from between the quarks. In spite of this recalcitrance there is substantial evidence for the existence of quarks, and now, thanks to a series of experiments, preliminary evidence for the existence of gluons.

25. Which of the following would be the most appropriate title for the passage?

(A) Linguistic Implications of Particle Physics
(B) Trends in Physics Research: Extracting the Gluon
(C) Quark Glue: The Particle That Binds
(D) The Influence of the Gluon on Particle Interactions
(E) The Impossible Dream: Obstacles to Proving the Existence of Gluons

26. The author refers to charms and quarks (line 3) primarily in order to

(A) demonstrate the similarity between these particles and the gluon
(B) make a distinction between apposite and inapposite terminology
(C) offer an objection to suggestions of similar frivolous names
(D) provide illustrations of idiosyncratic nomenclature in contemporary physics
(E) cite preliminary experimental evidence supporting the existence of gluons

27. The tone of the author's discussion of the neologisms coined by physicists is one of

   (A) scientific detachment
   (B) moderate indignation
   (C) marked derision
   (D) amused approbation
   (E) qualified skepticism

Directions: Each question below consists of a word
printed in capital letters, followed by five lettered words
or phrases. Choose the lettered word or phrase that is
most nearly opposite in meaning to the word in capital
letters.

Since some of the questions require you to distinguish
fine shades of meaning, be sure to consider all the
choices before deciding which one is best.

28. RECTIFY:
   (A) apologize
   (B) sanctify
   (C) make worse
   (D) rule illegal
   (E) rebuke

29. APEX:
   (A) smallest amount
   (B) clearest view
   (C) lowest point
   (D) broad plateau
   (E) bright color

30. PROSAIC:
   (A) imaginative
   (B) contradictory
   (C) hesitant
   (D) redundant
   (E) disorderly

31. DISSONANCE:
   (A) amalgamation
   (B) harmony
   (C) neutrality
   (D) resolution
   (E) proximity

32. DOLTISH:
   (A) immature
   (B) coarse
   (C) clever
   (D) stable
   (E) genial

33. CHAGRIN:
   (A) frown
   (B) disguise
   (C) make indifferent
   (D) make aware
   (E) please

34. DISINGENUOUS:
   (A) naive
   (B) accurate
   (C) hostile
   (D) witty
   (E) polite

35. RECALCITRANCE:
   (A) dependability
   (B) submissiveness
   (C) apathy
   (D) incongruity
   (E) eloquence

36. FECUNDITY:
   (A) consideration
   (B) comprehensibility
   (C) barrenness
   (D) gravity
   (E) sanity

37. LUGUBRIOUS:
   (A) transparent
   (B) sedulous
   (C) soporific
   (D) jocose
   (E) querulous

38. ANIMUS:
   (A) hospitality
   (B) probity
   (C) anonymity
   (D) amity
   (E) insularity

S T O P

**IF YOU FINISH BEFORE TIME IS CALLED, YOU MAY CHECK YOUR WORK ON THIS SECTION ONLY.
DO NOT WORK ON ANY OTHER SECTION IN THE TEST.**

SECTION 3

Time—30 minutes

30 Questions

Numbers: All numbers used are real numbers.

Figures: Position of points, angles, regions, etc. can be assumed to be in the order shown; and angle measures can be assumed to be positive.

Lines shown as straight can be assumed to be straight.

Figures can be assumed to lie in a plane unless otherwise indicated.

Figures that accompany questions are intended to provide information useful in answering the questions. However, unless a note states that a figure is drawn to scale, you should solve these problems NOT by estimating sizes by sight or by measurement, but by using your knowledge of mathematics (see Example 2 below).

Directions: Each of the Questions 1-15 consists of two quantities, one in Column A and one in Column B. You are to compare the two quantities and choose

A if the quantity in Column A is greater;
B if the quantity in Column B is greater;
C if the two quantities are equal;
D if the relationship cannot be determined from the information given.

Note: Since there are only four choices, NEVER MARK (E).

Common Information: In a question, information concerning one or both of the quantities to be compared is centered above the two columns. A symbol that appears in both columns represents the same thing in Column A as it does in Column B.

	Column A	Column B	Sample Answers
Example 1:	2×6	$2 + 6$	● Ⓑ Ⓒ Ⓓ Ⓔ

Examples 2-4 refer to △ PQR.

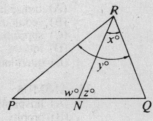

	Column A	Column B	Sample Answers
Example 2:	PN	NQ	Ⓐ Ⓑ Ⓒ ● Ⓔ

(since equal measures cannot be assumed, even though PN and NQ appear equal)

	Column A	Column B	Sample Answers
Example 3:	x	y	Ⓐ ● Ⓒ Ⓓ Ⓔ

(since N is between P and Q)

	Column A	Column B	Sample Answers
Example 4:	$w + z$	180	Ⓐ Ⓑ ● Ⓓ Ⓔ

(since PQ is a straight line)

A if the quantity in Column A is greater;
B if the quantity in Column B is greater;
C if the two quantities are equal;
D if the relationship cannot be determined from the information given.

Column A	Column B

$$\frac{1}{x} < 0$$

1.　　x　　　　　　　　1

$$x = y^2 - 1 = 3$$

2.　　x　　　　　　　　y

$$x^2 = 25$$

3.　　x　　　　　　　　5

4.　　$\dfrac{1}{x} \div \dfrac{1}{\frac{1}{x}}$　　　　$\dfrac{1}{x} \cdot \dfrac{1}{x}$

$$0 < x < 31$$
x is divisible by 3 and 9

5.　　x　　　　　　　　27

6.　　$\dfrac{1}{3}$ of (4 yards, 2 feet)　　　1 yard, 4 feet

$$x^n = 1$$

7.　　x　　　　　　　　1

$$x > 0$$

8.　　$\sqrt{\dfrac{2x}{y}} \times \sqrt{\dfrac{xy}{2}}$　　　　x

$$x = \frac{1}{2}$$

9.　　$\dfrac{\frac{3}{4}}{1 + x}$　　　　x

Column A	Column B

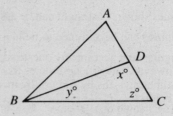

$$DC = \frac{1}{2}AC = \frac{1}{2}BC = \frac{1}{2}AB$$

10.　　$(BC)^2$　　　$(DC)^2 + (BD)^2$

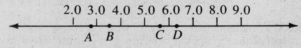

11.　Length of segment AC　　Length of segment BD

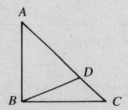

$$AB = BD = AD \text{ and } AB \perp BC$$

12.　　BC　　　　　　　DC

---

a and *b* are negative integers

13.　　$a + b$　　　　　　ab

$$x - z = 6$$
$$y + z = 9$$

14.　　$x + y$　　　　　　15

In triangle ABC, m$\angle A >$ m$\angle B$, and m$\angle C = 60°$.

15.　　Side CB　　　　　Side AB

Each of *Questions 16–30* has five choices. For each of these questions, select the best of the answer choices given.

16. A trailer carries 3, 4, or 5 crates on a trip. Each crate weighs no less than 125 pounds and no more than 250 pounds. What is the minimum weight (in pounds) of the crates on a single trip?

    (A)   375
    (B)   600
    (C)   625
    (D)   750
    (E) 1,250

17. In triangle *ABC*, angle *B* = angle *C*. *D* is any point on *BC*. Which of the following statement is true?

    (A) *AB* > *BC*
    (B) *AB* < *BC*
    (C) *BD* = *DC*
    (D) *AC* > *AD*
    (E) *AC* < *AD*

18. At a luncheon table where 12 men are seated, one-half of the men belong to Club *A*, one-third belong to Club *B*, and one-fourth belong to both clubs. How many men belong to neither?

    (A) 3
    (B) 4
    (C) 5
    (D) 6
    (E) 8

19. A lending library charges *c* cents for the first week that a book is loaned and *f* cents for each day over one week. What is the cost for taking out a book for *d* days, where *d* is greater than 7?

    (A) $c + fd$
    (B) $c + f(d - 7)$
    (C) cd
    (D) $7c + f(d - 7)$
    (E) $cd + f$

20. The numerator and denominator of a fraction are in the ratio of 2:3. If 6 is subtracted from the numerator, the result will be a fraction that has a value $\frac{2}{3}$ of the original fraction. The numerator of the original fraction is

    (A)   4
    (B)   6
    (C)   9
    (D) 18
    (E) 27

Questions 21–25 refer to the following graphs.

WEIGHT DISTRIBUTION IN AVERAGE ADULT	
(Total Body Weight 70,000 Grams)	
Organ	Weight (Grams)
Muscles	30,000
Skeleton	10,000
Blood	5,000
Gastro-intestinal tract	2,000
Lungs	1,000
Liver	1,700
Brain	1,500

USE OF WATER BY THE AVERAGE ADULT

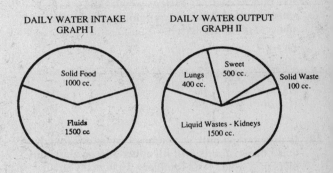

21. What percent (to the nearest $\frac{1}{10}$ of a percent) of total body weight is liver?

    (A)   .4
    (B)   1.2
    (C)   2.4
    (D)   4.1
    (E)   24

22. If the weight of the skeleton is represented as *g* grams, the total body weight is represented as

    (A) $7g$
    (B) $g + 6$
    (C) $60g$
    (D) $g + 60$
    (E) $70,000g$

23. What is the angle of the sector in Graph I representing daily water intake in solid food?

    (A) 51°
    (B) 72°
    (C) 103°
    (D) 120°
    (E) 144°

24. What percent of daily water output is water expired from the lungs?

(A) 1.6%
(B) 4%
(C) 16%
(D) 19%
(E) 40%

25. What percent of the daily water output through the kidneys is the daily water intake in fluids?

(A) 25%
(B) 33%
(C) 60%
(D) 100%
(E) 150%

26. If a eggs weigh b ounces, each c eggs weigh from d to e ounces each, and f eggs weigh from g to h ounces each, what is the minimum weight (in ounces) of all the eggs?

(A) $ab + ce + fg$
(B) $ab + cd + fg$
(C) $ab + ce + fh$
(D) $ab + cd + fh$
(E) $ab + de + gh$

27. In distributing milk at a summer camp it is found that a quart of milk will fill either 3 large glass tumblers or 5 small glass tumblers. How many small glass tumblers can be filled with one large glass tumbler?

(A) $\frac{3}{5}$ (B) $1\frac{2}{5}$ (C) $1\frac{2}{3}$ (D) 2   (E) $2\frac{1}{3}$

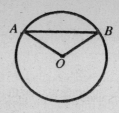

28. In Circle O above, $OA = 4$ and arc $AB = 112°$. How many degrees are in Angle ABO?

(A) 22   (B) 34   (C) 44   (D) 45   (E) 68

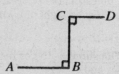

29. In the figure above, $AB \perp BC$, $BC \perp CD$, $AB = 8$, $BC = 5$, $CD = 4$. What is the shortest distance from A to D?

 (A) 12   (B) 13   (C) 15   (D) 16   (E) 17

30. There are 27 students in a chemistry class and 22 students in a physics class. Seven of these students take physics and chemistry. What is the ratio of the number of students taking only physics to those taking only chemistry?

(A)   3:4
(B)   4:3
(C)   7:6
(D)   22:27
(E)   34:29

S T O P

IF YOU FINISH BEFORE TIME IS CALLED, YOU MAY CHECK YOUR WORK ON THIS SECTION ONLY. DO NOT WORK ON ANY OTHER SECTION IN THE TEST.

SECTION 4

Time—30 minutes

30 Questions

Numbers: All numbers used are real numbers.

Figures: Position of points, angles, regions, etc. can be assumed to be in the order shown; and angle measures can be assumed to be positive.

Lines shown as straight can be assumed to be straight.

Figures can be assumed to lie in a plane unless otherwise indicated.

Figures that accompany questions are intended to provide information useful in answering the questions. However, unless a note states that a figure is drawn to scale, you should solve these problems NOT by estimating sizes by sight or by measurement, but by using your knowledge of mathematics (see Example 2 below).

Directions: Each of the Questions 1-15 consists of two quantities, one in Column A and one in Column B. You are to compare the two quantities and choose

> A if the quantity in Column A is greater;
> B if the quantity in Column B is greater;
> C if the two quantities are equal;
> D if the relationship cannot be determined from the information given.

Note: Since there are only four choices, NEVER MARK (E).

Common
Information: In a question, information concerning one or both of the quantities to be compared is centered above the two columns. A symbol that appears in both columns represents the same thing in Column A as it does in Column B.

	Column A	Column B	Sample Answers
Example 1:	2×6	$2 + 6$	● Ⓑ Ⓒ Ⓓ Ⓔ

Examples 2-4 refer to $\triangle PQR$.

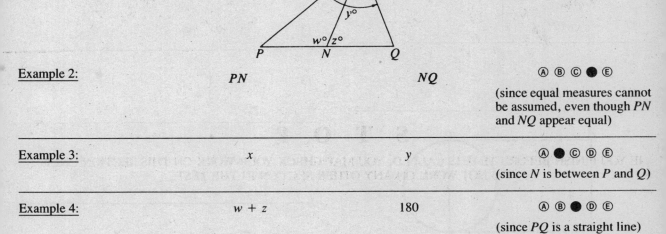

Example 2:	PN	NQ	Ⓐ Ⓑ Ⓒ ● Ⓔ
			(since equal measures cannot be assumed, even though PN and NQ appear equal)
Example 3:	x	y	Ⓐ ● Ⓒ Ⓓ Ⓔ
			(since N is between P and Q)
Example 4:	$w + z$	180	Ⓐ Ⓑ ● Ⓓ Ⓔ
			(since PQ is a straight line)

A if the quantity in Column A is greater;
B if the quantity in Column B is greater;
C if the two quantities are equal;
D if the relationship cannot be determined from the information given.

<u>Column A</u>   <u>Column B</u>   <u>Column A</u>   <u>Column B</u>

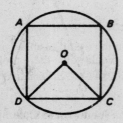

$$5 \times 5 \times 5 \times R = 3 \times 3 \times 3 \times 3$$

6.   5   R

$DO \perp OC$ and area of triangle $DOC = 12.5$

7. $(-3)^8$ $(-3)^9$

1.   Area of circle O 25π

8. $9 \times 682 \times 7$ $10 \times 682 \times 6$

The price of the item is equal to \$8 more than $\frac{8}{10}$ of its price.

$$-10 < r < -1$$

9. $\dfrac{1}{r^7}$ $\dfrac{1}{r^6}$

2.   The price of the item   \$40

10. $\dfrac{c^2 d^2 e^2}{c^3 d^3 e^3}$ $\dfrac{cde}{3}$

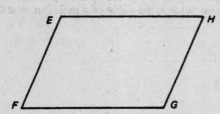

$$n^2 > 0$$

11. n 0

In parellelogram $EFGH$, $EF + EH = 20$

$$x \neq 0$$
$$x^2 = xy$$

3. EH FG

12. x y

$$a^2 = b^2 - 1$$
$$b \neq 0$$

13. $\dfrac{1}{2} + \dfrac{1}{3}$ $\dfrac{2}{5}$

4. a^4 $b^4 + 1$

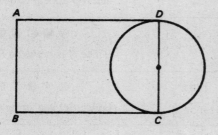

14.   0.4% $\dfrac{4}{1000}$

BC of rectangle $ABCD = 2.5\pi$
DC, diameter $= 10$

15.   .0005 $\dfrac{1}{2}\%$

5.   Area of $ABCD$ Area of circle

Directions: Each of the Questions 16–30 has five answer choices. For each of these questions, select the best of the answer choices given.

16. Which of the following fractions has the smallest value?

    (A) $\frac{1}{7}$ (B) $\frac{1}{8}$ (C) $\frac{2}{9}$ (D) $\frac{3}{11}$ (E) $\frac{4}{13}$

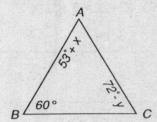

AB=BC=AC

17. In triangle ABC above, if $AB = BC = CA$, then $x + y =$

    (A) 7
    (B) 12
    (C) 19
    (D) 23
    (E) 60

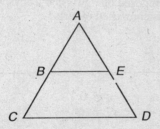

18. In triangle ACD above, the measure of $m\angle BAE = 50$; the length of BE equals the length AE; and $BE \parallel CD$. What is the measure of angle ADC?

    (A)   30
    (B)   50
    (C)   60
    (D)   80
    (E) 100

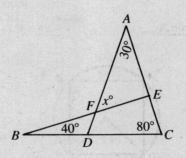

Note: Not drawn to scale.

19. In the figure above, $x =$

    (A) 30
    (B) 40
    (C) 45
    (D) 60
    (E) 80

20. If the operation $\oslash$ is defined by the equation $x \oslash y = 2x + y$, what is the value of a in $2 \oslash a = a \oslash 3$?

    (A) 0
    (B) -1
    (C) 1
    (D) 1.5
    (E) 4

Questions 21–25 are based on the following chart.

TEN LARGEST CITIES IN THE UNITED STATES

	Rank in 1960	Population 1960 (millions)	Population 1950 (millions)	Rank in 1950
New York City	1	7.71	7.89	1
Chicago	2	3.49	3.62	2
Los Angeles	3	2.45	1.97	4
Philadelphia	4	1.96	2.07	3
Detroit	5	1.67	1.85	5
Houston	6	0.93	0.60	14
Baltimore	7	0.92	0.95	6
Cleveland	8	0.87	0.91	7
District of Columbia	9	0.75	0.80	9
St. Louis	10	0.74	0.86	8

21. Which of the following cities had the largest percentage change in population between 1950 and 1960?

(A) New York City
(B) Chicago
(C) Los Angeles
(D) Houston
(E) District of Columbia

22. Which of the following cities had the same change in population between 1950 and 1960 as another of the ten largest cities?

(A) New York City
(B) Chicago
(C) Los Angeles
(D) Houston
(E) District of Columbia

23. If the total United States population was 170 million in 1950, approximately what percent of the population lived in the 5 largest cities in 1950?

(A) 5%
(B) 10%
(C) 17%
(D) 25%
(E) 85%

24. In 1960 how many times larger was Philadelphia than the District of Columbia?

(A) 1.2
(B) 1.5
(C) 2.0
(D) 2.6
(E) 3.2

25. If Detroit had a population of 1 million in 1922, what was the percentage increase between 1922 and 1960?

(A) 40
(B) 50
(C) 60
(D) 67
(E) 167

26. In a class composed of x girls and y boys what part of the class is composed of girls?

(A) $\dfrac{y}{x + y}$

(B) $\dfrac{x}{xy}$

(C) $\dfrac{x}{x + y}$

(D) $\dfrac{y}{xy}$

(E) $\dfrac{x + y}{y}$

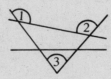

27. If $m\angle 1 = 145$ and $m\angle 2 = 125$, then $m\angle 3 =$

(A) 35
(B) 50
(C) 65
(D) 90
(E) 135

28. What is the maximum number of half-pint bottles of cream that can be filled with a 4-gallon can of cream? (2 pts. = 1 qt. and 4 qts. = 1 gallon)

    (A) 16
    (B) 24
    (C) 30
    (D) 32
    (E) 64

29. A coffee shop blends 2 kinds of coffee, putting in 2 parts of a 33¢ a pound grade to 1 part of a 24¢ grade. If the mixture is changed to 1 part of the 33¢ grade to 2 parts of the less expensive grade, how much will the shop save in blending 100 pounds?

    (A) $ .90
    (B) $1.00
    (C) $3.00
    (D) $8.00
    (E) $9.00

30. There are 200 questions on a 3-hour examination. Among these questions are 50 mathematics problems. It is suggested that twice as much time be allowed for each mathematics problem as for each of the other questions. How many minutes should be spent on the mathemetics problems?

    (A)   36
    (B)   60
    (C)   72
    (D) 100
    (E) 120

S T O P

IF YOU FINISH BEFORE TIME HAS ELAPSED, CHECK YOUR WORK ON THIS SECTION OF THE TEST ONLY. DO NOT GO ON TO THE NEXT SECTION OF THE TEST UNTIL TIME IS UP FOR THIS SECTION.

SECTION 5

Time—30 minutes

25 Questions

Directions: Each question or group of questions is based on a passage or set of conditions. In answering some of the questions, it may be useful to draw a rough diagram. For each question, select the best answer choice given.

Questions 1–4

For a motorist there are three ways of going from City A to City C. By way of a bridge the distance is 20 miles and the toll is 75¢. A tunnel between the two cities is a distance of 10 miles and the toll is $1.00 for the vehicle and driver plus 10¢ for each passenger. A two-lane highway without tolls goes east for 30 miles to City B and then 20 miles in a northwest direction to City C.

1. Which of the following is the shortest route from City B to City C?

   (A) directly on the toll-free highway to City C
   (B) the bridge
   (C) the tunnel
   (D) the tunnel or the bridge
   (E) the bridge only if traffic is heavy on the toll-free highway

2. The most economical way of going from City A to City B, in terms of tolls and distance, is to use the

   (A) tunnel
   (B) bridge
   (C) bridge or tunnel
   (D) toll-free highway
   (E) either one of these three depending upon traffic conditions

3. Martin usually drives alone from City C to City A every working day. Which factor would most probably influence his choice of the bridge or the tunnel?

   (A) whether his wife goes with him
   (B) traffic conditions on the toll-free road
   (C) traffic conditions on the bridge and tunnel
   (D) saving of 25¢ in tolls
   (E) price of gasoline consumed in covering the 10 additional miles on the bridge

4. In choosing between the use of the bridge and the tunnel, the chief factors would be

   I.   traffic and road conditions
   II. number of passengers in the car
   III. gasoline efficiency of the car
   IV. desire to save 25¢

   (A) I only
   (B) II only
   (C) II and III only
   (D) III and IV only
   (E) I and II only

Questions 5–6

A church found that their facilities were too small to accommodate the crowd for a special two-day religious service. They received a license to use the public park, and a public address system was promptly installed. Citizens who were not members of that church protested the action of the Park Department for having issued this license.

5. What is the best argument used by the church to retain its license?

   (A) Wide publicity had already been made to announce the location of special service.
   (B) The public address system was installed at great expense.
   (C) The church is a local taxpayer.
   (D) The park had been used before by religious organizations for rallies, concerts, and meetings.
   (E) No one would be excluded from entering the park during the service.

6. Which of the following is the best argument used by the citizens who protested the action by the Park Department?

   (A) Freedom of speech was violated.
   (B) Citizens would be denied the enjoyment of the public park during these two days.
   (C) There would be a violation of the noise-level standards.
   (D) A public referendum should have been held.
   (E) The town would incur expenses to clean up the park after the two-day service.

7. Wilbur is over six feet tall.

   The statement above can be logically deduced from which of the following statements?

   (A) The average height of the members of the basketball team is over six feet; Wilbur is the center on the basketball team.
   (B) If Wilbur was not asked to join the basketball team, then he is not over six feet tall; Wilbur was asked to join the basketball team.
   (C) If Wilbur is over six feet tall, then he can see the parade; Wilbur can see the parade.
   (D) In Dr. Gray's seminar, everyone who is not over six feet tall is seated in the first row; Dr. Gray seated Wilbur in the second row.
   (E) Everyone who is over six feet tall has to help stack cartons in the stockroom; Wilbur has to help stack cartons.

Questions 8–12

A project to consolidate the programs of a large university and a small college is set up. It is agreed that the representatives work in small committees of three, with two representatives of the large university. It was also agreed that no committee be represented by faculty members of the same subject area. The large university was represented by the following professors; *J*, who teaches English Literature, *K*, who is chairman of the Mathematics Department, and *L*, who is in the Department of Natural Sciences. The small college appointed the following: *M*, who teaches mathematics, *N*, who is a Latin teacher, and *O* and *P*, who teach English Literature.

8. Which of the following must be true?

    I.   If *J* serves on a committee, *P* must be assigned to that committee.
    II. If *J* cannot serve on a committee, then *M* cannot be assigned to that committee.
    III. If *J* cannot serve on a committee, then *L* must serve on that committee.

    (A) I only
    (B) II only
    (C) III only
    (D) I and II only
    (E) II and III only

9. Which of the following represents a committee properly composed?

    (A) *K, L, N*
    (B) *K, L, M*
    (C) *J, K, L*
    (D) *J, O, N*
    (E) *J, K, M*

10. Which of the following may serve with *P*?

    (A) *K* and *M*
    (B) *K* and *L*
    (C) *K* and *O*
    (D) *J* and *K*
    (E) *M* and *N*

11. If *L* is not available for service, which of the following must be on the committee?

    (A) *M* and *J*
    (B) *O* and *J*
    (C) *N* and *J*
    (D) *N* and *O*
    (E) *P* and *J*

12. Which of the following must be true?

    I.   *N* and *O* are always on the same committee.
    II. *M* and *O* never serve on the same committee.
    III. When *M* serves, *L* must serve.

    (A) I only
    (B) II only
    (C) I and II only
    (D) III only
    (E) II and III only

Quaestions 13–16

In a certain society, there are two marriage groups, Red and Brown. No marriage is permitted within a group. On marriage, males become part of their wife's group; women remain in their own group. Children belong to the same group as their parents. Widowers and divorced males revert to the group of their birth. Marriage to more than one person at the same time and marriage to a direct descendant are forbidden.

13. A Brown female could have had

    I.   a grandfather born Red
    II. a grandmother born Red
    III. two grandfathers born Brown

    (A) I only
    (B) III only
    (C) I and II only
    (D) II and III only
    (E) I, II, and III

14. A male born into the Brown group may have

    (A) an uncle in either group
    (B) a Brown daughter
    (C) a Brown son
    (D) a son-in-law born into the Red group
    (E) a daughter-in-law in the Red group

15. Which of the following is not permitted under the rules as stated?

    (A) A Brown male marrying his father's sister
    (B) A Red female marrying her mother's brother
    (C) A man born Red, who is now a widower, marrying his brother's widow
    (D) A widower marrying his wife's sister
    (E) A widow marrying her divorced daughter's ex-husband

16. If widowers and divorced males retained the group they had upon marrying, which of the following would be permissible? (Assume that no previous marriage occurred.)

    (A) A woman marrying her dead sister's husband
    (B) A woman marrying her divorced daughter's ex-husband
    (C) A widower marrying his brother's daughter
    (D) A woman marrying her mother's brother, who is a widower
    (E) A divorced male marrying his ex-wife's divorced sister

Questions 17–22

The letters A, B, C, D, E, F, and G, not necessarily in that order, stand for seven consecutive integers from 1 to 10.
D is 3 less than A.
B is the middle term.
F is as much less than B as C is greater than D.
G is greater than F.

17. The fifth integer is

    (A) A
    (B) C
    (C) D
    (D) E
    (E) F

18. A is a much greater than F as which integer is less than G?

    (A) A
    (B) B
    (C) C
    (D) D
    (E) E

19. If A = 7, the sum of E and G is

    (A) 8
    (B) 10
    (C) 12
    (D) 14
    (E) 16

20. A − F = ?

    (A) 1
    (B) 2
    (C) 3
    (D) 4
    (E) cannot be determined

21. An integer T is as much greater than C as C is greater than E. T can be written as A + E. What is D?

    (A) 2
    (B) 3
    (C) 4
    (D) 5
    (E) cannot be determined

22. The greatest possible value of C is how much greater than the smallest possible value of D?

    (A) 2
    (B) 3
    (C) 4
    (D) 5
    (E) 6

23. Ellen: I just heard that Julie flunked out of college.
    Nancy: That can't be true; she got straight A's in high school.

    From the conversation above, it can be inferred that

    (A) Nancy thinks Ellen is lying
    (B) Nancy assumes that no one who got straight A's in high school is likely to flunk out of college
    (C) Ellen thinks Julie has flunked out of college
    (D) Nancy thinks Julie is still in college
    (E) Ellen knows that Julie flunked out of college

24. President of the Company to the Board of Directors: We are being threatened by a union organizing drive. The workers are trying to wrest control from us. We must take any steps necessary to prevent this takeover, even if some of these measures may not be fully legal.

    If the statements above are true, it follows that

    (A) successful opposition to a union organizing drive must require illegal measures
    (B) the union organizing drive is being conducted illegally
    (C) the board of directors will refuse to recognize the union even if it wins a representation election
    (D) maintaining full control of the company is more important than obeying the law
    (E) successful unionization of any company deprives the company officers of control over the company

25. If you present a purple pass, then you may enter the compound.

    If the statement above is true, which of the following must also be true?

    I.   If you do not present a purple pass, then you may not enter the compound.
    II. If you may enter the compound, then you must have presented a purple pass.
    III. If you may not enter the compound, then you did not present a purple pass.

    (A) I only
    (B) II only
    (C) III only
    (D) I and II only
    (E) I, II, and III

S T O P

IF YOU FINISH BEFORE TIME IS CALLED, YOU MAY CHECK YOUR WORK ON THIS SECTION ONLY.
DO NOT WORK ON ANY OTHER SECTION IN THE TEST.

SECTION 6

Time—30 minutes

25 Questions

Directions: Each question or group of questions is based on a passage or set of conditions. In answering some of the questions, it may be useful to draw a rough diagram. For each question, select the best answer choice given.

Questions 1–4

In country X, the Conservative, Democratic, and Justice parties have fought three civil wars in twenty years. To restore stability, an agreement is reached to rotate the top offices—President, Prime Minister, and Army Chief of Staff—among the parties, so that each party controls one and only one Office at all times. The three top office holders must each have two deputies, one from each of the other parties. Each deputy must choose a staff composed equally of members of his or her chief's party and members of the third party.

1. When the Justice Party holds one of the top offices, which of the following cannot be true?

 (A) Some of the staff members within that Office are Justice Party members.
 (B) Some of the staff members within that Office are Democratic Party members.
 (C) Two of the deputies within the Offices are Justice Party members.
 (D) Two of the deputies within the Offices are Conservative Party members.
 (E) Some of the staff members within the other Offices are Justice Party members.

2. When the Democratic Party holds the Presidency, the staffs of the Prime Minister's deputies are composed

 I. one-fourth of Democratic Party members
 II. one-half of Justice Party members, one-fourth of Conservative Party members
 III. one-half of Conservative Party members, one-fourth of Justice Party members

 (A) I only
 (B) I and II only
 (C) II or III, but not both
 (D) I and II or I and III
 (E) Neither I, II, nor III

3. Which of the following is allowable under the rules as stated?

 (A) More than half of the staff within a given Office belonging to a single party
 (B) Half the staff members within a given Office belonging to a single party
 (C) Any person having a member of the same party as his or her immediate superior
 (D) Half the total number of staff members in all three Offices belonging to a single party
 (E) Half the staff members within a given Office belonging to parties different from that of the top office holder in that Office

4. The Office of the Army Chief of Staff passes from the Conservative to the Justice Party. Which of the following must be fired?

 (A) The Democratic deputy and all staff members belonging to the Justice Party
 (B) The Justice Party deputy and all his or her staff members
 (C) The Justice Party deputy and half of the Conservative staff members in the chief of staff office
 (D) The Conservative deputy and all of his or her staff members belonging to the Conservative Party
 (E) No deputies, and all staff members belonging to the Conservative Party

5. If Elaine is on the steering committee, then she is on the central committee. This statement can be logically deduced from which of the following statements?

 (A) All members of the central committee are on the steering committee.
 (B) Elaine is on either the central committee or the steering committee.
 (C) Everyone who is on the steering committee is also on the central committee.
 (D) Some members of the central committee are on the steering committee.
 (E) Elaine is on the steering committee.

6. Frank must be a football player; he is wearing a football jersey.

 The conclusion above is valid only if it is true that

 (A) football players often wear football jerseys
 (B) all football players wear football jerseys
 (C) football players never wear any kind of shirt other than football jerseys
 (D) football players are required to wear football jerseys
 (E) only football players wear football jerseys

7. Today's high school students are not being educated, they are being trained. Their teachers demand little of them other than they memorize facts and follow directions. The current emphasis on training in basic math and verbal skills, while a useful step, rarely leads to the essential second step: development of independent critical thinking.

The author would probably consider which of the following aspects of a student's term paper to be most praiseworthy?

(A) The choice of a challenging topic
(B) The use of grammatically correct sentence structure
(C) Evidence of extensive research prior to writing
(D) Avoidance of clichés and vagueness
(E) Evidence of original insights and freshly-developed concepts

Questions 8–11

Tom wishes to enroll in Latin AA, Sanskrit A, Armenian Literature 221, and Celtic Literature 701.

Latin AA meets five days a week, either from 9 to 11 a.m. or from 2 to 4 p.m.

Sanskrit A meets either Tuesday and Thursday from 12 noon to 3 p.m., or Monday, Wednesday, and Friday from 10 a.m. to 12 noon.

Armenian Literature 221 meets either Monday, Wednesday, and Friday from 12:30 to 2 p.m., or Tuesday and Thursday from 10:30 a.m. to 12:30 p.m.

Celtic Literature 701 meets by arrangement with the instructor, the only requirement being that it meet for one four-hour session or two two-hour sessions per week, between 9 a.m. and 4 p.m. from Monday to Friday, beginning on the hour.

8. Which combination is impossible for Tom?

(A) Latin in the morning, Sanskrit on Tuesday and Thursday, and Armenian Literature on Monday, Wednesday, and Friday
(B) Latin in the afternoon and Sanskrit and Armenian Literature on Monday, Wednesday, and Friday
(C) Latin in the afternoon, Sanskrit on Monday, Wednesday, and Friday, and Armenian Literature on Tuesday and Thursday
(D) Latin in the morning and Sanskrit and Armenian Literature on Monday, Wednesday, and Friday
(E) Latin in the afternoon, Armenian Literature on Monday, Wednesday, and Friday, and Celtic Literature on Tuesday

9. Which of the following gives the greatest number of alternatives for scheduling Celtic Literature, assuming that all other courses are scheduled without conflicts?

(A) Latin in the afternoon and Armenian Literature Monday, Wednesday, and Friday
(B) Sanskrit on Tuesday and Thursday and Armenian Literature on Monday, Wednesday and Friday
(C) Latin in the afternoon and Armenian Literature Tuesday and Thursday
(D) Latin in the morning and Sanskrit on Tuesday and Thursday
(E) Sanskrit on Monday, Wednesday, and Friday, and Armenian Literature on Tuesday and Thursday

10. If the Celtic instructor insists on holding at least one session on Friday, in which of the following can Tom enroll?

I.   Armenian Literature on Monday, Wednesday, and Friday
II. Sanskrit on Monday, Wednesday, and Friday

(A) I only
(B) II only
(C) both I and II
(D) I or II but not both
(E) neither I nor II

11. Which of the following additional courses, meeting as indicated, can Tom take?

(A) Old Church Slavonic—Monday, Wednesday, and Friday from 10 a.m. to 12 noon
(B) Intermediate Aramaic—Monday, Wednesday, and Friday from 11 a.m. to 12:30 p.m.
(C) Introductory Acadian—Tuesday and Thursday from 2 to 4 p.m.
(D) Fundamentals of Basque—Tuesday and Thursday from 1 to 3 p.m.
(E) Old Norse-Icelandic—Monday only from 12

Questions 12–18

Joe, Larry, Ned, Mary, Paul, Willy, Crystal, Albert, Bob, Frank, Ellen, and Rick all live in the same six-floor building. There are two apartments per floor. No more than two persons live in any apartment. Some apartments may be empty.

Larry and his roommate live two floors above Albert and his roommate Crystal.

Joe lives alone, three floors below Willy and two floors below Ellen.

Mary lives one floor below Albert and Crystal.

Ned lives three floors above the floor on which Bob and Frank have single apartments.

Rick and Paul live in single apartments two floors below Mary.

12. Which of the following lists the persons named in the correct order, going from the bottom floor to the top?

(A) Rick, Bob, Mary, Albert, Larry, Ned
(B) Rick, Frank, Ned, Ellen, Larry, Crystal
(C) Paul, Bob, Joe, Crystal, Ned, Larry
(D) Larry, Ellen, Albert, Mary, Frank, Rick
(E) Larry, Joe, Mary, Albert, Bob, Rick

13. Which of the following pairs must live on the same floor?

I.   Ned, Ellen
II. Joe, Mary
III. Albert, Larry

(A) I only
(B) III only
(C) I and II only
(D) II and III only
(E) I, II, and III

14. Larry's roommate, assuming that it is one of the persons mentioned, is

    (A) Ellen
    (B) Willy
    (C) Mary
    (D) Ned
    (E) Paul

15. Rick lives on the

    (A) first floor, below Bob or Frank
    (B) second floor, below Joe or Albert and Crystal
    (C) third floor, above Mary or Ellen
    (D) fourth floor, opposite Albert and Crystal
    (E) sixth floor, opposite Larry and his roommate

16. An empty apartment or empty apartments may be found on the

    (A) second floor only
    (B) fourth floor only
    (C) fifth floor only
    (D) third or sixth floor, but not both
    (E) fourth or sixth floor or both

17. Joe arranges to move into an apartment two floors down, whose occupant moves into an apartment one floor up. The occupant of this apartment moves into one three floors up, whose occupant takes Joe's old apartment. The new occupant of Joe's old apartment is

    (A) Bob or Frank
    (B) Ned or Ellen
    (C) Mary
    (D) Rick
    (E) Paul

18. Dorothy lives with a roommate. Her roommate could be any of the following EXCEPT

    (A) Willy
    (B) Mary
    (C) Ned
    (D) Ellen
    (E) Frank

Questions 19–22

(1) A causes B or C, but not both.
(2) F occurs only if B occurs.
(3) D occurs if B or C occurs.
(4) E occurs only if C occurs.
(5) J occurs only if E or F occurs.
(6) D causes G or H or both.
(7) H occurs if E occurs.
(8) G occurs if F occurs.

19. If A occurs, which may occur?

    I.   F and G
    II. E and H
    III. D

    (A) I only
    (B) II only
    (C) III only
    (D) I and III or II and III, but not both
    (E) I, II, and III

20. If B occurs, which must occur?

    (A) F and G
    (B) D and G
    (C) D
    (D) G and H
    (E) J

21. If J occurs, which must have occurred?

    (A) E
    (B) both E and F
    (C) either B or C
    (D) G
    (E) both B and C

22. Which may occur as a result of a cause not mentioned?

    I.   D
    II. A
    III. F

    (A) I only
    (B) II only
    (C) I and II only
    (D) II and III only
    (E) I, II, and III

23. In recommending to the board of trustees a tuition increase of $500 per year, the President of the university said: "There were no student demonstrations over the previous increases of $300 last year and $200 the year before."

    If the President's statement is accurate, which of the following can be validly inferred from the information given?

    I.   Most students in previous years felt that the increases were justified because of increased operating costs.
    II. Student apathy was responsible for the failure of students to protest the previous tuition increases.
    III. Students are not likely to demonstrate over the new tuition increases.

    (A) I only
    (B) II only
    (C) I or II, but not both
    (D) I, II, and III
    (E) neither I, II, nor III

24. A meadow in springtime is beautiful, even if no one is there to appreciate it.

The statement above would be a logical rebuttal to which of the following claims?

(A) People will see only what they want to see.
(B) Beauty is only skin deep.
(C) There's no accounting for taste.
(D) Beauty exists only in the eye of the beholder.
(E) The greatest pleasure available to mankind is the contemplation of beauty.

25. Since it is possible that substances contained in certain tree roots may provide a cure for cancer, the government must provide sufficient funds to allow thorough testing of this possibility.

The argument above assumes that

(A) substances contained in certain tree roots will probably cure cancer
(B) the line of research mentioned offers at present the most promising possibility for finding a cure for cancer
(C) the possibility of finding a cure is sufficient reason for funding research into possible cancer cures
(D) a cure for cancer would be extremely valuable to society
(E) the government is the only possible source of funds for the research described

S T O P

IF YOU FINISH BEFORE TIME IS CALLED, YOU MAY CHECK YOUR WORK ON THIS SECTION ONLY.
DO NOT WORK ON ANY OTHER SECTION IN THE TEST.

SECTION 7

Time—30 Minutes

38 Questions

Directions: Each sentence below has one or two blanks, each blank indicating that something has been omitted. Beneath the sentence are five lettered words or sets of words. Choose the word or set of words for each blank that best fits the meaning of the sentence as a whole.

1. The ------- of the apartment was unbelievable; it was difficult to realize that human beings could live in such -------.

   (A) disorder...isolation
   (B) squalor...filth
   (C) barrenness...confusion
   (D) stench...disarray
   (E) spaciousness...proximity

2. He had taken the shocking news quietly, neither ------- fate nor uttering any word of bitterness.

   (A) conspiring with
   (B) submitting to
   (C) railing against
   (D) dissenting from
   (E) mulling over

3. Old as the continents are, they are apparently not ------- features of the earth but rather secondary features that have formed and evolved during the earth's lifetime.

   (A) inherent
   (B) incongruous
   (C) primordial
   (D) isolated
   (E) unique

4. Although several details of the hypothesis are open to criticism, its general conclusion has not been -------.

   (A) refuted
   (B) determined
   (C) corroborated
   (D) disregarded
   (E) approximated

5. It is a great irony of contemporary history that those friends of judicial autonomy who argue most passionately for creative judicial intervention in the political sphere in effect advocate ------- of an independent, nonelected judiciary.

   (A) abolition
   (B) liberation
   (C) evaluation
   (D) inauguration
   (E) dissemination

6. There is a danger that because Mr. Peters' suggestions are so theatrically -------, readers may treat the book as a performance, enthralling but too ------- to take seriously.

   (A) striking...pedestrian
   (B) bold...overwrought
   (C) plausible...fantastic
   (D) conventional...disturbing
   (E) lacking...histrionic

7. As long as the acquisition of knowledge is rendered habitually -------, so long will there be a prevailing tendency to discontinue it when free from the ------- of parents and teachers.

   (A) repugnant...coercion
   (B) academic...authority
   (C) gratifying...restrictions
   (D) honorable...influence
   (E) irrelevant...custody

Directions: In each of the following questions, a related pair of words or phrases is followed by five lettered pairs of words or phrases. Select the lettered pair that best expresses a relationship similar to that expressed in the original pair.

8. MODERATOR : DEBATE::
   (A) legislator : election
   (B) chef : banquet
   (C) auditor : lecture
   (D) conspirator : plot
   (E) umpire : game

9. DELIRIUM : DISORIENTATION::
   (A) paralysis : immobility
   (B) anorexia : pain
   (C) insomnia : fretfulness
   (D) rash : vaccination
   (E) malaria : relapse

10. GLOSSARY : WORDS::
    (A) catalogue : dates
    (B) atlas : maps
    (C) almanac : synonyms
    (D) thesaurus : rhymes
    (E) lexicon : numbers

11. ARMATURE : STATUE::
    (A) landscape : painting
    (B) framework : building
    (C) arsenal : weapon
    (D) composer : symphony
    (E) apparatus : experiment

12. EPAULET : SHOULDER::
    (A) noose : neck
    (B) tiara : head
    (C) splint : arm
    (D) knapsack : back
    (E) palm : hand

13. LUMBER : BEAR::
    (A) roost : hen
    (B) bray : donkey
    (C) waddle : goose
    (D) swoop : hawk
    (E) chirp : sparrow

14. ENERVATED : VIGOR::
    (A) lax : rigor
    (B) profound : stupor
    (C) pallid : flavor
    (D) ravenous : appetite
    (E) nervous : energy

15. CELERITY : SNAIL::
    (A) indolence : sloth
    (B) cunning : weasel
    (C) curiosity : cat
    (D) humility : peacock
    (E) obstinacy : mule

16. ADULATION : FLATTERY::
    (A) humility : vanity
    (B) credulity : sincerity
    (C) emulation : rivalry
    (D) irascibility : provocation
    (E) castigation : admonishment

Directions: Each passage in this group is followed by questions based on its content. After reading a passage, choose the best answer to each question. Answer all questions following a passage on the basis of what is stated or implied in the passage.

The Quechua world is submerged, so to speak, in a cosmic magma that weighs heavily upon it. It possesses the rare quality of being as it were interjected into the midst of antagonistic forces, which in turn implies a whole body of social and aesthetic structures whose innermost meaning must be the administration of energy. This gives rise to the social organism known as the *ayllu*, the agrarian community that regulates the procurement of food. The *ayllu* formed the basic structure of the whole Inca empire.

The central idea of this organization was a kind of closed economy, just the opposite of our economic practices, which can be described as open. The closed economy rested on the fact that the Inca controlled both the production and consumption of food. When one adds to this fact the religious ideas noted in the Quechua texts cited by the chronicler Santa Cruz Pachacuti, one comes to the conclusion that in the Andean zone the margin of life was minimal and was made possible only by the system of magic the Quechua constructed through his religion. Adversities, moreover, were numerous, for the harvest might fail at any time and bring starvation to millions. Hence the whole purpose of the Quechua administrative and ideological system was to carry on the arduous task of achieving *abundance* and staving off shortages. This kind of structure presupposes a state of unremitting anxiety, which could not be resolved by action. The Quechua could not do so because his primordial response to problems was the use of magic, that is, recourse to the unconscious for the solution of external problems. Thus the struggle against the world was a struggle against the dark depths of the Quechua's own psyche, where the solution was found. By overcoming the unconscious, the outer world was also vanquished.

These considerations permit us to classify Quechua culture as absolutely static or, more accurately, as the expression of a mere state of being. Only in this way can

we understand the refuge that it took in the germinative center of the cosmic *mandala* as revealed by Quechua art. The Quechua empire was nothing more than a *mandala*, for it was divided into four zones, with Cuzco in the center. Here the Quechua ensconced himself to contemplate the decline of the world as though it were caused by an alien and autonomous force.

17. It can be inferred from the passage that the Quechua world

    (A) aimed at socio-economic interdependence
    (B) eliminated economic distress
    (C) may be placed in ancient South America
    (D) is located in contemporary Mexico
    (E) was a scene of dynamic activity

18. The term "mandala" as used in the last paragraph most likely means

    (A) an agrarian community
    (B) a kind of superstition
    (C) a closed economic pattern
    (D) a philosophy or way of regarding the world
    (E) a figure composed of four divisions

19. The author implies that the Quechua world was

    (A) uncivilized
    (B) highly introspective
    (C) vitally energetic
    (D) free of major worries
    (E) well organized

20. With which of the following statements would the author most likely agree?

    (A) Only psychological solutions can remedy economic ills.
    (B) The Quechua were renowned for equanimity and unconcern.
    (C) The Quechua limited themselves to realizable goals.
    (D) Much of Quechua existence was harsh and frustrating.
    (E) Modern Western society should adopt some Quechua economic ideas.

The explosion of a star is an awesome event. The most violent of these cataclysms, which produce supernovae, probably destroys a star completely. Within our galaxy of roughly 100 billion
(5) stars the last supernova was observed in 1604. Much smaller explosions, however, occur quite frequently, giving rise to what astronomers call novae and dwarf novae. On the order of 25 novae occur in our galaxy every year, but only two or
(10) three are near enough to be observed. About 100 dwarf novae are known altogether. If the exploding star is in a nearby part of the galaxy, it may create a "new star" that was not previously visible to the naked eye. The last new star of this sort that could
(15) be observed clearly from the Northern Hemisphere appeared in 1946. In these smaller explosions the star loses only a minute fraction of its mass and survives to explode again.

Astrophysicists are fairly well satisfied that they
(20) can account for the explosions of supernovae. The novae and dwarf novae have presented more of a puzzle. From recent investigations that have provided important new information about these two classes of exploding star, the picture that emerges
(25) is quite astonishing. It appears that every dwarf nova—and perhaps every nova—is a member of a pair of stars. The two stars are so close together that they revolve around a point that lies barely outside the surface of the larger star. As a result the
(30) period of rotation is usually only a few hours, and their velocities range upward to within a two-hundredth of the speed of light.

Astronomers use the term "cataclysmic variable" to embrace the three general classes of
(35) exploding star: dwarf novae, novae and supernovae. A cataclysmic variable is defined as a star that suddenly and unpredictably increases in brightness by a factor of at least 10. Dwarf novae are stars that increase in brightness by a factor of 10 to 100
(40) within a period of several hours and decline to their former brightness in two or three days. In this period they emit some 10.38 to 10.39 ergs of energy. At maximum brilliance a dwarf nova shines about as intensely as our sun; previously it
(45) had been only about a hundredth as bright. The number of outbursts ranges anywhere from three to 30 a year, but for any one star the intervals have a fairly constant value. Moreover, the maximum brightness from outburst to outburst is the same

(50) within a factor of two for a given star. The dwarf novae are often referred to, after their prototypes, as U Geminorum or SS Cygni stars. (The stars of each constellation are designated by letters or numbers.) A subgroup of dwarf novae, called Z Came-
(55) lopardalis stars, do not always descend to minimum brightness between outbursts but may stay at some intermediate level for several months.

21. The author's primary purpose in the passage is to

    (A) compare the characteristics of novae with those of other stars
    (B) explain why supernovae are so much less frequent than novae and dwarf novae
    (C) account for the unpredictability of cataclysmic variables as a class
    (D) describe the nature and range in scale of cataclysmic variables
    (E) explain what happens during the stages of a star's destruction

22. According to the passage, our observations of novae are hampered by their

    (A) extreme brightness
    (B) loss of mass
    (C) speed of rotation
    (D) distance from earth
    (E) tremendous violence

23. Dwarf novae differ from supernovae in which of the following aspects?

    I.   Magnitude of outburst
    II. Frequency of observation
    III. Periodicity of flare-ups

    (A) I only
    (B) II only
    (C) I and II only
    (D) I and III only
    (E) I, II, and III

24. By the term "new star" (line 13) the author means one that has

    (A) recently gained in mass
    (B) moved from a distant galaxy
    (C) become bright enough to strike the eye
    (D) not previously risen above the horizon
    (E) become visible by rotating in its orbit

25. The passage suggests which of the following about Z Camelopardalis stars?

    (A) They revert to their original level of brightness more readily than do U Geminorum stars.
    (B) Their number of outbursts is more frequent than that of other dwarf novae.
    (C) They may lose a proportionally greater fraction of their mass than do SS Cygni stars.
    (D) They may be less frequently observed by astronomers than are supernovae.
    (E) They are distinguishable from other dwarf novae by their lesser degree of brightness.

26. Which of the following topics would most probably be the subject of the paragraph immediately following the last paragraph above?

   (A) The likelihood of our sun's becoming a dwarf nova.
   (B) The manner in which the twin stars revolve.
   (C) The characteristics of the explosion of a nova.
   (D) The origin of the term "cataclysmic variable."
   (E) The nature of the explosions of supernovae.

27. The passage provides information that would answer which of the following questions?

   I.   In what century were astronomers last able to observe the explosion of a supernova?
   II. Why do the Z Camelopardalis stars remain at intermediate levels of brightness after some outbursts?
   III. How rapidly after outburst do dwarf novae achieve their maximum level of brilliance?

   (A) I only
   (B) III only
   (C) I and II only
   (D) I and III only
   (E) II and III only

Directions: Each question below consists of a word printed in capital letters, followed by five lettered words or phrases. Choose the lettered word or phrase that is most nearly opposite in meaning to the word in capital letters.

Since some of the questions require you to distinguish fine shades of meaning, be sure to consider all the choices before deciding which one is best.

28. FLUSTER:
   (A) soothe
   (B) diminish
   (C) strengthen
   (D) divert
   (E) allow

29. DELETION:
   (A) injury
   (B) delay
   (C) insertion
   (D) permission
   (E) pollution

30. DISPARAGE:
   (A) resemble
   (B) eulogize
   (C) vacillate
   (D) annoy
   (E) appear

31. BALEFUL:
   (A) meager
   (B) beneficent
   (C) indifferent
   (D) uncomfortable
   (E) original

32. SERVILITY:
   (A) resilience
   (B) wickedness
   (C) independence
   (D) righteousness
   (E) humility

33. FELICITOUS:
   (A) inappropriate
   (B) ineffable
   (C) irrational
   (D) atypical
   (E) uncertain

34. PRECIPITOUS:
   (A) cooperative
   (B) cautious
   (C) inaccurate
   (D) formal
   (E) simplistic

35. ASSUAGE:
   (A) wane
   (B) belie
   (C) worsen
   (D) intervene
   (E) presume

36. LATENT:
   (A) prior
   (B) tardy
   (C) devious
   (D) manifest
   (E) astronomical

37. BROACH:
   (A) seal off
   (B) vie with
   (C) unsettle
   (D) stint
   (E) enhance

38. ENCOMIUM:
   (A) prodigality
   (B) denunciation
   (C) sacrifice
   (D) disability
   (E) abbreviation

S T O P

IF YOU FINISH BEFORE TIME IS CALLED, YOU MAY CHECK YOUR WORK ON THIS SECTION ONLY.
DO NOT WORK ON ANY OTHER SECTION IN THE TEST.

Answer Key

Note: The answers to the quantitative sections are keyed to the corresponding review areas in the Mathematics Review (Chapter 11). The numbers in parentheses after each answer refer to the math topic(s) covered by that particular question.

Section 1   Verbal

1.	D	11.	B	21.	C	31.	D
2.	B	12.	C	22.	C	32.	A
3.	B	13.	E	23.	C	33.	B
4.	E	14.	E	24.	D	34.	D
5.	E	15.	C	25.	C	35.	C
6.	D	16.	A	26.	C	36.	A
7.	B	17.	E	27.	E	37.	D
8.	B	18.	C	28.	C	38.	B
9.	C	19.	E	29.	B		
10.	B	20.	C	30.	E		

Section 2   Verbal

1.	C	11.	C	21.	B	31.	B
2.	C	12.	A	22.	B	32.	C
3.	B	13.	B	23.	C	33.	E
4.	C	14.	C	24.	B	34.	A
5.	E	15.	A	25.	C	35.	B
6.	A	16.	B	26.	D	36.	C
7.	D	17.	B	27.	D	37.	D
8.	E	18.	D	28.	C	38.	D
9.	E	19.	E	29.	C		
10.	C	20.	C	30.	A		

Section 3   Quantitative

1.	B (II-G)	9.	C (I-B, II-A)	17.	D (III)	25.	D (II-E)
2.	A (II-B)	10.	C (III-A)	18.	C (I-B)	26.	B (II-A)
3.	D (II-B)	11.	C (I-F)	19.	B (II-B, C)	27.	C (II-E)
4.	C (I-B, II-A)	12.	A (III-D)	20.	D (I-B)	28.	B (III-F)
5.	D (II-G)	13.	B (II-A-3)	21.	C (IV-C)	29.	B (III-D)
6.	B (I)	14.	C (II-A-3)	22.	A (II-E)	30.	A (II-D)
7.	D (I-H)	15.	A (III-D, V)	23.	E (III-F, IV-B)		
8.	C (I-H)	16.	A (I)	24.	C (I-D, IV-B)		

Section 4   Quantitative

1.	C (III-F)	9.	B (II-G)	17.	C (III-D)	25.	D (IV-A)
2.	C (II-B)	10.	D (I-H)	18.	D (III-B, D)	26.	C (I-B)
3.	C (III-C)	11.	D (II-G)	19.	A (III-D)	27.	D (III-A)
4.	B (II-A-5)	12.	C (II-A)	20.	C (II-B)	28.	E (IV-B)
5.	C (III-G)	13.	A (I-B)	21.	D (IV-A)	29.	C (IV-B)
6.	A (I-A)	14.	C (I-B, D)	22.	A (IV-A)	30.	C (IV-B)
7.	A (I-H)	15.	B (I-C, D)	23.	B (I-D)		
8.	A (I-A)	16.	B (I-B)	24.	D (IV-A)		

Section 5 Analytical

1.	A	8.	E	15.	B	22.	D
2.	D	9.	A	16.	D	23.	B
3.	C	10.	B	17.	B	24.	D
4.	E	11.	C	18.	D	25.	C
5.	D	12.	E	19.	B		
6.	B	13.	C	20.	D		
7.	D	14.	A	21.	D		

Section 6 Analytical

1.	D	8.	D	15.	A	22.	C
2.	D	9.	A	16.	E	23.	E
3.	B	10.	D	17.	B	24.	D
4.	C	11.	B	18.	E	25.	C
5.	C	12.	C	19.	D		
6.	E	13.	C	20.	C		
7.	E	14.	B	21.	C		

Section 7 Verbal

1.	B	11.	B	21.	D	31.	B
2.	C	12.	B	22.	D	32.	C
3.	C	13.	C	23.	E	33.	A
4.	A	14.	A	24.	C	34.	B
5.	A	15.	D	25.	C	35.	C
6.	B	16.	E	26.	C	36.	D
7.	A	17.	C	27.	D	37.	A
8.	E	18.	E	28.	A	38.	B
9.	A	19.	B	29.	C		
10.	B	20.	D	30.	B		

Answer Explanations

Section 1

1. **D.** To the cynic (person who expect nothing but the worst of human actions and motives), human actions are *founded* or based upon selfish motives.

2. **B.** The author concedes that the big-bang theory has been changed somewhat: it has undergone *refinement* or polishing. However, he denies that its validity has been threatened seriously by any rival theories: it has *resisted* or defied all challenges.
    The use of the support signal *and* indicates that the first missing word is similar in meaning to "modification." The use of the contrast signal *but* indicates that the second missing word is contrary in meaning to "undergone modification."

3. **B.** Speech that is *hybrid* (made up of several elements) by definition *combines* these elements. The technical term *hybrid* best suits this context because it is a neutral term devoid of negative connotations (which *motley* and *mangled* possess).

4. **E.** Printing *propagates* or disseminates both error (bad books) and *knowledge* (good books).
    Note how the use of parallel structure demands that the second missing word be a positive term.

5. **E.** One would have to disentangle a *skein* or coiled and twisted bundle of yarn.
    Note how the presence of the verb *disentangle*, which may be used both figuratively and literally influences the writer's choice of words. In this case, while *line* and *strand* are possible choices, neither word possesses the connotations of twistings and tangled contortions that make *skein* the most suitable choice.

6. **D.** A man too wedded to *orthodox* theories or doctrines can best be described as *doctrinaire* or dogmatic.

7. **B.** The scholar was *eclectic* in his own approach, selecting what he thought was best from the different philosophic schools. However, he did not grant this freedom of selection to others: he was *intolerant of* his colleagues who preached (asserted, averred) what he practiced.
    Note that the use of *illogically* implicitly signals the contrast built into the sentence.

8. **B.** *Fans* or spectators are seated in the *bleachers*. An *audience* is seated in its seats.
    (Defining Characteristic)

9. **C.** An *auger* is a tool that pierces or *bores* holes. A *plane* is a tool that *smooths* surfaces.
    (Function)

10. **B.** A *chameleon*, a kind of lizard, is studied by a *herpetologist* (scientist who studies reptiles and amphibians). A *salmon*, a kind of fish, is studied by an *ichthyologist*.
    (Defining Characteristic)

11. **B.** To *scurry* is to *move* in a brisk and rapid manner. To *chatter* is to *talk* in a brisk and rapid manner.
    (Manner)

12. **C.** A *song* is part of a *cycle* or series of songs. A *sonnet* is part of a *sequence* or series of sonnets.
    (Group and Member)

13. **E.** Someone *obdurate* (unyielding, inflexible) is lacking in *flexibility*. Someone *adamant* (unshakable in opposition) is lacking in *submissiveness*.
    (Antonym Variant)

14. **E.** *Sartorial* by definition means pertaining to the *tailor's* art. *Terpsichorean* by definition means pertaining to the *dancer's* art.
    (Defining Characteristic)

15. **C.** To *skirt* an *issue* is to evade addressing or dealing with it. To *dodge* an *encounter* is to evade meeting the person.
    Beware eye-catchers. *Skirt* here is a verb meaning evade. *Vest* here is a verb meaning to have a legal right or interest in something. Neither here are nouns referring to garments.
    (Function)

16. **A.** A *feud* or war of revenge is a fight characterized by *acrimony* or bitterness. A *scuffle* or haphazard struggle is a fight characterized by *confusion*.
    (Defining Characteristic)

17. **E.** In this paragraph the author maintains that all forms of government tend to become somewhat dictatorial. He shows how society protects itself from this tendency. Throughout, he demonstrates how people tend to protect or *safeguard* their individual liberties.

18. **C.** The author says that the tendency for a government to encroach upon individual liberty to the extent to which it has the power to do so is "almost a natural law" of politics. Thus, government and individual liberty are *inherently* by their very natures in *opposition* to one another.

19. E. The final sentence states that the fascist dicta-tor-ships "destroyed (*eradicated*) all forms of social organization that were in any way rivals to the state."

20. C. If the fascist dictatorships "are the first truly tyrannical governments which western Europe has known for centuries," then it can be inferred that centuries ago there were tyranni-cal or *despotic* governments in western Europe. Thus, the fascist governments represent a *regression* or reversion to an earlier form of government.

21. C. The purpose of the passage is to answer the question raised at the end of the opening para-graph: "How does the egg breathe?" It does so by *explaining the processes of gas and water diffusion in eggs*.

22. C. The egg "breathes" by diffusion through microscopic pores in the shell. Thus, the egg-shell is permeable, cabable of being passed through without being broken, and this quality of *permeability* is what allows diffusion to take place.

23. C. You can arrive at the correct answer by the process of elimination.
Question I is answerable on the basis of the passage. Turning the fertilized egg prevents the embryo from adhering to the shell membranes (lines 6–8). Therefore, you can eliminate Choices B and D.
Question II is answerable on the basis of the passage (lines 47–64). The egg gains water as embryonic development takes place. It must lose water in order that its relative water con-tent at hatching be equal to its water content at laying. If it does not succeed in this, the hatch-ing will fail. Therefore, you can eliminate Choice A.
Question III is unanswerable on the basis of the passage. There is no information in the passage about such an eventuality. Therefore, you can eliminate Choice E.
Only Choice C is left. It is the correct answer.

24. D. The passage stresses the mechanisms of diffu-sion and metabolism to clarify the principles underlying the process of respiration of the developing bird embryo.
Choice A is incorrect. The passage is not his-torical in orientation.
Choice B is incorrect. The passage gives no technical instructions that would enable novice fowl breeders to master their trade.
Choice C is incorrect. The passage is exposi-tory, not persuasive.
Choice E is incorrect. The passage deals with the metabolic processes of common domestic fowl, not the breeding habits of exotic fowl.

25. C. Lines 59–60 state that the "relative water con-tent at hatching is to equal that of the freshly laid egg." Thus, every particle of water gained during incubation must be lost by hatching.

26. C. The passage states that the egg needs only warmth from the parents and "periodic turning to prevent the adhesion of the embryo to the shell membranes." If this adhesion must be prevented as part of the routine care of the embryo in the egg, then this suggests that if it were not prevented it would *threaten* the embryo in some way.

27. E. The author's presentation of the facts of diffu-sion is dispassionate and *objective*.

28. C. The opposite of to *disregard* or ignore is to *heed* or pay attention to.
Think of "disregarding a warning."

29. B. The opposite of *veracity* or truthfulness is *men-dacity* or dishonesty.
Word Parts Clue: *Ver-* means truth. *Veracity* means truthfulness.
Think of "trusting someone's veracity."

30. E. The opposite of to *bedeck* or ornament pro-fusely is to *strip*.
Think of someone "bedecked in diamonds and furs."

31. D. The opposite of *spurious* (false or fraudulent) is *genuine*.
Think of forgers selling "a spurious work of art."

32. A. The opposite of to *estrange* or alienate is to *reconcile*.
Think of "estranged couples" in a divorce.

33. B. The opposite of *provident* or frugal is *prodigal* or extravagant.
Think of the fable of the prodigal grasshopper and the provident ant.

34. D. The opposite of to *capitulate* or yield is to *resist*.
Think of "capitulating without a fight."

35. C. The opposite of *indigenous* or native is *alien* or foreign.
Beware eye-catchers. Choice A is incorrect.
Do not confuse *indigenous* or native with *indi-gent* or poor.

36. A. The opposite of *salubrity* or healthfulness is *unwholesomeness*.
Think of "the salubrity of mountain air."

37. D. The opposite of to *quail* or lose courage is to *become resolute* or firm.
Think of "quailing in fear."

38. B.   The opposite of *tantamount* or equivalent in value is *not equivalent*.
Context Clue: "Failure to publish is tantamount to suppression."

Section 2

1. C.   The key phrase here is "simplest in structure." In biology, *primitive* life forms are considered simple. Evolved forms are more specialized and do things in more complex ways.

2. C.   The leaders would be *apprehensive* in such circumstances that they could not achieve their goal of reconciliation.
Note that the phrase "negotiations have reached such a state" generally implies that they have reached a sorry state.

3. B.   If we are not *wary* or cautious, even we may be fooled by propaganda. One does not have to be *gullible* or easily deceived to fall for such tricks.

4. C.   *Charlatan* is another term for a *quack* or pretender to medical knowledge.

5. E.   The statement that "we do not know" whether a gesture indicates devotion or despair suggests that gestures are by their nature *ambiguous* or unclear.

6. A.   The common expectation is that *refined* or genteel people would reject evil while *coarse* people would tolerate it. However, the reverse holds true: *paradoxically*, the coarse word *condemns* an evil and the *refined* word excuses or condones it.
Watch out for words like *paradoxically* that signal the unexpected.

7. D.   The incongruity here is that one group finds Woolf too feminine for their tastes while another finds her not feminine (or perhaps feminist) enough for theirs.
Note that the word *peculiar* signals that Woolf's destiny is an unexpected one.

8. E.   A *dropcloth* protectively covers *furniture*. An *apron* protectively covers *clothing*.

(Function)

9. E.   An *archipelago* is a group or chain of *islands*. A *constellation* is a group of *stars*.
Beware eye-catchers. A *garden* does not by definition consist of *flowers*; a garden may comprise vegetables instead.

(Part to Whole)

10. C.   To *crow* is to express oneself in a *boastful* manner. To *pout* is to express oneself in a *sulky* manner.

(Defining Characteristic)

11. C.   By definition, an *ascetic* (one who practices severe self-discipline) is characterized by *self-denial*. A *zealot* (extreme enthusiast) is characterized by *fanaticism*.
Beware eye-catchers. A *miser* may hoard wealth, but he is not necessarily characterized by *affluence*. Even poor persons may be misers.

(Defining Characteristic)

12. A.   To *camouflage* something is to make it difficult to *discern* or perceive. To *encipher* or encode something is to make it difficult to *comprehend*.

(Function)

13. B.   A *seer* or prophet is by definition someone gifted in *prophecy*. A *sage* or wise person is by definition someone gifted in *wisdom*.

(Defining Characteristic)

14. C.   A *bracket* is a support for a *shelf*. A *strut* is a support for a *rafter*.
Note that you are being tested on an unfamiliar secondary meaning of *strut*. As always in dealing with the more difficult questions at the end of the analogy section, be suspicious when you come across what seems like a familiar word that is being used in an apparently incongruous context. You may be being tested on an unfamiliar secondary meaning of the word.

(Function)

15. A.   *Taxonomy* is the science or study of the *classification* of plants and animals. *Etymology* is the science or study of the *derivation* of words.

(Defining Characteristic)

16. B.   To be *brusque* or abrupt is to exhibit *unceremoniousness*. To be *obstinate* or stubborn is to exhibit *intractability*.

(Synonym Variant)

17. B.   In the third paragraph the author argues that women "have been unified by values, conventions, experiences, and behaviors impinging on each individual." To the extent that they have done this, they have come to constitute a subculture within our society. It is as part of such a subculture that women writers become conscious of their own female literary tradition. Thus, their *assimilation of the values* of their subculture furthers their ability to recognize the female literary tradition.

18. D.   The author opens the paragraph by stating that many literary critics have begun reinterpreting the study of women's literature. She then goes on to cite individual comments that support her assertion. Clearly, she is *receptive* or open to the ideas of these writers, for they and she share a common sense of the need to reinterpret their common field.
Choices A and B are incorrect. The author cites the literary critics straightforwardly, presenting their statements as evidence supporting her thesis.
Choice C is incorrect. The author does not *disparage* or belittle these critics. By quoting them respectfully she implicitly acknowledges their competence.
Choice E is incorrect. The author quotes the critics as acknowledged experts in the field. However, she is quite ready to disagree with their conclusions (as she disagrees with Moers' view of women's literature as an international movement). Clearly, she does not look on these critics with *awe*.

19. E.   Question E is answerable on the basis of the passage. According to lines 7–8, Mills disbelieved in the idea that women "have had a literature of their own all along."

20. C.   The gaps exist in the female literary tradition because once-famous female authors disappear from the records posthumously: they cease to be the subjects of critical discussion, and vanish as if they never had existed. Thus, there is no continuity in the female literary tradition.

21. B.   The writer neither lists (*enumerates*) nor sorts (*classifies*) anything in the opening paragraph.
Choice A is incorrect. The writer likens the female tradition to a lost continent and develops the metaphor by describing the continent "rising...from the sea of English literature."
Choice C is incorrect. The author refers or *alludes* to the classical legend of Atlantis.
Choice D is incorrect. The author quotes Colby and Thompson.
Choice E is incorrect. The author contrasts the revised view of women's literature with Mills' view.

22. B.   If women writers have no history, they have to rediscover the past. In process, they *create* or forge their consciousness of what their sex has achieved.
Here *forge* is used with its meaning of *fashion* or *make*, as blacksmiths forge metal by hammering it into shape. It is in this sense that James Joyce used *forge* in *A Portrait of the Artist as a Young Man*, whose hero goes forth to "forge in the smithy of (his) soul the uncreated conscience of (his) race."

23. C.   The author both cites Moers' work in support of her own assertions and argues against the validity of Moers' conclusion that women's literature is an international movement. Thus,

while she finds Moers' work basically *admirable* and worthy of respect, she considers it *inaccurate* in some of the conclusions it draws.
Choice A is incorrect. The author would not cite Moers as she does in the second paragraph if she believed Moers to be wholly *misleading*.
Choice B is incorrect. Since the author disagrees with at least one of Moers' conclusions, she obviously does not find Moers' work the *definitive* or final word.
Choices D and E are incorrect. Neither is supported by the author's mentions of Moers.

24. B.   Both the author's use of the phrase "a literature of their own" in the opening paragraph and her ongoing exploration of what she means by the female literary tradition in the English novel support this choice.
Choice A is incorrect. It is not the uniqueness of the phenomenon but the traditional nature of the phenomenon that interests the author.
Choice C is incorrect. The passage deals specifically with women's *literary* tradition.
Choice D is incorrect. The passage is concerned with the roots of female writing, not with its present day manifestations.
Choice E is incorrect. The author presents no such choice.

25. C.   The humorous tone of the opening sentence is matched by the whimsical title choice.

26. D.   The author provides them as examples of what he means by "whimsical terms" or *idiosyncratic nomenclature* in modern particle physics.

27. D.   Since the author considers the gluon to be *aptly* named, he clearly views this particular neologism or newly-coined term with *approbation*. However, he tempers his approval with *amusement*, for he finds the terms *whimsical* (capricious, fanciful) as well as apt.

28. C.   The opposite of to *rectify* or correct is to *make worse*.
Word Parts Clue: *Rect-* means right; *-ify* means to make. *Rectify* means to make right.
Think of "rectifying an error."

29. C.   The opposite of the *apex* or highest point is the *lowest point*.
Think of being at "the apex of one's career."

30. A.   The opposite of *prosaic* (dull, matter-of-fact) is *imaginative*.
Think of "being bored by a commonplace, prosaic job."

31. B.   The opposite of *dissonance* or discord is *harmony*.
Word Parts Clue: *Dis-* means apart; *son-* means sound. *Dissonance* is the state of sounding apart (that is, not in harmony).
Think of an instance of "jarring dissonance."

32. C. The opposite of *doltish* or stupid is *clever*.
Think of "a doltish blockhead."

33. E. The opposite of to *chagrin* (disappoint) is to *please*.
Beware eye-catchers. Choice A is incorrect. *Chagrin* is unrelated to *grin*.
Think of "being chagrined by a defeat."

34. A. The opposite of *disingenuous* or guileful (giving a false impression of naivete) is *naive* or unsophisticated.
Think of a "disingenuous appearance of candor."

35. B. The opposite of *recalcitrance* or stubbornness is *submissiveness*.
Think of "obstinate recalcitrance."

36. C. The opposite of *fecundity* or fruitfulness is *barrenness*.
Think of "the earth's abundant fecundity."

37. D. The opposite of *lugubrious* or melancholy is *jocose* or given to jesting.
Think of "lugubrious mourners."

38. D. The opposite of *animus* or hostility is *amity* or friendliness and good will.
Beware eye-catchers. Choice A, though tempting, is incorrect. *Hospitality* is an action (the enthusiastic reception of guests), not an emotion: when you speak of someone's hospitality, you are speaking of what he does, not of what he feels.

Section 3

1. B. Since the value of the fraction is negative, the denominator must be negative since the numerator has a positive value. Therefore the value of x is less than 1.

2. A. $y^2 - 1 = 3$
$y^2 = 4$
$y = \pm 2$
Since $x = 3$, the x is larger than y.

3. D. Since $x^2 = 25$, $x = \pm 5$. If $x = +5$, then the correct choice would be (C).
However, if $x = -5$, then the correct choice would be (A).

4. C.
In Column A, $\dfrac{1}{x} \div \dfrac{\frac{1}{1}}{x}$ or, $\dfrac{1}{x} \div \dfrac{x}{1}$ or, $\dfrac{1}{x} \cdot \dfrac{1}{x}$ or, $\dfrac{1}{x^2}$

In Column B, $\dfrac{1}{x} \cdot \dfrac{1}{x} = \dfrac{1}{x^2}$

5. D. x could be 9, 18, or 27.

6. B. $\frac{1}{3}$ of 4 yards = 1 yard and 1 foot
2 feet + 1 foot = 3 feet
$\frac{1}{3}$ of 3 feet = 1 foot
Therefore,
$\frac{1}{3}$ of 4 yards, 2 feet = 1 yard, 1 foot.

7. D. If n has a value of zero, then x could have any positive value.
If n has a value of 1, then x could be equal to 1.

8. C. $\sqrt{\dfrac{2x}{y}} \cdot \sqrt{\dfrac{xy}{2}} = \sqrt{\dfrac{2x^2y}{2y}} = \sqrt{x^2} = x$

9. C. $\dfrac{\frac{3}{4}}{1 + \frac{1}{2}}$ or $\dfrac{\frac{3}{4}}{\frac{3}{2}}$ or $\dfrac{3}{4} \div \dfrac{3}{2}$ or $\dfrac{3}{4} \cdot \dfrac{2}{3} = \dfrac{1}{2}$

10. C. If $\frac{1}{2} AC = \frac{1}{2} BC = \frac{1}{2} AB$, then $AC = AB = BC$. The triangle is equilateral and $z = 60$. Since BD divides AC so that $AD = DC$, it is also perpendicular, forming right triangle BDC, and $x = 90$. This question is an application of the Pythagorean theorem.

11. C. $A = 2.8$
$B = 3.4$
$C = 5.6$
$D = 6.2$
$AC = 5.6 - 2.8 = 2.8$
$BD = 6.2 - 3.4 = 2.8$

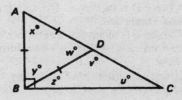

12. A. *ABD* is equilateral. $x = y = w = 60$. Since $AB \perp BC$, $y + z = 90$, and $z = 30$. BC lies opposite v which equals 120° and DC lies opposite the 30° angle. Therefore, $BC > DC$.

13. B. The sum of 2 negative integers is negative. The product of 2 negative integers is positive.

14. C. Adding the two equations gives you $x + y = 15$.

15. A.   Since the measure of angle C is 60, then the measure of angle A + angle B is 120, and therefore the measure of angle A is more than $\frac{1}{2}$ of 120, since A is larger than B (given). Side CB lies opposite the angle with a measure of more than 60 and is therefore larger than side AB, which lies opposite the angle with a measure of 60.

16. A.
Minimum crates = 3
Minimum weight = 125 pounds
3 × 125 = 375 pounds

17. D. $\angle ADC > \angle ABD$ (the exterior angle of a triangle is greater than either remote interior angle); $\angle ADC > \angle ACD$ (since $\angle ACD = \angle ABD$); $AC > AD$ (In a triangle the larger side is opposite the larger angle.)

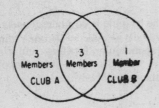

18. C.   Examine the problem graphically. $\frac{1}{2}$ of 12 (or 6) belong to Club A but note that 3 of these belong to both A and B. $\frac{1}{3}$ of 12 (or 4) belong to Club B but of these 3 also belong to Club A. We have thus accounted for 7 men who are club members Therefore, 5 men belong to neither club.

19. B.   Since $d > 7$, the charge for the first week, c cents, must be paid plus f cents for each additional day. The number of days over and above 1 week = $(d - 7)$. The charge for these days is $f(d - 7)$. Total cost = $c + f(d + 7)$.

20. D.   Let $\frac{2x}{3x}$ = the original fraction.

$$\frac{2x - 6}{3x} = \frac{2}{3}\left(\frac{2x}{3x}\right) \text{ [given]}$$
$$\frac{2x - 6}{3x} = \frac{4x}{9x}$$
$$\frac{2x - 6}{3x} = \frac{4}{9}$$
$$18x - 54 = 12x$$
$$6x = 54$$
$$x = 9$$
numerator = 2x or 18

21. C.   Total body weight = 70,000 grams
Weight of liver = 1,700 grams
$$\frac{1,700}{70,000} = \frac{17}{700} = .024 = 2.4\%$$

22. A.   Set up a proportion.
Let x = total body weight in terms of g.
$$\frac{\text{weight of skeleton}}{\text{total body weight}} - \frac{10,000 \text{ grams}}{70,000 \text{ grams}} = \frac{g}{x}$$
$$\frac{1}{7} = \frac{g}{x}$$
$$x = 7g$$

23. E. $\frac{1000}{2500} = \frac{\text{part}}{\text{entire}} = \frac{2}{5} = \frac{2}{5}$ of 360° = 144°

24. C. $\frac{\text{part}}{\text{whole}} = \frac{400}{2,500} = \frac{4}{25} = 16\%$

25. D.   Output through kidneys = 1500 cc. (Graph II)
Intake in fluids = 1500 cc. (Graph I)
$$\frac{1,500}{1,500} = 1 = 100\%$$

26. B.   a eggs must weigh ab ounces. Minimum weight for all c eggs = cd ounces. Minimum weight for all f eggs = fg ounces. Minimum weight of all eggs = $ab + cd + fg$.

27. C.   There is a direct proportion between the two types of tumblers.
$$\frac{3 \text{ large tumblers}}{5 \text{ small tumblers}} = \frac{1 \text{ large tumbler}}{x \text{ small tumblers}}$$
$$3x = 5$$
$$x = \frac{5}{3} \text{ or } 1\frac{2}{3}$$

28. B. $OA = OB = 4$
$m\angle AOB = \text{arc } AB = 112°$
$m\angle OAB + m\angle ABO = 68°$
$m\angle OAB = m\angle ABO = 34°$

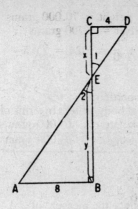

29. B. $\angle 1 = \angle 2$ (Vertical angles are equal.)
$\triangle AEB$ is similar to $\triangle DEC$.
Since $\dfrac{CD}{AB} = \dfrac{4}{8}$ or $\dfrac{1}{2}$, then $\dfrac{CE}{EB} = \dfrac{1}{2}$.
Let $x = CE$.
Let $y = EB$.
Then $\dfrac{x}{y} = \dfrac{1}{2}$ and $2x = y$. Since

$$x + y = 4$$
$$x + 2x = 5$$
$$3x = 5$$
and $x = \dfrac{5}{3}$ (CE)

In right triangle CED, leg $CD = 4$, leg $CE = \dfrac{5}{3}$.

By the Pythagorean theorem
$$(CE)^2 + (CD)^2 = (ED)^2$$
$$\left(\dfrac{5}{3}\right)^2 + 4^2 = (ED)^2$$
$$\dfrac{25}{9} + 16 = (ED)^2$$
$$\dfrac{169}{9} = (ED)^2$$
$$\dfrac{13}{3} = ED$$

If $ED = \dfrac{13}{3}$ then $AE = \dfrac{26}{3}$.

Therefore $AD = \dfrac{39}{3} = 13$.

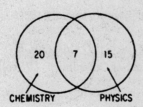

CHEMISTRY   PHYSICS

30. A. Note that 7 students take both subjects. 20 students take chemistry only and 15 students take physics only. The ratio of those taking physics only to those taking chemistry only is $\dfrac{15}{20}$ or $\dfrac{3}{4}$ or 3:4.

Section 4

1. C. Radii OD and OC are equal legs of right triangle DOC. Area of $DOC = \dfrac{1}{2}$ (leg) (leg) =

12.5 or (leg)$^2 = 25$. Therefore, leg = 5. Since leg (or radius) equals 5, the area of the circle equals 25π.

2. C. Let $x = $ the price of the item.
$$0.8x + 8 = x$$
$$8x + 80 = 10x$$
$$80 = 2x$$
$$x = 40$$

3. C. Since this is a parallelogram, $EH = FG$.

4. B. $a^2 = b^2 - 1$
$a^4 = (b^2 - 1)^2 = b^4 - 2b^2 + 1$ (Column A)
b^2 must be a positive quantity, hence $-2b^2$ is negative, making $b^4 - 2b^2 + 1$ less than $b^4 + 1$.

5. C. The area of $ABCD = (BC)(DC)$ or (2.5π) (10) or 25π. The area of the circle = πr^2. Since the diameter = 10, the radius = 5 and the area = πr^2, or 25π.

6. A. $125R = 81$
$$R = \dfrac{81}{125}$$
$$5 > R$$

7. A. $(-3)^9$ has a negative value (Column B)
$(-3)^8$ has a positive value (Column A)

8. A. Since both columns have 682 in common, consider only 9×7 in Column A and 10×6 in Column B. $63 > 60$.

9. B. The value of r is between -2 and -9. For any of these values r^7 would be negative. For example, if $r = -2$, then $\dfrac{1}{r^7} = -\dfrac{1}{128}$ or $-\dfrac{1}{128}$.
For any of these values for r, r^6 would have a positive value. For example, if $r = -2$, then $\dfrac{1}{r^6} = \dfrac{1}{64}$.
$$\dfrac{1}{64} > -\dfrac{1}{128}.$$

10. D. $\dfrac{c^2 d^2 e^2}{c^3 d^3 e^3}$ or $\dfrac{1}{cde}$ may be larger than, smaller than, or equal to $\dfrac{cde}{3}$ depending upon the values of c, d, and e.

11. D.   Since $n^2 > 0$, n may have a negative value, and $n < 0$. Since $n^2 > 0$, n may have a positive value in which case $n > 0$.

12. C. $x^2 = xy$. Divide by x and $x = y$.

13. A. $\frac{1}{2} + \frac{1}{3} = \frac{5}{6} = \frac{25}{30}$ $\frac{2}{5} = \frac{12}{30}$

14. C. $.4\% = \frac{.4}{100} = \frac{4}{1000}$

15. B. $\frac{1}{2}\% = .5\% = .005$
$.005 > .0005$

16. B.   To compare fractions, change all fractions to fractions with the same numerator or denominator.
$\frac{2}{9} = \frac{1}{4\frac{1}{2}}; \frac{3}{11} = \frac{1}{3\frac{2}{3}}; \frac{4}{13} = \frac{1}{3\frac{1}{3}}$
$\frac{1}{8}$ has the largest denominator.

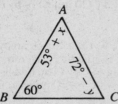

17. C.   Since ABC is equilateral, the measure of angle $BAC = 60$ and of $ACB = 60$.
$$53 + x = 60$$
$$x = 7$$
$$72 - y = 60$$
$$-y = -12$$
$$y = 12$$
$$x + y = 19$$

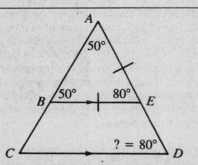

18. D.   Since $BE = AE$, the measure of angle $BAE = ABE = 50$. In triangle BAE, the measure of angle $AEB = 180 - 100 = 80$. Since $BE \parallel CD$, the measure of angle $ADC =$ the measure of angle $AEB = 80$.

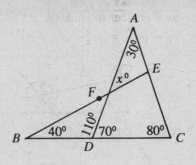

19. A.   In $\triangle ADC$, since the measure of $\angle A = 30$ and the measure of $\angle C = 80$, then the measure of $\angle ADC = 70$ and its supplement $\angle FDB = 110$. Then the measure of $\angle BFD = 30$ which $= \angle AFE$ (vertical angles).

20. C.
$$2 \oslash a = 4 + a$$
$$a \oslash 3 = 2a + 3 \cdot$$
$$4 + a = 2a + 3$$
$$1 = a$$

21. D.   Observe that in 1950 Houston ranked 14 while in 1960 it ranked 6. All the other cities listed among the largest 10 cities in 1950 were also among the largest 10 cities in 1960.

22. A.   For New York City the difference is $7.89 - 7.71 = 0.18$.
For Detroit the difference is $1.85 - 1.67 = 0.18$.

23. B.   Total population in the five largest cities in 1950 was
7.89
3.62
1.97
2.07
1.85
17.40 million
$\frac{17.4}{170}$ = approximately 10%

24. D.   Philadelphia = 1.96 million
District of Columbia = .75 million
$$.75x = 1.96$$
$$75x = 196$$
$$x = 2.6$$

25. D.   Change from 1 million to 1.67 million
difference
$= 0.67$
$\frac{\text{change}}{\text{original}} = \frac{0.67}{1.00} = \frac{67}{100} = 67\%$

26. C. $\dfrac{\text{number of girls}}{\text{total number of students}}$ = part of class made

up of girls = $\dfrac{x}{x + y}$.

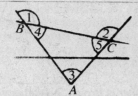

27. D. Angle 1 + angle 4 = 180°
145° + angle 4 = 180°
Angle 4 = 35°
Angle 2 + angle 5 = 180°
125° + angle 5 = 180°

Angle 5 = 55°
Angle 4 + angle 5 + angle 3 = 180°
(the sum of the angles of a triangle equals 180°)
35° + 55° + angle 3 = 180°
Angle 3 = 90°

28. E.

4 quarts = 1 gallon
16 quarts = 4 gallons
2 pints = 1 quart
32 pints = 16 quarts
or, 64 half pints = 16 quarts

29. C. First mixture
(33¢) (2 pounds) = 66¢
(24¢) (1 pound) = 24¢
90¢ is cost of 3 pounds or
30¢ is cost of one pound.

Second mixture
(33¢) (1 pound) = 33¢
(24¢) (2 pounds) = 48¢
81¢ is cost of 3 pounds or
27¢ is cost of one pound.

The shop will save 3¢ per pound or $3.00 for 100 pounds.

30. C. Let x = number of minutes allowed for each of the questions other than the mathematics problems. Then $2x$ = number of minutes allowed for each mathematics problem. $(50)(2x)$ or $100x$ = number of minutes allowed for all mathematics problems. $(150)(x)$ or $150x$ = number of minutes allowed for all other questions.

$100x + 150x$ = total time = 3 hours
= 180 minutes
$100x + 150x = 180$
$250x = 180$
$x = \dfrac{180}{250}$
$100x = \dfrac{180}{250}100 = 72$ minutes

Section 5

1–4. It would be helpful to make a sketch to summarize the information.

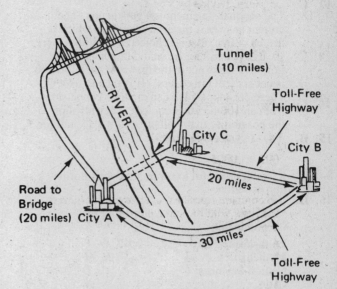

1. A. The mileage from City B to City C is 20 miles on the highway. For the other choices it would mean going to City A (30 miles) and then either by tunnel (10 miles) or by the bridge (20 miles).

2. D. The mileage on the toll-free highway from City A to City B is 30 miles. The other choices involve going to City C by bridge or tunnel, then from City C for 20 miles to City B.

3. C. The difference in cost between the bridge toll and the tunnel toll is negligible considering the possible saving in gasoline consumption, so that the most important factor would be traffic conditions.

4. E. Generally speaking the extra charge for using the tunnel can be compensated by the gasoline consumed on the extra 10 miles when crossing the bridge (IV). The gasoline efficiency can hardly account for the fuel used on 10 miles (III). Traffic and road conditions can be expected to influence a driver to choose one over the other since the difference in tolls can be compensated for by fuel consumption (I). However, if the car has many passengers, at 10¢ per passenger there could possibly be a saving of money by using the bridge, if road conditions are normal.

5. D. The established precedent is the best argument for permitting the church to use the park.

6. B. The argument in (A) could be used by the church. The correct answer is (B) since there would be some inconvenience to those who are

not members of that church. We cannot assume that the church meeting would be excessively noisy (C). We cannot assume that the church people will leave litter to be cleaned up (E).

7. D.   The original statement is a conclusion. The correct answer is the argument from which it can be drawn; that is, choice D. If Wilbur were six feet tall or less, he would be seated in the first row. He is not in the first row; therefore, he is not six feet tall or less. (If P, then Q. Not Q. Therefore, not P.) We can draw no conclusions from any of the other choices; They all allow the possibility that Wilbur is only 5′11″ tall (or 3′11″ tall, for that matter).

8–12.   It would be useful to summarize the information as follows:

| Large University | J, K, L |
| Small College | M, N, O, P |

English Literature	J, O, P
Mathematics	K, M
Natural Sciences	L
Latin	N

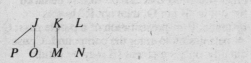

8. E.   J and P cannot serve on the same committee since they both teach English Literature I. If J cannot serve then K and L must serve. If K is serving, M may not represent the small college (II). Since L must serve, (III) is correct.

9. A.   Committee K, L, M has K and M on the same committee (B). J, K, L has no representative from the small college (C). J, O, N commits two errors. It has two representatives from the small college and it has J and O on the same committee (D). J, K, M has K and M on the same committee (E).

10. B.   K and M both teach mathematics (A). O cannot serve with P since they both represent the small college and they both teach English Literature (C). J cannot serve with P because they both teach English Literature (D). M and N cannot serve with P for they all represent the small college.

11. C.   If L is not available then J and K must serve. Since J is serving neither O nor P may serve.

12. E.   (I) is incorrect since N and O represent the small college. (II) is correct. M and O represent the small college. (III) is correct. When M serves, K may not serve.

13. C.   Both parents of a Brown female are Brown, but her father was born Red. Her mother's mother was Brown, and therefore that grandfather was born Red (I); her father's mother was Red (II), and therefore that grandfather was born Brown (III). Use the following logic: if the parents were born in different groups, and the grandmothers were in the same groups as the parents, the grandfathers must have been in different groups.

14. A.   His mother is Brown, his father was born Red. His mother's unmarried brother is Brown, his father's unmarried brother is Red—not to mention married brothers of his parents! Our friend may only marry a Red woman, and their children will be Red (B, C); any persons the children marry must be born Brown (D, E).

15. B.   Her mother is Red, and the brother, whether unmarried, divorced, or a widower, is also Red. No Red may marry a Red. The Brown male's father was born Red, so his sister is Red (A). The brother of the man born Red (who, as a widow, is Red again) was also born Red, so his wife (now his widow) is Brown (C). Any widower has reverted to his original group, while his wife's sister is in the same group as his wife was (D). Any widow's daughter is in her own group, and the ex-husband, having reverted to the group of his birth, will be eligible (E).

16. D.   The woman's mother has the same group as she; the mother's brother was born into this group, but married into the other and, as a widower, (according to the changed rules) remains in the second group, so marriage is possible. The dead sister's husband remains in the same group as the dead sister and is not eligible (A). The daughter is in the mother's group and the ex-husband remains in it and so is not eligible (B). The widower retains his married group; his brother, born in the same group as he was, is in the same married group; so is his daughter, and is not eligible (C). The divorced male now has his ex-wife's group; so does the sister, widowed or otherwise, so no marriage is possible (E).

17–22.   The trick here is to determine the relative positions of the letters on the basis of the clues, just as if this were a puzzle dealing with persons in a line or any similar situation. Questions 17 and 18 can then be answered immediately; Questions 19–22 involve simple arithmetic which is easy once the relative positions of the letters that stand for the integers are known. Start with the most definite statement, that B is the middle term, and diagram it like this:

$$\_ \ \_ \ \_ \ \underline{B} \ \_ \ \_ \ \_$$

The preceding statement, that D is 3 less than

A, gives two possible positions for A (A cannot be where B is or to the left; and it cannot be at the extreme right because then D would be where B is):

$$\underline{\;}\;\underline{D}\;\underline{\;}\;\underline{B}\;\underline{A}\;\underline{\;}\;\underline{\;}$$

or

$$\underline{\;}\;\underline{\;}\;\underline{D}\;\underline{B}\;\underline{\;}\;\underline{A}\;\underline{\;}$$

The third statement, F is as much less than B as C is greater than D, yields three possibilities: F is 1, 2, or 3 less than B. If F is 1 less than B, C is 1 greater than D. This is not possible in either of the two diagrams above. If F is 3 less than B, C is 3 greater than D. This, too, is not possible in either diagram. If F is 2 less than B, C is 2 greater than D. This is not possible in the first diagram, but it is possible in the second. This, then, must be the correct solution. The two end positions must therefore belong to E and G, and the last statement tells you G must be to the right of F. So you have:

$$\underline{E}\;\underline{F}\;\underline{D}\;\underline{B}\;\underline{C}\;\underline{A}\;\underline{G}$$

The questions are now easy.

17. B.   By inspection of the diagram.

18. D.   According to the diagram, A is four greater than F, and D is four less than G.

19. B.   Given a value for any of the letters, you can find the value of all the others. If A = 7, E = 2 and G = 8. Their sum is 10. Be careful that you don't assume that A = 7 in the other questions. That is given for this question only.

20. D.   You might choose E on the reasoning that, if no value is given for any letter, no numerical value can be found for A − F. But this is wrong. You *can* tell that A is 4 greater than F. When any number is subtracted from a number 4 greater than it, the result is 4, no matter what the numbers are.

21. D.   C is 4 greater than E, so T is four greater than C. But this means that T is 3 greater than A. If T = A + E and T = A + 3, E = 3. If E = 3, D = 5.

22. D.   If the seven integers all fall in the span from 1 to 10, then the highest possible value of C will occur if the seven letters represent the integers 4-10. In this case, C = 8. The smallest possible value of D will occur if the seven letters represent the integers 1-7. In this case, D = 3, and 8 − 3 = 5.

23. B.   Nancy says that what Ellen reports can't be true and offers, as evidence, Julie's high school grades. The assumption must be that no one who got such grades is likely to flunk out of college. Choice A is wrong because Ellen merely reports what she has heard; by disrupting it, Nancy does not brand her a liar. Nor does Ellen necessarily assume that the rumor is true (C). D is wrong because Nancy does not necessarily claim that Julie has not left college —only that she hasn't flunked out. Ellen has only *heard* something—she *knows* nothing (E).

24. D.   The president states that any measures required to defeat the "takeover," i.e., to maintain full control, are justified, whether legal or not. This implies D. The president does *not* say that illegal measures *will* definitely be required (A) or allege anything about the union (B). He or she states that *in this case* the workers are trying to take control; E is an unsupported generalization. The president's statements establish only what the president advocates, not what he or she and the Board of Directors will *actually* do if the union wins (C).

25. C.   Given the statement "If P, then Q," the *only* other statement that can be validly deduced from it is "If not Q, then not P." In this instance, P = presentation of a purple pass; Q = permission to enter the compound. Consequently, only statement III may be validly inferred. You cannot validly deduce "If not P, then not Q" (statement I) or "If Q, then P" (statement II).

Section 6

1-4.   The diagram shown here will make this puzzle much easier to follow.

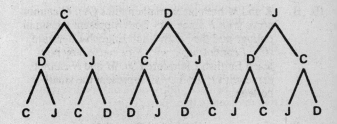

The top row shows the top office holders; the second row shows the deputies; the third row shows the staffs. Note that these relationships are true no matter which office a given party holds.

1. D.   Check the diagram, or reason as follows: the three Offices must always have two Democratic, two Conservative, and Two Justice Party deputies. When the Justice Party holds a top office, one of the deputies in that office must be a Conservative, so only one of the deputies in the other Offices can be a Conservative. A, B, C, and E all follow logically from the rules and must be true.

2. D.   Check the diagram—but remember that the staffs being asked about are not those under the Democratic President, but those under the Prime Minister, who can belong to *either* of the other parties. In each of the other offices, one of the deputies must be a Democratic Party member who can have no Democratic staff members, while the other deputy *must* have one-half Democratic staff members—for a total of one-fourth the staff members in each office. If the Prime Minister is a Justice Party member, one-half the staff members will be Justice and one-fourth Conservative; if the Prime Minister is Conservative, it will be the other way around. So I must be true, and either II or III must also be true.

3. B.   This must always be the case. Since the two deputies in any Office must each have a staff composed half of members of the top office holder's party, exactly half the staff members in any Office must always belong to one party. Choice E is, therefore, logically impossible. The rules for deputies and staffs exclude A and C. Exactly one-third of the total staff members in all three Offices must belong to each party (D).

4. C.   The Conservative Chief of Staff has a Justice Department deputy, while the Justice Party Chief of Staff must not; since a Conservative deputy must be brought in, all the Conservative staff members of the fired Justice Party deputy must also be fired; however, the Democratic deputy may retain his or her Conservative staff members, which means only half of the Conservative staff members must be fired. Looking at the diagram, you can see that the Democratic deputy and his or her Justice Party suffers can retain their posts (A); while the Justice deputy must be fired, his or her Democratic staffers can stay (B); the Conservative Chief of Staff had no Conservative deputy (D); one deputy must be fired, but some Conservative staffers may retain their posts (E).

5. C.   The statement given is true only is all members of the set "steering committee members" belong to the set "central committee members." (In a diagram, steering committee members would be a circle entirely inside a circle representing central committee members.) Choice A does not rule out the possibility that the steering committee has other members besides those who are on the central committee. B says that Elaine must belong to one of the committees, not necessarily to both. D is a weaker version of A; E establishes no link between central committee membership and steering committee membership.

6. E.   If anyone other than a football player wears a football jersey, the conclusion is not valid; so it is valid only if choice D is true. The other choices establish, in various ways, that football players probably or certainly wear football jerseys, but this does not mean that no one else does.

7. E.   Evidence of original insights (choice E) would best indicate the presence of what the author most stresses: independent critical thinking. Choice A may display ambition on the student's part; choice B evidences mastery of basic verbal skills; choice C shows a willingness to do hard work. But neither choice A, B, nor C is what the author would find *most* praiseworthy. Choice D is tempting, but simply avoiding clichés and vagueness does not necessarily display independent critical thinking.

8–11.   You could make a calendar for this one, but it would be very complicated. It's easier just to use the times given to make a table showing which possibilities can be scheduled without conflicts. State with Latin, since everything else has to be fitted around it:

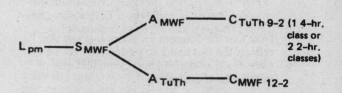

8. D.   The table will tell you that D is impossible; Sanskrit on MWF meets from 10 to 12, which conflicts with Latin. The others are all possible.

9. A.   This leaves the hours from 9 to 2 on Tuesday and Thursday free for Celtic Literature. Tom can schedule a 4-hour session at either 9 or 10 on either day (four possibilities), or two-hour sessions starting at 9, 10, 11, or 12 on Tuesday and Thursday (sixteen possible schedules), or two two-hour sessions in one day on either day (four possibilities). The other choices leave either MWF from 2 to 4 or MWF from 12 to 2. In either case, there are only six possibilities for scheduling Celtic Literature.

10. D. The Friday session must be either from 12 to 2 or from 2 to 4. No schedule leaves both these slots free. It can be 12 to 2 only if Tom takes Sanskrit on MWF and Armenian Literature on TuTh. It can be 2 to 4 only if he takes Sanskrit on TuTh and Armenian Literature on MWF.

11. B. This one may be hard without a calendar; you must look back at the times listed, unless you included them in your table. The MWF 11-12:30 slot is open if Tom takes morning Latin (out at 11) and MWF Armenian Literature (starts at 12:30). This doesn't interfere with Celtic Literature. Choice A, C, and D conflict with Sanskrit; E conflicts with Armenian and Celtic Literature.

12–18. To diagram this puzzle, start with several dashes in a column. These will represent the floors of the building. Start with more than six, so that a wrong guess doesn't push you off your diagram. Use initials and put one person or persons occupying an apartment on each side of a dash representing a given floor. Starting with L (and a blank for his roommate), A/C, M, and R and P fall into place easily. You now have six floors from top to bottom, so R and P must be on floor one. The only floors remaining with two blank spots are two and five; B and F must go on floor two and N must go three floors up, on floor five. The only remaining floor on which J can be three below anyone is floor three; W must be on floor six and E on floor five. You no have:

> L/W or L—W
> N/E or N—E
> —A/C
> J—M
> B—F
> R—P

Note that the diagram for floors five and six reflects the fact that Larry and Willy are on the same floor, as are Ned and Ellen, and may or may not be roommates.

12. C. By inspection of the diagram. Note that choice D gives a correct list from *top to bottom*—don't get careless and choose this answer.

13. C. Again by simple inspection of the diagram.

14. B. The only person mentioned who can live on floor six, and therefore be Larry's roommate, is Willy.

15. A. By inspection of the diagram, Choices B and C also have the wrong persons above or below; choices D and E list the right persons, but Rick can't live on floor four or floor six.

16. E. No one mentioned is on floor four; Willy *may* live with Larry on floor six.

17. B. Follow the diagram: Joe goes from floor three to floor one; Rick or Paul goes to floor two; Bob or Frank goes to Ned or Ellen's apartment on floor five, and one of them goes to Joe's old apartment.

18. E. Dorothy cannot possibly live with Frank, because we are told that he has a *single* apartment. All of the other persons mentioned as possibilities *may* have space available in their apartments.

19–22. A diagram like the one shown will make it possible to trace the events without becoming confused. The other point to bear in mind is that you must avoid unsupported assumptions; for example, statement (2) doesn't mean that F *always* occurs if B occurs—just that it never occurs without B having occurred. Similarly, statement (1) doesn't mean that B or C *cannot* occur without A—just that if A occurs, one of these (but not both) will occur. Finally, statement (3) doesn't mean that D occurs *only* this way—it *may* occur on its own, without B or C, but it will *certainly* occur if B or C occurs. Unless you're clear on this, you'll probably miss some questions.

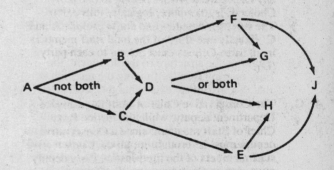

19. D. A causes B *or* C, but not both. In either case, D occurs (III). F and E can occur *only* if B or C occur, respectively, so they *cannot* both occur if A occurs (I, II). The other parts of I and II are consistent: G will occur if F occurs; H will occur if E occurs.

20. C. See statement (3). F *may* occur if B occurs, but may not (choice A); D will occur if B occurs, but D may cause H instead of G (choice B); G occurs if F occurs and may occur if D occurs, but F need not occur if B occurs, while D can lead to H; so G *or* H must occur, but both need not occur (choice D); J *may* not occur even if E or F occur (choice E).

21. C. If J occurs, E or F must have occurred—statement (5); thus either B or C must have occurred —statements (2), (4). Since E *or* F, but not both, are required for J, choices A and B are wrong. If E occurs and F does not, G need not occur (choice D). B and C *can* both occur (if one is not caused by A) but both aren't necessary for J; they can lead to E and F, but one of these is all that is required for J to occur (choice E).

22. C. D *may* occur without B or C; no cause for A is mentioned (I, II); but F occurs *only* if B occurs (statement 2) and so no other cause is possible (III).

23. E. Statements I and II are plausible explanations for the students' passivity in previous years, but neither one can be inferred definitely (choices A and B); you cannot conclude that one of them must be true (some third explanation is possible) or that they exclude each other (both could be true simultaneously) (choice C). From the students' previous behavior, *no* valid inferences about their response to a new, larger tuition hike are possible (choice D and E).

24. D. The original statement says that beauty has an objective existence; that is can exist independently of a person's perceiving it. This would be a rebuttal to the claim made in choice D that beauty is purely subjective and so entirely dependent on its perception by some viewer. None of the other choices is in opposition to the original statement.

25. C. Examine the structure of the argument: the only reason given for funding the research is that the possibility exists that the substances cure cancer. The unstated assumption is that this is a sufficient reason for providing funds. No probability is mentioned (choice A), and no comparison with other lines of research is made (choice B). D, while probably true, does not provide logical support for the argument about researching this specific possibility. The argument simply says that the government should provide the funds, not that they are definitely unavailable elsewhere (choice E).

Section 7

1. B. The structure of the sentence indicates that you are looking for two synonyms or near-synonyms, in this case *squalor* and *filth*.

2. C. To *rail against* fate would be to complain angrily about it or utter words of bitterness about it.
Note how the use of parallel structure (*neither...nor*) indicates that the two participial phrases linked together are similar in meaning.

3. C. If the continents have formed sometime in the course of the earth's lifetime, then they are not *primordial* features of the earth that have existed from the earth's beginning.
As in the present sentence, inverted word order may sometimes indicate a contrast. The inversion of normal word order in the sentence opening ("Old as the continents are") is concessive: the writer is conceding a point. Rewritten in normal word order, the sentence would begin "Although the continents are old."

4. A. Some aspects of the hypothesis can be criticized. However, its basic point still appears to hold true: it has not been *refuted* or disproved.

5. A. It would be *ironic* or the reverse of what was expected for friends of judicial *autonomy* or independence to support the *abolition* or destruction of an independent judiciary.
Note how the use of *irony* implicitly signals the reversal of normal expectations.

6. B. Readers would be disinclined to take seriously a work they considered *overwrought* or excessive in its *bold* theatricality.
Note how the use of *but* indicates that the second missing word contrasts with *enthralling* (absorbing) in meaning.

7. A. When an activity is *repugnant* or distasteful, people will discontinue it as soon as they are free to do so. If parents and teachers make the process of getting an education distasteful, children will quit school as soon as they are no longer *coerced* or forced to attend.
Note how the "as long as ... happens, so long will ... happen" structure indicates cause and effect.

8. E. A *moderator* presides over a *debate*. An *umpire* presides over a *game*.

(Function)

9. A. *Delirium* causes *disorientation* or confusion. *Paralysis* causes *immobility* or loss of movement.

(Cause and Effect)

10. B. A *glossary* or word list is composed of *words*. An *atlas* is composed of *maps*.

(Defining Characteristic)

11. B. An *armature* is the skeleton that supports a *statue*. A *framework* is the skeleton that supports a *building*.

(Function)

12. B. An *epaulet* is an ornament worn on the *shoulder*. A *tiara* is an ornament worn on the *head*.

(Defining Characteristic)

13. C.   A *bear* characteristically *lumbers* or moves heavily. A *goose* characteristically *waddles* or moves clumsily.

(Defining Characteristic)

14. A.   Someone *enervated* or weakened is lacking in *vigor* or strength. Someone *lax* or easy-going is lacking in *rigor* or severity.

(Antonym Variant)

15. D.   A *snail* is not noted for *celerity* or speed. A *peacock* is not noted for *humility* or modesty.

(Antonym Variant)

16. E.   *Adulation* or excessive flattery is more extreme than simple *flattery*. *Castigation* or severe reproof is more extreme than an *admonishment* or gentle reproof.

(Degree of Intensity)

17. C.   The references to the Inca empire and to the Andes Mountains, as well as to magical religions and chroniclers, suggest the Quechua world may be placed in ancient South America.

18. E.   The passage compare the Quechua empire to a *mandala* because "it was divided into four parts." Thus, a *mandala* is most likely a *figure composed of four divisions*.

19. B.   The author refers to the Quechua as existing in "a state of unremitting anxiety, which could not be resolved by action" and which the Quechua could only deal with by looking into himself and struggling with the depths of his own psyche. This suggests that the Quechua world was *highly introspective*.

20. D.   Both the unremitting anxiety of Quechua life and the recurring harvest failures that brought starvation to millions illustrate the *harshness and frustration* of Quechua existence.

21. D.   The author states what cataclysmic variables are and describes how the three general classes of exploding stars range in magnitude and other characteristics.
Choice A is incorrect. The author gives far more emphasis to dwarf novae than to novae.
Choice B is incorrect. The author offers no such explanation.
Choice C is incorrect. He states their unpredictability; he does not explain or account for it.
Choice E is incorrect. The author offers no such explanation.

22. D.   In the first paragraph, it says "25 novae occur in our galaxy every year, but only two or three are *near enough* to be observed." Thus, our observations of novae are hampered by their *distance*.

23. E.   You can arrive at the correct answer by the process of elimination.
Statement I is accurate. Dwarf novae explosions are less violent than are those of supernovae. Therefore, you can eliminate Choice B.
Statement II is accurate. Dwarf novae are observed far more frequently than are supernovae. Therefore, you can eliminate Choices A and D.
Statement III is accurate. Dwarf novae, unlike supernovae, flare up periodically rather than flaring up once and being totally consumed. Therefore, you can eliminate Choice C.
Only Choice E is left. It is the correct answer.

24. C.   Lines 11–14 state: "If the exploding star is in a nearby part of the galaxy, it may create a 'new star' that was not previously visible to the naked eye." Thus, a new star is one that has become bright enough to strike the eye.

25. C.   In each explosion, a dwarf nova loses "a minute fraction of its mass" (line 17). By staying at an intermediate level of brightness rather than descending to minimum brightness, Z Camelopardalis stars may use up a proportionally greater fraction of their mass than do the SS Cygni stars that descend to minimum brightness between outbursts.
Choice A is incorrect. Rather than reverting to some original level of brightness, Z Camelopardalis stars stay at an intermediate level of brightness for a time.
Choice B is incorrect. There is nothing in the passage to suggest it.
Choice D is incorrect. Z Camelopardalis stars are dwarf novae, which are far more frequently observed by astronomers than are supernovae.
Choice E is incorrect. Nothing in the passage suggests that they are less bright than other dwarf novae.

26. C.   In lines 19–21, the author states that although astrophysicists can account for the explosions of supernovae, "the novae and dwarf novae have presented more of a puzzle." He then proceeds to discuss dwarf novae in detail. He has yet to discuss novae, the other class of puzzling catastrophic variables.

27. D.   You can arrive at the correct answer by the process of elimination.
Question I is answerable on the basis of the passage. Line 5 states that the last supernova was observed in 1604. Therefore, you can eliminate Choices B and E.
Question II is unanswerable on the basis of the

passage. No reason for the phenomenon is given in the passage. Therefore, you can eliminate Choice C.

Question III is answerable on the basis of the passage. Lines 38–41 state that dwarf novae increase in brightness "within a period of several hours" and then decline from this maximum level of brilliance over a period of two to three days. Therefore, you can eliminate Choice A.

Only Choice D is left. It is the correct answer.

28. A.   The opposite of to *fluster* or discompose is to *soothe*.
Think of "being flustered by reporters' questions."

29. C.   The opposite of a *deletion* or removal of material is an *insertion* of material.
Think of "the deletion of objectionable material" from films.

30. B.   The opposite of to *disparage* or belittle is to *eulogize* or praise.
Think of "rival candidates disparaging each other."

31. B.   The opposite of *baleful* (malign, harmful) is *beneficent* or productive of good.
Think of "dangerous baleful influences."

32. C.   The opposite of *servility* or oversubmissiveness is *independence*.
Think of "cringing servility."

33. A.   The opposite of *felicitous* (happily suited to a situation; appropriate) is *inappropriate*.
Think of "a felicitous remark."

34. B.   The opposite of *precipitous* (hasty, rash; steep) is *cautious*.
Think of "a precipitous flight."

35. C.   The opposite of to *assuage* or ease is to *worsen*.
Think of "assuaging someone's grief."

36. D.   The opposite of *latent* (existing in potential; not manifest) is *manifest* or evident.
Think of "latent ability that needs bringing out."

37. A.   The opposite of to *broach* or open up something is to *seal it off*.
Think of "broaching a topic of conversation."

38. B.   The opposite of an *encomium* or statement of praise is a *denunciation* or condemnation.
Think of "a hero receiving an encomium."

Answer Sheet – MODEL TEST 2

Start with number 1 for each new section.
If a section has fewer than 38 questions, leave the extra spaces blank.

Section 1

1. Ⓐ Ⓑ Ⓒ Ⓓ Ⓔ	11. Ⓐ Ⓑ Ⓒ Ⓓ Ⓔ	21. Ⓐ Ⓑ Ⓒ Ⓓ Ⓔ	31. Ⓐ Ⓑ Ⓒ Ⓓ Ⓔ
2. Ⓐ Ⓑ Ⓒ Ⓓ Ⓔ	12. Ⓐ Ⓑ Ⓒ Ⓓ Ⓔ	22. Ⓐ Ⓑ Ⓒ Ⓓ Ⓔ	32. Ⓐ Ⓑ Ⓒ Ⓓ Ⓔ
3. Ⓐ Ⓑ Ⓒ Ⓓ Ⓔ	13. Ⓐ Ⓑ Ⓒ Ⓓ Ⓔ	23. Ⓐ Ⓑ Ⓒ Ⓓ Ⓔ	33. Ⓐ Ⓑ Ⓒ Ⓓ Ⓔ
4. Ⓐ Ⓑ Ⓒ Ⓓ Ⓔ	14. Ⓐ Ⓑ Ⓒ Ⓓ Ⓔ	24. Ⓐ Ⓑ Ⓒ Ⓓ Ⓔ	34. Ⓐ Ⓑ Ⓒ Ⓓ Ⓔ
5. Ⓐ Ⓑ Ⓒ Ⓓ Ⓔ	15. Ⓐ Ⓑ Ⓒ Ⓓ Ⓔ	25. Ⓐ Ⓑ Ⓒ Ⓓ Ⓔ	35. Ⓐ Ⓑ Ⓒ Ⓓ Ⓔ
6. Ⓐ Ⓑ Ⓒ Ⓓ Ⓔ	16. Ⓐ Ⓑ Ⓒ Ⓓ Ⓔ	26. Ⓐ Ⓑ Ⓒ Ⓓ Ⓔ	36. Ⓐ Ⓑ Ⓒ Ⓓ Ⓔ
7. Ⓐ Ⓑ Ⓒ Ⓓ Ⓔ	17. Ⓐ Ⓑ Ⓒ Ⓓ Ⓔ	27. Ⓐ Ⓑ Ⓒ Ⓓ Ⓔ	37. Ⓐ Ⓑ Ⓒ Ⓓ Ⓔ
8. Ⓐ Ⓑ Ⓒ Ⓓ Ⓔ	18. Ⓐ Ⓑ Ⓒ Ⓓ Ⓔ	28. Ⓐ Ⓑ Ⓒ Ⓓ Ⓔ	38. Ⓐ Ⓑ Ⓒ Ⓓ Ⓔ
9. Ⓐ Ⓑ Ⓒ Ⓓ Ⓔ	19. Ⓐ Ⓑ Ⓒ Ⓓ Ⓔ	29. Ⓐ Ⓑ Ⓒ Ⓓ Ⓔ	
10. Ⓐ Ⓑ Ⓒ Ⓓ Ⓔ	20. Ⓐ Ⓑ Ⓒ Ⓓ Ⓔ	30. Ⓐ Ⓑ Ⓒ Ⓓ Ⓔ	

Section 2

1. Ⓐ Ⓑ Ⓒ Ⓓ Ⓔ	11. Ⓐ Ⓑ Ⓒ Ⓓ Ⓔ	21. Ⓐ Ⓑ Ⓒ Ⓓ Ⓔ	31. Ⓐ Ⓑ Ⓒ Ⓓ Ⓔ
2. Ⓐ Ⓑ Ⓒ Ⓓ Ⓔ	12. Ⓐ Ⓑ Ⓒ Ⓓ Ⓔ	22. Ⓐ Ⓑ Ⓒ Ⓓ Ⓔ	32. Ⓐ Ⓑ Ⓒ Ⓓ Ⓔ
3. Ⓐ Ⓑ Ⓒ Ⓓ Ⓔ	13. Ⓐ Ⓑ Ⓒ Ⓓ Ⓔ	23. Ⓐ Ⓑ Ⓒ Ⓓ Ⓔ	33. Ⓐ Ⓑ Ⓒ Ⓓ Ⓔ
4. Ⓐ Ⓑ Ⓒ Ⓓ Ⓔ	14. Ⓐ Ⓑ Ⓒ Ⓓ Ⓔ	24. Ⓐ Ⓑ Ⓒ Ⓓ Ⓔ	34. Ⓐ Ⓑ Ⓒ Ⓓ Ⓔ
5. Ⓐ Ⓑ Ⓒ Ⓓ Ⓔ	15. Ⓐ Ⓑ Ⓒ Ⓓ Ⓔ	25. Ⓐ Ⓑ Ⓒ Ⓓ Ⓔ	35. Ⓐ Ⓑ Ⓒ Ⓓ Ⓔ
6. Ⓐ Ⓑ Ⓒ Ⓓ Ⓔ	16. Ⓐ Ⓑ Ⓒ Ⓓ Ⓔ	26. Ⓐ Ⓑ Ⓒ Ⓓ Ⓔ	36. Ⓐ Ⓑ Ⓒ Ⓓ Ⓔ
7. Ⓐ Ⓑ Ⓒ Ⓓ Ⓔ	17. Ⓐ Ⓑ Ⓒ Ⓓ Ⓔ	27. Ⓐ Ⓑ Ⓒ Ⓓ Ⓔ	37. Ⓐ Ⓑ Ⓒ Ⓓ Ⓔ
8. Ⓐ Ⓑ Ⓒ Ⓓ Ⓔ	18. Ⓐ Ⓑ Ⓒ Ⓓ Ⓔ	28. Ⓐ Ⓑ Ⓒ Ⓓ Ⓔ	38. Ⓐ Ⓑ Ⓒ Ⓓ Ⓔ
9. Ⓐ Ⓑ Ⓒ Ⓓ Ⓔ	19. Ⓐ Ⓑ Ⓒ Ⓓ Ⓔ	29. Ⓐ Ⓑ Ⓒ Ⓓ Ⓔ	
10. Ⓐ Ⓑ Ⓒ Ⓓ Ⓔ	20. Ⓐ Ⓑ Ⓒ Ⓓ Ⓔ	30. Ⓐ Ⓑ Ⓒ Ⓓ Ⓔ	

Section 3

1. Ⓐ Ⓑ Ⓒ Ⓓ Ⓔ	11. Ⓐ Ⓑ Ⓒ Ⓓ Ⓔ	21. Ⓐ Ⓑ Ⓒ Ⓓ Ⓔ	31. Ⓐ Ⓑ Ⓒ Ⓓ Ⓔ
2. Ⓐ Ⓑ Ⓒ Ⓓ Ⓔ	12. Ⓐ Ⓑ Ⓒ Ⓓ Ⓔ	22. Ⓐ Ⓑ Ⓒ Ⓓ Ⓔ	32. Ⓐ Ⓑ Ⓒ Ⓓ Ⓔ
3. Ⓐ Ⓑ Ⓒ Ⓓ Ⓔ	13. Ⓐ Ⓑ Ⓒ Ⓓ Ⓔ	23. Ⓐ Ⓑ Ⓒ Ⓓ Ⓔ	33. Ⓐ Ⓑ Ⓒ Ⓓ Ⓔ
4. Ⓐ Ⓑ Ⓒ Ⓓ Ⓔ	14. Ⓐ Ⓑ Ⓒ Ⓓ Ⓔ	24. Ⓐ Ⓑ Ⓒ Ⓓ Ⓔ	34. Ⓐ Ⓑ Ⓒ Ⓓ Ⓔ
5. Ⓐ Ⓑ Ⓒ Ⓓ Ⓔ	15. Ⓐ Ⓑ Ⓒ Ⓓ Ⓔ	25. Ⓐ Ⓑ Ⓒ Ⓓ Ⓔ	35. Ⓐ Ⓑ Ⓒ Ⓓ Ⓔ
6. Ⓐ Ⓑ Ⓒ Ⓓ Ⓔ	16. Ⓐ Ⓑ Ⓒ Ⓓ Ⓔ	26. Ⓐ Ⓑ Ⓒ Ⓓ Ⓔ	36. Ⓐ Ⓑ Ⓒ Ⓓ Ⓔ
7. Ⓐ Ⓑ Ⓒ Ⓓ Ⓔ	17. Ⓐ Ⓑ Ⓒ Ⓓ Ⓔ	27. Ⓐ Ⓑ Ⓒ Ⓓ Ⓔ	37. Ⓐ Ⓑ Ⓒ Ⓓ Ⓔ
8. Ⓐ Ⓑ Ⓒ Ⓓ Ⓔ	18. Ⓐ Ⓑ Ⓒ Ⓓ Ⓔ	28. Ⓐ Ⓑ Ⓒ Ⓓ Ⓔ	38. Ⓐ Ⓑ Ⓒ Ⓓ Ⓔ
9. Ⓐ Ⓑ Ⓒ Ⓓ Ⓔ	19. Ⓐ Ⓑ Ⓒ Ⓓ Ⓔ	29. Ⓐ Ⓑ Ⓒ Ⓓ Ⓔ	
10. Ⓐ Ⓑ Ⓒ Ⓓ Ⓔ	20. Ⓐ Ⓑ Ⓒ Ⓓ Ⓔ	30. Ⓐ Ⓑ Ⓒ Ⓓ Ⓔ	

Section 4

1. Ⓐ Ⓑ Ⓒ Ⓓ Ⓔ	11. Ⓐ Ⓑ Ⓒ Ⓓ Ⓔ	21. Ⓐ Ⓑ Ⓒ Ⓓ Ⓔ	31. Ⓐ Ⓑ Ⓒ Ⓓ Ⓔ
2. Ⓐ Ⓑ Ⓒ Ⓓ Ⓔ	12. Ⓐ Ⓑ Ⓒ Ⓓ Ⓔ	22. Ⓐ Ⓑ Ⓒ Ⓓ Ⓔ	32. Ⓐ Ⓑ Ⓒ Ⓓ Ⓔ
3. Ⓐ Ⓑ Ⓒ Ⓓ Ⓔ	13. Ⓐ Ⓑ Ⓒ Ⓓ Ⓔ	23. Ⓐ Ⓑ Ⓒ Ⓓ Ⓔ	33. Ⓐ Ⓑ Ⓒ Ⓓ Ⓔ
4. Ⓐ Ⓑ Ⓒ Ⓓ Ⓔ	14. Ⓐ Ⓑ Ⓒ Ⓓ Ⓔ	24. Ⓐ Ⓑ Ⓒ Ⓓ Ⓔ	34. Ⓐ Ⓑ Ⓒ Ⓓ Ⓔ
5. Ⓐ Ⓑ Ⓒ Ⓓ Ⓔ	15. Ⓐ Ⓑ Ⓒ Ⓓ Ⓔ	25. Ⓐ Ⓑ Ⓒ Ⓓ Ⓔ	35. Ⓐ Ⓑ Ⓒ Ⓓ Ⓔ
6. Ⓐ Ⓑ Ⓒ Ⓓ Ⓔ	16. Ⓐ Ⓑ Ⓒ Ⓓ Ⓔ	26. Ⓐ Ⓑ Ⓒ Ⓓ Ⓔ	36. Ⓐ Ⓑ Ⓒ Ⓓ Ⓔ
7. Ⓐ Ⓑ Ⓒ Ⓓ Ⓔ	17. Ⓐ Ⓑ Ⓒ Ⓓ Ⓔ	27. Ⓐ Ⓑ Ⓒ Ⓓ Ⓔ	37. Ⓐ Ⓑ Ⓒ Ⓓ Ⓔ
8. Ⓐ Ⓑ Ⓒ Ⓓ Ⓔ	18. Ⓐ Ⓑ Ⓒ Ⓓ Ⓔ	28. Ⓐ Ⓑ Ⓒ Ⓓ Ⓔ	38. Ⓐ Ⓑ Ⓒ Ⓓ Ⓔ
9. Ⓐ Ⓑ Ⓒ Ⓓ Ⓔ	19. Ⓐ Ⓑ Ⓒ Ⓓ Ⓔ	29. Ⓐ Ⓑ Ⓒ Ⓓ Ⓔ	
10. Ⓐ Ⓑ Ⓒ Ⓓ Ⓔ	20. Ⓐ Ⓑ Ⓒ Ⓓ Ⓔ	30. Ⓐ Ⓑ Ⓒ Ⓓ Ⓔ	

Section 5

1. Ⓐ Ⓑ Ⓒ Ⓓ Ⓔ	11. Ⓐ Ⓑ Ⓒ Ⓓ Ⓔ	21. Ⓐ Ⓑ Ⓒ Ⓓ Ⓔ	31. Ⓐ Ⓑ Ⓒ Ⓓ Ⓔ
2. Ⓐ Ⓑ Ⓒ Ⓓ Ⓔ	12. Ⓐ Ⓑ Ⓒ Ⓓ Ⓔ	22. Ⓐ Ⓑ Ⓒ Ⓓ Ⓔ	32. Ⓐ Ⓑ Ⓒ Ⓓ Ⓔ
3. Ⓐ Ⓑ Ⓒ Ⓓ Ⓔ	13. Ⓐ Ⓑ Ⓒ Ⓓ Ⓔ	23. Ⓐ Ⓑ Ⓒ Ⓓ Ⓔ	33. Ⓐ Ⓑ Ⓒ Ⓓ Ⓔ
4. Ⓐ Ⓑ Ⓒ Ⓓ Ⓔ	14. Ⓐ Ⓑ Ⓒ Ⓓ Ⓔ	24. Ⓐ Ⓑ Ⓒ Ⓓ Ⓔ	34. Ⓐ Ⓑ Ⓒ Ⓓ Ⓔ
5. Ⓐ Ⓑ Ⓒ Ⓓ Ⓔ	15. Ⓐ Ⓑ Ⓒ Ⓓ Ⓔ	25. Ⓐ Ⓑ Ⓒ Ⓓ Ⓔ	35. Ⓐ Ⓑ Ⓒ Ⓓ Ⓔ
6. Ⓐ Ⓑ Ⓒ Ⓓ Ⓔ	16. Ⓐ Ⓑ Ⓒ Ⓓ Ⓔ	26. Ⓐ Ⓑ Ⓒ Ⓓ Ⓔ	36. Ⓐ Ⓑ Ⓒ Ⓓ Ⓔ
7. Ⓐ Ⓑ Ⓒ Ⓓ Ⓔ	17. Ⓐ Ⓑ Ⓒ Ⓓ Ⓔ	27. Ⓐ Ⓑ Ⓒ Ⓓ Ⓔ	37. Ⓐ Ⓑ Ⓒ Ⓓ Ⓔ
8. Ⓐ Ⓑ Ⓒ Ⓓ Ⓔ	18. Ⓐ Ⓑ Ⓒ Ⓓ Ⓔ	28. Ⓐ Ⓑ Ⓒ Ⓓ Ⓔ	38. Ⓐ Ⓑ Ⓒ Ⓓ Ⓔ
9. Ⓐ Ⓑ Ⓒ Ⓓ Ⓔ	19. Ⓐ Ⓑ Ⓒ Ⓓ Ⓔ	29. Ⓐ Ⓑ Ⓒ Ⓓ Ⓔ	
10. Ⓐ Ⓑ Ⓒ Ⓓ Ⓔ	20. Ⓐ Ⓑ Ⓒ Ⓓ Ⓔ	30. Ⓐ Ⓑ Ⓒ Ⓓ Ⓔ	

Section 6

1. Ⓐ Ⓑ Ⓒ Ⓓ Ⓔ	11. Ⓐ Ⓑ Ⓒ Ⓓ Ⓔ	21. Ⓐ Ⓑ Ⓒ Ⓓ Ⓔ	31. Ⓐ Ⓑ Ⓒ Ⓓ Ⓔ
2. Ⓐ Ⓑ Ⓒ Ⓓ Ⓔ	12. Ⓐ Ⓑ Ⓒ Ⓓ Ⓔ	22. Ⓐ Ⓑ Ⓒ Ⓓ Ⓔ	32. Ⓐ Ⓑ Ⓒ Ⓓ Ⓔ
3. Ⓐ Ⓑ Ⓒ Ⓓ Ⓔ	13. Ⓐ Ⓑ Ⓒ Ⓓ Ⓔ	23. Ⓐ Ⓑ Ⓒ Ⓓ Ⓔ	33. Ⓐ Ⓑ Ⓒ Ⓓ Ⓔ
4. Ⓐ Ⓑ Ⓒ Ⓓ Ⓔ	14. Ⓐ Ⓑ Ⓒ Ⓓ Ⓔ	24. Ⓐ Ⓑ Ⓒ Ⓓ Ⓔ	34. Ⓐ Ⓑ Ⓒ Ⓓ Ⓔ
5. Ⓐ Ⓑ Ⓒ Ⓓ Ⓔ	15. Ⓐ Ⓑ Ⓒ Ⓓ Ⓔ	25. Ⓐ Ⓑ Ⓒ Ⓓ Ⓔ	35. Ⓐ Ⓑ Ⓒ Ⓓ Ⓔ
6. Ⓐ Ⓑ Ⓒ Ⓓ Ⓔ	16. Ⓐ Ⓑ Ⓒ Ⓓ Ⓔ	26. Ⓐ Ⓑ Ⓒ Ⓓ Ⓔ	36. Ⓐ Ⓑ Ⓒ Ⓓ Ⓔ
7. Ⓐ Ⓑ Ⓒ Ⓓ Ⓔ	17. Ⓐ Ⓑ Ⓒ Ⓓ Ⓔ	27. Ⓐ Ⓑ Ⓒ Ⓓ Ⓔ	37. Ⓐ Ⓑ Ⓒ Ⓓ Ⓔ
8. Ⓐ Ⓑ Ⓒ Ⓓ Ⓔ	18. Ⓐ Ⓑ Ⓒ Ⓓ Ⓔ	28. Ⓐ Ⓑ Ⓒ Ⓓ Ⓔ	38. Ⓐ Ⓑ Ⓒ Ⓓ Ⓔ
9. Ⓐ Ⓑ Ⓒ Ⓓ Ⓔ	19. Ⓐ Ⓑ Ⓒ Ⓓ Ⓔ	29. Ⓐ Ⓑ Ⓒ Ⓓ Ⓔ	
10. Ⓐ Ⓑ Ⓒ Ⓓ Ⓔ	20. Ⓐ Ⓑ Ⓒ Ⓓ Ⓔ	30. Ⓐ Ⓑ Ⓒ Ⓓ Ⓔ	

Section 7

1. Ⓐ Ⓑ Ⓒ Ⓓ Ⓔ	11. Ⓐ Ⓑ Ⓒ Ⓓ Ⓔ	21. Ⓐ Ⓑ Ⓒ Ⓓ Ⓔ	31. Ⓐ Ⓑ Ⓒ Ⓓ Ⓔ
2. Ⓐ Ⓑ Ⓒ Ⓓ Ⓔ	12. Ⓐ Ⓑ Ⓒ Ⓓ Ⓔ	22. Ⓐ Ⓑ Ⓒ Ⓓ Ⓔ	32. Ⓐ Ⓑ Ⓒ Ⓓ Ⓔ
3. Ⓐ Ⓑ Ⓒ Ⓓ Ⓔ	13. Ⓐ Ⓑ Ⓒ Ⓓ Ⓔ	23. Ⓐ Ⓑ Ⓒ Ⓓ Ⓔ	33. Ⓐ Ⓑ Ⓒ Ⓓ Ⓔ
4. Ⓐ Ⓑ Ⓒ Ⓓ Ⓔ	14. Ⓐ Ⓑ Ⓒ Ⓓ Ⓔ	24. Ⓐ Ⓑ Ⓒ Ⓓ Ⓔ	34. Ⓐ Ⓑ Ⓒ Ⓓ Ⓔ
5. Ⓐ Ⓑ Ⓒ Ⓓ Ⓔ	15. Ⓐ Ⓑ Ⓒ Ⓓ Ⓔ	25. Ⓐ Ⓑ Ⓒ Ⓓ Ⓔ	35. Ⓐ Ⓑ Ⓒ Ⓓ Ⓔ
6. Ⓐ Ⓑ Ⓒ Ⓓ Ⓔ	16. Ⓐ Ⓑ Ⓒ Ⓓ Ⓔ	26. Ⓐ Ⓑ Ⓒ Ⓓ Ⓔ	36. Ⓐ Ⓑ Ⓒ Ⓓ Ⓔ
7. Ⓐ Ⓑ Ⓒ Ⓓ Ⓔ	17. Ⓐ Ⓑ Ⓒ Ⓓ Ⓔ	27. Ⓐ Ⓑ Ⓒ Ⓓ Ⓔ	37. Ⓐ Ⓑ Ⓒ Ⓓ Ⓔ
8. Ⓐ Ⓑ Ⓒ Ⓓ Ⓔ	18. Ⓐ Ⓑ Ⓒ Ⓓ Ⓔ	28. Ⓐ Ⓑ Ⓒ Ⓓ Ⓔ	38. Ⓐ Ⓑ Ⓒ Ⓓ Ⓔ
9. Ⓐ Ⓑ Ⓒ Ⓓ Ⓔ	19. Ⓐ Ⓑ Ⓒ Ⓓ Ⓔ	29. Ⓐ Ⓑ Ⓒ Ⓓ Ⓔ	
10. Ⓐ Ⓑ Ⓒ Ⓓ Ⓔ	20. Ⓐ Ⓑ Ⓒ Ⓓ Ⓔ	30. Ⓐ Ⓑ Ⓒ Ⓓ Ⓔ	

MODEL TEST 2

SECTION 1

Time—30 Minutes

38 Questions

Directions: Each sentence below has one or two blanks, each blank indicating that something has been omitted. Beneath the sentence are five lettered words or sets of words. Choose the word or set of words for each blank that best fits the meaning of the sentence as a whole.

1. Criticism that tears down without suggesting areas of improvement is not ------- and should be avoided if possible.

    (A) representative
    (B) constructive
    (C) mandatory
    (D) pertinent
    (E) sagacious

2. As I am not an ardent admirer of the work of George Eliot, simple justice demands a prefatory ------- her many admirable qualities.

    (A) skepticism regarding
    (B) effusion over
    (C) denial of
    (D) tribute to
    (E) dismissal of

3. You may wonder how the expert on fossil remains is able to trace descent through teeth, which seem ------- pegs upon which to hang whole ancestries.

    (A) novel
    (B) reliable
    (C) specious
    (D) inadequate
    (E) academic

4. An essential purpose of the criminal justice system is to enable purgation to take place; that is, to provide a ------- by which a community expresses its collective ------- the transgression of the criminal.

    (A) catharsis...outrage at
    (B) disclaimer...forgiveness of
    (C) means...empathy with
    (D) procedure...distaste for
    (E) document...disapprobation of

5. In the tradition of scholarly -------, the poet and scholar A.E. Housman once assailed a German rival for relying on manuscripts "as a drunkard relies on lampposts, for ------- rather than illumination."

    (A) animosity...current
    (B) discourse...stability
    (C) erudition...shadow
    (D) invective...support
    (E) competition...assistance

6. According to the twelfth-century cosmologists, the natural philosopher must strive to ------- a state of detached objectivity in order to free his capacity for constructing useful hypotheses from the ------- of unquestioned assumptions and accepted opinions about nature.

    (A) capture...contemplation
    (B) achieve...tyranny
    (C) imitate...discipline
    (D) feign...pretense
    (E) attain...confusion

7. Unable to ------- his wholehearted distaste for media events and unnecessary publicity, Dean Brower continued to make ------- comments throughout the entire ceremony.

    (A) control...garbled
    (B) maintain...copious
    (C) conceal...effusive
    (D) disguise...caustic
    (E) express...vitriolic

Directions: In each of the following questions, a related pair of words or phrases is followed by five lettered pairs of words or phrases. Select the lettered pair that best expresses a relationship similar to that expressed in the original pair.

8. YOLK : EGG::
    (A) rind : melon
    (B) nucleus : cell
    (C) stalk : corn
    (D) duck : fowl
    (E) web : spider

9. WOOD : SAND::
    (A) coal : burn
    (B) brick : lay
    (C) oil : polish
    (D) metal : burnish
    (E) stone : quarry

10. VINDICTIVE : MERCY::
    (A) avaricious : greed
    (B) insightful : hope
    (C) modest : dignity
    (D) skeptical : trustfulness
    (E) pathetic : sympathy

469

11. RUFFLE : COMPOSURE::
    (A) flounce : turmoil
    (B) flourish : prosperity
    (C) provoke : discussion
    (D) adjust : balance
    (E) upset : equilibrium

12. BOUQUET : WINE::
    (A) chaff : wheat
    (B) aroma : coffee
    (C) yeast : bread
    (D) octane : gasoline
    (E) decanter : brandy

13. SEXTANT : NAUTICAL::
    (A) octet : musical
    (B) therapy : physical
    (C) forceps : surgical
    (D) comet : astronomical
    (E) blueprint : mechanical

14. REFRACTORY : MANAGE::
    (A) redoubtable : impress
    (B) lethargic : stimulate
    (C) pedantic : convince
    (D) officious : arrange
    (E) aggrieved : distress

15. LATENT : MANIFESTATION::
    (A) torpid : hibernation
    (B) patent : appearance
    (C) perfunctory : inspiration
    (D) punctilious : continuity
    (E) dormant : awakening

16. PRECIPICE : STEEPNESS::
    (A) defile : narrowness
    (B) well : shallowness
    (C) plateau : depth
    (D) mountain : range
    (E) marsh : aridity

Directions: Each passage in this group is followed by questions based on its content. After reading a passage, choose the best answer to each question. Answer all questions following a passage on the basis of what is stated or implied in the passage.

Given the persistent and intransigent nature of the American race system, which proved quite impervious to black attacks, Du Bois in his speeches and writings moved from one proposed solution to another, and the salience of various parts of his philosophy changed as his perceptions of the needs and strategies of black America shifted over time. Aloof and autonomous in his personality, Du Bois did not hesitate to depart markedly from whatever was the current mainstream of black thinking when he perceived that the conventional wisdom being enunciated by black spokesmen was proving inadequate to the task of advancing the race. His willingness to seek different solutions often placed him well in advance of his contemporaries, and this, combined with a strong-willed, even arrogant personality made his career as a black leader essentially a series of stormy conflicts.

Thus Du Bois first achieved his role as a major black leader in the controversy that arose over the program of Booker T. Washington, the most prominent and influential black leader at the opening of the twentieth century. Amidst the wave of lynchings, disfranchisement, and segregation laws, Washington, seeking the good will of powerful whites, taught blacks not to protest against discrimination, but to elevate themselves through industrial education, hard work, and property accumulation; then, they would ultimately obtain recognition of their citizenship rights. At first Du Bois agreed with this gradualist strategy, but in 1903 with the publication of his most influential book, *Souls of Black Folk*, he became the chief leader of the onslaught against Washington that polarized the black community into two wings—the "conservative" supporters of Washington and his "radical" critics.

17. The author's primary purpose in the passage is to

    (A) explain how Du Bois was influenced by Washington
    (B) compare the personalities of Du Bois and Washington
    (C) explain why Du Bois gained power in the black community
    (D) describe Du Bois' role in early twentieth century black leadership
    (E) correct the misconception that Du Bois shunned polarization

18. Which of the following statements about W.E.B. Du Bois does the passage best support?

    (A) He sacrificed the proven strategies of earlier black leaders to his craving for political novelty.
    (B) Preferring conflict to harmony, he followed a disruptive course that alienated him from the bulk of his followers.
    (C) He proved unable to change with the times in mounting fresh attacks against white racism.
    (D) He relied on the fundamental benevolence of the white population for the eventual success of his movement.
    (E) Once an adherent of Washington's policies, he ultimately lost patience with them for their inefficacy.

19. It can be inferred that Booker T. Washington in comparison with W.E.B. Du Bois could be described as all of the following EXCEPT

   (A) submissive to the majority
   (B) concerned with financial success
   (C) versatile in adopting strategies
   (D) traditional in preaching industry
   (E) respectful of authority

20. The author's attitude towards Du Bois' departure from conventional black policies can best be described as

   (A) skeptical
   (B) derisive
   (C) shocked
   (D) approving
   (E) resigned

Any successful theory in the physical sciences is expected to make accurate predictions. Given some well-defined experiment, the theory should correctly specify the outcome or should at least assign the correct probabilities to all the possible outcomes. From this point of view quantum mechanics must be judged highly successful. As the fundamental modern theory of atoms, of molecules, of elementary particles, of electromagnetic radiation and of the solid state it supplies methods for calculating the results of experiments in all these realms.

Apart from experimental confirmation, however, something more is generally demanded of a theory. It is expected not only to determine the results of an experiment but also to provide some understanding of the physical events that are presumed to underlie the observed results. In other words, the theory should not only give the position of a pointer on a dial but also explain why the pointer takes up that position. When one seeks information of this kind in the quantum theory, certain conceptual difficulties arise. For example, in quantum mechanics an elementary particle such as an electron is represented by the mathematical expression called a wave function, which often describes the electron as if it were smeared out over a large region of space.

This representation is not in conflict with experiment; on the contrary, the wave function yields an accurate estimate of the probability that the electron will be found in any given place. When the electron is actually detected, however, it is never smeared out but always has a definite position. Hence it is not entirely clear what physical interpretation should be given to the wave function or what picture of the electron one should keep in mind. Because of ambiguities such as this many physicists find it most sensible to regard quantum mechanics as merely a set of rules that prescribe the outcome of experiments. According to this view the quantum theory is concerned only with observable phenomena (the observed position of the pointer) and not with any underlying physical state (the real position of the electron).

It now turns out that even this renunciation is not entirely satisfactory. Even if quantum mechanics is considered to be no more than a set of rules, it is still in conflict with a view of the world many people would consider obvious or natural. This world view is based on three assumptions or premises that must be accepted without proof. One is realism, the doctrine that regularities in observed phenomena are caused by some physical reality whose existence is independent of human observers. The second premise holds that inductive inference is a valid mode of reasoning and can be applied freely, so that legitimate conclusions can be drawn from consistent observations. The third premise is called Einstein separability or Einstein locality, and it states that no influence of any kind can propagate faster than the speed of light. The three premises, which are often assumed to have the status of well-established truths, or even self-evident truths, form the basis of what I shall call local realistic theories of nature. An argument derived from these premises leads to an explicit prediction for the results of a certain class of experiments in the physics of elementary particles. The rules of quantum mechanics can also be employed to calculate the results of these experiments. Significantly, the two predictions differ, and so either the local realistic theories or quantum mechanics must be wrong.

21. This passage was most likely excerpted from a

   (A) physics textbook focused on the mathematical foundations of quantum mechanics
   (B) theoretical physics report urging further experiments to resolve current ambiguities
   (C) scientific journal article informing a general audience of new findings in quantum mechanics
   (D) pamphlet challenging the adequacy of quantum theory as a valid mathematical tool
   (E) student log of a series of controversial experiments in the physics of elementary particles

22. Describing an electron on the basis of its mathematical expression is most like describing a

   (A) paw from the cast of a pawprint
   (B) pebble from the ripples it makes in a pond
   (C) statue on the basis of its armature
   (D) tree trunk from the pattern of its rings
   (E) butterfly on the basis of its chrysalis

23. The author organizes the passage by

   (A) explaining the wide applicability of quantum theory and contrasting it with the inapplicability of local realistic theories
   (B) describing several assumptions underlying quantum theory and then refuting them consecutively
   (C) making distinctions between experimental and non-experimental methods of representing reality
   (D) making a generalization about scientific theory and then applying it to the theory of quantum mechanics
   (E) stating a specific idea and then moving from it to a sequence of generalizations about quantum theory

24. The author provides information that answers which of the following questions?

I. What are the presuppositions upon which the so-called local realistic theories are based?
II. Which premise of the local realistic theories of nature has been invalidated by current experimental predictions?
III. To what degree can one physically interpret a mathematical expression such as a wave function?

(A) I only
(B) III only
(C) I and II only
(D) I and III only
(E) I, II and III

25. All of the following can be found in the author's discussion of quantum theory EXCEPT

(A) a concrete example of a specific observable phenomenon
(B) a generalization about the criteria for judging the value of a given theory
(C) a hypothesis based on the invalidity of Einstein separability
(D) an enumeration of the fundamental assumptions underlying the local realistic theories of nature
(E) a statement setting the local realistic theories and the quantum theory at variance

26. In terms of its tone and form, this passage can best be described as

(A) a doctrinaire appraisal
(B) a concrete proposal
(C) an iconoclastic observation
(D) a systematic exposition
(E) a cursory examination

27. Which of the following statements concerning physicists is most directly suggested by the passage?

(A) Physicists who gloss over discrepancies between quantum theory and the local realistic theories have yet to account for current experiments in elementary particle physics.
(B) Physicists may have overestimated the ability of quantum mechanics to provide experimental confirmation for theories.
(C) Physicists have not been sufficiently orthodox in their adherence to the three fundamental premises of the local realistic theories.
(D) Physicists see little basis for the conceptual difficulties suffered by laymen in comprehending the underlying physical state of an observable phenomenon.
(E) Physicists exploring the physics of elementary particles fail to make explicit predictions about their experimental results.

Directions: Each question below consists of a word printed in capital letters, followed by five lettered words or phrases. Choose the lettered word or phrase that is most nearly opposite in meaning to the word in capital letters.

Since some of the questions require you to distinguish fine shades of meaning, be sure to consider all the choices before deciding which one is best.

28. ADULTERATED:
(A) solid
(B) immature
(C) exalted
(D) pure
(E) virtuous

29. DISTEND:
(A) deflate
(B) prolong
(C) commence
(D) forecast
(E) prevent

30. TRANSIENT:
(A) permanent
(B) desultory
(C) spontaneous
(D) subterranean
(E) obsequious

31. ELATED:
(A) crestfallen
(B) inebriated
(C) punctual
(D) insulted
(E) lamented

32. REVILE:
(A) compose
(B) awake
(C) deaden
(D) praise
(E) secrete

33. PROPITIOUS:
(A) adjacent
(B) clandestine
(C) contentious
(D) unfavorable
(E) coy

34. ENSUE:
(A) litigate
(B) precede
(C) arbitrate
(D) accentuate
(E) delay

35. RETROSPECTION:
   (A) introversion
   (B) deliberation
   (C) anticipation
   (D) gregariousness
   (E) equivocation

36. EGRESS:
   (A) deviation
   (B) entrance
   (C) approbation
   (D) dilemma
   (E) renown

37. MAUNDER:
   (A) speak purposefully
   (B) maintain silence
   (C) appear unaware
   (D) evade entanglement
   (E) seek consensus

38. HUBRIS:
   (A) impiety
   (B) insouciance
   (C) apathy
   (D) mendacity
   (E) humility

S T O P

IF YOU FINISH BEFORE TIME IS CALLED, YOU MAY CHECK YOUR WORK ON THIS SECTION ONLY.
DO NOT WORK ON ANY OTHER SECTION IN THE TEST.

SECTION 2

Time—30 Minutes

38 Questions

Directions: Each sentence below has one or two blanks, each blank indicating that something has been omitted. Beneath the sentence are five lettered words or sets of words. Choose the word or set of words for each blank that best fits the meaning of the sentence as a whole.

1. No volume on the history of economics can conclude without the hope that the subject will be ------- politics to form again the larger discipline of political economy.

   (A) vindicated by
   (B) segregated from
   (C) reunited with
   (D) recapitulated by
   (E) dependent on

2. Many educators believe that, far from being a temporary stopgap, useful only as a transitional measure, bilingual education has proved to have definite ------- education in any one tongue.

   (A) correlations with
   (B) advantages over
   (C) connotations for
   (D) limitations on
   (E) influence on

3. When facts are ------- and data hard to come by, even scientists occasionally throw aside the professional pretense of ------- and tear into each other with shameless appeals to authority and arguments that are unabashedly ad hominem.

   (A) elusive…objectivity
   (B) established…courtesy
   (C) demonstrable…neutrality
   (D) ineluctable…cooperation
   (E) hypothetical…scholarship

4. While the disease is in ------- state it is almost impossible to determine its existence by -------.

   (A) a dormant…postulate
   (B) a critical…examination
   (C) an acute…analysis
   (D) a suspended…estimate
   (E) a latent…observation

5. Woolf ------- conventional notions of truth: in her words, one cannot receive from any lecture "a nugget of pure truth" to wrap up between the pages of one's notebook and keep on the mantlepiece forever.

   (A) anticipates
   (B) articulates
   (C) neglects
   (D) mocks
   (E) rationalizes

6. The term "rare earths" is in fact a -------, for, paradoxically, the rare-earth elements are in actuality -------, being present in low concentration in virtually all minerals.

   (A) truism…essential
   (B) misnomer…ubiquitous
   (C) disclaimer…ephemeral
   (D) metaphor…figurative
   (E) mnemonic…unmemorable

7. That Clement would reclaim psychoanalysis as a healing profession is the ------- of her argument, but it is exactly in this part of her critique, translated to the American psychoanalytic milieu, that her shafts -------.

   (A) crux…fall down
   (B) implication…break down
   (C) basis…strike home
   (D) essence…dig in
   (E) thrust…glance away

Directions: In each of the following questions, a related pair of words or phrases is followed by five lettered pairs of words or phrases. Select the lettered pair that best expresses a relationship similar to that expressed in the original pair.

8. BLEAT : SHEEP ::
   (A) bask : lizard
   (B) preen : peacock
   (C) chirp : sparrow
   (D) slither : snake
   (E) butt : goat

9. CURDLE : MILK ::
   (A) flow : water
   (B) change : oil
   (C) brew : coffee
   (D) decant : wine
   (E) clot : blood

10. MOLT : FEATHERS ::
    (A) slough : skin
    (B) sharpen : talons
    (C) curry : hide
    (D) flutter : wings
    (E) bare : fangs

11. OFFHAND : PREMEDITATION ::
    (A) upright : integrity
    (B) aboveboard : guile
    (C) cutthroat : competition
    (D) backward : direction
    (E) underlying : foundation

12. LARVAL : INSECT ::
    (A) serpentine : snake
    (B) floral : plant
    (C) amphibian : reptile
    (D) embryonic : mammal
    (E) alate : bird

13. POLTERGEIST : APPARITION ::
    (A) dwarf : stature
    (B) witch : familiar
    (C) ogre : monster
    (D) sorceror : spell
    (E) gremlin : mischief

14. AUSTERE : STYLE ::
    (A) controlled : movement
    (B) affluent : wealth
    (C) subservient : demeanor
    (D) inspirational : faith
    (E) pragmatic : speech

15. AVER : AFFIRMATION ::
    (A) proclaim : objection
    (B) denounce : defiance
    (C) nonplus : resistance
    (D) refuse : distress
    (E) demur : protest

16. CHIDE : PILLORY ::
    (A) exalt : venerate
    (B) humor : mollycoddle
    (C) castigate : punish
    (D) quibble : cavil
    (E) sanctify : scourge

Directions: Each passage in this group is followed by questions based on its content. After reading a passage, choose the best answer to each question. Answer all questions following a passage on the basis of what is <u>stated</u> or <u>implied</u> in the passage.

At night, schools of prey and predators are almost always spectacularly illuminated by the bioluminescence produced by the microscopic and larger plankton. The reason for the ubiquitous production of light by the microorganisms of the sea remains obscure, and suggested explanations are controversial. It has been suggested that light is a kind of inadvertent by-product of life in transparent organisms. It has also been hypothesized that the emission of light on disturbance is advantageous to the plankton in making the predators of the plankton conspicuous to *their* predators! Unquestionably, it does act this way. Indeed, some fisheries base the detection of their prey on the bioluminescence that the fish excite. It is difficult, however, to defend the thesis that this effect was the direct factor in the original development of bioluminescence, since the effect was of no advantage to the individual microorganism that first developed it. Perhaps the luminescence of a microorganism also discourages attack by light-avoiding predators and is of initial survival benefit to the individual. As it then becomes general in the population, the effect of revealing plankton predators to their predators would also become important.

17. The primary topic of the passage is which of the following?

    (A) The origin of bioluminescence in plankton predators
    (B) The disadvantages of bioluminescence in microorganisms
    (C) The varieties of marine bioluminescent life forms
    (D) Symbiotic relationships between predators and their prey
    (E) Hypotheses on the causes of bioluminescence in plankton

18. The author mentions the activities of fisheries in order to provide an example of

    (A) how ubiquitous the phenomenon of bioluminescence is coastally
    (B) how predators do make use of bioluminescence in locating their prey
    (C) how human intervention imperils bioluminescent microorganisms
    (D) how nocturnal fishing expeditions are becoming more and more widespread
    (E) how limited bioluminescence is as a source of light for human use

19. The passage provides an answer to which of the following questions?

    (A) What is the explanation for the phenomenon of bioluminescence in marine life?
    (B) Does the phenomenon of plankton bioluminescence have any practical applications?
    (C) Why do only certain specimens of marine life exhibit the phenomenon of bioluminescence?
    (D) How does underwater bioluminescence differ from atmospheric bioluminescence?
    (E) What are the steps that take place as an individual microorganism becomes bioluminescent?

20. The author's attitude toward the hypothesis that plankton chiefly benefited from their bioluminescence because it made the plankton predators visible to their predators can best be described as

    (A) perplexed
    (B) derisive
    (C) intrigued
    (D) defensive
    (E) dispassionate

The curtain rises; the Cardinal and Daniel de Bosola enter from the right. In appearance, the Cardinal is something between an El Greco cardinal and a Van Dyke noble lord. He has the tall,
(5) spare form—the elongated hands and features—of the former; the trim pointed beard, the imperial repose, the commanding authority of the latter. But the El Greco features are not really those of asceticism or inner mystic spirituality. They are the
(10) index to a cold, refined but ruthless cruelty in a highly civilized controlled form. Neither is the imperial repose an aloof mood of proud detachment. It is a refined expression of satanic pride of place and talent.
(15)   To a degree, the Cardinal's coldness is artificially cultivated. He has defined himself against his younger brother Duke Ferdinand and is the opposite to the overwrought emotionality of the latter. But the Cardinal's aloof mood is not one of bland
(20) detachment. It is the deliberate detachment of a methodical man who collects his thoughts and emotions into the most compact and formidable shape—that when he strikes, he may strike with the more efficient and devastating force. His easy
(25) movements are those of the slowly circling eagle just before the swift descent with the exposed talons. Above all else, he is a man who never for a moment doubts his destined authority as a governor. He derisively and sharply rebukes his brother
(30) the Duke as easily and readily as he mocks his mistress Julia. If he has betrayed his hireling Bosola, he uses his brother as the tool to win back his "familiar." His court dress is a long brilliant scarlet cardinal's gown with white cuffs and a white collar
(35) turned back over the red, both collar and cuffs being elaborately scalloped and embroidered. He wears a small cape, reaching only to the elbows. His cassock is buttoned to the ground, giving a heightened effect to his already tall presence.
(40) Richelieu would have adored his neatly trimmed beard. A richly jeweled and oranamented cross lies on his breast, suspended from his neck by a gold chain.
     Bosola, for his part, is the Renaissance "familiar"
(45) dressed conventionally in somber black with a white collar. He wears a chain about his neck, a suspended ornament, and a sword. Although a "bravo," he must not be thought of as a leather-jacketed, heavy-booted tough, squat and swarthy.
(50) Still less is he a sneering, leering, melodramatic villain of the Victorian gaslight tradition. Like his black-and-white clothes, he is a colorful contradiction, a scholar-assassin, a humanist-hangman; introverted and introspective, yet ruthless in action;
(55) moody and reluctant, yet violent. He is a man of scholarly taste and subtle intellectual discrimination doing the work of a hired ruffian. In general effect, his impersonator must achieve suppleness and subtlety of nature, a highly complex, com-
(60) pressed, yet well restrained intensity of temperament. Like Duke Ferdinand, he is inwardly tormented, but not by undiluted passion. His dominant emotion is an intellectualized one: that of dis-

gust at a world filled with knavery and folly, but in
(65) which he must play a part and that a lowly, despicable one. He is the kind of rarity that Browning loved to depict in his Renaissance monologues.

21. The primary purpose of the passage appears to be to

(A) provide historical background on the Renaissance church
(B) describe ecclesiastical costuming and pageantry
(C) analyze the appearance and moral nature of two dramatic figures
(D) compare and contrast the subjects of two historical paintings
(E) denounce the corruption of the nobility in Renaissance Italy

22. It can be inferred from the passage that the Cardinal and Bosola

(A) are feuding brothers
(B) are noble lords
(C) together govern the church
(D) are characters in a play
(E) resemble one another in looks

23. In lines 25–27 the author most likely compares the movements of the Cardinal to those of a circling eagle in order to emphasize his

(A) flightiness
(B) love of freedom
(C) eminence
(D) sense of spirituality
(E) mercilessness

24. As used in line 48, the word *bravo* most nearly means

(A) a shout of approbation
(B) a medallion
(C) a clergyman
(D) a humanist
(E) a mercenary killer

25. The author of this passage assumes that the reader is

(A) familiar with the paintings of El Greco and Van Dyke
(B) disgusted with a world filled with cruelty and folly
(C) ignorant of the history of the Roman Catholic Church
(D) uninterested in psychological distinctions
(E) unacquainted with the writing of Browning

26. Which of the following best characterizes the author's attitude toward the Cardinal?

    (A) He deprecates his inability to sustain warm familial relationships.
    (B) He esteems him for his spiritual and emotional control.
    (C) He admires his grace in movement and sure sense of personal authority.
    (D) He finds him formidable both as an opponent and as a dramatic character.
    (E) He is perturbed by his inconsistencies in behavior.

27. According to the passage, the explanation of Bosola's inner suffering lies in his

    (A) highly overwrought excesses of feeling
    (B) resentment against his lack of appropriate rank
    (C) suppression of his intellectual ambitions
    (D) revulsion towards his involvement in ignoble acts
    (E) compassion for those victimized by the Cardinal

Directions: Each question below consists of a word printed in capital letters, followed by five lettered words or phrases. Choose the lettered word or phrase that is most nearly opposite in meaning to the word in capital letters.

Since some of the questions require you to distinguish fine shades of meaning, be sure to consider all the choices before deciding which one is best.

28. AMELIORATION:
    (A) cancellation
    (B) worsening
    (C) forgetfulness
    (D) bribe
    (E) consideration

29. DISARRAY:
    (A) neaten
    (B) empower
    (C) combine
    (D) oscillate
    (E) select

30. DISPUTATIOUS:
    (A) repugnant
    (B) coy
    (C) conciliatory
    (D) infamous
    (E) composed

31. RETICENCE:
    (A) irascibility
    (B) loquaciousness
    (C) quiescence
    (D) patience
    (E) surrender

32. INUNDATE:
    (A) uproot
    (B) channel
    (C) wallow
    (D) embroil
    (E) drain

33. INCONGRUOUS:
    (A) geometric
    (B) prudent
    (C) legitimate
    (D) harmonious
    (E) efficacious

34. APOSTATE:
    (A) laggard
    (B) loyalist
    (C) martinet
    (D) predecessor
    (E) skeptic

35. TOPICAL:
    (A) general
    (B) disinterested
    (C) chronological
    (D) fallacious
    (E) imperceptible

36. FULMINATE:
    (A) authorize
    (B) dominate
    (C) edify
    (D) illuminate
    (E) praise

37. TURBID:
    (A) vigorous
    (B) limpid
    (C) turgid
    (D) viscous
    (E) rancid

38. TYRO:
    (A) zealot
    (B) prodigal
    (C) braggart
    (D) expert
    (E) nihilist

S T O P

IF YOU FINISH BEFORE TIME IS CALLED, YOU MAY CHECK YOUR WORK ON THIS SECTION ONLY.
DO NOT WORK ON ANY OTHER SECTION IN THE TEST.

SECTION 3

Time—30 minutes

30 Questions

Numbers: All numbers used are real numbers.

Figures: Position of points, angles, regions, etc. can be assumed to be in the order shown; and angle measures can be assumed to be positive.

Lines shown as straight can be assumed to be straight.

Figures can be assumed to lie in a plane unless otherwise indicated.

Figures that accompany questions are intended to provide information useful in answering the questions. However, unless a note states that a figure is drawn to scale, you should solve these problems NOT by estimating sizes by sight or by measurement, but by using your knowledge of mathematics (see Example 2 below).

Directions: Each of the Questions 1-15 consists of two quantities, one in Column A and one in Column B. You are to compare the two quantities and choose

A if the quantity in Column A is greater;
B if the quantity in Column B is greater;
C if the two quantities are equal;
D if the relationship cannot be determined from the information given.

Note: Since there are only four choices, NEVER MARK (E).

Common
Information: In a question, information concerning one or both of the quantities to be compared is centered above the two columns. A symbol that appears in both columns represents the same thing in Column A as it does in Column B.

	Column A	Column B	Sample Answers
Example 1:	2×6	$2 + 6$	● Ⓑ Ⓒ Ⓓ Ⓔ

Examples 2-4 refer to $\triangle PQR$.

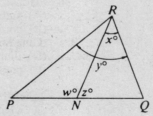

Example 2:	PN	NQ	Ⓐ Ⓑ Ⓒ ● Ⓔ

(since equal measures cannot be assumed, even though PN and NQ appear equal)

Example 3:	x	y	Ⓐ ● Ⓒ Ⓓ Ⓔ

(since N is between P and Q

Example 4:	$w + z$	180	Ⓐ Ⓑ ● Ⓓ Ⓔ

(since PQ is a straight line)

A if the quantity in Column A is greater;
B if the quantity in Column B is greater;
C if the two quantities are equal;
D if the relationship cannot be determined from the information given.

Column A	Column B

1. $3\frac{1}{2}\%$ $3\frac{35}{1000}$

2. The number of posts needed for a fence 144 feet long and posts are placed 12 feet apart.   12 posts

The houses on Jordan Drive are numbered as follows: west side (1801–1837), with consecutive odd numbers; east side has 18 houses.

3. Number of houses on the west side   Number of houses on the east side

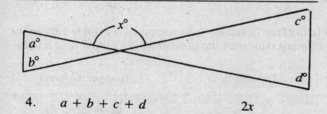

4. $a + b + c + d$ $2x$

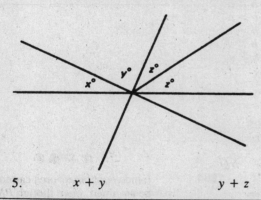

5. $x + y$ $y + z$

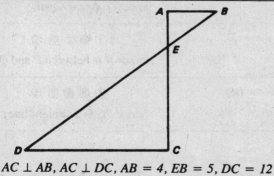

$AC \perp AB, AC \perp DC, AB = 4, EB = 5, DC = 12$

6. AC DC

Column A	Column B

Radius of circle $A = \frac{1}{2}$ radius of circle B

7. Circumference of circle B Twice the circumference of circle A

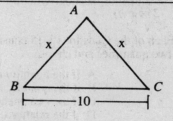

8. $\dfrac{BC}{AB} \cdot \dfrac{AC}{BC}$ 1

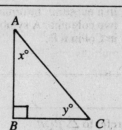

$x = 40$

9. Length of side AB Length of side BC

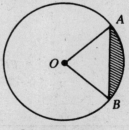

$OA = OB = 6$

10. Area of shaded portion $6\pi - 9\sqrt{3}$

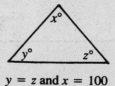

$y = z$ and $x = 100$

11. y 40

Perimeter of square $ABCD = 4a + 4$

12.   Length of side CD a

14.   Time elapsed from 2:55 $\frac{1}{3}$ hour
P.M. to 3:15 P.M. on
the same afternoon

In triangle ABC, side CA is extended forming an exterior angle which measures 80°.

13.   Length of side AB Length of side BC

$$\frac{(15)(16)}{x} = (5)(4)(3)$$

15. x 4

Directions: Each of Questions 16–30 has five answer choices. For each of these questions, select the best of the answer choices given.

16. If $K = \dfrac{1}{m + n}$, then $\dfrac{5}{K}$ is equal to

(A) $5(m + n)$

(B) $\dfrac{5}{m + n}$

(C) $\dfrac{m + n}{5}$

(D) $\dfrac{m + n}{5mn}$

(E) $\dfrac{5}{m} + \dfrac{5}{n}$

17. If $r = \sqrt{\dfrac{3V}{\pi h}}$, by what number must we multiply V in order to multiply r by 9?

(A) 3

(B) $\dfrac{9}{2}$

(C) 9

(D) 18

(E) 81

18. In a group of 15, 7 have studied Latin, 8 have studied Greek, and 3 have not studied either. How many of these have studied both Latin and Greek?

(A) 0   (B) 3   (C) 4   (D) 5   (E) 7

19. If $13 = \dfrac{13w}{1 - w}$; then $(2w)^2 =$

(A) $\dfrac{1}{4}$

(B) $\dfrac{1}{2}$

(C) 1

(D) 2

(E) 4

20. If a and b are positive integers and $\dfrac{a - b}{3.5} = \dfrac{4}{7}$, then

(A) $b < a$
(B) $b > a$
(C) $b = a$
(D) $b \gtreqless a$
(E) $b \lesseqgtr a$

Questions 21 and 22 refer to the following graphs.

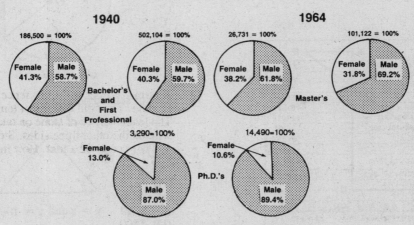

Distribution of Degrees
By Sex, 1940 and 1964
Per Cent Distribution

1940   **1964**

186,500 = 100%   502,104 = 100%   26,731 = 100%   101,122 = 100%

Female 41.3% | Male 58.7%   Female 40.3% | Male 59.7%   Female 38.2% | Male 61.8%   Female 31.8% | Male 69.2%

Bachelor's and First Professional   Master's

3,290=100%   14,490=100%

Female 13.0%   Female 10.6%

Ph.D.'s

Male 87.0%   Male 89.4%

Sources: U. S. Office of Education; The Conference Board

21. The number of women earning Ph.D.'s in 1964 (to the nearest hundred) was

(A) 200
(B) 500
(C) 1500
(D) 13,000
(E) 15,000

22. Which of the following statements best describes the distribution of Master's Degrees for the periods 1940 and 1964?

(A) Fewer women received Master's degrees in 1964 than in 1940.
(B) The increase in number of males who received Master's degrees in 1964 may be represented by the decimal .064.
(C) The increase in number of Master's Degrees received in 1964 was more than a 300% increase over the number received in 1940.
(D) The ratio of men to women receiving Master's Degrees was the same for both years.
(E) Fewer men received Master's Degrees in 1964 than in 1940.

Questions 23–25 refer to the following data.

Territorial Expansion

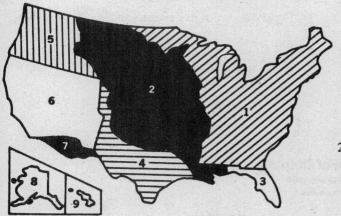

1	ORIGINAL 13 STATES 1790	888,685
2	LOUISIANA PURCHASE 1803	827,192
3	FLORIDA AND OTHER 1819	72,003
4	TEXAS 1845	390,144
5	OREGON TERRITORY 1846	285,580
6	MEXICAN CESSION 1848	529,017
7	GADSDEN PURCHASE 1853	29,640
8	ALASKA 1867	586,412
9	HAWAII 1898	6,450
	UNITED STATES TOTAL	3,615,123
	GUAM AND PUERTO RICO 1899	212 and 3,435
	AMERICAN SAMOA 1500	76
	VIRGIN ISLANDS 1917	133
	OTHER	9,083
	U.S. AND OUTLYING AREAS, TOTAL	3,678,062

GROSS AREA   Land and Water, square miles

23. After the Louisiana Purchase the area of the United States had

(A) roughly tripled
(B) roughly doubled
(C) increased slightly
(D) stayed the same
(E) decreased slightly

24. Which of the following percentages is closest to the percent of the United States total that is Alaska?

(A) 10
(B) 15
(C) 20
(D) 25
(E) 30

25. The area of the United States in 1900 was about x times the area of the United States in 1800, where x is

(A) $\frac{1}{4}$ (B) 3   (C) 4   (D) 5   (E) 6

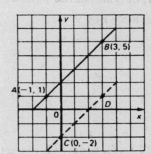

26. In the figure above, in order for the line segment AB to be parallel to the line segment CD, the coordinates of D must be $(3, x)$ with x equal to

(A) 1
(B) 2
(C) 3
(D) 4
(E) 5

27. A farmer wishes to build a fence around a rectangular field. The field is 100 feet long and 60 feet wide. The fence will be of stone on one long side and of wire on the other three sides. Stone costs $5 a foot, and wire costs $2 a foot. How much will the fence cost?

(A) $320
(B) $620
(C) $760
(D) $800
(E) $940

28. In June a baseball team that played 60 games had won 30% of its games played. After a phenomenal winning streak this team raised its average to 50%. How many games must the team have won in a row to attain this average?

    (A) 12   (B) 20   (C) 24   (D) 30   (E) 45

29. A train covers the distance d between two cities in h hours arriving 2 hours late. What rate would permit the train to arrive on schedule?

    (A) $h - 2$

    (B) $\dfrac{d}{h} - 2$

    (C) $\dfrac{d}{h - 2}$

    (D) $dh - 2$

    (E) $\dfrac{d}{h + 2}$

30. M men agreed to purchase a gift for $\$D$. If 3 men drop out, how much more will each have to contribute toward the purchase of the gift?

    (A) $\dfrac{D}{M - 3}$

    (B) $\dfrac{MD}{3}$

    (C) $\dfrac{3D}{M^2 - 3M}$

    (D) $\dfrac{3D}{3M - M^2}$

    (E) $\dfrac{2M + DM}{3M - M^2}$

S T O P

IF YOU FINISH BEFORE TIME IS CALLED, YOU MAY CHECK YOUR WORK ON THIS SECTION ONLY.
DO NOT WORK ON ANY OTHER SECTION IN THE TEST.

SECTION 4

Time—30 minutes

30 Questions

Numbers: All numbers used are real numbers.

Figures: Position of points, angles, regions, etc. can be assumed to be in the order shown; and angle measures can be assumed to be positive.

Lines shown as straight can be assumed to be straight.

Figures can be assumed to lie in a plane unless otherwise indicated.

Figures that accompany questions are intended to provide information useful in answering the questio However, unless a note states that a figure is drawn to scale, you should solve these problems NOT by estimating sizes by sight or by measurement, but by using your knowledge of mathematics (see Exam 2 below).

Directions: Each of the Questions 1-15 consists of two quantities, one in Column A and one in Column B. You are t compare the two quantities and choose

    A if the quantity in Column A is greater;
    B if the quantity in Column B is greater;
    C if the two quantities are equal;
    D if the relationship cannot be determined from the information given.

Note: Since there are only four choices, NEVER MARK (E).

Common Information: In a question, information concerning one or both of the quantities to be compared is centered above t two columns. A symbol that appears in both columns represents the same thing in Column A as it doe in Column B.

Column A	Column B	Sample Answers

Example 1: 2×6 $2 + 6$ ● Ⓑ Ⓒ Ⓓ Ⓔ

Examples 2-4 refer to $\triangle PQR$.

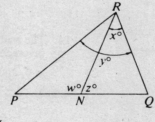

Example 2: PN NQ Ⓐ Ⓑ Ⓒ ● Ⓔ

(since equal measures cann be assumed, even though *P* and *NQ* appear equal)

Example 3: x y Ⓐ ● Ⓒ Ⓓ Ⓔ

(since *N* is between *P* and ᵩ

Example 4: $w + z$ 180 Ⓐ Ⓑ ● Ⓓ Ⓔ

(since *PQ* is a straight line)

A if the quantity in Column A is greater;
B if the quantity in Column B is greater;
C if the two quantities are equal;
D if the relationship cannot be determined from the information given.

Column A	Column B

$$\frac{1}{x} = \sqrt{.09}$$

1. x $3\frac{1}{3}$

$$a + 2b = 1\frac{1}{3}$$
$$a - b = \frac{1}{3}$$

2. $3b$ 1

---

3. $\dfrac{x - y}{-z}$ $\dfrac{y - x}{z}$

$x = 0$ and $y > 0$

4. $\dfrac{9x^2y^2}{27}$ $\dfrac{1}{3}$

---

5. $\dfrac{4}{5}$ quart $\dfrac{1}{5}$ gallon

$a:b = c:d$

6. $\dfrac{b}{a}$ $\dfrac{d}{c}$

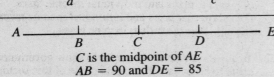

C is the midpoint of AE
$AB = 90$ and $DE = 85$

7.   Length of BC Length of CD

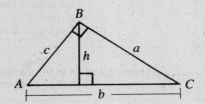

8. bh ac

Ten percent of the 2000 lottery tickets sold won prizes. Florence bought 20 tickets.

9. Number of prizes won   2 prizes
    by Florence

Column A	Column B

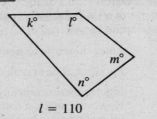

$l = 110$

10. l n

$a + b = 0$

11. a b

The area of triangle $ABC = 72$. The measure of angle A is equal to the measure of angle C, which is 45 degrees.

12.   Length of AB Length of BC

$$(a - 1)(a + 1) = 0$$
$$(b - 2)(b + 2) = 0$$

13. a^2 b^2

$x > 0$

14. The arithmetic mean x
     (average) of
     x, 0, and $\frac{3}{2}x$

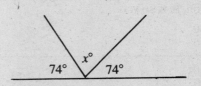

15. x 74

Directions: Each of Questions 16–30 has five answer choices. For each of these questions, select the best of the answer choices given.

16. A rectangular fish tank 25″ by 9″ has water in it to a level of 2″. This water is carefully poured into a cylindrical container with a diameter of 10″. How high (in terms of π) will the water reach in the cylindrical container?

(A) 18π

(B) $\dfrac{\pi}{18}$

(C) $\dfrac{18}{\pi}$

(D) $\dfrac{9}{2\pi}$

(E) $\dfrac{9\pi}{2}$

17. A triangular plot with sides of 28 feet, 35 feet, and 56 feet is to be surrounded by a fence built on posts set 7 feet apart. After posts are placed at each corner, how many additional posts will be needed?

(A) 14
(B) 15
(C) 16
(D) 17
(E) 20

18. A box is made in the form of a cube. If a second cubical box has inside dimensions three times those of the first box, how many times as much does it contain?

(A) 3
(B) 6
(C) 9
(D) 12
(E) 27

19. Two hours after a freight train leaves Circleville a passenger train leaves the same station traveling in the same direction at an average speed of 60 miles per hour. After traveling four hours, the passenger train overtakes the freight train. The average speed of the freight train was

(A) 30
(B) 40
(C) 58
(D) 60
(E) 120

20. Which of the following signs inserted in the parenthesis will make the statement following correct?

$$\frac{6}{14}\left(\right)\frac{9}{21}=\frac{3}{7}$$

(A) +
(B) −
(C) ×
(D) ÷
(E) =

Questions 21–25 refer to the following graphs.

**WHERE THE TAX
DOLLAR GOES**

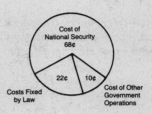

**WHERE THE TAX
DOLLAR COMES FROM**

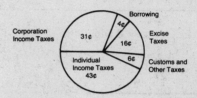

21. Which of the following is the source of most of the federal government revenue?

(A) excise taxes and corporate income taxes
(B) customs and excise taxes
(C) excise taxes and individual income taxes
(D) corporate taxes and individual income taxes
(E) all taxes other than income taxes

22. To accurately draw the sector to show government costs fixed by law the central angle of this sector should be

(A) 22°
(B) 44°
(C) 55°
(D) 60°
(E) 80°

23. What part of all taxes come from income taxes?

(A) $\dfrac{1}{3}$

(B) $\dfrac{1}{4}$

(C) $\dfrac{2}{5}$

(D) $\dfrac{1}{2}$

(E) $\dfrac{3}{4}$

24. What percent of the federal government income is derived from individual income taxes?

    (A) .0043%

    (B) .043%

    (C) .43%

    (D) 4.3%

    (E) 43%

25. Of every $1000 received by the federal government, how much is received from sources other than income taxes?

    (A) $260

    (B) $310

    (C) $430

    (D) $570

    (E) $740

26. To which of the following is $\frac{a}{b} - \frac{a}{c}$ equal?

    (A) $\frac{a}{b - c}$

    (B) $\frac{1}{b - c}$

    (C) $\frac{1}{bc}$

    (D) $\frac{ab - ac}{bc}$

    (E) $\frac{ac - ab}{bc}$

27. The two stars of a basketball team scored 416 points between them during a season. If one of them scored 192 points, what is the ratio of the points scored by this player to his teammate?

    (A) $\frac{6}{13}$ (B) $\frac{7}{13}$ (C) $\frac{6}{7}$ (D) $\frac{19}{22}$ (E) $\frac{7}{6}$

28. Nancy would like to complete all her homework before 10 P.M. in order to watch an important television program. She has 40-minute assignments in each of her five prepared subjects. What is the latest time at which she can start and still complete her homework in time for the program?

    (A) 6:30 P.M.

    (B) 6:40 P.M.

    (C) 7:10 P.M.

    (D) 7:20 P.M.

    (E) 8:00 P.M.

29. A club purchased novelties for $204.00 for resale at a benefit bazaar. During the first day they made sales amounting to $169.50. The inventory at the end of this day showed that they still had merchandise for which they paid $82.50. The gross profit at the end of the first day of the bazaar was

    (A) $ 34.60

    (B) $ 46.50

    (C) $ 48.00

    (D) $ 48.50

    (E) $121.50

30. Snowhite Paint Company contracts to paint three houses. Mr. Brown can paint a house in 6 days while Mr. Pinter would take 8 days and Mr. Slocum would take 12 days. After 8 days Mr. Brown goes on vacation and Mr. Pinter begins to work for a period of 6 days. How many days will it take Mr. Slocum to complete the contract?

    (A) 7

    (B) 8

    (C) 11

    (D) 12

    (E) 13

S T O P

IF YOU FINISH BEFORE TIME IS CALLED, YOU MAY CHECK YOUR WORK ON THIS SECTION ONLY. DO NOT WORK ON ANY OTHER SECTION IN THE TEST.

SECTION 5

Time—30 Minutes

25 Questions

Directions: Each question or group of questions is based on a passage or set of conditions. In answering some of the questions, it may be useful to draw a rough diagram. For each question, select the best answer choice given.

Questions 1–4

Eight varsity baseball players (*G,H,J,K,L,M,N,O*) are to be honored at a special ceremony. Three of these players (*H,M,* and *O*) are also varsity football players. Two of them (*K* and *N*) are also basketball players on the varsity team. In arranging the seats it was decided that athletes in two sports should not be seated next to another two-sport athlete.

1. Which of the following combinations is possible in order to have the arrangement of seat assignments as planned?

    (A) *H G K J*
    (B) *H K J L*
    (C) *J K M N*
    (D) *J L H K*
    (E) *L K N J*

2. To have the proper seating arrangement, *K* should sit between

    (A) *G* and *H*
    (B) *J* and *M*
    (C) *L* and *N*
    (D) *J* and *N*
    (E) *J* and *L*

3. Which of the following cannot sit next to *M*?

    (A) *G*
    (B) *J*
    (C) *G* and *J*
    (D) *K*
    (E) *L*

4. Before all athletes are seated there are two vacant seats on either side of *N*. Which two athletes may occupy these seats?

    (A) *G* and *K*
    (B) *G* and *L*
    (C) *J* and *H*
    (D) *L* and *O*
    (E) *M* and *J*

Questions 5–7

It takes a high degree of courage for a politician to risk his career by introducing federal legislation requiring registration and licensing of gun possession. While many say that the elimination of private ownership of firearms will cure the sociologic ills of our country, the gun lobby in Washington maintains that it is an invasion of personal liberty.

5. Which of the following is the best argument against national gun registration?

    (A) it would be difficult to enforce
    (B) murderers would ignore gun control legislation
    (C) it is a violation of rights granted in the Constitution
    (D) most murders occur between individuals that were acquainted with each other before the shooting
    (E) many homicides are committed without the use of guns

6. Which of the following is the best claim for banning firearms?

    (A) the root causes of violence lie deep in the nature of society
    (B) the state with the lowest crime rate has a stringent anti-gun law
    (C) many accidents occur in legal hunting and riflery
    (D) with fewer guns there would be fewer shootings
    (E) guns have no place in a civilized country

7. According to the statement in the passage, why would members of Congress hesitate to introduce gun-control legislation?

    (A) It would never pass.
    (B) It would be declared unconstitutional.
    (C) It would not decrease crime.
    (D) The gun lobby is very strong.
    (E) It is unpopular.

Questions 8–11

To obtain a visa for the Republic of Nimrod, an applicant must appear in person at the Nimrodian Consulate and show a U.S. birth certificate or naturalization papers, a certificate of vaccination for swamp fever, and a notorized bank statement showing a balance in excess of $1,000. Bank statements are available during normal business hours (Monday through Friday, 9 a.m. to 3 p.m. at most banks, which also have a notary on staff). Vaccinations are routinely performed at Alabaster Hospital, adjacent to the Nimrodian Consulate, on Wednesdays from noon to 5 p.m. They are also performed at Beryl Clinic, an hour's travel away from the consulate, on Mondays and Thursdays from 9 a.m. to noon and on Fridays from 4 to 5 p.m. Copies of U.S. birth certificates are issued on Mondays and Thursdays from 9 to 5 and copies of naturalization papers are issued on Tuesdays and Fridays from 9 to 5. The Nimrodian Consulate is open Mondays, Wednesdays, and Fridays from noon to 4 p.m.

8. Which of the following can complete the entire application procedure in the shortest time?

    (A) A native-born U.S. citizen starting Monday
    (B) A naturalized U.S. citizen starting Tuesday morning
    (C) A native-born U.S. citizen starting Wednesday morning
    (D) A naturalized U.S. citizen starting Thursday
    (E) A native-born U.S. citizen starting Friday

9. If a native-born U.S. citizen begins the application procedure by going for a copy of her birth certificate at noon on Thursday, the earliest she can finish will be

    (A) Friday morning
    (B) Friday afternoon
    (C) the following Monday afternoon
    (D) the following Tuesday afternoon
    (E) the following Wednesday afternoon

10. Mr. Nikto's bank, situated in the suburbs one hour's travel time from any other office that must be visited, issues statements only Tuesdays from 4 to 5 p.m. If Mr. Nikto completes the entire application procedure within 30 hours, he is

    (A) A naturalized U.S. citizen who began by getting vaccinated
    (B) A native-born U.S. citizen who began by getting a bank statement
    (C) A naturalized U.S. citizen who began by getting naturalization papers
    (D) A native-born U.S. citizen who began by getting a birth certificate
    (E) A naturalized U.S. citizen who began by getting a bank statement

11. Alabaster Hospital closes due to cuts in government funding. Thereafter, a naturalized U.S. citizen who begins the application procedure at noon on Tuesday can complete it no sooner than

    (A) Tuesday
    (B) Wednesday
    (C) Thursday
    (D) Friday
    (E) Monday

Questions 12–18

The organizer of Local 58 of the hospital workers is forming a five-person team to leaflet a nearby hospital. The team must contain two persons to distribute leaflets, one speaker to address the workers who stop, and a two-person defense squad. A, B, and C are possible leafletters; C, D, and E are possible speakers; F, G, and H are possible members of the defense guard. A and C prefer to go out together. E prefers to work only if F works.

12. Which choice of personnel is impossible if all preferences are respected?

    (A) A and B as leafletters, C as speaker
    (B) B and C as leafletters
    (C) A and C as leafletters, F and H on defense
    (D) Either D or E as speaker, with F on defense
    (E) G and H on defense

13. If A and B are leafletters and all preferences are respected, which is true?

    I.   C is the speaker.
    II. F is on defense.
    III. Either F or G is on defense.

    (A) I only
    (B) II only
    (C) III only
    (D) I and II only
    (E) I and III only

14. Which is a possible team if all preferences are respected?

    (A) A, B, C, D, F
    (B) A, C, D, E, F
    (C) A, B, C, F, G
    (D) A, C, E, G, H
    (E) B, C, D, F, G

15. If A is chosen as a member of the team and all preferences are respected, which must be true?

    (A) B must be a leafletter.
    (B) C must be a leafletter.
    (C) F must go.
    (D) Any of the three defense personnel may go.
    (E) Neither D nor E can go.

16. How many different possible teams can the organizer assemble, if all preferences are respected?

    (A) 5   (B) 8   (C) 9   (D) 13   (E) 15

17. Which person must be chosen as part of any team, if all preferences are respected?

    I.   A
    II. E
    III. F

    (A) I only
    (B) III only
    (C) I and II only
    (D) II and III only
    (E) I, II, and III

18. Which person can be part of the smallest number of different possible teams, if everyone's preferences are respected?

    (A) A

    (B) B

    (C) C

    (D) D

    (E) E

Questions 19–22

Delegations from Wallachia and Rumelia are meeting to discuss military, trade, and diplomatic problems. Each delegation consists of a chairperson, two military attachés, and two trade experts. The Wallachian delegation consists of A, B, C, D, and E; the Rumelian delegation of F, G, H, I, and J. Each chairperson is to occupy the middle seat in a row of five on two sides of a rectangular table.

(1) A insists on being seated at the opposite end of the table from B.

(2) G, who is deaf in his right ear, must be at the right end of the table.

(3) Neither D nor F is a chairperson.

(4) The Wallachian military attachées, one of whom is B, are seated together, and neither is opposite either of the Rumelian military attachés, neither of whom is G.

(5) C, a trade expert, is seated opposite H.

19. F may be a

    (A) trade expert seated next to I
    (B) military attaché seated next to I
    (C) military attaché seated next to J
    (D) trade expert seated next to H
    (E) trade expert seated opposite B

20. About which of the following do the stated conditions provide the least information?

    (A) The identity of the Wallachian chairperson
    (B) The identity of the Rumelian chairperson
    (C) The identity and seating position of the Wallachian military attachés
    (D) Which delegate is immediately to the right of the Wallachian chairperson
    (E) Which delegate is immediately to the right of the Rumelian chairperson

21. If J is a military attaché, which of the following must be true?

    I.   The Rumelian chairperson is I.
    II. F is a trade expert.
    III. I is a trade expert.

    (A) I only
    (B) II only
    (C) I and II only
    (D) I or III, but not both
    (E) II or III, but not both

22. Which of the following can be deduced from the introductory paragraph plus statements (1), (2), (4), and (5) only?

    (A) The identities of the Rumelian trade experts
    (B) The identities of the Wallachian military attachés
    (C) The identity of the Wallachian chairperson
    (D) Which two delegates are seated between G and H
    (E) Which two delegates are seated between B and C

Questions 23 and 24

In 1978 Thomas Malthus published "Essay on Population" in which he postulated that food supply can never keep pace with the rate of increase in human population.

23. Which of the following statements, if true, would tend to *weaken* Malthus's argument?

    I.   The total population of humans has risen at a rapid rate partly because of the removal of natural checks on population.
    II. In many nations, the increase of human population has far outstripped the food-producing capacity.
    III. Human population growth may be halted by the use of contraception.
    IV. For many ethnic and religious groups, artificial control of conception is morally unacceptable.

    (A) I only
    (B) I and II
    (C) II only
    (D) II and IV only
    (E) III only

24. Which of the following would be most likely to help limit the demands placed on food supplies?

    (A) wars
    (B) conservation of natural resources
    (C) better farming methods
    (D) better international relations
    (E) improved disease control

25. Most people who take the experimental medicine GRE/APT develop headaches; therefore, if Alice does not take GRE/APT, she will probably not develop headaches.

    The argument above most resembles which of the following?

    (A) Most Dobermans are easy to train, so Beth is sure to have no trouble training the Doberman she has just bought.
    (B) Most U.S.-built cars are poorly made; since this car is well made, it was probably not built in the U.S.
    (C) Most Broadway plays are very well acted, so *The Logic Game*, which is not a Broadway play, is probably not well acted.
    (D) Most engineers spent many years in school, so Sharon, who has spent many years in school, is probably an engineer.
    (E) All societies known to history have had clearly defined social hierarchies, so there will probably never be a truly non-hierarchical society.

S T O P

IF YOU FINISH BEFORE TIME IS CALLED, YOU MAY CHECK YOUR WORK ON THIS SECTION ONLY. DO NOT WORK ON ANY OTHER SECTION IN THE TEST.

SECTION 6

Time—30 Minutes

25 Questions

Directions: Each question or group of questions is based on a passage or set of conditions. In answering some of the questions, it may be useful to draw a rough diagram. For each question, select the best answer choice given.

Questions 1–4

Byram and Adoniram are code clerks at the Pentagon. One is in the pay of the Sulgravians and the other is in the pay of the Carolingians. If a document is stolen, it will take four days to reach the Sulgravian government and five days to reach the Carolingian government.

   Byram is given top-secret documents to encode on October 19 and 22.

   Adoniram is given a top-secret document to encode on October 21.

   Byram and Adoniram have lunch together on October 20.

   Agents of foreign governments do not transmit documents directly to governments that do not employ them, but may sell documents to an agent of another government. An agent who transmits a document always does so on the day he receives it.

1. If Adoniram is working for the Sulgravians, the Sulgravian government may receive documents on

   I.   October 24
   II. October 25
   III. October 26

  (A) I only
  (B) III only
  (C) I and II only
  (D) II and III only
  (E) I, II, and III

2. A top-secret document is received by the Carolingians on October 25. It could have been

  (A) stolen and transmitted by Byram
  (B) stolen and transmitted by Adoniram
  (C) stolen by Adoniram and sold to Byram, who transmitted it
  (D) stolen by Byram and sold to Adoniram, who transmitted it
  (E) stolen by either Byram or Adoniram and sold to the other, who transmitted it

3. If Adoniram is working for the Carolingians, which must be true?

  (A) The Sulgravians may receive documents only on October 23.
  (B) The Carolingians may receive documents only on October 26.
  (C) The Sulgravians may receive documents only on October 24, 26, and 27.
  (D) The Carolingians may receive documents only on October 24, 25, 26.
  (E) No documents received by the Sulgravians can have been bought at Byram and Adoniram's lunchtime meeting.

4. Which of the following is (are) possible given the conditions as stated?

   I.   Documents are received by one of the governments two days in a row.
   II. Documents are received by both governments two days in a row.
   III. Documents are received by one of the governments three days in a row.

  (A) I only
  (B) III only
  (C) I and III only
  (D) I, II, and III
  (E) neither I, II, nor III

5. Although there are no physical differences between the visual organs of the two groups, the inhabitants of the Bilge Islands, when shown a card displaying a spectrum of colors, perceive fewer colors than do most persons in the United States.

   Which of the following conclusions can most reliably be drawn from the information above?

  (A) Human color perception is at least partly determined by factors other than the physical structure of the visual organs.
  (B) The Bilge Islanders are probably taught in childhood to recognize fewer colors than are persons in the United States.
  (C) Differences in social structure probably affect color perception.
  (D) Color perception in humans is influenced by differences in physical environment.
  (E) Bilge Islanders may have fewer terms denoting colors in their language than do English-speaking persons.

Questions 6 and 7

Ms. Brady: Mr. Flynn insists that the only way for our company to increase its profits is to double the advertising budget. That obviously is not the answer. Our two major competitors have operations similar to ours. Both are showing increased profits while spending less on advertising than we presently spend.

6. Ms. Brady's primary method of making her point is to

  (A) suggest a different underlying cause of the problem
  (B) present evidence which was previously overlooked
  (C) point out a logical flaw in Mr. Flynn's reasoning
  (D) draw an analogy
  (E) question Mr. Flynn's competence

7. Which of the following statements would be Mr. Flynn's most effective rebuttal to Ms. Brady's argument?

(A) Our two major competitors do not need to advertise as much as we do, because they are already much better known and have larger shares of the market.
(B) I have been in this business for 30 years, during which time I have repeatedly proven my ability to identify and solve business problems.
(C) The only way for us to increase profits is to sell more of our products; the only way to sell more products is to convince people to buy them; the only way to convince people to buy them is through increased advertising.
(D) You have offered neither statistics to back up your claims nor any proposal for an alternative solution to our problem.
(E) My proposal is not "obviously" wrong. There is only one way to find out if it is wrong, and that is to try it.

Questions 8–12

(1) Ashland is north of East Liverpool and west of Coshocton.
(2) Bowling Green is north of Ashland and west of Fredericktown.
(3) Dover is south and east of Ashland.
(4) East Liverpool is north of Fredericktown and east of Dover.
(5) Fredericktown is north of Dover and west of Ashland.
(6) Coshocton is south of Fredericktown and west of Dover.

8. Which of the towns mentioned is furthest to the northwest?

(A) Ashland
(B) Bowling Green
(C) Coshocton
(D) East Liverpool
(E) Fredericktown

9. Which of the following must be both north and east of Fredericktown?

   I.   Ashland
   II. Coshocton
   III. East Liverpool

(A) I only
(B) II only
(C) III only
(D) I and II
(E) I and III

10. Which of the following towns must be situated both south and west of at least one other town?

(A) Ashland only
(B) Ashland and Fredericktown
(C) Dover and Fredericktown
(D) Dover, Coshocton, and Fredericktown
(E) Coshocton, Dover, and East Liverpool

11. Which of the following statements, if true, would make the information in the numbered statements more specific?

(A) Coshocton is north of Dover.
(B) East Liverpool is north of Dover.
(C) Ashland is east of Bowling Green.
(D) Coshocton is east of Fredericktown.
(E) Bowling Green is north of Fredericktown.

12. Which of the numbered statements gives information that can be deduced from one or more of the other statements?

(A) (1)
(B) (2)
(C) (3)
(D) (4)
(E) (6)

Questions 13–16

Spelunkers International offers exploring tours in eight caves: Abbott, Benny, Caesar, Dangerfield, Ewell, Fields, Guinness, and Hope.
(1) Class 1 spelunkers may not attempt caves Ewell, Fields, or Hope.
(2) Class 2 spelunkers may not attempt cave Hope.
(3) Class 3 spelunkers may attempt any cave.
(4) Cave Caesar may be attempted only by spelunkers who have previously explored cave Benny.
(5) Cave Fields may be attempted only by spelunkers who have previously explored cave Ewell.
(6) Only two of caves Benny, Caesar, Ewell, Fields, and Hope may be attempted by any explorer in a single tour.

13. Which tour is allowed for a class 2 spelunker who has never explored any of the eight caves before, if the caves are attempted in the order listed?

(A) Abbott, Fields, Ewell, Benny
(B) Dangerfield, Guinness, Caesar, Benny
(C) Guinness, Ewell, Dangerfield, Benny, Abbott
(D) Dangerfield, Ewell, Fields, Abbott, Caesar
(E) Guinness, Ewell, Fields, Dangerfield, Benny

14. A class 2 spelunker who has previously explored cave Ewell may be restricted in choosing a tour by which rule(s)?

    I.   Rule (4)
    II. Rule (5)
    III. Rule (6)

    (A) I only
    (B) II only
    (C) I and III only
    (D) II and III only
    (E) I, II, and III

15. In how many different ways may a class 1 spelunker who has never explored any of the eight caves before set up a tour of three caves, if she wishes to explore caves Abbott and Caesar?

    (A) 2
    (B) 3
    (C) 4
    (D) 5
    (E) 6

16. What is the maximum number of caves that a class 3 spelunker who has previously explored only cave Benny may include in a single tour?

    (A) 4
    (B) 5
    (C) 6
    (D) 7
    (E) 8

Questions 17–22

Mr. Pesth, foreman for Buda Construction Co., is hiring five persons to do wiring and plumbing on a site. He must have a minimum of two electricians. Nine persons are sent by the union hiring hall: Mike, Nick, and Olive are electricians, while Rich, Steve, Tom, Ulysses, Vic, and Wassily are plumbers.

Pesth is unwilling to hire Ulysses and Vic together, because he knows from past experience that they fight all the time.

Steve and Tom are buddies and will only work together.

Olive won't work with Rich, a Moravian, because she despises Moravians.

17. If Mike, Nick, and Olive are hired, the team of plumbers can consist of

    (A) Steve and Tom only
    (B) Steve and Tom or Ulysses and Vic
    (C) Ulysses and Wassily or Vic and Wassily
    (D) Steve and Tom, or Ulysses and Wassily or Vic and Wassily
    (E) Steve, Tom, and either Ulysses, Vic, or Wassily

18. Pesth has the greatest number of choices for hiring as plumbers if the electricians he chooses are

    (A) Mike, Nick, and Olive
    (B) Mike and Nick
    (C) Mike and Olive
    (D) Nick and Olive
    (E) Either Mike or Nick, plus Olive

19. If Rich is hired, the other persons hired must be

    (A) Mike, Nick, Steve, and Tom
    (B) Mike, Nick, Olive, and either Ulysses, Vic, or Wassily
    (C) Mike and Nick, together with either Steve and Tom or Ulysses and Wassily
    (D) Mike and Nick, together with either Ulysses and Vic or Vic and Wassily
    (E) Mike and Nick, together with either Steve and Tom, Ulysses and Wassily, or Vic and Wassily

20. Pesth can put together the rest of his crew in the greatest number of different ways if he hires

    (A) Steve and Tom
    (B) Olive
    (C) Ulysses
    (D) Vic
    (E) Wassily

21. If Mike is hired and Nick is not, which of the following statements must be true?

    I. Steve and Tom are hired.
    II. Either Ulysses or Vic is hired, but not both.

    (A) I only
    (B) II only
    (C) either I or II, but not both
    (D) both I and II
    (E) neither I nor II

22. Which of the following statements must be true?

    I.   If only two electricians are hired, the plumbers must include Steve and Tom.
    II. If Olive is not hired, Rich must be hired.
    III. If either Mike or Nick is not hired, Steve and Tom must be hired.

    (A) I only
    (B) II only
    (C) III only
    (D) I and III only
    (E) II and III only

23. The current trend toward specialization in nearly all occupational groups is exactly the opposite of what is needed. World problems today are so diverse, complex, and interrelated that only the generalist stands a chance of understanding the broad picture. Unless our schools stress a truly broad, liberal education, the world will crumble around us as we each expertly perform our own narrow functions.

Each of the following, if true, would weaken the conclusion drawn above, EXCEPT:

(A) Many of the world's problems can be solved only by highly specialized experts working on specific problems.
(B) Relatively few generalists are needed to coordinate the work of the many specialists.
(C) Specialization does not necessarily entail losing the ability to see the broad picture.
(D) Increasingly complex problems require a growing level of technical expertise which can only be acquired through specialization.
(E) Even the traditional liberal education is becoming more highly specialized today.

Questions 24 and 25

All good athletes want to win, and all athletes who want to win eat a well-balanced diet; therefore, all athletes who do not eat a well-balanced diet are bad athletes.

24. If the assumptions of the argument above are true, then which of the following statements must be true?

(A) No bad athlete wants to win.
(B) No athlete who does not eat a well-balanced diet is a good athlete.
(C) Every athlete who eats a well-balanced diet is a good athlete.
(D) All athletes who want to win are good athletes.
(E) Some good athletes do not eat a well-balanced diet.

25. Which of the following, if true, would refute the assumptions of the argument above?

(A) Ann wants to win, but she is not a good athlete.
(B) Bob, the accountant, eats a well-balanced diet, but he is not a good athlete.
(C) All the players on the Burros baseball team eat a well-balanced diet.
(D) No athlete who does not eat a well-balanced diet wants to win.
(E) Cindy, the basketball star, does not eat a well-balanced diet, but she is a good athlete.

S T O P

IF YOU FINISH BEFORE TIME IS CALLED, YOU MAY CHECK YOUR WORK ON THIS SECTION ONLY. DO NOT WORK ON ANY OTHER SECTION IN THE TEST.

SECTION 7
Time—30 Minutes
30 Questions

Numbers: All numbers used are real numbers.

Figures: Position of points, angles, regions, etc. can be assumed to be in the order shown; and angle measures can be assumed to be positive.

Lines shown as straight can be assumed to be straight.

Figures can be assumed to lie in a plane unless otherwise indicated.

Figures that accompany questions are intended to provide information useful in answering the questions. However, unless a note states that a figure is drawn to scale, you should solve these problems NOT by estimating sizes by sight or by measurement, but by using your knowledge of mathematics (see Example 2 below).

Directions: Each of the Questions 1-15 consists of two quantities, one in Column A and one in Column B. You are to compare the two quantities and choose

A if the quantity in Column A is greater;
B if the quantity in Column B is greater;
C if the two quantities are equal;
D if the relationship cannot be determined from the information given.

Note: Since there are only four choices, NEVER MARK (E).

Common
Information: In a question, information concerning one or both of the quantities to be compared is centered above the two columns. A symbol that appears in both columns represents the same thing in Column A as it does in Column B.

Column A	Column B	Sample Answers

| Example 1: | 2×6 | $2 + 6$ | ● Ⓑ Ⓒ Ⓓ Ⓔ |

Examples 2-4 refer to $\triangle PQR$.

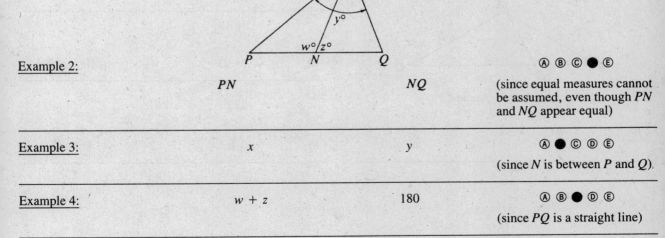

| Example 2: | PN | NQ | Ⓐ Ⓑ Ⓒ ● Ⓔ |
| | | | (since equal measures cannot be assumed, even though PN and NQ appear equal) |

| Example 3: | x | y | Ⓐ ● Ⓒ Ⓓ Ⓔ |
| | | | (since N is between P and Q) |

| Example 4: | $w + z$ | 180 | Ⓐ Ⓑ ● Ⓓ Ⓔ |
| | | | (since PQ is a straight line) |

A if the quantity in Column A is greater;
B if the quantity in Column B is greater;
C if the two quantities are equal;
D if the relationship cannot be determined from the information given.

Column A	Column B

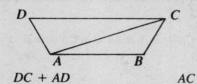

$a = 2$ and $b = 3$

1. $a - b$ $b - a$

2. $\sqrt{14.4}$ $\sqrt{1.44}$

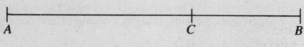

3. $DC + AD$ AC

4. Radius of a circle with   Radius of a circle with
    circumference of 9   area of 25

5. The length of the seg-   The length of the seg-
    ment joining the mid-   ment from point A to
    points of AC and CB the midpoint of AB

$\textcircled{X}$ is defined by the equation $\textcircled{X} = \dfrac{\sqrt{x}}{2}$.

6. $\textcircled{100}$ 10

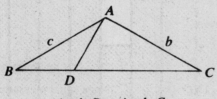

Angle B = Angle C

7. $\dfrac{x}{c}$ $\dfrac{x}{b}$

Column A	Column B

$a^2 + b^2 = 100$
$-6 \leqslant b \leqslant 0$

8. Lowest possible value   0
    of a

9. Distance covered by a   25 miles
    motorist going at 50
    miles per hour from
    10:55 P.M. to 11:25
    P.M. the same evening

$z > 5$

10. $\dfrac{1}{z}$ $\dfrac{1}{z-1}$

$\dfrac{a}{b} = \dfrac{c}{d}$

11. ad bc

$0 < x < y$

12. $3x$ y

13. $\dfrac{1}{4} \div \dfrac{3}{8}$ $1\dfrac{1}{2}$

$x > 0$

14. $(-2)^x$ $(1)^x$

$a = 2b$
$1 < b < 9$

15. a 6

Directions: Each of the Questions 16–30 has five answer choices. For each of these questions, select the best of the answer choices given.

---

16. If $9x - 3y = 12$ and $3x - 5y = 7$, then $6x - 2y$ equals

    (A) -5
    (B) 2
    (C) 4
    (D) 7
    (E) 8

17. The product of 8,754,896 and 48,933 equals

    (A) 428,403,325,965
    (B) 428,403,325,966
    (C) 428,403,325,967
    (D) 428,403,325,968
    (E) 428,403,325,969

18. If $2^{n+2} = 8$, then n equals

    (A) -1
    (B) $+1$
    (C) 2
    (D) 3
    (E) 4

19. If x is an odd integer, which of the following is even?

    (A) $2x + 1$
    (B) $2x - 1$
    (C) $x + x - 1$
    (D) $(x - 2)(x + 2)$
    (E) $2(x + 1)$

20. The price of a garment is reduced by 20 percent. During a special "early-bird" special all garments are marked "Take an additional 30 percent off the reduced price." The two reductions are equivalent to a single reduction of

    (A) 25%
    (B) 44%
    (C) 50%
    (D) 56%
    (E) 60%

Questions 21–25 refer to the following graphs.

FLORENCE DRESS SHOP
SALES AND EARNINGS REPORT (1980–1987)

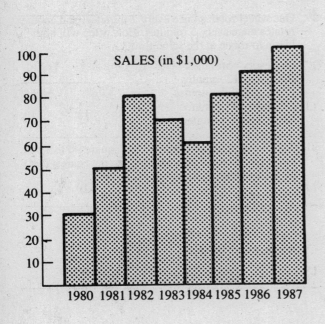

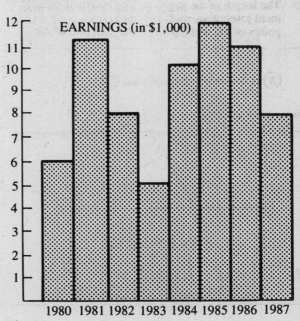

21. What is the average (arithmetic mean) in thousands of dollars of the sales for the period 1982–1985?

(A) $60.
(B) $70.
(C) $72.5
(D) $80.
(E) $80.5

22. Of the following, which year showed the greatest increase in sales over the previous year?

(A) 1980
(B) 1982
(C) 1984
(D) 1985
(E) 1986

23. What was the ratio of sales to earnings in 1980?

(A) $\frac{1}{2}$

(B) $\frac{2}{1}$

(C) $\frac{1}{5}$

(D) $\frac{5}{1}$

(E) $\frac{1}{6}$

24. What was the percentage increase in earnings from 1984 to 1985?

(A) 2%
(B) 6%
(C) 10%
(D) 12%
(E) 20%

25. If g represents the earnings in 1980 then the earnings in 1985 is expressed as

(A) $2g$

(B) $\frac{g}{2}$

(C) $g + 2$

(D) $\frac{2}{g}$

(E) $3g$

26. R and T are points on straight line PQ on which $PR = RT = TQ$. What percent of PT is PQ?

(A) $1\frac{1}{2}$%

(B) 50%

(C) $66\frac{2}{3}$%

(D) $33\frac{1}{3}$%

(E) 150%

27. Which of the following has the greatest value?

(A) 0.3
(B) $\sqrt{0.3}$

(C) $\frac{2}{5}$

(D) $\frac{1}{3}$

(E) 0.01π

28. Mr. Nichols, who owns $66\frac{2}{3}$% of a factory, sells half of his share for $33,333. The value of the entire factory is

(A) $9,999
(B) $66,666
(C) $99,999
(D) $100,000
(E) $133,332

29. One wheel rotates once every 7 minutes, and another rotates once every 5 minutes. How often will both begin to rotate at the same time?

(A) every 6 minutes
(B) every 12 minutes
(C) every 17.5 minutes
(D) every 35 minutes
(E) every 70 minutes

30. An official baseball diamond is a square 90 feet on each side. The shortest distance (to the nearest foot) from third base to first base is

(A) 90 feet
(B) 127 feet
(C) 135 feet
(D) 180 feet
(E) less than 90 feet

S T O P

IF YOU FINISH BEFORE TIME IS CALLED, YOU MAY CHECK YOUR WORK ON THIS SECTION ONLY.
DO NOT WORK ON ANY OTHER SECTION IN THE TEST.

Answer Key

Note: The answers to the quantitative sections are keyed to the corresponding review areas in the Mathematics Review (Chapter 11). The numbers in parentheses after each answer refer to the math topic(s) covered by that particular question.

Section 1   Verbal

1.	B	11.	E	21.	C	31.	A
2.	D	12.	B	22.	B	32.	D
3.	D	13.	C	23.	D	33.	D
4.	A	14.	B	24.	A	34.	B
5.	D	15.	E	25.	C	35.	C
6.	B	16.	A	26.	D	36.	B
7.	D	17.	D	27.	A	37.	A
8.	B	18.	E	28.	D	38.	E
9.	D	19.	C	29.	A		
10.	D	20.	D	30.	A		

Section 2   Verbal

1.	C	11.	B	21.	C	31.	B
2.	B	12.	D	22.	D	32.	E
3.	A	13.	C	23.	E	33.	D
4.	E	14.	A	24.	E	34.	B
5.	D	15.	E	25.	A	35.	A
6.	B	16.	B	26.	D	36.	E
7.	E	17.	E	27.	D	37.	B
8.	C	18.	B	28.	B	38.	D
9.	E	19.	B	29.	A		
10.	A	20.	B	30.	C		

Section 3   Quantitative

1.	C (I-B, D)	9.	A (III-D)	17.	E (I-H)	25.	C (IV-A)
2.	A (I)	10.	D (III-F)	18.	B (II-D)	26.	A (III-H, III-B)
3.	A (I)	11.	C (III-D)	19.	C (II-B)	27.	E (III-G)
4.	C (III-A)	12.	A (III-G)	20.	A (I-B, II-G)	28.	C (IV-B)
5.	D (III-A)	13.	B (III-A)	21.	C (IV-B)	29.	C (I, V)
6.	C (III-D)	14.	C (I)	22.	C (IV-B)	30.	C (I-B)
7.	C (III-F)	15.	C (I-B)	23.	B (IV-A)		
8.	C (III-D)	16.	A (I-B, II-B)	24.	B (I-D)		

Section 4   Quantitative

1. C (I-H)	9. D (I-D)	17. A (III-C)	25. A (IV)
2. C (II-A)	10. D (III-A)	18. E (III-G)	26. E (I-B)
3. C (I-B, II-A)	11. D (II-B)	19. B (II-C)	27. C (II-E)
4. B (II-A)	12. C (III-A, G)	20. E (I-B)	28. B (II-E)
5. C (I)	13. B (II-B)	21. D (IV)	29. C (I-C)
6. C (II-A, E)	14. B (I-G)	22. E (III, IV)	30. C (II-C)
7. B (III-B)	15. B (III-A)	23. E (I-B, IV)	
8. C (III-D, G)	16. C (III-G)	24. E (I-D, IV)	

Section 5   Analytical

1. A	8. A	15. D	22. E
2. E	9. C	16. B	23. E
3. D	10. C	17. A	24. A
4. B	11. D	18. E	25. C
5. C	12. B	19. A	
6. D	13. E	20. E	
7. D	14. C	21. C	

Section 6   Analytical

1. C	8. B	15. B	22. C
2. D	9. E	16. B	23. E
3. E	10. D	17. D	24. B
4. A	11. A	18. B	25. E
5. A	12. C	19. E	
6. D	13. C	20. A	
7. A	14. C	21. A	

Section 7   Quantitative

1. B (II-A)	9. C (II-C2)	17. D (I-E)	25. A (II-C, IV)
2. A (I-H)	10. B (I-B)	18. B (I-H)	26. E (I-D)
3. A (III)	11. C (II-E)	19. E (I-A)	27. B (I-B)
4. B (III-F)	12. D (II-G)	20. B (I-D)	28. C (I-D)
5. C (III-B)	13. B (I-B)	21. C (I-G, IV)	29. D (I-A)
6. B (III-A)	14. D (I-H)	22. B (IV)	30. B (III-D)
7. C (III-A)	15. D (II-A)	23. D (II-E, IV)	
8. B (II-A)	16. E (II-B)	24. E (I-D, IV)	

Answer Explanations

Section 1

1. **B.** Criticism that suggests areas of improvement is said to be *constructive*.
   Remember, before you look at the answer choices, read the sentence and try to think of a word that makes sense.

2. **D.** *Because* the writer does not personally enjoy Eliot's novels, before he criticizes her he feels he should, to be fair, pay *tribute* to her literary virtues.
   Look for signal words or phrases indicating that one thing causes another or logically determines another. In this instance, the conjunction *as* has the meaning *because*.

3. **D.** If "you may wonder" how the expert reaches his conclusions, it appears that it is questionable to rely on teeth for guidance in interpreting fossils. Choice D, *inadequate*, creates the element of doubt that the clause tries to develop. Choice C, *specious*, also creates an element of doubt; however, nothing in the context justifies the idea that the reasoning is specious or false. Note that here you are dealing with an extended metaphor. Picture yourself hanging a heavy winter coat on a slim wooden peg. Wouldn't you worry that the peg might prove inadequate or flimsy?

4. **A.** Here the task is to determine the communal reaction to crime. The writer maintains that the criminal justice system of punishments allows the community to purge itself of its anger, its sense of *outrage* at the criminal's acts. Thus, it provides a *catharsis* or purgation for the community.
   Remember, in double-blank sentences, go through the answers, testing the *first* word in each choice and eliminating those that don't fit. In this case, you can readily eliminate Choices B and E: it is unlikely that an *essential* purpose of the criminal justice system would be the provision of either a *disclaimer* (denial or disavowal, as in disavowing responsibility for a legal claim) or a *document*.

5. **D.** The key word here is *assailed*. Housman is attacking his rival. Thus he is in the tradition of scholarly *invective* (vehement verbal attack), criticizing his foe for turning to manuscripts merely for confirmation or *support* of old theories and not for enlightenment or illumination. Again, note the use of figurative language, in this case the simile of the drunkard.

6. **B.** Unquestioned assumptions and accepted opinions bind the natural philosopher, *tyrannically* restricting his ability to hypothesize freely. Thus, the philosopher must strive to *achieve* detachment in order to free himself from this *tyranny*.

7. **D.** Because the Dean was not able to *disguise* his distaste for the P.R. barrage, he failed to stifle his *caustic* or sarcastically biting remarks about the event.
   Note the implicit cause and effect relationship between the opening phrase and the central clause of the sentence.

8. **B.** Just as the *yolk* is central to the *egg*, the *nucleus* is central to the *cell*.
   (Part to Whole)

9. **D.** To *sand wood* is to smooth or polish it. To *burnish metal* is to polish it.
   (Function)

10. **D.** Someone *vindictive* or vengeful is lacking in *mercy*. Someone *skeptical* or suspicious is lacking in *trustfulness*.
    (Antonym Variant)

11. **E.** To *ruffle* someone's *composure* is to disturb or trouble his self-possession. To *upset* someone's *equilibrium* is to disturb or trouble his balance.
    (Function)

12. **B.** The *bouquet* of *wine* is its distinctive fragrance. It is analogous to the *aroma* of *coffee*.
    (Defining Characteristic)

13. **C.** By definition, a *sextant* is a piece of equipment that is *nautical*. Similarly, a *forceps* is a piece of equipment that is *surgical*.
    (Defining Characteristic)

14. **B.** Someone *refractory* (stubborn; unmanageable) by definition is hard to *manage*. Likewise, someone *lethargic* (sluggish; drowsy) by definition is hard to *stimulate*.
    (Definition)

15. **E.** Something *latent* has not yet emerged into view but has within it the potential for *manifestation*. Something *dormant* has not yet emerged from its sleep but has within it the potential for *awakening* into activity. As always, consider all the answer choices before making your selection. Choice C, for example, looks tempting: a *perfunctory* (mechanical; cursory) act lacks *inspiration*. However, something *perfunctory* does not necessarily have within it the potential for *inspiration*.

(Antonym Variant)

16. **A.** The defining characteristic of a *precipice* (very steep, sheer cliff) is *steepness*. The defining characteristic of a *defile* (long narrow pass through which one files) is *narrowness*. Note, by the way, that you are dealing with a secondary meaning of *defile*, a meaning in which *defile* is a noun, not a verb. Even if you do not know this meaning of the word, you can still arrive at the correct answer by eliminating those answer choices which are patently incorrect. You know that a *precipice* is by definition characterized by *steepness*. Therefore, you can eliminate Choices C and E: a broad *plateau* is not characterized by *depth*, nor is a damp *marsh* characterized by *aridity* or dryness. Similarly, you can eliminate Choice B: while wells may sometimes be shallow, a *well* is not *by definition* characterized by *shallowness*. Finally, you can eliminate Choice D: *range* is not something that characterizes a *mountain*; a *range* is a chain of *mountains*. Thus, even without knowing the meaning of the noun *defile* you can satisfy yourself that Choice A is the correct answer.

(Defining Characteristic)

17. **D.** The author first discusses Du Bois in relationship to black leaders in general and then provides the specific example of his relationship to Booker T. Washington.
Choice A is incorrect. The author mentions Du Bois' early support of Washington's gradualist approach in order to contrast it with his later departure from Washington's conservatism.
Choice B is incorrect. The author discusses Du Bois' personality only in passing; he discusses Washington's personality not at all.
Choice C is incorrect. The author's chief concern is to describe Du Bois' position, not analyze what lay behind his achieving this position. He spends more time showing why Du Bois angered his fellow blacks than he does showing why Du Bois attracted his fellow blacks.
Choice E is incorrect. It is unsupported by the passage.

18. **E.** The last sentence points out that Du Bois originally agreed with Washington's program.
Choice A is incorrect. Nothing in the passage suggests that Du Bois sacrificed effective strategies out of a desire to try something new.
Choice B is incorrect. Du Bois gained in influence, effectively winning away large numbers of blacks from Washington's policies.
Choice C is incorrect. Du Bois' quickness to depart from conventional black wisdom when it proved inadequate to the task of advancing the race shows him to be well able to change with the times.
Choice D is incorrect. Washington, not Du Bois, is described as seeking the good will of powerful whites.

19. **C.** The author does *not* portray Washington as versatile. Instead, he portrays Du Bois as versatile.
Choice A is incorrect. The author portrays Washington as submissive to the majority; he shows him teaching blacks not to protest.
Choice B is incorrect. The author portrays Washington as concerned with financial success; he shows him advocating property accumulation.
Choice D is incorrect. The author portrays Washington as traditional in preaching industry; he shows him advocating hard work.
Choice E is incorrect. The author portrays Washington as respectful of authority; he shows him deferring to powerful whites.

20. **D.** Although the author points out that Du Bois' methods led him into conflicts, he describes Du Bois as "often…well in advance of his contemporaries" and stresses that his motives for departing from the mainstream were admirable. Thus, his attitude can best be described as *approving*.

21. **C.** The extremely general opening paragraphs and the careful use of simple examples imply that the passage most likely has been taken from a scientific journal article intended for a lay audience.

22. **B.** The mathematical expression of an electron "as if it were smeared out over a large region of space" describes the electron dynamically. Only Choice B possesses an analogous dynamic quality.

23. **D.** The opening two paragraphs about what is demanded of a physical theory give way to a discussion of the theory of quantum mechanics as a successful physical theory.
Choice A is incorrect. While the author cites the wide applicability of quantum theory, nowhere does he openly assert that local realistic theories are inapplicable.
Choice B is incorrect. The author describes the

assumptions underlying local realistic theories, not those underlying quantum theory.

Choice C is incorrect. It is unsupported by the passage.

Choice E is incorrect. If anything, the author does the reverse.

24. **A.** Choice A is correct. You can arrive at it by the process of elimination.

Question I is answerable based on the passage. The fourth paragraph enumerates the premises underlying the local realistic theories of nature. Therefore you can eliminate Choice B.

Question II is unanswerable based on the passage. Nothing in the passage indicates that any premise of the local realistic theories has been invalidated. Therefore you can eliminate Choices C and E.

Question III is also unanswerable based on the passage. Though mathematical expressions such as wave formations are mentioned, no information is given regarding the degree to which one can interpret them physically. Therefore you can eliminate Choice D.

Only Choice A is left. It is the correct answer.

25. **C.** The author does *not* assume the premise of Einstein separability to be invalid.

Choice A is incorrect. The author gives the illustration of the position of a pointer on a dial as an example of an observed phenomenon.

Choice B is incorrect. The author's opening paragraph presents such a generalization.

Choice D is incorrect. The author lists the premises underlying local realistic theories.

Choice E is incorrect. The passage concludes with the statement that one theory or the other must be wrong.

26. **D.** In its explanation of the two conflicting theories and its enumeration of the premises underlying the local realistic theories of nature, the passage can best be described as a *systematic exposition*.

27. **A.** The author mentions that many physicists find it sensible to limit the scope of quantum mechanics by regarding it "as merely a set of rules that prescribe the outcome of experiments." He then describes this limitation as unsatisfactory, given quantum mechanics' conflict with the so-called local realistic theories of nature and given the differences in predictions resulting from the current experiments he cites. Thus, the physicists who ignore these differences have not yet explained the results of the current experiments in elementary particle physics he cites.

28. **D.** *Adulterated* (made impure) is the opposite of *pure*.
Think of "adulterated food."

29. **A.** To *distend* (enlarge, as by swelling) is the opposite of to *deflate*.
Word Parts Clue: *Tend-* means stretch; *dis-* means apart. Something distended is enlarged by being stretched apart.
Think of "a distended stomach."

30. **A.** *Transient* (fleeting; temporary) is the opposite of *permanent*.
Think of "transient youth."

31. **A.** *Elated* (joyful, in high spirits) is the opposite of *crestfallen* (dejected).
Think of "elated by her success."

32. **D.** To *revile* (verbally abuse) something is the opposite of *praising* it.
Think of "reviled as a traitor."

33. **D.** The opposite of *propitious* (favorable, advantageous) is *unfavorable*.
Think of being pleased by "propitious omens."

34. **B.** The opposite of to *ensue* (happen later, follow) is to *precede*.
Think of "the wedding that ensued."

35. **C.** *Retrospection* (looking backward; the act of surveying the past) is the opposite of *anticipation* (looking forward).
Word Parts Clue: *Retro-* means backward; *spect-* means look. *Retrospection* means looking backward.
Think of "an old man lost in retrospection."

36. **B.** The *egress* (exit) is the opposite of the *entrance*.
Word Parts Clue: *E-* means out; *gress-* means go. The *egress* is the way you go out.
Think of P. T. Barnum's sign, "This way to the egress."

37. **A.** To *maunder* (speak disconnectedly; talk without a clear purpose) is the opposite of to *speak purposefully*.
Think of "maundering at random."

38. **E.** *Hubris* (overweening arrogance; pride that offends the gods) is the opposite of *humility*.
Think of "conceited hubris."

Section 2

1. **C.** The writer hopes that economics and politics shall once more form the study known as political economy. Clearly, the subjects have been linked in the past. Thus, he hopes that the two separate fields shall be *reunited*.

2. **B.** If bilingual education is more than a mere stop-gap (a somewhat negative description), it must possess certain positive qualities. Thus it has *advantages over* education in a single tongue. Note the use of *far from* to signal the contrast between the negative and positive views on bilingual education presented in this sentence.

3. **A.** Under certain circumstances scientists attack each other with *ad hominem* arguments (personal attacks) and shameless appeals. When is this likely to occur? When facts are *established* or *demonstrable* or *ineluctable* (unavoidable)? Hardly. Under such circumstances they would rely on facts to establish their case. It is when facts prove *elusive* that they lose control and, in doing so, abandon their pretense of *objectivity*.

4. **E.** A disease in a *latent* state has yet to manifest itself and emerge into view. Therefore it is impossible to *observe*.
Remember, in double-blank sentences, go through the answers, testing the *first* word in each choice and eliminating those that don't fit. When a disease is in a *critical* or *acute* state, its existence is obvious. Therefore, you can eliminate Choices B and C.

5. **D.** The second clause presents an example of literary *mockery*. The abstract idea of preserving a nugget of pure truth is appealing; the concrete example of setting it up on the mantle makes fun of the whole idea.

6. **B.** If the rare earths are actually present to some degree in essentially all minerals, then they are not rare after all. Thus, the term "rare earths" is a *misnomer* (incorrect designation), for the rare earths are actually *ubiquitous* (omnipresence; found everywhere).
Watch out for words that signal the unexpected. Note the use of "paradoxically" here.

7. **E.** Although it is the *thrust* of Clement's argument that psychoanalysis must return to its healing offices, it is precisely here that her argument fails and her shafts *glance away*.
Be on the lookout for extended metaphors that influence the writer's choice of words. In this case, the use of "shafts" conjures up an image of javelins that do not strike home but instead glance off the foe.

8. **C.** A *sheep bleats* in its characteristic call. A *sparrow chirps* in its characteristic call.

(Defining Characteristic)

9. **E.** When *milk curdles*, by definition it coagulates or thickens. Likewise, when *blood clots*, it too coagulates.

(Definition)

10. **A.** A bird *molts* or sheds its *feathers*. A snake casts off or *sloughs* its *skin*.

(Defining Characteristic)

11. **B.** An *offhand* remark is made without forethought or *premeditation*. An *aboveboard* (open) deed is done without trickery or *guile*.

(Antonym Variant)

12. **D.** The *larval* (immature) stage of an *insect* best corresponds to the *embryonic* stage of a *mammal*.

(Defining Characteristic)

13. **C.** A *poltergeist* (noisy, mischievous spirit) is a kind of *apparition* or ghost. An *ogre* is a kind of *monster*.

(Class and Member)

14. **A.** An *austere style* is severely simple and restrained. *Controlled movement* is restrained as well.

(Defining Characteristic)

15. **E.** To *aver* or positively declare something is to indicate *affirmation*. To *demur* or object to something is to indicate *protest*.

(Action and Significance)

16. **B.** To *chide* or scold someone is less extreme than to *pillory* him, exposing him to public scorn. To *humor* or indulge someone is less extreme than to *mollycoddle* or inordinately baby him.

(Degree of Intensity)

17. **E.** The author first states that the reasons for bioluminescence in underwater microorganisms is obscure and then proceeds to enumerate various hypotheses.

18. **B.** The author does not deny that predators make use of bioluminescence in locating their prey. Instead, he gives an example of human predators (fishers) who are drawn to their prey (the fish that prey on plankton) by the luminescence of the plankton.

19. **B.** As the previous answer makes clear, the phenomenon of plankton bioluminescence does have practical applications. It is a valuable tool for fisheries interested in increasing their catch of fish that prey on plankton.

20. **B.** The author's use of both italics and an exclamation mark indicates his extreme scorn of the notion that bioluminescence originated in plankton because it allowed the plankton to expose their predators to the attention of those predators' predators. (Remember the rhyme about little fish having big fish to bite 'em, and so on *ad infinitum*?) Here he derides what he considers an untenable hypothesis.

21. **C.** The author provides the reader both with physical details of dress and bearing and with comments about the motivations and emotions of Bosola and the Cardinal.
Choice A is incorrect. The passage scarcely mentions the church.
Choice B is incorrect. The description of ecclesiastical costumes is only one item in the description of the Cardinal.
Choice D is incorrect. The persons described are characters in a play, not figures in paintings.
Choice E is incorrect. The author's purpose is description, not accusation.

22. **D.** From the opening lines, in which the curtain rises and the two men "enter from the right" (as a stage direction would say), and from the later references to gaslit Victorian melodrama, we can infer that Bosola and the Cardinal are characters in a play.
Choice A is incorrect. The Cardinal's brother is Duke Ferdinand.
Choices B and C are incorrect. Lines 55-66 describe Bosola as doing the work of a "hired ruffian" and playing a "lowly, despicable" role. He is a servant, not a noble lord or a lord of the church.
Choice E is unsupported by the passage.

23. **E.** The eagle is poised to strike "with exposed talons." It, like the Cardinal, collects itself to strike with greater force. The imagery accentuates the Cardinal's *mercilessness*.
Choice A is incorrect. The Cardinal is not *flighty* (light-headed and irresponsible); he is cold and calculating.
Choice B is incorrect. He loves power, not freedom.
Choice C is incorrect. An eagle poised to strike with bare claws suggests violence, not *eminence* (fame and high position).
Choice D is incorrect. Nothing in the passage suggests he is spiritual.
Beware eye-catchers. "Eminence" is a title of honor applied to cardinals in the Roman Catholic church. Choice D may attract you for this reason.

24. **E.** Although Bosola is not a leather-jacketed hoodlum, he is a hired assassin (despite his scholarly taste).

25. **A.** The casual references to the elongated hands and features in El Greco's work and to the trim beards and commanding stances in the work of Van Dyke imply that the author assumes the reader has seen examples of both painters' art.

26. **D.** The author's depiction of the Cardinal stresses his redoubtable qualities as a foe (calculation, duplicity, mercilessness) and as a challenge to an actor ("imperial repose," a commanding presence, smooth movements suggesting latent danger).
Choice A is incorrect. The author portrays the Cardinal's relations with his brother and mistress as cold, but he never apologizes for the Cardinal's lack of warmth. Indeed, the author somewhat savors it.
Choices B and C are incorrect. Neither esteem for a non-existent spirituality nor admiration for a villainous autocracy enters into the author's depiction of the Cardinal.
Choice E is incorrect. A cause of perturbation to others, the Cardinal is never perturbed.

27. **D.** Lines 62-66 indicate that his dominant emotion is disgust at an ignoble world and at himself for his despicable role in that world.
Choice A is incorrect. Not Bosola but Duke Ferdinand suffers from excessive emotionality.
Choice B is incorrect. It is not his lowly rank but his ignoble tasks that rankle Bosola.
Choices C and E are incorrect. They are unsupported by the passage.

28. **B.** The opposite of *amelioration* (improvement) is *worsening*.
Think of "a hoped-for amelioration."

29. **A.** The opposite of to *disarray* (throw into disorder) is to *neaten*.
Think of "disarraying the blankets."

30. **C.** The opposite of *disputatious* (argumentative) is *conciliatory* (pacific, soothing). Note that you can spot the familiar *dispute* in *disputatious*.
Think of "heated disputatious debates."

31. **B.** The opposite of *reticence* (uncommunicativeness; restraint in speech) is *loquaciousness* (talkativeness).
Think of "speaking without reticence."

32. **E.** The opposite of to *inundate* (flood) is to *drain*. Beware eye-catchers. Do not be tempted to choose Choice C simply because *inundate* and *wallow* both have something to do with water.
Think of "inundated by the rising flood."

33. **D.** The opposite of *incongruous* (inconsistent, not fitting) is *harmonious*.
Think of being startled by "incongruous behavior."

34. B.   An *apostate* (renegade; person faithless to an allegiance) is the opposite of a loyalist. Beware eye-catchers. Do not confuse *apostate* (renegade) with *apostle* (missionary; reformer). Think of "a faithless apostate."

35. A.   *Topical* (local, temporary) is the opposite of *general*. Remember that words may be used in several different ways. Here *topical* does not mean arranged according to topics (as in a topical index). Think of "a topical anesthetic," one applied locally, not generally.

36. E.   To *fulminate* (issue curses or censures; explode) is the opposite of to *praise*. Context Clue: "The wicked queen fulminated against Snow White."

37. B.   The opposite of *turbid* (muddy) is *limpid* (clear). Word Parts Clue: *Turb-* means disturb. A stream is turbid when the silt or sediment is disturbed. Think of "muddy, turbid waters."

38. D.   The opposite of *tyro* (beginner, novice) is *expert*. Think of "a mere tyro in the field."

Section 3

1. C. $3\frac{1}{2}\% = 3.5\% = \dfrac{3.5}{100} = \dfrac{35}{1000}$

2. A.   The length of the fence (144 feet) ÷ the distance between the posts (12 feet) equals 12 spaces between posts. However, the first space has 2 posts and an additional post will appear at each subsequent space.

3. A.   There are 37 houses on the west side. From #1 to #37 there are 19 odd numbers.

4. C.   The exterior angle of a triangle equals the sum of the measure of both remote interior angles. Therefore, $x = a + b$ and $x = c + d$. By addition, $2x = a + b + c + d$.

5. D. y is a common to both columns. Consider x and z. No information is given about their relationship.

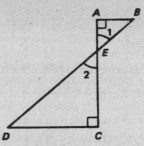

6. C.   Since vertical angles 1 and 2 are equal, right triangle ABE is similar to right triangle DEC, and $\dfrac{AB}{DC} = \dfrac{AE}{EC}$. In ABE, hypotenuse $BE = 5$, and $AB = 4$, then leg $AE = 3$. In DEC, if $AB = 4$, then $DC = 12$, and since $AE = 3$, then $EC = 9$, and $AC = AE + EC = 3 + 9 = 12$.

7. C.   Circumference $= 2\pi r$. If the radius of $A = \frac{1}{2}$ radius of B, then circumference of $A = \frac{1}{2}$ circumference of B. This may be stated as follows twice the circumference of $A = $ the circumference of B.

8. C. $\dfrac{BC}{AB} \times \dfrac{AC}{BC}$

   $\left(\dfrac{\cancel{10}}{\cancel{x}}\right)\left(\dfrac{\cancel{x}}{\cancel{10}}\right) = 1$

9. A.   Since $x = 40$, $y = 50$. Since AB lies opposite $\angle ACB$, the larger of the 2 acute angles, $AB > BC$.

10. D.   Since radius $= 6$, area of circle $= 36\pi$, but we do not know what part of the circle the segment AOB is.

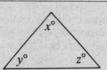

11. C. $z + y = 80$ since $x = 100$
    $y = z = 40$.

12. A.   Side of a square $= \frac{1}{4}$ of perimeter $\frac{1}{4}(4a + 4) = a + 1$ (length of any side) $a + 1 > a$

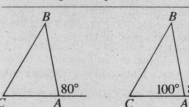

13. B. $m\angle B + m\angle C = 80°$
    $\angle BAC > \angle BCA$
    therefore $BC > AB$

14. C. Between 2:55 and 3:15, 20 minutes (or $\frac{1}{3}$ of an hour) elapse.

15. C. Since 15 is common to both columns, consider only $\frac{16}{x} = 4$. Since $4x = 16$, $x = 4$.

16. A. $K = \dfrac{1}{m + n}$

$\frac{1}{K} = m + n$ [reciprocals of equals are equal]

$\frac{5}{K} = 5(m + n)$ [multiply by 5]

17. E. If r is multiplied by 9, V must be multiplied by 81, since $\sqrt{81} = 9$. Recall: If equals are multiplied by equals, the results are equal.

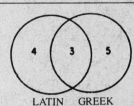

LATIN   GREEK

18. B. Observe the diagrammatic representation of the Latin and Greek students. Obviously we have accounted for 12 of these students. Three of them studied neither. Observe that 3 of these classical language students took Latin and Greek.

19. C. $\qquad 13 = \dfrac{13w}{1 - w}$

$13(1 - w) = 13w$
$13 - 13w = 13w$
$\qquad 13 = 26w$
$\qquad \frac{1}{2} = w$

$(2w)^2 = \left(2 \cdot \frac{1}{2}\right)^2 = (1)^2 = 1$

20. A. Since the relationship of the denominators is 1:2, the relationship of the numerators must be 1:2, so $a - b$ must be 2. Therefore, a is larger than b.

21. C. 10.6% of 14,490 = 1,534.94. The closest answer is 1,500.

22. C. 101,122 ÷ 26,731 = 3.78 or 378%.

23. B. The Louisiana Purchase added about 830,000 square miles. The previous area was about 890,000 square miles, so the area almost doubled.

24. B. Alaska is almost 600,000 square miles, which is about $\frac{1}{6}$ of 3,660,000 square miles. $\frac{1}{6}$ is $16\frac{2}{3}\%$ so the correct answer is 15%. Save time by estimating; don't perform the calculations exactly.

25. C. The area was about 3,600,000 square miles in 1900, and the area had been about 900,000 square miles in 1800. Since 4 times 900,000 is 3,600,000, x is about 4.

26. A. If two lines are parallel, then the distance between the two lines along parallel lines must be equal. The easiest lines to use to calculate distances are lines parallel to the y axis. The distance along the y axis from C to AB is 4. AB intersects the y axis at the point (0,2). The distance from D to AB along the line parallel to the y axis must also be 4. D must have coordinates (3,1). $x = 1$.

27. E. The fence will consist of 100 feet of stone and $100 + 60 + 60 = 220$ feet of wire. The cost will be $5(100) + $2(220) = $500 + $440 = $940.

28. C. To have averaged 30% of 60 games, the team must have won 18 out of 60 games. Let x = number of games played and won during winning streak.

New average: $\dfrac{18 + x}{60 + x} = 50\%$

$\dfrac{18 + x}{60 + x} = \dfrac{1}{2}$

$36 + 2x = 60 + x$

$\qquad\qquad x = 24$

29. C. The present time (h hours) must be reduced by 2 hours in order to insure promptness.

$\dfrac{\text{distance}}{\text{time}} = \text{rate}$

$\dfrac{d}{h - 2} = \text{new rate to insure promptness}$

30. C. $\dfrac{\$D}{M} = $ amount each will pay when there "are M" men

$\dfrac{\$D}{M - 3} = $ amount each will pay when "there are" $M - 3$ men

The difference is

$\dfrac{D}{M - 3} - \dfrac{D}{M}$

$\dfrac{DM - D(M - 3)}{M(M - 3)}$

$\dfrac{DM - DM + 3D}{M^2 - 3M}$

$\dfrac{3D}{M^2 - 3M}$

Section 4

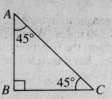

1. C. $\frac{1}{x} = \sqrt{.09}$ and $\frac{1}{x} = .3$
   $.3x = 1$
   $3x = 10$ and $x = 3\frac{1}{3}$

2. C. $a + 2b = 1\frac{1}{3}$
   $\underline{-a + b = -\frac{1}{3}}$ (Multiply by -1)
   $3b = 1$

3. C. Multiply by $\frac{-1}{-1} \cdot \frac{x-y}{-z} = \frac{-x+y}{z}$ or $\frac{y-x}{z}$

4. B. If $x =$ zero, the numerator equals 0 and the value of the fraction equals zero regardless of the value of y.

5. C. 4 quarts = 1 gallon
   1 quart = $\frac{1}{4}$ gallon
   $\frac{4}{5}$ quart = $\left(\frac{4}{5}\right)\left(\frac{1}{4}\right)$ or $\frac{1}{5}$ gallon

6. C. $a{:}b = c{:}d$ or $\frac{a}{b} = \frac{c}{d}$. Because reciprocals of equals are equal $\frac{b}{a} = \frac{d}{c}$.

7. B. $AC = CE$
   $AC - AB = BC; AC - 90 = BC$
   $CE - DE = CD; CE - 85 = CD$
   $CD > BC$

8. C. Area of $ABC = \frac{bh}{2}$ or $\frac{ac}{2}$. Therefore, $bh = ac$.

9. D. The 10% of 2,000 was calculated on all 2,000 tickets. Florence might *not* have any of those winning tickets or she might have 20.

10. D. We may not assume that this quadrilateral is a parallelogram and we have no basis for determining the value of n, the angle opposite the one with the measure given as 110. We do know that $k + l + m + n = 360$.

11. D. a, and/or b may be negative or equal to 0.

12. C. Since the measure of angle A equals the measure of angle C ($45°$), angle B must be a right angle. Sides AB and BC lie opposite equal angles.

13. B. $(a - 1)(a + 1) = a^2 - 1 = 0; a^2 = 1$ (Column A)
    $(b - 2)(b + 2) = b^2 - 4 = 0; b^2 = 4$ (Column B)

14. B. The sum of x, 0, and $\frac{3}{2}x = \frac{5}{2}x$.
    The average $= \frac{5}{2}x \div 3$ or $\frac{5}{6}x$. (Column A)

15. B. $74 + x + 74 = 180$
    $x = 180 - 148$
    $x = 32$ (Column A).

16. C. Volume of water in rectangular tank $= (25'')(9'')(2'')$
    Let $x =$ height of this volume of water in cylindrical container.
    Volume in cylindrical container $= (\pi)$ (radius)^2 (height) or $(\pi)(5)^2(x)$ or $(25)(x)(\pi)$
    Since volumes are equal.
    $(25'')(9'')(2'') = (25)(x)(\pi)$
    $18 = \pi x$
    $\frac{18}{\pi} = x$.

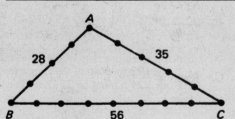

17. A. AB will need 3 additional posts.
    AC will need 4 additional posts.
    BC will need 7 additional posts.

18. E. Assume x, y, z, are, respectively, the sides of the original cube.
    Then $3x, 3y, 3z$ will be sides of enlarged box.
    Volume of original box $= xyz$
    Volume of enlarged box $= (3x)(3y)(3z)$ or $27xyz$

19. B. The passenger train traveled four hours and covered 240 miles. When it overtook the freight train, the freight train had also covered 240 miles, but it traveled for 6 hours. The average rate of the freight train was $\frac{240}{6}$ or 40 miles per hour.

20. E. Since $\frac{6}{14} = \frac{3}{7}$ and $\frac{9}{21} = \frac{3}{7}$, the sign to be inserted is $=$.

21. D. Seventy four cents of the tax dollar comes from the individual income tax (43¢) and the corporate income tax (31¢).

22. E. $\frac{22}{100}(360°) = 79.2°$. The closest correct choice is 80°.

23. E. The closest correct choice is $\frac{3}{4}$, since $\frac{74}{100}$ is close to 75%.

24. E. $\frac{43¢}{\$1.00} = \frac{43¢}{100¢} = \frac{43}{100} = 43\%$

25. A. Income taxes furnish 43¢ + 31¢ or 74¢ of each tax dollar. Therefore 26¢ of each tax dollar comes from other sources.
$$\frac{26¢}{\$1.00} = \frac{\$.26}{\$1.00} = \frac{\$260}{\$1000}$$

26. E. $\frac{a}{b} - \frac{a}{c} =$
$\frac{ac}{bc} - \frac{ab}{bc} =$
$\frac{ac - ab}{bc}$

27. C. Ratio $= \frac{192}{224} = \frac{6}{7}$

28. B. (5)(40 minutes) = 200 minutes
$= 3\frac{1}{3}$ hours
= 3 hours and 20 minutes
6:40 P.M. is 3 hours and 20 minutes before 10. P.M.

29. C. Cost of merchandise sold = $204 − $82.50
= $121.50.
Gross profit for day was $169.50 − $121.50 or $48.

30. C. Mr. Brown completes a house and $\frac{1}{3}$ of a second house in 8 days. Mr. Pinter does $\frac{6}{8}$ or $\frac{3}{4}$ of a house in 8 days. Together they have done $1\frac{1}{3} + \frac{3}{4}$ or $\frac{25}{12}$ or 2 houses and $\frac{1}{12}$ of the third house. Mr. Slocum must do $\frac{11}{12}$ of the third house. In one day Mr. Slocum does $\frac{1}{12}$ of a house. He will therefore need 11 days to do $\frac{11}{12}$ of the house.

Section 5

1–4. Analysis of this situation will indicate that G, J, L must not sit next to each other. The members of the football and the basketball teams must sit next to either G, J, or L.

1. A. In (A) G, J, and L are separated by varsity players on basketball or football teams.

2. E. K may not sit next to H as in (A). K may not sit next to M as in (B), nor N as in (C) or (D).

3. D. M May sit next to either G, J, or L. All others are two-sport athletes.

4. B. The only ones that may sit next to N are G, J, L.

5. C. The gun lobby maintains that our Constitution gives the people (not only the militia) the right to keep and bear arms. They also say the Fifth Amendment says that property may not be confiscated without due process and that the Ninth Amendment guarantees all unspecified rights.

6. D. (A) is incorrect since it suggests a cause of violence and not a solution. (B) is incorrect. The fact that a state has the lowest crime rate may be due to factors having nothing to do with anti-gun laws. In (C) a sport, not a crime, is mentioned. In (E) police protection is not taken into account.

7. D. The passage implies that the gun lobby might destroy the political future of a lawmaker who sponsors a gun control bill.

8–11.   You may want to sketch a calendar showing each day of the week and the offices that are open on that day. Or you may want to just make simple notes on the requirements listed and when they can be satisfied, like this:

Birth Cert.   MTh 9-5 ⎫
Nat. Papers   TuF 9-5 ⎬ One of these
                             ⎭
                    Wed 12-5
Hosp. ⎰ A   MTH 9-12, F 4-5
      ⎱ B
                    M-F 9-3
Bank   MWF 12-4
Consulate   (after all others)
   (after all others)

8. A.   By starting Monday morning at Beryl Clinic, getting a birth certificate and bank statement before 3 p.m, and proceeding to the Consulate, a native-born citizen can complete the procedure in less than eight hours. The naturalized citizen starting anytime Tuesday (the specification of Tuesday morning is simply a distracting detail) can't get to the Consulate until Wednesday at noon (B). The applicant in choice C can't get a birth certificate until Thursday; the applicant in choice D can't get naturalization papers until Friday; the applicant in choice E can't complete the procedure until Monday.

9. C.   This applicant may acquire a birth certificate and a bank statement on Thursday, but cannot get a vaccination until Friday at 4 (at Beryl Clinic), too late to go to the Consulate before Monday afternoon.

10. C. Mr. Nikto could have acquired naturalization papers as late as Tuesday afternoon and then gone to his bank; he can be vaccinated Wednesday afternoon and get to the Consulate that day. If Mr. Nikto is choice A, the procedure will take from Monday morning to Wednesday afternoon; if he is choice B, from Tuesday at 4 p.m. to Friday afternoon; if he is choice D, from Monday afternoon to Wednesday afternoon; if he is choice E, from Tuesday afternoon until Friday.

11. D. The naturalized citizen can get his or her naturalization papers and bank statement on Tuesday afternoon. Nothing can be accomplished on Wednesday. Thursday morning the applicant can be vaccinated at Beryl Clinic and the procedure could be completed when the Consulate office opens on Friday.

12–18. A "tree" diagram makes everything simple. BC is an impossible leafletting team, since C won't work without A; AC is a possible leafletting team, and so is AB, but only if C is the speaker. (Remember, F is not unwilling to work without E!)

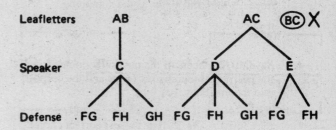

12. B. See the diagram. All other combinations are shown to be all right by the diagram.

13. E. C must be present, and necessarily as a speaker (I); three defense teams are possible—all contain either F or G (III), but one does not contain F (II).

14. C. From the diagram, or even without it—choices A and B contain two speakers, choice D violates E's wishes, and choice E violates both A's and C's wishes.

15. D. Either team involving A can involve any of the three defense personnel. The personnel listed in choices A, B, and C are all possible selections, but others are possible. Choice E is definitely false.

16. B. The bottom "branches" of the "tree" diagram all represent different possible teams, in combination with the other personnel shown.

17. A. Only A must be chosen. E is not necessary at all. F becomes a "must" only if E is the speaker.

18. E. Check the diagram—E appears in only two possible teams (ACEFG, ACEFH); A and C appear in all eight, B and D in three each.

19–22. Set up five lines symbolizing places at the table; A-E will be seated on one side and F-J on the other. The first three statements give you:

<u>A/B</u> ___ <u>C/E</u> ___ <u>A/B</u>
                 H/I/J   G

Statement (4) tells you, first, that the Walla-chian military attachés must be opposite the two Rumelian trade experts; second, that the latter must be at the right side of their table and the Wallachian military attachés opposite, on the *left* side from their point of view. From this, you can deduce where B and therefore A sit. You can now fill in this information, plus the uncertain possibilities:

Statement (5) allows you to cross a lot of this out:

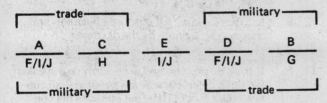

That's as much as you can do, but it's enough to answer all the questions.

19. A. We can't tell exactly who or where F is. But choice A is a possibility. Choices B, C and D are ruled out by the placing of H; choice E is ruled out by the placing of G.

20. E. Three persons are possibilities. Choices A, C, and D are known exactly; for choice B there are two possibilities, so more is known than in choice E.

21. C. This supposition eliminates J as Rumelian chairperson (I); since I must be the chairper-son, and J is a military attaché, F must be a trade expert (II); III therefore *cannot* be true.

22. E. Add back into your diagram the uncertainties that were eliminated by statement (3). The Wallachian chairperson can be either D or E; the military attaché seated to the Wallachian chairperson's left can also be either D or E, since only identifying the chairperson as E allowed you to identify the military attaché as D. The Rumelian chairperson can be F as well as I or J. Choice E can be definitely known under these conditions, even though you cannot tell who is in which of the two seats. Choice A cannot be known; it could not be, even *with* statement (3). For choices B and D, there is in each case more than one possibility for one of the slots; for choice C, there are two possibilities.

23. E. Statements I, II, and IV all tend to *strengthen* Malthus's argument, statements I and IV by helping to explain the causes of the phenome-non Malthus described, statement II by assert-ing that the phenomenon has, in fact, taken place. Statement III suggests that contraception might be used to invalidate Malthus's predic-tion; therefore, it does *weaken* Malthus's argument.

24. A. Malthus mentioned wars, famines, and other catastrophes as population checks. (B) and (C) would tend to increase food supply, but not to limit the demand for food. (D) and (E) would increase population.

25. C. The first part of the argument contains the premise: most people who do X (take GRE/APT) do Y (get headaches). From this, two possible incorrect conclusions can be drawn: if *anyone* does X, he/she must do Y; and, *only* those who do X can do Y. Choice A contains the first error, but the original argument and choice C both make the second error. Choice B makes a valid inference, whereas the original argument does not. Choice D has the basic structure: If X, then Y—if Y, then X. This is invalid, but it is a different error from the one made in the original argument. Choice E is an invalid inference from past to future, again a different kind of error from that in the original argument.

Section 6

1–4. To answer these questions, construct a calendar like the one below. The √ mark indicates opportunities for the acquisition of documents; S and C indicate when each government could have received documents acquired on the days shown. B/A indicates the lunchtime meeting of the two traitors.

	19	20	21	22	23	24	25	26	27
B	√			√	S	C		S	C
A			√				S	C	
B/A		√				S	C		

1. C. Adoniram could acquire documents from Byram (who acquired them on October 19) at their lunch October 20, or on his own on the 21st. The Sulgravians would receive them on the 24th or 25th, respectively (I, II). Adoniram cannot acquire and send any documents on the 22nd, so option III is out.

2. D.   Work backwards from the calendar. On the 25th, the Carolingians can receive a document only if it was acquired on the 20th at lunch. But in that case, Adoniram must have bought it from Byram, since he had then had no opportunity to acquire a document to sell to Byram.

3. E.   Adoniram can send documents only on the 20th or 21st; they could be received by the Carolingians only on the 25th or 26th. Choice B, therefore, is too narrow, while choice D includes an impossible date. Byram can send documents on the 19th, 20th, or 22nd—to the Sulgravians, who would receive them on the 23rd, 24th, or 26th. So choice A is too narrow and choice C includes an impossible date. But if Adoniram is working for the Carolingians and Byram for the Sulgravians, choice E is correct, since Adoniram had had no opportunity by the 20th to acquire anything to sell Byram.

4. A.   Adoniram can acquire documents from Byram on the 20th and on his own on the 21st, so whichever government he works for can receive documents two days in a row (I). But Byram cannot acquire anything two days in a row, so *both* governments cannot receive documents two days in a row (II). Finally, the calendar should show you that either government could receive documents three days in a row only if they were sent both by Byram and by Adoniram, which is impossible under the rules stated.

5. A.   The only inference that can logically be drawn is the one in choice A; since differences in perception do exist, but no physical differences, perception must depend partly on other factors. Choices B, C, and D all contain unsupported speculations about what those factors might be; choice E is irrelevant, since the data specify that the Bilge Islanders *perceive* fewer colors, not simply that they can name fewer colors. How this was determined we don't know.

6. D.   Brady's sole piece of evidence is the example of the two other companies that are *like* hers, i.e., that are analogous to hers (choice D). She never suggests what might be causing the problem of low profits (choice A). We do not know that the evidence she presents was previously overlooked (choice B). She discusses no flaw in Mr. Flynn's reasoning (choice C). And opposing Mr. Flynn is not the same as questioning his competence (choice E).

7. A.   Since Ms. Brady makes her point by drawing an analogy, Mr. Flynn's most effective rebuttal would be to undermine the strength of the analogy. He could do this by pointing out significant differences between the two situations that are supposed to be alike. That's exactly what he does in choice A. In choice B, he simply asserts his own expertise, and in choice C he simply restates his argument. In choice D, he merely suggests that Brady's argument may be weak, whereas in choice A he points out a specific weakness. In choice E, he does not even attempt a rebuttal.

8–12.   Your first instinct may be to draw a map and try to place the towns on it directly. You'll go hopelessly wrong if you try. (This is also true for other puzzles that contain *two* sets of ranked variables—John runs faster and jumps higher than Tom, and so on.) First place the towns on a north-south scale and on a separate east-west scale (Diagram 1). Then, if you wish, combine these into a two-dimensional map. This isn't necessary, but it may make the questions a little easier. We've included it (Diagram 2).

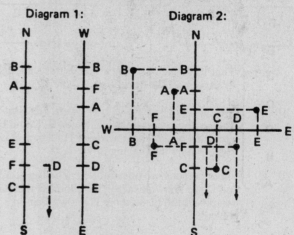

Diagram 1:   Diagram 2:

8. B.   Bowling Green is both farthest north and farthest west.

9. E.   Ashland and East Liverpool are north of Fredericktown, while Coshocton is to the south. All three towns are east of Fredericktown.

10. D.   This one may be easier to read from the two-dimensional map, but you can also read it from the two separate scales. Coshocton, Dover, and Fredericktown are all south and west of East Liverpool. Fredericktown is also south and west of Ashland. Bowling Green is not south of any town. Ashland is south of Bowling Green, but east of it.

11. A.   The only ambiguous information in the statements concerns the north-south position of Dover. Statements (5) and (6) tell us that Dover and Coshocton are both south of Fredericktown, but not their position in relation to each other. Choice A would clear this up. Choices B-E can all be deduced from the statements as given.

12. C.   Dover's north-south position with respect to Ashland can be deduced from statements (1), (4), and (5), without statement (3). Dover's east-west position with respect to Ashland can be deduced from statements (1) and (6). Each of the other choices is necessary to place the town it mentions either on the north-south scale, on the east-west scale, or on both.

13–16.   You may not need to create a diagram for this fairly simple problem. If you do, it might look something like this:

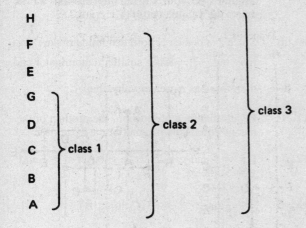

13. C.   Choice A violates rules (5) and (6). Choice B violates rule (4). Choice D violates rule (6). Choice E violates rules (4) and (6).

14. C.   If the spelunker wishes to explore cave Caesar, he or she must first explore cave Benny (I); he or she cannot explore more than two of those listed in rule (6). Rule (5) is no restriction, since it has already been satisfied.

15. B.   She must explore caves Abbott, Benny, and Caesar, and she must begin with either Abbott or Benny. If Abbott, she must explore Benny next and then Caesar; if Benny, she can explore Abbott and then Caesar or Caesar and then Abbott.

16. B.   He or she can explore any of the caves, provided the order is correct; but three out of the five caves Benny, Caesar, Ewell, Fields, and Hope may not be attempted in one tour. The spelunker may explore Abbott, Dangerfield, Guinness and any two of the restricted five.

17–22.   Make a table showing which plumbers can work with which teams of electricians. A useful (but not essential) preliminary is to diagram the permissible combinations. A line shows that two persons must work together; a line with a cross through it, that they *cannot* work together.

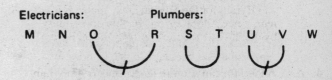

In any case, four teams of electricians are possible, with the following possibilities for plumbers in each case:

MNO   ST, UW, VW
MN   RST, RUW, RVW, STU, STV, STW
MO   STU, STV, STW
NO   STU, STV, STW

A total of fifteen different combinations are possible, as this table shows. Now read the answers to the questions from the table.

17. D.   By inspection of the table. Notice that Choice B has an impossible combination—U and V. Also, choice E has a six-person team, which is impossible.

18. B.   By inspection of the table.

19. E.   Since Olive is too prejudiced to work with Rich, he can only work with Mike and Nick as the two electricians; this eliminates choice B. The three possibilities for the other two plumbers are given in choice E.

20. A.   This answer may be surprising—it might seem that filling two slots right away would *reduce* the number of choices. But as the table shows, Steve and Tom appear in eleven possible teams. Olive appears in nine, Wassily in seven, Ulysses and Vic in five each.

21. A. The electricians are Mike and Olive. Steve and Tom appear in all teams (I), but one team can be made up with neither Ulysses nor Vic (II).

22. C. Mike, Nick, Rich, Ulysses, Wassily, and Mike, Nick, Rich, Vic, Wassily are two-electrician teams without Steve or Tom (I). There are three teams with neither Olive nor Rich (II). If Mike or Nick is not hired, the electricians must be Nick and Olive or Mike and Olive, respectively. Steve and Tom are in all teams which include Mike and Olive or Nick and Olive (III).

23. E. Choice A exposes the argument's failure to admit that many specific problems may be solved by persons who don't understand the broad picture; choice B exposes the assumption that because generalists are needed, *all* persons should be educated as generalists; choice C exposes the false dichotomy between specialization and seeing the broad picture; and choice D attacks the implicit assumption that fewer specialists are needed. Choice E, however, does not weaken the argument, because the argument is simply calling for a broad, liberal education, not necessarily the traditional liberal education.

24. B. The logic of the argument is valid, and choice B is simply a rephrasing of the conclusion. Therefore, it must be true if the argument is true. It is possible for there to be some bad athletes who want to win (choices A and D), and for some bad athletes to eat a well-balanced diet (choice C). Choice E contradicts the argument's conclusion.

25. E. The conclusion of the argument states that all good athletes eat a well-balanced diet. Choice E shows that this is not true; there is at least one good athlete who does not eat a well-balanced diet. Choices B and C are both possibly true, but do not weaken the original argument. Choice D can be deduced from the argument.

Section 7

1. B. $a - b = 2 - 3 = -1; b - a = 3 - 2 = 1;$ -1 is less than 1.

2. A. $\sqrt{14.4} = 3+$ and $\sqrt{1.44} = 1+$

3. A. A straight line is the shortest distance between two points.

4. B.
   Circumference $= \pi D$
   $\pi D = 9\pi$
   $D = 9$ and radius $= 4.5$
   Area $= \pi R^2$
   $\pi R^2 = 25\pi$
   $R^2 = 25$ and radius $= 5$

5. C. The segment joining the midpoint of AC to the midpoint of CB consists of $\frac{1}{2}$ of AC plus $\frac{1}{2}$ of CB, or a total of $\frac{1}{2}$ of AB (Column A). The segment from A to the midpoint of AB is also $\frac{1}{2}$ of AB (Column B).

6. B. $\boxed{100} = \dfrac{\sqrt{100}}{2} = \dfrac{10}{2} = 5$ (Column A)

7. C. Since $b = c$ both fractions have equal denominators.

8. B. The lowest possible value of a will be reached when b^2 is at a minimum. The minimum value of b^2 is zero, in which case a^2 could equal 100 and a could have a value of -10.

9. C. Between 10:55 PM and 11:25 PM 30 minutes or one-half hour elapses. Since the average rate is 50 miles per hour, the motorist covered 25 miles during this period.

10. B. Since z is positive, both denominators are positive, but $\dfrac{1}{z-1}$ has a smaller denominator and therefore has a greater value than $\dfrac{1}{z}$.

11. C. Recall than in a proportion, the product of the means equals the product of the extremes.

12. D. If $x = 1$ and $y = 2$, $3x > y$; but if $x = 1$ and $y = 5$, the $3x > y$.

13. B. $\dfrac{1}{4} \div \dfrac{3}{8}$ or $\dfrac{1}{4} \cdot \dfrac{8}{3} = \dfrac{2}{3}$ (Column A)
    $1\dfrac{1}{2}$ or $\dfrac{3}{2} > \dfrac{2}{3}$

14. D. $(-2)^x$ is negative if x is odd and positive if x is even. 1 raised to any power $= 1$. If x is even, them (-2^x) is greater than 1. If x is odd, then (-2^x) is negative.

15. D. Possible values of b range from 2 to 8. If $b = 2$, then $2b = 4$, which is less than 6. If $b = 3$, $2b = 6$. If $b = 4$, $2b = 8$, which is more than 6.

16. E. Call $9x - 3y = 12$ equation 1.
    Call $3x - 5y = 7$ equation 2.
       Divide equation 1 by 3:
          $3x - y = 4$
       Multiply by 2:
          $6x - 2y = 8$

17. D. There is no time for lengthy multiplication. Note simply that the correct answer must end with the digit 8.

18. **B.** Since $2^3 = 8$, then $n + 2 = 3$ and $n = 1$.

19. **E.** If 1 is added to an odd integer, the result is an even integer. Twice an even integer yields an even integer.

20. **B.** After a reduction of 20%, the price of the garment is 80% of the original price. The additional redution 30% of the 80% results in a price of 56% of the original price (note the incorrect Choice D). For the correct solution, consider that the price of 56% of the original is actually a 44% reduction of the original price.

21. **C.**

YEAR	SALES IN $1,000
1982	80
1983	70
1984	60
1985	80
SUM	$290

$$\text{AVERAGE} = \frac{\$290}{4} = \$72.5$$

22. **B.** In 1982 there was an increase from $50,000 to $80,000.

23. **D.** Sales in 1980 were $30,000.
Earnings in 1980 were $6,000.
$$\frac{30}{6} = \frac{5}{1}$$

24. **E.** Increase from $10,000 to $12,000.
$$\frac{2,000}{10,000} = \frac{1}{5} = 20\%.$$

25. **A.** If $g = \$6,000$, then $2g = \$12,000$.

26. **E.**

$$
\begin{array}{cccc}
P & R & T & Q \\
\bullet & \bullet & \bullet & \bullet
\end{array}
$$

$$\frac{PQ}{PT} = \frac{3 \text{ units}}{2 \text{ units}} = 1\frac{1}{2} = 150\%$$

27. **B.** (A) $0.3 = \frac{3}{10}$.

(B) $\sqrt{0.3} = 0.5+$ or more than $\frac{5}{10}$.

(C) $\frac{2}{5} = \frac{4}{10}$.

(D) $\frac{1}{3} = \frac{3\frac{1}{3}}{10}$.

(E) $\left(\frac{22}{7}\right)\left(\frac{1}{100}\right) = \frac{22}{700} = \frac{3+}{100}$ or $\frac{0.3+}{10}$.

28. **C.** $66\frac{2}{6}\% = \frac{2}{3}$

$\frac{1}{2}$ of $\frac{2}{3} = \frac{1}{3}$

Mr. Nichols sells $\frac{1}{3}$ of the value of the entire factory for $33,333.
Let x = value of entire factory.
$$\frac{1}{3}x = \$33,333 \quad x = \$99,999$$

29. **D.** The first wheel rotates once every 7, 14, 21, 28, 35, etc., minutes.
The second wheel rotates once every 5, 10, 15, 20, 25, 30, 35, etc., minutes.
They will both begin to rotate every 35 minutes.

30. **B.** Apply the Pythagorean theorem. Let x == distance from first base to third base.

$x^2 = 90^2 + 90^2$
$x^2 = 8100 + 8100$
$x^2 = 16200$
$x = \sqrt{16200}$
$x = 127$

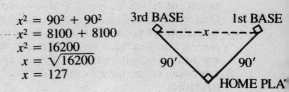

Answer Sheet – MODEL TEST 3

Start with number 1 for each new section.
If a section has fewer than 38 questions, leave the extra spaces blank.

Section 1

1. Ⓐ Ⓑ Ⓒ Ⓓ Ⓔ	11. Ⓐ Ⓑ Ⓒ Ⓓ Ⓔ	21. Ⓐ Ⓑ Ⓒ Ⓓ Ⓔ	31. Ⓐ Ⓑ Ⓒ Ⓓ Ⓔ
2. Ⓐ Ⓑ Ⓒ Ⓓ Ⓔ	12. Ⓐ Ⓑ Ⓒ Ⓓ Ⓔ	22. Ⓐ Ⓑ Ⓒ Ⓓ Ⓔ	32. Ⓐ Ⓑ Ⓒ Ⓓ Ⓔ
3. Ⓐ Ⓑ Ⓒ Ⓓ Ⓔ	13. Ⓐ Ⓑ Ⓒ Ⓓ Ⓔ	23. Ⓐ Ⓑ Ⓒ Ⓓ Ⓔ	33. Ⓐ Ⓑ Ⓒ Ⓓ Ⓔ
4. Ⓐ Ⓑ Ⓒ Ⓓ Ⓔ	14. Ⓐ Ⓑ Ⓒ Ⓓ Ⓔ	24. Ⓐ Ⓑ Ⓒ Ⓓ Ⓔ	34. Ⓐ Ⓑ Ⓒ Ⓓ Ⓔ
5. Ⓐ Ⓑ Ⓒ Ⓓ Ⓔ	15. Ⓐ Ⓑ Ⓒ Ⓓ Ⓔ	25. Ⓐ Ⓑ Ⓒ Ⓓ Ⓔ	35. Ⓐ Ⓑ Ⓒ Ⓓ Ⓔ
6. Ⓐ Ⓑ Ⓒ Ⓓ Ⓔ	16. Ⓐ Ⓑ Ⓒ Ⓓ Ⓔ	26. Ⓐ Ⓑ Ⓒ Ⓓ Ⓔ	36. Ⓐ Ⓑ Ⓒ Ⓓ Ⓔ
7. Ⓐ Ⓑ Ⓒ Ⓓ Ⓔ	17. Ⓐ Ⓑ Ⓒ Ⓓ Ⓔ	27. Ⓐ Ⓑ Ⓒ Ⓓ Ⓔ	37. Ⓐ Ⓑ Ⓒ Ⓓ Ⓔ
8. Ⓐ Ⓑ Ⓒ Ⓓ Ⓔ	18. Ⓐ Ⓑ Ⓒ Ⓓ Ⓔ	28. Ⓐ Ⓑ Ⓒ Ⓓ Ⓔ	38. Ⓐ Ⓑ Ⓒ Ⓓ Ⓔ
9. Ⓐ Ⓑ Ⓒ Ⓓ Ⓔ	19. Ⓐ Ⓑ Ⓒ Ⓓ Ⓔ	29. Ⓐ Ⓑ Ⓒ Ⓓ Ⓔ	
10. Ⓐ Ⓑ Ⓒ Ⓓ Ⓔ	20. Ⓐ Ⓑ Ⓒ Ⓓ Ⓔ	30. Ⓐ Ⓑ Ⓒ Ⓓ Ⓔ	

Section 2

1. Ⓐ Ⓑ Ⓒ Ⓓ Ⓔ	11. Ⓐ Ⓑ Ⓒ Ⓓ Ⓔ	21. Ⓐ Ⓑ Ⓒ Ⓓ Ⓔ	31. Ⓐ Ⓑ Ⓒ Ⓓ Ⓔ
2. Ⓐ Ⓑ Ⓒ Ⓓ Ⓔ	12. Ⓐ Ⓑ Ⓒ Ⓓ Ⓔ	22. Ⓐ Ⓑ Ⓒ Ⓓ Ⓔ	32. Ⓐ Ⓑ Ⓒ Ⓓ Ⓔ
3. Ⓐ Ⓑ Ⓒ Ⓓ Ⓔ	13. Ⓐ Ⓑ Ⓒ Ⓓ Ⓔ	23. Ⓐ Ⓑ Ⓒ Ⓓ Ⓔ	33. Ⓐ Ⓑ Ⓒ Ⓓ Ⓔ
4. Ⓐ Ⓑ Ⓒ Ⓓ Ⓔ	14. Ⓐ Ⓑ Ⓒ Ⓓ Ⓔ	24. Ⓐ Ⓑ Ⓒ Ⓓ Ⓔ	34. Ⓐ Ⓑ Ⓒ Ⓓ Ⓔ
5. Ⓐ Ⓑ Ⓒ Ⓓ Ⓔ	15. Ⓐ Ⓑ Ⓒ Ⓓ Ⓔ	25. Ⓐ Ⓑ Ⓒ Ⓓ Ⓔ	35. Ⓐ Ⓑ Ⓒ Ⓓ Ⓔ
6. Ⓐ Ⓑ Ⓒ Ⓓ Ⓔ	16. Ⓐ Ⓑ Ⓒ Ⓓ Ⓔ	26. Ⓐ Ⓑ Ⓒ Ⓓ Ⓔ	36. Ⓐ Ⓑ Ⓒ Ⓓ Ⓔ
7. Ⓐ Ⓑ Ⓒ Ⓓ Ⓔ	17. Ⓐ Ⓑ Ⓒ Ⓓ Ⓔ	27. Ⓐ Ⓑ Ⓒ Ⓓ Ⓔ	37. Ⓐ Ⓑ Ⓒ Ⓓ Ⓔ
8. Ⓐ Ⓑ Ⓒ Ⓓ Ⓔ	18. Ⓐ Ⓑ Ⓒ Ⓓ Ⓔ	28. Ⓐ Ⓑ Ⓒ Ⓓ Ⓔ	38. Ⓐ Ⓑ Ⓒ Ⓓ Ⓔ
9. Ⓐ Ⓑ Ⓒ Ⓓ Ⓔ	19. Ⓐ Ⓑ Ⓒ Ⓓ Ⓔ	29. Ⓐ Ⓑ Ⓒ Ⓓ Ⓔ	
10. Ⓐ Ⓑ Ⓒ Ⓓ Ⓔ	20. Ⓐ Ⓑ Ⓒ Ⓓ Ⓔ	30. Ⓐ Ⓑ Ⓒ Ⓓ Ⓔ	

Section 3

1. Ⓐ Ⓑ Ⓒ Ⓓ Ⓔ	11. Ⓐ Ⓑ Ⓒ Ⓓ Ⓔ	21. Ⓐ Ⓑ Ⓒ Ⓓ Ⓔ	31. Ⓐ Ⓑ Ⓒ Ⓓ Ⓔ
2. Ⓐ Ⓑ Ⓒ Ⓓ Ⓔ	12. Ⓐ Ⓑ Ⓒ Ⓓ Ⓔ	22. Ⓐ Ⓑ Ⓒ Ⓓ Ⓔ	32. Ⓐ Ⓑ Ⓒ Ⓓ Ⓔ
3. Ⓐ Ⓑ Ⓒ Ⓓ Ⓔ	13. Ⓐ Ⓑ Ⓒ Ⓓ Ⓔ	23. Ⓐ Ⓑ Ⓒ Ⓓ Ⓔ	33. Ⓐ Ⓑ Ⓒ Ⓓ Ⓔ
4. Ⓐ Ⓑ Ⓒ Ⓓ Ⓔ	14. Ⓐ Ⓑ Ⓒ Ⓓ Ⓔ	24. Ⓐ Ⓑ Ⓒ Ⓓ Ⓔ	34. Ⓐ Ⓑ Ⓒ Ⓓ Ⓔ
5. Ⓐ Ⓑ Ⓒ Ⓓ Ⓔ	15. Ⓐ Ⓑ Ⓒ Ⓓ Ⓔ	25. Ⓐ Ⓑ Ⓒ Ⓓ Ⓔ	35. Ⓐ Ⓑ Ⓒ Ⓓ Ⓔ
6. Ⓐ Ⓑ Ⓒ Ⓓ Ⓔ	16. Ⓐ Ⓑ Ⓒ Ⓓ Ⓔ	26. Ⓐ Ⓑ Ⓒ Ⓓ Ⓔ	36. Ⓐ Ⓑ Ⓒ Ⓓ Ⓔ
7. Ⓐ Ⓑ Ⓒ Ⓓ Ⓔ	17. Ⓐ Ⓑ Ⓒ Ⓓ Ⓔ	27. Ⓐ Ⓑ Ⓒ Ⓓ Ⓔ	37. Ⓐ Ⓑ Ⓒ Ⓓ Ⓔ
8. Ⓐ Ⓑ Ⓒ Ⓓ Ⓔ	18. Ⓐ Ⓑ Ⓒ Ⓓ Ⓔ	28. Ⓐ Ⓑ Ⓒ Ⓓ Ⓔ	38. Ⓐ Ⓑ Ⓒ Ⓓ Ⓔ
9. Ⓐ Ⓑ Ⓒ Ⓓ Ⓔ	19. Ⓐ Ⓑ Ⓒ Ⓓ Ⓔ	29. Ⓐ Ⓑ Ⓒ Ⓓ Ⓔ	
10. Ⓐ Ⓑ Ⓒ Ⓓ Ⓔ	20. Ⓐ Ⓑ Ⓒ Ⓓ Ⓔ	30. Ⓐ Ⓑ Ⓒ Ⓓ Ⓔ	

Section 4

1. Ⓐ Ⓑ Ⓒ Ⓓ Ⓔ
2. Ⓐ Ⓑ Ⓒ Ⓓ Ⓔ
3. Ⓐ Ⓑ Ⓒ Ⓓ Ⓔ
4. Ⓐ Ⓑ Ⓒ Ⓓ Ⓔ
5. Ⓐ Ⓑ Ⓒ Ⓓ Ⓔ
6. Ⓐ Ⓑ Ⓒ Ⓓ Ⓔ
7. Ⓐ Ⓑ Ⓒ Ⓓ Ⓔ
8. Ⓐ Ⓑ Ⓒ Ⓓ Ⓔ
9. Ⓐ Ⓑ Ⓒ Ⓓ Ⓔ
10. Ⓐ Ⓑ Ⓒ Ⓓ Ⓔ
11. Ⓐ Ⓑ Ⓒ Ⓓ Ⓔ
12. Ⓐ Ⓑ Ⓒ Ⓓ Ⓔ
13. Ⓐ Ⓑ Ⓒ Ⓓ Ⓔ
14. Ⓐ Ⓑ Ⓒ Ⓓ Ⓔ
15. Ⓐ Ⓑ Ⓒ Ⓓ Ⓔ
16. Ⓐ Ⓑ Ⓒ Ⓓ Ⓔ
17. Ⓐ Ⓑ Ⓒ Ⓓ Ⓔ
18. Ⓐ Ⓑ Ⓒ Ⓓ Ⓔ
19. Ⓐ Ⓑ Ⓒ Ⓓ Ⓔ
20. Ⓐ Ⓑ Ⓒ Ⓓ Ⓔ
21. Ⓐ Ⓑ Ⓒ Ⓓ Ⓔ
22. Ⓐ Ⓑ Ⓒ Ⓓ Ⓔ
23. Ⓐ Ⓑ Ⓒ Ⓓ Ⓔ
24. Ⓐ Ⓑ Ⓒ Ⓓ Ⓔ
25. Ⓐ Ⓑ Ⓒ Ⓓ Ⓔ
26. Ⓐ Ⓑ Ⓒ Ⓓ Ⓔ
27. Ⓐ Ⓑ Ⓒ Ⓓ Ⓔ
28. Ⓐ Ⓑ Ⓒ Ⓓ Ⓔ
29. Ⓐ Ⓑ Ⓒ Ⓓ Ⓔ
30. Ⓐ Ⓑ Ⓒ Ⓓ Ⓔ
31. Ⓐ Ⓑ Ⓒ Ⓓ Ⓔ
32. Ⓐ Ⓑ Ⓒ Ⓓ Ⓔ
33. Ⓐ Ⓑ Ⓒ Ⓓ Ⓔ
34. Ⓐ Ⓑ Ⓒ Ⓓ Ⓔ
35. Ⓐ Ⓑ Ⓒ Ⓓ Ⓔ
36. Ⓐ Ⓑ Ⓒ Ⓓ Ⓔ
37. Ⓐ Ⓑ Ⓒ Ⓓ Ⓔ
38. Ⓐ Ⓑ Ⓒ Ⓓ Ⓔ

Section 5

1. Ⓐ Ⓑ Ⓒ Ⓓ Ⓔ
2. Ⓐ Ⓑ Ⓒ Ⓓ Ⓔ
3. Ⓐ Ⓑ Ⓒ Ⓓ Ⓔ
4. Ⓐ Ⓑ Ⓒ Ⓓ Ⓔ
5. Ⓐ Ⓑ Ⓒ Ⓓ Ⓔ
6. Ⓐ Ⓑ Ⓒ Ⓓ Ⓔ
7. Ⓐ Ⓑ Ⓒ Ⓓ Ⓔ
8. Ⓐ Ⓑ Ⓒ Ⓓ Ⓔ
9. Ⓐ Ⓑ Ⓒ Ⓓ Ⓔ
10. Ⓐ Ⓑ Ⓒ Ⓓ Ⓔ
11. Ⓐ Ⓑ Ⓒ Ⓓ Ⓔ
12. Ⓐ Ⓑ Ⓒ Ⓓ Ⓔ
13. Ⓐ Ⓑ Ⓒ Ⓓ Ⓔ
14. Ⓐ Ⓑ Ⓒ Ⓓ Ⓔ
15. Ⓐ Ⓑ Ⓒ Ⓓ Ⓔ
16. Ⓐ Ⓑ Ⓒ Ⓓ Ⓔ
17. Ⓐ Ⓑ Ⓒ Ⓓ Ⓔ
18. Ⓐ Ⓑ Ⓒ Ⓓ Ⓔ
19. Ⓐ Ⓑ Ⓒ Ⓓ Ⓔ
20. Ⓐ Ⓑ Ⓒ Ⓓ Ⓔ
21. Ⓐ Ⓑ Ⓒ Ⓓ Ⓔ
22. Ⓐ Ⓑ Ⓒ Ⓓ Ⓔ
23. Ⓐ Ⓑ Ⓒ Ⓓ Ⓔ
24. Ⓐ Ⓑ Ⓒ Ⓓ Ⓔ
25. Ⓐ Ⓑ Ⓒ Ⓓ Ⓔ
26. Ⓐ Ⓑ Ⓒ Ⓓ Ⓔ
27. Ⓐ Ⓑ Ⓒ Ⓓ Ⓔ
28. Ⓐ Ⓑ Ⓒ Ⓓ Ⓔ
29. Ⓐ Ⓑ Ⓒ Ⓓ Ⓔ
30. Ⓐ Ⓑ Ⓒ Ⓓ Ⓔ
31. Ⓐ Ⓑ Ⓒ Ⓓ Ⓔ
32. Ⓐ Ⓑ Ⓒ Ⓓ Ⓔ
33. Ⓐ Ⓑ Ⓒ Ⓓ Ⓔ
34. Ⓐ Ⓑ Ⓒ Ⓓ Ⓔ
35. Ⓐ Ⓑ Ⓒ Ⓓ Ⓔ
36. Ⓐ Ⓑ Ⓒ Ⓓ Ⓔ
37. Ⓐ Ⓑ Ⓒ Ⓓ Ⓔ
38. Ⓐ Ⓑ Ⓒ Ⓓ Ⓔ

Section 6

1. Ⓐ Ⓑ Ⓒ Ⓓ Ⓔ
2. Ⓐ Ⓑ Ⓒ Ⓓ Ⓔ
3. Ⓐ Ⓑ Ⓒ Ⓓ Ⓔ
4. Ⓐ Ⓑ Ⓒ Ⓓ Ⓔ
5. Ⓐ Ⓑ Ⓒ Ⓓ Ⓔ
6. Ⓐ Ⓑ Ⓒ Ⓓ Ⓔ
7. Ⓐ Ⓑ Ⓒ Ⓓ Ⓔ
8. Ⓐ Ⓑ Ⓒ Ⓓ Ⓔ
9. Ⓐ Ⓑ Ⓒ Ⓓ Ⓔ
10. Ⓐ Ⓑ Ⓒ Ⓓ Ⓔ
11. Ⓐ Ⓑ Ⓒ Ⓓ Ⓔ
12. Ⓐ Ⓑ Ⓒ Ⓓ Ⓔ
13. Ⓐ Ⓑ Ⓒ Ⓓ Ⓔ
14. Ⓐ Ⓑ Ⓒ Ⓓ Ⓔ
15. Ⓐ Ⓑ Ⓒ Ⓓ Ⓔ
16. Ⓐ Ⓑ Ⓒ Ⓓ Ⓔ
17. Ⓐ Ⓑ Ⓒ Ⓓ Ⓔ
18. Ⓐ Ⓑ Ⓒ Ⓓ Ⓔ
19. Ⓐ Ⓑ Ⓒ Ⓓ Ⓔ
20. Ⓐ Ⓑ Ⓒ Ⓓ Ⓔ
21. Ⓐ Ⓑ Ⓒ Ⓓ Ⓔ
22. Ⓐ Ⓑ Ⓒ Ⓓ Ⓔ
23. Ⓐ Ⓑ Ⓒ Ⓓ Ⓔ
24. Ⓐ Ⓑ Ⓒ Ⓓ Ⓔ
25. Ⓐ Ⓑ Ⓒ Ⓓ Ⓔ
26. Ⓐ Ⓑ Ⓒ Ⓓ Ⓔ
27. Ⓐ Ⓑ Ⓒ Ⓓ Ⓔ
28. Ⓐ Ⓑ Ⓒ Ⓓ Ⓔ
29. Ⓐ Ⓑ Ⓒ Ⓓ Ⓔ
30. Ⓐ Ⓑ Ⓒ Ⓓ Ⓔ
31. Ⓐ Ⓑ Ⓒ Ⓓ Ⓔ
32. Ⓐ Ⓑ Ⓒ Ⓓ Ⓔ
33. Ⓐ Ⓑ Ⓒ Ⓓ Ⓔ
34. Ⓐ Ⓑ Ⓒ Ⓓ Ⓔ
35. Ⓐ Ⓑ Ⓒ Ⓓ Ⓔ
36. Ⓐ Ⓑ Ⓒ Ⓓ Ⓔ
37. Ⓐ Ⓑ Ⓒ Ⓓ Ⓔ
38. Ⓐ Ⓑ Ⓒ Ⓓ Ⓔ

Section 7

1. Ⓐ Ⓑ Ⓒ Ⓓ Ⓔ
2. Ⓐ Ⓑ Ⓒ Ⓓ Ⓔ
3. Ⓐ Ⓑ Ⓒ Ⓓ Ⓔ
4. Ⓐ Ⓑ Ⓒ Ⓓ Ⓔ
5. Ⓐ Ⓑ Ⓒ Ⓓ Ⓔ
6. Ⓐ Ⓑ Ⓒ Ⓓ Ⓔ
7. Ⓐ Ⓑ Ⓒ Ⓓ Ⓔ
8. Ⓐ Ⓑ Ⓒ Ⓓ Ⓔ
9. Ⓐ Ⓑ Ⓒ Ⓓ Ⓔ
10. Ⓐ Ⓑ Ⓒ Ⓓ Ⓔ
11. Ⓐ Ⓑ Ⓒ Ⓓ Ⓔ
12. Ⓐ Ⓑ Ⓒ Ⓓ Ⓔ
13. Ⓐ Ⓑ Ⓒ Ⓓ Ⓔ
14. Ⓐ Ⓑ Ⓒ Ⓓ Ⓔ
15. Ⓐ Ⓑ Ⓒ Ⓓ Ⓔ
16. Ⓐ Ⓑ Ⓒ Ⓓ Ⓔ
17. Ⓐ Ⓑ Ⓒ Ⓓ Ⓔ
18. Ⓐ Ⓑ Ⓒ Ⓓ Ⓔ
19. Ⓐ Ⓑ Ⓒ Ⓓ Ⓔ
20. Ⓐ Ⓑ Ⓒ Ⓓ Ⓔ
21. Ⓐ Ⓑ Ⓒ Ⓓ Ⓔ
22. Ⓐ Ⓑ Ⓒ Ⓓ Ⓔ
23. Ⓐ Ⓑ Ⓒ Ⓓ Ⓔ
24. Ⓐ Ⓑ Ⓒ Ⓓ Ⓔ
25. Ⓐ Ⓑ Ⓒ Ⓓ Ⓔ
26. Ⓐ Ⓑ Ⓒ Ⓓ Ⓔ
27. Ⓐ Ⓑ Ⓒ Ⓓ Ⓔ
28. Ⓐ Ⓑ Ⓒ Ⓓ Ⓔ
29. Ⓐ Ⓑ Ⓒ Ⓓ Ⓔ
30. Ⓐ Ⓑ Ⓒ Ⓓ Ⓔ
31. Ⓐ Ⓑ Ⓒ Ⓓ Ⓔ
32. Ⓐ Ⓑ Ⓒ Ⓓ Ⓔ
33. Ⓐ Ⓑ Ⓒ Ⓓ Ⓔ
34. Ⓐ Ⓑ Ⓒ Ⓓ Ⓔ
35. Ⓐ Ⓑ Ⓒ Ⓓ Ⓔ
36. Ⓐ Ⓑ Ⓒ Ⓓ Ⓔ
37. Ⓐ Ⓑ Ⓒ Ⓓ Ⓔ
38. Ⓐ Ⓑ Ⓒ Ⓓ Ⓔ

MODEL TEST 3

Time—30 minutes

38 Questions

Directions: Each sentence below has one or two blanks, each blank indicating that something has been omitted. Beneath the sentence are five lettered words or sets of words. Choose the word or set of words for each blank that best fits the meaning of the sentence as a whole.

1. The columnist was very gentle when he mentioned his friends, but he was bitter and even ------- when he discussed people who ------- him.
   (A) laconic...infuriated
   ✓(B) acerbic...irritated ✓
   (C) remorseful...encouraged
   (D) militant...distressed
   (E) stoical...alienated

2. Despite her ------- unwillingness, the promoters were still hopeful that, given sufficient diplomacy and flattery on their part, they could ------- her into signing the recording contract.
   (A) patent...entrap
   (B) extreme...intimidate
   (C) apparent...shame
   (D) painful...tantalize
   ✓(E) obvious...inveigle

3. Although he was generally considered an extremely ------- individual, his testimony at the trial revealed that he had been very -------.
   (A) intrepid...valiant
   (B) guileless...hypocritical
   (C) abstemious...temperate
   ✓(D) meek...timorous
   (E) ingenuous...obtuse

4. Reacting to Greene's critical satire by stating that henceforth he will write to please himself, Orlando chooses obscurity; even ------- would be welcome.
   (A) notoriety
   (B) adulation
   (C) parody
   ✓(D) anonymity
   (E) deprecation

5. Whereas off-Broadway theatre over the past several seasons has clearly ------- a talent for experimentation and improvisation, one deficiency in the commercial stage of late has been its marked incapacity for -------.
   ✓(A) manifested...spontaneity
   (B) lampooned...theatricality
   (C) cultivated...orthodoxy
   (D) disavowed...histrionics
   (E) betrayed...burlesque

6. The perpetual spinning of particles is much like that of a top, with one significant difference: unlike the top, the particles have no need to be wound up, for ------- is one of their ------- properties.
   (A) revolution...radical
   (B) motion...intangible
   ✓(C) rotation...intrinsic
   (D) acceleration...lesser
   (E) collision...hypothetical

7. She conducted the interrogation not only with dispatch but with -------, being a person who is ------- in manner yet subtle in discrimination.
   (A) elan...enthusiastic
   (B) equanimity...abrupt
   ✓(C) finesse...expeditious
   (D) zeal...doctrinaire
   (E) trepidation...cursory

Directions: In each of the following questions, a related pair of words or phrases is followed by five lettered pairs of words or phrases. Select the lettered pair that best expresses a relationship similar to that expressed in the original pair.

8. REAM : PAPER::
   (A) skin : tissue
   (B) envelope : letter
   ✓(C) cord : wood
   (D) swatch : cloth
   (E) chisel : stone

9. SMART : PAIN::
   (A) grieve : sorrow
   (B) wallow : misery
   ✓(C) afflict : torment
   (D) mollify : anger
   (E) weaken : intensity

10. BAMBOO : SHOOT::
    (A) heather : spray
    (B) holly : sprig
    ✓(C) bean : sprout
    (D) pepper : corn
    (E) oak : tree

11. DEFLECT : MISSILE::
    (A) defend : fortress
    (B) reflect : mirror
    (C) diversify : portfolio
    (D) dismantle : equipment
    ✓(E) distract : attention

519

12. CLOY : PALATE::
    (A) sniff : nose
    (B) slit : tongue
    √(C) surfeit : appetite
    (D) cling : touch
    (E) refine : taste

13. PRATFALL : EMBARRASSMENT::
    (A) deadlock : mortification
    (B) checkup : reluctance
    (C) downfall : penitence
    (D) diehard : grievance
    √(E) windfall : jubilation

14. MULISH : PLIANCY::
    (A) piggish : gluttony
    (B) sluggish : reluctance
    (C) kittenish : motility
    (D) apish : servility
    √(E) shrewish : amiability

15. MINATORY : THREATEN::
    (A) mandatory : complete
    (B) laudatory : praise
    √(C) salutary : greet
    (D) hortatory : listen
    (E) defamatory : publicize

16. CLOUD : SCUD::
    (A) fog : dissipate
    (B) mist : fall
    √(C) water : race
    (D) blood : clot
    (E) wave : break

Directions: Each passage in this group is followed by questions based on its content. After reading a passage, choose the best answer to each question. Answer all questions following a passage on the basis of what is *stated* or *implied* in the passage.

During the 1930's National Association for the Advancement of Colored People (NAACP) attorneys Charles H. Houston, William Hastie, James M. Nabrit, Leon Ransom, and Thurgood Marshall charted a legal strategy designed to end segregation in education. They developed a series of legal cases challenging segregation in graduate and professional schools. Houston believed that the battle against segregation had to begin at the highest academic level in order to mitigate fear of race mixing that could create even greater hostility and reluctance on the part of white judges. After establishing a series of favorable legal precedents in higher education, NAACP attorneys planned to launch an all-out attack on the separate-but-equal doctrine in primary and secondary schools. The strategy proved successful. In four major United States Supreme Court decisions precedents were established that would enable the NAACP to construct a solid legal foundation upon which the Brown case could rest: *Missouri ex rel. Gaines* v. *Canada*, Registrar of the University of Missouri (1938); *Sipuel* v. *Board of Regents of the University of Oklahoma* (1948); *McLaurin* v. *Oklahoma State Regents for Higher Education* (1950); and *Sweatt* v. *Painter* (1950).

In the Oklahoma case, the Supreme Court held that the plaintiff was entitled to enroll in the University. The Oklahoma Regents responded by separating black and white students in cafeterias and classrooms. The 1950 McLaurin decision ruled that such internal separation was unconstitutional. In the Sweatt ruling, delivered on the same day, the Supreme Court held that the maintenance of separate law schools for whites and blacks was unconstitutional. A year after Herman Sweatt entered the University of Texas law school, desegregation cases were filed in the states of Kansas, South Carolina, Virginia, and Delaware, and in the District of Columbia asking the courts to apply the qualitative test of the Sweatt case to the elementary and secondary schools and to declare the separate-but-equal doctrine invalid in the area of public education.

The 1954 *Brown* v. *Board of Education* decision declared that a classification based solely on race violated the 14th Amendment to the United States Constitution. The decision reversed the 1896 *Plessy* v. *Ferguson* ruling which had established the separate-but-equal doctrine. The *Brown* decision more than any other case launched the "equalitarian revolution" in American jurisprudence and signaled the emerging primacy of equality as a guide to constitutional decisions; nevertheless, the decision did not end state sanctioned segregation. Indeed, the second *Brown* decision, known as *Brown II* and delivered a year later, played a decisive role in limiting the effectiveness and impact of the 1954 case by providing southern states with the opportunity to delay the implementation of desegregation.

The intervention of the federal government and the deployment of the National Guard in the 1954 Little Rock crisis, and again in 1963 when the enrollment of James Meredith desegregated the University of Mississippi, highlights the role of federal power in promoting social change during this era. While black local and national leaders organized and orchestrated the legal struggles, and students joined in freedom rides and staged sit-ins, another equally important dimension of the rights quest took shape: the battle between federal and state authority and the evolution of the doctrine of federalism. The fact remains that the United States Supreme Court lacked the power to enforce its decisions. President Dwight D. Eisenhower's use of federal troops in Little Rock was a major departure from the reluctance of past presidents to display federal power in the south, especially to protect the lives and rights of black citizens.

17. According to the passage, Houston aimed his legis- lative challenge at the graduate and professional school level on the basis of the assumption that

   (A) the greatest inequities existed at the highest aca- demic and professional levels
   (B) the separate-but-equal doctrine applied solely to the highest academic levels
   (C) there were clear precedents for reform in exis- tence at the graduate school level
   X(D) the judiciary would feel less apprehension at desegregation on the graduate level
   (E) the consequences of desegregation would become immediately apparent at the graduate school level

18. The passage suggests that the reaction of the Okla- homa Regents to the 1948 Sipuel decision was one of

   (A) resigned tolerance
   (B) avowed uncertainty
   (C) moderate amusement
   X(D) distinct displeasure
   (E) unquestioning approbation

19. Which of the following best describes the relation- ship between the McLaurin decision and the 1954 *Brown* v. *Board of Education* decision?

   (A) The McLaurin decision superseded the Brown decision.
   (B) The Brown decision provided a precedent for the McLaurin decision.
   (C) The Brown decision reversed the McLaurin decision.
   (D) The McLaurin decision limited the application of the Brown decision.
   X(E) The McLaurin decision provided legal authority for the Brown decision.

20. To the claim that judicial decisions without executive intervention would have assured desegregation in education, the author would most probably respond with which of the following?

   X(A) Marked disagreement
   (B) Grudging acquiescence
   (C) Studied neutrality
   (D) Complete indifference
   (E) Unqualified enthusiasm

21. The passage suggests that *Brown* v. *Board of Educa- tion* might have had an even more significant impact on segregation if it had not been for which of the following?

   (A) The deployment of the National Guard
   (B) The *Plessy* v. *Ferguson* decision
   X(C) The 1955 *Brown II* decision
   (D) James Meredith's enrollment in Mississippi
   (E) The *Sweatt* v. *Painter* decision

22. Which of the following titles best describes the con- tent of the passage?

   (A) Executive Intervention in the Fight against Seg- regated Education
   (B) The *Brown* Decision and the Equalitarian Revolution
   X(C) A Long War: The Struggle to Desegregate American Education
   (D) The Emergence of Federalism and the Civil Rights Movement
   (E) Education Reform and the Role of the NAACP

23. Which of the following statements is most compati- ble with the principles embodied in *Plessy* v. *Fergu- son* as described in the passage?

   (A) Internal separation of whites and blacks within a given school is unconstitutional.
   X(B) Whites and blacks may be educated in separate schools so long as they offer comparable facilities.
   (C) The maintenance of separate professional schools for blacks and whites is unconstitutional.
   (D) The separate-but-equal doctrine is inapplicable to the realm of private education.
   (E) Blacks may be educated in schools with whites whenever the blacks and whites have equal institutions.

24. The aspect of Houston's work most extensively dis- cussed in the passage is its

   X(A) psychological canniness
   (B) judicial complexity
   (C) fundamental efficiency
   (D) radical intellectualism
   (E) exaggerated idealism

One simple physical concept lies behind the formation of the stars: gravitational instability. The concept is not new; Newton first perceived it late in the 17th century.

Imagine a uniform, static cloud of gas in space. Imag- ine then that the gas is somehow disturbed so that one small spherical region becomes a little denser than the gas around it so that the small region's gravitational field becomes slightly stronger. It now attracts more matter to it and its gravity increases further, causing it to begin to contract. As it contracts its density increases, which increases its gravity even more, so that it picks up even more matter and contracts even further. The process continues until the small region of gas finally forms a gravitationally bound object.

25. The primary purpose of the passage is to

   (A) demonstrate the evolution of the meaning of a term
   X(B) depict the successive stages of a phenomenon
   (C) establish the pervasiveness of a process
   (D) support a theory considered outmoded
   (E) describe a static condition

26. It can be inferred from the passage that the author views the information contained within it as

    (A) controversial but irrefutable
    (B) speculative and unprofitable
    X(C) uncomplicated and traditional
    (D) original but obscure
    (E) sadly lacking in elaboration

27. The author provides information that answers which of the following questions?

    I. How does the small region's increasing density affect its gravitational field?
    II. What causes the disturbance that changes the cloud from its original static state?
    III. What is the end result of the gradually increasing concentration of the small region of gas?

    (A) I only
    (B) II only
    (C) I and II only
    (D) I and III only
    X(E) I, II and III

Directions: Each question below consists of a word printed in capital letters, followed by five lettered words or phrases. Choose the lettered word or phrase that is most nearly opposite in meaning to the word in capital letters.

Since some of the questions require you to distinguish fine shades of meaning, be sure to consider all the choices before deciding which one is best.

28. HAMPER:
    (A) feed
    (B) animate
    X(C) facilitate
    (D) treat lightly
    (E) caution tactfully

29. URBANE:
    (A) civic
    (B) remote
    (C) deceptive
    (D) conventional
    X(E) naive

30. DEMISE:
    (A) integrity
    (B) irritation
    X(C) birth
    (D) excess
    (E) surmise

31. PARIAH:
    X(A) miser
    (B) nomad
    (C) servant
    (D) idol
    (E) renegade

32. PROSTRATE:
    (A) divert
    X(B) strengthen
    (C) depreciate
    (D) scrutinize
    (E) reassure

33. CONTENTIOUS:
    X(A) amenable
    (B) inactive
    (C) dispassionate
    (D) callow
    (E) severe

34. DEBACLE:
    (A) effort
    X(B) success
    (C) drought
    (D) transience
    (E) dominance

35. HAPLESS:
    (A) fortuitous
    X(B) fortunate
    (C) fortified
    (D) forbidden
    (E) forestalled

36. EXACERBATE:
    X(A) alleviate
    (B) bewilder
    (C) contemplate
    (D) intimidate
    (E) economize

37. PROBITY:
    (A) fallacy
    X(B) improbability
    (C) conviction
    (D) depravity
    (E) avidity

38. BANEFUL:
    (A) susceptible
    (B) incongruous
    (C) impulsive
    X (D) salubrious
    (E) desultory

S T O P

IF YOU FINISH BEFORE TIME IS CALLED, YOU MAY CHECK YOUR WORK ON THIS SECTION ONLY.
DO NOT WORK ON ANY OTHER SECTION IN THE TEST.

SECTION 2
Time—30 minutes
38 Questions

Directions: Each sentence below has one or two blanks, each blank indicating that something has been omitted. Beneath the sentence are five lettered words or sets of words. Choose the word or set of words for each blank that best fits the meaning of the sentence as a whole.

1. Even though previous reporters had lampooned the candidate throughout the campaign, he ------- further interviews.

    (A) resisted
    (B) halted
    (C) sidestepped
    (D) welcomed
    (E) dreaded

2. Soap operas and situation comedies, though given to distortion, are so derivative of contemporary culture that they are inestimable ------- the attitudes and values of our society in any particular decade.

    (A) contraventions of
    (B) antidotes to
    (C) indices of
    (D) prerequisites for
    (E) determinants of

3. Perry's critics in the scientific world ------- that many of the observations he has made during more than a decade of research in Costa Rica have been reported as ------- in popular magazines rather than as carefully documented case studies in technical journals.

    (A) intimate...hypotheses
    (B) charge...anecdotes
    (C) applaud...rumors
    (D) claim...scholarship
    (E) apologize...fabrications

4. The homeless wino crouched over the subway grating for warmth, the bag lady groping for recyclable bottles in the garbage can, the line of hungry men waiting at the soup kitchen's door—all these scenes of suffering ------- the ------- of the economic boom proclaimed by the prophets of affluence.

    (A) avouch...existence
    (B) belie...reality
    (C) challenge...legality
    (D) predicate...validity
    (E) minimize...gravity

5. Slander is like counterfeit money: many people who would not coin it ------- it without qualms.

    (A) waste
    (B) denounce
    (C) circulate
    (D) withdraw
    (E) invest

6. Compromise is ------- to passionate natures because it seems a surrender; and to intellectual natures because it seems a -------.

    (A) odious...confusion
    (B) inherent...fabrication
    (C) welcome...fulfillment
    (D) unsuited...submission
    (E) intimidating...dichotomy

7. Although we might ------- Milton's remark that he wrote prose with his left hand as characteristically ironic, we have tended to accept uncritically an apparent Renaissance prejudice against prose, using comments like Milton's to ------- our own prejudices against prose as a less immediately artful medium than poetry or drama.

    (A) refute...countervail
    (B) dismiss...invalidate
    (C) challenge...illuminate
    (D) expurgate...exacerbate
    (E) discount...buttress

Directions: In each of the following questions, a related pair of words or phrases is followed by five lettered pairs of words or phrases. Select the lettered pair that best expresses a relationship similar to that expressed in the original pair.

8. CONFINE : PRISONER::
    (A) impeach : governor
    (B) trace : fugitive
    (C) detain : suspect
    (D) testify : witness
    (E) ambush : sentry

9. SWATCH : FABRIC::
    (A) chip : paint
    (B) slag : metal
    (C) mortar : brick
    (D) essence : perfume
    (E) loaf : bread

10. TENDRIL : VINE::
    (A) trunk : tree
    (B) pollen : flower
    (C) pseudopod : amoeba
    (D) trellis : honeysuckle
    (E) cobra : snake

11. BATTEN : HATCH::
    (A) shatter : window
    (B) unload : cargo
    (C) pack : chest
    (D) latch : door
    (E) repair : cupboard

12. CONTEMPORANEOUS : EVENTS::
    (A) adjacent : objects
    (B) modern : times
    (C) temporary : measures
    (D) gradual : degrees
    (E) repetitive : steps

13. LIMERICK : POEM::
    (A) motif : symphony
    (B) prologue : play
    (C) catch : song
    (D) sequence : sonnet
    (E) epigraph : novel

14. RETAINER : RETINUE::
    (A) servant : mansion
    (B) witch : coven
    (C) director : corporation
    (D) miser : hoard
    (E) vassal : homage

15. HERO : ACCOLADE::
    (A) mentor : advice
    (B) suitor : proposal
    (C) clodhopper : grace
    (D) laughingstock : ridicule
    (E) defendant : indictment

16. RIDER : BILL::
    (A) purchase : receipt
    (B) endorsement : policy
    (C) violation : ordinance
    (D) consignment : invoice
    (E) summons : citation

Directions: Each passage in this group is followed by questions based on its content. After reading a passage, choose the best answer to each question. Answer all questions following a passage on the basis of what is *stated* or *implied* in the passage.

With Meredith's *The Egoist* we enter into a critical problem that we have not yet before faced in these studies. That is the problem offered by a writer of recognizably impressive stature, whose work is informed by a muscular intelligence, whose language has splendor, whose "view of life" wins our respect, and yet for whom we are at best able to feel only a passive appreciation which amounts, practically, to indifference. We should be unjust to Meredith and to criticism if we should, giving in to the inertia of indifference, simply avoid dealing with him and thus avoid the problem along with him. He does not "speak to us," we might say; his meaning is not a "meaning for us"; he "leaves us cold." But do not the challenge and the excitement of the critical problem as such lie in that ambivalence of attitude which allows us to recognize the intelligence and even the splendor of Meredith's work, while, at the same time, we experience a lack of sympathy, a failure of any enthusiasm of response?

17. According to the passage, the work of Meredith is noteworthy for its elements of
    (A) sensibility and artistic fervor
    (B) ambivalence and moral ambiguity
    (C) tension and sense of vitality
    (D) brilliance and linguistic grandeur
    (E) wit and whimsical frivolity

18. All of the following can be found in the author's discussion of Meredith EXCEPT
    (A) an indication of Meredith's customary effect on readers
    (B) an enumeration of the admirable qualities in his work
    (C) a selection of hypothetical comments at Meredith's expense
    (D) an analysis of the critical ramifications of Meredith's effect on readers
    (E) a refutation of the claim that Meredith evokes no sympathy

19. It can be inferred from the passage that the author finds the prospect of appraising Meredith's work critically to be
    (A) counterproductive
    (B) overly formidable
    (C) somewhat tolerable
    (D) markedly unpalatable
    (E) clearly invigorating

20. It can be inferred from the passage that the author would be most likely to agree with which of the following statements about the role of criticism?

(A) Its prime office should be to make our enjoyment of the things that feed the mind as conscious as possible.
(B) It should be a disinterested endeavor to learn and propagate the best that is known and thought in the world.
(C) It should enable us to go beyond personal prejudice to appreciate the virtues of works antipathetic to our own tastes.
(D) It should dwell upon excellences rather than imperfections, ignoring such deficiencies as irrelevant.
(E) It should strive both to purify literature and to elevate the literary standards of the reading public.

Genetic variation is also important in the evolution of lower organisms such as bacteria, and here too it arises from mutations. Bacteria have only one chromosome, however, so that different alleles
(5) or variant forms of a gene are not normally present within a single cell. The reshuffling of bacterial genes therefore ordinarily requires the introduction into a bacterium of DNA carrying an allele that originated in a different cell. One mechanism
(10) accomplishing this interbacterial transfer of genes in nature is transduction: certain viruses that can infect bacterial cells pick up fragments of the bacterial DNA and carry the DNA to other cells in the course of a later infection. In another process,
(15) known as transformation, DNA released by cell death or other natural processes simply enters a new cell from the environment by penetrating the cell wall and membrane. A third mechanism, conjugation, involves certain of the self-replicating cir-
(20) cular segments of DNA called plasmids, which can be transferred between bacterial cells that are in direct physical contact with each other.
   Whether the genetic information is introduced into a bacterial cell by transduction, transformation
(25) or conjugation, it must be incorporated into the new host's hereditary apparatus if it is to be propagated as part of that apparatus when the cell divides. As in the case of higher organisms, this incorporation is ordinarily accomplished by the
(30) exchange of homologous DNA; the entering gene must have an allelic counterpart in the recipient DNA. Because homologous recombination requires overall similarity of the two DNA segments, it can take place only between structurally
(35) and ancestrally related segments. And so, in bacteria as well as in higher organisms, the generation of genetic variability is limited to what can be attained by exchanges between different alleles of the same genes or between different genes that have
(40) stretches of similar nucleotide sequences. This requirement imposes severe constraints on the rate of evolution that can be attained through homologous recombination.

Until recently mutation and homologous recombina-
(45) tion nevertheless appeared to be the only important mechanisms for generating biological diversity. They seemed to be able to account for the degree of diversity observed in most species, and the implicit constraints of homologous recombination—which prevent the
(50) exchange of genetic information between unrelated organisms lacking extensive DNA-sequence similarity —appeared to be consistent with both a modest rate of biological evolution and the persistence of distinct species that retain their basic identity generation after
(55) generation.
   Within the past decade or so, however, it has become increasingly apparent that there are various "illegitimate" recombinational processes, which can join together DNA segments having little or no nucleotide-
(60) sequence homology, and that such processes play a significant role in the organization of genetic information and the regulation of its expression. Such recombination is often effected by transposable genetic elements: structurally and genetically discrete segments of DNA that
(65) have the ability to move around the chromosomes and the extrachromosomal DNA molecules of bacteria and higher organisms. Although transposable elements have been studied largely in bacterial cells, they were originally discovered in plants and are now known to exist in
(70) animals as well. Because illegitimate recombination can join together DNA segments that have little, if any, ancestral relationship, it can affect evolution in quantum leaps as well as in small steps.

21. The passage supplies information for answering which of the following questions?

I. Why are interbacterial transfer mechanisms important for genetic variation in bacteria?
II. What is the role of cell death in the interbacterial transfer of genes?
III. How do the so-called "illegitimate" recombinational processes differ from homologous recombination?

(A) I only
(B) II only
(C) I and II only
(D) II and III only
(E) I, II and III

22. The primary purpose of the passage is to

(A) examine the evidence supporting the existence of transposable genetic elements in bacteria
(B) report on the controversy over the use of illegitimate recombinational processes in bacteria
(C) discuss evolutionary theory and some hypotheses proposed to account for its anomalies
(D) explain established mechanisms for genetic change and introduce a newly-discovered one
(E) restrict the scope of the investigation of the causes of genetic variation in bacteria

23. The authors use the term "'illegitimate' recombinational processes" (lines 57–58) to refer to

(A) biological processes outlawed by federal regulation
(B) processes requiring similarity of nucleotide sequences
(C) processes that break the rules of homologous recombination
(D) processes that cannot be found among higher organisms
(E) processes exceeding the permissible amount of mutation

24. In terms of its tone and form, the passage can best be characterized as

(A) an angry refutation
(B) a partisan interpretation
(C) an equivocal endorsement
(D) a reflective meditation
(E) a dispassionate explication

25. A necessary precondition for the process known as transformation to take place is that the cell wall and membrane be

(A) contiguous
(B) pliant
(C) permeable
(D) homologous
(E) self-replicating

26. The function of viruses in the mechanism of transduction in bacteria is most like the function of

(A) caterpillars in the process of metamorphosis
(B) bees in the process of pollination
(C) germs in the process of immunization
(D) pores in the process of perspiration
(E) atoms in the process of fission

27. It can be inferred from the passage that the paragraph immediately preceding this excerpt most likely dealt with the

(A) probability of mutations in colonies of bacteria
(B) significance of genetic diversity in higher organisms
(C) discovery of transposable genetic elements in plants
(D) relationship between bacteria and higher organisms
(E) evidence supporting the theory of evolution

Directions: Each question below consists of a word printed in capital letters, followed by five lettered words or phrases. Choose the lettered word or phrase that is most nearly opposite in meaning to the word in capital letters.

Since some of the questions require you to distinguish fine shades of meaning, be sure to consider all the choices before deciding which one is best.

28. CONDONE:
(A) denounce
(B) endure
(C) imagine
(D) remember
(E) grieve

29. ANTITHETICAL:
(A) qualitative
(B) unnatural
(C) deceptive
(D) supportive
(E) noncommittal

30. OMNISCIENCE:
(A) power
(B) extravagance
(C) magnanimity
(D) conscience
(E) ignorance

31. MOLLIFY:
(A) acquit
(B) forbid
(C) embarrass
(D) provoke
(E) demolish

32. GAUCHE:
(A) grotesque
(B) tactful
(C) rightful
(D) fashionable
(E) inane

33. DIATRIBE:
  (A) medley
  (B) dilemma
  (C) afterthought
  (D) rebuttal
  (E) praise

34. GAINSAY:
  (A) estimate
  (B) corroborate
  (C) forfeit
  (D) expend
  (E) neglect

35. PROLIXITY:
  (A) proximity
  (B) disinclination
  (C) circuitousness
  (D) extremity
  (E) terseness

36. AVID:
  (A) veracious
  (B) forgetful
  (C) insignificant
  (D) turgid
  (E) loath

37. REPINE:
  (A) endure grudgingly
  (B) maintain composure
  (C) express satisfaction
  (D) arouse hostility
  (E) attract attention

38. SALIENCE:
  (A) insipidity
  (B) immutability
  (C) incongruity
  (D) intransigence
  (E) inconspicuousness

S T O P

**IF YOU FINISH BEFORE TIME IS CALLED, YOU MAY CHECK YOUR WORK ON THIS SECTION ONLY.
DO NOT WORK ON ANY OTHER SECTION IN THE TEST.**

SECTION 3

Time—30 Minutes

30 Questions

Numbers: All numbers used are real numbers.

Figures: Position of points, angles, regions, etc. can be assumed to be in the order shown; and angle measures can be assumed to be positive.

Lines shown as straight can be assumed to be straight.

Figures can be assumed to lie in a plane unless otherwise indicated.

Figures that accompany questions are intended to provide information useful in answering the questions. However, unless a note states that a figure is drawn to scale, you should solve these problems NOT by estimating sizes by sight or by measurement, but by using your knowledge of mathematics (see Example 2 below).

Directions: Each of the Questions 1-15 consists of two quantities, one in Column A and one in Column B. You are to compare the two quantities and choose

A if the quantity in Column A is greater;
B if the quantity in Column B is greater;
C if the two quantities are equal;
D if the relationship cannot be determined from the information given.

Note: Since there are only four choices, NEVER MARK (E).

Common
Information: In a question, information concerning one or both of the quantities to be compared is centered above the two columns. A symbol that appears in both columns represents the same thing in Column A as it does in Column B.

Column A	Column B	Sample Answers

Example 1: 2×6 $2 + 6$ ● Ⓑ Ⓒ Ⓓ Ⓔ

Examples 2-4 refer to $\triangle PQR$.

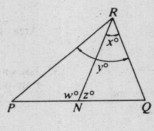

Example 2: PN NQ Ⓐ Ⓑ Ⓒ ● Ⓔ

(since equal measures cannot be assumed, even though PN and NQ appear equal)

Example 3: x y Ⓐ ● Ⓒ Ⓓ Ⓔ

(since N is between P and Q)

Example 4: $w + z$ 180   Ⓐ Ⓑ ● Ⓓ Ⓔ

(since PQ is a straight line)

A if the quantity in Column A is greater;
B if the quantity in Column B is greater;
C if the two quantities are equal;
D if the relationship cannot be determined from the information given.

Column A	Column B

1. $\sqrt{.04}$ $(.2)^2$

2. $\left(\dfrac{1}{2}\right)\left(\dfrac{7}{8}\right)$ $87\dfrac{1}{2}\%$

3. $\left(\dfrac{1}{2}\right)^2$ 23%

4. 0.3 $\dfrac{0.7}{2}$

5. $\dfrac{X}{Y}$ $\dfrac{X}{Y} \cdot \dfrac{Y}{X}$

$$-1 < a < 1$$
$$-1 < b < 0$$

6. a b

7. $\dfrac{2x - \dfrac{y-5}{6}}{\dfrac{y-5}{3}} - 4x$ -0.5

Circleville is 23 kilometers from Center City and Centerville is 46 kilometers from Center City

8.   Distance from Circle-ville to Centerville   23 kilometers

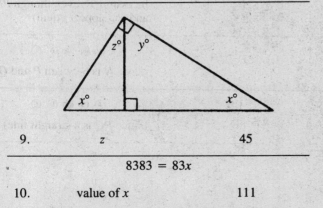

9. z 45

$$8383 = 83x$$

10.   value of x 111

Column A	Column B

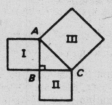

Squares I, II, and III are on the sides of isosceles right triangle ABC, whose area is 12.5.

11.   Area of square III   Twice the area of triangle ABC

$$x^2 - 5x + 6 = 0$$

12.   The sum of the roots of the equation   The product of the roots of the equation

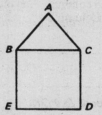

Area of triangle ABC + square $BCDE$ = 125 and perimeter of square = 40

13.   The shortest distance from point A to ED Twice the length of EB

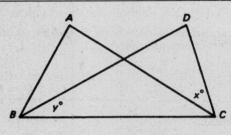

$BD = DC = AC$ and $x = 50$

14. x y

$$\dfrac{\text{Radius of circle } A}{\text{Radius of circle } B} = \dfrac{1}{2}$$

15.   Four times the area of circle A Area of circle B

Directions: Each of the Questions 16–30 has five answer choices. For each of these questions, select the best of the answer choices given.

16. An American tourist in Paris finds that he weighs 70 kilograms. When he left the United States he weighed 144 pounds. If 1 kilogram = 2.2 pounds, his net change in weight is

 (A) −31.8 lb
 (B) −10 lb
 (C) 0
 (D) +10 lb
 (E) +31.8 lb

17. The ratio of boys to girls in a class is $a:b$. What part of the class is made up of girls?

 (A) $\dfrac{b}{ab}$

 (B) $\dfrac{a}{ab}$

 (C) $\dfrac{b}{a+b}$

 (D) $\dfrac{a}{b+a}$

 (E) $\dfrac{a+b}{b}$

18. Which of the following is greater than $\dfrac{1}{4}$?

 (A) $(.25)^2$

 (B) $\sqrt{\dfrac{1}{4}}$

 (C) $\left(\dfrac{1}{4}\right)^4$

 (D) .04

 (E) $\dfrac{1}{250}$

19. A piece of paper with an area of 60 square inches is divided into two pieces so that the area of one is $\dfrac{2}{3}$ the area of the other. What is the area (in square inches) of one of the pieces?

 (A) 15
 (B) 20
 (C) 24
 (D) 30
 (E) 45

20. If $xyz = 240$, which of the following CANNOT be a value of y?

 (A) 0
 (B) 2
 (C) 5
 (D) 3
 (E) 8

Questions 21–25 refer to the following table.

OFFICE-VISIT FEES VARY WIDELY

	First-office-visit fee		Office-revisit fee	
	1986	1983	1986	1983
New York	$51	$36	$36	$25
New Jersey	50	41	31	25
California	49	41	31	26
Massachusetts	46	35	31	25
Florida	45	40	30	25
Texas	36	30	25	21
Georgia	35	31	25	21
Illinois	35	26	25	20
Pennsylvania	36	30	22	20
Ohio	31	28	23	20
Michigan	31	26	22	20
Virginia	31	25	22	19
North Carolina	31	25	21	19
All U.S.	**$37**	**$31**	**$25**	**$21**

Fees represent the most frequent charges of individual M.D.s in the spring of each year indicated. Anesthesiologists, pathologists, psychiatrists, and radiologists have been excluded from these tabulations.

The survey findings are copyrighted by Medical Economics Company, Inc. and were originally published in Medical Economics Magazine.

21. Of the 13 states listed which state had the highest first-office-visit fee and the highest office-revisit fee in 1983?

 (A) New York
 (B) New Jersey
 (C) California
 (D) Massachusetts
 (E) Florida

22. In 1986 how much more did patients in New York pay for first-office-visits than patients in North Carolina?

 (A) $20
 (B) $21
 (C) $31
 (D) $41
 (E) $51

23. How much less is the office-revisit fee than the first-office-visit fee in Georgia?

 (A) $ 4
 (B) $10
 (C) $21
 (D) $25
 (E) $31

24. What was the percentage increase for office revisit fees for all U.S. doctors from 1983 to 1986?

    (A) 4%
    (B) 16%
    (C) 19%
    (D) 21%
    (E) 25%

25. What was the arithmetic mean (average) office-revisit fee for 1986 in the following states: Pennsylvania, Michigan, and Virginia?

    (A) $11
    (B) $22
    (C) $33
    (D) $44
    (E) $55

26. A rectangle *l* inches long and *w* inches wide is made 3 inches longer. The area (in square inches) has increased by

    (A) $3w$
    (B) $3l$
    (C) $3lw$
    (D) $3(l + w)$
    (E) $3l + 3w + 9$

27. If $x + 2y = 1\frac{1}{3}$ and $x - y = \frac{1}{3}$, then $3y =$

    (A) $-\frac{1}{3}$

    (B) 0

    (C) $\frac{1}{3}$

    (D) 1

    (E) $1\frac{2}{3}$

28. City X is 200 miles east of City Y, and City Z is 150 miles directly north of City Y. What is the shortest distance (in miles) between X and Z?

    (A) $50\sqrt{7}$
    (B) 175
    (C) 200
    (D) 250
    (E) 300

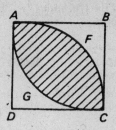

29. In the figure above, *ABCD* is a square of side 10. *AFC* is an arc of a circle with the center at *D* and radius 10. *AGC* is an arc of a circle with the center at *B* and radius 10. What is the area of the shaded region?

    (A) $50\pi - 100$
    (B) $25\pi - 100$
    (C) $100 - 25\pi$
    (D) $100 - 50\pi$
    (E) $100\pi - 100$

30. The price of a balcony seat in a theater is $\frac{1}{3}$ the price of a seat in the orchestra. When completely sold out the total receipts from the 600 orchestra seats and the 450 balcony seats are $4,500. What is the price of one orchestra seat?

    (A) $2.00
    (B) $2.30
    (C) $4.00
    (D) $6.00
    (E) $10.00

S T O P

IF YOU FINISH BEFORE TIME IS CALLED, YOU MAY CHECK YOUR WORK ON THIS SECTION ONLY. DO NOT WORK ON ANY OTHER SECTION IN THE TEST.

SECTION 4

Time—30 minutes

30 Questions

Numbers: All numbers used are real numbers.

Figures: Position of points, angles, regions, etc. can be assumed to be in the order shown; and angle measures can be assumed to be positive.

Lines shown as straight can be assumed to be straight.

Figures can be assumed to lie in a plane unless otherwise indicated.

Figures that accompany questions are intended to provide information useful in answering the questions. However, unless a note states that a figure is drawn to scale, you should solve these problems NOT by estimating sizes by sight or by measurement, but by using your knowledge of mathematics (see Example 2 below).

Directions: Each of the Questions 1-15 consists of two quantities, one in Column A and one in Column B. You are to compare the two quantities and choose

    A if the quantity in Column A is greater;
    B if the quantity in Column B is greater;
    C if the two quantities are equal;
    D if the relationship cannot be determined from the information given.

Note: Since there are only four choices, NEVER MARK (E).

Common
Information: In a question, information concerning one or both of the quantities to be compared is centered above the two columns. A symbol that appears in both columns represents the same thing in Column A as it does in Column B.

	Column A	Column B	Sample Answers
Example 1:	2×6	$2 + 6$	● Ⓑ Ⓒ Ⓓ Ⓔ

Examples 2-4 refer to $\triangle PQR$.

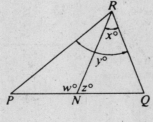

Example 2:	PN	NQ	Ⓐ Ⓑ Ⓒ ● Ⓔ
			(since equal measures cannot be assumed, even though PN and NQ appear equal)
Example 3:	x	y	Ⓐ ● Ⓒ Ⓓ Ⓔ
			(since N is between P and Q)
Example 4:	$w + z$	180	Ⓐ Ⓑ ● Ⓓ Ⓔ
			(since PQ is a straight line)

A if the quantity in Column A is greater;
B if the quantity in Column B is greater;
C if the two quantities are equal;
D if the relationship cannot be determined from the information given.

Column A	Column B

$$x + 5 = 5$$

1. $5 - x$ 5

2. $\frac{1}{2} + \frac{1}{3} + \frac{1}{4}$ 1

3. $\dfrac{1}{x} \div \dfrac{1}{\frac{1}{x}}$ $\dfrac{1}{x} \times \dfrac{1}{x}$

4. $\dfrac{\text{3 yards, 1 foot, 3 inches}}{3}$ 40 inches

5. 2^3 3^2

6. a^6 $6a^5$

$$0 < x < 99$$
x is divisible by 2, 5, 8

7. x 40

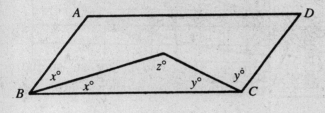

In parallelogram $ABCD$, $y = 50$

8. $x + y$ 90

In triangle ABC, the measure of angle A is greater than the measure of angle B, and angle C has a measure of $60°$.

9.   Length of side AC Length of side AB

Column A	Column B

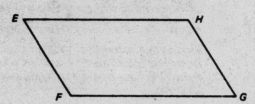

In parallelogram $EFGH$, $EF + EH = 20$

10. $HG + FG$ $\frac{1}{2}$ perimeter of $EFGH$

The arithmetic mean (average) of 4, 5, 6, 7, 8, and x is 6.

$$x > 0$$

11. x 6

$$x^2 = 100$$
$$y^2 = 25$$

12. $(x - y)(x + y)$ 125

13. $\dfrac{3}{\sqrt{3}}$ $\sqrt{3}$

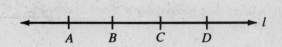

AB, BC, CD are equal lengths of l.

14. The length of $AB + BC$ The length of $AD -$
          on line l CD on line l

$$x\sqrt{0.01} = 1$$

15. x 10

Directions: Each of the Questions 16–30 has five answer choices. For each of these questions, select the best of the answer choices given.

16. The wheel of a bicycle is 28 inches in diameter. How many feet will it cover in 9 turns of the wheel? (Use $\pi = \frac{22}{7}$.)

(A) 66
(B) 252
(C) 396
(D) 462
(E) 792

17. If $A = \frac{2}{3} B$, $B = \frac{2}{3} C$, and $C = \frac{2}{3} D$, what part of D is B?

(A) $\frac{8}{27}$

(B) $\frac{4}{9}$

(C) $\frac{2}{3}$

(D) 75%

(E) $\frac{4}{3}$

18. The gasoline tank of an automobile can hold g gallons. If a gallons were removed when the tank was full, what part of the full tank was removed?

(A) $g - a$

(B) $\frac{g}{a}$

(C) $\frac{a}{g}$

(D) $\frac{g - a}{a}$

(E) $\frac{g - a}{g}$

19. A dress shop marked down all merchandise as follows:

GROUP	REGULAR PRICE	SALE PRICE
A	$60	$50
B	$65	$55
C	$70	$60
D	$75	$65
E	$80	$70

Which group of merchandise was offered at the greatest rate of discount from its original price?

(A) A
(B) B
(C) C
(D) D
(E) E

20. During one year, the highest temperature recorded in a certain city was 22°C, and the lowest temperature recorded was −41°C. What is the absolute value of the difference between the highest and lowest temperature?

(A) − 63
(B) − 19
(C) 19
(D) 41
(E) 63

Questions 21–25 are based on the following graph.

SOLUBILITY-TEMPERATURE RELATIONSHIP FOR VARIOUS SALTS

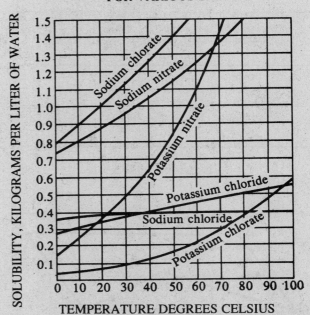

21. Which of the following salts has the greatest solubility?

(A) potassium chlorate at 81°C
(B) potassium chloride at 45°C
(C) potassium nitrate at 29°C
(D) sodium chloride at 85°C
(E) sodium chloride at 21°C

22. Approximately how many kilograms of potassium nitrate can be dissolved in ten liters of water at 23°C?

(A) .036
(B) .31
(C) .35
(D) 3.0
(E) 3.75

23. By what percent is the solubility of potassium chlorate in water increased as water is heated from 31°C to 65°C?

   (A) 15
   (B) 25
   (C) 35
   (D) 150
   (E) 250

24. If one mole of potassium chloride weighs .07456 kilograms, approximately how many moles of potassium chloride can be dissolved in 100 liters of water at 25°C?

   (A) .002
   (B) .2
   (C) 5
   (D) 50
   (E) 500

25. For which of the following pairs of salts is there *not* a temperature between 10°C and 90°C at which the salts have the same solubility?

   (A) potassium and sodium chlorides
   (B) potassium and sodium nitrates
   (C) potassium chlorate and nitrate
   (D) potassium chlorate and sodium chloride
   (E) potassium chloride and nitrate

26. If the perimeter of a square is 16, its area is

   (A) 4
   (B) 8
   (C) 16
   (D) 64
   (E) 256

27. A picture 16 inches × 24 inches has a frame 1 inch wide. About how many times greater than the area of the frame is the area of the picture?

   (A) 1.2
   (B) 4.5
   (C) 12
   (D) 45
   (E) 80

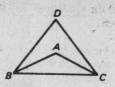

28. $AB = AC, DB = DC, \angle ABC = \frac{1}{2}\angle DBC$, and $m\angle D = 70$. How many degrees are there in $\angle A$?

   (A) 55
   (B) 70
   (C) 105
   (D) 110
   (E) 125

29. A graduating class of 356 votes to choose a president. With 5 candidates seeking office, what is the least number of votes a successful candidate could receive and yet have more votes than any other candidate?

   (A) 71
   (B) 72
   (C) 89
   (D) 178
   (E) 179

30. In a group of 15, 7 can speak Spanish, 8 can speak French, and 3 can speak neither. How much of the group can speak both French and Spanish?

   (A) $\frac{1}{5}$

   (B) $\frac{4}{15}$

   (C) $\frac{1}{3}$

   (D) $\frac{7}{15}$

   (E) $\frac{2}{3}$

S T O P

IF YOU FINISH BEFORE TIME HAS ELAPSED, CHECK YOUR WORK ON THIS SECTION OF THE TEST ONLY. DO NOT GO ON TO THE NEXT SECTION OF THE TEST UNTIL TIME IS UP FOR THIS SECTION.

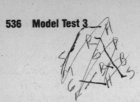
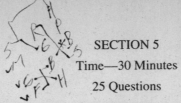

SECTION 5

Time—30 Minutes

25 Questions

Directions: Each question or group of questions is based on a passage or set of conditions. In answering some of the questions, it may be useful to draw a rough diagram. For each question, select the best answer choice given.

Questions 1–4

John is undecided which of the four popular novels to buy. He is considering a spy thriller, a murder mystery, a Gothic romance, and a science fiction novel. They are written by Rothko, Gorky, Burchfield, and Hopper, not necessarily in that order, and published by Heron, Pigeon, Bluejay, and Sparrow, not necessarily in that order.

(1) The book by Rothko is published by Sparrow.
(2) The spy thriller is published by Heron.
(3) The science novel is by Burchfield and is not published by Bluejay.
(4) The Gothic romance is by Hopper.

1. Pigeon publishes

   (A) the murder mystery
   (B) the science fiction novel
   (C) the spy thriller
   (D) the Gothic romance
   (E) the novel by Rothko

2. The novel by Gorky is

   (A) a science fiction novel published by Bluejay
   (B) a Gothic romance published by Bluejay
   (C) published by Heron and is a murder mystery
   (D) published by Pigeon and is a Gothic romance
   (E) published by Heron and is a spy thriller

3. John purchases books by the two authors whose names come first and third in alphabetical order. He does not buy

   (A) the murder mystery
   (B) the book published by Pigeon
   (C) the science fiction novel
   (D) the book published by Bluejay
   (E) the Gothic romance

4. On the basis of the first paragraph and statements (2), (3), and (4) only, it is possible to deduce that

   I.   Rothko wrote the murder mystery or the spy thriller
   II.   Sparrow published the murder mystery or the spy thriller
   III. the book by Burchfield is published by Sparrow or Pigeon

   (A) I only
   (B) II only
   (C) III only
   (D) I and III only
   (E) I, II, and II

Questions 5–7

When a farmer cultivates his land with an investment of $X for machinery, fertilizer, and labor, his average yield per dollar of investment is 10 bushels of potatoes. The next year he doubles his investment of labor and capital on the same land and he finds that his yield per dollar of investments is 15 bushels of potatoes. The next year he doubles that investment and his yield per dollar of investment is 12 bushels per dollar of investment.

5. The increase in yield per dollar of investment during the second year was most probably due to

   (A) better, more expensive equipment
   (B) more efficient use of all available soil
   (C) greater incentive to farm workers
   (D) better supervision of larger labor force
   (E) greater efficiency because of higher salaries

6. What accounts for the decrease in yield per dollar during the third year?

   (A) Bad weather reduces profits regardless of efficiency.
   (B) Poor irrigation with crowded crops reduces the size of a crop.
   (C) The limit of efficiency per unit of land was reached.
   (D) Increased costs of production decreased proportionate yield.
   (E) Inflation was a factor.

7. The situation in this passage illustrates the fact that

   (A) farmers must receive Federal subsidies
   (B) increasing capital investment results in lower cost of production per unit of product
   (C) there is a point in investment when a greater total yield results, but the increased yield is less than proportionate
   (D) many factors influence profitable farming
   (E) there is a limit to profit in agriculture

Questions 8–12

On Sunday, December 23, four ships were berthed at the New York City Municipal Pier at West 55 Street. All four ships were beginning their series of winter cruises to various ports in the Atlantic and the Caribbean.

Ship W left at 4 p.m. on Sunday, December 23, for a series of 8-day cruises to Bermuda and Nassau.

Ship X left at 4:30 p.m. on Sunday, December 23, for a series of alternating 11- and 13-day cruises.

Ship Y sailed at 5 p.m. on Sunday, December 23, for a series of 5-day cruises to Bermuda.

Ship Z sailed on Monday, December 24, for a series of 7-day cruises to Nassau.

All four ships are scheduled to return to New York City early in the morning and leave again late in the afternoon of the same day.

8. On December 31, which ships will be sailing from New York on a New Year's Eve cruise?

   (A) *W* and *X*
   (B) *X* and *Y*
   (C) *W* and *Z*
   (D) *X* and *Z*
   (E) *X, Y,* and *Z*

9. On how many sailing dates between Dec. 24 and Feb. 28 will ship *W* be moored alongside another ship?

   (A) 0
   (B) 2
   (C) 4
   (D) 5
   (E) 6

10. On how many occasions between Dec. 24 and Feb. 28 will three ships be moored at the pier?

    (A) 0
    (B) 1
    (C) 2
    (D) 3
    (E) 4

11. On which day of the week will these four ships make most of their departures?

    (A) Sunday
    (B) Monday
    (C) Tuesday
    (D) Thursday
    (E) Saturday

12. On which day or days of the week in the period between Dec. 24 and Feb. 28 will the pier be least crowded?

    (A) Tuesday and Friday
    (B) Tuesday and Thurdsay
    (C) Friday and Saturday
    (D) Wednesday and Thursday
    (E) Thursday and Saturday

Questions 13–16

Observance of Memorial Day, which falls on a Saturday this year, will be as follows for the Tri-State area (New Albion, New Shetland, New Wales):

   Banks and government departments which are normally open on Saturdays will close.

Those normally closed Saturdays will close as follows:

   Banks will close Friday in New Wales and Monday in New Shetland.

   State government offices will close Friday in New Albion and New Shetland.

Sanitation pick-up in Monday-Wednesday-Friday pickup areas will be cancelled Friday in New Albion and New Shetland, and Monday in New Wales; pickup in Tuesday-Thursday-Saturday areas will be cancelled Saturday in all three states.

   The post office and other federal offices, normally open Monday through Saturday, will be closed Saturday but open Friday and Monday in all three states.

   (Banks are normally open on Saturday only in New Albion; state government offices are normally open Saturday only in Wales.)

13. Which is not available Friday, Saturday, or Monday in New Wales?

    (A) Banking services
    (B) State government office services
    (C) Sanitation pickup in some areas
    (D) Postal services
    (E) Federal government office services

14. Mrs. Semkow goes to the post office, the bank, and the state income tax bureau on Monday. She may live in

    I.   New Albion
    II. New Shetland
    III. New Wales

    (A) I only
    (B) II only
    (C) I or III only
    (D) II or III only
    (E) I, II, or III

15. Mr. Rudolph finds but one of the listed services available Friday. He lives in

    (A) New Shetland or New Albion
    (B) a Monday-Wednesday-Friday pickup area in New Wales
    (C) any area in New Albion or New Wales
    (D) a Tuesday-Thursday-Saturday pickup area in any of the three states
    (E) a Monday-Wednesday-Friday area in New Albion

16. In which area(s) is there no deviation from normal service on Monday for any of the services listed?

    (A) All of New Albion
    (B) Monday-Wednesday-Friday pickup areas in New Albion and New Wales
    (C) Tuesday-Thursday-Saturday pickup areas in New Shetland and New Wales
    (D) All of New Wales
    (E) Mondays-Wednesday-Friday areas in New Shetland

Questions 17–22

(1) An Airedale, a boxer, a collie, and a Doberman win the top four prizes in the Kennel Show. Their owners are Mr. Edwards, Mr. Foster, Mr. Grossman, and Ms. Huntley, not necessarily in that order. Their dogs' names are Jack, Kelly, Lad, and Max, not necessarily in that order.
(2) Mr. Grossman's dog wins neither first nor second prize.
(3) The collie wins first prize.
(4) Max wins second prize.
(5) The Airedale is Jack.
(6) Mr. Foster's dog, the Doberman, wins fourth prize.
(7) Ms. Huntley's dog is Kelly.

17. First prize is won by

    (A) Mr. Edwards's dog
    (B) Ms. Huntley's dog
    (C) Max
    (D) Jack
    (E) Lad

18. Mr. Grossman's dog

    (A) is the collie
    (B) is the boxer
    (C) is the Airedale
    (D) wins second prize
    (E) is Kelly

19. Which statement correctly lists the dogs in descending order of their prizes?

    I.   Kelly; the Airedale; Mr. Edward's dog
    II. The boxer; Mr. Grossman's dog; Jack
    III. Mr. Edward's dog; the Airedale; Lad

    (A) I only
    (B) II only
    (C) III only
    (D) I and III only
    (E) II and III only

20. Lad

    (A) is owned by Mr. Foster
    (B) is owned by Mr. Edwards
    (C) is the boxer
    (D) is the collie
    (E) wins third prize

21. On the basis of statements (1), (3), (4), (5), and (6) only, which of the following may be deduced?

    I.   Max is the boxer.
    II. The Doberman is Kelly or Lad.
    III. Jack wins third prize.

    (A) I and II only
    (B) I and III only
    (C) II and III only
    (D) I, II, and III
    (E) Neither I, II, nor III

22. On the basis of statements (1), (2), (3), (4), and (7) only, which of the following may be deduced?

    I.   Mr. Grossman's dog is Jack or Lad.
    II. Mr. Edward's dog wins first or second prize.
    III. Kelly is the collie.

    (A) I only
    (B) II only
    (C) I and II only
    (D) II and III only
    (E) I, II, and III

Questions 23 and 24

(1) All students who major in philosophy wear Clavert Kreem jeans.
(2) None of the students in the Marching and Chowder Society wears Calvert Kreem jeans or majors in history.
(3) If Jack majors in philosophy, Mary majors in history.

23. If the statement above are all true, which of the following must also be true?

    (A) If Jack majors in philosophy, Mary does not wear Calvert Kreem jeans.
    (B) None of the students in the Marching and Chowder Society majors in philosophy.
    (C) If Jack wears Clavert Kreem jeans, he majors in philosophy.
    (D) If Mary majors in history, Jack is not in the Marching and Chowder Society.
    (E) Either Jack or Mary wears Calvert Kreem jeans.

24. The conclusion "Jack does not major in philosophy" could be validly drawn from the statements above if it were established that

    I.   Mary does not major in history
    II. Jack does not belong to the Marching and Chowder Society
    III. Jack does not wear Calvert Kreem jeans

    (A) I only
    (B) II only
    (C) III only
    (D) I and III only
    (E) II and III only

25. Spokesman for a chemical company to residents of a
    nearby town: We have conducted tests and have
    found no evidence that the fumes leaking from our
    waste disposal site are harmful to humans. There is
    no reason to be alarmed, much less to begin evacuat-
    ing people from their homes.

    Which of the following would be the least relevant
    question for the head of the residents' committee to
    direct to the chemical company spokesman?

    (A) What steps are being taken to correct the
        situation?
    (B) Are further tests being conducted?
    (C) How much will it cost you to stop the leaks?
    (D) Do the fumes have an adverse effect on plants
        or animals?
    (E) What are the possible long-term effects of expo-
        sure to the fumes?

S T O P

IF YOU FINISH BEFORE TIME IS CALLED, YOU MAY CHECK YOUR WORK ON THIS SECTION ONLY.
DO NOT WORK ON ANY OTHER SECTION IN THE TEST.

SECTION 6

Time—30 minutes

25 Questions

Directions: Each question or group of questions is based on a passage or set of conditions. In answering some of the questions, it may be useful to draw a rough diagram. For each question, select the best answer choice given.

Questions 1–4

(1) All G's are H's.
(2) All G's are J's or K's.
(3) All J's and K's are G's.
(4) All L's are K's.
(5) All N's are M's.
(6) No M's are G's.

1. Which of the following can be logically deduced from the conditions stated?

    (A) No M's are H's.
    (B) No M's that are not N's are H's.
    (C) No H's are M's.
    (D) Some M's are H's.
    (E) No N's are G's.

2. Which of the following is inconsistent with one or more of the conditions?

    (A) All H's are G's.
    (B) All H's that are not G's are M's.
    (C) Some H's are both M's and G's.
    (D) No M's are H's.
    (E) All M's are H's.

3. The statement "No L's are J's" is

    I. logically deducible from the conditions stated
    II. consistent with but not deducible from the conditions stated
    III. deducible from the stated conditions together with the additional statement "No J's are K's"

    (A) I only
    (B) II only
    (C) III only
    (D) II and III only
    (E) Neither I, II, nor III

4. If no P's are K's, which of the following must be true?

    (A) All P's are J's.
    (B) No P is a G.
    (C) No P is an H.
    (D) If any P is an H it is a G.
    (E) If any P is a G it is a J.

Questions 5 and 6

Ellen to Ralph: I'm not going to play with your cat because I'll be sneezing all afternoon if I do. I've played with your cat three times, and each time I've sneezed all afternoon.

5. The argument above is most like which of the following arguments?

    (A) Empiricism must have developed later than rationalism, because it developed as a reaction to rationalism.
    (B) Drug X increases fertility in humans. Every woman given the drug in tests gave birth to more than one child.
    (C) The dumping of chemicals into the lake two months ago caused the present dying off of the fish. No fish died in the lakes into which no chemicals were dumped.
    (D) The committee's report must have been valid, because it predicted that a crisis would develop, and that is exactly what has happened.
    (E) Joe's fiancee must be allergic to roses. Every time he takes her roses, she becomes weepy.

6. Ellen's argument would be most strengthened if it is also true that

    (A) Ralph also sneezes after playing with his cat.
    (B) Ellen never sneezes just before playing with Ralph's cat.
    (C) Ellen also sneezes after playing with Dan's dog.
    (D) Ellen sneezes only after playing with Ralph's cat.
    (E) Ralph's cat also sneezes after playing with Ellen.

7. But the number of flights has increased by 30% in the last ten years.

    The statement above would be a logical rebuttal to which of the following claims?

    (A) The airlines must be losing money. The cost of jet fuel has tripled in the last ten years.
    (B) Airline ticket prices have increased so fast in the last ten years that some people who could once afford to fly no longer can.
    (C) Flying is getting more unsafe. The number of airplane accidents per year has increased by over 10% in the last decade.
    (D) More air travelers are taking "short hop," commuter flights. The average number of miles traveled per flight has decreased by 20% in the last ten years.
    (E) The flight industry is being taken over by a few large airlines. There are 25% fewer airlines today than there were ten years ago.

Questions 8–11

At a formal dinner for eight, the host and hostess are
seated at opposite ends of a rectangular table, with three
persons along each side. Each man must be seated next
to at least one woman, and vice-versa.
  Allan is opposite Diane, who is not the hostess.
  George has a woman on his right and is opposite a
    woman.
  Helga is at the hostess's right, next to Frank.
  One person is seated between Belinda and Carol.

8. The eighth person present, Eric, must be

    I.   the host
    II. seated to Diane's right
    III. seated opposite Carol

    (A) I only
    (B) III only
    (C) I and II only
    (D) II and III only
    (E) I, II, and III

9. If each person is placed directly opposite his or her
    spouse, which of the following pairs must be
    married?

    (A) George and Helga
    (B) Belinda and Frank
    (C) Carol and Frank
    (D) George and Belinda
    (E) Eric and Helga

10. Which person is not seated next to a person of the
    same sex?

    (A) Allan
    (B) Belinda
    (C) Carol
    (D) Diane
    (E) Eric

11. George is bothered by the cigarette smoke of his
    neighbor and exchanges seats with the person four
    places to his left. Which of the following must be
    true following the exchange?

    I.   No one is seated between two persons of the
         opposite sex.
    II. One side of the table consists entirely of per-
         sons of the same sex.
    III. Either the host or the hostess has changed
         seats.

    (A) I only
    (B) III only
    (C) I and II only
    (D) II and III only
    (E) Neither I, II, not III

Questions 12–18

For a panel of professors to asses the State of the Union
Message on public TV, the producer must choose two
Republicans and two Democrats. At least one professor
must be an economist and at least one a military expert.
Available Republicans are Abbott, Bartlett, Catlett,
Dorset, and Everett; available Democrats are Fawcett,
Gantlet, Helfet, and Insett. Catlett, Fawcett, and Gantlet
are economists, Dorset and Insett are military experts.
Fawcett will not sit in the same room with Catlett, and
will take part only if Abbott is on the panel. Dorset
refuses to take part with Gantlet, and Everett refuses to
take part with Insett.

12. Which of the following is not an acceptable panel?

    (A) Fawcett, Helfet, Abbott, Dorset
    (B) Fawcett, Insett, Abbott, Dorset
    (C) Gantlet, Helfet, Abbott, Catlett
    (D) Gantlett, Insett, Abbott, Catlett
    (E) Helfet, Insett, Bartlett, Catlett

13. If Abbott and Bartlett are chosen as the Republicans,
    who can be chosen as the Democrats?

    (A) Fawcett and Insett only
    (B) Fawcett and Insett or Gantlet and Insett only
    (C) Fawcett and Gantlet or Gantlet and Helfet only
    (D) Fawcett and Insett, Gantlet and Insett, or Helfet
        and Insett
    (E) Gantlet and Helfet, Gantlet and Insett, or Helfet
        and Insett

14. If Gantlett is chosen, which of the following must be
    true?

    I.   Any acceptable panel must contain Insett.
    II. Any acceptable panel must contain Abbott.
    III. There is no acceptable panel which contains
         Bartlett.

    (A) I only
    (B) II only
    (C) I and II only
    (D) II and III only
    (E) I, II, and III

15. How many acceptable panels can the producer put
    together?

    (A) 6
    (B) 7
    (C) 8
    (D) 9
    (E) 10

16. Which of the following pairs cannot be part of an acceptable panel?

    I.   Fawcett and Gantlet
    II. Bartlett and Dorset
    III. Catlett and Dorset

    (A) I only
    (B) III only
    (C) I and II only
    (D) II and III only
    (E) I, II, and III

17. Which Republican belongs to the smallest number of different acceptable panels?

    (A) Abbott
    (B) Bartlett
    (C) Catlett
    (D) Dorset
    (E) Everett

18. Which professor belongs to the greatest number of different acceptable panels?

    (A) Abbott
    (B) Bartlett
    (C) Gantlet
    (D) Helfet
    (E) Insett

Questions 19–22

The Hotel Miramar has two wings, the East Wing and the West Wing. Some East Wing rooms, but not all, have an ocean view. All West Wing rooms have a harbor view. The charge for all rooms is identical, except as follows:
   There is an extra charge for all harbor view rooms on or above the third floor.
   There is an extra charge for all ocean view rooms, except those without balcony.
   Some harbor view rooms on the first two floor and some East Wing rooms without ocean view have kitchen facilities, for which there is an extra charge.
   Only the ocean view and harbor view rooms have balconies.

19. A guest may avoid an extra charge by requesting

    (A) a West Wing room on one of the first two floors
    (B) a West Wing room on the fourth floor without balcony
    (C) an East Wing room without an ocean view
    (D) an East Wing room without balcony
    (E) any room without kitchen facilities

20. Which of the following must be true if all the conditions are as stated?

    (A) All rooms above the third floor involve an extra charge.
    (B) No room without an ocean or harbor view or kitchen facilities involves an extra charge.
    (C) There is no extra charge for any East Wing room without an ocean view.
    (D) There is no extra charge for any room without kitchen facilities.
    (E) There is an extra charge for all rooms with an ocean or harbor view.

21. Which of the following must be false if all conditions are as stated?

    (A) Some ocean view rooms do not involve an extra charge.
    (B) All rooms with kitchen facilities involve an extra charge.
    (C) Some West Wing rooms above the second floor do not involve an extra charge.
    (D) Some harbor view rooms do not involve an extra charge.
    (E) Some rooms without a balcony or kitchen facilities involve an extra charge.

22. Which of the following cannot be determined on the basis of the information given?

    I.   Whether there are any rooms without a balcony for which an extra charge is imposed
    II. Whether any room without a kitchen or a view involves an extra charge
    III. Whether two extra charges are imposed for any room

    (A) I only
    (B) II only
    (C) I and III only
    (D) II and III only
    (E) I, II, and III

Question 23 and 24

The people do not run the country; neither do elected officials. The corporations run the country. Heads of corporations routinely and imperiously hand down decisions that profoundly affect millions of people. The people affected do not vote on the decisions, nor for the corporate oligarchs. Yet we are supposed to believe we live in a democracy.

23. Which of the following statements, if true, would support the author's views?

    I.   Corporate lobbies strongly influence the introduction and passage of legislation at all levels of government.
    II. Growing numbers of the most talented college graduates are going to work for private corporations rather than for the government.
    III. Few legal requirements are imposed on corporations as to the responsibilities they must fulfill to their employees and their communities.

    (A) I only
    (B) II only
    (C) I and III only
    (D) II and III only
    (E) I, II, and III

24. Which of the following statements most closely parallels the reasoning of the argument above?

    (A) The Police Department just laid off ten patrolmen. Yet we are supposed to believe this is a safe neighborhood.
    (B) He has lied to us many times. Yet we are supposed to believe he is now telling the truth.
    (C) The quality of television programs continues to decline. Yet we are supposed to believe they are still worth watching.
    (D) He has no training or experience in this profession. Yet we are supposed to believe he is qualified for this job.
    (E) We are asked to do nothing but regurgitate facts. Yet we are supposed to believe we are getting an education.

25. Anthony is standing to the right of Beth. Caroline is standing on the opposite side of Beth. Since the opposite of right is wrong, Caroline must be standing on the wrong side of Beth.

    Which of the following logical errors has the author of the argument above committed?

    (A) He has used a single term to mean two different things.
    (B) He has confused cause and effect.
    (C) He has assumed to be true what he wants to prove to be true.
    (D) He has provided no factual evidence for his conclusion.
    (E) He has drawn a general conclusion from an insufficient number of examples.

S T O P

**IF YOU FINISH BEFORE TIME IS CALLED, YOU MAY CHECK YOUR WORK ON THIS SECTION ONLY.
DO NOT WORK ON ANY OTHER SECTION IN THE TEST.**

SECTION 7

Time—30 minutes

30 Questions

Numbers: All numbers used are real numbers.

Figures: Position of points, angles, regions, etc. can be assumed to be in the order shown; and angle measures can be assumed to be positive.

Lines shown as straight can be assumed to be straight.

Figures can be assumed to lie in a plane unless otherwise indicated.

Figures that accompany questions are intended to provide information useful in answering the questions. However, unless a note states that a figure is drawn to scale, you should solve these problems NOT by estimating sizes by sight or by measurement, but by using your knowledge of mathematics (see Example 2 below).

Directions: Each of the Questions 1-15 consists of two quantities, one in Column A and one in Column B. You are to compare the two quantities and choose

> A if the quantity in Column A is greater;
> B if the quantity in Column B is greater;
> C if the two quantities are equal;
> D if the relationship cannot be determined from the information given.

Note: Since there are only four choices, NEVER MARK (E).

Common
Information: In a question, information concerning one or both of the quantities to be compared is centered above the two columns. A symbol that appears in both columns represents the same thing in Column A as it does in Column B.

	Column A	Column B	Sample Answers
Example 1:	2×6	$2 + 6$	● Ⓑ Ⓒ Ⓓ Ⓔ

Examples 2-4 refer to $\triangle PQR$.

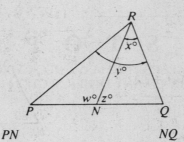

Example 2:	PN	NQ	Ⓐ Ⓑ Ⓒ ● Ⓔ
			(since equal measures cannot be assumed, even though PN and NQ appear equal)
Example 3:	x	y	Ⓐ ● Ⓒ Ⓓ Ⓔ
			(since N is between P and Q)
Example 4:	$w + z$	180	Ⓐ Ⓑ ● Ⓓ Ⓔ
			(since PQ is a straight line)

A if the quantity in Column A is greater;
B if the quantity in Column B is greater;
C if the two quantities are equal;
D if the relationship cannot be determined from the information given.

Column A	Column B

1. 3^2 2^3

2. $\dfrac{6 + \frac{3}{4}}{2 - \frac{5}{4}}$ $(3)^2$

3. $\frac{1}{3}$ of 8 $66\frac{2}{3}$% of 4

4. $\sqrt{\dfrac{1}{4}} + \sqrt{\dfrac{1}{25}}$ $\sqrt{\dfrac{1}{4} + \dfrac{1}{25}}$

$x = 3$ and $y = \dfrac{1}{6}$

5. $2x - 18y$ $3x - 36y$

6. the average of $\sqrt{.49}$,   75%
   $\frac{3}{4}$, and 0.8

$B = 0$
$A > 1$
$C > 1$

7. $2B(A + C)$ $A(B + C)$

8. $\dfrac{n + a}{a}$ $\dfrac{n}{a} + 1$

$x + y = 17$
$y + 3 = 13$

9. x y

$x < 0$ and $y < 0$

10. $x + y$ $x - y$

Column A	Column B

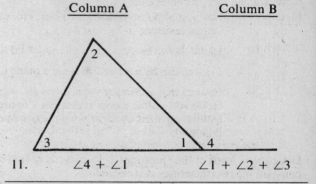

11. $\angle 4 + \angle 1$ $\angle 1 + \angle 2 + \angle 3$

Mark received either an 80% or a 90% on each of four physics tests.

12.   Mark's average   85%

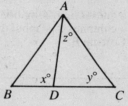

From D, any point on BC, AD is drawn

13. x y

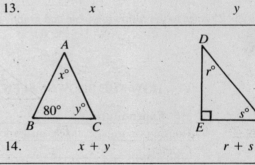

14. $x + y$ $r + s$

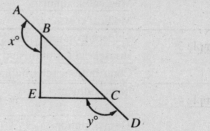

Legs EC and EB of right $\triangle BEC$ are equal in length and $ABCD$ is a straight line.

15. x y

Directions: Each of the Questions 16–30 has five answer choices. For each of these questions, select the best of the answer choices given.

16. If a roast that requires 1 hour and 40 minutes of roasting time has been in the oven for 55 minutes, how many more minutes of roasting time are required?

    (A) 15
    (B) 20
    (C) 30
    (D) 45
    (E) 50

17. City A is 200 miles west of City B and City C is 150 miles directly north of City B. What is the shortest distance (in miles) between City C and City A?

    (A) $50\sqrt{7}$
    (B) 175
    (C) 250
    (D) 300
    (E) 350

18. A square carpet with an area of 169 square feet must have 2 feet cut off one of its edges in order to be a perfect fit for a rectangular room. What is the area (in square feet) of this rectangular room?

    (A) 117
    (B) 121
    (C) 143
    (D) 165
    (E) 167

19. A lamp is manufactured to sell for $35.00, which yields a profit of 25% of cost. If the profit is to be reduced to 15% of cost, the new retail price will be

    (A) $21.00
    (B) $28.00
    (C) $31.50
    (D) $32.20
    (E) $43.00

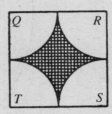

20. In the square $QRST$ above, $QR = 4$. Find the shaded area if Q, R, S, and T are the centers of the arcs that constitute the figure.

    (A) 16
    (B) 4π
    (C) $16 - 4\pi$
    (D) $16 - 2\pi$
    (E) $16 - 16\pi$

Questions 21–25 refer to the following table and graph.

HOW THE BROWNS SPENT THEIR MONEY LAST YEAR

Expenditures	
Housing (mortgage, taxes, insurance, utilities)	$13,750
Clothing	1,300
Medical insurance	1,500
Medical costs	2,600
Student loan repayments	4,200
Household furniture and appliances	1,700
Contributions (charitable, political)	750
Entertainment	2,200
Food	4,000
Transportation	3,000
Total expenditures	**$35,000**

HOW THE AVERAGE AMERICAN SPENDS MONEY

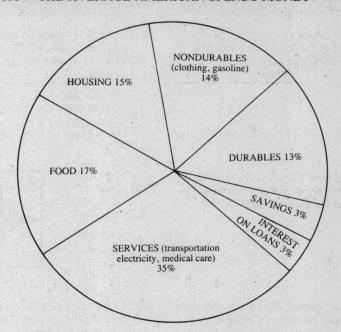

21. For a family with an annual income of $30,000, how much would be put into savings according to the figures for the average American?

    (A) $90
    (B) $300
    (C) $900
    (D) $3000
    (E) $9000

22. How much, out of every dollar spent, does the average American spend for housing?

    (A) 5¢

    (B) $7\frac{1}{2}$¢

    (C) 10¢

    (D) $12\frac{1}{2}$¢

    (E) 15¢

23. How does the expenditure for food by the Browns compare with the way the average American spends for food?

    (A) The Browns spend 5.6% less.
    (B) The Browns spend 5.6% more.
    (C) The Browns spend 9% less.
    (D) The Browns spend 13% less.
    (E) The Browns spend 13% more.

24. What part of the Browns expenditures is spent for medical care and medical insurance?

    (A) $\dfrac{15}{350}$

    (B) $\dfrac{41}{350}$

    (C) $\dfrac{26}{350}$

    (D) $\dfrac{35}{100}$

    (E) $\dfrac{41}{100}$

25. How does the spending for housing compare with the spending for food by the average American?

    (A) 2% more for housing
    (B) 2% less for food
    (C) Out of every dollar spent, two cents more is spent for food.
    (D) Out of every dollar spent, two cents less is spent for food.
    (E) Out of every dollar spent, two cents more is spent for housing.

26. When 6 gallons of gasoline are put into a car, the indicator goes from $\frac{1}{4}$ to $\frac{5}{8}$. The total capacity of the gasoline tank is

    (A) 12
    (B) 14
    (C) 15
    (D) 16
    (E) 30

27. A pile of steel plates is 2.75 feet high. If each plate is 0.375 inches thick, the number of steel plates in this pile is

    (A) 7
    (B) 8
    (C) 14
    (D) 88
    (E) more than 88

28. At c cents per orange, what is the price in dollars for 1 dozen oranges?

    (A) $12c$

    (B) $\frac{c}{12}$

    (C) $\frac{12}{100c}$

    (D) $\frac{c}{100}$

    (E) $\frac{12c}{100}$

29. A pipe can fill a swimming pool in h hours. What part of the pool is filled in x hours?

    (A) hx

    (B) $\frac{h}{x}$

    (C) $\frac{x}{h}$

    (D) $h + x$

    (E) $\frac{hx}{2}$

30. How many cc. of water must be added to 100 cc. of 80% solution of boric acid to reduce it to a 50% solution?

    (A) 30
    (B) 40
    (C) 50
    (D) 60
    (E) 84

S T O P

IF YOU FINISH BEFORE TIME HAS ELAPSED, CHECK YOUR WORK ON THIS SECTION OF THE TEST ONLY. DO NOT GO ON TO THE NEXT SECTION OF THE TEST UNTIL TIME IS UP FOR THIS SECTION.

Answer Key

Note: The answers to the quantitative sections are keyed to the corresponding review areas in the Mathematics Review (Chapter 11). The numbers in parentheses after each answer refer to the math topic(s) covered by that particular question.

Section 1   Verbal

1.	B	11.	E	21.	C	31.	D
2.	E	12.	C	22.	C	32.	B
3.	B	13.	E	23.	B	33.	A
4.	D	14.	E	24.	A	34.	B
5.	A	15.	B	25.	B	35.	B
6.	C	16.	C	26.	C	36.	A
7.	C	17.	D	27.	D	37.	D
8.	C	18.	D	28.	C	38.	D
9.	A	19.	E	29.	E		
10.	C	20.	A	30.	C		

Section 2   Verbal

1.	D	11.	D	21.	E	31.	D
2.	C	12.	A	22.	D	32.	B
3.	B	13.	C	23.	C	33.	E
4.	B	14.	B	24.	E	34.	B
5.	C	15.	D	25.	C	35.	E
6.	A	16.	B	26.	B	36.	E
7.	E	17.	D	27.	B	37.	C
8.	C	18.	E	28.	A	38.	E
9.	A	19.	E	29.	D		
10.	C	20.	C	30.	E		

Section 3   Quantitative

1.	A (I-H)	9.	C (III-A)	17.	C (I-B)	25.	B (I-G, IV)
2.	B (I-B, D)	10.	B (II-B)	18.	B (II-G)	26.	A (III-G)
3.	A (I-D, H)	11.	A (III-C, G)	19.	C (II-B)	27.	D (II-B)
4.	B (I-B, C)	12.	B (II-B-5)	20.	A (I-A)	28.	D (III-D)
5.	D (I-B)	13.	B (III-G)	21.	C (IV)	29.	A (III-G)
6.	D (II-G)	14.	B (III-C)	22.	A (IV)	30.	D (II-B)
7.	C (I-B, II-A)	15.	C (III-F)	23.	B (I, IV)		
8.	D (III-B)	16.	D (I-F)	24.	C (I-D, IX)		

Section 4   Quantitative

1.	C (II-B)	9.	B (III-D)	17.	B (I-B)	25.	C (IV-C)
2.	A (I-B)	10.	C (III-C)	18.	C (II-C)	26.	C (IV-C)
3.	C (II-A)	11.	C (I-G)	19.	A (I-D)	27.	B (III-G)
4.	A (I)	12.	B (II-A-5)	20.	E (I-F)	28.	E (III-D)
5.	B (I-H)	13.	C (I-H)	21.	C (IV-C)	29.	B (II-D)
6.	D (I-H)	14.	C (III-B)	22.	E (IV-C)	30.	A (II-D)
7.	D (II-G)	15.	C (I-H)	23.	D (IV-C)		
8.	C (III-C)	16.	A (III-G)	24.	E (II-E)		

Section 5   Analytical

1.	B	8.	C	15.	B	22.	C
2.	E	9.	D	16.	A	23.	B
3.	A	10.	A	17.	B	24.	D
4.	D	11.	B	18.	C	25.	C
5.	B	12.	A	19.	C		
6.	C	13.	C	20.	A		
7.	C	14.	C	21.	D		

Section 6   Analytical

1.	E	8.	C	15.	D	22.	A
2.	C	9.	A	16.	C	23.	C
3.	D	10.	D	17.	E	24.	E
4.	E	11.	A	18.	E	25.	A
5.	B	12.	C	19.	D		
6.	D	13.	B	20.	B		
7.	C	14.	A	21.	C		

Section 7   Quantitative

1.	A (I-H)	9.	B (I-H)	17.	C (III-D)	25.	C (I-D, IV)
2.	C (I-B, I-H)	10.	B (II-B)	18.	C (III-G)	26.	D (I-B)
3.	C (I-B, I-D)	11.	C (III-D)	19.	D (I-D)	27.	D (I-C)
4.	A (I-H)	12.	D (I-G)	20.	C (III-G)	28.	E (II-E)
5.	C (II-A)	13.	A (III-D)	21.	C (IV)	29.	C (II-C)
6.	C (I-B, I-C, I-G, I-H)	14.	A (III-D)	22.	E (IV)	30.	D (II-C)
7.	B (II-A)	15.	C (III-A)	23.	A (I-D, IV)		
8.	C (II-A)	16.	D (II-E)	24.	B (I-B, IV)		

Answer Explanations

Section 1

1. **B.** The columnist was *acerbic* (bitingly sarcastic) in writing of those who provoked or *irritated* him.
Note the use of *but* to establish the contrast between the two clauses, and the use of *even* to indicate that the missing word is stronger than *bitter*.

2. **E.** By using diplomacy and flattery, the promoters hope to *inveigle* (beguile; cajole) the *obviously* unwilling performer. *Inveigle* has overtones of persuading someone against his or her better judgment.
Choices B and C are clearly incorrect. The use of tact and flattery would not *intimidate* (frighten) or *shame* someone into taking an action. Similarly, Choices A and D are incorrect, since the use of tact and flattery would not necessarily lure the person into a hopeless or compromising position (*entrapment*) or tease and torment that person into giving in (*tantalization*).

3. **B.** In reputation he was a *guileless* or undeceitful person; in real life he showed himself to have been *hypocritical* or deceptive.
Note the use of *although* to signal the contrast.

4. **D.** Orlando shuns criticism, preferring *obscurity* or inconspicuousness. His reaction is so strong that even *anonymity* (obscurity carried to an extreme) would be preferable to further critical exposure.
Note how the intensifier *even* indicates that Orlando's desire is being taken to an extreme.

5. **A.** The off-Broadway and Broadway theatres are contrasted here. The former has *manifested* or shown a talent for improvisation, extemporaneous or spontaneous performance. The latter has manifested no such talent for *spontaneity*.
Note the use of *whereas* to establish the contrast.

6. C.   Particles have no need to be wound up because the property of spinning (*rotation*) is built into their makeup: it is *intrinsic*.

7. C.   That the interrogator is subtle in discrimination or judgment indicates her ability to conduct matters with *finesse*; that she is *expeditious* (efficient and prompt) in manner indicates her ability to conduct matters with "dispatch" (speed).

8. C.   A *ream* is a unit of quantity for *paper*; a *cord* is a unit of quantity for *wood*.

(Defining Characteristic)

9. A.   To *smart* is to feel *pain*; to *grieve* is to feel *sorrow*. Note that in this instance *smart* is a verb, not an adjective. Remember, you can always tell what parts of speech the capitalized words are by identifying the parts of speech in the answer choices.

(Action and Significance)

10. C.   A new growth of *bamboo* is a *shoot*; a new growth of a *bean* plant is a *sprout*.

(Defining Characteristic)

11. E.   By definition, a *missile* is *deflected* when it turns aside from its original direction. Likewise, someone's *attention* is *distracted* when it turns aside from its original direction.

(Definition)

12. C.   By definition, an excess of once-pleasing flavors *cloys* or sates the *palate* (seat of the sense of taste). An excess of once-tempting foodstuffs *surfeits* or sates the *appetite*.

(Definition)

13. E.   A *pratfall* is a humiliating mishap that causes you to feel *embarrassment*. A *windfall* is an unexpected piece of good fortune that causes you to feel *jubilation*.

(Cause and Effect)

14. E.   Someone *mulish* (stubborn) is not characterized by *pliancy* (readiness to yield). Someone *shrewish* (ill-tempered) is not characterized by *amiability*.

(Antonym Variant)

15. B.   By definition, a *minatory* statement menaces or *threatens*. A *laudatory* statement *praises* or commends.

(Definition)

16. C.   When *clouds scud*, they move swiftly, as if driven.
When *water races*, it moves swiftly as well.

(Definition)

17. D.   Houston believed that the battle had to begin at the graduate level "to mitigate fear" (relieve *apprehension*) of race-mixing and miscegenation that might otherwise have caused the judges to rule against the NAACP-sponsored complaints.

18. D.   Since the Regents responded to their defeat in *Sipuel* v. *Board of Regents of the University of Oklahoma* by separating black and white students in cafeterias and classrooms (thus subverting the effect of the decision), it seems likely that their reaction to the decision was one of *distinct displeasure*.

19. E.   The 1950 McLaurin decision was one of the decisions which provided legal precedents for the 1954 Brown decision.
Choice A is incorrect. *McLaurin* preceded *Brown I*. Therefore, it could not have superseded a decision that had yet to be made.
Choice B is incorrect. *Brown I* followed *McLaurin*. Therefore, it could not have set a precedent for *McLaurin*.
Choice C is incorrect. *Brown I* reversed *Plessy* v. *Ferguson*. It built on *Mclaurin*.
Choice D is incorrect. *McLaurin* preceded *Brown I*. Therefore, it could not have limited the application of a decision that had yet to be made.

20. A.   The author states plainly that the United States Supreme Court lacked the power to enforce its decisions and implies that without federal power (intervention by the executive) the desired social changes would not have taken place. Therefore, it seems probable that the author would view such a claim with *marked disagreement*.

21. C.   The author states that *Brown II* limited the effectiveness of *Brown I* by allowing southern states a chance to delay desegregating. This suggests that, but for *Brown II*, *Brown I* might have had a more significant impact on segregation.

22. C.   Taken as a whole, the passage deals with the entire struggle to desegregate American education, from the NAACP legal maneuvers of the 30's to the executive actions of the 50's and 60's. Only this title is broad enough to cover the passage as a whole.
Choice A is incorrect. The passage deals with the long legal maneuvers far more than it deals with executive intervention.
Choice B is incorrect. The passage deals with much more than *Brown* v. *Board of Education*.
Choices D and E are incorrect. They ignore the central subject of desegregation.

23. B.   The separate-but-equal doctrine established by *Plessy* v. *Ferguson* allows the existence of racially-segregated schools.

24. A.   In assessing the possible effects on judges of race-mixing in the lower grades, Houston was *psychologically canny*, shrewd in seeing potential dangers and in figuring strategies to avoid these dangers.

25. B.   The bulk of the passage records step by step what happens in the process of the formation of a star from a small region of interstellar gas. Thus, it *depicts the successive stages* of the process.

26. C.   To the author the concept is both simple and traditional, dating as it does from Newton's time.

27. D.   You can answer this question by the process of elimination.
Question I is answerable on the basis of the passage. As the region's density increases, its gravitational field increases in strength. Therefore, you can eliminate Choice B.
Question II is not answerable on the basis of the passage. The passage nowhere states what disturbs the gas. Therefore, you can eliminate Choices C and E.
Question III is answerable on the basis of the passage. The end result of the process is the formation of a gravitationally bound object. Therefore, you can eliminate Choice A.
Only Choice D is left. It is the correct answer.

28. C.   The opposite of to *hamper* (impede or hinder) is to *facilitate* (make easy).
Think of "hampering progress."

29. E.   The opposite of *urbane* (worldly; suave; sophisticated) is *naive* (unsophisticated).
Word Parts Clue: *Urb-* means city. *Urbane* means having the polish of a city-dweller.
Think of "an urbane suavity."

30. C.   The opposite of *demise* (death) is *birth*.
Think of "lamenting someone's demise."

31. D.   The opposite of a *pariah* or person rejected by society is an *idol* or person greatly loved by society.
Think of being "shunned as a pariah."

32. B.   To *prostrate* someone is to overcome him, to weaken him. Its opposite is to *strengthen*.
Note that a quick glance at the answer choices reveals that you are dealing with *prostrate* the verb, not *prostrate* the adjective.
Think of being "prostrated by grief."

33. A.   The opposite of *contentious* (quarrelsome, belligerent) is *amenable* (readily brought to yield, tractable).
Note that *contentious* derives from the verb to *contend* (to struggle or argue), not the adjective *content*.
Think of "a contentious argument."

34. B.   The opposite of a *debacle* (downfall; failure; collapse) is a *success*.
Think of "the Wall Street debacle of 1987."

35. B.   The opposite of *hapless* (unlucky) is *fortunate*.
Think of "hapless unfortunates."

36. A.   The opposite of to *exacerbate* (to worsen or make more harsh) is to *alleviate* or lighten.
Think of "exacerbating a quarrel."

37. D.   The opposite of *probity* (uprightness; integrity) is *depravity* (debasement; corruption).
Think of "unimpeachable probity."

38. D.   The opposite of *baneful* (pernicious; ruinous; deadly) is *salubrious* (healthful; beneficial).
Think of "the baneful effects of slander."

Section 2

1. D.   In contrast to what might have been expected, the candidate *welcomed* further interviews.
Note how the use of *even though* indicates a contrast between one idea and another, setting up a reversal of a thought.

2. **C.** Soap operas and situation comedies are derivative of contemporary culture: they take their elements from that culture. Therefore, they serve as *indices* (signs or indications) of what is going on in that culture; they both point to and point up the social attitudes and values they portray.

Note that the soap operas and comedies here cannot be *determinants of* our society's attitudes and values: they derive from these attitudes and values; they do not determine them.

3. **B.** The critics *charge* that Perry has published only *anecdotes* of his observations and not detailed analyses.

Note that *critics* would be unlikely to *applaud* the publication of *rumors* or *apologize* for Perry's publication of *fabrications* or lies. Thus, you can eliminate Choices C and E. Similarly, *popular magazines* would be unlikely to publish scientific *hypotheses* or examples of *scholarship*. You therefore can rule out Choices A and D as well.

4. **B.** The scenes of suffering *belie* (contradict) the *reality* of the proclamations of wealth.

5. **C.** Whatever word you choose here must apply equally well both to slander and to counterfeit money. People who would not make up a slanderous statement *circulate* slander by passing it on. So too people who would not coin or make counterfeit money *circulate* counterfeit money by passing it on.

Note how the extended metaphor here influences the writer's choice of words.

6. **A.** A passionate nature hates compromise (finds it *odious*) because it seems a surrender. An intellectual nature hates compromise because it seems a *confusion*, mixing together things that to the intellect are inherently distinct.

7. **E.** Milton's comment that he wrote prose with his left hand appears to belittle the writing of prose. We might *discount* or lessen the strength of this apparent criticism if we said Milton meant the remark ironically. However, we have not done so. Instead, we have used apparently negative comments like Milton's to *buttress* or support our own prejudices against prose.

8. **C.** One *confines* a *prisoner* to keep him in prison. One *detains* a *suspect* to keep him in custody.

(Function)

9. **A.** A *swatch* is a sample patch of *fabric*. A *chip* is a sample of *paint*.

(Function)

10. **C.** A *tendril* is a slender extension reaching out from a *vine*. A *pseudopod* is a slender extension reaching out from an *amoeba*.

(Part to Whole)

11. **D.** One *battens* or fastens a *hatch* (door leading down to a ship compartment) to close it. One *latches* a *door* to close it.

(Function)

12. **A.** *Events* that are *contemporaneous* (occurring within the same time frame) exist in temporal reference to one another. *Objects* that are *adjacent* exist in spatial reference to one another.

(Defining Characteristic)

13. **C.** A *limerick* is a kind of *poem*. A *catch* is a kind of *song*.

Note how simple the relationship of the original pair of words is. Questions toward the end of an analogy set seldom appear this easy. This should alert you to be on the lookout for something particularly deceptive among the answer choices. In this case, *catch* is used in an uncommon manner.

(Class and Member)

14. **B.** A *retainer* or attendant is part of a *retinue* (body of attendants). A *witch* is part of a *coven* (group of witches)

(Group and Member)

15. **D.** A *hero* is greeted with an *accolade* or laudatory notice. A *laughingstock* is greeted with *ridicule* or mockery.

(Defining Characteristic)

16. **B.** A *rider* is an attachment added to a legislative *bill* to meet a particular purpose. An *endorsement* is an attachment added to an insurance *policy* to meet a particular purpose.

Note the use of secondary meanings of *rider*, *endorsement*, and *bill*.

(Defining Characteristic)

17. **D.** The author cites Meredith's intelligence (*brilliance*) and his splendor of language (*linguistic grandeur*).

18. E.   Rather than refuting the claim, the author clearly acknowledges Meredith's inability to evoke the reader's sympathy.
Choice A is incorrect. From the start the author points out how Meredith leaves readers cold.
Choice B is incorrect. The author reiterates Meredith's virtues, citing muscular intelligence and literary merit.
Choice C is incorrect. The author quotes several such imagined criticisms.
Choice D is incorrect. The author indicates that if readers choose to avoid dealing with Meredith they shall be doing a disservice to the cause of criticism.
Only Choice E remains. It is the correct answer.

19. E.   Speaking of the "challenge and excitement of the critical problem as such," the author clearly finds the prospect of appraising Meredith critically to be stirring and *invigorating*.

20. C.   The author wishes us to be able to recognize the good qualities of Meredith's work while at the same time we continue to find it personally unsympathetic. Thus, she would agree that criticism should enable us to appreciate the virtues of works we dislike.
Choices A, B, and E are unsupported by the passage.
Choice D is incorrect. While the author wishes the reader to be aware of Meredith's excellences, she does not suggest that the reader should ignore those qualities in Meredith that make his work unsympathetic. Rather, she wishes the reader to come to appreciate the very ambivalence of his critical response.

21. E.   You can answer this question by the process of elimination.
Question I is answerable on the basis of the passage. Because different alleles of a gene are not normally present within a single cell, DNA carrying an allele that originated in a different cell must be introduced into a bacterium via interbacterial transfer mechanisms in order for genetic variation to take place. Therefore, you can eliminate Choices B and D.
Question II is answerable on the basis of the passage. Cell death releases DNA into the environment; this free-floating DNA then makes its way into a new cell through the mechanism of transformation. Therefore, you can eliminate Choice A.
Question III is answerable on the basis of the passage. The illegitimate recombinational processes differ from homologous recombination in their ability to join together DNA segments that have little, if any, ancestral relationship. Therefore, you can eliminate Choice C.
Only Choice E is left. It is the correct answer.

22. D.   The passage serves as an introduction to the concept of illegitimate recombination in cells. To introduce this concept properly, the authors first must explain the other mechanisms which previously seemed to be "the only important mechanisms for generating biological diversity."
Choice A is incorrect. The passage introduces the concept of transposable genetic elements; it does not examine the evidence for their existence.
Choice B is incorrect. The passage indicates no such controversy.
Choice C is incorrect. It is far too vague.
Choice E is incorrect. It is unsupported by the passage.

23. C.   The so-called illegitimate recombinational processes are illegitimate because they do not follow the "legitimate" or accepted patterns for generating biological diversity. They *break the rules* of homologous recombination by joining together DNA segments that are not closely linked by ancestral relationship.

24. E.   The passage objectively explains the nature of a scientific phenomenon. Thus, it can best be described as *a dispassionate explication* (detailed description or exposition).
Choice A is incorrect. The main thrust of the passage is not to *refute* or disprove anything. In addition, its tone is far from *angry*.
Choice B is incorrect. The passage takes no sides; it is not *partisan*.
Choice C is incorrect. The passage does not vacillate; it is not *equivocal*. Neither does it support a position; it is not an *endorsement*.
Choice D is incorrect. The passage is expository and descriptive rather than *meditative*.

25. C.   In transformation, "free-floating" DNA enters a new cell by *penetrating* the cell wall and membrane. Thus, for transformation to occur, the cell wall and membrane must be *permeable*, capable of being penetrated.

26. B.   In transduction, the function of the virus is to "pick up fragments of the bacterial DNA" of one cell and "carry the DNA to other cells." This is analogous to the function of the *bee*, who picks up fragments of pollen from one flower and carries the pollen to other flowers in the process known as *pollination*.

27. B.   The passage opens with the statement that "genetic variation is *also* important in the evolution of lower organisms such as bacteria." From this one can reasonably infer that the authors have just been discussing the importance of genetic variation in the evolution of other sorts of organisms, specifically higher organisms.

28. A. To *condone* is to excuse. Its opposite is to *denounce*.
Think of "condoning a minor offense."

29. D. The opposite of *antithetical* (opposing) is *supportive*.
Think of "warring antithetical elements."

30. E. The opposite of *omniscience* (the quality of knowing everything) is *ignorance*.
Word Parts Clue: *Omni-* means all. *Sci-* means to know. *Omniscience* is the quality of knowing all.
Think of "divine omniscience."

31. D. The opposite of to *mollify* or soothe is to *provoke*.
Think of "mollifying hurt feelings."

32. B. The opposite of *gauche* (awkward; lacking in social grace or tact) is *tactful*.
Think of being embarrassed by "a gauche remark."

33. E. The opposite of a *diatribe* (abusive criticism) is *praise*.
Think of "a bitter diatribe."

34. B. The opposite of to *gainsay* or contradict is to *corroborate* or support.
Beware eye-catchers. To gainsay derives from to say *against*, not from to gain.
Think of "gainsaying an assertion."

35. E. The opposite of *prolixity* (wordiness) is *terseness* or brevity.
Think of "long-winded prolixity."

36. E. The opposite of *avid* (very eager) is *loath* (reluctant). Note that Choice E is the relatively uncommon adjective *loath*, not the verb to *loathe* or detest.
Think of "an avid reader."

37. C. To *repine* is to complain or express discontent. Its opposite is to *express satisfaction*.
Think of "repining the pains of old age."

38. E. The opposite of *salience* (prominence; noticeableness; emphasis) is *inconspicuousness*.
Think of "striking salience."

Section 3

1. A. $\sqrt{.04} = .2$
$(.2)^2 = .04$
$.2 > .04$

2. B. $\frac{7}{8} = 87\frac{1}{2}\%$

$\left(\frac{1}{2}\right)\left(\frac{7}{8}\right) = 42 + \%$

3. A. $\left(\frac{1}{2}\right)^2 = \left(\frac{1}{4}\right) = 25\%$

4. B. $\frac{0.7}{2} = \frac{7}{20} = .35$
$.35 > 0.3$

5. D. $\frac{X}{Y} \cdot \frac{Y}{X} = 1$
$\frac{X}{Y}$ may be equal to, smaller than, or larger than 1.

6. D. a could be equal to zero, or some positive fraction less than 1.
b could be some negative fraction more than -1.

7. C. $2x - \frac{y-5}{6} \div \frac{y-5}{3} - 4x$

$\frac{12x - y + 5}{6} \div \frac{y - 5 - 12x}{3}$

$\frac{12x - y + 5}{2^{6}} \cdot \frac{3^{1}}{y - 5 - 12x}$

$\frac{12x - y + 5}{2} \cdot \frac{1}{-12x + y - 5}$

$\frac{12x - y + 5}{2} \cdot \frac{-1}{12x - y + 5}$

or, $-\frac{1}{2}$ or -0.5

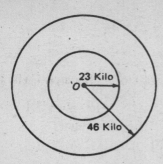

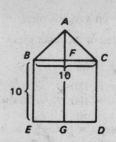

8. D. Center City is located at point O. Circleville could be located at any point on the circumference of the circle with the radius of 23 kilometers. Centerville could be located at any point on the circumference with radius of 46 kilometers. The distance from Circleville and Centerville could be the straight line distance from any point on the circumference of one of these circles to the other circle. Obviously there are innumerable possibilities.

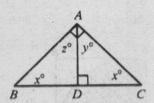

9. C. In right triangle ABC, $x = 45$. In right triangle ADC, $y = 45$. Therefore, $z = 45$.

10. B. $83x = 8383$
    $x = 101$ (Column A)

11. A. The area of triangle $ABC = \frac{1}{2}$ (leg × leg) = 12.5 or, (leg)² = 25. Therefore leg = 5. Area of square I or II = 5^2 or 25. Since $AB = BC = 5$, hypotenuse $AC = 5\sqrt{2}$. Area of square III = $(5\sqrt{2})^2$ or 50. Twice the area of ABC = 25 (given).

12. B. $x^2 - 5x + 6 = 0$
        $(x - 3)(x - 2) = 0$
            $x = 3, 2$
    The sum of the roots = 5.
    The product of the roots = 6.

13. B. Each side of square $BCDE = 10$
    Area of $ABC = 125 - 100$ or 25
    Area of $ABC = \frac{1}{2} (BC) (AF) = 25$
    $\frac{1}{2} (10) (AF) = 25$
    $AF = 5$
    $FG = BE = CD = 10$
    $AFG = 15$ and $2 (EB) = 20$

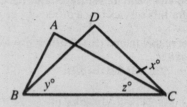

14. B. If $BD = DC$, then $y = x + z$ and $y > x$.

15. C. Area of circle $= \pi r^2$
    If the radius of circle B is twice the radius of circle A, then area of circle B is four times the area of circle A. Stated differently, four times the area of circle A = the area of circle B.

16. D. 1 kilogram = 2.2 pounds
    70 kilograms = (70) (2.2) or 154 pounds
    154 − 144 = 10 pounds increase

17. C. Class consists of $a + b$ pupils.
    Class consists of b girls.
    $\frac{b}{a + b}$ = part of class made of girls

18. B. (A) $(.25)^2 = .0625$

    (B) $\sqrt{\frac{1}{4}} = \frac{1}{2}$

    (C) $\left(\frac{1}{4}\right)^4 = \frac{1}{258}$

    (D) $.04 = \frac{4}{100}$

    (E) $\frac{1}{250} = \frac{1}{250}$

19. C. Let x = area of one piece.
$\frac{2}{3}x$ = area of the other piece.

$$x + \frac{2}{3}x = 60$$
$$3x + 2x = 180$$
$$5x = 180$$
$$x = 36$$

Other piece = $60 - 36 = 24$

20. A. The product of zero and any whole number is zero. If $y = 0$, then xyz cannot be equal to 240.

21. C. Note that New Jersey and California had the highest fees for first-office-visits in 1983 ($41), but New Jersey had a fee of $25 for the office-revisit while California had a $26 fee for the office-revisit.

22. A. In 1986 New York patients paid $51 for first-office-visits and in North Carolina patients paid $20 for this service, for a difference of $20.

23. B. Observe that there is a $10 difference for 1986 and 1983:
$35 - $25 and $31 - $21.

24. C. There was an increase of $4.00; $\frac{4}{21} = 19\%$.

Hint: Estimate the value of $\frac{4}{21}$ which is slightly

less than $\frac{4}{20}$ which equals $\frac{1}{5}$ or 20%.

25. B. There is no need for computation. Each had the same $22 fee.

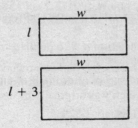

26. A. Area of original rectangle = lw
Area of new rectangle = $(l + 3)(w) =$
$lw + 3w$
Increase = $3w$

27. D. (1) $x + 2y = 1\frac{1}{3}$

(2) $x - y = \frac{1}{3}$

$-x + y = -\frac{1}{3}$ [multiply (2) by -1]

$x + 2y = 1\frac{1}{3}$ [equation (1)]

$3y = 1$ [addition]

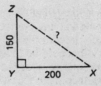

28. D. $(XZ)^2 = (150)^2 + (200)^2$
Or, note the ratio of legs
$$\frac{150}{200} = \frac{3}{4}$$
Therefore, the ratio of the sides of XYZ is
3:4:5. Since $YZ = 3(50)$ and $YX = 4(50)$, then
$XZ = 5(50)$ or 250.

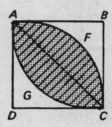

29. A. Draw AC.

Area of $\triangle ADC = \frac{10 \times 10}{2} = 50$

$ABCDFG$

$AFCD = \frac{1}{4}$ of circle

Area of this $\frac{1}{4}$ of circle $\frac{\pi(10)^2}{4} = 25\pi$

Shaded half above $AC = 25\pi - \triangle ADC$ or
$25\pi - 50$

Likewise shaded half below $AC = 25\pi - 50$

Entire shaded area = $50\pi - 100$

30. D. Let x = price of orchestra seat.

Then $\frac{x}{3}$ = price of balcony seat.

$600x$ = $ from all orchestra seats.

$450\left(\frac{x}{3}\right)$ = $ from all balcony seats.

$$600x + 150x = \$4,500$$
$$750x = \$4,500$$
$$x = \$6$$

Section 4

1. C. $x + 5 = 5$
    $x = 0$
    $5 - 0 = 5$ (Column A)

2. A. $\frac{1}{2} + \frac{1}{3} + \frac{1}{4} = \frac{13}{12} = 1\frac{1}{12}$

3. C. $\frac{1}{x} \div \frac{1}{\frac{1}{x}}$ or $\frac{1}{x} \div \frac{x}{1} = \frac{1}{x} \cdot \frac{1}{x} = \frac{1}{x^2}$

4. A. $\dfrac{3 \text{ yards, 1 foot, 3 inches}}{3} = 1$ yard, 5 inches
    or 41 inches.

5. B. $2^3 = (2)(2)(2) = 8$
    $3^2 = (3)(3) = 9$

6. D. $a^6 = (a)\,(a)\,(a)\,(a)\,(a)\,(a)$
    $6a^5 = (6)\,(a)\,(a)\,(a)\,(a)\,(a)$
    The quantity in Column A would be equal to
    the quantity in Column B only if the value of a
    were equal to 6.

7. D.   The value of x could be 40 or 80.

8. C.   If $y = 50$, then the measure of angle $DCB = $
    100, and the measure of angle $ABC = 80$, and
    $x = 40$. Therefore $x + y = 90$.

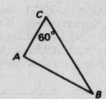

9. B.   The information given tells us that the measure
    of angle $A >$ the measure of angle B. Since A
    $+ B = 120$, the measure (in degrees) of angle
    A is greater than 60, and angle B has a measure
    of less than 60. Side AC lies opposite the small-
    est angle of the triangle.

10. C.   The sum of the lengths of 2 adjacent sides of a
    parallelogram equals one-half the perimeter.

11. C.   The sum $= 30 + x$
    The average $= \dfrac{30 + x}{6} = 6$
    $30 + x = 36$
    $x = 6$

12. B. $(x - y)(x + y) = x^2 - y^2$
    $x^2 - y^2 = 100 - 25 = 75$ (Column A)

13. C. $\dfrac{3}{\sqrt{3}} \cdot \dfrac{\sqrt{3}}{\sqrt{3}} = \dfrac{3\sqrt{3}}{3} = \sqrt{3}$

14. C. $AB + BC = 2$ units
    $AD - CD = 3$ units $- 1$ unit

15. C. $\sqrt{0.01} = 0.1$
    $(x)(0.1) = 1$
    $x = 10$

16. A.   The distance covered by a wheel when it makes
    one revolution is equal to the circumference of
    the wheel. Note 28 inches $= \dfrac{28}{12}$ feet.
    Circumference $= \pi(\text{diameter})$
    $\left(\dfrac{22}{7}\right)\left(\dfrac{28}{12}\right)\left(\dfrac{9}{1}\right) = $ distance (in feet) covered
    by nine turns
    $\dfrac{22}{7} \cdot \dfrac{28}{12} \cdot \dfrac{9}{1} = 66$ feet

17. B.   Find the value of D in terms of C.
    Since $C = \frac{2}{3}D$, then $\frac{3}{2}C = D$.
    Since $\frac{2}{3}C = B$ (given) we now have values of
    D and B in terms of C. What part of D is B
    requires
    $\dfrac{B}{D} = \dfrac{\frac{2}{3}C}{\frac{3}{2}C} = \dfrac{\frac{2}{3}}{\frac{3}{2}}$ or $\dfrac{2}{3} \cdot \dfrac{2}{3}$ or $\dfrac{4}{9}$

18. C. $\dfrac{\text{quantity removed}}{\text{capacity}} = $ part removed $= \dfrac{a}{g}$

19. A.   Notice that each group was reduced by $10.
    The greatest rate of discount would be for the
    group which was originally the least expensive.
    $\dfrac{10}{60} = 16.6\%$
    $\dfrac{10}{65} = 15.4\%$
    $\dfrac{10}{70} = 14.3\%$
    $\dfrac{10}{75} = 13.3\%$
    $\dfrac{10}{80} = 12.5\%$

20. E.   The difference is obtained by subtracting the lowest temperature, -41, from the highest, $+22$. In order to subtract -41, change its sign to $+$ and proceed as in addition:

$+22$
$+$
$\ominus41$
$+63$

The absolute value is the value without regard to sign; thus, the absolute value of $+63$ is 63. The absolute value of the difference is 63.

21. C. $(A) = .39$ kilograms per liter of water
$(B) = .42$ kilograms per liter of water
$(C) = .475$ kilograms per liter of water
$(D) = .4$ kilograms per liter of water
$(E) = .375$ kilograms per liter of water

22. E.   The graph indicates that at 23°C, 0.375 kilograms of potassium nitrate will dissolve in 1 liter of water. In 10 liters of water 3.75 kilograms will dissolve.

23. D.   Since the chart indicates the solubility of 0.1 kilograms per liter at 31°C and 0.25 kilograms per liter at 65°C, the difference is 0.15 kilograms per liter of water.

$$\frac{\text{difference}}{\text{original}} = \frac{0.15}{0.1} = \frac{15}{10} = 1\frac{1}{2} = 150\%$$

24. E.   If .35 kilograms dissolve in 1 liter of water at 25°C, then 35 kilograms dissolve in 100 liters of water at 25°C.
The rest of this problem involves a direct proportion.
Let $x = $ number of moles than can be dissolved in 100 liters at 25°C.

$$\frac{.07456 \text{ kilograms}}{1 \text{ mole}} = \frac{35 \text{ kilograms}}{x \text{ moles}}$$

$.07456x = 35$
$7456x = 3,500,000$
$x = 469 +$ moles,

or approximately 500 moles

25. C.   The salts mentioned in A, B, D, and E intersect on the graph somewhere between 15°C and 85°C.

26. C.   If the perimeter $= 16$, each side $= 4$ and the area $= (4)^2$
$(4)^2 = 16$

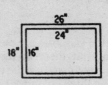

27. B.   Area of picture $= (24 \text{ inches}) (16 \text{ inches}) = 384$ sq. in.
Area of picture and frame $= (26 \text{ inches}) (18 \text{ inches}) = 468$ sq. in.
Area of frame $= 468 - 384 = 84$ sq. in.
Let $x = $ number of times the area of the picture is greater than the area of the frame.
$84x = 384$
$x = 4.5 +$

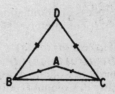

28. E. $\angle D = 70°$
$\angle B + \angle C = 110°$
$\angle B = \angle C = 55°$
$\angle ABC = 27°$
$\angle ABC = \angle ACB = 27°$
$\angle ABC = \angle ACB = 55°$
$\angle A = 180° - 55° = 125°$

29. B.   If a candidate received 71 votes, there could be a tie between 4 candidates. If one candidate received 72 votes there could be no tie and it is possible for that candidate to have thus received more votes than any other candidates.

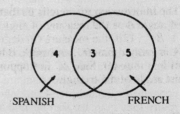

SPANISH   FRENCH

30. A.   We must account for 12 who speak these languages. Note that 3 must speak both languages.
$$\frac{3}{15} = \frac{1}{5}$$

Section 5

1–4. When all the variables are mentioned in a problem of this kind, there's a very easy way to attach the right names to the right things. Make a chart with three columns: type of book, author, and publisher. As you read through the puzzle, fill in the chart, putting names that belong together on the same line. After reading the four statements, your chart will look like this:

Type	Author	Publisher
	R	S
Spy		H
Sci Fi	B	not B
Gothic	H	

By the process of elimination, you can now fill in the chart completely. The result will look like this:

Type	Author	Publisher
Murder	R	S
Spy	G	H
Sci Fi	B	P
Gothic	H	B

1. B. By inspection of the completed chart shown above.

2. E. Can also be read directly from the chart.

3. A. John buys books by Burchfield and Hopper, and does not buy Gorky and Rothko. Choice A applies to Rothko, all others to Burchfield or Hopper.

4. D. The only disadvantage of the chart we constructed above is that you may have to construct it again to solve a question like this. If you do so, leaving out statement (1), you can get options I and III, but for option II, you can't get further than knowing that Sparrow published the mystery, the spy thriller, *or* the Gothic romance.

5–7. Basically this selection and its questions illustrate the general law of diminishing returns. If increasing amounts of capital are applied to constant amounts of land and labor, the total return may increase, but beyond a certain point the increase will not be in proportion to the inrease in investment.

5. B. The limit of diminishing returns has not yet been reached.

6. C. The limit of diminishing returns has been reached.

7. C. This actually states that the law of diminishing returns is operating in the situation described in the passage.

8–12. The construction of a calendar for the months of December, January and February may seem to be the best way to answer these questions. However, we may avoid this time-consuming activity by constructing the following table of the days when each ship will be in port. Thus,

Ship *W* will be in port on days 1, 9, 17, 25, 33, 41, 49, 57, and 65.

Ship *X* will be in port on days 1, 12, 25, 36, 49, 60, and 73.

Ship *Y* will be in port on days 1, 6, 11, 16, 21, 26, 31, 36, 41, 46, 51, 56, 61, and 66.

Ship *Z* will be in port on days 1, 2, 9, 16, 23, 30, 37, 44, 51, 58, and 65.

An examination of this list will enable the student to answer the questions.

8. C. Since December 23 was a Sunday, December 31 will be a Monday and will be the 9th day. Ships *W* and *Z* will be in port on December 31.

9. D. Ship *W* will be moored alongside ship *Z* on the 9th day, ship *X* on the 25th day, ship *Y* on the 41st day, ship *X* on the 49th day, and ship *Z* on the 65th day.

10. A. On no occasion will three ships be moored at the pier.

11. B. More departures will take place on Monday than on any other day. Sundays come on days 1, 8, 15, 22, 29, 36, 43, 50, 57, and 64. Including the sailings on December 23, there will be 7 Sunday sailings. Similarly, there will be 13 Monday sailings, 3 Tuesday sailings, 5 Wednesday sailings, 4 Thursday sailings, 3 Friday sailings, and 4 Saturday sailings.

12. A. From the chart above, we can see that Tuesday and Friday will be least busy.

13–16. This welter of confusing information can be reduced to a table showing what services are available on Friday and Monday in each state. You *don't* have to include Saturday—everything is closed Saturday everywhere.

	Friday:	Monday:
Banks	NA, NS	NA, NW
State gov't offices	NW	NA, NS, NW
Sanit—MWF areas	NW	NA, NS
Sanit—TTS areas	—	—
P.O./fed. offices	NA, NS, NW	NA, NS, NW

13. C. A glance at the table will show you that each service is available on either Friday or Monday, or both, in New Wales, except TTS sanitation pickup.

14. C. The post office and state government offices are open Monday in all three states, but banks are open only in New Albion and New Wales.

15. B. For MWF pickup areas in New Wales, all services are available Friday except banking. In MWF pickup areas in the other two states, neither trash pickup nor state government offices are available, though banking is. In TTS areas in all three states, sanitation pickup is not available Friday; banking is not available in new Wales, and state government offices are closed in the other two states. (The fact that sanitation pickup is not normally available Friday in TTS areas is irrelevant—the question states that Mr. Rudolph found all services but one available.)

16. A. This question is different. Everything is available Monday in New Albion except trash pickup in TTS areas—but this is *not* a "deviation from normal service." The table will confirm that there is some deviation from normal service for all of the other choices given.

17–22. A four-by-four grid listing prizes, breeds, owners, and dog names will be needed. Using the information given and the process of elimination, you can come up with the following chart:

PRIZE	BREED	OWNER	NAME
1	C	H	K
2	B	E	M
3	A	G	J
4	D	F	L

The questions themselves are fairly straightforward.

17. B. Once statement (6) identifies the 4th prize winner and you determine that Mr. Grossman's dog therefore won 3rd prize, it follows that, since Max won 2nd prize, Ms. Huntley's Kelly was the collie that won first prize.

18. C. The same reasoning process used in question 17 makes Mr. Grossman's dog the Airedale that won third prize.

19. C. Here it's possible for more than one statement to give correct information. It turns out that I is false because Mr. Edwards's dog won 2nd prize and the Airedale 3rd. II is false because Mr. Grossman's dog *is* Jack. III correctly identifies the winners of 2nd, 3rd, and 4th prizes.

20. A. This can be read from the diagram.

21. D. The easiest procedure is to jot down the information given in the specified statements:

PRIZE	BREED	OWNER	NAME
1	C		
2			M
	A		J
4	D	F	

Although much remains ambiguous without statements (2) and (7) (for example, who owns which dog), statements I, II, and III all follow by a process of elimination.

22. C. As for question 21, jot down a simple chart based only on the specified statements:

PRIZE	BREED	OWNER	NAME
1	C		
2			M
3 or 4		G	
1, 3 or 4		H	K

Given the ambiguities arising from the incomplete nature of the information, statement III cannot be deduced. Statements I and II may be deduced, however.

23-24. Engrave this in your memory indelibly: from a statement in the form "All A are B" or "If A, then B," *one and only one* valid conclusion can be drawn: "If not B, then not A." So: from statement (1), the only valid conclusion is, "A student who does not wear Calvert Kreem jeans does not major in philosophy," and from statement (3), the only valid conclusion is, "If Mary doesn't major in history, Jack doesn't major in philosophy." The statements, "If not A, then not B" and "If B, then A" are *not valid*.

23. B. Statement (2) says that none of the students in the Marching and Chowder Society wears Calvert Kreem jeans, so they are "not B" in statement (1); the conclusion that they do not major in philosophy is *valid*. Choice A is incorrect: it means only that Mary is not in the Marching and Chowder Society (statement 2) and says nothing about her jeans. Choice C is an "if B, then A" inference, "If Mary majors in history, Jack Majors in philosophy" (and therefore can't be in the Marching and Chowder Society because of his jeans). There's no basis for E.

24. D. I and III are correct "if not B, then not A" conclusions based on statements (3) and (1), respectively. II can establish only that Jack *may* wear Calvert Kreem Jeans or major in history, neither of which validly implies that he does not major in philosophy.

25. C.   The cost to the chemical company (choice C) would be a concern of the company, not of the residents. The residents are primarily concerned about the possible negative effects of the fumes. They might reasonably be expected to be concerned about stopping the fumes (choice A), the adequacy of the original tests (choice B), possible harm to plants and animals (choice D), and possible long-term effects of the fumes (choice E).

Section 6

1-4.   The conditions can be diagrammed as in the accompanying figure.

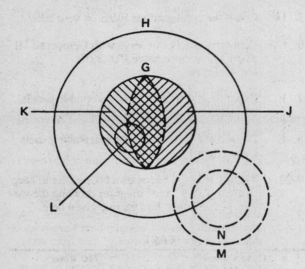

Notice that the positions of several elements (M,N, and whether there is an overlap between J and K) are uncertain; these are indicated by broken lines.

1. E.   From the diagram; statement (6) says that all M's must lie outside the G's; but all N's must lie inside the M's, according to statement (5). Since the only information about the M's is that they are *not* G's, none of the other statements, which attempt to put M's inside or outside the H's, can be deduced.

2. C.   This statement is inconsistent with the condition that no M's are G's. Choice A is possible—we could draw the G circle so that it coincided with the H circle. Choices B,D, and E are all possible, since we can draw M anywhere outside G.

3. D.   If you thought that statement (2) meant that no J's are K's, you were wrong; it states that all G's are J's or K's, but doesn't exclude the possibility that some G's are both and that J and K overlap. (Consider an analogous statement like "All voters in my town voted for Republicans or Democrats.") So statement (4) doesn't imply the statement given here, and I is out. It is *possible* that no L's are J's, however, even if J and K do overlap (II). Finally, the additional statement would mean that if L's were K's, they couldn't be J's (III).

4. E.   Choice A is not necessarily true, for the reasons given in the answer to number 3. Choices B and C are possible, but not necessarily true. Choice D fails to take the J's into account—it would be true only if the J's and K's overlapped completely. Choice E is correct; statement (2) means that any G that is not a K must be a J. Note that this choice is true even if J's and K's *do* overlap completely—in that case no P can be a G, but the 'if-then' statement in choice E remains true.

5. B.   Ellen assumes a causal relationship on the basis of inference (three times, therefore every time). She commits two logical errors: she fails to exclude alternative causes, and she uses too small a number of 'tests' for a valid conclusion. Choice B commits the first error, and may commit the second (we aren't told how many women took the drug). Choice A, a valid argument, concludes that an event must have occurred after its cause. Choice C includes evidence that does tend to rule out alternative explanations. Choice D fails to consider alternative explanations, but involves no inference. Choice E involves sufficient "tests" (she weeps every time) but fails to consider all possible explanations.

6. D.   This would tend to rule out alternative explanations (like the other lakes in choice C above), thereby strengthening the argument. Choice A is wrong because Ralph could sneeze for a different reason. Choice B does strengthen the argument (by suggesting that Ellen is not generally sneezy), but not as much as choice D. Choice C weakens the argument (Ellen is sneezy). Choice E implies that Ellen may make herself sneeze.

7. C.   If the number of accidents has increased by only 10%, while the number of flights has increased by 30%, then flying is actually getting safer. Thus, the original statement serves to rebut choice C. The increase in the number of flights need not imply that the airlines must be making more money (choice A), that all those who used to fly can still afford to fly (choice B), nor that a few large airlines are not taking over the industry (choice E). The only way the statement in choice D could be countered would be to dispute the figure given.

8-11. To diagram this, just fill in places around the table. Start with Helga, the first person who can be placed definitely. (Make an arbitrary choice as to which end the hostess is at—it will make no difference.) Frank must be at Helga's right. Diane must occupy the third place on Frank and Helga's side of the table because of the seating rule about the sexes, with Allan opposite Diane. You now have:

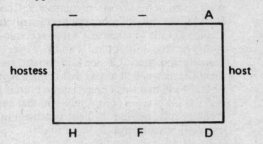

George cannot be the host, since a man is on the host's right, and he cannot be opposite Frank, so he must be opposite Helga. he is the one person between Belinda and Carol, but we don't know which of these is on his left and which is on his right (in the hostess's chair). But we can fill in this much information and answer the questions.

8. C. The only slot left for a male is the host's; the host is to Diane's right; but the person opposite him, the hostess, may be either Belinda *or* Carol.

9. A. George is definitely opposite Helga. He is *not* opposite Belinda (D), nor is Eric opposite Helga (E). Frank may be opposite Belinda *or* Carol, but we don't know which (B,C).

10. D. By inspection. All the others are next to at least one person of thesame sex, no matter where Belinda and Carol are sitting.

11. A. If you shift George four places to the left, he changes place with Diane. I can be verified, II and III ruled out by inspection of the new, altered diagram.

12-18. Your basic solution step is to make a table of the possible persons and qualifications on the Democratic side, with the possible combinations on the Republican side. Note that Fawcett insists on Abbott being present, but the reverse is not true. Remember that there *must* be at least one economist and at least one military expert. The valid combinations are as follows:

DEM.	REPUB.
FH	AD
FI	AB,AD
GI	AB, AC, BC
HI	AC, BC, CD

Note that no combinations containing Democrats FG or GH are acceptable. This is because the presence of G would rule out Republican D, the only available military expert. GI is an acceptable pair of Democrats, since I can fill the military expert's role.

12. C. By inspection of the table.

13. B. Democrats AB figure in acceptable panels with FI and GI.

14. A. GI is the *only* pair containing G that may be included in any acceptable panels (I). One of these does *not* contain A (II) and two *do* contain B (III).

15. D. Count the combinations listed on your table.

16. C. Republicans CD can serve with Democrats HI. There are no acceptable BD or FG combinations.

17. E. Republican E figures in *no* acceptable panels; all others can serve on more than one.

18. E. Democrat I serves on eight acceptable panels (count them).

19-22. The information becomes a little easier to keep straight with a "tree" diagram showing the various possibilities, like the one given here.

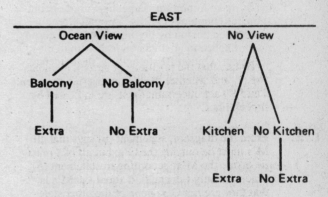

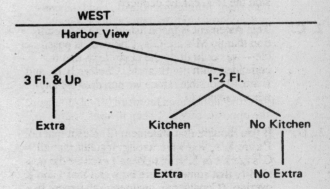

19. D.   Simply read the information from the diagram. Some rooms described in choices A and C have kitchen facilities; the rooms described in choice B *all* involve an extra charge; and ocean view rooms with balcony but without kitchen facilities (E) involve an extra charge.

20. B.   The only extra charges are for: ocean view with balcony; harbor view, third floor and up; and rooms with kitchen facilities, no matter where. But some ocean view rooms without balcony and some no-view, no-kitchen East Wing rooms *may* be above the third floor (A). Choices C,D, and E are all false.

21. C.   This directly contradicts the first extra-charge condition. The other choices are all definitely true.

22. A.   We don't know whether any West Wing rooms above the second floor or with kitchen facilities have balconies (I). But we do know that East Wing rooms without view or kitchen have no extra charge attached (II) and that all kitchen facilities are in rooms not otherwise subject to an extra charge (III). (Remember, the first paragraph says the charges are identical "except as follows." This means there are no extra charges we weren't told about.)

23. C.   The author asserts that the corporations, rather than people or elected officials, run the country. The author's evidence is that corporation heads make important decisions without being subject to popular controls. Option I strengthens the conclusion by giving evidence of corporate influence in an area not dealt with in the argument. Option III strengthens the evidence by giving additional data suggesting corporate autonomy. Option II is unrelated to either the evidence or the conclusion.

24. E.   The original argument contains an implicit but unstated definition of a term—democracy— and depends for its force on the contrast between the definition (popular control of all decisions affecting our lives) and the facts as alleged by the author. E also involves an implicit definition of education as involving more than "regurgitating facts," and depends on the contrast between this and the alleged facts. Choice A involves no definition of "safe neighborhood," implicit or otherwise. Choices B, C, and D all involve direct, explicit contrasts.

25. A.   First, the author uses the word "right" to mean "the opposite of left." Then he uses "right" to mean "correct" or "proper." This is illogical, as choice A points out. (Technically, this is known as the fallacy of equivocation.) There is no

cause or effect to be confused (choice B). And the author does provide evidence for his conclusion (choice D); it's just not very convincing evidence.

Section 7

1. A. $3^2 = (3)(3) = 9$ and $2^3 = (2)(2)(2) = 8$

2. C. $\left(6 + \dfrac{3}{4}\right) \div \left(2 - \dfrac{5}{4}\right)$

   $\left(6\dfrac{3}{4}\right) \div \left(\dfrac{3}{4}\right)$

   $\left(\dfrac{27}{4}\right) \div \left(\dfrac{3}{4}\right)$

   $\dfrac{\overset{9}{\cancel{27}}}{\cancel{4}} \cdot \dfrac{\cancel{4}}{\underset{1}{\cancel{3}}} = 9$

3. C. $\left(\dfrac{1}{3}\right)\left(8\right) = \dfrac{8}{3}$ and $66\frac{2}{3}\%$ or $\dfrac{2}{3}$ of $4 = \dfrac{8}{3}$

4. A. $\sqrt{\dfrac{1}{4}} = \dfrac{1}{2}; \sqrt{\dfrac{1}{25}} = \dfrac{1}{5}; \dfrac{1}{2} + \dfrac{1}{5} = \dfrac{7}{10}$

   $\sqrt{\dfrac{1}{4} + \dfrac{1}{25}} = \sqrt{\dfrac{25}{100} + \dfrac{4}{100}}$

   $= \sqrt{\dfrac{29}{100}} = \dfrac{5+}{10}$

5. C. $2x - 18y$

   $2(3) - (18)\left(\dfrac{1}{6}\right)$

   $6 - 3$

   $3x - 36y$

   $(3)(3) - (36)\left(\dfrac{1}{6}\right)$

   $9 - 6$

6. C. $\sqrt{0.49} = 0.7; \dfrac{3}{4} = 0.75$. Sum of 0.7, 0.75, and $0.8 = 2.25$. Average $= 0.75 = 75\%$

7. B.   Since $B = 0, 2B(A + C) = 0.$ In Column B, A is positive and C is positive. Therefore, $A(B + C)$ or $A(0 + C)$ is positive.

8. C. $\frac{n + a}{a} = \frac{n}{a} + \frac{a}{a}$ or $\frac{n}{a} + 1$

9. B. $y = 13 - 3$ or $y = 10$ (Column B)
      $x + 10 = 17$ or $x = 7$ (Column A)

10. B.   Since x and y have negative values, $x + y$ will be negative. However, in $-x - (-y)$, y will be positive.

11. C. $\angle 4 + \angle 1 = 180$ (supplementary angles)
      $\angle 1 + \angle 2 + \angle 3 = 180$ (the measure of the three angles of a triangle)

12. D.   Mark's average may possibly be more than, less than, or equal to 85%, depending upon whether he had more 80% scores or 90% scores.

13. A. $\angle ADB$ is an exterior angle of triangle ADC.
      $\angle ADB = \angle ACB + \angle BCA$, therefore $x = z + y$. Therefore $x > y$.

14. A. $x + y = 100$
      $r + s = 90$

15. C.   Since $EB = EC$,
      $\angle EBC = \angle ECB$
      $\angle ABE$ ($x°$) is the supplement of $\angle EBC$
      $\angle DCE$ ($y°$) is the supplement of $\angle ECB$
      Thus $x = y$ (supplements of equal angles are equal)

16. D.   1 hour 40 minutes = 100 minutes
      $100 - 55 = 45$ minutes

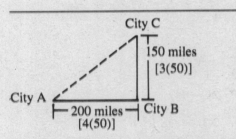

17. C.   The easiest way to do this type of problem is to draw a diagram like the one here. Note that a 3–4–5 right triangle is formed, with legs 3(50) and 4(50) and the hypotenuse of 5(50) or 250.

18. C.   Note that the dimensions of the cut carpet are (13)(11) = 143 square feet.

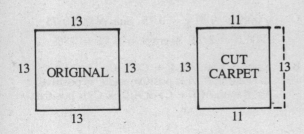

19. D.   Find cost and calculate new selling price.
      Let x = cost.
$$x + \frac{1}{4}x = \$35$$
$$4x + x = 140$$
$$5x = 140$$
$$x = \$28$$
      (Cost) \$28 + (profit) 15% of \$28 or \$4.20
      = \$32.20

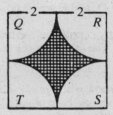

20. C.   The 4 arcs (unshaded portion of the square) together constitute 1 circle with radius = 2 and area = 4π. The shaded portion = area $QRST$ minus 4π, or $16 - 4\pi$.

21. C.   Either calculate \$30,000 (.03) = \$900 or note that 1% of \$30,000 = \$300 and 3% = \$900.

22. E.   If 15% = $\frac{15}{100}$ then $\frac{15¢}{100¢}$ or 15¢ out of every \$1.00 is the amount the average American spends for housing.

23. A.   The Browns spend $\frac{\$4,000}{\$35,000}$ or 11.4%. The average American spends 17%. The difference is 5.6%.

24. B.   Medical care includes medical insurance (\$1500) and medical costs (\$2600) for a total of \$4100 out of a total of \$35,000. $\frac{\$4,100}{\$35,000} = \frac{41}{350}$.

25. C.   Food = 17% and Housing = 15% for a difference of 2% or $\frac{2}{100}$.

26. D.   The rise is $\frac{3}{8}$, by the addition of 6 gallons.
      Let x = the total capacity.
$$\frac{3}{8}x = 6$$
$$x = 16 \text{ gallons}$$

27. D.   Note change in units. Change all to inches.

$$\frac{(2.75)(12)}{0.375} = \text{number of steel plates}$$

$$\frac{(2.75)(12)(10)}{0.375} = \frac{\overset{11}{\cancel{55}}\;\overset{4}{(2.75)}\cancel{(12)}\overset{2}{\cancel{(10)}}}{\underset{\underset{\cancel{5}}{\cancel{15}}}{\cancel{375}}} = 88$$

28. E.   This is a direct proportion. Observe shift in units. In dollars, price per orange is

$$\frac{\$}{\text{number of oranges}} = \frac{\frac{c}{100}}{1} = \frac{x}{12}$$

$$x = 12\left(\frac{c}{100}\right)$$

$$x = \frac{12c}{100}$$

29. C.   In one hour the pipe fills $\frac{1}{h}$ of pool.

In x hours the pipe fills $\frac{x}{h}$ of pool.

30. D.   The original solution of 100 cc. contains 80% boric acid or 80 cc.
Let $x =$ amount of water to be added to make a 50% solution.
Note that the amount of boric acid (80 cc.) remains the same.

$$\frac{80}{100 + x} = 50\%.$$

Answer Sheet — MODEL TEST 4

Start with number 1 for each new section.
If a section has fewer than 38 questions, leave the extra spaces blank.

Section 1

1. Ⓐ Ⓑ Ⓒ Ⓓ Ⓔ   11. Ⓐ Ⓑ Ⓒ Ⓓ Ⓔ   21. Ⓐ Ⓑ Ⓒ Ⓓ Ⓔ   31. Ⓐ Ⓑ Ⓒ Ⓓ Ⓔ
2. Ⓐ Ⓑ Ⓒ Ⓓ Ⓔ   12. Ⓐ Ⓑ Ⓒ Ⓓ Ⓔ   22. Ⓐ Ⓑ Ⓒ Ⓓ Ⓔ   32. Ⓐ Ⓑ Ⓒ Ⓓ Ⓔ
3. Ⓐ Ⓑ Ⓒ Ⓓ Ⓔ   13. Ⓐ Ⓑ Ⓒ Ⓓ Ⓔ   23. Ⓐ Ⓑ Ⓒ Ⓓ Ⓔ   33. Ⓐ Ⓑ Ⓒ Ⓓ Ⓔ
4. Ⓐ Ⓑ Ⓒ Ⓓ Ⓔ   14. Ⓐ Ⓑ Ⓒ Ⓓ Ⓔ   24. Ⓐ Ⓑ Ⓒ Ⓓ Ⓔ   34. Ⓐ Ⓑ Ⓒ Ⓓ Ⓔ
5. Ⓐ Ⓑ Ⓒ Ⓓ Ⓔ   15. Ⓐ Ⓑ Ⓒ Ⓓ Ⓔ   25. Ⓐ Ⓑ Ⓒ Ⓓ Ⓔ   35. Ⓐ Ⓑ Ⓒ Ⓓ Ⓔ
6. Ⓐ Ⓑ Ⓒ Ⓓ Ⓔ   16. Ⓐ Ⓑ Ⓒ Ⓓ Ⓔ   26. Ⓐ Ⓑ Ⓒ Ⓓ Ⓔ   36. Ⓐ Ⓑ Ⓒ Ⓓ Ⓔ
7. Ⓐ Ⓑ Ⓒ Ⓓ Ⓔ   17. Ⓐ Ⓑ Ⓒ Ⓓ Ⓔ   27. Ⓐ Ⓑ Ⓒ Ⓓ Ⓔ   37. Ⓐ Ⓑ Ⓒ Ⓓ Ⓔ
8. Ⓐ Ⓑ Ⓒ Ⓓ Ⓔ   18. Ⓐ Ⓑ Ⓒ Ⓓ Ⓔ   28. Ⓐ Ⓑ Ⓒ Ⓓ Ⓔ   38. Ⓐ Ⓑ Ⓒ Ⓓ Ⓔ
9. Ⓐ Ⓑ Ⓒ Ⓓ Ⓔ   19. Ⓐ Ⓑ Ⓒ Ⓓ Ⓔ   29. Ⓐ Ⓑ Ⓒ Ⓓ Ⓔ
10. Ⓐ Ⓑ Ⓒ Ⓓ Ⓔ   20. Ⓐ Ⓑ Ⓒ Ⓓ Ⓔ   30. Ⓐ Ⓑ Ⓒ Ⓓ Ⓔ

Section 2

1. Ⓐ Ⓑ Ⓒ Ⓓ Ⓔ   11. Ⓐ Ⓑ Ⓒ Ⓓ Ⓔ   21. Ⓐ Ⓑ Ⓒ Ⓓ Ⓔ   31. Ⓐ Ⓑ Ⓒ Ⓓ Ⓔ
2. Ⓐ Ⓑ Ⓒ Ⓓ Ⓔ   12. Ⓐ Ⓑ Ⓒ Ⓓ Ⓔ   22. Ⓐ Ⓑ Ⓒ Ⓓ Ⓔ   32. Ⓐ Ⓑ Ⓒ Ⓓ Ⓔ
3. Ⓐ Ⓑ Ⓒ Ⓓ Ⓔ   13. Ⓐ Ⓑ Ⓒ Ⓓ Ⓔ   23. Ⓐ Ⓑ Ⓒ Ⓓ Ⓔ   33. Ⓐ Ⓑ Ⓒ Ⓓ Ⓔ
4. Ⓐ Ⓑ Ⓒ Ⓓ Ⓔ   14. Ⓐ Ⓑ Ⓒ Ⓓ Ⓔ   24. Ⓐ Ⓑ Ⓒ Ⓓ Ⓔ   34. Ⓐ Ⓑ Ⓒ Ⓓ Ⓔ
5. Ⓐ Ⓑ Ⓒ Ⓓ Ⓔ   15. Ⓐ Ⓑ Ⓒ Ⓓ Ⓔ   25. Ⓐ Ⓑ Ⓒ Ⓓ Ⓔ   35. Ⓐ Ⓑ Ⓒ Ⓓ Ⓔ
6. Ⓐ Ⓑ Ⓒ Ⓓ Ⓔ   16. Ⓐ Ⓑ Ⓒ Ⓓ Ⓔ   26. Ⓐ Ⓑ Ⓒ Ⓓ Ⓔ   36. Ⓐ Ⓑ Ⓒ Ⓓ Ⓔ
7. Ⓐ Ⓑ Ⓒ Ⓓ Ⓔ   17. Ⓐ Ⓑ Ⓒ Ⓓ Ⓔ   27. Ⓐ Ⓑ Ⓒ Ⓓ Ⓔ   37. Ⓐ Ⓑ Ⓒ Ⓓ Ⓔ
8. Ⓐ Ⓑ Ⓒ Ⓓ Ⓔ   18. Ⓐ Ⓑ Ⓒ Ⓓ Ⓔ   28. Ⓐ Ⓑ Ⓒ Ⓓ Ⓔ   38. Ⓐ Ⓑ Ⓒ Ⓓ Ⓔ
9. Ⓐ Ⓑ Ⓒ Ⓓ Ⓔ   19. Ⓐ Ⓑ Ⓒ Ⓓ Ⓔ   29. Ⓐ Ⓑ Ⓒ Ⓓ Ⓔ
10. Ⓐ Ⓑ Ⓒ Ⓓ Ⓔ   20. Ⓐ Ⓑ Ⓒ Ⓓ Ⓔ   30. Ⓐ Ⓑ Ⓒ Ⓓ Ⓔ

Section 3

1. Ⓐ Ⓑ Ⓒ Ⓓ Ⓔ   11. Ⓐ Ⓑ Ⓒ Ⓓ Ⓔ   21. Ⓐ Ⓑ Ⓒ Ⓓ Ⓔ   31. Ⓐ Ⓑ Ⓒ Ⓓ Ⓔ
2. Ⓐ Ⓑ Ⓒ Ⓓ Ⓔ   12. Ⓐ Ⓑ Ⓒ Ⓓ Ⓔ   22. Ⓐ Ⓑ Ⓒ Ⓓ Ⓔ   32. Ⓐ Ⓑ Ⓒ Ⓓ Ⓔ
3. Ⓐ Ⓑ Ⓒ Ⓓ Ⓔ   13. Ⓐ Ⓑ Ⓒ Ⓓ Ⓔ   23. Ⓐ Ⓑ Ⓒ Ⓓ Ⓔ   33. Ⓐ Ⓑ Ⓒ Ⓓ Ⓔ
4. Ⓐ Ⓑ Ⓒ Ⓓ Ⓔ   14. Ⓐ Ⓑ Ⓒ Ⓓ Ⓔ   24. Ⓐ Ⓑ Ⓒ Ⓓ Ⓔ   34. Ⓐ Ⓑ Ⓒ Ⓓ Ⓔ
5. Ⓐ Ⓑ Ⓒ Ⓓ Ⓔ   15. Ⓐ Ⓑ Ⓒ Ⓓ Ⓔ   25. Ⓐ Ⓑ Ⓒ Ⓓ Ⓔ   35. Ⓐ Ⓑ Ⓒ Ⓓ Ⓔ
6. Ⓐ Ⓑ Ⓒ Ⓓ Ⓔ   16. Ⓐ Ⓑ Ⓒ Ⓓ Ⓔ   26. Ⓐ Ⓑ Ⓒ Ⓓ Ⓔ   36. Ⓐ Ⓑ Ⓒ Ⓓ Ⓔ
7. Ⓐ Ⓑ Ⓒ Ⓓ Ⓔ   17. Ⓐ Ⓑ Ⓒ Ⓓ Ⓔ   27. Ⓐ Ⓑ Ⓒ Ⓓ Ⓔ   37. Ⓐ Ⓑ Ⓒ Ⓓ Ⓔ
8. Ⓐ Ⓑ Ⓒ Ⓓ Ⓔ   18. Ⓐ Ⓑ Ⓒ Ⓓ Ⓔ   28. Ⓐ Ⓑ Ⓒ Ⓓ Ⓔ   38. Ⓐ Ⓑ Ⓒ Ⓓ Ⓔ
9. Ⓐ Ⓑ Ⓒ Ⓓ Ⓔ   19. Ⓐ Ⓑ Ⓒ Ⓓ Ⓔ   29. Ⓐ Ⓑ Ⓒ Ⓓ Ⓔ
10. Ⓐ Ⓑ Ⓒ Ⓓ Ⓔ   20. Ⓐ Ⓑ Ⓒ Ⓓ Ⓔ   30. Ⓐ Ⓑ Ⓒ Ⓓ Ⓔ

Section 4

1. Ⓐ Ⓑ Ⓒ Ⓓ Ⓔ
2. Ⓐ Ⓑ Ⓒ Ⓓ Ⓔ
3. Ⓐ Ⓑ Ⓒ Ⓓ Ⓔ
4. Ⓐ Ⓑ Ⓒ Ⓓ Ⓔ
5. Ⓐ Ⓑ Ⓒ Ⓓ Ⓔ
6. Ⓐ Ⓑ Ⓒ Ⓓ Ⓔ
7. Ⓐ Ⓑ Ⓒ Ⓓ Ⓔ
8. Ⓐ Ⓑ Ⓒ Ⓓ Ⓔ
9. Ⓐ Ⓑ Ⓒ Ⓓ Ⓔ
10. Ⓐ Ⓑ Ⓒ Ⓓ Ⓔ
11. Ⓐ Ⓑ Ⓒ Ⓓ Ⓔ
12. Ⓐ Ⓑ Ⓒ Ⓓ Ⓔ
13. Ⓐ Ⓑ Ⓒ Ⓓ Ⓔ
14. Ⓐ Ⓑ Ⓒ Ⓓ Ⓔ
15. Ⓐ Ⓑ Ⓒ Ⓓ Ⓔ
16. Ⓐ Ⓑ Ⓒ Ⓓ Ⓔ
17. Ⓐ Ⓑ Ⓒ Ⓓ Ⓔ
18. Ⓐ Ⓑ Ⓒ Ⓓ Ⓔ
19. Ⓐ Ⓑ Ⓒ Ⓓ Ⓔ
20. Ⓐ Ⓑ Ⓒ Ⓓ Ⓔ
21. Ⓐ Ⓑ Ⓒ Ⓓ Ⓔ
22. Ⓐ Ⓑ Ⓒ Ⓓ Ⓔ
23. Ⓐ Ⓑ Ⓒ Ⓓ Ⓔ
24. Ⓐ Ⓑ Ⓒ Ⓓ Ⓔ
25. Ⓐ Ⓑ Ⓒ Ⓓ Ⓔ
26. Ⓐ Ⓑ Ⓒ Ⓓ Ⓔ
27. Ⓐ Ⓑ Ⓒ Ⓓ Ⓔ
28. Ⓐ Ⓑ Ⓒ Ⓓ Ⓔ
29. Ⓐ Ⓑ Ⓒ Ⓓ Ⓔ
30. Ⓐ Ⓑ Ⓒ Ⓓ Ⓔ
31. Ⓐ Ⓑ Ⓒ Ⓓ Ⓔ
32. Ⓐ Ⓑ Ⓒ Ⓓ Ⓔ
33. Ⓐ Ⓑ Ⓒ Ⓓ Ⓔ
34. Ⓐ Ⓑ Ⓒ Ⓓ Ⓔ
35. Ⓐ Ⓑ Ⓒ Ⓓ Ⓔ
36. Ⓐ Ⓑ Ⓒ Ⓓ Ⓔ
37. Ⓐ Ⓑ Ⓒ Ⓓ Ⓔ
38. Ⓐ Ⓑ Ⓒ Ⓓ Ⓔ

Section 5

1. Ⓐ Ⓑ Ⓒ Ⓓ Ⓔ
2. Ⓐ Ⓑ Ⓒ Ⓓ Ⓔ
3. Ⓐ Ⓑ Ⓒ Ⓓ Ⓔ
4. Ⓐ Ⓑ Ⓒ Ⓓ Ⓔ
5. Ⓐ Ⓑ Ⓒ Ⓓ Ⓔ
6. Ⓐ Ⓑ Ⓒ Ⓓ Ⓔ
7. Ⓐ Ⓑ Ⓒ Ⓓ Ⓔ
8. Ⓐ Ⓑ Ⓒ Ⓓ Ⓔ
9. Ⓐ Ⓑ Ⓒ Ⓓ Ⓔ
10. Ⓐ Ⓑ Ⓒ Ⓓ Ⓔ
11. Ⓐ Ⓑ Ⓒ Ⓓ Ⓔ
12. Ⓐ Ⓑ Ⓒ Ⓓ Ⓔ
13. Ⓐ Ⓑ Ⓒ Ⓓ Ⓔ
14. Ⓐ Ⓑ Ⓒ Ⓓ Ⓔ
15. Ⓐ Ⓑ Ⓒ Ⓓ Ⓔ
16. Ⓐ Ⓑ Ⓒ Ⓓ Ⓔ
17. Ⓐ Ⓑ Ⓒ Ⓓ Ⓔ
18. Ⓐ Ⓑ Ⓒ Ⓓ Ⓔ
19. Ⓐ Ⓑ Ⓒ Ⓓ Ⓔ
20. Ⓐ Ⓑ Ⓒ Ⓓ Ⓔ
21. Ⓐ Ⓑ Ⓒ Ⓓ Ⓔ
22. Ⓐ Ⓑ Ⓒ Ⓓ Ⓔ
23. Ⓐ Ⓑ Ⓒ Ⓓ Ⓔ
24. Ⓐ Ⓑ Ⓒ Ⓓ Ⓔ
25. Ⓐ Ⓑ Ⓒ Ⓓ Ⓔ
26. Ⓐ Ⓑ Ⓒ Ⓓ Ⓔ
27. Ⓐ Ⓑ Ⓒ Ⓓ Ⓔ
28. Ⓐ Ⓑ Ⓒ Ⓓ Ⓔ
29. Ⓐ Ⓑ Ⓒ Ⓓ Ⓔ
30. Ⓐ Ⓑ Ⓒ Ⓓ Ⓔ
31. Ⓐ Ⓑ Ⓒ Ⓓ Ⓔ
32. Ⓐ Ⓑ Ⓒ Ⓓ Ⓔ
33. Ⓐ Ⓑ Ⓒ Ⓓ Ⓔ
34. Ⓐ Ⓑ Ⓒ Ⓓ Ⓔ
35. Ⓐ Ⓑ Ⓒ Ⓓ Ⓔ
36. Ⓐ Ⓑ Ⓒ Ⓓ Ⓔ
37. Ⓐ Ⓑ Ⓒ Ⓓ Ⓔ
38. Ⓐ Ⓑ Ⓒ Ⓓ Ⓔ

Section 6

1. Ⓐ Ⓑ Ⓒ Ⓓ Ⓔ
2. Ⓐ Ⓑ Ⓒ Ⓓ Ⓔ
3. Ⓐ Ⓑ Ⓒ Ⓓ Ⓔ
4. Ⓐ Ⓑ Ⓒ Ⓓ Ⓔ
5. Ⓐ Ⓑ Ⓒ Ⓓ Ⓔ
6. Ⓐ Ⓑ Ⓒ Ⓓ Ⓔ
7. Ⓐ Ⓑ Ⓒ Ⓓ Ⓔ
8. Ⓐ Ⓑ Ⓒ Ⓓ Ⓔ
9. Ⓐ Ⓑ Ⓒ Ⓓ Ⓔ
10. Ⓐ Ⓑ Ⓒ Ⓓ Ⓔ
11. Ⓐ Ⓑ Ⓒ Ⓓ Ⓔ
12. Ⓐ Ⓑ Ⓒ Ⓓ Ⓔ
13. Ⓐ Ⓑ Ⓒ Ⓓ Ⓔ
14. Ⓐ Ⓑ Ⓒ Ⓓ Ⓔ
15. Ⓐ Ⓑ Ⓒ Ⓓ Ⓔ
16. Ⓐ Ⓑ Ⓒ Ⓓ Ⓔ
17. Ⓐ Ⓑ Ⓒ Ⓓ Ⓔ
18. Ⓐ Ⓑ Ⓒ Ⓓ Ⓔ
19. Ⓐ Ⓑ Ⓒ Ⓓ Ⓔ
20. Ⓐ Ⓑ Ⓒ Ⓓ Ⓔ
21. Ⓐ Ⓑ Ⓒ Ⓓ Ⓔ
22. Ⓐ Ⓑ Ⓒ Ⓓ Ⓔ
23. Ⓐ Ⓑ Ⓒ Ⓓ Ⓔ
24. Ⓐ Ⓑ Ⓒ Ⓓ Ⓔ
25. Ⓐ Ⓑ Ⓒ Ⓓ Ⓔ
26. Ⓐ Ⓑ Ⓒ Ⓓ Ⓔ
27. Ⓐ Ⓑ Ⓒ Ⓓ Ⓔ
28. Ⓐ Ⓑ Ⓒ Ⓓ Ⓔ
29. Ⓐ Ⓑ Ⓒ Ⓓ Ⓔ
30. Ⓐ Ⓑ Ⓒ Ⓓ Ⓔ
31. Ⓐ Ⓑ Ⓒ Ⓓ Ⓔ
32. Ⓐ Ⓑ Ⓒ Ⓓ Ⓔ
33. Ⓐ Ⓑ Ⓒ Ⓓ Ⓔ
34. Ⓐ Ⓑ Ⓒ Ⓓ Ⓔ
35. Ⓐ Ⓑ Ⓒ Ⓓ Ⓔ
36. Ⓐ Ⓑ Ⓒ Ⓓ Ⓔ
37. Ⓐ Ⓑ Ⓒ Ⓓ Ⓔ
38. Ⓐ Ⓑ Ⓒ Ⓓ Ⓔ

Section 7

1. Ⓐ Ⓑ Ⓒ Ⓓ Ⓔ
2. Ⓐ Ⓑ Ⓒ Ⓓ Ⓔ
3. Ⓐ Ⓑ Ⓒ Ⓓ Ⓔ
4. Ⓐ Ⓑ Ⓒ Ⓓ Ⓔ
5. Ⓐ Ⓑ Ⓒ Ⓓ Ⓔ
6. Ⓐ Ⓑ Ⓒ Ⓓ Ⓔ
7. Ⓐ Ⓑ Ⓒ Ⓓ Ⓔ
8. Ⓐ Ⓑ Ⓒ Ⓓ Ⓔ
9. Ⓐ Ⓑ Ⓒ Ⓓ Ⓔ
10. Ⓐ Ⓑ Ⓒ Ⓓ Ⓔ
11. Ⓐ Ⓑ Ⓒ Ⓓ Ⓔ
12. Ⓐ Ⓑ Ⓒ Ⓓ Ⓔ
13. Ⓐ Ⓑ Ⓒ Ⓓ Ⓔ
14. Ⓐ Ⓑ Ⓒ Ⓓ Ⓔ
15. Ⓐ Ⓑ Ⓒ Ⓓ Ⓔ
16. Ⓐ Ⓑ Ⓒ Ⓓ Ⓔ
17. Ⓐ Ⓑ Ⓒ Ⓓ Ⓔ
18. Ⓐ Ⓑ Ⓒ Ⓓ Ⓔ
19. Ⓐ Ⓑ Ⓒ Ⓓ Ⓔ
20. Ⓐ Ⓑ Ⓒ Ⓓ Ⓔ
21. Ⓐ Ⓑ Ⓒ Ⓓ Ⓔ
22. Ⓐ Ⓑ Ⓒ Ⓓ Ⓔ
23. Ⓐ Ⓑ Ⓒ Ⓓ Ⓔ
24. Ⓐ Ⓑ Ⓒ Ⓓ Ⓔ
25. Ⓐ Ⓑ Ⓒ Ⓓ Ⓔ
26. Ⓐ Ⓑ Ⓒ Ⓓ Ⓔ
27. Ⓐ Ⓑ Ⓒ Ⓓ Ⓔ
28. Ⓐ Ⓑ Ⓒ Ⓓ Ⓔ
29. Ⓐ Ⓑ Ⓒ Ⓓ Ⓔ
30. Ⓐ Ⓑ Ⓒ Ⓓ Ⓔ
31. Ⓐ Ⓑ Ⓒ Ⓓ Ⓔ
32. Ⓐ Ⓑ Ⓒ Ⓓ Ⓔ
33. Ⓐ Ⓑ Ⓒ Ⓓ Ⓔ
34. Ⓐ Ⓑ Ⓒ Ⓓ Ⓔ
35. Ⓐ Ⓑ Ⓒ Ⓓ Ⓔ
36. Ⓐ Ⓑ Ⓒ Ⓓ Ⓔ
37. Ⓐ Ⓑ Ⓒ Ⓓ Ⓔ
38. Ⓐ Ⓑ Ⓒ Ⓓ Ⓔ

MODEL TEST FOUR

Time—30 minutes

38 Questions

Directions: Each sentence below has one or two blanks, each blank indicating that something has been omitted. Beneath the sentence are five lettered words or sets of words. Choose the word or set of words for each blank that best fits the meaning of the sentence as a whole.

1. The dean tried to retain control of the situation on campus, but his attempt was ------- by the board of trustees.

   (A) endorsed   (B) frustrated   (C) disclosed
   (D) witnessed   (E) justified

2. The current dispute between analytic and non-analytic philosophers ------- mere ideas, for in academia success in such disputes leads to position and prestige, which lead to control over jobs, money, and publication.

   (A) accentuates
   (B) transcends
   (C) invalidates
   (D) exacerbates
   (E) precedes

3. Book publishing has long been ------- profession, partly because for younger editors the best way to win a raise or a promotion was to move on to another publishing house.

   (A). an innovative
   (B) a prestigious
   (C) an itinerant
   (D) a rewarding
   (E) an insular

4. For centuries, physicists have had good reason to believe in the principle of equivalence propounded by Galileo: it has ------- many rigorous tests that ------- its accuracy to extraordinary precision.

   (A) endured...compromised
   (B) passed...presupposed
   (C) borne...postulated
   (D) survived...proved
   (E) inspired...equated

5. Among contemporary writers of fiction, Mrs. Woolf is ------- figure, in some ways as radical as James Joyce, in others no more modern than Jane Austen.

   (A) a doctrinaire
   (B) an introspective
   (C) a peripheral
   (D) a disinterested
   (E) an anomalous

6. To the embittered ex-philanthropist, all the former recipients of his charity were -------, as stingy with their thanks as they were wasteful of his largesse.

   (A) louts   (B) misers   (C) ingrates
   (D) prigs   (E) renegades

7. Physicists dream of a unified theory of matter that could replace the current ------- of mutually inconsistent theories that clutter the field.

   (A) bonanza   (B) concord   (C) dearth
   (D) integration   (E) welter

Directions: In each of the following questions, a related pair of words or phrases is followed by five lettered pairs of words or phrases. Select the lettered pair that best expresses a relationship similar to that expressed in the original pair.

8. FOOTBALL : GRIDIRON::
   (A) soccer : goal
   (B) rugby : arena
   (C) wrestling : mat
   (D) baseball : diamond
   (E) bowling : pin

9. LAUREL WREATH : VICTORY::
   (A) rosebud : charity
   (B) maple leaf : sweetness
   (C) blindfold : visibility
   (D) palm tree : idleness
   (E) olive branch : peace

10. GEOLOGIST : GNEISS::
    (A) herpetologist : liver
    (B) archaeologist : architectonics
    (C) entomologist : anteater
    (D) meteorologist : asteroid
    (E) botanist : zinnia

11. AGITATOR : FIREBRAND::
    (A) miser : spendthrift
    (B) renegade : turncoat
    (C) anarchist : backslider
    (D) maverick : scapegoat
    (E) reprobate : hothead

12. CALLOW : MATURITY::
    (A) incipient : fruition
    (B) eager : anxiety
    (C) youthful : senility
    (D) apathetic : disinterest
    (E) pallid : purity

569

13. INOCULATION : IMMUNITY::
    (A) talisman : charm
    (B) serum : antidote
    (C) exposure : weathering
    (D) indoctrination : disloyalty
    (E) invasion : fortification

14. DISPASSIONATE : PARTISANSHIP::
    (A) enthusiastic : zealousness
    (B) disconsolate : sorrow
    (C) intemperate : moderation
    (D) volatile : immobility
    (E) ardent : involvement

15. GRISLY : RECOIL::
    (A) sudden : rebound
    (B) tainted : purify
    (C) flagging : invigorate
    (D) heartrending : weep
    (E) craven : quail

16. TOCSIN : DANGER::
    (A) antitoxin : cure
    (B) augury : warning
    (C) oracle : mystery
    (D) clarion : battle
    (E) knell : death

Directions: Each passage in this group is followed by questions based on its content. After reading a passage, choose the best answer to each question. Answer all questions following a passage on the basis of what is stated or implied in the passage.

Mary Shelley herself was the first to point to her fortuitous immersion in the literary and scientific revolutions of her day as the source of her novel *Frankenstein*. Her extreme youth, as well as her sex, have contributed to the generally held opinion that she was not so much an author in her own right as a transparent medium through which passed the ideas of those around her. "All Mrs. Shelley did," writes Mario Praz, "was to provide a passive reflection of some of the wild fantasies which were living in the air about her."

Passive reflections, however, do not produce original works of literature, and *Frankenstein*, if not a great novel, was unquestionably an original one. The major Romantic and minor Gothic tradition to which it *should* have belonged was to the literature of the overreacher: the superman who breaks through normal human limitations to defy the rules of society and infringe upon the realm of God. In the Faust story, hypertrophy of the individual will is symbolized by a pact with the devil. Byron's and Balzac's heroes; the Wandering Jew; the chained and unchained Prometheus: all are overreachers, all are punished by their own excesses—by a surfeit of sensation, of experience, of knowledge and, most typically, by the doom of eternal life.

But Mary Shelley's overreacher is different. Frankenstein's exploration of the forbidden boundaries of human science does not cause the prolongation and extension of his own life, but the creation of a new one. He defies mortality not by living forever, but by giving birth.

17. The primary purpose of the passage is to

    (A) discount Mary Shelley's contribution to the realm of fantastic literature
    (B) trace Mary Shelley's familiarity with the scientific and literary theories of her day
    (C) rehabilitate Mary Shelley's reputation by stressing the innovative qualities in her work
    (D) clarify the nature of the literary tradition to which *Frankenstein* belonged
    (E) demonstrate the influence of Shelley's *Frankenstein* on other examples of the genre

18. The author quotes Mario Praz primarily in order to

    (A) support her own perception of Mary Shelley's uniqueness
    (B) illustrate recent changes in scholarly opinions of Shelley
    (C) demonstrate Praz's unfamiliarity with Shelley's *Frankenstein.*
    (D) provide an example of the predominant critical view of Shelley
    (E) contrast Praz's statement about Shelley with Shelley's own self-appraisal

19. The author of the passage concedes which of the following about Mary Shelley as an author?

    (A) She was unaware of the literary and mythological traditions of the overreacher.
    (B) She intentionally parodied the scientific and literary discoveries of her time.
    (C) She was exposed to radical artistic and scientific concepts which influenced her work.
    (D) She lacked the maturity to create a literary work of absolute originality.
    (E) She was not so much an author in her own right as an imitator of the literary works of others.

20. According to the author, Frankenstein parts from the traditional figure of the overreacher in

    (A) his exaggerated will
    (B) his atypical purpose
    (C) the excesses of his method
    (D) the inevitability of his failure
    (E) his defiance of the deity

The distinction often made between learning and instinct is exemplified by two theoretical approaches to the study of behavior: ethology and behaviorist psychology. Ethology is usually
(5)   thought of as the study of instinct. In the ethological world view most animal behavior is governed

by four basic factors: sign stimuli (instinctively recognized cues), motor programs (innate responses to
cues), drive (controlling motivational impulses)
(10) and imprinting (a restricted and seemingly aberrant
form of learning).

   Three of these factors are found in the egg-rolling response of geese, a behavior studied by Kon-
rad Z. Lorenz and Nikolaas Tinbergen, who
(15) together with Karl Frisch were the founders of ethology. Geese incubate their eggs in mound-shaped
nests built on the ground, and it sometimes happens that the incubating goose inadvertently knocks
an egg out of the nest. Such an event leads to a
(20) remarkable behavior. After settling down again on
its nest, the goose eventually notices the errant
egg. The animal then extends its neck to fix its eyes
on the egg, rises and rolls the egg back into the nest
gently with its bill. At first glance this might seem
(25) to be a thoughtful solution to a problem. As it happens, however, the behavior is highly stereotyped
and innate. Any convex object, regardless of color
and almost regardless of size, triggers the response;
beer bottles are particularly effective.
(30)   In this example the convex features that trigger
the behavior are the ethologists' sign stimuli. The
egg-rolling response itself is the motor program.
The entire behavior is controlled by a drive that
appears about two weeks before the geese lay eggs
(35) and persists until about two weeks after the eggs
hatch. Geese also exhibit imprinting: during a sensitive period soon after hatching, goslings will follow almost any receding object that emits an
innately recognized "kum-kum" call and thereafter
(40) treat the object as a parent.

   Classical behaviorist psychologists see the world
quite differently from ethologists. Behaviorists are
primarily interested in the study of learning under
strictly controlled conditions and have traditionally
(45) treated instinct as irrelevant to learning. Behaviorists believe nearly all the responses of higher
animals can be divided into two kinds of learning
called classical conditioning and operant
conditioning.
(50)   Classical conditioning was discovered in dogs by
the Russian physiologist Ivan P. Pavlov. In his
classic experiment he showed that if a bell is rung
consistently just before food is offered to a dog,
eventually the dog will learn to salivate at the
(55) sound of the bell. The important factors in classical
conditioning are the unconditioned stimulus (the
innately recognized cue, equivalent to the ethological sign stimulus, which in this case is food), the
unconditioned response (the innately triggered
(60) behavioral act, equivalent to the ethological motor
program, which in this case is salivation) and the
conditioned stimulus (the stimulus the animal is
conditioned to respond to, which in this case is the
bell). Early behaviorists believed any stimulus an
(65) animal was capable of sensing could be linked, as a
conditioned stimulus, to any unconditioned
response. In operant conditioning, the other major
category of learning recognized by most behaviorists, animals learn a behavior pattern as the result

(70) of trial-and-error experimentation they undertake in
order to obtain a reward or avoid a punishment. In
the classic example a rat is trained to press a lever
to obtain food. The experimenter shapes the behavior by rewarding the rat at first for even partial per-
(75) formance of the desired response. For example, at
the outset the rat might be rewarded simply for facing the end of the cage in which the lever sits.
Later the experimenter requires increasingly precise behavior, until the response is perfected. Early
(80) behaviorists thought any behavior an animal was
capable of performing could be taught, by means
of operant conditioning, as a response to any cue or
situation.

21. The passage is chiefly concerned with

   (A) comparing the effectiveness of ethology with
       that of other behavioral theories
   (B) presenting a new theory to replace ethology and
       behaviorist psychology
   (C) discussing how two differing theories explain
       behavioral processes
   (D) disputing the hypotheses of Pavlov and other
       classical behaviorists
   (E) explaining the processes that control innate
       behavior

22. The author cites Lorenz, Tinbergen, and Frisch for
    their

   (A) studies of the egg-rolling response in geese
   (B) pioneering work studying instinctual behavior
   (C) rejection of imprinting as a form of learning
   (D) use of stringently controlled laboratory settings
   (E) invalidation of the behaviorist approach

23. It can be inferred from lines 24 – 29 that the goose's
    behavior in replacing the egg is "remarkable"
    because it

   (A) appears purposeful and intelligent
   (B) is triggered by the egg
   (C) refutes current ethological theories
   (D) is a response to sign stimuli
   (E) lasts for only four weeks

24. According to the passage, behaviorist learning theo-
    ries take into account which of the following charac-
    teristics of animals?

   I.   Their unconditioned response to certain funda-
        mental stimuli, such as food.
   II. Their ability to learn through being imprinted
        at an early age.
   III. Their tendency to shun negative stimuli.

   (A) I only
   (B) II only
   (C) III only
   (D) I and II only
   (E) I and III only

25. In exploring these two theoretical approaches to the study of behavior, the author does all of the following EXCEPT

    (A) define a term
    (B) point out functional parallels
    (C) refer to an experimental study
    (D) illustrate through an example
    (E) settle an argument

26. According to the passage, the experimental nature of operant conditioning necessarily involves

    (A) the exposure to punishment of the subject of the experiment
    (B) the introduction of increasingly greater rewards by the experimenter
    (C) an increasing refinement of behavior on the part of the experimental animal
    (D) the use of increasingly subtle cues to trigger the behavioral pattern
    (E) an unwillingness to accept marginal execution of the desired behavior

27. The tone of the author's discussion of the egg-rolling response as an example of instinct is one of

    (A) derision   (B) condescension   (C) neutrality
    (D) exasperation   (E) enthusiasm

Directions: Each question below consists of a word printed in capital letters, followed by five lettered words or phrases. Choose the lettered word or phrase that is most nearly <u>opposite</u> in meaning to the word in capital letters.

Since some of the questions require you to distinguish fine shades of meaning, be sure to consider all the choices before deciding which one is best.

28. SEDATE:
    (A) unify
    (B) immunize
    (C) recuperate
    (D) stimulate
    (E) injure

29. APATHETIC:
    (A) healthy
    (B) sincere
    (C) enthusiastic
    (D) untroubled
    (E) hasty

30. DISLODGE:
    (A) restore
    (B) secure
    (C) wander
    (D) transport
    (E) anticipate

31. CELIBACY:
    (A) informality
    (B) promiscuity
    (C) gluttony
    (D) garrulity
    (E) vanity

32. FLEDGLING:
    (A) experienced
    (B) shy
    (C) cautious
    (D) pedestrian
    (E) fleeting

33. INSIPIDNESS:
    (A) wisdom
    (B) cowardice
    (C) lividity
    (D) savoriness
    (E) tentativeness

34. SEQUESTER:
    (A) precede in sequence
    (B) permit to mingle
    (C) alter in composition
    (D) free from doubt
    (E) attempt to better

35. EQUANIMITY:
    (A) clamor
    (B) disparity
    (C) agitation
    (D) propensity
    (E) indivisibility

36. ANATHEMATIZE:
    (A) appraise
    (B) reciprocate
    (C) patronize
    (D) insinuate
    (E) bless

37. MORIBUND:
    (A) mortal
    (B) vital
    (C) transient
    (D) precarious
    (E) tangential

38. DISTILL:
    (A) provoke
    (B) subordinate
    (C) adulterate
    (D) conjure
    (E) deflate

S T O P

IF YOU FINISH BEFORE TIME IS CALLED, YOU MAY CHECK YOUR WORK ON THIS SECTION ONLY.
DO NOT WORK ON ANY OTHER SECTION IN THE TEST.

SECTION 2

Time—30 minutes

38 Questions

Directions: Each sentence below has one or two blanks, each blank indicating that something has been omitted. Beneath the sentence are five lettered words or sets of words. Choose the word or set of words for each blank that best fits the meaning of the sentence as a whole.

1. Bernard Shaw's goal as an anchorman is ------: when he covered the attempted assassination of President Reagan in 1981, his eyes were not enlarged and his voice was not high-pitched.

    (A) accuracy   (B) eloquence   (C) dispassion
    (D) credibility   (E) sensitivity

2. The epiphyte plants of the rain forest use trees for physical support but do not, like ------, sap nutrients from their hosts.

    (A) fauna   (B) predators   (C) parasites
    (D) insectivores   (E) stumps

3. Although he did not consider himself ------, he felt that the inconsistencies in her story ------ a certain degree of incredulity on his part.

    (A) an apostate...justified
    (B) an optimist...intimated
    (C) a hypocrite...demonstrated
    (D) a charlatan...dignified
    (E) a skeptic...warranted

4. Her employers could not complain about her work because she was ------ in the ------ of her duties.

    (A) derelict...performance
    (B) importunate...observance
    (C) meticulous...postponement
    (D) assiduous...execution
    (E) hidebound...conception

5. Critics have been misled by Williams' obvious ------ exaggerated theatrical gestures into ------ his plays as mere melodramas, "full of sound and fury, signifying nothing."

    (A) disinclination for...disparaging
    (B) repudiation of...misrepresenting
    (C) indulgence in...acclaiming
    (D) penchant for...denigrating
    (E) indifference to...lauding

6. Mr. Southern is a historian who has entered so thoroughly into the spirit of the age that even its paradoxes leave him ------.

    (A) nonplussed
    (B) indifferent
    (C) undaunted
    (D) ambivalent
    (E) intransigent

7. What is at the heart of Korzybski's thought is the perception that language, far from being a tool ------ thought and communication, carries within itself a whole body of assumptions about the world and ourselves which go a long way toward shaping and ------ the kinds of thoughts we are able to have.

    (A) incidental to...determining
    (B) requisite for...interpreting
    (C) subordinate to...invalidating
    (D) independent of...correlating
    (E) fundamental to...expurgating

Directions: In each of the following questions, a related pair of words or phrases is followed by five lettered pairs of words or phrases. Select the lettered pair that best expresses a relationship similar to that expressed in the original pair.

8. BARGE : VESSEL::
    (A) cargo : hold
    (B) brake : automobile
    (C) shovel : implement
    (D) squadron : plane
    (E) link : chain

9. RAMSHACKLE : SOUNDNESS::
    (A) garbled : clarity
    (B) decrepit : demolition
    (C) humdrum : monotony
    (D) flimsy : transparency
    (E) steadfast : speed

10. DAMPEN : ENTHUSIASM::
    (A) moisten : throat
    (B) test : commitment
    (C) distract : attention
    (D) reverse : direction
    (E) mute : sound

11. BURST : SOUND::
    (A) ebb : tide
    (B) tinder : fire
    (C) blast : wind
    (D) glimmer : light
    (E) shard : pottery

12. DOVE : COTE::
    (A) sheep : fleece
    (B) pig : sty
    (C) goose : flock
    (D) duck : bill
    (E) fox : den

13. SHOT : SALVO::
    (A) sword : hilt
    (B) ball : musket
    (C) arrow : volley
    (D) flint : powder
    (E) wound : ointment

14. CRAB : CRUSTACEAN::
    (A) salamander : marsupial
    (B) horse : palomino
    (C) swan : cygnet
    (D) spider : arachnid
    (E) aphid : insectivore

15. SKULDUGGERY : SWINDLER::
    (A) surgery : quack
    (B) quandary : craven
    (C) chicanery : trickster
    (D) forgery : speculator
    (E) cutlery : butcher

16. SELF-RESPECTING : VAINGLORIOUS::
    (A) loyal : perfidious
    (B) healthful : salubrious
    (C) querulous : cantankerous
    (D) modest : lascivious
    (E) careful : punctilious

Directions: Each passage in this group is followed by questions based on its content. After reading a passage, choose the best answer to each question. Answer all questions following a passage on the basis of what is stated or implied in the passage.

There can be no doubt that the emergence of the Negro writer in the post-war period stemmed, in part, from the fact that he was inclined to exploit the opportunity to write about himself. It was more
(5) than that, however. The movement that has variously been called the "Harlem Renaissance," the "Black Renaissance," and the "New Negro Movement" was essentially a part of the growing interest of American literary circles in the immediate and
(10) pressing social and economic problems. This growing interest coincided with two developments in Negro life that fostered the growth of the New Negro Movement. These two factors, the keener realization of injustice and the improvement of the
(15) capacity for expression, produced a crop of Negro writers who constituted the "Harlem Renaissance."
The literature of the Harlem Renaissance was, for the most part, the work of a race-conscious group. Through poetry, prose, and song, the writ-
(20) ers cried out against social and economic wrongs. They protested against segregation and lynching. They demanded higher wages, shorter hours, and better conditions of work. They stood for full social equality and first-class citizenship. The new
(25) vision of social and economic freedom which they had did not force them to embrace the several foreign ideologies that sought to sink their roots in some American groups during the period.
The writers of the Harlem Renaissance, bitter
(30) and cynical as some of them were, gave little attention to the propaganda of the socialists and communists. The editor of the *Messenger* ventured the opinion that the New Negro was the "product of the same world-wide forces that have brought into
(35) being the great liberal and radical movements that are now seizing the reins of power in all the civilized countries of the world." Such forces may have produced the New Negro, but the more articulate of the group did not resort to advocating the
(40) type of political action that would have subverted American constitutional government. Indeed, the writers of the Harlem Renaissance were not so much revolting against the system as they were protesting its inefficient operation. In this approach

(45) they proved as characteristically American as any writers of the period. Like his contemporaries, the Negro writer was merely becoming more aware of America's pressing problems; and like the others, he was willing to use his art, not only to contribute
(50) to the great body of American culture but to improve the culture of which he was a part.
It seems possible, moreover, for the historian to assign to the Negro writer a role that he did not assume. There were doubtless many who were not
(55) immediately concerned with the injustices heaped on the Negro. Some contrived their poems, novels, and songs merely for the sake of art, while others took up their pens to escape the sordid aspects of their existence. If there is an element of race in
(60) their writings, it is because the writings flow out of their individual and group experiences. This is not to say that such writings were not effective as protest literature, but rather that not all the authors were conscious crusaders for a better world. As a
(65) matter of fact, it was this detachment, this objectivity, that made it possible for many of the writers of the Harlem Renaissance to achieve a nobility of expression and a poignancy of feeling in their writings that placed them among the masters of recent
(70) American literature.

17. The author is primarily concerned with

    (A) arguing that the literature of the Harlem Renaissance arose from the willingness of black writers to portray their own lives
    (B) depicting the part played by socially-conscious black writers in a world-wide ideological and literary crusade
    (C) providing examples of the injustices protested by the writers of the Harlem Renaissance
    (D) describing the social and political background that led to the blossoming of the Harlem Renaissance
    (E) analyzing stages in the development of the New Negro Movement into the Harlem Renaissance

18. In reference to the achievements of the Harlem Renaissance, the passage conveys primarily a sense of

(A) protest   (B) betrayal   (C) nostalgia
(D) urgency   (E) admiration

19. Which of the following is implied by the statement
that the writers of the Harlem Renaissance "were not
so much revolting against the system as they were
protesting its inefficient operation" (lines 41 – 44)?

(A) Black writers played only a minor part in protesting the injustices of the period.
(B) Left to itself, the system was sure to operate
efficiently.
(C) Black writers in general were not opposed to the
system as such.
(D) In order for the system to operate efficiently,
blacks must seize the reins of power in
America.
(E) Black writers were too caught up in aesthetic
philosophy to identify the true nature of the
conflict.

20. With which of the following statements regarding
the writers of the Harlem Renaissance would the
author most likely agree?

(A) They needed to increase their commitment to
international solidarity.
(B) Their awareness of oppression caused them to
reject American society.
(C) They transformed their increasing social and
political consciousness into art.
(D) Their art suffered from their over-involvement
in political crusades.
(E) Their detachment from their subject matter lessened the impact of their works.

21. The information in the passage suggests that the
author is most likely

(A) a historian concerned with presenting socially
conscious black writers of the period as loyal
Americans
(B) a literary critic who questions the conclusions of
the historians about the Harlem Renaissance
(C) an educator involved in fostering creative writing projects for minority youths
(D) a Black writer of fiction interested in discovering new facts about his literary roots
(E) a researcher with questions about the validity of
his sources

22. Which of the following statements best describes the
organization of lines 29 – 41 of the passage ("The
writers... constitutional government")?

(A) The author cites an authority supporting a previous statement and then qualifies the original
statement to clarify its implications.
(B) The author makes a point, quotes an observation
apparently contradicting that point, and then
resolves the inconsistency by limiting the
application of his original statement.

(C) The author makes a negative comment and then
modifies it, first by quoting a statement that
qualifies its impact and then by rephrasing his
original comment to eliminate its negative
connotations.
(D) The author summarizes an argument, quotes an
observation in support of that argument, and
then advances an alternate hypothesis to
explain potential contradictions in that
argument.
(E) The author states a thesis, quotes a statement
relevant to that thesis, and then presents two
cases, both of which corroborate the point of
the original statement.

23. The passage supplies information for answering
which of the following questions?

(A) What factors led to the stylistic improvement in
the literary works of black writers in the post-
war period?
(B) Who were the leading exponents of protest literature during the Harlem Renaissance?
(C) Why were the writers of the Harlem Renaissance in rebellion against foreign ideological
systems?
(D) How did black writers in the post-war period
define the literary tradition to which they
belonged?
(E) With what specific socioeconomic causes did
the Black writers of the post-war period associate themselves?

(The passage was written prior to 1967)

The coastlines on the two sides of the Atlantic Ocean
present a notable parallelism: the easternmost region of
Brazil, in Pernambuco, has a convexity that corresponds
almost perfectly with the concavity of the African Gulf
of Guinea, while the contours of the African coastline
between Rio de Oro and Liberia would, by the same
approximation, match those of the Caribbean Sea.
    Similar correspondences are also observed in many
other regions of the Earth. This observation began to
awaken scientific interest about sixty years ago, when
Alfred Wegener, a professor at the University of Ham-
burg, used it as a basis for formulating a revolutionary
theory in geological science. According to Wegener,
there was originally only one continent or land mass,
which he called Pangea. Inasmuch as continental masses
are lighter than the base on which they rest, he reasoned,
they must float on the substratum of igneous rock,
known as sima, as ice floes float on the sea. Then why,
he asked, might continents not be subject to drifting?
The rotation of the globe and other forces, he thought,
had caused the cracking and, finally, the breaking apart
of the original Pangea, along an extensive line represented today by the longitudinal submerged mountain
range in the center of the Atlantic. While Africa seems
to have remained static, the Americas apparently drifted
toward the west until they reached their present position

after more than 100 million years. Although the phenomenon seems fantastic, accustomed as we are to the concept of the rigidity and immobility of the continents, on the basis of the distance that separates them it is possible to calculate that the continental drift would have been no greater than two inches per year.

24. The primary purpose of the passage is to

   (A) describe the relative speed of continental movement
   (B) predict the future configuration of the continents
   (C) refute a radical theory postulating continental movement
   (D) describe the reasoning behind a geological theory
   (E) explain how to calculate the continental drift per year

25. The author's attitude toward Wegener's theory can best be described as

   (A) derisive
   (B) indignant
   (C) judicious
   (D) partisan
   (E) naive

26. It can be inferred from the passage that evidence for continental drift has been provided by the

   (A) correspondences between coastal contours
   (B) proof of an original solitary land mass
   (C) level of sima underlying the continents
   (D) immobility of the African continent
   (E) relative heaviness of the continental masses

27. The passage presents information that would answer which of the following questions?

   (A) In what ways do the coastlines of Africa and South America differ from one another?
   (B) How much lighter than the substratum of igneous rock below them are the continental masses?
   (C) Is the rotation of the globe affecting the stability of the present day continental masses?
   (D) According to Wegener's theory, in what direction have the Americas tended to move?
   (E) How does Wegener's theory account for the apparent immobility of the African continent?

Directions: Each question below consists of a word printed in capital letters, followed by five lettered words or phrases. Choose the lettered word or phrase that is most nearly <u>opposite</u> in meaning to the word in capital letters.

Since some of the questions require you to distinguish fine shades of meaning, be sure to consider all the choices before deciding which one is best.

28. SMART:
   (A) soothe
   (B) tickle
   (C) support
   (D) shorten
   (E) question

29. LUCID:
   (A) ornate
   (B) arrogant
   (C) embroiled
   (D) hapless
   (E) obscure

30. PERIPHERY:
   (A) authority
   (B) distance
   (C) velocity
   (D) center
   (E) sequence

31. ENIGMATIC:
   (A) frenetic
   (B) genuine
   (C) unambiguous
   (D) vulnerable
   (E) antagonistic

32. REPUDIATE:
   (A) mislead
   (B) minimize
   (C) ascertain
   (D) isolate
   (E) accept

33. ALOOFNESS:
    (A) exaggeration
    (B) simplicity
    (C) concern
    (D) complacency
    (E) disingenuousness

34. EXHUME:
    (A) decay
    (B) inhale
    (C) fertilize
    (D) restrain
    (E) inter

35. DESPOTIC:
    (A) erratic
    (B) impertinent
    (C) reflective
    (D) insouciant
    (E) humble

36. OBFUSCATE:
    (A) insinuate
    (B) exacerbate
    (C) protract
    (D) clarify
    (E) placate

37. PAEAN:
    (A) dirge
    (B) prologue
    (C) chorale
    (D) anthem
    (E) coda

38. CONCATENATE:
    (A) disclaim
    (B) impede
    (C) unlink
    (D) derail
    (E) vacillate

S T O P

OU FINISH BEFORE TIME IS CALLED, YOU MAY CHECK YOUR WORK ON THIS SECTION ONLY.
DO NOT WORK ON ANY OTHER SECTION IN THE TEST.

SECTION 3

Time—30 minutes

30 Questions

Numbers: All numbers used are real numbers.

Figures: Position of points, angles, regions, etc. can be assumed to be in the order shown; and angle measures can be assumed to be positive.

Lines shown as straight can be assumed to be straight.

Figures can be assumed to lie in a plane unless otherwise indicated.

Figures that accompany questions are intended to provide information useful in answering the questions. However, unless a note states that a figure is drawn to scale, you should solve these problems NOT by estimating sizes by sight or by measurement, but by using your knowledge of mathematics (see Example 2 below).

Directions: Each of the Questions 1-15 consists of two quantities, one in Column A and one in Column B. You are to compare the two quantities and choose

A if the quantity in Column A is greater;
B if the quantity in Column B is greater;
C if the two quantities are equal;
D if the relationship cannot be determined from the information given.

Note: Since there are only four choices, NEVER MARK (E).

Common Information: In a question, information concerning one or both of the quantities to be compared is centered above the two columns. A symbol that appears in both columns represents the same thing in Column A as it does in Column B.

	Column A	Column B	Sample Answers
Example 1:	2×6	$2 + 6$	● Ⓑ Ⓒ Ⓓ Ⓔ

Examples 2-4 refer to $\triangle PQR$.

	Column A	Column B	Sample Answers
Example 2:	PN	NQ	Ⓐ Ⓑ Ⓒ ● Ⓔ

(since equal measures cannot be assumed, even though *PN* and *NQ* appear equal)

	Column A	Column B	Sample Answers
Example 3:	x	y	Ⓐ ● Ⓒ Ⓓ Ⓔ

(since *N* is between *P* and *Q*)

	Column A	Column B	Sample Answers
Example 4:	$w + z$	180	Ⓐ Ⓑ ● Ⓓ Ⓔ

(since *PQ* is a straight line)

A if the quantity in Column A is greater;
B if the quantity in Column B is greater;
C if the two quantities are equal;
D if the relationship cannot be determined from the information given.

Column A	Column B

1. $\dfrac{1}{2}$ $\left(\dfrac{1}{2}\right)^3$

2. $10 - \dfrac{10}{.1}$ 0

3. $\dfrac{x}{4}\%$ of 400 x

4. $\dfrac{0.1}{2}$ $\dfrac{1}{0.2}$

5. The average of $\sqrt{.81}$, 60%, $1\dfrac{1}{2}$ 3

$7x = 196$

6. $\dfrac{x}{7}$ 4

7. $(2)(4)(6)(8)(10)(12)(14)$ $(16)(14)(12)(10)(8)(6)$

$A > B$
$B > C$

8. $2A$ $B + C$

$5 \times 5 \times 5 \times 5 = 10 \times 10 \times T$

9. T 10

$\dfrac{\text{Area of circle } A}{\text{Area of circle } B} = \dfrac{1}{4}$

10. Four times the radius of circle A The radius of circle B

Point O (5,3) is the center of a circle. Point P (5,7) lies on the circle.

11. The circumference of the circle 8π

Column A	Column B

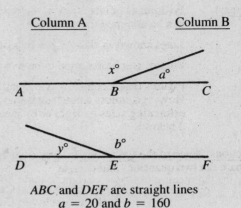

ABC and DEF are straight lines
$a = 20$ and $b = 160$

12. $a + x$ $x + y$

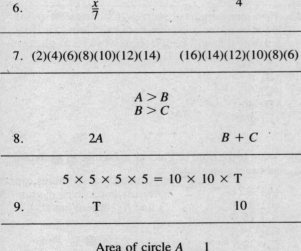

13. x 5

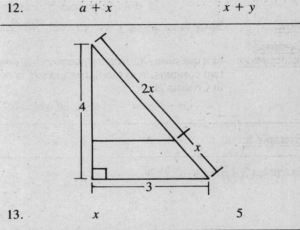

The area of ABC is 12.5.

14. Length of BC 5

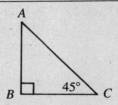

15. $\left(\dfrac{X}{Z}\right)\left(\dfrac{Z}{Y}\right)$ 0

Directions: Each of Questions 16–30 has five answer choices. For each of these questions, select the best of the answer choices given.

16. If $3x - 6 = 1$, then $x - 2 =$

   (A) $\frac{1}{3}$

   (B) $\frac{1}{2}$

   (C) 2

   (D) $2\frac{1}{3}$

   (E) 3

17. If the hypotenuse of isosceles right triangle *ABC* is $6\sqrt{2}$, then the area of *ABC* equals

   (A) 6
   (B) 9
   (C) 12
   (D) 18
   (E) 36

18. $(146 \times 117) + (173 \times 146) + (146 \times 210)$ equals

   (A) 69,000
   (B) 70,000
   (C) 71,000
   (D) 72,000
   (E) 73,000

19. If $7x - 5y = 13$, and $2x - 7y = 26$,
    then $5x + 2y =$

   (A) -39
   (B) -13
   (C) 13
   (D) 19.5
   (E) 39

20. A man covers *d* miles in *t* hours. At that rate how long (in hours) will it take him to cover *m* miles?

   (A) dmt

   (B) $\frac{md}{t}$

   (C) $\frac{mt}{d}$

   (D) $\frac{dt}{m}$

   (E) $\frac{d}{t}$

Questions 21–25 refer to the following table.

RELATIVE SWEETNESS OF DIFFERENT SUBSTANCES	
Lactose	.16
Maltose	.32
Glucose	.74
Sucrose	1.00
Fructose	1.70
Saccharin	675.000

21. About how many times sweeter than lactose is fructose?

   (A) .09
   (B) .1
   (C) 1.54
   (D) 1.86
   (E) 10.6

22. What percent increase in sweetness is obtained by substituting equal amounts of maltose for lactose?

   (A) 16
   (B) 50
   (C) 100
   (D) 200
   (E) 500

23. How many grams of sucrose (to the nearest gram) must be added to one gram of saccharin to make a mixture that will be 100 times as sweet as glucose?

   (A) 7
   (B) 8
   (C) 9
   (D) 10
   (E) 100

24. What is the ratio of glucose to lactose in a mixture as sweet as maltose?

   (A) 8:21
   (B) 21:8
   (C) 25:9
   (D) 29:8
   (E) 32:5

25. Approximately how many times sweeter than sucrose is a mixture of glucose, sucrose, and fructose in the ratio of 1:2:3?

   (A) 0.6
   (B) 1
   (C) 1.3
   (D) 2.3
   (E) 2.9

26. One-half of the student body at Cetco School study French and one-third of the others study Spanish. The remaining 300 do not study any foreign language. How many students are there in this school?

    (A) 360
    (B) 550
    (C) 900
    (D) 1350
    (E) 1800

27. Mr. Jones can mow his lawn in x hours. After 2 hours it begins to rain. What part of the lawn is left unmowed?

    (A) $\dfrac{2-x}{x}$

    (B) $\dfrac{x}{2}$

    (C) $x - 2$

    (D) $\dfrac{x-2}{2}$

    (E) $\dfrac{x-2}{x}$

28. In right triangle ABC, if $\angle A > \angle B > \angle C$, then

    (A) $\angle C > 45°$
    (B) $\angle B = 90°$
    (C) $\angle A > 170°$
    (D) $\angle A > 90°$
    (E) $\angle A = 90°$

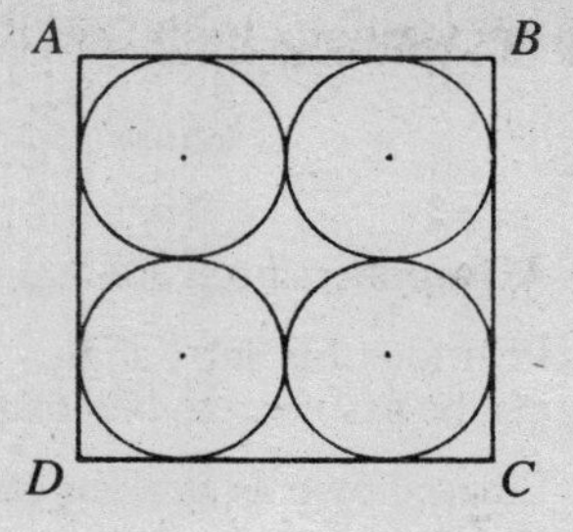

29. In the figure above, the area of each circle is 4π. The perimeter of $ABCD =$

    (A) 16
    (B) 16π
    (C) 32π
    (D) 32
    (E) 64π

30. The area of a square 18 feet on a side is equal to the area of a rectangle with a length of 3 yards. The width of this rectangle (in feet) is

    (A) 2
    (B) 9
    (C) 18
    (D) 27
    (E) 36

S T O P

**IF YOU FINISH BEFORE TIME IS CALLED, YOU MAY CHECK YOUR WORK ON THIS SECTION ONLY.
DO NOT WORK ON ANY OTHER SECTION IN THE TEST.**

SECTION 4

Time—30 minutes

30 Questions

Numbers: All numbers used are real numbers.

Figures: Position of points, angles, regions, etc. can be assumed to be in the order shown; and angle measures can be assumed to be positive.

Lines shown as straight can be assumed to be straight.

Figures can be assumed to lie in a plane unless otherwise indicated.

Figures that accompany questions are intended to provide information useful in answering the questions. However, unless a note states that a figure is drawn to scale, you should solve these problems NOT by estimating sizes by sight or by measurement, but by using your knowledge of mathematics (see Example 2 below).

Directions: Each of the Questions 1-15 consists of two quantities, one in Column A and one in Column B. You are to compare the two quantities and choose

A if the quantity in Column A is greater;
B if the quantity in Column B is greater;
C if the two quantities are equal;
D if the relationship cannot be determined from the information given.

Note: Since there are only four choices, NEVER MARK (E).

Common
Information: In a question, information concerning one or both of the quantities to be compared is centered above the two columns. A symbol that appears in both columns represents the same thing in Column A as it does in Column B.

Column A	Column B	Sample Answers

Example 1: 2×6 $2 + 6$ ● Ⓑ Ⓒ Ⓓ Ⓔ

Examples 2-4 refer to $\triangle PQR$.

Example 2: PN NQ Ⓐ Ⓑ Ⓒ ● Ⓔ
(since equal measures cannot be assumed, even though PN and NQ appear equal)

Example 3: x y Ⓐ ● Ⓒ Ⓓ Ⓔ
(since N is between P and Q)

Example 4: $w + z$ 180   Ⓐ Ⓑ ● Ⓓ Ⓔ
(since PQ is a straight line)

A if the quantity in Column A is greater;
B if the quantity in Column B is greater;
C if the two quantities are equal;
D if the relationship cannot be determined from the information given.

Column A	Column B

Questions 1 and 2 refer to the following figure.

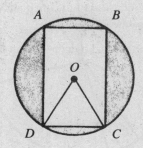

Perimeter of equilateral triangle $ODC = 12$

AD of rectangle $ABCD = 7$

1. Perimeter of $ABCD$ 22

2. Area of shaded area $16\pi - 28$

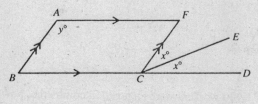

$x = 20$

3. $6x$ y

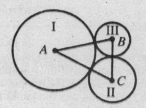

A, C, and B are centers of circles I, II, and III, respectively
Area of circle I $= 25\pi$, area of circle II $= 16\pi$, area of circle III $= 9\pi$

4. Perimenter of triangle ABC 12

Column A	Column B

5. $\dfrac{\frac{1}{4} - \frac{3}{16}}{\frac{1}{8}}$ 2

6. $\sqrt{\frac{1}{9} + \frac{1}{16}}$ $\sqrt{\frac{1}{16}} + \sqrt{\frac{1}{9}}$

7. $\dfrac{1}{.5}$ $\sqrt{4}$

8. $\left(\dfrac{1}{.07}\right)^2$ $\dfrac{1}{7}$

$3^{n+2} = 27$

9. n 3

10. $\sqrt{.16}$ 0.1π

11. $\dfrac{1}{\sqrt{25}}$ $\dfrac{1}{(0.5)}$

$3 - 2x < 9$

12. x -3

$a < 0$ and $b < 0$

13. $a - b$ $a + b$

$x > 0$ and $y > 0$

$\frac{x}{y} > 2$

14. $2y$ x

15. $\sqrt{.25}$ $\dfrac{1}{4}$

Directions: Each of the Questions 16–30 has five answer choices. For each of these questions, select the best of the answer choices given.

16. If $xyz = 1$ and $x = z$, $y =$

(A) $1 - x^2$

(B) x^2

(C) $1 - 2x$

(D) $\dfrac{1}{x^2}$

(E) $\dfrac{1}{2x}$

17. A piece of cloth y yards long had f feet cut from one end and i inches cut from the other end. The present length (in feet) of the piece of cloth is

(A) $\dfrac{y}{3}(f + 12i)$

(B) $3y - f + \dfrac{1}{12}i$

(C) $3y - \left(f + \dfrac{i}{12}\right)$

(D) $36y - 12f - i$

(E) $\dfrac{y}{3} - f + 12i$

18. A sports jacket marked $48 is offered at a discount of 25 percent during a storewide sale. At this reduced price the dealer makes a profit of 20 percent on the cost. The cost to the dealer is

(A) $29
(B) $30
(C) $32
(D) $36
(E) $40

19. A company reports that 2,000 electronic parts are found defective. If this represents 6.25 percent of the total shipment, how many of these parts were shipped?

(A) 3,200
(B) 17,000
(C) 32,000
(D) 34,000
(E) 320,000

20. On a diagram of a camp site drawn to scale of 1:120, the size of a building is $7\frac{1}{5}$ inches. The actual length (in feet) of this building is

(A) 7.2
(B) 72
(C) 120
(D) 720
(E) 864

Questions 21–23 refer to the following graph.

PORTION OF WAGE EARNERS ENGAGED
IN VARIOUS OCCUPATIONS
IN BONNEVILLE CITY IN 1986
(Number of degrees represent angles on circle graph.)

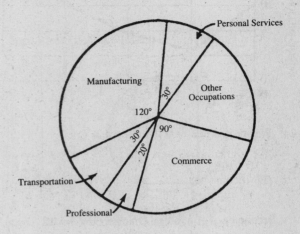

21. What percent of the wage earners in Bonneville were engaged in transportation in 1986?

(A) 6

(B) $8\frac{1}{3}$

(C) $16\frac{2}{3}$

(D) 30

(E) 60

22. If 1,980 workers were engaged in commerce, how many were engaged in manufacturing?

(A) 1,485
(B) 1,782
(C) 2,200
(D) 2,640
(E) 7,920

23. The average income of professional workers was 50 percent greater than that of the transportation workers. If the total income of the tranportation workers was $2,376,000, what was the total income of the professional workers?

(A) $1,056,000
(B) $2,376,000
(C) $3,168,000
(D) $3,564,000
(E) $7,128,000

Questions 24–25 refer to the following graph.

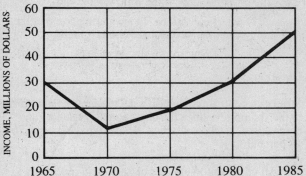

YEARLY INCOME IN BONNEVILLE MANUFACTURING COMPANY

24. We are justified in concluding that

   (A) higher prices were charged by the company in 1985
   (B) income of the company increased more rapidly in the 1980–1985 period than in the preceding five years
   (C) the number of sales of the company have been increasing since 1970
   (D) there was a depression in 1970
   (E) none of the above

25. About what was the average annual income of the company from 1970 to 1980?

   (A) \$15,000,000
   (B) \$20,000,000
   (C) \$25,000,000
   (D) \$30,000,000
   (E) \$35,000,000

26. The number of feet in c inches is

   (A) $\dfrac{1}{12c}$

   (B) $12c$

   (C) $\dfrac{12}{c}$

   (D) $36c$

   (E) $\dfrac{c}{12}$

27. Which of the following represents the area of a rectangle whose length is $x + 1$ and whose width is $x - 1$?

   (A) $x^2 + 1$
   (B) $2x$
   (C) $x^2 - 1$
   (D) $4x$
   (E) x^2

28. Which of the following must be added to $2x - 4$ to produce a sum of 0?

   (A) 0
   (B) $x + 4$
   (C) $2x + 4$
   (D) $x + 2$
   (E) $-2x + 4$

29. The expression $\dfrac{6}{x} \div \dfrac{3}{x}$ is equivalent to

   (A) $\dfrac{1}{2}$

   (B) $2x$

   (C) $\dfrac{x^2}{18}$

   (D) $\dfrac{18}{x^2}$

   (E) 2

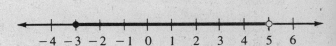

30. The number line above shows the solution set of which of the following inequalities?

   (A) $-3 < x < 5$
   (B) $3 \leqq x < 5$
   (C) $-3 \leqq x < 5$
   (D) $-3 < x \leqq 5$
   (E) $-3 \leqq x \leqq 5$

S T O P

IF YOU FINISH BEFORE TIME IS CALLED, YOU MAY CHECK YOUR WORK ON THIS SECTION ONLY.
DO NOT WORK ON ANY OTHER SECTION IN THE TEST.

SECTION 5

Time — 30 minutes

25 Questions

Directions: Each question or group of questions is based on a passage or set of conditions. In answering some of the questions, it may be useful to draw a rough diagram. For each question, select the best answer choice given.

Questions 1–4

In order to conduct the work of a mail order concern it is necessary to have a minimum of three workers each day. The staff consists of five persons who work on a part-time basis. Alice can work on Mondays, Wednesdays, and Fridays. Betty cannot report for work on Wednesdays. Carol can report for work on Tuesdays and Wednesdays only. Dorothy cannot work on Fridays. Edith is available anytime except on the first Monday and Thursday of the month.

1. Which three are available on any Monday?

   (A) Dorothy, Betty, and Alice
   (B) Alice, Edith, and Carol
   (C) Betty, Edith, and Carol
   (D) Edith, Carol, and Dorothy
   (E) Betty, Carol, and Dorothy

2. Which three could you count on to report for work on Friday?

   (A) Alice, Betty, and Dorothy
   (B) Alice, Carol, and Dorothy
   (C) Betty, Carol, and Edith
   (D) Carol, Betty, and Alice
   (E) Alice, Betty, and Edith

3. During which day of the week might it be impossible to obtain a full complement of workers?

   (A) Monday
   (B) Tuesday
   (C) Wednesday
   (D) Thursday
   (E) Friday

4. During which day of the week would it be necessary to call on Edith to complete the full complement of workers?

   (A) Monday
   (B) Tuesday
   (C) Wednesday
   (D) Thursday
   (E) Friday

Questions 5–7

Strict gun control laws cause a decrease in violent crime; in the six months since the city council passed a gun control law, armed robberies in City X have dropped by 18 percent.

5. All of the following, if true, are valid objections to the argument above except:

   (A) A decrease in crime in one city does not mean that such a decrease would occur anywhere a gun control law was enacted.
   (B) Other factors may have caused the drop in armed robberies.
   (C) Armed robbery is only one category of violent crime that might be affected by a gun control law.
   (D) The gun control law has made it more difficult for citizens to purchase guns for legitimate purposes of self-defense.
   (E) Since the law was passed, murders involving guns in City X have increased by 22 percent.

6. Which of the following statements, if true, would strengthen the argument above?

   I. Before the law was passed, the number of armed robberies had been steadily increasing.
   II. The more severe the punishment mandated for a crime, the less likely that crime is to occur.
   III. Three-fourths of all violent crimes involve the use of a gun.

   (A) I only
   (B) III only
   (C) I and II only
   (D) II and III only
   (E) I, II, and III

7. Which of the following statements, if true, would weaken the argument above?

   I. In the six months since the law was passed, 40 percent more police have been hired.
   II. In the six months since the law was passed, accidental deaths by firearms have increased by 10 percent.
   III. Only 30 percent of those indicted under the new law have been convicted.

   (A) I only
   (B) III only
   (C) I and II only
   (D) I and III only
   (E) II and III only

Questions 8–11

(1) Each word in a horizontal row must begin with a successive letter.
(2) Each word in a vertical column must begin with a different letter.
(3) Each word in a horizontal row must have the same number of letters.
(4) Each word in a vertical column must have a different number of letters.
(5) Each word in a vertical column must be the same part of speech. (NOTE: many English words are more than one part of speech; for example, *cry* is both a noun and a verb.)

	I.	II.	III.	IV.	V.
1.	endear	filter	garish	hotter	intake
2.	chatter	destiny	endless	fester	gradual
3.	bend	calf	death	edge	flow
4.	dread	elbow	fetid	greed	heave
5.	ask	bet	coy	dam	ebb

8. How many rules are not violated by any row or column in the grid?

(A) 2   (B) 3   (C) 4   (D) 5   (E) 6

9. How many rows and columns satisfy all rules for rows and columns, respectively?

(A) Four rows and three columns
(B) Four rows and two columns
(C) Three rows and two columns
(D) Three rows and four columns
(E) Two rows and two columns

10. Word 3 in column III would satisfy all rules if it were changed to

(A) deter   (B) dirty   (C) deaf
(D) dash   (E) dry

11. What is the minimum number of words that must be changed for the grid to satisfy all rules?

(A) 2   (B) 3   (C) 4   (D) 5   (E) 6

Questions 12–18

Only July 4, the Pops Orchestra will perform ten works by nine U.S. composers.
Beach's *Quintet* will be heard immediately after Della Joio's *Fantasies*
Ives's *Fourth of July* will be heard later than the Della Joio. It will be followed immediately by Foster's *Summer Longings*.
The third selection following Copland's *Lincoln Portrait* will be Ellington's *New World A-Coming;* the next will be an aria from Hanson's *Merry Mount*.
Gottschalk's *Grand Tarantelle* will be heard earlier than the Della Joio.
Antes's *Trio* is the second work following the Hanson, and does not end the program.

12. Which of the following lists the composers mentioned in the order in which their works are heard?

(A) Foster, Ives, Antes, Ellington, Beach, Gottschalk
(B) Copland, Della Joio, Beach, Ellington, Hanson, Foster
(C) Gottschalk, Della Joio, Beach, Foster, Antes, Ives
(D) Copland, Gottschalk, Della Joio, Beach, Ellington, Hanson
(E) Beach, Ellington, Hanson, Foster, Ives, Antes

13. The Della Joio *Fantasies* is

(A) the second work on the program
(B) the second work after the Copland
(C) the work immediately preceding the Ellington
(D) followed by two other works before the Hanson aria is heard
(E) heard immediately following the Gottschalk

14. If the intermission occurs immediately after the Beach *Quintet,* the fourth work after the intermission is by

(A) Antes   (B) Copland   (C) Ives
(D) Foster   (E) Hanson

15. The number of works to be heard between the Beach and the Foster is

(A) 1   (B) 2   (C) 3   (D) 4   (E) 5

16. The soloist who will perform during the Antes, the Gottschalk, and the Ellington must begin tuning up just prior to the start of her first performance. She will begin tuning up

(A) during the fourth work on the program
(B) during the Della Joio
(C) during the sixth work on the program
(D) during the Hanson
(E) prior to the start of the program

17. One composer is represented by two works, separated by four other selections. This composer is

(A) Antes   (B) Beach   (C) Copland
(D) Della Joio   (E) Ellington

18. If the total number of works played were eleven instead of ten, which of the following would be possible without violating the stated conditions?

I.   The Copland *Lincoln Portrait* being played first
II. The Antes *Trio* being played after Foster's *Summer Longings*
III. The Antes *Trio* being played before Gottschalk's *Grand Tarantelle*

(A) I only
(B) III only
(C) I and II only
(D) II and III only
(E) I, II, and III

Questions 19–22

A,B,C, or W may cause D.
B,C, or W may cause E.
W or X may cause F.
D or E may cause G or H only if they are caused by B or C; they may cause I only if they are caused by C.
Only E and F together may cause M or N.
F may cause H only if it is caused by W or X.

19. Which can result from the largest number of immediately preceding events?

    (A) D
    (B) E
    (C) F
    (D) M
    (E) N

20. Which can result in the smallest number of subsequent events, counting both those that follow immediately and those that follow after another event?

    (A) A
    (B) B
    (C) C
    (D) W
    (E) X

21. How many different events or combinations of events may cause H?

    (A) 5
    (B) 6
    (C) 7
    (D) 8
    (E) 9

22. Which may be a result of the smallest number of different combinations of events?

    (A) G
    (B) H
    (C) I
    (D) M
    (E) N

Questions 23–25

Statistics indicate that, on the average, women executives' salaries are about 20% lower than those of men in comparable jobs. This is true in spite of the job discrimination suits filed by the U.S. government against firms such as A.T.&T. and the Bank of America in the early 1970s, as well as the passage of laws forbidding job discrimination by gender in many states and localities. In the face of this unrelenting prejudice against women, it is plain that only an amendment to the U.S. Constitution can fully remedy the iniquities under which today's women are laboring.

23. Which of the following is assumed by the author of the above argument?

    (A) All women executives are at least as well qualified as their male counterparts.
    (B) A constitutional amendment is more likely to influence employment practices than separate state laws and court actions.
    (C) Legal remedies for discrimination can only be effective when coupled with a sincere desire for reform.
    (D) Average salaries are often misleading as indicators of the real status of a particular social group.
    (E) Discrimination against women is as serious and widespread as discrimination against members of racial and ethnic minorities.

24. Which of the following would be the most relevant question to ask the author of the above argument?

    (A) What employment practices are currently followed by A.T.&T. and the Bank of America in relation to their female executives?
    (B) Don't female executives in the U.S. have a far better lot than the millions of impoverished women now living in the underdeveloped nations of the Third World?
    (C) Which states and localities have passed laws forbidding job discrimination by gender?
    (D) Isn't "equal pay for equal work" a cardinal principle of law in Slavonia, a well-known totalitarian and repressive state?
    (E) Is a constitutional amendment the most effective way to remedy the problem of job discrimination by gender?

25. All of the following are weaknesses of the above argument except that

    (A) it makes generalizations concerning the status of women based on the plight of a single group of women
    (B) it draws conclusions from statistical evidence which the data themselves may not support
    (C) it disregards efforts being made by some employers to end job discrimination within their own firms
    (D) it fails to fully consider possible remedies other than the one proposed
    (E) it ignores other possible explanations for the cited difference in average salaries

S T O P

IF YOU FINISH BEFORE TIME IS CALLED, YOU MAY CHECK YOUR WORK ON THIS SECTION ONLY.
DO NOT WORK ON ANY OTHER SECTION IN THE TEST.

Section 6

Time — 30 minutes

25 Questions

Directions: Each question or group of questions is based on a passage or set of conditions. In answering some of the questions, it may be useful to draw a rough diagram. For each question, select the best answer choice given.

Questions 1–4

Lance is selecting carpeting, wallpaper, and drapes for four rooms in Mrs. March's apartment. For one room, he chooses maroon carpeting and purple drapes; for another, he chooses striped drapes and fleur-de-lis wallpaper. For the dining room he selects green carpeting and does *not* use fleur-de-lis wallpaper. For the bedroom he chooses lavender drapes and pink walls. For one room, he uses carpeting, wallpaper, and drapes, once each in a different room. The den is adjacent to the living room and must not repeat any of its colors.

1. If one room has yellow walls, it must also have

   (A) white drapes
   (B) maroon carpeting
   (C) purple drapes
   (D) white carpeting
   (E) striped drapes

2. Which correctly lists the colors of carpeting, wallpaper, and drapes, in that order, for one room?

   (A) maroon, green, purple
   (B) green, fleur-de-lis, striped
   (C) green, white, white
   (D) green, pink, lavender
   (E) white, fleur-de-lis, striped

3. Which room has white walls?

   I. Living room
   II. Dining room
   III. Den

   (A) I only
   (B) II only
   (C) III only
   (D) I or III
   (E) II or III

4. If Lance wishes to avoid repetition of any colors between the living room and the dining room, he can do so by changing the color of

   (A) the carpeting in the dining room
   (B) the wallpaper in the living room or the dining room
   (C) the wallpaper or the carpeting in the living room
   (D) the drapes in the dining room
   (E) the drapes in the dining room or the wallpaper in the living room

5. Gary: I wish you wouldn't drink so much beer. It's bad for your health.
   Nancy: How can you say that? I don't weigh a pound more than I did a year ago.

   Which of the following responses would most strengthen Gary's argument?

   (A) You weigh ten pounds more than you did six years ago.
   (B) Most people who drink a lot of beer do put on weight.
   (C) If you keep drinking so much beer, you will soon put on weight.
   (D) Putting on weight is not the only harmful effect of drinking beer.
   (E) You can put on weight in other ways than by drinking beer.

Questions 6 and 7

Students who are excused from Freshman Composition write better than those who take the course. Thus, we can encourage better writing by our students by dropping the Freshman Composition course.

6. The major flaw in the reasoning used in the argument above is that the author

   (A) bases the argument on a purely subjective judgment
   (B) does not cite evidence for the statements given
   (C) confuses cause and effect
   (D) fails to take into account any long-term effects of the course
   (E) assumes that all freshman composition courses are essentially alike

7. Each of the following, if true, would weaken the argument above EXCEPT

   (A) schools with no freshman composition course do not generally produce better student writers
   (B) most students who take the Freshman Composition course do not appreciably improve their writing skills
   (C) to be excused from Freshman Composition, a student must pass a rigorous writing test
   (D) each of the English department's best instructors teaches at least one Freshman Composition class each semester
   (E) 65 percent of the students surveyed reported that they learned a great deal about grammar and rhetoric from taking Freshman Composition

Questions 8–12

Five executives of a European corporation hold a conference in Rome.

Mr. A converses in Spanish and Italian.
Mr. B converses in Spanish and English
Mr. C converses in English and Italian
Mr. D converses in French and Spanish
Mr. E, a native Italian, can also converse in French.

8. Which, of the following, can act as interpreter when Mr. C and Mr. D wish to confer?

   (A) only Mr. A   (B) only Mr. B
   (C) only Mr. E   (D) Mr. A or Mr. B
   (E) any of the other three executives

9. Which of the following, cannot converse between them without an interpreter?

   (A) Mr. B and Mr. E
   (B) Mr. A and Mr. B
   (C) Mr. A and Mr. C
   (D) Mr. B and Mr. D
   (E) Mr. A and Mr. E

10. Besides Mr. E, which of the following can converse with Mr. D without an interpreter?

    (A) only Mr. A
    (B) only Mr. B
    (C) only Mr. C
    (D) Messrs. A and B
    (E) Messrs. A, B, and C

11. If a sixth executive is brought in, to be understood by the maximum number of the original five, he should be fluent in

    (A) English and French
    (B) Italian and English
    (C) French and Italian
    (D) Italian and Spanish
    (E) English and Spanish

12. Of the languages spoken at this conference, choose the two least common languages.

    (A) English and Spanish
    (B) English and French
    (C) Italian and Spanish
    (D) English and Italian
    (E) French and Spanish

Questions 13–16

All A's, B's, C's, D's, E's, and F's are Q's.
All A's are B's.
No B that is not an A is an F.
Some C's are A's.
All D's are C's.
Some C's are not B's.
No D is an A.
All Q's and only Q's that are neither B's nor C's are E's.

13. Which of the following can be deduced from the information given?

    (A) All F's are A's.
    (B) Some F's are A's.
    (C) Some F's are E's.
    (D) Some F's are C's.
    (E) All F's are A's, C's, or E's.

14. Which must be false if the information given is true?

    (A) No D's are B's.
    (B) Some B's are D's.
    (C) Some F's are both B's and C's.
    (D) Some Q's are neither B's nor E's.
    (E) Some F's are D's.

15. Which cannot be shown to be true or false on the basis of the information given?

    I.   No B or C is an E.
    II. Some C's are B's but not A's.
    III. No B is both an A and a D.

    (A) I only
    (B) II only
    (C) III only
    (D) I and II
    (E) II and III

16. P is not a B. Which of the following must be true?

    (A) P is an E.
    (B) If P is a C, it is neither and A nor a D.
    (C) If P is a Q, it is an E or a C.
    (D) If P is not an E, it is a C.
    (E) If P is a Q, it may be a C or an A, but not both.

Questions 17–22

At a congress of the Progressive Federal Party, the seven top party leaders, who are all cabinet ministers, are seated on the platform in order of rank. The Prime Minister, the party leader, is in the center. The closer a person is to the Prime Minister, the higher is his or her rank, with a person on the Prime Minister's right outranking one equidistant from the Prime Minister on her left. The seven leaders are Arning, Brenner, Civili, Dorner, Eckland, Fentz, and Grell.
Fentz is four places to the left of the Minister of Agriculture, who is two places to the right of Civili.
Brenner's neighbors are Arning and the Minister of Agriculture.
Grell is two places to the left of Dorner.
The Ministers of Education, Mining, and Culture are seated together, in that order, from left to right.
The remaining ministers are those of Social Welfare and Defense.

17. The Minister of Culture is

    (A) Arning
    (B) Brenner
    (C) Civili
    (D) Dorner
    (E) Eckland

18. The fifth-ranking person in the party hierarchy is

    (A) Grell, the Minister of Mining
    (B) Fentz, the Minister of Culture
    (C) Dorner, the Prime Minister
    (D) Eckland, the Minister of Defense
    (E) Arning, the Minister of Education

19. The Minister of Social Welfare

    I. outranks the Minister of Defense
    II. is outranked by the Minister of Mining

    (A) I only
    (B) II only
    (C) I and II only
    (D) I or II, but not both
    (E) Neither I nor II

20. How many of the seven party leaders outrank the Minister of Education

    (A) 2
    (B) 3
    (C) 4
    (D) 5
    (E) 6

21. If, during the congress, the Minister of Agriculture and the Minister of Education are ordered to exchange positions, which is true?

    (A) Arning will move to a seat six places away from his original seat.
    (B) Fentz will move up five places in the leadership ranking.
    (C) Eckland will move to a seat three places away from his original seat.
    (D) Grell will move up four places in the leadership ranking.
    (E) Eckland will move from the Prime Minister's left side to his right.

22. If, during the congress, Eckland is demoted two places in the party leadership ranking, which is true?

    (A) The Minister of Defense moves up one place in the leadership ranking.
    (B) Civili becomes the second-ranking leader in the party.
    (C) The Minister of Mining moves up two places in the leadership ranking.
    (D) Dorner is demoted within the leadership.
    (E) The positions of five persons within the leadership remain unchanged.

23. Lillian, who has just celebrated her 107th birthday, attributes her longevity to her lifelong habit of drinking a double shot of whiskey each night and smoking three cigars each morning.

    The best way to counter her argument would be to point out that

    (A) smoking has been proved to be a causative factor in several life-threatening diseases
    (B) other factors besides those mentioned may have caused her to live 107 years
    (C) not all centenarians drink alcohol and smoke tobacco
    (D) Lillian should not be consuming the substances mentioned without medical advice
    (E) alcohol has been shown to kill brain cells

Questions 24 and 25

If Dr. Seymour's theory is correct, then the events she predicts will happen. The events she predicted did happen. Therefore, her theory must be correct.

24. Which of the following arguments has a logical structure that most nearly resembles that of the argument above?

    (A) If we win the game, we will be the league champions. We won the game; therefore, we are the league champions.
    (B) If the fan is running, then the electricity must be on. The electricity is on; therefore, the fan must be running.
    (C) If the store is open, I will buy a shirt. I think the store is open; therefore, I should be able to buy a shirt.
    (D) If Alice answers her phone, then my prediciton is correct. I predict that she is at home; therefore, she will answer her phone.
    (E) If Ted's flight is delayed, he will miss his appointment. He kept his appointment; therefore, his flight must have been on time.

25. The conclusion drawn in the argument above would be valid if which of the following were true?

    (A) Only Dr. Seymour's theory full explains the events which happened.
    (B) If the events Dr. Seymour predicted happen, then her theory is correct.
    (C) If Dr. Seymour's theory is correct, then the events she predicted may happen.
    (D) Only Dr. Seymour predicted the events which happened.
    (E) If the events Dr. Seymour predicted happen, then Dr. Seymour's theory may be correct.

S T O P

IF YOU FINISH BEFORE TIME IS CALLED, YOU MAY CHECK YOUR WORK ON THIS SECTION ONLY.
DO NOT WORK ON ANY OTHER SECTION IN THE TEST.

SECTION 7

Time - 30 Minutes

38 Questions

Directions: Each sentence below has one or two blanks, each blank indicating that something has been omitted. Beneath the sentence are five lettered words or sets of words. Choose the word or set of words for each blank that best fits the meaning of the sentence as a whole.

1. Because the ice grains in slush are so loosely bonded, it is ------ and thus can cause an avalanche even on gentle slopes.

   (A) compact
   (B) flexible
   (C) interdependent
   (D) paradoxical
   (E) unstable

2. While some of the drawings are well rendered, others are mere ------; nonetheless, nearly all possess a sort of rude ------ that catches the eye.

   (A) portraits...grandeur
   (B) illustrations...finesse
   (C) daubs...vigor
   (D) caricatures...polish
   (E) mementoes...familiarity

3. With their pea-sized brains and giant bodies, dinosaurs became a symbol of lumbering stupidity; their extinction seemed only to ------ their ------ design.

   (A) betray...fundamental
   (B) hypothesize...incongruous
   (C) invalidate...conscious
   (D) embody...ultimate
   (E) confirm...flawed

4. The shortcomings of Mr. Brooks' analysis are ------ his ------ in explaining financial complexity and the sheer importance of his text.

   (A) alleviated by...ineptitude
   (B) offset by...clarity
   (C) magnified by...precision
   (D) demonstrated by...adroitness
   (E) mitigated by...incompetence

5. To a person ------ natural history, his country or seaside stroll is a walk through a gallery filled with wonderful works of art, nine-tenths of which have their faces turned to the wall.

   (A) enamored of
   (B) uninstructed in
   (C) responsive to
   (D) disillusioned with
   (E) dependent on

6. Do not be ------ by that fiery formula which springs from the lips of so many ------ old gentlemen: "I shall write to *The Times* about this outrage!"

   (A) dissuaded...indefatigable
   (B) daunted...irresolute
   (C) intimidated...choleric
   (D) discredited...crotchety
   (E) exasperated...apathetic

7. Despite John's somewhat ------ undergraduate career, as undistinguished by academic brilliance as by dissolute excesses, nothing could convince his anxious though doting mother that her son was neither a genius nor a ------.

   (A) ordinary...prodigy
   (B) colorful...profligate
   (C) anomalous...zealot
   (D) lackluster...libertine
   (E) indifferent...miser

Directions: In each of the following questions, a related pair of words or phrases is followed by five lettered pairs of words or phrases. Select the lettered pair that best expresses a relationship similar to that expressed in the original pair.

8. STAR : CLUSTER::
   (A) orange : rind
   (B) comet : orbit
   (C) tree : clump
   (D) mirror : reflection
   (E) bulb : lamp

9. GUFFAW : LAUGH::
   (A) sip : drink
   (B) squabble : quarrel
   (C) whimper : cry
   (D) sneeze : cough
   (E) lope : run

10. LOBSTER : POT::
    (A) sardine : tin
    (B) goldfish : bowl
    (C) sparrow : nest
    (D) oyster : shell
    (E) rabbit : snare

11. PISTON : CYLINDER::
    (A) elevator : shaft
    (B) vertex : triangle
    (C) bullet : revolver
    (D) kitchen : colander
    (E) valve : bearing

12. ERUDITE : SCHOLAR::
    (A) remote : hermit
    (B) pliant : beggar
    (C) meandering : traveler
    (D) mendacious : liar
    (E) vindictive : conqueror

13. DRUM : TYMPANI::
    (A) cornet : percussion
    (B) oboe : woodwind
    (C) piano : orchestra
    (D) violin : concerto
    (E) coda : symphony

14. GIBBER : SENSE::
    (A) jabber : noise
    (B) toddle : mobility
    (C) dawdle : deference
    (D) vacillate : resolution
    (E) disobey : order

15. MITIGATE : PUNISHMENT::
    (A) aggregate : wealth
    (B) execute : mandate
    (C) commute : sentence
    (D) collect : fine
    (E) set : penalty

16. SENTENTIOUS : APHORISM::
    (A) redundant : criticism
    (B) deprecatory : panegyric
    (C) allegorical : maxim
    (D) symbolic : adage
    (E) laudatory : eulogy

Directions: Each passage in this group is followed by questions based on its content. After reading a passage, choose the best answer to each question. Answer all questions following a passage on the basis of what is stated or implied in the passage.

(This passage was written prior to 1950.)

We now know that what constitutes practically all of matter is empty space; relatively enormous voids in which revolve with lightning velocity infinitesimal particles so utterly small that they
(5) have never been seen or photographed. The existence of these particles has been demonstrated by mathematical physicists and their operations determined by ingenious laboratory experiments. It was not until 1911 that experiments by Sir Ernest Ruth-
(10) erford revealed the architecture of the mysterious atom. Moseley, Bohr, Fermi, Millikan, Compton, Urey, and others have also worked on the problem.
Matter is composed of molecules whose average diameter is about 1/125 millionth of an inch. Mole-
(15) cules are composed of atoms so small that about 5 million could be placed in a row on the period at the end of this sentence. Long thought to be the ultimate, indivisible constituent of matter, the atom has been found to consist roughly of a proton, the

(20) positive electrical element in the atomic nucleus, surrounded by electrons, the negative electric elements swirling about the proton.

17. The primary purpose of the passage is to
    (A) honor the pioneering efforts of Sir Ernest Rutherford and this followers
    (B) refute the existence of submicroscopic particles
    (C) illustrate how scientists measure molecular diameter
    (D) summarize the then current findings on the composition of matter
    (E) analyze evidence against one theory of atomic structure

18. According to the passage, all of the following were true of the center of the atom EXCEPT that it
    (A) had not yet been seen by the naked eye
    (B) contained elements that were positively charged
    (C) was very little larger than a molecule
    (D) followed experimentally determinable processes
    (E) was smaller than 1/125 millionth of an inch

19. By referring to the period at the end of the sentence (lines 16–17), the author intends to point up the atom's
    (A) density
    (B) mystery
    (C) velocity
    (D) consistency
    (E) minuteness

20. Which of the following relationships most closely parallels the relationship between the proton and the electrons described in the passage?
    (A) A hawk to its prey
    (B) A blueprint to a framework
    (C) A planet to its satellites
    (D) A magnet to iron filings
    (E) A compound to its elements

No one can be a great thinker who does not realize that as a thinker it is her first duty to follow her intellect to whatever conclusions it may lead. Truth gains more even by the errors of one who, with due
(5) study and preparation, thinks for herself, than by the true opinions of those who only hold them because they do not suffer themselves to think. Not that it is solely, or chiefly, to form great thinkers that freedom of thinking is required. On the con-
(10) trary, it is as much or even more indispensable to enable average human beings to attain the mental stature which they are capable of. There have been, and may again be, great individual thinkers in a general atmosphere of mental slavery. But there
(15) never has been, nor ever will be, in that atmosphere an intellectually active people. Where any people has made a temporary approach to such a character, it has been because the dread of heterodox speculation was for a time suspended. Where

(20) there is a tacit convention that principles are not to
be disputed; where the discussion of the greatest
questions which can occupy humanity is considered to be closed, we cannot hope to find that generally high scale of mental activity which has made
(25) some periods of history so remarkable. Never when
controversy avoided the subjects which are large
and important enough to kindle enthusiasm was the
mind of a people stirred up from its foundations
and the impulse given which raised even persons of
(30) the most ordinary intellect to something of the
dignity of thinking beings.
  She who knows only her own side of the case
knows little of that. Her reasons may be good, and
no one may have been able to refute them. But if
(35) she is equally unable to refute the reasons of the
opposite side; if she does not so much as know
what they are, she has no ground for preferring
either opinion. The rational position for her would
be suspension of judgment, and unless she contents
(40) herself with that, she is either led by authority, or
adopts, like the generality of the world, the side to
which she feels the most inclination. Nor is it
enough that she should hear the arguments of
adversaries from her own teachers, presented as
(45) they state them, and accompanied by what they
offer as refutations. That is not the way to do justice to the arguments, or bring them into real contact with her own mind. She must be able to hear
them from persons who actually believe them; who
(50) defend them in earnest, and do their very utmost
for them. She must know them in their most plausible and persuasive form: she must feel the whole
force of the difficulty which the true view of the
subject has to encounter and dispose of; else she
(55) will never really possess herself of the portion of
truth which meets and removes that difficulty.
Ninety-nine in a hundred of what are called educated persons are in this condition; even of those
who can argue fluently for their opinions. Their
(60) conclusion may be true, but it might be false for
anything they know: they have never thrown themselves into the mental position of those who think
differently from them and considered what such
persons may have to say; and consequently they do
(65) not, in any proper sense of the word, know the doctrines which they themselves profess. They do not
know those parts of it which explain and justify the
remainder; the considerations which show that a
fact which seemingly conflicts with another is
(70) reconcilable with it, or that, of two apparently
strong reasons, one and not the other ought to be
preferred.

21. According to the author, it is always advisable to

(A) have opinions which cannot be refuted
(B) adopt the point of view to which one feels the
    most inclination
(C) be acquainted with the arguments favoring the
    point of view with which one disagrees
(D) suspend heterodox speculation in favor of doc-
    trinnaire approaches
(E) ignore the accepted opinions of the vast majority

22. According to the author, in a great period such as the
Renaissance we may expect to find

(A) acceptance of truth
(B) controversy over principles
(C) inordinate enthusiasm
(D) a dread of heterodox speculation
(E) a suspension of judgment

23. According to the author, which of the following
statements is true?

(A) Most educated people study both sides of a
    question.
(B) Heterodox speculation will lead to many unnec-
    essary errors of thinking.
(C) In debatable issues, we should rely on the opi-
    nions of the experts for guidance.
(D) It is wise to hear both sides of a debatable issue
    from one's teachers.
(E) The majority of those who argue eloquently
    truly know only one side of an issue.

24. As it is used in line 7 of the passage, the word "suffer" most nearly means

(A) endure
(B) undergo
(C) permit
(D) support
(E) force

25. It can be inferred from the passage that a person who
knows only her own side of an issue is regarded by
the author as

(A) timorous
(B) opinionated
(C) heterodox
(D) educated
(E) rational

26. According to the author, the person who holds orthodox beliefs without examination may be described in
all of the following ways EXCEPT as

(A) enslaved by tradition
(B) less than fully rational
(C) determined on controversy
(D) having a closed mind
(E) unwilling to adopt new ideas

27. It can be inferred from the passage that the author
would be most likely to agree with which of the following statements?

(A) A truly great thinker makes no mistakes.
(B) Periods of intellectual achievement are periods
    of unorthodox reflection.
(C) The refutation of accepted ideas can best be
    provided by one's own teachers.
(D) Excessive controversy prevents clear thinking.
(E) In a period of mental slavery, no true intellectual
    thought is possible.

Directions: Each question below consists of a word printed in capital letters, followed by five lettered words or phrases. Choose the lettered word or phrase that is most nearly opposite in meaning to the word in capital letters.

Since some of the questions require you to distinguish fine shades of meaning, be sure to consider all the choices before deciding which one is best.

28. RECOLLECT:
(A) comprise
(B) misplace
(C) settle
(D) forget
(E) administer

29. MISAPPREHENSION:
(A) indignation
(B) derision
(C) intense speculation
(D) approximate estimation
(E) correct interpretation

30. ABIDE:
(A) retract an offer
(B) refuse to endure
(C) shield from harm
(D) exonerate
(E) welcome

31. BENEVOLENT:
(A) tense
(B) intrepid
(C) malicious
(D) prominent
(E) disinterested

32. PRECIPITATE:
(A) intricate
(B) devious
(C) posthumous
(D) dilatory
(E) contradictory

33. ACERBITY:
(A) noteworthiness
(B) hypocrisy
(C) mildness of temperament
(D) lack of anxiety
(E) thirst for pleasure

34. EXTIRPATE:
(A) dilate
(B) implicate
(C) proliferate
(D) expostulate
(E) incriminate

35. TORTUOUS:
(A) merciful
(B) direct
(C) dangerous
(D) legal
(E) tawdry

36. APLOMB:
(A) discomposure
(B) righteousness
(C) temerity
(D) disapprobation
(E) parsimoniousness

37. BEATIFIC:
(A) unattractive
(B) arrhythmic
(C) enormous
(D) fiendish
(E) radical

38. ODIUM:
(A) fragrance
(B) monotony
(C) idiosyncrasy
(D) veneration
(E) vigilance

S T O P

IF YOU FINISH BEFORE TIME IS CALLED, YOU MAY CHECK YOUR WORK ON THIS SECTION ONLY.
DO NOT WORK ON ANY OTHER SECTION IN THE TEST.

Answer Key

Note: The answers to the quantitative sections are keyed to the corresponding review areas in the Mathematics Review (Chapter 11). The numbers in parentheses after each answer refer to the math topic(s) covered by that particular question.

Section 1 Verbal

1.	B	11.	B	21.	C	31.	B
2.	B	12.	B	22.	B	32.	A
3.	C	13.	C	23.	A	33.	D
4.	D	14.	C	24.	E	34.	B
5.	E	15.	D	25.	E	35.	C
6.	C	16.	E	26.	C	36.	E
7.	E	17.	C	27.	C	37.	B
8.	D	18.	D	28.	D	38.	C
9.	E	19.	C	29.	C		
10.	E	20.	B	30.	B		

Section 2 Verbal

1.	C	11.	C	21.	A	31.	C
2.	C	12.	B	22.	B	32.	E
3.	E	13.	C	23.	E	33.	C
4.	D	14.	D	24.	D	34.	E
5.	D	15.	C	25.	C	35.	E
6.	C	16.	E	26.	A	36.	D
7.	A	17.	D	27.	D	37.	A
8.	C	18.	E	28.	A	38.	C
9.	A	19.	C	29.	E		
10.	E	20.	C	30.	D		

Section 3 Quantitative

1.	A (I-B, H)	9.	B (I)	17.	D (III-D, G)	25.	C (II-E)
2.	B (I-B)	10.	A (III-F)	18.	E (II-A)	26.	C (I-B)
3.	C (I-D)	11.	C (III-H)	19.	B (II-B)	27.	E (II-A)
4.	B (I-C, D)	12.	C (III-A)	20.	C (II-C)	28.	E (III-D)
5.	B (I-G)	13.	B (III-D)	21.	E (I-C)	29.	D (III-G)
6.	C (II-A)	14.	C (III-H)	22.	C (I-D)	30.	E (III-G)
7.	B (I-A)	15.	A (III-A, D)	23.	B (II-B)		
8.	A (II-G)	16.	A (II-B)	24.	A (II-E)		

Section 4 Quantitative

1.	C (III-G)	9.	B (I-H)	17.	C (II-A)	25.	B (IV-C)
2.	C (III-G)	10.	A (I-C, H)	18.	B (I-D)	26.	E (H-E)
3.	B (III-AC)	11.	B (I-B, C, H)	19.	C (I-D)	27.	C (II-A, III-G)
4.	A (III-G)	12.	A (II-G)	20.	B (II-E)	28.	E (II-A)
5.	B (I-B)	13.	A (II-A)	21.	B (II-E)	29.	E (I-B)
6.	B (I-H)	14.	B (II)	22.	D (IV-B)	30.	C (I-F)
7.	C (I-C)	15.	A (I-B, C, H)	23.	B (IV-A)		
8.	A (I-B, C, H)	16.	D (II-B)	24.	B (IV-C)		

Section 5   Analytical

1.	A	8.	A	15.	E	22.	C
2.	E	9.	C	16.	E	23.	B
3.	D	10.	C	17.	C	24.	E
4.	E	11.	C	18.	C	25.	C
5.	D	12.	B	19.	A		
6.	C	13.	D	20.	A		
7.	A	14.	A	21.	B		

Section 6   Analytical

1.	A	8.	E	15.	B	22.	B
2.	B	9.	A	16.	C	23.	B
3.	D	10.	D	17.	C	24.	B
4.	C	11.	D	18.	A	25.	B
5.	D	12.	B	19.	D		
6.	C	13.	E	20.	E		
7.	B	14.	D	21.	B		

Section 7 Verbal

1.	E	11.	A	21.	C	31.	C
2.	C	12.	D	22.	B	32.	D
3.	E	13.	B	23.	E	33.	C
4.	B	14.	D	24.	C	34.	C
5.	B	15.	C	25.	B	35.	B
6.	C	16.	E	26.	C	36.	A
7.	D	17.	D	27.	B	37.	D
8.	C	18.	C	28.	D	38.	D
9.	B	19.	E	29.	E		
10.	E	20.	C	30.	B		

Answer Explanations

Section 1

1. B. The use of *but* indicates that the dean's attempt to keep control failed. It did so because it was *frustrated* by the board of trustees. None of the other possible actions of the board of trustees would necessarily have caused the dean's attempt to fail.

2. B. The dispute goes beyond or *transcends* mere ideas, for it influences the financial and professional futures of the disputants.
   Note the use of *mere* to downplay the importance of ideas to the essence of the dispute.

3. C. The key phrase here is "move on." If editors have to travel from firm to firm to succeed in their field, then publishing can be classified as an *itinerant* profession, a profession marked by traveling.

4. D. The physicists have had good reason to believe in the principle because it has *survived* rigorous or strict tests. These tests have *proved* that the principle is accurate.
   Note how the second clause supports the first, explaining why the physicists have had reason to be confident in the principle.

5. E. If Mrs. Woolf combines both radical and nonradical elements in her fictions, then she presents *an anomalous* or contradictory image.

6. C. The embittered benefactor thinks of them as *ingrates* (ungrateful persons) because they do not thank him sufficiently for his generosity. He does not think of them as *misers* (hoarders of wealth): although they are stingy in expressing thanks, they are extravagant in spending money. He certainly does not think of them as *louts* (clumsy oafs), *prigs* (self-righteous fussbudgets), or *renegades* (traitors) : the specific attribute he resents in them is ingratitude, not cloddishness, self-satisfaction, or perfidy.

7. E. The field is cluttered by a *welter* or chaotic jumble of contradictory theories.
   Choice A is incorrect. While *bonanza* means abundance, it is an abundance of good things, a desired abundance. Here the abundance of theories is undesired; it is a confusion, not a blessing.

8. D. The playing field in *football* is called the *gridiron*. The playing field in *baseball* is called the *diamond*.

   (Defining Characteristic)

9. E. A *laurel wreath* is the symbol of *victory*. An *olive branch* is the symbol of *peace*.
   Beware eye-catchers. We may associate *idleness* with the notion of lying under a *palm tree*; however, this is not an essential or necessary relationship.

   (Symbol and Abstraction It Represents)

10. E. A *geologist* studies rocks; *gneiss* is a type of rock. A *botanist* studies plants; a *zinnia* is a type of plant.
    Beware eye-catchers. A *meteorologist* deals with weather and other atmospheric phenomena, not with *asteroids* and other astronomical phenomena. Likewise, an *entomologist* deals with ants, not *anteaters*.

    (Defining Characteristic)

11. B. *Agitator* (trouble-maker) is a synonym for *firebrand*. *Renegade* (traitor) is a synonym for *turncoat*.

    (Synonym)

12. B. Someone *callow* is immature and will not reach full development till *maturity*. Something *incipient* is beginning to become apparent and will not reach full development till *fruition*.

    (Antonym Variant)

13. C. *Inoculation* (introduction of a serum or vaccine into a living creature) results in *immunity*. *Exposure* to the elements results in *weathering*.

    (Cause and Effect)

14. C. Someone *dispassionate* or temperate in judgment is lacking in *partisanship* or bias. Someone *intemperate* or immoderate is lacking in *moderation*.

    (Antonym Variant)

15. D. Something *grisly* or gruesome causes one to *recoil* or flinch. Something *heartrending* or severely distressing causes one to *weep*.

    (Cause and Effect)

16. E. A *tocsin* is the ringing of a bell that signals *danger*. A *knell* is the ringing of a bell that signals *death*.
    Beware eye-catchers. *Tocsin* and *toxin* sound alike but are unrelated. Similarly, beware tempting marginal relationships. A *clarion* call of a trumpet may summon one to *battle*; it does not *by definition* do so.

    (Function)

17. C. The author first establishes the general picture
        of unoriginal, passive Mary Shelley and then
        goes about demolishing it by bringing out just
        how innovative Shelley was in departing from
        the traditional model of the overreacher. Thus,
        the author's purpose is to *rehabilitate* Shelley's
        literary reputation.
        Choice A is incorrect. Others have discounted
        Shelley's contribution; this author esteems it.
        Choice B is incorrect. The author mentions,
        but does not trace, Shelley's familiarity with
        the then current scientific and literary
        revolution.
        Choice D is incorrect. While the author deals
        with this question, she does so as part of her
        general attempt to reevaluate Shelley.
        Choice E is incorrect. It is unsupported by the
        passage.

18. D. Immediately before quoting Praz, the author
        states that the general view of Shelley depicts
        her as "a transparent medium through which
        passed the ideas of those around her." The quo-
        tation from Praz provides an excellent example
        of this particular point of view.
        To answer this question correctly, you do not
        need to reread the passage in its entirety.
        Quickly scan the passage for the name Praz;
        reread only the context in which it appears.

19. C. The opening sentence points out that Shelley
        herself acknowledged the influence of her
        unplanned immersion in the scientific and liter-
        ary revolutions of her time. Clearly, the author
        of the passage concedes this as true of Shelley.

20. B. The concluding paragraph distinguishes Fran-
        kenstein from the other overreachers in his
        desire not to extend his own life but to impart
        life to another (by creating his monster). Thus,
        his purpose is *atypical* of the traditional
        overreacher.
        To say that someone *parts from* the traditional
        figure of the overreacher is to say that he *differs*
        from it. Thus, to answer this question quickly,
        scan the passage looking for *overreacher* and
        different (or their synonyms).

21. C. Choice C is correct. The opening sentence
        states that ethology and behaviorist psychology
        (*two differing theories*) illustrate the distinction
        between learning and instinct (*behavioral proc-
        esses*). The discussion of these two theories
        that follows explains the behavioral processes.
        Choice A is incorrect. The passage does not
        suggest that one behavioral theory is more
        effective than another.
        Choice B is incorrect. The passage sums up
        current theories; it does not propose a new one
        in their place.
        Choice D is incorrect. The passage presents
        Pavlov's arguments in the course of explaining
        behaviorist psychology; it does not dispute
        them.

        Choice E is incorrect. The passage is con-
        cerned with learned behavior as well as instinc-
        tive or innate behavior.

22. B. Choice B is correct. In lines 13-16, the author
        states that Lorenz and Tinbergen were, with
        Frisch, the founders of ethology (the study of
        instinct).
        Choice A is incorrect. Only Lorenz and Tin-
        bergen are cited for their work with the egg-
        rolling response in geese; nothing in the pas-
        sage suggests that Frisch worked with egg-
        rolling.
        Choice C is incorrect. It is unsupported by the
        passage.
        Choice D is incorrect. Behaviorists, not etholo-
        gists, are cited as favoring strictly controlled
        conditions (lines 42-44).
        Choice E is incorrect. Nothing in the passage
        suggests the ethologists have invalidated the
        behaviorists' approach.

23. A. Choice A is correct. What is remarkable about
        the goose's response is that "at first glance (it)
        might seem to be a thoughtful solution to a
        problem." This suggests that the appearance of
        purpose and intelligence is what makes the act
        remarkable or noteworthy.
        Choice B is incorrect. This is an aspect of the
        goose's response; it is not what makes the
        goose's response noteworthy. It is not remarka-
        ble for an egg-rolling response to be triggered
        by an egg.
        Choice C is incorrect. The egg-rolling
        response supports ethological theories; it does
        not refute or disprove them.
        Choice D is incorrect. This is an aspect of the
        goose's response, not what makes the goose's
        response noteworthy.
        Choice E is incorrect. It is both inaccurate fac-
        tually (the response lasts longer than four
        weeks) and not an aspect of the goose's
        response that would be noteworthy.

24. E. Choice E is correct. You can arrive at it by the
        process of elimination.
        Statement I is true. Behaviorists such as Pavlov
        worked with the unconditioned responses of
        animals. Therefore, you can eliminate Choices
        B and C.
        Statement II is untrue. Imprinting is a term cur-
        rent among ethologists, not behaviorists (lines
        36-40). Therefore, you can eliminate Choice D.
        Statement III is true. Behaviorists assume ani-
        mals act in order to obtain rewards or avoid
        punishments (*shun negative stimuli*). There-
        fore, you can eliminate Choice A.
        Only Choice E is left. It is the correct answer.

25. E. The author does *not* settle any arguments; he
        merely presents differing theories without
        attempting to resolve their differences.
        Choice A is incorrect. The author defines terms
        throughout the entire passage.

Choice B is incorrect. The author points out equivalents (*functional parallels*) between the two systems (lines 55-64).

Choice C is incorrect. The author refers to experimental studies involving both classical and operant conditioning.

Choice D is incorrect. The author uses the example of beer bottles to illustrate what sort of convex objects evoke the egg-rolling response from geese (lines 27-29).

26. C.   The trial-and-error method of experimentation first rewards the animal for even partial performance of the desired response but later rewards only increasingly precise behavior. Thus, this method requires *an increasing refinement of behavior* from the experimental animal.

Choice A is incorrect. Although both rewards and punishments may be used in operant conditioning, the animal does not have to be exposed to punishment for the experiment to succeed.

Choice B is incorrect. The experimenter asks for increasingly precise behavior. Nothing suggests he or she gives increasingly greater rewards.

Choice D is incorrect. Nothing suggests that the cues necessarily change.

Choice E is incorrect. At the onset of the experiment, the experimenter rewards *even partial performance* of the desired behavior.

27. C.   Although the author reports that behaviorists view instinct as "irrelevant to learning," his description of the egg-rolling process shows no such bias against the ethologists' point of view. Instead, he focuses on pointing out correspondences between the two approaches to behavior in an unbiased, dispassionate manner; the tone of his discussion is one of *neutrality*.

28. D.   The opposite of to *sedate* or *tranquillize* is to *stimulate* or arouse.
Beware eye-catchers. Note the abundance of medical terms among the answer choices here.
Think of "sedating a restless patient."

29. C.   The opposite of *apathetic* or indifferent is *enthusiastic*.
Word Parts Clue: *A-* means without; *path-* means feeling. Someone *apathetic* is without feeling; he or she does not care.
Think of "sadly apathetic voters."

30. B.   The opposite of to *dislodge* or cause something to shift is to *secure* or fasten it in place.
Think of "dislodging a boulder" from its position.

31. B.   The opposite of *celibacy* or chastity is *promiscuity* or indiscriminate sexual union.
Think of "vows of celibacy."

32. A.   The opposite of *fledgling* or untried is *experienced*. The image is of a young bird just capable of leaving the nest.
Think of "fledgling pilots trying their wings."

33. D.   The opposite of *insipidness* or lack of flavor is *savoriness*, the quality of being flavorsome.
Think of the "insipidness of overcooked boiled cabbage."

34. B.   The opposite of to *sequester* or segregate is to *permit to mingle*.
Word Parts Clue: *Se-* means apart. To *sequester* someone means to set him apart.
Think of "sequestered jurors."

35. C.   The opposite of *equanimity* (emotional balance or composure) is *agitation*.
Word Parts Clue: *Equ-* means even; *anim-* means mind or spirit. *Equanimity* is an evenness of mind; composure.
Think of "something shattering one's equanimity."

36. E.   The opposite of to *anathematize* or curse is to *bless*.
Think of "anathematizing one's foes."

37. B.   The opposite of *moribund* or approaching death is *vital* or full of life.
Word Parts Clue: *Mori-* means die. *Moribund* means dying.
Think of "a moribund patient."

38. C.   The opposite of to *distill* or concentrate in purity is to *adulterate* or make impure (as by adding inessentials).
Think of "distilling strong brandy."

Section 2

1. C.   While all the answer choices are plausible goals for an anchorman, only one is acceptable in light of the second clause: *dispassion* or calm. Shaw's maintenance of his composure is illustrated by his ability to maintain the normal pitch of his voice.

2. C.   By definition, *parasites* sap or drain nutrients from their hosts.

3. E.   Inconsistencies in a story would *warrant* or justify disbelief or incredulity on anyone's part, whether or not he considered himself a *skeptic* (doubter).

4. D.   The *assiduous* or diligent *execution* of one's job would give one's employer no cause for complaint.

5. D. It is Williams' *penchant* or liking for theatrical-ity that causes critics to *denigrate* or belittle his plays as mere melodrama.
Note how the use of *mere* and the sense of the Shakespearean quotation convey the idea that Williams' plays have been sullied or belittled.

6. C. Because Mr. Southern so understands the spirit of the age, he is unafraid of or *undaunted by* its paradoxes.
To say that a historian has entered thoroughly into the spirit of an age is a compliment. Thus, the missing word must be complimentary in meaning.

7. A. If language shapes and *determines* the very thoughts we are able to have, then it is certainly far more than merely *incidental* to or acciden-tally linked with thought and communication. Note how the phrase *far from being* signals the basic contrast of the sentence.

8. C. A *barge* is a kind of *vessel* or ship. A *shovel* is a kind of *implement* or tool.

(Class and Member)

9. A. Something *ramshackle* or rickety lacks *sound-ness* or solidity. Something *garbled* or jumbled lacks *clarity*.

(Antonym Variant)

10. E. To *dampen enthusiasm* is to diminish it. To *mute* (muffle) *sound* is to diminish it.
Note that Choice C is incorrect: to *distract attention* is not to diminish it but to divert it in a new direction.

(Defining Characteristic)

11. C. A *burst* is a sudden violent outbreak of *sound*. A *blast* is a sudden violent outbreak (heavy gust) of wind.
Beware eye-catchers. Choice D is incorrect. A *glimmer* is a feeble or intermittent *light*, not a sudden violent flare or blast of light.

(Degree of Intensity)

12. B. Domesticated *doves* are kept in an enclosure called a *cote*. Domesticated *pigs* are kept in an enclosure called a *sty*.
Note that Choice E is incorrect. While *foxes* live in *dens*, foxes are not domestic animals and dens are not manmade enclosures.

(Defining Characteristic)

13. C. A *shot* is part of a *salvo* (a simultaneous dis-charge of shots). An *arrow* is part of a *volley* (a simultaneous discharge of arrows).
Beware eye-catchers. *Salvo* is unrelated to salve or *ointment*.

(Part to Whole)

14. D. A *crab* is an example of a *crustacean*. A *spi-der* is an example of an *arachnid*.

(Class and Member)

15. C. *Skulduggery* or dishonest, unscrupulous behav-ior is the mark of the *swindler*. *Chicanery* or trickery is the mark of the *trickster*.

(Defining Characteristic)

16. E. *Self-respecting* is less extreme than *vainglo-rious* or excessively proud. *Careful* is less extreme than *punctilious* or excessively atten-tive to fine points.

(Degree of Intensity)

17. D. The concluding sentence of the opening para-graph mentions factors that produced the crop of black writers who made up the Harlem Ren-aissance. The subsequent paragraph continues the discussion of these social and political factors.
Choice A is incorrect. Although the opening sentence indicates that the willingness of black writers to portray their own lives was a contrib-uting factor to the Harlem Renaissance, the next sentence makes it clear that this willing-ness was only *part* of what was going on.
Choice B is incorrect. The author is concerned with these writers as part of an American liter-ary movement, not a worldwide crusade.
Choice C is incorrect. The author cites exam-ples of specific injustices in passing.
Choice E is incorrect. It is unsupported by the passage.

18. E. The author's use of such terms as "nobility of expression" and "masters of recent American literature" makes it clear his attitude is one of *admiration*.

19. C. The fact that the writers were more involved with fighting problems in the system than with attacking the system itself suggests that funda-mentally they *were not opposed to* the demo-cratic system of government.
Choice A is incorrect. The fact that they did not revolt against the system does not necessar-ily imply that they played a minor part in fight-ing abuses of the system.
Choices B, D, and E are incorrect. None are suggested by the statement.

20. C.   In lines 8-10, the author mentions the growing interest in social and economic problems
among the writers of the Harlem Renaissance.
They used poetry, prose, and song to cry out
against social and economic wrongs. Thus,
they transformed their growing social and
political interest into art.
Choice A is incorrect. The author distrusts the
"foreign ideologies" (line 27) with their commitment to international solidarity.
Choice B is incorrect. The author states they
wished to improve American culture.
Choices D and E are incorrect. Neither is
implied by the author.

21. A.   Both the author's reference to historical interpretations of the Negro writer's role (lines 52-
54) and the author's evident concern to distinguish Negro writers from those who
"embraced" socialist and communist propaganda (lines 24-28) suggest he is a historian
interested in presenting these writers as loyal
Americans.
Choice B is incorrect. The author touches on
literature only in relationship to historical
events.
Choices C, D and E are incorrect. There is
nothing to suggest any of these interpretations
in the passage.

22. B.   The author's point is that the writers essentially
ignored socialist and communist propaganda.
This is apparently contradicted by the *Messenger* quote asserting that the New Negro (and
thus the new black writer) was *produced* by the
same forces that produced socialism and com-
munism. The author gives qualified assent to
that assertion ("Such forces *may* have produced
the New Negro").

23. E.   The passage cites the battles for better working
conditions, desegregation, and social and political equality, among others.
Choice A is unanswerable on the basis of the
passage. The passage mentions an "improvement in the capacity for expression" in the
period, but cites no factors leading to this stylistic improvement.
Choice B is unanswerable on the basis of the
passage. It mentions no specific names.
Choice C is unanswerable on the basis of the
passage. The passage states the writers did not
"embrace the several foreign ideologies that
sought to sink their roots" in America. However, it nowhere suggests that the writers were
in rebellion against these foreign ideologies.
Choice D is unanswerable on the basis of the
passage. No such information is supplied.

24. D.   The author takes the reader through Wegener's
reasoning step by step, describing what led
Wegener to reach his conclusions.

25. C.   The author both notes that Wegener's theory is
revolutionary and indicates that it defies our
conventional notions of the rigidity and immobility of the continents. At the same time, he
presents Wegener's reasoning fully and objectively, neither mocking him nor adulating him.
Thus, the author displays a *judicious* attitude, a
level-headed, academically respectable
approach to a then controversial theory.

26. A.   Since the existence of the correspondences
between the various coastal contours was used
by Wegener as a basis for formulating his theory of continental drift, it can be inferred that
the correspondences provide evidence for the
theory.
Choice B is incorrect. The passage does not
indicate that Pangea's existence has been
proved.
Choice C is incorrect. It is the relative heaviness of sima, not the level or depth of sima,
that suggested the possibility of the lighter continents drifting.
Choice D is incorrect. Mobility rather than
immobility would provide evidence for continental drift.
Choice E is incorrect. The continents are
lighter than the underlying sima.

27. D.   Choice D is answerable on the basis of the passage. The next-to-the-last sentence of the second paragraph states that the Americas
"apparently drifted toward the west."

28. A.   The opposite of to *smart* or cause a sharp stinging pain is to *soothe*.
Think of "a cut that smarts."

29. E.   The opposite of *lucid* (clear) is *obscure*.
Think of "lucid thinking."

30. D.   The opposite of the *periphery* (outward boundary) is the *center*.
Think of the "periphery or outskirts of a city."

31. C.   The opposite of *enigmatic* (puzzling; mysterious) is *unambiguous* or clear.
Think of the Mona Lisa's "enigmatic smile."

32. E.   The opposite of to *repudiate* (disown; refuse to
acknowledge) is to *accept*.
Think of "repudiating a debt."

33. C.   The opposite of *aloofness* (remoteness, indifference) is *concern*.
Think of "haughty aloofness."

34. E.   The opposite of to *exhume* or disinter is to bury
or *inter*.
Word Parts Clue: *Ex-* means out. *Humus* means
earth. To *exhume* is to dig out of the earth.
Think of "exhuming a corpse."

35. E.   The opposite of *despotic* (imperious, domineering) is *humble*.
Think of "a despotic tyrant."

36. D.   The opposite of to *obfuscate* or confuse is to
clarify.
Word Parts Clue: *Ob-* means completely; *fusc-*
means dark; *-ate* means to make. To *obfuscate*
is to becloud or make completely dark.
Think of "obfuscating the issue."

37. A.   The opposite of a *paean* or song expressing
exultation is a *dirge* or song expressing grief.
Think of "a triumphant paean."

38. C.   The opposite of to *concatenate* or link together
is to detach or *unlink*.
Word Parts Clue: *Con-* means together; *catena-*
means chain. *Concatenate* means to link
together as in a chain.
Think of "sonnets concatenated in a sequence."

Section 3

1. A. $\left(\frac{1}{2}\right)^3 = \frac{1}{2} \cdot \frac{1}{2} \cdot \frac{1}{2} = \frac{1}{8}$

2. B. $10 - \frac{10}{.1} = 10 - \frac{100}{1} = 10 - 100 = -90$

3. C. $\frac{x}{4}\% = \frac{x}{400}$

$\frac{x}{400}$ of 400 = x

4. B. $\frac{0.1}{2} = \frac{1}{20}$

$\frac{1}{.02} = \frac{10}{2} = 5$

5. B. $\sqrt{.81} = .9$
$60\% = .6$
$1\frac{1}{2} = \frac{1.5}{3.0}$
Sum
Average = 1

6. C. $7x = 196$
$x = 28$
$\frac{x}{7} = 4$

7. B.   Both columns have in common: 14, 12, 10, 8,
and 6. Column A has, in addition, (2)(4) or 8.
Column B has, in addition, 16.

8. A.   From the given information $2A > 2B$. But $2B > B + C$, since $C < B$.

9. B. $5^4 = 625$
$625 = 100T$
$6.25 = T$
Therefore, $10 > T$.

10. A.   If the area of a circle is four times a smaller circle its radius is two times as much.

11. C.   The distance from 5,3 to 5,7 = 4. The radius
of the circle is 4 and the circumference is 8π.

12. C.   If $a = 20$ then $x = 160$
If $b = 160$ then $y = 20$
$a + x = 180$
$y + x = 180$

13. B.   The triangle is a 3-4-5 triangle.
Hypotenuse $= 2x + x = 3x$
Hypotenuse $= 5$
$3x = 5$
$x = \frac{5}{3}$ (Column A)

14. C.   Since the measure of angle $C = 45°$, the
measure of angle $A = 45°$ and $AB = BC$.
Let $x = AB = BC$
Area $ABC = \frac{1}{2}(x)(x) = 12.5$
$x^2 = 25$ and $x = 5$
$AB = 5; BC = 5$

15. A. $\left(\frac{X}{Z}\right)\left(\frac{Z}{Y}\right) = \frac{X}{Y}$

X and Y are opposite equal angles and therefore
$X = Y$ and $\frac{X}{Y} = 1$

16. A.   (1) $3x - 6 = 1$
(2) $x - 2 = ?$
Observe equation (2) $= \frac{1}{3}$ of equation (1)
$x = \frac{1}{3}(3x)$
$-2 = \frac{1}{3}(-6)$
$? = \frac{1}{3}(1)$
$? = \frac{1}{3}$

17. D.   Let $x = AB = BC$.
By the Pythagorean theorem,
$x^2 + x^2 = (6\sqrt{2})^2$
$2x^2 = (36)(2)$
$x^2 = (36)$
$x = 6$
Area $= \frac{(6)(6)}{2}$ or 18
Or, recall that in 45°, 45° right triangles, the
hypotenuse = leg $\sqrt{2}$.

18. E.   Factor out 146.
146(117 + 173 + 210)
146(500) = 73,000

19. B.   (1) $7x - 5y = 13$
(2) $2x - 7y = 26$
(3) $5x + 2y =$
Observe equation (3) is the difference between
equation (1) and (2). Therefore $13 - 26 = -13$.

20. C.   Rate $= \dfrac{\text{distance}}{\text{time}}$ or $\dfrac{d}{t}$
Let x = time required to cover m miles.
Distance = rate $\times$ time
$m = \dfrac{d}{t} \times x$
$m = \dfrac{dx}{t}$ or $\dfrac{mt}{d} = x$

21. E.   Lactose = 0.16
Fructose = 1.70
Fructose is about 10.6 times sweeter.

22. C.   The increase is from .16 to .32.
Change is .16.
$\dfrac{\text{change}}{\text{original}} = \dfrac{.16}{.16} = 1 = 100\%$

23. B.   100 times as sweet as glucose = 74
Let x = number of grams of sucrose to be
added to saccharin.
1 gram of saccharin = 675
x grams of sucrose = $(1.00)(x) = x$
$\dfrac{\text{sweetness}}{\text{number of grams}} = \dfrac{x + 675}{1 + x} = 74$
$74 + 74x = x + 675$
$74x = 601$
$x = 8.2$ grams

24. A.   Obviously we must use less of the glucose than
lactose to get .32, since glucose is sweeter than
lactose. Observe the answers.

25. C.   To make mixture:
1 gram glucose = .74
2 grams sucrose = 2.00
3 grams fructose = 5.10
Total of 6 grams = 7.84
1 gram sucrose = 1.00
6 grams sucrose = 6.00
Let x = number of times mixture is sweeter
than sucrose.
$7.84 = 6x$
$1.3 = x$

26. C. $\frac{1}{2}$ study French.
$\frac{1}{3}$ of $\frac{1}{2}$ or $\frac{1}{6}$ study Spanish.
The remainder $\left(\dfrac{2}{6}\right)$ or $\frac{1}{3}$ do not study any foreign language.

Let x = the total number of students in this
school.
$\frac{1}{3}x = 300$
$x = 900$

27. E.   In 2 hours Mr. Jones completed $\frac{2}{x}$ part of the
lawn. He left unmowed $1 - \dfrac{2}{x}$ or $\dfrac{x - 2}{x}$.

28. E.   Since $\angle A$ is the largest angle and since this is a
right triangle, $\angle A = 90°$.

29. D.   Since the area of each circle is 4π, the radius
of each circle is 2. ($\pi r^2 = 4\pi$). The diameter
of each circle is 4. Since each side of $ABCD$
equals two diameters, $AB = BC = DC = AD$
= 8 and the perimeter of $ABCD = (4)(8)$ or 32.

30. E.   Area of square = 324 square feet
Area of rectangle = 324 square feet
Length of rectangle = 3 yards = 9 feet
Let x = width of rectangle.
Area of rectangle = $9x = 324x = 36$.

Section 4

1. C.   Since ODC is equilateral, $DC = \frac{1}{3}$ of 12 or 4.
Since $AB = DC$, and $BC = AD$, perimeter
$ABCD = 22$.

2. C.   Shaded area = area of circle ($\pi r^2 = 16\pi$)
minus area of rectangle (7×4 or 28).

3. B.   Since $x = 20$, $\angle FCD = 40$
$\angle FCB = 140$ (supplement)
$\angle FAB = \angle FCB$ (opposite angles of a
parallelogram)
Therefore, $y = 140$ and $y > 6x$

4. A.   Radius of $I = 5$
Radius of $II = 4$
Radius of $III = 3$
$AB = 5 + 3 = 8$
$BC = 3 + 4 = 7$
$AC = 5 + 4 = 9$
Perimeter of $ABC = 24$

5. B. $\dfrac{\frac{1}{4} - \frac{3}{16}}{\frac{1}{8}} = \dfrac{\frac{4}{16} - \frac{3}{16}}{\frac{1}{8}} = \dfrac{\frac{1}{16}}{\frac{1}{8}} = \dfrac{1}{\overset{2}{\cancel{16}}} \cdot \dfrac{\overset{1}{\cancel{8}}}{1} = \dfrac{1}{2}$

6. B. $\sqrt{\dfrac{1}{9} + \dfrac{1}{16}} = \sqrt{\dfrac{16}{144} + \dfrac{9}{144}} = \sqrt{\dfrac{25}{144}} = \dfrac{5}{12}$
$\sqrt{\dfrac{1}{16}} = \dfrac{1}{4}; \sqrt{\dfrac{1}{9}} = \dfrac{1}{3}, \dfrac{1}{4} + \dfrac{1}{3} = \dfrac{7}{12}$
$\dfrac{7}{12} > \dfrac{5}{12}$

7. **C.** $\frac{1}{5} = \frac{10}{5} = 2$ and $\sqrt{4} = 2$

8. **A.** $\left(\frac{1}{.07}\right)^2 = \frac{1}{0.0049} = 204 +$

   $204 > \frac{1}{7}$

9. **B.** $3^{n+2} = 27$ or, $3^3 = 27$
   Since $n + 2 = 3$, the $n = 1$
   $3 > 1$

10. **A.** $\sqrt{.16} = 0.4$ and $0.1\pi = (0.1)(3.14)$ or 0.314
    $0.4 > 0.3$

11. **B.** $\frac{1}{\sqrt{25}} = \frac{1}{5}$ and, $\frac{1}{(0.5)} = 2$

    $2 > \frac{1}{5}$

12. **A.** Recall these basic principles involving inequalities. Subtracting the same expression from each side of an inequality gives an equivalent inequality. Dividing each side of an inequality by the same negative expression *reverses* the inequality.
    $3 - 2x < 9$
    $-2x < 6$ (subtracting 3 from each side)
    $x > -3$ (dividing by -2)

13. **A.** Since both a and b are negative, the expression $a + b$ will always have a negative value, and the expression $a - b$ will have a positive value.

14. **B.** The fraction $\frac{x}{y}$ has a positive value since the numerator and the denominator are positive. If this fraction were equal to 2, then x would equal $2y$. However, since the fraction is equal to more than 2, then x is greater than $2y$.

15. **A.** $\sqrt{.25} = 0.5 = \frac{1}{2}$

    $\frac{1}{2} > \frac{1}{4}$

16. **D.** $xyz = 1$
    Since $x = z$
    $xyz = 1$
    $x^2 y = 1$
    $y = \frac{1}{x^2}$

17. **C.** Change all dimensions to feet.

    Piece of cloth was $3y$ feet long f feet and $\frac{i}{12}$

    feet were cut.

    The present length is $3y - \left(f + \frac{i}{12}\right)$

18. **B.** 48.00 (market price) $- \frac{1}{4}$ (48.00) or
    $12.00 = 36.00$ selling price
    Let $x = $ cost.

    (cost) $x +$ profit $\left(\frac{1}{5}x\right) = \$36$

    $x + \frac{x}{5} = 36$
    $5x + x = 180$
    $6x = 180$
    $x = \$30$

19. **C.** Let $x = $ number of articles shipped.
    $.0625x = 2,000$
    $625x = 20,000,000$
    $x = 32,000$

20. **B.** $\left(7\frac{1}{5}\text{ inches}\right)(120) = 864$ inches $= 72$ feet

21. **B.** $30° = \frac{30°}{360°} = \frac{1}{12} = 8\frac{1}{3}\%$

22. **D.** This is a direct proportion. Let $x = $ number of workers engaged in transportation.
    $\frac{90°}{1980} = \frac{120°}{x}$
    $90x = (120)(1980)$
    $x = \frac{(120)(1980)}{(90)}$

    $x = \frac{\overset{4}{\cancel{(120)}}\overset{660}{\cancel{(1980)}}}{\underset{3}{\cancel{90}}} = 2640$

23. **B.** There are 50% more transportation workers (30° on chart) than professional workers (20° on chart). The 50% greater income of the professional workers makes their total income equal to the transportation workers' total income.

24. **B.** The increase from 1980–1985 was $20 million, and the preceding 5 years, from 1975–1980 was $10 million.

25. **B.** $30 million + $11 million = $41 million $\div$ 2
    $= \$20\frac{1}{2}$ million. The closest choice is (B).

26. **E.** There are 12 inches in one foot. To change inches to feet, we would have to divide the inches into groups of 12. Thus, 36 inches contains $36 \div 12$, or 3 groups of 12, or 3 feet. In like manner, c inches contains $c \div 12$ or
    $\frac{c}{12}$ feet.

27. **C.** $(x + 1)(x - 1) = x^2 - 1$

28. E. If the sum of two numbers is known (here it is 0), subtracting one of the numbers from the sum will give the other number: Subtract:

$$\begin{array}{r} 0 \\ 2x - 4 \\ \hline \end{array}$$

To subtract polynomials, change the signs of the subtrahend (polynomial being subtracted) and proceed as in addition:

$$\begin{array}{r} 0 \\ -2x + 4 \\ \hline \end{array}$$

The other number is: $-2x + 4$

29. E. To divide two fractions, invert the divisor $\left(\text{here, the divisor is } \dfrac{3}{x}\right)$, and change the operation to multiplication:

$$\frac{6}{x} \cdot \frac{x}{3}$$

"Cancel" or divide numerator and denominator by factors that will go evenly into both. In this case, 3 and x are such factors. Note that $x \div x = 1$:

$$\frac{\overset{2}{\cancel{6}}}{\cancel{x}} \cdot \frac{\cancel{x}}{\cancel{3}}$$

Multiply together the remaining factors of the numerator to obtain the numerator of the answer and multiply together the remaining factor of the denominator to obtain the denominator of the answer:

$$\frac{2}{1} \cdot \frac{1}{1}$$

Simplify: 2

30. C. The darkened line extends to the right of -3 and includes -3. Therefore, the solution set contains numbers greater than or equal to 3. The darkened line extends to the left of 5, but the open, unshaded dot at 5 indicates that 5 is not included in the solution set; therefore, numbers less than 5 but not including 5 are in the solution set.

If x stands for any member of the solution set, the two conditions above may be represented by $-3 \leqq x < 5$.

Section 5

1-4. Summarize the availability of the staff.

Monday Alice, Betty, Dorothy, Edith (except first Monday of month)
Tuesday Carol, Betty, Dorothy, Edith
Wednesday Alice, Carol, Dorothy, Edith
Thursday Betty, Dorothy, Edith (except first Thursday of month)
Friday Alice, Betty, Edith

1. A. Observe that Alice, Betty, and Dorothy are available on any Monday.

2. E. Observe summary above.

3. D. Dorothy and Betty are available on any Thursday but Edith is available on all Thursdays except the first Thursday of the month.

4. E. Observe summary. Only Alice, Betty, and Edith are available on Fridays.

5. D. The argument states that gun control laws reduce violent crime; the evidence is a drop in armed robberies in one city. This involves unwarranted generalization (A, C), a failure to consider alternative explanations (B), and a possible failure to consider contrary evidence (E). D, however, raises an objection to gun control laws unrelated to either the validity of the evidence or the validity of the conclusion in the argument.

6. C. Option I partly answers the objection given in choice B above; this makes it appear more likely that the law directly caused the drop in armed robberies. Option II strengthens the argument in a somewhat more general way; if this statement is true, those violent crimes committed with a gun will be more strongly deterred by the additional punishment mandated for violation of the gun control law. Option III would strengthen the argument *only if* an additional assumption were made, that gun control laws make gun crimes less likely.

7. A. Option I weakens the argument by suggesting an alternative explanation for the drop in the crime rate. Option II has nothing to do with the crime rate. Option III does not, in itself, suggest that the gun control law is an ineffective *deterrent*.

8-11. You might first examine the grid and circle the words which seem to violate one or more rules. They are: *death* [violates rules (3) and (4), as well as (5), because it is not an adjective]; *hotter* [violates rule (5), since all other words in column IV are either nouns or verbs; violates rule (4) unless *fester* is changed]; *fester* [violates rule (3); violates rule (4) unless *hotter* is changed — but if *fester* is changed to satisfy rule (3), it will no longer violate rule (4), may violate rule (5), depending on whether *dam* and *edge* are read as nouns or verbs]; *greed* [may violate rule (5), depending, again, on *dam* and *edge*]; *gradual* [violates rule (5)]. Now you should be able to answer the questions dealing only with the trouble spots in the grid.

8. A. Rules (1) and (2) are not violated by any row or column; the others are (see above).

9. C.   Two rules, (1) and (3), apply to rows; rule (1) is satisfied by all rows, rule (3) by rows 1, 4, and 5. Three rules, rules (2), (4), and (5), apply to columns. Rule (2) is satisfied by all columns; rules (4) and (5) only by columns I and II.

10. C.   *Death* must be changed to a four-letter word, according to rule (3); this will also bring it into conformity with rule (4); and the new word must be an adjective, according to rule (5).

11. C.   This is tricky. *Death* and *gradual* must be changed (*deaf* and *glitter* will do). *Hotter* must be changed to the right part of speech—but what is that? If *dam* and *edge* are verbs, *hotter* can become *hanker*, but *greed* must become a verb (*groan*), while *fester* must become a seven-letter verb (*flicker*). This is a total of five changes. But if *dam* and *edge* are nouns, *hotter* can be a noun (*heater*), *fester* can become a seven-letter noun (*failure*), and *greed* can remain unchanged. This is a total of four changes. Of course, you are not required to supply words which will fit the rules; the examples we've given are simply to clarify the puzzle for you.

12-18.   The various statements result in two lists of musical works, which can then be put together because the total number of works is specified. This also becomes important in the last question. The statements about Beach, Ives, and Gottschalk give you:

G . . . D B . . . I F

The dots indicate that we don't know how many works intervene. The other statements yield:

C — — E H — A

The three dashes indicate that a precise number of works intervene. *Within a limit of ten works in all*, these two patterns can be put together in only one way:

G C D B E H — A I F

Note that one space is still blank. We know that ten works will be heard, but only nine composers and works are named, so this is logical.

12. B.   This can be answered by inspection of the diagram. Note that choice A is correct *in reverse order*.

13. D.   This can also be answered by inspection. Note that choice C contradicts a stated condition.

14. A.   This can also be answered by inspection.

15. E.   Again, simply inspect the diagram. Five works, including one whose name we don't know, will be heard between the Beach and the Foster.

16. E.   Since the soloist's first performance will be during the Gottschalk—the first work to be heard—she will begin tuning up prior to the start of the program.

17. C.   This is just a matter of counting back from the blank space. Works H, E, B, and D are the four that intervene.

18. C.   This is the only really hard item in this set. Inserting G into the blank following C, we would have: C G—E H—A D B I F, a total of 11 (I). Inserting I and F into the blanks after C, we would have: G D B C I F E H—A—, a total of 11 (remember that Antes can't end the program) (II). But if A preceded G (III), six composers would precede A five would follow, for a total of 12.

19-22.   A diagram showing which events may lead to which will help you here. We have used broken and dotted lines with B, C, and the events which follow from them in order to distinguish which combinations lead to which results. Your diagram need not be this elaborate (or neat); you are the only person who must be able to read it.

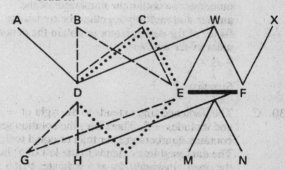

19. A.   D results from A, B, C, or W. E results from B, C, or W; F from W or X; M or N from E + F. Your only problem might have come if you failed to notice the stipulation of *immediately preceding* events—so you can't count C or W among the causes of M in this question.

20. A.   A results in D only; but D may cause another event only if it is caused by B or C, so no subsequent event follows after the AD sequence. B, C, and W all have more than one immediate result; X has only one, F, but F caused by X may cause H.

21. B.   BDH, BEH, CDH, CEH, WFH, and XFH are the combinations that cause H. Notice that H may not result from any of the immediately preceding events unless these resulted from an earlier event.

22. C.   I results from two combinations only—CDI and CEI. G results from four combinations—BDG, BEG, CDG, CEG. H results from six, as we just saw. M and N result from either five or six combinations—in the case of M, BEXFM, CEXFM, WEXFM, BEWFM, CEWFM, and possibly WEWFM (we don't know if W can act twice, but it doesn't matter —choice C is still lowest by far).

23. B.   This can be deduced from the fact that the author believes that a constitutional amendment will succeed where lawsuits and local statutes have failed.

24. E.   This question raises an issue the author has failed to address adequately: given the fact that job discrimination by gender is a real problem, does it necessarily follow that only a constitutional amendment can solve the problem?

25. C.   The fact that some employers do not discriminate against women does not undermine the argument as presented, since it does not imply that no problem of discrimination exists.

Section 6

1-4.   There is so much ambiguous information in this that it's best to start by simply jotting down the information in shorthand and see what develops. You get:

ROOM	CARPETING	WALLPAPER	DRAPES
(1)	M		P
(2)	G?	FdL	S
DR	G		
BR	G?	P	L

Now this information begins to come together. The white drapes must be in the dining room. The white wallpaper cannot be there, so it must be in room 1, which may be either the living room or the den. The white carpeting *cannot* be in room 2, as this is either the living room or den; in either case, a color would be repeated, which Lance will not tolerate. So the white carpeting is in the bedroom and the second room with green carpeting is room 2. We still don't know which room is the living room and which the den, or what color the wallpaper is in the dining room, but if we fill in the above information we can answer all the questions.

1. A.   The room with the unknown wallpaper is the dining room, which has white drapes.

2. B.   This is room 2. The correctly filled-in diagram rules out all other choices.

3. D.   Room 1 has white walls. It is either the living room (I) or the den (III).

4. C.   We are concerned with room 1 and room 2, either of which may be the living room, or the dining room. Maroon, purple, fleur-de-lis, and stripes don't bother us. Our problems are the white wallpaper in room 1, the white drapes in the dining room, and the green carpeting in room 2 and the dining room. Since either room 1 or room 2 is the living room, changing the wallpaper or the carpeting in that room will avoid color repetition. Each of the other choices will work if the living room is room 1 but not if it is room 2, or vice-versa.

5. D.   Analyze Nancy's logic: she assumes that the only harmful effect of beer drinking is gaining weight. The best way to strengthen Gary's argument, and refute Nancy's, is to dispute this assumption. D points out the obvious and explodes her argument. The other choices all fail to challenge Nancy's illogical logic.

6. C.   It is most likely that students are excused from Freshman Composition if they demonstrate superior writing ability. Thus, being excused is an effect, not a cause, of their writing well; but the argument, in assuming that dropping the course will improve everyone's writing, treats it as if it were a cause. Choice A is incorrect— the first sentence in the argument is a factual statement, whether true or false. Choice B is incidental—the reasoning would be invalid even if the statements were backed by miles of evidence. Choices D and E similarly focus on incidental features which might be important *if* the basic reasoning were valid.

7. B.   All choices except choice B suggest that Freshman Composition has educational value and can help to improve writing skills. Choice B suggests just the opposite.

8-12.   Summarize the facts.
Spanish is spoken by 3 – (A,B,D)
Italian is spoken by 3 – (A,C,E)
English is spoken by 2 – (B,C)
French is spoken by 2 – (D,E)

8. E.   When C and D converse they can use English, Italian, French, and Spanish between them. Mr. A speaks Spanish and Italian. Mr. B speaks English and Spanish. Mr. E speaks French and Italian.

9. A.   Mr. B understands English and Spanish, while Mr. E speaks two other languages, French and Italian.

10. D.   Mr. A and Mr. B can converse in Spanish.

11. D.   Three executives speak Spanish (Messrs. A, B, and D). The other executives (Messrs. C and E) speak Italian.

12. B. English is spoken by two executives (Messrs. B and C) and French is spoken by two executives (Messrs. D and E). English and Spanish are spoken by 5. Italian and Spanish are spoken by 6. English and Italian are spoken by 5. French and Spanish are spoken by 5.

13-16. Problems like this, which are almost impossible to figure out without a diagram, become relatively simple with a circle diagram like the one shown. Broken lines are used for uncertain relations; shading is used for E; F is shown in various possible positions.

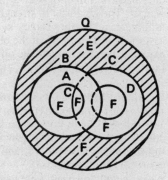

13. E. All we know about F's is that they are Q's and that the non-A part of the B circle does not contain any. They must be A's, C's, or E's because these groups define the rest of the Q's. Choice A can be seen to be wrong from the diagram. Choices B, C, and D are all possible, but not necessarily true.

14. D. B's, C's, and E's define all the Q's. Choices A and B are possible, but not necessarily true. Choice C would fit an F that was within the A/C overlap. Choice E seems false only if you are hypnotized by the F we have drawn in the A circle, which is also a B. Remember that F is only one possibility.

15. B. E's are defined as not B or C, so I is definitely true. III is true because no D is an A. II cannot be known; the fact that C's appear both outside the B's and inside the A's does not mean that there are any in the non-A part of B, where our broken line shows them.

16. C. The question does not say that P is a Q, so choice A is out. Choice B is only a possibility —P could be in the non-B portion of the D circle as drawn. Choice C is correct—E and C together define the non-B portions of Q (remember that A's are B's). Choice D fails to account for the fact that P may be outside Q altogether. If not a B, P, *cannot* be an A (choice E).

17-22. As usual with puzzles about seating arrangements, begin with a series of blanks—at first, more than you will eventually need. You might put initials above the blanks and cabinet positions below. The statement about Fentz gives:

$$\underline{}\ \underline{\text{F}}\ \underline{}\ \underline{}\ \underline{}\ \underline{\text{C}}\ \underline{}\ \underline{}\ \underline{}$$
$$\text{Ag.}$$

Brenner must be to the right of the Minister of Agriculture since, if he or she were to the left, Civili would be one of his or her neighbors. This gives you a stretch of seven persons between Fentz and Arning, and so you can trim the ends of your diagram. Put the Prime Minister in the center spot. Grell can be two places to the left of Dorner only if Dorner is the Prime Minister. The three ministers seated in a row must be on the left of the Prime Minister, since the Agriculture Minister is on the right. Eckland is placed by elimination. We cannot determine which of the two right-hand places the last two ministers occupy. The completed diagram looks like this:

F	G	C	D	E	B	A
Educ.	Min.	Cult.	P.M.	Ag.	SW or D	SW or D

17. C. This information may be easily gleaned from the diagram.

18. A. Remember the rules about rank. The top five leaders are Dorner, Eckland, Civili, Brenner, and Grell.

19. D. We don't know whether Brenner or Arning is Minister of Social Welfare. If Brenner, he outranks the Minister of Defense, who (by elimination) is Arning. If Arning, he is outranked by the Minister of Mining, Grell. Thus, either I or II may be true. Both together (C) is impossible.

20. E. The extreme left-hand seat is the lowest in rank.

21. B. According to the question, Minister of Education Fentz will exchange positions with Minister of Agriculture Eckland. As a result, Fentz will move up from seventh to second in the leadership ranking. Choice E would be correct if the directions mentioned were reversed.

22. B. Eckland, previously second in rank, becomes fourth; Civili, previously third, becomes second, and Brenner, previously fourth, becomes third. The positions of the Ministers of Defense, Mining, and Education, who rank lower than fourth, and Dorner, who ranks first, are unaffected.

23. **B.** Lillian's argument is flawed because she fails to consider all the possible factors that could explain her longevity; B points this out. Choices A and C do not weaken Lillian's argument, because they do not prove that tobacco and whiskey have bad effects in all cases (choice E may even be considered an *ad hominem* argument!). Choice C doesn't directly answer Lillian, because it proves only that other factors may explain *other* centenarians' survival. Choice D does not get to the flaw in Lillian's reasoning—and besides, she may have had medical advice.

24. **B.** The logical structure of the argument is: If P, then Q; Q, therefore P. This is fallacious reasoning, and we're asked to find the same fallacious reasoning in one of the choices. Choice B commits exactly the same error. Choice A says: If P, then Q; P, therefore Q (which is valid). Choice E says: If P, then Q; Not Q, therefore not P (also valid). Neither of these structures matches that of the original argument. Neither choice C nor choice D can be symbolized using just two letters, thus neither can match the original.

25. **B.** Choice B states the hidden assumption on which the original, fallacious argument was based. If it were true, the original conclusion ("her theory must be correct") would be valid.

Section 7

1. **E.** The *unstableness* of slush makes it unlikely to cling to even gentle slopes. Instead, it starts to slide; it may even cause an avalanche.
Things that are tightly bonded stick together securely; things that are loosely bonded stick together less well. Note that the loose bonding of the ice grains lessens their stability.

2. **C.** The writer contrasts well-rendered works of art with poorly executed *daubs* or crude pictures. However, he qualifies his criticism by stating that almost all these artworks possess a *vigor* or liveliness that attracts the viewer.

3. **E.** Extinction or destruction of the species appears to *confirm* a *flawed* design that combines an overly small brain in an overly huge body. (Actually, current studies of reptiles indicate that the dinosaur's brain was in proper proportion to its body mass.)

4. **B.** *Clarity* in explaining complicated financial matters would do a great deal to *offset* or compensate for shortcomings in a text.
Note the use of *and* linking the positive phrase "sheer importance of his text" with the second blank. This indicates that the second missing word must be a positive term.

5. **B.** If nine tenths of the works of art in the gallery have their faces turned to the wall, then the visitor to the gallery has no clue whatsoever to what wonders they contain. Similarly, a person *uninstructed in* natural history wanders through the world with no clue whatsoever to nine tenths of the natural wonders that surround him.

6. **C.** *Choleric* or irascible old men are likely to issue fiery proclamations. However, such formulas should not *intimidate* or frighten anyone.
The use of terms such as "fiery formula" and "outrage" conveys the image of an elderly gentleman who gets hot under the collar or *choleric*.

7. **D.** John's mother is at once excessively optimistic and excessively pessimistic. Optimistically she thinks her son is a genius (person showing "academic brilliance"). Pessimistically she thinks he is a *libertine* (person given to "dissolute excesses"). In both instances she is wrong: John's career has not been distinguished by genius or depravity; it has merely been *lackluster* (dull, uninspired).
Note that an undergraduate career undistinguished by genius and depravity would not be likely to be described as either *colorful* or *anomalous* (abnormal). Thus, you could immediately eliminate Choices B and C.

8. **C.** A *cluster* is a group of *stars*. A *clump* is a group of *trees*.

(Group and Member)

9. **B.** To *guffaw* is to *laugh* in a noisy manner. To *squabble* is to *quarrel* in a noisy manner.

(Manner)

10. **E.** A *lobster* is trapped by lobstermen in a *pot*. A *rabbit* is trapped by hunters in a *snare*.

(Function)

11. **A.** A *piston* moves up and down within a *cylinder*. An *elevator* moves up and down within a *shaft*. Beware eye-catchers. A *bullet* is fired from a *revolver*; it does not merely move up and down the barrel of the revolver.

(Location)

12. **D.** *Erudition* or learnedness characterizes the scholar. *Mendacity* or dishonesty characterizes the *liar*.

(Defining Characteristic)

13. B. A *drum* is an instrument in the *tympani* or percussion section of an orchestra. An *oboe* is an instrument in the *woodwind* section of an orchestra.

(Class and Member)

14. D. To *gibber* (chatter foolishly) is to speak without *sense*. To *vacillate* (waver) is to act without *resolution* (firmness of resolve).

(Antonym Variant)

15. C. To *mitigate* a *punishment* is to lessen or reduce it. To *commute* a *sentence* is to lessen or reduce it.

(Function)

16. E. An *aphorism* or concise formulation of a truth is by definition *sententious* (pithy; concise). A *eulogy* or expression of praise is by definition *laudatory*.

(Defining Characteristic)

17. D. In the opening and closing sentences of the passage, the author sums up what "we now know" and informs the reader what "has been found" about the composition of matter (what constitutes matter).

18. C. The passage states that molecules are made of atoms; logically, therefore, an atom is smaller, not larger, than the molecule to which it belongs.
Choice A is incorrect. Line 5 states atoms "have never been seen or photographed."
Choice B is incorrect. Lines 19-20 mentions the presence of positive electric elements.
Choice D is incorrect. Lines 5-8 note the ingenious laboratory experiments that determine its operations or processes.
Choice E is incorrect. Lines 13-14 mentions the average diameter of a molecule is 1/125 millionth of an inch. Atoms are smaller yet.

19. E. The comparison emphasizes the smallness or *minuteness* of atoms.

20. C. The satellites *circle* the planet. The electrons *swirl around* the proton. As depicted, the relationships are comparable.
Choice A is incorrect. A hawk *swoops down* upon its prey. The proton does not swoop down upon the electrons.
Choice B is incorrect. A blueprint is an outline or plan. A framework is a skeletal structure, possibly constructed in accordance with a blueprint. The relationships are not comparable.
Choice D is incorrect. Iron filings are *drawn or attracted* to a magnet. Electrons *swirl around* a proton.
Choice E is incorrect. A compound is *made up of* elements. A proton is not made up of electrons.

21. C. In the second paragraph, the author emphasizes the need for being able to refute the arguments of the opponents of the side of an issue which an individual supports.

22. B. In the next-to-the-last sentence of the first paragraph we are told that when principles cannot be disputed, a period of history cannot achieve the level of brilliance which has made some periods of history so noteworthy.

23. E. The second paragraph states that "ninety-nine in a hundred" of so-called educated people do not have a full sense of the force of the arguments that favor their opponents' side.

24. C. The opening sentence states that it is a duty to follow one's intellect to whatever conclusions it may lead. Those who do not do so are not suffering or *permitting* themselves to think.

25. B. The third sentence of the second paragraph states that the kind of person described in this question "has no ground for preferring either opinion." If she chooses either side, she is acting out of bias or prejudice, and so is opinionated.

26. C. A person who holds orthodox ideas without subjecting them to examination cannot be *determined on controversy* (bent on getting into an argument), for her ideas will not be in conflict with those of a majority of her contemporaries.

27. B. If it is the suspension of the dread of heterodox speculation that characterizes such periods of intellectual achievement, then such periods must be characterized by unorthodox thought and reflection.

28. D. The opposite of to *recollect* or remember is to *forget*.
Think of "recollecting someone's name."

29. E. The opposite of a *misapprehension* or incorrect understanding is a *correct interpretation*.
Think of "being under an unfortunate misapprehension."

30. B. The opposite of to *abide* or bear patiently is to *refuse to endure*.
Think of being "unable to abide punk rock."

31. C. The opposite of *benevolent* or well-meaning is *malicious* or wicked.
Word Parts Clue: *Bene-* means well; *vol-* means wish. Someone *benevolent* wishes people well.
Think of "a benevolent philanthropist."

32. D. The opposite of *precipitate* or hasty is *dilatory* or tardy.
Think of "a precipitate departure."

33. C.   The opposite of *acerbity* or sharpness of temper is *mildness of temperament*.
Think of "biting acerbity."

34. C.   The opposite of to *extirpate* or eradicate is to
proliferate or cause to increase in numbers.
Think of "extirpating endangered species."

35. B.   The opposite of *tortuous* or winding is *direct*.
Beware eye-catchers. *Tortuous* has nothing to
do with *torture*.
Think of "a tortuous mountain road."

36. A.   The opposite of *aplomb* (equanimity or poise)
is *discomposure* or agitation.
Think of "the aplomb of a diplomat."

37. D.   The opposite of *beatific* or saintly is *fiendish*.
Beware eye-catchers. Choice A is incorrect.
Beatific is not a synonym for beautiful.
Think of "beatific angels."

38. D.   The opposite of *odium* or detestation is *venera-
tion* or great respect.
Beware eye-catchers. Choice A is incorrect.
Odium is unrelated to odor.
Think of "despicable odium."

Answer Sheet – MODEL TEST 5

Start with number 1 for each new section.
If a section has fewer than 38 questions, leave the extra spaces blank.

Section 1

1. Ⓐ Ⓑ Ⓒ Ⓓ Ⓔ	11. Ⓐ Ⓑ Ⓒ Ⓓ Ⓔ	21. Ⓐ Ⓑ Ⓒ Ⓓ Ⓔ	31. Ⓐ Ⓑ Ⓒ Ⓓ Ⓔ
2. Ⓐ Ⓑ Ⓒ Ⓓ Ⓔ	12. Ⓐ Ⓑ Ⓒ Ⓓ Ⓔ	22. Ⓐ Ⓑ Ⓒ Ⓓ Ⓔ	32. Ⓐ Ⓑ Ⓒ Ⓓ Ⓔ
3. Ⓐ Ⓑ Ⓒ Ⓓ Ⓔ	13. Ⓐ Ⓑ Ⓒ Ⓓ Ⓔ	23. Ⓐ Ⓑ Ⓒ Ⓓ Ⓔ	33. Ⓐ Ⓑ Ⓒ Ⓓ Ⓔ
4. Ⓐ Ⓑ Ⓒ Ⓓ Ⓔ	14. Ⓐ Ⓑ Ⓒ Ⓓ Ⓔ	24. Ⓐ Ⓑ Ⓒ Ⓓ Ⓔ	34. Ⓐ Ⓑ Ⓒ Ⓓ Ⓔ
5. Ⓐ Ⓑ Ⓒ Ⓓ Ⓔ	15. Ⓐ Ⓑ Ⓒ Ⓓ Ⓔ	25. Ⓐ Ⓑ Ⓒ Ⓓ Ⓔ	35. Ⓐ Ⓑ Ⓒ Ⓓ Ⓔ
6. Ⓐ Ⓑ Ⓒ Ⓓ Ⓔ	16. Ⓐ Ⓑ Ⓒ Ⓓ Ⓔ	26. Ⓐ Ⓑ Ⓒ Ⓓ Ⓔ	36. Ⓐ Ⓑ Ⓒ Ⓓ Ⓔ
7. Ⓐ Ⓑ Ⓒ Ⓓ Ⓔ	17. Ⓐ Ⓑ Ⓒ Ⓓ Ⓔ	27. Ⓐ Ⓑ Ⓒ Ⓓ Ⓔ	37. Ⓐ Ⓑ Ⓒ Ⓓ Ⓔ
8. Ⓐ Ⓑ Ⓒ Ⓓ Ⓔ	18. Ⓐ Ⓑ Ⓒ Ⓓ Ⓔ	28. Ⓐ Ⓑ Ⓒ Ⓓ Ⓔ	38. Ⓐ Ⓑ Ⓒ Ⓓ Ⓔ
9. Ⓐ Ⓑ Ⓒ Ⓓ Ⓔ	19. Ⓐ Ⓑ Ⓒ Ⓓ Ⓔ	29. Ⓐ Ⓑ Ⓒ Ⓓ Ⓔ	
10. Ⓐ Ⓑ Ⓒ Ⓓ Ⓔ	20. Ⓐ Ⓑ Ⓒ Ⓓ Ⓔ	30. Ⓐ Ⓑ Ⓒ Ⓓ Ⓔ	

Section 2

1. Ⓐ Ⓑ Ⓒ Ⓓ Ⓔ	11. Ⓐ Ⓑ Ⓒ Ⓓ Ⓔ	21. Ⓐ Ⓑ Ⓒ Ⓓ Ⓔ	31. Ⓐ Ⓑ Ⓒ Ⓓ Ⓔ
2. Ⓐ Ⓑ Ⓒ Ⓓ Ⓔ	12. Ⓐ Ⓑ Ⓒ Ⓓ Ⓔ	22. Ⓐ Ⓑ Ⓒ Ⓓ Ⓔ	32. Ⓐ Ⓑ Ⓒ Ⓓ Ⓔ
3. Ⓐ Ⓑ Ⓒ Ⓓ Ⓔ	13. Ⓐ Ⓑ Ⓒ Ⓓ Ⓔ	23. Ⓐ Ⓑ Ⓒ Ⓓ Ⓔ	33. Ⓐ Ⓑ Ⓒ Ⓓ Ⓔ
4. Ⓐ Ⓑ Ⓒ Ⓓ Ⓔ	14. Ⓐ Ⓑ Ⓒ Ⓓ Ⓔ	24. Ⓐ Ⓑ Ⓒ Ⓓ Ⓔ	34. Ⓐ Ⓑ Ⓒ Ⓓ Ⓔ
5. Ⓐ Ⓑ Ⓒ Ⓓ Ⓔ	15. Ⓐ Ⓑ Ⓒ Ⓓ Ⓔ	25. Ⓐ Ⓑ Ⓒ Ⓓ Ⓔ	35. Ⓐ Ⓑ Ⓒ Ⓓ Ⓔ
6. Ⓐ Ⓑ Ⓒ Ⓓ Ⓔ	16. Ⓐ Ⓑ Ⓒ Ⓓ Ⓔ	26. Ⓐ Ⓑ Ⓒ Ⓓ Ⓔ	36. Ⓐ Ⓑ Ⓒ Ⓓ Ⓔ
7. Ⓐ Ⓑ Ⓒ Ⓓ Ⓔ	17. Ⓐ Ⓑ Ⓒ Ⓓ Ⓔ	27. Ⓐ Ⓑ Ⓒ Ⓓ Ⓔ	37. Ⓐ Ⓑ Ⓒ Ⓓ Ⓔ
8. Ⓐ Ⓑ Ⓒ Ⓓ Ⓔ	18. Ⓐ Ⓑ Ⓒ Ⓓ Ⓔ	28. Ⓐ Ⓑ Ⓒ Ⓓ Ⓔ	38. Ⓐ Ⓑ Ⓒ Ⓓ Ⓔ
9. Ⓐ Ⓑ Ⓒ Ⓓ Ⓔ	19. Ⓐ Ⓑ Ⓒ Ⓓ Ⓔ	29. Ⓐ Ⓑ Ⓒ Ⓓ Ⓔ	
10. Ⓐ Ⓑ Ⓒ Ⓓ Ⓔ	20. Ⓐ Ⓑ Ⓒ Ⓓ Ⓔ	30. Ⓐ Ⓑ Ⓒ Ⓓ Ⓔ	

Section 3

1. Ⓐ Ⓑ Ⓒ Ⓓ Ⓔ	11. Ⓐ Ⓑ Ⓒ Ⓓ Ⓔ	21. Ⓐ Ⓑ Ⓒ Ⓓ Ⓔ	31. Ⓐ Ⓑ Ⓒ Ⓓ Ⓔ
2. Ⓐ Ⓑ Ⓒ Ⓓ Ⓔ	12. Ⓐ Ⓑ Ⓒ Ⓓ Ⓔ	22. Ⓐ Ⓑ Ⓒ Ⓓ Ⓔ	32. Ⓐ Ⓑ Ⓒ Ⓓ Ⓔ
3. Ⓐ Ⓑ Ⓒ Ⓓ Ⓔ	13. Ⓐ Ⓑ Ⓒ Ⓓ Ⓔ	23. Ⓐ Ⓑ Ⓒ Ⓓ Ⓔ	33. Ⓐ Ⓑ Ⓒ Ⓓ Ⓔ
4. Ⓐ Ⓑ Ⓒ Ⓓ Ⓔ	14. Ⓐ Ⓑ Ⓒ Ⓓ Ⓔ	24. Ⓐ Ⓑ Ⓒ Ⓓ Ⓔ	34. Ⓐ Ⓑ Ⓒ Ⓓ Ⓔ
5. Ⓐ Ⓑ Ⓒ Ⓓ Ⓔ	15. Ⓐ Ⓑ Ⓒ Ⓓ Ⓔ	25. Ⓐ Ⓑ Ⓒ Ⓓ Ⓔ	35. Ⓐ Ⓑ Ⓒ Ⓓ Ⓔ
6. Ⓐ Ⓑ Ⓒ Ⓓ Ⓔ	16. Ⓐ Ⓑ Ⓒ Ⓓ Ⓔ	26. Ⓐ Ⓑ Ⓒ Ⓓ Ⓔ	36. Ⓐ Ⓑ Ⓒ Ⓓ Ⓔ
7. Ⓐ Ⓑ Ⓒ Ⓓ Ⓔ	17. Ⓐ Ⓑ Ⓒ Ⓓ Ⓔ	27. Ⓐ Ⓑ Ⓒ Ⓓ Ⓔ	37. Ⓐ Ⓑ Ⓒ Ⓓ Ⓔ
8. Ⓐ Ⓑ Ⓒ Ⓓ Ⓔ	18. Ⓐ Ⓑ Ⓒ Ⓓ Ⓔ	28. Ⓐ Ⓑ Ⓒ Ⓓ Ⓔ	38. Ⓐ Ⓑ Ⓒ Ⓓ Ⓔ
9. Ⓐ Ⓑ Ⓒ Ⓓ Ⓔ	19. Ⓐ Ⓑ Ⓒ Ⓓ Ⓔ	29. Ⓐ Ⓑ Ⓒ Ⓓ Ⓔ	
10. Ⓐ Ⓑ Ⓒ Ⓓ Ⓔ	20. Ⓐ Ⓑ Ⓒ Ⓓ Ⓔ	30. Ⓐ Ⓑ Ⓒ Ⓓ Ⓔ	

Section 4

1. Ⓐ Ⓑ Ⓒ Ⓓ Ⓔ	11. Ⓐ Ⓑ Ⓒ Ⓓ Ⓔ	21. Ⓐ Ⓑ Ⓒ Ⓓ Ⓔ	31. Ⓐ Ⓑ Ⓒ Ⓓ Ⓔ
2. Ⓐ Ⓑ Ⓒ Ⓓ Ⓔ	12. Ⓐ Ⓑ Ⓒ Ⓓ Ⓔ	22. Ⓐ Ⓑ Ⓒ Ⓓ Ⓔ	32. Ⓐ Ⓑ Ⓒ Ⓓ Ⓔ
3. Ⓐ Ⓑ Ⓒ Ⓓ Ⓔ	13. Ⓐ Ⓑ Ⓒ Ⓓ Ⓔ	23. Ⓐ Ⓑ Ⓒ Ⓓ Ⓔ	33. Ⓐ Ⓑ Ⓒ Ⓓ Ⓔ
4. Ⓐ Ⓑ Ⓒ Ⓓ Ⓔ	14. Ⓐ Ⓑ Ⓒ Ⓓ Ⓔ	24. Ⓐ Ⓑ Ⓒ Ⓓ Ⓔ	34. Ⓐ Ⓑ Ⓒ Ⓓ Ⓔ
5. Ⓐ Ⓑ Ⓒ Ⓓ Ⓔ	15. Ⓐ Ⓑ Ⓒ Ⓓ Ⓔ	25. Ⓐ Ⓑ Ⓒ Ⓓ Ⓔ	35. Ⓐ Ⓑ Ⓒ Ⓓ Ⓔ
6. Ⓐ Ⓑ Ⓒ Ⓓ Ⓔ	16. Ⓐ Ⓑ Ⓒ Ⓓ Ⓔ	26. Ⓐ Ⓑ Ⓒ Ⓓ Ⓔ	36. Ⓐ Ⓑ Ⓒ Ⓓ Ⓔ
7. Ⓐ Ⓑ Ⓒ Ⓓ Ⓔ	17. Ⓐ Ⓑ Ⓒ Ⓓ Ⓔ	27. Ⓐ Ⓑ Ⓒ Ⓓ Ⓔ	37. Ⓐ Ⓑ Ⓒ Ⓓ Ⓔ
8. Ⓐ Ⓑ Ⓒ Ⓓ Ⓔ	18. Ⓐ Ⓑ Ⓒ Ⓓ Ⓔ	28. Ⓐ Ⓑ Ⓒ Ⓓ Ⓔ	38. Ⓐ Ⓑ Ⓒ Ⓓ Ⓔ
9. Ⓐ Ⓑ Ⓒ Ⓓ Ⓔ	19. Ⓐ Ⓑ Ⓒ Ⓓ Ⓔ	29. Ⓐ Ⓑ Ⓒ Ⓓ Ⓔ	
10. Ⓐ Ⓑ Ⓒ Ⓓ Ⓔ	20. Ⓐ Ⓑ Ⓒ Ⓓ Ⓔ	30. Ⓐ Ⓑ Ⓒ Ⓓ Ⓔ	

Section 5

1. Ⓐ Ⓑ Ⓒ Ⓓ Ⓔ	11. Ⓐ Ⓑ Ⓒ Ⓓ Ⓔ	21. Ⓐ Ⓑ Ⓒ Ⓓ Ⓔ	31. Ⓐ Ⓑ Ⓒ Ⓓ Ⓔ
2. Ⓐ Ⓑ Ⓒ Ⓓ Ⓔ	12. Ⓐ Ⓑ Ⓒ Ⓓ Ⓔ	22. Ⓐ Ⓑ Ⓒ Ⓓ Ⓔ	32. Ⓐ Ⓑ Ⓒ Ⓓ Ⓔ
3. Ⓐ Ⓑ Ⓒ Ⓓ Ⓔ	13. Ⓐ Ⓑ Ⓒ Ⓓ Ⓔ	23. Ⓐ Ⓑ Ⓒ Ⓓ Ⓔ	33. Ⓐ Ⓑ Ⓒ Ⓓ Ⓔ
4. Ⓐ Ⓑ Ⓒ Ⓓ Ⓔ	14. Ⓐ Ⓑ Ⓒ Ⓓ Ⓔ	24. Ⓐ Ⓑ Ⓒ Ⓓ Ⓔ	34. Ⓐ Ⓑ Ⓒ Ⓓ Ⓔ
5. Ⓐ Ⓑ Ⓒ Ⓓ Ⓔ	15. Ⓐ Ⓑ Ⓒ Ⓓ Ⓔ	25. Ⓐ Ⓑ Ⓒ Ⓓ Ⓔ	35. Ⓐ Ⓑ Ⓒ Ⓓ Ⓔ
6. Ⓐ Ⓑ Ⓒ Ⓓ Ⓔ	16. Ⓐ Ⓑ Ⓒ Ⓓ Ⓔ	26. Ⓐ Ⓑ Ⓒ Ⓓ Ⓔ	36. Ⓐ Ⓑ Ⓒ Ⓓ Ⓔ
7. Ⓐ Ⓑ Ⓒ Ⓓ Ⓔ	17. Ⓐ Ⓑ Ⓒ Ⓓ Ⓔ	27. Ⓐ Ⓑ Ⓒ Ⓓ Ⓔ	37. Ⓐ Ⓑ Ⓒ Ⓓ Ⓔ
8. Ⓐ Ⓑ Ⓒ Ⓓ Ⓔ	18. Ⓐ Ⓑ Ⓒ Ⓓ Ⓔ	28. Ⓐ Ⓑ Ⓒ Ⓓ Ⓔ	38. Ⓐ Ⓑ Ⓒ Ⓓ Ⓔ
9. Ⓐ Ⓑ Ⓒ Ⓓ Ⓔ	19. Ⓐ Ⓑ Ⓒ Ⓓ Ⓔ	29. Ⓐ Ⓑ Ⓒ Ⓓ Ⓔ	
10. Ⓐ Ⓑ Ⓒ Ⓓ Ⓔ	20. Ⓐ Ⓑ Ⓒ Ⓓ Ⓔ	30. Ⓐ Ⓑ Ⓒ Ⓓ Ⓔ	

Section 6

1. Ⓐ Ⓑ Ⓒ Ⓓ Ⓔ	11. Ⓐ Ⓑ Ⓒ Ⓓ Ⓔ	21. Ⓐ Ⓑ Ⓒ Ⓓ Ⓔ	31. Ⓐ Ⓑ Ⓒ Ⓓ Ⓔ
2. Ⓐ Ⓑ Ⓒ Ⓓ Ⓔ	12. Ⓐ Ⓑ Ⓒ Ⓓ Ⓔ	22. Ⓐ Ⓑ Ⓒ Ⓓ Ⓔ	32. Ⓐ Ⓑ Ⓒ Ⓓ Ⓔ
3. Ⓐ Ⓑ Ⓒ Ⓓ Ⓔ	13. Ⓐ Ⓑ Ⓒ Ⓓ Ⓔ	23. Ⓐ Ⓑ Ⓒ Ⓓ Ⓔ	33. Ⓐ Ⓑ Ⓒ Ⓓ Ⓔ
4. Ⓐ Ⓑ Ⓒ Ⓓ Ⓔ	14. Ⓐ Ⓑ Ⓒ Ⓓ Ⓔ	24. Ⓐ Ⓑ Ⓒ Ⓓ Ⓔ	34. Ⓐ Ⓑ Ⓒ Ⓓ Ⓔ
5. Ⓐ Ⓑ Ⓒ Ⓓ Ⓔ	15. Ⓐ Ⓑ Ⓒ Ⓓ Ⓔ	25. Ⓐ Ⓑ Ⓒ Ⓓ Ⓔ	35. Ⓐ Ⓑ Ⓒ Ⓓ Ⓔ
6. Ⓐ Ⓑ Ⓒ Ⓓ Ⓔ	16. Ⓐ Ⓑ Ⓒ Ⓓ Ⓔ	26. Ⓐ Ⓑ Ⓒ Ⓓ Ⓔ	36. Ⓐ Ⓑ Ⓒ Ⓓ Ⓔ
7. Ⓐ Ⓑ Ⓒ Ⓓ Ⓔ	17. Ⓐ Ⓑ Ⓒ Ⓓ Ⓔ	27. Ⓐ Ⓑ Ⓒ Ⓓ Ⓔ	37. Ⓐ Ⓑ Ⓒ Ⓓ Ⓔ
8. Ⓐ Ⓑ Ⓒ Ⓓ Ⓔ	18. Ⓐ Ⓑ Ⓒ Ⓓ Ⓔ	28. Ⓐ Ⓑ Ⓒ Ⓓ Ⓔ	38. Ⓐ Ⓑ Ⓒ Ⓓ Ⓔ
9. Ⓐ Ⓑ Ⓒ Ⓓ Ⓔ	19. Ⓐ Ⓑ Ⓒ Ⓓ Ⓔ	29. Ⓐ Ⓑ Ⓒ Ⓓ Ⓔ	
10. Ⓐ Ⓑ Ⓒ Ⓓ Ⓔ	20. Ⓐ Ⓑ Ⓒ Ⓓ Ⓔ	30. Ⓐ Ⓑ Ⓒ Ⓓ Ⓔ	

Section 7

1. Ⓐ Ⓑ Ⓒ Ⓓ Ⓔ	11. Ⓐ Ⓑ Ⓒ Ⓓ Ⓔ	21. Ⓐ Ⓑ Ⓒ Ⓓ Ⓔ	31. Ⓐ Ⓑ Ⓒ Ⓓ Ⓔ
2. Ⓐ Ⓑ Ⓒ Ⓓ Ⓔ	12. Ⓐ Ⓑ Ⓒ Ⓓ Ⓔ	22. Ⓐ Ⓑ Ⓒ Ⓓ Ⓔ	32. Ⓐ Ⓑ Ⓒ Ⓓ Ⓔ
3. Ⓐ Ⓑ Ⓒ Ⓓ Ⓔ	13. Ⓐ Ⓑ Ⓒ Ⓓ Ⓔ	23. Ⓐ Ⓑ Ⓒ Ⓓ Ⓔ	33. Ⓐ Ⓑ Ⓒ Ⓓ Ⓔ
4. Ⓐ Ⓑ Ⓒ Ⓓ Ⓔ	14. Ⓐ Ⓑ Ⓒ Ⓓ Ⓔ	24. Ⓐ Ⓑ Ⓒ Ⓓ Ⓔ	34. Ⓐ Ⓑ Ⓒ Ⓓ Ⓔ
5. Ⓐ Ⓑ Ⓒ Ⓓ Ⓔ	15. Ⓐ Ⓑ Ⓒ Ⓓ Ⓔ	25. Ⓐ Ⓑ Ⓒ Ⓓ Ⓔ	35. Ⓐ Ⓑ Ⓒ Ⓓ Ⓔ
6. Ⓐ Ⓑ Ⓒ Ⓓ Ⓔ	16. Ⓐ Ⓑ Ⓒ Ⓓ Ⓔ	26. Ⓐ Ⓑ Ⓒ Ⓓ Ⓔ	36. Ⓐ Ⓑ Ⓒ Ⓓ Ⓔ
7. Ⓐ Ⓑ Ⓒ Ⓓ Ⓔ	17. Ⓐ Ⓑ Ⓒ Ⓓ Ⓔ	27. Ⓐ Ⓑ Ⓒ Ⓓ Ⓔ	37. Ⓐ Ⓑ Ⓒ Ⓓ Ⓔ
8. Ⓐ Ⓑ Ⓒ Ⓓ Ⓔ	18. Ⓐ Ⓑ Ⓒ Ⓓ Ⓔ	28. Ⓐ Ⓑ Ⓒ Ⓓ Ⓔ	38. Ⓐ Ⓑ Ⓒ Ⓓ Ⓔ
9. Ⓐ Ⓑ Ⓒ Ⓓ Ⓔ	19. Ⓐ Ⓑ Ⓒ Ⓓ Ⓔ	29. Ⓐ Ⓑ Ⓒ Ⓓ Ⓔ	
10. Ⓐ Ⓑ Ⓒ Ⓓ Ⓔ	20. Ⓐ Ⓑ Ⓒ Ⓓ Ⓔ	30. Ⓐ Ⓑ Ⓒ Ⓓ Ⓔ	

MODEL TEST 5

SECTION 1

Time—30 Minutes

38 Questions

Directions: Each sentence below has one or two blanks, each blank indicating that something has been omitted. Beneath the sentence are five lettered words or sets of words. Choose the word or set of words for each blank that best fits the meaning of the sentence as a whole.

1. Language, culture, and personality may be considered independently of each other in thought, but they are ------ in fact.

   (A) autonomous   (B) pervasive   (C) equivocal
   (D) inseparable   (E) immutable

2. Since depression seems to result when certain cells in the brain receive too little of two key chemicals, the neurotransmitters norepinephrine and serotonin, one goal of treatment is to make more of the chemicals ------ the nerve cells that need them.

   (A) analogous to   (B) dependent on
   (C) available to   (D) regardless of
   (E) interchangeable with

3. Wildlife managers and conservationists have gradually come to recognize that ------ methods of protecting the flock by maintaining refuges and regulating hunting are no longer sufficient, and in their dissatisfaction they are ------ a new approach.

   (A) radical...incapable of
   (B) innovative...cognizant of
   (C) conventional...pressing for
   (D) previous...chagrined by
   (E) conservative...dubious of

4. Neutron stars are believed to be the highly compressed remnants of exploding stars (supernovas) and thus ------ of one of the most ------ processes in nature.

   (A) causes...cataclysmic
   (B) products...violent
   (C) examples...equivocal
   (D) justifications...harsh
   (E) precursors...dynamic

5. The sudden shift from ------ to ------ in Hugo's novels can startle readers, especially when he abruptly juxtaposes a scene of chaste and holy love with one of coarse and profane licentiousness.

   (A) devotion...frivolity
   (B) piety...ribaldry
   (C) vulgarity...adultery
   (D) decorum...salubrity
   (E) purity...maturity

6. Isozaki's eye for detail is apparent everywhere in the new museum, but fortunately the details are ------ to the building's larger formal composition, which is ------ by the busyness of much recent architecture.

   (A) important...harmed
   (B) irrelevant...fragmented
   (C) appropriate...echoed
   (D) subordinated...unencumbered
   (E) incidental...nullified

7. Instead of taking exaggerated precautions against touching or tipping or jarring the costly bottle of wine, the waitress handled it quite ------, being careful only to use a napkin to keep her hands from the cool bottle itself.

   (A) fastidiously
   (B) capriciously
   (C) nonchalantly
   (D) tentatively
   (E) imprudently

Directions: In each of the following questions, a related pair of words or phrases is followed by five lettered pairs of words or phrases. Select the lettered pair that best expresses a relationship similar to that expressed in the original pair.

8. LODGE : BEAVER::
   (A) sty : pig
   (B) nest : bird
   (C) shell : turtle
   (D) pelt : rabbit
   (E) walnut : squirrel

9. RUSTLE : CATTLE::
   (A) bleat : sheep
   (B) swim : fish
   (C) pan : gold
   (D) speculate : stock
   (E) hijack : cargo

10. GLAND : ENZYME::
    (A) muscle : spasm
    (B) generator : current
    (C) organ : kidney
    (D) brain : cortex
    (E) silo : grain

11. JUG : CROCKERY::
   (A) wine : vineyard
   (B) hospital : surgery
   (C) hat : millinery
   (D) tankard : brewery
   (E) kiln : ceramics

12. GLINT : LIGHT::
   (A) blare : sound
   (B) whiff : scent
   (C) shade : color
   (D) glut : food
   (E) wave : tide

13. DOGGEREL : POET::
   (A) symphony : composer
   (B) easel : painter
   (C) caption : cartoonist
   (D) soliloquy : playwright
   (E) potboiler : novelist

14. FERAL : DOMESTICATION::
   (A) arable : cultivation
   (B) viral : infection
   (C) crude : refinement
   (D) frugal : economy
   (E) pliable : molding

15. SCOTCH : RUMOR::
   (A) divert : traffic
   (B) broach : topic
   (C) quash : riot
   (D) singe : fire
   (E) spread : gossip

16. QUALIFY : PARTICULAR::
   (A) restrain : effusive
   (B) flout : arbitrary
   (C) acknowledge : specific
   (D) mollify : agreeable
   (E) burnish : dull

Directions: Each passage in this group is followed by questions based on its content. After reading a passage, choose the best answer to each question. Answer all questions following a passage on the basis of what is stated or implied in that passage.

The lithosphere, or outer shell, of the earth is made up of about a dozen rigid plates that move with respect to one another. New lithosphere is created at mid-ocean ridges by the upwelling and cooling of magma from the earth's interior. Since new lithosphere is continuously being created and the earth is not expanding to any appreciable extent, the question arises: What happens to the "old" lithosphere?

The answer came in the late 1960's as the last major link in the theory of sea-floor spreading and plate tectonics that has revolutionized our understanding of tectonic processes, or structural deformations, in the earth and has provided a unifying theme for many diverse observations of the earth sciences. The old lithosphere is subducted, or pushed down, into the earth's mantle (the thick shell of red-hot rock beneath the earth's thin, cooler crust and above its metallic, partly melted core). As the formerly rigid plate descends it slowly heats up, and over a period of millions of years it is absorbed into the general circulation of the earth's mantle.

The subduction of the lithosphere is perhaps the most significant phenomenon in global tectonics. Subduction not only explains what happens to old lithosphere but also accounts for many of the geologic processes that shape the earth's surface. Most of the world's volcanoes and earthquakes are associated with descending lithospheric plates. The prominent island arcs-chains of islands such as the Aleutians, the Kuriles, the Marianas, and the islands of Japan—are surface expressions of the subduction process. The deepest trenches of the world's oceans, including the Java and Tonga trenches and all others associated with island arcs, mark the seaward boundary of subduction zones. Major mountain belts, such as the Andes and the Himalayas, have resulted from the convergence and subduction of lithospheric plates.

To understand the subduction process it is necessary to look at the thermal regime of the earth. The temperatures within the earth at first increase rapidly with depth, reaching about 1,200 degrees Celsius at a depth of 100 kilometers. Then they increase more gradually, approaching 2,000 degrees C. at about 500 kilometers. The minerals in peridotite, the major constituent of the upper mantle, start to melt at about 1,200 C., or typically at a depth of 100 kilometers. Under the oceans the upper mantle is fairly soft and may contain some molten material at depths as shallow as 80 kilometers. The soft region of the mantle, over which the rigid lithospheric plate normally moves, is the asthenosphere. It appears that in certain areas convection currents in the asthenosphere may drive the plates, and that in other regions the plate motions may drive the convection currents.

Several factors contribute to the heating of the lithosphere as it descends into the mantle. First, heat simply flows into the cooler lithosphere from the surrounding warmer mantle. Since the conductivity of the rock increases with temperature, the conductive heating becomes more efficient with increasing depth. Second, as the lithospheric slab descends it is subjected to increasing pressure, which introduces heat of compression. Third, the slab is heated by the radioactive decay of uranium, thorium and potassium, which are present in the earth's crust and add heat at a constant rate to the descending material. Fourth, heat is provided by the energy released when the minerals in the lithosphere change to denser phases, or more compact crystal structures, as they are subjected to higher pressures during descent. Finally, heat is generated by friction, shear stresses and the dissipation of viscous motions at the boundaries between the moving lithospheric plate and the surrounding mantle. Among all these sources the first and fourth contribute the most toward the heating of the descending lithosphere.

17. The primary purpose of the passage is to

   (A) refute a current theory
   (B) describe a process
   (C) analyze a technique
   (D) debate a point
   (E) predict a development

18. Each of the following geological phenomena is mentioned in the passage as being relevant to the subduction of the lithosphere EXCEPT

   (A) principal archipelagoes
   (B) significant rifts in the sea bottom
   (C) deserts in process of formation
   (D) prominent mountain ranges
   (E) volcanic eruptions

19. The style of the passage can best be described as

   (A) oratorical
   (B) argumentative
   (C) expository
   (D) meditative
   (E) deprecatory

20. According to the passage, which of the following statements is (are) true of the earth's mantle?

   I.   It is in a state of flux.
   II. Its temperature far exceeds that of the lithosphere.
   III. It eventually incorporates the subducted lithosphere.

   (A) I only
   (B) II only
   (C) I and III only
   (D) II and III only
   (E) I, II, and III

21. It can be inferred from the passage that the author regards current knowledge about the relationship between lithospheric plate motions and the convection currents in the asthenosphere as

   (A) obsolete
   (B) unfounded
   (C) derivative
   (D) definitive
   (E) tentative

22. The author is most probably addressing which of the following audiences?

   (A) Geothermal researchers investigating the asthenosphere as a potential energy source.
   (B) Historians of science studying the origins of plate tectonic theory.
   (C) College undergraduates enrolled in an introductory course on geology.
   (D) Graduate students engaged in analyzing the rate of sea-floor spreading.
   (E) Geologists involved in reformulating the theory of plate tectonics.

23. Which of the following is NOT true of the heating of the lithosphere as it is described in the passage?

   (A) The temperature gradient between the lithosphere and the surrounding mantle enables heat to be transferred from the latter to the former.
   (B) Minerals in the lithospheric slab release heat in the course of phase changes that occur during their descent into the mantle.
   (C) The more the temperature of the lithospheric slab increases, the more conductive the rock itself becomes.
   (D) A significant contributor to the increasing heat of the descending lithospheric slab is its increasing efficiency as a conductor.
   (E) The further the lithospheric slab descends into the mantle, the faster the radioactive decay of elements within it adds to its heat.

   Unlike the carefully weighted and planned compositions of Dante, Goethe's writings have always the sense of immediacy and enthusiasm. He was a constant experimenter with life, with ideas, and with forms of writing. For the same reason, his works seldom have the qualities of finish or formal beauty which distinguish the masterpieces of Dante and Virgil. He came to love the beauties of classicism but these were never an essential part of his make-up. Instead, the urgency of the moment, the spirit of the thing, guided his pen. As a result, nearly all his works have serious flaws of structure, of inconsistencies, of excesses and redundancies and extraneities.
   In the large sense, Goethe represents the fullest development of the romanticist. It has been argued that he should not be so designated because he so clearly matured and outgrew the kind of romanticism exhibited by Wordsworth, Shelley, and Keats. Shelley and Keats died young; Wordsworth lived narrowly and abandoned his early attitudes. In contrast, Goethe lived abundantly and developed his faith in the spirit, his understanding of nature and human nature, and his reliance on feelings as man's essential motivating force. The result was an all-encompassing vision of reality and a philosophy of life broader and deeper than the partial visions and attitudes of other romanticists. Yet the spirit of youthfulness, the impatience with close reasoning or "logic-chopping," and the continued faith in nature remained his to the end, together with an occasional waywardness and impulsiveness and a disregard of artistic or logical propriety which savor strongly of romantic individualism. Since so many twentieth-century thoughts and attitudes are similarly based on the stimulus of the Romantic Movement, Goethe stands as particularly the poet of modern times as Dante stood for medieval times and as Shakespeare for the Renaissance.

24. The title that best expresses the ideas of this passage is

   (A) Goethe and Dante
   (B) The Characteristics of Romanticism
   (C) Classicism versus Romanticism
   (D) Goethe, the Romanticist
   (E) Goethe's Abundant Life

25. A characteristic of romanticism NOT mentioned in this passage is its

    (A) elevation of nature
    (B) preference for spontaneity
    (C) modernity of ideas
    (D) unconcern for artistic decorum
    (E) simplicity of language

26. It can be inferred from the passage that classicism has which of the following characteristics?

    I.   Sensitivity towards emotional promptings
    II. Emphasis on formal aesthetic criteria
    III. Meticulous planning of artistic works

    (A) II only   (B) III only   (C) I and II
    (D) II and III   (E) I, II, and III

27. The author's attitude towards Goethe's writings is best described as

    (A) unqualified endorsement
    (B) lofty indifference
    (C) reluctant tolerance
    (D) measured admiration
    (E) undisguised contempt

Directions: Each question below consists of a word printed in capital letters, followed by five lettered words or phrases. Choose the lettered word or phrase that is most nearly opposite in meaning to the word in capital letters.

Since some of the questions require you to distinguish fine shades of meaning, be sure to consider all the choices before deciding which one is best.

28. SUPERFICIAL:
    (A) profound
    (B) exaggerated
    (C) subjective
    (D) spirited
    (E) dense

29. NAIVETE:
    (A) originality
    (B) sensitivity
    (C) sophistication
    (D) antipathy
    (E) vigor

30. TETHER:
    (A) fetch
    (B) demand
    (C) estrange
    (D) neglect
    (E) loose

31. PANDEMONIUM:
    (A) amusement
    (B) indolence
    (C) deceleration
    (D) tranquillity
    (E) tolerance

32. ENERVATE:
    (A) aggravate
    (B) stimulate
    (C) edify
    (D) applaud
    (E) disregard

33. DESTITUTION:
    (A) civilization
    (B) recompense
    (C) affluence
    (D) reformation
    (E) parsimony

34. BEREAVE:
    (A) commiserate
    (B) antagonize
    (C) restore
    (D) evade
    (E) clarify

35. ESCHEW:
    (A) gnaw
    (B) reproach
    (C) transform
    (D) preserve
    (E) seek

36. RECONDITE:
    (A) immediate
    (B) opportune
    (C) inherent
    (D) obvious
    (E) diverse

37. OBVIATE:
    (A) becloud
    (B) necessitate
    (C) rationalize
    (D) execute
    (E) assuage

38. CONTUMACIOUS:
    (A) laudatory
    (B) taciturn
    (C) fastidious
    (D) impassive
    (E) tractable

S T O P

IF YOU FINISH BEFORE TIME IS CALLED, YOU MAY CHECK YOUR WORK ON THIS SECTION ONLY.
DO NOT WORK ON ANY OTHER SECTION IN THE TEST.

SECTION 2

Time - 30 Minutes

38 Questions

Directions: Each sentence below has one or two blanks, each blank indicating that something has been omitted. Beneath the sentence are five lettered words or sets of words. Choose the word or set of words for each blank that best fits the meaning of the sentence as a whole.

1. With few exceptions, explorers now are not individuals setting out alone or in pairs to some remote destination but are instead members of ------, often international, undertaking.

   (A) a singular
   (B) a collaborative
   (C) an objective
   (D) an insular
   (E) a private

2. Anthropologists who have dismissed Villa's notion of prehistoric "social cannibalism" ------ that Villa's research was carefully done but stress that other interpretations of the evidence are possible.

   (A) deny
   (B) ignore
   (C) preclude
   (D) refute
   (E) grant

3. Surprisingly to those who view the ocean floor as a uniformly ------ waste, each vent in the floor, where sea water is heated by the earth's interior magma, has been found to be an island-like ------ with its own distinctive fauna.

   (A) teeming...habitat
   (B) lifeless...enclave
   (C) barren...oasis
   (D) sunken...grotto
   (E) hazardous...environment

4. Rather than allowing these dramatic exchanges between her characters to develop fully, Ms. Norman unfortunately tends to ------ the discussions involving the two women.

   (A) exacerbate
   (B) protract
   (C) augment
   (D) truncate
   (E) elaborate

5. A ------ of recent cases of scientific fraud in which gross errors of fact and logic have slipped past the review panels that scrutinize submissions to journals suggests that the review system is seriously ------.

   (A) plethora...intended
   (B) lack...strained
   (C) dearth...compromised
   (D) spate...taxed
   (E) preponderance...substantiated

6. Egocentric, at times vindictive when he believed his authority was being questioned, White could also be kind, gracious, and even ------ when the circumstances seemed to require it.

   (A) authoritarian
   (B) taciturn
   (C) vainglorious
   (D) self-deprecating
   (E) self-assured

7. Many of Updike's characters live to ------ the assurances they give one another glibly or sincerely; they define themselves by their betrayals of their spouses or their children or their parents.

   (A) flaunt   (B) underscore   (C) fulfill
   (D) deplore   (E) belie

Directions: In each of the following questions, a related pair of words or phrases is followed by five lettered pairs of words or phrases. Select the lettered pair that best expresses a relationship similar to that expressed in the original pair.

8. BOOK : CHAPTER::
   (A) painting : frame
   (B) sentence : verb
   (C) building : story
   (D) tree : root
   (E) movie : scenario

9. INAUGURATE : PRESIDENT::
   (A) abdicate : king
   (B) promote : student
   (C) campaign : candidate
   (D) install : officer
   (E) succeed : governor

10. ADJUST : TINKER::
    (A) invent : design
    (B) improve : hamper
    (C) throw : hurl
    (D) analyze : repair
    (E) write : scribble

11. ZINC : ELEMENT::
    (A) gold : bullion
    (B) uranium : fission
    (C) quark : particle
    (D) electron : molecule
    (E) light : photosynthesis

12. UPROARIOUS : AMUSING::
    (A) treacherous : steadfast
    (B) tumultuous : windy
    (C) menacing : aghast
    (D) repugnant : disagreeable
    (E) devious : clever

13. FORENSIC : DEBATE::
    (A) empirical : argument
    (B) judicious : law
    (C) histrionic : theatre
    (D) sophomoric : humor
    (E) philosophic : temperament

14. LIMPET : DETACH::
    (A) porpoise : sound
    (B) hummingbird : hover
    (C) chameleon : disguise
    (D) tick : extract
    (E) eel : wriggle

15. COUNTENANCE : APPROVAL::
    (A) uphold : delay
    (B) disclaim : obligation
    (C) traduce : reputation
    (D) propound : distinction
    (E) air : expression

16. INSOUCIANT : DISTURB::
    (A) supererogatory : require
    (B) laconic : interpret
    (C) distraught : ruffle
    (D) incredulous : convince
    (E) egregious : obtrude

Directions: Each passage in this group is followed by questions based on its content. After reading a passage, choose the best answer to each question. Answer all questions following a passage on the basis of what is stated or implied in that passage.

Paralleling the growth of interest among professional historians during the early 1960s was a simultaneous groundswell of popular interest in the Afro-American past that was directly stimulated by the drama of the protest movement. Sensing the "Negro Mood," the journalist Lerone Bennett wrote a series of articles on Afro-American history for *Ebony* and soon after brought them together in his popular volume, *Before the Mayflower* (1962). As the nonviolent direct action movement attained its crest in 1963-64, movement activists introduced black history units into the curricula of the "freedom schools" that accompanied the school integration boycotts. Meanwhile, boards of education began to address themselves to "the racial imbalance and neutralism of pusillanimous textbooks designed to appeal to Southern as well as Northern school adoption committees." In 1964 New York City's school board published *The Negro in American History*; Detroit's social studies teachers produced *The Struggle for Freedom and Rights: Basic Facts about the Negro in American History*. Franklin, surveying the activities among publishers, teachers, and school boards, called these beginnings of curriculum revision "one of the most significant by-products of the current Civil Rights Revolution."

The relationship between these developments at the grass roots level and what was occurring in the scholarly world is of course indirect. Yet given the context of social change in the early 1960s, Negro history was now the object of unprecedented attention among wide segments of the American population, black and white. In academe nothing demonstrated this growing legitimacy of black history better than the way in which certain scholars of both races, who had previously been ambivalent about being identified as specialists in the field, now reversed themselves.

Thus Frenise Logan, returning to an academic career, decided to attempt to publish his doctoral dissertation on blacks in late nineteenth-century North Carolina. A 1960 award encouraged him to do further research, and his expanded *The Negro in North Carolina, 1876–1894* appeared in 1964. It is true that as late as 1963 a white professor advised John W. Blassingame to avoid black history if he wanted to have "a future in the historical profession." Yet more indicative of how things were going was that 1964–65 marked a turning point for two of Kenneth Stampp's former students—Nathan Huggins and Leon Litwack. The changing intellectual milieu seems to have permitted Huggins, whose original intention of specializing in African and Afro-American history had been overruled by practical concerns, to move into what became his long-range commitment to the field. By 1965 when his interest in intellectual history found expression in the idea of doing a book on the Harlem Renaissance, the factors that earlier would have discouraged him from such a study had dissipated. For Litwack the return to Negro history was an especially vivid experience, and he recalls the day he spoke at the University of Rochester, lecturing on Jacksonian democracy. Some students in the audience, sensing that his heart was just not in that topic, urged him to undertake research once again in the field to which he had already contributed so significantly. He settled on the study that became *Been in the Storm So Long* (1979). In short, both Huggins and Litwack now felt able to dismiss the professional considerations that had loomed so large in their earlier decision to work in other specialties and to identify themselves with what had hitherto been a marginal field of inquiry.

17. The author indicates that the growth of scholarly involvement in the study of black history was

    (A) unappreciated in academic circles
    (B) encouraged by the civil rights movement
    (C) systematically organized
    (D) unaffected by current events
    (E) motivated by purely financial concerns

18. The author's account is based on all of the following EXCEPT

    (A) personal anecdotes
    (B) magazine articles
    (C) curricular materials
    (D) public opinion polls
    (E) scholarly publications

19. The author cites Logan, Huggins, and Litwack for their

   (A) work on curriculum reform in the public schools
   (B) participation in the Freedom Summer in Mississippi
   (C) return to the field of Afro-American history
   (D) research on blacks in nineteenth century North Carolina
   (E) identification with nonviolent direct action

20. The author suggests that the advice given to John W. Blassingame was

   (A) meant maliciously
   (B) inappropriate to the times
   (C) acted on in good faith
   (D) vital to his career
   (E) verified by research

21. Which of the following best describes the purpose of the passage?

   (A) To document the sacrifices made by black and white scholars in the field
   (B) To defend the validity of black history as a legitimate scholarly pursuit
   (C) To investigate the origins of Afro-American studies in American universities
   (D) To encourage the return to the study of black history at the grass roots level
   (E) To describe black history's coming of age as an academically respectable field

22. The passage suggests that Bennett's work was similar to Logan's work in which of the following ways?

   I.   Both Bennett's and Logan's books recorded a then relatively unfamiliar aspect of Afro-American history.
   II. Both Bennett's and Logan's work were designed to appeal to a primarily academic audience.
   III. Both Bennett's and Logan's work were published in a variety of formats.

   (A) I only
   (B) III only
   (C) I and II only
   (D) I and III only
   (E) II and III only

23. It can be inferred that prior to 1950 for a historian to choose to specialize in black history

   (A) was encouraged by the academic establishment
   (B) established his academic conventionality
   (C) afforded him special opportunities for publication
   (D) was detrimental to his professional career
   (E) enhanced his contact with his colleagues

An oft-used, but valuable, analogy compares the immune system with an army. The defending troops are the white blood cells called lymphocytes, born in the bone marrow, billeted in the lymph nodes and spleen, and on exercise in the blood and lymph systems. A body can muster some 200m cells, making the immune system comparable in mass to the liver or brain.

The lymphocytes are called to action when the enemy makes itself known. They attack anything foreign. Their job is to recognize the enemy for what it is, and then destroy it. One of the key features of the immune system is its specificity. Inoculation with smallpox provokes an attack on any smallpox virus, but on nothing else. This specificity of response depends on the lymphocyte's ability to identify the enemy correctly by the molecules on its surface, called antigens.

An antigen is an enemy uniform. It can be a protein on the surface of a cold virus, or it can be a protein on the surface of a pollen grain, in which case the immune response takes the form of an allergy. An antigen can also be a protein on the surface of a transplanted organ, in which case the immune response "rejects" the transplant. Organs can therefore be transplanted only between closely related people—in whom the antigens are the same—or into people treated with a drug that suppresses the immune system, such as cyclosporin.

24. The author's primary purpose in the passage is to do which of the following?

   (A) Demonstrate the inadequacy of an analogy.
   (B) Propose a method to strengthen the immune system.
   (C) Compare the immune system to the brain.
   (D) Clarify the workings of the body's defense system.
   (E) Merge two differing views of a bodily process.

25. The author provides information to answer which of the following questions?

   (A) What is the process by which antigens are produced?
   (B) What is the mechanism by which cyclosporin suppresses the immune system?
   (C) What is the process that prevents closely related persons from developing dissimilar antigens?
   (D) How does inoculation with smallpox wear off over a period of years?
   (E) Where do the body's lymphocytes originate?

26. It can be inferred from the passage that treatment with cyclosporin might result in which of the following?

   I.   An increased susceptibility to invasion by disease
   II. The rejection of a transplanted organ
   III. An increased effectiveness of antigens

   (A) I only
   (B) II only
   (C) I and II only
   (D) I and III only
   (E) I, II and III

27. In describing the immune system, the author does all of the following EXCEPT

    (A) define a term
    (B) illustrate through a comparison
    (C) refer to an authority
    (D) give an approximation
    (E) develop an extended metaphor

Directions: Each question below consists of a word printed in capital letters, followed by five lettered words or phrases. Choose the lettered word or phrase that is most nearly opposite in meaning to the word in capital letters.

Since some of the questions require you to distinguish fine shades of meaning, be sure to consider all the choices before deciding which one is best.

28. SAP:
    (A) divert
    (B) educate
    (C) invigorate
    (D) liquify
    (E) polish

29. UNFEIGNED:
    (A) pretentious
    (B) cautious
    (C) simulated
    (D) controlled
    (E) designed

30. VACILLATION:
    (A) coarseness
    (B) simplicity
    (C) retraction
    (D) firmness
    (E) tedium

31. SWATHE:
    (A) fondle
    (B) nourish
    (C) anoint
    (D) unwrap
    (E) refresh

32. COGNIZANCE:
    (A) ignobility
    (B) disbelief
    (C) impotence
    (D) illegality
    (E) unawareness

33. NEBULOUS:
    (A) hypothetical
    (B) querulous
    (C) lamentable
    (D) piquant
    (E) distinct

34. DENIGRATE:
    (A) emancipate
    (B) examine
    (C) desecrate
    (D) mollify
    (E) extol

35. DECORUM:
    (A) lucidity
    (B) flexibility
    (C) impropriety
    (D) duplicity
    (E) severity

36. CONDIGN:
    (A) intentional
    (B) unbiased
    (C) obdurate
    (D) inevitable
    (E) unmerited

37. PUISSANCE:
    (A) effortlessness
    (B) powerlessness
    (C) recklessness
    (D) timeliness
    (E) wholeness

38. PALLIATE:
    (A) exacerbate
    (B) immunize
    (C) oscillate
    (D) rarefy
    (E) precipitate

S T O P

IF YOU FINISH BEFORE TIME IS CALLED, YOU MAY CHECK YOUR WORK ON THIS SECTION ONLY.
DO NOT WORK ON ANY OTHER SECTION IN THE TEST.

SECTION 3

Time—30 Minutes

30 Questions

Numbers: All numbers used are real numbers.

Figures: Position of points, angles, regions, etc. can be assumed to be in the order shown; and angle measures can be assumed to be positive.

Lines shown as straight can be assumed to be straight.

Figures can be assumed to lie in a plane unless otherwise indicated.

Figures that accompany questions are intended to provide information useful in answering the questions. However, unless a note states that a figure is drawn to scale, you should solve these problems NOT by estimating sizes by sight or by measurement, but by using your knowledge of mathematics (see Example 2 below).

Directions: Each of the <u>Questions 1-15</u> consists of two quantities, one in Column A and one in Column B. You are to compare the two quantities and choose

> A if the quantity in Column A is greater;
> B if the quantity in Column B is greater;
> C if the two quantities are equal;
> D if the relationship cannot be determined from the information given.

Note: Since there are only four choices, NEVER MARK (E).

Common Information: In a question, information concerning one or both of the quantities to be compared is centered above the two columns. A symbol that appears in both columns represents the same thing in Column A as it does in Column B.

	Column A	Column B	Sample Answers
Example 1:	2×6	$2 + 6$	● Ⓑ Ⓒ Ⓓ Ⓔ

Examples 2-4 refer to △ *PQR*.

	Column A	Column B	Sample Answers
Example 2:	*PN*	*NQ*	Ⓐ Ⓑ Ⓒ ● Ⓔ (since equal measures cannot be assumed, even though *PN* and *NQ* appear equal)
Example 3:	*x*	*y*	Ⓐ ● Ⓒ Ⓓ Ⓔ (since *N* is between *P* and *Q*)
Example 4:	*w* + *z*	180	Ⓐ Ⓑ ● Ⓓ Ⓔ (since *PQ* is a straight line)

A if the quantity in Column A is greater;
B if the quantity in Column B is greater;
C if the two quantities are equal;
D if the relationship cannot be determined from the information given.

Column A	Column B

1. $\dfrac{7 + 7 + 7}{-7 - 7 - 7}$ 1

$0 < x < 100$
x is divisible by 2,3,5

2.   30 x

---

3.   109 inches   3 yards, 1 inch

There are 30 members on the varsity football squad, 20 on the varsity baseball squad, and 10 varsity players who are on both squads.

4. The ratio of the number on both squads to the number on the baseball squad
     | The ratio of the number on the baseball squad but not on the football squad to the number on the football squad but not on the baseball squad

---

$57x = 3,306$
$58y = 3,306$

5. x y

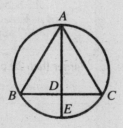

$\overarc{AB} = \overarc{AC} = \overarc{BC}$
$BD = DC$

6. $\dfrac{AC}{DC}$ 2

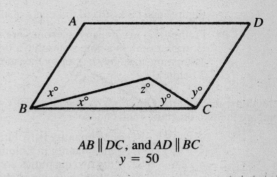

$AB \parallel DC$, and $AD \parallel BC$
$y = 50$

7. z 90

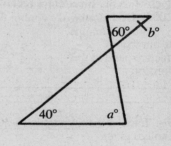

8. a b

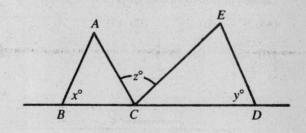

$AB = AC$ and $EC = ED$
$x = 40$ and $y = 80$

9. $3x$ $2z$

$8 < x$
$y < 3$

10. x y

A if the quantity in Column A is greater;
B if the quantity in Column B is greater;
C if the two quantities are equal;
D if the relationship cannot be determined from the information given.

<u>Column A</u>	<u>Column B</u>	<u>Column A</u>	<u>Column B</u>

$AB = BC = AC$
$BD \perp AC$

11. $\dfrac{x}{y}$ 3

In a shipment of electronic parts 0.01 percent is defective. ABC Electronics received a shipment of 10,000 of these parts.

12. The number of   1
    defective parts in this
    shipment

$x = -3$

13. $x^2 + x$ $-2x$

14. $\dfrac{1}{100} + \dfrac{3}{100}$ 0.04

$x > \dfrac{y}{3} > 0$

15. x y

<u>Directions:</u> Each of the Questions 16-30 has five answer choices. For each of these questions, select the best of the answer choices given.

16. What is the radius of the largest circular disc that can be cut from a strip of metal $15'' \times 21''$?

(A) $7''$ (B) $7\frac{1}{2}''$ (C) $15''$

(D) $15\frac{1}{2}''$ (E) $157\frac{1}{2}''$

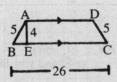

17. In the figure above, if $BC = 26$, $AE = 4$, $AB = DC = 5$, $AE \perp BC$ and AD is parallel to BC; $AD = ?$

(A) 3
(B) 6
(C) 20
(D) 23
(E) none of these

18. How many 5¢ stamps can be purchased for c cents?

(A) $5c$

(B) $\dfrac{c}{5}$

(C) $\dfrac{5}{c}$

(D) $500c$

(E) $\dfrac{5c}{100}$

19. By how much is $\dfrac{3}{7}$ larger than 20 percent of 2?

(A) $\dfrac{1}{35}$

(B) $\dfrac{1}{7}$

(C) $\dfrac{4}{7}$

(D) $3\dfrac{3}{7}$

(E) $3\dfrac{4}{7}$

20. Points *B* and *C* lie on line *AD* so that *AB* = *BC* = *CD*. What part of *AD* is *AC*?

   (A) $\frac{1}{4}$ (B) $\frac{1}{3}$ (C) $\frac{2}{4}$ (D) $\frac{2}{3}$ (E) $\frac{3}{4}$

Questions 21-25 refer to the following table and graph.

YOUR PROPERTY TAX BILL

Tax Levy Description	Tax Rate per $100 of Taxable Value
School	24.856
Community College	0.654
Library	1.458
Police	6.815
Water Supply	0.380
Sewer Maintenance	0.674
Sewage Disposal	1.211
Parks	0.039
General County	3.683
General Town	0.860
Fire	0.640

WHERE THE SCHOOL TAX GOES

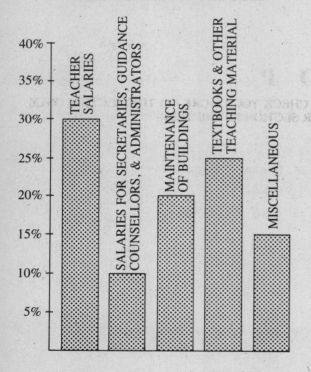

21. What is the ratio of taxpayers' money spent for teachers salaries to the salaries of other school personnel?

   (A) 1:2
   (B) 1:3
   (C) 3:1
   (D) 2:3
   (E) 3:2

22. How many times more is the money taxed for schools than for the community college?

   (A) 4
   (B) 6
   (C) 24
   (D) 38
   (E) 48

23. What is the annual tax paid for schools by a property owner whose house has a taxable value of $10,000?

   (A) $24.85
   (B) $248.50
   (C) $2,485.00
   (D) $24,850.00
   (E) $248,500.00

24. If the amount of money spent for maintenance of school buildings is represented by $D, then the amount of money spent for miscellaneous school items is expressed as

   (A) $20D

   (B) $15D

   (C) $\$\frac{3}{4}D$

   (D) $\$\frac{4}{3}D$

   (E) $\$1\frac{1}{3}D$

25. What part of the school budget is allocated for textbooks and other teaching material?

   (A) $\frac{1}{25}$

   (B) $\frac{1}{5}$

   (C) $\frac{1}{4}$

   (D) $\frac{1}{8}$

   (E) $\frac{3}{8}$

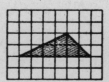

26. In the figure above, how many square units are there in the shaded triangle?

   (A) 4
   (B) 6
   (C) 8
   (D) 9
   (E) 12

27. How many 3-gallon cans can be filled with the milk from 165 one-pint containers? (2 pints = 1 quart; 4 quarts = 1 gallon)

    (A) 3
    (B) 4
    (C) 5
    (D) 6
    (E) 7

28. If $3x = \frac{5}{6}y$, then $5y =$

    (A) $\frac{1}{2}x$

    (B) $2x$

    (C) $3.6x$

    (D) $5x$

    (E) $18x$

29. The size of the smaller angle between the hands of the clock at half past six, expressed in degrees, is

    (A) $7\frac{1}{2}°$

    (B) $15°$

    (C) $22\frac{1}{2}°$

    (D) $30°$

    (E) more than $22\frac{1}{2}°$ but less than $30°$

30. How many ounces of water must be added to 48 ounces of alcohol to make a solution that is 25% alcohol?

    (A) 16
    (B) 48
    (C) 64
    (D) 144
    (E) 192

S T O P

IF YOU FINISH BEFORE TIME IS CALLED, YOU MAY CHECK YOUR WORK ON THIS SECTION ONLY.
DO NOT WORK ON ANY OTHER SECTION IN THE TEST.

SECTION 4

Time—30 Minutes

30 Questions

Numbers: All numbers used are real numbers.

Figures: Position of points, angles, regions, etc. can be assumed to be in the order shown; and angle measures can be assumed to be positive.

Lines shown as straight can be assumed to be straight.

Figures can be assumed to lie in a plane unless otherwise indicated.

Figures that accompany questions are intended to provide information useful in answering the questions. However, unless a note states that a figure is drawn to scale, you should solve these problems NOT by estimating sizes by sight or by measurement, but by using your knowledge of mathematics (see Example 2 below).

Directions: Each of the Questions 1-15 consists of two quantities, one in Column A and one in Column B. You are to compare the two quantities and choose

        A if the quantity in Column A is greater;
        B if the quantity in Column B is greater;
        C if the two quantities are equal;
        D if the relationship cannot be determined from the information given.

Note: Since there are only four choices, NEVER MARK (E).

Common
Information: In a question, information concerning one or both of the quantities to be compared is centered above the two columns. A symbol that appears in both columns represents the same thing in Column A as it does in Column B.

	Column A	Column B	Sample Answers
Example 1:	2×6	$2 + 6$	● Ⓑ ⒸⒹⒺ

Examples 2-4 refer to $\triangle PQR$.

Example 2:	PN	NQ	ⒶⒷⒸ ● Ⓔ

(since equal measures cannot be assumed, even though PN and NQ appear equal)

Example 3:	x	y	Ⓐ ● ⒸⒹⒺ

(since N is between P and Q)

Example 4:	$w + z$	180	ⒶⒷ ● ⒹⒺ

(since PQ is a straight line)

A if the quantity in Column A is greater;
B if the quantity in Column B is greater;
C if the two quantities are equal;
D if the relationship cannot be determined from the information given.

<u>Column A</u>	<u>Column B</u>	<u>Column A</u>	<u>Column B</u>

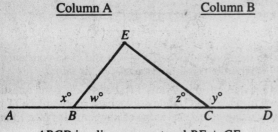

ABCD is a line segment and $BE \perp CE$

1. $x + y$ 90

2. $\dfrac{1}{\dfrac{3}{2}}$ .... $\dfrac{3}{2}$

$$a = b = c$$

3. $a + b$ .... $b + c$

4. The time elapsed from 9:55 AM to 10:15 AM on the same morning .... $\dfrac{1}{3}$ hour

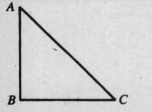 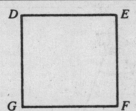

$AB = BC$, and $DE = EF = FG = DG$
Area of right triangle ABC
equals area of square $DEFG$

5. $\dfrac{AB}{DG}$ .... $\sqrt{2}$

6. The positive value of $\sqrt{\dfrac{1}{25}}$ 20%

7. The positive value of $\sqrt{14.4}$ 4

8. The time required to cover $\dfrac{1}{2}$ mile traveling at 20 miles per hour .... The time required to cover $\dfrac{1}{3}$ mile traveling at 30 miles per hour

9. The number of revolutions made by the wheel of a bicycle (diameter of $\dfrac{7}{\pi}$ feet) covering a distance of 70 feet .... The number of revolutions made by the wheel of a motorcycle (diameter of $\dfrac{10}{\pi}$ feet) covering a distance of 100 feet

$$X + Y + Z = 350$$
$$X + Y = 100$$
All unknowns > 0

10. Z X

Distance from X to $Y = 3$ miles
Distance from Y to $Z = 2$ miles

11. Distance from X to Z ...... Distance from X to Y

$$9x^2 = y$$
x is a nonzero integer

12. x .... y

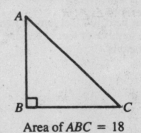

Area of $ABC = 18$

13. AB .... BC

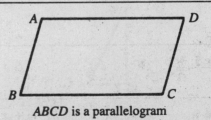

ABCD is a parallelogram

14. $AD + BC$ .... $AB + DC$

$$\dfrac{48}{x} = 4$$

15. $16\dfrac{2}{3}\%$ of 72 x

Directions: Each of the Questions 16–30 has five answer choices. For each of these questions, select the best of the answer choices given.

16. The ingredients for making 5 dozen cookies, as given in a recipe, are 1 egg, $\frac{1}{2}$ cup shortening, $\frac{3}{4}$ cup sugar, 1 teaspoon flavoring, $1\frac{1}{2}$ cup sifted flour. How much flour would be needed in order to make 20 cookies?

(A) $\frac{1}{4}$ cup

(B) $\frac{1}{2}$ cup

(C) $3\frac{3}{4}$ cups

(D) $4\frac{1}{2}$ cups

(E) 6 cups

17. Potassium nitrate is composed of 39 parts potassium, 14 parts nitrogen, and 48 parts oxygen. Find the percentage (to the nearest %) of potassium in potassium nitrate.

(A) 14
(B) 39
(C) 45
(D) 48
(E) 62

18. A rectangular field 100 feet long is twice as long as it is wide. The number of feet of fencing needed to enclose the field is

(A) 150
(B) 300
(C) 400
(D) 500
(E) 600

19. In the triangle above, BC equals one half of AB. The area of right triangle ABC equals 64 square feet. To the nearest foot, what is hypotenuse AC?

(A) 12
(B) 14
(C) 18
(D) 24
(E) 32

x	5	$\frac{5}{9}$
y	3	?

20. In the figure above, if $x = ky$, and k is a constant, what is the missing value of y in the table?

(A) $\frac{1}{27}$ (B) $\frac{1}{3}$ (C) $\frac{25}{27}$

(D) $\frac{27}{25}$ (E) 3

Questions 21–25 refer to the following chart.

NUTRITIONAL VALUE OF SOME
DAIRY PRODUCTS

	SIZE OF PORTION	CALO-RIES	PROTEIN (grams)
Milk, whole	1 glass (8 oz.)	160	9
Milk, skim or buttermilk	1 glass (8 oz.)	90	9
Milk, chocolate drink . . .	1 glass (8 oz.)	190	8
Cheese, American or	1" cube or med. slice		
Swiss	(1 oz.)	110	8
Cheese oods, Cheddar-type	2 tablespoons (1 oz.)	90	6
Cheese, cottage, creamed	2 tablespoons (1 oz.)	30	4
Cheese, cream	2 x 1 x ½" or 2 tbsp.	110	2
Butter	1 tablespoon (½ oz.)	100	–
Butter	1 teaspoon or small pat . .	35	–
Cream, light, table	2 tablespoons	60	1
Cream, heavy, whipped	1 heaping tablespoon	50	–
Half-and-half	¼ cup	80	2
Ice cream, vanilla	¼ pint (½ cup)	145	3
Ice cream, as for a la mode	Medium scoop (⅓ pint) . .	115	2
Sherbert	½ cup	130	1

21. How many tablespoons of light cream have the same number of calories as 8 ounces of buttermilk?

(A) 2
(B) 3
(C) 4
(D) 5
(E) 6

22. How many calories of cream cheese would there be in the amount needed to furnish the same number of grams of protein as there are in 4 ounces of chocolate milk?

(A) 55
(B) 95
(C) 110
(D) 220
(E) 330

23. Which of the following has the greatest number of calories per pound?

    (A) whole milk
    (B) buttermilk
    (C) Swiss cheese
    (D) cottage cheese
    (E) chocolate milk

24. Which of the following has the smallest number of calories per ounce?

    (A) cottage cheese
    (B) cheddar-type cheese
    (C) Swiss cheese
    (D) butter
    (E) whole milk

25. Which of the following furnishes the greatest number of grams of protein per unit weight?

    (A) whole milk
    (B) cottage cheese
    (C) butter
    (D) chocolate milk
    (E) American cheese

26. Which of the following statements is always true?

    I.   A root of a negative number may be a real number.
    II. The positive square root of a number is smaller than the number.
    III. A binomial multiplied by a binomial yields a trinomial

    (A) I only
    (B) II only
    (C) III only
    (D) II and III only
    (E) all are true

27. Which of the following numbers does *not* have a reciprocal?

    (A) 1
    (B) -2
    (C) $\frac{1}{3}$
    (D) 0
    (E) 3

28. If $x + y = 16$, then $x - z =$

    (A) $z + 16$
    (B) 8
    (C) $16 - y$
    (D) $z(16 - y)$
    (E) $16 - y - z$

29. If a and b are positive integers and $\frac{a - b}{3.5} = \frac{4}{7}$, then

    (A) $b < a$
    (B) $b > a$
    (C) $b = a$
    (D) $b \gtrless a$
    (E) $b \lessgtr a$

30. 10^x means that 10 is to be used as a factor x times, and 10^{-x} means $\frac{1}{10^x}$. Very large and very small numbers, therefore, are frequently written as a decimal multiplied by 10^x where x is a positive or a negative integer. Which, if any, of the following is false?

    (A) $470,000 = 4.7 \times 10^5$
    (B) 450 billion $= 4.5 \times 10^{11}$
    (C) $.00000000075 = 7.5 \times 10^{-10}$
    (D) 86 hundred-thousandths $= 8.6 \times 10^{-2}$
    (E) none of these

S T O P

IF YOU FINISH BEFORE TIME IS CALLED, YOU MAY CHECK YOUR WORK ON THIS SECTION ONLY. DO NOT WORK ON ANY OTHER SECTION IN THE TEST.

SECTION 5

Time—30 Minutes

25 Questions

Directions: Each question or group of questions is based on a passage or set of conditions. In answering some of the questions, it may be useful to draw a rough diagram. For each question, select the best answer choice given.

Questions 1–4

Mrs. F, official hostess of New York City, has invited several wives of delegates to the United Nations for an informal luncheon. She plans to seat her eleven guests so that each lady will be able to converse with at least the person directly to her right or left. She has prepared the following list.

Mrs. F speaks English only.
Mrs. G speaks English and French.
Mrs. H speaks English and Russian.
Mrs. J speaks Russian only.
Mrs. K speaks English only.
Mrs. L speaks French only.
Mrs. M speaks French and German.
Mrs. N speaks English and German.
Mrs. O speaks English and French.
Mrs. P speaks German and Russian.
Mrs. Q speaks French and German.
Mrs. R speaks English only.

1. Which of the following arrangements will meet Mrs. F's requirement?

    I.   FOLMPJHKGQNR
    II. FRNLPKHJGMQO
    III. FRGJHOLMPQPKN

    (A) I only
    (B) II only
    (C) III only
    (D) I and II only
    (E) I and III only

2. If the ladies seated to the right of Mrs. P are respectively *MGHKFO*, who must sit at Mrs. P's left hand?

    (A) J
    (B) L
    (C) N
    (D) Q
    (E) R

3. If seven of the ladies have seated themselves in the following order, *NGFROMQ*, who must be the next lady seated?

    (A) H
    (B) J
    (C) K
    (D) L
    (E) P

4. Mrs. F has decided upon the following seating arrangement:
    R K G Q N F O L M P J H
    At the last minute, Mrs. H and Mrs. P inform the hostess that they will not be able to attend. Which of the following adjustments will allow Mrs. F's seating requirements to be met?

    I.   Seat Mrs. J between Mrs. K and Mrs. G
    II. Seat Mrs. J between Mrs. Q and Mrs. F
    III. Seat Mrs. J to the right of Mrs. N

    (A) I only
    (B) III only
    (C) I or II only
    (D) II or III only
    (E) Neither I, II, not III

5. Senator Johnson: No argument for this bill is valid, because no one would argue for this bill without having an ulterior motive: namely, the desire for personal gain.

    The bill's sponsors would be committing the same error in reasoning as Senator Johnson if they responded by saying:

    (A) Of course we have ulterior motives. It is perfectly reasonable to support a bill in order to promote our personal interests.
    (B) The fact that passing a bill would benefit its sponsors does not mean that the bill should not be passed.
    (C) The fact that Senator Johnson has substituted a personal attack for a discussion of the merits of the bill leads us to suspect that he can offer no strong arguments against it.
    (D) Senator Johnson has no valid reason for opposing our bill; he is only doing so because we helped defeat his pork-barrelling bill last month.
    (E) Everyone is always motivated in part by a desire for personal gain; Senator Johnson is no exception.

6. Father: My daughter could be a star on Broadway if she could only get one big break. Why, you should see the rave reviews she received when she was the lead in her high school play.

The best way to counter the argument above would be to point out that

(A) big breaks are hard to come by on Broadway
(B) one big break does not ensure continued success in the theatre
(C) the standards on Broadway are much higher than they are at the high school level
(D) fewer plays are being produced on Broadway today than in the past
(E) relatively few aspiring actors ever become Broadway stars

7. Most persons who oppose gun control are conservatives; therefore, since Kathleen favors gun control, she is probably not a conservative.

The above argument most resembles which of the following?

(A) Most sociology professors are liberals; therefore Dr. Williams, who is a liberal, is probably a sociology professor.
(B) Most corporation presidents own a country home; if Ms. Steeples is a corporation president, she may or may not have a country home.
(C) Few major publishing firms publish much poetry; since Flame Press publishes only poetry, it is probably not a major publishing firm.
(D) Most sports cars are extremely expensive; since the new Venus Leopard is not a sports car, it is probably inexpensive.
(E) Most desert plants are cacti; therefore the cholla, a desert plant, is probably a cactus.

Questions 8–11

The Homer Museum of American Art is open daily except Monday from 11 a.m. to 5 p.m. Tuesdays and Thursdays the museum remains open until 8 p.m. The spring special exhibitions are: "Albert Pinkham Ryder, A Retrospective," which is on view from Friday, April 24, through Sunday, May 31, in the Pollock Wing; "Precursors of Thomas Eakins," from Friday, May 8, through Sunday, July 6, in the Third Floor Gallery; and "The Hudson River School," in the John Twachtman Gallery, which is closed Tuesdays, from Friday, May 1, through Sunday, May 24 only. The Pollock wing is closed Thursdays during May.

8. If Dan can visit the museum only after 5 p.m. or on Saturday, and does not wish to view more than one special exhibition in a day, he can see all three special exhibitions in the briefest time by starting with

(A) "The Hudson River School" on a Thursday
(B) the Ryder Retrospective on a Saturday
(C) "Precursors of Eakins" or the Ryder Retrospective on a Tuesday
(D) "Precursors of Eakins" on a Thursday
(E) any exhibition on a Saturday

9. Ellen wishes to visit the three special exhibitons on successive Thursdays. This is only possible if she visits

I. the Ryder Retrospective in April
II. "The Hudson River School" second
III. "Precursors of Eakins" immediately following the Ryder Retrospective

(A) I only
(B) II only
(C) I and II only
(D) II and III only
(E) I, II, and III

10. Ralph can visit all three special exhibitions on one day if he goes on

I. any Saturday in May
II. the second, third, or fourth Saturday in May
III. any Tuesday or Friday between May 5 and May 22

(A) I only
(B) II only
(C) III only
(D) I and III only
(E) II and III only

11. Terry visits the museum on an afternoon six days after the opening of "The Hudson River School." Which of the special exhibitions may he visit?

I. The Ryder Retrospective
II. "Precursors of Eakins"
III. "The Hudson River School"

(A) I only
(B) III only
(C) I and II only
(D) II and III only
(E) I, II, and III

Questions 12–18

At a symposium on the possible dangers of the industrial chemical PBX, three pro-industry spokespersons are to be seated to the left of the moderator and three critics of PBX to the right of the moderator. The speakers are Drs. Albert, Burris, Cathode, Durand, Ettis, and Felsenstein.

(1) The person delivering the paper "Epidemiological Aspects of PBX" is seated immediately between Dr. Albert and Dr. Durand.
(2) The persons delivering "Public Health and PBX" and "Radiological Aspects of PBX" are close friends and insist on sitting together.
(3) Felsenstein is placed two seats to the left of the moderator.
(4) As heavy smoking is repugnant to the moderator, she insists that the person delivering "PBX: Benign or Malignant," a heavy smoker, be seated at one end of the table.
(5) Cathode, delivering "The Impact of PBX on the Environment," is seated to the left of Felsenstein.
(6) Albert, a critic of PBX, is seated to the left of Ettis.

12. The pro-industry spokespersons are

   (A) Albert, Felsinstein, Durand
   (B) Felsenstein, Burris, Albert
   (C) Cathode, Felsenstein, Ettis
   (D) Albert, Burris, Durand
   (E) Cathode, Felsenstein, Burris

13. The person seated immediately to the left of the moderator is

   (A) Albert
   (B) Burris
   (C) Cathode
   (D) Durand
   (E) Ettis

14. Assuming it is one of the papers delivered at the symposium, "PBX and the Digestive Tract" must be by

   (A) Albert
   (B) Burris
   (C) Durand
   (D) Ettis
   (E) Felsenstein

15. Which of the following cannot be determined on the basis of the information given?

   I.   The author of "Public Health and PBX"
   II. The title of the paper delivered by Durand
   III. The identity of the two friends who insist on being together

   (A) I only
   (B) I only
   (C) III only
   (D) I and II only
   (E) II and III only

16. Given the seating rules as stated, which of the numbered statements are logically sufficient to establish the position of Dr. Ettis and the title of the paper she delivers?

   (A) 1, 3, 4
   (B) 1, 2, 3, 4
   (C) 1, 3, 5; 6
   (D) 1, 4, 5, 6
   (E) 1, 3, 4, 5

17. The symposium is expanded to include a seventh speaker. If he is seated exactly midway between Cathode and the moderator, he will sit

   (A) to the left of the author of "Radiological Aspects of PBX"
   (B) one seat to the right of the moderator
   (C) two seats to the right of Durand
   (D) three seats to the left of Albert
   (E) four seats to the left of the author of "PBX: Benign or Malignant"

18. The symposium is further expanded to include an eighth speaker. If she is seated exactly midway between Durand and the author of "Public Health and PBX," which of the following must be true?

   (A) The eighth speaker must be seated to the right of the moderator.
   (B) Burris must be the author of "Radiological Aspects of PBX."
   (C) The eighth speaker must be seated on the same side of the moderator as Felsenstein.
   (D) The moderator must be seated next to the author of "Public Health and PBX."
   (E) The eighth speaker must be seated immediately to the left of Ettis.

Questions 19–22

A is the father of two children. B and D, who are of different sexes.
C is B's spouse
E is the same sex as D.
B and C have two children: F, who is the same sex as B, and G, who is the same sex as C.
E's mother, H, who is married to L, is the sister of D's mother, M.
E and E's spouse, I, have two children, J and K, who are the same sex as I.
No persons have married more than once and no children have been born out of wedlock. The only restrictions on marriage are that marriage to a sibling, to a direct descendant, or to more than one person at the same time are forbidden.

19. F is

   (A) G's brother
   (B) G's sister
   (C) B's daughter
   (D) D's niece or nephew
   (E) the same sex as H

20. According to the rules, D can marry

    (A) F only
    (B) G only
    (C) J only
    (D) J or K only
    (E) F, J, or K

21. If L and H divorced, H could marry

    I.   D only
    II. F
    III. D or G

    (A) I only
    (B) II only
    (C) III only
    (D) I or II, but not both
    (E) II or III, but not both

22. If the generation of F and K's parents and their siblings contains more females than males, which of the following must be true?

    (A) There are more females than males in F and K's generation.
    (B) J is male.
    (C) A is the same sex as D
    (D) K and G are the same sex.
    (E) D is H's nephew.

Questions 23–25

The internal combustion engine, which powers all private motorized vehicles, should be banned. It burns up petroleum products that are needed to produce plastics, synthetics, and many medicines. Once all the oil is gone, we will no longer be able to produce these valuable commodities. Yet we do not have to burn gasoline to satisfy our transportation needs. Other kinds of engines could be developed if the oil companies would stop blocking research efforts.

23. The argument above depends on which of the following assumptions?

    I.   We are in imminent danger of running out of oil.
    II. Alternative methods of producing plastics will not be found before the oil runs out.
    III. If they so desired, the oil companies could develop methods of transporation not based on the burning of petroleum.

    (A) I only
    (B) II only
    (C) I and II only
    (D) II and III only
    (E) I, II and III

24. The argument above would be most weakened by the development of which of the following?

    (A) An internal combustion engine that operated on one-tenth the gasoline used in a normal engine
    (B) A car that operated on solar energy stored in special batteries
    (C) A method of producing plastic that used no petroleum products
    (D) A synthetic oil with all the properties of natural oil
    (E) A means of locating numerous undiscovered oil fields

25. The argument above would be most strengthened if which of the following were true?

    (A) One of the oil companies has suppressed the discovery of an engine that burns only alcohol.
    (B) Some of the medicines that require petroleum for their production help to control and cure several of the world's most deadly diseases.
    (C) The world's current oil reserves are about half of what they were 30 years ago.
    (D) In high pollution areas, automobile exhaust fumes have been shown to cause high rates of lung cancer and heart disease.
    (E) When gasoline is burned inside an auto engine, less than one-fourth of the energy produced is used to propel the vehicle.

S T O P

IF YOU FINISH BEFORE TIME IS CALLED, YOU MAY CHECK YOUR WORK ON THIS SECTION ONLY.
DO NOT WORK ON ANY OTHER SECTION IN THE TEST.

SECTION 6

Time - 30 Minutes

25 Questions

Directions: Each question or group of questions is based on a passage or set of conditions. In answering some of the questions, it may be useful to draw a rough diagram. For each question, select the best answer choice given.

Questions 1–5

In a certain society, only two forms of marriage are recognized. In *Prahtu* marriage, several brothers marry a single woman, while in *Brihtu* marriage, several sisters marry a single man. All members of a given married group are regarded as the parents of any children of the marriage. Marriage between male and female children of the same parents is forbidden.

E is a son of A.
G is a daughter of B.
F is a daughter of C.
E, F, M, and N have a daughter, H.
E and F have the same paternal grandmother, Q.
A and B are the only grandfathers of H; C, J, K, and L are the only grandmothers of H.
No one has married more than once; all children were born in wedlock.

1. G is a sister of

   (A) N only
   (B) M only
   (C) E
   (D) F
   (E) E or F, but not both

2. N is a sibling of

   I.   M only
   II. M and E
   III. M and F

   (A) I only
   (B) II only
   (C) III only
   (D) II or III, but not both
   (E) Neither I, II, nor III

3. One of Q's children may be

   (A) A
   (B) C
   (C) J
   (D) K
   (E) M

4. Which of the following is an offspring of a *Brihtu* marriage?

   (A) H
   (B) E
   (C) A
   (D) B
   (E) J

5. If E, F, M, and N had not married, which would be a permissible marriage?

   (A) N marries M and others of M's sex.
   (B) N and M marry E.
   (C) N and M marry G and F.
   (D) G marries E only.
   (E) E marries G and F.

Questions 6–9

Seven varsity basketball players are to be honored at a special luncheon. The players will be seated on the dais along one side of a single rectangular table.
Adams and Goldberg have to leave the luncheon early and so must be seated at the extreme right end of the table, which is closest to the exit.
Baker will receive the Most Valuable Player's trophy and so must be in the center chair to facilitate the presentation.
Cooper and D'Amato, who were bitter rivals for the position of center during the basketball season, dislike one another and should be seated as far apart as is convenient.
Edwards and Farley are best friends and want to sit together.

6. Which of the following may not be seated at either of the table?

   (A) Cooper
   (B) D'Amato
   (C) Goldberg
   (D) Farley
   (E) Adams

7. Which of the following pairs may not be seated together?

   (A) Cooper and Farley
   (B) Baker and D'Amato
   (C) Edwards and Adams
   (D) Goldberg and D'Amato
   (E) Edwards and Cooper

8. Which of the following pairs may not occupy the seats on either side of Baker?

   (A) Farley and D'Amato
   (B) D'Amato and Edwards
   (C) Edwards and Goldberg
   (D) Farley and Cooper
   (E) Cooper and Edwards

9. If neither Edwards nor D'Amato is seated next to Baker, how many *different* seating arrangements are possible?

    (A) 1
    (B) 2
    (C) 3
    (D) 4
    (E) 5

Questions 10–15

Number series questions provide psychologists with a means of testing a person's ability to determine quantitative patterns. Below are seven number series:

     I.   4, 64, 5, 125, 6, x
    II.   6, 37, 7, 50, 8, 65, 9, x
   III.   5, 25, 125, 7, 49, 343, 9, 81, x
    IV.   9, −7, 18, −18, 31, x
     V.   4, 16, 80, 480, 3360, x
    VI.   25, 24, 22, 19, 15, 10, x
   VII.   100, 81, 64, 49, 36, x

10. In which of the above number series is the third power of a number the determining factor?

    (A) I and III
    (B) I, IV, and V
    (C) I, III, and VII
    (D) II, III, and VI
    (E) I, III, IV, and VII

11. In which of the above number series is the use of powers of a number *NOT* a determining factor?

    (A) I
    (B) II
    (C) IV
    (D) V
    (E) VII

12. In which of the above number series is the determining factor the addition and subtraction of squares?

    (A) II
    (B) IV
    (C) VI
    (D) VII
    (E) None

13. In which of the above number series is $n^2 + 1$ the determining factor?

    (A) II
    (B) III
    (C) V
    (D) VII
    (E) None

14. In which of the above number series is the recognition of increasing multiples significant?

    (A) II
    (B) V
    (C) VI
    (D) II and IV
    (E) II and VI

15. In which of the above number series is it necessary to consider a pattern of three elements?

    (A) I
    (B) II
    (C) III
    (D) IV
    (E) V

Questions 16–20

Mr. Pict must accommodate seven tour group passengers in two four-person cabins on the S.S. *Gallia*. The passengers in each cabin must all be able to converse with one another, though not necessarily all in the same language. A, an Etruscan, also speaks Gothic and Hittite. B and F are Hittites and speak only that language. C, an Etruscan, also speaks Gothic. D and G are Goths and speak only Gothic. E, and Etruscan, also speaks Hittite. Hittites refuse to share rooms with Goths.

16. Which combination of passengers in one of the cabins will result in a rooming arrangement that satisfies all condition?

    (A) B, C, F
    (B) D, E, G,
    (C) A, D, E, G
    (D) C, D, E, G
    (E) A, B, C, F

17. Which can be true given the conditions as stated?

     I.   C cannot room with A.
    II.   A cabin containing three persons must include A.
   III.   E can always room with a Hittite.

    (A) I only
    (B) II only
    (C) I and III only
    (D) II and III only
    (E) I, II, and III

18. How many different combinations of cabin mates satisfy all conditions?

    (A) 2
    (B) 3
    (C) 4
    (D) 5
    (E) 6

19. If E objects to sharing a cabin with A, whom can Mr. Pict place him with in order to arrive at an arrangement that satisfies all conditions?

   I. D and G, with no fourth cabin mate
  II. B and F, with no fourth cabin mate
 III. C, D, and G

   (A) I only
   (B) II only
   (C) I and III only
   (D) II and III only
   (E) Neither I, II, nor III

20. At the last minute, a new person applies to join the group. Mr. Pict can place her with any of the following except

   (A) C, D, and G if she is a Goth
   (B) A, B, and F is she is an Etruscan
   (C) B, E, and F if she is a Hittite
   (D) C, D, and G if she is an Etruscan
   (E) B, E, and F is she is a Goth

Questions 21–25

In the days of sailing ships fresh food was not available, and at the end of long trips many sailors came down with scurvy. Many attempts were made to seek a cure for this condition.
1. John Hall cured several cases of scurvy by administering a sour brew made of a certain grass and watercress.
2. William Harvey suggested that the sailors take lemon juice to prevent scurvy. He thought the acid (citric acid) in lemon juice would prevent the disease.
3. James Lind experimented with 12 sick sailors to find out whether the acid was responsible for the cure. Each was given the same diet except four of the men were given small amounts of dilute sulfuric acid, four others were given vinegar (acetic acid), and the remaining four were given lemons. Only those given lemons recovered from the scurvy.

21. Credit for solving the problem described in the passage belongs to

   (A) Hall because he devised a cure for scurvy.
   (B) Harvey because he first proposed a solution of the problem.
   (C) Lind because he used the scientific experimental method.
   (D) Harvey and Lind, because they found that lemons are more effective than Hall's brew.
   (E) All three men because each made some contribution.

22. How many controls did James Lind use?

   (A) one
   (B) two
   (C) three
   (D) four
   (E) none

23. The hypothesis tested by Lind was

   (A) lemons contain some substance not present in vinegar
   (B) citric acid of lemons is effective in treating scurvy
   (C) lemons contain some unknown acid that cures scurvy
   (D) the substance to cure scurvy is found only in lemons
   (E) some specific substance, rather than acids in general, is needed to cure scurvy

24. Lind's experiment did *not* answer the question:

   (A) Will lemons cure scurvy?
   (B) Will either sulfuric acid or vinegar cure scurvy?
   (C) Will citric acid alone cure scurvy?
   (D) Are lemons more effective than either sulfuric acid or vinegar in the treatment of scurvy?
   (E) Are all substances that contain acids equally effective as a treatment for scurvy?

25. A possible cause of scurvy is

   (A) lack of watercress
   (B) lack of acidity
   (C) lack of fresh food
   (D) lengthy sea voyages
   (E) lack of lemon juice

S T O P

IF YOU FINISH BEFORE TIME IS CALLED, YOU MAY CHECK YOUR WORK ON THIS SECTION ONLY. DO NOT WORK ON ANY OTHER SECTION IN THE TEST.

SECTION 7

Time—30 Minutes

30 Questions

Numbers: All numbers used are real numbers.

Figures: Position of points, angles, regions, etc. can be assumed to be in the order shown; and angle measures can be assumed to be positive.

Lines shown as straight can be assumed to be straight.

Figures can be assumed to lie in a plane unless otherwise indicated.

Figures that accompany questions are intended to provide information useful in answering the questions. However, unless a note states that a figure is drawn to scale, you should solve these problems NOT by estimating sizes by sight or by measurement, but by using your knowledge of mathematics (see Example 2 below).

Directions: Each of the Questions 1-15 consists of two quantities, one in Column A and one in Column B. You are to compare the two quantities and choose

> A if the quantity in Column A is greater;
> B if the quantity in Column B is greater;
> C if the two quantities are equal;
> D if the relationship cannot be determined from the information given.

Note: Since there are only four choices, NEVER MARK (E).

Common
Information: In a question, information concerning one or both of the quantities to be compared is centered above the two columns. A symbol that appears in both columns represents the same thing in Column A as it does in Column B.

Column A	Column B	Sample Answers

Example 1: 2×6 $2 + 6$ ● Ⓑ Ⓒ Ⓓ Ⓔ

Examples 2-4 refer to $\triangle PQR$.

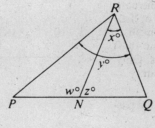

Example 2:

PN NQ Ⓐ Ⓑ Ⓒ ● Ⓔ

(since equal measures cannot be assumed, even though PN and NQ appear equal)

Example 3: x y Ⓐ ● Ⓒ Ⓓ Ⓔ

(since N is between P and Q)

Example 4: $w + z$ 180   Ⓐ Ⓑ ● Ⓓ Ⓔ

(since PQ is a straight line)

Column A	Column B	Column A	Column B

$a = 3b$

1. $a{:}b$ $b{:}a$

2. 8^2 2^8

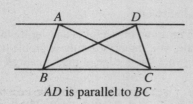

AD is parallel to BC

3. Area of ABC Area of DBC

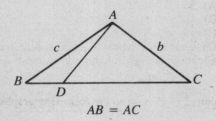

$AB = AC$

4. $\dfrac{b}{c}$ $\dfrac{c}{b}$

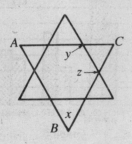

$BA = BC$, $\angle x = 60°$, and $\angle y = 100°$

5. value of z 140°

$a = 3, \quad b = 9$

6. $a^2 - b$ $b - a^2$

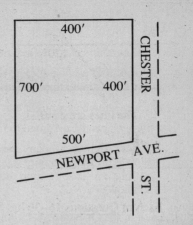

7. The area of the lot on the corner of Chester Street and Newport Avenue   200,000 square feet

$a < b$

8. $-2a$ $-2b$

q is the smallest of nine consecutive numbers.

9. The average of these nine numbers $q + 4$

10. $(1813)\left(\dfrac{1}{2} + \dfrac{1}{3}\right)$ 1813

$x > 0$
$y > 0$
$xy = 1$

11. $\dfrac{x}{y}$ x^2

$x < 0$

12. $\dfrac{1}{x}$ x^2

13. $\dfrac{1}{200}$ $\dfrac{1}{2}\%$

Column A	Column B

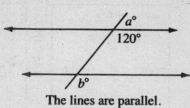

The lines are parallel.

14. a b

Column A	Column B

$$2a - b = 3$$
$$a + b = -6$$

15. a b

Directions: Each of Questions 16–30 has five answer choices. For each of these questions, select the best of the answer choices given.

16. A $41\frac{1}{2}$-foot string is to be cut into 6 approximately equal lengths. The average length of each piece will be

(A) 6'1"
(B) 6'9"
(C) 6'11"
(D) 7'9"
(E) 8'3"

17. A shirt marked $12.50 was sold for $10.00. The rate of discount on the marked price was

(A) 2%
(B) 2.5%
(C) 20%
(D) 25%
(E) 80%

18. A radio marked $96 is offered for $72. The percent discount is

(A) 4%
(B) 24%
(C) 25%
(D) $33\frac{1}{3}$%
(E) $66\frac{2}{3}$%

19. A car uses a gallon of gasoline in traveling 15 miles. Another automobile can travel m miles on a gallon of gasoline. How many miles can the second travel on the amount of gasoline required by the first car in going 60 miles?

(A) $\frac{m}{4}$
(B) m
(C) $4m$
(D) $\frac{m}{9}$
(E) $9m$

20. How many gallons of paint should be purchased to cover 760 square feet if a gallon will cover 200 square feet?

(A) 3
(B) 4
(C) 5
(D) 6
(E) 7

Questions 21–25 refer to the following graphs.

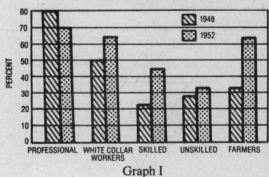

Graph I

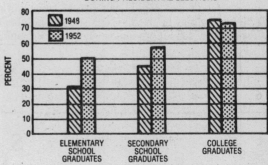

Graph II

21. Which of the following groups showed the smallest percent increase of Republican voters between the elections of 1948 and 1952?

(A) professional
(B) white collar workers
(C) skilled
(D) farmers
(E) elementary school graduates

22. Which of the following groups showed an increase of almost 100% between the two presidential election years?

(A) elementary school graduates
(B) college graduates
(C) professional
(D) skilled
(E) farmers

24. If w represents the percent of white collar workers, who voted Republican in 1948, which of the following may not be used to represent the percent of white collar workers who voted Republican in 1952?

(A) 130% w
(B) $w + 15\%$
(C) $2w - 35\%$
(D) $\frac{w}{2} + 40\%$
(E) $(w - 30\%)^2$

25. What percent of the elementary school-educated unskilled workers voted Republican in 1952?

(A) 18%
(B) 33%
(C) 42%
(D) 84%
(E) cannot be determined from the information furnished by the graph

26. What is a percent of b divided by b percent of a?

(A) a
(B) b
(C) 1
(D) 10
(E) 100

23. If h represents the number of secondary school graduates who voted Republican in 1948, which of the following may be used to represent the number of secondary school graduates who voted Republican in 1952?

(A) $\frac{29}{23} h$ (C) $\frac{25}{28} h$ (E) $\frac{3}{25} h$

(B) $\frac{28}{25} h$ (D) $h + 12$

27. Which of the following fractions is next smaller in value than one-half?

(A) $\frac{1}{5}$

(B) $\frac{1}{4}$

(C) $\frac{2}{5}$

(D) $\frac{16}{25}$

(E) $\frac{3}{10}$

28. The fraction $\frac{t + n}{n}$ equals

(A) $\frac{t}{n} + n$

(B) $\frac{t + n}{t}$

(C) $\frac{t}{n} + 1$

(D) $t^2 + 1$

(E) t

29. A cow is grazing in a pasture bordered by two fences more than 10 feet long that meet at an angle of 60°. If the cow is tethered by a ten-foot-long rope to the post at which the two fences meet, it can graze in an area of

(A) 20π

(B) $\frac{5\pi}{3}$

(C) $\frac{20\pi}{3}$

(D) $\frac{50\pi}{3}$

(E) 100π

30. A certain recipe makes enough dough to fill two cake tins, each 7 inches in diameter and 1 inch deep. How many inches deep will the cake dough be if put into one cake tin 10 inches in diameter?

(A) 0.51
(B) 0.71
(C) 0.98
(D) 1.02
(E) 1.40

S T O P

IF YOU FINISH BEFORE TIME IS CALLED, YOU MAY CHECK YOUR WORK ON THIS SECTION ONLY.
DO NOT WORK ON ANY OTHER SECTION IN THE TEST.

Answer Key

Note: The answers to the quantitative sections are keyed to the corresponding review areas in the Mathematics Review (Chapter 11). The numbers in parentheses after each answer refer to the math topic(s) covered by that particular question.

Section 1   Verbal

1.	D	11.	C	21.	E	31.	D
2.	C	12.	B	22.	C	32.	B
3.	C	13.	E	23.	E	33.	C
4.	B	14.	C	24.	D	34.	C
5.	B	15.	C	25.	E	35.	E
6.	D	16.	D	26.	D	36.	D
7.	C	17.	B	27.	D	37.	B
8.	B	18.	C	28.	A	38.	E
9.	E	19.	C	29.	C		
10.	B	20.	E	30.	E		

Section 2   Verbal

1.	B	11.	C	21.	E	31.	D
2.	E	12.	D	22.	D	32.	E
3.	C	13.	C	23.	D	33.	E
4.	D	14.	D	24.	D	34.	E
5.	D	15.	E	25.	E	35.	C
6.	D	16.	D	26.	A	36.	E
7.	E	17.	B	27.	C	37.	B
8.	C	18.	D	28.	C	38.	A
9.	D	19.	C	29.	C		
10.	E	20.	B	30.	D		

Section 3   Quantitative

1.	B (I-B)	9.	C (III-A, D)	17.	C (III-G)	25.	C (I-B, IV)
2.	D (I-A)	10.	A (II-G)	18.	B (II-E)	26.	B (III-H)
3.	C (I)	11.	C (III-A, D)	19.	A (I-D)	27.	D (II-E)
4.	C (II-E)	12.	C (I-D)	20.	D (I-B, III)	28.	E (II-B)
5.	A (II-A)	13.	C (II-B)	21.	C (II-E, IV)	29.	B (III-F)
6.	C (III-F)	14.	C (I-B, C)	22.	D (I, IV)	30.	D (I-D)
7.	C (III-A, C)	15.	D (I-B, II-A)	23.	C (I-A, IV)		
8.	D (III-A)	16.	B (III-F)	24.	C (II-ED, IV)		

Section 4   Quantitative

1.	A (III-A, D)	9.	C (III-G)	17.	B (I-D)	25.	E (III-D)
2.	B (I-B)	10.	A (II-A)	18.	B (III-G)	26.	A (I-H, II-A)
3.	C (II-B)	11.	D (III-B)	19.	C (III-D)	27.	D (I-B)
4.	C (I-A)	12.	B (II-A)	20.	B (II-E)	28.	E (II-A)
5.	C (III-G)	13.	D (III-G)	21.	B (II-B)	29.	A (II-G)
6.	C (I-C, H)	14.	D (III-C)	22.	D (II-C)	30.	D (I-H)
7.	B (I-H)	15.	C (I-D, II-A)	23.	C (I-B)		
8.	A (II-C2)	16.	B (II-E)	24.	E (II-A)		

Section 5   Analytical

1.	E	8.	C	15.	A	22.	B
2.	A	9.	C	16.	C	23.	B
3.	D	10.	B	17.	D	24.	D
4.	E	11.	B	18.	B	25.	B
5.	D	12.	E	19.	D		
6.	C	13.	B	20.	E		
7.	D	14.	A	21.	E		

Section 6   Analytical

1.	D	8.	C	15.	C	22.	B
2.	D	9.	B	16.	D	23.	E
3.	A	10.	A	17.	E	24.	C
4.	B	11.	D	18.	C	25.	C
5.	E	12.	B	19.	D		
6.	D	13.	A	20.	E		
7.	C	14.	B	21.	E		

Section 7   Quantitative

1.	A (II-A)	9.	C (I-G)	17.	C (I-D)	25.	E (IV)
2.	B (I-H)	10.	B (I-B)	18.	C (I-D)	26.	C (I-D)
3.	C (III-G)	11.	C (II-A)	19.	C (II-E)	27.	C (I-B)
4.	C (IV-D)	12.	B (II-A)	20.	B (I-A)	28.	C (II-A)
5.	C (III-A)	13.	C (I-B, D)	21.	B (IV)	29.	D (III-G)
6.	C (I-A)	14.	B (III-A)	22.	E (IV)	30.	C (III-G)
7.	A(III-G)	15.	A (II-B)	23.	A (II-B, E, IV)		
8.	A (II-G)	16.	C (I-A)	24.	E (I-D, IV)		

Answer Explanations

Section 1

1. **D.** The statement asserts that the three are not in fact independent or separate but are instead *inseparable*.

2. **C.** If depression arises when nerve cells get too little of certain chemicals, it makes sense to have these cells get more of the chemicals. This can be done by making more of the chemicals *available to* the cells.

3. **C.** *Conventional* or traditional methods no longer are adequate to protect wild creatures. Conservationists wish to protect wildlife. Therefore, they are *pressing for* a new approach.

4. **B.** If neutron stars are the remnants or remaining traces of exploding stars, then they are the *products* or results of *violent* natural processes. Choice A is incorrect. The neutron stars did not cause the explosions; they were *caused by* the explosions.
Choice C is incorrect. There is nothing *equivocal* or inconclusive about the explosion of a star.
Choice D is incorrect. Nothing in the statement suggests that the creation of neutron stars *justifies* or vindicates the explosion of a star. In addition *harsh* is far too weak a word to describe a stellar explosion.
Choice E is incorrect. Neutron stars come into existence *after* a supernova explodes. Thus, they are not *precursors* or forerunners of the explosion.

5. **B.** The contrast in Hugo is between *piety* or devotion ("a scene of chaste and holy love") and *ribaldry* or indecency (a scene of "coarse and profane licentiousness").
Note that the sentence's parallelism demands that the two missing words be antonyms or near-antonyms.

6. **D.** The key word here is *busyness*, used to indicate a state of having many intricate details that do not coordinate into a harmonious whole. Because the details were *subordinated* or made less important than the building's total design, the building was *unencumbered* or unhampered by a sense of busyness.

7. **C.** The waitress omits taking *exaggerated* precautions. However, this does not imply that in doing so she was either rash (*imprudent*) or erratic (*capricious*). She was merely being *nonchalant* or poised, undisturbed by any untoward agitation over the performance of an everyday task.

8. **B.** A *lodge* is a place of shelter constructed by a *beaver*. A *nest* is a place of shelter constructed by a *bird*.

(Defining Characteristic)

9. **E.** To *rustle cattle* is to steal them. To *hijack cargo* is to steal it. Note that you are dealing with a secondary meaning of the verb *rustle* here.

(Defining Characteristic)

10. **B.** A *gland* produces *enzymes*. A *generator* produces electrical *current*.
Beware eye-catchers. Choices A, C, and D are incorrect although they contain biological terms.

(Function)

11. **C.** A *jug* is an example of *crockery* or earthenware. A *hat* is an example of *millinery* or the hatmaker's ware.

(Class and Member)

12. **B.** A *glint* is a small gleam of *light*. A *whiff* is a slight puff of *scent*.

(Degree of Intensity)

13. **E.** *Doggerel* is trivial or inferior verse produced by a *poet*. A *potboiler* is a trivial or inferior literary work produced by a *novelist*.

(Defining Characteristic)

14. **C.** Something *feral* or wild lacks *domestication* or taming. Something *crude* or rough lacks *refinement* or polish.

(Antonym Variant)

15. **C.** To *scotch* or block a *rumor* is to suppress it. To *quash* or quell a *riot* is to suppress it.

(Defining Characteristic)

16. **D.** To *qualify* something is to make it less general and more *particular*. To *mollify* something is to make it less harsh and more *agreeable*.

(Defining Characteristic)

17. **B.** The author's purpose is to *describe* the geological process known as the subduction of the lithosphere.
Choice A is incorrect. The author is not refuting or disproving a theory.
Choice C is incorrect. The author is dealing with a process, not a technique.
Choice D is incorrect. The author is being descriptive and expository, not argumentative.
Choice E is incorrect. The author makes no predictions about things that may occur in the future; he describes a process that is taking place in the present.

18. C.   Only deserts are not mentioned as related to the subduction of the lithosphere.

19. C.   The author is concerned with explaining what happens in a geological phenomenon. His style is by definition expository.

20. E.   All three statements are true. The general circulation or flow of the earth's mantle mentioned in the second paragraph is an indication that the mantle is in a state of flux or flow. The second paragraph also indicates that the lithosphere or crust is cooler than the mantle and that the subducted lithosphere is absorbed or incorporated by the mantle.

21. E.   In the last sentence of the fourth paragraph, the author states that *it appears* that convection currents may in some regions drive the plates and in other regions be driven by the plates. However, this is merely a hypothesis. Thus, current knowledge of the relationship between the plate motions and the currents is clearly *tentative* or hypothetical.
         To locate this information in the body of the text, scan the passage for the key words *asthenosphere* and *convection*.

22. C.   Only undergraduates enrolled in an introductory course would need both the historical orientation to the field presented in the second paragraph and the detailed explanation of the subduction process that follows. Graduate students in geology, professional geologists, and geothermal researchers would all be well aware of something as fundamental as the subduction phenomenon; they would need no introduction to it. Historians of science, for their part, would want more information about the individuals who first formulated the theory; they would have little need for details about the process of subduction itself.

23. E.   Statement E is untrue. The passage states that the radioactive decay of uranium, thorium and potassium "add(s) heat *at a constant rate* to the descending material." The statements in Choices A, B, C and D, however, are all true: each is noted in the final paragraph.

24. D.   In the two paragraphs of this passage, we find the justification for Choice D. In the first paragraph, we are told that Goethe loved the elements of classicism but could not adhere to its requirements. In the second paragraph we are shown how Goethe embodied the elements of romanticism in his writings.

Choice A is incorrect. The passage fails to give equal weight to both writers.
Choice B is incorrect. The passage focuses on Goethe, not on romanticism.
Choice C is incorrect. The passage refers to the differences between classicism and romanticism in order to explain Goethe's writings.
Choice E is incorrect. The passage deals with Goethe's art, not his life.

25. E.   The author never mentions *simplicity of language* as a characteristic of romanticism.
         Choice A is incorrect. The passage refers to a "continued faith in nature" as one aspect of Goethe's romanticism.
         Choice B is incorrect. The passage refers to impulsiveness or *spontaneity* as savoring strongly of romantic individualism.
         Choice C is incorrect. Since romanticism has *formed* so many modern attitudes, one finds in romanticism ideas that seem noteworthy for their modernity.
         Choice D is incorrect. The passage refers to "a disregard of artistic or logical propriety" as characteristic of romanticism.

26. D.   You can arrive at the correct answer by the process of elimination.
         Sensitivity towards emotional promptings is characteristic of romanticism; it is an unlikely characteristic of classicism. Therefore, you can eliminate Choices C and E.
         Emphasis on formal aesthetic criteria is a likely characteristic of classicism. The passage talks of the formal beauty that distinguishes the classical works of Dante and Virgil. Therefore, you can eliminate Choice B.
         Meticulous planning of artistic works is a likely characteristic of classicism. The passage talks of the carefully planned compositions of the classicist Dante; it also tells of the structurally flawed compositions of the romantic Goethe. Therefore, you can eliminate Choice A.
         Only Choice D is left. It is the correct answer.

27. D.   The author both admires Goethe's writings and notes their flaws; his attitude is one of *measured admiration*.

28. A.   The opposite of *superficial* or shallow is *profound*.
         Think of "superficial ideas."

29. C.   The opposite of *naivete* or lack of worldliness is *sophistication*.
         Think of "innocent naivete."

30. E. The opposite of to *tether* or fasten is to *loose*. Think of "tethering a horse to the hitching post."

31. D. The opposite of *pandemonium* or tumultuous uproar is *tranquillity* or calm.
Word Parts Clue: *Pan-* means all; *demon-* means evil spirit. Hell or *Pandemonium*, the place where all the evil spirits dwell, is a place of noise and uproar.
Think of "pandemonium breaking loose."

32. B. To *enervate* (weaken or enfeeble) is the opposite of to *stimulate* or energize.
Think of being "enervated by the heat."

33. C. The opposite of *destitution* (privation; lack of life's necessities) is *affluence* or wealth.
Think of "the poor living in destitution."

34. C. The opposite of to *bereave* (deprive or dispossess, especially by death) is to *restore*.
Think of being "bereaved of all hope."

35. E. The opposite of to *eschew* or shun is to *seek*. Beware eye-catchers. Choice A is incorrect. *Eschew* is unrelated to chewing or gnawing.
Think of "eschewing violence and seeking peace."

36. D. The opposite of *recondite* (obscure; difficult to comprehend) is *obvious*.
Context Clue: "Many consider quantum theory a recondite subject."

37. B. The opposite of to *obviate* something (make it unnecessary) is to require or *necessitate* it.
Think of "obviating a need."

38. E. The opposite of *contumacious* (insubordinate; stubbornly disobedient) is *tractable* (docile; obedient).
Think of "contumacious rebels."

Section 2

1. B. The writer contrasts the individualistic nature of early explorations with the *collaborative* nature of present day ones.

2. E. The anthropologists have dismissed Villa's theory. Nevertheless, they still must stress that other interpretations of the evidence are possible. Why? Because they have not been able to dismiss his evidence. Thus, they are forced to *grant* or concede that his research was carefully done.

3. C. Rather than being *barren* or devoid of life, the vent regions are like *oases* that support life.
Choice A is incorrect. A *waste* by definition is not *teeming* but *barren*.
Choice B is incorrect. The vent region would not be described as an *enclave* (tract enclosed within a foreign territory).
Choice D is incorrect. A *grotto* would not be described as island-like.
Choice E is incorrect. Nothing in the sentence justifies the use of the term *hazardous*.

4. D. Instead of allowing the exchanges to develop fully, the playwright cuts short or *truncates* them.

5. D. A *spate* or flood of examples of fraud suggests that the review system intended to catch such frauds is severely *taxed* or burdened.

6. D. Despite his self-centeredness, White could be kind to others. He could even go beyond kindness and do what for someone egocentric was harder still—*deprecate* or belittle himself. Note the use of *even* as an intensifier here.

7. E. Characters who define themselves by their betrayals *belie* or contradict any assurances they have given others of their good faith.
Choices A, B and D are incorrect. Nothing in the sentence suggests they *flaunt* (parade), *underscore* (emphasize) or *deplore* (lament) the promises they have made.
Choice C is incorrect. Updike's characters break their promises; they do not *fulfill* them.

8. C. A *book* consists of several *chapters*. A *building* consists of several *stories*.

(Part to Whole)

9. D. To *inaugurate* a *president* is to introduce him or her into office. To *install* an *officer* is to do the same.

(Function)

10. E. To *tinker* is to *adjust* or repair something in an unskilled manner. To *scribble* is to *write* or draw something in an unskilled manner.

(Manner)

11. C. *Zinc* is a specific example of an *element*. A *quark* is a specific example of a *particle*.

(Class and Member)

12. D. Something *uproarious* is by definition extremely *amusing*. Something *repugnant* is by definition extremely *disagreeable*.

(Degree of Intensity)

13. C. *Forensic* means pertaining to the art of *debate*. *Histrionic* means pertaining to the art of the theatre.
Beware eye-catchers. Choice A is incorrect. An argument may be empirical or based on fact; however, arguments are not necessarily empirical.

(Defining Characteristic)

14. D. A *limpet* (mollusk that adheres strongly when disturbed) is difficult to *detach*. A *tick* (parasite that burrows into its host) is difficult to *extract*.

(Defining Characteristic)

15. E. To *countenance* or allow something is to give it *approval*. To *air* or voice something is to give it *expression*.
Note that *air* here is used with a less familiar, secondary meaning.

(Synonym Variant)

16. D. Someone *insouciant* (nonchalant; unconcerned) is difficult to *disturb*. Someone *incredulous* (skeptical; disbelieving) is difficult to *convince*.

(Antonym Variant)

17. B. The opening sentence maintains the growth of scholarly activity was stimulated by the protest movement. The protest movement caused an upsurge of popular interest in the Afro-American past. It also created a climate in which professional studies of black history were legitimized.

18. D. The author cites no public opinion polls in the passage. However, he does cite personal anecdotes (Logan's and Litwack's experiences), magazine articles (Bennett's series in *Ebony*), curricular materials (both the freedom schools' materials and those developed for the New York and Detroit public schools) and scholarly publications (Logan's and Litwack's texts).

19. C. The three men are cited as examples of scholars who were encouraged to resume their earlier researches in black history.
Choices A, B and E are incorrect. None of the three men were identified in the passage with these concerns.
Choice D is incorrect. Only Logan is identified with research on blacks in nineteenth-century North Carolina.

20. B. Since the advice was not actually "indicative of how things were going" in the field, it was inappropriate to the times or out of keeping with the current state of cultural and professional development.

21. E. The author is describing what occurred during the period to change black history from a marginal field to a vital field of specialization.

22. D. You can arrive at the correct answer by the process of elimination.
Statement I is supported by the passage. At the time Bennett and Logan wrote, both the pre-Mayflower period of black history and the nineteenth-century life of blacks in North Carolina were relatively unexplored. Therefore, you can eliminate Choices B and E.
Statement II is unsupported by the passage. Bennett's work was a popularization intended for a wide general audience. It was not aimed at academics. Therefore, you can eliminate Choice C.
Statement III is supported by the passage. Bennett's work appeared first as a series of magazine articles, then as a book. Logan's work first appeared as a doctoral thesis, then (with revisions) as a book. Therefore, you can eliminate Choice A.
Only Choice D is left. It is the correct answer.

23. D. According to the passage, prior to the early 1960s Negro history was not an object of particularly great renown in academe. In the 1950s, the advice given to Blassingame to avoid black history if he desired "a future in the historical profession" seemed wise —graduate students of the caliber of Huggins and Litwack felt an ambivalence about entering the field because of "practical concerns." What these concerns boiled down to was the sense that to choose black history as one's specialization would be *detrimental* or harmful to one's career.

24. D. The author is developing the military analogy in order to clarify the workings of the immune system, the body's system of defense.
Choice A is incorrect. The author is not critical of the analogy; he draws on it in order to explain a complex system.
Choice B is incorrect. The passage is expository, not persuasive.
Choice C is incorrect. The author compares the mass of the immune system to that of the brain. However, this is only a passing reference.
Choice E is incorrect. In developing the military analogy, the author offers only one view of the immune system.

25. E. The second sentence states that lymphocytes are "born in the bone marrow." This answers the question as to where the body's lymphocytes *originate*.

26. A. Cyclosporin is a drug that suppresses the body's immune system. Since the immune system protects the body from foreign invaders, such

as viruses, suppression or inhibition of the immune system might well make the body more susceptible to invasion by disease. It would not, however, make the body more likely to reject a transplanted organ, nor would it be likely to increase the efficacy of antigens. Indeed, treatment by cyclosporin tends to make the body less likely to reject a transplanted organ and presumably makes the immune system less responsive to the presence of antigens.

27. C. The author never cites or quotes any medical authorities to support his statements about the immune system.
Choice A is incorrect. The author identifies *lymphocytes* as white blood cells and *antigens* as protein molecules on a substance's surface that trigger the immune response.
Choice B is incorrect. The passage is based on the comparison made between the immune system and an army.
Choice D is incorrect. The author estimates the number of white blood cells available for mustering at approximately 200m.
Choice E is incorrect. By the use of military terminology ("troops," "billeted," "muster," "uniform") the author develops the central metaphor comparing the immune system to an army.

28. C. The opposite of to *sap* or weaken is to *invigorate* or stengthen.
Think of "sapping one's energy."

29. C. The opposite of *unfeigned* or not pretended is *simulated* or feigned.
Beware eye-catchers. Choice A is incorrect. *Pretentious* means ostentatious, showy, or ambitious. It does not mean pretended or feigned.
Think of welcoming someone "with unfeigned delight."

30. D. The opposite of *vacillation* or wavering is *firmness*. Think of "indecisive vacillation."

31. D. The opposite of to *swathe* or cover up is to *unwrap*.
Beware eye-catchers. Though babies are sometimes described as *swathed* in swaddling clothes and injured persons are sometimes described as *swathed* in bandages, *swathing* is related to wrapping, not to nurturing or anointing.
Think of "swathed in blankets."

32. E. The opposite of *cognizance* (conscious knowledge, awareness) is *unawareness*.
Word Parts Clue: *Cogn-* means know. *Cognizance* means knowledge.
Context Clue: "He had no cognizance of the crime."

33. E. The opposite of *nebulous* (vague, cloudy) is *distinct*.
Think of "a nebulous memory."

34. E. The opposite of to *denigrate* (belittle or defame) is to *extol* or praise.
Think of "denigrating someone's efforts."

35. C. The opposite of *decorum* (correctness, good taste) is *impropriety* or unseemliness.
Think of "a proper degree of decorum."

36. E. The opposite of *condign* or due (as in exactly deserved) is *unmerited*.
Think of "condign punishment."

37. B. The opposite of *puissance* or power is *powerlessness*.
Beware eye-catchers. Choice A is incorrect. The opposite of power is a lack of power, not a lack of effort.
Think of "the puissance of the emperor."

38. A. The opposite of to *palliate* or moderate in severity or intensity is to *exacerbate* or increase in severity.
Think of "efforts to palliate a disease."

Section 3

1. B. $\dfrac{7 + 7 + 7}{-7 - 7 - 7} = \dfrac{21}{-21} = -1$
$1 > -1$

2. D. x may be 30 or 60 or 90.

3. C. 3 yards, 1 inch = 109 inches.

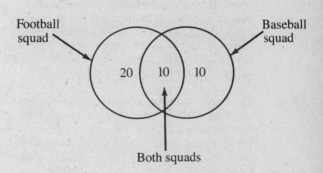

Football squad

Baseball squad

20 10 10

Both squads

4. C. The number of those on both squads = 10.
The number on the baseball squad = 20.
The number on the baseball squad but not on the football squad = 10.
The number on the football squad but not on the baseball squad = 20.
Column A   10:20 or 1:2
Column B   10:20 or 1:2

5. A. There is no need for computation. The product is the same in both cases. The value of x is larger than the value of y because the multiplier of x is smaller than the multiplier of y.

6. C. Because the arcs are equal, ABC is an equilateral triangle. AE bisects BC (given); therefore, DC is $\frac{1}{2}$ any of the sides of ABC.

7. C. Since $y = 50$, the measure of angle $DBC = 100$. Since this is a parallelogram the measure of angle $ABC = 80$ and $x = 40$. In the triangle formed, since $x + y = 90$, the measure of z, the vertex angle, is 90 because the sum of all the angles is a straight angle.

8. D. We may conclude that $a = 80$ but we have no information to determine the value of b, since we may not assume that any lines are parallel.

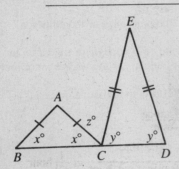

9. C. $x + y + z = 180$
$40 + 80 + z = 180$
$z = 60$
$3x = 120$
$2z = 120$

10. A. The symbols indicate that x is greater than 8 and y is less than 3.

11. C. Since $BD \perp AC$, $x = 90$
Since ABC is equilateral, $z = 60$
Therefore, $y = 30$
$\frac{x}{y} = \frac{90}{30} = 3$

12. C. .01 percent = 0.0001
$(0.0001)(10,000) = 1.0$

13. C. $x^2 + x = (-3)^2 + (-3) = 9 - 3 = 6$
$-2x = (-3)(-2) = 6$

14. C. $\frac{1}{100} + \frac{3}{100} = \frac{4}{100} = 0.04$

15. D. We may assume that x and y have positive values but only that x is greater than $\frac{1}{3}y$. Note the many possibilities.
If $x = 3$ and $y = 2$, 3 is greater than $\frac{2}{3}$.
If $x = 4$ and $y = 5$, 4 is greater than $\frac{5}{3}$.

16. B. (See diagram)

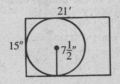

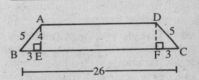

17. C. Draw $DF \perp BC$
$DF = AE = 4$
Therefore, $FC = 3$

$BE = 3$
$EF = 26 - 6 = 20$
$AD = 20$

18. B. This is a direct proportion. Let x = number of postage stamps that can be purchased for c cents.
$$\frac{1 \text{ stamp}}{.5\ \cancel{c}} = \frac{x \text{ stamps}}{c\ \cancel{c}}$$
$5x = c$
$x = \frac{c}{5}$

19. A. 20% (or $\frac{1}{5}$) or $2 = \frac{2}{5}$
$\frac{3}{7} - \frac{2}{5}$
$\frac{15}{35} - \frac{14}{35} = \frac{1}{35}$
$A \qquad B \qquad C \qquad D$

20. D.
$\frac{AC}{AD} = \frac{2 \text{ equal segments}}{3 \text{ equal segments}} = \frac{2}{3}$

21. C. Teachers' salaries represent 30% of the budget. Salaries of other school personnel represent 10% of the budget. 30%:10% or 3:1

22. D. Tax rate per $100 for schools = 24.856
Tax rate per $100 for community college
= 0.654

$$\frac{24.856}{0.654} = 38.+$$

23. C. $10,000 = $100 hundreds
($100)(24.856) = $2485.60

24. C. If $D = 20% of the budget then

$$\frac{\$D}{20\%} = \frac{?}{15\%}$$

$$(20\%)(?) = 15(\$D)$$

$$? = \$\frac{15}{20}D = \$\frac{3}{4}D$$

25. C. $25\% = \frac{1}{4}$

26. B. Area of triangle $= \frac{1}{2}$ (base)(altitude)

Area of triangle $= \frac{1}{2}$ (6 units)(2 units) = 6 units

27. D. 3 gallons = 12 quarts = 24 pints
165 pints = 6.8 (3-gallon cans)
Only six 3-gallon cans will be *filled*.

28. E. A time-consuming method would be to solve
for y in terms of x and to substitute that value in
$5y$. A superior method would be to multiply
both sides of the equation by 6 in order to
obtain a value of $5y$.

$$3x = \frac{5}{6}y$$

$$(6)(3x) = \left(\frac{5}{6}y\right)(6)$$

$$18x = 5y$$

29. B. One-minute unit on the clock $= \frac{360°}{60°} = 6°$

At half-past six the large hand of the clock is
midway between 6 and 7 ($2\frac{1}{2}$ units) or 15°.

30. D. Let x = number of ounces of water to be added
to make a 25% alcohol solution.

$$\frac{\text{amount of alcohol}}{\text{amount of solution}} = \frac{1}{4}$$

$$\frac{48}{48 + x} = \frac{1}{4}$$

$$48 + x = 192$$

$$x = 144$$

Section 4

1. A. Angle *BEC* is a right angle. Therefore $w + z$
= 90. Since $w + x + z + y = 360$ and $w + z = 90$, then $x + y = 270$.

2. B. $1 \div \frac{3}{2} = (1)\left(\frac{2}{3}\right) = \frac{2}{3}$

3. C. If equal quantities are added to equal quantities
the sums are equal.

4. C. The time elapsed is 20 minutes $= \frac{1}{3}$ hour.

5. C. Let s = side of square
then, area of square $= s^2$
s^2 = area of triangle *ABC* (given)
Therefore, $AB = BC = s\sqrt{2}$ for $s^2 =$
$$\frac{(s\sqrt{2})(s\sqrt{2})}{2}$$
Therefore, $\frac{AB}{DG} = \frac{s\sqrt{2}}{s}$ or $\sqrt{2}$

6. C. $\sqrt{\frac{1}{25}} = \frac{1}{5} = 20\%$

7. B. $\sqrt{14.4} > 3$
$\sqrt{14.4} < 4$

8. A. Time $= \frac{\text{distance}}{\text{rate}}$

Time $= \frac{\frac{1}{2} \text{ mile}}{20 \text{ miles per hour}} = \frac{1}{40}$ hour

Time $= \frac{\frac{1}{3} \text{ mile}}{30 \text{ miles per hour}} = \frac{1}{90}$ hour

9. C. $\frac{\text{Distance}}{\text{Circumference}}$ = number of revolutions

$\frac{70 \text{ feet}}{7 \text{ feet}} = 10$ revolutions

$\frac{100 \text{ feet}}{10 \text{ feet}} = 10$ revolutions

Circumference $= \pi D$

Circumference $= (\pi) \cdot \frac{7}{(\pi)} = 7$ (Column A)

Circumference $= (\pi) \cdot \frac{10}{(\pi)} = 10$ (Column B)

10. A. If $X + Y = 100$
then $100 + Z = 350$
and $Z = 250$
if $X + Y = 100$
then $X < 100$ and $Z > X$

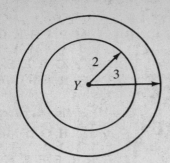

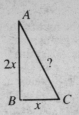

11. D.   If Y is at the center of both circles, then Z could be anywhere on the circumference of the circle with radius $= 2$, and X could be at any point on the circumference with radius $= 3$. There are many possibilities for the location of X in respect to the location of Z.

12. B. $x < y$ because when it is squared and multiplied by 9 it has the same value of y.

13. D.   From the information given, we can only deduce that $\frac{1}{2}$ the product of these two values equals 18.

14. D.   We may conclude only that $AD = BC$ and $AB = DC$.

15. C. $$4x = 48$$
$$x = 12$$
$$16\tfrac{2}{3}\% = \frac{1}{6}$$
$$\frac{1}{6} \text{ of } 72 = 12$$

16. B.   Since the recipe is given for 60 cookies and only 20 cookies are to be made, the ingredients must be cut by $\frac{1}{3}$.
$$\frac{1}{3} \cdot 1\frac{1}{2} = \frac{1}{3} \cdot \frac{3}{2} = \frac{1}{2} \text{ cup of sifted flour}$$

17. B. $$\frac{\text{potassium}}{\text{potassium} + \text{nitrogen} + \text{oxygen}} =$$
$$\frac{39}{39 + 14 + 48} = \frac{39}{101} =$$
approximately 39%

18. B.   The width is 50, since the length is twice the width. Perimeter $= 50 + 50 + 100 + 100 = 300$ feet.

19. C.   Let $x = BC$; then $AB = 2x$.
Area of triangle $ABC = \frac{1}{2}(b)(h)$
or $\left(\frac{1}{2}\right)(x)(2x)$ or x^2.

Area is given equal to 64 square feet.
$x^2 = 64$
$x = 8$
$BC = 8; AB = 16$
$(8)^2 + (16)^2 = (AC)^2$ (Pythagorean theorem)
$64 + 256 = (AC)^2$
$(AC)^2 = 320$
$AC = \sqrt{320}$
or approximately 18 feet

20. B. $x = ky$
$5 = 3k$
$k = \frac{5}{3}$

$\therefore \dfrac{5}{9} = \dfrac{5}{3} \cdot y$

$y = \dfrac{1}{3}$

21. B.   8 ounces buttermilk $= 90$ calories
2 tablespoons light cream $= 60$ calories
3 tablespoons light cream $= 90$ calories

22. D.   4 ounces chocolate milk $= 4$ grams of protein
4 tablespoons cream cheese $= 4$ grams of protein
4 tablespoons cream cheese $= 220$ calories

23. C.   (A) whole milk 320
(B) buttermilk 180
(C) Swiss cheese 1760
(D) cottage cheese 480
(E) chocolate milk 380

24. E.   (A) cottage cheese $= 30$ calories
(B) cheddar-type cheese $= 90$ calories
(C) Swiss cheese $= 110$ calories
(D) butter $= 200$ calories
(E) whole milk $= 20$ calories

25. E. In 8 ounces, the number of grams of protein is:
whole milk, 9 grams;
cottage cheese, 32 grams;
butter, none;
chocolate milk, 8 grams;
American cheese, 64 grams.

26. A. I is true, e.g., $\sqrt[3]{-8} = -2$

II is false; $\sqrt{\frac{1}{4}}$ is not smaller than $\frac{1}{4}$;

$\sqrt{\frac{1}{4}} = \frac{1}{2}; \frac{1}{2}$ is larger than $\frac{1}{4}$

III is false; $(A - B)(A + B) = A^2 - B^2$

27. D. The reciprocal of 0 is $\frac{1}{0}$. Any number with a zero in the denominator does not exist, since division by zero is meaningless or undefined. Therefore, 0 does not have a reciprocal.

(A) The reciprocal of 1 or $\frac{1}{1}$ is 1.

(B) The reciprocal of -2 or $\frac{-2}{1}$ is $\frac{1}{-2}$.

(C) The reciprocal of $\frac{1}{3}$ is $\frac{3}{1}$ or 3.

(E) The reciprocal of 3 is $\frac{1}{3}$.

28. E. $x + y = 16$
$x = 16 - y$
$(16 - y) - z = 16 - y - z$

29. A. $\frac{a - b}{3.5} = \frac{4}{7}$

Since $3.5 = \frac{1}{2}$ of 7, then $a - b = \frac{1}{2}$ of $4 = 2$.
Since $a - b = 2, b < a$.

30. D. $10^x = \underbrace{(10)(10)(10) \ldots \ldots \ldots \ldots \ldots \ldots 10}_{x \text{ times}}$

$10^{-x} = \dfrac{1}{\underbrace{(10)(10)(10) \ldots \ldots \ldots (10)}_{x \text{ times}}}$

(A) is true.
$470,000 = (4.7)(10)(10)(10)(10)(10)$
$= 4.7 \times 10^5$
(B) is true. 450 billion $= 4.5 \times 10^{11}$
(C) is true. $.00000000075 = 7.5 \times 10^{-10}$
(D) is not true. $\frac{86}{100,000} = \frac{8.6}{10,000} 8.6^{-4}$

Section 5

1-3. A quick reading of the three questions will reveal that the student is not asked to prepare a seating arrangement. The student should examine what is presented.

1. E Choice I is satisfactory.

Lady— F O L M P J H K G Q N R
Language or Languages Spoken E F F G R E E E F G E
E G R R F G E

Choice III is also satisfactory.

Lady— F R G J H O L M Q P K N
Language or Languages Spoken E E E R E F F F G E G
F R E G G R E

Choice II is unsatisfactory.

Lady— F R N L P
Language or Languages Spoken E E E F G
G R

Having discovered that Mrs. L will not be able to communicate with either Mrs. N or Mrs. P, the student need not continue examining the remaining ladies' abilities to communicate with their neighbors.

2. A. Since Mrs. J speaks Russian only, she must sit alongside Mrs. P or Mrs. H. Mrs. H is already seated; the only place left is alongside P.

3. D. An examination of the list of guests reveals that five ladies speak French. Four have already seated themselves in this group of seven. L speaks only French and therefore must be seated alongside Q.

4. E. It is not really necessary to examine statements I, II, and III. A glance at the chart should reveal that Mrs. J, who speaks Russian only, will have no one to converse with, since the only other Russian-speaking women—Mrs. H and Mrs. P—will not be in attendance. Choice E is the only possible answer.

5. D. Johnson makes two claims: (1) anyone supporting the bill must have an ulterior motive, and (2) therefore, there are no valid grounds for supporting the bill. Choice D makes the same two claims about Johnson. Choice B is the best response to Johnson, and does *not* make the error in reasoning that he makes; choice A grants Johnson's claims and does not attack him; choice C attacks Johnson's argument rather than attacking his motives; and choice E attacks Johnson but doesn't claim that this discredits his argument.

6. C.   This deluded father is basing his whole argument about his daughter's talents on the rave reviews from a single high school play. The best way to counter his argument would be to point out the inadequacy of that evidence, which is what choice C does. All the other choices refer to the stiff competition for jobs on Broadway and the high odds against succeeding. They do not directly counter the father's line of reasoning.

7. D.   The original argument states that most X (opponents of gun control) are Y (conservatives); therefore, someone who is not X is probably not Y. The flaw in this reasoning is that many persons other than X may also be Y. D makes the same error: most X (sports cars) are Y (expensive), so a non-X is probably not Y. But many kinds of cars other than sports cars may be expensive. The other arguments have logical structures different from that of the original argument. Choice A wrongly argues: most X are Y, therefore a Y is probably X. Choices B, C, and E are all logically valid.

8-11.   Since this problem involves both days of the week and calendar dates, make a calendar. Keep it simple. It doesn't have to show all days of the week—only one choice in one question involves a day other than Tuesday, Thursday, or Saturday—and it doesn't have to go all the way through May. It will look like this:

	RYDER	EAKINS	HUDSON RIVER
Th. 4-30	√	—	—
Sat. 5-2	√	—	√
Tu. 5-5	√	—	—
Th. 5-7	—	—	√
Sat. 5-9	√	√	√
Tu. 5-12	√	√	—
Th. 5-14	—	√	√
Sat. 5-16	√	√	√
Tu. 5-19	√	√	—
Th. 5-21	—	√	√
Sat. 5-23	√	√	√

(ends 5-24)

8. C.   The conditions mean Dan can go to the museum only on Tuesday, Thursday, or Saturday. By starting on Tuesday, he can complete the three visits in five days, whereas by starting on Thursday or Saturday he must take six days. This is enough to get you to choice C. Dan must go to the Eakins or Ryder exhibitions first, since the Twachtman Gallery is closed Tuesdays.

9. C.   Since the Pollock Wing is closed Thursdays during May, Ellen must see the Ryder exhibition first, on Thursday, April 30 (I); she must, then, see "The Hudson River School" second, on May 7, since the "Precursors of Eakins" does not open until May 8 (II). This excludes choice III.

10. B.   Your calendar tells you that all three exhibitions can be seen on Saturday, May 9, 16, or 23 (II) —not on Saturday, May 2, because the "Eakins" is not yet open, and not on May 30, because "The Hudson River School" is closed (I). III is out both because the Twachtman Gallery is closed Tuesdays and because Eakins does not open until May 8.

11. B.   Terry's visit falls on Thursday, May 7 (six days after the May 1 opening of "The Hudson River School"). A glance at the calendar shows that "The Hudson River School" is the only special exhibition open on that date.

12-18.   To diagram this one, start with seven blanks for the seats. Put the moderator in the middle; put the initials of the speakers under the blanks and abbreviated titles over the blanks. (Of course, your diagram may be slightly different. Any clear and readable system will do.) Starting with statements (3) and (5), you have:

Impact						
C	F		Mod.			

The person delivering "Epidemiological Aspects" must be in a middle seat, and it must be on the right because Cathode, not Albert or Durand, is in an end seat on the left. Given this information, Albert and Durand must be in the two other seats on the right, while the two friends in statement (2) must be in the two remaining seats on the left, although in each case we don't know who is in which seat. Since the person in statement (4) is delivering "Benign," not "Impact," he or she must be in the end seat on the right. Finally, statement (6) tells us that Ettis is in the middle on the right, with Albert to his or her left. You now have:

Impact	Pub/Rad	Pub/Rad			Epidem	Benign
C	F		Mod.	A	E	D

By elimination, Burris is in the last available seat. We still don't know the title of Albert's paper, nor do we know which paper is to be delivered by Felsenstein, which by Burris.

12. E.   By inspection of the diagram. Notice that choices A and B include Albert as pro-industry, while statement (6) says that he or she is a critic.

13. B.   By inspection of the diagram.

14. A.   Albert is the only person the title of whose paper is unknown.

15. A.   We've seen that I remains ambiguous. II and III can be read from the diagram.

16. C.   Statement (1) establishes the title of the paper. Statements (3) and (5), along with (1), put the author in the middle seat on the right. Statement (6) establishes the name of the person in that seat. Statements (2) and (4) aren't needed.

17. D.   The diagram shows that, if the seventh speaker is to sit midway between Cathode and the moderator, he must sit between Felsenstein and Burris.

18. B.   If the eighth speaker is to sit exactly midway between Durand and the author of "Public Health and PBX," then the latter must be Felsenstein, not Burris, since otherwise there would be no vacant spot *exactly* midway between the two. Therefore, Burris must be the author of "Radiological Aspects of PBX." The eighth speaker will sit between the moderator and Albert.

19-22.   We've drawn a diagram similar to the traditional "family tree" diagram used in history books and genealogies. Since so many persons are of uncertain sex, we've used m for male, f for female, and x and y for unknowns. We know, for example, that G is the same sex as C, so we label both x; B and therefore F are the opposite sex from C, so we label both y, and so on. Horizontal lines indicate marriage, vertical or diagonal lines indicate children.

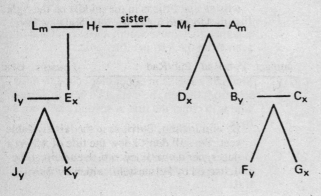

19. D.   This question orients you, in case you made an unwarranted assumption about the sexes. Since we do not know B's sex for sure, we don't know F's; this rules out all the wrong choices —including E, since we *do* know H's sex. As the child of D's sibling B, F is D's niece or nephew.

20. E.   D is an x, and can therefore marry any unmarried y.

21. E.   H is female. If x = male, H can marry D *or* G, so I is out. If y = male, H can marry F. Clearly H cannot marry both. (J and K are ruled out, since they are H's direct descendants.)

22. B.   This generation (the middle generation) contains three x's and two y's. If the more numerous x's are female, J, a y, must be male. If x = female, choices A, C, and E are untrue. Choice D can never be true.

23. B.   Statement I is *not* assumed. The author assumes only that we are in danger of running out of oil *eventually*. Statement II *is* assumed. The author's claim is that we *must* use oil to produce plastics and other goods. Statement III is *not* assumed. The author assumes only that *someone* could develop alternative methods of transportation, not that the oil companies are in a position to do this themselves.

24. D.   The author's only basis for advocating the banning of the internal combustion engine is that the oil it burns is needed for other purposes. If a synthetic oil were developed that did everything natural oil does, the author's complaint would lose its force. All the other choices describe events which would ameliorate the problem without eliminating it.

25. B.   The author claims that the oil we are burning is needed to produce many important commodities. Choice B underscores both the value of some of those items and the necessity of using oil to produce them. Choice A supports the author's secondary point that other methods of transportation could be developed, but does not directly support the main conclusion that the internal combustion engine should be banned. Choice C emphasizes the urgency of the problem, but the original argument makes no claims about time. Choices D and E provide bases of other arguments for the banning of gasoline-burning cars, but have no effect on the original argument.

Section 6

1-5. In this extremely tricky problem, the first five statements will tell you only who is in what generation and some of the relationships, but the last two statements clarify everything. Using solid horizontal lines for marriages, circles for married groups, broken lines for sibling relationships, and vertical lines for parent-child relationships, we first get the following Diagram:

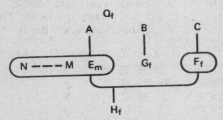

We know that N and M must be brothers of E *or* sisters of F, but we never find out which. We don't yet know the relationships among A, B, and C, although we *do* know that C and A aren't married (because their male and female children marry). We don't know exactly who Q's children are. The next two statements tell us. A and B are male; the paternal grandmother of E and F must be the mother of their fathers, so A and B must be brothers. *But* if they are the only grandfathers of H, they must be the fathers of her father E and her mother F. Since C is F's mother, B and C must be married, and G must be F's sister. Since A and C can't be married, A must be married in *Brihtu* marriage to several sisters (remember, A and B are H's *only* grandfathers), while B is married in *Brihtu* marriage to C and her sister or sisters. J, K, and L are the wives of A and B, but we don't know who is the wife of which of them. All this gives us the following completed diagram:

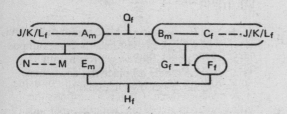

The questions are now easy.

1. D. This can be read from the diagram. G is definitely *not* a sister of E, since she is a sister of F who is married to E. Since F may be the sister of N and M, G may be their sister as well; but she would be the sister of both, which eliminates choices A and B.

2. D. N *must* be the sibling of more than one person, since he or she is married to three people. The possibilities are: M and E, if N is male; M and F, if N is female—but not both.

3. A. A is definitely one of Q's children; C, J, and K cannot be, since they are married to Q's children (A and B); M must be a sibling of one of Q's grandchildren

4. B. The only *Brihtu* marriages we are sure of are those of A and B. The marriage of N, M, E, and F, of which H is the daughter, could be either. We don't know whom Q married, so we can't tell what kind of marriage A and B are children of. We don't know who J's parents might have been.

5. E. We know that E is eligible to marry F, and that G is F's sister. N cannot marry M (choice A), since they are the same sex—there would be either no male or no female in the resulting marriage. Choice B *may* be permissible, but we don't know. Choice C is impermissible: assuming that N and M are E's brothers, this would mean that two brothers married two sisters, which is neither *Brihtu* nor *Prahtu* marriage. Choice D is a monogamous marriage, which is definitely out in the society under consideration.

6-9. The players must be seated as shown in the following diagram:

Cooper *or* D'Amato	Edwards *or* Farley	Edwards *or* Farley	Baker
Cooper *or* D'Amato	Adams *or* Goldberg	Adams *or* Goldberg	

Note that all the seats except for the center seat *may* be occupied by either of two individuals. Take this into account when answering the questions.

6. D. In order for Farley and Edwards to be seated together, they must occupy the second and third seats from the left, in either order.

7. C. Since Edwards is in either the second or third seat from the left, he cannot be next to Adams, who is in either the first or second seat from the right.

8. C. Goldberg is in one of the two seats nearest the exit, and therefore cannot be on either side of Baker.

9. B.   If neither Edwards nor D'Amato is seated next to Baker, then Baker must be flanked by Farley on the left and Cooper on the right. This means that the table must be seated as follows (left to right): D'Amato, Edwards, Farley, Baker, Cooper, and, in the last two seats, Adams and Goldberg in either order. The fact that Adams and Goldberg may be seated in either order results in the two possible seating arrangements for the table as a whole.

10-15.   An examination of the seven number series reveals

I.   64 is the third power of 4 (4 × 4 × 4); 125 is the third power of 5 (5 × 5 × 5). The next number should be the third power of 6 (6 × 6 × 6).

II.   This is a more difficult series. The square of 6 is 36. 37 is the square of 6 + 1. The square of 7 is 49. 50 is the square of 7 + 1. The square of 8 is 64. 65 is the square of 8 + 1. We may assume that x in this series will equal 9 × 9 + 1 or 82.

III.   Here we find a pattern of three elements. 25 = 5 × 5; 125 = 5 × 5 × 5. Similarly 49 = 7 × 7; 343 = 7 × 7 × 7. We may assume that x will equal 9 × 9 × 9.

IV.   The difference between 9 and −7 is 16 (4 × 4). The difference between −7 and 18 is 25 (5 × 5). The difference between 18 and −18 is 36 (6×6). The difference between −18 and 31 is 49 (7×7). We should also notice that these squares alternately use plus and minus signs. The next number should be 31 − (8 × 8) or 33.

V.   16 = 4 × 4. 80 = 16 × 5. 480 = 80 × 6. 3360 = 480 × 7. The next number should be 3360 × 8. Here the pattern is increasing multipliers of the preceding number.

VI.   Increasing units of subtraction. The pattern is number −1, −2, −3, −4, etc.

VII.   Descending order of squares. 100 is 10 × 10. 81 is 9 × 9. 64 = 8 × 8. 49 = 7 × 7. 36 = 6 × 6. The next number should be 25 (5 × 5).

10. A.   Questions involving the third power occur in I and III.

11. D.   Choice V does not involve the use of second or third powers of numbers.

12. B.   See analysis of IV above.

13. A.   See analysis of II above.

14. B.   See analysis of V above.

15. C.   Example III cannot be solved unless we see that 5, 25, and 125 make a pattern which is repeated with 7, 49, and 343.

16-20.   Make a table of the rooming possibilities. Since Hittites and Goths must be separated, D and G must always be in one cabin, while B and F are in the other. In the first three lines of the following table, D and G are placed consecutively with A, C, and E, while whichever two of these three remain are placed in the other cabin with B and F. Then, B and F are put with A, B, and C in turn, the two remaining being put with D and G in the other cabin. The √ mark shows combinations in which everyone in each cabin can talk, whether directly or with one person translating. The X mark shows combinations where this is impossible.

DGA	BFGE	√
DGC	BFAE	√
DGE	BFAC	X
DGCE	BFA	√
DGAE	BFC	X
DGAC	BFE	√

16. D.   The combination of DGCE and BFA is satisfactory. BFC is impossible, because B and F speak only Hittite and C speaks only Etruscan and Gothic. Likewise, DGE is out, because E speaks no Gothic. The other two choices are fine by themselves, since A speaks all languages; but they represent the four-person second cabins corresponding to the two impossible choices given in choices A and B.

17. E.   There is one acceptable rooming arrangement that places C with A (I). There are two acceptable arrangements in which A is not in the three-person cabin (II). In one acceptable arrangement, DGCE and BFA, E does not room with a Hittite (III).

18. C.   If your table has been set up correctly, just count.

19. D.   D, E, and G are *not* part of any acceptable arrangement (I); B, E, F and C, D, E, G are (II, III).

20. E.   B, E, and F—an acceptable combination previously, since E speaks Hittite—becomes impossible now, since Goths won't room with Hittites. The others all place the newcomer with persons of her own nationality.

21. E.   While Lind used the scientific method, the contributions of Hall and Harvey set the stage for his experiment. Credit for the discovery must be given to all three men.

22. B.   The group receiving the dilute sulfuric acid and the group receiving vinegar, were the control groups. These sailors received the same diets as the third group except for the substance tested.

23. E. Hall and Harvey seemed to have established the fact that acids are effective, but Lind's experiment was to find out whether it was acidity or some specific substance perhaps associated with acids that cured scurvy. Today we know this substance is ascorbic acid. Hall's brew and Harveys's lemon juice must have contained ascorbic acid.

24. C. Lind did not use pure citric acid. Lemon juice contains other substances besides citric acid.

25. C. The passage indicates that lack of fresh food was the cause of scurvy.

Section 7

1. A. $\frac{a}{b} = 3$; $\frac{b}{a} = \frac{1}{3}$

2. B. $(8)^2 = (8)(8) = 64$
   $(2)^8 = (2)(2)(2)(2)(2)(2)(2)(2) = 256$

3. C. Both triangles share the same base and they have equal altitudes, since AD is parallel to BC.

4. C. Since $b = c$, each fraction equals 1.

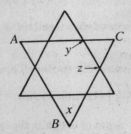

5. C. Since $BA = BC$,
   $\angle A = \angle C$. Since $\angle x = 60°$, $\angle A + \angle C = 120°$. (The sum of the angles of a triangle equals 180°.) Therefore $\angle C = 60°$. Since $\angle y = 100°$, $\angle CGH = 80°$, because these angles are supplementary. In triangle CGH, since $\angle C = 60°$ and $\angle CGH = 80°$, the $\angle CHG$ must equal 40°. Since $\angle z$ is the supplement of $\angle CHG$, then $\angle z = 180° - 40°$, or 140°.

   A B C D E F G H

   x y z

6. C. $a^2 = 9, b = 9; a^2 - b = 0.$
   $b = 9; a^2 = 9; b - a^2 = 0.$

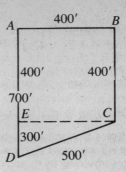

7. A. Draw EC. $EC = AB = 400$ feet. Area of square $ABCE = (400)^2$, or 160,000 square feet. Area of triangle $EDC = \frac{1}{2}(400)(300)$, or 60,000 square feet. Area of entire lot = 160,000 + 60,000, or 220,000 square feet. (Column A)

8. A. Multiply the expression $a < b$ by -2. The result is $-2a > -2b$. Recall that when you multiply each side of an inequality by the same negative expression, the inequality is reversed.

9. C. The numbers are $q, q + 1, q + 2, q + 3, q + 4, q + 5, q + 6, q + 7, q + 8$. The sum of the numbers is $9q + 36$. The average is $\frac{9q + 36}{9}$, which is $q + 4$.

10. B. $\frac{1}{2} + \frac{1}{3} = \frac{5}{6}$
    $\left(\frac{5}{6}\right)(1813) < 1813$

11. C. $xy = 1$
    $y = \frac{1}{x}$ (divide by x)
    $\frac{x}{y} = \frac{x}{\frac{1}{x}}$ (substitution)
    $\frac{x}{y} = x^2$

12. B. Since x is negative, $\frac{1}{x}$ is negative and x^2 is positive.

13. C. $\frac{1}{2}\% = \frac{\frac{1}{2}}{100} = \frac{1}{200}$

14. B. $b° = 120$ (corresponding angles of parallel lines)
    $a° + 120 = 180°$
    $a° = 60$

15. A. Add the two equations.
$3a = -3$ and $a = -1$.
$-1 + b = -6$
$b = -5$
-1 is greater than -5, so a is greater than b.

16. C. $\dfrac{41.5 \text{ feet}}{6} = 6.91 +$ feet, or each string is just under 7 feet. Checking each answer for the closest figure is more rapid than changing 41 feet to 498 inches, dividing by 6, and converting the answer to feet and inches.

17. C. $\dfrac{\text{difference}}{\text{original}} = \dfrac{\$2.50}{\$12.50} = \dfrac{1}{5} = 20\%$

18. C. $\dfrac{\text{difference}}{\text{original}} = \dfrac{\$24}{\$96} = \dfrac{1}{4} = 25\%$

19. C. Since the first car uses 1 gallon for 15 miles, it will use 4 gallons for 60 miles. Since the second car uses 1 gallon for m miles, it will go $4m$ miles on 4 gallons.

20. B. $\dfrac{760}{200} = 3.8$ gallons. It will be necessary to purchase 4 gallons.

21. B. Recall that the percent increase is the difference divided by the original times 100.
(A) is a decrease. (B) is an increase of $\dfrac{15}{30}$ or $\dfrac{3}{10}$ or 30%. (C) and (D) have increases of about 100%. (E) has an increase of about 66%.

22. E. The farmers show an increase from 32% to 62%.

23. A. If h represents 46%, then let x represent 58%.
$\dfrac{h}{46} = \dfrac{x}{58}$
$46x = 58h$
$x = \dfrac{58h}{46}$ or $\dfrac{29h}{23}$

24. E. $w = 50\% (1948)$
$65\% = (1952)$.
(A) an increase of 15% over the original 50% equals an increase of 30% of the original. Original + 30% = 130%.
(B) Shows an arithmetic increase of 15%.
(C) Since $w = 50\%$, $2w = 100\%$ and $100\% - 35\% = 65\%$.
(D) $\dfrac{w}{2} = 25\%$, $25\% + 40\% = 65\%$
(E) $(50\% - 30\%)^2 = (20\%)^2$, which does NOT equal 65%.

25. E. Some of the unskilled workers may be secondary school graduates.

26. C. $\left(\dfrac{ab}{100}\right) \div \left(\dfrac{ba}{100}\right) = \left(\dfrac{ab}{100}\right) \cdot \left(\dfrac{100}{ba}\right) = 1$

27. C. (A) $\dfrac{1}{5} = 0.2$
(B) $\dfrac{1}{4} = 0.25$
(C) $\dfrac{2}{5} = 0.4$
(D) $\dfrac{16}{25} = 0.64 \left(\text{which is more than } \dfrac{1}{2}\right)$
(E) $\dfrac{3}{10} = 0.3$

28. C. $\dfrac{t + n}{n} = \dfrac{t}{n} + \dfrac{n}{n}$ or $\dfrac{t}{n} + 1$

29. D. If the cow were tethered by a ten-foot-rope in a pasture without fences, it could graze in a circular area of 100π. Since the fences form an angle of 60°, the cow will be confined to $\dfrac{60}{360}$ or $\dfrac{1}{6}$ of that circle, or $\dfrac{1}{6}$ of $\pi 100$ or $\dfrac{50\pi}{3}$.

30. C. Radius $= \dfrac{7}{2}$ inches, and the area of the bottom of the smaller tin $= \pi\left(\dfrac{7}{2}\right)\left(\dfrac{7}{2}\right)$ square inches.
The volume of each small tin $= \pi\left(\dfrac{7}{2}\right)\left(\dfrac{7}{2}\right)$ (1) cubic inches.
The volume of the two small tins $= 2\pi\left(\dfrac{7}{2}\right)\left(\dfrac{7}{2}\right)$ (1) cubic inches.
Let $x =$ depth of dough in the larger tin. Since the radius of the larger tin $= 5$ inches, the volume of dough in the larger tin $= (5)(5)(\pi)(x)$ or $25\pi x$.
$25\pi x = \dfrac{49}{2}\pi$ (the amount of dough is the same);
$25x = \dfrac{49}{2}$;
$x = \dfrac{49}{50}$ or 0.98.